ADVANCED

ACCOUNTING

SIXTH EDITION

Paul M. Fischer, PhD, CPA
Professor of Accounting
University of Wisconsin, Milwaukee

William J. Taylor, PhD, CPA
Assistant Professor of Accounting
University of Wisconsin, Milwaukee

SOUTH-WESTERN College Publishing

An International Thomson Publishing Company

Sponsoring Editor: Elizabeth A. Bowers
Developmental Editor: Sara E. Bates
Production Editor: Peggy A. Williams
Production House: Matrix Productions Inc.
Cover Designer: Siebert Design
Cover Illustrator: McCrystle Wood
Interior Designer: Joseph M. Devine
Marketing Manager: Sharon C. Oblinger

AD90FA

Library of Congress Cataloging-in-Publication Data

Fischer, Paul M.
    Advanced accounting / Paul M. Fischer, William J. Taylor. --
6th ed.
        p.   cm.
    ISBN 0-538-84126-5
    1. Accounting.   I. Taylor, William James.   II. Title.
    HF5635.F5389   1994
    657'.046--dc20   94-28895
                                                          CIP

    2 3 4 5 6 7 8 D 1 0 9 8 7 6 5

Printed in the United States of America

I(T)P
International Thomson Publishing
South-Western College Publishing is an ITP Company. The ITP trademark is used under
license.

Preface

The sixth edition of ADVANCED ACCOUNTING contains significant revisions in the areas of business combinations, governmental and not-for-profit accounting, and multinational accounting. The full coverage of earnings per share calculations found in the first four editions returns by popular demand.

This text is known for its close linking of accounting theory and practice and for its "learn by example" approach to teaching. Every topic contains complete and realistic examples. Students learn best by applying concepts directly to examples. End-of-chapter materials provide a variety of means to accomplish this. Questions are used to reinforce theory. Exercises are short, focused applications of specific topics in the chapter and make great assignments to be done prior to class. Problems tend to be more comprehensive than exercises, often combining topics. They work well as after-class assignments. New to this edition, in the business combinations chapters, are selected cases which provide a new opportunity to blend theoretical and numerical analysis. The authors have found that these work really well when used as group projects. Be aware that the instructor's solutions manual contains precise descriptions of every exercise, problem, and case to aid the instructor's choice of assignment material. All end-of-chapter materials are in the order in which the topics are developed in the chapter narrative.

The STUDENT COMPANION ENRICHMENT MANUAL, available for students, provides several advantages to users. First, it contains a second copy of every consolidated worksheet in the text. This allows the student to set the text narrative explaining a worksheet procedure right next to the worksheet in the enrichment manual to which it applies. Second, it contains a review outline of each chapter and other supporting materials to reinforce the chapter. Third, it contains a blend of questions and efficient problems for each chapter. The problems are structured so that each concept in the chapter is applied to a short example. Answers are provided for student feedback. Finally, it provides additional enrichment material in the areas of branch accounting and the Securities and Exchange Commission.

HIGHLIGHTS OF CHANGES IN THE SIXTH EDITION

The following changes from the fifth edition are most notable:

1. The flow of topics in business combinations has been modified to place the most critical topics in the first six chapters. These are the topics most often needed in practice and are more frequently tested on the CPA Exam. The seventh and eighth chapters in this section contain a variety of advanced consolidation issues. Each topic within Chapters 7 and 8 is treated separately so that an instructor may choose which topics are to be covered when time is limited.

2. Chapter 1, which deals with business combinations accomplished through an acquisition of assets has been modified to include the 1993 change in tax law that permits a deduction for goodwill using a 15-year amortization period. The comparison of purchase and pooling and the accounting for the costs of a busi-

ness combination have been made easier to understand.

3. We have modified our exclusive "Determination and Distribution of Excess Schedule" to include debit and credit labels to ease the distribution of the excess of cost or book value on the worksheet. This strengthens the importance of this schedule in providing all support for the elimination of the investment account and the resulting account adjustments.

4. The impact of deferred tax liabilities that result from a tax-free exchange is an important topic but is troublesome to students. We have found that it becomes a blockage to the understanding of more important topics in Chapters 2 and 3. The material on deferred tax liabilities resulting from a tax-free exchange has thus been moved to an appendix following Chapter 3. The coverage considers the new change in the deductibility of goodwill.

5. Regarding intercompany transactions in Chapters 4 and 5, users of the text asked that we add journal entry format eliminations to the narrative in addition to their inclusion in sample worksheets. We have done this.

6. Chapter 11 includes an end-of-chapter problem that requires students to translate a foreign subsidiary's financial statements and prepare a consolidated worksheet. A follow-up problem uses the same basic facts except that the functional currency is the dollar. This requires the remeasurement of the foreign subsidiary's financial statements. These problems provide an excellent opportunity to compare and contrast translation and remeasurement.

7. Chapter 13 deals with the disclosure of earnings per share data. This topic was not covered in the previous edition of the text but had been in all other editions. Many adopters of the text felt that the coverage of this topic was excellent and that it was a logical topic to be included in an advanced financial accounting course. As before, the computation of primary and fully diluted earnings per share is treated in a comprehensive manner.

8. Wherever possible, the text has included footnote disclosures from actual financial statements in order to help students understand how accounting information is communicated.

9. The importance of developing critical thinking skills is addressed in the end-of-chapter materials. These materials include questions that require the student to do more than merely "push the numbers." Students are asked to evaluate the accounting effect of various alternatives. For example: "Would it be better to hedge a foreign currency transaction with a forward contract or a foreign loan?"

10. We have incorporated FASB Statements No. 116 and 117 as well as the latest GASB pronouncements in the extensive revision of the governmental and not-for-profit chapters. This new material keeps students up to date on the current changes occurring in these areas of financial reporting.

ORGANIZATION OF THE BOOK

The sixth edition remains flexible in terms of the order in which topics are covered. There are no dependencies between major sections of the text except that coverage of consolidations should precede multinational accounting if one is to understand accounting for foreign subsidiaries. Clearly, the text contains more topics than can be covered in a single semester. The book contains adequate coverage to fill two advanced courses. Where only one semester is available, a careful selection of topics can be made. It would be our advice to cover only the first six chapters in business combinations when only a single semester is available.

The text is divided into the following major topics:

BUSINESS COMBINATIONS—BASIC TOPICS (CHAPTERS 1–6)

This advanced book is unique in that it devotes an initial chapter to the basic issues of purchase and pooling of interests accounting in the context of direct asset acquisitions. This provides an opportunity to focus on theoretical concepts without being concerned about the mechanics of consolidations. The most difficult concept in the chapter is the combining of stockholders' equities in a pooling of interests, and this is aided by a unique "equity transfer diagram."

Chapters 2 through 5 cover the basics of preparing a consolidated income statement and balance sheet. In 1977 we introduced the "Determination and Distribution of Excess Schedule" and the "Income Distribution Schedule." These schedules are much appreciated by students and faculty. The determination and distribution schedule (quickly termed the D&D schedule by students) analyzes the difference between the price paid in a purchase and the underlying equity of the subsidiary. It provides a check figure for all subsequent years' worksheets, provides all information for the distribution of differences between book and market values, and provides all data for the amortization of the differences. The schedule provides rules for all types of purchase situations and for alternative consolidation theories. The income distribution schedule (known as the IDS) is a set of T accounts that distributes income between the minority and controlling interest. It also provides a useful check function to assure that all intercompany eliminations are accounted for properly. Covering these chapters will provide the student with all topics needed for the CPA Exam. In fact, Chapter 5 goes beyond the current content of the exam. The exam is very limited in its coverage of intercompany bonds and has not tested intercompany leases despite their popularity in practice as of the publication date of this text.

With regard to the alternative worksheet methods and why we follow the approaches we do: First, consider the method used to record the investment in the subsidiary's and the parent's books. There are two key points of general agreement. The first is that it doesn't really matter which method is used since the investment account is eliminated! Second, when the course is over a student should know how to handle each method:

simple equity, full (we call it sophisticated) equity, and cost. The real issue is which method is the easiest one to learn first. We believe the winner is simple equity since it is totally symmetric with the equity accounts of the subsidiary. It simplifies elimination of subsidiary equity against the investment account. Every change in subsidiary equity is reflected, on a pro rata basis, in the parent's investment account. Thus, the simple equity method becomes the mainline method of the text. We teach the student to convert investments maintained under the cost method to the simple equity method. In practice, most firms and the majority of the problems in the text use the cost method. This means that the simple equity method is employed to solve problems that begin as either simple equity or cost method problems.

We also cover the sophisticated equity method which amortizes the excess of cost or book value through the investment account. This method should also adjust for intercompany profits through the investment account. The method is cumbersome because it requires the student to deal with amortizations of excess and intercompany profits in the investment account before getting to the consolidated worksheet, which is designed to handle these topics. You end up teaching consolidating procedures without the benefit of a worksheet! We cover this method after the student is proficient with a worksheet and the other methods. Thorough understanding of the sophisticated method is important so that it can be applied to influential investments that are not consolidated.

The second major concern among advanced-text professors has to do with the worksheet style used. There are three choices: the horizontal (trial balance) format, the vertical (stacked) method, and the balance sheet only. Again, we do cover all three, but our mainline method is the horizontal format. Horizontal is by far the most appealing to students. They have used it in both introductory and intermediate accounting. It is also the most likely method to be found in practice. On this basis, we use it initially to develop all topics. We do cover the vertical format, but not until the student is proficient with the horizontal format. There is no difference in the elimination entries; only the worksheet logistics differ. It takes only one problem assignment to teach the students this approach so they are prepared for its possible appearance on the CPA Exam. The balance-sheet-only format has no reason to exist other than its use as a CPA Exam testing shortcut. We cover it in an appendix.

Chapter 6 (Chapter 8 in the fifth edition) is more critical for those entering practice than it is for the CPA Exam. It contains cash flow for consolidated firms, taxation issues, and the use of the sophisticated equity method for influential investments. Taxation is the most difficult topic in consolidation, especially where the parent and subsidiary are taxed separately as opposed to filing a consolidated return. Every intercompany transaction is a tax allocation issue. Teaching the tax allocation issues with every topic as it is introduced is very confusing to students. We prefer to have the students fully understand worksheet procedures without taxes and then introduce taxes.

BUSINESS COMBINATIONS— SPECIALIZED TOPICS (CHAPTERS 7, 8, AND APPENDICES)

These chapters deal with topics that occasionally surface in practice and have not appeared on the CPA Exam for over 10 years. Studying these chapters perfects the students' understanding of consolidations and stockholders' equity accounting, thus affording a valuable experience. Chapter 7 (Chapter 6 in the fifth edition) deals with piecemeal acquisitions of an investment in a subsidiary, sale of the parent's investment, and the impact of preferred stock in the subsidiary's equity structure. Chapter 8 deals with the impact of subsidiary equity transactions including stock dividends, sale of common stock shares, and subsidiary reacquisitions of shares. The chapter also considers indirect or three-tier ownership structures and reciprocal holdings where the subsidiary owns parent shares.

The Appendices to the Consolidations Chapters should not be dismissed from the study plan for a semester. The material on alternative consolidation theories is conceptually important. It summarizes the FASB's 1991 Discussion Memorandum and compares alternative theories to current practice. Studying it reinforces the students' understanding and prepares them for changes that may occur. The students enjoy this material more than any other in consolidations. We are really pleased with how well our techniques adapt to alternative theories.

The other topic in the Appendices is accounting for leveraged buyouts. This is a popular topic and is easily mastered using consolidation techniques. Students enjoy mastering it since it is a common business phenomenon that sounds difficult but really isn't. It particularly appeals to students with an interest in financial management.

MULTINATIONAL ACCOUNTING (CHAPTERS 9–11)

As business has developed beyond national boundaries, the discipline of accounting also has evolved internationally. As our global economy develops, so does the demand for reliable and comparable financial information. Chapter 9 discusses the international accounting environment and compares accounting principles among several countries. This comparison illustrates the need for the harmonization of accounting standards. Approaches to the harmonization of standards and the various organizations involved are identified. Chapter 10 discusses accounting for foreign currency transactions. The basic mechanics of exchange rates and the business risks resulting from exchange rate changes are set forth. The use of forward contracts as a hedge against rate change fluctuations is discussed and the accounting for such hedges is demonstrated. Chapter 11 demonstrates the remeasurement and/or translation of a foreign entity's financial statements into a U.S. investor's currency. Whenever possible, examples of footnote disclosure relating to international accounting issues are presented.

SPECIAL REPORTING CONCERNS (CHAPTERS 12 AND 13)

The utility of financial information is increased if it is communicated on a timely basis. Therefore, interim financial statements and reporting requirements have become widely accepted. In Chapter 12 the concept of an interim period as an integral part of a larger annual accounting period is set forth as a basis for explaining the specialized accounting principles of interim reporting. Particular attention is paid to the determination of the interim income tax provision including the tax implications of net operating losses. The topic of segmental reporting is also discussed in Chapter 12 and the various disclosure requirements as well. A worksheet format for developing segmental data is used, and students are able to review the segmental footnote disclosure for a large public company.

In Chapter 13 students are given a comprehensive discussion of the disclosure of earnings per share data. Supporting schedules are used to facilitate the calculation of per share amounts. The calculation of primary earnings per share is developed, and then with that background, students are exposed to the calculation of fully diluted earnings per share. The chapter concludes with a comprehensive illustration dealing with the calculation of both primary and fully diluted earnings per share.

ACCOUNTING FOR PARTNERSHIPS (CHAPTERS 14 AND 15)

Chapters 14 and 15 take the student through the entire life cycle of a partnership beginning with formation and ending in liquidation. Although new forms of organization such as the limited liability corporation are available, partnerships continue to be a common form of organization. Practicing accountants must be aware of the characteristics of this form of organization and the unique accounting principles. The accounting aspects of profit and loss agreements, changes in the composition of partners (admissions and withdrawals), and partnership liquidations are fully illustrated. In addition to accounting principles, certain income tax principles relating to partnerships are set forth. The end-of-chapter material in this area focuses on evaluating various alternative strategies available to partners, for example, deciding whether it would be better to liquidate a partnership or admit a new partner.

GOVERNMENTAL AND NOT-FOR-PROFIT ACCOUNTING (CHAPTERS 16–19)

Chapters 16 and 17 have been updated to include recent Governmental Accounting Standards Board (GASB) pronouncements. Chapter 16 includes a complete discussion of measurement focus and basis of accounting issues for state and local governments. The deferral of GASB Statement No. 11 and the issues involved in its implementation are outlined for the reader.

In Chapter 16 we introduce the unique accounting and financial reporting issues of state and local governments. The chapter also covers the basics of accounting and financial reporting for the general fund and the two account groups. This order emphasizes the "working capital" focus of the general fund and the resulting need to account for fixed assets and long-term liabilities elsewhere.

Chapter 17 covers the accounting and financial reporting of the specialized funds of government: those established to account for restricted operating resources, long-term construction projects or acquisition of major fixed assets, and servicing of principal and interest on long-term debt. The chapter also covers the unique accounting issues of various trust funds and proprietary (business-type) funds.

Chapters 18 and 19 have been completely rewritten to include recent Financial Accounting Standards Board (FASB) standards on accounting and financial reporting for such organizations as private not-for-profit health care entities, private universities, and voluntary health and welfare organizations. The new FASB standards represent the most comprehensive change in the history of financial reporting by not-for-profit organizations. The standards define how the resources of a private not-for-profit organization are to be divided into unrestricted, temporarily restricted, or permanently restricted net asset classifications. Financial statements also are based on net asset classifications. A statement of cash flows is now required. The new standards represent a shift away from fund accounting to organization-wide financial reporting. As such, they supersede sections of the existing individual industry audit guides that have been accepted as generally accepted accounting practices to date.

In Chapter 18 we provide an overall summary of the new accounting and financial reporting standards as they apply to all not-for-profit organizations. We then offer a complete description of accounting and illustrations of the financial reports of public universities. Since the GASB has not changed accounting for public universities, these organizations will continue to follow the AICPA audit guidance. The next section in this chapter illustrates accounting and financial reporting for private not-for-profits following the new FASB guidance. For ease of presentation, these illustrations are presented without regard to a fund structure. However, since the new FASB guidance does not preclude funds-based reporting, an appendix is included incorporating the new standards within the existing funds structure. This gives the instructor the option of teaching the material for private universities with or without funds.

Chapter 19 covers accounting and financial reporting for health care entities and voluntary health and welfare organizations. The chapter also incorporates for each type of organization the most recent FASB standards in addition to existing AICPA audit guidance that has not been superseded. In this chapter, funds are viewed as internal control and management tools. External financial statements are illustrated without a funds structure. As in Chapter 18, however, a funds-based illustration is included in the appendix for both health care organizations and voluntary health and welfare organizations.

FIDUCIARY ACCOUNTING (CHAPTERS 20 AND 21)

The role of estate planning and the use of trusts are important to many individuals and present some unique accounting principles. The tax implications of estate planning are discussed so that the student has a basic understanding of this area. Various accounting reports necessary for the administration of an estate or trust are illustrated in Chapter 20.

No business is immune from financial difficulty. Chapter 21 discusses various responses to such difficulties including: troubled debt restructuring, quasi-reorganizations, corporate liquidations, and corporate reorganizations.

SUPPLEMENTARY MATERIALS

The materials supporting this text include a solutions manual, transparencies, an examination book, and templates, with solutions, for use with Lotus 1-2-3. For the student, the STUDENT COMPANION ENRICHMENT MANUAL, which includes a study guide and preprinted consolidation working papers, is available.

FOR THE INSTRUCTOR

Solutions Manual. The manual accompanying this text provides descriptions of all exercises and problems with their estimated completion time. The manual contains answers to all end-of-chapter questions and solutions to all exercises and problems, along with the logic for the solutions when appropriate. In particular, answers to multiple-choice questions include supporting explanations and computations.

Transparencies. The set of transparencies contains blank worksheets, solutions for all of the consolidation problems, and selected solutions from the remainder of the text.

Examination Book. The test bank contains multiple-choice questions and examination problems for each chapter along with the solutions. These materials may be reproduced by the instructor.

Templates. Both student and solution templates for use with Lotus 1-2-3 are available. They are accompanied by problem instructions in ASCII form for easy conversion to most word processing programs. The templates are for use with selected nonconsolidation chapters as well as the consolidation chapters. General instructions and a complete summary of the problems are provided. The diskettes are for use with IBM hardware.

FOR THE STUDENT

Student Companion Enrichment Manual.
This book is composed of three main sections: the Text Companion (TC), the Enrichment (E), and the Study Guide (SG). Reproduced on removable pages within the TC are the ends of Chapters 2–8 plus appendix worksheets to allow the students easy reference as they study the related text narrative. Also in the TC section are several supporting examples, diagrams, and illustrations to assist understanding of complex topics. The E section contains coverage of branch accounting and the SEC as background information for the students. The SG section contains a detailed outline and several learning activities (such as true/false, multiple choice, matching, and short problems) for each chapter of the text. The solutions for these activities appear at the end of the section. The SG material assists students in their mastery of subject areas.

Working Papers for Consolidations. The working papers for solving the consolidation problems in Chapters 2–8 and Chapter 11 contain pre-printed trial balances as a means of saving time. The pages are bound in a single volume and are perforated for easy removal. Blank worksheets are included at the end for extra assignments. These may be duplicated if more are needed.

ACKNOWLEDGMENTS

On this, our sixth edition, we are grateful to Rita Cheng of the University of Wisconsin—Milwaukee for her work as a consulting editor on the governmental and not-for-profit chapters. We appreciate her depth of knowledge in these areas and the new ideas that she has brought to the text.

Special appreciation and acknowledgment is due to Carol Fischer, Jill Patten, and Vivian Adashek. Their meticulous proofing aided the revision of the text by detecting errors and inconsistencies.

To our families and friends for their understanding, support, and tolerance, we are truly thankful.

Thank you to the following educators who, through reviews, have provided pertinent information for improving the text: Gene Bucciarelli, Golden Gate University; Chula G. King, University of West Florida; David Medved, Detroit College of Business; David Meeting, Cleveland State University; Thomas Schaefer, Florida State University; and John Sherman, University of Texas at Dallas.

Many colleagues in the teaching profession have been generous in devoting their time and talents as verifiers of the text's ancillaries. In particular, we wish to acknowledge the contributions of: Joseph Botana, Lakeland College; Michael Chase, California State University—Long Beach; John Cheever, California Polytechnic State University; Mary L. Fischer, University of Texas at Tyler; Daniel Flaherty, University of Texas of the Permian Basin; Philip Kentzele, Central Michigan University; Kenneth Macur, University of Wisconsin—Whitewater; David Medved, Detroit College of Business; Walter Moore, Cleveland State University; and Bruce Swindle, McNeese State University.

Thank you to Eric Carlsen, Kean College of New Jersey; Richard Griffin, University of Tennessee at Martin; Lucille Montondon, Southwest Texas State University; Ronald Pawliczek, Boston College; and Walter K. Rutledge, University of West Florida—for their special efforts in revising and improving the test bank.

We would like to thank the South-Western College Publishing Accounting Team for their dedication throughout the entire publishing process. Their passion for excellence helped us attain the highest level of quality and accuracy.

To all who have communicated with us either directly or through South-Western with feedback, thank you. We welcome questions, suggestions, and comments from all users of this text as we endeavor to provide you with the highest-quality materials.

Paul M. Fischer
William James Taylor

About the Authors

William James Taylor primarily teaches financial accounting and auditing at both the undergraduate and graduate levels. In addition he is involved in teaching a CPA review course and continuing professional education seminars. He has been recognized for his teaching excellence and has received both the Amoco Outstanding Professor Award and the School of Business Administration Advisory Council Teaching Award. He earned his PhD from Georgia State University and is a CPA. His professional experience includes working for Deloitte and Touche and Arthur Andersen & Co. in their audit practices. His private consulting activities include business valuations, litigation services, and issues affecting closely held businesses.

Dr. Taylor is actively involved in the Wisconsin Institute of Certified Public Accountants and chairs several task forces dealing with the 150-hour educational requirement and minority issues. He is also a member of the American Institute of CPAs and the American Accounting Association. He serves as a director and officer for a number of organizations.

Paul M. Fischer is the Jerry Leer Professor of Accounting at the University of Wisconsin—Milwaukee. He teaches intermediate and advanced financial accounting and has received both the AMOCO Outstanding Professor Award and the School of Business Administration Advisory Council Teaching Award. He also teaches CPA review classes and continuing education classes, and provides executive training courses for several large corporations. He earned his undergraduate accounting degree at Milwaukee and earned an MBA and PhD at the University of Wisconsin—Madison. Dr. Fischer is a CPA and is a member of the American Institute of CPAs, the Wisconsin Institute of CPAs and the American Accounting Association. He is a past president of the Midwest Region of the American Accounting Association.

Dr. Fischer has previously authored Cost Accounting: Theory and Applications (with Frank), Financial Dimensions of Marketing Management (with Crissy and Mossman), journal articles, and computer software. He actively pursues research and consulting interests in the areas of leasing, pension accounting, and business combinations.

Contents in Brief

Contents

PART 1

Combined Corporate Entities and Consolidations

The acquisition of one business by another is one of the most common types of major financial transactions. In some cases, a firm may obtain control over another firm by acquiring all of the assets and liabilities of another firm and merge the assets and liabilities into its own chart of accounts. This is viewed as a "direct asset acquisition" and is studied in Chapter 1. Once properly recorded, the transactions of both the predecessor firms are recorded on the single set of remaining books. Financial statements automatically reflect the operations of the new combined firm.

When one firm acquires control of another, it is more common to treat the acquisition as an investment on the parent company books and to allow the subsidiary to retain its own accounting records. This means that there still will be two accounting entities, each with its own accounting statements. When the level of ownership indicates that control has been achieved, accounting theory dictates that the separate statements be consolidated into a single set of financial statements. Worksheet procedures are developed in this text to derive consolidated statements from the separate statements of a parent and its subsidiary. The accountant must deal with procedures to handle the intercompany investment and the wide variety of intercompany transactions that may continue to occur between the parent and the subsidiary.

CHAPTER 1

Introduction to Business Combinations

The acquisition of one firm by another has been a common business transaction since the beginning of commercial activity. Business acquisitions are, in essence, a group purchase of assets for a single price. The magnitude of many transactions draws the attention of the business press. Generally, the public has viewed business combinations as being sound business practice which create economies of scale. There have, however, been some "dark sides" to business combinations. The first problem began during the 1940s when alternative methods started to evolve to record business combinations. Recording combinations as a purchase versus a pooling of interests led to dramatic differences in financial reports and began to build skepticism.

There have been many waves of business combination activity in the past 100 years. There were periods of increased levels of combinations in the 1890s, the 1920s, and the 1960s as many prosperous firms attempted to achieve greater domination of their industry. There was a decline in combination activity in the 1970s. This was very likely due to several factors including the recession of the period, energy shortages, and inflation. The 1980s into the early 1990s has been termed by many to be a period of "merger mania." Combining with other firms was defended as being critical to economic survival. Smaller firms felt the need to better position themselves to deal with large domestic firms as well as the onslaught of foreign competition. There are, however, concerns that the high prices paid in some business combinations may place a real burden on the acquiring firm. In addition, there can be an adverse impact on the national economy caused by possible lower employment, reduced research and development activities, and an increased vulnerability to poor decision-making due to a reduced number of key executives.[1] Consider the acquisition of American

---

[1]Henry F. Meyers, "The Outlook: Will Mergers Help or Hurt in the Long Run?" *Wall Street Journal*, May 2, 1988.

Motors by the Chrysler Corporation. This combination reduced the number of large American automakers from four to three and had a devastating impact on the economy of southeastern Wisconsin. For those reasons and others, many combinations are not desired by the management of the acquired firm. A whole series of strategies have evolved to thwart hostile takeovers.

The accountant may be involved in various activities surrounding a business combination. Accountants often will do a "preacquisition audit" to confirm the existence and value of the assets and liabilities of the target firm (firm to be acquired). Frequently, the accountant will aid the buyer or seller in arriving at a tentative price. The accountant will advise the client on how to structure the transaction to achieve the desired tax and financial reporting objectives. Finally, the transaction must be recorded in a manner that conforms to generally accepted accounting principles and must present the effects of the combination in the accounting statements of the current and subsequent periods.

ECONOMIC ADVANTAGES OF COMBINATIONS

A business combination is often a group acquisition of all of the assets of another firm. In most cases the acquiring firm also assumes the liabilities of the acquired firm and pays them as they become due. Assets acquired as a part of the combination usually are recorded at fair market value. It is common that the price paid for the entire firm will exceed the sum of the separate asset market values. This extra payment is considered the purchase of goodwill. The payment normally is based on the expectation that the future income of the acquired firm is higher than normal for its type of industry. *Goodwill* is an intangible asset that should be amortized over its anticipated useful life.

Savings may result from the elimination of duplicative assets. Perhaps both firms will utilize common facilities and share fixed costs. There may be economies of scale as one management team replaces two separate sets of managers. It may be possible to better coordinate production, marketing, and administrative actions. *Horizontal combinations* involve those where competitors serving similar functions hope to economize by combining similar functions. *Vertical combinations* involve firms that were at different levels in the marketing chain, such as a manufacturer acquiring a wholesaler that will market its goods. The intended benefit here is the closer coordination of the different level of activities in a given industry.

Perhaps the most universal economic benefit in business combinations is the possible tax advantages. The owners of a small business, whether sole proprietors, partners, or shareholders, may wish to retire from the active management of their firm. If they were to sell their interest for cash or accept debt instruments, they would have an immediate taxable gain. If, however, they accept common stock of another firm in exchange for their interest and carefully structure the transaction, they may account for the transaction as a tax-free exchange. No taxes are paid until they ultimately sell the shares received in the combination. The shares received are recorded, for tax purposes, at the book value of the interest traded for the shares.

Further tax advantages exist when the firm to be acquired has reported losses on its tax returns in prior periods. Section 172 (b) of the Internal Revenue Code provides that operating losses can be carried back three years to obtain a refund of taxes paid in previous years. Should the loss not be offset by income in the three prior years, the loss may be carried forward fifteen years to offset future taxable income, thus eliminating or reducing income taxes that would otherwise be payable. These loss maneuvers have little or no value to a target firm that has not had income in the three prior years and does not expect profitable operations in the near future. However, tax losses are transferable in a business combination. To an acquiring firm that has had profit in the three prior years and/or expects profitable periods in the near future, the tax losses of a target firm may have real value. That value, viewed as an asset by the acquiring firm, will be reflected in the price paid. However, the acquiring firm must exercise caution in anticipating the benefits of tax loss carryovers. The realization of the tax benefits may be denied if it can be shown that the primary motivation for the combination was the transfer of the tax loss benefit.

There also may be a tax benefit in a subsequent period as a single consolidated tax return is filed by the single remaining corporation. The losses of one of the affiliated firms can be used to offset the net income of another affiliated firm to lessen the taxes that would otherwise be paid by the profitable firm. In some cases, there may be disadvantages to filing as a consolidated firm. Firms with low incomes may fare better being taxed separately due to the progressive income tax rate structure. The marginal tax rate of each firm may be lower than that resulting when the incomes of the two firms are combined.[2]

OBTAINING CONTROL

Control of another firm may be achieved by either an asset or a stock acquisition. In an asset acquisition, *all* the firm's assets are acquired *directly* from the company. In most cases, existing liabilities of the acquired firm also are assumed. When assets are acquired and liabilities are assumed, we refer to the transaction as an acquisition of "net assets." Payment could be made in cash, exchanged property, or issuance of either debt or equity securities. It is common to issue securities since it avoids depleting cash or other assets that may be needed in future operations. Legally, a *statutory consolidation* refers to the combining of two or more previously independent legal entities into one new legal entity. Each of the previous firms is dissolved and is replaced by a single continuing firm. A *statutory merger* refers to the absorption of one or more former legal entities into another firm that continues as the sole surviving legal entity. The absorbed firm ceases to exist as a legal entity but may continue as a division of the surviving firm.

In a *stock acquisition*, a controlling interest (more than 50%) of another company's voting common stock is acquired. The firm making the acquisition is

---

[2]See Chapter 6, "Taxation of Consolidated Firms," pages 360–368.

termed the *parent*, and the firm acquired is termed a *subsidiary*. Both the parent and the subsidiary remain separate legal entities and maintain their own financial records and statements. However, for external financial reporting purposes, the firms usually will combine their individual financial statements into a single set of statements called *consolidated statements*. Thus, a consolidation may refer to a special type of combination or, more commonly, to the consolidated statements of a parent and its subsidiary.

There may be several advantages to obtaining control by purchasing a controlling interest in stock. Most obvious is that the total cost is lower, since only a controlling interest in the assets, and not the total assets, must be acquired. In addition, control through stock ownership may be simpler to achieve since no formal negotiations or transactions with the acquired firm's management are necessary. Further advantages may result from maintaining the separate legal identity of the former firm. First of all, risk is lowered because the legal liability of any one corporation is limited to its own assets. Secondly, separate legal entities may be desirable when only one of the firms is subject to government control. Lastly, there may be tax advantages resulting from the preservation of the legal entities.

Stock acquisitions are said to be "friendly" when the stockholders of the target firm, as a group, decide to sell or exchange their shares. In such a case, an offer may be made to the board of directors by the acquiring firm. If the directors approve, they will recommend acceptance of the offer to the shareholders, who may approve the transaction. Often, a two-thirds vote is required. Once approval is gained, the exchange of shares will be made with the individual shareholders. Where the shareholders decline the offer or no offer is made, the acquiring firm may deal directly with individual shareholders in an attempt to secure a controlling interest. Frequently, the acquiring firm may make a formal *tender offer*. The tender offer, typically, will be published in newspapers and will offer a greater than market price for shares made available by a stated date. The acquiring firm may reserve the right to withdraw the offer if an insufficient number of shares are made available to it. Where management and/or a significant number of shareholders oppose the purchase of the firm by the intended buyer, the acquisition is viewed as *hostile*. Unfriendly offers are so common that there have evolved several standard defensive mechanisms. The common terms used to describe these defensive moves are:

Greenmail.   The target firm may pay a premium price ("greenmail") to purchase treasury shares. It may either buy shares already owned by a potential acquiring firm or purchase shares from a current owner who, it is feared, would sell to the acquiring firm. The price paid for these shares in excess of their market price may not be deducted from stockholders' equity; instead, it is expensed.[3]

---

[3]Financial Accounting Standards Board, FASB Technical Bulletin, Nos. 85 and 86, *Accounting for a Purchase of Treasury Shares at a Price Significantly in Excess of the Current Market Price of the Shares* and the *Income Statement Classification of Costs Incurred in Defending Against a Takeover Attempt* (Norwalk, CT, 1985).

White Knight.   The target firm locates a different firm to acquire a controlling interest. This could occur when the original acquiring firm is in a similar industry, and it is feared that current management of the target firm would be displaced. The replacement acquiring firm, the "white knight," might be in a different industry and could be expected to keep current management intact.

Poison Pill.   The "poison pill" involves the issuance of stock rights to existing shareholders to purchase additional shares at a price far below market value. However, the rights are exercisable only when an acquiring firm purchases or makes a bid to purchase a stated number of shares. The effect of the options is to substantially raise the cost to the acquiring firm. If the attempt fails, there is at least a greater gain for the original shareholders.

Selling the Crown Jewels.   This approach has the management of the target firm selling vital assets (the "crown jewels") of the target firm to others to make the firm less attractive to the acquiring firm.

Leveraged Buyouts.   The management of the existing target firm attempts to purchase a controlling interest in that firm. Often, substantial debt will be incurred to raise the funds needed to purchase the stock, hence the term "leveraged buyout." When bonds are sold to provide this financing, the bonds may be referred to as "junk bonds" since they are often high interest and high risk due to the thin equity of the resulting corporation.

Further protection against takeovers is offered by federal and state law. The Clayton Act of 1914 (section 7) is a federal law that prohibits business combinations in which "the effect of such acquisition may be substantially to lessen competition or to tend to create a monopoly." The Williams Act of 1968 is a federal law that regulates tender offers; it is enforced by the SEC. Several states also have enacted laws to discourage hostile takeovers. These laws are motivated, in part, by the fear of losing employment and taxes.

ACCOUNTING RAMIFICATIONS

When control is achieved through an asset acquisition, the acquiring firm records on its books the assets and assumed liabilities of the acquired firm. From the acquisition date on, all transactions of both the acquiring and acquired firm are recorded in one combined set of accounts. The only new skill one needs to master is the proper recording of the acquisition when it occurs. Once the initial acquisition is recorded properly, *subsequent accounting procedures are the same as for any single accounting entity.* Combined statements of the new larger firm for periods following the combination are automatic.

Accounting procedures are more involved when control is achieved through a stock acquisition. The controlling firm, the parent, will record only an investment account to reflect its interest in the controlled firm, the subsidiary.

Both the parent and the subsidiary remain separate legal entities with their own separate sets of accounts and separate financial statements. Accounting theory holds that where one firm has effective control over another, there is only one economic entity, and there should be only one set of financial statements that combines the activities of the entities under common control. The accountant will prepare a worksheet, referred to as the *consolidated worksheet*, that starts with the separate accounts of the parent and the subsidiary. Various adjustments and eliminations will be made on this worksheet to merge the separate accounts of the two firms into a single set of financial statements, the consolidated statements.

This chapter will discuss business combinations resulting from asset acquisitions, since the accounting principles are more easily understood in this context. The principles developed are applied directly to business combinations resulting from stock acquisitions that are studied in the chapters that follow. Our first mission is to understand the two basic theoretical models used to record business combinations, the *pooling* and the *purchase* methods. These two models apply to all business combinations where one firm achieves control over another, whether this control is achieved through an asset or a stock acquisition.

POOLING VS. PURCHASE

APB Opinion No. 16, *Business Combinations*, provides the basic principles for accounting for business combinations. The vast majority of combinations will be accounted for under the *purchase method*. Purchases are characterized as situations where one firm tends to achieve control over another, often displacing former owners and/or management. In essence, there has been a group purchase of assets which should be recorded at fair market value. In most cases, the price paid is clear; it will be the cash given or the fair market value of the equity or debt instruments issued. In some cases, the payment may be made using securities that have no clear market value. In these cases, the price will have to be inferred from the fair market value of the assets acquired. When the acquired firm has liabilities that will be assumed and later paid by the purchasing firm, these liabilities are recorded at their current market value based on current interest rates on the purchase date. Goodwill is recorded when the price paid exceeds the market value of the separate assets (minus liabilities assumed). Goodwill is, in theory, a payment for anticipated above-average earnings, and its cost should be amortized over the period of anticipated benefits. This amortization period should consider the underlying cause of the extra earnings. A reputation for "great service" will not last long if not maintained. A superior location advantage could, on the other hand, be very long lasting. It is customary to amortize goodwill on a straight-line basis. The maximum amortization period allowed is 40 years.

According to APB Opinion No. 16 (par. 47), the only exception to the accounting for a business combination as a purchase may apply to situations where the surviving company issues only voting common stock for all the assets of an acquired firm in an asset acquisition or issues only voting common stock for at least 90% of the voting common stock of the acquired firm in a stock acquisition. The term "pooling of interests" is used to describe the fusion of two separate stockholder groups into a single accounting entity. The exchange of voting common stock and meeting other required pooling criteria support the argument that *no sale has occurred*. Instead, the stockholders of the acquired firm are merely exchanging their interest in the former firm for an interest in the combined corporation. The absence of a sale means there is no cause to record market values for the assets received or the securities issued. The acquiring firm combines the book value of the acquired firm's assets and liabilities with its own. The only exceptions to maintaining those book values occur when lower market values are acknowledged according to the lower-of-cost-or-market rule, and changes in accounting principles may be made to afford consistency of accounting methods for the two former firms. The total paid-in capital of the acquired firm is assigned to the paid-in capital recorded for the shares issued by the acquiring firm. The retained earnings of the acquired firm is added to the retained earnings of the acquiring firm, except in some rare cases where it is needed to meet the par value requirements of the shares issued. (Detailed coverage of pooling of interest requirements and accounting procedures is presented later in this chapter.)

EFFECT ON FUTURE STATEMENTS

The consequences of the purchase versus pooling methods on the accounting statements may be very pronounced. The following chart compares the impact of the two accounting methods on future balance sheets of the combined company:

Item	Purchase Method	Pooling Method
1. Assets and liabilities of acquired firm	Recorded at current fair market values with a possibility of goodwill.	Recorded at book value of acquired firm (a). No additional goodwill acknowledged (b).
2. Equity securities issued	Market value of shares issued is added to paid-in capital.	Paid-in capital of acquired firm is assigned as paid-in value of shares issued (c).
3. Retained earnings of acquired firm	Not acknowledged.	Added to retained earnings (c).

(a)   Where the book values of assets exceed fair market value, the assets are recorded at the lower fair market value, and the retained earnings of the acquired firm is reduced.

(b)   Goodwill previously recorded by the acquired firm would be recorded at its remaining book value.

(c)   The retained earnings of the acquired firm may be reduced to meet the issuer's par or stated value requirement.

Future income statements are affected by the differing values assigned to assets under the purchase and pooling methods. The purchase method will record individual assets at fair market values that exceed book values that would be recorded under the pooling method. The higher market values will lead to higher depreciation charges in future periods. In most cases the added depreciation cannot be deducted for tax purposes. The purchase method usually will require the recording of goodwill that must be amortized over a period not to exceed 40 years for financial reporting purposes. Before 1993, goodwill usually was not deductible for tax purposes. However, with the enactment of Section 197 as part of the 1993 Omnibus Budget Reconciliation Act, goodwill is now deductible for tax purposes over a 15-year period. This provision applies to purchases after July 10, 1990.[4] Consider the following income statement comparison resulting from the use of the purchase versus the pooling method:

	Purchase	Pooling
Revenue	$250,000	$250,000
Less:		
All expenses other than depreciation on acquired firm's assets and goodwill amortization	100,000	100,000
Depreciation of acquired firm's building:		
Purchase, 1/10 of $500,000 fair market value	50,000	
Pooling, 1/10 of $200,000 net book value		20,000
Goodwill amortization:		
Purchase, $250,000 divided by anticipated life of 10 years	25,000	
Pooling—no goodwill created		0
Net income	$ 75,000	$130,000

The major difference in the above incomes is caused solely by the recognition of fair market values in a purchase and the likely recording of goodwill in a purchase. Remember that, in most cases, the added depreciation charges are not tax deductible and thus, the differences in income caused by depreciation are not reduced to an "after tax" amount.

A common measure of a firm's profitability is the return on assets statistic. This is calculated by dividing net income by total assets. Return on assets can be doubly inflated for a pooling of interests. First, income is inflated by lower depreciation charges and a lack of goodwill amortization. Second, the asset values usually are understated since they are recorded at historical cost. The combination of greater income and lesser asset values may overstate severely the return on assets under a pooling as compared to the purchase method.

It is possible that past purchase accounting rules provide an advantage to foreign corporations that compete with domestic corporations to purchase U.S. companies. Prior to 1993 the United States was unique among major nations in

---

[4]Section 197 of the Internal Revenue Code.

that it required the amortization of goodwill but did not allow a tax deduction for it. Other countries either allowed a tax deduction for the amortization or did not require amortization. This put domestic acquiring firms at a competitive disadvantage. Their future incomes from the acquired firm were less than those of a foreign buyer; thus, the price they could afford to pay for a firm might have been less. This may help to explain why foreign acquisitions of U.S. corporations have increased dramatically in recent years.[5] The upsurge in combinations activity after the tax law change of firms acquiring others that offer long-term synergy (e.g., Northrop-Grumman and GE-Kemper) may be an offshoot of this effect.

The income statements of both the current and prior periods also benefit from the retroactive application of the pooling concept. If a company purchases another firm midway through the year, it may add to its own income only the purchased firm's income from the purchase date to year-end. In a pooling, income may be added for the entire year no matter when during the year the combination occurred. When a purchase occurs, the prior years' comparative statements of the acquiring firm do not include the income of the acquired firm. In a pooling, prior years' comparative statements of the acquiring firm are restated to include the income of the acquired firm. (Additional information on the effects of purchases and poolings on financial statements will be covered at the end of the chapter.)

EXPENSES TO ACCOMPLISH A COMBINATION

There may be significant expenses involved in negotiating and consummating a business combination. There are three categories of expenses:

1. Direct acquisition costs—These are payments made to third parties for costs such as audit and legal expenses.
2. Indirect acquisition costs—These are allocations of internal costs that probably would have existed without a combination but reflect management time allocated to acquisition activities.
3. Security issuance costs—These include bond and stock issue costs incurred by the decision to use securities rather than cash as consideration.

Purchase accounting rules add the direct acquisition costs to the price paid for the acquired firm. It is a cost necessary to purchase the assets, much like legal fees incurred to buy real estate, and should be added to the cost of the assets purchased. Indirect acquisition costs are hard to attribute directly to the combination and must be expensed when incurred. The cost of issuing securities is deducted from the value assigned to the debt or equity securities issued. This is the normal procedure for issue costs, and it remains unchanged in a purchase.

Pooling rules require that all three types of costs be expensed at the time of the combination. Since no sale is considered to have occurred, there is no basis upon which to increase asset values. The stock issued is viewed as a continuation of the original shares. The likely account used for all expenses connected with a pooling would be Professional Service Expenses.

---

[5]See Chapters 9–11 for additional information regarding international accounting implications.

SUMMARY

If given a choice, most firms would choose to account for combinations under the pooling method. Where assets are undervalued and/or goodwill exists, the pooling method will produce higher incomes and a higher return on assets in future years. In addition, the balance sheet of the continuing firm is enhanced when the retained earnings of the acquired firm is added to existing retained earnings. The only likely disadvantage of the pooling method is that acquired assets may not be shown on the balance sheet at their full value. Therefore, the total worth of the combined firms may be considerably less than would have resulted under the purchase method. There are a limited number of cases where a firm may not prefer the pooling method. This may occur in acquisitions of firms with low or negative amounts of income and retained earnings.

Even with these advantages of the pooling method, it is difficult to justify its continued use. The distortions it causes, as compared to the purchase method, are disturbing to many accountants and financial analysts. It seems that the careful structuring of an acquisition to meet arbitrary criteria (see pages 27–32) is a shallow excuse for ignoring the true value of the assets over which control is achieved. It should be noted that the United States is the only country of the ten major industrial nations that allows the use of the pooling method for business combinations.[6]

Prior to the issuance of APB Opinion No. 16 in 1970, firms frequently chose the pooling method even though the transactions did not have the characteristics of a pooling. As a result, APB Opinion No. 16 provided very restrictive criteria for the use of the pooling method. All combinations not meeting the criteria must be accounted for as purchases. Thus, there are no criteria for the use of the purchase method in accounting for combinations other than the failure to have the combinations qualify as poolings. If the pooling method is desired by the acquiring firm, the combination must be structured carefully in order to be classified as such. Currently, very few combinations meet the criteria. In recent years, under 10% of the firms surveyed in *Accounting Trends and Techniques* used the pooling method.[7] Coverage of the application of the more popular purchase method is presented below and is followed by coverage of the criteria and application of the pooling method.

ASSET ACQUISITION AS A PURCHASE

When the acquisition of an existing company's assets is being considered, the current value of the firm's assets and the amount of its liabilities must be appraised carefully. Such an evaluation usually precedes negotiations. Generally, the prospective purchaser will seek permission to conduct a pre-

[6]Choi and Mueller, *International Accounting* (New York: Prentice-Hall, 1984), p. 74.
[7]Jack Shohet and Richard Rikert, eds., *Accounting Trends and Techniques*, 47th ed. (New York: American Institute of Certified Public Accountants, 1993), p. 53.

acquisition audit to determine whether all assets and liabilities are recorded properly. The purchaser knows that, while book values may be indicative of the current value of some current assets, these values may not represent a reasonable market value for inventories, plant assets, or intangibles. Inventories priced on a LIFO basis will have little relationship to current market value. Inventories priced on a FIFO or average cost basis may be closer to market value but may still depart significantly when prices fluctuate quickly. Plant assets and intangibles are presented at historical cost less an arbitrary depreciation or amortization allowance, with no relationship to current market value. Even liabilities to be assumed may not be stated at their current market value in light of changes in market interest rates. For example, 10-year bonds issued at par 4 years ago when the prevailing interest rate was 8% now would sell at a premium if the current market rate of interest is 6%.

Acknowledging the limitations of book values, the purchaser may engage an independent consultant to estimate the current market values of the assets to be acquired and the liabilities to be assumed. Market values are an estimate of the price to which a willing buyer and seller would agree. These estimates provide only a guide to establishing the price to be paid for the entire firm.

Assume that Acquisitions Inc. is considering the purchase of Jacobs Company and has secured the following audited condensed balance sheet:

Jacobs Company			
Balance Sheet			
December 31, 19X3			
Accounts receivable ...	$ 20,000	Current liabilities.................	$ 20,000
Inventory.............	40,000	Capital stock 1,000 shares $10 par..	10,000
Land.................	10,000	Paid-in capital in excess of par.....	50,000
Buildings (net)	40,000	Retained earnings................	50,000
Equipment (net).......	20,000		
Total assets...........	$130,000	Total liabilities and equity	$130,000

Aware of the deficiencies of book values, management obtains the following appraisal of market values:

Accounts receivable...........................	$ 20,000
Inventory.....................................	45,000
Land...	10,000
Buildings	50,000
Equipment....................................	40,000
Current liabilities	(20,000)
Total market value of net assets	$145,000

If the market values are accurate, Acquisitions Inc. will expect to pay at least $145,000 for the net assets (total assets less liabilities assumed) of Jacobs Company. The purchase of net assets means that Acquisitions Inc. will assume the liabilities of Jacobs Company. Perhaps a deal could be struck for less than $145,000, but, very likely, more will be paid. Acquisitions may be willing to pay a premium for Jacobs' assets, since Jacobs is a functioning firm with an established trade. If the assets were purchased individually from other sources, time would be required to combine them into a viable, profitable firm. The payment for this advantage is considered the purchase of goodwill. The amount of the payment depends on the expected future profitability of the assets to be acquired and the outcome of the negotiating process.

CALCULATING AND RECORDING GOODWILL

The purchaser may attempt to estimate the value of goodwill in order to arrive at a logical purchase price. Goodwill is a payment for above-normal expected future earnings. An estimate of future income may be made by projecting recent years' incomes into the future. When this is done, it is important to factor out "one time" occurrences that will not likely reoccur in the near future. Examples would include the cumulative effect of changes in accounting principles, extraordinary items, discontinued operations, or any other unusual event. Expected future income is compared to "normal" income. Normal income is the product of the appropriate industry rate of return on assets times the fair market value of the assets of the acquired firm (not including goodwill). The following calculation of earnings in excess of normal might be made for Jacobs Company:

Expected average future income.		$ 21,000
Less normal return on assets:		
Market value of total identifiable assets	$165,000	
Industry normal rate of return	10%	
Normal return on assets.		16,500
Expected annual earnings in excess of normal.		$ 4,500

There are several methods that use the expected annual earnings in excess of normal to estimate goodwill. A common approach is to pay for a given number of years' excess earnings. For instance, Acquisitions might offer to pay for 4 years of excess earnings, which would total $18,000. Alternatively, the excess earnings could be viewed as an annuity. The most optimistic purchaser might expect the excess earnings to continue forever. If so, the buyer might capitalize the excess earnings as a perpetuity at the normal industry rate of return according to the following formula:

$$\text{Goodwill} = \frac{\text{Annual excess earnings}}{\text{Industry normal rate of return}}$$

$$= \frac{\$4,500}{.10}$$

$$= \$45,000$$

Another purchaser might feel that the factors producing excess earnings are of limited duration, such as 10 years, for example. This purchaser would calculate goodwill as follows:

Goodwill = discounted present value of a $4,500-per-year annuity for
            10 years at 10%
       = $4,500 × 10-years, 10% present value of annuity factor
       = $4,500 × 6.145
       = $27,653

Other purchasers might feel that the normal industry earning rate is appropriate only for tangible assets and not goodwill. Thus, they might capitalize excess earnings at a higher rate of return to reflect the higher risk inherent in goodwill.

All calculations of goodwill are estimates used to assist in the determination of the price to be paid for a firm. For example, Acquisitions might add the $27,653 estimate of goodwill to the $145,000 market value of Jacobs' other net assets to arrive at a tentative maximum price of $172,653. However, estimates of goodwill may differ from actual negotiated goodwill. If the final agreed-upon price for Jacobs' assets was $160,000, the actual negotiated goodwill would be $15,000, which is the price paid less the market value of the net assets acquired.

RECORDING A PURCHASE

To continue the previous example, assume that the combining firms agree to a value of $160,000 for Jacobs Company's net assets, including goodwill. If Acquisitions paid $1,000 in direct legal costs, this would raise the price paid for the net assets of Jacobs to $161,000, and the following entry would be made by Acquisitions to record the net asset purchase:

Accounts Receivable (market value)	20,000	
Inventory (market value)	45,000	
Land (appraised market value)	10,000	
Buildings (appraised market value)	50,000	
Equipment (appraised market value)	40,000	
Goodwill (price minus sum of net asset market values)	16,000	
Current Liabilities (market value)		20,000
Cash (includes direct acquisition costs)		161,000

Each identifiable asset and assumed liability is recorded at its estimated fair market value. Fixed assets are recorded at net market value with no accumulated depreciation since they are beginning as "new" assets to the acquiring firm. Goodwill is recorded at the negotiated price, which, again, is always the excess of the total consideration given for the net assets ($161,000 in the example) over the sum of the values assigned to all identifiable net assets acquired. If an acquired firm already has goodwill on its books, such goodwill is ignored except as it is confirmed by the purchase price. For example, if Jacobs Company had previously recorded goodwill of $25,000, Acquisitions still would assign $145,000 to the net identifiable assets and assign the extra $16,000 paid to the goodwill. In this case, only $16,000 of the $25,000 recorded former goodwill would be confirmed by the current purchase price.

It should be noted that the selling firm's entries do not parallel those of the purchaser. The seller records the removal of net assets at their book values. The excess of the price received for the net assets by the seller ($160,000)[8] over the sum of the net asset book values ($130,000 assets – $20,000 liabilities = $110,000) is recorded as a gain on the sale. In this case, the gain is $50,000. The entry on Jacobs' books would be:

Cash	160,000	
Current Liabilities	20,000	
Accounts Receivable		20,000
Inventory		40,000
Land		10,000
Buildings (net)		40,000
Equipment (net)		20,000
Gain on Sale		50,000

RECORDING BARGAIN PURCHASES

Occasionally, a firm will be purchased at a "bargain" price. A bargain price is a price that is less than the sum of the estimated market values of a firm's separate identifiable assets and liabilities. Naturally, when this situation occurs, any goodwill existing on the books of the seller is ignored since the price paid does not confirm it. The least reliable estimates of market values are assumed to be those applicable to long-lived assets because a ready market often does not exist for such assets. Consequently, according to APB Opinion No. 16 (par. 87), *all current assets, long-term investments in marketable securities, and liabilities assumed are recorded at their full market value, regardless of the total price paid for the firm.* Any excess of the sum of the market values of the net identifiable assets over the price paid is to be deducted only from long-lived assets other than investments in marketable securities.

For example, assume that Acquisitions Inc. acquired Jacobs Company by paying $132,000 ($152,000 total asset value – $20,000 of liabilities) to the seller and $1,000 for direct acquisition costs. The excess of the market value of the net assets over cost (often referred to as *negative goodwill*) would be determined as follows:

Total estimated market value of separate net assets	$145,000
Less price paid (including direct acquisition costs)	133,000
Excess of market value over cost	$ 12,000

---

[8]Remember, the $1,000 in direct costs is paid by the purchaser to a third party, not to the seller.

The excess must be deducted from the total estimated market value of the long-lived assets to arrive at the purchase cost assignable to these assets. The assignable cost then is allocated to the individual long-lived assets in proportion to their fair market values.

The total estimated market value of the long-lived assets and the percentage of the estimated market value of each of these assets to the total estimated market value are calculated first:

Asset	Estimated Market Value	Percent of Total Market Value
Land	$ 10,000	10%
Buildings.	50,000	50
Equipment	40,000	40
Total market value	$100,000	100%

The cost assignable to the long-lived assets is the $100,000 total market value less the $12,000 excess of market value over cost, or $88,000. This cost is assigned to the individual assets according to their relative market values as follows:

Asset	Percent of Total Market Value		Total Cost Assignable		Assigned Value
Land	10%	×	$88,000	=	$ 8,800
Buildings	50	×	88,000	=	44,000
Equipment	40	×	88,000	=	35,200
	100%				$88,000

The entry to record the bargain purchase is:

Accounts Receivable (market value)	20,000	
Inventory (market value).	45,000	
Land (assigned purchase cost).	8,800	
Buildings (assigned purchase cost)	44,000	
Equipment (assigned purchase cost).	35,200	
Cash (includes direct acquisition costs).		133,000
Current Liabilities (market value)		20,000

Occasionally, some long-lived assets are given current asset status and recorded at net realizable value, regardless of the price paid for the firm. This situation occurs only when the purchaser intends to sell these assets soon after the date of the combination, as in the case of acquired assets that duplicate those already owned by the purchaser.

Though a rare occurrence, the price paid for a firm could be less than the market value of the current assets and any long-term investment in marketable securities less liabilities. Since accounts in these three categories must be recorded at their market values, no value would remain to be assigned to long-lived assets. According to APB Opinion No. 16 (par. 91), the excess of the values assigned to the current assets, marketable securities, and liabilities over the price paid is to be recorded as a deferred credit in the account Excess of Market Value of Net Current Assets over Cost. The credit is to be amortized to income over a period not to exceed 40 years.

To illustrate this situation, assume that Acquisitions Inc. paid $30,000 for the net assets of Jacobs Company and paid $1,000 in direct acquisition costs. Since the market value of the net assets is $145,000, there is a bargain of $114,000 ($145,000 net assets at market – $31,000 total price for the net assets). The bargain exceeds the market value of the land, buildings, and equipment by $14,000 ($114,000 bargain – $100,000 combined market value of land, buildings, and equipment accounts). The remaining $14,000 bargain may not be subtracted from the remaining assets which must be recorded at market value. Instead, the remaining bargain becomes the deferred credit which will be amortized to income in future periods. The entry would be as follows:

Accounts Receivable (market value)	20,000	
Inventory (market value)	45,000	
Land (no value available)	0	
Buildings (no value available)	0	
Equipment (no value available)	0	
Cash (includes direct acquisition costs)		31,000
Current Liabilities (market value)		20,000
Excess of Market Value of Net Current Assets over Cost		14,000

In summary, when a bargain purchase occurs:

1. Current assets, long-term investments in marketable securities, and liabilities assumed always are recorded at fair market value.
2. Previously recorded goodwill on the seller's books is reduced to zero and no new goodwill exists.
3. Long-lived assets are recorded at fair market value less a reduction for the bargain.
4. A deferred credit is recorded only after *all* long-lived assets are reduced to *zero*. The deferred credit is amortized over a period of 40 years or less.

ALLOCATING THE PURCHASE PRICE—SPECIAL CONCERNS

There are several situations that may complicate the recording of a purchase. There may be long-term liabilities that need to be revalued based on market values that differ from the recorded amounts on the books of the selling firm. Also, there may be lease agreements to which the seller was a party that must be recorded. In addition, tax law may require the purchasing firm to use the selling firm's book value for depreciation on future tax returns instead of the higher market value on the purchase date. Furthermore, the firm purchased may have tax loss carryovers available to the purchasing firm which become one of the assets being acquired. Lastly, there may be contingent assets, liabilities, or asset impairments that exist on the purchase date. Each of these situations is examined separately.

Revaluation of Long-Term Liabilities.   Liabilities that are assumed by the buyer in a purchase transaction must also be recorded at their current market value. When interest rates have increased since the original issue of the debt, the market value of the debt will be less than book value and a discount will be recorded. If interest rates have decreased since issuance of the debt, the debt will have a value in excess of book value and a premium will be recorded. For large corporations with publicly traded debt securities, the market value of the debt is easily secured. In those cases where quoted market prices are not available, the current value of the debt instrument is imputed using the market rate of interest for similar debt instruments. Consider the following example of imputing the current value of an existing bond. The firm being acquired has outstanding a $100,000, 8% bond with 5 years remaining to maturity. Interest is paid annually each December 31. The acquisition date is January 1, 19X1. The current interest rate for a similar bond is 6%. The current value of the debt would be imputed:

Present value of interest payments at 6%
  ($8,000 annual interest × 5-year, 6% present value of annuity factor
  of 4.2124) . . . . $ 33,699
Present value of principal ($100,000 × 5-year present value factor of .7473)   74,730
Imputed market value of liability $108,429

The purchase entry would include the following credits:

Bonds Payable.   100,000
Premium on Bonds Payable   8,429

The premium will be amortized over the remaining 5-year term. Had the current interest rate exceeded the original face rate of 8%, the bonds would have a market value below $100,000, and a discount would result.

Lease Agreements.   As mentioned earlier, special analysis of the purchase price in a business combination is necessary when the firm acquired in a purchase transaction is bound contractually by existing leases as either a lessee or lessor. Sometimes, the terms of the lease may be modified as a result of the combination. These modifications would require the consent of a third party— either the lessor, when the selling firm is the lessee, or the lessee, when the selling firm is the lessor. When the terms of the lease are modified to the extent that a new lease is created, the new lease is classified and recorded according to the requirements of FASB Statement No. 13.[9] It is more common, however, to find that the contractual terms of a lease are not altered as a result of the purchase. In such cases, it is necessary to record only the market value of the seller's existing rights and obligations under the lease.

    When the firm acquired is a lessee under an operating lease, it has recorded rent as an expense but has not recorded any asset or long-term liability. Thus, there is no existing recorded asset or liability to adjust. At acquisition, if the

---

[9]Statement of Financial Accounting Standards No. 13, *Accounting for Leases* (Stamford, CT: Financial Accounting Standards Board, 1976), par. 9.

contractual rent under the remaining lease term is materially below fair market rental value, an asset should be recorded equal to the value of the rent savings. The asset should be amortized over the lease term as an adjustment to rent expense. If the contractual rent exceeds the market rental value, a liability should be credited, equal to the value of the excess rent, using an appropriate market interest rate. The liability should be amortized as a reduction of rent expense in future periods. Under both situations, future rent expense would reflect market rental value as of the date of the combination.[10]

When the acquired firm is a lessee under a capital lease, it has recorded the asset as well as the liability under that lease. At the time of the purchase, both the asset and the liability should be analyzed independently and recorded at their separate market values.

When the acquired firm is a lessor under an operating lease, it has recorded the cost of the leased asset less accumulated depreciation. In the purchase transaction, the asset should be recorded at its current market value. However, the market value may be based partly on the present value of the rents due under existing leases.

When the firm acquired is a lessor under a capital lease, it has recorded only a receivable due for future rents and perhaps an unguaranteed residual value. In the purchase transaction, the receivable should be recorded at its fair market value based on prevailing current interest rates. The unguaranteed residual value should be estimated and discounted to its present value, using the same current interest rate.

Nontaxable Exchanges.   The selling firm may wish to structure the purchase so as to avoid a taxable gain at the time of the combination. This is accomplished by exchanging the common stock of the purchasing firm for the assets of the selling firm. The owners of the selling firm do not record a gain for tax purposes until the shares received are sold. The purchasing firm in a nontaxable exchange inherits the book values of the assets purchased for use in future tax calculations. This means that only the net book value on the books of the selling firm may be used as the tax basis of the assets acquired when they are sold or depreciated later. This results in the recording of a deferred tax liability for the added tax burden caused by the inability of the purchasing firm to deduct the excess of the value assigned to the assets over the selling firm's book value.

As an example, assume that in a nontaxable exchange the tax basis of a given fixed asset is $50,000, and its fair market value at acquisition is $150,000. Depreciation on the $100,000 difference is not deductible on future tax returns. Therefore, if the purchasing firm is in a 35% tax bracket, there will be a $35,000 difference between what is recognized as tax expense and what is paid in taxes over the asset's depreciable life. The purchasing firm will record a deferred tax liability of $35,000 at the same time that it records the asset at $150,000. This tax

---

[10]Accounting Principles Board Opinion No. 16, *Business Combinations* (New York: American Institute of Certified Public Accountants, 1970), par. 88.

liability will be reversed in future periods when taxable income exceeds financial ("book") income because of the lack of deductibility for the depreciation on the $100,000 excess of market over book value. The goodwill arising in a nontaxable exchange is not deductible. This means that a deferred tax liability also arises applicable to the goodwill. Suppose that after recording all other assets and liabilities at market value, $65,000 of unallocated cost remains. The net of tax value of the goodwill is $65,000. Thus, the goodwill is recorded at a gross value of $100,000 ($65,000 ÷ .65) and a deferred tax liability of $35,000 is recorded.

Tax Loss Carryovers.   Tax law provides that a firm with a tax loss first may carry the loss back to the previous three years to offset income and thus receive a refund of taxes paid in the preceding years. If the loss exceeds income available in the prior three-year period, the loss can be carried forward up to fifteen years to offset future income and therefore reduce the taxes which otherwise would be paid. The selling firm may have unused tax loss carryovers which it has not been able to utilize due to an absence of sufficient income in prior years. This becomes a benefit for which the purchasing firm will pay. The purchaser is allowed to use the seller's tax loss carryovers to offset its own income in the current, prior, or if necessary, future periods. To the extent that the buyer can use the carryover to offset current income or income of the three prior years, the asset "tax refunds receivable" is recorded.

If the tax carryover is to be carried forward to offset future taxes, the asset Deferred Tax Expense is recorded. It is, however, necessary to attempt to determine whether there will be adequate future tax liabilities to consume the deferred tax asset. The accountant would have to consider existing evidence to make this determination. If it is likely (over 50% probability) that some or all of the deferred tax asset will not be realized, the contra-account Allowance for Unrealizable Tax Assets would be used to reduce the deferred tax asset to an estimated amount to be realized.[11] This may have the practical effect of the contra-account's totally offsetting the deferred tax asset to the extent that no net deferred tax asset is recorded. It may occur that the tax loss carryforward is considered in arriving at a purchase price and that value is given for it. Yet, it may be necessary to offset it with an allowance. The inability to record a net deferred tax asset often will result in the consideration paid for that asset being assigned to goodwill. This occurs because the price paid will exceed the value of the assets that are allowed to be recorded.

In a subsequent period, there may be evidence that the allowance for unrealizable tax assets is not needed since it is more likely that the asset will be realized. The allowance would be reduced in the period in which this information is available. The credit would be used first to reduce remaining goodwill recorded in the purchase. Any credit still remaining would be used to reduce other noncurrent intangible assets. If the credit cannot be absorbed by goodwill or

---

[11]Statement of Financial Accounting Standards No. 109, *Accounting for Income Taxes* (Norwalk, CT: Financial Accounting Standards Board, 1992), par. 17.

other intangible assets, it would become a reduction of income tax expense of the period.

Consider an example of a purchase that includes both of the previous tax ramifications. Farlow Inc. is purchasing Granada Company which has the following balance sheet on the purchase date:

Assets		Liabilities and Equity	
Inventory	$ 50,000	Liabilities	$180,000
Land	100,000	Common stock ($10 par)	100,000
Building	270,000	Retained earnings	70,000
Accum. depreciation	(70,000)		
		Total liabilities	
Total assets	$350,000	and equity	$350,000

The market values of the land and the building are $100,000 and $300,000, respectively. Granada Company has a tax loss carryforward totaling $200,000 in operating losses. Farlow Inc. paid $325,000 for the net assets of Granada in a transaction structured as a nontaxable exchange. Farlow has an effective tax rate of 30% and believes that tax loss carryforwards will be realized. The price paid would be compared first to market values. The market values include the deferred tax liability caused by the excess of the building's market value over its book value.

Farlow would allocate its purchase price to the accounts in the following manner:

Price paid			$325,000
Market values of net assets:			
Inventory		$ 50,000	
Land		100,000	
Building		300,000	
Deferred tax liability, 30% × ($300,000 market value of building − $200,000 book value)		(30,000)	
Recorded liabilities		(180,000)	
Deferred tax expense (an asset), value of carryforward is 30% × $200,000 = $60,000		60,000	300,000
Goodwill (Net of deferred tax liability)			$ 25,000

Recorded as follows:

Goodwill ($25,000 ÷ 70%)	$ 35,714
Deferred tax liability (30% × $35,714)	(10,714)
Net goodwill	$ 25,000

The following entry would be made assuming that Farlow paid $325,000 cash:

Inventory	50,000	
Land	100,000	
Building	300,000	
Deferred Tax Expense	60,000	
Goodwill	35,714	
Liabilities		180,000
Deferred Tax Liability ($30,000 building, $10,714 goodwill)		40,714
Cash		325,000

Notice that the deferred tax expense and deferred tax liability are recorded separately, though they are offset in the statements. In future periods, the tax loss carryforward realized will be credited to the deferred tax expense account.

Contingencies.   Special procedures should be followed when the seller has a contingent asset, liability, or asset impairment which exists on the date of the purchase. A contingency is "an existing condition, situation, or set of circumstances involving uncertainty as to possible gain or loss to an enterprise that will ultimately be resolved when one or more future events occur or fail to occur."[12] An example would be a lawsuit that existed before the purchase, or was filed shortly after the purchase, but that involved an event that occurred prior to the purchase date.

When the existence of the contingent asset, liability, or asset impairment is probable and can be reasonably estimated, it should be recorded at the estimated amount as part of the allocation of the purchase price.[13] It is not necessary that the amount be probable and estimable on the date of the purchase. The assessments may be made subsequent to the purchase date during what is called the "allocation period," which is the time period when noncontingent assets and liabilities acquired in the purchase are quantified and valued. Normally, this period should not exceed one year. Amounts not recorded during the allocation period should be included in the income calculations for the period in which the amounts are determined.[14]

ISSUING SECURITIES AS CONSIDERATION

Many major business acquisitions involve the issuance of the purchaser's securities as payment. As previously stated, the use of securities preserves cash for the future operations of the buyer and may allow the transaction to qualify as a tax-free exchange for the seller. The principles for recording the purchase are not changed; only the recording of the consideration differs. The market value of the securities issued becomes the total consideration to be assigned to the acquired firm. The purchaser also must add the market value of the securities issued to its debt or paid-in capital. Using an earlier example which involved a $160,000

---

[12]Statement of Financial Accounting Standards No. 5, *Accounting for Contingencies* (Stamford: Financial Accounting Standards Board, 1975), par. 1.

[13]Statement of Financial Accounting Standards No. 38, *Accounting for Preacquisition Contingencies of Purchased Enterprises* (Stamford: Financial Accounting Standards Board, 1980), par. 5.

[14]*Ibid.*, par. 6.

acquisition price for the net assets of Jacobs Company, assume that Acquisitions Inc. will issue its $2 par common stock as consideration. The total market value of the shares issued to Jacobs Company must equal the agreed-upon net price of $160,000. Assuming a market value of $20 per share for its stock, Acquisitions Inc. must issue 8,000 shares ($160,000 ÷ $20). The following entry to record the purchase is identical to the entry on page 14, except that the addition to Acquisitions paid-in capital accounts is substituted for the cash payment.

Accounts Receivable (market value)	20,000	
Inventory (market value)	45,000	
Land (appraised market value)	10,000	
Buildings (appraised market value).	50,000	
Equipment (appraised market value)	40,000	
Goodwill ($160,000 price minus sum of net market values plus		
$1,000 of acquisition costs)	16,000	
Current Liabilities (market value)		20,000
Common Stock (8,000 shares × $2 par)		16,000
Paid-In Capital in Excess of Par ($160,000 – $16,000 par		
value)		144,000
Cash (for acquisition costs).		1,000

Another form of consideration involves the issuance of the purchasing company's bonds for the assets of the acquired firm. Market values are recorded in the same manner as in the preceding entry. However, care must be taken to record properly the market value of the bonds issued. The applicable bond premium or discount must be recorded. For instance, assume that Acquisitions Inc. plans to issue $1,000, 8% bonds in exchange for the $160,000 net assets of Jacobs Company. Normally, the purchaser would exchange 160 bonds ($160,000 ÷ $1,000 per bond) for the net assets of Jacobs Company. However, on the settlement date, the bonds have a market value of $990 each. Therefore, a discount of $1,600 ($10 per bond × 160 bonds) should be recorded. If the discount is settled by cash payment to the Jacobs Company, the purchase would be recorded as follows:

Accounts Receivable.	20,000	
Inventory	45,000	
Land	10,000	
Buildings.	50,000	
Equipment	40,000	
Goodwill	16,000	
Discount on Bonds Payable	1,600	
Current Liabilities.		20,000
Cash (acquisition cost plus discount on bonds)		2,600
Bonds Payable.		160,000

The resulting discount (or premium) must be amortized over the life of the bond issue. As an alternative to the cash payment, additional bonds could have been issued to compensate for the discount.

Any direct costs incurred to register and issue the securities are subtracted from the value assigned to the securities and are not treated as a direct acquisition cost. Had there been a $500 bond issuance cost in this example, a $500 deferred charge or increase in the discount would have been recorded.

MIXING SECURITIES AS CONSIDERATION

The purchaser may exchange different types of securities in a single transaction. The differing securities may reflect the nature of the assets acquired. For example, the seller initially may desire debt or preferred equity securities equal to the market value of all assets, excluding goodwill. These securities provide a senior claim on earnings as well as on assets should foreclosure become necessary. In this way, a preference in dissolution equal to the asset contribution of the purchased firm is provided. Typically, common stock is issued as payment for goodwill, reflecting the uncertainty involved in estimating this intangible asset.

Low-risk securities, however, have the disadvantage of lacking a long-run speculative appeal. Very likely the seller will prefer to become a common stockholder if, at a later date, the acquiring firm prospers. Therefore, convertible debt or convertible equity securities may be used to satisfy both the seller's short-run security concern and long-run speculative interest. As an alternative to convertible securities, participating preferred stock may be used, since it offers a permanent preference on both assets and income by allowing full or limited participation with common stockholders in dividend distributions.

INCLUDING CONTINGENT CONSIDERATION IN A PURCHASE AGREEMENT

A purchase agreement may provide that the purchaser will transfer additional consideration to the seller, contingent upon the occurrence of specified future events or transactions. This consideration could involve the transfer of cash or other assets or the issuance of additional securities. During the period preceding the date on which the contingency is resolved, the purchaser has a contingent liability that is disclosed in a footnote to the financial statements but is not recorded.[15] On the date that the contingency is resolved, the contingent liability ceases, and the purchaser records any additional consideration as an adjustment to the original purchase transaction. The method used to make the adjustment is dependent upon the nature of the contingency.

Contingent Consideration Based on Earnings.   A purchaser may agree to make a final payment contingent upon the earnings of the acquired firm during a specified future time period. If, during this period, the earnings of the acquired firm reach or exceed an agreed amount, further payment will be made at the end of the contingency period. In essence, the value of all or part of the goodwill is to be confirmed before full payment is made. Clearly, when an

---

[15]APB Opinion No. 16 (par. 78) provides that a liability is to be recorded if the amount of the contingent liability is determinable at the date of the acquisition. Of course, doing so would increase the price paid for the firm and would impact values assigned to the assets.

earnings contingency exists, the total price to be paid for the acquired firm is not known until the end of the contingency period. As is the case for the initial payment, the purchaser must record the fair market value of the consideration given, including the market value of additional securities issued. Normally, the amount of the additional payment will result in an increased amount of good-will.[16] Adjustments to other assets would be made only if the contingency was based on their value.

To illustrate, assume that Company A acquires the assets of Company B on January 1, 19X2, in exchange for Company A common stock under conditions that require the acquisition to be recorded as a purchase. Also, Company A agrees to issue 10,000 additional common shares to the former stockholders of Company B on January 1, 19X5, if the acquired firm's average annual income before taxes for the three years reaches or exceeds $50,000. During the contin-gency period, Company A will disclose the contingent liability in the footnotes to its financial statements. If the earnings condition is met, Company A will record the final payment on January 1, 19X5, by increasing the goodwill account. Assuming the 10,000 shares have a par value of $1 and a market value of $8 per share on January 1, 19X5, the following entry would be made:

Goodwill ($8 market value × 10,000 shares).................	80,000	
Common Stock ($1 par × 10,000 shares)		10,000
Paid-In Capital in Excess of Par		70,000

Goodwill recorded as a result of a contingency payment must be amortized over the *remaining* life of the original goodwill. The period of amortization must end within 40 years of the original date of the combination. If a contingency involving goodwill is resolved 5 years after the original purchase, the added goodwill recorded can be amortized over a maximum of only 35 (40 – 5) years. No retroactive adjustment may be made for amortization applicable to prior periods.[17]

Contingent Consideration Based on Issuer's Security Prices.   In exchange for its assets, a seller may be reluctant to accept the securities of the purchasing firm. This reluctance is caused by the seller's fear of a possible future decline in the market value of the securities. When a stock issuance is involved, the concern may be based, in part, on the dilutive effect of a significant increase in the number of shares outstanding. To combat this apprehension, the purchaser may guarantee the total value of the securities as of a given future date. The purchaser agrees to transfer additional assets or issue additional securities on that date for the amount by which the guaranteed value exceeds the market value on the date selected. For example, on January 1, 19X2, Company C issues

---

[16]When the contingency involves the value of an asset other than goodwill, that asset's value is to be adjusted as a result of the contingent payment. For example, with a contingency involving the value of a building, the value would be adjusted at the time the contingency was resolved and the added payment made.

[17]Accounting Principles Board Opinion No. 16, *Business Combinations* (New York: American Institute of Certified Public Accountants, 1970), par. 80.

*Is it purchase b +
cash , or assets
or through C∆ stock*

100,000 shares of its common stock, which has a $1 par value and a $12 market value per share, in exchange for the assets of Company D. The conditions of the exchange require the acquisition to be recorded as a purchase. The following summarized entry would be recorded:

```
Net Assets ($12 market value × 100,000 shares) . . . . . . . . . .   1,200,000
    Common Stock ($1 par × 100,000 shares) . . . . . . . . . . . . .              100,000
    Paid-In Capital in Excess of Par . . . . . . . . . . . . . . . . . . . . . . .            1,100,000
```

Company C guarantees the value of the stock at $12 per share as of January 1, 19X3. If necessary, additional consideration will be paid in cash. During the contingency period, Company C must disclose the contingent liability. Should the market price of the common stock be less than $12 per share on January 1, 19X3, additional consideration will be recorded.

Assume that on January 1, 19X3, the market value is $10 per share. Then $200,000 (100,000 shares × $2 per share deficiency) is the amount by which the guaranteed value of the shares exceeds the total market value. Company C will have to pay an additional $200,000 in cash. How should the payment be recorded? The payment is not based on a revaluation of the goodwill account, as is the case with an earnings contingency. Instead, the payment reflects the fact that the value assigned to the original security issuance was only an estimate, with the final amount to be determined later. To record the adjustment of the estimate, the original credit to Paid-In Capital should be decreased as shown by the following entry:

```
Paid-In Capital in Excess of Par . . . . . . . . . . . . . . . . . . . . . . . . .   200,000
    Cash . . . . . . . . . . . . . . . . . . . . . . . . . . . . . . . . . . . . . . . . . . . . .              200,000
```

In the preceding example, the value guaranteed was satisfied in cash. More often, the satisfaction will involve the issuance of additional securities. In that case, Company C would issue 20,000 additional shares ($200,000 market value deficiency ÷ $10 current market value per share). Company C needs 120,000 shares to equate to the $1,200,000 original consideration, rather than the 100,000 shares previously issued. Accordingly, the $1,200,000 originally assigned to the 100,000 shares must be reassigned to 120,000 shares. The following entry will accomplish the reassignment:

```
Paid-In Capital in Excess of Par . . . . . . . . . . . . . . . . . . . . . . . . .   20,000
    Common Stock ($1 par × 20,000 shares) . . . . . . . . . . . . . . . . .              20,000
```

Less frequently, price guarantees may apply to debt securities issued in a purchase transaction. Since bond prices react more to general money market conditions than to the operating performance of a particular firm, it is not common to guarantee their value. But when a price guarantee is used for bonds issued in a purchase, recording procedures parallel those used for stock. The settlement of a guarantee results in allocating the value assigned to the original bonds to a greater number of bonds. This allocation will decrease or eliminate an original premium and/or will increase or create a discount.

ASSET ACQUISITION AS A POOLING OF INTERESTS

A pooling of interests is a combination that must meet very strict criteria to ensure that there is a true bonding of existing interests. Since the firm being acquired must fully cooperate to assure the pooling treatment, it is unlikely that the pooling method could ever be applied to a hostile takeover. When the pooling criteria are met, it is held that there has not been a purchase or sale, and thus there is no cause to recognize market values. Please understand that the negotiation of the combination will consider market values of assets and liabilities; they just are not recorded.

CRITERIA FOR THE USE OF THE POOLING METHOD

As previously mentioned, prior to the issuance of APB Opinion No. 16, many firms tended to ignore the then loosely defined criteria for the use of the purchase and pooling methods. A choice between the methods often was based on the impact of the methods on future financial statements. However, APB Opinion No. 16 states that the purchase and pooling methods are not alternative recording methods available for any given combination. Any combination not meeting *all* of the criteria for a pooling of interests must be designated as a purchase. Thus, the criteria seek to ensure that only a true fusion of previous stockholder interests and assets will be accorded the pooling treatment. APB Opinion No. 16 classifies the criteria according to the attributes of the combining firms, the agreement as to how interests are to be combined, and the absence of planned subsequent transactions. The Opinion also introduces special terminology for referring to firms combining under the pooling method. The acquiring firm (the one that will issue the stock) that will continue in existence is termed the *issuer,* while the acquired firm is termed the *combiner.* These terms will be used in subsequent discussions to avoid any connotation of a purchase–sale's having occurred when the pooling method is appropriate.

Attributes of the Combining Firms.   APB Opinion No. 16 (par. 46) provides two criteria that establish essential attributes of the combining firms.

> *Criterion 1.   Each of the combining firms may not have been a subsidiary or division of another firm for two years preceding the date on which a plan of combination is initiated. The initiation date is the earliest date at which the stockholders of the combining firms are informed of the terms of the combination (including the stock exchange ratio) either through a public announcement or through written notification.*

The intent of this condition is that a company should not be able to fragment a business enterprise and pool only part of it. For new firms created within the two years, this condition is applicable only to the firm's period of existence. For the purposes of this condition, a former subsidiary that was separated from the parent by government order is considered a "new" firm.

> *Criterion 2.   Each of the combining firms must be independent of one another. On the date of initiation of the plan and until its consummation, no*

firm may own more than 10% of the voting common stock of any other combining firm. Shares acquired as a part of the plan of combination are exempted.

Agreement on How Interests Are to Be Combined.   APB Opinion No. 16 (par. 47) provides seven criteria that relate to the manner in which interests are combined.

> *Criterion 1.   The combination must be accomplished in a single transaction or in accordance with a specific plan, in which case the plan must be executed within one year of its initiation. One exception is allowed when there is a delay that is beyond the control of the combining firms. The only delays considered uncontrollable are (1) proceedings and deliberations of a federal or state regulatory agency on whether to approve or disapprove a combination where the combination cannot be effected without approval and (2) litigation aimed at prohibiting the combination.*

The intent of this condition is to prevent a piecemeal, selective displacement of stockholders on possibly different terms.

> *Criterion 2.   Subsequent to the initiation date, the issuer must issue its common stock for either all the assets of the combiner or at least 90% of the outstanding voting common shares of the combiner in a stock acquisition. The shares issued must have rights identical to those of the majority of the issuer's outstanding voting common shares.*

In an asset acquisition, there is a minor modification of the requirement that all assets be acquired. The combining firm may retain cash or other assets on a temporary basis to settle existing liabilities, contingencies, or items in dispute. Once these matters are settled, any remaining assets should be transferred to the issuer in exchange for common stock.

For poolings accomplished as a stock acquisition, the 90% requirement must be carefully analyzed. For the purposes of this requirement, the computation of combiner shares received excludes:

a. Shares held by the issuer or its subsidiaries prior to the initiation date, and
b. Shares acquired after the initiation date by giving any consideration other than the voting common shares of the issuer. Fractional shares acquired for cash cannot be considered in meeting the 90% provision.

To illustrate, assume that Company C (combiner) has 20,000 shares of voting common stock outstanding and Company I (issuer) exchanges 8,500 shares of its voting common stock for 17,000 shares of Company C stock. Company I, prior to the date of initiation, acquired 1,000 shares of Company C stock in exchange for its own shares. In addition, Company I paid cash for 500 shares of Company C stock as a part of the combination plan. Even though Company I holds 92.5% (18,500 ÷ 20,000) of Company C shares at the consummation date, the 90% rule is not met, and the combination must be accounted for as a purchase. The computations are as follows:

Shares owned by Company I   18,500
Less disqualified shares:
   Company C shares owned prior to initiation date   1,000
   Company C shares acquired after initiation date for cash   500
Shares meeting the pooling requirement   17,000

Ownership interest for pooling criteria
   (17,000 shares ÷ 20,000 outstanding shares) **85%**

The application of the 90% rule becomes more complex when the combiner holds shares of the issuer. To illustrate, assume that Company I issues 9,250 shares of its stock for 18,500 of the 20,000 shares of outstanding Company C stock subsequent to the initiation date of a plan of combination. In addition, Company C previously acquired 500 shares of Company I stock. The following diagram summarizes the interfirm stock transactions:

	Company I	Company C
Prior to initiation date.		Owns 500 shares of Company I stock
Subsequent to initiation date	Issues 9,250 shares of its stock to Company C ⟶ In exchange for 18,500 shares of ⟵ Company C stock	

According to the exchange ratio, 1 share of Company I stock is equal in value to 2 shares of Company C stock.[18] Thus, 1,000 (500 × 2) shares of Company C stock represent an equity in Company I. Viewed in another manner, the 1,000 shares of Company C stock support the investment in 500 shares of Company I stock. APB Opinion No. 16 would hold that on an equivalent share basis, 1,000 of the shares of Company C stock received by Company I are in essence a return of its own shares. Therefore, the equivalent shares must be subtracted from the total combiner shares held by the issuer on the consummation date. The 90% test is not met, and the combination must be accounted for as a purchase. The calculations are as follows:

Shares owned by Company I.   18,500
Less disqualified shares:
   Equivalent number of Company C shares represented by Company C
     investment in Company I (500 × 2)   1,000
Shares meeting the pooling requirement.   17,500

Ownership interest for pooling criteria
   (17,500 shares ÷ 20,000 outstanding shares). **87.5%**

---

[18]The exchange rate used is the actual resulting ratio at the consummation date. Any cash given for fractional shares will diminish the exchange rate.

If the combiner acquires shares of the issuer subsequent to the initiation date, these shares also are subtracted on an equivalent share basis from the total shares acquired by the issuer in determining compliance with the 90% rule.

The 90% criterion does allow partial payment using cash or other consideration for a minor portion of the shares. However, each combiner shareholder that is participating in the combination agreement must exchange *all* shares for those of the issuer. Cash or other consideration can be used only for fractional shares or for dissenting shareholders who will not be shareholders in the surviving firm.[19]

Criterion 3.   The combining companies may not change their equity interests in contemplation of a combination for the period of time beginning two years before the initiation date and extending through the consummation date.

The intent of this provision is to prevent a combiner from purchasing and reselling common shares in an attempt to create a group of shareholders who own 90% of the shares and who agree to combine. It is also the intent of the provision that the issuer be prevented from realigning its shareholders in an attempt to create a majority group who are willing to combine. Treasury stock purchases must be defended as normal and motivated by other purposes in order not to violate this condition. "Other purposes" would include, for example, acquisition of shares to satisfy employee stock option plans.

Criterion 4.   Dividend distributions (other than in common stock) must be no greater than normal for two years before the initiation date through the consummation date.

"Normal" is defined by reference to past dividend policy and earnings of the period. Greater than normal dividends would allow a firm to distribute part of its assets to shareholders and to pool only the residual. Thus, shareholders would receive part assets and part equity of the pooled firm, which is counter to the concept of pooling as a fusion of existing interests.

Criterion 5.   The voting common stockholders of the combiner must receive voting shares of the issuer proportionate to their holdings in the combiner.

For instance, Mr. X., who owned 30% of Company Q voting common stock obtained by the issuer, must receive 30% of the issuer's voting common stock in exchange for shares of Company Q. In this way, the proportionate stockholder interests of the combiner are preserved.

Criterion 6.   The voting rights of the resulting ownership interests are exercisable. There may be no deprivation or restriction of these rights for any time period.

---

[19]Accounting Principles Board Opinion No. 16, *Business Combinations* (New York: American Institute of Certified Public Accountants, 1970), par. 47b; Accounting Interpretation No. 25 of APB Opinion No. 16, *Business Combinations* (New York: AICPA, 1971).

An attempt to place the shares issued in a voting trust, for example, would violate this criterion.

Criterion 7.   There can be no contingent consideration agreements based on events subsequent to the consummation date.

As addressed earlier, two types of contingent considerations are those involving future payments based on profits in subsequent periods and those involving an agreement that provides that the acquiring firm will compensate the acquired firm's shareholders for a decline in the value of the securities they receive as payment. Neither is allowed under the pooling criteria.

While contingent consideration is not allowed in a pooling, contingency agreements are permitted. The most common type of agreement that is allowed is a "general management representation," which is found in most business combinations. In such an agreement, the management of the acquired company warrants that the assets exist and are worth their agreed value, and all liabilities are recorded. These contingencies involve the values assigned to assets and liabilities existing on the consummation date and do not involve subsequent events. The agreement usually calls for an adjustment of the shares issued up to about 10%, but actual adjustments are rare.[20]

Absence of Planned Subsequent Transactions.   Stipulations exist to prevent planned subsequent transactions that would counteract the conditions of a pooling of interests and allow a purchase to appear in the guise of a pooling. The pooling treatment is denied by APB Opinion No. 16 (par. 48) if any *one* of the following conditions is included explicitly or by intent in the negotiations and/or terms of the agreement to combine:

1. An agreement by which the issuer will retire or reacquire the common shares issued to effect the combination.
2. An agreement to aid financially a faction of the stockholders of the former combiner.
3. A plan to dispose of a significant part of the assets of the combining firms within two years of the consummation of the combination.[21]

Disposal of combining firm assets is objectionable since it could allow large gains to be recorded on the sales. This would occur since only book values were recorded in the pooling.

Added SEC Requirements.   There are several added stipulations required of firms which are both desiring to pool and subject to regulation by the Securities and Exchange Commission. The major additional requirements imposed by the SEC are:

---

[20]*Interpretations of APB Opinion Nos. 16 and 17,* 7th Ed. (Chicago: Arthur Andersen & Co., 1988), p. 114.

[21]APB Opinion No. 16 (par. 60) provides that if there is a material gain or loss on a sale of the assets of the previously separate firms within two years of a pooling, the gain or loss is shown as an extraordinary item.

1. The firms being pooled must be viable operating companies; that is, the combination cannot be simply a pool of assets. For example, an operating lumber company was not allowed to pool with a timber company that owned timber tracts but had not actually operated in the current and preceding years.
2. The SEC will not allow a significant sale of assets in contemplation of the combination. Any asset disposals in the six to nine months preceding the combination must be defended as being done in the ordinary course of business.[22]
3. The SEC requires that the issuer obtain at least 90% of all combiner company voting stock, including class B common and preferred stock with voting rights. The SEC also requires obtaining 90% of any securities judged to be "substantially the same" as common stock. This includes common stock options and warrants as well as convertible securities that are currently convertible and where conversion is likely to be due to the value of the common stock.

POOLING OF INTERESTS ACCOUNTING

A pooling of interests is viewed as a fusion of existing accounting entities; there has been no purchase or sale. Thus, there is no cause to record market values. Assets, liabilities, and equities are recorded at their existing book values. Adjustments to the accounts of the combiner are allowed only if they would be appropriate in the course of normal operations. An example of this would be the write-down of inventory from cost to market value or the write-down of a fixed asset that has suffered a permanent impairment of value. Any adjustment to the accounts of the combiner will result in an adjustment to the combiner's retained earnings prior to carrying the retained earnings to the issuer's books.

The combiner may have recorded a deferred tax expense for the benefits of a tax loss carryforward. The deferred tax asset, however, may be offset by a contravaluation account to reflect a probable lack of full realization of the benefits. The issuer may have additional future tax liabilities that will be more able to offset the deferred tax asset. This allows the existing valuation account to be reduced or eliminated. The reduction in the valuation account becomes an increase in the combiner's retained earnings prior to its transfer to the issuer. There may be some cases where the deferred tax credit may not have been recorded by the combiner. In such a case, the net amount of the deferred tax asset, the carryforward less the valuation account (if any), is an adjustment to combiner retained earnings prior to transfer to the issuer.

To illustrate the recording of a pooling of interests, the example used in an earlier purchase analysis is revised. Assume that Expansion Inc. (formerly Acquisitions Inc.) is going to pool with Jacobs Company by issuing common stock and that Expansion will be the surviving accounting entity. Expansion is the issuer, not the purchaser, and Jacobs is the combiner, not the seller. These

---

[22]*Interpretation of APB Opinion Nos. 16 and 17*, 7th ed., p. 77.

terms emphasize that the firms are joint owners in a pooling and are not parties to an exchange. When the pooling is consummated, the *book values* of Jacobs Company will be recorded on the books of Expansion Inc. The only exception to this rule is for assets that have book values in excess of market values; in that case, the lower market values are recorded.

The fact that market values are not recorded does not mean that they are ignored during negotiations preceding the combination. Both parties to a pooling must agree on the market values of the items involved in order to arrive at the number of issuer shares to be exchanged for the combiner's net assets.

The firms agree on the following values for the net assets of Jacobs Company:

	Book Value	Market Value
Accounts receivable	$ 20,000	$ 20,000
Inventory	40,000	45,000
Land	10,000	10,000
Buildings (net)	40,000	50,000
Equipment (net)	20,000	40,000
Current liabilities	(20,000)	(20,000)
Total	$110,000	$145,000

Expansion agrees that the value of the goodwill is $15,000. To satisfy the $160,000 net asset value, Expansion will issue common stock with a par value of $2 and a market value of $20. Expansion will issue 8,000 shares ($160,000 net asset value divided by $20 per share). It is common to state the stock exchange ratio in a business combination. In this example, the ratio would be 8 to 1, or 8,000 Expansion shares for 1,000 Jacobs Company shares. While the negotiation and settlement of the pooling are based on market values, the recording of the transaction is based on book values. This would include the recording of goodwill that is present on the books of the combiner at the time of the pooling. The book values of the Jacobs Company are transferred to Expansion Inc. by recording the following entry:[23]

Accounts Receivable	20,000	
Inventory	40,000	
Land	10,000	
Buildings	40,000	
Equipment	20,000	
Current Liabilities		20,000
Common Stock (8,000 shares × $2 par)		16,000
Paid-In Capital in Excess of Par		44,000*
Retained Earnings		50,000

*($60,000, the total paid-in capital of Jacobs on the consummation date, less $16,000 assigned to par value.)

One difficult aspect of recording a pooling of interests is the combining of stockholders' equities. The total paid-in capital of the combiner must be carried

---

[23]See Jacobs balance sheet, p. 12.

as a unit to the total paid-in capital of the issuer. The composition of the combiner paid-in capital is ignored and is redistributed between the par or stated value and the additional paid-in capital of the issuer. In addition, recall that in a pooling of interests, incomes of the combiner and issuer are combined retroactively for periods prior to the combination. This means that retained earnings balances of the combiner and issuer also are combined. Normally, the retained earnings of the combiner is added directly to the retained earnings of the issuer. The following chart summarizes the equity transfer of the previous entry:

Jacobs Company (combiner) Balances			Increase in Expansion Inc. (issuer) Balances	
Capital stock ($10 par)........	$ 10,000		Capital stock ($2 par)........	$ 16,000
Paid-in capital in excess of par	50,000		Paid-in capital in excess of par	44,000
Total paid-in capital........	$ 60,000	→	Total paid-in capital........	$ 60,000
Retained earnings	50,000	→	Retained earnings	50,000
Total equity...............	$110,000		Total equity...............	$110,000

Equity transfer rules must accommodate combinations in which the par or stated value of the shares issued exceeds the total paid-in capital of the combiner. This is a rare occurrence, since most firms have no par or very low par value shares. When this situation occurs, the issuer first must use its *own* paid-in capital in excess of par to cover the deficiency. Only when such an excess is depleted, or when it does not exist, may the combiner retained earnings be reduced. This is the only exception to the general rule that the retained earnings of the firms are combined. As an example, assume that in the previous situation Expansion was issuing $10 par stock and all the other facts were unchanged. The issuer must add $80,000 (8,000 shares × $10 par) to its par value, while the total paid-in capital of the combiner is only $60,000. If the issuer has sufficient additional paid-in capital upon which to draw, the $20,000 deficiency would be met by reducing that account's balance as shown in the following chart:

Jacobs Company (combiner) Balances			Increase (Decrease) in Expansion Inc. (issuer) Balances	
Capital stock ($10 par)........	$ 10,000		Capital stock ($10 par)........	$ 80,000
Paid-in capital in excess of par	50,000		Paid-in capital in excess of par	(20,000)
Total paid-in capital........	$ 60,000	→	Total paid-in capital........	$ 60,000
Retained earnings	50,000	→	Retained earnings	50,000
Total equity...............	$110,000		Total equity...............	$110,000

Expansion's entry to record the pooling in this case would be:

Accounts Receivable	20,000	
Inventory	40,000	
Land	10,000	
Buildings	40,000	
Equipment	20,000	
Paid-In Capital in Excess of Par (existing on Expansion's books)	20,000	
Current Liabilities		20,000
Common Stock ($10 par)		80,000
Retained Earnings		50,000

If the issuer has no additional paid-in capital with which to meet the deficiency, the combiner retained earnings account would be used as shown in the following chart:

Jacobs Company (combiner) Balances		Reassignment	Increase in Expansion Inc. (issuer) Balances	
Capital stock ($10 par)	$ 10,000		Capital stock ($10 par)	$ 80,000
Paid-in capital in excess of par	50,000			
Total paid-in capital	$ 60,000	+ 20,000	Total paid-in capital	$ 80,000
Retained earnings	50,000	– 20,000	Retained earnings	30,000
Total equity	$110,000		Total equity	$110,000

The entry to record the pooling then would be:

Accounts Receivable	20,000	
Inventory	40,000	
Land	10,000	
Buildings	40,000	
Equipment	20,000	
Current Liabilities		20,000
Common Stock ($10 par)		80,000
Retained Earnings		30,000

In some cases, it may be necessary to consume all of the combiner retained earnings and draw upon the retained earnings of the issuer.

In a pooling, shareholders of the combiner must become shareholders of the continuing issuer. To accomplish the continuity of ownership, the combiner usually will dissolve itself by distributing the shares it receives from the issuer to its shareholders.

Pooling principles require that the assets of the combiner be recorded at book values and combined assets may not be increased through the combination. Consequently, the direct costs of consummating the combination may not be capitalized as an asset. Similarly, the issuance cost of new securities may not be deducted from the value assigned to the securities. Assume that in the previous example, Expansion paid $1,000 in direct acquisition costs. A separate entry would expense the cost as follows:

Professional Services Expense	1,000	
Cash		1,000

Another complication arises when an issuer uses previously issued and reacquired stock (treasury stock) to accomplish a pooling. In contemplation of the combination, this treasury stock may not have been acquired in the two-year period preceding the business combination, since such an acquisition of treasury shares would defeat a pooling criterion.[24] Pooling principles require that the book value of the combiner capital be assigned to stock issued in a pooling. Clearly, the issuer would violate these principles if it could reacquire previously issued shares and use their cost as the value assigned to the shares exchanged in the pooling. The problem that arises is: How does the issuer dispose of the difference between the price paid for the treasury shares and the value that must be assigned to them in a pooling of interests? The answer is: The treasury shares are treated as though they are retired. For instance, suppose Company E reacquired 10,000 shares of its common stock for $250,000 and later exchanged these shares for the assets of Company F. The summarized balance sheets of Companies E and F immediately prior to the pooling are as follows:

Company E (Issuer)

	Liabilities.	$200,000
	Common stock (50,000 shares, $2 par)	100,000
	Retained earnings	700,000
	Less treasury stock at cost	(250,000)
Total assets. $750,000	Total liabilities and equity	$750,000

Company F (Combiner)

	Liabilities.	$ 50,000
	Common stock (20,000 shares, $1 par)	20,000
	Paid-in capital in excess of par	40,000
	Retained earnings	40,000
Total assets. $150,000	Total liabilities and equity	$150,000

In this case, the shares to be used in the combination were purchased for $25 each, but must carry a book value of $10 each (combiner equity of $100,000 ÷ 10,000 shares issued). *Since shares issued to accomplish a pooling must be treated as newly issued*, APB Opinion No. 16 (par. 54) requires that previously acquired shares be accounted for as though they were first retired. Therefore, Company E first should make a retirement entry for the 10,000 treasury shares as follows:

Common Stock (10,000 shares × $2 par)	20,000	
Retained Earnings	230,000	
Treasury Stock (at cost)		250,000

---

[24]Accounting Interpretation No. 20 of Accounting Principles Board Opinion No. 16, *Business Combinations* (New York: American Institute of Certified Public Accountants, 1971).

Then, the shares released to accomplish the pooling are recorded as newly issued:

Assets	150,000	
Liabilities		50,000
Common Stock (10,000 shares × $2 par).................		20,000
Paid-In Capital in Excess of Par		
($60,000 total paid-in – $20,000 par)...................		40,000
Retained Earnings.....................................		40,000

REPORTING REQUIREMENTS

As is true of all asset acquisitions, the purchase of another firm affects the financial statements of the purchaser only for periods following the purchase date. The comparability of current statements with statements of periods prior to the purchase is provided only by footnote disclosure of the estimation of what the financial information would have been had the purchase occurred at the beginning of the earliest period presented. Poolings of interests, however, require retroactive restatement. Thus, all of the comparative financial statements are presented as they would have appeared had the pooled companies always been combined.

In a purchase or a pooling situation, the firms involved may have used different accounting principles to account for similar types of transactions. One company might use LIFO inventory valuation, while the other may use FIFO. To achieve uniformity or to improve future reporting, it might be desirable to change the accounting principles of one or both members of the combination.

The following table summarizes the reporting requirements for business combinations:

Item	Purchase Method	Pooling Method
1. Change in accounting principles	Financial statements for previous periods restated retroactively. This procedure is an exception to the usual requirement to include in current income the cumulative effect of the change.[25]	Same as for a purchase.
2. Income earned in current year, prior to date of acquisition	Income of purchased firm included only as of purchase date. Disclose in footnote estimated income as if purchase had occurred at beginning of year. Estimate includes adjustments for asset and liability revaluations and goodwill amortization.	Income of both firms combined for entire period. Include in footnotes each firm's operating results for period prior to the combination.
3. Prior periods included in comparative statements	Only separate statements of parent shown. Disclose in footnote the estimated results as if purchase had occurred at the beginning of the comparative periods presented. Estimate includes adjustments for asset and liability revaluations and goodwill amortization.	Statements restated as if pooling occurred at beginning of the comparative periods presented. Intercompany transactions eliminated. Must disclose that statements of previously separate firms have been combined.

---

[25]Accounting Principles Board Opinion No. 20, *Accounting Changes* (New York: American Institute of Certified Public Accountants, 1971), pars. 29 and 30.

Let us study two examples of the impact of business combinations on comparative financial statements. Exhibit 1 below is a footnote from the 1987 financial statements of the Chrysler Corporation concerning its purchase of the American Motors Corporation. Notice that the terms of the purchase, the allocation of the price paid to the assets acquired, and the liabilities assumed are disclosed. Also, note that had the purchase occurred at the first period included in the comparative statements, there is a pro forma disclosure of the impact the purchase would have made on the 1986 and 1987 income statements. The footnote also explains that the income of American Motors is not included in the body of the 1987 income statement prior to the purchase date.

Exhibit 2 on page 39 is a footnote from the 1992 financial statements of Unifi, Inc., the year in which it was the issuer in a pooling with Macfield, Inc. The footnote explains that the statements of the periods presented have been restated to account retroactively for the pooling.

Exhibit 1
Chrysler Corporation
Notes to Consolidated Financial Statements

Note 2 (in part): Acquisitions
Acquisition of American Motors Corporation (AMC)

On August 5, 1987, Chrysler acquired AMC for 14.9 million shares of Chrysler Corporation Common Stock and 0.3 million shares of Chrysler Corporation $2.375 Cumulative Convertible Preferred Stock having a combined value of $518 million and a cash payment of $200 million, plus related expenses. Additionally, as part of Chrysler's purchase of Regie Nationale des Usines Renault's (Renault) interest in AMC, Chrysler has agreed to make a contingent payment to Renault of up to $350 million, depending on the profitability and volume of sales of certain vehicles manufactured by AMC. Such payment, if any, will be recorded as an adjustment of intangible assets.

Chrysler accounted for the acquisition as a purchase. AMC's assets and liabilities are included in the accompanying consolidated balance sheet at values representing a preliminary allocation of the purchase cost. The excess of the purchase cost over the preliminary valuation of the tangible assets and liabilities of AMC was assigned principally to the Jeep trademark and technology, dealer network and other intangible assets, and is being amortized principally over 40 years using the straight-line method. The preliminary allocation is summarized as follows (in millions of dollars):

Current assets	$ 934.9
Intangible assets	1,514.7
Other noncurrent assets	185.9
Net property, plant and equipment	1,105.6
Current liabilities	(1,118.1)
Accrued employee benefits	(437.0)
Other noncurrent liabilities	(681.8)
Long-term debt	(763.2)
Total	$ 741.0

continued

The consolidated statement of earnings includes the operations of AMC from August 6, 1987. Unaudited pro forma results of operations, assuming the acquisition of AMC had occurred at the beginning of 1986, are as follows:

	Pro Forma Year Ended December 31	
	1987	1986
	(In millions of dollars)	
Net sales	$28,872.7	$26,048.8
Net earnings	$ 1,318.3	$ 1,287.6
Net earnings per share—primary (in dollars)	$5.67	$5.43

This pro forma information does not purport to be indicative of the results that actually would have been obtained if the operations had been combined during the periods presented and is not intended to be a projection of future results.

Source: Chrysler Corporation's 1987 Annual Report.

Exhibit 2
Unifi, Inc.

Business Combinations

On April 23, 1993, Vintage Yarns, Inc. (Vintage) was merged with and became a wholly-owned subsidiary of the Company, and 7,891,800 shares of the Company's common stock were issued in exchange for all of the outstanding common stock of Vintage. Additionally, 496,832 shares of the Company's common stock were reserved for issuance pursuant to outstanding options on Vintage common stock. On August 8, 1991, Macfield, Inc. (Macfield) was merged with and into the Company, and 16,263,644 shares of the Company's common stock were issued in exchange for all of the outstanding common stock of Macfield. Both mergers were accounted for as a pooling of interests, and accordingly, the accompanying financial statements for the years ended June 28, 1992 and June 30, 1991 have been restated to include the accounts and operations of Vintage and Macfield for all periods prior to the mergers.

Prior to the mergers, Vintage used a fiscal year ending September 30 and Macfield used a fiscal year ending on the Saturday nearest April 30. Accordingly, the restated financial statements combine the June 28, 1992 financial statements of the Company with the September 30, 1992 financial statements of Vintage and the June 30, 1991 financial statements combine the Company's financial statements at such date with the September 30, 1991 financial statements of Vintage, and the April 28, 1991 financial statements of Macfield. Net sales and net income of Vintage for the three months ended September 30, 1992 were $42.8 million and $7.2 million, respectively and have been included in the results of operations of the Company for fiscal 1993 and 1992. Accordingly, an adjustment for the net income of the three month period has been reflected as an adjustment to the June 29, 1992 consolidated retained earnings and an adjustment of $1.8 million has been reflected to conform the accounting policies of the previously separate companies. Additionally, net sales and net income of Macfield for

continued

the two months ended June 30, 1991 were $105.7 million and $2.8 million, respectively, with such net income reflected as an adjustment to retained earnings effective July 1, 1991. Separate results of the combining entities for each of the three years in the period ended June 27, 1993 are as follows (in 000's):

	June 27, 1993	June 28, 1992	June 30, 1991
Net sales:			
Unifi.	$1,133,863	$1,091,368	$ 441,826
Vintage	198,331	169,601	122,040
Macfield			523,691
Less intercompany sales . . .			(3,135)
	$1,332,194	$1,260,969	$1,084,422
Net income:			
Unifi.	$ 94,839	$ 62,570	$ 38,272
Vintage[1]	33,214	26,277	8,011
Macfield			20,250
	$ 128,053	$ 88,847	$ 66,533

[1]For all periods prior to the merger, to the date of the acquisition, Vintage was taxed as an S Corporation and, therefore, federal and state taxes were assessed to the shareholders. For purposes of the consolidated financial statements, income taxes have been provided on Vintage's earnings at the rates which would have been applicable had such earnings been taxed to it. Distributions to S Corporation shareholders have been adjusted for the effects of corporate, federal and state taxes payable on an annualized basis.

In connection with the merger with Macfield, approximately $24.8 million of merger costs and expenses ($18.4 million net of income taxes, or $.27 per share) were incurred and have been charged to expense in the Company's first quarter of fiscal 1992.

Source: Unifi, Inc. 1993 Annual Report.

QUESTIONS

1. Income tax issues may be a motivation for firms to enter into a business combination. Suggest how income tax considerations may influence the desire of both parties in a combination.

2. Describe the two basic methods by which control of another firm's assets might be obtained. Which method would most likely involve a lower total cost? What are the ramifications of each method on accounting procedures in future periods?

3. The management of Local Control Inc. is unhappy about a possible tender offer being made for a controlling interest in its shares by a large conglomerate. What actions might the firm take to avoid the hostile takeover?

4. Compare the balance sheet ramifications of a purchase versus a pooling of interests. Include the effects on assets, liabilities, and equity. Why might a pooling of interests create a balance sheet with a more profitable appearance?

5. Explain the likely advantage the pooling method will have on income statements for periods subsequent to the combination as compared to the purchase method.

6. The firm being purchased has the total market values of $150,000 and $30,000 for its assets and liabilities, respectively. The acquiring firm issues 2,000 shares of common stock with a $10 par and a $60 market value per share for the net assets. What entry would be needed by the acquiring firm to record this transaction under the purchase method?

7. The firm being purchased has long-lived assets with a market value of $200,000. What are the accounting consequences of paying a price that is $50,000 in excess of the market value of the identifiable net assets? What happens if the price paid is $40,000 less than the value of the identifiable net assets?

8. Under the purchase method, which accounts always are recorded at full market value by the acquiring firm? Why are only these accounts given this priority? What procedure is used when the price paid for the firm is less than the total market value of these "priority" accounts?

9. What procedures should be followed in recording long-term bonds assumed in the purchase of another firm when interest rates have increased substantially since the bonds were issued?

10. A company that has been acquired is a party to several leases, in the capacity of both a lessee and a lessor. In each of the following situations, indicate which accounts should be used and state how to arrive at an amount:

    (a) The company is a lessee on a 2-year operating lease. The rent is below that which would be paid if currently negotiated.

    (b) The company is a lessee under a capital lease with a 6-year remaining term.

    (c) The company is a lessor under an operating lease with a remaining term of 3 years. The rents are below current rental value.

    (d) The company is a lessor under a direct financing (capital) lease with a 4-year remaining term. Title to the asset passes to the lessee at the end of the term.

11. A firm is contemplating the purchase of another company in a transaction that qualifies as a nontaxable exchange for tax purposes. The market values of the assets purchased are in excess of their book values. What are the accounting ramifications of purchasing this firm at a price high enough to result in the recording of goodwill?

12. The company being purchased has a tax loss carryover of $300,000 that it has not been able to utilize. The purchasing firm has an effective tax rate of 30%. The purchasing firm will be able to carry back $100,000 to obtain a tax refund, and the balance will be carried forward. How will the purchasing firm record the tax loss carryforward assuming that it (a) will have deferred future tax liabilities available to offset and (b) anticipates no deferred tax liabilities?

13. Company P acquired Company S at a price far in excess of the market value of its identifiable net assets. Pursuant to an earnings contingency, an additional payment is made 10 years later. How is this payment recorded, and what are the limitations concerning the allocation of the added amount to future periods?

14. An acquiring firm guaranteed that if the total market value of the 2,000 shares of $10 par stock issued in an acquisition fell below $120,000 on January 1, 19XX, additional shares would be issued to make up the deficiency. What entry would be made on January 1, 19XX, if the market value of the stock dropped to $40 per share?

15. How are the voting common stockholders of the combiner assured "equality of treatment" by the pooling of interests criteria?

16. One of the criteria to be met in order to use the pooling method is the 90% stock acquisition rule. Specifically, how and when must the stock of the combiner be obtained if it is to be included in the qualifying 90% of the combiner outstanding stock?

17. What uses are made of market values in a business combination accomplished through a pooling of interests versus a combination accomplished through a purchase?

18. In a pooling of interests, how are the market values of the combiner used to arrive at the stock exchange ratio? Are these market values recorded?

19. Under the purchase and pooling methods, what recognition is given to previously recorded goodwill (goodwill already recorded on the books of the acquired firm) by the acquiring firm?

20. In a pooling of interests, how are the total paid-in capital and retained earnings of the combiner recorded on the books of the issuer? Describe the "basic equity transfer" rule.

21. How are direct acquisition costs, indirect acquisition costs, and issue costs recorded under (a) the purchase method and (b) the pooling method?

22. Assuming that a business combination occurs at midyear, contrast the reporting requirements of a purchase versus pooling concerning income earned during the year.

23. Company A is acquiring Company B on the last day of the fiscal reporting period of both firms. Company B has had substantial income in previous periods. What is the basic impact of the combination on the three years of comparative income and retained earnings statements to be provided if the combination is recorded as (a) a purchase and (b) a pooling? Include mention of related footnote disclosures.

EXERCISES

Exercise 1. Kimberly Company is considering acquiring the assets of Clark Corporation by assuming Clark's liabilities and by making a cash payment. Clark Corporation has the following balance sheet on the date negotiations occur:

Clark Corporation
Balance Sheet
December 31, 19X7

Assets		Liabilities and Equity	
Current assets	$200,000	Total liabilities	$200,000
Land	100,000	Capital stock ($10 par)	100,000
Buildings (net)	220,000	Paid-in capital in excess of par	200,000
Equipment (net)	280,000	Retained earnings	300,000
Total assets	$800,000	Total liabilities and equity	$800,000

Appraisals indicate that the building is undervalued by $80,000 and the equipment is overstated by $30,000. Past earnings have been considered above average and were as follows:

Year	Net Income
19X3	$ 90,000
19X4	110,000
19X5	120,000
19X6	60,000*
19X7	130,000

*includes extraordinary loss of $40,000

It is assumed that the average operating income of the past 5 years will continue. In this industry, the average return on assets is 10% on the market value of the total identifiable assets.

(1) Prepare an estimate of goodwill based on each of the following assumptions:
 — (a) The purchasing company paid for 5 years of excess earnings.
 — (b) Excess earnings will continue forever and are to be capitalized at the industry normal return.
 — (c) Excess earnings will continue for only 5 years and should be capitalized at a higher rate of 16%, which reflects the risk applicable to goodwill.

(2) Determine the actual goodwill recorded if Kimberly pays $750,000 cash for the net assets of Clark Corporation and assumes all existing liabilities.

Exercise 2. Benz Company is contemplating the purchase of the net assets of Cardinal Company for $800,000 cash. To complete the transaction, direct acquisition costs are $15,000. The balance sheet of Cardinal Company on the purchase date is as follows:

Cardinal Company
Balance Sheet
December 31, 19X1

Assets		Liabilities and Equity	
Current assets	$ 80,000	Liabilities	$100,000
Land	50,000	Common stock	
Building	450,000	($10 par)	100,000
Accumulated depreciation,		Paid-in capital in	
building.	(200,000)	excess of par	150,000
Equipment	300,000	Retained earnings.	230,000
Accumulated depreciation,			
equipment	(100,000)		
Total assets	$580,000		$580,000

The following market values have been obtained for Cardinal's assets and liabilities:

Current assets	$100,000
Land	75,000
Building	300,000
Equipment	275,000
Liabilities.	102,000

(1) Record the purchase of the net assets of Cardinal Company on Benz Company's books.
(2) Record the sale of the net assets on the books of Cardinal Company.
(3) Record the purchase of 100% of the common stock of Cardinal Company on Benz's books. Cardinal Company will remain a separate legal entity.

Exercise 3. Feldmen Company was acquired by Robertson International on July 1, 19X1. This combination does not meet the pooling criteria and must be accounted for as a purchase. Robertson exchanged 60,000 shares of its $5 par stock, with a market value of $20 per share, for the net assets of Feldmen Company.

Robertson incurred the following costs as a result of this transaction:

Direct acquisition costs	$25,000
Indirect acquisition costs.	30,000
Stock registration and issuance costs.	10,000
Total costs	$65,000

The balance sheet of Feldmen Company, on the day of the acquisition, was as follows:

Feldmen Company
Balance Sheet
July 1, 19X1

Assets			Liabilities and Equity		
Cash		$ 100,000	Current liabilities............		$ 80,000
Inventory		300,000	Liability under capital		
Equipment under			lease		150,000
capital lease (net)..........		200,000	Bonds payable		400,000
Property, plant, and			Stockholders' equity:		
equipment:			Common stock	$200,000	
Land	$200,000		Paid-in capital in		
Buildings (net)............	250,000	450,000	excess of par.............	100,000	
			Retained earnings	120,000	420,000
			Total liabilities and		
Total assets		$1,050,000	equity		$1,050,000

The appraised market values as of July 1, 19X1 are:

Inventory	$250,000
Equipment under capital lease................	220,000
Land	180,000
Buildings......................................	300,000
Liability under capital lease	140,000
Bonds payable................................	270,000

Record the purchase of Feldmen Company on the books of Robertson Corporation.

Exercise 4. Santo Corporation has agreed to purchase the net assets of Barnet Corporation. Just prior to the purchase, Barnet's balance sheet was as follows:

Barnet Corporation
Balance Sheet
January 1, 19X1

Assets			Liabilities and Equity		
Current assets.....................		$220,000	Current liabilities		$ 80,000
Equipment (net)		100,000	Stockholders' equity:		
			Common stock ($10 par)	$100,000	
			Retained earnings	140,000	240,000
Total assets		$320,000	Total liabilities and equity...........		$320,000

Market values agree with book values except for the equipment which has an estimated market value of $40,000. Santo Corporation paid $10,000 in direct acquisition costs and $15,000 in indirect acquisition costs to consummate the transaction.

Record the purchase on the books of Santo Corporation assuming the cash paid to Barnet Corporation was (a) $160,000 and (b) $90,000.

Exercise 5. Everett Company is purchasing the net assets of Green Company on December 31, 19X6, when Green Company has the following balance sheet:

Assets		Liabilities and Equity	
Current assets	$100,000	Liabilities	$ 90,000
Land	50,000	Common stock ($10 par)......	200,000
Buildings (net)..............	200,000	Retained earnings............	140,000
Equipment (net)	60,000		
Goodwill...................	20,000		
Total assets	$430,000	Total liabilities and equity	$430,000

Everett has obtained the following market values for Green Company accounts:

Current assets	$120,000
Land	100,000
Buildings....................................	250,000
Equipment	150,000
Liabilities...................................	92,000

Direct acquisition costs are $18,000 and indirect acquisition costs are $5,000.

Prepare the entries to record the purchase of Green Company assuming the cash payment by Everett Company to Green Company is $450,000. Everett Company will assume the liabilities of Green Company.

Exercise 6. Your client, Lewison International, has informed you that they have reached an agreement with Herro Company for the purchase of all of Herro's assets. This transaction is considered to be a purchase and will be accomplished through the issue of Lewison's common stock.

After your examination of the financial statements and the purchase agreement, you have discovered the following important facts.

The Lewison common stock issued has a market value of $800,000. The market value of Herro's assets net of all liabilities is $700,000. All asset book values equaled their market values except for one machine valued at $200,000. This machine was originally purchased two years ago by Herro for $180,000. This machine has been depreciated using the straight-line method with an assumed useful life of 10 years and no salvage value. The acquisition is to be considered a nontaxable exchange for tax purposes.

Assuming a 30% tax rate, what amounts will be recorded for the machine, deferred tax liability, and goodwill?

Exercise 7. Reis Company had the following balance sheet on December 31, 19X1, when it was purchased for $900,000 in cash by Watermark Corporation:

Reis Company
Balance Sheet
December 31, 19X1

Assets		Liabilities and Equity		
Current assets..........	$100,000	Current liabilities		$ 60,000
Equipment (net)	200,000	Stockholders' equity:		
Building (net)	270,000	Common stock		
		($5 par)...........	$100,000	
		Retained earnings	410,000	510,000
		Total liabilities		
Total assets	$570,000	and equity		$570,000

The equipment has a market value of $280,000; all other assets have market values equal to their book values. The combination is structured as a tax-free exchange. Reis Company has a tax loss carryforward of $400,000 which it has not recorded. Watermark Corporation can use $100,000 of the tax loss carryforward to offset past income and generate a refund. The balance of the $400,000 is considered realizable. Watermark is taxed at a rate of 30%.

Record the purchase of Reis Company by Watermark Corporation.

Exercise 8. Gonring Company purchased the net assets of Helm Company on January 1, 19X1, and made the following entry to record the purchase:

Current Assets	100,000	
Equipment	150,000	
Land	50,000	
Buildings	300,000	
Goodwill	100,000	
Liabilities		80,000
Common Stock ($1 par)		100,000
Paid-In Capital in Excess of Par		520,000

Make the required entry on January 1, 19X3, for each of the two following independent contingency agreements:

(1) An additional cash payment would be made on January 1, 19X3, equal to twice the amount by which average annual earnings of the Helm Division exceed $25,000 per year, prior to January 1, 19X3. Net income was $50,000 in 19X1 and $60,000 in 19X2.
(2) Added shares would be issued on January 1, 19X3, to compensate for any fall in the value of Gonring common stock below $6 per share. The settlement would be to cure the deficiency by issuing added shares based on their market value on January 1, 19X3. The market price of the shares on January 1, 19X3, was $4.

Exercise 9. Onan Company intends to engage in a pooling of interests with General Company. General Company has 50,000 shares of common stock outstanding on the initiation date. Onan will issue one of its shares for every two General shares. On the initiation date, Onan already owns 1,000 General shares and a wholly owned subsidiary of Onan owns another 1,500 shares.

By the consummation date, Onan issued 22,000 of its shares in accord with the predetermined exchange rate. Onan also purchased 1,000 General shares from dissident shareholders of General Company for cash.

Determine the number of General Company shares that are eligible to meet the 90% test which is required to record the acquisition as a pooling of interests. Has the 90% test been satisfied?

Exercise 10. Company P holds 96,000 shares of Company S common stock on December 31, 19X6. Of these shares, 92,000 were acquired after the initiation date of the business combination by issuing 1 share of Company P stock in exchange for every 5 shares of Company S stock, 2,000 shares were purchased after the initiation date using cash, and 2,000 shares were acquired prior to the initiation date on the 1-for-5 exchange basis. On the initiation date, Company S held 500 shares of Company P stock. At all times, there were 100,000 shares of Company S common stock outstanding.

Analyze the combination to see if it qualifies as a pooling of interests.

Exercise 11. After lengthy negotiations, Fischer Industries and Taylor International have decided to merge on January 1, 19X2. This transaction meets the requirements for a pooling of interests and Fischer will be the issuer.

Immediately prior to the pooling, Taylor International prepared the following balance sheet:

Taylor International
Balance Sheet
December 31, 19X1

Assets		Liabilities and Equity		
Current assets	$ 400,000	Current liabilities		$ 100,000
Property, plant, and		Bonds payable		800,000
equipment	2,200,000	Stockholders' equity:		
Accum. depreciation	(500,000)	Common stock ($10 par)	$ 200,000	
		Retained earnings	1,000,000	1,200,000
Total assets	$2,100,000	Total liabilities and equity		$2,100,000

Negotiations revolved around what Taylor felt his business was worth and what Fischer was willing to pay. It was finally agreed that the value of Taylor's net assets, including company goodwill was $1,800,000 and would be paid with $5 par common stock having a market value of $50. Fischer Industries will issue the required number of previously unissued shares in exchange for all of the net assets of Taylor International. The following independent appraisals have been made:

Property, plant, and equipment	2,000,000
Bonds payable	750,000

In consummating the transaction, Fischer Industries incurred $5,000 of direct acquisition costs and $20,000 for stock registration and issuance.

(1) Determine the number of shares of stock that Fischer Industries will issue.

(2) Record the pooling of interests on the books of Fischer Industries.

(3) What entry would Taylor International make to record the receipt of the shares and their distribution to the shareholders in order to liquidate the company?

Exercise 12. Echo Company is issuing 100,000 shares of its common stock for the 100,000 outstanding shares of Fox Company in a pooling of interests. Echo's stockholders' equity is as follows:

Common stock	$1,000,000
Paid-in capital in excess of par	200,000
Retained earnings	600,000

The balance sheet of Fox Company at the time of the pooling is as follows:

Assets

Current assets	$ 100,000
Equipment (net)	100,000
Plant (net)	200,000
Total	$ 400,000

Liabilities and Equity

Liabilities	$ 50,000
Common stock, $1 par	100,000
Paid-in capital in excess of par	100,000
Retained earnings	150,000
Total	$ 400,000

Prepare the pooling entry for each of the following independent cases:
(1) The par value of the Echo Company shares is $2.
(2) The par value of the Echo Company shares is $5.

Exercise 13. On December 31, 19X5, Lumina Company has the following balance sheet:

Assets		Liabilities and Equity	
Cash	$100,000	Liabilities	$150,000
Receivables	150,000	Common stock ($5 par)	50,000
Inventory	200,000	Paid-in capital in excess	
Land	50,000	of par	450,000
Buildings (net)	280,000	Retained earnings	210,000
Equipment (net)	80,000		
Total assets	$860,000	Total liabilities and equity	$860,000

Zeeco Company will issue its $10 par value shares on a 1-for-1 basis to accomplish a pooling of interests. There are, however some adjustments that may need to be acknowledged before the pooling can be recorded.

The inventory of Lumina Company is recorded on a LIFO basis. Zeeco uses the FIFO method and will also convert Lumina's inventory to FIFO. This will increase the inventory cost to $250,000. The building is obsolete and has an appraised value of only $100,000. The recorded liabilities do not include accrued interest of $5,000.
(1) Prepare the adjusting entries needed on the books of Lumina Company prior to the pooling of interests.
(2) Prepare the entry that Zeeco Company will make to record the pooling of interests. Support the entry with an equity transfer chart.

Exercise 14. Marcus Company is going to exchange its 10,000 of treasury shares for all 50,000 outstanding shares of Koempfer Company in a business combination to be recorded as a pooling of interests. Just prior to the pooling, the two companies had the following balance sheets:

Assets		Marcus		Koempfer
Current assets		$ 310,000		$ 200,000
Property, plant, and equipment (net)		1,400,000		800,000
Total assets		$1,710,000		$1,000,000
Liabilities and Equity				
Current liabilities		$ 170,000		$ 90,000
Common stock	($5 par)	500,000	($2 par)	100,000
Paid-in capital in excess of par		800,000		170,000
Retained earnings		360,000		640,000
Treasury stock at cost, 10,000 shares		(120,000)		
Total liabilities and equity		$1,710,000		$1,000,000

Prepare the journal entries for Marcus Company to record the pooling of interests with Koempfer Company. (Prepare a retirement entry for the treasury stock prior to recording the pooling.)

Exercise 15. End Company acquired the net assets of Carol Corporation on January 1, 19X1. End Company agreed to issue, at face, 10%, $1,000, 10-year bonds in an amount equal to the market value of Carol's net assets. Compensation for goodwill arising from the acquisition will be satisfied through the issuance of common stock. End's common stock has a par value of $5 and a current market value of $20.

End Company will capitalize any excess net income as a perpetuity at 20%. Carol's operating net income has been $60,000 per year, and the normal return is 12% of the market value of total identifiable assets.

Carol Corporation had the following balance sheet on January 1, 19X1:

Carol Corporation
Balance Sheet
January 1, 19X1

Assets		Liabilities and Equity		
Current assets......................	$ 50,000	Current liabilities		$ 40,000
Property, plant, and equipment:		Stockholders' equity:		
Equipment (net)....................	300,000	Common stock ($5 par)	$ 50,000	
		Paid-in capital in excess of par	150,000	
		Retained earnings	110,000	310,000
Total assets	$350,000	Total liabilities and equity...........		$350,000

End Company arrived at the following market values for Carol Corporation's assets:

Current assets.............................	$ 60,000
Property, plant, and equipment...............	$400,000

(1) Calculate the price paid for the net assets of Carol Corporation.
(2) Record the acquisition on the books of End Company.

PROBLEMS

Problem 1-1. Gantner Company is contemplating the acquisition of Mallow Inc. on January 1, 19X1. Gantner wishes to explore the consequences of recording the acquisition as a purchase versus as a pooling of interests. Gantner would like you to predict the pro forma income of the new, combined firms under the alternative methods.

If Gantner proceeded to acquire Mallow as a purchase, it would pay $600,000 cash to Mallow and would pay direct acquisition costs of $20,000. If Gantner were to pool with Mallow, it would issue 20,000 shares of its $10 par stock which has a market value of $30 per share. Direct acquisition costs would still be $20,000.

The January 1, 19X1, balance sheet of Mallow Inc. is anticipated to be as follows:

Mallow Inc.
Pro Forma Balance Sheet
January 1, 19X1

Assets		Liabilities and Equity	
Cash equivalents.............	$100,000	Current liabilities.............	$ 30,000
Accounts receivable..........	120,000	Long-term liabilities	165,000
Inventory	50,000	Common stock ($10 par)......	80,000
Property, plant, and		Retained earnings............	115,000
equipment	200,000		
Accum. depreciation	(80,000)		
Total assets	$390,000	Total liabilities and equity	$390,000

Market values agree with book values except for the inventory and the property, plant, and equipment which have a market value of $70,000 and $400,000, respectively.

Your projections of the combined operations for 19X1 are as follows:

Combined sales.	$200,000
Combined cost of goods sold, including beginning inventory of Mallow at book value which will be sold in 19X1.	120,000
Other expenses not including depreciation of Mallow assets or goodwill amortization	25,000

Depreciation on Mallow fixed assets is straight line using a 20-year life. Goodwill, if existent, is amortized over 10 years.

Required:
(1) In good form, prepare the entry to record the acquisition of Mallow first as a purchase and then as a pooling of interests. Gantner has paid-in excess of par of $200,000.
(2) Prepare a pro forma income statement for the combined firm for 19X1 under both the purchase and pooling of interests methods. Prepare support for all calculation of consolidated income. Ignore tax issues.

Problem 1-2. Dixon Corporation has been looking to expand its operations and has decided to acquire the assets of Bruce Company and Grambow Company. Dixon will issue 25,000 shares of its $10 par common stock to acquire the net assets of Bruce Company and will issue 12,000 shares to acquire the net assets of Grambow Company.

Bruce Company and Grambow Company have the following balance sheets as of December 31, 19X1:

Assets	Bruce	Grambow
Inventory	$120,000	$ 80,000
Other current assets.	140,000	50,000
Long-term investment in marketable securities (at cost)	220,000	35,000
Property, plant, and equipment:		
Land.	120,000	50,000
Building.	500,000	300,000
Accumulated depreciation	(150,000)	(110,000)
Total assets.	$950,000	$ 405,000

Liabilities and Equity		
Current liabilities.	$160,000	$ 55,000
Bonds payable.	200,000	100,000
Stockholders' equity:		
Common stock ($10 par).	300,000	100,000
Retained earnings.	290,000	150,000
Total liabilities and equity	$950,000	$ 405,000

The following market values are agreed upon by the two firms:

Assets	Bruce	Grambow
Inventory	$120,000	$ 100,000
Current assets	140,000	50,000
Marketable securities.	270,000	30,000
Land.	100,000	60,000
Buildings.	400,000	350,000

Dixon's stock is currently trading at $40 per share. Dixon will incur $10,000 of direct acquisition costs, $13,000 of indirect acquisition costs, and $15,000 of registration and issue costs.

Required:

Record the acquisition on the books of Dixon Corporation, using purchase accounting principles.

Problem 1-3. Use the facts of problem 1-2 for the acquisition of Bruce and Grambow by Dixon. Assume that the pooling criteria are met. Be sure to record assets at their lower of cost or market.

Required:

Record the acquisition on the books of Dixon Corporation, using pooling of interest accounting principles.

Problem 1-4. Caswell Company is contemplating the purchase of LaBelle Company as of January 1, 19X8. LaBelle Company has provided the following current balance sheet:

Assets		Liabilities and Equity	
Cash and receivables.....	$150,000	Current liabilities................	$120,000
Inventory	180,000	9% bonds payable	300,000
Land	50,000	Common stock ($5 par)..........	100,000
Building	600,000	Paid-in capital in excess of par.....	200,000
Accum. depreciation ...	(150,000)	Retained earnings...............	150,000
Goodwill................	40,000		
Total assets	$870,000	Total liabilities and equity........	$870,000

The following information exists relative to balance sheet accounts:
(a) The inventory has a fair market value of $200,000.
(b) The land is appraised at $100,000 and the building at $600,000.
(c) The 9% bonds payable have 5 years to maturity and pay annual interest each December 31. The current interest rate for similar bonds is 8% per year.
(d) It is likely that there will be a payment for goodwill based on projected income in excess of the industry average which is 10% on total assets. Caswell will project the average past 5 years' operating income and will pay for excess income based on an assumption of a 5-year life and a risk rate of return of 16%. The past 5 years' net incomes for LaBelle are:

19X3	$120,000
19X4	$140,000
19X5	$150,000
19X6	$200,000 (includes $40,000 extraordinary gain)
19X7	$180,000

Required:
(1) Provide an estimate of fair value for the bonds and for goodwill.
(2) Using the values derived in (1), record the purchase on the Caswell books.

Problem 1-5. Jay Taylor Records is considering the purchase of Rose Records Incorporated. Jay has asked you, his accountant, to evaluate the various offers he might make to Rose Records Incorporated. The December 31, 19X1, balance sheet of Rose Records Incorporated is as follows:

Rose Records Incorporated
Balance Sheet
December 31, 19X1

Assets			Liabilities and Equity			
Current assets:			Accounts payable			$ 40,000
Accounts receivable	$ 50,000					
Inventory...................	200,000					
		$250,000	Stockholders' equity:			
Noncurrent assets:			Common stock..............	$ 40,000		
Land......................	$ 20,000		Paid-in capital in excess of par ..	110,000		
Buildings (net)	70,000	90,000	Retained earnings	150,000	300,000	
Total assets.................		$340,000	Total liabilities and equity		$340,000	

The following market values differ from existing book values:

Inventory	$250,000
Land	40,000
Building	120,000

Required:

Record the purchase entry for Jay Taylor Records that would result under each of the alternative offers.

(1) Jay Taylor Records issues 20,000 of its $10 par common stock with a market value of $25 per share for the net assets of Rose Records Incorporated.

(2) Jay Taylor Records issues 400, $1,000 face value 8% bonds to Rose Records Incorporated for its net assets. Other bonds are issued the same day at 98% of face value.

(3) Jay Taylor Records pays $225,000 in cash.

Problem 1-6. Sensor Inc. purchased for $1,800,000 in cash the net assets of All-Equipment Leasing Company. The purchase was made on December 31, 19X1, at which time All-Equipment had prepared the following balance sheet:

All-Equipment Leasing Company
Balance Sheet
December 31, 19X1

Assets		Liabilities and Equity	
Current assets	$ 100,000	Current liabilities	$ 150,000
Assets under		Obligation under capital	
operating leases	520,000	lease of equipment	35,000
Net investment in direct		Common stock ($5 par)	100,000
financing			
(capital leases)	730,000	Paid-in capital in excess	
Leased equipment under		of par	400,000
capital lease (net).........	40,000		
Buildings (net)	200,000	Retained earnings	955,000
Land......................	50,000		
Total assets...............	$1,640,000	Total liabilities and equity ...	$1,640,000

The following information is available concerning the assets and liabilities of All-Equipment:

(a) Current assets and liabilities are stated fairly. No payments resulting from leases are included in current accounts, since all payments are due each December 31 and payment for 19X1 has been made.

(b) Assets under operating leases have an estimated value of $580,000. This figure includes consideration of remaining rents and the value of the assets at the end of the lease terms.

(c) The net investment in direct financing leases represents receivables at their discounted present values. All leases are written at the current market interest rate of 12%, except one equipment lease requiring payments of $50,000 per year for 5 remaining years. The $50,000 payments include interest at 8%.

(d) The buildings and the land have appraised market values of $400,000 and $100,000, respectively.

(e) The leased equipment under the capital lease pertains to a computer used by All-Equipment. The obligation under the capital lease of equipment includes the present value of 5 remaining payments of $9,233 due at the end of each year and discounted at 10%. The current interest rate for this type of transaction is 12%. The market value of the equipment under the lease is $60,000.

(f) All-Equipment has been named in a $200,000 lawsuit involving an accident by a lessee using its equipment. It is likely that All-Equipment will be found liable in the amount of $50,000.

Required:
Record the purchase of All-Equipment Leasing Company by Sensor Inc. Carefully support your entry.

Problem 1-7.   Gusty Company issued 10,000 shares of $10 par common stock for the net assets of Marco Incorporated on December 31, 19X2. The stock has a market value of $60 per share. Direct acquisition costs were $10,000 and the cost of issuing the stock was $3,000. At the time of the purchase, Marco had the following summarized balance sheet:

Assets

Current assets	$150,000
Equipment (net).	200,000 *300,000*
Land and buildings (net)	250,000
Total assets.	$600,000

Liabilities and Stockholders' Equity

Bonds payable.	$200,000
Common stock, $10 par.	100,000
Retained earnings.	300,000
Total liabilities and equity	$600,000

The only market value differing from book value is equipment, which is worth $300,000. Marco has $120,000 in operating losses in prior years. The previous asset values are also the tax basis of the assets which, since the acquisition is a tax-free exchange, will be the tax basis for Gusty. Gusty is confident that it will recover the entire tax loss carryforward applicable to the past losses of Marco. The applicable tax rate is 30%.

Required:
Record the purchase of the net assets of Marco Incorporated by Gusty Company.

Problem 1-8. Dodd Corporation is purchasing the net assets, exclusive of cash, of Walsh Company as of January 1, 19X1, at which time Walsh Company's balance sheet is as follows:

Assets

Current assets:

Cash..	$ 30,000	
Accounts receivable	50,000	$ 80,000

Noncurrent assets:

Investments in marketable securities	$ 120,000	
Land..	600,000	
Buildings (net)	450,000	
Equipment (net).....................................	800,000	
Goodwill	100,000	2,070,000
Total assets..		$2,150,000

Liabilities and Stockholders' Equity

Current liabilities:

Accounts payable	$ 150,000	
Income tax payable..................................	190,000	$ 340,000

Equity:

Common stock, $5 par...............................	$1,200,000	
Retained earnings	610,000	1,810,000
Total liabilities and equity		$2,150,000

Dodd Corporation feels that the following market values should be substituted for Walsh's book values:

Accounts receivable	$ 60,000
Investment in marketable securities	150,000
Land..	450,000
Buildings...	450,000
Equipment	600,000
Accounts payable	120,000

Dodd will issue 20,000 shares of its common stock with a $2 par value and a quoted market value of $60 per share on January 1, 19X1, to Walsh Company to acquire the net assets, exclusive of cash. Dodd also agrees that two years later it will issue additional securities to compensate Walsh for any decline in value below that on the date of issue.

Required:

(1) Record the purchase on the books of Dodd Corporation on January 1, 19X1. Include support for calculations used to arrive at the values assigned to the assets and liabilities.

(2) Indicate the disclosure that would be necessary in the financial statements of Dodd Corporation on December 31, 19X1, assuming the quoted value of the stock is $62 per share.

(3) Record payment (if any) of contingent consideration on January 1, 19X3, assuming that the quoted value of the stock is $57.50. (Round shares to nearest whole share.)

Problem 1-9. Boyd Company wishes to obtain total control over one of its suppliers, Konkol Corporation. Boyd Company is offering to exchange 100,000 shares of its common stock on a one-to-one basis for Konkol's common stock.

Konkol Corporation has the following balance sheet on December 31, 19X1:

Konkol Corporation
Balance Sheet
December 31, 19X1

in excess of mkt value?

Assets			Liabilities and Equity		
Accounts receivable		$ 150,000	Accounts payable		$ 200,000
Inventory.		340,000	Stockholders' equity:		
Property, plant, and			Common stock ($5 par 100,000		
equipment:			shares outstanding).	$500,000	600k
Land.	$ 150,000		Paid-in capital in excess of par . . .	100,000	
Building.	900,000		Retained earnings	496,000	1,096,000
Accum. depreciation. . . .	(244,000)	806,000			
Total assets		$1,296,000	Total liabilities and equity.		$1,296,000

Konkol Corporation has been depreciating its building using the double-declining-balance method. Boyd Company intends to use the straight-line method, ensuring that all assets are depreciated uniformly. Had the straight-line method been used by Konkol Corporation, the depreciation charges would have been $135,000.

This transaction meets all of the pooling criteria. The stockholders' equity of Boyd Company on January 1, 19X1 is as follows:

Common stock ($2 par value, 300,000 shares outstanding).	$600,000
Paid-in capital in excess of par.	100,000
Retained earnings.	800,000

Required:
(Ignore tax effects)
(1) Record the pooling of interests on the books of Boyd Company.
(2) Assume, instead, that Boyd Company has 100,000 shares of $6 par value common stock outstanding. Record the pooling of interests on the books of Boyd Company.
(3) Assume, instead, that Boyd Company has 50,000 shares of $12 par value common stock outstanding. Record the pooling of interests on the books of Boyd Company if it then issues 60,000 shares to acquire Konkol. All other equity items remain unchanged.

Problem 1-10. Gazzola Company is a corporation that was organized on July 1, 19X1. The June 30, 19X6 balance sheet for Gazzola is as follows:

Assets

Investments.		$ 400,500
Accounts receivable	$1,250,000	
Allowance for doubtful accounts	(300,000)	950,000
Inventory.		1,500,000
Prepaid insurance		18,000
Land		58,000
Machinery and equipment (net)		1,473,500
Goodwill		100,000
Total assets		$4,500,000

Liabilities and Equity

Current liabilities	$1,475,000
Common stock, $10 par	1,200,000
Retained earnings	1,825,000
Total liabilities and equity.	$4,500,000

Machinery was purchased in fiscal years 19X2, 19X4, and 19X5 for $500,000, $850,000, and $660,000, respectively. The straight-line method of depreciation and a 10-year esti-mated life with no salvage value have been used for all machinery, with a half-year of depreciation taken in the year of acquisition. The experience of other companies over the last several years indicates that the machinery can be sold at 125% of its book value.

An analysis of the accounts receivable indicates that the allowance for doubtful accounts should be increased to $337,500. An independent appraisal made in June 19X1 valued the land at $70,000. Using the lower cost or market rule, inventory is to be restated at $1,200,000.

To be exchanged are 14,500 shares of Hayes Corporation for 120,000 Gazzola shares. During June 19X6, the market value of a share of Hayes Corporation was $265. The stockholders' equity account balances of Hayes Corporation as of June 30, 19X6, were as follows:

Common stock, $100 par	$2,000,000
Additional paid-in capital	580,000
Retained earnings	2,496,400
Total stockholders' equity.	$5,076,400

Direct acquisition costs are $12,000.

Required:

Assuming the books of Hayes Corporation are to be retained, prepare the necessary journal entry (or entries) to effect the business combination on July 1, 19X6 as (1) a pooling of interests and (2) a purchase. All supporting schedules should be in good form.

Problem 1-11. In a business combination to be accounted for as a pooling of interests, Hawk Corporation will issue on December 31, 19X6, 50,000 shares of its $5 par common stock, which has a market value of $20 per share, in exchange for the net assets, including cash, of Rogers Corporation.

The two firms decided that Rogers should change from the FIFO method of valuing inventory to the LIFO method. The board of directors of Rogers Corporation agreed that these adjustments will be made on a retroactive basis.

The following end-of-year inventory information has been supplied by Rogers:

	FIFO	LIFO
19X5.	$170,000	$150,000
19X6.	200,000	146,000

Income statement data for both companies before any effect of changes in principal, cumulative effects, and extraordinary items were:

	19X5		19X6	
	Hawk	Rogers	Hawk	Rogers
Sales	$900,000	$ 600,000	$1,100,000	$650,000
Cost of sales.	480,000	400,000	596,000	430,000
Operating expenses	150,000	100,000	200,000	110,000

Hawk Corporation also discovered that Rogers Corporation has been using the cash method to account for warranties. Hawk Corporation uses the accrual warranty treatment and will make the necessary adjustments to account for Rogers warranties in this manner. A review of products sold and still under warranty suggests the following liability status:

	19X5	19X6
Actual liability for the year	$40,000	$65,000
Amount recorded by Rogers Corporation	20,000	25,000

Just prior to the exchange, Hawk and Rogers had the following balance sheets:

Assets	Hawk	Rogers
Cash	$ 160,000	$ 80,000
Accounts receivable.	420,000	200,000
Inventory	350,000	200,000
Property, plant, and equipment (net)	1,200,000	500,000
Total assets	$2,130,000	$980,000

Liabilities and Equity		
Current liabilities.	$ 250,000	$100,000
Bonds payable		350,000
Stockholders' equity:		
Common stock ($5 par).	500,000	100,000
Paid-in capital in excess of par.	600,000	250,000
Retained earnings.	780,000	180,000
Total liabilities and equity	$2,130,000	$980,000

Required:
(1) Prepare a pro forma balance sheet to give effect to the business combination regarded as a pooling of interests.
(2) Prepare a comparative income statement for the years 19X5 and 19X6 for the combined corporation. (Ignore income taxes.)

CASE 1   PURCHASE OR POOL

Snow Parts Inc. is a mail order retailer of snowmobile parts. The firm now has an opportunity to expand its operations into the all-terrain vehicle parts business by acquiring Off-Roaders Inc. The deal can be structured as a pooling of interests or as a purchase. While Off-Roaders would prefer a cash payment, they are willing to take Snow Parts common stock in exchange. The president of Snow Parts asks your advice on whether to purchase or pool from the standpoint of impact on future year's income. He also is concerned about the reasonableness of the price Off-Roaders is seeking.

The following balance sheet was provided by Off-Roaders for the year just ended:

Assets		Liabilities and Equity	
Accounts receivable	$ 400,000	Current liabilities..............	$ 300,000
Inventory..............	400,000	8% bonds payable	600,000
Land.................	400,000	Common stock ($1 par)........	100,000
Building (net)	700,000	Paid-in capital in excess of par...	600,000
Equipment (net)........	200,000	Retained earnings.............	500,000
Total assets	$2,100,000	Total liabilities and equity	$2,100,000

Your research has found the following information about the above accounts:
(a) The accounts receivable and all liabilities are close enough to market value so that purchase accounting would not require any adjustment.
(b) The inventory has a market value of $500,000 and would clearly be sold by the end of the next year.
(c) The land is close to market value, but the building is worth $1,500,000 and the equipment is worth $500,000. The building has a 20-year remaining life and the equipment a 10-year remaining life.
(d) It is common to pay for 5 years of excess earnings. Normal earnings in this industry is 12% of the market value of total assets. The average annual income of Off-Roaders has been $500,000. If goodwill is to be recorded, it would be appropriate to amortize it over 10 years.

You have received pro forma income statements for both firms for the coming year. Of course, the income statement of Off-Roaders is based on existing book values. Projected results are:

	Snow Parts	Off-Roaders
Sales revenue.......................................	$3,000,000	$1,400,000
Cost of goods sold....................................	1,500,000	600,000
General and administrative expense	300,000	200,000
Depreciation expense	200,000	55,000
Net income	$1,000,000	$ 545,000

You have the following summaries of the two proposals that are acceptable to Off-Roaders:

Deal 1   The price being asked is $3,000,000 cash. Off-Roaders agrees that Snow Parts common stock is trading at $33 but fears dilution because of the major new issue that would be used as payment. Thus, Off-Roaders is using an assumed market value per share of $30 and is asking for 100,000 shares under this option.

Deal 2   Pay $3,000,000 cash. The funds would be borrowed by issuing long-term bonds.

In either event, direct acquisition costs covering accountants' and lawyers' fees are expected to be $100,000. The president of Snow Parts feels the use of the low $30 stock price is basically a premium being charged for the pooling of interests accounting treatment. You are convinced that the pooling criteria would not be violated if Deal 1 is accomplished.

Required:
Draft a memo to the president of Snow Parts covering the fairness of the price and advising of the impact of purchase versus pooling on the following years' combined incomes of the newly merged firm. Include with the memo all needed supporting schedules.

CASE 2   BOOKING A BARGAIN

The controller of one of your primary clients has called upon you for assistance in analyzing a major business acquisition that his firm is considering. The client is a firm called Your Office Inc. The firm runs a chain of unique shops in a major city. The shops derive their revenue from doing high quality copying and artwork and by selling customized office supplies. Due to their convenience to customers, they also sell some common generic supplies. Your Office Inc. has found an opportunity to purchase a four-store chain of traditional office supply stores in a nearby city.

The chain does business as Smith Office Supplies. It has been losing money in recent years since it has had problems competing with a large new discount office supply store in the same city. The chain is in serious enough financial trouble that it is under pressure from the bank holding its notes payable. The bank involved has brought the opportunity to your client's attention.

You have been provided the following balance sheet:

Smith Office Supply
Balance Sheet
December 31, 19X4

Assets

Current assets:

Cash equivalents	$100,000	
Accounts receivable	260,000	
Inventories	220,000	$ 580,000

Property, plant, and equipment:

	Cost	Accumulated Depreciation	Net	
Property A	$ 310,000	$160,000	$150,000	
Property B	370,000	170,000	200,000	
Property C	480,000	180,000	300,000	
Property D	250,000	150,000	100,000	
	$1,410,000	$660,000		750,000
Total assets				$1,330,000

Liabilities and Stockholders' Equity

Accounts payable		$ 100,000
Notes payable		400,000
Stockholders' equity:		
Common stock, 500,000 shares authorized and		
outstanding ($1 par)	$500,000	
Paid-in capital in excess of par	100,000	
Retained earnings	230,000	830,000
Total liabilities and stockholders' equity		$1,330,000

You have also secured the following information:

(a) Aging of the accounts receivable suggests that a $50,000 allowance for bad debts is needed.

(b) Much of the inventory is obsolete and other inventory is not compatible with Your Office Inc.'s product line. The inventory would be sold at a special liquidation sale and has a net realizable value of $150,000.

(c) There are four stores, shown as A through D on the balance sheet. Three, A through C, are in good locations and would be remodeled into Your Office shops. Store D is in a poor location and would be sold as soon as possible. A reputable realtor said that you would net $120,000 for store D. The estimated value of the other stores are: Store A at $200,000, store B at $180,000 and store C at $150,000. These values for stores A through C are questionable if a fast sale were desired.

(d) The notes payable are held by the bank, are overdue and in default. There is $40,000 of accrued interest that has not been recorded. The accounts payable are fairly stated.

Your client has met with the owners of Smith Office Supplies and the bank. There is a tentative agreement. Your Office Inc. would assume all liabilities of Smith and would pay only $400,000 cash to the owners of the firm. Smith has no interest in taking back stock of your client and thus pooling of interests is out of the question. Your client wants to know how the transaction would be accounted for, the major concern being the asset values recorded and the impact of the values assigned on future income statements. Your client's controller is concerned about management's possible misperceptions. Management has heard two opinions from friends. One is that since the deal is a bargain, the company could take an immediate gain at the time of the purchase. The other opinion is that "negative goodwill" would be recorded and allocated over 40 years.

Required:

Provide a report to your client indicating the values you would assign to all accounts if the purchase were to occur. The report should also directly address the accuracy of the two opinions management has received from friends.

CHAPTER 2

Consolidated Statements at the Date of Acquisition

The preceding chapter provided the accounting methods used to record business combinations that are asset acquisitions. This chapter applies the theories, developed in Chapter 1, to stock acquisitions. Legally, the controlling parent firm only has an investment in another firm and that is all it will record on its accounting records. However, the parent is able to control the subsidiary's operations, and the subsidiary's operations often will become integrated with those of the parent. When control through stock ownership exists, consolidated statements are necessary to erase the legal boundaries between the parent and the subsidiary and to present the financial statements of the affiliated firms as those of a single economic entity. This chapter is the first of several that will attempt to build a comprehensive set of principles and methods for the preparation of consolidated statements.

THE FUNCTION OF CONSOLIDATED STATEMENTS

Consolidated financial statements are designed to present the results of operations, cash flow, and the financial position of the parent and its subsidiaries as if they were a single firm. Generally, consolidated statements are most informative to the stockholders of the controlling firm. Yet, consolidated statements do have their shortcomings. The rights of minority shareholders are limited to only the subsidiary company whose shares they own. Minority stockholders get little value from consolidated statements; they need the separate statements of the subsidiary. Creditors may look only to the legal entity that is indebted to them for the satisfaction of their claims. The creditors of the minority firm need the statements of the subsidiary to assess their position. The creditors of the parent should be content with consolidated statements since the investment in the subsidiary is an asset that produces cash flow that may be used to service their claim.

Consolidated statements have been criticized for being too aggregated. Unprofitable subsidiaries may not be obvious since, when consolidated, their performance is combined with that of other affiliates. This shortcoming is easily overcome. One option is to prepare separate statements for the subsidiaries as supplements to the consolidated statements. The second option, which may be required, is to provide disclosure for major business segments. Where subsidiaries are in businesses distinct from the parent, the definition of a segment may parallel that of a subsidiary.

TRADITIONAL CRITERIA FOR CONSOLIDATED STATEMENTS

Generally, statements are to be consolidated when a parent firm owns over 50% of the voting common stock of another company. There may be instances where consolidation is appropriate even though less than 51% of the voting common stock is owned by the parent. SEC Regulation S-X defines control in terms of power to direct or cause the direction of management and policies of a person, whether through the ownership of voting securities, by contract, or otherwise. Thus, control has been said to exist when a less than 51% ownership interest exists but where there is no other large ownership interest that can exert influence on management. The exception to consolidating when control exists is if control is only temporary or does not rest with the majority owner. Control would be presumed not to reside with the majority owner, for example, when the subsidiary is in bankruptcy or in legal reorganization, or when foreign exchange restrictions or foreign government controls cast doubt on the ability of the parent to exercise control over the subsidiary.

Prior to 1988, it was acceptable to exclude subsidiaries from consolidation when their operations were not homogeneous with those of the parent. It was common for a manufacturing-based parent to exclude from consolidations those subsidiaries involved in banking, financing, real estate, or leasing activities, but this exception for "nonhomogeneity" came under criticism. Frequently, firms diversified and excluded some types of subsidiaries from consolidation. This meant that a significant amount of assets, liabilities, and cash flows were not presented. The option of not consolidating selected subsidiaries often was considered a form of "off-balance sheet" financing. For instance, Ford, General Motors, and Chrysler did not consolidate their financing company subsidiaries; this meant that millions of dollars of debt did not appear on the consolidated balance sheets of these firms. Stockholders are interested in the total financial position of the corporation, regardless of how diversified the operations have become. Based on their concerns and the divergence in practice as to consolidation policy, the nonhomogeneity exception was eliminated by FASB Statement No. 94.[1] In addition, the statement eliminated less commonly used exceptions for

---

[1]Statement of Financial Accounting Standards No. 94, *Consolidation of All Majority-Owned Subsidiaries* (Stamford: Financial Accounting Standards Board, 1987).

large minority interests and foreign locations. There is a concern that the combining of unlike operations will cloud the interpretation of financial statements. In response to this concern, many corporations are preparing classified balance sheets that separate the assets and liabilities of the nonhomogeneous operations. Ford Motor Company segregates their financial services subsidiaries, which in the past had not been consolidated.

Nonconsolidated subsidiaries now have become a rarity. When they do exist, they are accounted for as an investment under the equity method. The accounting methods for such an investment are discussed in Chapter 6.

CONSOLIDATION WITH OR WITHOUT MAJORITY OWNERSHIP

It already has been noted that the SEC has suggested that where control exists without majority ownership of voting shares, consolidation may be appropriate. The FASB, in Statement No. 94, also suggested this possibility. A Discussion Memorandum (DM), "Consolidation Policies and Procedures," issued by the FASB in September of 1991 continues to study the issue of consolidating without majority ownership. This discussion memorandum, like others, does not take a position on issues but, rather, raises and studies relevant issues.

The DM first defines control as "the power to direct or cause the direction of the management and the operating and financing policies of another entity."[2] It goes on to state that to accomplish this objective, the parent must have the ability to decide how the subsidiary's resources are obtained, used, and financed in much the same manner as it would control its own resources. The DM takes the position that this control requires the parent to have the ability to elect or remove a majority of the board of directors or to otherwise control the majority of the votes. Since many of the decisions involving the obtaining, using, and financing of resources require stockholder approval, the DM suggests that control usually would include the ability to obtain stockholder approval. The memorandum makes it clear that control requires the ability to secure approval for actions, not just the ability to block actions.

The DM states that control might be achieved in three alternative fashions: (1) possession of the ability to exercise a majority of the voting rights, (2) ownership of enough minority interest to achieve control, or (3) acquisition of control through a contractual arrangement or a lease.

CONTROL BY OWNERSHIP OF, OR ABILITY TO EXERCISE, A MAJORITY OF VOTING RIGHTS

Ownership sufficient to control a majority of voting rights frequently is termed "legal control" since it is enforceable under the law. Legal control is most obvious

---

[2]FASB Discussion Memorandum, *Consolidation Policy and Procedures* (Norwalk, CT: Financial Accounting Standards Board, September 1991).

when the parent owns a majority of a single class of common stock. There are, however, other means of achieving such control. The first is the practice of "pyramiding," whereby there are several tiers of corporations and each tier is controlled by the corporation above it. For example, Company A owns a 51% interest in Company B and Company B, in turn, owns a 51% interest in Company C. Even though Company A owns an effective 26% (51% × 51%) interest in Company C, it indirectly controls it. Traditionally, this type of control, termed "indirect" in this text, has led to consolidated statements.

Typically, control is achieved by owning a greater than 50% interest in the single class of common stock. There are, however, corporations that have multiple classes of common stock, where a given class may have the majority of voting rights even though it has a limited right to distributions of profits. In some cases, preferred shareholders may be granted the majority of the voting rights; control may be achieved by securing ownership of a majority of voting rights without owning a majority of the firm's residual interest. Finally, there may be situations where a voting trust is established. Voting trusts may be used voluntarily to unify control or involuntarily as a result of legal actions by creditors or stockholders. Where the trust has title to sufficient shares to control the corporation and the trust is controlled by the parent company, control is attained.

CONTROL BY OWNERSHIP OF A LARGE MINORITY OF VOTING RIGHTS

It may be possible to control the voting rights of a corporation by owning less than 50% of the voting shares. This is true especially when the ownership of the remaining shares is dispersed into small holdings of apathetic owners. Here the ability to control rests on the inability of other stockholders to unite and override the large minority interest. In other cases, there may be some shareholders who always vote with or give their proxies (rights to vote) to the large minority interest. Establishing control with only minority interest is a judgment call. There is the danger that such control could end quickly if inactive shareholders were to spring into action. It is very likely that in the future guidelines will be developed by the FASB to aid in the determination of when control without majority ownership exists. At the present time, consolidation of less than a 51% ownership interest is rare.

CONTROL THROUGH MANAGEMENT CONTRACT, LEASE, OR OTHER CONTRACTUAL ARRANGEMENT

Federal securities laws and court decisions state that control of another entity can be achieved through contract or lease without any ownership of the stock of the involved corporation. Sometimes a company is created by another firm to serve a specific function for the founder, such as financing its receivables. Typically, there would be contractual control of the new firm even in the absence of any significant ownership interest. Control by contract or lease may not be as pervasive as control through ownership of voting rights. However, it could be sufficient to judge that effective control does exist, and as a result, consolidation of the firm may be warranted. This is another area where the FASB can be expected to establish guidelines.

TECHNIQUES OF CONSOLIDATION

This chapter builds an understanding of the techniques used to consolidate the separate balance sheets of a parent and its subsidiary immediately subsequent to the acquisition. To focus on the combining of the balance sheet accounts without the complication of subsequent operating transactions, the consolidated balance sheet as of the acquisition date is discussed first. The impact of consolidations on operations after the acquisition date is discussed in Chapters 3 through 8.

Chapter 1 emphasized that there are two means of achieving control over the assets of another firm. A firm may acquire directly the assets of another firm, or it may acquire a controlling interest in the other firm's voting common stock. In an asset acquisition, the firm whose assets were purchased is dissolved. The assets acquired are recorded directly on the books of the purchaser; consolidation of balance sheet amounts is automatic. Where control is achieved through a stock acquisition, the acquired firm (the subsidiary) remains as a separate legal entity with its own financial statements. While the initial accounting for the two types of acquisitions differs significantly, a 100% stock purchase and an asset acquisition have the same effect of creating one larger single reporting entity and should produce the same consolidated balance sheet. There is, however, a difference if the stock acquisition is less than 100%. Then, there will be a minority interest in the consolidated balance sheet which is not possible when the assets are purchased directly.

In the following discussion, the recording of an asset acquisition and a 100% stock acquisition are compared, and the balance sheets that result from each type of acquisition are studied. Then the chapter deals with the accounting procedures needed when there is less than 100% stock ownership and a minority interest exists.

REVIEWING AN ASSET ACQUISITION

Illustration 2-1 demonstrates an asset acquisition of Company S by Company P for cash. Part A of the exhibit presents the balance sheets of the two firms just prior to the acquisition. Part B shows the entry to record Company P's payment of $500,000 in cash for the net assets of Company S. The book values of the assets and liabilities acquired are assumed to be representative of their market values, and no goodwill is acknowledged. The assets and liabilities of Company S are added to those of Company P to produce the balance sheet for the combined firm, shown in Part C. Since account balances are combined in recording the acquisition, statements for the single combined reporting entity are produced automatically, and *no consolidation process is needed*.

Illustration 2-1
Asset Acquisition

A. Balance sheets of Companies P and S prior to acquisition:

Company P Balance Sheet

Assets		Liabilities and Equity	
Cash....................	$ 600,000	Current liabilities..........	$ 150,000
Accounts receivable.......	300,000	Bonds payable............	300,000
Inventory	100,000	Common stock	100,000
Equipment (net)	150,000	Retained earnings.........	600,000
Total..................	$1,150,000	Total..................	$1,150,000

Company S Balance Sheet

Assets		Liabilities and Equity	
Accounts receivable.......	$ 200,000	Current liabilities..........	$ 100,000
Inventory	100,000	Common stock	200,000
Equipment (net)	300,000	Retained earnings.........	300,000
Total..................	$ 600,000	Total..................	$ 600,000

B. Entry on Company P's books to record acquisition of the net assets of Company S by Company P:

Accounts Receivable................................	200,000	
Inventory..	100,000	
Equipment...	300,000	
Current Liabilities...................................		100,000
Cash		500,000

C. Balance sheet of Company P subsequent to asset acquisition:

Company P Balance Sheet

Assets		Liabilities and Equity	
Cash....................	$ 100,000	Current liabilities..........	$ 250,000
Accounts receivable.......	500,000	Bonds payable............	300,000
Inventory	200,000	Common stock	100,000
Equipment (net)	450,000	Retained earnings.........	600,000
Total..................	$1,250,000	Total..................	$1,250,000

CONSOLIDATING A STOCK ACQUISITION

In a stock acquisition, the acquiring firm deals with existing stockholders only, not the firm itself. Assuming the same facts as those used in Illustration 2-1, except that Company P purchases all of the outstanding stock of Company S for $500,000, Company P would make the following entry:

Investment in Subsidiary S. 500,000
      Cash   500,000

    This entry does not acknowledge the individual underlying net assets over which control is achieved. Instead, the acquisition is recorded as an investment that represents controlling interest in the net assets. If no further action is taken, the investment in the subsidiary account would appear as a long-term investment on the balance sheet of Company P. However, this presentation is permitted only if one of the rare exceptions to the requirement for consolidated statements exists.

    Assuming consolidated statements are required, the balance sheets of the separate firms must be combined into a consolidated balance sheet for the single resulting reporting entity. The consolidation process is a supplement to the existing accounting records of the firms. The process begins with the two firms' individual balance sheets from which the accounts representing the intercompany investment must be eliminated.

    The consolidation process is demonstrated in Worksheet 2-1, pages 108–109. (Worksheets referred to in a chapter are at the end of the chapter and in the Student Companion Enrichment Manual, as indicated by the icon in the margin.) The stockholders' equity accounts of the subsidiary are eliminated against the investment in subsidiary account of the parent. These accounts do *not* appear on a consolidated balance sheet. The equity accounts of the subsidiary have no economic substance, since the only common stock owned by parties outside the consolidated firm are the shares issued by the parent company. The investment in subsidiary account is not needed, as it will be replaced by the specific assets and liabilities of the subsidiary.

    After the intercompany investment accounts are eliminated, the account balances of the two firms are combined. Worksheet 2-1 leads to the following formal consolidated balance sheet of Companies P and S:

Company P and Subsidiary Company S
Consolidated Balance Sheet
December 31, 19X1

Assets			Liabilities and Equity		
Current assets:			Current liabilities		$ 250,000
Cash	$100,000		Bonds payable		300,000
Accounts			Stockholders' equity:		
receivable	500,000		Common stock	$100,000	
Inventory	200,000	$ 800,000	Retained earnings	600,000	700,000
Equipment (net)		450,000			
Total assets		$1,250,000	Total liabilities and equity . . .		$1,250,000

    The accounts and amounts on this balance sheet are exactly the same as those on the balance sheet prepared for the asset acquisition in Part C of Illustration 2-1. *This result is the objective of the consolidation process.*

The format of Worksheet 2-1 should be analyzed carefully since it will be used in subsequent examples. It is acceptable to use a single line for like accounts of both firms. However, stockholders' equity accounts are shown on separate lines because the subsidiary equity is partially or entirely eliminated, while the equity of the parent survives as the controlling interest in the consolidated firm. Thus, separation of the equities will avoid confusion when the elimination entries are made.

It must be emphasized again that the consolidated financial statements are only a supplement to the statements of the separate firms. Eliminations are made *only* on the *worksheet* and are *not* recorded on the books of either firm. Since consolidation eliminations are *never recorded*, the consolidation process starts anew *each year* from the statements of the separate firms.

More detailed processes for preparing a consolidated balance sheet will be examined as follows in the remainder of this chapter:

Consolidating a purchase:
　　Parent owns 100% (no minority interest exists).
　　Parent owns less than 100% (a minority interest exists).
Consolidating a pooling of interests.

STOCK ACQUISITION ACCOUNTED FOR AS A PURCHASE

The acquisition of a controlling interest in another firm must be analyzed before it can be recorded. When 90% or more of another firm's voting common stock is obtained and all other pooling criteria are met, the transaction must be recorded according to pooling procedures. All stock acquisitions not meeting the pooling criteria must be recorded under purchase procedures. Since most stock acquisitions do not qualify for the pooling treatment, the purchase treatment is discussed first.

When a subsidiary stock acquisition is to be accounted for as a purchase, the investment should be recorded at fair market value. In most cases, the investment would be recorded at the fair market value of the shares issued by the purchasing firm. For publicly traded firms, this should always be the case. There may be purchases by corporations whose shares do not trade publicly and thus where the market value of the shares is not clear. In these cases, the purchase would be recorded at the estimated fair market value of the net assets over which control is achieved.

To illustrate, assume Company P purchases a 100% interest in Company S by issuing common stock. The summarized balance sheets prepared for Company P and Company S just prior to the purchase are shown in Illustration 2-2.

On December 31, 19X1, Company P issues 20,000 shares of its $10 par stock to acquire all the common stock of Company S and pays $10,000 in direct acquisition costs. Assuming Company P shares have a market value of $50 each, the investment is recorded on Company P's books by the following entry:

Investment in Subsidiary S (20,000 shares × $50 market value
    + $10,000 direct acquisition costs).................... 1,010,000
    Common Stock (20,000 shares × $10 par)   200,000
    Paid-In Capital in Excess of Par........................   800,000
    Cash (for acquisition costs)   10,000

    This entry must acknowledge the market value of the shares exchanged, regardless of the underlying book value of the interest acquired in the subsidiary. As in the case of an asset acquisition, direct acquisition costs are considered part of the total cost of the interest acquired. Thus, in summary, *when deemed to be a purchase, the investment is recorded at fair market value plus direct acquisition costs. In most cases, the market value recorded is that of the consideration given.*

Illustration 2-2
Company P
Balance Sheet
December 31, 19X1

Assets		Liabilities and Equity	
Cash.....................	$ 210,000	Current liabilities..........	$ 300,000
Accounts receivable.......	300,000	Bonds payable............	500,000
Inventory	500,000	Common stock ($10 par)...	500,000
Land.....................	100,000	Paid-in capital in	
Building (net).............	900,000	excess of par	500,000
Equipment (net)	650,000	Retained earnings.........	860,000
Total assets..............	$2,660,000	Total liabilities and equity ..	$2,660,000

Company S
Balance Sheet
December 31, 19X1

Assets		Liabilities and Equity	
Cash.....................	$ 150,000	Current liabilities..........	$ 100,000
Accounts receivable.......	250,000	Bonds payable............	300,000
Inventory	300,000	Common stock ($5 par)....	50,000
Equipment (net)	400,000	Paid-in capital in excess	
		of par..................	350,000
		Retained earnings.........	300,000
Total assets..............	$1,100,000	Total liabilities and equity ..	$1,100,000

CONSOLIDATION OF THE PURCHASE OF 100% INTEREST

The example used for Worksheet 2-1 portrayed a stock purchase where the price paid for its interest in the subsidiary was equal to the book value of the equity acquired. It was also assumed that assets and liabilities had book values equal to their market values. Seldom will this be the case. The price paid will be indicative of the market value of the net assets over which control is achieved. Normally the market value of the net assets will not agree with their book values.

The rules for assigning value to assets and liabilities remain as in Chapter 1. Recall that there are "priority accounts," comprised of current assets, all investments in marketable securities, and all liabilities, that always are recorded at market value. Remaining long-lived assets are raised to market value if the price allows it. Otherwise, the bargain is subtracted from these long-lived assets. In extreme cases, there may be no value to assign to long-lived assets and a deferred credit is recorded.

A "Determination and Distribution of Excess Schedule" will be used to make the assignment of the price paid to subsidiary accounts and to guide worksheet eliminations and adjustments. Tests are built into the schedule to assure allocation of price according to the above principles.

Let us return to the example used in Illustration 2-2 where Company P issued common stock with a market value of $1,000,000 and paid $10,000 in direct acquisition costs to purchase a 100% interest in the common stock of Company S. Assume that the fair market value of Company S's inventory and equipment are estimated to be $350,000 and $550,000, respectively, and the accounts receivable are fairly stated. The following determination and distribution of excess schedule begins by comparing the price paid to the book value of the interest acquired. The cost of the investment exceeds book value by $310,000. Note that the parentheses following the "Excess of cost over book value" indicate that the investment account will have a debit balance after elimination of the parent portion of subsidiary equity. Refer to Worksheet 2-2, pages 110–111, after elimination 1 is made. This balance means that the net assets of Company S must be increased $310,000 to reflect market values when the consolidated statements are prepared.

Company P and Subsidiary Company S Determination and Distribution of Excess Schedule December 31, 19X1			
Price paid for investment in Co. S including direct acquisition costs		$1,010,000	
Less book value of interest acquired:			
Common stock ($5 par)	$ 50,000		
Paid-in capital in excess of par	350,000		
Retained earnings	300,000		
Total stockholders' equity	$700,000		
Interest acquired	100%	700,000	
Excess of cost over book value (debit balance)........		$ 310,000	
Adjustment of priority accounts:			
Inventory..		50,000	Dr
Adjustment of long-lived assets:			
Equipment		150,000	Dr
Goodwill		$ 110,000	Dr

Regardless of the excess, all priority accounts are adjusted to fair market value. In this example, inventory is raised $50,000, leaving $260,000 available for long-lived assets. At this point a test is proposed: *Is the excess available for long-lived assets enough to adjust them all the way to market value?* In this example, the answer is yes, and the equipment is adjusted to market value; the remaining excess goes to goodwill. Had the test not been passed, we would have a "bargain purchase" which requires special allocation procedures included in our next example.

The Dr (debit) designations following the asset adjustments indicated the assets will be debited (increased) in the process of consolidating. Refer to step (2) in the Eliminations & Adjustment columns of Worksheet 2-2 to see these adjustments. As a results of steps (1) and (2):

(1) The investment account of the parent and the underlying stockholders' equity of the subsidiary are eliminated as follows:

Common Stock ($5 par), Co. S	50,000	
Paid-In Capital in Excess of Par, Co. S	350,000	
Retained Earnings, Co. S	300,000	
Investment in Subsidiary S		700,000

(2) The subsidiary's assets are restated on the consolidated balance sheet at fair market value. Goodwill also is acknowledged as follows:

Inventory	50,000	
Equipment	150,000	
Goodwill	110,000	
Investment in Subsidiary S (remaining balance)		310,000

BARGAIN PURCHASE PROCEDURES

A bargain purchase is a purchase at a price too low to allow long-lived assets to be adjusted to *full* market value. Some accountants refer to the element of the bargain as "negative goodwill." The danger of using this term is that it could imply that such an account is recorded, which is not the case. The element of the bargain is subtracted from the value assigned to the long-lived assets. Let us change the preceding example by assuming that Company P issued only 16,000 of its $50 market value ($10 par) common stock to acquire a 100% interest in the common stock of Company S and paid $10,000 in direct acquisition costs. Company P's entry to record the purchase would be:

Investment in Subsidiary S (16,000 shares × $50 market value + $10,000 direct acquisition costs)	810,000	
Common Stock (16,000 shares × $10 par)		160,000
Paid-in Capital in Excess of Par		640,000
Cash (for acquisition costs)		10,000

The acquisition would lead to the following trial balances of Companies P and S. Note that both the investment in subsidiary and the paid-in capital accounts of Company P reflect the above entry.

	Company P		Company S	
Cash	200,000		150,000	
Accounts Receivable.	300,000		250,000	
Inventory	500,000		300,000	
Land	100,000			
Buildings (net)	900,000			
Equipment (net).	650,000		400,000	
Investment in Subsidiary S.	810,000			
Current Liabilities.		300,000		100,000
Bonds Payable.		500,000		300,000
Common Stock ($10 par)		660,000		
Common Stock ($5 par)				50,000
Paid-In Capital in Excess of Par . .		1,140,000		350,000
Retained Earnings		860,000		300,000
Total	3,460,000	3,460,000	1,100,000	1,100,000

Let us again assume that the inventory and equipment have fair market values of $350,000 and $550,000, respectively. The following determination and distribution schedule would be prepared:

Company P and Subsidiary Company S Determination and Distribution of Excess Schedule December 31, 19X1		
Price paid for investment in Co. S including direct acquisition costs		$810,000
Less book value of interest acquired:		
Common stock ($5 par).	$ 50,000	
Paid-in capital in excess of par.	350,000	
Retained earnings	300,000	
Total stockholders' equity.	$700,000	
Interest acquired.	100%	700,000
Excess of cost over book value (debit balance)		$110,000
Adjustment of priority accounts:		
Inventory		50,000 Dr
Adjustment of long-lived assets:		
Equipment		60,000 Dr
Goodwill.		$ 0

As always, adjust the *priority accounts* to market value whatever the excess available. After adjusting the inventory, $60,000 is available for long-lived assets. The test of whether enough excess is available to raise long-lived assets to the full market value is not passed since only $60,000 is available to adjust the equipment. Note that equipment is less than full market value on the consolidated worksheet.

In Worksheet 2-3, pages 112–113, step (1) eliminates the intercompany accounts, and step (2) distributes the excess of the cost of the investment over the book value of the subsidiary equity according to the determination and distribution of excess schedule. After these two steps are completed, the account balances can be added to arrive at the consolidated balance sheet amounts.

Note that the preceding example has been concerned with only one subsidiary long-lived asset; thus, the assignment of the $60,000 excess was straightforward. The preparation of the determination and distribution of excess schedule for a bargain purchase is complicated when there exist multiple long-lived assets. In such a case, the sum of the recorded book values of those assets plus the remaining excess of cost over book value attributable to the long-lived assets must be apportioned to each of them, since the price paid is not sufficient to increase all of the long-lived assets to their full market values. The following procedures are used:

1. The total assigned value of the subsidiary's long-lived assets will be the sum of their existing book values plus the remaining excess of cost attributable to long-lived assets.
2. Allocate this total assigned value to each long-lived asset in proportion to its share of the total market value of the long-lived assets.
3. Apportion to each long-lived asset the difference between its allocated assigned value and its existing book value.

Be sure to note that *all* long-lived assets are placed into the allocation process, including those that have equal market and book values. This is required since, when the allocation process is completed, all long-lived assets must be stated at the same percentage of their market values.

As an example, assume the excess cost attributable to the long-lived assets of subsidiary Company S remains at $60,000, as shown in the determination and distribution of excess schedule on page 72, and Company S has three long-lived assets with the following values:

	Book Value	Market Value
Land.	$140,000	$206,250
Buildings (net).	180,000	275,000
Equipment (net)	80,000	68,750
Total	$400,000	$550,000

The following steps apportion the $460,000 of assigned value ($400,000 + $60,000 excess cost):

1. Calculate the total assigned value: $400,000 book value + $60,000 excess cost = $460,000
2. Allocate the total assigned value:

	Market Value	Fraction of Market Value	×	Total Assigned Value	=	Allocated Assigned Value
Land	$206,250	3/8*	×	$460,000	=	$172,500
Buildings	275,000	4/8	×	460,000	=	230,000
Equipment . . .	68,750	1/8	×	460,000	=	57,500
Total.	$550,000					$460,000

3. Apportion to each asset the difference between its allocated assigned value and its book value:

	Allocated Assigned Value	−	Book Value	=	Increase (Decrease)
Land....................	$172,500	−	$140,000	=	$ 32,500
Buildings..................	230,000	−	180,000	=	50,000
Equipment	57,500	−	80,000	=	(22,500)
Total..................	$460,000	−	$400,000	=	$ 60,000

*3/8 is calculated $206,250 ÷ $550,000

As a result of the allocation, the determination and distribution of excess schedule would be prepared as follows:

Company P and Subsidiary Company S Determination and Distribution of Excess Schedule December 31, 19X1			
Price paid for investment in Co. S including direct acquisition costs................................		$810,000	
Less book value of interest acquired:			
Common stock ($5 par).........................	$ 50,000		
Paid-in capital in excess of par...................	350,000		
Retained earnings	300,000		
Total stockholders' equity.....................	$700,000		
Interest acquired.............................	100%	700,000	
Excess of cost over book value (debit balance)		$110,000	
Adjustment of priority accounts:			
Inventory.....................................		50,000	**Dr**
Adjustment of long-lived assets:			
Land		32,500	**Dr**
Building		50,000	**Dr**
Equipment..................................		(22,500)	**Cr**
Goodwill.......................................		$ 0	

The following entry would be made *on the worksheet* to adjust the current asset, Inventory, to its full market value and to distribute the $60,000 excess attributable to long-lived assets:

Inventory (adjust to full market value)	50,000	
Land (partial adjustment to market)........................	32,500	
Building (partial adjustment to market)	50,000	
Equipment (partial adjustment to market).................		22,500
Investment in Subsidiary S (excess after elimination of subsidiary equity)...................................		110,000

The procedure results in each long-lived asset's sharing the same percentage of its market value. For example, each long-lived asset in the preceding illustration received 83.64% of its market value. It may be tempting to shorten the procedure by allocating the $60,000 excess of cost by relative market values and then adding each asset's allocated portion of the excess to its recorded book value. The shortcut, however, will not result in each asset's being recorded at the same percentage of its market value unless the original book value of each asset was an equal percentage of its market value. It is highly unlikely that book values would be so aligned.

Bargain purchases may occur at a price low enough to result in the book value of the interest acquired being greater than the price paid. Let us return to the original example where Company S had only one long-lived asset, equipment. Assume that the price paid for the interest in Company S was only $610,000. To illustrate, assume that Company P acquired 100% of the common stock of Company S by issuing 12,000 shares of its $50 market ($10 par) common stock and paying $10,000 in direct acquisition costs. The entry to record the purchase would be:

Investment in Subsidiary S (12,000 shares × $50 market value		
+ $10,000 acquisition costs)............................	610,000	
Common Stock (12,000 shares × $10 par)		120,000
Paid-In Capital in Excess of Par		480,000
Cash (for acquisition costs).............................		10,000

This investment would lead to the following trial balances for Companies P and S. Note that both the investment in subsidiary and the paid-in capital accounts of Company P reflect the new lower acquisition cost.

	Company P		Company S	
Cash	200,000		150,000	
Accounts Receivable................	300,000		250,000	
Inventory	500,000		300,000	
Land	100,000			
Buildings (net)	900,000			
Equipment (net).....................	650,000		400,000	
Investment in Subsidiary S............	610,000			
Current Liabilities....................		300,000		100,000
Bonds Payable......................		500,000		300,000
Common Stock ($10 par)		620,000		
Common Stock ($5 par)				50,000
Paid-In Capital in Excess of Par		980,000		350,000
Retained Earnings		860,000		300,000
Total	3,260,000	3,260,000	1,100,000	1,100,000

Assume the recorded book values of Company S are equal to the market value except for the inventory and equipment that are worth $350,000 and $300,000, respectively. The determination and distribution of excess schedule would show an excess of book value over cost:

Company P and Subsidiary Company S
Determination and Distribution of Excess Schedule
December 31, 19X1

Price paid for investment in Co. S including direct acquisition costs		$610,000	
Less book value of interest acquired:			
Common stock ($5 par).	$ 50,000		
Paid-in capital in excess of par.	350,000		
Retained earnings	300,000		
Total stockholders' equity.	$700,000		
Interest acquired.	100%	700,000	
Excess of book value over cost (credit balance)		**$ 90,000**	
Adjustment of priority accounts:			
Inventory		**50,000**	**Dr**
Adjustment of long-lived assets:			
Equipment.		**(140,000)**	**Cr**
Goodwill.		$ 0	

The excess of book value means that, in total, assets must be written down. Despite that, the priority accounts are increased to market value. This means the total required write-down of the long-lived asset becomes $140,000. *The write-down of long-lived assets cannot exceed their book value.* In this case, the book value of the only long-lived asset, equipment, is $400,000. Had the required write-down exceeded $400,000, the equipment would have been reduced to zero, and a deferred credit, *Excess of Market Value of Subsidiary Current Assets Over Cost*, would have been recorded. Do not confuse the deferred credit with the term "negative goodwill." Negative goodwill is really the "bargain" element defined as the deficiency of cost available for fixed assets. The deferred credit is the remainder when the bargain exceeds the value of the long-lived assets. For example, if the bargain was $300,000 and if the market value of the long-lived assets were $250,000, the bargain or negative goodwill is $300,000 while the deferred credit is $50,000 ($300,000 bargain – $250,000 market value of long-lived assets).

In Worksheet 2-4, pages 114–115, the subsidiary stockholders' equity is eliminated against the investment account in step (1). Step (2) distributes the resulting *credit* balance of the investment account to the specific subsidiary assets according to the determination and distribution of excess schedule. As in previous illustrations, the intercompany accounts are eliminated, and the consolidated balance sheet amounts are determined.

An added complication may arise in handling an investment at a price below the book value of the subsidiary. There may be several subsidiary long-lived assets whose market values differ from their book values. In this case, the excess of book value attributable to long-lived assets must be apportioned among all long-lived assets. The procedure for apportionment is as follows:

1. The total assigned value of all long-lived assets will be the sum of the existing long-lived assets' book values *reduced* by the excess of *book value over the cost* of the investment attributable to the long-lived assets, as computed in the determination and distribution of excess schedule. The excess attributable to long-lived assets is the original excess of book value for the investment plus or minus any market value adjustment made for current assets, long-term investments in marketable securities, and liabilities.

2. Allocate this total assigned value to each long-lived asset in proportion to its share of the total market value of the long-lived assets.

3. Apportion to each long-lived asset the difference between its allocated assigned value and its existing book value.

SUBSIDIARY WITH PREVIOUSLY RECORDED GOODWILL

It should be recalled from the Chapter 1 discussion of direct asset acquisitions that goodwill on the books of an acquired firm is disregarded. In the case of a stock acquisition, however, a subsidiary's recorded goodwill is included in the subsidiary's balance sheet which is to be consolidated. But *no goodwill should appear on the consolidated balance sheet until all long-lived assets are stated at full market value.* Thus, the procedure will be to reassign the amount of existing goodwill to the extent that it is needed in order to bring long-lived assets to market value. Any portion of the previously recorded goodwill not required for the adjustment of other accounts will be extended to the consolidated balance sheet. To illustrate, assume that Company P pays $920,000 for Company S which has the following balance sheet:

Assets		Liabilities and Equity	
Receivables...............	$140,000	Liabilities	$100,000
Inventory	150,000	Common stock ($5 par)	100,000
Land	20,000	Paid-in capital in excess	
Buildings	340,000	of par	200,000
Equipment................	50,000	Retained earnings	400,000
Goodwill	100,000		
Total assets	$800,000	Total liabilities and equity....	$800,000

Market values exceed book values for the inventory, buildings, and equipment which are worth $200,000, $490,000, and $100,000, respectively. The determination and distribution of excess schedule would be as follows:

Company P and Subsidiary Company S
Determination and Distribution of Excess Schedule
December 31, 19X1

Price paid for investment in Co. S including direct acquisition costs.		$920,000	
Less book value of interest acquired:			
Common stock ($5 par).	$100,000		
Paid-in capital in excess of par.	200,000		
Retained earnings	400,000		
Total stockholders' equity.	$700,000		
Interest acquired.	100%	700,000	
Excess of cost over book value (debit balance)		$220,000	
Adjustment of priority accounts:			
Inventory		50,000	**Dr**
Remaining excess available for long-lived assets		170,000	
Add goodwill needed to bring long-lived assets			
to market value ($100,000 available)		(30,000)	**Cr**
Available for long-lived assets.		200,000	
Adjustment of long-lived assets:			
Building		150,000	**Dr**
Equipment.		50,000	**Dr**
Goodwill (new)		$ 0	

The *worksheet entry* to distribute the excess, adjust goodwill, and write up the assets would be as follows:

Inventory	50,000	
Building	150,000	
Equipment.	50,000	
Goodwill.		30,000
Investment in Subsidiary S (excess cost elimination of subsidiary equity)		220,000

When there is existing goodwill on the books of the subsidiary, the test *Is the excess available for long-lived assets enough to adjust them all the way to market value?* must be modified by adding to the excess available, existing goodwill. The amount of goodwill added is the amount needed to bring all long-lived assets to market value. In this example, $200,000 was needed to bring the buildings and equipment to market. The excess available was only $170,000, thus $30,000 of the $100,000 goodwill was redirected to long-lived assets. If the available goodwill was not sufficient to bring the long-lived assets to full market value, the procedures for a bargain purchase allocation would be used. All goodwill would be eliminated when consolidating. Goodwill can only be recorded after all other assets and liabilities are at market value.

DEPRECIABLE ASSETS

Previous examples have used "net" values for depreciable assets to simplify explanations. In reality, the subsidiary will list original cost less accumulated depreciation. According to *purchase theory*, there is little justification for carrying to the consolidated balance sheet an amount for accumulated depreciation on a subsidiary's asset existing prior to the purchase. To do so would imply that the asset was used by the new owner prior to the purchase date. Thus, the preferable practice is to have the consolidated amounts reflect the market value, with no accumulated depreciation. Future depreciation charges on consolidated worksheets will be based on the new market value and the estimated remaining useful life.

To illustrate, assume an acquired firm has a building on its books at an original cost of $650,000 less $400,000 accumulated depreciation. Also, the building has a $300,000 market value on the purchase date. The net write-up required is $50,000. The preferable procedure is to produce a net asset value of $300,000 as shown in the following partial worksheet:

	Partial Trial Balance		Eliminations & Adjustments		Consolidated Balance Sheet
	Co. P	Co. S	Dr.	Cr.	
Building		650,000		350,000	300,000
Accumulated Depreciation		(400,000)	400,000		—
Investment in Subsidiary S				50,000*	—

*The $50,000 is the balance remaining after the elimination of the subsidiary equity accounts.

A less theoretically correct but common procedure is to not eliminate all accumulated depreciation, but rather to adjust the plant asset by:

1. Increasing its net book value through a reduction of the existing accumulated depreciation, or
2. Decreasing its net book value through a reduction of the original cost of the asset.

Unless otherwise stated, this practical approach will be used in this text when the parent owns less than a 100% interest.

ADJUSTMENT OF ASSUMED LIABILITIES

Liabilities assumed in a purchase may have market values that are at variance with their recorded book values. This situation could exist as a result of failing to record accrued interest or as a result of changing interest rates. If interest rates decrease and the market value of the debt increases, the net assets of the firm are reduced, and the excess of cost available for long-lived assets increases. The impact on the remaining excess is the same as a decrease in the value of a current asset. On the other hand, if interest rates increase and the market value of the debt decreases, the net assets are adjusted upwards, and the excess available for long-lived assets decreases.

Remember, liabilities are adjusted to reflect their full market values, regardless of the price paid in a business combination. For example, assume Company P pays $500,000 for all of the outstanding common stock of Company S at a time when Company S has the following balance sheet:

Assets		Liabilities and Equity	
Current assets.	$250,000	Bonds payable	$200,000
Long-lived assets	350,000	Common stock. . . . .⋅.	100,000
		Retained earnings.	300,000
Total assets	$600,000	Total liabilities and equity	$600,000

Also, the subsidiary's current assets have a book value equal to market value. However, certain equipment is undervalued by $40,000, and due to a decrease in the interest rates, bond liability has a market value of $208,000. A determination and distribution of excess schedule would be prepared as follows:

Company P and Subsidiary Company S
Determination and Distribution of Excess Schedule
December 31, 19X1

Price paid for investment		$500,000	
Less book value of interest acquired:			
Common stock	$100,000		
Retained earnings	300,000		
Total stockholders' equity	$400,000		
Interest acquired	100%	400,000	
Excess of cost over book value (debit balance)		$100,000	
Add undervaluation of bonds payable		(8,000)	**Cr**
Adjustment of long-lived assets:			
Equipment		40,000	**Dr**
Goodwill		$ 68,000	**Dr**

The *worksheet entry* to adjust the bonds to market value and to distribute the excess attributable to long-lived assets would be as follows:

Equipment (to market value)	40,000	
Goodwill (balance of excess)	68,000	
Premium on Bonds Payable (to market value)		8,000
Investment in Subsidiary S (excess cost after elimination of		
subsidiary equity)		100,000

CONSOLIDATION OF THE PURCHASE OF LESS-THAN-100% INTEREST

When control of a firm is achieved through the purchase of common stock and consolidated statements are required, consolidation procedures are applied. Control may be secured by purchasing less than 100% but usually over 50% of the subsidiary's voting common stock. In those cases in which a less-than-100% interest is purchased, only a portion of the subsidiary stockholders' equity is eliminated against the parent's investment in the subsidiary account. The remaining portion of the subsidiary common stock interest belongs to the minority interest, represented by stockholders of the subsidiary other than the parent. From a consolidated viewpoint, these shareholders are a special group of owners of the consolidated firm. However, their ownership rights are limited to their interest in the subsidiary as a separate legal entity. For instance, minority stockholders receive only those dividends that are paid by the subsidiary. In liquidation, the only assets of the subsidiary that are available to minority stockholders are those assets remaining after creditor and preferred stockholder claims have been satisfied.

To illustrate, assume that Company P purchased an 80% interest in Company S for $400,000 in cash. The entry to record the purchase would be:

Investment in Subsidiary S. 400,000
    Cash   400,000

Immediately following the acquisition, the account balances of Companies P and S would be as follows:

	Company P		Company S	
Cash.	200,000			
Accounts Receivable	300,000		200,000	
Inventory	100,000		100,000	
Investment in Subsidiary S	400,000			
Equipment (net).	150,000		300,000	
Current Liabilities.		150,000		100,000
Bonds Payable.		300,000		
Common Stock.		100,000		200,000
Retained Earnings.		600,000		300,000
Total	1,150,000	1,150,000	600,000	600,000

In the following determination and distribution of excess schedule, the total subsidiary stockholders' equity is multiplied by the 80% ownership interest in calculating the interest acquired:

Company P and Subsidiary Company S Determination and Distribution of Excess Schedule December 31, 19X1		
Price paid for investment in Co. S.		$400,000
Less book value of interest acquired:		
Common stock	$200,000	
Retained earnings	300,000	
Total stockholders' equity.	$500,000	
Interest acquired	**80%**	400,000
Excess.		$ 0

In Worksheet 2-5, pages 116–117, the intercompany balances are eliminated. That portion of the subsidiary stockholders' equity not eliminated is extended to the Minority Interest column of the worksheet. The remaining balances are added to arrive at the amounts for the consolidated balance sheet. Thus, the worksheet is the source for the formal balance sheet.

The following balance sheet illustration summarizes the total minority interest and includes it as a component of stockholders' equity. This presentation of the minority interest of a subdivision of stockholders' equity is in keeping with the *economic unit concept* found in the 1991 FASB Discussion Memorandum. The concept views the consolidated statements as the reports of a single economic entity with an ownership equity divided into a controlling and minority interest. As an alternative, the paid-in capital and retained earnings elements of the minority interest may be shown. It is not common to do so since the shareholders of the minority interest should look to the subsidiary's separate statements for detail.

Company P and Subsidiary Company S
Consolidated Balance Sheet
December 31, 19X1

Assets

Current assets:		
Cash..	$200,000	
Accounts receivable	500,000	
Inventory..	200,000	$ 900,000
Equipment (net)....................................		450,000
Total assets......................................		$1,350,000

Liabilities

Current liabilities...................................	$250,000	
Bonds payable.....................................	300,000	$ 550,000

Stockholders' Equity

Minority interest		**100,000**
Controlling interest:		
Common stock	**$100,000**	
Retained earnings................................	**600,000**	**700,000**
Total liabilities and stockholders' equity.................		$1,350,000

The published financial statements of many consolidated firms exclude the minority interest from the stockholders' equity section of the balance sheet. This is a manifestation of the *parent company concept* of consolidations which emphasizes the controlling interest's position. The minority interest is viewed as a claim against the assets available to the controlling ownership group. Some consolidated balance sheets show the minority interest under the long-term liability caption. This presentation is discouraged by Statement of Financial Accounting Concepts No. 6 which states, "Minority interests in net assets of consolidated subsidiaries do not represent present obligations of the enterprise to pay cash or distribute other assets to minority shareholders. Rather, those shareholders have ownership or residual interests in the components of a consolidated enterprise."[3] If the minority interest is not to be included under the caption "stockholders' equity," it is more acceptable to show it as a separate item placed between

---

[3]Statement of Financial Accounting Concepts No. 6, *Elements of Financial Statements* (Stamford: Financial Accounting Standards Board, 1985), par. 254.

liabilities and equity. Total exclusion of the minority equity from the consolidated balance sheet is a third possibility identified by the discussion memorandum. The *proportionate consolidation concept* includes only the parent company's owner-ship interest in subsidiary assets and liabilities. This means that the minority interest percentage of subsidiary assets and liabilities are not shown on the consolidated balance sheet. This text will include the minority interest as a separate nonitemized line item within the stockholders' equity section of the balance sheet. This is in keeping with the *economic unit concept* of consolidation which focuses on the entire consolidated firm and all of its owners.

(The appendix to all consolidation chapters, which follows Chapter 8, re-views in detail the alternative concepts contained in the FASB Discussion Memo-randum and lists the possible implications of the concepts on each chapter of this text. The appendix prepares comparative determination and distribution of excess schedules and worksheet eliminations for the alternative concepts.)

ADJUSTMENT OF SUBSIDIARY ACCOUNTS TO REFLECT MARKET VALUE

The price paid for a less-than-100% interest in a subsidiary will usually differ from the underlying book value of the interest purchased. For consolidated reporting purposes, the book value of the subsidiary assets must be adjusted to reflect the purchase price paid by the parent.

The only change from the previous 100% acquisition illustrations is that assets are adjusted on the worksheet by multiplying the parent's ownership percentage by the difference between the book and market values. For example, assume a parent pays $40,000 above the book value for an 80% interest in the stockholders' equity of a subsidiary. Also, the subsidiary has one long-lived asset to which the excess is attributable. Logic might dictate that if a $40,000 excess was paid for an 80% interest in the asset, a $50,000 ($40,000 ÷ 80%) excess would be paid for a 100% interest. Even though the asset appears to be undervalued by $50,000, only the $40,000 increase is acknowledged. Again, the parent company's purchase confirms only its portion (80% in this example) of the difference between the book and market values. Thus, the worksheet adjustment acknowl-edges only the interest acquired. Recognition of the full increase, in essence, would require the recognition of a gain for the minority shareholders prior to its realization through a bargained exchange.

The purchase example on page 68 will be revised in order to apply what might be termed the "pro rata market value" adjustments. Assume Company P purchases only an 80% interest in Company S and all other facts, including the market value of the subsidiary's assets, remain the same. Since Company P was willing to issue 20,000 shares of its $50 market value ($10 par) common stock for a 100% interest in Company S, assume it now issues 16,000 shares (80% × 20,000 shares) for the 80% interest and pays $10,000 in direct acquisition costs. The entry to record the acquisition would be:

Investment in Subsidiary S (16,000 shares × $50 market value + $10,000 direct acquisition costs)	810,000	
Common Stock (16,000 shares × $10 par).................		160,000
Paid-In Capital in Excess of Par		640,000
Cash (for acquisition costs).............................		10,000

The trial balance for each company immediately following the acquisition is as follows:

	Company P		Company S	
Cash	200,000		150,000	
Accounts Receivable	300,000		250,000	
Inventory	500,000		300,000	
Land	100,000			
Buildings (net)	900,000			
Equipment (net)	650,000		400,000	
Investment in Subsidiary S	810,000			
Current Liabilities		300,000		100,000
Bonds Payable		500,000		300,000
Common Stock ($10 par)		660,000		
Common Stock ($5 par)				50,000
Paid-In Capital in Excess of Par		1,140,000		350,000
Retained Earnings		860,000		300,000
Total	3,460,000	3,460,000	1,100,000	1,100,000

 The worksheet adjustments made on the basis of the following determination and distribution of excess schedule are shown in Worksheet 2-6, pages 118–119. The subsidiary's book values are assumed to be equal to market values, except for the inventory and the equipment which have market values of $350,000 and $550,000, respectively.

Company P and Subsidiary Company S Determination and Distribution of Excess Schedule December 31, 19X1		
Price paid for investment in Co. S including direct acquisition costs		$810,000
Less book value of interest acquired:		
Common stock ($5 par)	$ 50,000	
Paid-in capital in excess of par	350,000	
Retained earnings	300,000	
Total stockholders' equity	$700,000	
Interest acquired	80%	560,000
Excess of cost over book value (debit balance)		$250,000
Adjustment of priority accounts:		
Inventory ($50,000 total × 80%)		40,000 Dr
Adjustment of long-lived assets:		
Equipment ($150,000 total × 80%)		120,000 Dr
Goodwill		$ 90,000 Dr

Note the following unique features of a determination and distribution of excess schedule for a less-than-100% interest:

1. The excess of cost over book value is based on a comparison of the price paid and a pro rata share of the stockholders' equity of the subsidiary.
2. Priority accounts (current assets, long-term marketable securities, and assumed liabilities) are adjusted by multiplying the ownership interest acquired by the difference between their book and market values.

3. Only the parent's ownership interest in the already recorded goodwill of the subsidiary is available for reassignment, if necessary, to long-lived assets.

The pro rata market value method of preparing a consolidated worksheet is a feature of the *parent company concept* of business combinations identified by the FASB Discussion Memorandum. This concept limits the adjustments of subsidiary assets and liabilities to the interest purchased by the controlling firm. The Discussion Memorandum also considers the *economic unit concept* of business combinations which focuses on the value of the entire firm and would increase subsidiary accounts to 100% of market value regardless of the percentage of parent company ownership. One approach to the concept raises all identifiable assets and goodwill to 100% of market value, while another raises all identifiable assets to 100% of market value but only recognizes the controlling interest in goodwill. Early drafts of APB Opinion No. 16 did consider this alternative, but the final statement did not endorse it. Current accounting practice tends to follow the pro rata market value approach under the *parent company concept* which will be the method used in this text.

BARGAIN PURCHASE PROCEDURES

A bargain purchase may occur when a less-than-100% interest in the common stock of a subsidiary is purchased. A bargain purchase occurs when the excess available for long-lived assets is not sufficient to fully adjust them to reflect the *parent's interest* in their market values.

The following determination and distribution of excess schedule uses the same facts as those used on the schedule on page 72 except that it applies to an 80% interest:

Company P and Subsidiary Company S
Determination and Distribution of Excess Schedule
December 31, 19X1

Price paid for investment in Co. S including direct acquisition costs		$650,000
Less book value of interest acquired:		
Common stock ($5 par)	$ 50,000	
Paid-in capital in excess of par	350,000	
Retained earnings	300,000	
Total stockholders' equity	$700,000	
Interest acquired	80%	560,000
Excess of cost over book value (debit balance)		$ 90,000
Adjustment of priority accounts:		
Inventory ($50,000 × 80%)		40,000 Dr
Adjustment of long-lived assets:		
Equipment*		50,000 Dr
Goodwill		$ 0

*The maximum increase would be $120,000 (80% × $150,000 excess of market value). Since the excess available is less than this amount, all of the excess is added to the equipment account, leaving no excess for goodwill.

The worksheet entry to distribute the excess of cost over book value would be:

```
Inventory (80% of value difference)........................  40,000
Equipment (up to 80% of value difference) ...................  50,000
    Investment in Subsidiary S (excess after elimination of 80% of
        subsidiary equity).......................................          90,000
```

Note that priority accounts are adjusted by the amount of their undervaluation or overvaluation multiplied by the parent's ownership percentage, regardless of the price paid for the interest.

In a bargain purchase, goodwill recorded by the subsidiary should be reassigned to long-lived assets. However, the maximum amount of goodwill available for reassignment is the subsidiary's previously recorded goodwill multiplied by the parent's ownership interest.

In those cases where there is a bargain purchase and several long-lived assets exist, the excess of cost attributable to those assets should be apportioned according to the procedure described on page 73. The market values of the separate long-lived assets should continue to be used as the weights for distributing the total assigned value of the long-lived assets. The assigned value is the parent company's share of the subsidiary book value plus the available excess. Suppose that in the above determination and distribution of excess schedule there were several long-lived assets with a total book value of $200,000. The assigned value to be allocated would be $160,000 (the parent's share of book value) plus the $50,000 excess available. The $40,000 of the long-lived assets' total book value applicable to the minority interest is *not* available for assignment since it has not been purchased. The difference between the assigned and book values of each long-lived asset should be entered in the determination and distribution of excess schedule. This difference is *not* multiplied by the controlling ownership percentage, since the assignable value includes only the excess applicable to the controlling interest.

There may be cases where the controlling interest in the subsidiary's stockholders' equity exceeds the price paid for the investment. This means that the determination and distribution of excess schedule will show an excess of book value over cost. In total, subsidiary assets will have to be written down when consolidating. All adjustments, however, will be limited to the controlling interests percentage of the difference between book and market values. Regardless of the price paid, the priority accounts still will be adjusted for the controlling interest's percentage of the difference between book and market values.

To illustrate the consolidation procedures applicable to purchases with an excess of book value over cost, let us reconstruct the determination and distribution of excess schedule on page 76 to reflect an 80% purchase:

Company P and Subsidiary Company S Determination and Distribution of Excess Schedule December 31, 19X1		
Price paid for 80% investment in Co. S including		
direct acquisition costs		$490,000
Less book value of interest acquired:		
Common stock ($5 par).	$ 50,000	
Paid-in capital in excess of par.	350,000	
Retained earnings	300,000	
Total stockholders' equity.	$700,000	
Interest acquired.	80%	560,000
Excess of book value over cost (credit balance).		$ (70,000)
Adjustment of priority accounts:		
Inventory (80% × $50,000)		**40,000** Dr
Adjustment of long-lived assets:		
Equipment*.		**(110,000)** Cr
Goodwill.		$ 0

*The maximum reduction of equipment is $320,000 (80% of $400,000). If the credit amount remaining after the adjustment of the priority accounts exceeded $320,000, a deferred credit would be recorded.

The worksheet entry to distribute the excess of book value over cost would be:

Inventory (80% of value difference)	40,000	
Investment in Subsidiary S (excess after elimination of		
80% of subsidiary equity)	70,000	
Equipment (remaining excess of book value)		110,000

If several long-lived assets exist, the previously illustrated apportionment procedure would be applied. In addition, a special procedure is required if previously recorded goodwill appears on the subsidiary's books. As in the case of a 100% acquisition, previously recorded goodwill may have to be reassigned to identifiable long-lived assets on the determination and distribution of excess schedule. However, for a less-than-100% acquisition, only a portion equal to the ownership percentage may be made available for reassignment; the minority portion of goodwill is not available for reassignment.

PUSH-DOWN ACCOUNTING

Thus far, it has been assumed that the subsidiary's statements are unaffected by the parent's purchase of subsidiary shares so that no asset or liability adjustment is reflected on the subsidiary's separate records. In all preceding examples, revaluations first occur on the consolidated worksheet. This method is the most common, but it is not the only generally accepted method.

Some accountants object to the inconsistency of using book values in the subsidiary's separate statements and using market-adjusted values where the same operations are included in the consolidated statements. These accountants advocate *push-down* accounting, whereby the subsidiary's records are adjusted to reflect the market value increases. In essence, it is argued that the purchase of a controlling interest gives rise to a new basis of accountability for the interest traded. It is argued further that the subsidiary retained earnings applicable to the controlling interest should be moved to paid-in capital.

In December 1991, the FASB issued a discussion memorandum, New Basis Accounting, that studied the circumstances under which it might be appropriate to adjust the accounts of a firm to reflect market value.[4] The option of applying push-down accounting is considered for all instances where there has been a change in controlling interest. In addition, consideration is given to adjusting accounts to reflect market value when there is no change in control but there are significant sales of stock or borrowing transactions that provide support for market values materially different from the existing book values.

The discussion memorandum looks at the issues of when it might be appropriate to apply push-down accounting.

If the push-down method is applied to the determination and distribution of excess schedule example on page 70, the following entry would be made by the subsidiary on its books:

Inventory	50,000	
Equipment	150,000	
Goodwill	110,000	
Retained Earnings (previous subsidiary balance)	300,000	
Paid-In Capital in Excess of Par (previous retained earnings plus revaluations)		610,000

This entry would raise the subsidiary total stockholders' equity to $1,010,000 and would mean a simple elimination of the $1,010,000 investment account, with no excess on the consolidated worksheet.

In the case of a less-than-100% purchase under the *parent company concept*, adjustments would be limited to the controlling interest's percentage. Only the controlling interest's percentage of retained earnings would be transferred to paid-in capital.

The SEC staff has adopted a policy of requiring the push-down method in some cases for the separately published statements of the subsidiary. The existence of any significant minority interest (usually above 5%) and/or significant publicly held debt or preferred stock generally eliminates the requirement to use push-down accounting. *Note that the consolidated statements are unaffected by this issue.* The only difference is in the placement of the adjustments from the determination and distribution of excess schedule. The conventional approach, which is used in this text, makes the adjustments on the consolidated worksheet; the push-down method makes them on the subsidiary's books. Thus, they are in

---

[4]FASB Discussion Memorandum, *New Basis Accounting* (Norwalk, CT: Financial Accounting Standards Board, December 1991).

place when consolidation procedures are applied. This difference affects the presentation of the subsidiary's separate statements.

INVESTMENT IN A SUBSIDIARY ACCOUNTED FOR AS A POOLING OF INTERESTS

When the pooling criteria are met, as discussed in Chapter 1, the acquisition of a controlling interest in the common stock of another firm is recorded as a pooling of interests. Consolidated financial statements also will be required when the operations of the pooled firms are integrated.

CONSOLIDATING A 100% INTEREST UNDER POOLING

The recording and consolidation of a pooling achieved through a stock acquisition can be better understood by first reviewing the recording of a pooling achieved through an asset acquisition. Assume Company C (the combiner) had the following balance sheet just prior to pooling with Company I (the issuer):

Company C			
Balance Sheet			
December 31, 19X1			
Current assets.......... $10,000	Liabilities		$10,000
Property, plant,	Stockholders' equity:		
and equipment	Common stock		
(net)................ 30,000	($10 par)..........	$10,000	
	Retained earnings	20,000	30,000
	Total liabilities		
Total assets $40,000	and equity		$40,000

Also, Company I is willing to issue 3,000 shares of its stock for the $30,000 net assets of Company C. Company I stock has a par value of $2 and a market value of $15 per share. Since pooling principles ignore market values and combine book balances, the entry to record the pooling on Company I's books would be:

Current Assets...	10,000	
Property, Plant, and Equipment (net)	30,000	
Liabilities...		10,000
Common Stock ($2 per share × 3,000 shares)		6,000
Paid-In Capital in Excess of Par............................		4,000
Retained Earnings		20,000

The original amount of the Company C total paid-in capital is preserved, although it is redistributed between the par value and paid-in capital in excess of par accounts of Company I. The full amount in the Company C retained earnings account is transferred to the Company I retained earnings account, since a reduction was not necessary to meet a par or stated value requirement of the issuer.

In this example which portrays a pooling through an asset acquisition, the combiner was dissolved and its accounts were merged with those of the issuer. Assume now that Company I exchanges its shares for the shares of Company C by dealing with stockholders and that all other pooling criteria are met. In addition, Company I elects not to dissolve Company C but to let Company C continue as a separate legal entity with its own accounting records. In effect, a pooling through a stock acquisition occurs. Since the assets and liabilities of Company C remain on Company C's books, Company I can record only an investment in Company C. However, this investment must be recorded at the book value of the underlying net assets in order to comply with pooling principles. The market value of the securities exchanged is ignored. Normally, Company I must add to its paid-in capital an amount equal to the paid-in capital of Company C. The issuer must acknowledge as retained earnings its equity in the Company C retained earnings, unless it is needed to meet a par or stated value requirement and Company I has no additional paid-in capital available for redistribution. From these principles, the following entry is derived:

Investment in Subsidiary C	**30,000**	
Common Stock ($2 per share × 3,000 shares)		6,000
Paid-In Capital in Excess of Par		4,000
Retained Earnings		20,000

This entry would lead to the separate trial balances for Companies I and C shown in the first two columns of Worksheet 2-7, pages 120–121. In this worksheet, intercompany balances are eliminated, and the balance sheets of the parent and subsidiary are consolidated as of the date of the pooling.

When properly recorded, the investment in the subsidiary account *always* will be eliminated against the stockholders' equity of the subsidiary *with no excess of any type* remaining after the elimination. This procedure must be followed, since the recorded value of the investment account equals the subsidiary stockholders' equity multiplied by the parent's ownership percentage (100% in this example). As a result of this equality, no determination and distribution of excess schedule is needed when pooling.

CONSOLIDATING A LESS-THAN-100% INTEREST UNDER POOLING

Often the issuer will not acquire 100% of the combiner stock, although it must acquire at least 90% in exchange for its voting common stock to pool. In such a case, the issuer records only the pro rata book value acquired. If Company I of the previous example exchanges only 2,700 shares ($2 par) for 90% of Company C stock, the entry to record the investment would be:

Investment in Subsidiary C	27,000	
Common Stock ($2 per share × **2,700** shares)		5,400
Paid-In Capital in Excess of Par (90% × $4,000)		3,600
Retained Earnings (90% × $20,000)		18,000

Subsequent worksheet eliminations would cancel the investment in the subsidiary account against 90% of the Company C equities, with a 10% minority interest remaining. Procedures for displaying the minority interest parallel those previously discussed.

There is a lack of clarity in the accounting literature for the procedures used to account for the possible acquisition of shares not a part of the original exchange of voting common shares. There is agreement that they are not to be recorded or consolidated under pooling principles. APB Opinion No. 16 states a given combination cannot be recorded as a part purchase, part pooling.[5] However, APB Opinion No. 16 also states that the acquisition of a minority interest subsequent to a pooling is to be recorded as a purchase.[6] The position of this text is that the acquisition of fractional shares for cash and/or the cash payment for the shares of dissenting minority shareholders who will not exchange for parent shares should be treated as a retirement of the shares if it is accomplished as a part of the original combination. This would be accomplished by recording the shares at cost on the parent's books and retiring them on the consolidated worksheet. Where the cost exceeds the original issue price, there would be a decrease in parent retained earnings. Where the cost is less than the issue price, there would be an increase in parent paid-in capital in excess of par.

When minority shares are acquired at a later date, in a transaction not a part of the original combination, they should be recorded under purchase rules. The parent would record the shares at cost, prepare a determination and distribution of excess schedule for the small interest, and consolidate it as a purchase. This would result in minor adjustments on the worksheet to reflect the market value increase applicable to the minor interest. In this case, we will be preparing a worksheet part pooling, part purchase. The mixed accounting, however, is not being applied to a single transaction, which was the concern of APB Opinion No. 16.

RECOGNIZING AND CORRECTING THE IMPROPERLY RECORDED INVESTMENT ACCOUNT

Ordinarily, when a corporation issues stock, it must increase its total paid-in capital by the entire amount of consideration received. When it issues stock to acquire noncash assets, including shares of another firm's stock, the consideration received is the market value of the assets received or the shares given, whichever is more readily determinable. The only exception to these principles is an investment in a subsidiary to effect a pooling. In this case, only the net book value of the assets received should be recorded, as was previously illustrated. However, it is common to find a firm that ignores this exception. Such a firm will increase both its investment and paid-in capital accounts by an amount equal to the market value of the shares given or received. When this mistake is found,

---

[5]Accounting Principles Board Opinion No. 16, *Business Combinations* (New York: American Institute of Certified Public Accountants, 1970), par. 5.
[6]*Ibid.*, par. 43.

the issuer's accounts should be corrected prior to preparing the consolidated worksheet.[7]

To illustrate, assume Company I made the following incorrect investment entry when it acquired 90% of the stock of Company C, although pooling criteria were met:

Investment in Subsidiary C ($15 per share market value × 2,700 shares)	40,500	
Common Stock ($2 per share × 2,700 shares)		5,400
Paid-In Capital in Excess of Par.............................		35,100

Prior to preparing the consolidated worksheet, the *issuer's books* would be corrected by reversing the original incorrect entry and recording the investment as a pooling. The following entries would be made:

Common Stock ($2 per share × 2,700 shares)	5,400	
Paid-In Capital in Excess of Par..............................	35,100	
Investment in Subsidiary C..................................		40,500
Investment in Subsidiary C (90% of Company C equity)..........	27,000	
Common Stock ($2 per share × 2,700 shares)		5,400
Paid-In Capital in Excess of Par ($9,000 – $5,400)		3,600
Retained Earnings (90% × $20,000)		18,000

When these corrections have been made and the proper amounts have been recorded by the issuer, the subsequent worksheet eliminations would be identical to those for a less-than-100% interest pooling.

QUESTIONS

1. What are "nonhomogeneous" subsidiaries? What recent change has occurred with respect to accounting for them and why will this change improve disclosure?

2. A company may gain control over the assets of another firm by acquiring the assets of the firm or by purchasing a controlling interest in its stock. Under which method is the acquired firm dissolved? Under which method is the acquired firm preserved as a separate legal and accounting entity? Under which method may there be a minority interest?

3. What is the purpose of the consolidation process, and why does it start anew each year?

4. Are the eliminations that are made on a consolidated worksheet really journal entries that are recorded in the journals and ledgers? If not, what purpose do they serve?

5. Describe the two ways a stock acquisition may be recorded. At what value is the investment in the stock of the subsidiary recorded under each method?

6. What are the functions of the determination and distribution of excess schedule? Is it used for both a pooling and a purchase?

7. Under the purchase method, several accounts always are adjusted to their market value in consolidating, regardless of the price paid for the interest in the subsidiary. What are these accounts?

---

[7]Some states require the investment to be recorded at market value. Where this is true, the "correction" entries would be made on the worksheet as part of the elimination.

8.   What is a bargain purchase, and what complications does it present to the consolidation process?

9.   In a bargain purchase, describe how the value assigned to long-lived assets is determined when more than one long-lived asset exists.

10.   Explain the meaning of the account Excess of Market Value of Subsidiary Current Assets over Cost. How does it arise in the consolidation process? Is it the same thing as negative goodwill?

11.   What are the acceptable ways of disclosing the minority interest on a consolidated balance sheet, and what are the theories that support these alternatives?

12.   Under the pooling method, the investment in subsidiary account should be eliminated against the parent's share of the subsidiary stockholders' equity, with no excess. If this result does not occur, what is the likely cause and how is it corrected?

13.   A parent acquired a 90% interest in a subsidiary by exchanging its voting common stock in a transaction that met the criteria for a pooling of interests. On the same date, it also purchased a 5% interest in the subsidiary from a dissenting shareholder that would not accept the parent common stock in exchange for their shares. How will the 5% interest be reflected in the consolidated statements?

14.   A parent acquired a 90% interest in a subsidiary by exchanging its voting common stock in a transaction that met the criteria for a pooling of interests. A year later, it also purchased a 5% interest in the subsidiary from a minority shareholder by paying cash for the shares. How will the 5% interest be reflected in the consolidated statement?

EXERCISES

Exercise 1.   Red Company is thinking about acquiring Black Company. Red Company is considering two methods of accomplishing control and is wondering how the accounting treatment will differ under each method. Red Company has estimated that the market values of Black's net assets are equal to their book values, except for the equipment which is understated by $20,000. *acquisition purchase at fmv*

The following balance sheets have been prepared on the date of acquisition:

Assets	Red	Black
Cash	$460,000	$ 40,000
Accounts receivable..	50,000	70,000
Inventory	50,000	100,000
Property, plant, and equipment (net)	250,000	250,000
Total assets	$810,000	$460,000

Liabilities and Equity		
Current liabilities	$140,000	$ 80,000
Bonds payable	250,000	100,000
Stockholders' equity:		
Common stock ($100 par)	200,000	150,000
Retained earnings	220,000	130,000
Total liabilities and equity.................................	$810,000	$460,000

(1)   Assume Red Company purchased the net assets directly from Black Company for $450,000. *cost purchase*

(a) Prepare the entry that Red Company would make to record the purchase.
(b) Prepare the balance sheet for Red Company immediately following the purchase.

(2) Assume that 100% of the outstanding stock of Black Company is purchased from the former stockholders for a total of $450,000.

(a) Prepare the entry that Red Company would make to record the purchase.
(b) State how the investment would appear on Red's unconsolidated balance sheet prepared immediately after the purchase.
(c) Indicate how the consolidated balance sheet would appear.

Exercise 2. Roland Company is considering the cash purchase of 100% of the outstanding stock of Burton Company. The terms are not set and alternative prices are being considered for negotiation. The balance sheet of Burton Company shows the following values:

Assets		Liabilities and Equity	
Cash equivalents.........	$ 60,000	Current liabilities.................	$ 60,000
Inventory	120,000	Common stock ($5 par)...........	100,000
Land	50,000	Paid-in capital in excess of par.....	150,000
Building (net)...........	200,000	Retained earnings................	120,000
Total assets	$430,000	Total liabilities and equity.........	$430,000

Appraisals reveal that the inventory has a market value of $160,000 and that the land nd building have market values of $100,000 and $300,000, respectively. The questions to be answered concern the price to be paid for Burton's common stock:

(1) Above what price would goodwill be recorded?
(2) Below what price would long-lived assets be recorded at less-than-full market value?
(3) Below what price would a deferred credit be recorded?

Exercise 3. Edmund Company purchased all the outstanding stock of Benco Inc. for $600,000. Edmund also paid $10,000 in direct acquisition costs and $3,000 for indirect acquisition costs. Just before the investment, the two firms had the following balance sheets:

Assets	Edmund	Benco
Other current assets.....................................	$ 900,000	$200,000
Inventory	400,000	120,000
Property, plant, and equipment (net)	1,200,000	600,000
Total assets	$2,500,000	$920,000

Liabilities and Equity	Edmund	Benco
Current liabilities.......................................	$ 800,000	$400,000
Bonds payable	500,000	200,000
Common stock ($10 par).................................	200,000	100,000
Paid-in capital in excess of par...........................	400,000	250,000
Retained earnings......................................	600,000	(30,000)
Total liabilities and equity..............................	$2,500,000	$920,000

Appraisals for the assets of Benco Inc. indicate that market values differ from recorded book values for the inventory and for the property, plant, and equipment which have market values of $150,000 and $700,000, respectively.

Only a portion is recorded

(1) Prepare the entry to record the purchase of the Benco Inc. common stock including all acquisition costs.
(2) Prepare a determination and distribution of excess schedule for the investment in Benco Inc.
(3) Prepare the elimination entries that would be made on a consolidated worksheet.

Exercise 4. Patton Company is purchasing 100% of the outstanding stock of Sandy Company which has the following balance sheet on the date of acquisition:

Assets		Liabilities and Equity	
Inventory	$100,000	Current liabilities	$150,000
Other current assets	200,000	Bonds payable	200,000
Property, plant, and		Common stock ($5 par)	100,000
equipment (net)	500,000	Paid-in capital in	
Goodwill	50,000	excess of par	300,000
		Retained earnings	100,000
Total assets	$850,000	Total liabilities and equity	$850,000

Appraisals indicate that the following market values should be acknowledged:

Inventory	$150,000
Property, plant, and equipment	700,000
Bonds payable	210,000

Prepare the determination and distribution of excess schedule and the worksheet elimination entries that would be made if:
(1) The price paid for the 100% interest was $850,000.
(2) The price paid for the 100% interest was $700,000.

Exercise 5. Arcadia Company is purchasing 100% of the outstanding common stock of Hancock Mining Company for $400,000 plus $20,000 of direct acquisition costs. The following balance sheet was prepared for Hancock Mining on the date of the purchase:

Assets		Liabilities and Equity	
Inventory	$ 50,000	Current liabilities	$150,000
Mineral rights	250,000	Common stock ($5 par)	100,000
Equipment (net)	150,000	Paid-in capital in	
Goodwill	50,000	excess of par	300,000
		Retained earnings	(50,000)
Total assets	$500,000	Total liabilities and equity	$500,000

Appraisals are as follows for the assets of Hancock Mines:

Inventory	$ 10,000
Mineral rights	700,000
Equipment	100,000

Based on the above facts:
(1) Prepare a determination and distribution of excess schedule.
(2) Prepare the elimination entries that would be made on a consolidated worksheet prepared on the date of purchase.

Exercise 6. Quincy Company purchased 80% of the common stock of Calumet Company for $700,000 plus direct acquisition costs of $30,000. At the time of the purchase, Calumet Company had the following balance sheet:

Assets		Liabilities and Equity	
Cash equivalents	$ 120,000	Current liabilities	$ 200,000
Inventory	200,000	Bonds payable	400,000
Land	100,000	Common stock ($5 par)	100,000
Building (net)	450,000	Paid-in capital	
Equipment (net)	230,000	in excess of par	150,000
		Retained earnings	250,000
Total assets	$1,100,000	Total liabilities and equity . . .	$1,100,000

Market values differ from book values for all assets other than cash equivalents. The market values are:

Inventory	$300,000
Land	200,000
Building	600,000
Equipment	200,000

Based on the above facts:
(1) Prepare a determination and distribution of excess schedule.
(2) Prepare the elimination entries that would be made on a consolidated worksheet prepared on the date of purchase.

Exercise 7. Black Company purchased 8,000 shares of Wright Company for $74 per share. Just prior to the purchase, Wright Company had the following balance sheet:

Assets		Liabilities and Equity	
Cash	$ 20,000	Current liabilities	$250,000
Inventory	280,000	Common stock ($5 par)	50,000
Property, plant, and		Paid-in capital in excess	
equipment (net)	400,000	of par	130,000
Goodwill	100,000	Retained earnings	370,000
Total assets	$800,000	Total liabilities and equity	$800,000

Black Company believes that the inventory has a market value of $400,000 and that the property, plant, and equipment is worth $500,000. Business consultants have suggested that the goodwill is worth no more than $50,000. Based on these facts:
(1) Prepare a determination and distribution of excess schedule.
(2) Prepare the elimination entries that would be made on a consolidated worksheet prepared on the date of acquisition.

Exercise 8. On January 1, 19X7, Knight Corporation purchased all the outstanding shares of Craig Company for $950,000. It has been decided that Craig Company will use push-down accounting principles to account for this transaction. The current balance sheet is stated at historical cost.

The following balance sheet was prepared for Craig Company on January 1, 19X7:

Assets			Liabilities and Equity		
Current assets:			Current liabilities		$ 90,000
Cash	$ 80,000		Long-term liabilities:		
Accounts receivable	260,000		Bonds payable	$300,000	
			Deferred taxes	50,000	350,000
Prepaid expenses	20,000	$ 360,000	Stockholders' equity:		
Property, plant, and equipment:			Common stock ($10 par)	$300,000	
Land	$200,000		Retained earnings	420,000	720,000
Building (net)	600,000	800,000			
Total assets		$1,160,000	Total liabilities and equity		$1,160,000

Knight Corporation received the following appraisals for Craig Company assets and liabilities:

Accounts receivable........................	$280,000
Land	230,000
Building (net)..............................	700,000
Bonds payable.............................	280,000
Deferred tax liability.......................	40,000

(1) Record the investment.
(2) Record the adjustments on the books of Craig Company.
(3) Prepare the entries that would be made on the consolidated worksheet to eliminate the investment.

Exercise 9. Afram Company and Carlos Company are planning to combine their operations through a pooling of interests. Afram Company will exchange one share of its common stock for every two shares of Carlos Company stock. All of the Carlos shares will be exchanged by their owners for Afram shares. Prior to the pooling of interests, the two firms have the following balance sheets:

Assets	Afram	Carlos	Liabilities and Equity	Afram	Carlos
Current assets	$250,000	$100,000	Liabilities.....................	$120,000	$ 80,000
Property, plant, and			Common stock ($10 par)	200,000	
equipment (net).............	450,000	160,000	Common stock ($1 stated		
Goodwill		40,000	value)......................		10,000
			Additional paid-in capital.......	50,000	90,000
			Retained earnings.............	330,000	120,000
Total assets..................	$700,000	$300,000	Total liabilities and equity	$700,000	$300,000

(1) Prepare the entry to record the investment as a pooling of interests. Support your entry with an equity transfer schedule.
(2) Prepare a consolidated balance sheet immediately after the investment.

Exercise 10. Varsity Company and Top Company had the following balance sheets prior to a pooling of interests:

Assets	Varsity	Top	Liabilities and Equity	Varsity	Top
Current assets	$ 500,000	$ 300,000	Liabilities..................	$ 300,000	$ 500,000
Property, plant, and			Common stock ($2 par)	400,000	
equipment (net)..........	1,200,000	800,000			
			Common stock ($1 par)		150,000
			Paid-in capital in excess of		
			par	150,000	50,000
			Retained earnings..........	850,000	400,000
Total assets................	$1,700,000	$1,100,000	Total liabilities and equity ...	$1,700,000	$1,100,000

Varsity will exchange its stock for all of the outstanding stock of Top Company. On Varsity's books, record the investment for each of the following situations. Support each entry with an equity transfer schedule.
(1) Varsity issues 80,000 shares.
(2) Varsity issues 100,000 shares.
(3) Varsity issues 150,000 shares.
(4) Varsity issues 250,000 shares.

Exercise 11. Williams Corporation is considering the acquisition of Bay Mills Company. The following balance sheet was prepared for Bay Mills as of December 31, 19X5:

Assets		Liabilities and Equity	
Cash......................	$ 20,000	Current liabilities	$120,000
Inventory..................	150,000	Common stock ($5 par)	50,000
Property, plant, and		Paid-in capital in excess	
equipment (net)..........	500,000	of par....................	150,000
		Retained earnings...........	350,000
Total assets...............	$670,000	Total liabilities and equity	$670,000

Appraisals, upon which both firms agree, show the inventory to have a market value of $200,000 and the property, plant, and equipment to have a market value of $600,000.

Williams Corporation has the following stockholders' equity:

Common stock ($10 par).....................	$200,000
Paid-in capital in excess of par.................	300,000
Retained earnings..........................	450,000
Total equity	$950,000

Any acquisition that would occur would be based on the above market values and the assumption of a $50 market price per share for the Williams Corporation stock.

(1) Assume that Williams exchanges a sufficient number of its shares to purchase an 80% interest in Bay Mills:
   (a) Determine how many shares of Williams common stock will be exchanged.
   (b) Record the investment in the Bay Mills shares.
   (c) Prepare a determination and distribution of excess schedule.
   (d) Prepare the elimination entries that would be made on a consolidated worksheet prepared on the acquisition date.
(2) Assume that Williams exchanges a sufficient number of its shares to acquire a 90% interest in Bay Mills and that the transaction meets the criteria for a pooling of interests.
   (a) Determine how many shares of Williams common stock will be exchanged.
   (b) Record the investment in Bay Mills shares and provide an equity transfer schedule.
   (c) Prepare the elimination entries that would be made on a consolidated worksheet prepared on the acquisition date.

Exercise 12. Subtra Inc. had the following balance sheet on December 31, 19X7:

Assets		Liabilities and Equity	
Current assets...............	$ 50,000	Liabilities	$150,000
Land	70,000	Common stock ($10 par)......	50,000
Buildings (net)..............	230,000	Retained earnings...........	400,000
Equipment (net)	200,000		
Goodwill...................	50,000		
Total assets	$600,000	Total liabilities and equity	$600,000

Prior to a pooling of interests in which Parma was the issuer, Parma had the following stockholders' equity:

Common stock ($10 par)	$ 500,000
Retained earnings	2,000,000
	$2,500,000
Less treasury stock, 5,000 shares at cost	300,000
Total stockholders' equity	$2,200,000

Parma exchanged the 5,000 shares of treasury stock plus 5,000 new shares of common stock for 90% of the common stock of Subtra. Parma paid $10,000 in direct acquisition costs.

Record the acquisition of Subtra as a pooling of interests. Prepare an equity transfer schedule as support.

Exercise 13. Wright Enterprises has given you the following balance sheet on December 31, 19X5:

Wright Enterprises
Balance Sheet
December 31, 19X5

Assets			Liabilities and Equity		
Current assets	$ 856,000		Liabilities........................		$ 900,000
Investment in Mazurek Company ..	800,000		Common stock ($5 stated value) ...	$1,000,000	
Property, plant, and equipment			Additional paid-in capital..........	950,000	
(net)	2,150,000		Retained earnings	956,000	2,906,000
			Total liabilities and stockholders'		
Total assets.....................	$3,806,000		equity.........................		$3,806,000

Wright Enterprises acquired a 90% interest of Mazurek Company on October 1, 19X5, by exchanging 20,000 shares of $40 market value ($5 par) common stock directly with Mazurek's stockholders. On the exchange date, Mazurek Company had the following stockholders' equity:

Common stock ($2 par)......................	$ 50,000
Paid-in capital in excess of par................	250,000
Retained earnings..........................	300,000
	$600,000

Initially, the transaction was erroneously recorded as a purchase. No entries have been made in the investment account since the inception of the pooling.

Prepare the necessary journal entry to correctly portray the above combination as a pooling of interests. Provide an equity transfer schedule as support.

PROBLEMS

Problem 2-1. On July 1, 19X6, Holley Company exchanged 18,000 of its $25 market value ($10 par value) shares for all the outstanding shares of Budd Company. The transaction did not meet the criteria for a pooling of interests since Holley Company was only recently divested by its parent company. Holley paid direct acquisition costs of $20,000 and paid $5,000 in stock issuance costs. The two firms had the following balance sheets on July 1, 19X6:

Assets	Holley	Budd
Other current assets.	$ 50,000	$ 70,000
Inventory	120,000	60,000
Land	100,000	40,000
Buildings (net).	300,000	120,000
Equipment (net)	430,000	110,000
Total assets	$1,000,000	$400,000

Liabilities and Equity		
Current liabilities.	$ 180,000	$ 60,000
Common stock ($10 par).	400,000	200,000
Retained earnings.	420,000	140,000
Total liabilities and equity	$1,000,000	$400,000

The following market values differ from book values for Budd's assets:

Inventory	$ 65,000
Land	100,000
Building	150,000
Equipment	75,000

Required:

(1) Record the investment in Budd Company and any other entry necessitated by the purchase.
(2) Prepare a determination and distribution of excess schedule.
(3) Prepare a consolidated balance sheet for July 1,19X6, immediately subsequent to the purchase.

Problem 2-2. Balance sheets for Abbott Company, Bristol Company, and Costello Company on December 31, 19X1, are as follows:

	Abbott	Bristol	Costello
Cash.	$ 200,000	$100,000	$ 50,000
Inventory.	300,000	150,000	100,000
Property, plant, and equipment (net).	500,000	200,000	150,000
Goodwill	100,000	50,000	25,000
Total assets.	$1,100,000	$500,000	$325,000
Liabilities.	$ 300,000	$100,000	$150,000
Common stock ($10 par)	200,000	100,000	50,000
Paid-in capital in excess of par	400,000	50,000	75,000
Retained earnings.	200,000	250,000	50,000
Total liabilities and equity	$1,100,000	$500,000	$325,000

On this date, Abbott purchased all of the common stock of Bristol Company by issuing 600, 11% bonds with a face value of $1,000 each. (On the day of the sale, 11% was the prevailing rate for similar bonds.) Abbott also exchanged 5,000 shares of its common stock, with a market value of $30 each, for 80% of the common stock of Costello Company.

Required:

Prepare a determination and distribution of excess schedule and a consolidated balance sheet for December 31, 19X1, under each of the following assumptions.

(1) Bristol's inventory has a market value of $175,000, and its property, plant, and equipment is appraised at $325,000. Costello's inventory is understated by $50,000.

(2) Bristol's inventory is understated by $100,000, and the market value of its property, plant, and equipment is $500,000. Costello's liabilities are overstated by $10,000. Costello's inventory is grossly understated; its fair market value is $250,000.

Suggestion: Make goodwill available for reassignment in both determination and distribution schedules. Notice that it is needed in some cases and not in others.

Problem 2-3. Bolsun Company purchased 90% of the common stock of Mate Company for $400,000 when Mate Company had the following balance sheet:

Assets

Current assets	$100,000
Land	50,000
Building (net)	100,000
Equipment (net)	120,000
Total.	$370,000

Liabilities and Equity

Bonds payable.	$100,000
Common stock, $5 par.	50,000
Paid-in capital in excess of par.	70,000
Retained earnings.	150,000
Total.	$370,000

The market values of the long-lived assets are as follows: Land, $80,000; Building, $240,000; Equipment, $160,000.

Required:

(1) Prepare a determination and distribution of excess schedule.

(2) Prepare the elimination entries that would be made on a consolidated worksheet prepared on the date of acquisition.

Problem 2-4. On March 1, 19X5, Collier Enterprises purchased a 100% interest in Robby Corporation for $480,000. It was decided that Robby Corporation will apply push-down accounting principles to account for this acquisition.

Robby Corporation had the following balance sheet on February 29, 19X5:

Robby Corporation
Balance Sheet
For the Month Ended February 29, 19X5

Assets		Liabilities and Equity	
Accounts receivable.	$ 60,000	Current liabilities.	$ 50,000
Inventory	80,000	Bonds payable.	100,000
Land	40,000	Common stock	50,000
Buildings	300,000	Paid-in capital in excess of par. . . .	250,000
Accum. depr.—blg	(120,000)	Retained earnings.	70,000
Equipment.	220,000		
Accum. depr.—equip.	(60,000)		
Total assets	$520,000	Total liabilities and equity	$520,000

Collier Enterprises received an independent appraisal on the market values of Robby Corporation's assets. The controller has reviewed the figures and accepts them as reasonable.

Inventory	$100,000
Land	55,000
Building	200,000
Equipment	150,000
Bonds payable	98,000

Required:
(1) Record the investment in Robby Corporation.
(2) Prepare a determination and distribution of excess schedule.
(3) Give Robby Corporation's adjusting entry showing the conversion of Retained Earnings to Paid-In Capital.

Problem 2-5. The balance sheets of Martin Company and Freeze Company are as follows on December 31, 19X4:

Assets	Martin	Freeze
Current assets	$ 250,000	$ 300,000
Property, plant, and equipment	1,100,000	500,000
Accumulated depreciation	(300,000)	(200,000)
Total assets	$1,050,000	$ 600,000

Liabilities and Equity		
Current liabilities	$ 250,000	$ 200,000
Common stock ($10 par)	300,000	
Common stock ($1 par)		50,000
Paid-in capital in excess of par	200,000	100,000
Retained earnings	300,000	250,000
Total liabilities and equity	$1,050,000	$ 600,000

On this date, Martin exchanged one share of its newly issued common stock for every two shares of Freeze stock. Martin acquired all outstanding shares of Freeze Company. The market value of a share of Martin stock was $30 on the acquisition date. Freeze's assets are fairly stated except for the property, plant, and equipment which has a market value of $450,000.

Required:
(1) Assume the acquisition does not meet the pooling of interests criteria.
   (a) Record the investment in Freeze stock.
   (b) Prepare a determination and distribution of excess schedule.
   (c) Prepare a consolidated balance sheet for December 31, 19X4, immediately subsequent to the purchase.
(2) Assume that the acquisition does meet the pooling of interests criteria.
   (a) Record the investment in Freeze stock.
   (b) Prepare a consolidated balance sheet for December 31, 19X4, immediately subsequent to the pooling.

Problem 2-6. On December 31, 19X7, Beatem Company purchased on the open market 80% of the outstanding shares of Cheatem Company common stock and 75% of the outstanding shares of Run Company common stock. The following unconsolidated balance sheets of the companies were prepared immediately subsequent to the purchase:

	Beatem	Cheatem	Run
Cash	$ 100,000	$ 50,000	$ 80,000
Inventory	250,000	170,000	200,000
Property, plant, and equipment (net)	500,000	200,000	320,000
Investment in Cheatem......................	400,000		
Investment in Run	300,000		
Total assets	$1,550,000	$420,000	$600,000
Current liabilities	$ 150,000	$ 50,000	$ 80,000
Common stock ($10 par)	500,000		
Common stock ($5 par).......................		100,000	
Common stock ($1 par).......................			10,000
Paid-in capital in excess of par	700,000	100,000	290,000
Retained earnings	200,000	170,000	220,000
Total liabilities and equity....................	$1,550,000	$420,000	$600,000

Beatem Company feels that the inventory and property, plant, and equipment accounts of the subsidiaries do not reflect market values. Beatem Company has secured the following market values:

	Cheatem	Run
Inventory	$230,000	$260,000
Property, plant, and equipment	250,000	400,000

Required:
(1) Prepare a determination and distribution of excess schedule for each investment.
(2) Prepare a worksheet for a consolidated balance sheet for December 31, 19X7.
(3) Prepare the formal consolidated balance sheet for December 31, 19X7.

Problem 2-7. On December 31, 19X1, Party Company purchased 80% of the common stock of Sparten Company for $280,000. On this date, any excess of cost over book value was attributed to accounts with market values that differed from book value. These accounts of the Sparten Company had the following market values:

Inventory	$140,000
Land	45,000
Buildings and equipment	225,000
Bonds payable.............................	105,000

The following balance sheets were prepared for the two firms immediately after the purchase:

	Party	Sparten
Cash	$160,000	$ 50,000
Accounts receivable	70,000	30,000
Inventory	130,000	120,000
Investment in Sparten Company	280,000	
Land	50,000	35,000
Building and equipment	350,000	230,000
Accumulated depreciation	(100,000)	(50,000)
Other intangibles	40,000	
Total assets	$980,000	$415,000
Current liabilities	$192,000	$ 65,000
Bonds payable		100,000
Common stock ($10 par), Party	100,000	
Common stock ($5 par), Sparten		50,000
Paid-in capital in excess of par	150,000	70,000
Retained earnings	538,000	130,000
Total liabilities and equity	$980,000	$415,000

Required:

(1) Prepare a determination and distribution of excess schedule for the investment in Sparten Company.
(2) Complete a consolidated worksheet for Party Company and its subsidiary Sparten Company as of December 31, 19X1.

Problem 2-8. Metro International has approached the management of ACME Company and has made an offer to acquire 90% of ACME's outstanding stock on July 1, 19X6. Metro International will give 20,000 shares of its previously unissued, $1 par, $35 market value, common stock in exchange for a 90% ownership interest. If this offer is accepted, it is unclear whether *all* the criteria for a pooling of interests will be met.

Out-of-pocket costs of the acquisition incurred by Metro International would be as follows:

Direct acquisition costs (legal fees and finder's fees)	$27,000
Stock issuance costs	18,000

Comparative balance sheets for the two companies just prior to the combination are as follows:

	Metro	ACME
Cash	$ 200,000	$ 80,000
Other assets	650,000	180,000
Marketable securities	180,000	50,000
Property, plant, and equipment (net)	2,500,000	800,000
Patents	240,000	60,000
Total assets	$3,770,000	$1,170,000

Current liabilities	$ 410,000	$ 320,000
Bonds payable	1,000,000	300,000
Common stock ($1 par)	300,000	
Common stock ($25 par)		25,000
Paid-in capital in excess of par	1,200,000	275,000
Retained earnings	860,000	250,000
Total liabilities and equity	$3,770,000	$1,170,000

On July 1, 19X6, ACME Company's book values approximate market values, except for the following:

Marketable securities	$ 60,000
Property, plant, and equipment	950,000 — 800,000 — 150,000
Patents	80,000
Bonds payable	296,000

Required:
(1) Prepare the entry that Metro International would make on July 1, 19X6, to record the investment in stock of ACME Company as: (a) a purchase and (b) a pooling of interests.
(2) Prepare a consolidated balance sheet for July 1, 19X6, immediately subsequent to the acquisition assuming that the acquisition is regarded as: (a) a purchase and (b) a pooling of interests.
(3) Compare the differences on the 19X6 fiscal year income statement that would occur as a result of the purchase versus a pooling treatment.

Problem 2-9. Comparative balance sheets of Edward Corporation and its subsidiary Hinkley Corporation on June 30, 19X7, are as follows:

	Edward Corporation	Hinkley Corporation
Cash	$ 153,200	$ 40,000
Accounts receivable	416,100	110,000
Prepayments	48,000	5,500
Land	750,000	160,000
Buildings	690,000	147,000
Accumulated depreciation	(50,000)	(12,000)
Delivery trucks	515,500	190,000
Accumulated depreciation	(35,000)	(10,000)
Investment in Hinkley Corporation	722,000	
Total assets	$3,209,800	$630,500
Accounts payable	$ 152,210	$ 80,500
Accrued expenses	16,100	3,600
Bonds payable	400,000	
Common stock ($2 par)	412,000	
Common stock ($10 par)		400,000
Paid-in capital in excess of par	755,000	
Retained earnings	1,474,490	146,400
Total liabilities and equity	$3,209,800	$630,500

On June 27, 19X7, Edward exchanged 18,000 of its shares, with a market value of $35 each, for 90% of the shares of Hinkley Corporation, using a 1-for-2 exchange rate. The transaction qualified as a pooling of interests. Edward Corporation paid $20,000 in direct acquisition costs which were capitalized in the investment account. Assume the Hinkley equity at the pooling was the same as shown above.

On June 30, 19X7, Edward acquired another 5% of Hinkley stock in exchange for 2,000 shares of Edward common stock which had a per share market value of $36 on that date.

Any payment in excess of book value is considered a payment for goodwill.

Required:

Prepare the correcting entries to be made on Edward's books and a worksheet for a June 30, 19X7, consolidated balance sheet.

Suggestion: The first acquisition is a pooling of interests and requires a correction entry for the investment account. It should be supported by an equity transfer diagram. The second acquisition cannot meet the criteria for a pooling of interests and should be accounted for as a purchase. Be careful with the direct acquisition costs in the pooling.

CASE   CONSOLIDATING A BARGAIN PURCHASE

Your client, Best Value Hardware Stores, has come to you to assist in evaluating an opportunity to purchase a controlling interest in a hardware store in a neighboring city. The store under consideration is a closely held family corporation. Owners of 60% of the shares are willing to sell you the 60% interest, 30,000 common stock shares in exchange for 7,500 of Best Value shares which have a market value of $40 each and a par value of $10 each.

Your client sees this as a good deal and a good way to enter a new market. The controller of Best Value knows, however, that all is not well with the store being considered. The store, Al's Hardware, has not kept pace with the market and has been losing money. It also has a major lawsuit against it stemming from alleged faulty electrical components it supplied which caused a fire. The store is not insured for the loss. Legal counsel advises that the store will likely pay $300,000 in damages.

The following balance sheet was provided by Al's Hardware as of December 31, 19X4:

Assets		Liabilities and Equity	
Cash	$ 180,000	Current liabilities	$ 425,000
Accounts receivable	460,000	8% Mortgage payable	600,000
Inventory	730,000	Common stock ($5 par)	250,000
Land	120,000	Paid in capital in	
Building	630,000	excess of par	750,000
Accum. depr.—bldg.	(400,000)	Retained earnings	(80,000)
Equipment	135,000		
Accum. depr.—equip.	(85,000)		
Goodwill	175,000		
Total assets	$1,945,000		$1,945,000

Your analysis raises substantial concerns about the values shown. You have gathered the following information:

(1) Aging of the accounts receivable reveals the need for a $110,000 allowance for bad debts.

(2) The inventory has many obsolete items; the market value is $600,000.

(3) Appraisals for long-lived assets are as follows:

Land....................................	$100,000
Building................................	300,000
Equipment	100,000

(4) The goodwill resulted from the purchase of another hardware store that has since been consolidated into the existing location. The goodwill was attributed to customer loyalty.

(5) Liabilities are fairly stated except that there should be a provision for the estimated loss on the lawsuit.

On the basis of your research, you are convinced that the statements of Al's Hardware are not representative and need major restatement. Your client is not interested in being associated with statements that are not accurate.

Your client asks you to make recommendations on two concerns:

(1) Does the price asked seem to be a real bargain? It is suggested that you consider the market value of the entire equity of Al's Hardware and then decide if the price is reasonable for a 60% interest.

(2) If the deal were completed, what accounting methods would you recommend either on the books of Al's Hardware or in the consolidation process? Al's Hardware would remain a separate legal entity with a substantial minority interest.

WORKSHEET 2-1

100% Interest; Price Equals Book Value
Company P and Subsidiary Company S
Worksheet for Consolidated Balance Sheet
December 31, 19X1

		Trial Balance	
		Company P	Company S
1	Debits:		
2	Cash	100,000	
3	Accounts Receivable	300,000	200,000
4	Inventory	100,000	100,000
5	**Investment in Subsidiary S**	**500,000**	
6	Equipment (net)	150,000	300,000
7	Total	1,150,000	600,000
8	Credits:		
9	Current Liabilities	150,000	100,000
10	Bonds Payable	300,000	
11	Common Stock, Co. P	100,000	
12	Retained Earnings, Co. P	600,000	
13	**Common Stock, Co. S**		**200,000**
14	**Retained Earnings, Co. S**		**300,000**
15	Total	1,150,000	600,000

Worksheet 2-1 (see page 67)

| Eliminations & Adjustments | | Consolidated Balance Sheet | | |
Dr.	Cr.	Dr.	Cr.	
				1
		100,000		2
		500,000		3
		200,000		4
	(1) 500,000			5
		450,000		6
				7
				8
			250,000	9
			300,000	10
			100,000	11
			600,000	12
(1) 200,000				13
(1) 300,000				14
500,000	500,000	1,250,000	1,250,000	15

Eliminations and Adjustments:
(1) Eliminate the investment in the subsidiary account against the subsidiary equity accounts.

WORKSHEET 2-2

100% Interest; Price Exceeds Market Value
Company P and Subsidiary Company S
Worksheet for Consolidated Balance Sheet
December 31, 19X1

		Trial Balance	
		Company P	Company S
1	Debits:		
2	Cash	200,000	150,000
3	Accounts Receivable	300,000	250,000
4	**Inventory**	500,000	**300,000**
5	Land	100,000	
6	Buildings (net)	900,000	
7	**Equipment (net)**	650,000	**400,000**
8	**Investment in Subsidiary S**	**1,010,000**	
9			
10	**Goodwill**		
11	Total	3,660,000	1,100,000
12	Credits:		
13	Current Liabilities	300,000	100,000
14	Bonds Payable	500,000	300,000
15	Common Stock ($10 par), Co. P	700,000	
16	Paid-In Capital in Excess of Par, Co. P	1,300,000	
17	Retained Earnings, Co. P	860,000	
18	Common Stock ($5 par), Co. S		50,000
19	Paid-In Capital in Excess of Par, Co. S		350,000
20	Retained Earnings, Co. S		300,000
21	Total	3,660,000	1,100,000

Worksheet 2-2 (see page 70)

Eliminations & Adjustments				Consolidated Balance Sheet			
Dr.		Cr.		Dr.		Cr.	
							1
				350,000			2
				550,000			3
(2)	50,000			850,000			4
				100,000			5
				900,000			6
(2)	150,000			1,200,000			7
		(1)	700,000				8
		(2)	310,000				9
(2)	110,000			110,000			10
							11
							12
						400,000	13
						800,000	14
						700,000	15
						1,300,000	16
						860,000	17
(1)	50,000						18
(1)	350,000						19
(1)	300,000						20
	1,010,000		1,010,000	4,060,000		4,060,000	21

Eliminations and Adjustments:
(1) Eliminate intercompany accounts. The investment in subsidiary account includes a 100% interest in the stockholders' equity of Company S. Therefore, the entire stockholders' equity of Company S is eliminated against the investment account. The balance of the investment account, $310,000, has no intercompany counterpart, but rather reflects the total undervaluation of Company S's assets. This balance is distributed in step (2).
(2) Distribute the $310,000 undervaluation of Company S's assets to the proper asset accounts. The following information for this distribution is taken from the determination and distribution of excess schedule:

Excess of cost over book value		$310,000
Distribute to:		
Inventory	$ 50,000	
Equipment.	150,000	
Goodwill	110,000	310,000
		$ 0

WORKSHEET 2-3

100% Interest; Bargain Purchase: Market Value Exceeds Price
Company P and Subsidiary Company S
Worksheet for Consolidated Balance Sheet
December 31, 19X1

		Trial Balance	
		Company P	Company S
1	Debits:		
2	Cash	200,000	150,000
3	Accounts Receivable	300,000	250,000
4	**Inventory**	500,000	**300,000**
5	Land	100,000	
6	Buildings (net)	900,000	
7	**Equipment (net)**	650,000	**400,000**
8	Investment in Subsidiary S	810,000	
9			
10	Total	3,460,000	1,100,000
11	Credits:		
12	Current Liabilities	300,000	100,000
13	Bonds Payable	500,000	300,000
14	Common Stock ($10 par), Co. P	660,000	
15	Paid-In Capital in Excess of Par, Co. P	1,140,000	
16	Retained Earnings, Co. P	860,000	
17	Common Stock ($5 par), Co. S		50,000
18	Paid-In Capital in Excess of Par, Co. S		350,000
19	Retained Earnings, Co. S		300,000
20	Total	3,460,000	1,100,000

Worksheet 2-3 (see page 72)

Eliminations & Adjustments				Consolidated Balance Sheet			
Dr.		Cr.		Dr.	Cr.		
							1
				350,000			2
				550,000			3
(2)	50,000			850,000			4
				100,000			5
				900,000			6
(2)	60,000			1,110,000			7
		(1)	700,000				8
		(2)	110,000				9
							10
							11
					400,000		12
					800,000		13
					660,000		14
					1,140,000		15
					860,000		16
(1)	50,000						17
(1)	350,000						18
(1)	300,000						19
	810,000		810,000	3,860,000	3,860,000		20

Eliminations and Adjustments:
(1) Eliminate intercompany accounts. The investment in subsidiary account includes a 100% interest in the stockholders' equity of Company S. Thus, the entire stockholders' equity of Company S is eliminated against the investment account.
(2) The balance of the investment account, $110,000, represents the total undervaluation of Company S's assets. Distribute the undervaluation amount to the proper asset accounts in the following manner, as prescribed by the determination and distribution of excess schedule:

Excess of cost over book value.....................................			$110,000
Distribute to:			
Inventory..		**$50,000**	
Equipment		**60,000**	110,000
			$ 0

WORKSHEET 2-4

100% Interest; Bargain Purchase: Book Value Exceeds Price
Company P and Subsidiary Company S
Worksheet for Consolidated Balance Sheet
December 31, 19X1

		Trial Balance	
		Company P	Company S
1	Debits:		
2	Cash	200,000	150,000
3	Accounts Receivable	300,000	250,000
4	**Inventory**	500,000	**300,000**
5	Land	100,000	
6	Buildings (net)	900,000	
7	**Equipment (net)**	650,000	**400,000**
8	**Investment in Subsidiary S**	**610,000**	
9	Total	3,260,000	1,100,000
10	Credits:		
11	Current Liabilities	300,000	100,000
12	Bonds Payable	500,000	300,000
13	Common Stock ($10 par), Co. P	620,000	
14	Paid-In Capital in Excess of Par, Co. P	980,000	
15	Retained Earnings, Co. P	860,000	
16	Common Stock ($5 par), Co. S		50,000
17	Paid-In Capital in Excess of Par, Co. S		350,000
18	Retained Earnings, Co. S		300,000
19	Total	3,260,000	1,100,000

Worksheet 2-4 (see page 76)

Eliminations & Adjustments				Consolidated Balance Sheet			
Dr.		Cr.		Dr.		Cr.	
							1
				350,000			2
				550,000			3
(2)	50,000			850,000			4
				100,000			5
				900,000			6
		(2)	140,000	910,000			7
(2)	90,000	(1)	700,000				8
							9
							10
						400,000	11
						800,000	12
						620,000	13
						980,000	14
						860,000	15
(1)	50,000						16
(1)	350,000						17
(1)	300,000						18
	840,000		840,000	3,660,000		3,660,000	19

Eliminations and Adjustments:
(1) Eliminate intercompany accounts. Since the entire stockholders' equity of Company S is owned by Company P, it must be completely eliminated against the investment account. The negative or credit balance of $90,000 which results from the elimination represents the net overvaluation of Company S's assets.
(2) Distribute the credit balance of the investment account to the specific subsidiary accounts according to the determination and distribution of excess schedule. In this example, the net decrease in asset value is distributed so as to increase the inventory by $50,000 and decrease the equipment by $140,000.

Excess of **book** value **over cost**		$90,000
Distribute to:		
Inventory.	$ 50,000	
Equipment	(140,000)	90,000
		$ 0

WORKSHEET 2-5

80% Interest; Price Equals Book Value
Company P and Subsidiary Company S
Worksheet for Consolidated Balance Sheet
December 31, 19X1

		Trial Balance	
		Company P	Company S
1	Debits:		
2	Cash	200,000	
3	Accounts Receivable	300,000	200,000
4	Inventory	100,000	100,000
5	**Investment in Subsidiary S**	**400,000**	
6	Equipment (net)	150,000	300,000
7	Total	1,150,000	600,000
8	Credits:		
9	Current Liabilities	150,000	100,000
10	Bonds Payable	300,000	
11	Common Stock, Co. P	100,000	
12	Retained Earnings, Co. P	600,000	
13	**Common Stock, Co. S**		**200,000**
14	**Retained Earnings, Co. S**		**300,000**
15	**Minority Interest**		
16	Total	1,150,000	600,000

Worksheet 2-5 (see page 81)

Eliminations & Adjustments		Minority Interest	Consolidated Balance Sheet		
Dr.	Cr.		Dr.	Cr.	
					1
			200,000		2
			500,000		3
			200,000		4
	(1) 400,000				5
			450,000		6
					7
					8
				250,000	9
				300,000	10
				100,000	11
				600,000	12
(1) 160,000		40,000			13
(1) 240,000		60,000			14
		100,000		100,000	15
400,000	400,000		1,350,000	1,350,000	16

Eliminations and Adjustments:
(1)   Eliminate 80% of the subsidiary equity accounts against the investment in subsidiary account.

WORKSHEET 2-6

80% Interest; Price Exceeds Market Value
Company P and Subsidiary Company S
Worksheet for Consolidated Balance Sheet
December 31, 19X1

		Trial Balance	
		Company P	Company S
1	Debits:		
2	Cash	200,000	150,000
3	Accounts Receivable	300,000	250,000
4	**Inventory**	500,000	**300,000**
5	Land	100,000	
6	Buildings (net)	900,000	
7	**Equipment (net)**	650,000	**400,000**
8	**Investment in Subsidiary S**	**810,000**	
9			
10	**Goodwill**		
11	Total	3,460,000	1,100,000
12	Credits:		
13	Current Liabilities	300,000	100,000
14	Bonds Payable	500,000	300,000
15	Common Stock ($10 par), Co. P	660,000	
16	Paid-In Capital in Excess of Par, Co. P	1,140,000	
17	Retained Earnings, Co. P	860,000	
18	**Common Stock ($5 par), Co. S**		50,000
19	**Paid-In Capital in Excess of Par, Co. S**		350,000
20	**Retained Earnings, Co. S**		300,000
21	**Minority Interest**		
22	Total	3,460,000	1,100,000

Worksheet 2-6 (see page 84)

Eliminations & Adjustments		Minority Interest	Consolidated Balance Sheet		
Dr.	Cr.		Dr.	Cr.	
					1
			350,000		2
			550,000		3
(2) 40,000			840,000		4
			100,000		5
			900,000		6
(2) 120,000			1,170,000		7
	(1) 560,000				8
	(2) 250,000				9
(2) 90,000			90,000		10
					11
					12
				400,000	13
				800,000	14
				660,000	15
				1,140,000	16
				860,000	17
(1) 40,000		10,000			18
(1) 280,000		70,000			19
(1) 240,000		60,000			20
		140,000		140,000	21
810,000	810,000		4,000,000	4,000,000	22

Eliminations and Adjustments:
(1)   Eliminate 80% of the subsidiary equity accounts against the investment account.
(2)   Distribute the balance of the investment account, $250,000, to the specific subsidiary accounts according to the determination and distribution of excess schedule:

Excess of cost over book value.....................................		$250,000
Distribute to:		
Inventory..	$ 40,000	
Equipment	120,000	
Goodwill	90,000	250,000
		$ 0

WORKSHEET 2-7

100% Interest; Pooling of Interests
Company I and Subsidiary Company C
Worksheet for Consolidated Balance Sheet
December 31, 19X1

		Trial Balance	
		Company I	Company C
1	Debits:		
2	Current Assets	20,000	10,000
3	Property, Plant, and Equipment (net)	70,000	30,000
4	**Investment in Subsidiary C**	**30,000**	
5	Total	120,000	40,000
6	Credits:		
7	Liabilities	15,000	10,000
8	Common Stock, Co. I	56,000	
9	Paid-In Capital in Excess of Par, Co. I	4,000	
10	Retained Earnings, Co. I	45,000	
11	**Common Stock, Co. C**		**10,000**
12	**Retained Earnings, Co. C**		**20,000**
13	Total	120,000	40,000

Worksheet 2-7 (see page 90)

Eliminations & Adjustments		Consolidated Balance Sheet		
Dr.	Cr.	Dr.	Cr.	
				1
		30,000		2
		100,000		3
	(1) 30,000			4
				5
				6
			25,000	7
			56,000	8
			4,000	9
			45,000	10
(1) 10,000				11
(1) 20,000				12
30,000	30,000	130,000	130,000	13

Eliminations and Adjustments:
(1)   Eliminate the investment account against the subsidiary equity accounts.

CHAPTER 3

Consolidated Statements Subsequent to Acquisition

This chapter's mission is to teach the procedures needed to prepare consolidated income statements, retained earnings statements, and balance sheets in periods subsequent to the acquisition of a subsidiary. There are a variety of worksheet models to master. This variety is caused primarily by the alternative methods available to a parent for maintaining its investment in a subsidiary account. Accounting principles do not address the method used by a parent to record its investment in a subsidiary that is to be consolidated. The method used is of no concern to standard setters since the investment account always is eliminated when consolidating. Thus, the method chosen to record the investment usually is based on convenience.

In the preceding chapter, worksheet procedures for a combination deemed to be a purchase included asset and liability adjustments to reflect market values on the date of the purchase. This chapter discusses the subsequent depreciation and amortization of these asset and liability revaluations in conjunction with its analysis of worksheet procedures for preparing consolidated financial statements. Appendix A, pages 147–148, explains the vertical worksheet as an alternative approach to the horizontal worksheet used in this chapter for developing consolidated statements.

This chapter does not deal with the income tax issues of the consolidated firm except to the extent that they are reflected in the original acquisition price. Appendix B, pages 148–152, considers tax issues that arise as part of the original purchase. These include recording procedures for deferred tax liabilities arising in a tax-free exchange and tax loss carryovers. A full discussion of tax issues in consolidations is included in Chapter 6.

ACCOUNTING FOR THE INVESTMENT IN A SUBSIDIARY

A parent may choose one of two basic methods when accounting for its investment in a subsidiary: the *equity method* or the *cost method.* The equity method records as income an ownership percentage of the reported income of the subsidiary, whether or not it was received by the parent. The cost method treats the investment in the subsidiary as a normal stock investment by recording income only when dividends are declared by the subsidiary.

EQUITY METHOD

The equity method views the earning of income by a controlled subsidiary as sufficient reason to record the parent's share of that income. The parent has the power to demand the payment of dividends. Clearly, the decision to require the payment of dividends should not be the cause to record income. The receipt of a dividend is just the conversion into cash of a claim on income that already has been recorded.

The equity method records as income the parent's ownership interest percentage times the subsidiary reported net income. The income is added to the parent's investment account. In a like manner, the parent records its share of a subsidiary loss and lowers its investment account for its share of the loss. Dividends received from the parent are viewed as a conversion of a portion of the investment account into cash; thus dividends reduce the investment account balance. The investment account at any point in time can be summarized as follows:

Investment in Subsidiary (equity method)

Original cost plus: Ownership interest × reported income of subsidiary since acquisition	less: Ownership interest × reported losses of subsidiary since acquisition less: Ownership interest × dividends declared by subsidiary since acquisition
equals: Equity-adjusted balance	

The *simple equity method* makes no adjustment to the parent's share of subsidiary income for any amortizations resulting from differences between the book and market values of the investment on the date of acquisition. There is no danger in omitting these amortizations from the investment account when consolidated statements are prepared since the investment account is eliminated entirely in the preparation of those statements. The real advantage of using the simple equity method when consolidating is that every dollar of change in the stockholders' equity of the subsidiary is recorded on a pro rata basis in the investment account. This method expedites the elimination of the investment account in the consolidated worksheets in future periods. It is favored in this text because of its simplicity.

For some unconsolidated investments, the *sophisticated equity method* is required by APB Opinion No. 18, *The Equity Method of Accounting for Investments in Common Stock*. According to this Opinion, a firm's investment should be adjusted for amortizations when the investor has an "influential" investment of 20% or more of another firm's voting stock. For example, assume that the price paid for an investment in a subsidiary exceeded underlying book value and that the determination and distribution of excess schedule attributed the entire excess to goodwill. Just as goodwill will decrease in value and should be amortized, so should that portion of the price paid for the investment attributed to goodwill also be amortized. If the estimated life of the goodwill is 10 years, then the portion of the investment price attributed to goodwill should be amortized over 10 years. This would be accomplished by reducing the investment income each year by the amortization, which means that the income posted to the investment account each year is also less by the amount of the amortization.

The sophisticated equity method is required for influential investments (normally 20% to 50% interests) and for those rare subsidiaries that are not consolidated. Its use for these types of investments is fully discussed in Chapter 6. The sophisticated equity method also is used by some parent companies to maintain the investment in a subsidiary that is to be consolidated. This better reflects the investment account in the parent-only statements, but such statements may not be used as the primary statements for external reporting purposes. Parent-only statements may be used as supplemental statements only when the criteria for consolidated statements are met. The use of this method for investments to be consolidated makes recording the investment income and the elimination of the investment account more difficult than under the simple equity method.

COST METHOD

When the cost method is used, the investment in subsidiary account is retained at its original cost-of-acquisition balance. No adjustments are made to the account for income as it is earned by the subsidiary. Income on the investment is limited to dividends received from the subsidiary. An exception is made for subsidiary dividends that are based on income *earned prior to the acquisition date*. Such dividends are viewed as a partial liquidation and are deducted from the original investment. For example, assume that an 80%-owned subsidiary that was acquired at the start of the year earned $10,000 and paid $15,000 in dividends. The parent would record dividend income of $8,000 (80% of the income earned) and reduce its investment account by $4,000 (80% of the dividends in excess of income). The cost method is acceptable for subsidiaries that are to be consolidated since, in the consolidation process, the investment account is eliminated entirely.

The cost method is the most common method used in practice by parent companies. It is simple to use during the accounting period and avoids the risk of incorrect adjustments. Typically, the correct income of the subsidiary is not known until after the end of the accounting period. Awaiting its determination would delay the parent company's closing procedures. Firms that use the cost method simply convert to the simple equity method as part of the consolidation process. This text emphasizes the application of the simple equity method because it is the method used to convert cost method investments so that they may be eliminated in the consolidation process.

EXAMPLE OF THE EQUITY AND COST METHODS

The simple equity, sophisticated equity, and cost methods will be illustrated by an example covering two years. This example, which will become the foundation for several consolidated worksheets in this chapter, is based on the following facts:

1. The following determination and distribution of excess schedule was pre- pared on the date of purchase. This schedule is similar to that of the preceding chapter but is modified to indicate the period over which adjust- ments to the subsidiary book values will be allocated. This expanded format will be used in preparing all future worksheets.

Price paid, January 1, 19X1		$145,000
Less interest acquired:		
Common stock ($10 par)	$100,000	
Retained earnings	50,000	
Total stockholders' equity	$150,000	
Interest acquired	90%	135,000
Excess of cost over book value (debit balance)		10,000
Goodwill (10-year amortization)		$ 10,000 **Dr**

2. Income during 19X1 was $30,000 for Company S; dividends declared by Company S at the end of 19X1 totaled $10,000.
3. During 19X2, Company S had a loss of $10,000 and declared dividends of $5,000.

The journal entries and resulting investment account balances shown on pages 126 and 127 record this information on the books of Company P using the simple equity, cost, and sophisticated equity methods. Note that the only differ- ence between the sophisticated and simple equity methods is that the former reduces investment income each year for an amount equal to the amortization of goodwill.

The balance in the simple-equity-adjusted investment account of a parent easily can be tested for its correctness. Under the simple equity method, every change in the retained earnings account of the subsidiary leads to an equity adjustment in the investment account for an amount equal to the change multi- plied by the ownership interest. *At any time, the balance in a simple-equity-adjusted investment account can be stated as follows:*

Balance = Cost + (Ownership Interest × Change in Subsidiary Retained Earnings since Acquisition)

In the illustration, the December 31, 19X2 balance in the simple-equity-adjusted Investment in Company S would be verified as follows:

Balance = Cost + (.90 × change in Company S retained earnings since acquisition)
= $145,000 + [.90 × ($55,000 December 31, 19X2 balance − $50,000 January 1, 19X1 balance)]
= $145,000 + (.90 × $5,000)
= $149,500

This procedure will be valuable in checking the balance in an investment account prior to consolidating. Later in the chapter, this technique becomes the basis for converting investments recorded under the cost method to the simple equity method. If it is desired, the sophisticated equity balance can be obtained by adjusting the simple equity balance for the cumulative amortizations of excess.

Most presentations of worksheet elimination procedures in subsequent chapters are based on the use of the simple equity method. Rather than mastering a separate set of procedures for investments carried at cost, such investments will be converted to the simple equity method prior to the application of elimination procedures.

Event		Simple Equity Method		
19X1 Jan. 1	Purchase of stock	Investment in Company S................ Cash	145,000	145,000
Dec. 31	Subsidiary income of $30,000 reported to parent	Investment in Company S Subsidiary Income	27,000	27,000
31	Dividends of $10,000 declared by subsidiary	Dividends Receivable...................... Investment in Company S................	9,000	9,000
		Investment balance, Dec. 31, 19X1........		**$163,000**
19X2 Dec. 31	Subsidiary loss of $10,000 reported to parent	Loss on Subsidiary Operations............. Investment in Company S................	9,000	9,000
31	Dividends of $5,000 declared by subsidiary	Dividends Receivable...................... Investment in Company S................	4,500	4,500
		Investment balance, Dec. 31, 19X2........		**$149,500**

ELIMINATION PROCEDURES

Worksheet procedures necessary to prepare consolidated income statements, retained earnings statements, and balance sheets are examined in the following section. It must be recalled that the consolidation procedure is used each year as it is applied to each period's separate parent and subsidiary accounts. The consolidation process is performed independently each year since the worksheet eliminations of previous years are never recorded by the parent or subsidiary.

The illustrations that follow are based on the facts concerning the investment in Company S, as detailed in the previous example. The procedures for consolidating an investment maintained under the simple equity method will be discussed first, followed by an explanation of how procedures would differ under the cost and sophisticated equity methods.

EFFECT OF SIMPLE EQUITY METHOD ON CONSOLIDATION

The trial balances of Company P and Company S at the end of 19X1 appear in the first two columns of Worksheet 3-1, pages 182–183. The balances reflect the simple equity adjustments for 19X1, which were just illustrated. Be sure to pay close attention to step (1). It is this elimination step that creates what this text refers to as *date alignment*. On the trial balance, the investment account already has been adjusted to its year-end balance. However, the subsidiary retained earnings still reflects its beginning-of-the-year balance. Remaining eliminations may not proceed until the investment account and the subsidiary equity accounts, against which the former is eliminated, are at *the same point in time*. Step (1) eliminates the equity adjustments made and intercompany dividends

Cost Method			Sophisticated Equity Method		
Investment in Company S.......	145,000		Investment in Company S.......	145,000	
Cash		145,000	Cash		145,000
No entry.			Investment in Company S.......	26,000[a]	
			Subsidiary Income		26,000
Dividends Receivable..........	9,000		Dividends Receivable..........	9,000	
Subsidiary (Dividend) Income ..		9,000	Investment in Company S.....		9,000
Investment balance,			**Investment balance,**		
Dec. 31, 19X1		**$145,000**	**Dec. 31, 19X1**		**$162,000**
No entry.			Loss on Subsidiary Operations...	10,000[b]	
			Investment in Company S.....		10,000
Dividends Receivable..........	4,500		Dividends Receivable..........	4,500	
Subsidiary (Dividend) Income ..		4,500	Investment in Company S.....		4,500
Investment balance,			**Investment balance,**		
Dec. 31, 19X2		**$145,000**	**Dec. 31, 19X2**		**$147,500**

[a] Parent's share of subsidiary income less amortization of excess of $1,000 per year.
[b] Parent's share of subsidiary loss plus amortization of excess of $1,000 per year.

declared during the year, thereby returning the investment account to its balance at *the start of the year.* Now that date alignment exists, the subsidiary equity at the start of the year can be eliminated against the investment account in step (2), and the excess cost can be distributed and amortized for the current year in steps (3) and (4), respectively.

Let us review the worksheet eliminations in journal entry form:

(1) Create date alignment and eliminate current year subsidiary income:

Subsidiary Income (Co. P account)	27,000	
Investment in Company S (Co. P account)		27,000
Investment in Company S (Co. P account)	9,000	
Dividend Declared (Co. S account)		9,000

(2) Eliminate investment account, now at beginning-of-the-year balance:

Common Stock, Company S	90,000	
Retained Earnings, Jan. 1, 19X1, Co. S.	45,000	
Investment in Company S (Co. P account)		135,000

(3) Distribute excess of cost (goodwill):

Goodwill (created when consolidating)	10,000	
Investment in Co. S (balance of		
Co. P's investment account).		10,000

(4) Amortize goodwill for the current year:

Expenses (charged to Co. P share of consolidated income)	1,000	
Goodwill.		1,000

The Consolidated Income Statement column follows the Eliminations & Adjustments columns. The adjusted nominal accounts of the constituent firms are used to calculate the *combined net income* of $69,000. This income is distributed to the controlling and minority interests. Note that the minority receives 10% of the $30,000 reported net income of the subsidiary, or $3,000. The controlling interest receives the balance of the combined net income, or $66,000, which this text terms *consolidated net income.*

The distribution of income is handled best by using *income distribution schedules* which appear at the end of Worksheet 3-1. The subsidiary income distribution schedule is a "T account" which begins with the reported net income of the subsidiary. This income is termed "internally generated net income" which connotes the income of only the firm being analyzed without consideration of income derived from other members of the affiliated group. Until Chapter 8, when the subsidiary owns an interest in the parent, the subsidiary's internally generated net income is the same as its net income. In Worksheet 3-1, the subsidiary net income is multiplied by the minority ownership percentage to calculate the minority interest in income. A similar T account is used for the parent income distribution schedule. The parent's share of subsidiary net income is added to the internally generated net income of the parent, and amortizations of excess are deducted. Goodwill amortization is borne entirely by the controlling interest. Note that this is true for *all* excess cost over book value situations. Under the parent company concept, only the portion applicable to the purchaser's interest is acknowledged; thus, the amortization of excess affects only the controlling interest. The balance in the parent T account is the controlling share of the combined net income (called consolidated net income). The income distribution is a valuable self-check procedure since the sum of the income distributions should equal the combined net income on the worksheet.

The Minority Interest column of the worksheet summarizes the total ownership interest of the minority stockholders at the close of the period. The column includes the minority's interest in each of the following: subsidiary paid-in capital balance, subsidiary retained earnings balance at the beginning of the period, combined net income, and dividends declared by the subsidiary during the period.

The Controlling Retained Earnings column produces the controlling interest's retained earnings balance at the close of the period. The column includes the parent retained earnings balance at the beginning of the period plus the parent's share of combined net income. If the parent had declared dividends, the dividends would have been shown as a deduction in this column.

The Consolidated Balance Sheet column includes the combined asset and liability balances. The paid-in equity balances of the parent are extended as the consolidated paid-in capital balance. Usually, the net minority interest is extended to the balance sheet without enumeration of its components. Also, the total of the Controlling Retained Earnings column is extended to the balance sheet.

Separate debit and credit columns may be used for the consolidated balance sheet. This arrangement may minimize errors and aid analysis. Single columns are not advocated, but are used to facilitate the inclusion of lengthy worksheets in a summarized fashion.

The information for the following formal statements is taken directly from Worksheet 3-1:

Company P and Subsidiary Company S
Consolidated Income Statement
For Year Ended December 31, 19X1

Revenue	$180,000
Expenses (includes $1,000 goodwill amortization)	(111,000)
Combined net income	$ 69,000
Minority interest	(3,000)
Consolidated net income	$ 66,000

Company P and Subsidiary Company S
Consolidated Retained Earnings Statement
For Year Ended December 31, 19X1

	Minority	Controlling
Retained earnings, January 1, 19X1	$5,000	$123,000
Distribution of combined net income	3,000	66,000
Dividends declared	(1,000)	
Balance, December 31, 19X1	$7,000	$189,000

Company P and Subsidiary Company S Consolidated Balance Sheet December 31, 19X1				
Assets		**Stockholders' Equity**		
Net tangible assets	$397,000	Minority interest		$ 17,000
Goodwill	9,000	Controlling interest:		
		Common stock......	$200,000	
		Retained earnings ...	189,000	389,000
		Total stockholders'		
Total assets..........	$406,000	equity.............		$406,000

There are two features of these statements that deserve added attention. The first concerns the reporting procedures for consolidated net income. Technically, consolidated net income is the income available to both the parent and minority interests. This is the approach used by the *economic unit concept* which views consolidated net income as available to the controlling and minority interests and merely allocates it to these interests below the net income line. However, it has become common practice to view consolidated net income as just the income available to the controlling interest. Unfortunately, this suggests that the minority interest in income is an expense which, of course, it is not. Many firms go so far as to show the minority interest in income as an expense. Exhibit 1 presents the minority interest in income as a deduction to arrive at consolidated net income. It is an implied expense by its location. Exhibit 2 includes an income statement and an accompanying footnote that show the minority interest in income as an expense. Showing the minority interest as an expense is a result of using the *parent company concept*,[1] which holds that the focus of the income statement should be on the income owned by the controlling interest. Any income not available to the controlling interest takes on the appearance of an expense to the controlling interest. This text uses the most common practice of applying the *parent company concept*[2] which subtracts the minority interest in the subsidiary's adjusted net income from the combined net income to arrive at the controlling firm's share of combined net income, or consolidated net income.

The second feature of the consolidated statements is that the balance sheet includes the minority shareholders' equity as a part of the total stockholders' equity. As was explained in Chapter 2, some firms treat the minority interest as a liability or place it in a separate category.

Now consider consolidation procedures for 19X2 as they would apply to Companies P and S under the simple equity method. This will provide added practice in preparing worksheets and will emphasize that, at the end of each year, consolidation procedures are applied to the separate statements of the constituent firms. In essence, *each year's consolidation procedures begin as if there never had been a previous consolidation.* However, reference to past worksheets is used commonly to save time.

---

[1]See the appendix following Chapter 8 for a comparison of consolidation concepts.
[2]*Ibid.*

Exhibit 1
McDermott International, Inc.
Consolidated Statement of Income (Loss) and Retained Earnings (Deficit)
for the Three Fiscal Years Ended March 31, 1993

	1993	1992	1991
		(in thousands)	
Revenues	$3,172,555	$3,524,482	$3,069,849
Costs and Expenses:			
Cost of operations	2,742,260	3,025,998	2,756,950
Depreciation and amortization	121,508	125,812	99,857
Selling, general and administrative expenses	237,468	258,859	226,426
	3,101,236	3,410,669	3,083,233
	71,319	113,813	(13,384)
Equity in Income (Loss) of Investees	94,058	7,242	(29,685)
Operating Income (Loss)	165,377	121,055	(43,069)
Other Income (Expense):			
Interest income	40,391	53,768	73,094
Interest expense	(90,340)	(102,321)	(111,595)
Minority interest	(18,203)	(19,065)	(1,220)
Other—net	10,197	70,369	9,590
	(57,955)	2,751	(30,131)
Income (Loss) from Continuing Operations before Provision for Income Taxes, Extraordinary Items, and Cumulative Effect of Accounting Changes	107,422	123,806	(73,200)
Provision for Income Taxes	40,099	43,269	14,497
Income (Loss) from Continuing Operations before Extraordinary Items and Cumulative Effect of Accounting Changes	67,323	80,537	(87,697)
Income (Loss) from Discontinued Operations		(3,368)	18,172
Income (Loss) before Extraordinary Items and Cumulative Effect of Accounting Changes	67,323	77,169	(69,525)
Extraordinary Items	(10,431)		
Cumulative Effect of Accounting Changes	(245,624)		
Net Income (Loss)	(188,732)	77,169	(69,525)
Retained Earnings — Beginning of Year	114,204	82,919	196,415
Deduct Cash Dividends — Common	51,736	45,884	43,971
Retained Earnings (Deficit) — End of Year	$ (126,264)	$ 114,204	$ 82,919

continued

PRIMARY AND FULLY DILUTED:	1993	1992	1991
Earnings (Loss) Per Common and Common Equivalent Share:			
Continuing operations before extraordinary items and cumulative effect of accounting changes	$ 1.29	$ 1.75	$ (2.00)
Discontinued operations		(0.08)	0.42
Extraordinary items	(0.20)		
Accounting changes	(4.72)		
Net income (loss)	$ (3.63)	$ 1.67	$ (1.58)

Source: 1993 annual report for McDermott International, Inc.

Exhibit 2
Partial Consolidated Statements of Income and Retained Earnings
Overseas Shipholding Group, Inc. and Subsidiaries

In thousands, except per share amounts, for the year ended December 31,	1993	1992	1991
Total Shipping Revenues	$389,421	$370,885	$419,105
Total Shipping Expenses	349,938	341,471	317,059
Income from Vessel Operations	39,483	29,414	102,046
Other Income (Net) — Note K	30,674	12,337	33,354
	70,157	41,751	135,400
Interest Expense	43,311	44,580	55,574
Income/(Loss) before Federal Income Taxes and Cumulative Effect of Accounting Change	26,846	(2,829)	79,826
Provision/(Credit) for Federal Income Taxes — Note J	8,900	(2,900)	24,750
Income before Cumulative Effect of Accounting Change	17,946	71	55,076
Cumulative Effect of Change in Accounting for Income Taxes — Note A6		16,000	
Net Income	17,946	16,071	55,076
Retained Earnings at Beginning of Year	766,647	770,265	733,349
	784,593	786,336	788,425
Cash Dividends Declared and Paid	19,606	19,689	18,160
Retained Earnings at End of Year	$764,987	$766,647	$770,265

continued

Note K — Other Income (Net):	1993	1992	1991
Other income (net) consists of:			
Interest	$ 4,017	$ 5,293	$ 11,820
Dividends	3,473	6,502	8,322
Gain on sales of securities — net			
(based on first-in, first-out method)	9,128	14,112	5,453
Provision for loss on investment in GPA Group plc		(20,000)	
Gain/(loss) on disposal of vessels	12,088	(1,259)[a]	4,067
Foreign currency exchange gains/(losses)	(1,647)	4,830	(1,223)
Minority interest	(116)	735	20
Miscellaneous — net	3,731	2,124	4,895
	$ 30,674	$ 12,337	$ 33,354

[a]Represents a provision for loss on a vessel sold subsequent to year-end.

Gross realized gains on sales of securities were $10,802,000 (1993), $15,728,000 (1992), and $6,931,000 (1991), and gross realized losses were $1,674,000 (1993), $1,616,000 (1992), and $1,478,000 (1991).

Source: 1993 annual report of Overseas Shipholding Group, Inc.

The separate trial balances of Companies P and S are displayed in the first two columns of Worksheet 3-2, pages 184–185. The investment in subsidiary account includes the simple-equity-adjusted investment balance as calculated on page 126. Note that the balances in the retained earnings accounts of Companies P and S are calculated as follows:

Company P: January 1, 19X1 balance $123,000
 Net income, 19X1 (including Company P's
 share of subsidiary income under simple equity method)   67,000
 Balance, January 1, 19X2 . . . . $190,000

Company S: January 1, 19X1 balance . . . . $ 50,000
 Net income, 19X1 30,000
 Dividends declared. . . . . (10,000)
 Balance, January 1, 19X2 . . . . $ 70,000

Again, step (1) is used to create the needed date alignment. The equity adjustment made during the year and the intercompany dividends are eliminated. This returns the investment account to its balance at the start of the second year so that the account is at a common point in time with the subsidiary equity accounts, against which the investment account is eliminated in step (2). Notice that step (4) amortizes the excess for both the current and past periods.

In journal entry form this elimination is:

Retained Earnings, Jan. 1, 19X2, Co. P   1,000
Expenses (charged to Co. P share of consolidated income)   1,000
 Goodwill (2 years of amortization)   2,000

Note, again, the amortization of goodwill for both the prior and current year is borne only by the parent, since only its interest in goodwill was recorded. Be sure to understand that the amortization of excess done the prior year appeared only on that year's worksheet and was *not recorded* on either firms' accounting records. This emphasizes that consolidation starts from the separate statements of the two companies each year and that *the statements do not reflect the prior periods' consolidation procedures.*

Note that the original determination and distribution of excess schedule prepared on the date of acquisition becomes the foundation for *all* subsequent worksheets. Once prepared, the schedule is used without modification.

EFFECT OF COST METHOD ON CONSOLIDATON

Recall that parent firms most often may choose to record their investments in a subsidiary under the cost method, whereby the investments are maintained at their original costs, with income from the investments recorded when dividends are declared by the subsidiary. The use of the cost method means that the investment account does not reflect changes in subsidiary equity. Rather than develop a new set of procedures for the elimination of an investment under the cost method, *the cost method investment will be converted to its simple equity balance at the beginning of the period* to create date alignment. Then, the elimination procedures developed earlier can be applied.

Worksheet 3-3, pages 186–187, is a consolidated financial statements worksheet for Companies P and S for the first year of combined operations. The worksheet is based upon the entries made under the cost method, as shown on page 127. Reference to Company P's Trial Balance column in Worksheet 3-3 reveals that the investment in the subsidiary account at year end still is stated at the original $145,000 cost and the income recorded by the parent as a result of subsidiary ownership is limited to $9,000, or 90% of the dividends declared by the subsidiary. When the cost method is used, the account title *Dividend Income* may be used in place of Subsidiary Income.

At the end of the first year of operations, there would be no need for an equity conversion entry. Date alignment exists since the Company P investment account and the Company S equity accounts already are stated as of a common point in time, January 1, 19X1. For step (1), it is necessary to eliminate the intercompany dividends only. The remaining eliminations, steps (2) through (4), are identical to their corresponding entries in Worksheet 3-1. The last four columns of Worksheet 3-3 also are identical to their counterparts in Worksheet 3-1.

For periods subsequent to the first year of combined operations, an entry converting the investment in the subsidiary account to its simple-equity-method balance will be needed on the consolidated worksheets in order to create date alignment. To illustrate, Worksheet 3-4, pages 188–189, covers the second year of operations for Companies P and S. This worksheet is identical to Worksheet 3-2 except that here the cost method is used to account for the investment in Company S. Thus, the balance of the investment account is the original $145,000 cost as of the January 1, 19X1 purchase date. However, the retained earnings account of Company S carries the January 1, 19X2 balance. Because these accounts do not share a common point in time, eliminations cannot proceed. Note that in Worksheet 3-4 the balance of the parent retained earnings account is $18,000 less than its balance in Worksheet 3-2 since it does not include the undistributed 19X1 income of the subsidiary. The conversion step, step (C) in Worksheet 3-4, converts the investment account to its simple-equity-method balance on January 1, 19X2, so that the account shares a common date with the subsidiary equity accounts against which the investment account now can be eliminated. In journal entry form, the conversion step is:

```
Investment in Company S (to bring account
    to equity balance on Jan. 1, 19X2). . . . . . . . . . . . . . . . . . . . . . .   18,000
    Retained Earnings, Jan. 1, 19X2, Co. P. . . . . . . . . . . . . . . . . . . .                18,000
```

The conversion entry simultaneously updates the Company P retained earnings account to its simple-equity-method balance as of January 1, 19X2. The dollar amount of the conversion is calculated by multiplying the ownership interest by the change in the subsidiary retained earnings account between the date of acquisition and the beginning of the current year. In this case, the adjustment is made as follows:

$$
\begin{aligned}
\text{Conversion} &= [.90 \times (\text{Company S Retained Earnings, January 1, 19X2} - \\
&\qquad \text{Company S Retained Earnings, January 1, 19X1})] \\
&= [.90 \times (\$70,000 - \$50,000)] = .90 \times \$20,000 \\
&= \$18,000
\end{aligned}
$$

The simplicity of this technique of converting from the cost to the simple equity method should be appreciated. At any future date, in order to convert to the simple equity method, it is only necessary to compare the balance of the subsidiary retained earnings account on the worksheet trial balance with the balance of that account on the original date of acquisition (included in the determination and distribution of excess schedule). Specific reference to income earned and dividends paid by the subsidiary in each intervening year is unnecessary. The only complications occur when stock dividends have been issued by the subsidiary or when the subsidiary has issued or retired stock. These complications are examined in Chapter 8.

After the conversion, the eliminations may proceed. Since the cost method is being used, the first elimination is confined to intercompany dividends. Steps (2) through (4) are identical to the corresponding steps in Worksheet 3-2. Note that step (2) is possible only after the conversion step brings the account balances to a common point in time.

EFFECT OF SOPHISTICATED EQUITY METHOD ON CONSOLIDATION

In some cases, a parent may desire to prepare its own separate statements as a supplement to the consolidated statements. In this situation, the investment in the subsidiary must be shown on the parent's separate statements at the sophisticated equity balance. This requirement may lead the parent to maintain its subsidiary investment account under the sophisticated equity method. Two ramifications occur when such an investment is consolidated. First, the current year's equity adjustment is net of excess amortizations; second, the investment account contains only the remaining unamortized excess applicable to the investment.

The use of the sophisticated equity method complicates the elimination of the investment account in that the worksheet distribution and amortization of the excess procedures are altered. However, there is no impact on the other consolidation procedures. To illustrate, the information given in Worksheet 3-2 will be used as the basis for an example. The trial balance of Company P will show the following changes as a result of using the sophisticated equity method:

1. The Investment in Company S will be carried at $147,500 ($149,500 simple equity balance less 2 years' amortization of excess at $1,000 per year).
2. The January 1, 19X2 balance for Company P Retained Earnings will be $189,000 ($190,000 under simple equity less 1 year's amortization of excess of $1,000).
3. The subsidiary loss account of the parent will have a balance of $10,000 ($9,000 share of the subsidiary loss plus $1,000 amortization of excess).

Based on these changes, a partial worksheet under the sophisticated equity method follows:

Company P and Subsidiary Company S
Partial Worksheet for Consolidated Financial Statements
For Year Ended December 31, 19X2

(Credit balance amounts are in parentheses.)	Trial Balance		Eliminations & Adjustments	
	Company P	Company S	Dr.	Cr.
Investment in Company S	147,500		(1) 10,000	(2) 153,000
			(1) 4,500	(3) 9,000
Goodwill			(3) 9,000	(4) 1,000
Retained Earnings, Jan. 1, 19X2, Co. P	(189,000)			
Common Stock ($10 par), Co. S		(100,000)	(2) 90,000	
Retained Earnings, Jan. 1, 19X2, Co. S		(70,000)	(2) 63,000	
Revenue	(100,000)	(50,000)		
Expenses	80,000	60,000	(4) 1,000	
Subsidiary Loss	10,000			(1) 10,000
Dividends Declared		5,000		(1) 4,500

Eliminations and Adjustments:
(1) Eliminate the current-year entries made in the investment account and the subsidiary loss account. The loss account now includes the $1,000 excess amortization.
(2) Using the balances at the beginning of the year, eliminate 90% of the Company S equity balances against the remaining investment account.
(3) Distribute the remaining unamortized excess on January 1, 19X2, ($10,000 on purchase date less $1,000 19X1 amortization) to the goodwill account.
(4) Amortize goodwill for the current year.

The sophisticated equity method essentially is a modification of simple equity procedures. The major difference in the consolidation procedures under the two methods is that, subsequent to the acquisition, the original excess calculated on the determination and distribution of excess schedule does not appear when the sophisticated equity method is used. Only the remaining unamortized excess appears. Since the investment account is eliminated in the consolidation process, the added complexities of the sophisticated method are not justified for most firms and seldom are applied to consolidated subsidiaries.

DETERMINATION OF THE METHOD BEING USED

Before you attempt to prepare a consolidated worksheet, you need to know which of the three methods is being used by the parent to record its investment in the subsidiary. You cannot begin to eliminate the intercompany investment until that is determined. The most efficient approach is to:

1. Test for the use of the cost method. If the cost method is used:
   a. The investment account will be at the original cost shown on the determination and distribution of excess schedule.
   b. The parent will have recorded as its share of subsidiary income its ownership interest times the *dividends declared* by the subsidiary. In most cases, this income will be called "subsidiary dividend income," but some may call it "subsidiary income" or "dividend income."
2. If the method used is not cost, check for the use of simple equity as follows:
   a. The investment account will not be at the original cost.
   b. The parent will have recorded as subsidiary income its ownership percentage times the *reported net income* of the subsidiary.
3. If the method used is neither cost nor simple equity, it must be the sophisticated equity method. Confirm that it is by noting that:
   a. The investment account will not be at the original cost.
   b. The parent will have recorded as subsidiary income its ownership percentage times the reported net income of the subsidiary *minus the amortizations of excess for the current period.*

COMPLICATED PURCHASE, SEVERAL CAUSES OF EXCESS

In Worksheets 3-1 through 3-4, it was assumed that the entire excess of cost over book value was attributable to goodwill. In reality, this assumption seldom will be true. The following example illustrates a more complicated purchase.

Paulos Company paid $790,000 to obtain 8,000 shares (80% interest) of Carlos Company on January 1, 19X1. In addition, $10,000 of direct acquisition costs were paid by Paulos Company. At the time of the purchase, Carlos Company had the following summarized balance sheet:

| Carlos Company |
| Balance Sheet |
| January 1, 19X1 |

Assets			Liabilities and Equity	
Inventory........................		$ 75,000	Current liabilities	$ 50,000
Land...........................		150,000	Bonds payable, 6%, due	
Building........................	$600,000		Dec. 31, 19X4	200,000
Less accumulated depreciation	300,000	300,000	Common stock ($10 par)	100,000
			Paid-in capital in excess of par	150,000
Equipment	$150,000		Retained earnings................	250,000
Less accumulated depreciation	50,000	100,000		
Goodwill		125,000		
Total assets....................		$750,000	Total liabilities and equity	$750,000

The market values for Carlos Company's tangible assets and long-term liabilities on January 1, 19X1, are as follows:

	Market Values
Inventory	$ 80,000
Land	200,000
Building (20-year remaining life)	500,000
Equipment (5-year remaining life).............................	80,000
Bonds payable based on current 8% market interest rate as follows:	
Present value of interest payment at 8% ($12,000 annual interest	
× 4-year, 8% present value of annuity factor of 3.31213) ...... $ 39,746	
Present value of principal ($200,000 × 4-year, 8% present value	
factor of .73503) 147,006	186,752

Based on these market values, the following determination and distribution of excess schedule is prepared. This schedule calculates an excess of cost of $400,000 on the interest acquired; $14,598 of this excess is consumed by the revaluation of the current assets and liabilities. Previously recorded goodwill was not added to the excess available for long-lived assets since only $184,000 was needed to adjust these assets to market value. The balance of the excess, $201,402, was allocated to additional goodwill.

Price paid (including $10,000 direct acquisition costs)		$800,000
Less interest acquired:		
Capital stock ($10 par)	$100,000	
Paid-in capital in excess of par	150,000	
Retained earnings.................................	250,000	
Total stockholders' equity	$500,000	
Interest acquired....................................	80%	400,000
Excess of cost over book value of subsidiary interest		
(debit balance).....................................		**$400,000**

Less adjustments to current assets and debt:

Inventory undervalued $5,000; 80% × $5,000.	$ 4,000	Dr
Discount on bonds overstated by $13,248; record		
discount of 80% × $13,248 (4-year life)	10,598	Dr
Excess available to adjust long-lived assets:		
Land understated $50,000; increase land 80% × $50,000	40,000	Dr
Building (20-year life) understated $200,000;		
decrease accumulated depreciation 80% × $200,000 . . .	160,000	Dr
Equipment (5-year life) overstated $20,000;		
reduce equipment 80% × $20,000.	(16,000)	Cr
Balance of excess reflecting *additional* goodwill		
(10-year life).	$201,402	Dr

Theoretically, the plant asset adjustments required by the determination and distribution of excess schedule should be made in a manner that would eliminate all accumulated depreciation applicable to the controlling interest as of the purchase date. This procedure would complicate future worksheets. As a practical alternative, when possible, the plant asset adjustments should be made in such a way as to reduce accumulated depreciation, and adjustments should never increase accumulated depreciation. Therefore, the increase in the net value of the building was accomplished by decreasing its accumulated depreciation account, not by increasing the asset account. The reduction in the equipment was accomplished by decreasing the asset account rather than increasing its accumulated depreciation account.

In this example, additional goodwill is recorded. Recall from Chapter 2 that existing goodwill is made available for distribution. The amortization of goodwill adjustment is always based on the net change in goodwill.

Worksheet 3-5, pages 190–193, is a consolidated financial statements worksheet for Paulos Company and Carlos Company one year after the acquisition. During the year, Carlos had a net income of $60,000 and declared $20,000 in dividends. Paulos Company shows the following simple-equity-adjusted balance for its investment in Carlos:

Original cost.	$800,000
80% of 19X1 income of $60,000	48,000
80% of $20,000 dividends declared by Carlos.	(16,000)
Investment balance, December 31, 19X1	$832,000

The worksheet is completed by using income distribution schedules to allocate the combined net income of $108,708 to the minority and controlling interests, with the minority interest receiving 20% of the subsidiary's reported $60,000 net income. Note once again that none of the amortizations resulting from revaluations affect the minority interest, because only the adjustments relating to the 80% controlling interest in the assets and liabilities were recorded initially. Therefore, all the amortizations pertain only to the controlling interest and are reflected only in the parent company income distribution schedule.

At this point, it should be understood that the amortizations of excess cost applicable to long-lived assets could become more complex than they are in Worksheet 3-5. The amortization adjustments found in steps (4c) and (4d) divide the applicable excess by the assets' remaining lives as shown in the determination and distribution of excess schedule. It was implicitly assumed that the amortization periods were the assets' remaining lives used by the subsidiary and the subsidiary used straight-line depreciation. If the subsidiary had used an alternative depreciation method, that method would have been applied to the excess. It may occur that the parent company does not wish to use the subsidiary's depreciation method and/or remaining life. In this case, the parent would recompute depreciation, based on its ownership interest in the asset. The recomputed amount would be compared to the parent's ownership interest in the subsidiary's recorded depreciation expense, and the difference would become the amortization adjustment for the period.

Worksheet 3-6, pages 194–197, is the worksheet for the second year of combined operations for the purchase that was analyzed in Worksheet 3-5. The second year is included to emphasize that *each year the consolidation starts anew from the separate trial balances of the two firms.* None of the eliminations made on the previous period's worksheet are reflected in the 19X2 separate trial balances of Paulos Company and Carlos Company.

The following information may be inferred from the trial balance figures in Worksheet 3-6:

1. Carlos reported a net income of $100,000 for 19X2 and declared $20,000 in dividends. This income is based on the asset values maintained on Carlos' books, and does not reflect revaluations caused by the 80% purchase by Paulos.

2. The investment in Carlos' account reflects:

Investment balance, December 31, 19X1	$832,000
80% of 19X2 net income of $100,000	80,000
80% of $20,000 dividends declared by Carlos.	(16,000)
Balance, December 31, 19X2	$896,000

3. Paulos recorded subsidiary income of $80,000, which is 80% of Carlos' reported net income.

4. The January 1, 19X2 balance in the Paulos retained earnings account is derived as follows:

Balance, January 1, 19X1.	$700,000
19X1 income generated by Paulos Company	80,000
Subsidiary income under the simple equity method	48,000
Balance, January 1, 19X2.	$828,000

5. The $828,000 balance in the Paulos retained earnings account reflects 80% of the reported net income of Carlos and does not include adjustments resulting from the amortizations of the excess of the price paid for the 80% interest. These amortizations appear only on the consolidated worksheet.

INTRAPERIOD PURCHASE UNDER THE SIMPLE EQUITY METHOD

The accountant will be required to apply specialized procedures when consolidating a controlling investment in common stock that is acquired during the fiscal year. When such an acquisition is deemed to be a purchase, the determination and distribution of excess schedule must be based on the subsidiary stockholders' equity on the interim purchase date, including the subsidiary retained earnings balance on that date. A further complication under purchase accounting is that the combined net income of the consolidated firm, as derived on the worksheet, is to include only subsidiary income earned subsequent to the purchase date.

There are two options available for consolidating an intraperiod purchase. The first option is to require the subsidiary to close its books as of the purchase date. This procedure would make retained earnings on the acquisition date available for use in the determination and distribution of excess schedule and would mean that the consolidated worksheet would include only the operations of the subsidiary subsequent to the purchase date. The second and more realistic option is to modify the determination and distribution of excess schedule to include the purchased share of undistributed income for the portion of the year prior to the purchase. Then, it is possible to include the operations of the subsidiary for the entire fiscal year in the consolidated worksheet.

Option 1: Subsidiary Books Closed. Company S has the following trial balance on July 1, 19X1, the date of an 80% purchase by Company P:

Current Assets	68,000	
Equipment	80,000	
Accumulated Depreciation		30,000
Liabilities		10,000
Common Stock ($10 par)		50,000
Retained Earnings, January 1, 19X1		45,000
Dividends Declared	5,000	
Sales		90,000
Cost of Goods Sold	60,000	
Expenses	12,000	
Total	225,000	225,000

If Company P requires Company S to close its nominal accounts as of July 1, Company S would increase its retained earnings account by $13,000 with the following entries:

Sales	90,000	
Cost of Goods Sold		60,000
Expenses		12,000
Retained Earnings		18,000
Retained Earnings	5,000	
Dividends Declared		5,000

Assume Company P pays $106,400 for its 80% interest in Company S. Assume also that the equipment is undervalued by $40,000 and has a 10-year remaining life. The determination and distribution of excess schedule would be as follows:

Price paid.		$106,400
Less interest acquired:		
Common stock ($10 par)	$ 50,000	
Retained earnings, July 1, 19X1	58,000	
Total stockholders' equity, **July 1, 19X1**.	$108,000	
Interest acquired	80%	**86,400**
Excess of cost over book value (debit balance)		**20,000**
Equipment, 10-year life (maximum asset increase		
would be 80% × $40,000, or $32,000).		**20,000** **Dr**
Goodwill		$ 0

    Proceeding to the end of the year, assume that the operations of Company S for the last six months result in a net income of $20,000 and dividends of $5,000 are declared by Company S on December 31. Worksheet 3-7, pages 198–199, includes Company S nominal accounts for the second six-month period only, since the nominal accounts were closed on July 1. Company S Retained Earnings shows the July 1, 19X1 balance. The trial balance of Company P includes operations for the entire year. The subsidiary income listed by Company P includes 80% of the subsidiary's $20,000 second six-months' income. Company P's investment account balance shows:

Original cost.	$106,400
80% of subsidiary's second six-months' income of $20,000.	16,000
80% of $5,000 dividends declared by subsidiary on Dec. 31.	(4,000)
Investment balance, December 31, 19X1	$118,400

    In conformance with purchase theory, the Consolidated Income Statement column of Worksheet 3-7 includes only subsidiary income earned after the acquisition date. Likewise, only subsidiary income earned after the purchase date is distributed to the minority and controlling interests. Income earned and dividends declared prior to the purchase date by Company S are reflected in its July 1, 19X1 retained earnings balance, of which the minority is granted its share. The notes to the statements would have to disclose what the income of the consolidated firm would have been had the purchase occurred at the start of the year.

Option 2: Subsidiary Books Not Closed.   Usually, a subsidiary does not close its books as a result of the parent company's securing a controlling interest in its stock. Normally the parent company is able to ascertain the income earned by the subsidiary between the beginning of the year and the date control is achieved. If the subsidiary already has declared dividends as of the time of the acquisition, these dividends would be deducted in arriving at the total subsidiary equity interest as of that date.

Assume the parent had access to the Company S trial balance shown on page 141, but Company S did not close its books as of July 1, 19X1. Company P would prepare its determination and distribution of excess schedule as follows:

Price paid		$106,400
Less interest acquired:		
Common stock ($10 par).........................	$ 50,000	
Retained earnings, January 1, 19X1................	45,000	
Income of Company S, January 1–July 1	**18,000**	
Dividends declared, January 1–July 1	**(5,000)**	
Total stockholders' equity, **July 1, 19X1**	$108,000	
Interest acquired	80%	86,400
Excess of cost over book value (debit balance)........		**20,000**
Equipment, 10-year life (maximum asset increase		
would be 80% × $40,000, or $32,000)		**20,000** **Dr**
Goodwill		$ 0

Since the subsidiary did not close its books as of July 1, 19X1, Worksheet 3-8, pages 200–203, includes the Company S trial balance reflecting the entire year's operations. The Company S retained earnings account is dated January 1, 19X1. The Company P investment and subsidiary income accounts are identical to those in Worksheet 3-7.

The challenge is to create date alignment. The investment account balance and the retained earnings of the subsidiary must be adjusted to the same point in time. The investment account is as of July 1, 19X1, while the retained earnings of the subsidiary is as of January 1, 19X1. This problem is solved by using a temporary account, Purchased Income, to record the current year income already earned by the subsidiary as of July 1 that was purchased by the parent. This would be 80% of the $18,000 subsidiary income earned during the first six months. Purchased income is included in step (2), which can be explained in journal entry form as follows:

Common Stock, Company S	40,000	
Retained Earnings, **Jan. 1, 19X1**, Company S..................	36,000	
Purchased Income[1].....................................	14,400	
Dividends declared[2]		4,000
Investment in Company S		86,400

[1] Parent share of income earned in the first six months which was included in the equity interest purchased (80% × $18,000)

[2] Prior to the purchase date and deducted from subsidiary equity at time of purchase (80% × $5,000)

In Worksheet 3-8, the nominal accounts of the subsidiary for the entire year are included in the consolidated income column. Since 80% of the income earned in the first half of the year belonged to outside interests (shareholders that are no longer members of the affiliated group), Purchased Income must be deleted to arrive at the combined net income that belongs to current members of the affiliated group. As with the income, 80% of the dividends declared by the subsidiary prior to the purchase also belonged to outside interests and must be eliminated. However, this elimination does *not* affect the consolidated income statement. Note that the minority interest existed for the entire year; thus it is permitted a *20% share* of subsidiary income for the *full* year. Worksheet 3-8 leads to the following unique income statement:

Company P and Subsidiary Company S Consolidated Income Statement For Year Ended December 31, 19X1	
Sales.	$682,000
Cost of goods sold	(470,000)
Gross profit.	$212,000
Other expenses	(95,000)
Total net income of Company P and Company S for year 19X1	$117,000
Income earned by outside interests existing prior to Company P purchase	**(14,400)**
Combined net income	$102,600
Minority interest.	(7,600)
Consolidated net income.	$ 95,000

The format of this income statement has the advantage of disclosing the total net income of the two firms for the year and the consolidated net income. The total net income for the year becomes the basis for a pro forma statement of what income would have been if the combination had occurred at the beginning of the year. This figure would need to be supplemented only by a disclosure that there would have been an additional $1,000 of equipment depreciation for the first six months of the year. The disclosure is required by APB Opinion No. 16 (par. 96) for intraperiod purchases.

Special care must be taken in consolidating an intraperiod purchase in subsequent periods. It is common to find that a firm has made an error by taking a full year's share of equity income in the period of acquisition rather than including only income earned after the date of acquisition. When this error is found, a correcting entry should be recorded by the parent.

INTRAPERIOD PURCHASE UNDER THE COST METHOD

There are only two variations of the procedures discussed in the preceding section if the cost method is used by the parent firm to record its investment in the subsidiary:

1. During the year of acquisition, the parent would record as income only its share of dividends declared by the subsidiary. Thus, eliminating entries would be confined to the intercompany dividends.
2. In subsequent years, the cost-to-equity conversion adjustment would be based on the change in the subsidiary retained earnings balance *from the*

intraperiod purchase date to the beginning of the year for which the worksheet is being prepared.

POOLING OF INTERESTS: SUBSEQUENT TO ACQUISITION

In a pooling of interests, worksheet procedures in subsequent periods are simple if the original acquisition is recorded properly. Since there is no excess of cost over book value in a pooling, the amortizations of the excess are not present. For example, assume that on January 1, 19X1, Company I issued 2,700 shares of its $2 par stock ($15 market value) for a 90% interest in Company C. As presented in the example on page 89, Company C had the following condensed balance sheet:

Assets		Liabilities and Equity	
Current assets..............	$10,000	Liabilities	$10,000
Property, plant, and		Common stock ($10 par)........	10,000
equipment (net).............	30,000	Retained earnings..............	20,000
Total assets	$40,000	Total liabilities and equity	$40,000

The following net income figures were reported by Company C subsequent to the acquisition date:

19X1..	$20,000
19X2..	15,000
19X3 (current year)...........................	25,000

Pooling rules require the issuer to record the investment at the book value of the underlying equity. Thus, Company I would have recorded the original acquisition as follows:

Investment in Company C (90% × $30,000 total Company C equity)	27,000	
Common Stock (2,700 shares × $2 par)		5,400
Paid-In Capital in Excess of Par (90% of Company C Paid-In		
Capital = $9,000, less $5,400 assigned to par)..................		3,600
Retained Earnings (90% × $20,000 Company C January 1, 19X1		
Retained Earnings)...		18,000

 Worksheet 3-9, pages 205–206, is a consolidated financial statements worksheet for Companies I and C on December 31, 19X3. The balance in the investment in Company C account is the result of Company I's use of the equity method, as follows:

Original recorded value on January 1, 19X1................................	$27,000
90% × Company C 19X1 income of $20,000	18,000
90% × Company C 19X2 income of $15,000	13,500
90% × Company C 19X3 income of $25,000	22,500
Equity-adjusted balance, December 31, 19X3	$81,000

An investment initially might be recorded properly as a pooling and not be equity adjusted in subsequent periods. When an investment deemed to be a pooling is maintained at cost, a simple equity conversion entry may be made to update the investment account to its beginning-of-the-period balance. After the conversion, eliminations proceed as under the simple equity method, except that the elimination entry is limited to the intercompany dividends. The conversion procedures follow those used in Worksheets 3-3 and 3-4 for an investment recorded at cost. The sophisticated equity method is not used since there are no amortizations of excess.

Also, it may occur that the investment originally was recorded incorrectly at market value. This complication was discussed in Chapter 2. If this situation is encountered, it is suggested that the investment account be corrected to reflect the book value of the investment prior to proceeding to the consolidated worksheet. The investment account should be adjusted to the correct balance under either the cost or equity method, depending on the issuer's desires.

INTRAPERIOD POOLING

Recall that under pooling theory, the incomes of the parent and the subsidiary are to be *consolidated at the beginning of the year, regardless of when control is achieved during the year.* Thus, there is no reason to close the subsidiary's books on the date control is achieved. Closing the books would, in fact, hinder the preparation of consolidated statements. Worksheets for consolidated financial statements must begin with a trial balance of the subsidiary that includes the entire year's operations and the beginning-of-the-year balance for the subsidiary retained earnings account. Since consolidation procedures are applied *retroactively to the beginning of the year,* the entire incomes of the parent and the subsidiary are distributed to the controlling and minority interests. No income is regarded as earned by outside interests. In summary, the consolidation procedures are identical to those used when the controlling investment has been made at the beginning of the year.

SUMMARY: WORKSHEET TECHNIQUE

At this point, it is wise to review the overall mechanical procedures used to prepare a consolidated worksheet. It will help you to have this set of procedures at your side for the first few worksheets you do. Later, the process will become automatic. The following procedures are designed to provide for both efficiency and correctness:

1. When recopying the trial balances, always sum them before you proceed with the eliminations. At this point, you want to be sure that there are no errors in transporting figures to the worksheet. An amazing number of students' consolidated balance sheets are out of balance because their trial balances did not balance to begin with.

2.   Carefully key all eliminations to aid future reference. It is suggested that a symbol, such as an asterisk, a line, or a circle, be used to identify each worksheet adjustment entry that affects combined net income. This identification will make it easier to locate the adjustments that must be posted later to the income distribution schedules. Recall that any adjustment to income must be assigned to one of the firm's income distribution schedules. This second step will become particularly important in the next two chapters where there will be many adjustments to income.

3.   Sum the eliminations to be sure that they balance before you begin to extend the account totals.

4.   Now that the eliminations are completed, horizontally determine account totals and then extend them to the appropriate worksheet column. Extend each account in the order that it appears on the trial balance. Do not select just the accounts needed for a particular statement. For example, do not work only on the income statement. This can lead to errors. There may be some accounts that you will forget to extend, and you may not be aware of the errors until your balance sheet column total fails to equal zero. Extending each account in order assures that none will be overlooked and allows careful consideration of the appropriate destination of each account balance.

5.   Calculate combined net income.

6.   Prepare income distribution schedules. Verify that the sum of the distributions equals the combined net income on the worksheet. Distribute the minority interest in income to the Minority Interest column and distribute the controlling interest in income to the Controlling Retained Earnings column.

7.   Sum the Minority Interest column and extend that total to the Consolidated Balance Sheet column. Sum the Controlling Retained Earnings column and extend that total to the Consolidated Balance Sheet column as well.

8.   Verify that the Consolidated Balance Sheet column total equals zero (or that the totals are equal if two columns are used).

APPENDIX A: THE VERTICAL WORKSHEET

This chapter has used the *horizontal worksheet format* for its examples. Columns for eliminations and adjustments, consolidated income, minority interest, controlling retained earnings, and the balance sheet are arranged horizontally in adjacent columns. This format makes it convenient to extend account balances from one column to the next. This is the format that you used for trial balance working papers in introductory and intermediate accounting. It is also the most common worksheet format used in practice. The horizontal format will be used in all nonappendix worksheets in subsequent chapters and in all worksheet problems unless otherwise stated.

The alternative format is the *vertical format*. Rather than beginning the worksheet with the trial balances of the parent and the subsidiary, this format begins with the completed income statements, statements of retained earnings, and the balance sheets of the parent and subsidiary. This method, which is seldom used in practice and harder to master, commonly is used on the CPA Exam. Its appeal to the CPA Exam probably is that it fits on a single page and eliminates the need for foldout worksheets.

The vertical format is used in Worksheet 3-10 on pages 206–207. This worksheet is based on the same facts used for Worksheet 3-6 (an equity method example for the second year of a purchase with a complicated distribution of excess cost). Worksheet 3-10 is based on the determination and distribution of excess schedule shown on pages 138 and 139.

Note that the original separate statements are stacked vertically upon each other. Be sure to follow the *carrydown* procedure as it is applied to the separate statements. The net income from the income statement is carried down to the retained earnings statement. Then, the ending retained earnings balance is carried down to the balance sheet. Later, this same carrydown procedure is applied to the eliminations and to the consolidated statements.

Understand that there are no differences in the elimination and adjustment procedures as a result of this alternative format. Compare the elimination steps to those in Worksheet 3-6. Even though there is no change in the eliminations, there are two areas of caution. First, the order in which the accounts appear is reversed; that is, nominal accounts precede balance sheet accounts. This difference in order will require care in making eliminations. Second, the eliminations to retained earnings must be made against the January 1 beginning balances, not the December 31 ending balances. The ending retained earnings balances are never adjusted but are derived after all eliminations have been made.

The complicated aspect of the vertical worksheet is the carrydown procedure used to create the retained earnings statement and the balance sheet. Arrows are used in Worksheet 3-10 to emphasize the carrydown procedure. Note that the net income line in the retained earnings statement and the retained earnings lines on the balance sheet are never available to receive eliminations. These balances are always carried down. The net income balances are derived from the same income distribution schedules used in Worksheet 3-6.

APPENDIX B: TAX-RELATED ADJUSTMENTS

Recall from Chapter 1 that a deferred tax liability results when the market value of an asset may not be used in future depreciation calculations for tax purposes. (This occurs when the purchase is a tax-free exchange as to the seller.) In this situation, future depreciation charges for tax purposes must be based on the book value of the asset, and a liability should be acknowledged in the determination and distribution of excess schedule by creating a deferred tax liability account. Consider the following determination and distribution of excess schedule for a subsidiary that has a building with a book value for tax purposes of $120,000 and a market value of $200,000. Assuming a tax rate of 30%, there is a deferred tax liability of $24,000 ($80,000 excess of market value over tax basis × 30%).

Price paid for investment.	$600,000	
Less interest acquired:		
Common stock. $100,000		
Retained earnings. 400,000		
Total stockholders' equity $500,000		
Interest acquired. 100%	500,000	
Excess of cost over book value (debit balance).	**$100,000**	
Available for long-lived assets:		
Building	**$ 80,000**	**Dr**
Deferred tax liability, building	**(24,000)**	**Cr**
Goodwill (net of deferred tax liability)	**$ 44,000**	**Dr**
Distributed as follows:		
Goodwill ($44,000 ÷ 70%).	$ 62,857	
Deferred tax liability (30% × $62,857)	(18,857)	
Net goodwill	$ 44,000	

The worksheet entry to distribute the excess of cost over book value would be as follows:

Building (to market value)	80,000	
Goodwill (balance of excess)	62,857	
Deferred Tax Liability ($24,000 + $18,857)		42,857
Investment in Subsidiary S (excess cost after elimination of		
subsidiary equity).		100,000

Worksheet eliminations will be simpler if each deferred tax liability is recorded below the asset to which it relates. It is possible that inventory could have a market value in excess of its book value used for tax purposes. This, too, would require the recognition of a deferred tax liability.

Recall the general rule that the market values of the liabilities are acknowledged in full even in a bargain purchase. There is an exception to this rule with respect to the deferred tax liability that results from recording the market value adjustments made in a purchase: *The deferred tax liability has the same priority as the asset to which it relates.* For instance, since inventory always is adjusted to full market value, the deferred tax liability related to inventory is recognized fully as well. In the case of a long-lived asset, only a portion of the difference between book and market value is recorded in a bargain purchase; thus, the deferred tax liability is limited to the portion of the market–book value disparity that is recorded.

The need to recognize the deferred tax liability may complicate the distribution of the excess. Assume we have an asset that has a market value estimated to exceed its book value by $150,000, but there is only $70,000 of excess available to distribute to the asset. Assuming a 30% tax rate, the excess would be divided by 70%, or the net-of-tax percentage, to arrive at the amount to allocate to the asset itself—in this case, $100,000 ($70,000 ÷ 70%)—and 30% of the $100,000 would be recognized as related deferred tax liability. The $70,000 excess of cost would be distributed as follows:

Excess of cost over book value available		$70,000
Adjustment of long-lived assets:		
Asset	$100,000	
Deferred tax liability	(30,000)	70,000
		$ 0

A second tax complication arises when the subsidiary has tax loss carryovers. To the extent that the tax loss carryovers are not recorded or are reduced by a valuation allowance by the subsidiary on its balance sheet, the carryovers may be an asset to be considered in the determination and distribution of excess schedule. If the parent has income in the prior three years that is available for offsetting some or all of the tax loss, a carryback is recognized as a current asset (Tax Refund Receivable) that would receive its full value allocation even in a bargain purchase. Any remaining carryover is carried forward and recorded as an asset. If it is probable that the deferred tax asset will not be fully realized, a contra-valuation allowance is provided. The tax loss carryforward and any valuation allowance should be recognized as a current asset if it will be realized within one year; otherwise, it should be shown as a noncurrent asset. When the tax loss carryforward is a noncurrent asset, it should not be recorded at full market value in a bargain purchase. Instead, it should be one of several possible long-lived assets that is subject to the allocation procedure.

Let us consider the example of a subsidiary that has the following tax loss carryovers:

Tax loss carryback	$200,000
Tax loss carryforward to be used within 1 year	100,000
Tax loss carryforward to be used after 1 year	50,000

Assume the parent has anticipated future tax liabilities against which the tax loss carryforwards may be offset and has a 30% tax rate. A determination and distribution of excess schedule might appear as follows:

Price paid for investment		$900,000	
Less interest acquired:			
Common stock.	$300,000		
Retained earnings	400,000		
Total stockholders' equity	$700,000		
Interest acquired	100%	700,000	
Excess of cost over book value (debit balance)		**$200,000**	
Tax refund receivable (30% × $200,000)		60,000	**Dr**
Current deferred tax expense (30% × $100,000)		30,000	**Dr**
Available for long-lived assets.		$110,000	
Adjustment to long-lived assets:			
Noncurrent deferred tax expense (30% × $50,000)		15,000	**Dr**
Goodwill (net of deferred tax liability)		**$ 95,000**	**Dr**

Distributed as follows:

Goodwill ($95,000 ÷ 70%)............................	$135,714
Deferred tax liability (30% × $135,714)	(40,714)
Net goodwill......................................	$ 95,000

The *worksheet entry* would be as follows:

Tax Refund Receivable	60,000	
Deferred Tax Expense—Current........................	30,000	
Deferred Tax Expense—Noncurrent.....................	15,000	
Goodwill...	135,714	
Investment in Subsidiary S (excess after elimination of		
subsidiary equity).................................		200,000
Deferred tax liability.................................		40,714

Both of the preceding tax issues will complicate the consolidated worksheet. Our example will consider the distribution of the tax adjustments on the worksheet and the resulting amortization adjustments needed to calculate consolidated net income. We will consider a nontaxable exchange with fixed asset and goodwill adjustments in addition to a tax loss carryover.

    Assume that Paro Company purchased an 80% interest in Sunstran Corporation on January 1, 19X1, at which time the following determination and distribution of excess schedule was prepared:

Price paid (including $20,000 direct acquisition costs) ...		$920,000	
Less interest acquired:			
Capital stock ($10 par).............................	$100,000		
Paid-in capital in excess of par	300,000		
Retained earnings	400,000		
Total stockholders' equity.......................	$800,000		
Interest acquired	80%	640,000	
Excess of cost over book value (debit balance)		$280,000	
Building (20-year life) understated $200,000			
(decrease accumulated depreciation 80% ×			
$200,000)		$160,000	**Dr**
Deferred tax liability (30% tax rate × $160,000)		(48,000)	**Cr**
Deferred tax expense (30% tax rate × 80%			
× $300,000 loss carryforward)....................		72,000*	**Dr**
Goodwill (15-year life)(net of deferred tax liability)......		$ 96,000	**Dr**
Distributed as follows:			
Goodwill ($96,000 ÷ 70%).........................		$137,143	
Deferred tax liability (30% × $137,143)..............		(41,143)	
Net goodwill		$ 96,000	

*For this example, assume there is assurance of adequate 19X1 income to offset fully the tax loss carryforward.

Worksheet 3-11 pages 208–211, is the consolidated worksheet for Paro Company and its subsidiary, Sunstran Corporation, at the end of 19X1. Unlike previous worksheets, the nominal accounts of both firms include a provision for tax. The calculation of the tax liabilities for affiliated firms is discussed in Chapter 6. For now, accept the amounts shown as given. It should be noted, however, that Paro has reduced its tax provision for the benefit of the tax loss carryforward of $72,000 that it purchased in the combination. The tax provision recorded by the subsidiary was calculated using the assets' book values as the bases for depreciation.

The procedures to eliminate the investment account are the same as for previous examples using the equity method. Notice that step (3a) distributes the excess to the accumulated depreciation account to increase the net value of the building by $160,000, and step (3b) records the related deferred tax liability resulting from the inability to depreciate for tax purposes the increase. Step (3c) records the tax loss carryforward which was included in the determination and distribution of excess schedule. The goodwill resulting from the purchase is recorded in step (3d). Step (3e) records the deferred tax liability applicable to the goodwill which is not amortizable for tax purposes when the original purchase is a nontaxable exchange.

As a result of the increase in the net value of the building, step (4a) increases depreciation by $8,000 for the year. Given the 30% tax rate, step (4b) reduces the provision for the tax account by $2,400 as a result of the depreciation adjustment. This step is not a reduction of the current taxes payable; instead, it is a reduction of the deferred tax liability recorded as part of the distribution of the excess cost. Remember that the deferred tax liability reflects the loss of future tax deductions caused by the difference between the building's higher market value and its lower book value on the date of purchase. Thus, the net result of this entry is to record the tax provision as if the tax deductions were allowable without changing the tax payable for the year. Step (4c) reflects the fact that the tax loss carryforward is used to reduce the current year's tax liability. Paro reduced its provision for tax directly on its books when it recorded the taxes payable. Paro had no choice since the tax loss carryforward account did not exist on its separate books. Such an account is first acknowledged in the consolidation process. The tax loss carryforward account is established through the distribution of the investment excess (step 3c). Step (4c) eliminates the tax loss carryforward and increases the provision for tax for the current year to its position prior to the offsetting for the carryover amount. Step (4d) amortizes goodwill based on a 15-year life. Step (4e) amortizes the deferred tax liability applicable to the goodwill amortization. Again, that step, like (4b), reduces the current year's tax provision. The parent company income distribution schedule reflects all the amortizations of the excess cost made on the worksheet as adjustments to the controlling interest's share of combined net income. This approach is consistent with previous worksheets.

QUESTIONS

1. What is the difference between the simple equity method and the cost method? How can you tell which is being used by the parent?
2. Why doesn't it matter whether the cost method or the equity method is used to account for an investment when the consolidation process is required?
3. Describe the difference between the simple and sophisticated equity methods of accounting for an investment in a subsidiary. Explain why the difference is irrelevant when consolidated statements are to be prepared.
4. A parent company acquired an 85% interest in a subsidiary on Jan. 1, 19X1, at a cost of $178,000. The subsidiary declared and paid cash dividends on its stock totaling $10,000 in early January of 19X2. Clearly, the dividends were paid out of income earned prior to the purchase of a controlling interest by the parent. How will the parent record the dividend assuming it records its investment under the cost method?
5. Describe the eliminations and adjustments to be made on the worksheet when the investment in a subsidiary is accounted for under the equity method.
6. What comprises the minority interest on a consolidated balance sheet? What is the most common way to disclose the minority interest on a consolidated balance sheet?
7. Describe the eliminations and adjustments to be made on the worksheet when the investment in a subsidiary is carried at cost.
8. In a purchase, the parent's share of the liabilities of the subsidiary is adjusted to reflect current market values at the time of acquisition. How are an undervalued and an overvalued subsidiary liability treated on the determination and distribution of excess schedule?
9. Under the proprietary theory approach, why is the minority's share of subsidiary income unaffected by amortizations that result from the revaluation of the subsidiary's assets and liabilities?
10. Prepare a skeleton outline of the parent company income distribution schedule for a parent that owns a 90% interest in a subsidiary. Assume that the price paid for the interest exceeded book value and the excess is attributable to goodwill.
11. What effect does an intraperiod purchase have on the determination and distribution of excess schedule and on the worksheet covering the period of acquisition? What special disclosure is required on the consolidated income statement due to the intraperiod purchase?
12. In an intraperiod purchase, subsidiary income is allocated to three different interest groups in the year of acquisition. What are these groups?
13. How do the problems created by an intraperiod pooling differ from those created by an intraperiod purchase?

EXERCISES

Exercise 1. Barnes Company purchased an 80% interest in Crane Company common stock for $320,000 cash on January 1, 19X1. At that time, Crane Company had the following balance sheet:

Assets		Liabilities and Equity	
Current assets	$ 60,000	Accounts payable	$ 60,000
Land........................	100,000	Common stock ($5 par)	50,000
Equipment	350,000	Paid-in capital in	
Accumulated depreciation....	(150,000)	excess of par	100,000
		Retained earnings...........	150,000
Total assets................	$360,000	Total liabilities and equity	$360,000

Appraisals indicated that accounts are fairly stated except for the equipment which has a fair market value of $225,000 and a remaining life of 5 years. Any goodwill that results has an estimated life of 10 years.

Crane Company experienced the following changes in retained earnings during 19X1 and 19X2:

Retained earnings, January 1, 19X1		$120,000
Net income, 19X1	$60,000	
Dividends paid in 19X1....................................	(10,000)	50,000
Balance, December 31, 19X1.................................		170,000
Net income, 19X2	$40,000	
Dividends paid in 19X2....................................	(10,000)	30,000
Balance, December 31, 19X2.................................		$200,000

Prepare a determination and distribution of excess schedule for the investment in Crane Company. Prepare journal entries that Barnes Company would make on its books to record income earned and/or dividends received on its investment in Crane Company during 19X1 and 19X2 under the following methods: (a) simple equity, (b) sophisticated equity, and (c) cost.

Exercise 2. Parsons Corporation purchased a 75% interest in the common stock of Lake 'n' Sea Boat Company on January 1, 19X4, for $400,000 cash. Lake 'n' Sea had the following balance sheet on that date:

Assets		Liabilities and Equity	
Current assets	$ 80,000	Current liabilities	$ 50,000
Inventory...................	40,000	Common stock ($5 par)	50,000
Land.......................	100,000	Paid-in capital in	
Buildings and		excess of par	150,000
equipment (net)...........	200,000	Retained earnings...........	200,000
Goodwill	30,000		
Total assets................	$450,000	Total liabilities and equity	$450,000

Appraisals indicated that the book values for inventory and buildings and equipment are below fair market values. The inventory had a market value of $50,000 and was sold during 19X4. The buildings and equipment have an appraised market value of $300,000 and a remaining life of 20 years. Any goodwill, existing or new, has an estimated life of 10 years.

Lake 'n' Sea Boat Company reported the following income earned and dividends paid during 19X4 and 19X5:

Retained earnings, January 1, 19X4		$200,000
Net income, 19X4	$70,000	
Dividends paid in 19X4.	(20,000)	50,000
Balance, December 31, 19X4.		$250,000
Net income, 19X5	$48,000	
Dividends paid in 19X5.	(20,000)	28,000
Balance, December 31, 19X5.		$278,000

Prepare a determination and distribution of excess schedule for the investment in Lake 'n' Sea Boat Company and determine the balance in the Investment in Lake 'n' Sea Boat Company on Parsons Company's books as of December 31, 19X5 under the following methods that could be used by the parent, Parsons Company: (a) simple equity, (b) sophisticated equity, and (c) cost.

Exercise 3. Aron Company purchased an 80% interest in Brewer Company for $230,000 in cash on January 1, 19X1, when Brewer Company had the following balance sheet:

Assets		Liabilities and Equity	
Current assets	$100,000	Current liabilities	$ 50,000
Property, plant, and		Common stock ($10 par)	100,000
equipment (net)	200,000	Retained earnings	150,000
Total assets	$300,000	Total liabilities and equity	$300,000

Any excess of the price paid over book value is attributable only to the plant assets, which have a 10-year remaining life. Aron Company uses the simple equity method to record its investment in Brewer Company.

The following trial balances of the two companies were prepared on December 31, 19X1:

	Aron	Brewer
Current Assets	80,000	130,000
Property, Plant, and Equipment	400,000	200,000
Accumulated Depreciation.	(106,000)	(20,000)
Investment in Brewer Company	246,000	
Current Liabilities.	(60,000)	(40,000)
Common Stock ($10 par)	(300,000)	(100,000)
Retained Earnings, January 1, 19X1	(200,000)	(150,000)
Sales.	(150,000)	(100,000)
Expenses.	110,000	75,000
Subsidiary Income	(20,000)	
Dividends Declared		5,000
Total	0	0

(1) Prepare a determination and distribution of excess schedule for the investment.
(2) Prepare all the eliminations and adjustments that would be made on the 19X1 consolidated worksheet.
(3) Prepare the 19X1 consolidated income statement and its related income distribution schedules.
(4) Prepare the 19X1 consolidated balance sheet.

Exercise 4. The trial balances of Aron and Brewer companies of Exercise 3 for December 31, 19X2, are presented as follows:

	Aron	Brewer
Current Assets	172,000	105,000
Property, Plant, and Equipment.	400,000	200,000
Accumulated Depreciation.	(130,000)	(40,000)
Investment in Brewer Company	242,000	
Current Liabilities.	(80,000)	
Common Stock ($10 par)	(300,000)	(100,000)
Retained Earnings, January 1, 19X2	(260,000)	(170,000)
Sales.	(200,000)	(100,000)
Expenses	160,000	95,000
Subsidiary Income.	(4,000)	
Dividends Declared		10,000
Total	0	0

Aron Company continued to use the simple equity method.
(1) Prepare all the eliminations and adjustments that would be made on the 19X2 consolidated worksheet.
(2) Prepare the 19X2 consolidated income statement and its related income distribution schedules.

Exercise 5. *(Note: read carefully. This is not the same as Exercise 3.)* Aron Company purchased an 80% interest in Brewer Company for $230,000 on January 1, 19X1, when Brewer Company had the following balance sheet:

Assets		Liabilities and Equity	
Current assets	$100,000	Current liabilities.	$ 50,000
Property, plant, and		Common stock ($10 par)	100,000
equipment (net)	200,000	Retained earnings.	150,000
Total assets	$300,000	Total liabilities and equity	$300,000

Any excess of the price paid over book value is attributable only to the plant assets, which have a 10-year remaining life. Aron uses the sophisticated equity method to record the investment in Brewer Company.
The following trial balances of the two companies were prepared on December 31, 19X1:

	Aron	Brewer
Current Assets	80,000	130,000
Property, Plant, and Equipment.	400,000	200,000
Accumulated Depreciation.	(106,000)	(20,000)
Investment in Brewer Company	243,000	
Current Liabilities.	(60,000)	(40,000)
Common Stock ($10 par)	(300,000)	(100,000)
Retained Earnings, January 1, 19X1	(200,000)	(150,000)
Sales.	(150,000)	(100,000)
Expenses	110,000	75,000
Subsidiary Income (from Brewer Company)	(17,000)	
Dividends Declared		5,000
Total	0	0

(1) If you did not solve Exercise 3, prepare a determination and distribution of excess schedule for the investment.
(2) Prepare all the eliminations and adjustments that would be made on the 19X1 consolidated worksheet.
(3) If you did not solve Exercise 3, prepare the 19X1 consolidated income statement and its related income distribution schedule.
(4) If you did not solve Exercise 3, prepare the 19X1 consolidated balance sheet.

Exercise 6. The trial balances of Aron and Brewer companies of Exercise 5 for December 31, 19X2, are presented as follows:

	Aron	Brewer
Current Assets	172,000	105,000
Property, Plant, and Equipment.	400,000	200,000
Accumulated Depreciation	(130,000)	(40,000)
Investment in Brewer Company	236,000	
Current Liabilities	(80,000)	
Common Stock ($10 par)	(300,000)	(100,000)
Retained Earnings, January 1, 19X2	(257,000)	(170,000)
Sales	(200,000)	(100,000)
Expenses	160,000	95,000
Subsidiary Income (from Brewer Company)	(1,000)	
Dividends Declared		10,000
Total	0	0

Aron Company continued to use the sophisticated equity method.
(1) Prepare all the eliminations and adjustments that would be made on the 19X2 consolidated worksheet.
(2) If you did not solve Exercise 4, prepare the 19X2 consolidated income statement and its related income distribution schedules.

Exercise 7. *(Note: read carefully. This is not the same as Exercise 3 or 5.)* Aron Company purchased an 80% interest in Brewer Company for $230,000 in cash on January 1, 19X1, when Brewer Company had the following balance sheet:

Assets		Liabilities and Equity	
Current assets	$100,000	Current liabilities	$ 50,000
Property, plant, and		Common stock ($10 par)	100,000
equipment (net)	200,000	Retained earnings	150,000
Total assets	$300,000	Total liabilities and equity	$300,000

Any excess of the price paid over book value is attributable only to the plant assets, which have a 10-year remaining life. Aron Company uses the cost method to record its investment in Brewer Company.

The following trial balances of the two companies were prepared on December 31, 19X1:

	Aron	Brewer
Current Assets	80,000	130,000
Property, Plant, and Equipment.............................	400,000	200,000
Accumulated Depreciation...................................	(106,000)	(20,000)
Investment in Brewer Company	230,000	
Current Liabilities..	(60,000)	(40,000)
Common Stock ($10 par)	(300,000)	(100,000)
Retained Earnings, January 1, 19X2	(200,000)	(150,000)
Sales...	(150,000)	(100,000)
Expenses	110,000	75,000
Dividend Income (from Brewer Company).....................	(4,000)	
Dividends Declared		5,000
Total	0	0

(1) If you did not solve Exercise 3 or 5, prepare a determination and distribution of excess schedule for the investment.

(2) Prepare all the eliminations and adjustments that would be made on the 19X1 consolidated worksheet.

(3) If you did not solve Exercise 3 or 5, prepare the 19X1 consolidated income statement and its related income distribution schedules.

(4) If you did not solve Exercise 3 or 5, prepare the 19X1 consolidated balance sheet.

Exercise 8. The trial balances of Aron and Brewer companies of Exercise 7 for December 31, 19X2, are presented as follows:

	Aron	Brewer
Current Assets	172,000	105,000
Property, Plant, and Equipment.............................	400,000	200,000
Accumulated Depreciation...................................	(130,000)	(40,000)
Investment in Brewer Company	230,000	
Current Liabilities..	(80,000)	
Common Stock ($10 par)	(300,000)	(100,000)
Retained Earnings, January 1, 19X2	(244,000)	(170,000)
Sales...	(200,000)	(100,000)
Expenses	160,000	95,000
Dividend Income (from Brewer Company).....................	(8,000)	
Dividends Declared		10,000
Total	0	0

Aron Company continued to use the cost method.

(1) Prepare all the eliminations and adjustments that would be made on the 19X2 consolidated worksheet.

(2) If you did not solve Exercise 4 or 6, prepare the 19X2 consolidated income statement and its related income distribution schedules.

Exercise 9. Karen Company had the following balance sheet on January 1, 19X2:

Assets		Liabilities and Equity	
Current assets	$200,000	Current liabilities.............	$100,000
Equipment (net)	300,000	Common stock ($10 par)......	100,000
		Retained earnings............	300,000
Total assets	$500,000	Total liabilities and equity	$500,000

Between January 1 and July 1, 19X2, Karen Company estimated its net income to be $30,000. On July 1, 19X2, Neiman Company purchased 80% of the outstanding common stock of Karen Company for $320,000. Any excess of book value over cost was attributed to the equipment which had a estimated 5-year life. Karen Company did not close its books on July 1.

On December 31, 19X2, Neiman Company and Karen Company prepared the following trial balances:

	Neiman	Karen
Current Assets	210,000	250,000
Equipment	500,000	300,000
Accumulated Depreciation—Equipment	(140,000)	(20,000)
Investment in Karen Company	320,000	
Current Liabilities	(200,000)	(70,000)
Common Stock ($10 par)	(200,000)	(100,000)
Retained Earnings, 1/1/X2	(430,000)	(300,000)
Sales	(300,000)	(200,000)
Cost of Goods Sold	180,000	90,000
General Expenses	60,000	50,000
Total	0	0

(1) Prepare a determination and distribution of excess schedule for the investment.
(2) Prepare all the eliminations and adjustments that would be made on the December 31, 19X2 consolidated worksheet.
(3) Prepare the 19X2 consolidated income statement and its related income distribution schedules.

Exercise 10. On January 1, 19X4, LaRusso Company issued 12,000 shares of its common stock in exchange for 9,000 shares of Preston Company in a transaction that met the pooling of interests criteria. LaRusso shares have a par value of $10 and a market value of $30 per share. On January 1, 19X4, Preston Company had the following balance sheet:

Assets		Liabilities and Equity	
Current assets	$ 95,000	Bonds payable	$100,000
Buildings and equipment	350,000	Common stock ($5 par)	50,000
Accumulated depreciation	(125,000)	Paid-in capital	
Goodwill	50,000	in excess of par	70,000
		Retained earnings	150,000
Total assets	$370,000	Total liabilities and equity	$370,000

The market value of the buildings and equipment is $300,000. The balance of the market value of the interest acquired is attributed to additional goodwill with a 10-year life.

LaRusso Company had the following stockholders' equity accounts on the date of the combination:

Common stock ($10 par)	$200,000
Paid-in capital in excess of par	300,000
Retained earnings	420,000

The separate income statements of LaRusso and Preston companies contained the following information for 19X4:

	LaRusso	Preston
Sales	$140,000	$90,000
Cost of goods sold	80,000	60,000
General expenses	30,000	18,000

Prepare a consolidated income statement for 19X4 and the stockholders' equity section of a consolidated balance sheet prepared on December 31, 19X4.

Exercise 11. On January 1, 19X6, Pluto Inc. issued 200,000 additional shares of its voting common stock in exchange for 100,000 shares of the outstanding voting common stock of Sherry Company in a business combination appropriately accounted for by the pooling-of-interests method. The market value of the voting common stock of Pluto was $40 per share on the date of the business combination. Immediately prior to the acquisition, the balance sheets of Pluto and Sherry contained the following information:

Pluto Inc.

Common stock $5 par; authorized 1,000,000 shares; issued and outstanding 600,000 shares.	$ 3,000,000
Additional paid-in capital	6,000,000
Retained earnings	11,000,000
Total stockholders' equity	$20,000,000

Sherry Company

Common stock, $10 par; authorized 250,000 shares; issued and outstanding 100,000 shares.	$ 1,000,000
Additional paid-in capital	2,000,000
Retained earnings	4,000,000
Total stockholders' equity	$ 7,000,000

Additional information is as follows:
(a) Net income for the year ended December 31, 19X6, was $1,150,000 for Pluto and $350,000 for Sherry.
(b) During 19X6, Pluto paid $900,000 in dividends to its stockholders, and Sherry paid $210,000 in dividends to Pluto.

Prepare the consolidated stockholders' equity section of the balance sheet of Pluto Inc. and its subsidiary, Sherry Company, at December 31, 19X6.

(AICPA adapted)

APPENDIX EXERCISES

Exercise B-1. Rainman Corporation is considering the acquisition of Lamb Company through the purchase of Lamb's common stock. Rainman Corporation will issue 20,000 shares of its $5 par common stock, with a market value of $20 per share, in exchange for all 10,000 outstanding shares of Lamb Company's voting common stock.

This acquisition doesn't meet all the criteria for a pooling of interests; therefore, it must be accounted for as a purchase. The acquisition does, however, meet the criteria for a tax-free exchange as to the seller. Because of this, Rainman Corporation will be limited for future tax returns to the book value of the depreciable assets. Rainman Corporation falls into the 30% tax bracket.

The appraisal of the assets of Lamb Company showed that the inventory has a market value of $120,000, and the property, plant, and equipment has a market value of $270,000. Lamb Company had the following balance sheet just before the acquisition:

Lamb Company
Balance Sheet
December 31, 19X5

Assets		Liabilities and Equity		
Cash	$ 40,000	Current liabilities		$ 70,000
Accounts receivable ..	150,000	Bonds payable		100,000
Inventory	100,000	Stockholders' equity:		
Property, plant, and		Common stock ($10 par)	$100,000	
equipment (net)	210,000	Retained earnings	230,000	330,000
Total assets	$500,000	Total liabilities and equity..		$500,000

(1) Record the acquisition of Lamb Company by Rainman Corporation.
(2) Prepare a determination and distribution of excess schedule.
(3) Prepare the elimination entries that would be made on the consolidated worksheet.

Exercise B-2.   Fargo Company will issue securities with a market value of $400,000 for a 90% interest in Dakota Company on January 1, 19X1, at which time Dakota Company had the following balance sheet:

Assets		Liabilities and Equity	
Accounts receivable	$ 50,000	Current liabilities	$ 70,000
Inventory	80,000	Common stock ($5 par)	100,000
Land	20,000	Paid-in capital in excess	
Building (net)	200,000	of par	130,000
		Retained earnings	50,000
Total assets	$350,000	Total liabilities and equity.....	$350,000

It was believed that the inventory and the building were undervalued by $20,000 and $50,000, respectively. The building had a 10-year remaining life; the inventory on hand January 1, 19X1, was sold during the year. The deferred tax liability associated with the asset revaluations was to be reflected in the consolidated statements. Each firm has an income tax rate of 30%. Goodwill, if any, would be amortized over 15 years.

The separate income statements of the two companies prepared for 19X1 are shown below.

(1) Prepare a determination and distribution of excess schedule for the investment.
(2) Prepare the 19X1 consolidated income statement and its related income distribution schedules.

	Fargo	Dakota
Sales..	$ 400,000	$150,000
Cost of goods sold...	(200,000)	(90,000)
Gross profit	$ 200,000	$ 60,000
General expenses...	(50,000)	(25,000)
Depreciation expense	(60,000)	(15,000)
Operating income..	$ 90,000	$ 20,000
Subsidiary income..	18,000	
Net income before income tax	$ 108,000	$ 20,000
Provision for tax (does not include tax on subsidiary income)..	(27,000)	(6,000)
Net income	$ 81,000	$ 14,000

PROBLEMS

Problem 3-1. On January 1, 19X1, Polar Company purchased an 80% interest in Solar Company by issuing 10,000 of its common stock shares with a par value of $10 per share and a market value of $60 per share. The direct acquisition costs were $20,000. At the time of the purchase, Solar had the following balance sheet:

Assets		Liabilities and Equity	
Current assets	$100,000	Current liabilities	$ 80,000
Investments	150,000	Bonds payable	250,000
Land	120,000	Common stock ($10 par)	100,000
Building (net)	350,000	Paid-in capital in excess	
Equipment (net)	160,000	of par	200,000
		Retained earnings	250,000
Total assets	$880,000	Total liabilities and equity	$880,000

Appraisals indicate that book values are representative of market values with the exception of land and buildings. The land has a fair market value of $190,000 and the building is appraised at $450,000. The building has an estimated remaining life of 20 years. Any goodwill arising from the purchase would be amortized over 10 years.

The following summary of Solar's retained earnings applies to 19X1 and 19X2:

Balance, January 1, 19X1	$250,000
Net income for 19X1	60,000
Dividends paid in 19X1	(10,000)
Balance, December 31, 19X1	$300,000
Net income for 19X2	45,000
Dividends paid in 19X2	(10,000)
Balance, December 31, 19X2	$335,000

Required:

(1) Prepare a determination and distribution of excess schedule for the investment in Solar Company. As a part of the schedule, indicate annual amortization of excess adjustments.

(2) For 19X1 and 19X2, prepare the entries that Polar would make concerning its investment in Solar under the simple equity, sophisticated equity, and cost methods. It is suggested that you set up a worksheet with side-by-side columns for each method so that you can easily compare the entries.

(3) For 19X1 and 19X2, prepare the worksheet elimination that would be made on a consolidated worksheet under the simple equity, sophisticated equity, and cost methods. It is suggested that you set up a worksheet with side-by-side columns for each method so that you can easily compare the entries.

Problem 3-2. On January 1, 19X1, Parent Company purchased 80% of the common stock of Subsidiary Company for $308,000. On this date, Subsidiary had common stock, other paid-in capital, and retained earnings of $50,000, $100,000, and $150,000, respectively. Net income dividends for 2 years for Subsidiary Company were as follows:

	19X1	19X2
Net income	$60,000	$90,000
Dividends	20,000	30,000

On January 1, 19X1, the only tangible assets of Subsidiary that were undervalued were inventory and building. Inventory, for which FIFO is used, was worth $10,000 more than cost. The inventory was sold in 19X1. Building, which was worth $25,000 more than book value, has a remaining life of 10 years, and straight-line depreciation is used. Goodwill, if any, is to be amortized over the maximum period permitted.

Required:
(1) Using this information or the information in the following trial balances, prepare a determination and distribution of excess schedule.
(2) Parent Company carries the Investment in Subsidiary Company under the simple equity method. In general journal form, record the entries that would be made to apply the equity method in 19X1 and 19X2.
(3) Compute the balance that should appear in Investment in Subsidiary Company and in Subsidiary Income on December 31, 19X2 (the second year). Fill in these amounts on Parent Company's trial balance for 19X2.
(4) Complete a worksheet for consolidated financial statements for 19X2. Include columns for eliminations and adjustments, consolidated income, minority interest, controlling retained earnings, and balance sheet.

	Parent Company	Subsidiary Company
Inventory, December 31	100,000	50,000
Other Current Assets	148,000	180,000
Investment in Subsidiary Company	388,000	
Land	50,000	50,000
Buildings and Equipment	350,000	320,000
Accumulated Depreciation	(100,000)	(60,000)
Goodwill		
Other Intangibles	20,000	
Current Liabilities	(120,000)	(40,000)
Bonds Payable		(100,000)
Other Long-Term Liabilities	(200,000)	
Common Stock — P Co.	(200,000)	
Other Paid-In Capital — P Co.	(100,000)	
Retained Earnings — P Co.	(214,000)	
Common Stock — S Co.		(50,000)
Other Paid-In Capital — S Co.		(100,000)
Retained Earnings — S Co.		(190,000)
Net Sales	(520,000)	(450,000)
Cost of Goods Sold	300,000	260,000
Operating Expenses	120,000	100,000
Subsidiary Income	(72,000)	
Dividends Declared — P Co.	50,000	
Dividends Declared — S Co.		30,000 80%

Problem 3-3. (This is the same as Problem 3-2, except the sophisticated equity method is used.) On January 1, 19X1, Parent Company purchased 80% of the common stock of Subsidiary Company for $308,000. On this date, Subsidiary had common stock, other paid-in capital, and retained earnings of $50,000, $100,000, and $150,000, respectively. Net income dividends for 2 years for Subsidiary Company were as follows:

	19X1	19X2
Net income	$60,000	$90,000
Dividends...........................	20,000	30,000

On January 1, 19X1, the only tangible assets of Subsidiary that were undervalued were inventory and building. Inventory, for which FIFO is used, was worth $10,000 more than cost. The inventory was sold in 19X1. Building, which was worth $25,000 more than book value, has a remaining life of 10 years, and straight-line depreciation is used. Goodwill, if any, is to be amortized over the maximum period permitted.

Required:
(1) Using this information or the information in the following trial balances, prepare a determination and distribution of excess schedule.
(2) Parent Company carries the Investment in Subsidiary Company under the sophisticated equity method. In general journal form, record the entries that would be made to apply the equity method in 19X1 and 19X2.
(3) Compute the balance that should appear in Investment in Subsidiary Company and in Subsidiary Income on December 31, 19X2 (the second year). Fill in these amounts on Parent Company's trial balance for 19X2.
(4) Complete a worksheet for consolidated financial statements for 19X2. Include columns for eliminations and adjustments, consolidated income, minority interest, controlling retained earnings, and balance sheet.

	Parent Company	Subsidiary Company
Inventory, December 31................................	100,000	50,000
Other Current Assets	148,000	180,000
Investment in Subsidiary Company	374,000	
Land...	50,000	50,000
Buildings and Equipment	350,000	320,000
Accumulated Depreciation	(100,000)	(60,000)
Goodwill		
Other Intangibles..	20,000	
Current Liabilities	(120,000)	(40,000)
Bonds Payable...		(100,000)
Other Long-Term Liabilities.............................	(200,000)	
Common Stock — P Co.	(200,000)	
Other Paid-In Capital — P Co...........................	(100,000)	
Retained Earnings — P Co...............................	(203,000)	
Common Stock — S Co.		(50,000)
Other Paid-In Capital — S Co...........................		(100,000)
Retained Earnings — S Co...............................		(190,000)
Net Sales...	(520,000)	(450,000)
Cost of Goods Sold......................................	300,000	260,000
Operating Expenses	120,000	100,000
Subsidiary Income	(69,000)	
Dividends Declared — P Co..............................	50,000	
Dividends Declared — S Co..............................		30,000

Problem 3-4. The trial balances of Errol Company and its subsidiary, Crystal Inc., are as follows on December 31, 19X3:

	Errol Company	Crystal Inc.
Current Assets.	530,000	130,000
Property, Plant, and Equipment.	1,805,000	440,000
Accumulated Depreciation	(405,000)	(70,000)
Investment in Crystal Inc	300,000	
Liabilities	(900,000)	(225,000)
Common Stock ($1 par)	(220,000)	
Common Stock ($5 par)		(50,000)
Paid-In Capital in Excess of Par	(880,000)	(15,000)
Retained Earnings, January 1, 19X3.	(230,000)	(170,000)
Revenues.	(460,000)	(210,000)
Investment Income		
Expenses	450,000	170,000
Dividends Declared	10,000	
Total	0	0

On January 1, 19X1, Errol Company exchanged 20,000 shares of its common stock, with a market value of $15 per share, for all the outstanding stock of Crystal Inc. in a transaction that did not meet the criteria for a pooling of interests. Any excess of cost over book value was attributed to goodwill and is being amortized over a 40-year period. The stockholders' equity of Crystal Inc. on the purchase date was:

Common stock ($5 par).	$ 50,000
Paid-in capital in excess of par.	15,000
Retained earnings.	135,000
Total equity	$200,000

Required:
(1) Prepare a determination and distribution of excess schedule for the investment.
(2) Prepare the 19X3 consolidated statements, including the income statement, retained earnings statement, and balance sheet. (A worksheet is not required.)

Problem 3-5. On January 1, 19X3, Jack Corporation exchanged 45,000 shares of newly issued common stock, with a market value of $10 per share, for all the outstanding stock of Bob Company. The combination meets the criteria for a pooling of interests. Jack Corporation maintains its investment in the subsidiary under the cost method.

The stockholders' equity of Bob Company on January 1, 19X3, was as follows:

Common stock ($10 par).	$200,000
Paid-in capital in excess of par.	75,000
Retained earnings.	175,000
Total stockholders' equity	$450,000

The trial balances of the two companies on December 31, 19X3, are as follows:

	Jack	Bob
Cash.	350,000	115,400
Accounts Receivable	75,000	45,000
Inventory	80,000	55,000
Land.	100,000	65,000
Buildings.	750,000	275,000
Accumulated Depreciation—Buildings.	(395,000)	(28,400)

Equipment	2,150,000	426,000
Accumulated Depreciation—Equipment	(750,000)	(63,000)
Investment in Subsidiary.	450,000	
Accounts Payable	(740,000)	(400,000)
Common Stock	(1,000,000)	(200,000)
Paid-In Capital in Excess of Par	(560,000)	(75,000)
Retained Earnings.	(495,000)	(175,000)
Sales	(440,000)	(210,000)
Cost of Goods Sold	315,000	100,000
Other Expenses.	100,000	40,000
Subsidiary Dividend Income.	(30,000)	
Dividends Declared.	40,000	30,000
Total.	0	0

Required:

(1) Prepare the elimination entries that would be made on the consolidated worksheet.
(2) Prepare the December 31, 19X3 consolidated statements, including the income statement, retained earnings statement, and balance sheet. (A worksheet is not required.)

Problem 3-6. Sam Corporation purchased all the outstanding stock of Goodman Corporation for $200,000 in cash on January 1, 19X7. On the purchase date, Goodman Corporation had the following condensed balance sheet:

Assets		Liabilities and Equity	
Cash	$ 60,000	Liabilities.	$150,000
Inventory	40,000	Common stock ($10 par).	100,000
Land	120,000	Paid-in capital in excess of par. . . .	50,000
Building (net).	180,000	Retained earnings (deficit)	100,000
Total assets	$400,000	Total liabilities and equity	$400,000

Any excess of cost over book value was attributable to the building, which is currently overstated on Goodman's books. All other assets and liabilities have book values equal to market values. The building has an estimated 10-year life with no salvage value.

The trial balances of the two firms on December 31, 19X7, appear as follows:

	Sam	Goodman
Cash	200,000	143,000
Inventory	60,000	30,000
Land	120,000	120,000
Buildings (net)	600,000	162,000
Investment in Goodman Corp.	200,000	
Accounts Payable	(405,000)	(210,000)
Common Stock ($3 par)	(300,000)	
Common Stock ($10 par)		(100,000)
Paid-In Capital in Excess of Par.	(180,000)	(50,000)
Retained Earnings 1/1/X7.	(255,000)	(100,000)
Sales.	(210,000)	(40,000)
Cost of Goods Sold	120,000	35,000
Other Expenses	45,000	10,000
Dividends Declared	5,000	
Total	0	0

Required:

(1) Prepare a determination and distribution of excess schedule for the investment.

(2) Prepare the 19X7 consolidated worksheet. Include columns for the eliminations and adjustments, the consolidated income statement, the controlling retained earnings, and the consolidated balance sheet.

(3) Prepare the 19X7 consolidated statements, including the income statement, retained earnings statement, and balance sheet.

Problem 3-7. Sauer Company prepared the following balance sheet on January 1, 19X1:

Assets		Liabilities and Equity	
Current assets...............	$ 50,000	Liabilities	$140,000
Land	75,000	Common stock ($10 par)	100,000
Buildings	350,000	Paid-in capital	
Accumulated depreciation—		in excess of par............	120,000
buildings	(140,000)	Retained earnings (deficit)	(25,000)
Total assets	$335,000	Total liabilities and equity.....	$335,000

On this date, Roland Company purchased 8,000 shares of Sauer Company's outstanding stock for a total price of $270,000. Also on this date, the buildings were understated by $40,000 and were felt to have a 10-year remaining life. Any remaining discrepancy between the price paid and book value was attributed to goodwill and estimated to have a 20-year life. Since the purchase, Roland Company has used the cost method to record the investment and its related income.

Roland Company and Sauer Company have prepared the following separate trial balances on December 31, 19X2:

	Roland	Sauer
Current Assets	180,000	115,000
Land	150,000	75,000
Buildings	590,000	350,000
Accumulated Depreciation—Buildings	(265,000)	(182,000)
Investment in Sauer Company	270,000	
Liabilities	(175,000)	(133,000)
Common Stock ($10 par)	(200,000)	(100,000)
Paid-In Capital in Excess of Par		(120,000)
Retained Earnings, January 1, 19X2	(495,000)	15,000
Sales...	(360,000)	(120,000)
Dividend Income (from Sauer Company)	(4,000)	
Cost of Goods Sold	179,000	50,000
Expenses	120,000	45,000
Dividends Declared	10,000	5,000
Total	0	0

Required:

(1) Prepare a determination and distribution of excess schedule for the investment.

(2) Prepare the 19X2 consolidated worksheet. Include columns for the eliminations and adjustments, the consolidated income statement, the minority interest, the controlling retained earnings, and the consolidated balance sheet. Prepare supporting income distribution schedules.

(3) Prepare the 19X2 consolidated statements including the income statement, retained earnings statement, and the balance sheet.

Problem 3-8. On January 1, 19X1, Fordum Corporation exchanged 90,000 shares of its $5 par stock, with a market value of $15 per share, for 90% of the outstanding common stock of Rice Corporation in a transaction qualifying as a pooling of interests. Direct acquisition costs were $50,000 and are included in the investment account. The account Investment in Rice Corporation reflects the market value of the shares exchanged and the issuance cost related to the common stock of Fordum Corporation.

Immediately prior to the exchange, Rice Corporation had the following owners' equity:

Common stock ($2 par)......................	$200,000
Paid-in capital in excess of par.................	400,000
Retained earnings (deficit)	(50,000)
Total equity	$550,000

Since the exchange, Fordum has used the cost method to account for its investment in Rice. No intercompany transactions have ever occurred.

Fordum Corporation and Rice Corporation have the following trial balances on December 31, 19X3:

	Fordum Corporation	Rice Corporation
Current Assets	840,000	360,000
Property, Plant, and Equipment	4,800,000	1,570,000
Accumulated Depreciation	(1,600,000)	(520,000)
Investment in Rice Corporation	1,400,000	
Liabilities..	(1,830,000)	(790,000)
Common Stock ($5 par).............................	(1,000,000)	
Common Stock ($2 par).............................		(200,000)
Paid-In Capital in Excess of Par......................	(1,650,000)	(400,000)
Retained Earnings, January 1, 19X3	(900,000)	10,000
Sales...	(1,050,000)	(440,000)
Cost of Goods Sold................................	600,000	250,000
Expenses...	350,000	160,000
Dividends Declared................................	40,000	
Total	0	0

Required:
(1) Prepare the journal entries that should be made to reflect properly this investment on the books of the parent company.
(2) Prepare the 19X3 consolidated worksheet. Include columns for the eliminations and adjustments, the consolidated income statement, the minority interest, the controlling retained earnings, and the consolidated balance sheet. Prepare supporting income distribution schedules as well.

Problem 3-9. Tom Corporation purchased 80% of the outstanding stock of Foster Company for $240,000 on January 1, 19X1, at which time Foster Company had the following stockholders' equity:

Common stock ($5 par)......................	$150,000
Retained earnings...........................	50,000
Total equity	$200,000

The market values of Foster's assets and liabilities agreed with the book values, except for the equipment and the building. The equipment was undervalued by $10,000 and was thought to have a 5-year life; the building was undervalued by $50,000 and was thought to have a 20-year life. Any goodwill that results is being amortized over 40 years. Tom Corporation uses the sophisticated equity method to record its investments.

Since the purchase date, both firms have operated separately and no intercompany transactions have occurred.

The separate trial balances of the firms on December 31, 19X2, are as follows:

	Tom Corp.	Foster Co.
Cash..	319,600	110,000
Land..	160,000	90,000
Buildings...	225,000	135,000
Accumulated Depreciation—Building........................	(100,000)	(50,000)
Equipment..	450,000	150,000
Accumulated Depreciation—Equipment	(115,000)	(60,000)
Investment in Foster Co.	251,200	
Liabilities...	(480,000)	(150,000)
Common Stock ($100 par).....................................	(400,000)	
Common Stock ($5 par)..		(150,000)
Paid-In Capital in Excess of Par.............................	(40,000)	
Retained Earnings 1/1/X2.....................................	(247,200)	(65,000)
Sales...	(460,000)	(120,000)
Cost of Goods Sold...	220,000	60,000
Other Expenses	210,000	50,000
Subsidiary Income	(3,600)	
Dividends Declared..	10,000	
Total	0	0

Required:
(1) Prepare a determination and distribution of excess schedule for the investment.
(2) Prepare the 19X2 consolidated worksheet. Include columns for the eliminations and adjustments, the consolidated income statement, the minority interest, the controlling retained earnings, and the consolidated balance sheet. Prepare supporting income distribution schedules as well.
(3) Prepare the 19X2 consolidated statements, including the income statement, retained earnings statement, and balance sheet.

Suggestion: The sophisticated equity method is used; this means that the investment account is net of amortizations. The parent retained earnings account does not need an adjustment for amortizations of excess since that has been recorded already on the parent's books.

Problem 3-10. Dallman International purchased 80% of the outstanding stock of the Highland Company for $1,600,000 plus $8,000 of direct acquisition costs on January 1, 19X5. At the purchase date, the inventory, the equipment, and the patents of Highland Company had fair market values of $10,000, $50,000, and $100,000, respectively, in excess of their book values. The other assets and liabilities of Highland Company had book values equal to their market values. The inventory was sold during the month following the purchase. The two companies agreed that the equipment had a remaining life of 8 years and the patents 10 years. On the purchase date, the owners' equity of Highland Company was as follows:

Common stock ($10 stated value)	$1,000,000
Additional paid-in capital	300,000
Retained earnings	400,000
Total equity	$1,700,000

During the next two years, Highland Company had income and paid dividends as follows:

	Income	Dividends
19X5	$ 90,000	$30,000
19X6	150,000	30,000

The trial balances of the two corporations as of December 31, 19X7, are as follows:

	Dallman International	Highland Company
Current Assets	624,000	505,000
Equipment (net)	1,320,000	940,000
Patents	100,000	35,000
Other Assets	1,620,000	730,000
Investment in Highland.	1,608,000	
Accounts Payable.	(658,000)	(205,000)
Common Stock ($5 par)	(2,000,000)	
Common Stock ($10 par)		(1,000,000)
Paid-In Capital in Excess of Par	(1,200,000)	(300,000)
Retained Earnings 1/1/X7	(1,255,000)	(580,000)
Sales.	(905,000)	(425,000)
Cost of Goods Sold	470,000	170,000
Other Expenses	250,000	100,000
Dividend Income	(24,000)	
Dividends Declared	50,000	30,000
Total	0	0

Required:

Assume that any resulting goodwill is being amortized over 40 years and no intercompany transactions occurred.

(1) Prepare the original determination and distribution of excess schedule for the investment.

(2) Prepare the 19X7 consolidated worksheet for December 31, 19X7. Include columns for the eliminations and adjustments, the consolidated income statement, the controlling retained earnings, and the consolidated balance sheet.

Problem 3-11. On July 1, 19X5, Punch Inc. purchased 90% of the common stock of Sun Inc. for $1,127,000 plus $16,000 in direct acquisition costs. Sun had the following stockholders' equity on January 1, 19X5:

Common stock ($10 par value)	$200,000
Paid-in capital in excess of par.	300,000
Retained earnings.	300,000
Total equity	$800,000

Sun's estimated income for the first 6 months of 19X5 was $40,000, including the $30,000 depreciation on the building, $20,000 depreciation on the equipment, and $1,000 goodwill amortization. Following is a summary of the book and market values of Sun's asset and liability accounts on July 1, 19X5. Book values include the above amortizations.

Account	Book Value	Market Value	Punch's Life Assumption
Cash...	$150,000	$150,000	
Accounts Receivable...........................	200,000	200,000	Collected by year end
Inventory......................................	250,000	270,000	Sold by year end
Land..	100,000	200,000	
Building.......................................	700,000	600,000	20-year life, no salvage, straight-line*
Accumulated Depreciation—Building.............	(300,000)		
Equipment	300,000	250,000	5-year life, no salvage, straight-line*
Accumulated Depreciation—Equipment	(160,000)		
Goodwill	50,000	?	25 years
Mortgage Payable..............................	(450,000)	(400,000)	10-year, straight-line amortization

*Life and method do not agree with those used by Sun Inc.

Sun's books were not closed on July 1, 19X5; thus, the following December 31, 19X5 trial balances of Punch and Sun include the results from operations for all of 19X5:

	Punch	Sun
Cash...	323,000	261,000
Accounts Receivable...........................	200,000	230,000
Inventory......................................	400,000	220,000
Land..	200,000	100,000
Building.......................................	1,000,000	700,000
Accumulated Depreciation—Building.............	(500,000)	(330,000)
Equipment	400,000	300,000
Accumulated Depreciation—Equipment	(100,000)	(180,000)
Goodwill (net)		49,000
Investment in Sun Inc..........................	1,143,000	
Mortgage Payable..............................		(450,000)
Common Stock	(1,800,000)	(200,000)
Paid-In Capital in Excess of Par...............		(300,000)
Retained Earnings, Jan. 1, 19X5...............	(1,066,000)	(300,000)
Sales	(2,000,000)	(900,000)
Cost of Goods Sold............................	1,500,000	600,000
General Expense...............................	100,000	98,000
Depreciation Expense..........................	200,000	100,000
Goodwill Amortization.........................		2,000
Total	0	0

Note that Sun's Depreciation Expense includes $60,000 on the building and $40,000 on the equipment.

Required:

(1) Prepare the original determination and distribution of excess schedule for the investment.

(2) Prepare the consolidated worksheet for December 31, 19X5. Include columns for the eliminations and adjustments, the consolidated income statement, the minority interest, the controlling retained earnings, and the consolidated balance sheet. Prepare supporting income distribution schedules as well.

(3) Prepare the 19X5 consolidated statements, including the income statement, retained earnings statement, and balance sheet.

Suggestion: Due to the minority interest, it is difficult to restate long-lived assets with no accumulated depreciation. It is recommended that the adjustments be made by decreasing accumulated depreciation. However, using the parent's estimates it is first necessary to recalculate what depreciation should be. Remember that in this example, the parent is using different life assumptions and depreciation methods from those of the subsidiary. The parent's estimate (for 90% of the asset's value) should replace 90% of the depreciation now recorded by the subsidiary. Also, remember to reduce goodwill amortization when existing goodwill is consumed and allocated to other assets.

Problem 3-12. On January 1, 19X4, Harpoon Corporation purchased 80% of the outstanding common stock of Largo Company for $6,000,000 in cash. The book and market values for Largo Company were as follows:

	Recorded Book Value	Market Value
Cash	1,305,000	1,305,000
Inventory	790,000	850,000
Land	2,500,000	4,000,000
Buildings	2,400,000	1,200,000
Accumulated Depreciation—Building	(1,600,000)	
Equipment.	2,750,000	2,000,000
Accumulated Depreciation—Equipment	(1,850,000)	
Goodwill	120,000	300,000*
Liabilities	(580,000)	(580,000)
Bonds payable	(2,000,000)	(1,800,000)
Common Stock ($5 par)	(3,000,000)	
Retained Earnings 1/1/X4.	(835,000)	
Total	0	

*Estimate, final value dependent upon total purchase price.

By the end of 19X4 the January 1, 19X4 inventory of Largo Company had been sold. At the purchase date, the building and equipment were estimated to have remaining lives of 10 years and 5 years, respectively. It was also decided that any goodwill resulting from the purchase shall be amortized over the next 20 years. As of January 1, 19X4, the 6% bonds had 5 years remaining to maturity.

The trial balances of Harpoon Corporation and Largo Company on December 31, 19X4, are as follows:

	Harpoon Corp.	Largo Co.
Cash...	1,700,000	2,137,000
Inventory......................................	1,600,000	800,000
Land...	4,000,000	2,500,000
Building.......................................	6,900,000	2,400,000
Accumulated Depreciation—Building....................	(3,400,000)	(1,680,000)
Equipment......................................	10,000,000	2,750,000
Accumulated Depreciation—Equipment	(5,000,000)	(2,000,000)
Investment in Largo Co.............................	6,456,000	
Goodwill	200,000	108,000
Liabilities......................................	(1,300,000)	(610,000)
Bonds Payable	(6,000,000)	(2,000,000)
Common Stock ($5 par)	(13,000,000)	(3,000,000)
Retained Earnings 1/1/X4..........................	(1,550,000)	(835,000)
Sales..	(3,000,000)	(1,500,000)
Cost of Goods Sold..............................	1,900,000	700,000
Other Expenses	900,000	200,000
Subsidiary Income	(480,000)	
Dividends Declared..............................	74,000	30,000
Total	0	0

Required:

(1) Prepare a determination and distribution of excess schedule for the investment.
(2) Prepare the 19X4 consolidated worksheet. Include columns for the eliminations and adjustments, the consolidated income statement, the minority interest, the controlling retained earnings, and the consolidated balance sheet. Prepare supporting income distribution schedules as well.

(AICPA adapted)

Suggestion: Be sure to limit your adjustment for goodwill amortization to only the net increase in goodwill (some goodwill exists already at the time of purchase and will have been amortized by the subsidiary).

Problem 3-13. On April 1, 19X1, Jansen Inc. purchased 100% of the common stock of Murdock Company for $5,850,000. At the date of purchase, the book and market values of Murdock's assets and liabilities were as follows:

	Book Value	Market Value
Cash..	$ 200,000	$ 200,000
Notes Receivable (net)	85,000	85,000
Accounts Receivable (net)	980,000	980,000
Inventories.......................................	828,000	700,000
Land...	1,560,000	2,100,000
Machinery and Equipment	7,850,000	10,600,000
Accumulated Depreciation...........................	(3,250,000)	(4,000,000)
Other Assets	140,000	50,000
Total assets	$8,393,000	$10,715,000

Notes Payable.	$ 115,000	$ 115,000
Accounts Payable	1,150,000	1,150,000
Subordinated Debentures (7%).	5,000,000	5,000,000
Common Stock ($10 par)	1,000,000	
Paid-In Capital in Excess of Par.	122,000	
Retained Earnings	1,006,000	
Total liabilities and equity.	$8,393,000	

By year's end, December 31, 19X1, the following transactions had occurred:

(a) The balance of Murdock's net accounts receivable account at April 1, 19X1, had been collected.

(b) The inventory on hand at April 1, 19X1, had been charged to the cost of goods sold. Murdock used a perpetual inventory system in accounting for the inventories.

(c) Included in Jansen's investment account is $1,500,000 of Daley Corporation 7% subordinated debentures. These debentures mature on October 31, 19X7, with interest payable annually on October 31.

(d) As of April 1, 19X1, Jansen viewed the machinery and equipment as having an estimated remaining life of 6 years. Murdock used the straight-line method of depreciation and a different remaining life. Murdock's depreciation expense calculation for the 9 months ended December 31, 19X1, was based upon the old depreciation rates.

(e) The other assets consist entirely of long-term investments made by Murdock and do not include any investment in Jansen.

(f) Accrued interest on debt is recorded by both companies in their respective accounts receivable and accounts payable accounts.

(g) Jansen's policy is to amortize intangible assets over a 20-year period.

Murdock Company closed its books on April 1, 19X1. Therefore, the following December 31, 19X1 trial balances provide revenue and expense figures for 12 months for Jansen and 9 months for Murdock.

	Jansen Inc.	Murdock Company
Cash	972,000	530,000
Notes Receivable.		85,000
Accounts Receivable (net)	2,758,000	1,368,400
Inventories	3,204,000	1,182,000
Land	4,000,000	1,560,000
Buildings	1,286,000	
Accumulated Depreciation—Buildings	(372,000)	
Machinery and Equipment	15,875,000	7,850,000
Accumulated Depreciation—Machinery and Equipment . . .	(6,301,000)	(3,838,750)
Investments	7,350,000	
Other Assets.	263,000	140,000
Notes Payable		(115,000)
Accounts Payable	(1,364,000)	(954,000)
Long-Term Debt.	(10,000,000)	
Subordinated Debentures, 7%		(5,000,000)
Common Stock	(2,400,000)	(1,000,000)
Paid-In Capital in Excess of Par.	(240,000)	(122,000)
Retained Earnings	(12,683,500)	(1,006,000)
Sales.	(18,200,000)	(5,760,000)
Cost of Goods Sold.	10,600,000	3,160,000
Selling, General, and Administrative Expenses.	3,448,500	1,063,900

Depreciation Expense—Buildings	127,000	
Depreciation Expense—Equipment.	976,000	588,750
Interest Revenue	(105,000)	(1,700)
Interest Expense	806,000	269,400
Total	0	0

Required:

(1) Prepare a determination and distribution of excess schedule for the investment in the common stock of Murdock Company. Jansen Inc. desires that the consolidated statements reflect the replacement cost and related depreciation as shown in the market value information.

(2) Prepare a consolidated worksheet that converts the separate trial balances into a consolidated trial balance. This worksheet should have the following columns:

Trial Balance		Eliminations & Adjustments		Consolidated Trial Balance
Jansen Inc.	Murdock Company	Dr.	Cr.	

(AICPA adapted)

Suggestion: This is a "short-cut" format that is often used on the CPA Exam. It is really the horizontal format, but it does not require the extension of amounts to the income statement, minority interest, controlling retained earnings, and balance sheet columns. This relieves you from having to allocate combined net income to the minority and controlling interests. Very likely, the grader of the exam will focus on the consolidated totals. This allows for variety in how an individual can make eliminations.

APPENDIX PROBLEMS

Problem 3A-1.   (Same as Problem 3-2 except vertical format worksheet is used.)
On January 1, 19X1, Parent Company purchased 80% of the common stock of Subsidiary Company for $308,000. On this date, Subsidiary had common stock, other paid-in capital, and retained earnings of $50,000, $100,000, and $150,000, respectively. Net income dividends for 2 years for Subsidiary Company were as follows:

	19X1	19X2
Net income	$60,000	$90,000
Dividends	20,000	30,000

On January 1, 19X1, the only tangible assets of Subsidiary that were undervalued were inventory and building. Inventory, for which FIFO is used, was worth $10,000 more than cost. The inventory was sold in 19X1. Building, which was worth $25,000 more than book value, has a remaining life of 10 years, and straight-line depreciation is used. Goodwill, if any, is to be amortized over the maximum period permitted.

Required:
(1) Using this information or the information in the following statements, prepare a determination and distribution of excess schedule.
(2) Parent Company carries the Investment in Subsidiary Company under the simple equity method. In general journal form, record the entries that would be made to apply the equity method in 19X1 and 19X2.
(3) Complete the vertical worksheet for consolidated financial statements for 19X2.

Statement — Accounts	Parent Company	Subsidiary Company
Income Statement		
Net Sales..	(520,000)	(450,000)
Cost of Goods Sold.................................	300,000	260,000
Operating Expenses................................	120,000	100,000
Subsidiary Income.................................	72,000	
Minority Interest in Income.........................		
Net Income..	(172,000)	(90,000)
Retained Earnings Statement		
Balance, Jan. 1, 19X2 — P Co.	(214,000)	
Balance, Jan. 1, 19X2 — S Co.		(190,000)
Net Income (from above)	(172,000)	(90,000)
Dividends Declared — P Co.........................	50,000	
Dividends Declared — S Co.........................		30,000
Balance, December 31, 19X2	(336,000)	(250,000)
Consolidated Balance Sheet		
Inventory, December 31............................	100,000	50,000
Other Current Assets..............................	148,000	180,000
Investment in Subsidiary Company	388,000	
Land..	50,000	50,000
Building and Equipment	350,000	320,000
Accumulated Depreciation	(100,000)	(60,000)
Goodwill..		
Other Intangibles.................................	20,000	
Current Liabilities	(120,000)	(40,000)
Bonds Payable....................................		(100,000)
Other Long-Term Liabilities.......................	(200,000)	
Common Stock — P Co.	(200,000)	
Other Paid-in Capital — P Co......................	(100,000)	
Common Stock — S Co.		(50,000)
Other Paid-in Capital — S Co......................		(100,000)
Retained Earnings — 12/31/X2	(336,000)	(250,000)
(from above)		
Totals...	0	0

Problem 3A-2. Brandt Enterprises purchased an 80% interest in Wagner International for $800,000 on January 1, 19X5. Brandt Enterprises also paid $4,000 in direct acquisition costs. On the purchase date, Wagner International had the following stockholders' equity:

Common stock ($10 par)....................	$150,000
Paid-in capital in excess of par..........	200,000
Retained earnings.........................	400,000
	$750,000

Also on the purchase date, it was determined that Wright International's assets were understated as follows:

Equipment, 10-year remaining life	$80,000
Land.....................................	20,000
Building, 20-year remaining life.........	60,000

Any remaining excess of cost over book value was attributed to goodwill which is being amortized over 20 years.

The following summarized statements of Brandt Enterprises and Wagner International are for the year ended December 31, 19X7:

	Brandt Enterprises	Wagner International
Income Statements:		
Sales	(650,000)	(320,000)
Cost of Goods Sold	260,000	240,000
Operating Expenses.....................	170,000	70,000
Depreciation Expense	65,000	30,000
Subsidiary (Income)/Loss	16,000	
Net (Income)/Loss......................	(139,000)	20,000
Retained Earnings:		
Retained Earnings, Jan. 1, 19X7, Brandt .	(625,000)	
Retained Earnings, Jan. 1, 19X7, Wagner .		(460,000)
Net (Income)/Loss......................	(139,000)	20,000
Dividends Declared		10,000
Retained Earnings 12/31/19X7............	(764,000)	(430,000)
Balance Sheets:		
Cash	334,000	170,000
Inventory	135,000	400,000
Land	145,000	150,000
Buildings	900,000	500,000
Accum. Depreciation—Building	(345,000)	(360,000)
Equipment..............................	350,000	250,000
Accum. Depreciation—Equipment	(135,000)	(90,000)
Investment in Wagner International	828,000	
Liabilities	(248,000)	(40,000)
Bonds Payable		(200,000)
Common Stock—Brandt....................	(1,200,000)	
Common Stock—Wagner...................		(150,000)
Paid-In Capital in Excess of Par		(200,000)
Retained Earnings 12/31/X7	(764,000)	(430,000)
Balance................................	0	0

Required:

Using the vertical format, prepare a consolidated worksheet for December 31, 19X7. Precede the worksheet with a determination and distribution of excess schedule. Include income distribution schedules to allocate the combined net income to the minority and controlling interests.

Suggestion: Remember that all adjustments to retained earnings are to beginning retained earnings, and it is the beginning balance of the subsidiary retained earnings account which is subject to elimination. Carefully follow the "carry-down" procedure to calculate the ending retained earnings balances.

Problem 3A-3. Ixonia Company purchased a 90% interest in Sullivan Company for $700,000 on January 1, 19X1. The investment account includes $20,000 of indirect acquisition costs. The investment has been accounted for under the cost method. At the time of the purchase, a building owned by Sullivan was understated by $180,000; it had a 20-year remaining life on the purchase date. Any remaining excess was attributed to goodwill with a 10-year life. The stockholders' equity of Sullivan Company on the purchase date was as follows:

Common stock ($10 par).....................	$350,000
Retained earnings...........................	200,000
Total equity	$550,000

The following summarized statements are for the year ending December 31, 19X2:

(Credit balance amounts are in parentheses.)

	Ixonia	Sullivan
Income Statements:		
Sales...	(580,000)	(280,000)
Cost of Goods Sold	285,000	155,000
Operating Expenses	140,000	55,000
Depreciation Expense	72,000	30,000
Dividend Income	(9,000)	
Net Income	(92,000)	(40,000)
Retained Earnings Statements:		
Retained Earnings, Jan. 1, 19X2, Ixonia....................	(484,000)	
Retained Earnings, Jan. 1, 19X2, Sullivan...................		(320,000)
Net Income	(92,000)	(40,000)
Dividends Declared	20,000	10,000
Retained Earnings, Dec. 31, 19X2........................	(556,000)	(350,000)
Balance Sheets:		
Cash	330,000	170,000
Inventory	260,000	340,000
Land	99,000	150,000
Building	800,000	500,000
Accumulated Depreciation—Building	(380,000)	(360,000)
Equipment...	340,000	250,000
Accumulated Depreciation—Equipment.....................	(190,000)	(90,000)
Investment in Sullivan Company	720,000	
Current Liabilities......................................	(123,000)	(60,000)
Bonds Payable		(200,000)
Common Stock, Ixonia	(800,000)	
Paid-In Capital in Excess of Par, Ixonia....................	(500,000)	
Common Stock, Sullivan		(350,000)
Retained Earnings, Dec. 31, 19X2........................	(556,000)	(350,000)
Balance...	0	0

Required:

Using the vertical format, prepare a consolidated worksheet for December 31, 19X2. Precede the worksheet with a determination and distribution of excess schedule. Include income distribution schedules to allocate the combined net income to the minority and controlling interests.

Suggestion: Remember that all adjustments to retained earnings are to beginning retained earnings, and it is the beginning balance of the subsidiary retained earnings account which is subject to elimination. One of the adjustments to the parent retained earnings account is the cost-to-equity conversion entry. Be sure to follow the carry-down procedure to calculate the ending retained earnings balances.

Problem 3B-1. On December 31, 19X5, Holder Company exchanged 10,000 of its $10 par value shares for a 90% interest in Jessica Company. The transaction did not meet the criteria for a pooling of interests and thus was recorded at the $70 per share market value of Holder shares. Jessica Company had the following balance sheet on the date of the purchase:

Assets		Liabilities and Equity	
Cash	$ 100,000	Current liabilities...........	$ 130,000
Accounts receivable........	200,000	Deferred rental income	120,000
Inventory	150,000	Bonds payable	250,000
Investment in marketable		Common stock ($10 par)....	100,000
securities	150,000	Paid-in capital in excess	
Property, plant, and		of par	150,000
equipment (net)	400,000	Retained earnings	250,000
Total assets	$1,000,000	Total liabilities and equity...	$1,000,000

It was determined that the following market values differed from book values for the assets of Jessica Company:

Inventory $200,000
Property, plant, and equipment (net) 500,000
Investment in marketable securities 170,000

The purchase is a tax-free exchange to the seller, which means Holder Company will use the book value of Jessica's assets for tax purposes. Jessica Company has $150,000 of tax loss carryovers. Holder will be able to carry back its 90% share of $100,000 of the losses to offset taxes paid. The balance of the tax loss carryover will not be used within a year but is considered fully realizable in the future. The tax rate for both firms is 30%.

Required:

Record the investment and prepare a determination and distribution of excess schedule.

Suggestion: The tax loss carryback is a current asset and the tax loss carryforward is a long-lived asset. Asset adjustments should be accompanied by the appropriate deferred tax liability.

Special Challenge: Solve this problem assuming the market value per share of stock exchanged by Holder was $50 per share. Recall that the deferred tax asset (realizable after 1 year) is not a priority account.

Problem 3B-2. The balance sheets of Spock Company and Kirk Company as of December 31, 19X6, are as follows:

	Spock	Kirk
Cash.	$ 1,200,000	$ 50,000
Accounts receivable	2,400,000	300,000
Inventory.	11,200,000	1,500,000
Prepayments	422,000	47,000
Equipment (net).	18,978,000	2,100,000
Investment in Kirk Co	2,400,000	
Total assets.	$36,600,000	$3,997,000
Payables	$ 7,200,000	$1,750,000
Accruals.	1,615,000	400,000
Common stock ($100 par)	10,000,000	1,000,000
Retained earnings.	17,785,000	847,000
Total liabilities and equity	$36,600,000	$3,997,000

An appraisal on December 31, 19X6, which was considered carefully and approved by the boards of directors of both firms, placed a total replacement value, less depreciation, of $3,200,000 on Kirk's property, plant, and equipment.

Spock Company offered to purchase all the assets of Kirk Company, subject to its liabilities, as of December 31, 19X6, for $3,000,000. However, 20% of the stockholders of Kirk Company objected to the price because it did not include any consideration for goodwill, which they believed to be worth at least $500,000. A counterproposal was made, and a final agreement was reached. In exchange for its own shares, Spock acquired 80% of the common stock of Kirk at the agreed-upon market value of $300 per share. The purchase is structured as a tax-free exchange to the seller; thus Spock will use the book value of the assets for future tax purposes. The tax rate for both firms is 30%.

Required:

Prepare a consolidated worksheet and a consolidated balance sheet as of December 31, 19X6.

(AICPA adapted)

Problem 3B-3. The trial balances of Crivitz Corporation and Dillon Corporation as of December 31, 19X1, are as follows:

	Crivitz Corporation	Dillon Corporation
Current Assets	167,000	80,000
Land	400,000	100,000
Building and Equipment (net)	900,000	240,000
Investment in Dillon Corporation	425,600	
Current Tax Liability.	(15,000)	(6,000)
Other Current Liabilities	(130,000)	(100,000)
Common Stock ($5 par)	(500,000)	
Common Stock ($50 par)		(200,000)
Paid-In Capital in Excess of Par.	(550,000)	
Retained Earnings, January 1, 19X1	(650,000)	(100,000)
Sales.	(309,000)	(150,000)
Subsidiary Income.	(12,600)	
Cost of Goods Sold	170,000	80,000
Expenses	89,000	50,000
Provision for Tax	15,000	6,000
Total	0	0

On January 1, 19X1, Crivitz purchased 90% of the outstanding stock of Dillon Corporation for $400,000, plus direct acquisition costs of $13,000. The acquisition was a tax-free exchange as to the seller. At the purchase date, Dillon's equipment was undervalued by $100,000 and had a remaining life of 10 years. All the other assets had book values that approximated their market values. Any resulting goodwill is being amortized over 15 years. A tax rate of 30% applies to both firms.

Required:
(1) Prepare a determination and distribution of excess schedule for the investment.
(2) Prepare the 19X1 consolidated worksheet. Include columns for the eliminations and adjustments, the consolidated income statement, the minority interest, the controlling retained earnings, and the consolidated balance sheet. Prepare supporting income distribution schedules as well.
(3) Prepare the 19X1 consolidated statements, including the income statement, retained earnings statement, and balance sheet.

Suggestion: A deferred tax liability results from the increase in the market value of the equipment. As the added depreciation is recognized on the equipment, the deferred tax liability becomes payable. Note that income distribution schedules record net-of-tax income. Therefore, be sure that any adjustments to the income distribution schedules consider tax where appropriate.

WORKSHEET 3-1

Simple Equity Method
Company P and Subsidiary Company S
Worksheet for Consolidated Financial Statements
For Year Ended December 31, 19X1

	(Credit balance amounts are in parentheses.)	Trial Balance	
		Company P	Company S
1	**Investment in Company S**	163,000	
2			
3			
4	**Goodwill**		
5	Other Assets (Net of Liabilities)	227,000	170,000
6	Common Stock ($10 par), Co. P	(200,000)	
7	Retained Earnings, Jan. 1, 19X1, Co. P	(123,000)	
8	Common Stock ($10 par), Co. S		(100,000)
9	Retained Earnings, Jan. 1, 19X1, Co. S		(50,000)
10	Revenue	(100,000)	(80,000)
11	**Expenses**	60,000	50,000
12	**Subsidiary Income**	(27,000)	
13	**Dividends Declared**		10,000
14		0	0
15	**Combined Net Income**		
16	**To Minority Interest (see distribution schedule)**		
17	**Balance to Controlling Interest (see distribution schedule)**		
18	Total Minority Interest		
19	Retained Earnings, Controlling Interest, Dec. 31, 19X1		
20			

Eliminations and Adjustments:
(1) Eliminate the current-year entries made in the investment account and in the subsidiary income account. It should be noted that when this step is completed, the balance in the investment account is the balance *at the beginning of the year*. At this point, the investment account and the Company S equity accounts are *adjusted to a common point in time* and are ready for elimination. Only dividends paid to outside minority stockholders remain on the worksheet.
(2) Eliminate the pro rata share of Company S equity balances *at the beginning of the year* against the investment account. The elimination of the parent's share of subsidiary stockholders' equity leaves only the minority interest in eacʻ। element of the equity.
(3) Distribute the $10,000 excess cost as required by the determination and distribution of excess schedule on page 125. In this example, Goodwill is recorded for $10,000.
(4) Amortize the resulting goodwill over the 10-year period. The current portion is $1,000 per year ($10,000 ÷ 10 years).

Worksheet 3-1 (see page 127)

Eliminations & Adjustments				Consolidated Income Statement	Minority Interest	Controlling Retained Earnings	Consolidated Balance Sheet	
Dr.		Cr.						
(1)	9,000	(1)	27,000					1
		(2)	135,000					2
		(3)	10,000					3
(3)	10,000	(4)	1,000				9,000	4
							397,000	5
							(200,000)	6
						(123,000)		7
(2)	90,000				(10,000)			8
(2)	45,000				(5,000)			9
				(180,000)				10
(4)	1,000			111,000				11
(1)	27,000							12
		(1)	9,000		1,000			13
	182,000		182,000					14
				(69,000)				15
				3,000*	(3,000)			16
				66,000*		(66,000)		17
					(17,000)		(17,000)	18
						(189,000)	(189,000)	19
							0	20

Subsidiary Company S Income Distribution

Internally generated net income........	$30,000	
Adjusted income.....................	$30,000	
Minority share	10%	
Minority interest	$ 3,000*	

Parent Company P Income Distribution

Goodwill amortization ....(4) **$ 1,000**	Internally generated net income........	$40,000
	90% × Company S adjusted income of $30,000	27,000
	Controlling interest	**$66,000***

WORKSHEET 3-2

Simple Equity Method, Second Year
Company P and Subsidiary Company S
Worksheet for Consolidated Financial Statements
For Year Ended December 31, 19X2

	(Credit balance amounts are in parentheses.)	Trial Balance	
		Company P	Company S
1	**Investment in Company S**	149,500	
2			
3	**Goodwill**		
4	Other Assets (Net of Liabilities)	251,500	155,000
5	Common Stock ($10 par), Co. P	(200,000)	
6	**Retained Earnings, Jan. 1, 19X2, Co. P**	(190,000)	
7	Common Stock ($10 par), Co. S		(100,000)
8	Retained Earnings, Jan. 1, 19X2, Co. S		(70,000)
9	Revenue	(100,000)	(50,000)
10	Expenses	80,000	60,000
11	**Subsidiary Loss**	9,000	
12	**Dividends Declared**		5,000
13		0	0
14	**Combined Net Income**		
15	**To Minority Interest (see distribution schedule)**		
16	**Balance to Controlling Interest (see distribution schedule)**		
17	Total Minority Interest		
18	Retained Earnings, Controlling Interest, Dec. 31, 19X2		
19			

Eliminations and Adjustments:
(1) Eliminate the current-year entries made in the investment account and in the subsidiary loss account. This step returns the investment in Company S account to its January 1, 19X2 balance. The investment account and the subsidiary equity accounts now are *stated at a common point in time*, which will facilitate their elimination.
(2) Using balances *at the beginning of the year*, eliminate 90% of the Company S equity balances against the remaining investment account.
(3) Distribute the $10,000 excess cost as indicated by the determination and distribution of excess schedule that was prepared on the date of acquisition.
(4) Amortize the goodwill over the selected 10-year period. It is necessary to record the amortization *for current and past periods*, because asset adjustments resulting from the consolidation process do not appear on the separate statements of the constituent firms. Thus, step (4) reduces Goodwill by $2,000 for the 19X1 and 19X2 amortization. The amount for the current year is expensed, while the cumulative amortization for prior years is deducted from the beginning controlling retained earnings account. The minority interest does not share in the adjustments, since the only goodwill originally acknowledged is that which is applicable to the controlling interest.

Worksheet 3-2 (see page 133)

Eliminations & Adjustments				Consolidated Income Statement	Minority Interest	Controlling Retained Earnings	Consolidated Balance Sheet	
Dr.		Cr.						
(1)	9,000	(2)	153,000					1
(1)	4,500	(3)	10,000					2
(3)	10,000	(4)	2,000				8,000	3
							406,500	4
							(200,000)	5
(4)	1,000					(189,000)		6
(2)	90,000				(10,000)			7
(2)	63,000				(7,000)			8
				(150,000)				9
(4)	1,000			141,000				10
		(1)	9,000					11
		(1)	4,500		500			12
	178,500		178,500					13
				(9,000)				14
				(1,000)*	1,000			15
				10,000*		(10,000)		16
				(15,500)			(15,500)	17
						(199,000)	(199,000)	18
							0	19

Subsidiary Company S Income Distribution

Internally generated loss	$10,000
Adjusted loss	$10,000
Minority share	10%
Minority interest	$ 1,000*

Parent Company P Income Distribution

Goodwill amortization . . . .(4) $ 1,000	Internally generated net income	$20,000
90% × Company S adjusted loss of		
$10,000 9,000		
	Controlling interest	**$10,000***

WORKSHEET 3-3

Cost Method
Company P and Subsidiary Company S
Worksheet for Consolidated Financial Statements
For Year Ended December 31, 19X1

	(Credit balance amounts are in parentheses.)	Trial Balance	
		Company P	Company S
1	**Investment in Company S**	**145,000**	
2			
3	Goodwill		
4	Other Assets (Net of Liabilities)	227,000	170,000
5	Common Stock ($10 par), Co. P	(200,000)	
6	Retained Earnings, Jan. 1, 19X1, Co. P	(123,000)	
7	Common Stock ($10 par), Co. S		(100,000)
8	Retained Earnings, Jan. 1, 19X1, Co. S		(50,000)
9	Revenue	(100,000)	(80,000)
10	Expenses	60,000	50,000
11	**Subsidiary (Dividend) Income**	**(9,000)**	
12	**Dividends Declared**		**10,000**
13		0	0
14	Combined Net Income		
15	To Minority Interest (see distribution schedule)		
16	Balance to Controlling Interest (see distribution schedule)		
17	Total Minority Interest		
18	Retained Earnings, Controlling Interest, Dec. 31, 19X1		
19			

Eliminations and Adjustments:
(1)   Eliminate intercompany dividends.
(2)   Eliminate 90% of the Company S equity balances at the beginning of the year against the investment account.
(3)   Distribute the $10,000 excess cost as indicated by the determination and distribution of excess schedule on page 125.
(4)   Amortize the goodwill for the current year.

Worksheet 3-3 (see page 134)

Eliminations & Adjustments				Consolidated Income Statement	Minority Interest	Controlling Retained Earnings	Consolidated Balance Sheet	
Dr.		Cr.						
		(2)	135,000					1
		(3)	10,000					2
(3)	10,000	(4)	1,000				9,000	3
							397,000	4
							(200,000)	5
						(123,000)		6
(2)	90,000				(10,000)			7
(2)	45,000				(5,000)			8
				(180,000)				9
(4)	1,000			111,000				10
(1)	9,000							11
		(1)	9,000		1,000			12
	155,000		155,000					13
				(69,000)				14
				3,000*	(3,000)			15
				66,000*		(66,000)		16
					(17,000)		(17,000)	17
						(189,000)	(189,000)	18
							0	19

Subsidiary Company S Income Distribution

Internally generated net income	$30,000
Adjusted income	$30,000
Minority share	10%
Minority interest	$ 3,000*

Parent Company P Income Distribution

Goodwill amortization...............(4) $ 1,000	Internally generated net income.........	$40,000
	90% × Company S adjusted income of	
	$30,000	27,000
	Controlling interest	$66,000 *

WORKSHEET 3-4

Cost Method, Second Year
Company P and Subsidiary Company S
Worksheet for Consolidated Financial Statements
For Year Ended December 31, 19X2

	(Credit balance amounts are in parentheses.)	Trial Balance	
		Company P	Company S
1	**Investment in Company S**	145,000	
2			
3	Goodwill		
4	Other Assets (Net of Liabilities)	251,500	155,000
5	Common Stock ($10 par), Co. P	(200,000)	
6	**Retained Earnings, Jan. 1, 19X2, Co. P**	(172,000)	
7	Common Stock ($10 par), Co. S		(100,000)
8	Retained Earnings, Jan. 1, 19X2, Co. S		(70,000)
9	Revenue	(100,000)	(50,000)
10	Expenses	80,000	60,000
11	**Subsidiary (Dividend) Income** ·	(4,500)	
12	**Dividends Declared**		5,000
13		0	0
14	Combined Net Income		
15	To Minority Interest (see distribution schedule)		
16	Balance to Controlling Interest (see distribution schedule)		
17	Total Minority Interest		
18	Retained Earnings, Controlling Interest, Dec. 31, 19X2		
19			

Eliminations and Adjustments:
(C) Convert to simple equity method as of January 1, 19X2.
(1) Eliminate the current-year intercompany dividends.
(2) Eliminate 90% of the Company S equity balances at the beginning of the year against the investment account.
(3) Distribute the $10,000 excess cost as indicated by the determination and distribution of excess schedule that was prepared on the date of acquisition.
(4) Amortize the goodwill for the current year and one previous year.

Worksheet 3-4 (see page 134)

Eliminations & Adjustments				Consolidated Income Statement	Minority Interest	Controlling Retained Earnings	Consolidated Balance Sheet	
Dr.		Cr.						
(C)	18,000	(2)	153,000					1
		(3)	10,000					2
(3)	10,000	(4)	2,000				8,000	3
							406,500	4
							(200,000)	5
(4)	1,000	(C)	18,000			(189,000)		6
(2)	90,000				(10,000)			7
(2)	63,000				(7,000)			8
				(150,000)				9
(4)	1,000			141,000				10
(1)	4,500							11
		(1)	4,500		500			12
	187,500		187,500					13
				(9,000)				14
				(1,000)*	1,000			15
				10,000*		(10,000)		16
					(15,500)		(15,500)	17
						(199,000)	(199,000)	18
							0	19

Subsidiary Company S Income Distribution

Internally generated **loss**	$10,000
Adjusted income	$10,000
Minority share	10%
Minority interest	**$ 1,000***

Parent Company P Income Distribution

Goodwill amortization..............(4)	$ 1,000	Internally generated net income	$20,000
90% × Company S adjusted loss of			
$10,000	9,000		
		Controlling interest....................	**$10,000***

WORKSHEET 3-5

Simple Equity Method, First Year
Paulos Company and Subsidiary Carlos Company
Worksheet for Consolidated Financial Statements
For Year Ended December 31, 19X1

	(Credit balance amounts are in parentheses.)	Trial Balance	
		Paulos	Carlos
1	Cash	100,000	50,000
2	Inventory	226,000	62,500
3	Land	200,000	150,000
4	Building	800,000	600,000
5	**Accumulated Depreciation—Building**	(80,000)	(315,000)
6	Equipment	400,000	150,000
7	**Accumulated Depreciation—Equipment**	(50,000)	(70,000)
8	**Investment in Carlos Company**	832,000	
9			
10			
11	Goodwill		112,500
12	Current Liabilities	(100,000)	
13	Bonds Payable		(200,000)
14	**Discount on Bonds**		
15	Common Stock, Paulos	(1,500,000)	
16	Retained Earnings, Jan. 1, 19X1, Paulos	(700,000)	
17	Common Stock ($10 par), Carlos		(100,000)
18	Paid-In Capital in Excess of Par, Carlos		(150,000)
19	Retained Earnings, Jan. 1, 19X1, Carlos		(250,000)
20	Sales	(350,000)	(200,000)
21	**Cost of Goods Sold**	150,000	80,000
22	**Expenses**	120,000	60,000
23			
24			
25	**Subsidiary Income**	(48,000)	
26	**Dividends Declared**		20,000
27		0	0
28	Combined Net Income		
29	To Minority Interest (see distribution schedule)		
30	Balance to Controlling Interest (see distribution schedule)		
31	Total Minority Interest		
32	Retained Earnings, Controlling Interest, Dec. 31, 19X1		
33			

Eliminations & Adjustments				Consolidated Income Statement	Minority Interest	Controlling Retained Earnings	Consolidated Balance Sheet	
Dr.		Cr.						
							150,000	1
							288,500	2
(3e)	40,000						390,000	3
							1,400,000	4
(3d)	160,000	(4d)	8,000				(243,000)	5
		(3c)	16,000				534,000	6
(4c)	3,200						(116,800)	7
(1)	16,000	(1)	48,000					8
		(2)	400,000					9
		(3)	400,000					10
(3f)	201,402	(4f)	20,140				293,762	11
							(100,000)	12
							(200,000)	13
(3b)	10,598	(4b)	2,352				8,246	14
							(1,500,000)	15
						(700,000)		16
(2)	80,000				(20,000)			17
(2)	120,000				(30,000)			18
(2)	200,000				(50,000)			19
				(550,000)				20
(3a)	4,000			234,000				21
(4b)	2,352	(4c)	3,200	207,292				22
(4d)	8,000							23
(4f)	20,140							24
(1)	48,000							25
		(1)	16,000		4,000			26
	913,692		913,692					27
				(108,708)				28
				12,000*	(12,000)			29
				96,708*		(96,708)		30
						(108,000)	(108,000)	31
						(796,708)	(796,708)	32
							0	33

(continued)

Eliminations and Adjustments:

(1)   Eliminate the current-year entries made in the investment in Carlos Company account and in the subsidiary income account. The investment account now is adjusted to its January 1, 19X1 balance so that it may be eliminated.

(2)   Eliminate the 80% ownership portion of the subsidiary equity accounts against the investment. A $400,000 excess cost remains.

(3)   Distribute the $400,000 excess cost as follows, in accordance with the determination and distribution of excess schedule:

   (a)   Increase the beginning inventory by $4,000. However, the beginning inventory has been closed to the cost of goods sold; thus, the cost of goods sold is increased by $4,000. If the inventory had not been sold, the inventory account would be adjusted. The cost of goods sold in the later period of sale then would be adjusted on a subsequent worksheet.

   (b)   Record discount of $10,598 on the bonds payable.

   (c)   Reduce the equipment by $16,000 by reducing the asset account directly.

   (d)   Increase the building by $160,000 by decreasing its accumulated depreciation account.

   (e)   Increase the land by $40,000.

   (f)   Increase the goodwill by $201,402.

(4)   Record amortizations resulting from the asset and liability revaluations of step (3). The adjustments are lettered (a) through (f) to correspond with the revaluations in step (3):

   (a)   No amortization required; adjustment already charged to the cost of goods sold.

   (b)   Amortize the discount as follows:

   Net present value of controlling interest in Carlos bonds, January 1, 19X1:

Face, 80% × $200,000..	$160,000	
Discount...	10,598	$149,402
Multiply by 8% effective interest rate........................		.08
Effective interest expense....................................		$ 11,952
Nominal interest, 6% × $160,000..............................		9,600
Discount amortization..		$ 2,352

(c) Record annual decrease in equipment depreciation expense; $16,000 net decrease in the equipment divided by 5-year life equals $3,200.

(d) Record annual increase in building depreciation expense; $160,000 net increase in the building divided by 20-year life equals $8,000.

(e) No amortization results from adjustment of the land.

(f) Record additional annual amortization of the goodwill; $201,402 net increase in the goodwill divided by 10-year life equals $20,140. It is assumed that the previously recorded goodwill of $125,000 on January 1, 19X1, also is being amortized over 10 years.

Subsidiary Carlos Company Income Distribution

Internally generated net income	$60,000
Adjusted income......................	$60,000
Minority share.......................	20%
Minority interest	**$12,000***

Parent Paulos Company Income Distribution

Inventory adjustment..............**(3a)**	**$ 4,000**	Internally generated net income	$80,000
Discount amortization ....**(4b)**	**2,352**	80% × Carlos Company adjusted	
Building depreciation ....**(4d)**	**8,000**	income of $60,000	48,000
Goodwill amortization .... (4f)	20,140	**Equipment depreciation** .... **(4c)**	**3,200**
		Controlling interest...................	**$96,708***

WORKSHEET 3-6

Simple Equity Method, Second Year
Paulos Company and Subsidiary Carlos Company
Worksheet for Consolidated Financial Statements
For Year Ended December 31, 19X2

	(Credit balance amounts are in parentheses.)	Trial Balance	
		Paulos	Carlos
1	Cash	322,000	160,000
2	Inventory	210,000	120,000
3	Land	200,000	150,000
4	Building	800,000	600,000
5	Accumulated Depreciation—Building	(120,000)	(330,000)
6	Equipment	400,000	150,000
7	Accumulated Depreciation—Equipment	(100,000)	(90,000)
8	Investment in Carlos Company	896,000	
9			
10			
11	Goodwill		100,000
12	Current Liabilities	(150,000)	(40,000)
13	Bonds Payable		(200,000)
14	Discount on Bonds		
15	Common Stock, Paulos	(1,500,000)	
16	**Retained Earnings, Jan. 1, 19X2, Paulos**	(828,000)	
17			
18			
19			
20	Common Stock, Carlos		(100,000)
21	Paid-In Capital in Excess of Par, Carlos		(150,000)
22	Retained Earnings, Jan. 1, 19X2, Carlos		(290,000)
23	Sales	(400,000)	(300,000)
24	Cost of Goods Sold	200,000	120,000
25	Expenses	150,000	80,000
26			
27			
28	**Subsidiary Income**	(80,000)	
29	**Dividends Declared**		20,000
30		0	0
31	Combined Net Income		
32	To Minority Interest (see distribution schedule)		
33	**Balance to Controlling Interest** (see distribution schedule)		
34	Total Minority Interest		
35	Retained Earnings, Controlling Interest, Dec. 31, 19X2		
36			

Worksheet 3-6 (see page 140)

Eliminations & Adjustments				Consolidated Income Statement	Minority Interest	Controlling Retained Earnings	Consolidated Balance Sheet	
Dr.		Cr.						
							482,000	1
							330,000	2
(3e)	40,000						390,000	3
							1,400,000	4
(3d)	160,000	(4d)	16,000				(306,000)	5
		(3c)	16,000				534,000	6
(4c)	6,400						(183,600)	7
(1)	16,000	(1)	80,000					8
		(2)	432,000					9
		(3)	400,000					10
(3f)	201,402	(4f)	40,280				261,122	11
							(190,000)	12
							(200,000)	13
(3b)	10,598	(4b)	4,892				5,706	14
							(1,500,000)	15
(3a)	4,000	(4c)	3,200			(796,708)		16
(4b)	2,352							17
(4d)	8,000							18
(4f)	20,140							19
(2)	80,000				(20,000)			20
(2)	120,000				(30,000)			21
(2)	232,000				(58,000)			22
				(700,000)				23
				320,000				24
(4b)	2,540	(4c)	3,200	257,480				25
(4d)	8,000							26
(4f)	20,140							27
(1)	80,000							28
		(1)	16,000		4,000			29
	1,011,572		1,011,572					30
				(122,520)				31
				20,000*	(20,000)			32
				102,520*		(102,520)		33
					(124,000)		(124,000)	34
						(899,228)	(899,228)	35
							0	36

(continued)

Eliminations and Adjustments (the steps are keyed to correspond with those in Worksheet 3-5):

(1) Eliminate the current-year entries made in the investment in Carlos Company account and in the subsidiary income account. The investment account now is adjusted back to its January 1, 19X2 balance so that it may be eliminated.

(2) Eliminate the 80% ownership portion of the January 1, 19X2 subsidiary equity accounts against the investment. A $400,000 excess cost remains.

(3) Distribute the $400,000 excess cost as required by the determination and distribution of excess schedule. The distribution is identical to that shown in Worksheet 3-5, except for the January 1, 19X1 inventory adjustment of $4,000. The inventory adjustment now is carried to the purchaser's January 1, 19X2 retained earnings balance since it is an adjustment to 19X1 income.

(4) Record amortizations resulting from the asset and liability revaluations of step (3). The amortizations include those for the current and previous periods because the trial balances of the separate firms do not reflect the amortizations on the December 31, 19X1 consolidated worksheet. The adjustments are lettered (a) through (f) to correspond with the revaluations in step (3) of Worksheet 3-5:

(a) No amortization required; adjustment already charged to January 1, 19X2 controlling retained earnings account.

(b) Amortize the discount as follows:

Face, 80% × $200,000	$160,000	
Discount, December 31, 19X1 (see Worksheet 3-5)	(8,246)	$151,754
Multiply by 8% effective interest rate		.08
Effective interest expense		$ 12,140
Nominal interest, 6% × $160,000		9,600
19X2 discount amortization		**$ 2,540**
Add 19X1 discount amortization (from page 192)		2,352
Total amortization to date		$ 4,892

The current-year amortization is charged to expense, while the 19X1 amortization is charged to January 1, 19X2 controlling Retained Earnings.

(c) Record $3,200 annual decrease in equipment depreciation for 19X1 and 19X2. The 19X1 portion is carried to January 1, 19X2 controlling Retained Earnings, while the 19X2 adjustment is reflected in current expense.

(d) Record $8,000 annual increase in 19X1 and 19X2 building depreciation; the 19X1 adjustment reduces the January 1, 19X2 controlling retained earnings account; the 19X2 adjustment increases current expense.

(e) No amortization results from adjustment of the land.

(f) Amortize the goodwill for the current year by increasing expenses and for the past year by reducing the January 1, 19X2 controlling retained earnings account.

Subsidiary Carlos Company Income Distribution

Internally generated net income	$100,000
Adjusted income.	$100,000
Minority share.	20%
Minority interest	$ 20,000*

Parent Paulos Company Income Distribution

Discount amortization . . . . **(4b)**	**$ 2,540**	Internally generated net income.	$ 50,000
Building depreciation . . . . **(4d)**	**8,000**	80% × Carlos Company adjusted	
Goodwill amortization . . . .(4f)	20,140	income of $100,000.	80,000
		Equipment depreciation. . . . . (4c)	**3,200**
		Controlling interest	$102,520*

WORKSHEET 3-7

Intraperiod Purchase; Subsidiary Books Closed on Purchase Date
Company P and Subsidiary Company S
Worksheet for Consolidated Financial Statements
For Year Ended December 31, 19X1

	(Credit balance amounts are in parentheses.)	Trial Balance	
		Company P	Company S
1	Current Assets	187,600	87,500
2	**Investment in Company S**	118,400	
3			
4			
5	Equipment	400,000	80,000
6	Accumulated Depreciation	(200,000)	(32,500)
7	Liabilities	(60,000)	(12,000)
8	Common Stock, Co. P	(250,000)	
9	Retained Earnings, **Jan. 1, 19X1, Co. P**	(100,000)	
10	Common Stock, Co. S		(50,000)
11	Retained Earnings, **July 1, 19X1, Co. S**		(58,000)
12	Sales	(500,000)	(92,000)
13	Cost of Goods Sold	350,000	60,000
14	Expenses	70,000	12,000
15	**Subsidiary Income**	**(16,000)**	
16	Dividends Declared		5,000
17		0	0
18	Combined Net Income		
19	To Minority Interest (see distribution schedule)		
20	Balance to Controlling Interest (see distribution schedule)		
21	Total Minority Interest		
22	Retained Earnings, Controlling Interest, Dec. 31, 19X1		
23			

Eliminations and Adjustments:
(1) Eliminate the entries made in the investment in Company S account and in the subsidiary income account to record the parent's 80% controlling interest in the subsidiary's *second six-months' income and the subsidiary dividends*, restoring the investment account to its *balance as of the July 1, 19X1 investment date*.
(2) Eliminate 80% of the subsidiary's *July 1, 19X1* equity balances against the balance of the investment account.
(3) Distribute the excess of cost over book value of $20,000 to the accumulated depreciation account in accordance with the determination and distribution of excess schedule.
(4) Amortize *for one-half year* the excess attributable to the equipment.

Worksheet 3-7 (see page 142)

Eliminations & Adjustments			Consolidated Income Statement	Minority Interest	Controlling Retained Earnings	Consolidated Balance Sheet	
Dr.		Cr.					
						275,100	1
(1)	4,000	(1)	16,000					2
		(2)	86,400					3
		(3)	20,000					4
						480,000	5
(3)	20,000	(4)	1,000				(213,500)	6
						(72,000)	7
						(250,000)	8
					(100,000)		9
(2)	40,000				(10,000)			10
(2)	46,400				(11,600)			11
				(592,000)				12
				410,000				13
(4)	1,000			83,000				14
(1)	16,000							15
		(1)	4,000		1,000			16
	127,400		127,400					17
				(99,000)				18
				4,000*	(4,000)			19
				95,000*		(95,000)		20
					(24,600)		(24,600)	21
						(195,000)	(195,000)	22
							0	23

Subsidiary Company S Income Distribution

Internally generated net income **second half of year**	**$20,000**
Adjusted income	$20,000
Minority share	20%
Minority interest.......................	**$ 4,000***

Parent Company P Income Distribution

Equipment depreciation............. (4) $1,000	Internally generated net income.........	$80,000
	80% × Company S adjusted income of $20,000 **(last 6 mo.)**	16,000
	Controlling interest	**$95,000***

WORKSHEET 3-8

Intraperiod Purchase; Subsidiary Books Not Closed on Purchase Date
Company P and Subsidiary Company S
Worksheet for Consolidated Financial Statements
For Year Ended December 31, 19X1

	(Credit balance amounts are in parentheses.)	Trial Balance	
		Company P	Company S
1	Current Assets	187,600	87,500
2	**Investment in Company S**	118,400	
3			
4			
5	Equipment	400,000	80,000
6	Accumulated Depreciation	(200,000)	(32,500)
7	Liabilities	(60,000)	(12,000)
8	Common Stock, Co. P	(250,000)	
9	Retained Earnings, **Jan. 1, 19X1, Co. P**	(100,000)	
10	Common Stock, Co. S		(50,000)
11	Retained Earnings, **Jan. 1, 19X1, Co. S**		(45,000)
12	Sales	(500,000)	(182,000)
13	Cost of Goods Sold	350,000	120,000
14	Expenses	70,000	24,000
15	**Subsidiary Income**	**(16,000)**	
16	**Dividends Declared**		**10,000**
17			
18	**Purchased Income**		
19		0	0
20	Combined Net Income		
21	To Minority Interest (see distribution schedule)		
22	Balance to Controlling Interest (see distribution schedule)		
23	Total Minority Interest		
24	Retained Earnings, Controlling Interest, Dec. 31, 19X1		
25			

Eliminations and Adjustments:
(1)   Eliminate the entries made in the investment account and in the subsidiary income account (same as Worksheet 3-7). Notice that Company P's share of the subsidiary dividends declared are from those declared *after* the purchase.
(2)   Eliminate 80% of the subsidiary equity balances at the beginning of the year plus 80% of Company S's income earned *as of July 1, 19X1,* against the investment account. The share of preacquisition income is entered as *Purchased Income* to emphasize that this income was earned prior to the date of purchase by Company P. For

Worksheet 3-8 (see page 143)

Eliminations & Adjustments		Consolidated Income Statement	Minority Interest	Controlling Retained Earnings	Consolidated Balance Sheet	
Dr.	Cr.					
					275,100	1
(1) 4,000	(1) 16,000					2
	(2) 86,400					3
	(3) 20,000					4
					480,000	5
(3) 20,000	(4) 1,000				(213,500)	6
					(72,000)	7
					(250,000)	8
				(100,000)		9
(2) 40,000			(10,000)			10
(2) 36,000			(9,000)			11
		(682,000)				12
		470,000				13
(4) 1,000		95,000				14
(1) 16,000						15
	(1) 4,000		2,000			16
	(2) 4,000					17
(2) 14,400		14,400				18
131,400	131,400					19
		(102,600)				20
		7,600*	(7,600)			21
		95,000*		(95,000)		22
			(24,600)		(24,600)	23
				(195,000)	(195,000)	24
					0	25

elimination purposes, this account may be viewed as a supplement to retained earnings. Since the subsidiary also declared dividends *prior to* July 1, 19X1, the controlling percentage of those dividends should be eliminated in this entry by crediting Dividends Declared.

(3)   Distribute the $20,000 excess of cost over book value (same as Worksheet 3-7).

(4)   Amortize for *one-half year* the excess attributable to the equipment (same as Worksheet 3-7).

(continued)

Subsidiary Company S Income Distribution

Internally generated net income **entire year**.........................	**$38,000**
Adjusted income	$38,000
Minority share	20%
Minority interest......................	**$ 7,600***

Parent Company P Income Distribution

Equipment depreciation............ (4)	$1,000	Internally generated net income.........	$80,000
		80% × Company S adjusted income of $20,000 **(last 6 mo.)**	16,000
		Controlling interest	**$95,000***

WORKSHEET 3-9

Pooling of Interests
Company I and Subsidiary Company C
Worksheet for Consolidated Financial Statements
For Year Ended December 31, 19X3

	(Credit balance amounts are in parentheses.)	Trial Balance	
		Company I	Company C
1	Current Assets	46,000	35,000
2	Property, Plant, and Equipment (net)	64,500	60,000
3	Investment in Company C	81,000	
4			
5	Liabilities		(5,000)
6	Common Stock ($2 par), Co. I	(55,400)	
7	Paid-In Capital in Excess of Par, Co. I	(3,600)	
8	Retained Earnings, Jan. 1, 19X3, Co. I	(60,000)	
9	Common Stock ($10 par), Co. C		(10,000)
10	Retained Earnings, Jan. 1, 19X3, Co. C		(55,000)
11	Sales	(150,000)	(100,000)
12	Cost of Goods Sold	70,000	50,000
13	Expenses	30,000	25,000
14	Subsidiary Income	(22,500)	
15		0	0
16	Combined Net Income		
17	To Minority Interest (see distribution schedule)		
18	Balance to Controlling Interest (see distribution schedule)		
19	Total Minority Interest		
20	Retained Earnings, Controlling Interest, Dec. 31, 19X3		
21			

Eliminations and Adjustments:
(1)   Eliminate the current-year entries in the investment in Company C account and in the subsidiary income account, restoring the investment account to its January 1, 19X3 balance, so that it may be eliminated.
(2)   Eliminate 90% of the balances in the Company C stockholders' equity accounts against the investment account. No excess results.

Worksheet 3-9 (see page 145)

Eliminations & Adjustments			Consolidated Income Statement	Minority Interest	Controlling Retained Earnings	Consolidated Balance Sheet	
Dr.		Cr.					
						81,000	1
						124,500	2
	(1)	22,500					3
	(2)	58,500					4
						(5,000)	5
						(55,400)	6
						(3,600)	7
					(60,000)		8
(2)	9,000			(1,000)			9
(2)	49,500			(5,500)			10
			(250,000)				11
			120,000				12
			55,000				13
(1)	22,500						14
	81,000	81,000					15
			(75,000)				16
			2,500*	(2,500)			17
			72,500*		(72,500)		18
				(9,000)		(9,000)	19
					(132,500)	(132,500)	20
						0	21

Subsidiary Company C Income Distribution

Internally generated net income	$25,000
Adjusted income.....................	$25,000
Minority share.......................	10%
Minority interest	$ 2,500*

Parent Company I Income Distribution

Internally generated net income	$50,000
90% × Company C adjusted income of $25,000........................	22,500
Controlling interest...................	$72,500*

WORKSHEET 3-10

Vertical Format, Equity Method
Paulos Company and Subsidiary Carlos Company
Worksheet for Consolidated Financial Statements
For Year Ended December 31, 19X2

		Financial Statements	
	Compare this worksheet to Worksheet 3-6. Note that eliminations and adjustments, explanations as well as the income distribution schedules are the same for Worksheet 3-10 as for Worksheet 3-6.	Paulos	Carlos
1	**Income Statement**		
2	Sales	(400,000)	(300,000)
3	Cost of goods sold	200,000	120,000
4	Expenses	150,000	80,000
5			
6			
7	Subsidiary income	(80,000)	
8	Net income	(130,000)	(100,000)
9	Minority interest (see distribution schedule)		
10	Controlling interest (see distribution schedule)		
11			
12	**Retained Earnings Statement**		
13	Retained earnings, Jan. 1, 19X2, Paulos	(828,000)	
14			
15			
16			
17	Retained earnings, Jan. 1, 19X2, Carlos		(290,000)
18	Net income (carrydown)	(130,000)	(100,000)
19	Dividends declared		20,000
20	Retained earnings, Dec. 31, 19X2	(958,000)	(370,000)
21	Retained earnings, minority interest, Dec. 31, 19X2		
22	Retained earnings, controlling interest, Dec. 31, 19X2		
23			
24	**Balance Sheet**		
25	Cash	322,000	160,000
26	Inventory	210,000	120,000
27	Land	200,000	150,000
28	Building	800,000	600,000
29	Accumulated depreciation—building	(120,000)	(330,000)
30	Equipment	400,000	150,000
31	Accumulated depreciation—equipment	(100,000)	(90,000)
32	Investment in Carlos	896,000	
33			
34			
35	Goodwill		100,000
36	Current liabilities	(150,000)	(40,000)
37	Bonds payable		(200,000)
38	Discount on bonds		
39	Common stock, Paulos	(1,500,000)	
40	Common stock, Carlos		(100,000)
41	Paid-in capital in excess of par, Carlos		(150,000)
42	Retained earnings, Dec. 31, 19X2 (carrydown)	(958,000)	(370,000)
43	Retained earnings, controlling interest, Dec. 31, 19X2		
44	Retained earnings, minority interest, Dec. 31, 19X2		
45	Total minority interest		
46	Total	0	0

Worksheet 3-10 (see page 148)

Eliminations & Adjustments				Minority Interest	Consolidated	
Dr.		Cr.				
						1
					(700,000)	2
					320,000	3
(4b)	2,540	(4c)	3,200		257,480	4
(4d)	8,000					5
(4f)	20,140					6
(1)	80,000					7
					(122,520)	8
				(20,000)		9
					(102,520)	10
						11
						12
(3a)	4,000	(4c)	3,200		(796,708)	13
(4b)	2,352					14
(4d)	8,000					15
(4f)	20,140					16
(2)	232,000			(58,000)		17
				(20,000)	(102,520)	18
		(1)	16,000	4,000		19
						20
				(74,000)		21
					(899,228)	22
						23
						24
					482,000	25
					330,000	26
(3e)	40,000				390,000	27
					1,400,000	28
(3d)	160,000	(4d)	16,000		(306,000)	29
		(3c)	16,000		534,000	30
(4c)	6,400				(183,600)	31
(1)	16,000	(1)	80,000			32
		(2)	432,000			33
		(3)	400,000			34
(3f)	201,402	(4f)	40,280		261,122	35
					(190,000)	36
					(200,000)	37
(3b)	10,598	(4b)	4,892		5,706	38
					(1,500,000)	39
(2)	80,000			(20,000)		40
(2)	120,000			(30,000)		41
						42
					(899,228)	43
				(74,000)		44
					(124,000)	45
	1,011,572		1,011,572	(124,000)	0	46

WORKSHEET 3-11

Equity Method, Tax Issues
Paro Company and Subsidiary Sunstran Corporation
Worksheet for Consolidated Financial Statements
For Year Ended December 31, 19X1

	(Credit balance amounts are in parentheses.)	Trial Balance	
		Paro	Sunstran
1	Cash	300,000	60,000
2	Accounts Receivable (net)	376,000	65,000
3	Inventory, Dec. 31, 19X1	540,000	100,000
4	Investment in Sunstran Corporation	988,000	
5			
6			
7	Land	100,000	30,000
8	Building	1,300,000	950,000
9	Accumulated Depreciation	(400,000)	(300,000)
10	**Tax Loss Carryforward**		
11	Goodwill		
12	Accounts Payable	(248,000)	(20,000)
13	**Deferred Tax Liability**		
14			
15	Common Stock, Paro	(510,000)	
16	Paid-In Capital in Excess of Par, Paro	(100,000)	
17	Retained Earnings, Jan. 1, 19X1, Paro	(1,750,000)	
18	Common Stock, Sunstran		(100,000)
19	Paid-In Capital in Excess of Par, Sunstran		(300,000)
20	Retained Earnings, Jan. 1, 19X1, Sunstran		(400,000)
21	Sales	(3,400,000)	(900,000)
22	Cost of Goods Sold	2,070,000	600,000
23	Selling and General Expense	530,000	150,000
24			
25	Subsidiary Income	(84,000)	
26	Provision for Tax	188,000	45,000
27			
28	Dividends Declared	100,000	20,000
29		0	0
30	Combined Net Income		
31	To Minority Interest (see distribution schedule)		
32	Balance to Controlling Interest (see distribution schedule)		
33	Total Minority Interest		
34	Retained Earnings, Controlling Interest, Dec. 31, 19X1		
35			

Worksheet 3-11 (see page 152)

Eliminations & Adjustments		Consolidated Income Statement	Minority Interest	Controlling Retained Earnings	Consolidated Balance Sheet	
Dr.	Cr.					
					360,000	1
					441,000	2
					640,000	3
(1) 16,000	(1) 84,000					4
	(2) 640,000					5
	(3) 280,000					6
					130,000	7
					2,250,000	8
(3a) 160,000	(4a) 8,000				(548,000)	9
(3c) 72,000	(4c) 72,000					10
(3d) 137,143	(4d) 9,143				128,000	11
					(268,000)	12
(4b) 2,400	(3b) 48,000				(84,000)	13
(4e) 2,743	(3e) 41,143					14
					(510,000)	15
					(100,000)	16
				(1,750,000)		17
(2) 80,000			(20,000)			18
(2) 240,000			(60,000)			19
(2) 320,000			(80,000)			20
		(4,300,000)				21
		2,670,000				22
(4a) 8,000		697,143				23
(4d) 9,143						24
(1) 84,000						25
(4c) 72,000	(4b) 2,400	299,857				26
	(4e) 2,743					27
	(1) 16,000		4,000	100,000		28
1,203,429	1,203,429					29
		(633,000)				30
		21,000*	(21,000)			31
		612,000*		(612,000)		32
			(177,000)		(177,000)	33
				(2,262,000)	(2,262,000)	34
					0	35

(continued)

Eliminations and Adjustments:
(1) Eliminate the current-year entries made in the investment in Sunstran Corporation account and in the subsidiary income account. The investment account is adjusted now to its January 1, 19X1 balance so that it may be eliminated.
(2) Eliminate the 80% ownership portion of the subsidiary equity accounts against the investment. A $280,000 excess cost remains.
(3) Distribute the $280,000 excess cost as follows, in accordance with the determination and distribution of excess schedule:
   (a) Increase the building by $160,000 by lowering its accumulated depreciation account.
   (b) Record the tax deferred liability relative to the building adjustment.
   (c) Record the tax loss carryforward.
   (d) Record the goodwill.
   (e) Record the deferred tax liability applicable to goodwill.
(4) Record amortizations resulting from the asset and liability revaluations of step (3). The adjustments are lettered (a) through (d) to correspond with the revaluations in step (3).
   (a) Record the annual increase in building depreciation; $160,000 net increase in the building divided by its 20-year life equals $8,000.
   (b) Reduce the provision for tax account by 30% of the increase in depreciation expense ($2,400).
   (c) The tax loss carryforward is used in the current period and is added to the provision for tax account. The parent company has already recorded the benefit of the tax loss carryforward by decreasing the liability and the provision for tax. This adjustment restores the amount of the decrease to the provision for tax account. The tax loss carryforward is the result of the asset created in the consolidations process and not a reduction of the current provision for tax.
   (d) Amortize the goodwill for the current year; $137,143 divided by the 15-year life equals $9,143.
   (e) Reduce the provision for tax account by 30% of the goodwill amortization.

Subsidiary Sunstran Corporation Income Distribution

	Internally generated net income........	$105,000
	Adjusted income	$105,000
	Minority share	20%
	Minority interest....................	$ 21,000*

Parent Paro Company Income Distribution

Increase in depreciation expense.....(4a)	$ 8,000	Internally generated net income........		$612,000
Increase in provision for tax ....(4c)	**72,000**	80% × Sunstran Corporation		
Goodwill amortization ....(4d)	9,143	adjusted income of $105,000..........		84,000
		Decrease in provision for tax		
		(4b)........................	$2,400	
		(4e)........................	2,743	5,143
		Controlling interest.............		$612,000*

CHAPTER 4

Intercompany Transactions: Merchandise, Plant Assets, and Notes

The elimination of the parent's investment in a subsidiary and the adjustments that may result from the elimination process are only the start of the procedures that are necessary to consolidate a parent and a subsidiary. It is common for affiliated firms to transact business with one another. The more integrated the affiliates are with respect to operations, the more common intercompany transactions become. This chapter considers the most often encountered types of intercompany transactions. These include intercompany sales of merchandise and fixed assets as well as loans between members of the consolidated group.

Transactions between the separate legal and accounting entities must be recorded on each affiliate's books. The consolidation process starts with the assumption that these transactions are recorded properly on the separate books of the parent and the subsidiary. However, consolidated statements are the set of statements that portray the parent and its subsidiary as a single economic entity. There should not be any intercompany transactions found in these consolidated statements. Only those transactions between the consolidated firm and the firms outside the consolidated firm should survive to the consolidated statements. Intercompany transactions must be eliminated as part of the consolidation process. For each type of intercompany transaction, sound reasoning will be developed to support the worksheet procedures. The guiding principle shall come from answering the question: *From the standpoint of a single consolidated firm, what accounts and amounts should remain in the financial statements?*

The worksheet eliminations for intercompany transactions are the same no matter what method is used by the parent to maintain its investment in the subsidiary account. The examples in this chapter assume the use of the simple equity method. This is done because any investment that is maintained under the cost method is converted to the simple equity method. The impact of intercompany transactions on the investment account under the sophisticated equity method is considered in the appendix to this chapter. Note, however, that even where the sophisticated equity method is used, there is no change in the procedures for the individual intercompany transactions.

INTERCOMPANY MERCHANDISE SALES

It is common to find that the goods sold by one member of an affiliated group have been purchased from another member of the group. One firm may produce component parts that are assembled by its affiliate that sells the final product. In other cases, the product may be produced entirely by one member firm and sold on a wholesale basis to another member firm that is responsible for selling and servicing the product to the final users. Taken as a whole, these different examples of merchandise sales represent the most common type of intercompany transaction and must be understood as a basic feature of consolidated reporting.

Sales between affiliated firms will be recorded in the normal manner on the books of the separate firms. Remember that each firm is a separate legal entity maintaining its own accounting records. Thus sales to and purchases from an affiliated firm are recorded as if they were transactions made with a firm outside the consolidated group, and the separate financial statements of the affiliated firms will include these purchase and sale transactions. However, when the statements of the affiliates are consolidated, such sales become transfers of goods within the consolidated entity. Since these sales do not involve parties outside the consolidated group, they cannot be acknowledged in consolidated statements.

Following are the procedures for consolidating affiliated firms engaged in intercompany merchandise sales:

1. The intercompany sale must be eliminated to avoid double counting. To understand this requirement, assume that Company P sells merchandise costing $1,000 to a subsidiary, Company S, for $1,200. Company S, in turn, sells the merchandise to an outside party for $1,500. If no elimination is made, the consolidated income statement would show the following with respect to the two transactions:

Sales	$2,700	($1,500 outside sale plus $1,200 sale to Company S)
Less cost of goods sold.	2,200	($1,000 cost to Company P plus $1,200 purchase by Company S)
Gross profit.	$ 500	(18.5% gross profit rate)

While the gross profit is correct, sales and the cost of goods sold are inflated. As a result, the gross profit percentage is understated, since the $500 gross profit appears to relate to $2,700 of sales. The intercompany sale must be eliminated from the consolidated statements. All that should remain on the consolidated income statement with respect to the two transactions is:

Sales	$1,500	(only the final sale to the outside party)
Less cost of goods sold............	1,000	(only the purchase from the outside party)
Gross profit.....................	$ 500	(33⅓% gross profit rate)

When the goods sold between the affiliated firms are manufactured by the selling affiliate, the consolidated cost of goods sold includes only those costs that can be inventoried, such as labor, materials, and overhead, and may not include any profit.

The intercompany sale, though eliminated, does have an effect on the distribution of combined net income to the controlling and minority interests. This is true because the reported net income of the subsidiary reflects the intercompany sales price, and the subsidiary's separate income statement becomes the base from which the minority share of income is calculated. In effect, the intercompany transfer price becomes an agreement as to how a portion of combined net income will be divided. For example, if Company S is an 80%-owned subsidiary, the minority interest will receive 20% of the $300 profit made on the final sale by Company S, or $60. If the intercompany transfer price is increased from $1,200 to $1,300 and the final sales price remains at $1,500, Company S would earn only $200, and the minority interest would receive 20% of $200, or $40.

2. Often, intercompany sales will be made on credit. Thus, intercompany trade balances will appear in the separate accounts of the affiliated firms. From a consolidated viewpoint, intercompany receivables and payables represent internal agreements to transfer funds. As such, this internal debt has no effect on consolidated statements and must be eliminated. Only debt transactions with entities *outside* the consolidated group should appear on the consolidated balance sheet.

3. No profit on intercompany sales may be recognized until the profit is realized by a sale to an *outside* party. This means that any profit contained in the ending inventory of intercompany goods must be eliminated and its recognition deferred until the period in which the goods are sold to outsiders. In the example described in (1), assume that the sale by Company P to Company S was made on December 30, 19X1, and that Company S did not sell the goods until March of 19X2. From a consolidated viewpoint, there can be no profit recognized until the outside sale occurs in March of 19X2. At that time, consolidation theory will acknowledge a $500 profit, of which $200 will be distributed to Company P and $300 will be distributed to Company S as part of the 19X2 combined net income. However, until that time, the $200 profit on the intercompany sale recorded by Company P must be deferred. In addition, not only must the $1,200 intercompany sale be eliminated, but the inventory on December 31, 19X1, must be reduced by $200 (the amount of the intercompany profit) to its $1,000 cost to the consolidated firms.

Care must be taken in calculating the profit applicable to inventory. It is most convenient when the gross profit rate is provided so that it can be multiplied by the inventory value to arrive at the intercompany profit. In some instances, however, the profit on sales may be stated as a percentage of cost. For example, one might be told that the cost of units are "marked up" 25% to arrive at the intercompany sales price. If the inventory value is $1,000, it cannot be multiplied by 25% to calculate the intercompany profit because the 25% applies to the cost, and not the sales price, at which the inventory is stated. Instead, the gross profit rate, which is a percentage of sales price, must be calculated. The easiest method of accomplishing this is to pick the theoretical cost of $1 and mark it up by 25% (the given percentage of cost) to $1.25 and ask: "What is the gross profit percentage?" In this example, it is $.25 ÷ $1.25, or 20%. From this point, the $1,000 inventory value can be multiplied by 20% to arrive at the intercompany profit of $200.

The worksheet procedures to eliminate the effects of intercompany inventory sales are discussed in the next three sections as follows:

1. There are no intercompany goods in the beginning or ending inventories.
2. Intercompany goods remain in the ending inventory.
3. There are intercompany goods in the ending inventory and there were intercompany goods in the beginning inventory. This is the most common situation.

NO INTERCOMPANY GOODS
IN PURCHASING FIRM'S INVENTORIES

 In the simplest case, which is illustrated in Worksheet 4-1, pages 260–261, all goods sold between the affiliates have been sold, in turn, to outside parties by the end of the accounting period. Worksheet 4-1 is based on the following assumptions:

1. Company S is an 80%-owned subsidiary of Company P. On January 1, 19X1, Company P purchased its interest in Company S at a price equal to its pro rata share of Company S book value. Company P uses the equity method to record the investment. Worksheet steps (1) and (2) eliminate the investment account.
2. Companies P and S had the following separate income statements for 19X1:

	Company P	Company S
Sales	$700,000	$500,000
Less cost of goods sold	510,000	350,000
Gross profit.	$190,000	$150,000
Other expenses	(90,000)	(75,000)
Subsidiary income	60,000	
Net income.	$160,000	$ 75,000

Note that under the equity method, Company P's income includes 80% of the reported income of Company S.

3. During the year, Company S sold goods that cost it $80,000 to Company P for
    $100,000 (a 20% gross profit). Company P then sold all of the goods pur-
    chased from Company S to outside parties for $150,000 (a 33¹/₃% gross profit).
    Company P had not paid $25,000 of the invoices received from Company S
    for the goods. (Note that it is assumed in this and Worksheets 4-2 and 4-3 that
    a perpetual inventory system is used.) Consider the journal entries made by
    each affiliate:

Company S

Accounts Receivable (from Company P)	100,000	
Sales (to Company P)		100,000
Cost of Goods Sold (to Company P)	80,000	
Inventory		80,000
Cash	75,000	
Accounts Receivable (from Company P)		75,000

Company P

Inventory	100,000	
Accounts Payable (to Company S)		100,000
Accounts Receivable (from outside parties)	150,000	
Sales (to outside parties)		150,000
Cost of Goods Sold (to outside parties)	100,000	
Inventory		100,000
Accounts Payable (to Company S)	75,000	
Cash		75,000

   Worksheet step (3) eliminates the intercompany sale and its effects on the
Company P accounts. Step (3) is a simplified summary entry that can be further
analyzed with the following entry:

Sales (to Company P)	100,000	
Cost of Goods Sold (by Company S to Company P—the intercompany sale)		80,000
Cost of Goods Sold (by Company P to outside parties—the profit recorded by Company S)		20,000

The expanded entry above removes the cost of goods sold with respect to the
intercompany sale and removes the intercompany profit from the sales made by
the parent to outside parties. Note that the parent recorded the cost of the goods
sold to outside parties at $100,000. However, the true cost of the goods to the
consolidated firm is less a 20% gross profit of $20,000. Thus, the real cost was only
$80,000.

   Step (4) eliminates the intercompany receivables/payables still remaining
unpaid at the end of the year. Income distribution schedules are used in Worksheet 4-1 to distribute the $175,000 of combined net income to the minority and
controlling interests. It should be noted that all of the above procedures remain
unchanged if the parent is the seller of the intercompany goods.

INTERCOMPANY GOODS IN PURCHASING FIRM'S ENDING INVENTORY

Let us now change the example in Worksheet 4-1 to assume that Company P did not resell $40,000 of total of $100,000 of goods it purchased from Company S. This means that $40,000 of goods purchased from Company S remain in Company P's ending inventory. Consider the following revised entries for the two affiliates:

Company S

Accounts Receivable (from Company P)	100,000	
Sales (to Company P)		100,000
Cost of Goods Sold (to Company P)	80,000	
Inventory		80,000
Cash	75,000	
Accounts Receivable (from Company P)		75,000

Company P

Inventory	100,000	
Accounts Payable (to Company S)		100,000
Accounts Receivable (from outside parties)	90,000	
Sales (to outside parties)		90,000
Cost of Goods Sold (to outside parties)	60,000	
Inventory		60,000
Accounts Payable (to Company S)	75,000	
Cash		75,000

Let us now consider what has happened to the $100,000 of goods sold to Company P by Company S:

$80,000 is the original cost of the goods sold by Company S which should be removed from the cost of goods sold since it is just the intercompany sale and not the outside sale.

$12,000 is the intercompany profit on the goods sold by Company P to outside parties. The cost of these sales should be reduced by $12,000 ($20\% \times \$60,000$) to arrive at the true cost of the goods to the consolidated firm.

$8,000 is the intercompany profit remaining in the Company P ending inventory. This inventory, now at $40,000 should be reduced $8,000 ($20\% \times \$40,000$) to $32,000. Another way to view this is that 60% of the original intercompany goods have been sold to outside parties. Thus, only 60% of the intercompany profit ($\$20,000 \times 60\% = \$12,000$) has been realized.

If we follow the above analysis to the letter, we would make the following elimination in entry form:

Sales (by Company S to Company P)	100,000	
Cost of Goods Sold (by Company S)		80,000
Cost of Goods Sold (by Company P)		12,000
Inventory, December 31, 19X1 (held by Company P)		8,000

In practice, this entry is cumbersome in that it requires an analysis of the destiny of all intercompany sales. The approach used in Worksheet 4-2, pages 262–263, is simplified first to eliminate the intercompany sales under the assumption that all goods have been resold, and then to adjust for those goods still remaining in the inventory. This method simplifies worksheet procedures including the distribution of combined net income. In journal form, the simplified entries are:

(3)   Sales (by Company S to Company P)   100,000
         Cost of Goods Sold ($80,000 cost of Company S sales +
            $20,000 possible intercompany profit on goods sold by
            Company P)   100,000

(4)   Cost of Goods Sold (unrealized intercompany profit)   8,000
         Inventory, December 31, 19X1
            (held by Company P)   8,000

The $8,000 is viewed as the unrealized intercompany inventory profit that may not be realized until a later period when the goods are sold to outside parties.

The unrealized intercompany profit is subtracted from the seller's income distribution. In the income distribution schedules for Worksheet 4-2, the unrealized profit of $8,000 is deducted from the subsidiary's internally generated net income of $75,000. The adjusted net income of $67,000 is apportioned, with $13,400 (20%) distributed to the minority interest and $53,600 (80%) distributed to the controlling interest.

There is no change in worksheet elimination procedures if the parent is the seller and the subsidiary has intercompany goods in its ending inventory. Only the distribution of combined net income changes. To illustrate, assume the parent, Company P, is the seller of the intercompany goods. The income distribution schedules would be prepared as follows:

Subsidiary Company S Income Distribution

Internally generated net income	$ 75,000
Adjusted income	$ 75,000
Minority share.	20%
Minority interest	$ 15,000

Parent Company P Income Distribution

Unrealized profit in ending inventory . . . . (5)	**$ 8,000**	Internally generated net income	$100,000
		80% × Company S adjusted income of $75,000	60,000
		Controlling interest.	$152,000

INTERCOMPANY GOODS IN PURCHASING FIRM'S BEGINNING AND ENDING INVENTORIES

When intercompany goods are included in the purchaser's beginning inventory, the inventory value includes the profit made by the seller. The intercompany seller of the goods has included in the prior period such sales in its separate income statement as though the transactions were consummated. Thus, the beginning retained earnings balance of the seller also includes the profit on these goods. While this profit should be reflected on the separate books of the affiliates, it should not be recognized when a consolidated view is taken. Remember: *Profit must not be recognized until it is realized in the subsequent period through the sale of goods to an outside party.* Therefore, in the consolidating process, the beginning inventory of intercompany goods must be reduced to its cost to the consolidated firm. Likewise, the retained earnings of the consolidated entity must be reduced by deleting the profit that was recorded in prior periods on intercompany goods contained in the buyer's beginning inventory.

To illustrate, using the example of Company P and Company S from Worksheet 4-3 on pages 264–267, assume the two companies have the following individual income data for 19X2:

	Company P	Company S
Sales	$800,000	$600,000
Less cost of goods sold	610,000	440,000
Gross profit.	$190,000	$160,000
Other expenses	(120,000)	(100,000)
Subsidiary income	48,000	
Net income.	$118,000	$ 60,000

Assume the following additional facts:

1. Company P's 19X2 beginning inventory includes $40,000 of the goods purchased from Company S in 19X1. The gross profit rate on the sale was 20%.
2. Company S sold $120,000 of goods to Company P during 19X2.
3. Company S recorded a 20% gross profit on these sales.
4. At the end of 19X2, Company P still owed $60,000 to Company S for the purchases. Company P also had $30,000 of the intercompany purchases in its 19X2 ending inventory.

Worksheet 4-3 contains the 19X2 year-end trial balances of Company P and Company S. Steps (1) and (2) again eliminate the investment account. Step (3) adjusts for the intercompany profit contained in the beginning inventory. At the start of 19X2, Company P included $40,000 of goods purchased from Company S in its beginning inventory. During 19X2, the inventory was debited to the cost of goods sold at $40,000. The cost of goods sold must now be reduced to cost by removing the $8,000 intercompany profit. The intercompany profit also was included in last year's income by the subsidiary. That income was closed to retained earnings. Thus, the beginning retained earnings of Company S is overstated by $8,000. That $8,000 is divided between the minority and controlling interest in retained earnings. Subsidiary retained earnings has been 80% eliminated and only the 20% minority interest remains. The other 80% of beginning retained earnings is included in Company P's retained earnings through the use of the equity method. In entry form the adjustment is explained:

(3) Retained Earnings, Jan. 1, 19X2, Company P (80% controlling
     interest) 6,400
     Retained Earnings, Jan. 1, 19X2, Company S (20% minority
     interest) 1,600
     Cost of Goods Sold (by Company P to outside parties)   8,000

Note that once the controlling share of subsidiary retained earnings is eliminated, there is a transformation of what was *subsidiary* retained earnings into what now is *minority interest* in retained earnings. Steps (4) through (6) eliminate the intercompany sales, ending inventory, and trade accounts in the same manner as was done in Worksheet 4-2. After all eliminations and adjustments are made, the combined net income of $132,000 is distributed as shown in the income distribution schedules. The adjustments for intercompany inventory profits are reflected in the *selling company's schedule.*

It might appear that the intercompany goods in the beginning inventory are always assumed to be sold in the current period, since the deferred profit of the previous period is realized during the current period as reflected by the seller's income distribution schedule. That assumption need not be made, however. Even if part of the beginning inventory is unsold at year end, it still would be a part of the $30,000 ending inventory, on which $6,000 of profit is deferred. Note that the use of the LIFO method for inventories could cause a given period's inventory profit to be deferred indefinitely. Unless otherwise stated, the examples and problems of this text will assume a FIFO flow.

Worksheet 4-3 assumed the intercompany merchandise sales were made by the subsidiary. Procedures would differ as follows if the sales were made by the parent:

1. The beginning inventory profit would be subtracted entirely from the beginning controlling retained earnings since only the parent recorded the profit.
2. The adjustments for the beginning and ending inventory profits would be included in the parent income distribution schedule and not in the subsidiary schedule.

ELIMINATIONS FOR PERIODIC INVENTORIES

In Worksheets 4-1 through 4-3, the cost of goods sold was included in the trial balances, since both the parent and the subsidiary used a perpetual inventory system. However, in Worksheet 4-4 on pages 268–271, a periodic inventory system is used. In this illustration, which is based on the same facts as Worksheet 4-3, the following differences in worksheet procedures result from the use of a periodic inventory system:

1. The 19X2 beginning inventories of $70,000 and $40,000, rather than the ending inventories, appear as assets in the trial balances. The beginning

inventories less the intercompany profit in Company P's beginning inventory are extended to the consolidated income statement column as a debit.

2.   The purchases accounts, rather than the cost of goods sold, appear in the trial balances and, after adjustment, are extended to the consolidated income statement column.

3.   Step (3) credits the January 1 inventory to eliminate the intercompany profit.

4.   Step (4) credits the purchases account, which is still open under the periodic method, and makes the usual debit to the sales account.

5.   The ending inventories of Company P and Company S have not yet been entered on the consolidated worksheet, thus there is an opportunity to reduce the inventory held by the buyer to its cost to the consolidated firm. Step (5) records the consolidated ending inventory, net of intercompany profits, as both a debit and a credit. The amount of the combined ending inventories less the intercompany profit in Company P's ending inventory is extended to the consolidated balance sheet column as a debit and the consolidated income statement column as a credit, where it is deducted in order to arrive at the consolidated net income. The formal income statement will show the adjusted ending inventory as a deduction from purchases plus the beginning inventory in order to arrive at the cost of goods sold.

The net amount is determined as follows:

Company S recorded inventory	$ 50,000
Company P recorded inventory	60,000
Deduct intercompany inventory profit, 20% × $30,000	(6,000)
Consolidated inventory	$104,000

EFFECT OF LOWER-OF-COST-OR-MARKET METHOD ON INVENTORY PROFIT

Intercompany inventory in the hands of the purchaser may have been written down by the purchaser to a market value below its intercompany transfer cost. Assume that for $50,000 Company S purchased goods that cost its parent company $40,000. Assume further that Company S has all the goods in its ending inventory but has written them down to $42,000, the lower market value at the end of the period. As a result of this markdown, the inventory needs to be reduced by only another $2,000 to reflect its cost to the consolidated firm ($40,000). The only remaining issue is how to defer the $2,000 inventory profit in the income distribution schedules. As before, such profit is deferred by entering it as a debit on the intercompany seller's schedule. In the subsequent period, the profit will be realized by the seller.

It may seem strange that the $8,000 of profit written off is realized, in effect, by the seller, since it is not deducted in the seller's distribution schedule. This procedure is proper, however, since the loss recognized by the buyer is offset. Had the inventory been written down to $40,000 or less there would be no need to defer the offsetting profit in the consolidated worksheet or in the income distribution schedules.

LOSSES ON INTERCOMPANY SALES

Assume a parent sells goods to a subsidiary for $5,000 and the goods cost the parent $6,000. If the market value of the goods is $5,000 or less, the loss may be recognized in the consolidated income statement, even if the goods remain in the subsidiary's ending inventory. Such a loss can be recognized under the lower-of-cost-or-market principle that applies to inventory. However, if the intercompany sales price is below market value, the part of the loss that results from the price being below market value cannot be recognized until the subsidiary sells the goods to an outside party. Elimination procedures would be similar but opposite in direction to those used for unrealized gains.

INTERCOMPANY PLANT ASSET SALES

Any plant asset may be sold between members of an affiliated group, and such a sale may result in a gain for the seller. The buyer will record the asset at a price that includes the gain, and when the sale involves a depreciable asset, the buyer will base future depreciation charges on the price paid. While these recordings are proper for the firms as separate entities, they must not be reflected in the consolidated statements. Consolidation theory views the sale as an *internal transfer of assets*. There is no basis for recognizing a gain at the time of the internal transfer. Unlike the case of merchandise sales, however, recognition of the gain on the transfer does not have to await sale of the asset to an outside party. The buyer's normal intent is to use the asset, not to resell it. Since the asset is overstated by the amount of the intercompany gain, subsequent depreciation is overstated as well. The consolidation process reduces depreciation in future years so that depreciation charges in the consolidated statements reflect the original cost of the asset to the consolidated firm. While the gain is deferred in the year of sale, it is realized later through the increased combined net income resulting from the reduction in depreciation expense in subsequent periods. The decrease in depreciation expense for each and every period is equal to the difference between the depreciation based on the intercompany sales price and the depreciation based on the book value of the asset on the sale date.

INTERCOMPANY SALE OF A NONDEPRECIABLE ASSET

One member of an affiliated group may sell land to another affiliate and record a gain. For consolidating purposes, there has been no sale; thus, there is no cause to recognize a gain. Since the asset is not depreciable, the entire gain must be deferred until the land is sold to an outside party. This deferment may be permanent if there is no intent to sell at a later date. For example, assume that in 19X1 Company S (80% owned) sells land to its parent firm, Company P. The sale price is $30,000, and the original cost of the land to Company S was $20,000. Consolidation theory would rule that, until Company P sells the land to an outside party, recognition of the profit must be deferred. The following worksheet elimination is made in the year of sale:

	Partial Trial Balance		Eliminations & Adjustments	
	Company P	Company S	Dr.	Cr.
Land	30,000			10,000
Gain on Sale of Land		(10,000)	10,000	

As usual, the selling firm's income distribution schedule would reflect the deferment of the gain.

In subsequent years, assuming the land is not sold by Company P, the gain must be removed from the consolidated retained earnings. Since the sale was made by Company S, which is an 80%-owned subsidiary of Company P, the controlling interest must absorb 80% of the deferment, while the minority interest must absorb 20%. For example, the adjustments in 19X2 would be:

	Partial Trial Balance		Eliminations & Adjustments	
	Company P	Company S	Dr.	Cr.
Land	30,000			10,000
Retained Earnings, Jan. 1, 19X2, Company P	(100,000)*		8,000	
Retained Earnings, Jan. 1, 19X2, Company S		(20,000)*	2,000	

*arbitrary balance

Now assume Company P sells the land in 19X3 to an outside party for $45,000, recording a gain of $15,000. When this sale occurs, the $10,000 intercompany gain also is realized. The following elimination would remove the previously unrealized gain from the consolidated retained earnings and would add it to the gain already recorded by Company P. The retained earnings adjustment is allocated 80% to the controlling interest and 20% to the minority interest, since the original sale was made by the subsidiary.

	Partial Trial Balance		Eliminations & Adjustments	
	Company P	Company S	Dr.	Cr.
Gain on Sale of Land	(15,000)			10,000
Retained Earnings, Jan. 1, 19X3, Company P	(120,000)*		8,000	
Retained Earnings, Jan. 1, 19X3, Company S		(15,000)*	2,000	

*arbitrary balance

The income distribution schedule would add the $10,000 gain to the 19X3 internally generated net income of Company S. At this point, it should be clear that the gain on the intercompany sale was deferred, not eliminated. The original gain of $10,000 eventually is credited to the subsidiary. Thus, the gain does affect the minority share of combined net income at a future date. Any sale of a nondepreciable asset should be viewed as an agreement between the controlling and minority interests regarding the future distribution of combined net income.

When a parent sells a nondepreciable asset to a subsidiary, the worksheet procedures are the same, except that:

1. The deferment of the gain in the year of the intercompany sale and the recognition of the gain in the year of the sale of the asset to an outside party flow through only the parent company income distribution schedule.
2. In the years subsequent to the intercompany sale through the year the land is sold to an external company, the related adjustment is made exclusively through the controlling retained earnings.

INTERCOMPANY SALE OF A DEPRECIABLE ASSET

Turning to the case where a depreciable plant asset is sold between affiliates, the following example illustrates the worksheet procedures necessary for the deferment of a gain on the sale *over the asset's useful life*. Assume that the parent, Company P, sells a machine to a subsidiary, Company S, for $30,000 on January 1, 19X1. Originally, the machine cost $32,000. Accumulated depreciation as of January 1, 19X1, is $12,000. Therefore, the book value of the machine is $20,000, and the reported gain on the sale is $10,000. Further assume that Company S (*the buyer*) believes the asset has a 5-year remaining life; thus, it records straight-line depreciation of $6,000 annually.

The eliminations spread the gain over the 5-year life of the asset by reducing annual depreciation charges. For consolidated reporting purposes, depreciation is based on the asset's $20,000 book value to the consolidated firm. Worksheet 4-5, pages 272–273, is based on the following additional facts:

1. Company P owns an 80% investment in Company S. The amount paid for the investment was equal to the book value of Company S underlying equity.

The simple equity method is used by Company P to record its investment. Steps (1) and (2) eliminate the investment account.

2. There were no beginning or ending inventories, and the firms had the following separate income statements for 19X1:

	Company P	Company S
Sales.	$200,000	$100,000
Cost of goods sold	(150,000)	(59,000)
Gross profit	$ 50,000	$ 41,000
Depreciation expense.	(30,000)	(16,000)
Gain on sale of machine.	10,000	
Subsidiary income (80%)	20,000	
Net income	$ 50,000	$ 25,000

Step (3) eliminates the intercompany gain, restates the asset at cost, and restores the accumulated depreciation on the date of the intercompany sale as follows:

Gain on Sale of Machinery.	10,000	
Machinery	2,000	
Accumulated Depreciation, Machinery.		12,000

Step (4) reduces the depreciation expense for the year by the difference between depreciation based on:

• The book value [($32,000 – $12,000 = $20,000 depreciable base) ÷ 5 years = $4,000] and

• The intercompany sales price ($30,000 depreciable base ÷ 5 years = $6,000).

The following elimination results:

Accumulated Depreciation, Machinery.	2,000	
Depreciation Expense, Machinery ($6,000 – $4,000)		2,000

The allocation of combined net income of $47,000 is shown in the income distribution schedules. Note that Company S (the buyer in this example) must absorb depreciation based on the agreed sales price, and it is the controlling interest that realizes the benefit of the reduced depreciation as the asset is used. Also, note that the realizable profit for Company P (the seller) in any year is the depreciation absorbed by the buyer minus the depreciation for consolidating purposes ($6,000–$4,000). If the sale had been made by Company S, the profit deferment and recognition entries would flow through its income distribution schedule.

          Worksheets for periods subsequent to the sale of the machine must correct the current-year nominal accounts and remove the unrealized profit in the beginning consolidated retained earnings. Worksheet 4-6, pages 274–277, portrays a consolidated worksheet for 19X2, based on the following separate income statements of Company P and Company S:

	Company P	Company S
Sales	$250,000	$120,000
Cost of goods sold	(180,000)	(80,000)
Gross profit	$ 70,000	$ 40,000
Depreciation expense	(20,000)	(16,000)
Subsidiary income (80%)	19,200	
Net income	$ 69,200	$ 24,000

Step (3) in this worksheet corrects the asset's cost and restates the accumulated depreciation account as of the *beginning* of the year. In entry form, the adjustment is explained:

Machinery (restate the asset at cost)		2,000
Accumulated Depreciation (reduce		
19X1 depreciation recognized as profit)		2,000
Retained Earnings, Jan. 1, 19X2, Co. P		
(unrealized gain on Jan. 1, 19X2)		8,000
Accumulated depreciation (restore		
accumulated depreciation as of		
date of sale)		12,000

Since the sale was by the parent, only the controlling interest in beginning retained earnings is adjusted. Had the sale been by the subsidiary, the adjustment would have been split 20/80 to the minority and controlling interests in beginning retained earnings.

Step (4) corrects the depreciation expense and the accumulated depreciation accounts for the current year. The resulting combined net income of $76,000 is distributed as shown in the income distribution schedules that follow Worksheet 4-6. During each year, Company S must absorb the larger depreciation expense that resulted from its purchase of the asset. Company P has the right to realize $2,000 more of the original deferred profit.

It may occur that an asset purchased from an affiliate is sold before it is depreciated fully. To illustrate this possibility, assume that Company S of the previous example sells the asset to a third party for $14,000 at the end of the second year. Since Company S's asset cost is $30,000, with $12,000 of accumulated depreciation, the loss recorded by Company S is $4,000 ($14,000 − $18,000 net book value). However, on a consolidated basis, the $4,000 loss becomes a $2,000 gain, determined as follows:

	On Books of Company S		For Consolidated Entity	
Selling price of machine sold				
by Company S		$14,000		$14,000
Less book value at end of second year				
following sale to Company S:				
Cost of machine	$30,000		$32,000	
Accumulated depreciation	(12,000)	18,000	(20,000)	12,000
Gain (loss)		$ (4,000)		$ 2,000

Worksheet 4-7, pages 278–279, is a revision of the previous worksheet so that Company S's subsequent sale of the depreciable asset at the end of the second year is included. Step (3) removes the $8,000 remaining intercompany profit on the asset sale from controlling retained earnings, adjusts current depreciation by $2,000, and converts the $4,000 loss on the sale recorded by the subsidiary into a $2,000 gain on the consolidated statements.

The eliminations for the sale of a new asset purchased or manufactured by one affiliate and sold to another affiliate are less complicated than the eliminations for the sale of a used asset. In the previous examples involving the sale of a used asset, the adjustments were affected by the seller's depreciation that had accumulated before the sale and the resulting book value of the asset. When a new asset is sold, however, the seller has not depreciated the asset prior to its sale; therefore, the eliminations involve only restating the asset to its cost to the consolidated firm. Depreciation adjustments in subsequent years are made by allocating the gain on the sale over the asset's life.

A loss on an intercompany sale of plant assets does not have to be deferred if the loss could have been recorded in the absence of a sale. Where there has been a permanent decline in the utility of a fixed asset, it may be written down to a lower market value. In this case, utility is defined as the benefits the asset provides the firm. Where, however, the asset is sold to an affiliated firm at a price below fair market value, the loss is to be deferred in the same manner as an intercompany gain. The loss would be deferred over the depreciation life of the asset. If the asset were sold to a nonaffiliated firm, the remaining deferred loss would be recognized at the time of the sale.

INTERCOMPANY LONG-TERM CONSTRUCTION CONTRACTS

One member of an affiliated group of companies may construct a plant asset for another affiliate over an extended period of time. The firm constructing the asset will record progress under the completed-contract method or the percentage-of-completion method. During construction, special adjustments may be necessary when consolidating, depending on which of the two methods is used to record the contract by the constructing affiliate. From a consolidated viewpoint, such activity amounts to the self-construction of an asset to be used by the consolidated entity. Once the asset has been sold to an affiliate, consolidation procedures are similar to those used for a normal intercompany sale of a plant asset.

Completed-Contract Method.   The constructing affiliate using the completed-contract method records no profit on the asset until it is completed and transferred to the purchasing affiliate. However, costs incurred to date on the contract are capitalized in a special account, such as *Cost of Construction in Progress*. This account will appear on the trial balance of the constructing affiliate. This account should be eliminated and rerecorded as *Assets Under Construction*, which is the usual account for the cost of an asset being constructed for a firm's own use.

The constructing affiliate may bill the purchasing affiliate for work done prior to the completion of the asset. When this occurs, the constructing affiliate will record billed amounts by debiting *Contracts Receivable* and crediting *Billings on Long-Term Contracts.* The billings account acts as a contra-account to Cost of Construction in Progress. The purchasing affiliate would debit *Assets Under Construction* and credit *Contracts Payable* for billings received. Consolidation procedures require that the constructing affiliate's account Billings on Long-Term Contracts be eliminated against Cost of Construction in Progress. Any excess of cost incurred over the amount of billings is closed to the purchaser's account, Assets Under Construction. In addition, it is necessary to eliminate any remaining intercompany receivable and payable amounts recorded on the long-term contract.

Percentage-of-Completion Method.   This method allows the constructing firm to recognize a portion of the total estimated profit on the contract as construction progresses. During the construction period, the contracting firm debits an account usually entitled *Construction in Progress* for costs that are incurred to outside firms. The contractor also debits Construction in Progress and credits *Earned Income on Long-Term Contracts* for the estimated profit earned during each accounting period. Thus, the construction in progress account includes accumulated costs and estimated earnings. When the purchaser is billed, the contractor will debit the amount billed to Contracts Receivable and credit Billings on Construction in Progress, while the purchaser will debit Assets Under Construction and credit Contracts Payable.

To illustrate the elimination procedures when the percentage-of-completion method is used, assume a subsidiary, Company S, enters into a contract to construct a building for its parent firm, Company P, for $500,000 and Company S estimates the cost of the building to be $400,000. During 19X1, the building is 50% completed and $200,000 of cost has been incurred as of December 31, 19X1, but only $150,000 has been billed. The contract is completed in 19X2 at an additional cost of $200,000. The entries on the books of the separate affiliates for December, 19X1 are as follows:

Company P

Assets Under Construction	150,000	
Contracts Payable		150,000
To record billing from subsidiary for amount due.		

Company S

Construction in Progress	200,000	
Payables (to outsiders)		200,000
To record costs incurred for the long-term contract under		
the percentage-of-completion method.		
Construction in Progress	50,000	
Earned Income on Long-Term Contracts		50,000
To record pro rata share of estimated profit		
[50% × ($500,000 − $400,000)].		
Contracts Receivable	150,000	
Billings on Construction in Progress		150,000
To record billing to parent for the portion of amount due		
under the contract.		

The subsidiary's balance sheet prepared at the end of 19X1 would list a net current asset of $100,000, as the $150,000 balance in Billings on Construction in Progress would be offset against the $250,000 balance in Construction in Progress. If billings exceed the amount recorded for construction in progress, a net current liability would be shown on the balance sheet.

The following partial consolidated worksheet for 19X1 shows the relevant accounts and the eliminations that would appear for this example. The elimination procedures are complex and involve answering the question: What should remain on the consolidated statements? From a consolidated viewpoint, a self-constructed asset is in progress and $200,000 has been spent to date. All that should remain on the consolidated statements is a $200,000 asset under construction and a $200,000 payable to outside interests. The income distribution schedule of the constructing affiliate would reflect the profit deferral through a debit for $50,000.

Company P and Subsidiary Company S
Partial Worksheet for Consolidated Financial Statements
For Year Ended December 31, 19X1

(Credit balance amounts are in parentheses.)	Trial Balance		Eliminations & Adjustments	
	Company P	Company S	Dr.	Cr.
Assets Under Construction	150,000		(3) 50,000	
Contracts Receivable		150,000		(1) 150,000
Billings on Construction in Progress		(150,000)	(3) 150,000	
Construction in Progress		250,000		(2) 50,000
				(3) 200,000
Earned Income on Long-Term Contracts		(50,000)	(2) 50,000	
Contracts Payable	(150,000)		(1) 150,000	
Payables (to outsiders)		(200,000)		

Eliminations and Adjustments:
(1)   Eliminate the intercompany debt and receivable resulting from the long-term contract.
(2)   Eliminate the income recorded on the long-term intercompany contract and remove the profit from Construction in Progress.
(3)   Eliminate the balances of Construction in Progress and Billings on Construction in Progress, and increase Assets Under Construction for the unbilled costs on the long-term intercompany contract.

As is true with all intercompany sales of plant assets, any intercompany profit is deferred until realized through the subsequent sale or use of the asset. Thus, the intercompany profit resulting from a long-term construction contract should be realized as the asset is depreciated. The unrealized profit will result in an adjustment to retained earnings in subsequent years.

INTERCOMPANY DEBT

Typically, a parent firm is larger than any one of its subsidiaries and can secure funds under more favorable terms. Because of this, a parent firm often will advance cash to a subsidiary. The parent may accept a note from the subsidiary as security for the loan, or the parent may discount a note that the subsidiary received from a customer. In most cases, the parent will charge a competitive interest rate for the funds advanced to the subsidiary.

In the examples that follow, the more common situation in which the parent is the lender is assumed. If the subsidiary were the lender, the theory and practice would be identical, with the only differences being the books on which the applicable accounts appear and the procedure for the distribution of combined net income.

Assume that on July 1, 19X1, an 80%-owned subsidiary, Company S, borrows $10,000 from its parent, Company P, signing a 1-year, 8% note, with interest payable on the due date. This intercompany loan will cause the following accounts and their balances to appear on the December 31, 19X1 trial balances of the separate affiliated firms:

Parent Company P		Subsidiary Company S	
Notes Receivable	10,000	Notes Payable	(10,000)
Interest Income	(400)	Interest Expense	400
Interest Receivable	400	Interest Payable	(400)

While this information is required on the books of the separate firms, it should not appear on the consolidated statements. The procedures needed to eliminate this intercompany note and its related interest amounts are demonstrated in Worksheet 4-8, pages 280–281. Step (3) eliminates the intercompany receivable and payable for the note and the accrued interest on the note. Step (4) eliminates the intercompany interest income and expense amounts. In this worksheet, it is assumed that the intercompany note is the only note recorded. However, it may occur that an intercompany note and its related interest expense, revenue, and accruals are commingled with notes to outside parties. Before the trial balances are entered on the worksheet and before consolidation is attempted, intercompany interest expense and revenue must be accrued properly on the books of the parent and subsidiary.

After all the necessary worksheet eliminations are made, the effect of the note on the distribution of combined net income must be considered. There might be a temptation to increase the minority share of combined net income by $400 as a result of eliminating the interest expense on the intercompany note, but it is not correct to do so. Even though the interest does not appear on the consolidated income statement, it is a legitimate expense for Company S as a separate entity and a legitimate revenue for Company P as a separate entity. In essence, Company S has agreed to transfer $400 to Company P for interest during 19X1, and the minority must respect this agreement when calculating its share of combined net income. Thus, the basis for calculating the minority share is the net income of Company S as a separate entity. The minority receives 20% of this $10,000 net income which includes the $400 of intercompany interest expense.

A parent receiving a note from a subsidiary subsequently may discount the note at a nonaffiliated financial institution in order to receive immediate cash. This results in a note receivable discounted being recorded by the parent. From a consolidated viewpoint, there is a note payable to outside parties. Consolidation procedures should eliminate the internal note receivable against the note receivable discounted. This elimination will result in the note, now payable to an outside party, being extended to the consolidated balance sheet. Intercompany interest accrued prior to the discounting is eliminated. Interest paid by the subsidiary subsequent to the discounting is paid to the outside party and is not eliminated. The net interest expense or revenue on the discounting of the note is a transaction between the parent and the outside party and thus is not eliminated. When consolidated statements are prepared, however, it is desirable to net the interest expense on the note recorded by the maker subsequent to the discounting of the note against the net interest expense or revenue on the discounting transaction.

SOPHISTICATED EQUITY METHOD: INTERCOMPANY TRANSACTIONS

Chapter 3 demonstrated the use of the sophisticated equity method for the parent's recording of its investment in a subsidiary. Recall that one major difference between the simple and sophisticated equity methods was that the latter records subsidiary income net of amortizations of excess. In contrast, the simple equity method ignores amortizations and records as income for the parent the subsidiary reported income multiplied by the parent's percentage of ownership. Some firms using the sophisticated equity method will proceed to the next level of complexity. Instead of adjusting for their share of the income reported by the subsidiary (as under the simple equity method), they will adjust for their share of subsidiary income after it is adjusted for intercompany profits. This means that before the parent can make an equity adjustment for income of the subsidiary, it must prepare an income distribution schedule for the subsidiary company. The adjusted net income derived in the income distribution schedule will become the income to which the parent ownership percentage is applied to arrive at equity income.

The added complexity of the sophisticated equity method is unwarranted when statements are to be consolidated, since the subsidiary income and the investment in subsidiary accounts are eliminated entirely. However, this procedure must be used in the rare case when a subsidiary is not to be consolidated or when parent-only statements are to be prepared as a supplement to the consolidated statements.

UNREALIZED PROFITS OF THE CURRENT PERIOD

The case of intercompany profits generated only during the current period will be considered first. Although the same procedure applies to all types of subsidiary-generated unrealized intercompany profits and losses of the current period, the impact of the sophisticated equity method will be demonstrated assuming only the existence of inventory profits.

The following example is based on the information presented in Worksheet 4-2, but this time the parent is using the sophisticated equity method. Because of this fact, the parent has to prepare a subsidiary income distribution schedule before it can record its share of subsidiary income. This schedule is shown below. Note that instead of recording *on its books* a subsidiary income of $60,000, the parent would have recorded $53,600:

Equity Income: Subsidiary Company S

Unrealized profit in ending inventory	$8,000	Internally generated net income		$75,000
		Adjusted income		$67,000
		Controlling share		80%
		Controlling interest		$53,600*

*This is the same amount that is shown in the parent's income distribution schedule for Worksheet 4-2.

The only elimination procedure in this example that differs from Worksheet 4-2 is step (1), which eliminates the entry made by the parent to record its share of the subsidiary current period income. There is no impact on the other worksheet procedures, and the balance of Worksheet 4-2 would be unchanged. A portion of the revised worksheet is shown on page 233.

UNREALIZED PROFITS OF CURRENT AND PRIOR PERIODS

The effect of the sophisticated equity method when there are intercompany profits from current and prior periods is demonstrated in the following example, which is based on the information given in Worksheet 4-3. The subsidiary income reported by the parent in 19X2 under the sophisticated equity method is calculated as follows:

Equity Income: Subsidiary Company S

Unrealized profit in ending inventory	$6,000	Internally generated net income		$60,000
		Realized profit in beginning inventory		$ 8,000
		Adjusted income		$62,000
		Controlling share		80%
		Controlling interest		$49,600

The elimination procedures illustrated in the following partial worksheet are applicable to all types of subsidiary-generated intercompany profits and losses of prior and current periods. The differences in the parent's trial balance are explained in the notes that follow the partial worksheet on page 234.

When the sophisticated equity method is used, the worksheet elimination of the parent's investment account against the stockholders' equity of the subsid-

(Credit balance amounts are in parentheses.)	Trial Balance		Eliminations & Adjustments	
	Company P	Company S	Dr.	Cr.
Accounts Receivable	110,000	150,000		(5) 25,000
Inventory, Dec. 31, 19X1	70,000	40,000		(4) 8,000
Investment in Company S	(b) 189,600			(1) 53,600
				(2) 136,000
Other Assets	314,000	155,000		
Accounts Payable	(80,000)	(100,000)	(5) 25,000	
Common Stock ($10 par), Co. P	(200,000)			
Retained Earnings, Jan. 1, 19X1, Co. P	(250,000)			
Common Stock ($10 par), Co. S		(100,000)	(2) 80,000	
Retained Earnings, Jan. 1, 19X1, Co. S		(70,000)	(2) 56,000	
Sales	(700,000)	(500,000)	(3) 100,000	
Cost of Goods Sold	510,000	350,000	(4) 8,000	(3) 100,000
Expenses	90,000	75,000		
Subsidiary Income	(a) (53,600)		(1) 53,600	
	0	0	322,600	322,600

Company P and Subsidiary Company S
Partial Worksheet
For Year Ended December 31, 19X1

Notes to Trial Balance:
(a)   See the previously prepared distribution schedule.
(b) $136,000 beginning-of-year balance + $53,600 sophisticated equity method income

Eliminations and Adjustments:
(1)   Eliminate the entry recording the parent's share (80%) of the subsidiary net income under the sophisticated equity method.
(2-5)   Same as Worksheet 4-2.

iary is more complicated because there is an inconsistency between the parent's accounts and those of the subsidiary. In the partial worksheet illustrated, the parent's investment and retained earnings accounts do not reflect the $8,000 beginning inventory profit recorded by the subsidiary. The intercompany profit was removed in the prior period before the parent's share of the subsidiary's net income was recorded. The subsidiary's trial balance does include the $8,000 beginning inventory profit in the January 1 retained earnings balance, and the parent's beginning inventory, now in the cost of goods sold, does include the profit. The inconsistency is removed on the worksheet by making an adjustment, coded "Adj," that removes the intercompany profit from the subsidiary's begin-

Company P and Subsidiary Company S
Partial Worksheet
For Year Ended December 31, 19X2

(Credit balance amounts are in parentheses.)	Trial Balance		Eliminations & Adjustments	
	Company P	Company S	Dr.	Cr.
Accounts Receivable	160,000	170,000		(6) 60,000
Inventory, Dec. 31, 19X2	60,000	50,000		(5) 6,000
Investment in Company S	(c) 239,200			(1) 49,600
				(2) 189,600
Other Assets	354,000	165,000		
Accounts Payable	(90,000)	(80,000)	(6) 60,000	
Common Stock ($10 par), Co. P	(200,000)			
Retained Earnings, Jan. 1, 19X2, Co. P	**(b) (403,600)**			
Common Stock ($10 par), Co. S		(100,000)	(2) 80,000	
Retained Earnings, Jan. 1, 19X2, Co. S		(145,000)	(Adj) 8,000	
			(2) 109,600	
Sales	(800,000)	(600,000)	(4) 120,000	
Cost of Goods Sold	610,000	440,000	(5) 6,000	(Adj) 8,000
				(4) 120,000
Expenses	120,000	100,000		
Subsidiary Income	**(a) (49,600)**		**(1) 49,600**	
	0	0	433,200	433,200

Notes to Trial Balance:
(a)   See the previously prepared distribution schedule.
(b) $410,000 simple equity balance – (80% × $8,000 subsidiary beginning inventory profit).
(c) $136,000 original balance + $53,600 sophisticated equity method income for 19X1 + $49,600 sophisticated equity method income for 19X2.

Eliminations and Adjustments:
(Adj)   Eliminate the $8,000 beginning inventory profit from the cost of goods sold and the subsidiary beginning retained earnings accounts. This step replaces step (3) of Worksheet 4-3.
(1)   Eliminate the entry recording the parent's share (80%) of the subsidiary net income under the sophisticated equity method.
(2)   Eliminate 80% of the subsidiary equity balances against the investment account. The elimination of Retained Earnings is 80% of the adjusted balance of $137,000 ($145,000 – $8,000).
(4-6)   Same as Worksheet 4-3.

ning retained earnings and the parent's beginning inventory. This step replaces step (3) in Worksheet 4-3.

Step (1) of the partial worksheet removes the subsidiary income as recorded by the parent. Step (2) reflects the adjustment of the subsidiary's Retained Earnings. The remaining steps and worksheet procedures are identical to those in Worksheet 4-3.

APPENDIX: INTERCOMPANY PROFIT ELIMINATIONS ON THE VERTICAL WORKSHEET

In keeping with the overall worksheet format approach of this text, all previous examples in this chapter have been presented using the horizontal worksheet style. Worksheet 4-9, pages 282–285, provides the reader an opportunity to study the vertical worksheet when intercompany merchandise and plant asset transactions are involved. This worksheet is based on the following facts:

1. Company P purchased an 80% interest in Company S on January 1, 19X1. At that time, the following determination and distribution of excess schedule was prepared:

Price paid		$500,000
Less interest acquired:		
Common stock ($5 par)	$200,000	
Retained earnings, January 1, 19X1	350,000	
Total stockholders' equity	$550,000	
Interest acquired	80%	440,000
Excess of cost over book value attributed to goodwill		
(40-year life)		$ 60,000

2. Company P accounts for the investment under the simple equity method.
3. Company S sells merchandise to Company P at cost plus 25%. Sales totaled $150,000 during 19X2. There were $40,000 of such goods in Company P's beginning inventory and $50,000 of such goods in Company P's ending inventory. As of December 31, 19X2, Company P had not paid the $20,000 owed for the purchases.
4. On July 1, 19X1, Company P sold a new machine that cost $20,000 to Company S for $25,000. At that time, both companies believed that the machine had a 5-year remaining life; both companies use straight-line depreciation.
5. Company S declared and paid $20,000 in dividends during 19X2.

Notice that the eliminations in Worksheet 4-9 are identical to those required for the horizontal format. Also, when working with the vertical format, keep in mind the cautions that are stated in Appendix A of Chapter 3: (1) the nominal accounts are presented above the balance sheet accounts, and (2) the eliminations are made only to the *beginning* retained earnings accounts. The carrydown procedures for the vertical worksheet are the same as those presented in this appendix.

QUESTIONS

1. What types of intercompany transactions may result in a profit's being recorded by a parent or subsidiary? What is the basic theoretical approach to recognizing such profits?

2. A subsidiary sold merchandise, which cost $40,000, to the parent firm at cost plus 25%. A perpetual inventory system is used. The parent, during the same period, sold three-fourths of the merchandise. What adjustments will be needed as a result of these transactions when consolidating?

3. Explain why the intercompany sale of merchandise has an influence on the distribution of combined net income, even though the sale is eliminated on the consolidated statements.

4. A parent company sold to its subsidiary merchandise costing $80,000 for $100,000. Half of the goods were unsold at year end and had been written down to $45,000, the lower market value. What adjusting entries are required in the consolidation process assuming the use of a perpetual inventory system and that a separate account is used for the loss?

5. Provide the worksheet entries needed to delete the unrealized profit on intercompany sales from beginning and ending inventories for the following situations assuming the parent has a 90%-ownership interest in the subsidiary:

   (a) Subsidiary's beginning inventory includes $20,000 of goods purchased from the parent company. Parent sells all merchandise at a 25% markup on cost. Subsidiary purchased goods at a price of $150,000 from parent during the year and had $45,000 of the goods in ending inventory.

   (b) Parent's beginning inventory includes $36,000 of goods purchased from the subsidiary company. Subsidiary sells all merchandise at a 20% markup on cost. Parent purchased goods at a price of $280,000 from subsidiary during the year and had $25,000 of the goods in ending inventory.

6. How does the recognition of the deferred gain on the intercompany sale of a depreciable asset at a profit differ from the recognition of the deferred gain on an intercompany land sale?

7. Under what circumstances is a loss on the intercompany sale of a depreciable fixed asset deferred, and what are the procedures for its deferment?

8. Prepare parent and subsidiary income distribution schedules and enter each of the following items in the correct column: (a) intercompany profit on unsold ending inventory—parent seller; (b) realized intercompany profit on beginning inventory—subsidiary seller; (c) internally generated net income of parent; (d) internally generated net income of subsidiary; (e) unrealized gain on intercompany sale of depreciable asset—subsidiary seller; (f) gain on intercompany sale of depreciable asset realized through use—subsidiary seller; (g) realized intercompany profit on beginning inventory—parent seller; and (h) retirement loss on bonds—bonds issued by subsidiary, purchased by parent.

9. Hiller Construction Company is a 90%-owned subsidiary of Chain O'Lakes Properties Inc. Hiller is building an office complex for Chain O'Lakes and is accounting for the contract under the percentage-of-completion method. To date, Hiller has billed

CGS   45M—(45÷1.25)   9000

     Inv   9000

but not collected $1,450,000, recorded costs of $1,200,000, and recorded earned income of $250,000.

No adjustments or eliminations were made concerning this transaction in the process of preparing the consolidated statements. What misstatements can be found on the consolidated income statement and balance sheet?

10. Frequently, related firms will have outstanding intercompany loan balances. What effect do intercompany interest revenue and expense have on the consolidation process, including the distribution of combined net income?

RE   20 M - (20M ÷ 1.25)   4000

C6S   4000

EXERCISES

Exercise 1. Sandborn Company is a wholly owned subsidiary of Malcom Enterprises. Sandborn is a just-in-time supplier of goods to Malcom and thus, Sandborn maintains no inventories. Sandborn consistently sells to Malcom to realize a gross profit of 25%. Sandborn supplies goods only to Malcom. Sales for the past three years were:

	Sandborn	Malcom
19X1	$250,000	$350,000
19X2	300,000	400,000
19X3	420,000	475,000

All goods sold by Malcom are purchases from Sandborn. Malcom's inventory and purchases information is:

Year	Beginning Inventory	Purchases	Ending Inventory
19X1	$ 0	$250,000	$25,000
19X2	25,000	300,000	60,000
19X3	60,000	420,000	84,000

19X1 was the first year of operations for both firms.

Prepare schedules covering 19X1 through 19X3 that calculate for each year:
(1) The gross profit recorded by the Sandborn Company.
(2) The gross profit recorded by Malcom Enterprises as a separate entity.
(3) The gross profit to be reported by the consolidated firm.

Exercise 2. Gander Corporation is a wholly owned subsidiary of Mountain Company. During 19X1, Gander sold all of its production to Mountain Company for $400,000, a price that includes a 20% gross profit. 19X1 is the first year that such intercompany sales were made. By year end, Mountain sold 80% of the goods it had purchased at a markup on cost of 25%. The balance of the intercompany goods, $80,000, remained in the ending inventory and were adjusted to a lower market value $70,000. The adjustment was a charge to the cost of goods sold.
(1) Determine the gross profit on sales recorded by both Gander and Mountain companies.
(2) Determine the gross profit to be shown on the consolidated income statement.

Exercise 3. Nutone Company is a 80%-owned subsidiary of Volks Corporation. The separate income statements of the two firms for 19X6 are as follows:

RE Min.   600
RE Con. I.t   5400
C6S   10000
C6S 25m - (25 ÷ 1.20)   4167
Inv.   4167

	Volks Corp.	Nutone Co.
Sales..	$210,000	$120,000
Cost of goods sold	(150,000)	(90,000)
Gross profit......................................	$ 60,000	$ 30,000
Other expenses	(40,000)	(12,000)
Other income	5,000	
Operating income	$ 25,000	$ 18,000
Subsidiary income	14,400	
Net income......................................	$ 39,400	$ 18,000

The following facts apply to 19X6:
(a) Nutone Company sold $60,000 of goods to Volks Corporation. The gross profits on sales to Volks and to unrelated firms are equal and have not changed from the previous years.
(b) Volks Corporation held $10,000 of the goods purchased from Nutone Company in its beginning inventory and $20,000 of such goods in ending inventory.
(c) Volks Corporation billed Nutone Company $5,000 for consulting services. The charge was expensed by Nutone Company and treated as other income by Volks Corporation.

Prepare the consolidated income statement for 19X6, including the distribution of the combined net income to the controlling and minority interests. The supporting income distribution schedules should be prepared as well.

Exercise 4. On January 1, 19X2, Furey Company sold a machine to Bardon Company for $20,000. The machine had an original cost of $24,000, and depreciation on the asset had accumulated to $9,000 at the time of the sale. The machine has a 5-year remaining life and will be depreciated on a straight-line basis with no salvage value. Bardon Company is an 80%-owned subsidiary of Furey Company.
(1) Explain the adjustments that would have to be made to arrive at combined net income for the years 19X2 through 19X6 as a result of this sale.
(2) Prepare the elimination that would be required on the December 31, 19X3 consolidated worksheet as a result of this sale.
(3) Assuming Bardon Company was the seller of the machine and all the other facts remained constant, prepare the elimination that would be required on the December 31, 19X3 consolidated worksheet as a result of this sale.

Exercise 5. Wavemasters Inc. owns an 80% interest in Sayner Development Co. In a prior period, Sayner Development purchased a parcel of land for $50,000 which it will now develop and sell to the parent company, Wavemasters Inc. Sayner agreed to sell the land for $100,000 and constructed a building on the land during 19X1 at a cost of $500,000. The building was sold to Wavemasters at the very end of 19X1 for $600,000. It is estimated that the building has a 40-year life with no salvage value.
(1) Prepare all worksheet eliminations that would be made on the 19X1 consolidated worksheet as a result of the real estate sales.
(2) Prepare all worksheet eliminations that would be made on the **19X3** consolidated worksheet as a result of the 19X1 real estate sale.

Exercise 6. Hilton Corporation sold a press to its 80%-owned subsidiary, Agri Fab Inc., for $5,000 on January 1, 19X2. The press originally was purchased by Hilton on January 1,

19X1, for $20,000, and $6,000 of depreciation for 19X1 had been recorded. The fair market value of the press on January 1, 19X2, was $10,000. Agri Fab proceeded to depreciate the press on a straight-line basis, using a 5-year life and no salvage value. On December 31, 19X3, Agri Fab, having no further need for the machine, sold it for $2,000 and recorded a loss on the sale.

Explain the adjustments that would have to be made to the separate income statements of the two firms to arrive at the consolidated income statements for 19X2 and 19X3.

Exercise 7. Janis Company contracted with its 80%-owned subsidiary, Essuman Equipment Company, for the construction of two stamping machines. The first machine was completed and put into operation on July 1, 19X9. It cost Essuman $60,000 and has a 5-year estimated life with no salvage value. The contract price was $75,000. The machine is being depreciated on a straight-line basis. The second machine, with an estimated total cost of $90,000 and a contract price of $120,000, was 80% complete on December 31, 19X9. To date, costs on the second contract total $72,000. By the statement date, Janis had completely paid for the first machine and still owed $3,000 of the $60,000 billed to date on the second machine. Essuman uses the completed contract method to account for its long-term construction contracts.

(1) Prepare the necessary eliminations for the consolidated worksheet on December 31, 19X9.

(2) What are the effects of these contracts on the income distribution schedules?

Exercise 8. Donner Contractors, an 80%-owned subsidiary, is constructing a warehouse for its parent, Fast-Parts Corporation. The following information is available at December 31, 19X5:

Percent of completion	60%
Costs incurred to date	$120,000
Estimated costs to complete	80,000
Contract price	240,000
Amount billed to date (no amounts collected) . . .	135,000

Donner uses the percentage-of-completion method to account for its long-term contracts.

Record the journal entries that each of the two firms would have made relative to the construction. Prepare a partial trial balance using the data from your entries, and show the eliminations relating to the contract for the December 31, 19X5 consolidated worksheet.

Exercise 9. The separate income statements of Diggem Construction Company and its 90%-owned subsidiary, Blastem Demolition Inc., for the year ended December 31, 19X6, are as follows:

	Diggem Co.	Blastem Inc.
Sales.	$700,000	$280,000
Cost of goods sold.	(450,000)	(190,000)
Gross profit.	$250,000	$ 90,000
Other expenses	(180,000)	(70,000)
Other income	70,000	20,000
Operating income	$140,000	$ 40,000
Subsidiary income.	36,000	
Net income	$176,000	$ 40,000

The following additional facts apply:

(a) On January 1, 19X5, Blastem Demolition purchased a building, with a book value of $100,000 and an estimated 25-year life, from Diggem Construction for $150,000. The building was being depreciated on a straight-line basis with no salvage value. On December 31, 19X6, Blastem Demolition sold the building to the nonaffiliated Grant Company for $160,000.

(b) On January 1, 19X6, Blastem Demolition sold a machine with a book value of $50,000 to Diggem Construction for $60,000. The machine had an expected life of 5 years and is being depreciated on a straight-line basis with no salvage value.

Prepare the December 31, 19X6 consolidated income statement and supporting income distribution schedules.

Exercise 10. Edmund Company has consistently sold merchandise to its 80%-owned subsidiary, Temple Inc., at cost plus 25%. Edmund sales to Temple were $80,000 during 19X4. Temple had Edmund goods in its beginning and ending inventories for which it was invoiced $10,000 and $6,000, respectively. However, the ending inventory was adjusted to $4,000 using the lower-of-cost or market method.

On January 1, 19X2, Temple sold an unused machine with a net book value of $8,000 to Edmund for $10,000. Edmund Company used 5-year straight-line depreciation with no salvage value. Edmund sold the machine for $4,600 on December 31, 19X4.

Prepare the worksheet elimination entries with the accompanying explanations needed for the December 31, 19X4 consolidated trial balance worksheet. Assume the use of the perpetual inventory method.

Exercise 11. Saratoga Company owns 80% of the outstanding common stock of Windsor Company. On May 1, 19X3, Windsor Company arranged a 1-year, $50,000 loan from Saratoga Company. The loan agreement specified that interest would accrue at the rate of 6% per annum and that all interest would be paid on the maturity date of the loan. The financial reporting period ends on December 31, 19X3, and the note originating from the loan remains outstanding.

(1) Prepare the entries that both firms would have made on their separate books including the accrual of interest.

(2) Prepare the eliminations, in entry form, that would be made on a consolidated worksheet prepared as of December 31, 19X3.

Exercise 12. Assume the same facts as in Exercise 11 but, in addition, assume that Saratoga was itself in need of cash. It discounted the note received from Windsor at the First Bank on July 1, 19X3, at a discount rate of 8% per annum.

(1) Prepare the entries that both firms would make on their separate books including interest accruals.

(2) Prepare the eliminations, in entry form, that would be made on a consolidated worksheet prepared as of December 31, 19X3.

PROBLEMS

Problem 4-1. On January 1, 19X6, 100% of the outstanding stock of Sampson Company was purchased by Perlberg Corp. for $3,000,000. At that time, the fair market value and book value of Sampson's net assets both equaled $2,800,000. The excess is being amortized as goodwill over a 20-year period.

The following trial balances of Perlberg Corp. and Sampson Company were prepared on December 31, 19X6:

	Perlberg Corp.	Sampson Co.
Cash	1,010,000	170,000
Accounts Receivable	425,000	365,000
Inventory	600,000	275,000
Property, Plant, and Equipment (net)	4,000,000	2,300,000
Investment in Sampson Co.	3,210,000	
Accounts Payable	(35,000)	(100,000)
Common Stock ($10 par)	(1,000,000)	(400,000)
Paid-In Capital in Excess of Par	(1,500,000)	(200,000)
Retained Earnings 1/1/X6	(5,500,000)	(2,200,000)
Sales	(12,000,000)	(1,000,000)
Cost of Goods Sold	7,000,000	750,000
Other Expenses	4,000,000	40,000
Subsidiary Income	(210,000)	
Total	0	0

Throughout 19X6, sales to Perlberg Corp. made up 40% of Sampson's revenue and produced a 20% gross profit rate. At year end, Perlberg Corp. had sold 90% of the goods purchased from Sampson Company and still owed Sampson $25,000. None of the Sampson products were in Perlberg's January 1, 19X6 beginning inventory.

Required:
Prepare the worksheet necessary to produce the consolidated income statement and balance sheet of Perlberg Corp. and its subsidiary for the year ended December 31, 19X6. Include the determination and distribution of excess schedule.

Problem 4-2. On April 1, 19X1, Mooney Corporation purchased 80% of the outstanding stock of Tripper Company for $425,000. A condensed balance sheet of Tripper Company at the purchase date follows:

Assets		Liabilities and Equity	
Current assets	$180,000	Liabilities	$100,000
Long-lived assets (net)	320,000	Equity	400,000
Total assets	$500,000	Total liabilities and equity	$500,000

All book values approximated market values on the purchase date. Mooney Corporation amortizes its intangibles over 20 years or their legal life, whichever is shorter.

The following information has been gathered pertaining to the first two years of operation since Mooney's purchase of Tripper Company stock:

(a) Intercompany merchandise sales are summarized as follows:

Date	Transaction	Sales	Gross Profit	Merchandise Remaining in Purchaser's Ending Inventory
April 1, 19X1 to	Mooney to Tripper	$35,000	15%	$9,000
March 31, 19X2	Tripper to Mooney	20,000	20	3,500
April 1, 19X2 to	Mooney to Tripper	32,000	22	6,000
March 31, 19X3	Tripper to Mooney	30,000	25	3,000

(b) On March 31, 19X3, Mooney owed Tripper $10,000, and Tripper owed Mooney $5,000 as a result of the intercompany sales.

(c) Mooney paid $25,000 in cash dividends on March 20, 19X2 and 19X3. Tripper paid its first cash dividend on March 10, 19X3, giving each share of outstanding common stock a $0.15 cash dividend.

(d) The trial balances of the two companies as of March 31, 19X3, follow:

	Mooney Corporation	Tripper Company
Cash	216,200	44,300
Accounts Receivable (net)	290,000	97,000
Inventory	310,000	80,000
Investment in Tripper Company	425,000	
Land	1,081,000	150,000
Building and Equipment.	1,850,000	400,000
Accumulated Depreciation.	(940,000)	(210,000)
Intangibles (net)	60,000	
Accounts Payable.	(242,200)	(106,300)
Bonds Payable	(400,000)	
Common Stock ($.50 par).	(250,000)	
Common Stock ($1 par)		(200,000)
Paid-In Capital in Excess of Par	(1,250,000)	(100,000)
Retained Earnings, April 1, 19X2.	(1,105,000)	(140,000)
Sales.	(880,000)	(630,000)
Dividend Income (from Tripper Company)	(24,000)	
Cost of Goods Sold	704,000	504,000
Other Expenses	130,000	81,000
Dividends Declared	25,000	30,000
Total	0	0

Required:

(1) Prepare the worksheet necessary to produce the consolidated financial statements of Mooney Corporation and its subsidiary for the year ended March 31, 19X3. Include the determination and distribution of excess schedule and the income distribution schedules.

(2) Prepare the formal consolidated income statement for the fiscal year 19X2–19X3.

Problem 4-3. Muskegon Corporation purchased 80% of the common stock of Shannon Ltd. on Jan. 1, 19X1, for $600,000 in order to ensure its raw material supply would be consistently available. At the time of the purchase, Shannon's net assets had a market value equal to the book value of $600,000. Also at that time, the Shannon retained earnings account had a balance of $300,000. Muskegon amortizes its intangible assets over 10 years.

Since the acquisition, 60% of Shannon's sales have been to the Muskegon Corporation. Muskegon's ending inventories on December 31, 19X1 and 19X2 contained $127,000 and $163,000, respectively, in goods purchased from Shannon. Shannon has maintained a 33¹/₃% markup on cost. At the end of 19X1 and 19X2 Muskegon's Accounts Payable contained $36,000 and $43,000, respectively, in liabilities to Shannon for purchases of goods.

The December 31, 19X2 total inventories were $750,000 for Muskegon and $100,000 for Shannon. The firms use the periodic inventory method.

Trial balances as of December 31, 19X2, are as follows:

	Muskegon Corporation	Shannon Ltd.
Cash	275,000	60,000
Accounts Receivable (net)	575,000	65,000
Inventory, Jan. 1, 19X2	720,000	90,000
Investment in Shannon Ltd	600,000	
Land	100,000	30,000
Building and Equipment (net)	1,200,000	650,000
Accounts Payable	(280,000)	(72,500)
Bonds Payable, 10%, due Jan. 1, 19X8		(100,000)
Common Stock ($15 par)	(510,000)	(180,000)
Paid-In Capital in Excess of Par	(100,000)	(120,000)
Retained Earnings, Jan. 1, 19X2	(1,750,000)	(375,140)
Sales	(3,450,000)	(750,000)
Purchases	2,100,000	572,640
Selling and General Expenses	420,000	120,000
Interest Expense		10,000
Dividends Declared	100,000	
Total	0	0

Required:

(1) Prepare the worksheet necessary to produce the consolidated financial statements of Muskegon Corporation and its subsidiary for the year ended December 31, 19X2. Include the determination and distribution of excess schedule and the income distribution schedules.

(2) Prepare the formal consolidated financial statements, including the income statement, retained earnings statement, and balance sheet.

Problem 4-4. On January 1, 19X3, Stephen Corporation exchanged on a one-for-three basis common stock it held in its treasury for 80% of the outstanding stock of James Company. Stephen Corporation common stock had a market price of $40 per share on the exchange date.

On the date of the acquisition, the stockholders' equity section of James Company was as follows:

Common stock ($5 par)	$ 450,000
Paid-in capital in excess of par	180,000
Retained earnings	370,000
Total	$1,000,000

Also on that date, James Company's book values approximated market values, except for the land, which was undervalued by $75,000. Any goodwill recognized from the acquisition is being amortized over 40 years.

Information regarding intercompany transactions for 19X5 follows:

(a) Stephen Corporation sells merchandise to James Company, realizing a 30% gross profit. Sales during 19X5 were $140,000. James had $25,000 of the 19X4 purchases in its beginning inventory for 19X5 and $35,000 of the 19X5 purchases in its ending inventory for 19X5.

(b) James signed a 12%, 4-month, $10,000 note to Stephen in order to cover the remaining balance of its payables on November 1, 19X5. No new merchandise was purchased after this date.

(c) James wrote down to $28,000 the merchandise purchased from Stephen Corporation and remaining in its 19X5 ending inventory.

The trial balances of Stephen Corporation and James Company as of December 31, 19X5, are as follows:

	Stephen Corp.	James Co.
Cash	140,000	205,200
Accounts Receivable	285,000	110,000
Interest Receivable....................................	1,500	
Notes Receivable	50,000	
Inventory	470,000	160,000
Land	350,000	300,000
Property, Plant, and Equipment........................	1,110,000	810,000
Accumulated Depreciation.............................	(500,000)	(200,000)
Intangibles..	60,000	
Investment in James Company	1,128,000	
Accounts Payable....................................	(611,500)	(175,000)
Interest Payable		(200)
Common Stock ($1 par)	(400,000)	
Common Stock ($5 par)		(450,000)
Paid-In Capital in Excess of Par	(1,235,000)	(180,000)
Retained Earnings 1/1/X5.............................	(958,500)	(470,000)
Treasury Stock (at cost)...............................	315,000	
Sales..	(1,020,000)	(500,000)
Interest Income......................................	(1,500)	
Subsidiary Income...................................	(88,000)	
Cost of Goods Sold	705,000	300,000
Other Expenses	200,000	90,000
Total	0	0

Required:

Prepare the worksheet necessary to produce the consolidated financial statements of Stephen Corp. and its subsidiary for the year ended December 31, 19X5. Include the determination and distribution of excess schedule and the income distribution schedules.

Problem 4-5. On September 1, 19X1, Glen Corporation purchased 80% of the outstanding common stock of Symba Corporation for $152,000. On that date, Symba's net book values equaled market values and there was no excess of cost or book value resulting from the purchase. Glen has been maintaining its investment under the simple equity method.

Over the next three years, the intercompany transactions between the firms were as follows:

(a) On December 1, 19X1, Symba sold its four-year-old delivery truck to Glen for $12,200 *upstream →* in cash. At that time, Symba had depreciated the truck, which had cost $15,000, to its $5,000 salvage value. Glen estimated on the date of the sale that the asset had a remaining useful life of 3 years and an estimated salvage value of $200.

(b) On March 1, 19X3, Glen sold a building to Symba for $103,000. Glen originally paid $80,000 for the building and planned to depreciate it over 20 years, assuming a *downstream →* $10,000 salvage value. However, Glen had the property for only 10 years and carried it at a net book value of $45,000 on the sale date. Symba will use the building for 10 years, at which time Symba expects to sell the asset for $13,000.

Both companies use straight-line depreciation for all assets. One-half year's depreciation is taken for all assets in the year they are purchased and in the year they are sold.

Trial balances of Glen Corporation and Symba Corporation as of the August 31, 19X3 year end are as follows:

	Glen Corporation	Symba Corporation
Cash	120,000	50,000
Accounts Receivable (net)	115,000	18,000
Notes Receivable	10,000	
Inventory	175,000	34,000
Investment in Symba Corporation	217,440	
Plant and Equipment.	990,700	295,000
Accumulated Depreciation.	(175,000)	(85,000)
Other Assets	28,000	
Accounts Payable.	(80,000)	(50,200)
Notes Payable.	(25,000)	
Bonds Payable, 12%	(300,000)	
Common Stock ($10 par)	(290,000)	(70,000)
Paid-In Capital in Excess of Par	(110,000)	(62,000)
Retained Earnings, Sept. 1, 19X2	(498,850)	(118,000)
Sales.	(920,000)	(240,000)
Cost of Goods Sold	598,000	132,000
Selling and General Expenses.	108,000	80,000
Investment Income	(23,040)	
Interest Income.		(800)
Interest Expense.	37,750	
Gain on Sale of Building.	(58,000)	
Dividends Declared	90,000	7,000
Total	0	0

Required:

Prepare the worksheet necessary to produce the consolidated financial statements of Glen Corporation and its subsidiary for the year ended August 31, 19X3. Include the income distribution schedules.

Problem 4-6. Pardon Inc. purchased 100% of the common stock of Slarno Corporation for $150,000 in cash on June 30, 19X6. At that date, Slarno's stockholders' equity was as follows:

Common stock ($1 par)	$100,000
Retained earnings.	50,000
Total.	$150,000

The fair market values of the assets and liabilities did not differ materially from their book values. Slarno has made no adjustments on its books to reflect the purchase by Pardon. On December 31, 19X6, Pardon and Slarno prepared consolidated financial statements.

The transactions that occurred between Pardon and Slarno during the next year included the following:

(a) On January 3, 19X7, land with a $10,000 book value was sold by Pardon to Slarno for $15,000. Slarno made a $3,000 down payment and signed an 8% mortgage note, payable in 12 equal quarterly payments of $1,135, including interest, beginning March 31, 19X7.

(b) Slarno produced equipment for Pardon under two separate contracts. The first contract, which was for office equipment, was begun and completed during the year at a cost to Slarno of $17,500. Pardon paid $22,000 in cash for the equipment on April 17, 19X7. The second contract was begun on February 15, 19X7, but will not be completed until May, 19X8. Slarno has incurred $45,000 of costs as of December 31, 19X7, and anticipates an additional $30,000 of costs to complete the $95,000 contract. Slarno accounts for all contracts under the percentage-of-completion method. Pardon has made no account on its books for this uncompleted contract as of December 31, 19X7.

(c) Pardon depreciates all of its equipment over a 10-year estimated economic life, with no salvage value. Pardon takes a half-year's depreciation in the year of purchase.

(d) Pardon sells merchandise to Slarno at an average markup of 12% on cost. During the year, Pardon charged Slarno $238,000 for merchandise purchased, of which Slarno paid $211,000. Slarno has $11,200 of this merchandise on hand on December 31, 19X7.

Trial balances of Pardon Inc. and its subsidiary as of December 31, 19X7, are as follows:

	Pardon Inc.	Slarno Corp.
Cash	45,000	31,211
Accounts Receivable	119,000	73,500
Billings on Construction in Progress		(1,201,900)
Mortgage Receivable	8,311	
Unsecured Notes Receivable	18,000	
Inventories	217,000	117,500
Land	34,000	42,000
Building and Equipment (net)	717,000	408,000
Investment in Slarno Corporation	150,000	
Accounts Payable	(203,000)	(147,000)
Mortgages Payable	(592,000)	(397,311)
Common Stock	(250,000)	(100,000)
Retained Earnings, Jan. 1, 19X7	(139,311)	(70,000)
Sales	(1,800,000)	
Earned Income on Long-Term Contracts		(437,000)
Cost of Goods Sold	1,155,000	
Construction in Progress		1,289,000
Selling, General, and Administrative Expenses	497,000	360,000
Interest Income	(20,000)	
Interest Expense	49,000	32,000
Gain on Sale of Land	(5,000)	
Total	0	0

Required:

Prepare the worksheet necessary to produce the consolidated financial statements of Pardon Inc. and its subsidiary for the year ended December 31, 19X7. Assume both companies have made all of the adjusting entries required for separate financial statements, unless an obvious discrepancy exists. Include the determination and distribution of excess schedule.

Problem 4-7. The December 31, 19X6 trial balances of the Paul Corporation and its 90%-owned subsidiary Sara Corporation are as follows:

	Paul Corp.	Sara Corp.
Cash	75,000	45,500
Accounts and Other Current Receivables	410,900	170,000
Inventory	920,000	739,400
Property, Plant, and Equipment (net)	1,000,000	400,000
Investment in Sara Corp.	1,200,000	
Accounts Payable and Other Current Liabilities	(140,000)	(305,900)
Common Stock ($10 par)	(500,000)	
Common Stock ($10 par)		(200,000)
Retained Earnings 1/1/X5	(2,800,000)	(650,000)
Dividends Declared		1,000
Sales	(2,000,000)	(650,000)
Dividend Income	(900)	
Interest Expense		5,000
Interest Income	(5,000)	
Cost of Goods Sold	1,500,000	400,000
Other Expenses	340,000	45,000
Totals	0	0

Paul's investment in Sara was purchased for $1,200,000 in cash on January 1, 19X5, and is accounted for by the cost method. On January 1, 19X5, Sara had the following equity balances:

Common stock	$200,000
Retained earnings	600,000
	$800,000

Paul's excess of cost over book value on Sara's investment has been identified appropriately as goodwill and is to be amortized over 10 years.

Sara borrowed $100,000 from Paul on June 30, 19X6, with the note maturing on June 30, 19X7, at 10% interest. Correct accruals have been recorded by both companies.

During 19X6, Paul sold merchandise to Sara at an aggregate invoice price of $300,000, which included a profit of $60,000. As of December 31, 19X6, Sara had not paid Paul for $90,000 of these purchases, and 10% of the total merchandise purchased from Paul still remained in Sara's inventory.

Sara declared a $1,000 cash dividend in December 19X6 payable in January 19X7.

Required:
Prepare the worksheet required to produce the consolidated statements of Paul Corporation and its subsidiary Sara Corporation for the year ending December 31, 19X6. Include the determination and distribution of excess schedule and the income distribution schedule.

Problem 4-8. The following trial balances were prepared after completion of the examination of the December 31, 19X4 financial statements of Presidential Corporation and its subsidiaries, Sublenee Corporation and Submariner Corporation. The subsidiary investments are accounted for by the cost method.

	Presidential Corp.	Sublenee Corp.	Submariner Corp.
Cash	73,000	21,000	47,000
Accounts Receivable	104,000	31,000	123,000
Inventory	241,000	70,000	78,000
Investments (other)	185,000		
Property, Plant, and Equipment..........	375,000	58,000	99,000
Accumulated Depreciation..............	(96,000)	(7,000)	(21,000)
Investment in Sublenee Corp	150,000		
Investment in Submariner Corp	184,000		
Accounts Payable.....................	(46,000)	(33,000)	(24,000)
Common Stock ($20 par)	(500,000)		
Common Stock ($20 par)		(200,000)	
Common Stock ($20 par)			(100,000)
Retained Earnings	(563,000)		(22,000)
Sales................................	(960,000)	(275,000)	(570,000)
Cost of Goods Sold	820,000	300,000	350,000
Other Expenses	60,000	35,000	40,000
Dividend Income	(18,000)		
Gain on Sale of Assets	(9,000)		
Total	0	0	0

The audit working papers provided the following additional information:

(a) Sublenee Corporation was formed by Presidential Corporation on January 1, 19X4. To secure additional capital, 25% of the common stock of Sublenee was sold at par value in the securities market. Presidential Corporation purchased the remaining stock at par for cash.

(b) On July 1, 19X4, Presidential acquired from stockholders 4,000 shares of Submariner Corporation common stock for $184,000. Any excess paid was attributed to goodwill and is being amortized over a 10-year period. A condensed trial balance of Submariner Corporation at July 1, 19X4, was as follows:

Current Assets	165,000
Property, Plant, and Equipment (net)............	60,000
Current Liabilities............................	(45,000)
Common Stock ($20 par)......................	(100,000)
Retained Earnings	(36,000)
Sales.......................................	(200,000)
Cost of Goods Sold...........................	140,000
Operating Expenses	16,000
Total	0

(c) The following intercompany product sales were made in 19X4:

	Sales	Gross Profit on Sales	Included in Purchaser's Inventory on 12/31/X4 at LCM
Presidential to Submariner	$ 50,000	30%	$20,000
Sublenee to Submariner	35,000	20%	15,000
Submariner to Presidential	60,000	30%	20,000
	$145,000		$55,000

In valuing Presidential Corporation's inventory at the lower-of-cost-or-market, the portion of the inventory purchased from Submariner Corporation was written down by $2,000.

(d) On January 2, 19X4, Presidential Corporation sold a punch press to Sublenee Corporation. The machine originally was purchased on January 1, 19X2, and was being depreciated by the straight-line method over a 10-year life (8 years remaining). Sublenee Corporation planned to compute depreciation by the same method based on the remaining useful life of the press. Details of the intercompany sale are as follows:

Sales price		$29,000
Less book value of the press:		
Cost of the press.	$30,000	
Accumulated depreciation	(6,000)	24,000
Gain on sale.		$ 5,000

(e) Cash dividends were paid on the following dates in 19X4:

	Presidential	Submariner
June 30	$22,000	$ 6,000
December 31	26,000	14,000
	$48,000	$20,000

(f) Presidential Corporation billed $5,000 to each subsidiary at year end for executive services in 19X4. Presidential treated it as sales and the subsidiary recorded it as an operating expense. The invoices were paid in January 19X5.

Required:

Prepare the worksheet necessary to produce the consolidated financial statements of Presidential Corporation and subsidiaries for the year ended December 31, 19X4. The consolidated income statement is to contain the nominal accounts of Submariner for the entire year. Include any necessary determination and distribution of excess schedule and income distribution schedules.

(AICPA adapted)

Suggestion: Allowing amounts in the nominal accounts of Submariner for the period preceding its purchase will require the use of "purchased income" in the worksheet. Also, retained earnings of all firms should be restored to the balances on January 1 to aid elimination. This means that dividend declared accounts should be established.

Problem 4-9. On January 1, 19X1, Pepper Company acquired 80% of the common stock of Salt Company for $220,000. On this date, Salt had total owners' equity of $200,000. During 19X1 and 19X2, Pepper has appropriately accounted for its investment in Salt using the simple equity method.

Any excess of cost over book value is attributable to inventory (worth $12,500 more than cost), to equipment (worth $25,000 more than book value), and to goodwill. FIFO is used for inventories. The equipment has a remaining life of 4 years, and straight-line depreciation is used. Goodwill is to be amortized over 10 years. On January 1, 19X2, Pepper held merchandise acquired from Salt for $20,000. During 19X2, Salt sold merchandise to Pepper for $40,000, $10,000 of which is still held by Pepper on December 31, 19X2. Salt's usual gross profit is 50%.

On December 31, 19X1, Pepper sold equipment to Salt at a gain of $15,000. During 19X2, the equipment was used by Salt. Depreciation is being computed using the straight-line method, a 5-year life, and no salvage value.

The following trial balances were prepared for the Pepper and Salt companies for December 31, 19X2.

	Pepper Co.	Salt Co.
Inventory, December 31	110,000	50,000
Other Current Assets	241,000	235,000
Investment in Salt Company	328,000	
Other Long-Term Investments	20,000	
Land	140,000	80,000
Buildings and Equipment	375,000	200,000
Accumulated Depreciation	(120,000)	(30,000)
Other Intangibles		20,000
Current Liabilities	(150,000)	(70,000)
Bonds Payable		(100,000)
Other Long-Term Liabilities	(200,000)	(50,000)
Common Stock—Pepper Company	(200,000)	
Other Paid-In Capital—Pepper Company	(100,000)	
Retained Earnings—Pepper Company	(320,000)	
Common Stock—Salt Company		(50,000)
Other Paid-In Capital—Salt Company		(50,000)
Retained Earnings—Salt Company		(150,000)
Net Sales	(600,000)	(315,000)
Cost of Goods Sold	350,000	150,000
Operating Expenses	150,000	60,000
Subsidiary Income	(84,000)	
Dividends Declared—Pepper Company	60,000	
Dividends Declared—Salt Company		20,000
Totals	0	0

Required:

Complete the worksheet for consolidated financial statements for the year ended December 31, 19X2. Include any necessary determination and distribution of excess schedule and income distribution schedules.

Problem 4-10. (This is the same as Problem 4-9 except for use of the cost method.) On January 1, 19X1, Pepper Company acquired 80% of the common stock of Salt Company for $220,000. On this date, Salt had total owners' equity of $200,000, which included retained earnings of $100,000. During 19X1 and 19X2, Pepper has accounted for its investment in Salt using the cost method.

Any excess of cost over book value is attributable to inventory (worth $12,500 more than cost), to equipment (worth $25,000 more than book value), and to goodwill. FIFO is used for inventories. The equipment has a remaining life of 4 years, and straight-line depreciation is used. Goodwill is to be amortized over 10 years.

On January 1, 19X2, Pepper held merchandise acquired from Salt for $20,000. During 19X2, Salt sold merchandise to Pepper for $40,000, $10,000 of which is still held by Pepper on December 31, 19X2. Salt's usual gross profit is 50%.

On December 31, 19X1, Pepper sold equipment to Salt at a gain of $15,000. During 19X2, the equipment was used by Salt. Depreciation is being computed using the straight-line method, a 5-year life, and no salvage value.

The following trial balances were prepared for the Pepper and Salt companies for December 31, 19X2.

	Pepper Co.	Salt Co.
Inventory, December 31	110,000	50,000
Other Current Assets	241,000	235,000
Investment in Salt Company	220,000	
Other Long-Term Investments	20,000	
Land	140,000	80,000
Buildings and Equipment	375,000	200,000
Accumulated Depreciation	(120,000)	(30,000)
Other Intangibles		20,000
Current Liabilities	(150,000)	(70,000)
Bonds Payable		(100,000)
Other Long-Term Liabilities	(200,000)	(50,000)
Common Stock—Pepper Company	(200,000)	
Other Paid-In Capital—Pepper Company	(100,000)	
Retained Earnings—Pepper Company	(280,000)	
Common Stock—Salt Company		(50,000)
Other Paid-In Capital—Salt Company		(50,000)
Retained Earnings—Salt Company		(150,000)
Net Sales	(600,000)	(315,000)
Cost of Goods Sold	350,000	150,000
Operating Expenses	150,000	60,000
Dividend Income	(16,000)	
Dividends Declared—Pepper Company	60,000	
Dividends Declared—Salt Company		20,000
Totals	0	0

Required:

Complete the worksheet for consolidated financial statements for the year ended December 31, 19X2. Include any necessary determination and distribution of excess schedule and income distribution schedules.

Sophisticated

Problem 4-11. (This is the same as Problem 4-9 except for use of the sophisticated equity method.) On January 1, 19X1, Pepper Company acquired 80% of the common stock of Salt Company for $220,000. On this date, Salt had total owners' equity of $200,000. During 19X1 and 19X2, Pepper has appropriately accounted for its investment in Salt using the sophisticated equity method.

Any excess of cost over book value is attributable to inventory (worth $12,500 more than cost), to equipment (worth $25,000 more than book value), and to goodwill. FIFO is used for inventories. The equipment has a remaining life of 4 years, and straight-line depreciation is used. Goodwill is to be amortized over 10 years.

On January 1, 19X2, Pepper held merchandise acquired from Salt for $20,000. During 19X2, Salt sold merchandise to Pepper for $40,000, $10,000 of which is still held by Pepper on December 31, 19X2. Salt's usual gross profit is 50%.

On December 31, 19X1, Pepper sold equipment to Salt at a gain of $15,000. During 19X2, the equipment was used by Salt. Depreciation is being computed using the straight-line method, a 5-year life, and no salvage value.

The following trial balances were prepared for the Pepper and Salt companies for December 31, 19X2.

	Pepper Co.	Salt Co.
Inventory, December 31.	110,000	50,000
Other Current Assets	241,000	235,000
Investment in Salt Company	298,000	
Other Long-Term Investments	20,000	
Land.	140,000	80,000
Buildings and Equipment	375,000	200,000
Accumulated Depreciation	(120,000)	(30,000)
Other Intangibles		20,000
Current Liabilities	(150,000)	(70,000)
Bonds Payable.		(100,000)
Other Long-Term Liabilities.	(200,000)	(50,000)
Common Stock—Pepper Company	(200,000)	
Other Paid-In Capital—Pepper Company	(100,000)	
Retained Earnings—Pepper Company.	(294,000)	
Common Stock—Salt Company		(50,000)
Other Paid-In Capital—Salt Company		(50,000)
Retained Earnings—Salt Company.		(150,000)
Net Sales	(600,000)	(315,000)
Cost of Goods Sold	350,000	150,000
Operating Expenses.	150,000	60,000
Subsidiary Income	(80,000)	
Dividends Declared—Pepper Company.	60,000	
Dividends Declared—Salt Company.		20,000
Totals.	0	0

Required:

Complete the worksheet for consolidated financial statements for the year ended December 31, 19X2. Include any necessary determination and distribution of excess schedule and income distribution schedules.

Problem 4-12. *(Review of Chapters 3 and 4.)* Print Company purchased 80% of the common stock of Slow Ink Company for $368,000 on January 2, 19X1. At that time, Slow Ink had the following balance sheet:

Assets		Liabilities and Stockholders' Equity	
Cash	$ 60,000	Accounts payable	$ 50,000
Accounts receivable	65,000	Bonds payable	200,000
Inventory	125,000	Common stock ($5 par)	50,000
Land	50,000	Paid-in capital in excess of par	100,000
Buildings (net)	250,000	Retained earnings	200,000
Goodwill (net)	50,000		
Total assets	$600,000	Total liabilities and equity	$600,000

The following information was available for the accounts where market values differed from book values on the date of the acquisition:

Account	Market Value	Life at Jan. 2, 19X1
Inventory	$150,000	Sold in 19X1
Land	100,000	
Buildings	400,000	20 years of 40-year original life
Bonds payable	190,000	5 years to maturity
Goodwill	?	20 years

The bond discount is to be amortized using the straight-line method.

The following transactions have occurred since the purchase and may be of concern in preparing the 19X3 consolidated financial statements:

upstream (1) Print's 19X3 beginning inventory includes $30,000 of the goods purchased from Slow Ink. Slow Ink always sells to Print at cost plus 25%.

(2) Slow Ink made sales to Print during 19X3 totaling $90,000. $10,000 still was unpaid at upstream year end. Print had $35,000 of such goods in its 19X3 ending inventory; however, the goods were adjusted to the lower market value of $31,000.

(3) Slow Ink sold a piece of equipment to Print on January 2, 19X2, for $12,000. The upstream equipment had a book value of $8,000 and a 5-year remaining life at the time of the sale.

The following trial balances of Print Company and its subsidiary were prepared on December 31, 19X3:

	Print Company	Slow Ink Company
Cash	72,000	100,000
Accounts Receivable	120,000	100,000
Inventory	180,000	120,000
Investment in Slow Ink Company	368,000	
Land	60,000	50,000
Building (net)	340,000	230,000
Equipment (net)	40,000	
Goodwill (net)		42,500
Accounts Payable	(100,000)	(60,000)
Bonds Payable		(200,000)
Common Stock	(300,000)	(50,000)
Paid-In Capital in Excess of Par.		(100,000)
Retained Earnings, Jan. 1, 19X3	(712,000)	(222,500)
Sales	(300,000)	(120,000)
Cost of Goods Sold	200,000	80,000
Other Expenses	40,000	20,000
Dividends Declared		10,000
Dividend Income (from Slow Ink Company)	(8,000)	
Total	0	0

Required:

Prepare the worksheet necessary to produce the consolidated financial statements of Print Company and its subsidiary for the year ended December 31, 19X3. Include the determination and distribution of excess schedule and the income distribution schedules.

Suggestion: Print's acquisition of Slow Ink Company is a bargain purchase and will require an allocation of available market value to long-lived assets. Eighty percent of the book value plus any excess available to fixed assets should be allocated to Slow Ink Company's fixed assets. Also, this is a cost–method problem that will require a cost-to-equity conversion.

Problem 4-13. Pine Corporation issued 200,000 shares of its $10 par common stock on March 31, 19X1, to acquire all of the outstanding $25 par value common stock of Strand Inc. The business combination meets all conditions for a pooling of interests. On March 31, 19X1, the market price of Pine's common stock was $35 a share. Both corporations continued to operate as separate businesses, maintaining separate accounting records with years ending December 31.

On March 31, 19X1, immediately before the combination, the stockholders' equities were:

	Pine	Strand
Common stock.	$ 5,500,000	$2,500,000
Additional paid-in capital	4,200,000	470,000
Retained earnings	7,360,000	2,430,000
	$17,060,000	$5,400,000

Additional information is as follows:
(a) During March 19X1, Pine paid $720,000 for expenditures relating to the business combination with Strand.
(b) Pine accounts for its investment in Strand using the sophisticated equity method.
(c) On March 31, 19X1, the fair values of Strand's assets and liabilities equaled their book values, except for its long-term investment in marketable equity securities, for which the aggregate market value exceeded aggregate cost by $600,000.
(d) On March 10, 19X1, Strand paid a cash dividend totaling $250,000 on its common stock.
(e) On November 15, 19X1, Pine paid a cash dividend totaling $1,500,000 on its common stock.
(f) During August 19X1, Pine sold merchandise to Strand at a profit of $800,000. At December 31, 19X1, one-fourth of this merchandise remained in Strand's inventory.
(g) For the period April 1 through December 31, 19X1, Strand paid Pine management fees totaling $150,000.
(h) Strand's 19X1 net income was $1,450,000. Pine's 19X1 income was $2,240,000, before considering equity in Strand's net income.
(i) The balances in retained earnings at January 1, 19X1, were $6,820,000 and $2,290,000 for Pine and Strand, respectively.

Required:
(1) Prepare Pine Corporation's journal entries to record the business combination with Strand Inc. and the expenditures relating to the business combination. Provide an equity transfer schedule.
(2) Prepare a schedule to compute the investment in Strand Inc., at sophisticated equity, at December 31, 19X1.
(3) Prepare a formal consolidated statement of changes in retained earnings of Pine Corporation and its subsidiary Strand Inc. for the year ended December 31, 19X1.

(AICPA adapted)

APPENDIX PROBLEMS

Problem 4A-1. Arther Corporation acquired all of the outstanding $10 par voting common stock of Trent Inc. on January 1, 19X2, in exchange for 50,000 shares of its $10 par voting common stock. On December 31, 19X1, the common stock of Arther had a closing market price of $15 per share on a national stock exchange. The retained earnings balance of Trent Inc. was $156,000 on the date of the acquisition. The acquisition was accounted for appropriately as a purchase. Both companies continued to operate as separate business entities maintaining separate accounting records with years ending December 31.

On December 31, 19X4, after year-end adjustments but before the nominal accounts were closed, the companies had the following condensed statements:

	Arther Corporation	Trent Inc.
Income Statement:		
Sales	(1,900,000)	(1,500,000)
Dividend Income (from Trent Inc.)	(40,000)	
Cost of Goods Sold.	1,180,000	870,000
Operating Expenses		
(includes depreciation).	550,000	440,000
Net Income.	(210,000)	(190,000)
Retained Earnings:		
Retained Earnings, Jan. 1, 19X4.	(250,000)	(206,000)
Net Income.	(210,000)	(190,000)
Dividends Paid.		40,000
Balance, Dec. 31, 19X4	(460,000)	(356,000)
Balance Sheet:		
Cash.	285,000	150,000
Accounts Receivable (net)	430,000	350,000
Inventories	530,000	410,000
Land, Plant, and Equipment	660,000	680,000
Accumulated Depreciation	(185,000)	(210,000)
Investment in Trent Inc. (at cost)	750,000	
Accounts Payable and Accrued Expenses	(670,000)	(544,000)
Common Stock ($10 par).	(1,200,000)	(400,000)
Additional Paid-In Capital	(140,000)	(80,000)
Retained Earnings, Dec. 31, 19X4	(460,000)	(356,000)
Total.	0	0

Additional information is as follows:

(a) There have been no changes in the common stock and additional paid-in capital accounts since the one necessitated in 19X2 by Arther's acquisition of Trent Inc.

(b) At the acquisition date, the market value of Trent's machinery exceeded book value by $54,000. This excess is being amortized over the asset's estimated average remaining life of 6 years. The fair market values of Trent's other assets and liabilities were equal to book values. Any goodwill resulting from the purchase is being amortized over a 20-year period.

(c) On July 1, 19X2, Arther sold a warehouse facility to Trent for $129,000 in cash. At the date of sale, Arther's book values were $33,000 for the land and $66,000 for the undepreciated cost of the building. Trent allocated the $129,000 purchase price to the land for $43,000 and to the building for $86,000. Trent is depreciating the building over its estimated 5-year remaining useful life by the straight-line method with no salvage value.

(d) During 19X4, Arther purchased merchandise from Trent at an aggregate invoice price of $180,000, which included a 100% markup on Trent's cost. At December 31,

19X4, Arther owed Trent $75,000 on these purchases, and $36,000 of the merchandise purchased remained in Arther's inventory.

Required:
Complete the vertical worksheet necessary to prepare the consolidated income statement and retained earnings statement for the year ended December 31, 19X4, and a consolidated balance sheet as of December 31, 19X4, for Arther Corporation and its subsidiary. Formal consolidated statements and journal entries are not required. Include the determination and distribution of excess schedule and the income distribution schedules.

(AICPA adapted)

Problem 4A-2.   Pate Corporation purchased a 90% interest in Sun Inc. for $800,000 on January 1, 19X4, when the stockholders' equity of Sun was as follows:

Common stock ($10 par).....................	$200,000
Retained earnings...........................	500,000
Total stockholders' equity	$700,000

On this date, it was determined that Sun's plant assets were undervalued by $100,000 and had a 10-year remaining life. Any remaining excess purchase price was attributed to goodwill. Pate Corporation uses the maximum write-off period for its intangibles.

Sun sold a machine to Pate Corporation for $25,000 on July 1, 19X4. The machine originally cost Sun $30,000, and $20,000 of accumulated depreciation had been recorded as of the sale date. Also on the sale date, the machine had a 5-year remaining life and no salvage value. Pate uses straight-line depreciation computed to the nearest month.

Pate Corporation sells merchandise to Sun at cost plus 50%. Sales totaled $300,000 during 19X5. Sun had $90,000 of such goods in its ending inventory, which was an increase of $30,000 from the previous year. Sun had not paid Pate for $25,000 of the purchases made during the year.

Pate Corporation uses the simple equity method to record its investment in Sun. At December 31, 19X5, Pate Corporation and its subsidiary, Sun Inc., had the following trial balances:

	Pate Corp.	Sun Inc.
Income Statement:		
Sales...	(822,000)	(500,000)
Cost of Goods Sold.................................	300,000	200,000
Other Expenses	60,000	50,000
Depreciation Expense..............................	20,000	40,000
Subsidiary Income.................................	(189,000)	
Net Income	(631,000)	(210,000)
Retained Earnings:		
Retained Earnings, Jan. 1, 19X5, Pate.................	(900,000)	
Retained Earnings, Jan. 1, 19X5, Sun		(800,000)
Net Income	(631,000)	(210,000)
Dividends Declared.................................	20,000	10,000
Retained Earnings 12/31/19X5	(1,511,000)	(1,000,000)
Balance Sheet:		
Cash	150,000	125,000
Inventory..	135,000	175,000
Accounts Receivable...............................	65,000	180,000

	Pate Corp.	Sun Inc.
Plant Assets	600,000	1,000,000
Accumulated Depreciation...........................	(189,000)	(150,000)
Investment in Sun Inc...............................	1,250,000	
Accounts Payable	(50,000)	(30,000)
Other Liabilities	(150,000)	(100,000)
Common Stock ($5 par).............................	(300,000)	
Common Stock ($10 par)............................		(200,000)
Retained Earnings 12/31/X5	(1,511,000)	(1,000,000)
Balances	0	0

Required:

Complete the vertical worksheet necessary to prepare the consolidated income statement and retained earnings statement for the year ended December 31, 19X5, and consolidated balance sheet as of December 31, 19X5, for Pate Corporation and its subsidiary. Formal consolidated statements and journal entries are not required. Include the determination and distribution of excess schedule and the income distribution schedules.

Problem 4A-3. (This is similar to Problem 4-9; it uses the simple equity method and vertical worksheet format.) On January 1, 19X1, Pepper Company acquired 80% of the common stock of Salt Company for $220,000. On this date, Salt had total owners' equity of $200,000, which included retained earnings of $100,000. During 19X1 and 19X2, Pepper has accounted for its investment in Salt using the cost method.

Any excess of cost over book value is attributable to inventory (worth $12,500 more than cost), to equipment (worth $25,000 more than book value), and to goodwill. FIFO is used for inventories. The equipment has a remaining life of 4 years, and straight-line depreciation is used. Goodwill is to be amortized over 10 years.

On January 1, 19X2, Pepper held merchandise acquired from Salt for $20,000. During 19X2, Salt sold merchandise to Pepper for $40,000, $10,000 of which is still held by Pepper on December 31, 19X2. Salt's usual gross profit is 50%.

On December 31, 19X1, Pepper sold equipment to Salt at a gain of $15,000. During 19X2, the equipment was used by Salt. Depreciation is being computed using the straight-line method, a 5-year life, and no salvage value.

The following trial balances were prepared for the Pepper and Salt companies for December 31, 19X2.

	Pepper Co.	Salt Co.
Income Statement:		
Net Sales	(600,000)	(315,000)
Cost of Goods Sold	350,000	150,000
Operating Expenses.....................................	150,000	60,000
Subsidiary Income	(84,000)	
Net Income...	(184,000)	(105,000)
Retained Earnings Statement:		
Balance, Jan. 1, 19X2—Pepper Company...................	(320,000)	
Balance, Jan. 1, 19X2—Salt Company......................		(150,000)
Net Income (from above)	(184,000)	(105,000)
Dividends Declared—Pepper Company......................	60,000	
Dividends Declared—Salt Company........................		20,000
Balance, December 31, 19X2	(444,000)	(235,000)

	Pepper Co.	Salt Co.
Consolidated Balance Sheet:		
Inventory, December 31....................................	110,000	50,000
Other Current Assets	241,000	235,000
Investment in Salt Company...............................	328,000	
Other Long-Term Investments	20,000	
Land...	140,000	80,000
Building and Equipment	375,000	200,000
Accumulated Depreciation	(120,000)	(30,000)
Other Intangibles..		20,000
Current Liabilities	(150,000)	(70,000)
Bonds Payable...		(100,000)
Other Long-Term Liabilities................................	(200,000)	(50,000)
Common Stock—Pepper Company	(200,000)	
Other Paid-In Capital—Pepper Company...................	(100,000)	
Common Stock—Salt Company		(50,000)
Other Paid-In Capital—Salt Company......................		(50,000)
Retained Earnings—12/31/X2	(444,000)	(235,000)
Totals...	0	0

Required:

Complete the worksheet for consolidated financial statements for the year ended December 31, 19X2. Include any necessary determination and distribution of excess schedule and income distribution schedules.

CASE   THE MINORITY'S CONCERN WITH INTERCOMPANY TRANSACTIONS

Henderson Window Company was a privately held corporation until January 1, 19X4. On January 1, 19X4, Cool Glass Company purchased a 70% interest in Henderson at a price well in excess of book value. There were some minor differences between book and market values, but the bulk of the excess was attributed to goodwill. In its consolidated statements, Cool Glass is amortizing the goodwill over 10 years.

Harvey Henderson did not sell his shares to Cool Glass as a part of the January 1, 19X4 Cool Glass purchase. He wanted to remain a Henderson shareholder since he felt Henderson was a more profitable and stable company than was Cool Glass. Harvey remains an employee of Henderson Window, working in an accounting capacity.

Harvey is concerned about some accounting issues that he feels are detrimental to his ownership interest. Harvey told you that Henderson always bought most of its glass from Cool Glass. He never felt the prices charged for the glass were unreasonable. Since the purchase of Henderson by Cool Glass, he feels the price charged to Henderson by Cool Glass has risen dramatically, and it is out of step with what would be paid to other glass suppliers.

The second concern is the sale of a large Henderson warehouse to Cool Glass for less than what Harvey would consider the market value to be. Harvey agrees that the sale is reasonable since the new just-in-time order system has made the space unnecessary. He just feels the sale price is below market.

Harvey did make his concerns known to the president of Cool Glass. The president made several points. First, she said that the price charged for the glass was a little high, but Harvey should consider its high quality. She went on to say the transfer price washes out in the annual report, and it has no impact on reported net income of the corporation. She also stated that the warehouse sale was at a low price, but there was a reason. It was a good year and a large gain wasn't needed. She would rather have lower depreciation in future years. Her last point was: "We paid a big price for Henderson, and we are stuck with big goodwill amortization expenses. We should get some benefits from it!"

Required:

Write a memo to Harvey Henderson suggesting how he might respond to the president's comments.

WORKSHEET 4-1

Intercompany Sales; No Intercompany Goods in Inventories
Company P and Subsidiary Company S
Worksheet for Consolidated Financial Statements
For Year Ended December 31, 19X1

	(Credit balance amounts are in parentheses.)	Trial Balance	
		Company P	Company S
1	**Accounts Receivable**	**110,000**	**150,000**
2	Inventory, Dec. 31, 19X1	70,000	40,000
3	Investment in Company S	196,000	
4			
5	Other Assets	314,000	155,000
6	**Accounts Payable**	**(80,000)**	**(100,000)**
7	Common Stock ($10 par), Co. P	(200,000)	
8	Retained Earnings, Jan. 1, 19X1, Co. P	(250,000)	
9	Common Stock ($10 par), Co. S		(100,000)
10	Retained Earnings, Jan. 1, 19X1, Co. S		(70,000)
11	**Sales**	**(700,000)**	**(500,000)**
12	**Cost of Goods Sold**	**510,000**	**350,000**
13	Expenses	90,000	75,000
14	Subsidiary Income	(60,000)	
15		0	0
16	Combined Net Income		
17	To Minority Interest (see distribution schedule)		
18	Balance to Controlling Interest (see distribution schedule)		
19	Total Minority Interest		
20	Retained Earnings, Controlling Interest, Dec. 31, 19X1		
21			

Eliminations and Adjustments:
(1)   Eliminate the entry recording the parent's share of subsidiary net income.
(2)   Eliminate against the investment in Company S account the pro rata portion of the subsidiary equity balances
      (80%) owned by the parent. To simplify the elimination, there is no discrepancy between the cost and book
      values of the investment in this example. Also note that the worksheet process is expedited by always
      eliminating the intercompany investment first.
(3)   Eliminate the intercompany sales to avoid double counting. Now only Company S's original purchase from
      third parties and Company P's final sale to third parties remain in the consolidated income statement.
(4)   Eliminate the $25,000 intercompany trade balances resulting from the intercompany sale.

Worksheet 4-1 (see page 215)

| Eliminations & Adjustments | | Consolidated Income Statement | Minority Interest | Controlling Retained Earnings | Consolidated Balance Sheet | |
Dr.	Cr.					
	(4) 25,000				235,000	1
					110,000	2
	(1) 60,000					3
	(2) 136,000					4
					469,000	5
(4) 25,000					(155,000)	6
					(200,000)	7
				(250,000)		8
(2) 80,000			(20,000)			9
(2) 56,000			(14,000)			10
(3) 100,000		(1,100,000)				11
	(3) 100,000	760,000				12
		165,000				13
(1) 60,000						14
321,000	321,000					15
		(175,000)				16
		15,000*	(15,000)			17
		160,000*		(160,000)		18
			(49,000)		(49,000)	19
				(410,000)	(410,000)	20
					0	21

Subsidiary Company S Income Distribution

Internally generated net income	$ 75,000
Adjusted income....................	$ 75,000
Minority share	20%
Minority interest	$ 15,000*

Parent Company P Income Distribution

Internally generated net income	$100,000
80% × Company S adjusted income of $75,000	60,000
Controlling interest..................	$160,000*

WORKSHEET 4-2

Intercompany Goods in Ending Inventory
Company P and Subsidiary Company S
Worksheet for Consolidated Financial Statements
For Year Ended December 31, 19X1

	(Credit balance amounts are in parentheses.)	Trial Balance	
		Company P	Company S
1	Accounts Receivable	110,000	150,000
2	**Inventory, Dec. 31, 19X1**	**70,000**	**40,000**
3	Investment in Company S	196,000	
4			
5	Other Assets	314,000	155,000
6	Accounts Payable	(80,000)	(100,000)
7	Common Stock ($10 par), Co. P	(200,000)	
8	Retained Earnings, Jan. 1, 19X1, Co. P	(250,000)	
9	Common Stock ($10 par), Co. S		(100,000)
10	Retained Earnings, Jan. 1, 19X1, Co. S		(70,000)
11	Sales	(700,000)	(500,000)
12	**Cost of Goods Sold**	**510,000**	**350,000**
13	Expenses	90,000	75,000
14	Subsidiary Income	(60,000)	
15		0	0
16	Combined Net Income		
17	To Minority Interest (see distribution schedule)		
18	Balance to Controlling Interest (see distribution schedule)		
19	Total Minority Interest		
20	Retained Earnings, Controlling Interest, Dec. 31, 19X1		
21			

Eliminations and Adjustments:
(1) Eliminate the entry recording the parent's share of subsidiary net income.
(2) Eliminate 80% of the subsidiary equity balances against the investment in Company S account. There is no excess of cost or book value in this example.
(3) Eliminate the intercompany sale.
(4) Eliminate the profit in the ending inventory.
(5) Eliminate the intercompany trade balances.

Worksheet 4-2 (see page 218)

Eliminations & Adjustments		Consolidated Income Statement	Minority Interest	Controlling Retained Earnings	Consolidated Balance Sheet	
Dr.	Cr.					
	(5) 25,000				235,000	1
	(4) 8,000				102,000	2
	(1) 60,000					3
	(2) 136,000					4
					469,000	5
(5) 25,000					(155,000)	6
					(200,000)	7
				(250,000)		8
(2) 80,000			(20,000)			9
(2) 56,000			(14,000)			10
(3) 100,000		(1,100,000)				11
(4) 8,000	(3) 100,000	768,000				12
		165,000				13
(1) 60,000						14
329,000	329,000					15
		(167,000)				16
		13,400*	(13,400)			17
		153,600*		(153,600)		18
			(47,400)		(47,400)	19
				(403,600)	(403,600)	20
					0	21

Subsidiary Company S Income Distribution

Unrealized profit in ending inventory . . . .(4) $ 8,000	Internally generated net income . . . . $ 75,000
	Adjusted income. $ 67,000
	Minority share 20%
	Minority interest . . . . $ 13,400*

Parent Company P Income Distribution

	Internally generated net income $100,000
	80% × Company S adjusted income of $67,000 53,600
	Controlling interest. $153,600*

WORKSHEET 4-3

Intercompany Goods in Beginning and Ending Inventories
Company P and Subsidiary Company S
Worksheet for Consolidated Financial Statements
For Year Ended December 31, 19X2

	(Credit balance amounts are in parentheses.)	Trial Balance	
		Company P	Company S
1	Accounts Receivable	160,000	170,000
2	**Inventory, Dec. 31, 19X2**	**60,000**	**50,000**
3	Investment in Company S	244,000	
4			
5	Other Assets	354,000	165,000
6	Accounts Payable	(90,000)	(80,000)
7	Common Stock ($10 par), Co. P	(200,000)	
8	**Retained Earnings, Jan. 1, 19X2, Co. P**	**(410,000)**	
9	Common Stock ($10 par), Co. S		(100,000)
10	**Retained Earnings, Jan. 1, 19X2, Co. S**		**(145,000)**
11			
12	Sales	(800,000)	(600,000)
13	**Cost of Goods Sold**	**610,000**	**440,000**
14			
15	Expenses	120,000	100,000
16	Subsidiary Income	(48,000)	
17		0	0
18	Combined Net Income		
19	To Minority Interest (see distribution schedule)		
20	Balance to Controlling Interest (see distribution schedule)		
21	Total Minority Interest		
22	Retained Earnings, Controlling Interest, Dec. 31, 19X2		
23			

Eliminations and Adjustments:
(1)   Eliminate the entry recording the parent's share of subsidiary net income.
(2)   Eliminate 80% of the subsidiary equity balances against the investment in account. There is no excess of cost or book value in this example.
(3)   Eliminate the intercompany profit of $8,000 (20% × $40,000) in the beginning inventory by reducing both the cost of goods sold and the beginning retained earnings accounts. 20% of the decrease in retained earnings is shared by the minority interest, since, in this case, *the selling firm was the subsidiary*. If the parent had been the seller, only the controlling interest in retained earnings would be decreased. It should be noted that the $8,000 profit is shifted from 19X1 to 19X2, since, as a result of the entry, the 19X2 consolidated cost of goods sold

Worksheet 4-3 (see page 219)

Eliminations & Adjustments				Consolidated Income Statement	Minority Interest	Controlling Retained Earnings	Consolidated Balance Sheet	
Dr.		Cr.						
		(6)	60,000				270,000	1
		(5)	**6,000**				104,000	2
		(1)	48,000					3
		(2)	196,000					4
							519,000	5
(6)	60,000						(110,000)	6
							(200,000)	7
(3)	6,400					(403,600)		8
(2)	80,000				(20,000)			9
(2)	116,000							10
(3)	1,600				(27,400)			11
(4)	120,000			(1,280,000)				12
(5)	6,000	(3)	8,000					13
		(4)	120,000	928,000				14
				220,000				15
(1)	48,000							16
	438,000		438,000					17
				(132,000)				18
				12,400*	(12,400)			19
				119,600*		(119,600)		20
					(59,800)		(59,800)	21
						(523,200)	(523,200)	22
							0	23

balance is reduced $8,000. This procedure emphasizes the concept that intercompany inventory profit is not eliminated but only deferred until inventory is sold to an outsider.

(4) Eliminate the intercompany sales to prevent double counting.

(5) Eliminate the intercompany profit of $6,000 (20% × $30,000) recorded by Company S for the intercompany goods contained in Company P's ending inventory, and increase the cost of goods sold balance by this same amount.

(6) Eliminate the intercompany trade balances.

(continued)

Subsidiary Company S Income Distribution

Unrealized profit in ending inventory,		Internally generated net income	$60,000
20% × **$30,000** . . . .(5) $ 6,000		**Realized profit in beginning inventory,**	
		20% × **$40,000** . . . .(3)	8,000
		Adjusted income	$62,000
		Minority share	20%
		Minority interest	$12,400*

Parent Company P Income Distribution

Internally generated net income	$ 70,000
80% × Company S adjusted income of $62,000	49,600
Controlling interest	**$119,600***

WORKSHEET 4-4

Intercompany Goods in Beginning and Ending Inventories; Periodic Inventory
Company P and Subsidiary Company S
Worksheet for Consolidated Financial Statements
For Year Ended December 31, 19X2

	(Credit balance amounts are in parentheses.)	Trial Balance	
		Company P	Company S
1	Accounts Receivable	160,000	170,000
2	**Inventory, Jan. 1, 19X2**	**70,000**	**40,000**
3	Investment in Company S	244,000	
4			
5	Other Assets	354,000	165,000
6	Accounts Payable	(90,000)	(80,000)
7	Common Stock ($10 par), Co. P	(200,000)	
8	**Retained Earnings, Jan. 1, 19X2, Co. P**	**(410,000)**	
9	Common Stock ($10 par), Co. S		(100,000)
10	**Retained Earnings, Jan. 1, 19X2, Co. S**		**(145,000)**
11			
12	Sales	(800,000)	(600,000)
13	**Purchases**	**600,000**	**450,000**
14	**Inventory, Dec. 31, 19X2**		
15			
16	Expenses	120,000	100,000
17	Subsidiary Income	(48,000)	
18		0	0
19	Combined Net Income		
20	To Minority Interest (see distribution schedule)		
21	Balance to Controlling Interest (see distribution schedule)		
22	Total Minority Interest		
23	Retained Earnings, Controlling Interest, Dec. 31, 19X2		
24			

Eliminations and Adjustments:
(1) Eliminate the entry recording the parent's share of subsidiary net income.
(2) Eliminate 80% of the subsidiary equity balances against the investment account. There is no excess of cost or book value in this example.
(3) Eliminate the intercompany profit of $8,000 (20% × $40,000) in the beginning inventory by reducing both the January 1 inventory and the beginning retained earnings balances. 20% of the decrease in retained earnings is shared by the minority interest, since, in this case, *the selling firm was the subsidiary*. If the parent had been the seller, only the controlling interest in retained earnings would be decreased. It should be noted that the $8,000 profit is shifted from 19X1 to 19X2, since, as a result of the entry, the 19X2 consolidated cost of goods

Worksheet 4-4 (see page 220)

Eliminations & Adjustments			Consolidated Income Statement	Minority Interest	Controlling Retained Earnings	Consolidated Balance Sheet	
Dr.	Cr.						
	(6)	60,000				270,000	1
	(3)	8,000	102,000				2
	(1)	48,000					3
	(2)	196,000					4
						519,000	5
(6) 60,000						(110,000)	6
						(200,000)	7
(3) 6,400					(403,600)		8
(2) 80,000				(20,000)			9
(2) 116,000							10
(3) 1,600				(27,400)			11
(4) 120,000			(1,280,000)				12
	(4)	120,000	930,000				13
(5) 104,000						104,000	14
	(5)	104,000	(104,000)				15
			220,000				16
(1) 48,000							17
536,000	536,000						18
			(132,000)				19
			12,400*	(12,400)			20
			119,600		(119,600)		21
				(59,800)		(59,800)	22
					(523,200)	(523,200)	23
						0	24

sold will be reduced $8,000. This procedure emphasizes the concept that intercompany inventory profit is not eliminated but only deferred until inventory is sold to an outsider.

(4) Eliminate the intercompany sales to prevent double counting of purchases and sales.

(5) Enter the combined ending inventories of Company P and Company S, $60,000 and $50,000, respectively, less the intercompany profit of $6,000 (20% × $30,000) recorded by Company S for the intercompany goods contained in Company P's ending inventory.

(6) Eliminate the intercompany trade balances.

(continued)

Subsidiary Company S Income Distribution

Unrealized profit in ending inventory, 20% × $30,000 . . . . (5)	$ 6,000	Internally generated net income	$60,000[a]
		Realized profit in beginning inventory, 20% × $40,000 . . . . (3)	8,000
		Adjusted income	$62,000
		Minority share	20%
		Minority interest	$12,400*

[a] [$600,000 − ($40,000 + $450,000 − $50,000) − $100,000 = $60,000]

Parent Company P Income Distribution

Internally generated net income	$ 70,000[b]
80% × Company S adjusted income of $62,000	49,600
Controlling interest	$119,600*

[b] [$800,000 – ($70,000 + $600,000 – $60,000) – $120,000 = $70,000]

WORKSHEET 4-5

Intercompany Sale of Depreciable Asset
Company P and Subsidiary Company S
Worksheet for Consolidated Financial Statements
For Year Ended December 31, 19X1

	(Credit balance amounts are in parentheses.)	Trial Balance	
		Company P	Company S
1	Current Assets	15,000	20,000
2	**Machinery**	50,000	(a) **230,000**
3	**Accumulated Depreciation—Machinery**	(25,000)	(b) **(100,000)**
4	Investment in Company S	120,000	
5			
6	Common Stock ($10 par), Co. P	(100,000)	
7	Retained Earnings, Jan. 1, 19X1, Co. P	(10,000)	
8	Common Stock ($10 par), Co. S		(50,000)
9	Retained Earnings, Jan. 1, 19X1, Co. S		(75,000)
10	Sales	(200,000)	(100,000)
11	Cost of Goods Sold	150,000	59,000
12	**Depreciation Expense**	30,000	(b) **16,000**
13	**Gain on Sale of Machine**	**(10,000)**	
14	Subsidiary Income	(20,000)	
15		0	0
16	Combined Net Income		
17	To Minority Interest (see distribution schedule)		
18	Balance to Controlling Interest (see distribution schedule)		
19	Total Minority Interest		
20	Retained Earnings, Controlling Interest, Dec. 31, 19X1		
21			

Notes to Trial Balance:
(a) Includes machine purchased for $30,000 *from Company P* on January 1, 19X1.
(b) Includes $6,000 depreciation on machine purchased from Company P on January 1, 19X1.

Eliminations and Adjustments:
(1) Eliminate the entry recording the parent's share of subsidiary net income for the current year.
(2) Eliminate 80% of the subsidiary equity balances against the investment account. There is no excess to be distributed.
(3) Eliminate the $10,000 gain on the intercompany sale of the machine. In addition, adjust the machine to $32,000 and restore its related accumulated depreciation to $12,000 in order to reflect the book value of the asset to the consolidated firm on January 1, 19X1.
(4) Reduce the depreciation expense and accumulated depreciation accounts to reflect the depreciation ($4,000 per year) based on the consolidated book value of the machine, rather than the depreciation ($6,000 per year) based on the sales price.

Worksheet 4-5 (see page 224)

Eliminations & Adjustments			Consolidated Income Statement	Minority Interest	Controlling Retained Earnings	Consolidated Balance Sheet	
Dr.		Cr.					
						35,000	1
(3)	2,000						282,000	2
(4)	2,000	(3)	12,000				(135,000)	3
		(1)	20,000					4
		(2)	100,000					5
							(100,000)	6
						(10,000)		7
(2)	40,000				(10,000)			8
(2)	60,000				(15,000)			9
				(300,000)				10
				209,000				11
		(4)	2,000	44,000				12
(3)	10,000							13
(1)	20,000							14
	134,000		134,000					15
				(47,000)				16
				5,000*	(5,000)			17
				42,000*		(42,000)		18
					(30,000)		(30,000)	19
						(52,000)	(52,000)	20
							0	21

Subsidiary Company S Income Distribution

	Internally generated net income	$25,000
	Adjusted income......................	$25,000
	Minority share	20%
	Minority interest	$ 5,000*

Parent Company P Income Distribution

Unrealized gain on sale of machine . . .(3) $10,000	Internally generated net income (including sale of machine)...........	$30,000
	80% × Company S adjusted income of $25,000	20,000
	Gain realized through use of machine sold to subsidiary.................(4)	**2,000**
	Controlling interest....................	$42,000*

WORKSHEET 4-6

Intercompany Sale of Depreciable Asset
Company P and Subsidiary Company S
Worksheet for Consolidated Financial Statements
For Year Ended December 31, 19X2

	(Credit balance amounts are in parentheses.)	Trial Balance			
		Company P		Company S	
1	Current Assets	85,000			60,000
2	**Machinery**	50,000	**(a)**	**230,000**	
3	**Accumulated Depreciation—Machinery**	(45,000)	**(b)**	**(116,000)**	
4					
5	Investment in Company S	139,200			
6					
7	Common Stock ($10 par), Co. P	(100,000)			
8	**Retained Earnings, Jan. 1, 19X2, Co. P**	**(60,000)**			
9	Common Stock ($10 par), Co. S				(50,000)
10	Retained Earnings, Jan. 1, 19X2, Co. S				(100,000)
11	Sales	(250,000)			(120,000)
12	**Cost of Goods Sold**	180,000			80,000
13	**Depreciation Expense**	20,000	**(c)**	**16,000**	
14	Subsidiary Income	(19,200)			
15		0			0
16	Combined Net Income				
17	To Minority Interest (see distribution schedule)				
18	Balance to Controlling Interest (see distribution schedule)				
19	Total Minority Interest				
20	Retained Earnings, Controlling Interest, Dec. 31, 19X2				
21					

Notes to Trial Balance:
(a) Includes machine purchased for $30,000 *from Company P* on January 1, 19X1.
(b) Includes $12,000 accumulated depreciation ($6,000 per year) on machine purchased from Company P on January 1, 19X1.
(c) Includes $6,000 depreciation on machine purchased from Company P on January 1, 19X1.

Eliminations and Adjustments:
(1) Eliminate the entry recording the parent's share of subsidiary net income for the current year.
(2) Eliminate 80% of the subsidiary equity balances against the investment account. There is no excess to be distributed.
(3) Eliminate the gain on the intercompany sale as it is reflected in beginning retained earnings on the parent's trial balance. This entry adjusts the machine account to $32,000 and restates accumulated depreciation as of the

Worksheet 4-6 (see page 225)

Eliminations & Adjustments			Consolidated Income Statement	Minority Interest	Controlling Retained Earnings	Consolidated Balance Sheet	
Dr.		**Cr.**					
						145,000	1
(3)	2,000					282,000	2
(3)	2,000	(3)	12,000					3
(4)	2,000					(169,000)	4
		(1)	19,200					5
		(2)	120,000					6
						(100,000)	7
(3)	8,000				(52,000)		8
(2)	40,000			(10,000)			9
(2)	80,000			(20,000)			10
			(370,000)				11
			260,000				12
		(4)	2,000	34,000				13
(1)	19,200						14
	153,200		153,200					15
			(76,000)				16
			4,800*	(4,800)			17
			71,200*		(71,200)		18
				(34,800)		(34,800)	19
					(123,200)	(123,200)	20
						0	21

beginning of the year. Thus, the adjustment to accumulated depreciation includes a $12,000 increase in order to acknowledge the $12,000 balance on the sale date and a $2,000 reduction for the profit element of the 19X1 depreciation. Since the sale was made by the *parent*, Company P, the entire unrealized gain at the beginning of the year (now $8,000) is removed from the controlling retained earnings beginning balance. If the sale had been made by the subsidiary, the adjustment of beginning retained earnings would be split 80% to the controlling interest and 20% to the minority interest.

(4) Reduce the depreciation expense and accumulated depreciation accounts to reflect the depreciation based on the consolidated book value of the asset on the date of sale. This entry will bring the accumulated depreciation account to its correct consolidated year-end balance.

(continued)

Subsidiary Company S Income Distribution

Internally generated net income	$24,000
Adjusted income	$24,000
Minority share	20%
Minority interest	$ 4,800*

Parent Company P Income Distribution

Internally generated net income	$50,000
80% of Company S adjusted income of $24,000	19,200
Gain realized through use of machine sold to subsidiary . . . .**(4)**	**2,000**
Controlling interest	$71,200*

WORKSHEET 4-7

Intercompany Sale of a Depreciable Asset; Subsequent Sale of Asset to an Outside Party
Company P and Subsidiary Company S
Worksheet for Consolidated Financial Statements
For Year Ended December 31, 19X2

	(Credit balance amounts are in parentheses.)	Trial Balance	
		Company P	Company S
1	Current Assets	85,000	74,000
2	Machinery	50,000	200,000
3	Accumulated Depreciation—Machinery	(45,000)	(104,000)
4	Investment in Company S	136,000	
5			
6	Common Stock ($10 par), Co. P	(100,000)	
7	**Retained Earnings, Jan. 1, 19X2, Co. P**	**(60,000)**	
8	Common Stock ($10 par), Co. S		(50,000)
9	Retained Earnings, Jan. 1, 19X2, Co. S		(100,000)
10	Sales	(250,000)	(120,000)
11	Cost of Goods Sold	180,000	80,000
12	**Depreciation Expense**	20,000	**16,000**
13	**Loss on Sale of Machine**		**4,000**
14	Subsidiary Income	(16,000)	
15	**Gain on Sale of Machine**		
16		0	0
17	Combined Net Income		
18	To Minority Interest (see distribution schedule)		
19	Balance to Controlling Interest (see distribution schedule)		
20	Total Minority Interest		
21	Retained Earnings, Controlling Interest, Dec. 31, 19X2		
22			

Eliminations and Adjustments:
(1) Eliminate the entry recording the parent's share of subsidiary net income for the current year.
(2) Eliminate 80% of the subsidiary equity balances against the investment account. There is no excess to be distributed.
(3) Eliminate the gain on the intercompany sale as it is reflected in the parent's beginning retained earnings account, adjust the current year's depreciation expense, and revise the recording of the sale of the equipment to an outside party to reflect the net book value of the asset to the consolidated firm.

Subsidiary Company S Income Distribution

Internally generated net income	$20,000
Adjusted income	$20,000
Minority share	20%
Minority interest	$ 4,000*

Worksheet 4-7 (see page 227)

Eliminations & Adjustments		Consolidated Income Statement	Minority Interest	Controlling Retained Earnings	Consolidated Balance Sheet	
Dr.	Cr.					
					159,000	1
					250,000	2
					(149,000)	3
	(1) 16,000					4
	(2) 120,000					5
					(100,000)	6
(3) 8,000				(52,000)		7
(2) 40,000			(10,000)			8
(2) 80,000			(20,000)			9
		(370,000)				10
		260,000				11
	(3) 2,000	34,000				12
	(3) 4,000					13
(1) 16,000						14
	(3) 2,000	(2,000)				15
144,000	144,000					16
		(78,000)				17
		4,000*	(4,000)			18
		74,000*		(74,000)		19
			(34,000)		(34,000)	20
				(126,000)	(126,000)	21
					0	22

Parent Company P Income Distribution

Internally generated net income	$50,000	
80% × Company S adjusted income of $20,000..........................	16,000	
Gain realized on sale of machine.....(3)	**8,000**[a]	
Controlling interest	$74,000*	

[a] $10,000 original gain – $2,000 realized in 19X1

WORKSHEET 4-8

Intercompany Notes
Company P and Subsidiary Company S
Worksheet for Consolidated Financial Statements
For Year Ended December 31, 19X1

	(Credit balance amounts are in parentheses.)	Trial Balance	
		Company P	Company S
1	Cash	35,000	20,400
2	**Note Receivable from Company S**	**10,000**	
3	**Interest Receivable**	**400**	
4	Property, Plant, and Equipment (net)	140,000	150,000
5	Investment in Company S	128,000	
6			
7	**Note Payable to Company P**		**(10,000)**
8	**Interest Payable**		**(400)**
9	Common Stock, Co. P	(100,000)	
10	Retained Earnings, Jan. 1, 19X1, Co. P	(200,000)	
11	Common Stock, Co. S		(50,000)
12	Retained Earnings, Jan. 1, 19X1, Co. S		(100,000)
13	Sales	(120,000)	(50,000)
14	**Interest Income**	**(400)**	
15	Subsidiary Income	(8,000)	
16	Cost of Goods Sold	75,000	20,000
17	Other Expenses	40,000	19,600
18	**Interest Expense**		**400**
19		0	0
20	Combined Net Income		
21	To Minority Interest (see distribution schedule)		
22	Balance to Controlling Interest (see distribution schedule)		
23	Total Minority Interest		
24	Retained Earnings, Controlling Interest, Dec. 31, 19X1		
25			

Eliminations and Adjustments:
(1) Eliminate the parent's share (80%) of subsidiary net income.
(2) Eliminate the controlling portion (80%) of the Company S January 1, 19X1 stockholders' equity against the investment in Company S account. No excess results.

Subsidiary Company S Income Distribution

Internally generated net income	$10,000
Adjusted income......................	$10,000
Minority share	20%
Minority interest	$ 2,000*

Worksheet 4-8 (see page 230)

Eliminations & Adjustments		Consolidated Income Statement	Minority Interest	Controlling Retained Earnings	Consolidated Balance Sheet	
Dr.	Cr.					
					55,400	1
	(3) 10,000					2
	(3) 400					3
					290,000	4
	(1) 8,000					5
	(2) 120,000					6
(3) 10,000						7
(3) 400						8
					(100,000)	9
				(200,000)		10
(2) 40,000			(10,000)			11
(2) 80,000			(20,000)			12
		(170,000)				13
(4) 400						14
(1) 8,000						15
		95,000				16
		59,600				17
	(4) 400					18
138,800	138,800					19
		(15,400)				20
		2,000*	(2,000)			21
		13,400*		(13,400)		19
			(32,000)		(32,000)	23
				(213,400)	(213,400)	24
					0	22

(3) Eliminate the intercompany note and accrued interest applicable to the note. This step removes the *internal note* from the consolidated balance sheet.

(4) Eliminate the intercompany interest expense and revenue. Since an equal amount of expense and revenue is eliminated, there is no change in the combined net income as a result of this step.

Parent Company P Income Distribution

Internally generated net income	$ 5,400
80% × Company S adjusted income of $10,000	8,000
Controlling interest....................	$13,400*

WORKSHEET 4-9

Vertical Worksheet Alternative
Company P and Subsidiary Company S
Worksheet for Consolidated Financial Statements
For Year Ended December 31, 19X2

	(Credit balance amounts are in parentheses.)	Financial Statements	
		Company P	Company C
1	**Income Statement**		
2	Sales	(600,000)	(530,000)
3	Cost of goods sold	400,000	280,000
4			
5	Depreciation expense	40,000	50,000
6	Other expenses	60,000	70,000
7	Subsidiary income	(104,000)	
8	**Net income**	(204,000)	(130,000)
9	Minority interest (see distribution schedule)		
10	Controlling interest (see distribution schedule)		
11			
12	**Retained Earnings Statement**		
13	Retained earnings, Jan. 1, 19X2, Co. P	(600,000)	
14			
15			
16	Retained earnings, Jan. 1, 19X2, Co. S		(400,000)
17			
18	**Net income (carrydown)**	(204,000)	(130,000)
19	Dividends declared		20,000
20	**Retained earnings, Dec. 31, 19X2**	(804,000)	(510,000)
21	Minority interest, retained earnings, Dec. 31, 19X2		
22	Controlling interest, retained earnings, Dec. 31, 19X2		
23			
24	**Balance Sheet**		
25	Inventory	300,000	250,000
26	Accounts receivable	120,000	180,000
27	Plant assets	236,000	400,000
28	Accumulated depreciation	(100,000)	(60,000)
29			
30	Investment in Company S	628,000	
31			
32			
33	Goodwill		
34	Current liabilities	(80,000)	(60,000)
35	Common stock ($5 par), Co. S		(200,000)
36	Common stock ($10 par), Co. P	(300,000)	
37	**Retained earnings (carrydown)**	(804,000)	(510,000)
38	Retained earnings, controlling interest, Dec. 31, 19X2		
39	Retained earnings, minority interest, Dec. 31, 19X2		
40	Total minority interest		
41	Total	0	0

Worksheet 4-9 (see page 235)

Eliminations & Adjustments Dr.		Eliminations & Adjustments Cr.		Minority Interest	Consolidated	
						1
(6)	150,000				(980,000)	2
(7)	10,000	(6)	150,000			3
		(5)	8,000		532,000	4
		(10)	1,000		89,000	5
(4)	1,500				131,500	6
(1)	104,000					7
					(227,500)	8
				(25,600)*		9
					(201,900)*	10
						11
						12
(4)	1,500					13
(5)	6,400					14
(9)	4,500				(587,600)	15
(2)	320,000					16
(5)	1,600			(78,400)		17
				(25,600)	(201,900)	18
		(1)	16,000	4,000		19
						20
				(100,000)		21
					(789,500)	22
						23
						24
		(7)	10,000		540,000	25
		(8)	20,000		280,000	26
		(9)	5,000		631,000	27
(9)	500					28
(10)	1,000				(158,500)	29
		(1)	88,000			30
		(2)	480,000			31
		(3)	60,000			32
(3)	60,000	(4)	3,000		57,000	33
(8)	20,000				(120,000)	34
(2)	160,000			(40,000)		35
					(300,000)	36
						37
					(789,500)	38
				(100,000)		39
				(140,000)	(140,000)	40
	841,000		841,000		0	41

(continued)

Eliminations and Adjustments:
 (1) Eliminate the current year entries recording the parent's share (80%) of subsidiary net income and the dividends declared.
 (2) Eliminate the pro rata portion of the subsidiary equity balances owned by the parent (80%) against the balance of the investment account.
 (3) Distribute the excess to the goodwill account according to the determination and distribution of excess schedule.
 (4) Amortize the goodwill at $1,500 per year for the past year and current year.
 (5) Eliminate the intercompany profit in the beginning inventory, 20% (.25 ÷ 1.25) multiplied by $40,000. Since it was a subsidiary sale, the profit is shared 20% by the minority interest.
 (6) Eliminate the intercompany sales made during 19X2.
 (7) Eliminate the intercompany profit (20%) applicable to the $50,000 of intercompany goods in the ending inventory.
 (8) Eliminate the intercompany trade balances.
 (9) Eliminate the intercompany gain remaining on January 1, 19X2, applicable to the sale of the machine by Company P ($5,000 original gain less one-half year's gain of $500).
(10) Reduce the depreciation expense and accumulated depreciation accounts ($1,000 for the current year) in order to reflect depreciation based on the original cost.

Subsidiary Company S Income Distribution

Unrealized profit in ending inventory (20% × $50,000)..................(7) $10,000	Internally generated net income.........	$130,000
	Realized profit in beginning inventory (20% × $40,000)..................(5)	8,000
	Adjusted income......................	$128,000
	Minority share	20%
	Minority interest	**$ 25,600***

Parent Company P Income Distribution

Goodwill amortization...............(4) $ 1,500	Internally generated net income.........	$100,000
	Gain realized on sale of machine ....(10)	1,000
	80% × Company S adjusted income of $128,000	102,400
	Controlling interest	**$201,900***

CHAPTER 5

Intercompany Transactions: Bonds and Leases

This chapter focuses on intercompany transactions that create a long-term debtor–creditor relationship between the members of a consolidated group. The usual impetus for these transactions is the parent's ability to borrow larger amounts of capital at more favorable terms than would be available to the subsidiary. In addition, the parent company may desire to manage all capital needs of the consolidated firm for better control of all capital sources. Intercompany leasing with the parent as the lessor also may be motivated by centralized credit control.

Intercompany bond holdings will be analyzed first. Here, one member of the consolidated group, usually the subsidiary, has issued bonds which appear on its balance sheet as long-term liabilities. Another member may purchase the bonds and list them on its balance sheet as an investment. However, when consolidated statements are prepared, the intercompany purchase, in effect, should be viewed as a retirement of the bonds. Consideration of intercompany leasing of assets will follow the bond coverage. In this case, one member of the consolidated group purchases the asset and leases it to another member. While the leasing transaction is recorded as such on the separate books of the affiliates, the lease has no substance from a consolidated viewpoint. Only a lease that involves a nonaffiliated firm may appear in the consolidated statements.

INTERCOMPANY INVESTMENT IN BONDS

To secure long-term funds, one member of a consolidated group may sell its bonds directly to another member of the group. Clearly, such a transaction results in intercompany debt which must be eliminated from the consolidated statements. On the worksheet, the investment in bonds recorded by one firm must be eliminated against the bonds payable of the other. In addition, the applicable interest expense recorded by one affiliate must be eliminated against the applicable interest revenue recorded by the other affiliate. Interest accruals recorded on the books of the separate firms must be eliminated as well.

There are situations where one affiliate (usually the subsidiary) has outstanding bonds that have been purchased by parties that are not members of the affiliated group, and a decision is made by another affiliate (usually the parent) to obtain these bonds. The simplest way to accomplish the removal of subsidiary bonds from outsiders is for the parent to advance funds to the subsidiary so that the subsidiary may retire the bonds. From an accounting standpoint, this transaction is easy to record. The former debt is retired and a new, long-term intercompany debt originates. The only procedures required on future consolidated worksheets involve the elimination of the resulting intercompany debt.

A more complicated method is to have the parent purchase the subsidiary bonds from the outside parties and to hold them as an investment. This method creates an intercompany investment in bonds, where each affiliate continues to accrue and record interest on the bonds. While the intercompany bonds are treated as a liability on one set of books and as an investment on the other set, from a consolidated viewpoint the bonds have been retired, and the debt to outside parties has been liquidated. The purchase of intercompany bonds has the following ramifications when consolidating:

1. Consolidated statements prepared for the period in which the bonds are purchased must portray the intercompany purchase as a retirement of the bonds. It is possible, but unlikely, that the bonds will be purchased at book value. There usually will be a gain or loss on retirement; this gain or loss is deemed to be *extraordinary* and is recognized on the consolidated income statement.
2. For all periods during which the intercompany investment exists, the intercompany bonds, interest accruals, and interest expense/revenue must be eliminated since the bonds no longer exist from a consolidated viewpoint.

The complexity of the elimination procedures depends on whether the bonds originally were issued at face value or at a premium or discount. Additionally, one must exercise extra care in the application of elimination procedures when only a portion of the outstanding bonds are purchased intercompany.

BONDS ORIGINALLY ISSUED AT FACE VALUE

When bonds are sold at face value by a subsidiary to outside parties, contract (nominal) interest agrees with the effective, or market, interest, and no amortizations of issuance premiums or discounts need to be recorded. However, subsequent to the issuance, the market rate of interest most likely will deviate from the contract rate. Thus, while there is no original issuance premium or discount, there will be what could be termed an *investment premium or discount* resulting from the intercompany purchase of the bonds.

To illustrate the procedures required for intercompany bonds originally issued at face value, assume a subsidiary, Company S, issued 5-year, 8% bonds at face value of $100,000 to outside parties on January 1, 19X1. Interest is paid on January 1 for the preceding year. On January 2, 19X3, the parent, Company P, purchased the bonds from the outside parties for $103,600.

Company S will continue to list the $100,000 bonded debt and to record interest expense of $8,000 during 19X3, 19X4, and 19X5. However, Company P will record a bond investment of $103,600 and will amortize $1,200 per year by reducing the investment account and adjusting interest revenue. (Though the interest method of amortization is preferable, the straight-line method is permitted if results are not materially different. This initial example and most others in this chapter use the straight-line method in order to simplify analysis. A summary example is used to demonstrate the interest method of amortization.)

Although the investment and liability accounts continue to exist on the separate books of the affiliated firms, retirement has occurred from a consolidated viewpoint. Debt with a book value of $100,000 was retired by a payment of $103,600, and there is a $3,600 extraordinary loss on retirement. If a consolidated worksheet is prepared on the day the bonds are purchased, Bonds Payable would be eliminated against Investment in Company S Bonds, and an extraordinary loss on retirement would be reported on the consolidated income statement. The following abbreviated worksheet displays the procedures used to retire the bonds as part of the elimination process:

	Partial Trial Balance		Eliminations & Adjustments	
	Company P	Company S	Dr.	Cr.
Investment in Company S Bonds	103,600			103,600
Bonds Payable		(100,000)	100,000	
Extraordinary Loss on Bond Retirement			3,600	

This partial worksheet, prepared on January 2, 19X3, is only hypothetical, since, in reality, there will be no consolidated worksheet prepared until December 31, 19X3, the end of the period. During 19X3, Companies P and S will record the transactions for interest as follows:

Company P		
Interest Receivable........	8,000	
Investment in Company S Bonds..............		1,200
Interest Income........		6,800
To record interest revenue net of $1,200 per year premium amortization.		

Company S		
Interest Expense..........	8,000	
Interest Payable........		8,000
To record interest expense.		

These entries will be reflected in the trial balances of the December 31, 19X3 consolidated worksheet, shown in Worksheet 5-1 on pages 324–327. Note that Investment in Company S Bonds reflects the premium amortization, since the balance is $102,400 ($103,600 original cost − $1,200 amortization). In this work-sheet, it is assumed that Investment in Company S Stock reflects a 90% interest purchased at a price equal to the book value of the underlying equity and the simple equity method is used by Company P to record the investment in stock.

Steps (1) and (2) eliminate the intercompany stock investment. Step (3) eliminates the intercompany bonds at their year-end balances and the intercompany interest expense and revenue recorded during the year. In entry form, elimination step (3) is as follows:

Bonds Payable, 8% (on Company S books)	$100,000	
Interest Income (recorded by Company P)	6,800	
Extraordinary Loss on Retirement (created in the		
consolidation process)	3,600	
Investment in Company S Bonds (on Company P books)		102,400
Interest Expense (on Company S books)		8,000

The amount of the extraordinary gain or loss is the sum of the difference between the remaining book value of the investment on bonds compared to the debt and the difference between interest expense and debt. For this example:

Investment in Bonds Balance, December 31, 19X3	$102,400	
Bonds Payable, December 31, 19X3	100,000	$ 2,400
Interest Expense, 19X3	8,000	
Interest Revenue, 19X3	6,800	1,200
Extraordinary Loss, January 2, 19X3		$ 3,600

Step (4) of Worksheet 5-1 eliminated the intercompany interest accruals. In entry form, the elimination is:

Interest Payable (recorded by Company S)	8,000	
Interest Receivable (recorded by Company P)		8,000

As a result of the elimination steps, the consolidated income statement will include the extraordinary retirement loss but will exclude intercompany interest payments and accruals. The consolidated balance sheet will not list the intercompany bonds payable or investment in bonds accounts.

The only remaining problem is the distribution of combined net income to the controlling and minority interests. The income distribution schedule shows Company S absorbing all of the retirement loss. It is most common to view the purchasing affiliate as a mere agent of the issuing affiliate. Therefore, it is the issuer, not the purchaser, that must bear the entire gain or loss on retirement. Even though the debt is retired from a consolidated viewpoint, it still exists internally. Company P has a right to collect the interest as part of its share of Company S's operations. Based on the value of the debt on January 2, 19X3, the interest expense/revenue is $6,800. The interest cost of $8,000 recorded by Company S must be corrected to reflect the internal interest expense of $6,800. The income distribution schedule increases the income of Company S to reflect the adjustment ($1,200) to interest expense. It should be noted that the retirement loss borne by Company S will offset entirely the adjustments to interest expense by the time the bonds mature. If the parent, Company P, had issued the bonds to outside parties and if the subsidiary, Company S, later had purchased them, the only change would be that the income distribution schedule of Company P would absorb the loss on retirement and the interest adjustment.

The worksheet procedures that would be needed at the end of 19X4 are shown in Worksheet 5-2 on pages 328–331. The interest revenue and expense have been recorded on the books of the separate firms. The investment in Company S bonds account on the parent's books reflects its book value at the end of 19X4. Step (3) eliminates the intercompany bonds at their year-end balances and the intercompany interest expense and revenue. Recall that the original retirement loss was $3,600 when the bonds had 3 years to maturity. By the start of the second period, 19X2, $1,200 of that loss already was amortized on the separate books of the affiliates. The loss remaining is $2,400 (it is verified in the explanation to step (3) in Worksheet 5-2). This remaining loss is debited to retained earnings since the retirement occurred in a prior period. The adjustment is allocated to minority and controlling beginning retained earnings since the bonds were issued by the subsidiary. Step (4) eliminates intercompany interest accruals.

The 19X4 consolidated income statement will not include intercompany interest. The income distribution schedules for Worksheet 5-2 reflect the fact that the debt still existed internally during the period. However, the interest expense recorded by Company S is reduced to reflect the interest cost based on the January 2, 19X3 purchase price.

If Company S was the purchaser and Company P the issuer of the bonds, Worksheet 5-2 would differ as follows:

1. The January 1, 19X4 retained earnings adjustment would be absorbed completely by the controlling retained earnings, since the parent company would be the issuer absorbing the loss.
2. The income distribution schedule of the parent would contain the interest adjustment.

BONDS NOT ORIGINALLY ISSUED AT FACE VALUE

The principles of eliminating intercompany investments in bonds are not altered by the existence of a premium or discount stemming from original issuance. The numerical calculations just become more complex. To illustrate, assume Company S issued $100,000 of 5-year, 8% bonds on January 1, 19X1. The market interest rate approximated 9% and, as a result, the bonds sold at a discount of $3,890. Interest is paid each December 31. On each interest payment date, the discount is amortized $778 ($3,890 ÷ 5 years) by decreasing the discount and by increasing interest expense. On December 31, 19X3, the balance of the discount is $1,556 [$3,890 − (3 × $778 annual amortization)].

The parent, Company P, purchased the bonds for $103,600 on December 31, 19X3, after interest had been paid. The parent will amortize $1,800 of the investment each subsequent December 31, reducing the parent's interest income to $6,200 ($8,000 cash – $1,800 amortization) for 19X4 and 19X5.

The following abbreviated December 31, 19X3 (date of purchase) worksheet lists the investment in Company S bonds account, the bonds payable account, and the remaining issuance discount. Eliminating the $103,600 price paid for the bonds by Company P against the book value of $98,444 ($100,000 – $1,556) creates an extraordinary loss on retirement of $5,156 which is carried to combined net income. Worksheet procedures may be aided by linking the bonds payable and the related discount or premium on the worksheet. This is done on our worksheets by circling the amounts in the trial balance and in the eliminations.

	Partial Trial Balance		Eliminations & Adjustments	
	Company P	Company S	Dr.	Cr.
Investment in Company S Bonds	103,600			103,600
Bonds Payable, 8%		(100,000)	100,000	
Discount on Bonds Payable		1,556		1,556
Extraordinary Loss on Bond Retirement			5,156	
Interest Expense		8,778*		

*$8,000 cash + $778 straight-line amortization.

Interest expense on the books of Company S is extended to the consolidated income statement, since this interest was incurred as a result of transactions with outside parties. There would be no interest adjustment for 19X3, since the bonds were not purchased by the parent until December 31, 19X3. The income distribution schedules accompanying the worksheet would assess the retirement loss against the issuer, Company S.

The implications of these intercompany bonds on the 19X4 consolidated worksheet are reflected in Worksheet 5-3 on pages 332–335. Assume Company P acquired a 90% interest in the common stock of Company S at a price equal to the book value of the underlying equity. The simple equity method is used by the parent to record the investment in the stock of Company S. The trial balances include the following items:

1. The investment in Company S bonds at its amortized December 31, 19X4 balance of $101,800 ($103,600 – $1,800 amortization),

2. The interest revenue (adjusted for amortization) of $6,200 on the books of Company P,

3. The discount on bonds account at its amortized December 31, 19X4 balance of $778, and

4. The interest expense (adjusted for discount amortization) of $8,778 ($8,000 cash + $778 amortization) on the books of Company S.

Step (3) eliminates the investment in bonds against the bonds payable and the applicable remaining discount. Step (3) also eliminates interest expense and revenue. Be sure to understand the calculation of the adjustment to beginning retained earnings which is explained in the step (3) information. The loss at the start of the year is the sum of the loss remaining at year end and that amortized on the books of the separate affiliates during the year.

Again, the consolidated income statement does not include intercompany interest. However, the Company S income distribution schedule does reflect the adjustment of Company S's interest expense. The original $8,778 interest expense has been replaced by a $6,200 expense, based on the purchase price paid by Company P. The smaller interest expense compensates the subsidiary for the retirement loss absorbed in a previous period.

PURCHASE OF ONLY A PORTION OF THE BONDS

The examples in this chapter assume that the parent company purchases all of the outstanding bonds of the subsidiary. In such cases, all of the bonds are retired on the worksheet. There may be cases, however, where the parent purchases only a portion of the subsidiary's outstanding bonds. Suppose, for example, that the parent purchased 80% of the subsidiary's outstanding bonds. Only the 80% interest in the bonds would be eliminated on the consolidated worksheet, and only the interest expense and revenue applicable to 80% of the bonds would be eliminated on the worksheet. The 20% interest in the subsidiary bonds owned by persons outside the control group remains as a valid debt of the consolidated firm and should not be eliminated. It is a common error for students to eliminate the 80% interest in intercompany bonds owned by a parent against 100% of the bonds issued by the subsidiary. Such a mistake improperly eliminates valid debt and greatly miscalculates the extraordinary gain or loss on retirement. It also should be noted that the interest paid to persons outside the control group should remain a part of the consolidated statements. Only the interest paid to the affiliated firm is to be eliminated.

INTEREST METHOD OF AMORTIZATION

The procedures used to eliminate intercompany bonds are not altered by the interest method of amortization; only the dollar values change. To illustrate the calculations, assume that Company S issued $100,000 of 5-year, 8% bonds on January 1, 19X1. The market interest rate on that date was 9%, so that the bonds sold at a discount of $3,890. Interest on the bonds is paid each December 31. The discount amortization for the term of the bonds follows:

Year	Balance January 1	Effective Interest	Nominal Interest	Discount Amortization
1	$96,110	$8,650 (.09 × $96,110)	$8,000	$ 650
2	96,760 ($96,110 + $650)	8,708 (.09 × $96,760)	8,000	708
3	97,468 ($96,760 + $708)	8,772 (.09 × $97,468)	8,000	772
4	98,240 ($97,468 + $772)	8,842 (.09 × $98,240)	8,000	842
5	99,082 ($98,240 + $842)	8,918* (.09 × $99,082)	8,000	918
*Includes $1 rounding error.				$3,890

On December 31, 19X3, after interest had been paid, the bonds were purchased by parent Company P at a price to yield 6%. Based on present value computations, $103,667 was paid for the bonds. The premium on the bonds would be amortized by Company P as follows:

Year	Investment Balance, January 1	Effective Interest	Nominal Interest	Premium Amortization
4	$103,667	$6,220 (.06 × $103,667)	$8,000	$1,780
5	101,887 ($103,667 − $1,780)	6,113 (.06 × $101,887)	8,000	1,887
				$3,667

The abbreviated December 31, 19X3 (date of purchase) worksheet at the top of the following page lists the investment in Company S bonds account, the bonds payable account, and the remaining issuance discount. Eliminating the $103,667 price paid by Company P against the book value of $98,240 ($100,000 − $1,760) creates an extraordinary loss on retirement of $5,427 that is carried to combined net income.

The differences in the 19X4 consolidated worksheet caused by the interest method of amortization are shown in Worksheet 5-4 on pages 336–339. Note particularly the change in the Company S income distribution schedule. The original 9% interest, totaling $8,842, has been replaced by the $6,220 of interest calculated using the 6% rate.

	Partial Trial Balance		Eliminations & Adjustments	
	Company P	Company S	Dr.	Cr.
Investment in Company S Bonds	103,667			103,667
Bonds Payable, 8%		(100,000)	100,000	
Discount on Bonds Payable		1,760		1,760
Extraordinary Loss on Bond Retirement			5,427	
Interest Expense		8,772*		

*See preceding discount amortization schedule for issuer.

INTERCOMPANY LEASES

Intercompany leases have become one of the most frequently encountered types of transactions between affiliated firms. It is particularly common for parent firms with substantial financial resources to acquire major assets and to lease the assets to their subsidiaries. This action may occur because the financially stronger parent may be able to both purchase and finance assets on more favorable terms. Also, the parent company may desire close control over plant assets and may prefer centralized ownership and management of assets. Leasing becomes a mechanism through which the parent can convey the use of centrally owned assets to subsidiaries. Some firms achieve centralized asset management by forming separate leasing subsidiaries whose major function is to lease assets to affiliated firms. When such subsidiaries exist, they are consolidated automatically with the parent regardless of the ownership percentage of the parent.[1]

OPERATING LEASES

Consolidation procedures for intercompany leases depend on the original recording of the lease by the separate firms. When an operating lease exists, the lessor has recorded the purchase of the asset and depreciates it. The lessor records rent revenue, while the lessee records rent expense. In such cases, it is necessary to eliminate in the consolidation process the intercompany rent expense/revenue and any related rent receivable/payable. The lessor's asset and related accumulated depreciation should be reclassified as a normal productive asset rather than as property under an operating lease. As an example, assume the parent, Company P, has both productive equipment used in its own operations and equipment that is under operating lease to a subsidiary, Company S. The following partial worksheet may be used to analyze required consolidation procedures:

---

[1]Statement of Financial Accounting Standards No. 13, *Accounting for Leases* (Stamford: Financial Accounting Standards Board, 1976), par. 31.

	Partial Trial Balance		Eliminations & Adjustments	
	Company P	Company S	Dr.	Cr.
Equipment	800,000		(3) 100,000	
Accumulated Depreciation—Equipment	(300,000)			(3) 40,000
Equipment Under Operating Lease	100,000			(3) 100,000
Accumulated Depreciation—Equipment Under Operating Lease	(40,000)		(3) 40,000	
Rent Receivable	1,200			(2) 1,200
Rent Payable		(1,200)	(2) 1,200	
Rent Income	(14,400)		(1) 14,400	
Rent Expense		14,400		(1) 14,400
Depreciation Expense	50,000			

Eliminations and Adjustments:
(1)   Eliminate intercompany rent expense and revenue of $1,200 per month.
(2)   Eliminate one month's accrued rent.
(3)   Reclassify the asset under the intercompany operating lease and its related accumulated depreciation as a normal productive asset.

No adjustments are made in the income distribution schedules as a result of operating leases. The eliminations made on the worksheet do not change the amount of income or the distribution of income between the minority and controlling interests.

CAPITALIZABLE LEASES

Consolidation procedures become more complicated when the lease is recorded as a capital lease by the lessee and as a direct-financing or sales-type lease by the lessor. The lessee records both an asset and intercompany long-term debt. Generally, the criteria for determining when a lease requires such accounting treatment are the same for affiliated firms as for independent firms. However, when the terms of the lease are significantly affected by the fact that the lessee and lessor are affiliates, the usual criteria for classification of leases do not apply. Lease terms could be considered "significantly affected" when they could not reasonably be expected to occur between independent firms.[2] For example, a parent might lease to its subsidiary at a rent far below the market rate, or a parent might rent a highly specialized machine to its subsidiary on a month-to-month basis. Typically, such specialized machinery would be leased only on a long-term lease promising a full recovery of cost to the lessor, since there would be no use for the machine by other lessees if it were returned to the lessor. The month-to-

----
[2]*Ibid.*, par. 29.

month lease is possible only because the parent's control of the subsidiary assures a continued flow of rent payments. When, in the accountant's judgment, the terms of the lease are affected significantly by the parent–subsidiary relationship, the normal criteria are not used, and the transaction is recorded so as to reflect its true economic substance.[3] Usually in these circumstances, the lessee is viewed as having purchased the asset using funds borrowed from the lessor.

Consolidation Procedures for Direct-Financing Leases.

A direct-financing lease is viewed as a unique type of asset transfer by the lessor, who accepts a long-term receivable from the lessee as consideration for the asset received by the lessee. There is no profit or loss to the lessor on the transfer, only future interest revenue as payments become due.

Prior to studying consolidated worksheet procedures, the entries made by the affiliated lessee and lessor will be analyzed. In its simplest form, a direct-financing lease is recorded by the lessee as an asset, and debt is recorded to recognize the lease obligation. The lessor records the lease as a receivable from the lessee. If all payments to be received by the lessor will come from or are guaranteed by the original lessee, the present value of the net receivable recorded by the lessor will equal the present value of the payable recorded by the lessee, and the interest rates used to amortize the debt will be equal.

To illustrate, assume Company S is an 80%-owned subsidiary of Company P. On January 1, 19X1, Company P purchased a machine for $5,851 and leased it to Company S. The terms of the direct-financing lease provide for rental payments of $2,000 per year at the beginning of each period and allow the lessee to exercise an option to purchase the machine for $1,000 at the end of 19X3. The $1,000 purchase option is considered a bargain purchase option that will be exercised and is included in the minimum lease payments. The implicit interest rate (which equates all payments, including the bargain purchase option, to the lessor's purchase cost) is 16%. The lessee will depreciate the capitalized cost of the machine over 5 years, using the straight-line method. The lessee may use a 5-year life, despite the 3-year lease term, because it is assumed that the bargain purchase option will be exercised and that the asset will be used for 5 years.

The amortization of the debt at the implicit 16% interest rate is as follows:

Date	Payment	Interest at 16% on Previous Balance	Reduction of Principal	Principal Balance
Jan. 1, 19X1	$2,000		$2,000	$3,851*
Jan. 1, 19X2	2,000	$ 616	1,384	2,467
Jan. 1, 19X3	2,000	395	1,605	862
Dec. 31, 19X3	1,000	138	862	
Total	$7,000	$1,149	$5,851	

*Purchase price of $5,851 – $2,000 initial payment.

---

[3]*Ibid.*

The journal entries for the separate firms would be as follows for the first two years:

Date	Company S (Lessee)		Company P (Lessor)	
19X1				
Jan. 1	Assets Under Capital Lease............. 5,851		Minimum Lease Payments Receivable ... 5,000	
	Obligations Under Capital Lease	3,851	Cash 2,000	
	Cash	2,000	Unearned Interest Income	1,149
			Accounts Payable (for asset)	5,851
Dec. 31	Interest Expense (at 16%) 616		Unearned Interest Income 616	
	Interest Payable.....................	616	Interest Income (at 16%)	616
	Depreciation Expense (1/5 × $5,851) 1,170			
	Accumulated Depreciation—Assets			
	Under Capital Lease	1,170		
19X2				
Jan. 1	Obligations Under Capital Lease 1,384		Cash 2,000	
	Interest Payable..................... 616		Minimum Lease Payments	
	Cash	2,000	Receivable	2,000
Dec. 31	Interest Expense (at 16%) 395		Unearned Interest Income 395	
	Interest Payable.....................	395	Interest Income (at 16%)	395
	Depreciation Expense.................. 1,170			
	Accumulated Depreciation—Assets			
	Under Capital Lease	1,170		

At the end of each period, consolidation procedures would be needed to eliminate the intercompany transactions. In substance, there appears on the separate records of the affiliates an intercompany transfer of a plant asset with resulting intercompany debt. The intercompany debt, related interest expense/revenue, and interest accruals must be eliminated. Also, it is necessary to reclassify the assets under capital leases as productive assets owned by the consolidated group. The adjusted partial worksheets (pages 298 and 299) illustrate consolidation procedures at the end of 19X1 and 19X2.

A review of the worksheet eliminations and adjustments reveals that combined net income is not changed because equal amounts of interest expense and revenue were eliminated. Therefore, *no adjustments are required in the income distribution schedules.*

Some capital leases will designate a portion of the annual rent as being applicable to executory costs, such as property taxes or maintenance, incurred by the lessor. Such payments for executory costs are not included in the obligation of the lessee or the minimum lease payments receivable recorded by the lessor. Instead, such payments are recorded as rent expense and revenue in each period. In the consolidation process, that portion of rent applicable to executory costs is eliminated like any other charge for intercompany services.

The preceding example has a bargain purchase option. This means that all payments to be received by the lessor would come from the original lessee. Equality of payments for both parties to a lease between affiliates is the most common case. However, there may be intercompany leases where there is an unguaranteed residual value for the lessor. This means that a portion of the total payments to be received by the lessor will come from parties outside the control

Partial Worksheet
For Year Ended December 31, 19X1

	Trial Balance		Eliminations & Adjustments	
	Company P	Company S	Dr.	Cr.
Assets Under Capital Lease		5,851		(3) 5,851
Accumulated Depreciation—Assets Under Capital Lease		(1,170)	(3) 1,170	
Property, Plant, and Equipment	200,000	120,000	(3) 5,851	
Accumulated Depreciation—Property, Plant, and Equipment	(80,000)	(50,000)		(3) 1,170
Obligations Under Capital Lease		(3,851)	(2) 3,851	
Interest Payable		(616)	(2) 616	
Minimum Lease Payments Receivable	5,000			(2) 5,000
Unearned Interest Income	(533)		(2) 533	
Interest Expense		616		(1) 616
Interest Income	(616)		(1) 616	

Eliminations and Adjustments:
(1) Eliminate intercompany interest expense/revenue of $616.
(2) Eliminate the intercompany debt recorded by the lessee (obligation under capital lease plus accrued interest payable) against the net intercompany receivable of the lessor (minimum lease payments receivable less unearned interest income).
(3) Reclassify the asset under capital lease and its related accumulated depreciation as a productive asset owned by the consolidated firm.

group. Therefore, the stream of payments to be received by the lessor exceeds the stream of payments to be paid by the lessee. This complicates the consolidation process. (The appendix to this chapter illustrates a revised version of the preceding example that deals with an unequal stream of payments.)

Consolidation Procedures for Sales-Type Leases.   Under a sales-type lease, a lessor records a sales profit or loss at the inception of the lease. The sales profit or loss is the difference between the fair market value of the asset at the inception of the lease and the cost of the asset to the lessor. Consolidation procedures do not allow recognition of this profit or loss at the inception of the lease. Instead, the profit or loss is deferred and then amortized over the lessee's period of usage. This period will be the lease term unless there is a bargain purchase or bargain renewal option, in which case the asset's useful life would be used.

To illustrate, assume that in the previous example the asset leased to Company S had a cost to Company P of $4,951. Company P would have recorded the following entry at the inception of the sales-type lease:

Partial Worksheet
For Year Ended December 31, 19X2

	Trial Balance		Eliminations & Adjustments	
	Company P	Company S	Dr.	Cr.
Assets Under Capital Lease		5,851		(3) 5,851
Accumulated Depreciation—Assets Under Capital Lease		(2,340)	(3) 2,340	
Property, Plant, and Equipment	200,000	120,000	(3) 5,851	
Accumulated Depreciation—Property, Plant, and Equipment	(100,000)	(60,000)		(3) 2,340
Obligations Under Capital Lease		(2,467)	(2) 2,467	
Interest Payable		(395)	(2) 395	
Minimum Lease Payments Receivable	3,000			(2) 3,000
Unearned Interest Income	(138)		(2) 138	
Interest Expense		395		(1) 395
Interest Income	(395)		(1) 395	

Eliminations and Adjustments:
(1)   Eliminate intercompany interest expense/revenue of $395.
(2)   Eliminate intercompany debt and net receivable.
(3)   Reclassify the asset under capital lease and its related accumulated depreciation as a productive asset owned by the consolidated firm.

Minimum Lease Payments Receivable	5,000	
Cash	2,000	
Unearned Interest Income		1,149
Asset (cost of asset leased)		4,951
Sales Profit on Leases		900

This entry differs from that of the previous example only to the extent of recording the gain and transferring an existing asset. None of the lessor's subsequent entries recording the earning of interest and the payment of the receivable would change. The lessee's entries are unaffected by the existence of the sales profit.

Consolidation procedures for a sales-type lease, however, do require added steps to those already illustrated. The sales profit is similar to a profit on the sale of a plant asset. The $900 profit in this example must be deferred over the 3-year lease term. Thus, the asset and its related depreciation accounts must be adjusted to reflect the original sales profit.

The following added adjustments on the 19X1 partial worksheet (p. 298) would be needed for the original $900 sales profit:

Sales Profit on Leases	900	
Property, Plant, and Equipment		900

To reduce cost of asset for gain on sales-type lease.

Accumulated Depreciation—Property, Plant, and Equipment 300
   Depreciation Expense   300
      To reduce depreciation expense at the rate of $300 per year.

The income distribution schedule of the parent (lessor) would reflect the deferral of the original $900 profit in the year of the sale and would recognize $300 per year during the asset's life.

For the 19X2 partial worksheet (p. 299), the following added adjustments would be required if a sales-type lease was involved:

Retained Earnings—Controlling Interest 600
Accumulated Depreciation—Property, Plant, and Equipment 300
   Property, Plant, and Equipment.   900
      To adjust the remaining sales profit at the beginning of the period.

Accumulated Depreciation—Property, Plant, and Equipment 300
   Depreciation Expense   300
      To reduce depreciation expense at the rate of $300 per year.

INTERCOMPANY TRANSACTIONS PRIOR TO BUSINESS COMBINATION

It is possible that the firms involved in a business combination may have had dealings with each other prior to the consummation of the acquisition. The ramifications of such dealings on the consolidation process depend on whether the combination is a purchase or a pooling of interests.

When the acquisition is a purchase, there is no need to be concerned with intercompany sales occurring prior to the acquisition. It is assumed that the sales were arm's-length transactions between unrelated parties. Even though assets containing the profit are on the balance sheet on the acquisition date, no adjustments are needed when consolidating. When one affiliate previously purchased the other affiliate's bonds, a complication does arise. The bonds become an intercompany debt as of the purchase date and thus are viewed as retired on the purchase date when consolidating.

Acquisitions deemed to be a pooling of interests create a need for eliminating intercompany transactions occurring prior to the acquisition date. Recall that poolings are retroactive to the entire current period and to earlier periods. This means that all intercompany transactions during the period in which a pooling occurs must be eliminated, no matter when the pooling occurs. In essence, consolidated statements for the period during which a pooling occurs are the same as they would appear if the pooling had occurred at the beginning of the period. When comparative statements are prepared, pooling is retroactive for all such statements. This means that transactions between the firms during those previous periods must be eliminated. In summary, consolidation procedures are applied as they would be if the firms had been pooled from their inception.

APPENDIX: INTERCOMPANY LEASES
WITH UNGUARANTEED RESIDUAL VALUE

The intercompany lease may contain an unguaranteed residual value. This means that the original intercompany lessee will supply only a portion of the total cash flow to be received by the lessor. At the end of the original lease term, the lessor may lease the asset again or sell it. In either case, there is no obligation on the part of the lessee to renew the lease or to purchase the asset. Since the original lessee is contractually bound to provide only a portion of the payments to be received by the lessor, the lessee will record as its lease obligation only the present value of the minimum lease payments for which it is obligated. The present value of these minimum lease payments is computed using the lessee's incremental borrowing rate, unless the lessor's implicit interest rate in the lease is known or is reasonably estimable and is lower, in which case the lessor's implicit rate is used.[4] Usually, the lessor's implicit rate will be available since the lessee and lessor are members of the same control group. Therefore, the lessor's implicit rate will be used for leases between affiliates of the consolidated group. Leases using any other rate should be adjusted to the implicit rate prior to consolidating.

The lessor records the gross investment in the lease, which is the sum of the minimum lease payments receivable and the unguaranteed residual value. Unearned interest income is recorded as a contra-account at an amount that reduces the gross investment to the market value of the asset at the inception of the lease. Unearned interest is amortized using the implicit rate of the lessor. The implicit rate of the lessor thus equates the present value of all payments expected, including the unguaranteed residual value, to the market value of the asset.

The recording methods used by the lessee and lessor for leases with an unguaranteed residual value present a complication to the consolidation process. The amount of the asset under the capital lease recorded by the lessee will be less than the asset's market value, since the present value of the lease payments recorded by the lessee will not include the asset's unguaranteed residual value. To understand this complication, the previous example may be used with one change. Instead of the $1,000 bargain purchase option that was included in the set of minimum lease payments, assume there is a $1,000 unguaranteed residual value. Since the residual value is not guaranteed, it is not part of the minimum lease payments. The revised facts are as follows:

1. Cost of asset to lessor: $5,851.
2. Lease terms: Three annual payments of $2,000 due at the start of each year. Unguaranteed residual value of $1,000 to lessor at the end of 19X3.
3. Lessor implicit rate: 16% equates the three $2,000 payments plus the unguaranteed residual value to $5,851.
4. Lessee interest rate: 16% (lessor implicit rate) which, when applied to only the lease payments, results in a present value of $5,210.
5. Depreciation: Straight-line over the 3-year lease term, since the contractual use of the asset is for three years.
6. Amortization tables:

---

[4]When the present value of the minimum lease payments using the incremental borrowing rate exceeds the market value of the asset, the asset and the obligation are recorded at the market value of the asset. The interest rate that equates the present value of the payments to the market value of the asset is used then to amortize the debt.

Lessor (16%)

Date	Payment	Interest at 16% on Previous Balance	Reduction of Principal	Principal Balance
Jan. 1, 19X1	$2,000		$2,000	$3,851*
Jan. 1, 19X2	2,000	$ 616	1,384	2,467
Jan. 1, 19X3	2,000	395	1,605	862
Dec. 31, 19X3	1,000	138	862	
Total	$7,000	$1,149	$5,851	

*Purchase price of $5,851 – $2,000 initial payment.

Lessee (16%)

Date	Payment	Interest at 16% on Previous Balance	Reduction of Principal	Principal Balance
Jan. 1, 19X1	$2,000		$2,000	$3,210**
Jan. 1, 19X2	2,000	$ 514	1,486	1,724
Jan. 1, 19X3	2,000	276	1,724	
Total	$6,000	$ 790	$5,210	

**Present value of $5,210 – $2,000 initial payment.

The journal entries for the separate firms would be as follows for the first two years:

Date	Company S (Lessee)			Company P (Lessor)		
19X1						
Jan. 1	Assets Under Capital Lease	5,210		Minimum Lease Payments Receivable...	4,000	
	Cash		2,000	Unguaranteed Residual Value	1,000	
	Obligations Under Capital Lease		3,210	Cash	2,000	
				Unearned Interest Income		1,149
				Accounts Payable (for asset)		5,851
Dec. 31	Interest Expense (at 16%)	514		Unearned Interest Income	616	
	Interest Payable		514	Interest Income (at 16%)		616
	Depreciation Expense (1/3 × $5,210)	1,737				
	Accumulated Depreciation—Assets Under Capital Lease		1,737			
19X2						
Jan. 1	Obligations Under Capital Lease	1,486		Cash	2,000	
	Interest Payable	514		Minimum Lease Payments Receivable		2,000
	Cash		2,000			
Dec. 31	Interest Expense (at 16%)	276		Unearned Interest Income	395	
	Interest Payable		276	Interest Income (at 16%)		395
	Depreciation Expense	1,737				
	Accumulated Depreciation—Assets Under Capital Lease		1,737			

A comparison of the lessor's and lessee's amortization tables shows the following difference between the lessee's interest expense and the lessor's interest income each period:

Year Ending December 31	16% Lessor Implicit Interest	16% Lessee Interest	Difference
19X1	$ 616	$514	$102
19X2	395	276	119
19X3	138		138
Total	$1,149	$790	$359

The difference is the interest on the unguaranteed residual value, which is recorded only by the lessor. This can be demonstrated as follows:

Date	16% Implicit Interest	Difference in Principal Balances
Jan. 1, 19X1		$ 641*
Dec. 31, 19X1	$102	743
Dec. 31, 19X2	119	862
Dec. 31, 19X3	138	1,000
Total	$359	

*$5,851 − $5,210.

In the consolidation process, the intercompany debt and all interest applicable to the lease are eliminated. Even the interest income recorded on the unguaranteed residual value is eliminated, since it is a ramification of a lease that, from a consolidated viewpoint, does not exist. The asset recorded by the lessee and the unguaranteed residual value recorded by the lessor are eliminated and replaced by a productive asset recorded by the consolidated firm.

 Worksheet 5-5, pages 340–343, contains the detailed steps for the elimination of the intercompany lease at the end of 19X1. In this worksheet, it is assumed that the interest in the 80%-owned subsidiary was purchased at its book value. Steps (1) and (2) eliminate the investment. Step (3) eliminates the $616 of interest income against the $514 of interest expense. The $102 disparity reflects the interest applicable to the unguaranteed residual value and is returned to unearned interest income. Step (4) eliminates the intercompany debt applicable to the lease. The $359 disparity reflects the interest applicable to the unguaranteed residual value over the life of the lease. This amount is used to reduce the unguaranteed residual value to its original present value of $641. The $641, combined with the $5,210 asset under capital lease, is eliminated and replaced by an owned asset and recorded at the $5,851 original cost to the consolidated firm. Step (5) adjusts the depreciation to reflect the cost and the residual value of the asset to the consolidated firm. The accumulated depreciation also is reclassified as that applicable to an owned asset.

 In Worksheet 5-6 on pages 344–346, the consolidation procedures for the second year of the lease term are illustrated.

1. What are the alternative methods available to affiliated firms of extinguishing debt in the hands of outside parties, and how is the consolidation process affected by each method? When the parent purchases bonds issued by the subsidiary from an outside party, why is the resulting gain or loss borne entirely by the issuer?

2. What is the effect on combined net income in the year of acquisition and in subsequent periods of the following parent purchases of 8% subsidiary bonds?
    (a) Issued at 9%, purchased to yield 7%
    (b) Issued at 7%, purchased to yield 9%
    (c) Issued at 9%, purchased to yield 10%
    (d) Issued at 10%, purchased to yield 9%

3. Why would the amounts of interest expense and revenue recorded by affiliated firms relative to intercompany bondholdings not agree? How is the disparity dealt with in the consolidation process?

4. Assume that a subsidiary company's outstanding bonds are purchased at a gain by the parent company.
    (a) Explain why a gain on bond retirement appears on the consolidated statements, even though the subsidiary has not retired the bonded debt.
    (b) The income distribution schedule for the subsidiary company shows internally generated net income and adjusted income. Assuming no other intercompany transactions, compare these two income figures:
        (1) In the year of bond acquisition,
        (2) Each succeeding year until maturity, and
        (3) In the aggregate for the periods during which the bonds are outstanding.
    Briefly justify each answer.

5. Company P purchased Company S's $50,000, 5-year, 6% bonds three years after issuance. The bonds originally were issued at face value and later purchased by Company P at a market rate of 5% for $50,928. Using the straight-line method of amortization, compute the income distribution schedule interest adjustments over the remaining term of the bonds and explain their relationship to the original consolidated gain or loss on retirement. On whose income distribution schedule do these items appear?

6. What are the benefits of leasing among affiliated firms?

7. Why are no adjustments made on the income distribution schedules of controlling and minority interests as a result of operating and direct-financing leases?

8. Distinguish between a direct-financing lease and a sales-type lease from the standpoint of the lessor.

9. Company X is leasing several plant assets from its parent firm, Company T. Which of the following items should Company X include in minimum lease payments if the lease is classified as an operating lease? As a capital lease?
    (a) Annual rental payments
    (b) Amounts reimbursing the lessor for executory costs, such as insurance, maintenance, and taxes
    (c) Guaranteed residual value
    (d) Penalties paid for failure to renew
    (e) Bargain purchase option

10. Designate whether the following accounts normally are recorded on the books of the lessor or the lessee. Indicate which accounts are eliminated, reclassified, or adjusted in the consolidation process.
    (a) Equipment Operating Lease
    (b) Rent Expense—Executory Costs
    (c) Accounts Payable (for asset)
    (d) Depreciation Expense—Operating Lease
    (e) Depreciation Expense—Capital Lease
    (f) Unearned Interest Income
    (g) Assets Under Capital Lease

11. Parent Company purchased an asset for $30,850 and has agreed to lease the asset to its subsidiary over a 5-year period. The fair market value of the leased asset at the inception of the lease term was $32,000. Record the adjustments pertaining to the sales profit on the lease that would be made on the consolidated worksheet for the first and final years of the lease term.

EXERCISES

Exercise 1. Midwest Trucking is a large corporation with the ability to obtain financing by selling bond issuances at favorable rates. Currently it pays 8% interest on its 10-year bond issues. In the past year Midwest purchased an 80% interest in a subsidiary, Route 151 Line. Route 151 has $1,000,000 of bonds outstanding that mature in 6 years. Interest is paid annually at a stated rate of 11%. The bonds were issued at face value. Interest rates have come down, but Route 151 could still expect to pay 9% to 9.5% interest on a long-term issue. Route 151 is a smaller firm with a lower credit rating than Midwest.

Midwest would like to reduce interest costs on the Route 151 debt. It has asked your advice on whether it should purchase the bonds or loan Route 151 the money to retire its own debt. Compare the options with a focus on the impact on consolidated statements.

Exercise 2. Hartwig Company is an 80%-owned subsidiary of Ney Industries. Hartwig Company issued 10-year, 8% bonds in the amount of $500,000 on January 1, 19X1. The bonds were issued at face value and interest is payable each January 1. On January, 1, 19X3, Ney Industries purchased all of the Hartwig bonds for $484,000. Ney will amortize the discount on a straight-line basis. For the years ending (a) December 31, 19X3, and (b) December 31, 19X4, determine the effects of this transaction:
    (1) On combined net income.
    (2) On the distribution of income to the controlling and minority interest.

Exercise 3. Kelly Company is an 80%-owned subsidiary of Brown Corporation. Kelly Company issued $100,000 of 10%, 8-year bonds for $102,400 on January 1, 19X1. Annual interest is paid on January 1. Brown Corporation purchased the bonds on January 2, 19X5, for $99,200. Both firms are using the straight-line method to amortize the premium/discount on the bonds.
    (1) Prepare the eliminations and adjustments that would be made on the December 31, 19X5 consolidated worksheet as a result of this purchase.
    (2) Prepare the eliminations and adjustments that would be made on the December 31, 19X6 consolidated worksheet.

Exercise 4. On January 1, 19X4, Dunbar Corporation, an 85%-owned subsidiary of Garfield Industries, received $48,055 for $50,000 of 8%, five-year bonds it issued when the market rate was 9%. When Garfield Industries purchased these bonds for $47,513 on January 2, 19X6, the market rate was 10%. Given the following effective interest amortization schedules for both firms, calculate the gain or loss on retirement and the interest adjustments to the issuer's income distribution schedules over the remaining term of the bonds.

Dunbar (issuer)

Date	Effective Interest (9%)	Nominal Interest	Discount Amortization	Balance
1/1/X4				$48,055
1/1/X5	$4,325	$4,000	$ 325	48,380
1/1/X6	4,354	4,000	354	48,734
1/1/X7	4,386	4,000	386	49,120
1/1/X8	4,421	4,000	421	49,541
1/1/X9	4,459*	4,000	459	50,000

Garfield (purchaser)

Date	Effective Interest (10%)	Nominal Interest	Discount Amortization	Balance
1/1/X6				$47,513
1/1/X7	$4,751	$4,000	$ 751	48,264
1/1/X8	4,826	4,000	826	49,091
1/1/X9	4,909	4,000	909	50,000

Exercise 5. Real Meat Products is an 80%-owned subsidiary of Foremost Meat Packers Inc. On January 1, 19X8, Real Meat sold $100,000 of 10-year, 9% bonds for $102,000. Interest is paid annually on January 1. The market rate for this type of bond was 12% on January 2, 19Y0, when Foremost purchased 40% of the Real Meat bonds for $36,000. Discounts may be amortized on a straight-line basis.
(1) Prepare the eliminations and adjustments required for this bond purchase on the December 31, 19Y0 consolidated worksheet.
(2) Prepare the eliminations and adjustments required on the December 31, 19Y1 consolidated worksheet.

Exercise 6. Largo Industries, a 90%-owned subsidiary of Shallow Incorporated, issued $150,000 of 12-year, 13% bonds on January 1, 19X5, to yield 12% interest. Interest is paid annually on January 1. The interest method is used to amortize the premium. Shallow purchased the bonds for $175,915 on January 2, 19X8, when the market rate of interest was 10%. On the purchase date, the remaining premium on the bonds was $7,999. Largo's 19X8 net income was $500,000.
(1) Prepare the eliminations and adjustments required for this purchase on the December 31, 19X8 consolidated worksheet.
(2) Prepare the 19X8 income distribution schedule for the minority interest.

Exercise 7. Prime Machinery Company purchased, for cash, an $80,000 custom machine on January 1, 19X1. The machine has an estimated 10-year life and will be depreciated straight-line with no salvage value. The machine was then leased to Superia Engineering Company, an 80%-owned subsidiary, under a five-year operating lease for $12,000 per year, payable each January 1.
(1) Record the 19X1 entries for the purchase of the machine and the lease to Superia Engineering Company on the books of Prime Machinery Company.
(2) Record the 19X1 entries for the transaction on the books of Superia Engineering Company.

(3) Provide the elimination entries that would be made on the 19X1 consolidated work-sheet.

Exercise 8. On January 1, 19X0, Adams Company, an 80%-owned subsidiary of Beatrix Electronics Inc., signed a 4-year direct-financing lease with its parent for the rental of electronic equipment. The lease agreement requires a $6,000 payment on January 1 of each year, and Adams may purchase the equipment under a bargain purchase option for $2,000 on January 1, 19X4. The equipment originally cost $21,682 and had an estimated remaining life of six years at the start of the lease term. The lessor's implicit interest rate is 12%. The lessee also uses the 12% rate to record the transaction.

(1) Prepare the eliminations and adjustments required for this lease on the December 31, 19X0 consolidated worksheet.
(2) Prepare the eliminations and adjustments for the December 31, 19X1 consolidated worksheet.

Exercise 9. The Auto Clinic is a wholly owned subsidiary of Fast Check Equipment Company. Fast Check Equipment sells and leases four-wheel alignment machines. The usual selling price of the machine is $35,000; it has a cost to Fast Check Equipment of $25,000. On January 1, 19X1, Fast Check Equipment leased such a machine to Auto Clinic. The lease provided for payments of $9,096 at the start of each year for 5 years. The payments include $1,000 per year for maintenance to be provided by the seller. There is a bargain purchase price of $2,000 at the end of the fifth year. The implicit interest rate in the lease is 10% per year. The equipment is being depreciated over eight years.

The amortization schedule for the lease prepared by Fast Check Equipment is as follows.

Date	Payment	Interest at 10% on Previous Balance	Reduction of Principal	Principal Balance
1/1/X1	$ 8,096		$ 8,096	$26,904
1/1/X2	8,096	$2,691	5,405	21,499
1/1/X3	8,096	2,150	5,946	15,553
1/1/X4	8,096	1,556	6,540	9,013
1/1/X5	8,096	901	7,195	1,818
12/31/X5	2,000	182	1,818	0

Prepare the eliminations and adjustments, in entry form, that would be required on a consolidated worksheet prepared on December 31, 19X1.

PROBLEMS

Problem 5-1. Since its 100% acquisition of Mink Corporation stock on December 31, 19X2, Jewel Corporation has maintained its investment under the cost method. However, due to Mink's earning potential, the price included a $20,000 payment for goodwill to be amortized over 10 years. At the time of the purchase, the fair market value of Mink's assets equaled their book value. Mink Corporation's retained earnings balance was $50,000 on the purchase date.

On January 2, 19X4, Mink Corporation issued 10-year, 9% bonds at a face value of $50,000. The bonds pay interest each December 31. Mink amortizes the discount using the straight-line method. On January 2, 19X6, Jewel Corporation purchased all of Mink Corporation's outstanding bonds for $51,000. They have been included in Jewel's long-term investment in bonds account.

Below are the trial balances of both firms on December 31, 19X6:

	Jewel Corp.	Mink Corp.
Cash	88,500	67,500
Accounts Receivable	450,000	75,000
Inventory	200,000	65,000
Investment in Bonds	50,875	
Plant and Equipment (net)	2,420,000	196,000
Investment in Mink Corp.................................	300,000	
Accounts Payable.......................................	(275,000)	(18,000)
Bonds Payable (9%)....................................		(50,000)
Common Stock—Jewel ($10 par)........................	(1,000,000)	
Paid-In Capital in Excess of Par—Jewel....................	(750,000)	
Retained Earnings—Jewel, 1/1/X6	(700,000)	
Common Stock—Mink ($10 par).........................		(100,000)
Paid-In Capital in Excess of Par—Mink		(130,000)
Retained Earnings—Mink, 1/1/X6.........................		(80,000)
Sales...	(2,500,000)	(540,000)
Cost of Goods Sold	1,000,000	405,000
Other Expenses..	720,000	105,000
Interest Income..	(4,375)	
Interest Expense.......................................		4,500
Total...	0	0

Required:

Prepare the worksheet necessary to produce the consolidated balance sheet and income statements of the Jewel Corporation and its subsidiary for the year ended December 31, 19X6.

Problem 5-2. On January 1, 19X1, Parts Hut Company purchased 90% of the common stock of Swift Company for $335,000. On this date, Swift had common stock, other paid-in capital, and retained earnings of $100,000, $40,000, and $210,000, respectively. Any excess of cost over book value is due to goodwill, to be amortized over 5 years. In both 19X1 and 19X2, Parts Hut has accounted for the investment in Swift using the cost method.

On July 1, 19X1, Swift sold $100,000 par value of 10-year, 8% bonds for $94,000. The bonds pay interest semiannually on January 1 and July 1 of each year. On December 31, 19X1, Parts Hut purchased all of Swift's bonds for $96,200, plus accrued interest. The bonds are still held on December 31, 19X2. Both companies have correctly recorded all entries relative to bonds and interest, using straight-line amortization for premium or discount.

The trial balances of Parts Hut Company and its subsidiary were as follows on December 31, 19X2:

	Parts Hut Company	Swift Company
Interest Receivable....................................	4,000	
Other Current Assets..................................	264,400	314,900
Investment in Swift Company..........................	335,000	
Investment in Swift Bonds............................	96,600	
Land	80,000	60,000
Buildings and Equipment.............................	400,000	280,000
Accumulated Depreciation............................	(120,000)	(60,000)
Interest Payable		(4,000)

	Parts Hut Company	Swift Company
Other Current Liabilities	(98,000)	(56,000)
Bonds Payable, 8%		(100,000)
Discount on Bonds Payable		5,100
Other Long-Term Liabilities	(200,000)	
Common Stock—Parts Hut	(100,000)	
Other Paid-In Capital—Parts Hut	(200,000)	
Retained Earnings—Parts Hut	(365,000)	
Common Stock—Swift		(100,000)
Other Paid-In Capital—Swift		(40,000)
Retained Earnings—Swift		(260,000)
Net Sales	(640,000)	(350,000)
Cost of Goods Sold	360,000	200,000
Operating Expenses	168,400	71,400
Interest Expense		8,600
Interest Income	(8,400)	
Dividend Income	(27,000)	
Dividends Declared	50,000	30,000
Total	0	0

Required:

Prepare the worksheet necessary to produce the consolidated financial statements of Parts Hut and its subsidiary Swift for the year ended December 31, 19X2. Round all computations to the nearest dollar.

Problem 5-3. On January 1, 19X3, Warehouse Outlets had the following balances in its stockholders' equity accounts: Common Stock ($10 par), $800,000; Paid-In Capital in Excess of Par, $625,000; and Retained Earnings, $450,000. General Appliances purchased 64,000 shares of Warehouse Outlets common stock for $1,700,000 on that date. Any excess of cost over book value was attributed to goodwill and given a 10-year life.

Warehouse Outlets issued $500,000 of 8-year, 11% bonds on December 31, 19X2. The bonds sold for $476,000. General Appliances purchased one-half of these bonds in the market on January 1, 19X5, for $259,000. Both firms use the straight-line method of amortization of premiums and discounts.

On July 1, 19X6, General Appliances sold to Warehouse Outlets an old building with a book value of $167,500, remaining life of 10 years, and $30,000 salvage value, for $195,000. The building is being depreciated on a straight-line basis. Warehouse Outlets paid $20,000 in cash and signed a mortgage note with its parent for the balance. Interest, at 11% of the unpaid balance, and principal payments are due annually beginning July 1, 19X7. (For convenience, the mortgage balances are not divided into current and long-term portions.)

The trial balances of the two firms at December 31, 19X6, are as follows:

	General Appliances	Warehouse Outlets
Cash	401,986	72,625
Accounts Receivable (net)	752,500	105,000
Interest Receivable	9,625	
Inventory	1,950,000	900,000
Investment in Warehouse Outlets	1,700,000	
Investment in 11% Bonds	256,000	
Investment in Mortgage	175,000	
Property, Plant, and Equipment	9,000,000	2,950,000

	General Appliances	Warehouse Outlets
Accumulated Depreciation	(1,695,000)	(940,000)
Accounts Payable	(670,000)	(80,000)
Interest Payable	(18,333)	(9,625)
Bonds Payable, 11%	(2,000,000)	(500,000)
Discount on Bonds Payable	10,470	12,000
Mortgage Payable		(175,000)
Common Stock ($5 par)	(3,200,000)	
Common Stock ($10 par)		(800,000)
Paid-In Capital in Excess of Par	(4,550,000)	(625,000)
Retained Earnings, Jan. 1, 19X6	(1,011,123)	(770,000)
Sales	(9,800,000)	(3,000,000)
Gain on Sale of Building	(27,500)	
Interest Income	(35,625)	
Dividend Income	(48,000)	
Cost of Goods Sold	4,940,000	1,700,000
Depreciation Expense	717,000	95,950
Interest Expense	223,000	67,544
Other Expenses	2,600,000	936,506
Dividends Declared	320,000	60,000
Total	0	0

Required:

Prepare the worksheet necessary to produce the consolidated financial statements of General Appliances and its subsidiary for the year ended December 31, 19X6. Include the determination and distribution of excess and income distribution schedules.

Problem 5-4.   Erin Incorporated acquired all of the outstanding $25 par value common stock of Sturm Incorporated on January 1, 19X7, in exchange for 40,000 shares of its $25 par value common stock. The business combination meets all the conditions for a pooling of interests. On June 30, 19X7, Erin's common stock closed at $65 per share on the national stock exchange. Both corporations continued to operate as separate businesses, maintaining separate accounting records with fiscal years ending December 31.

On December 31, 19X7, the companies had condensed balance sheet accounts as follows:

	Erin Incorporated	Sturm Incorporated
Cash	925,000	326,000
Other Current Assets	2,300,000	835,000
Inventory	2,310,000	1,045,000
Land	600,000	330,000
Property, Plant, and Equipment (net)	4,525,000	1,980,000
Long-Term Investments and Other Assets	865,000	385,000
Investment in Sturm Inc.	2,010,000	
Current Liabilities	(2,465,000)	(1,145,000)
Long-term Debt	(1,900,000)	(1,300,000)
Common Stock ($25 par)	(3,200,000)	
Common Stock ($25 par)		(1,000,000)
Additional Paid-in Capital	(1,850,000)	(190,000)
Retained Earnings	(3,326,000)	(820,000)
Sales	(2,500,000)	(2,000,000)

	Erin Incorporated	Sturm Incorporated
Cost of Goods Sold..............................	1,200,000	970,000
Other Expenses...................................	429,500	320,000
Dividend Income..................................	(160,000)	
Dividends Declared...............................	256,000	160,000
Interest Income	(19,500)	
Interest Expense		104,000
Total..	0	0

Additional information is as follows:
(a) Erin uses the cost method of accounting for its investment in Sturm.
(b) On June 15, 19X7, Sturm paid a cash dividend of $4 per share on its common stock.
(c) On December 10, 19X7, Erin paid a cash dividend totaling $256,000 on its common stock.
(d) Sturm's long-term debt consisted of 8%, ten-year bonds issued at face value on March 31, 19X1. Interest is payable semiannually on March 31 and September 30. On March 31, 19X7 Erin purchased $300,000 of face value Sturm bonds for $292,000. The purchase discount is amortized using the straight-line method.
(e) During October 19X7, Erin sold merchandise to Sturm at an aggregate invoice price of $720,000, which included profit of $180,000. On December 31, 19X7, one-half of the merchandise remained in Sturm's inventory, and Sturm had not paid Erin for the merchandise purchased.
(f) Sturm's 19X7 net income was $606,000. Erin's 19X7 income before considering equity in Sturm's net income was $851,000.
(g) The balances in retained earnings on December 31, 19X6, were $2,506,000 and $820,000 for Erin and Sturm, respectively.

Required:
Prepare the December 31, 19X7 consolidated worksheet for Erin Incorporated and its subsidiary Sturm Incorporated.

(AICPA adapted)

Problem 5-5. On January 1, 19X4, Kaeppler Corporation purchased 80% of the outstanding stock of Hacker Company for $1,000,000 in cash.
A condensed January 1, 19X4 Hacker Company balance sheet follows:

Assets		Liabilities and Stockholders' Equity	
Current assets	$ 450,000	Liabilities, net..............	$ 760,000
Property, plant, and equipment (net)..........	1,100,000	Common stock ($8 par)	640,000
Other assets	50,000	Retained earnings..........	200,000
		Total liabilities and	
Total assets..............	$1,600,000	equity................	$1,600,000

At the purchase date, Hacker Company's inventory and land accounts were understated by $25,000 and $100,000, respectively. Any remaining excess was attributed to goodwill and given a 40-year life. The inventory on hand January 1, 19X4, was sold during 19X4.

On January 1, 19X1, Hacker Company issued $500,000 of 20-year, 8% bonds. The bonds, which sold at a price to yield 7%, pay interest on each December 31. The premium on these bonds was $47,233 on January 1, 19X5.

On January 1, 19X5, Kaeppler Corporation purchased $200,000 (face value) of these bonds for $168,705, to yield 10%.

Trial balances of the two firms as of December 31, 19X5, are as follows:

	Kaeppler Corporation	Hacker Company
Cash.	386,024	147,789
Accounts and Notes Receivable (net)	495,000	225,000
Inventory	510,000	235,000
Investment in 8% Bonds	169,576	
Investment in Hacker Company	1,146,000	
Land.	1,000,000	400,000
Building and Equipment	3,650,000	1,400,000
Accumulated Depreciation	(1,400,000)	(650,000)
Other Assets		40,250
Accounts and Notes Payable	(475,000)	(230,000)
Bonds Payable, 7%.	(2,000,000)	
Bonds Payable, 8%.		(500,000)
Premium on Bonds Payable		(45,539)
Common Stock ($5 stated value)	(2,500,000)	
Common Stock ($8 par)		(640,000)
Retained Earnings, Jan. 1, 19X5	(705,000)	(300,000)
Sales	(2,400,000)	(1,050,000)
Subsidiary Income	(90,000)	
Other Income.	(46,600)	(12,000)
Cost of Goods Sold	1,560,000	693,000
Other Expenses.	600,000	256,500
Dividends Declared.	100,000	30,000
Total.	0	0

Interest income and expense related to Hacker Company's bonds are included in the other income and other expenses accounts. Amounts included reflect amortization of premiums or discounts, using the interest method of amortization.

Required:

Prepare the worksheet necessary to produce the consolidated financial statements of Kaeppler Corporation and its subsidiary for the year ended December 31, 19X5. Support should be provided for amounts pertaining to interest on Hacker Company's 8% bonds. Include the determination and distribution of excess and income distribution schedules.

Problem 5-6. *(Note: This problem is designed to be worked using the vertical worksheet format introduced in the appendix to Chapter 3.)* In a transaction that meets the pooling rules, Prin Company acquired 90% of the outstanding common stock of Sand Company on January 1, 19X0. Sand stockholders' equity on January 1, 19X0, consisted of $200,000 in Common Stock and $120,000 in Retained Earnings.

Sand issued $100,000 of 10-year, 10% bonds for $90,000 on January 1, 19W9, when the market rate was 12%.

On January 2, 19X2, Prin purchased 60% of Sand's bonds for $64,900, to yield 8%. Prin purchased the remaining bonds for $45,400 on January 2, 19X3, when the market rate was 6%. Straight-line amortization is used for all premiums or discounts on bonds.

Prin routinely sells merchandise inventory to Sand at a price to yield a gross profit of 30%. Intercompany merchandise sales in 19X3 were $100,000. Purchases from Prin accounted for $20,000 of Sand's beginning inventory and $15,000 of its ending inventory.

Separate statements prepared by the two firms at December 31, 19X3, showed the following information:

	Prin Company	Sand Company
Income Statement:		
Sales...	(900,000)	(390,000)
Interest income......................................	(8,400)	
Cost of goods sold..................................	580,000	210,000
Interest expense....................................		11,000
Other expenses	234,850	136,802
Subsidiary income..................................	(28,978)	
Combined net income.............................	(122,528)	(32,198)
Retained Earnings Statement:		
Retained earnings, Jan. 1, 19X3—Prin..................	(265,000)	
Retained earnings, Jan. 1, 19X3—Sand		(202,000)
Net income	(122,528)	(32,198)
Dividends declared	30,000	
Retained earnings, Dec. 31, 19X3....................	(357,528)	(234,198)
Balance Sheet:		
Cash	24,950	40,000
Accounts receivable (net)............................	68,800	58,000
Inventory..	70,000	67,000
Investment in Sand	390,778	
Investment in 10% bonds............................	108,000	
Property, plant, and equipment.......................	700,000	500,000
Accumulated depreciation	(210,000)	(92,000)
Accounts payable...................................	(70,000)	(43,802)
Bonds payable, 10%		(100,000)
Discount on bonds payable...........................		5,000
Common stock ($10 par)—Prin........................	(300,000)	
Common stock ($2 par)—Sand........................		(200,000)
Paid-in capital in excess of par—Prin..................	(425,000)	
Retained earnings, Dec. 31, 19X3—Prin	(357,528)	
Retained earnings, Dec. 31, 19X3—Sand		(234,198)
Total	0	0

Required:

Prepare the worksheet necessary to produce the consolidated financial statements of Prin Company and its subsidiary for the year ended December 31, 19X3. Use the vertical format. Include income distribution schedules.

Problem 5-7. The problem below is an example of a question of the CPA "Other Objective Format" type as it was applied to the consolidations area. A mark-sensing answer sheet was used on the exam. You may just supply the answer which should be accompanied by calculations where appropriate.

Presented below are selected amounts from the separate unconsolidated financial statements of Poe Corporation and its 90%-owned subsidiary, Shaw Company, at December 31, 19X2. Additional information follows:

	Poe Corporation	Shaw Company
Selected income statement amounts:		
Sales	$710,000	$530,000
Cost of goods sold	490,000	370,000
Gain on the sale of equipment.		21,000
Earnings from investment in subsidiary (sophisticated equity)	61,000	
Interest expense		16,000
Depreciation.	25,000	20,000
Selected balance sheet amounts:		
Cash.	$ 50,000	$ 15,000
Inventories	229,000	150,000
Equipment	440,000	360,000
Accumulated depreciation	(200,000)	(120,000)
Investment in Shaw (sophisticated equity balance). . . .	189,000	
Investment in bonds.	100,000	
Discount on bonds	(9,000)	
Bonds payable.		(200,000)
Common stock	(100,000)	(10,000)
Additional paid-in capital.	(250,000)	(40,000)
Retained earnings.	(402,000)	(140,000)
Selected statement of retained earnings amounts:		
Beginning balance, Dec. 31, 19X1	$272,000	$100,000
Net income.	210,000	70,000
Dividends paid.	80,000	30,000

Additional information is as follows:
- On January 2, 19X2, Poe purchased 90% of Shaw's 100,000 outstanding common stock for cash of $155,000. On that date, Shaw's stockholders' equity equaled $150,000 and the fair values of Shaw's assets and liabilities equaled their carrying amounts. Poe has accounted for the acquisition as a purchase. Poe's policy is to amortize intangibles over 10 years.
- On September 4, 19X2, Shaw paid cash dividends of $30,000.
- On December 31, 19X2, Poe recorded its equity in Shaw's earnings.

Required:
(1) Items (a) through (c) below represent transactions between Poe and Shaw during 19X2. Determine the dollar amount effect of the consolidating adjustment on 19X2 consolidated income before considering minority interest (combined net income). Ignore income tax considerations.

Items to be answered:
(a) On January 3, 19X2, Shaw sold equipment with an original cost of $30,000 and a carrying value of $15,000 to Poe for $36,000. The equipment had a remaining life of three years and was depreciated using the straight-line method by both companies.
(b) During 19X2, Shaw sold merchandise to Poe for $60,000, which included a profit of $20,000. At December 31, 19X2, half of this merchandise remained in Poe's inventory.
(c) On December 31, 19X2, Poe paid $91,000 to purchase 50% of the outstanding bonds issued by Shaw. The bonds mature on December 31, 19X8, and were

originally issued at par. The bonds pay interest annually on December 31 of each year, and the interest was paid to the prior investor immediately before Poe's purchase of the bonds.

(2) Determine the amount recorded by Poe as amortization of Goodwill for 19X2.

(3) **Items (a) through (l)**. Items (a) through (l) below refer to accounts that may or may not be included in Poe's and Shaw's consolidated financial statements. The list on the right refers to the various possibilities of those amounts to be reported in Poe's consolidated financial statements for the year ended December 31, 19X2. Consider all transactions stated above in determining your answer. Ignore income tax considerations.

Items to be answered:

(a) Cash
(b) Equipment
(c) Investment in subsidiary
(d) Bonds payable
(e) Minority interest
(f) Common stock
(g) Beginning retained earnings
(h) Dividends paid
(i) Gain on retirement of bonds
(j) Cost of goods sold
(k) Interest expense
(l) Depreciation expense

Responses to be selected:

1. Sum of amounts on Poe's and Shaw's separate unconsolidated financial statements.
2. Less than the sum of amounts on Poe's and Shaw's separate unconsolidated financial statements but not the same as the amount on either.
3. Same as amount for Poe only.
4. Same as amount for Shaw only.
5. Eliminated entirely in consolidation.
6. Shown in consolidated financial statements but not in separate unconsolidated financial statements.
7. Neither in consolidated nor in separate unconsolidated financial statements.

(AICPA adapted)

Problem 5-8. Paro Company acquired a 90% interest in Sandman Company on January 1, 19X1, for $660,000. Any excess of cost over book value was due to goodwill, which is being amortized over the maximum period.

Capital balances of Sandman Company on January 1, 19X1, were:

Common stock ($10 par)	$200,000
Paid-in capital in excess of par	100,000
Retained earnings	300,000
Total equity	$600,000

Sandman Company sold a machine to Paro for $30,000 on January 1, 19X4. It cost Sandman $20,000 to build the machine, which had a 5-year remaining life on the date of the sale and is subject to straight-line depreciation.

Paro purchased one-half of the outstanding 9% bonds of Sandman for $89,183 (to yield 12%) on December 31, 19X5. The bonds were sold originally by Sandman to yield 10% to outside parties. The discount on the bonds was $7,586 on December 31, 19X5. The effective interest method of amortization is used.

During 19X6, Paro Company sold merchandise to Sandman for $50,000. Paro recorded a 30% gross profit on the sales price. $20,000 of the merchandise purchased from Paro remains unsold at the end of the year.

The trial balances of Paro and its subsidiary, Sandman, are as follows on December 31, 19X6:

	Paro Company	Sandman Company
Inventory	40,000	80,000
Equipment	371,193	1,522,414
Accumulated Depreciation	(200,000)	(600,000)
Investment in Sandman Stock	660,000	
Investment in Sandman Bonds	90,885	
Bonds Payable, 9%		(200,000)
Discount on Bonds Payable		6,345
Common Stock ($10 par)	(200,000)	(200,000)
Paid-In Capital in Excess of Par	(300,000)	(100,000)
Retained Earnings, Jan. 1, 19X6	(401,376)	(500,000)
Sales	(300,000)	(260,000)
Cost of Goods Sold	100,000	72,000
Interest Income	(10,702)	
Other Expenses	150,000	160,000
Interest Expense		19,241
Total	0	0

Required:

Prepare the worksheet necessary to produce the consolidated financial statements of Paro Company and its subsidiary for the year ended December 31, 19X6. Include the determination and distribution of excess and income distribution schedules.

Problem 5-9. Sym Corporation, a wholly owned subsidiary of Paratec Corporation, leased equipment from its parent company on August 1, 19X6. The terms of the agreement clearly do not require the lease to be accounted for as a capital lease. Both entities are accounting for the lease as an operating lease. The lease payment is $12,000 per year paid in advance each August 1.

Paratec purchased its investment in Sym on December 31, 19X1 when Sym had a retained earnings balance of $150,000. Paratec is accounting for its investment in Sym under the cost method. Included in the original purchase price was a $50,000 premium attributable to Sym's history of exceptional earnings. Intangible assets are amortized over a 10-year period.

The December 31, 19X8 trial balances of Paratec and its subsidiary are presented below:

	Paratec Corporation	Sym Corporation
Cash	190,000	40,000
Accounts Receivable (net)	738,350	142,000
Inventory	500,000	75,000
Prepaid Rent on Equipment		7,000
Investment in Bonds	250,000	65,000
Investment in Sym Corporation	400,000	
Land	250,000	85,000
Plant and Equipment	1,950,000	295,000
Accumulated Depreciation—Plant and Equipment	(250,000)	(60,000)
Equipment Under Operating Lease	120,000	
Accumulated Depreciation—Assets Under Operating Lease	(36,000)	
Accounts Payable	(385,000)	(52,000)
Deferred Rent Revenue	(7,000)	
Common Stock (no par)	(2,000,000)	(200,000)

	Paratec Corporation	Sym Corporation
Retained Earnings, Jan. 1, 19X8	(1,076,350)	(310,000)
Sales..	(4,720,000)	(500,000)
Rent Income	(12,000)	
Cost of Goods Sold	3,068,000	300,000
Rent Expense		12,000
Other Expenses	725,000	101,000
Dividends Declared	295,000	
Total	0	0

Required:

Prepare the worksheet necessary to produce the consolidated income statement and balance sheet of Paratec Corporation and its subsidiary for the year ended December 31, 19X8.

Problem 5-10. On January 1, 19X1, Train Distributing Company acquired an 80% interest in Trac Warehousing Inc. for $1,200,000. Trac's Retained Earnings at that date was $320,000. Its book values approximated market values, and any excess was attributed to goodwill and given a 10-year life.

Train is leasing a warehouse from Trac that originally cost Trac $850,000. On July 1, 19X1, the date the lease agreement was signed, the warehouse had an estimated total life of 20 years, a salvage value of $50,000, and accumulated depreciation of $200,000 under the straight-line method. The terms of the 10-year lease require an $8,000 rental payment on the first of each month, including executory costs of $300 per month. Trac has other lease contracts.

In conjunction with its warehousing operations, Trac purchases and sells merchandise to distributors. Sales to Train, at the usual 25% above cost, totaled $260,000 for 19X2. At year end, Train owed $15,000 on these purchases. Train's beginning inventory balance included $60,000 in merchandise purchased from Trac, and its ending inventory balance included $45,000.

The following trial balances were prepared by the separate firms on December 31, 19X2:

	Train Distributing Company	Trac Warehousing Inc.
Cash..	61,000	40,000
Receivables (net).................................	106,600	85,000
Inventory.......................................	180,000	100,000
Investment in Trac Warehousing Inc.	1,304,000	
Property, Plant, and Equipment	2,580,000	2,000,000
Accumulated Depreciation—Property, Plant, and Equipment	(1,249,000)	(1,550,000)
Assets Under Operating Lease......................		1,975,000
Accumulated Depreciation—Assets Under Operating Lease		(990,000)
Accounts Payable	(125,000)	(70,000)
Bonds Payable, 10%..............................	(400,000)	
Common Stock ($10 par)..........................	(1,000,000)	

	Train Distributing Company	Trac Warehousing Inc.
Common Stock ($5 par).............................		(600,000)
Paid-In Capital in Excess of Par	(720,000)	(540,000)
Retained Earnings, Jan. 1, 19X2.....................	(526,000)	(380,000)
Sales	(2,400,000)	(1,000,000)
Rent Income.......................................		(150,000)
Cost of Goods Sold................................	1,390,000	600,000
Rent Expense.....................................	96,000	
Interest Expense	40,000	
Other Expenses...................................	662,400	450,000
Subsidiary Income	(80,000)	
Dividends Declared................................	80,000	30,000
Total...	0	0

Required:

Prepare the worksheet necessary to produce the consolidated financial statements of Train Distributing Company and its subsidiary for the year ended December 31, 19X2. Include the determination and distribution of excess and income distribution schedules.

Problem 5-11. Plessor Industries acquired 80% of the outstanding common stock of Slessee Company on January 1, 19X1, for $320,000. On that date, Slessee's book values approximated market values, and the balance of its retained earnings account was $80,000. Any excess was attributed to goodwill and given a 5-year life. Slessee's net income was $20,000 for 19X1 and $30,000 for 19X2. No dividends were paid in either year.

On January 1, 19X2, Slessee signed a 5-year lease with Plessor for the rental of a small factory building with a 10-year life. Payments of $25,000 are due each January 1, and Slessee is expected to exercise the $5,000 bargain purchase option at the end of the fifth year. The market value of the factory was $103,770 at the start of the lease term. Plessor's implicit rate on the lease is 12%.

A second lease agreement, for the rental of production equipment with an 8-year life, was signed by Slessee on January 1, 19X3. The terms of this 4-year lease require a payment of $15,000 each January 1. The present value of the lease payments at Plessor's 12% implicit rate was equal to the market value of the equipment, $52,298, when the lease was signed. The cost of the equipment to Plessor was $45,000, and there is a $2,000 bargain purchase option. Eight-year, straight-line depreciation is being used, with no salvage value.

The following trial balances were prepared by the separate firms at December 31, 19X3:

	Plessor Industries	Slessee Company
Cash...	60,000	40,745
Accounts Receivable....................................	97,778	76,000
Inventory...	140,000	120,000
Minimum Lease Payments Receivable....................	127,000	
Unearned Interest Income..............................	(14,417)	
Investment in Slessee Company	320,000	
Assets Under Capital Lease.............................		156,068
Accumulated Depreciation—Assets Under Capital Lease.....		(27,291)

	Plessor Industries	Slessee Company
Property, Plant, and Equipment	1,900,000	310,000
Accumulated Depreciation—Property, Plant, and Equipment	(1,077,000)	(72,000)
Accounts Payable	(148,000)	(45,065)
Obligations Under Capital Lease		(100,520)
Common Stock ($10 par)	(700,000)	(300,000)
Paid-In Capital in Excess of Par.	(325,000)	
Retained Earnings, Jan. 1, 19X3	(295,000)	(130,000)
Sales	(1,400,000)	(600,000)
Sales Profit on Leases	(7,298)	
Interest Income	(12,063)	
Cost of Goods Sold	780,000	380,000
Interest Expense		12,063
Other Expenses	510,000	165,000
Dividend Income	(12,000)	
Dividends Declared	56,000	15,000
Total	0	0

Required:

Prepare the worksheet necessary to produce the consolidated financial statements of Plessor Industries and its subsidiary for the year ended December 31, 19X3. Include the determination and distribution of excess and income distribution schedules.

Problem 5-12. Pantro Inc. purchased an 80% interest in Simpson Company for $480,000 on January 1, 19X1, when Simpson had the following stockholders' equity:

Common stock ($10 par)	$100,000
Additional paid-in capital	300,000
Retained earnings	100,000
Total equity	$500,000

Any excess was attributed to goodwill and given a 40-year life.

The trial balances of Pantro Inc. and Simpson Company were prepared on December 31, 19X5.

	Pantro Inc.	Simpson Company
Cash	91,013	26,050
Inventory	70,000	20,000
Property, Plant, and Equipment	320,000	50,000
Accumulated Depreciation—Property, Plant, and Equipment . .	(70,000)	(20,000)
Assets Under Capital Lease	40,676	
Accumulated Depreciation—Assets Under Capital Lease	(10,796)	
Assets Under Operating Lease		420,000
Accumulated Depreciation—Assets Under Operating Lease . . .		(80,000)
Minimum Lease Payments Receivable		412,000
Unearned Interest Income on Leases		(4,000)
Investment in Simpson Company	480,000	
Accounts Payable	(130,000)	(180,000)
Obligations Under Capital Lease	(24,560)	

	Pantro Inc.	Simpson Company
Interest Payable	(4,440)	
Common Stock ($10 par)	(200,000)	(100,000)
Paid-In Capital in Excess of Par	(300,000)	(300,000)
Retained Earnings, Jan. 1, 19X5	(278,333)	(226,610)
Sales.	(300,000)	(130,000)
Rent Income		(34,000)
Interest Income—Capital Lease		(4,440)
Depreciation Expense	41,000	23,000
Interest Expense.	4,440	
Selling and General Expense	70,000	38,000
Cost of Goods Sold	190,000	90,000
Rent Expense	11,000	
Total	0	0

The following intercompany leases have been written by Simpson since the acquisition:
1. On January 1, 19X3, Simpson purchased for $140,000 land and a building, which it leased to Pantro Inc. under a 5-year operating lease. Payments of $11,000 per year are required at the beginning of each year. The $120,000 building cost is being depreciated over 20 years on a straight-line basis.
2. On January 1, 19X4, Simpson purchased a machine for $14,000 and leased it to Pantro Inc. The 4-year lease qualifies as a capital lease. The rentals are $5,000 per year, payable at the beginning of each year. There is a bargain purchase option whereby Pantro will purchase the machine at the end of 4 years for $2,000.

    The market value of the machine was $17,560 at the start of the lease term. The lease payments, including the purchase option, yield an implicit rate of 15% to the lessor. Pantro is depreciating the machine over 7 years on a straight-line basis with no salvage value.
3. On January 1, 19X5, Simpson purchased a truck for $23,116 and leased it to Pantro Inc. under a 3-year capital lease. Payments of $8,000 per year are required at the beginning of each year. There is a bargain purchase agreement for $5,000. Pantro Inc. is depreciating the truck over 4 years, straight-line with no salvage value. The lease has a lessor implicit rate of 20%.
4. Pantro Inc. has accrued interest in 19X5 on its capital lease obligations. Simpson has recognized earned interest for the year on its capital leases.

Required:
Prepare the worksheet necessary to produce the consolidated financial statements of Pantro Inc. and its subsidiary for the year ended December 31, 19X5. Include the determination and distribution of excess and income distribution schedules.

CASE METHODS OF ELIMINATING SUBSIDIARY DEBT

Power Pro Inc. is a large manufacturer of marine engines. In recent years, Power Pro, like other engine manufacturers has purchased independent boat builders. The intent of the acquisitions is to control the engine choice of the boat builder. By including the outboard engine in the boat package, it is not necessary to sell to and finance many small dealers.

Power Pro purchased Swift-Craft during the last year. Swift-Crafts are built in California and are sold only in western states. Power Pro wants to build the boats in the Midwest as well so as to expand sales without paying major shipping costs from the West. A new plant will cost $1,000,000 to build and another $1,500,000 to equip for production.

Currently, Swift-Craft has $800,000 in long-term debt. It has 11% annual interest bonds outstanding in the hands of local investors. Current investors have no interest in lending any more funds. The interest rate Swift-Craft pays is high due to its size and credit rating.

Power Pro has ready access to the bond market and borrows at 7.5% annual interest. Power Pro also has expertise in constructing and equipping new facilities since it has built many new plants. Power Pro also has a sophisticated fixed asset accounting system. Power Pro would prefer to build the new plant and turn it over to Swift-Craft when it is complete. It is considering either selling the building to Swift-Craft and taking back the mortgage or leasing the asset to Swift-Craft under a long-term capital lease.

Power Pro would like you to cover the options it has in using its borrowing ability and asset management experience in assisting Swift-Craft. There is a concern as to existing debt and with respect to funds needed to finance the new plant. Your discussion should consider the impact of alternatives on the consolidation process and on minority shareholders.

APPENDIX PROBLEMS

Problem 5A-1. Steven Truck Company has been an 80%-owned subsidiary of Paulz Heavy Equipment since January 1, 19X3, when Paulz purchased 128,000 shares of Steven common stock for $832,000, an amount equal to the book value of Steven's net assets at that date. Steven's net income and dividends paid since acquisition are as follows:

Year	Net Income	Dividends
19X3	$70,000	$25,000
19X4	75,600	25,000
19X5	81,650	30,000

On January 1, 19X5, Paulz leased a truck from Steven. The 3-year financing-type lease provides for payments of $10,000 each January 1. On January 1, 19X5, the present value of the truck at Steven's 8% implicit rate, including the unguaranteed residual value of $6,000 at the end of the third year, was $32,596. Paulz also has used the 8% implicit rate to record the lease. The truck is being depreciated on a straight-line basis.

On January 1, 19X6, Steven signed a 4-year financing-type lease with Paulz for the rental of specialized production machinery with an 8-year life. There is a $7,000 purchase option at the end of the fourth year. The lease agreement requires lease payments of $30,000 each January 1 plus $1,500 for maintenance of the equipment. It also calls for contingent payments equal to 10% of Steven's cost savings through the use of this equipment, as reflected in any increase in net income (excluding gains or losses on sale of assets) above the previous growth rate of Steven's net income. The present value of the equipment on January 1, 19X6, at Paulz's 10% implicit rate was $109,388.

On October 1, 19X6, Steven sold Paulz a warehouse having a 20-year remaining life, a book value of $135,000, and an estimated salvage value of $20,000. Paulz paid $195,000 for the building, which is being depreciated on a straight-line basis.

The trial balances were prepared by the separate firms on December 31, 19X6.

	Paulz Heavy Equipment	Steven Truck Company
Cash	90,485	123,307
Accounts Receivable (net)	228,000	120,000
Inventory	200,000	140,000
Minimum Lease Payments Receivable	97,000	10,000
Unguaranteed Residual Value....................		6,000
Unearned Interest Income	(9,673)	(444)
Assets Under Capital Lease	27,833	109,388
Accumulated Depreciation—Assets Under Capital Lease	(18,556)	(13,674)
Property, Plant, and Equipment	2,075,000	1,145,000
Accumulated Depreciation—Property, Plant, and Equipment	(713,000)	(160,000)
Investment in Steven Truck Company.............	1,045,800	
Accounts Payable..............................	(100,000)	(85,000)
Interest Payable	(740)	(7,939)
Obligations Under Capital Lease	(9,260)	(79,388)
Common Stock ($5 par)	(1,800,000)	(800,000)
Retained Earnings, Jan. 1, 19X6.................	(864,834)	(387,250)
Sales...	(3,200,000)	(1,400,000)
Gain on Sale of Assets		(60,000)
Interest Income................................	(7,939)	(1,152)
Rent Income	(2,182)	
Cost of Goods Sold	1,882,000	770,000
Interest Expense...............................	740	7,939
Depreciation Expense..........................	135,000	45,000
Other Expenses	924,326	483,213
Subsidiary Income.............................	(124,000)	
Dividends Declared	144,000	35,000
Total	0	0

Required:

Prepare the worksheet necessary to produce the consolidated financial statements of Paulz Heavy Equipment and its subsidiary for the year ended December 31, 19X6. Include income distribution schedules.

Problem 5A-2. Penn Company leased a production machine to its 80%-owned subsidiary, Smith Company. The lease agreement, dated January 1, 19X1, requires Smith to pay $18,000 each January 1 for three years. There is an unguaranteed residual value of $5,000. The machine cost $50,098. The present value of the machine at Penn's 16% implicit interest rate was $50,098 on January 1, 19X1. Smith also uses the 16% lessor implicit rate to record the lease. The machine is being depreciated over 3 years on a straight-line basis with a $5,000 salvage value. Lease payment amortization schedules are as follows:

Penn (16%)

Date	Payment	Interest at 16% on Previous Balance	Reduction of Principal	Principal Balance
Jan. 1, 19X1	$18,000		$18,000	$32,098
Jan. 1, 19X2	18,000	$5,136	12,864	19,234
Jan. 1, 19X3	18,000	3,078	14,922	4,312
Jan. 1, 19X4	5,000	688	4,312	
Total	$59,000	$8,902	$50,098	

Smith (16%)

Date	Payment	Interest at 16% on Previous Balance	Reduction of Principal	Principal Balance
Jan. 1, 19X1	$18,000		$18,000	$28,894
Jan. 1, 19X2	18,000	$4,623	13,377	15,517
Jan. 1, 19X3	18,000	2,483	15,517	
Total	$54,000	$7,106	$46,894	

Required:

(1) Prepare the eliminations and adjustments required for this lease on the December 31, 19X1 consolidated worksheet.

(2) Prepare the eliminations and adjustments for the December 31, 19X2 consolidated worksheet.

WORKSHEET 5-1

Intercompany Investment in Bonds, Year of Acquisition; Straight-Line Method of Amortization
Company P and Subsidiary Company S
Worksheet for Consolidated Balance Sheet
For Year Ended December 31, 19X3

	(Credit balance amounts are in parentheses.)	Trial Balance	
		Company P	Company S
1	Other Assets	56,400	220,000
2	**Interest Receivable**	8,000	
3	Investment in Company S Stock (90%)	100,800	
4			
5	**Investment in Company S Bonds (100%)**	102,400	
6	**Interest Payable**		(8,000)
7	**Bonds Payable, 8%**		(100,000)
8	Common Stock ($10 par), Co. P	(100,000)	
9	Retained Earnings, Jan. 1, 19X3, Co. P	(120,000)	
10	Common Stock ($10 par), Co. S		(80,000)
11	Retained Earnings, Jan. 1, 19X3, Co. S		(20,000)
12	Operating Revenue	(100,000)	(80,000)
13	Operating Expense	70,000	60,000
14	**Interest Income**	(6,800)	
15	**Interest Expense**		8,000
16	Subsidiary Income	(10,800)	
17	**Extraordinary Loss on Bond Retirement**		
18		0	0
19	Combined Net Income		
20	To Minority Interest (see distribution schedule)		
21	Balance to Controlling Interest (see distribution schedule)		
22	Total Minority Interest		
23	Retained Earnings, Controlling Interest, Dec. 31, 19X3		
24			

Eliminations and Adjustments:
(1) Eliminate the entry recording the parent's share of subsidiary net income for the current year. This step returns the investment in Company S stock account to its January 1, 19X3 balance to aid the elimination process.
(2) Eliminate 90% of the subsidiary equity balances of January 1, 19X3, against the investment in stock account. No excess results.
(3) Eliminate intercompany interest revenue and expense. Eliminate the balance of the investment in bonds against the bonds payable. Note that the investment in bonds is at its end-of-year amortized balance. The loss on retirement at the date the bonds were purchased is calculated as follows:

Worksheet 5-1 (see page 288)

Eliminations & Adjustments			Consolidated Income Statement	Minority Interest	Controlling Retained Earnings	Consolidated Balance Sheet	
Dr.		Cr.					
						276,400	1
	(4)	8,000					2
	(1)	10,800					3
	(2)	90,000					4
	(3)	102,400					5
(4)	8,000						6
(3)	100,000						7
						(100,000)	8
					(120,000)		9
(2)	72,000			(8,000)			10
(2)	18,000			(2,000)			11
			(180,000)				12
			130,000				13
(3)	6,800						14
	(3)	8,000					15
(1)	10,800						16
(3)	3,600		3,600				17
	219,200	219,200					18
			(46,400)				19
			960*	(960)			20
			45,440*		(45,440)		21
				(10,960)		(10,960)	22
					(165,440)	(165,440)	23
						0	24

Loss remaining at year end:
Investment in bonds at Dec. 31, 19X3 . . . . $102,400
Carrying value of bonds at Dec. 31, 19X3 . . . .   100,000 $2,400

Loss amortized during year:
Interest expense eliminated   8,000
Interest revenue eliminated   6,800   1,200
Loss at Jan. 2, 19X3 . . . . $3,600

(4)   Eliminate intercompany interest payable and receivable.

(continued)

Subsidiary Company S Income Distribution

Extraordinary loss on
  bond retirement . . . .(3)   **$3,600**
	Internally generated net income,
	  including interest expense. . . . .
		$12,000

	Interest adjustment **($3,600 ÷ 3)** . . . .(3)	**1,200**
	Adjusted income	$ 9,600
	Minority share.	10%
	Minority interest.	$ 960*

Parent Company P Income Distribution

Internally generated net income, **including interest revenue**	$36,800
90% × Company S adjusted income of $9,600	8,640
Controlling interest.	$45,440*

WORKSHEET 5-2

Intercompany Investment in Bonds, Year Subsequent to Acquisition; Straight-Line Method of Amortization
Company P and Subsidiary Company S
Worksheet for Consolidated Financial Statements
For Year Ended December 31, 19X4

| | (Credit balance amounts are in parentheses.) | Trial Balance | |
		Company P	Company S
1	Other Assets	94,400	242,000
2	Interest Receivable	8,000	
3	Investment in Company S Stock (90%)	120,600	
4			
5	**Investment in Company S Bonds (100%)**	**101,200**	
6	Interest Payable		(8,000)
7	Bonds Payable, 8%		(100,000)
8	Common Stock ($10 par), Co. P	(100,000)	
9	**Retained Earnings, Jan. 1, 19X4, Co. P**	**(167,600)**	
10	Common Stock ($10 par), Co. S		(80,000)
11	**Retained Earnings, Jan. 1, 19X4, Co. S**		**(32,000)**
12			
13	Operating Revenue	(130,000)	(100,000)
14	Operating Expense	100,000	70,000
15	Subsidiary Income	(19,800)	
16	Interest Expense		8,000
17	Interest Income	(6,800)	
18		0	0
19	Combined Net Income		
20	To Minority Interest (see distribution schedule)		
21	Balance to Controlling Interest (see distribution schedule)		
22	Total Minority Interest		
23	Retained Earnings, Controlling Interest, Dec. 31, 19X4		
24			

Eliminations and Adjustments:
(1) Eliminate the entry recording the parent's share of subsidiary net income for the current year.
(2) Eliminate the pro rata share of subsidiary equity balances against the investment in stock account. There is no excess to be distributed.
(3) Eliminate intercompany interest revenue and expense. Eliminate the balance of the investment in bonds against the bonds payable. Note that the investment in bonds is at its end-of-year amortized balance. The remaining unamortized loss on retirement at the start of the year is calculated as follows:

Worksheet 5-2 (see page 290)

Eliminations & Adjustments		Consolidated Income Statement	Minority Interest	Controlling Retained Earnings	Consolidated Balance Sheet	
Dr.	Cr.					
					336,400	1
	(4) 8,000					2
	(1) 19,800					3
	(2) 100,800					4
	(3) 101,200					5
(4) 8,000						6
(3) 100,000						7
					(100,000)	8
(3) 2,160				(165,440)		9
(2) 72,000			(8,000)			10
(2) 28,800			(2,960)			11
(3) 240						12
		(230,000)				13
		170,000				14
(1) 19,800						15
	(3) 8,000					16
(3) 6,800						17
237,800	237,800					18
		(60,000)				19
		2,320*	(2,320)			20
		57,680*		(57,680)		21
			(13,280)		(13,280)	22
				(223,120)	(223,120)	23
					0	24

Loss remaining at year end:
  Investment in bonds at Dec. 31, 19X4. . . . . $101,200
  Carrying value of bonds at Dec. 31, 19X4. . . . .   100,000 $1,200

Loss amortized during year:
  Interest expense eliminated.   8,000
  Interest revenue eliminated   6,800   1,200
    Remaining loss at Jan. 1, 19X4. . . . . $2,400

The remaining unamortized loss of $2,400 on January 1, 19X4, is allocated 90% to the controlling retained earnings and 10% to the minority retained earnings since the bonds were issued by the subsidiary.
(4) Eliminate intercompany interest payable and receivable.

(continued)

Subsidiary Company S Income Distribution

Internally generated net income, including interest expense.............	$22,000
Interest adjustment ($3,600 ÷ 3).......................(3)	1,200
Adjusted income.......................	$23,200
Minority share.........................	10%
Minority interest.......................	$ 2,320*

Parent Company P Income Distribution

Internally generated net income including interest revenue	$36,800
90% × Company S adjusted income of $23,200	20,880
Controlling interest.	$57,680*

WORKSHEET 5-3

Intercompany Bonds, Subsequent Period; Straight-Line Method of Amortization
Company P and Subsidiary Company S
Worksheet for Consolidated Financial Statements
For Year Ended December 31, 19X4

	(Credit balance amounts are in parentheses.)	Trial Balance	
		Company P	Company S
1	Other Assets	59,400	259,082
2	Investment in Company S Stock	143,874	
3			
4	Investment in Company S Bonds	101,800	
5	Bonds Payable		(100,000)
6	**Discount on Bonds**		778
7	Common Stock, Co. P	(100,000)	
8	**Retained Earnings, Jan. 1, 19X4, Co. P**	(160,000)	
9	Common Stock, Co. S		(40,000)
10	**Retained Earnings, Jan. 1, 19X4, Co. S**		(110,000)
11			
12	Sales	(80,000)	(50,000)
13	**Interest Income**	(6,200)	
14	Cost of Goods Sold	50,000	31,362
15	**Interest Expense**		8,778
16	Subsidiary Income	(8,874)	
17		0	0
18	Combined Net Income		
19	To Minority Interest (see distribution schedule)		
20	Balance to Controlling Interest (see distribution schedule)		
21	Total Minority Interest		
22	Retained Earnings, Controlling Interest, Dec. 31, 19X4		
23			

Eliminations and Adjustments:
(1) Eliminate the entry recording the parent's share of subsidiary net income for the current year.
(2) Eliminate 90% of the January 1, 19X4 subsidiary equity balances against the January 1, 19X4 investment in Company S stock balance. No excess results.
(3) Eliminate intercompany interest revenue and expense. Eliminate the balance of the investment in bonds against the bonds payable. Note that the investment in bonds and the discount on bonds are at their end-of-year amortized balances. The remaining unamortized loss on retirement at the start of the year is calculated as follows:

Worksheet 5-3 (see page 291)

Eliminations & Adjustments		Consolidated Income Statement	Minority Interest	Controlling Retained Earnings	Consolidated Balance Sheet	
Dr.	Cr.					
					318,482	1
	(1) 8,874					2
	(2) 135,000					3
	(3) 101,800					4
(3) 100,000						5
	(3) 778					6
					(100,000)	7
(3) 4,640				(155,360)		8
(2) 36,000			(4,000)			9
(2) 99,000			(10,484)			10
(3) 516						11
		(130,000)				12
(3) 6,200						13
		81,362				14
	(3) 8,778					15
(1) 8,874						16
255,230	255,230					17
		(48,638)				18
		1,244*	(1,244)			19
		47,394*		(47,394)		20
					(15,728)	21
				(202,754)	(202,754)	22
					0	23

Loss remaining at year end:
Investment in bonds at Dec. 31, 19X4 .... $101,800
Bonds payable at Dec. 31, 19X4 100,000
Discount on bonds at Dec. 31, 19X4...   (778) $2,578

Loss amortized during year:
Interest expense eliminated 8,778
Interest revenue eliminated 6,200   2,578

Remaining loss at Jan. 1, 19X4 .... $5,156

Since from the consolidated viewpoint the bonds were retired in the prior year and since the bonds were issued by the subsidiary, the remaining unamortized loss of $5,156 on January 1, 19X4 is allocated 90% to the controlling retained earnings and 10% to the minority retained earnings.

(continued)

Subsidiary Company S Income Distribution

Internally generated net income, including interest expense.............	$ 9,860
Interest adjustment ($8,778 – $6,200) ....(3)	2,578
Adjusted income	$12,438
Minority share	10%
Minority interest.......................	$ 1,244*

Parent Company P Income Distribution

Internally generated net income, including interest revenue	$36,200
90% × Company S adjusted income of $12,438	11,194
Controlling interest.	$47,394*

WORKSHEET 5-4

Intercompany Bonds; Interest Method of Amortization
Company P and Subsidiary Company S
Worksheet for Consolidated Financial Statements
For Year Ended December 31, 19X4

	(Credit balance amounts are in parentheses.)	Trial Balance	
		Company P	Company S
1	Other Assets	59,333	259,082
2	Investment in Company S Stock	144,000	
3			
4	**Investment in Company S Bonds**	**101,887**	
5	**Bonds Payable**		**(100,000)**
6	**Discount on Bonds**		**918**
7	Common Stock, Co. P	(100,000)	
8	Retained Earnings, Jan. 1, 19X4, Co. P	(160,180)	
9	Common Stock, Co. S		(40,000)
10	Retained Earnings, Jan. 1, 19X4, Co. S		(110,200)
11			
12	Sales	(80,000)	(50,000)
13	**Interest Income**	**(6,220)**	
14	Cost of Goods Sold	50,000	31,358
15	**Interest Expense**		**8,842**
16			
17	Subsidiary Income	(8,820)	
18		0	0
19	Combined Net Income		
20	To Minority Interest (see distribution schedule)		
21	Balance to Controlling Interest (see distribution schedule)		
22	Total Minority Interest		
23	Retained Earnings, Controlling Interest, Dec. 31, 19X4		
24			

Eliminations and Adjustments:
(1)   Eliminate the entry recording the parent's share of subsidiary net income for the current year.
(2)   Eliminate 90% of the January 1, 19X4 subsidiary equity balances against the January 1, 19X4 investment in Company S stock balance. No excess results.
(3)   Eliminate intercompany interest revenue and expense. Eliminate the balance of the investment in bonds against the bonds payable. Note that the investment in bonds and the discount on bonds are at their end-of-year amortized balances. The remaining unamortized loss on retirement at the start of the year is calculated as follows:

Worksheet 5-4 (see page 293)

Eliminations & Adjustments		Consolidated Income Statement	Minority Interest	Controlling Retained Earnings	Consolidated Balance Sheet	
Dr.	Cr.					
					318,415	1
	(1) 8,820					2
	(2) 135,180					3
	(3) **101,887**					4
(3) **100,000**						5
	(3) **918**					6
					(100,000)	7
(3) 4,884				(155,296)		8
(2) 36,000			(4,000)			9
(2) 99,180			(10,477)			10
(3) 543						11
		(130,000)				12
(3) 6,220						13
		81,358				14
	(3) 8,842					15
						16
(1) 8,820						17
255,647	255,647					18
		(48,642)				19
		1,242*	(1,242)			20
		47,400*		(47,400)		21
			(15,719)		(15,719)	22
				(202,696)	(202,696)	23
					0	24

Loss remaining at year end:
Investment in bonds at Dec. 31, 19X4 . . . . $101,887
Bonds payable at Dec. 31, 19X4   100,000
Discount on bonds at Dec. 31, 19X4 . . . .   (918) $2,805

Loss amortized during year:
Interest expense eliminated   8,842
Interest revenue eliminated   6,220   2,622
Remaining loss at Jan. 1, 19X4 . . . . $5,427

Since from the consolidated viewpoint the bonds were retired in the prior year and since the bonds were issued by the subsidiary, the remaining unamortized loss of $5,427 on January 1, 19X4 is allocated 90% to the controlling retained earnings and 10% to the minority retained earnings.

(continued)

Subsidiary Company S Income Distribution

Internally generated net income, including interest expense.............	$ 9,800
Interest adjustment **($8,842 − $6,220)** ....(3)	2,622
Adjusted income	$12,422
Minority share	10%
Minority interest.......................	$ 1,242*

Parent Company P Income Distribution

Internally generated net income, including interest revenue	$36,220
90% × Company S adjusted income of $12,422	11,180
Controlling interest.	$47,400*

WORKSHEET 5-5

Intercompany Capital Lease
Worksheet for Consolidated Financial Statements
For Year Ended December 31, 19X1

	(Credit balance amounts are in parentheses.)	Trial Balance	
		Company P	Company S
1	Accounts Receivable	30,149	44,793
2	**Minimum Lease Payments Receivable**	**4,000**	
3	**Unguaranteed Residual Value**	**1,000**	
4	**Unearned Interest Income**	**(533)**	
5	**Assets Under Capital Lease**		**5,210**
6	**Accumulated Depreciation—Assets Under Capital Lease**		**(1,737)**
7	Property, Plant, and Equipment	200,000	120,000
8	Accumulated Depreciation—Property, Plant, and Equipment	(80,000)	(50,000)
9	Investment in Company S	87,634	
10			
11	Accounts Payable	(21,000)	(5,000)
12	**Obligations Under Capital Lease**		**(3,210)**
13	**Interest Payable**		**(514)**
14	Common Stock ($10 par), Co. P	(50,000)	
15	Retained Earnings, Jan. 1, 19X1, Co. P	(120,000)	
16	Common Stock ($5 par), Co. S		(40,000)
17	Retained Earnings, Jan. 1, 19X1, Co. S		(50,000)
18	Sales	(120,000)	(70,000)
19	**Interest Income**	**(616)**	
20	Subsidiary Income	(15,634)	
21	Operating Expense	65,000	38,207
22	**Interest Expense**		**514**
23	Depreciation Expense	20,000	11,737
24		0	0
25	Combined Net Income		
26	To Minority Interest (see distribution schedule)		
27	Balance to Controlling Interest (see distribution schedule)		
28	Total Minority Interest		
29	Retained Earnings, Controlling Interest, Dec. 31, 19X1		
30			

Worksheet 5-5 (see page 303)

Eliminations & Adjustments			Consolidated Income Statement	Minority Interest	Controlling Retained Earnings	Consolidated Balance Sheet	
Dr.		Cr.					
						74,942	1
	(4)	4,000					2
	(4)	1,000					3
(4) 635	(3)	102					4
	(4)	5,210					5
(5) 1,737							6
(4) 5,851						325,851	7
	(5)	1,617				(131,617)	8
	(1)	15,634					9
	(2)	72,000					10
						(26,000)	11
(4) 3,210							12
(4) 514							13
						(50,000)	14
					(120,000)		15
(2) 32,000				(8,000)			16
(2) 40,000				(10,000)			17
			(190,000)				18
(3) 616							19
(1) 15,634							20
			103,207				21
	(3)	514					22
	(5)	120	31,617				23
100,197		100,197					24
			(55,176)				25
			3,908*	(3,908)			26
			51,268*		(51,268)		27
				(21,908)		(21,908)	28
					(171,268)	(171,268)	29
						0	30

(continued)

Eliminations and Adjustments:
(1) Eliminate the parent company's entry recording its share of Company S net income. This step returns the investment account to its January 1, 19X1 balance to aid the elimination process.
(2) Eliminate 80% of the January 1, 19X1 Company S equity balances against the investment in Company S balance.
(3) Eliminate the interest income recorded by the lessor, $616, and the interest expense recorded by the lessee, $514. The $102 disparity reflects the interest recorded on the unguaranteed residual value. This amount is returned to the unearned interest income.
(4) Eliminate the intercompany debt and the unguaranteed residual value. Eliminate the asset under capital lease and record the owned asset. The amounts are reconciled as follows:

Disparity in recorded debt:

Lessor balance, **$4,000 – $635** unearned interest income.	$3,365
Lessee balance, **$3,210 + $514** accrued interest	3,724
Interest applicable to unguaranteed residual value.	$ (359)
Unguaranteed residual value.	**1,000**
Net original present value of unguaranteed residual value	$ 641
Asset under capital lease	**5,210**
Owned asset at original cost	$5,851

(5) Reclassify accumulated depreciation and adjust the depreciation expense to acknowledge cost of asset. The adjustment to depreciation expense is determined as follows:

Capitalized cost by lessee		$5,210
Depreciable cost:		
Cost	$5,851	
Less residual (salvage) value.	1,000	4,851
Decrease in depreciable cost.		$ 359
Adjustment to depreciation expense ($359 ÷ 3-year lease term)		**$ 120**

Subsidiary Company S Income Distribution

Internally generated net income, **including interest income on lease**	$19,542
Adjusted income	$19,542
Minority share	20%
Minority interest.......................	$ 3,908*

Parent Company P Income Distribution

Interest eliminated ....(3) **$102**	Internally generated net income, **including interest income on lease**		$35,616
	80% × Company S adjusted income of $19,542............................		15,634
	Decrease in depreciation..............(5)		**120**
	Controlling interest		$51,268*

WORKSHEET 5-6

Intercompany Capital Lease, Subsequent Period
Company P and Subsidiary Company S
Worksheet for Consolidated Financial Statements
For Year Ended December 31, 19X2

	(Credit balance amounts are in parentheses.)	Trial Balance	
		Company P	Company S
1	Accounts Receivable	102,149	82,925
2	**Minimum Lease Payments Receivable**	**2,000**	
3	**Unguaranteed Residual Value**	**1,000**	
4	**Unearned Interest Income**	**(138)**	
5			
6	**Assets Under Capital Lease**		**5,210**
7	**Accumulated Depreciation—Assets Under Capital Lease**		**(3,474)**
8	Property, Plant, and Equipment	200,000	120,000
9	Accumulated Depreciation—Property, Plant, and Equipment	(100,000)	(60,000)
10	Investment in Company S	102,129	
11			
12	Accounts Payable	(41,000)	(15,000)
13	**Obligations Under Capital Lease**		**(1,724)**
14	**Interest Payable**		**(276)**
15	Common Stock ($10 par), Co. P	(50,000)	
16	**Retained Earnings, Jan. 1, 19X2, Co. P**	**(171,250)**	
17	Common Stock ($5 par), Co. S		(40,000)
18	Retained Earnings, Jan. 1, 19X2, Co. S		(69,542)
19	Sales	(150,000)	(80,000)
20	**Interest Income**	**(395)**	
21	Subsidiary Income	(14,495)	
22	Operating Expense	100,000	49,868
23	**Interest Expense**		**276**
24	Depreciation Expense	20,000	11,737
25		0	0
26	Combined Net Income		
27	To Minority Interest (see distribution schedule)		
28	Balance to Controlling Interest (see distribution schedule)		
29	Total Minority Interest		
30	Retained Earnings, Controlling Interest, Dec. 31, 19X2		
31			

Worksheet 5-6 (see page 303)

Eliminations & Adjustments				Consolidated Income Statement	Minority Interest	Controlling Retained Earnings	Consolidated Balance Sheet	
Dr.		Cr.						
							185,074	1
		(5)	2,000					2
		(5)	1,000					3
(5)	359	(3)	119					4
		(4)	102					5
		(5)	5,210					6
(6)	3,474							7
(5)	5,851						325,851	8
		(6)	3,234				(163,234)	9
		(1)	14,495					10
		(2)	87,634					11
							(56,000)	12
(5)	1,724							13
(5)	276							14
							(50,000)	15
(4)	102	(6)	120			(171,268)		16
(2)	32,000				(8,000)			17
(2)	55,634				(13,908)			18
				(230,000)				19
(3)	395							20
(1)	14,495							21
				149,868				22
		(3)	276					23
		(6)	120	31,617				24
114,310		114,310						25
				(48,515)				26
				3,624*	(3,624)			27
				44,891*		(44,891)		28
					(25,532)		(25,532)	29
						(216,159)	(216,159)	30
							0	31

(continued)

Eliminations and Adjustments:
(1) Eliminate the parent company's entry recording its share of Company S net income.
(2) Eliminate 80% of the January 1, 19X2 Company S equity balances against the investment in Company S balance.
(3) Eliminate the interest income recorded by the lessor, $395, and the interest expense recorded by the lessee, $276. The $119 disparity reflects the interest recorded on the unguaranteed residual value. This amount is returned to the unearned interest income.
(4) Adjust the unearned income and the parent's retained earnings for the $102 interest recorded in 19X1 on the unguaranteed residual value.
(5) Eliminate the intercompany debt and the unguaranteed residual value. Eliminate the asset under capital lease and record the owned asset. The amounts are reconciled as follows:

Disparity in recorded debt:
Lessor balance, **$2,000 – $359** unearned interest income.	$1,641
Lessee balance, **$1,724 + $276** accrued interest.	2,000
Interest applicable to unguaranteed residual value.	$ (359)
Unguaranteed residual value.	**1,000**
Net original present value of unguaranteed residual value.	$ 641
Asset under capital lease.	**5,210**
Owned asset at original cost.	$5,851

(6) Reclassify accumulated depreciation. Adjust the depreciation expense for the current year and the controlling retained earnings for the preceding year to acknowledge cost of asset. The adjustment to the depreciation expense and the retained earnings is determined as follows:

Capitalized cost by lessee		$5,210
Depreciable cost:		
Cost	$5,851	
Less residual (salvage) value.	1,000	4,851
Decrease in depreciable cost.		$ 359
Adjustment to depreciation expense and retained earnings ($359 ÷ 3-year lease term)		$ 120

Subsidiary Company S Income Distribution

Internally generated net income, **including interest on lease**	$18,119
Adjusted income	$18,119
Minority share	20%
Minority interest.	$ 3,624*

Parent Company P Income Distribution

Interest eliminated ....(3) **$119**	Internally generated net income, **including interest income on lease**	$30,395
	80% × Company S adjusted income of $18,119.	14,495
	Decrease in depreciation.........(6)	**120**
	Controlling interest	$44,891*

CHAPTER 6

Cash Flow, EPS, Taxation, and Unconsolidated Investments

This chapter contains the remaining consolidation issues that affect the vast majority of consolidated firms and extends consolidation concepts to nonconsolidated investments that are accounted for under the sophisticated equity method.

This chapter begins with the procedures necessary to prepare a consolidated statement of cash flows. Fortunately, this requires only minor changes in the procedures used in your prior accounting courses. Also, only minor adjustments of typical earnings per share procedures are needed for consolidated firms. The final consolidation issue is taxation of the consolidated firm. Prior worksheets are now enhanced to include the provision for tax. This is quite simple when the affiliated firms are taxed as a single entity. Procedures are a bit more involved when the individual firms are taxed separately.

This chapter concludes with a discussion of the use of the sophisticated equity method for investments that are not consolidated. These investments require the use of procedures that parallel those used in consolidations. The end result is that the income reported from the investee is the same as if the investee were consolidated and the controlling interest in subsidiary income was calculated.

CONSOLIDATED STATEMENT OF CASH FLOWS

FASB Statement of Financial Accounting Standards No. 95 requires that a statement of cash flows accompany a firm's published income statement and balance sheet. The process of preparing a consolidated statement of cash flows is similar to that which is used for a single firm, a topic covered in depth in intermediate accounting texts. Since the analysis of changes in cash of a consolidated entity begins with consolidated statements, intercompany transactions will have been eliminated and thus will not cause any complications. However, because of the parent–subsidiary relationship, there are some situations that require special consideration. These situations are discussed in the following paragraphs.

CASH ACQUISITION OF CONTROLLING INTEREST

The cash purchase of a controlling interest in a firm is considered an *investing activity* and would appear as a cash outflow in the cash flows from investing activities section of the statement of cash flows. It also is necessary to explain the total increase in consolidated assets and the addition of the minority interest to the consolidated balance sheet. This is a result of the requirement that the statement of cash flows disclose investing and *financing activities* that affect the firm's financial position even though they do not impact cash.

To illustrate the disclosure required, consider an example of a cash purchase of an 80% interest in a firm. Assume Company S had the following balance sheet on January 1, 19X1, when Company P acquired an 80% interest for $540,000 in cash:

Assets		Liabilities and Equity	
Cash and cash equivalents	$ 50,000	Long-term liabilities.	$150,000
Inventory	60,000	Common stock ($10 par)	200,000
Equipment (net)	190,000	Retained earnings.	350,000
Building (net)	400,000		
Total assets.	$700,000	Total liabilities and equity	$700,000

Assuming the market values of the inventory, equipment, and building are $60,000, $250,000, and $425,000, respectively, and any remaining excess of cost is attributed to goodwill with a 20-year life, the following determination and distribution of excess schedule would be prepared:

Price paid		$540,000	
Less interest acquired:			
Common stock ($10 par).	$200,000		
Retained earnings	350,000		
Total stockholders' equity	$550,000		
Interest acquired	80%	440,000	
Excess of cost over book value (debit balance).		$100,000	
Excess of cost attributable to long-lived assets:			
Equipment, 80% × $60,000		$ 48,000	Dr
Building, 80% × $25,000.		20,000	Dr
Goodwill (20-year amortization).		$ 32,000	Dr

The effect of the purchase on the balance sheet accounts of the consolidated firm for 19X1 would be as follows:

	Debit	Credit
Cash ($540,000 paid – $50,000 subsidiary cash)		490,000
Inventory.	60,000	
Equipment ($190,000 book value + $48,000 excess)	238,000	
Building ($400,000 book value + $20,000 excess).	420,000	
Goodwill	32,000	
Long-term liabilities		150,000
Minority interest (20% × $550,000 subsidiary equity)		110,000
Total.	750,000	750,000

The disclosure of the purchase on the statement of cash flows would be summarized as follows:

Under the heading "Cash flows from investing activities":

Payment for purchase of Company S, net of cash
acquired. . . . . $(490,000)

In the supplemental schedule of noncash financing and investing activity:

Company P purchased 80% of the common stock of Company S for $540,000. In conjunction with the acquisition, liabilities were assumed and a minority interest was created as follows:

Adjusted value of assets acquired ($700,000 book value + $100,000 excess)	$800,000
Cash paid for common stock.	540,000
Balance	$260,000
Liabilities assumed	$150,000
Minority interest	$110,000

NONCASH ACQUISITION OF CONTROLLING INTEREST

Suppose that instead of paying cash for its controlling interest, Company P issued 10,000 shares of its $10-par stock for the controlling interest. Further assume the shares had a market value of $54 each. Since the acquisition price is the same ($540,000), the determination and distribution of excess schedule would not change. The analysis of balance sheet account changes would be as follows:

	Debit	Credit
Cash ($50,000 subsidiary cash)	50,000	
Inventory.	60,000	
Equipment ($190,000 book value + $48,000 excess)	238,000	
Building ($400,000 book value + $20,000 excess).	420,000	
Goodwill	32,000	
Long-term liabilities		150,000
Minority interest (20% × $550,000 subsidiary equity)		110,000
Common stock, $10 par, Company P		100,000
Paid-in capital in excess of par, Company P		440,000
Total.	800,000	800,000

The disclosure of the purchase on the statement of cash flows would be summarized as follows:

Under the heading "Cash flows from investing activities":

> Cash acquired in purchase of Company S $50,000

In the supplemental schedule of noncash financing and investing activity:

> Company P acquired 80% of the common stock of Company S in exchange for 10,000 shares of Company P common stock valued at $540,000. In conjunction with the acquisition, liabilities were assumed and a minority interest was created as follows:

> | Adjusted value of assets acquired ($700,000 book value + $100,000 excess) . . . . . . | $800,000 |
> |---|---|
> | Common stock issued. . . . . | $540,000 |
> | Liabilities assumed . . . . | $150,000 |
> | Minority interest . . . . | $110,000 |

When an acquisition qualifies as a pooling of interests, all prior financial statements are consolidated retroactively which requires that cash flow analyses proceed from a comparison of the consolidated balance sheets of the current and previous periods. Due to the retroactive application of the pooling of interests, there will be no difference between the comparative statements as a result of the pooling. The impact of the pooling on the consolidated stockholders' equity is disclosed in the period the pooling is consummated.

ADJUSTMENTS RESULTING FROM BUSINESS COMBINATIONS

A business combination will have ramifications on the statements of cash flows prepared in subsequent periods. A purchase may create amortizations of excess deductions (noncash items) which need to be adjusted. In addition, there may be impact resulting from additional purchases of subsidiary shares and/or dividend payments by the subsidiary. Intercompany bonds and nonconsolidated investments also need to be considered for their impact.

Amortization of Excesses. Income statements prepared for periods including or following a purchase of another firm will include the amortization of the excesses that are shown on the determination and distribution of excess schedule as well as book value depreciation and amortization recorded by both the parent and subsidiary. These amortizations of the excesses, while reflected in consolidated net income, do not require the use of cash; thus, they must be included as an adjustment to consolidated net income to arrive at cash flows from operating activities. For example, if the building and equipment of Company S have useful lives of 20 years and 5 years, respectively, the following adjustments would appear on the cash flows statement for 19X1:

Cash from operating activities:
  Combined net income . . . . $XXXXXX
  Add amortizations resulting from business combination:
    Depreciation [(1/5 × $48,000) + (1/20 × $20,000)]   10,600
    Goodwill amortization (1/20 × $32,000)   1,600

In addition, cash from operating activities would be adjusted for depreciation and amortizations of book value recorded by the constituent firms on their separate books.

Purchase of Additional Subsidiary Shares. The purchase of additional shares directly from the subsidiary results in no added cash flowing into the consolidated firm. The transfer of cash within the consolidated firm would not appear in the consolidated statement of cash flows. However, the purchase of additional shares from the minority does result in an outflow of cash. From a consolidated viewpoint, it is the equivalent of purchasing treasury shares. Thus, it would be listed under financing activities.

Subsidiary Dividends. Dividends paid by the subsidiary to the parent are a transfer of cash within the consolidated entity and thus would not appear in the consolidated statement of cash flows. However, dividends paid by the subsidiary to minority shareholders represent a flow of cash to parties outside the consolidated group and would appear as an outflow under the cash flows from financing activities heading of the consolidated statement of cash flows.

Purchase of Intercompany Bonds. The purchase of intercompany bonds from parties outside the consolidated firm effects a cash flow from one member of the consolidated group to parties outside the consolidated entity. Recall that the purchase of intercompany bonds is viewed as a retirement of the bonds on the consolidated worksheet. The consolidated statement of cash flows also treats the purchase of the bonds as a retirement of the consolidated firm's debt, and includes the cash outflow under cash flows from financing activities. Since the process of constructing a cash flows statement starts with the consolidated income statement and balance sheet, intercompany interest payments and amortizations of premiums and/or discounts already are eliminated and will not enter into the analysis of consolidated cash flows. Only cash interest payments to bondholders outside the consolidated entity are important to the analysis and should be included in cash flows from *operating* activities.

Nonconsolidated Investments.   Investments in the stock of firms not included in the consolidated group result in income to the consolidated entity. Where the investment is accounted for under the cost method, cash dividends received are included in cash flows from operating activities. However, where the equity method is applied, only that portion of the income received in cash may be included in cash from operating activities. For example, the investee may report income of $50,000 and pay dividends of $10,000. Assume further that the consolidated firm paid $20,000 more than book value for its 30% interest and regards the excess as attributable to goodwill with a 40-year life. Investment income under the equity method would be calculated as follows:

30% of reported income of $50,000 . . . . $15,000
Less amortization of excess cost ($20,000 ÷ 40)   500
    Equity income $14,500

Only $3,000 (30% × $10,000) was received in the form of cash dividends; thus, the $14,500 of income would be reduced to only $3,000 of cash from operating activities. The $11,500 of undistributed income would be adjusted out of net income to arrive at cash from operating activities.

PREPARATION OF CONSOLIDATED STATEMENT OF CASH FLOWS

A complete example of the process of preparing a consolidated statement of cash flows is presented in this section. Assume Company P originally purchased an 80% interest in Company S on January 1, 19X1. In addition, Company P purchased a 20% interest in Company E on January 2, 19X2, and accounts for the investment under the sophisticated equity method. The following determination and distribution of excess schedules were prepared for each investment:

For the January 1, 19X1, 80% investment in subsidiary Company S:

Price paid $365,000
Less interest acquired:
    Common stock. . . . . $ 50,000
    Paid-in capital in excess of par   150,000
    Retained earnings   100,000
        Total equity $300,000
        Interest acquired 80%   240,000
Excess of cost over book value (debit balance) $125,000
Excess of cost attributable to equipment (5-year life).   25,000   Dr
Goodwill (10-year life) . . . . $100,000   Dr

For the January 2, 19X2, 20% investment in nonconsolidated Company E:

Price paid.	$255,000
Less interest acquired:	
Common stock. . . . . $ 500,000	
Retained earnings. 750,000	
Total equity $1,250,000	
Interest acquired. 20% 250,000	
Goodwill (10-year life).	$ 5,000

Since this investment is not consolidated, there will be no recording of the goodwill. This information is used only to amortize the excess cost in future income statements. Because of this, there are no debits or credits accompanying the distribution of the excess. The following consolidated statements were prepared for Company P and its subsidiary, Company S, for 19X3:

Company P and Subsidiary Company S
Consolidated Income Statement
For Year Ended December 31, 19X3

Sales.		$900,000
Less cost of goods sold		525,000
Gross profit.		$375,000
Less expenses:		
General and administrative.	$150,500	
Depreciation.	70,000[a]	
Goodwill amortization.	10,000[b]	230,500
Operating income		$144,500
Investment income (equity method).		15,500[c]
Combined net income of Companies P and S.		$160,000
Less minority interest.		11,200
Consolidated net income.		$148,800

[a]Includes $5,000 of depreciation resulting from the excess of the subsidiary equipment's market value over book value on January 1, 19X1, the date on which the 80% interest was acquired.
[b]Consists of the $10,000 goodwill amortization on the 80% interest acquired January 1, 19X1.
[c]20% of Company E net income of $80,000 less $500 amortization of goodwill. (Dividends received were $2,000.)

Company P and Subsidiary Company S
Consolidated Retained Earnings Statement
For Year Ended December 31, 19X3

	Minority	Controlling
Retained earnings, January 1, 19X3	$32,000*	$420,000
Add distribution of combined net income	11,200	148,800
Less dividends declared.	(4,000)	(50,000)
Balance, December 31, 19X3	$39,200	$518,800

*The retained earnings balance for Company S on January 1, 19X3, was $160,000; $32,000 represents the minority's 20% remaining interest.

Company P and Subsidiary Company S
Consolidated Balance Sheet
December 31, 19X2 and 19X3

Assets	19X3	19X2
Cash and cash equivalents.	$ 179,000	$ 160,000
Inventory	210,000	180,000
Accounts receivable	154,000	120,000
Property, plant, and equipment.	1,330,000	1,250,000
Accumulated depreciation	(370,000)	(300,000)
Goodwill	70,000	80,000
Investment in Company E (20%).	333,500	320,000
Total assets	$1,906,500	$1,810,000

Liabilities and Stockholders' Equity		
Accounts payable.	$ 156,500	$ 166,000
Bonds payable	300,000	300,000
Minority interest.	79,200	72,000
Controlling interest:		
Common stock, par	200,000	200,000
Paid-in capital in excess of par	652,000	652,000
Retained earnings	518,800	420,000
Total liabilities and stockholders' equity	$1,906,500	$1,810,000

The following additional facts are available to aid in the preparation of a consolidated statement of cash flows:

1. Company P purchased a new piece of equipment during 19X3 for $80,000.
2. In 19X3, Company P declared and paid $50,000 in dividends, and Company S declared and paid $20,000 in dividends.

Illustration 6-1 is a worksheet approach to calculating a statement of cash flows under the *indirect method*. Explanations 1 through 8 use changes in balance sheet accounts to analyze cash from operations. This information is taken from the income statement and is implied from changes in current assets and current liabilities. Explanation 9 reflects the only investing activity in this example. Explanations 10 and 11 show the financing activities. The worksheet provides the information needed to develop the statement of cash flows located on page 356.

If the *direct method* of disclosing cash from operating activities is used, the cash flows from operating activities section of the statement of cash flows would be prepared as follows:

Cash flows from operating activities:
Cash from customers ($900,000 sales – $34,000 increase in accounts receivable)	$866,000
Cash from investments (dividends received)	2,000
Cash to suppliers ($525,000 cost of goods sold + $30,000 inventory increase + $9,500 decrease in accounts payable)	(564,500)
Cash for general and administrative expenses	(150,500)
Net cash provided by operating activities	$153,000

Illustration 6-1
Company P and Subsidiary Company S
Worksheet for Analysis of Cash: Indirect Approach
For Year Ended December 31, 19X3

	Account Change			Explanations			Balance
	Debit	Credit		Debit		Credit	
Inventory...................................	30,000		6)	30,000			0
Accounts receivable	34,000		5)	34,000			0
Property, plant, and equipment	80,000		9)	80,000			0
Accumulated depreciation..................		70,000			3)	70,000	0
Goodwill.....................................		10,000			4)	10,000	0
Investment in Company E (20%)	13,500		8)	13,500			0
Accounts payable	9,500		7)	9,500			0
Bonds payable..............................							0
Minority interest		7,200	11)	4,000	2)	11,200	0
Controlling interest:							
Common stock, par							0
Paid-in excess of par.....................							0
Retained earnings........................		98,800	10)	50,000	1)	148,800	0
	167,000	186,000		221,000		240,000	
Net change in cash.......................	19,000	0		19,000		0	

Cash from Operations:

Consolidated net income......................................	1)	148,800				
Minority interest in net income..............................	2)	11,200				
Depreciation expense..	3)	70,000				
Amortization of goodwill.....................................	4)	10,000				
Increase in accounts receivable			5)	34,000		
Increase in inventory			6)	30,000		
Decrease in accounts payable...............................			7)	9,500		
Equity income in excess of dividends.........................			8)	13,500		
Net cash provided by operating activities		153,000				

Cash from Investing:

Purchase of equipment			9)	80,000
Net cash used in investing activities				80,000

Cash from Financing:

Dividend payment to controlling interest......................			10)	50,000
Dividend payment to minority interest.........................			11)	4,000
Net cash used in investing activities				54,000
Net cash provided..		19,000		

**Company P and Subsidiary Company S
Consolidated Statement of Cash Flows
For Year Ended December 31, 19X3**

Cash flows from operating activities:		
Consolidated net income.		$148,800
Adjustments to reconcile net income to net cash:		
Minority interest in combined net income	$11,200	
Depreciation expense.	70,000	
Amortization of goodwill	10,000	
Increase in accounts receivable	(34,000)	
Increase in inventory	(30,000)	
Decrease in accounts payable	(9,500)	
Equity income from Company E in excess of dividends received	(13,500)	
Total adjustments		4,200
Net cash provided by operating activities		$153,000
Cash flows from investing activities:		
Purchase of equipment		(80,000)
Cash flows from financing activities:		
Dividend payments to controlling interests	(50,000)	
Dividend payments to minority interest	(4,000)	
Net cash used in financing activities		(54,000)
Net increase in cash and cash equivalents		$ 19,000
Cash and cash equivalents at beginning of year		160,000
Cash and cash equivalents at year end		$179,000

CONSOLIDATED EARNINGS PER SHARE

The computation of consolidated earnings per share (EPS) remains virtually the same as that for single entities (see Chapter 13). For the purpose of this discussion, all calculations will be made only on an annual basis. The calculation of EPS is not altered when applied to the consolidated firm providing that the subsidiary firm has *no dilutive securities*. As long as no such securities exist, the consolidated net income is divided by the number of outstanding parent company shares, and numerator and denominator adjustments caused by parent company dilutive securities can be considered in the normal manner. When the subsidiary has dilutive securities, the calculation of consolidated EPS becomes a two-stage process. First, the EPS of the subsidiary must be calculated. Then the consolidated EPS is calculated using as a component of the calculation the adjusted EPS of the subsidiary. This two-stage process handles subsidiary dilutive securities which require the possible issuance of subsidiary company shares. A further complication occurs when the subsidiary has outstanding dilutive options, warrants, and/or convertible securities which may require the issuance of parent company shares.

First consider the calculation of consolidated EPS when the subsidiary has outstanding dilutive securities which may require the issuance of subsidiary company shares only. The EPS model for a single entity is modified in two ways:

1. Only the parent's adjusted (for intercompany transactions) income, the parent's income adjusters, and the parent's share adjusters enter the formula directly.
2. The subsidiary's income is entered indirectly by carrying over the parent's ownership percentage of subsidiary EPS.

The basic model by which to compute consolidated EPS in this situation is as follows:

This model may be used to compute either primary or fully diluted EPS. The parent's internally generated net income should be adjusted for unrealized profits recorded during the current period and for realization of profits deferred from previous periods. Likewise, the income used to compute the subsidiary EPS must be adjusted for intercompany transactions. To illustrate, assume the following data concerning the subsidiary:

Net income (adjusted for intercompany profits)................................ $22,000
Preferred stock dividend.. $ 2,000
Interest on convertible bonds .... $ 3,000
Common stock shares outstanding 5,000
Warrants to purchase one share of common stock 1,000
  Warrants held by parent.. 500
Convertible bonds outstanding (convertible into 10 shares of common stock) 200
  Convertible bonds held by parent 180

$$\text{Subsidiary Primary EPS} = \frac{\$22,000 - \overset{(1)}{\$2,000} + \overset{(2)}{\$3,000}}{5,000 + \underset{(3)}{2,000} + \underset{(4)}{500}} = \$3.07$$

(1) Dividend on nonconvertible preferred stock, none of which is owned by the parent.

(2) Income adjustment for convertible debentures which are considered a common stock equivalent.

(3) Share adjustment associated with convertible debentures, 200 bonds × 10 shares per bond.

(4) Share adjustment (treasury stock method) associated with the warrants. It is assumed that, using the average market value of the stock, 500 shares could be purchased with the proceeds of the sale and that 500 additional new shares would be issued.

Assume the parent owns 80% of the subsidiary and has internally generated net income of $40,000 and 10,000 shares of common stock outstanding. Also assume the parent has dilutive bonds outstanding which are convertible into 3,000 shares of common stock and the interest paid on these bonds was $5,000. The consolidated primary EPS would be computed as follows:

$$\text{Consolidated Primary EPS} = \frac{\$40,000 + \overset{(1)}{\$5,000} + \overset{(2)}{\$18,574}}{\underset{(3)}{10,000 + 3,000}} = \$4.89$$

(1) Income adjustment from interest on parent company convertible bonds, which are considered a common stock equivalent (CSE).

(2) Subsidiary common shares owned by parent
   (80% × 5,000) 4,000
   Parent-owned equivalent shares applicable to convertible
   debentures (90% × 2,000)[1] 1,800
   Parent-owned equivalent shares applicable to warrants
   (50% × 500)[2]   250
   Total parent-owned equivalent shares..................... 6,050

   Parent's interest in subsidiary income
   (6,050 shares × $3.07 subsidiary PEPS) $18,574

(3) Shares assumed to be issued in exchange for parent company convertible bonds (a CSE).

If the dilutive subsidiary securities enable the holder to acquire common stock of the parent, these securities are not included in the computation of subsidiary EPS. However, these securities must be included in the parent's share adjustment in computing consolidated EPS. The basic model by which to compute consolidated EPS in this situation is as follows:

Consolidated EPS =

(Parent's adjusted internally generated net income + Parent's income adjustments + (Parent-owned equivalent shares × Subsidiary EPS) + Income adjustment resulting from subsidiary securities that enable holder to acquire parent stock) / (Parent's common stock outstanding + Parent's share adjustments)

---

[1] Parent owns 180 (or 90%) of 200 subsidiary convertible bonds.
[2] Parent owns 500 (or 50%) of 1,000 subsidiary warrants.

To illustrate, assume the following facts for a parent owning 90% of the outstanding subsidiary shares:

Parent internally adjusted net income.	$20,000
Parent company common stock shares outstanding	10,000
Parent company dilutive convertible bonds:	
Interest expense.	$ 1,000
Shares to be issued in conversion.	2,000
Subsidiary net income	$ 7,000
Subsidiary common stock shares outstanding	4,000
Subsidiary preferred stock convertible into parent common stock:	
Dividend requirement.	$ 1,200
Number of preferred shares	1,000
Number of parent company common shares required.	2,000
Subsidiary common stock warrants to acquire 100 parent shares	100

The first step is to calculate the subsidiary's EPS as follows:

$$\text{Subsidiary EPS} = \frac{\$7,000 - \$1,200 \text{ preferred dividends}}{4,000 \text{ outstanding shares}} = \$1.45$$

Note that the subsidiary convertible preferred stock and stock warrants are not satisfied with subsidiary shares and thus are not considered converted for the purpose of calculating subsidiary EPS. The consolidated primary EPS would be computed as follows:

$$\text{Consolidated Primary EPS} = \frac{\overset{(1)}{\$20,000} + \$1,000 + \overset{(2)}{(3,600 \times \$1.45)} + \overset{(3)}{\$1,200}}{\underset{(4)}{10,000 + (2,000 + 2,000 + 50)}} = \$1.95$$

(1) $1,000 income adjustment associated with the parent company convertible security.

(2) The parent's share of subsidiary EPS. Again, since the subsidiary's preferred stock and warrants are not convertible into subsidiary shares, the total parent-owned equivalent shares is 90% × 4,000.

(3) Income adjustment representing the dividend on subsidiary preferred shares that would not be paid if the shares were converted into common stock of the parent. Note that 100% of the adjustment is added back, even though the parent's interest in the subsidiary is less than 100%.

(4) The parent's share adjustment consisting of 2,000 shares traceable to the parent company convertible security; 2,000 shares traceable to the subsidiary preferred stock that is convertible into parent common stock; and 50 incremental shares traceable to the subsidiary warrants to acquire parent common stock. It is assumed that 50 of the 100 shares required to satisfy the warrants can be purchased with the proceeds of the exercise and 50 new shares must be issued.

Special analysis is required in computing consolidated EPS when an acquisition occurs during a reporting period. When the acquisition is a pooling of interests, the computation of EPS includes subsidiary income and securities for the entire period. However, when the acquisition is a purchase, only subsidiary income since the acquisition date is included, and the number of subsidiary shares is weighted for the partial period.

TAXATION OF CONSOLIDATED FIRMS

Consolidated firms that do not meet the requirements to be an *affiliated group*, as defined by the tax law, must pay their taxes as separate entities. The tax definition of an affiliated group is less inclusive than that used in accounting theory. The Tax Reform Act of 1984 does not allow two or more corporations to file a consolidated return or to be considered an affiliated group for tax purposes unless the parent owns:

1. 80% of the voting power of all classes of stock and
2. 80% of the fair market value of all the outstanding stock of the other corporation.

For these provisions, preferred stock is not included if it (1) is not entitled to vote, (2) is limited and preferred as to dividends, and (3) does not have redemption rights beyond its issue price plus a reasonable redemption or liquidation premium and is not convertible into the other class of stock. Comparison of these criteria with those required for consolidated financial reporting indicates that many consolidated firms have no choice but to submit to separate taxation of the member firms.

Consolidated firms that meet the tax law requirements to be an affiliated group may elect to be taxed as a single entity or as separate entities. Once the election is made to file as a single entity, the permission of the Internal Revenue Service is required before the firms can be taxed separately again. Firms that elect to be taxed as a single entity file a consolidated tax return which may provide several tax advantages. For example, a consolidated return generally permits the offset of operating profits and losses and of capital gains and losses. Also, intercompany profits are not taxed until realized in later periods.

When firms that comprise an affiliated group elect not to file a consolidated return, each firm within the group computes and pays its taxes independently. In some cases there could be advantages in doing so. The first is that the firms do not have to use the same fiscal period or the same accounting method if separate tax returns are filed. Secondly, there may be intercompany losses that could be deducted in separate returns but not in consolidated returns. This is, however, quite rare since most intercompany losses are not deductible even when preparing separate returns.

Members of consolidated groups, when filing separate returns, must sum their incomes when applying graduated corporate tax rates. The lower tax rates available for low income levels can only be used once and cannot be applied by each of the firms individually.

CONSOLIDATED TAX RETURN

When an affiliated group elects to be taxed as a single entity, combined income as determined on the worksheet is the basis for the tax calculation. The affiliated firms should not record a provision for income tax based on their own separate incomes. Rather, the income tax expense is calculated as part of the consolidated worksheet process. The tax provision is based on consolidated net income; intercompany profits will have been eliminated already. Thus no special procedures are needed to deal with intercompany transactions when computing the tax provision. Once calculated, the tax provision may be recorded on the books of the separate firms.

As an example of an affiliated group's choosing to be taxed as a single entity, assume Company P purchased an 80% interest in Company S on January 1, 19X1, at which time the following determination and distribution of excess schedule was prepared:

Price paid		$795,000
Less interest acquired:		
Common stock....................................	$500,000	
Retained earnings, January 1, 19X1...................	400,000	
Total stockholders' equity	$900,000	
Interest acquired	80%	720,000
Goodwill, 15-year life ($5,000 per year)		$ 75,000 Dr

The following income statements are for companies P and S for 19X3. Since the firms desire to file a consolidated tax return, neither firm has recorded a provision for income tax.[3] The corporate tax rate is 30%.

	Company P	Company S
Sales...	$600,000	$400,000
Less cost of goods sold	350,000	200,000
Gross profit	$250,000	$200,000
Less operating expenses	100,000	100,000
Operating income	$150,000	$100,000
Subsidiary income....................................	80,000	
Income before tax...................................	$230,000	$100,000

On January 1, 19X2, Company P sold a piece of equipment, with a book value of $40,000, to Company S for $60,000. The equipment is depreciated by Company S on a straight-line basis over a 5-year life.

The following applies to 19X3 intercompany merchandise sales to Company P by Company S:

---

[3]Another term for "provision for income tax" is "income tax expense."

Intercompany sales in beginning inventory of Company P. $ 50,000
Intercompany sales in ending inventory of Company P   70,000
Sales to Company P during 19X3   100,000
Gross profit rate 50%

Worksheet 6-1, pages 396–399, contains the trial balances of Companies P and S on December 31, 19X3. Since the income tax is to be calculated on the worksheet, no provision exists on the separate books. If separate provisions appear in the trial balances, they should be eliminated as an initial procedure in consolidating.

The balance of the investment in Company S account results from the use of the simple equity method. All eliminations should be made prior to calculating the provision for tax. This will assure that the combined net income, upon which the provision is based, is adjusted for all intercompany transactions. Steps (1) through (9) are identical to the procedures used in all prior worksheets; they are unchanged by taxation issues. Combined net income before tax is calculated on the worksheet and becomes the base for the tax provision. Step (10) is not entered until this calculation is made. In journal entry form the entry is:

Provision for Income Tax 71,700
   Income Tax Payable   71,700
Explanation:
Combined income before tax (from the consolidated
   worksheet). $239,000
Tax rate. 30%
Tax provision and liability. . . . . $ 71,700

In this case, it was assumed that the purchase was a taxable exchange as to the seller and that all asset adjustments, including goodwill, are deductible. For tax purposes, goodwill is amortized over 15 years. As indicated in Chapter 1, there are some combinations that are nontaxable exchanges and amortizations of excess are then not deductible.[4]

The final complexity caused by a consolidated return involves the distribution of combined income. In the schedules that accompany Worksheet 6-1, the income distributions start with internally generated income before taxes. All adjustments to the worksheet are entered before tax effects. This procedure results in an adjusted income before tax for each firm.

The income tax expense of the member firms then is calculated. The income distribution schedules allocate the income tax expense and proceed to calculate each firm's adjusted net income. The subsidiary adjusted net income is distributed to the controlling and minority interests according to ownership percentages.

---

[4]When there are nondeductible amortizations of excess cost, there also may be a recorded deferred tax liability. Recall that an excess of market value over cost relative to an identifiable asset requires the recording of a deferred tax liability for the amount of the tax rate times the excess. This deferred tax liability would be amortized to tax expense in proportion to the amortization of the excess.

It will be necessary for each member firm to record its share of the tax provision on its own books. The subsidiary, Company S, would record the following:

Provision for Income Tax. 27,000
   Income Tax Payable 27,000
      To record the allocated portion of the tax provision.

The parent, Company P, would record the following:

Subsidiary Income (80% × $27,000 tax provision). 21,600
   Investment in Company S 21,600
      To adjust Subsidiary Income for the tax expense recorded by
      Company S.

Provision for Income Tax. 44,700
   Income Tax Payable 44,700
      To record the allocated portion of the tax provision.

In review: Consolidated returns are consistent with consolidated reporting procedures and do not alter in any way the procedures that have been discussed in previous chapters. It is necessary only to add new procedures to the worksheet to provide for income taxes. The procedures were explained in our example assuming the use of the simple equity method. There would not be any impact on the tax step if the cost or sophisticated equity method were used.

SEPARATE TAX RETURNS

When separate returns are required or are elected to be filed, each member of the consolidated group must base its provision for tax on its own reported income. For the parent, taxable income may include dividends received from other corporations. When the members of the consolidated firm meet the requirements of an affiliated firm (this requires at least an 80% ownership interest), 100% of the dividends received are excluded from reported income. For ownership interests of at least 20% but less than 80%, 80% of the dividends received are excluded from reported income.[5] For ownership interests less than 20%, 70% of the dividends received are excluded from reported income. The full or partial exclusion of dividends applies only to dividends from domestic corporations and is intended to reduce multiple taxation of the same income.

A major complication arises in consolidating. The provision for tax recorded by each firm is based on their reported separate net incomes **prior to eliminating intercompany transactions.** That means that there are timing differences that are created when consolidating. For example: Suppose that the parent sells inventory to the subsidiary at a price that includes a 25% gross profit. If $40,000 of intercompany sales remains in the subsidiary's ending inventory, consolidation procedures defer $10,000 of intercompany profit. The problem is

---

[5]The exclusion rate is determined by current tax law and is subject to change.

that the subsidiary already recorded a 30% or $3,000 tax provision on the profit as a separate firm. This $3,000 now becomes a deferred tax asset when the profit to which it attaches is deferred (prepaid) on the consolidated worksheet. In the following period, the intercompany profit on the inventory is realized (assuming the inventory is sold in that period). The deferred tax asset relative to the inventory profit then is expensed as part of the current year's provision for tax. The adjustments required as a result of these tax issues are examples of applying interperiod tax allocation procedures.

The use of separate tax returns for a consolidated group leads to a complicated application of interperiod tax allocation techniques. The calculations may become cumbersome even when only intercompany sales of plant assets and merchandise are involved. To illustrate, assume Company P purchased a 75% interest in Company S on January 1, 19X1, at which time the following determination and distribution of excess schedule was prepared:

Price paid		$285,000
Less interest acquired:		
Common stock	$250,000	
Retained earnings, Jan. 1, 19X1	100,000	
Total stockholders' equity	$350,000	
Interest acquired	75%	262,500
Goodwill, 15-year life ($1,500 per year)		$ 22,500 Dr

On January 1, 19X3, Company S sold equipment, with a book value of $60,000, to Company P for $100,000. Company P is depreciating the asset over 5 years on a straight-line basis.

During 19X4, Companies P and S reported the following operating incomes before tax:

	Company P	Company S
Sales	$430,000	$240,000
Less cost of goods sold	280,000	150,000
Gross profit	$150,000	$ 90,000
Less operating expenses	70,000	30,000
Operating income before tax	$ 80,000	$ 60,000

A 30% corporate tax rate is assumed for both firms. The following data apply to the 19X4 intercompany merchandise sales to Company S by the parent, Company P:

Intercompany sales in beginning inventory of Company S	$ 60,000
Intercompany sales in ending inventory of Company S	40,000
Sales to Company S during 19X4	100,000
Gross profit rate	40%

Taxation of Separate Entities.   Before Companies P and S can be consolidated, it is necessary to calculate their separate tax liabilities since the 80% test of an affiliated group for tax purposes is not met. The tax provision of the subsidiary is $18,000 (30% × $60,000 Company S income before tax). Company S would record its tax provision as follows:

Provision for Income Tax.	18,000	
Income Tax Payable		18,000

The tax provision for Company P requires consideration of the tax status of subsidiary income. When the conditions for an affiliated group are not met, the parent company must include in its taxable income 20% of the dividends it receives from a subsidiary. When an affiliated group *elects* separate taxation, no dividends are included and no additional tax needs to be calculated. According to APB Opinion No. 23, subsidiary income included in the pretax income of a parent leads to a temporary difference between the earning of the income and its inclusion in the tax return as dividend income.[6] It is not necessary to account for the temporary difference if the tax law provides a means by which the investment can be recovered tax free. Accordingly, Company P will provide for tax expense equal to its tax rate times 20% of its share of the total subsidiary net income. It is assumed that the parent records its tax provision based on the income it records from the subsidiary. In this example, the parent records the investment under the simple equity method. Thus, the tax accrual is based on 20% of the simple equity income without any reduction for amortization of excesses. A parent using the cost method would record the tax only on dividends received and would need to accrue tax on the worksheet based on the cost-to-equity conversion.

This tax may be viewed as a *secondary tax* since it is the second taxation of subsidiary income. For 19X4, this tax liability would be calculated as follows:

Subsidiary net income	$42,000
Controlling interest, 75% × $42,000	31,500
Provision for tax on subsidiary income, 30% × (20% × $31,500)	1,890

Company P would add this amount to the tax it has provided for its internally generated income to arrive at its total tax provision for the period:

Tax on internally generated income, 30% × $80,000	$24,000
Secondary tax provision for subsidiary income	1,890
Total Company P provision for tax.	$25,890

Since Company P has not received its share of the income of Company S, the secondary tax is not immediately payable, and a deferred tax liability for $1,890 is created. Assuming that the tax on internally generated income is

---

[6]Opinions of the Accounting Principles Board No. 23, *Accounting for Income Taxes—Special Areas* (New York: American Institute of Certified Public Accountants, 1971), pars. 9–12.

currently payable, Company P would make the following entry to record its 19X4 tax provision:

Provision for Income Tax.	25,890	
Income Tax Payable		24,000
Deferred Tax Liability.		1,890

If dividends had been paid by the subsidiary, the secondary tax applicable to the dividends received by Company P would be included in the current tax liability. Note that the secondary tax only applies to consolidated firms that do not qualify as an affiliated group. Firms that do meet the requirements would only calculate a single tax on each firm's adjusted net income.

Worksheet Procedures.   Worksheet 6-2, pages 400–403, includes the trial balances of companies P and S. The firms do not qualify as an affiliated group for tax purposes. Several observations should be made regarding the amounts listed:

1. The balance in Investment in Company S is computed according to the simple equity method, as follows:

Original cost		$285,000
Subsidiary income, 19X1-19X3 (*after tax*):		
Company S retained earnings, Jan. 1, 19X4	$350,000	
Company S retained earnings, Jan. 1, 19X1	100,000	
Net increase	$250,000	
Controlling interest	75%	187,500
Controlling interest in subsidiary net income, 19X4 (75% × $42,000)		31,500
Equity-adjusted balance, Dec. 31, 19X4		$504,000

2. Since the parent's share of subsidiary undistributed income has been recorded from the date of acquisition, a deferred tax liability has been recorded by Company P each year to recognize the secondary tax provision. The total deferred tax liability on December 31, 19X4, is calculated as follows:

Deferred tax liability on 19X1–19X3 income (20% × 30% × $187,500 19X1–19X3 undistributed income)	$11,250
Current year's additional deferment (20% × 30% × $31,500)	1,890
Total deferred tax liability	$13,140

3. The trial balances of both companies include their separate provisions for income tax and the current tax liabilities. *These provisions do not reflect adjustments for intercompany transactions.*

Worksheet steps (1) through (9) are identical to those that would be prepared in the absence of any consideration of taxes. The first special procedure to consider is step (10). Its purpose is to adjust for the tax impact of the adjustments that affect beginning retained earnings. Step (5) reduced retained earnings for the intercompany profit on the equipment sale. Now it is necessary to increase retained earnings for the tax expense previously recorded by the separate firms concerning this profit. Not only has a tax provision relative to this sale been recorded by the subsidiary, but the parent also has recorded the secondary tax applicable to the sale. Both sets of taxes are viewed now as deferred (prepaid). Since the taxes have been expensed previously, they also are removed from retained earnings. In addition, step (10) defers the tax that has been recorded by Company P relative to the intercompany inventory profit at the start of the year. Since the sale was made and the tax recorded by the parent company, there is no secondary tax. Step (10) also records the tax deduction for goodwill in the prior 3 years. The tax accrual for simple equity income recorded by the parent did not consider amortizations of excess. The goodwill amortization reduces the parent's deferred tax liability.

Step (11) deals with the tax impact of adjustments to the current-year income. Since part of the intercompany profit on the equipment sale will be recognized this year, the deferred tax (including the secondary tax) now is expensed. Likewise, the tax deferred relative to the beginning inventory profit is expensed. It then becomes necessary to defer the tax applicable to the intercompany profit in the ending inventory. Again, since the inventory profit was recorded by the parent and not the subsidiary, there is no secondary tax. The tax deduction relative to the goodwill amortization is included.

When the steps in Worksheet 6-2 are completed, the resulting combined net income is $106,008, which is distributed to the controlling and minority interests. The distribution schedules start with internally generated net income *after tax*, since the tax expense is calculated by each firm separately. Thus, each adjustment must be on an after-tax basis when made to the internally generated net income.

Let us revisit Worksheet 6-2 to discuss how it would be simplified if the consolidated firm met the requirements of an affiliated firm. The following procedures would be omitted from the worksheet:

1. Company P would not have recorded the deferred tax liability of $13,140 on its books. If the firms are an affiliated group, there is no tax due on the parent's share of subsidiary income. The parent's current-year provision for income tax would only be $24,000 since there would not be the secondary tax of $1,890 on the parent's share of subsidiary income.
2. Step (10) would not include the secondary tax of $1,008 applicable to the intercompany equipment sale.
3. Step (11) would not include the secondary tax of $252 applicable to the intercompany equipment sale.
4. The parent's income distribution schedule would not deduct the secondary tax on the parent's share of subsidiary income. Instead, the parent would just include 75% of the subsidiary's after-tax income of $47,600, or $35,700.

There are some additional minor worksheet modifications required if the cost or sophisticated equity methods are used by the parent company. If the cost method is used, there needs to be a recording of the deferred tax liability for prior years' subsidiary income. The adjustment would be to multiply the net amount of the cost-to-equity conversion adjustment by the effective tax rate and to debit the parent's retained earnings and to credit a deferred tax liability account. If the sophisticated equity method is used, the parent company's retained earnings and current-year tax provision are correct and need no adjustment. The only steps needed in consolidating is to adjust the beginning retained earnings of the subsidiary for any intercompany profits on a net-of-tax basis. The adjustment of subsidiary retained earnings on the consolidated worksheet was covered in the partial worksheet on page 234. It still would be necessary to calculate the minority and controlling interest in combined net income on an after-tax basis when preparing the income distribution schedules.

EQUITY METHOD FOR UNCONSOLIDATED INVESTMENTS

Prior to the 1971 issuance of APB Opinion No. 18, "The Equity Method of Accounting for Investments in Common Stock," investors could freely choose between the equity and cost methods to recognize income on their investments. When the equity method was used, it tended to be a simple equity method that recognized only a pro rata share of the investee's income, without any attempt to amortize an excess of cost or book value on the investment or to defer intercompany gains and losses. The choice between these two divergent methods is not significant when consolidation is required since the investment and investment income accounts are eliminated in the consolidation process. However, the accounting profession did become concerned with the use of the cost method for major investments not subject to consolidation. The APB reasoned that, in such cases, the investor may have significant influence over the investee's dividend policy and the payment of dividends often would be unrelated to the investee's income during a given period. For example, dividend payments would be level over a period of years during which income varied significantly. This reasoning led the APB to state:

> The equity method tends to be most appropriate if an investment enables the investor to influence the operating or financial decisions of the investee. The investor then has a degree of responsibility for the return on its investment, and it is appropriate to include in the results of operations of the investor its share of earnings or losses of the investee. Influence tends to be more effective as the investor's percent of ownership in the voting stock of the investee increases. Investments of relatively small percentages of voting stock of an investee tend to be passive in nature and enable the investor to have little or no influence on the operations of the investee.[7]

---

[7]Opinions of the Accounting Principles Board No. 18, *The Equity Method of Accounting for Investments in Common Stock* (New York: American Institute of Certified Public Accountants, 1971), par. 12.

APB Opinion No. 18 requires the use of the sophisticated equity method for the following types of investments:

1. *Influential investments.* The APB defines influence as "representation on the board of directors, participation in policy-making processes, material intercompany transactions, interchange of managerial personnel, or technological dependency."[8] When the investor holds 20% or more of the voting shares of an investee, influence is assumed, and the sophisticated equity method is required unless the investor takes on the burden of proof to show that influence does not exist, in which case the cost method would be used.[9] When the investment falls below 20%, the presumption is that influence does not exist, and the cost method is to be used unless the investor can show that influence does exist despite the low percentage of ownership. Since the most common use of the sophisticated equity method is for influential (20% to 50%) investments, such investments are used in subsequent illustrations.

2. *Corporate joint ventures.* A corporate joint venture is a separate, specific project organized for the benefit of several corporations. An example would be a research project undertaken jointly by several members of a given industry. The member firms typically participate in the management of the venture and share the gains and losses. Since such an arrangement does not involve passive investors, the sophisticated equity method is required.

3. *Unconsolidated subsidiaries.* A parent may own over 50% of the shares of a subsidiary but may meet one of the exceptions (control is temporary or does not rest with the majority owner) to the requirement that subsidiaries be consolidated. However, if influence does exist, the sophisticated equity method would be used for the investment.

As defined by APB Opinion No. 18, the use of the equity method requires that the investment in common stock appear as a single, equity-adjusted amount on the balance sheet of the investor. The investor's income statement will include the investor's share of the investee ordinary income as a single amount in the ordinary income section. The investor's share of investee discontinued operations, extraordinary items, and cumulative effects of changes in accounting principles will appear as single amounts in the sections of the investor's income statement that correspond to the placement of these items in the investee's statement.

CALCULATION OF EQUITY INCOME

In its basic form, the equity method requires the investor to recognize its pro rata share of investee reported income. Dividends, when received, do not constitute income, but are viewed instead as a partial liquidation of the investment. In

---

[8]*Ibid.*, par. 17.
[9]For examples of situations that may overcome the presumption of influence, see FASB Interpretation No. 35, *Criteria for Applying the Equity Method of Accounting for Investments in Common Stock* (Stamford: Financial Accounting Standards Board, 1981).

reality, however, the price paid for the investment usually will not agree with the underlying book value of the investee, which requires that any amortization of an excess of cost or book value be treated as an adjustment of the investor's pro rata share of investee income. It is very likely that the reported income of the investee will include gains and losses on transactions with the investor. As was true in consolidations, these gains and losses cannot be recognized until they are confirmed by a transaction between the affiliated group and unrelated parties. The proper application of the sophisticated equity method will mean that the income recognized by the investor will be the same as it would be under consolidation procedures. In fact, the sophisticated equity method sometimes is referred to as "one-line consolidation."

In the next two sections, the sophisticated equity method will be presented without consideration of the tax implications. Following that, the tax effect on such an investment will be addressed.

Amortization of Excesses.   A determination and distribution of excess schedule is prepared for a sophisticated equity method investment just as it would be if the investment was to be consolidated. For example, assume the following schedule was prepared by Excel Corporation for a 25% interest in Flag Company acquired on January 1, 19X1:

Price paid		$300,000
Less interest acquired:		
Common stock ($10 par)	$200,000	
Retained earnings, January 1, 19X1	600,000	
Total stockholders' equity	$800,000	
Interest acquired	25%	200,000
Excess of cost over book value		$100,000
Less excess attributable to equipment with a 5-year remaining life		
and undervalued by $80,000, 25% × $80,000		20,000
Goodwill (40-year life)		$ 80,000

As a practical matter, APB Opinion No. 18 states that it may not be possible to relate the excess to specific assets, in which case the entire excess may be considered goodwill. However, an attempt should be made to allocate the excess in the same manner as would be done for the purchase of a controlling interest in a subsidiary.

The determination and distribution of excess schedule indicates the pattern of amortization to be followed. The required amortizations must be made directly through the investment account since the distributions shown on the schedule are not recorded in the absence of consolidation procedures. The debit and credit indicators have been dropped from the determination and distribution of excess schedule since there will not be any worksheet adjustments in the absence of consolidation. Assuming Flag Company reported net income of $50,000 for 19X1, Excel Corporation would make the following entry for 19X1:

Investment in Flag Company...............................	6,500	
Investment Income.....................................		6,500

Income is calculated as follows:

25% × Flag reported net income of $50,000		$12,500
Less amortizations of excess cost:		
Equipment, $20,000 ÷ 5	$4,000	
Goodwill, $80,000 ÷ 40	2,000	6,000
Investment income, net of amortizations		$ 6,500

If an investment is acquired for less than book value, the excess of book value over cost would be amortized over a period not to exceed 40 years. This procedure would increase investment income in the years of amortization.

Intercompany Transactions by Investee.   The investee may sell inventory to the investor. As would be true if the investment were consolidated, the share of the investee's profit on goods still held by the investor at the end of a period cannot be included in income of that period. Instead, the profit must be deferred until the goods are sold by the investor. Since the two firms are separate reporting entities, the intercompany sales and related debt cannot be eliminated. Only the investor's share of the investee's profit on unsold goods in the hands of the investor is deferred. In a like manner, the investor may have plant assets that were purchased from the investee. The investor's share of the investee's gains and losses on these sales also must be deferred and allocated over the depreciable life of the asset. Profit deferments should be handled in an income distribution schedule similar to that used for consolidated worksheets. To illustrate, assume the following facts for the example of the 25% investment in Flag by Excel. Again, note that income tax is not being considered in this illustration:

1. Excel had the following merchandise acquired from Flag Company in its ending inventories:

Year	Amount	Gross Profit of Flag Company
19X1	$30,000	40%
19X2	40,000	45

2. Excel purchased a truck from Flag Company on January 1, 19X1, for $20,000. The truck is being depreciated over a 4-year life on a straight-line basis with no salvage value. The truck had a net book value of $16,000 when it was sold by Flag.
3. Flag Company had an income of $50,000 in 19X1 and $70,000 in 19X2.
4. Flag declared and paid $10,000 in dividends in 19X2.

Based on these facts, Excel Corporation would prepare the following income distribution schedules:

19X1 Income Distribution for Investment in Flag Company

Gain on sale of truck, to be amortized over 4 years .... $ 4,000	Reported income of Flag Company......................		$50,000
Profit in Excel ending inventory, 40% × $30,000 12,000	Realization of 1/4 of profit on sale of truck........................		1,000
	Adjusted income of Flag Company		$35,000
	Ownership interest, 25%		$ 8,750
	Less amortization of excess cost:		
	Equipment	$4,000	
	Goodwill	2,000	6,000
	Investment income, net of amortizations		$ 2,750

19X2 Income Distribution for Investment in Flag Company

Profit in Excel ending inventory, 45% × $40,000 .... $18,000	Reported income of Flag Company......................		$70,000
	Profit in Excel beginning inventory, 40% × $30,000		12,000
	Realization of 1/4 of profit on sale of truck.......................		1,000
	Adjusted income of Flag Company		$65,000
	Ownership interest, 25%		$16,250
	Less amortization of excess cost:		
	Equipment	$4,000	
	Goodwill	2,000	6,000
	Income from investment		$10,250

The schedules would lead to the following entries to record investment income:

19X1	Investment in Flag Company.........................	2,750	
	Investment Income...............................		2,750
19X2	Investment in Flag Company.........................	10,250	
	Investment Income...............................		10,250

In addition, the following entry would be made in 19X2 to record dividends received:

Cash	2,500	
Investment in Flag Company		2,500

It should be noted that only the investor's share of intercompany gains and losses is deferred. The investee's remaining stockholders are not affected by the Excel Corporation investment.

TAX EFFECTS OF EQUITY METHOD

The investor not meeting the requirements of affiliation as defined by the tax law pays income taxes on dividends received. In the case of a domestic corporation, 20% of the dividends are includable in taxable income. However, a temporary difference is created through the use of the equity method for financial reporting.[10] As a result, *the provision for tax must be based on the equity income, and a deferred tax liability must be created for undistributed investment income.* The provision may be based on the assumption that investment income will be distributed in dividends, or it will be realized via the sale of the investment. In the latter case, it is likely that the income would be taxed in the form of a capital gain. The assumption used will determine the rate to be applied to the undistributed income. The provision for tax is based on the investor's net investment income after adjustments and amortizations. However, amortizations of excess cost are not deductible since they have no impact on the income that could be distributed to the investor and thus must be added back to the net investment income to compute the tax.

The following entries are based on the previous example of Flag Company and Excel Corporation, but it is assumed that each firm is subject to a 30% income tax. Excel Corporation's share of Flag Company *net* income would now be calculated as follows:

	19X1	19X2
Adjusted income of Flag Company, before tax*	$35,000	$65,000
Tax provision (30%)	10,500	19,500
Adjusted net income of Flag Company	$24,500	$45,500
Ownership interest in adjusted net income (25%)	$ 6,125	$11,375
Less amortizations of excess*	6,000	6,000
Net income from investment	$ 125	$ 5,375

*See the income distribution schedules in the previous section.

Note that the tax provision calculated by the investor will not agree with the provision for tax on the books of the investee. This is due to the adjustments made in the income distribution schedules to recognize the profit deferrals.

The 19X1 and 19X2 entries to record investment income and the applicable tax provision would be:

19X1	Investment in Flag Company	125	
	Investment Income		125
	Provision for Income Tax [20% × 30% × ($125 net income + $6,000 nondeductible amortizations of excess)]	368	
	Deferred Tax Liability		368

---

[10] Opinions of the Accounting Principles Board No. 24, *Accounting for Income Taxes—Investments in Common Stock Accounted for by the Equity Method (Other than Subsidiaries and Corporate Joint Ventures)* (New York: American Institute of Certified Public Accountants, 1972), par. 7.

19X2	Investment in Flag Company	5,375	
	Investment Income		5,375
	Cash	2,500	
	Investment in Flag Company		2,500
	Provision for Income Tax [20% × 30% × ($5,375 net income		
	+ $6,000 nondeductible amortizations of excess)]	683	
	Income Tax Payable (20% × 30% × $2,500 dividends)		150
	Deferred Tax Liability ($683 − $150)		533

UNUSUAL EQUITY ADJUSTMENTS

There are several unusual situations involving the investee that require special procedures for the proper recording of investment income. These situations are described in the following paragraphs.

Investee with Preferred Stock. In the absence of consolidation, an investment in preferred stock does not require elimination. However, the existence of preferred stock in the capital structure of the investee requires that the investor's equity adjustment be based on only that portion of investee income available for common stockholders. Dividends declared on preferred stock must be subtracted from income of the investee. When the preferred stock has cumulative or participation rights, the claim of preferred stockholders must be subtracted from the investee income each period to arrive at the income available for common stockholders. The procedures for calculating this income are contained in Chapter 7.

Investee Stock Transactions. The investee corporation may engage in transactions with its common stockholders, such as issuing additional shares, retiring shares, or engaging in treasury stock transactions. Each of these transactions affects the investor's equity interest. A comparison is made of the investor's ownership interest before and after the investee stock transaction. An increase in the investor's interest is treated as a gain, while a decrease is recorded as a loss.

Write-Down to Market Value. The investment in another firm is subject to reduction to a lower market value if it appears that a relatively permanent fall in value has occurred. The fact that the current market value of the shares is temporarily less than the equity-adjusted cost of the shares is not sufficient cause for a write-down. When the sophisticated equity method is used and a permanent decline in value occurs, a reduction would be made to the equity-adjusted cost. The equity method would continue to be applied subsequent to the write-down. There can be no subsequent write-ups, however, other than through normal equity adjustments.

Zero Investment Balance. It is possible that an investee will suffer losses to the extent that the continued application of the equity method would produce a negative balance in the investment account. Equity adjustments are to be discon-

tinued when the investment balance becomes zero.[11] Further losses are acknowledged only by memo entries, which are needed to maintain the total unrecorded
share of losses. If the investee again becomes profitable, the investor must not
record income on the investment until its subsequent share of income equals the
previously unrecorded share of losses.

To illustrate these procedures, assume Grate Corporation has a 35% investment in Dittmar Company, with a sophisticated-equity-adjusted cost of $30,000
on January 1, 19X1, and Dittmar reports the following results:

Period	Income (loss)
19X1	$(80,000)
19X2	(50,000)
19X3	(20,000)
19X4	90,000

The following T account summarizes entries for 19X1 through 19X4 (taxes
are ignored):

Investment in Dittmar Company

Equity-adjusted balance, Jan. 1, 19X1	$30,000	Equity loss for 19X1, 35% × $80,000 Dittmar loss	$28,000
		Recorded equity loss for 19X2, 35% × $50,000 Dittmar loss = $17,500; loss limited to investment balance	2,000
Balance	$ 0		
		Memo entries:	
Memo entry:		Unrecorded 19X2 loss, $17,500 – $2,000	$15,500
Unrecorded share of 19X4 Dittmar income	22,500	Unrecorded loss for 19X3, 35% × $20,000 Dittmar loss	7,000
Actual entries resumed: Recorded equity income, 19X4, 35% × $90,000 Dittmar income, less amount to cover unrecorded losses ($15,500 + $7,000)	$ 9,000		
Balance, Dec. 31, 19X4	$ 9,000		

Intercompany Transactions by Investor.   An investor may sell merchandise and/or plant assets to an investee at a gain or loss. When influence is
deemed to exist, it might seem appropriate to defer the entire gain or loss until

---

[11]According to APB Opinion No. 18 (par. 19i), any net advance to the investee that the investor
may have on its books also is available to offset the investor's share of investee losses until the
receivable is reduced to a zero balance.

the asset is resold or depreciated by the investee. However, an interpretation of APB Opinion No. 18 requires the entire gain or loss to be deferred only when the transaction is with a controlled (over 50%-owned) investee and is not at arm's length. In all other cases, it is appropriate to defer only a gain or loss that is in proportion to the investor's ownership interest.[12]

To illustrate, assume Grant Corporation, which owns a 35% interest in Hartwig Company, sold $50,000 of merchandise to Hartwig at a gross profit of 40%. Of this merchandise, $20,000 is still in Hartwig's 19X1 ending inventory. Grant needs to defer only profit equal to the $8,000 (40% × $20,000) unrealized gross profit multiplied by its 35% interest, or $2,800. Grant would make the following entry on December 31, 19X1:

Sales	2,800	
Deferred Gross Profit on Sales to Investee		2,800

Assuming the investor recorded the provision for income tax prior to this adjustment, the tax applicable to the unrealized gain would be deferred by the following entry, which is based on a 30% tax rate:

Deferred Tax Expense (30% × $2,800)	840	
Provision for Income Tax.		840

The deferred gross profit and the related tax deferment would be realized in the period in which the goods are sold to outside parties. The deferred profit and related tax effects on plant asset sales would be realized in proportion to the depreciation recorded by the investee company.

It may occur that the investor will purchase outstanding bonds of the investee. Unlike consolidation procedures, the bonds are not assumed to be retired since the investor and investee are separate reporting entities. Similarly, a purchase of investor bonds by the investee is not a retirement of the bonds. Thus, no adjustments to income are necessary as a result of intercompany bondholdings.

Gain or Loss of Influence.   An investor may own less than a 20% interest in an investee, in which case the cost method ordinarily would be used to record investment income. If the investor subsequently buys sufficient additional shares to have its total interest equal or exceed 20%, the investor must apply retroactively the sophisticated equity method to the total holding period of the investment. APB Opinion No. 18 requires an adjustment of retained earnings for the period prior to the time the 20% interest is achieved.

It is possible that an investor will own 20% or more of the voting shares of the investee but will sell a portion of the shares so that the ownership interest falls below 20%. In such a case, the sophisticated equity method is discontinued as of the sale date. However, there is no adjustment back to the cost method. The balance of the investment account remains at its equity-adjusted balance on the

---

[12]Accounting Interpretations, *The Equity Method of Accounting for Investments in Common Stock: Accounting Interpretations of APB Opinion No. 18* (New York: American Institute of Certified Public Accountants, 1971), par. 1.

sale date. Should influence be attained again, a retroactive ("catch-up") equity adjustment would be made.

When all or part of an investment recorded under the sophisticated equity method is sold, the gain or loss is based on the equity-adjusted balance as of the sale date. An adjustment also would be necessary for deferred tax balances applicable to the investment.

DISCLOSURE REQUIREMENTS

Since a significant portion of the investor's income may be derived from investments, added disclosures are required in order to inform properly the readers of the financial statements. For investments of 20% or more, the investor must disclose the name of each investee, the percentage of ownership in each investee, and the disparity between the cost and underlying book value for each investment. If the sophisticated equity method is not being applied, the reasons must be given. When investments are material with respect to the investor's financial position or income, the financial statements of the investees should be included as supplemental information.

When a market value for the investment is available, it should be disclosed. However, if the investor owns a relatively large block of a subsidiary's shares, quoted market values would have little relevance because the sale of an entire controlling interest would involve different motivations and would result in a unique value.

QUESTIONS

1. During the current period, a company purchased an 80% interest in another firm. What is the impact of the purchase on the consolidated statement of cash flow in the period of the purchase assuming (a) the interest was acquired for cash? (b) bonds were issued in exchange for the interest? (c) the parent firm issued common stock in exchange for the interest?

2. What are the possible ramifications on the current period's consolidated statement of cash flows of a purchase of a subsidiary that occurred in a prior period?

3. Which of the following items would be included in a consolidated statement of cash flows and, if they are included, in what section would they appear?
   (a) Amortization of excesses relative to the investment.
   (b) Parent company investment in subsidiary bonds purchased directly from the subsidiary.
   (c) Parent company acquisition that meets the pooling criteria.
   (d) Cash acquisition of remaining interest in a subsidiary following a pooling of interests.
   (e) Minority interest in subsidiary equity in year of acquisition.
   (f) Parent company sale of a part of its interest in a subsidiary.
   (g) Cash dividends paid by a 90%-owned subsidiary.

4. Indicate how the computation of consolidated earnings per share is influenced by the minority interest in a subsidiary's equity.

5. Discuss the need for interperiod tax allocation as a part of the consolidation process when members of a consolidated group file separate tax returns.

6. Company S has operating income of $100,000 before tax. Company P has a 70% ownership interest in Company S. Assuming Companies P and S are taxed as separate entities, what provision for tax must P make for its share of S income? Assume a 30% tax rate for both companies.

7. Briefly describe when the APB Opinion No. 18 sophisticated equity method must be used in accounting for an investment.

8. Why is the APB Opinion No. 18 sophisticated equity method viewed as requiring a "one-line" consolidation?

9. Is it possible for the investment account to have a negative balance under the sophisticated equity method?

10. Hummer Corporation owns a 30% interest in Canfield Company. How much profit would you adjust for and how would you make the adjustment if (a) Hummer sold merchandise to Canfield during the year, and Canfield has in its ending inventory goods purchased for $5,000 which were sold by Hummer at a 30% gross profit? (b) Canfield sold merchandise to Hummer during the year and Hummer has in its ending inventory goods purchased for $8,000 which were sold by Canfield at a 25% gross profit?

11. Discuss the use of lower-of-cost-or-market values in regard to investments carried under the APB Opinion No. 18 equity method.

12. Describe the accounting procedures for (a) an investor who owns less than a 20% interest in an investee and subsequently purchases enough stock to exceed 20%, and (b) an investor whose ownership interest exceeds 20%, but who subsequently sells a portion of the investment to cause the interest to fall below 20%.

13. What disclosures concerning material investments must be made on the financial statements?

EXERCISES

Exercise 1. Bark Company purchased a 90% interest in Rite-Line Company for $520,000 cash on January 1, 19X3. Any excess of cost over book value was attributed to goodwill with a 10-year life. To help pay for the acquisition, Bark Company issued 300, $1,000 face value, 10-year, 8% bonds. Rite-Line's balance sheet on the date of the purchase was as follows:

Assets		Liabilities and Equity	
Cash	$ 20,000	Current liabilities............	$110,000
Inventory	140,000	Bonds payable	100,000
Property, plant,		Common stock ($10 par)......	200,000
and equipment	550,000	Retained earnings............	300,000
		Total liabilities and	
Total assets	$710,000	equity	$710,000

Consolidated net income for 19X3 was $119,000, net of the minority's interest of $8,000. Bark declared and paid dividends of $10,000 and Rite-Line declared and paid dividends of $5,000. There were no purchases or sales of property, plant, or equipment during the year. Based on the following information, prepare a statement of cash flows using the indirect method for Bark Company and its subsidiary for the year ended December 31, 19X3. Any supporting schedules should be in good form.

	Bark Company Dec. 31, 19X2	Consolidated Dec. 31,19X3
Cash	$100,000	$ 63,500
Inventory	220,000	454,000
Property, plant, and equipment	800,000	1,230,000
Goodwill		63,000
Current liabilities	(160,000)	(284,000)
Bonds payable	(200,000)	(600,000)
Minority interest		(57,500)
Controlling common stock, $10 par	(200,000)	(200,000)
Controlling paid-in capital in excess of par	(300,000)	(300,000)
Retained earnings	(260,000)	(369,000)
Totals	0	0

Exercise 2. Duckworth Corporation purchased an 80% interest in Poladna Corporation on January 1, 19X3, in exchange for 5,000 Duckworth shares (market value of $18) plus $155,000 cash. The appraisal showed that some of Poladna's equipment, with a 4-year estimated remaining life, was undervalued $20,000. Goodwill is to be amortized over a 10-year period. The following is Poladna Corporation's balance sheet on December 31, 19X2:

Assets

Cash	$ 30,000
Inventory	30,000
Property, plant, and equipment	300,000
Accumulated depreciation	(90,000)
Total assets	$ 270,000

Liabilities and Equity

Current liabilities	$ 30,000
Long-term liabilities	40,000
Common stock ($10 par)	150,000
Retained earnings	50,000
Total liabilities and equity	$ 270,000

Comparative balance sheet data are as follows:

	December 31, 19X2 (Parent only)	December 31, 19X3 (Consolidated)
Cash	$ 100,000	$ 95,000
Inventory	60,000	84,200
Property, plant, and equipment	950,000	1,342,000
Accumulated depreciation	(360,000)	(574,000)
Goodwill		62,100
Current liabilities	(80,000)	(115,000)
Long-term liabilities	(100,000)	(130,000)
Minority interest		(43,000)
Controlling interest:		
Common stock ($10 par)	(350,000)	(400,000)
Additional paid-in capital	(50,000)	(90,000)
Retained earnings	(170,000)	(231,300)
	0	0

The following information relates to the activities of the two firms for 19X3:
(a) Poladna paid off $10,000 of its long-term debt.
(b) Duckworth purchased production equipment for $76,000.
(c) Combined net income was $97,300; the minority interest's share was $6,000. Depreciation expense taken by Duckworth and Poladna on their separate books was $92,000 and $28,000, respectively.
(d) Duckworth paid $30,000 in dividends; Poladna paid $15,000.

Prepare the consolidated statement of cash flows for the year ended December 31, 19X3, for Duckworth Corporation and its subsidiary, Poladna Corporation.

Exercise 3. Paridon Motors purchased an 80% interest in Super Battery Company on January 1, 19X2, for $700,000 cash. At that date, Super Battery Company had the following stockholders' equity:

Common stock ($10 par)	$100,000
Paid-in capital in excess of par	300,000
Retained earnings	250,000
Total stockholders' equity	$650,000

Any excess of cost over book value was attributed to goodwill with a 20-year amortization period. A statement of cash flows is being prepared for 19X5. For each of the following situations, indicate the impact on the cash flow statement for 19X5.
(a) Adjustment resulting from the original purchase of the controlling interest.
(b) Super Battery Company issued 2,000 shares of common stock for $90 per share on January 1, 19X5. At the time, the stockholders' equity of Super Battery was $800,000. Paridon Motors purchased 1,000 shares.
(c) Paridon Motors purchased at 102, $100,000 of face value, 10% annual interest bonds issued by Super Battery Company at face value on January 1, 19X3. Paridon purchased the bonds on January 1, 19X5.
(d) Super Battery purchased a production machine from Paridon Motors on July 1, 19X5, for $80,000. Paridon's cost was $60,000 and accumulated depreciation was $20,000.

Exercise 4. On May 1, 19X6, Kern Company purchased a 70% interest in Boston Company for $350,000. The following determination and distribution of excess schedule was prepared:

Price paid		$355,000
Less interest acquired:		
Common stock ($12 par)	$300,000	
Retained earnings	100,000	
Total stockholders' equity	$400,000	
Interest acquired	70%	280,000
Excess of cost over book value attributable to goodwill (15-year life)		$ 75,000

Kern Company and Boston Company had the following separate income statements for the year ended December 31, 19X8:

	Kern Company	Boston Company
Sales..	$750,000	$550,000
Less cost of goods sold	440,000	357,500
Gross profit..	$310,000	$192,500
Less other expenses	200,000	140,000
Income before dividends	$110,000	$ 52,500
Dividends received	17,500	
Income before tax	$127,500	$ 52,500

During 19X8, Boston Company paid cash dividends of $1 per share of common stock.

Prepare the entry to record income tax payable on each firm's books. Assume a 30% corporate income tax rate.

Exercise 5. Dills Company purchased an 80% interest in the common stock of Sarada Company for $850,000 on January 1, 19X7. The price was $75,000 in excess of the book value of the underlying equity, and the excess was attributed to goodwill with a 15-year life.

During 19X9, Dills Company and Sarada Company reported the following internally generated income before taxes:

	Dills Company	Sarada Company
Sales..	$ 300,000	$ 120,000
Cost of goods sold....................................	(200,000)	(90,000)
Gain on machine	5,000	
Expenses...	(40,000)	(20,000)
Income before taxes	$ 65,000	$ 10,000

Sarada Company sold goods to Dills Company for $50,000. Dills Company had $20,000 of Sarada Company's goods in its beginning inventory and $6,000 of Sarada's goods in its ending inventory. Sarada Company sells goods to Dills Company at cost plus 25%.

Dills Company sold a new machine to Sarada Company on January 1, 19X9, for $30,000. The cost of the machine was $25,000. It has a 5-year life.

The affiliated group files a consolidated tax return and is taxed at 30%.

Prepare a consolidated income statement for 19X9. Include income distribution for both firms.

Exercise 6. (*This is the same as Exercise 5, but with separate taxation.*) Dolls Company purchased an 80% interest in the common stock of Sarah Company for $850,000 on January 1, 19X7. The price was $75,000 in excess of the book value of the underlying equity, and the excess was attributed to goodwill with a 15-year life.

During 19X9, Dolls Company and Sarah Company reported the following internally generated income before taxes:

	Dolls Company	Sarah Company
Sales..	$ 300,000	$ 120,000
Cost of goods sold....................................	(200,000)	(90,000)
Gain on machine	5,000	
Expenses...	(40,000)	(20,000)
Income before taxes	$ 65,000	$ 10,000

Sarah Company sold goods to Dolls Company for $50,000. Dolls Company had $20,000 of Sarah Company's goods in its beginning inventory and $6,000 of Sarah's goods in its ending inventory. Sarah Company sells goods to Dolls Company at cost plus 25%.

Dolls Company sold a new machine to Sarah Company on January 1, 19X9, for $30,000. The cost of the machine was $25,000. It has a 5-year life.

The firms file separate tax returns. Both are subject to a 30% tax rate. Dolls receives an 80% dividend deduction.

Prepare a consolidated income statement for 19X9. Include income distribution for both firms.

Exercise 7. The separate income statements of Casper Company and its 60%-owned subsidiary, Varsity Company, for the year ended December 31, 19X7, are as follows:

	Casper Company	Varsity Company
Sales.	$520,000	$300,000
Less cost of goods sold	350,000	180,000
Gross profit.	$170,000	$120,000
Less operating expenses	100,000	90,000
Operating income	$ 70,000	$ 30,000
Subsidiary income.	12,600	
Income before tax	$ 82,600	$ 30,000
Provision for income tax	21,756	9,000
Net income	$ 60,844	$ 21,000

The following additional information is available:
(a) Casper Company purchased its interest in Varsity Company on July 1, 19X5. There was no excess of cost or book value associated with the original purchase.
(b) Varsity Company sold a piece of equipment to Casper Company on December 31, 19X6, for $10,000. This piece of equipment had a book value of $5,000 and an estimated future life of four years at the purchase date. Straight-line depreciation is assumed.
(c) Casper Company sold $15,000 worth of merchandise to Varsity Company during 19X7. Casper sells its merchandise at a price that enables it to realize a gross profit of 30%.
(d) Varsity Company had $2,000 worth of this merchandise in its ending inventory.
(e) A corporate income tax rate of 30% is assumed.

Prepare the worksheet adjustments pertaining to the intercompany transactions, and prepare the interperiod tax allocations that result from the elimination of the intercompany transactions. The firms do not qualify as an affiliated group under the tax code.

Exercise 8. Trailer Corporation purchased a 25% interest in Like Company for $110,000 on January 1, 19X7. The following determination and distribution of excess schedule was prepared:

Price paid.		$110,000
Less interest acquired:		
Common stock ($10 par)	$200,000	
Retained earnings	100,000	
Total stockholders' equity	$300,000	
Interest acquired	25%	75,000

Excess of cost over book value..............................	$ 35,000
Less excess attributable to equipment, 25% × $40,000	
(10-year life)	10,000
Goodwill (20-year life).......................................	$ 25,000

Like Company earned income of $20,000 in 19X7 and $24,000 in 19X8. Like Company declared a 25-cent per share cash dividend on December 22, 19X8, payable January 12, 19X9, to stockholders of record on December 30, 19X8.

During 19X8, Like sold merchandise costing $10,000 to Trailer for $15,000. 20% of the merchandise was still in Trailer's ending inventory on December 31, 19X8.

Prepare the equity adjustment required by APB Opinion No. 18 on Trailer's books on December 31, 19X7, and December 31, 19X8, to account for its investment in Like Company. Assume Trailer Corporation makes no adjustment except at the end of each calendar year. Ignore income tax considerations.

Exercise 9. Barq Company purchased a 30% interest in Morse Company for $80,000 on January 1, 19X1, when Morse had the following stockholders' equity:

Common stock ($10 par)......................	$100,000
Paid-in capital in excess of par.................	20,000
Retained earnings...........................	130,000
Total.......................................	$250,000

Any excess cost was due to goodwill that is being amortized over 5 years.

Since the investment, Barq has consistently sold goods to Morse to realize a 30% profit. Such sales totaled $50,000 during 19X3. Morse had $10,000 of such goods in its beginning inventory and $40,000 in its ending inventory.

On January 1, 19X3, Morse sold a machine with a book value of $10,000 to Barq for $20,000. The machine has a 5-year life and is being depreciated on a straight-line basis.

Morse reported a net income of $60,000 before taxes for 19X3. Both firms are subject to a 30% corporate tax rate. Morse paid no dividends in 19X3.

Prepare all entries caused by Barq's investment in Morse for 19X3 (including tax ramifications). Assume that Barq has recorded the tax on its internally generated income. Barq has properly recorded the investment in previous periods.

Exercise 10. Spancrete Corporation acquired a 30% interest in the outstanding stock of Werl Corporation on January 1, 19X5. At that time, the following determination and distribution of excess schedule was prepared:

Price paid...		$125,000
Less interest acquired:		
Common stock...	$150,000	
Retained earnings	160,000	
Total stockholders' equity	$310,000	
Interest acquired	30%	93,000
Excess of cost over book value attributable to goodwill		
(10-year life)		$ 32,000

During 19X5, Spancrete purchased $200,000 of goods from Werl. $20,000 of these purchases were in the December 31, 19X5 ending inventory. During 19X6, Spancrete purchased $250,000 of goods from Werl. $30,000 of these purchases were in the December 31, 19X6 ending inventory. Werl's gross profit rate is 30%. Also, Spancrete purchased a machine from Werl for $15,000 on January 1, 19X6. The machine had a book value of $10,000 and a 5-year remaining life. Werl reported net income of $90,000 and paid $20,000 on dividends during 19X6.

Prepare an income distribution schedule for Werl, and record the entries to adjust the investment in Werl for 19X6.

Exercise 11. Hanson Corporation purchased a 10% interest in Novic Company on January 1, 19X6, and an additional 15% interest on January 1, 19X8. These investments cost Hanson Corporation $80,000 and $110,000, respectively.

The following stockholders' equities of Novic Company are available:

	December 31, 19X5	December 31, 19X7
Common stock ($10 par)	$500,000	$500,000
Retained earnings.....................	250,000	300,000
Total equity........................	$750,000	$800,000

Any excess of cost over book value on the original investment was attributed to goodwill and given a 5-year life. Any excess on the second purchase is attributable to equipment with a 4-year life.

Novic Company had income of $30,000, $30,000, and $40,000, for 19X6, 19X7, and 19X8, respectively. Novic paid dividends of $.20 per share in 19X7 and 19X8.

Ignore income tax considerations, and assume adjusting entries are made at the end of the calendar year only.

(1) Prepare the equity "catch-up" entry, as required by APB Opinion No. 18, on January 1, 19X8, when Hanson's investment in Novic Company first exceeded 20%. Any supporting schedules should be in good form.

(2) Prepare the December 31, 19X8 equity adjustment on Hanson's books. Provide supporting calculations in good form.

Exercise 12. On January 1, 19X7, Lund Corporation purchased a 30% interest in Aluma-Boat Company for $200,000. At the time of the purchase, Aluma-Boat had total stockholders' equity of $400,000. Any excess of cost over the equity purchased was attributed in part to machinery worth $50,000 more than book value with a remaining useful life of 5 years. Any remaining excess would be allocated to goodwill with an assumed life of 10 years.

Aluma-Boat reported the following income and dividend distributions in 19X7 and 19X8:

	19X7	19X8
Income............................	$50,000	$45,000
Dividends declared and paid..........	10,000	10,000

Lund sold its investment in Aluma-Boat Company on January 2, 19X9, for $230,000. Record the sale of the investments. You may ignore income taxes. Carefully schedule the investment account balance at the time of the sale.

PROBLEMS

Problem 6-1. Anton Company is an 80%-owned subsidiary of Roland Company. The interest in Anton was purchased on January 1, 19X0, for $620,000 cash. At that date, Anton had a stockholders' equity of $650,000. The excess price was attributed to equipment with a 5-year life undervalued by $25,000 and to goodwill with an estimated life of 10 years.

The following comparative consolidated trial balances apply to Roland Company and its subsidiary, Anton:

	December 31, 19X0	December 31, 19X1
Cash	$ 34,000	$ 55,500
Inventory	120,000	160,000
Accounts receivable	200,000	300,000
Property, plant, and equipment	3,000,000	3,350,000
Accumulated depreciation	(1,080,000)	(1,280,000)
Investment in Charles Corp. (30%)		244,500
Goodwill	72,000	64,000
Accounts payable	(117,000)	(200,000)
Bonds payable	(100,000)	(400,000)
Minority interest	(138,000)	(151,000)
Controlling interest:		
Common stock, par	(1,000,000)	(1,000,000)
Additional paid-in capital	(650,000)	(650,000)
Retained earnings	(341,000)	(493,000)
Total	$ 0	$ 0

The following 19X1 information is available for the Roland and Anton companies:
(a) Anton purchased equipment for $50,000.
(b) Anton issued $300,000 of long-term bonds and later used the proceeds to purchase a new building
(c) On January 1, 19X1, Roland purchased 30% of the outstanding common stock of Charles Corporation for $230,000. This is an influential investment. Charles's stockholders' equity was $700,000 on the date of the purchase. Any excess cost is attributed to goodwill with a 10-year life. Charles reported net income of $80,000 in 19X1 and paid dividends of $25,000.
(d) Consolidated net income (controlling interest) for 19Xl was $252,000; the minority interest in combined net income was $16,000. Roland paid $100,000 in dividends in 19X1; Anton paid $15,000 in dividends in 19X1.

Required:

Prepare the consolidated statement of cash flows for 19X1 using the indirect method. Any supporting calculations should be in good form.

Problem 6-2. Billing Enterprises purchased a 90% interest in the common stock of Raush Corporation on January 1, 19X0, for an agreed price of $500,000. Billing issued $400,000 of bonds to Raush shareholders plus $100,000 cash as payment. Raush's balance sheet on the acquisition date was as follows:

Assets		Liabilities and Equity	
Cash	$ 60,000	Accounts payable	$ 45,000
Accounts receivable	95,000	Long-term liabilities	120,000
Plant assets (net)	460,000	Common stock ($10 par)	150,000
		Retained earnings	300,000
Total assets	$615,000	Total liabilities and equity	$615,000

Raush's equipment was understated by $20,000 and had a remaining depreciable life of 5 years. Any remaining excess was attributed to goodwill with a 10-year life.

In addition to the bonds issued as part of the purchase, Billing sold additional bonds in the amount of $100,000.

Combined net income for 19X0 was $85,000. The controlling interest was $80,000 and the minority interest was $5,000. Raush paid $10,000 in dividends to all shareholders, including Billing Enterprises.

No plant assets were purchased or sold during 19X0.

Comparative balance sheet data are as follows:

	December 31, 19W9 Parent Only	December 31, 19X0 Consolidated
Cash..................................	$ 82,000	$ 182,700
Accounts receivable	120,000	161,000
Plant assets (net).....................	870,000	1,276,000
Goodwill		69,300
Accounts payable	(52,000)	(80,000)
Bonds payable........................		(500,000)
Long-term liabilities	(80,000)	(40,000)
Minority interest		(49,000)
Controlling interest:		
Common stock ($10 par)	(200,000)	(200,000)
Additional paid-in capital.............	(300,000)	(300,000)
Retained earnings...................	(440,000)	(520,000)
Total.................................	$ 0	$ 0

Required:

Prepare a consolidated statement of cash flows using the indirect method for the year ended December 31, 19X0. Supporting schedules should be in good form.

Problem 6-3. Presented below are the consolidated workpaper balances of Bush Inc. and its subsidiary, Dorr Corporation, as of December 31, 19X6 and 19X5:

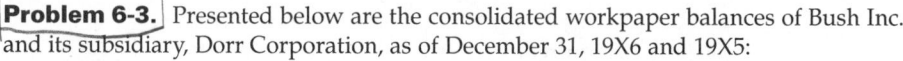

Assets	19X6	19X5	Net Change Incr. (Decr.)
Cash	$ 313,000	$ 195,000	$118,000
Marketable equity securities (at cost)........	175,000	175,000	
Allowance to reduce marketable equity			
securities to market	(13,000)	(24,000)	11,000
Accounts receivable (net)	418,000	440,000	(22,000)
Inventories..............................	595,000	525,000	70,000
Land	385,000	170,000	215,000
Plant and equipment......................	755,000	690,000	65,000
Accumulated depreciation	(199,000)	(145,000)	(54,000)
Goodwill (net)...........................	57,000	60,000	(3,000)
Total assets	$2,486,000	$2,086,000	$400,000

Liabilities and Stockholders' Equity

Current portion of long-term note...........	$ 150,000	$ 150,000	$
Accounts payable and accrued liabilities.....	595,000	474,000	121,000
Note payable, long-term..................	300,000	450,000	(150,000)
Deferred income taxes	44,000	32,000	12,000
Minority interest in net assets of subsidiary ..	179,000	161,000	18,000
Common stock ($10 par)...................	580,000	480,000	100,000
Additional paid-in capital	303,000	180,000	123,000
Retained earnings........................	335,000	195,000	140,000
Treasury stock (at cost)		(36,000)	36,000
Total liabilities and stockholders' equity ...	$2,486,000	$2,086,000	$400,000

Additional information:

(a) On January 20, 19X6, Bush Inc. issued 10,000 shares of its common stock for land having a fair market value of $215,000.

(b) On February 5, 19X6, Bush reissued all of its treasury stock for $44,000.

(c) On May 15, 19X6, Bush paid a cash dividend of $58,000 on its common stock.

(d) On August 8, 19X6, equipment was purchased for $127,000.

(e) On September 30, 19X6, equipment was sold for $40,000. The equipment cost $62,000 and had a net book value of $34,000 on the date of the sale.

(f) On December 15, 19X6, Dorr Corporation paid a cash dividend of $50,000 on its common stock.

(g) Deferred income taxes represent timing differences relating to the use of accelerated depreciation methods for income tax reporting and the straight-line method for financial reporting.

(h) Net income for 19X6 was as follows:

Controlling interest in combined net income	$198,000
Dorr Corporation.............................	110,000

(i) Bush Inc. owns 70% of Dorr Corporation. There was no change in ownership interest in Dorr during 19X5 and 19X6. There were no intercompany transactions other than the dividend paid to Bush by its subsidiary.

Required:

Prepare the statement of cash flows for the consolidated firm using the indirect method. A cash analysis worksheet should be prepared to aid in the development of the statement. Any other supporting schedules should be in good form.

Problem 6-4. On January 1, 19X2, Peabody Corporation acquired an 80% interest in Summers Corporation. Information regarding the income and equity structure of the two companies as of the year ended December 31, 19X4, is as follows:

	Peabody	Summers
Internally generated net income..........................	$50,500	$56,000
Common shares outstanding during the year..............	20,000	12,000
Warrants to acquire Peabody stock,		
outstanding during the year	2,000	1,000
5% convertible $100 par preferred shares		
outstanding during the year		800
Nonconvertible preferred shares outstanding..............	1,000	

Additional information is as follows:
(a) The warrants to acquire Peabody stock were issued in 19X3. Each warrant can be exchanged for one share of Peabody common stock at an exercise price of $12 per share. The three-month test was met in 19X3.
(b) Each share of convertible preferred stock can be converted into two shares of Summers common stock. The preferred stock pays an annual dividend totaling $4,000. When issued in 19X2, the Aa bond yield was 6%. Peabody owns 60% of the convertible preferred stock.
(c) The nonconvertible preferred stock was issued on July 1, 19X4, and paid a six-month dividend totaling $500.
(d) Relevant market prices per share of Peabody common stock during 19X4 are as follows:

	Average	Ending
1st Quarter	$10	$11
2d Quarter	12	14
3d Quarter	13	15
4th Quarter	16	15

Required:
Compute the primary and fully diluted consolidated EPS for the year ended December 31, 19X4.

Problem 6-5. On January 1, 19X1, Delta Corporation exchanged 12,000 shares of its common stock for an 80% interest in Moore Company. The stock issued had a par value of $10 per share and a market value of $20 per share. On the date of purchase, Moore had the following balance sheet:

Common stock ($2 par)	$ 20,000
Paid-in capital in excess of par	50,000
Retained earnings	100,000
Total equity	$170,000

On the purchase date, Moore had equipment with an 8-year remaining life that was undervalued by $20,000. Any remaining excess cost was attributed to goodwill with a 15-year remaining life.

There are intercompany merchandise sales. During 19X2, Delta sold $20,000 of merchandise to Moore. Moore sold $30,000 of merchandise to Delta. Moore had $2,000 of Delta goods in its beginning inventory and $4,200 of Delta goods in its ending inventory. Delta had $2,500 of Moore goods in its beginning inventory and $3,000 of Moore goods in its ending inventory. Delta's gross profit rate is 40%. Moore's is 25%.

On July 1, 19X1, Delta sold a machine to Moore for $90,000. The book value of the machine on Delta's books was $50,000 at the time of the sale. The machine has a 5-year remaining life. Depreciation on the machine is included in expenses.

The consolidated group meets the requirements of an affiliated group under the tax law but has opted for **separate taxation.** The original purchase was not structured as a nontaxable exchange.

Delta uses the cost method to record its investment in Moore. Since Moore has never paid dividends, Delta has not recorded any income on its investment in Moore. The two firms prepared the following income statements for 19X2:

	Delta	Moore
Sales..............................	$1,000,000	$600,000
Less cost of goods sold.............	800,000	375,000
Gross profit	$ 200,000	$225,000
Less expenses.......................	80,000	185,000
Income before tax	$ 120,000	$ 40,000

Required:

Prepare the 19X2 consolidated net income in schedule form. Include eliminations and adjustments. Provide income distribution schedules to allocate combined net income to the controlling and minority interests.

Problem 6-6. On January 1, 19X1, Panther Company purchased 90% of the common stock of Sultan Company for $582,000. On this date, Sultan had total owner's equity of $550,000, including retained earnings of $250,000.

On January 1, 19X1, the only tangible asset of Sultan that was undervalued was building, which was worth $30,000 more than book value. The building has a remaining life of 9 years and is depreciated using the straight-line method. Goodwill, if any, is to be amortized over 15 years.

During 19X1 and 19X2, Panther has appropriately accounted for its investment in Sultan using the cost method.

On January 1, 19X2, Panther held merchandise acquired from Sultan for $15,000. During 19X2, Sultan sold merchandise to Panther for $80,000, of which $20,000 is held by Panther on December 31, 19X2. Sultan's usual gross profit on affiliated sales is 40%.

On December 31, 19X1, Panther sold some equipment to Sultan with a cost of $50,000 and a book value of $25,000. The sales price was $40,000. Sultan is depreciating the equipment over a 3-year life, assuming no salvage value and using the straight-line method.

Panther and Sultan qualify as an affiliated group for tax purposes and thus will file a consolidated tax return. Assume a 30% corporate income tax rate. Assume that amortizations of excess cost are deductible.

The following trial balances were prepared on December 31, 19X2:

	Panther Company	Sultan Company
Inventory, December 31	$ 80,000	$ 80,000
Other Current Assets..................	166,000	450,000
Investment in Sultan Company..........	582,000	
Land	140,000	100,000
Buildings and Equipment...............	315,000	400,000
Accumulated Depreciation..............	(120,000)	(110,000)
Current Liabilities....................	(150,000)	(100,000)
Long-Term Liabilities.................	(200,000)	(150,000)
Common Stock—Panther	(200,000)	
Other Paid-In Capital—Panther.........	(100,000)	
Retained Earnings—Panther............	(434,000)	
Common Stock—Sultan.................		(100,000)
Other Paid-In Capital—Sultan		(200,000)
Retained Earnings—Sultan		(300,000)
Net Sales	(600,000)	(380,000)

(continued)

	Panther Company	Sultan Company
Cost of Goods Sold	$350,000	$180,000
Operating Expenses	130,000	120,000
Dividend Income	(9,000)	
Dividends Declared	50,000	10,000
Total	$ 0	$ 0

Required:

Complete the worksheet for consolidated financial statements for the year ended December 31, 19X2.

Problem 6-7. On January 1, 19X6, Pankow Company purchased an 80% interest in Johnson Company for $420,000. Pankow Company prepared the following determination and distribution of excess schedule for its investment:

Price paid		$420,000
Less interest acquired:		
Common stock ($10 par)	$100,000	
Paid-in capital in excess of par	150,000	
Retained earnings	200,000	
Total stockholders' equity	$450,000	
Interest acquired	80%	360,000
Excess of cost over book value		$ 60,000
Less excess attributable to building, 80% × $30,000		
undervaluation (20-year life)		24,000
Goodwill (15-year life)		$ 36,000

Additional information:

(a) On July 1, 19X6, Pankow sold a machine to Johnson Company for $40,000. The machine had a net book value of $24,000 and an estimated future life of 8 years as of the sale date. Straight-line depreciation is assumed.

(b) Pankow and Johnson had intercompany merchandise sales since January 1, 19X6. A summary of the 19X8 intercompany merchandise sales follows:

	Pankow to Johnson	Johnson to Pankow
Seller's merchandise in buyer's January 1, 19X8 inventory	$ 3,000	$ 1,000
19X8 sales	20,000	30,000
Seller's merchandise in buyer's December 31, 19X8 inventory	2,000	3,000
Outstanding intercompany payables, December 31, 19X8	1,500	2,000
Gross profit on sales	25%	30%

(c) Trial balances of the two firms as of December 31, 19X8, are as follows:

	Pankow Company	Johnson Company
Cash	$ 112,600	$ 35,000
Accounts Receivable	180,000	84,000
Inventory	200,000	100,000
Investment in Johnson Company	420,000	
Property, Plant, and Equipment	1,800,000	750,000
Accumulated Depreciation	(1,180,000)	(365,500)
Accounts Payable	(136,000)	(68,000)
Other Liabilities	(46,000)	(6,000)
Common Stock ($10 par)	(1,000,000)	(100,000)
Paid-In Capital in Excess of Par		(150,000)
Retained Earnings, Jan. 1, 19X7	(260,000)	(250,000)
Sales	(1,200,000)	(400,000)
Subsidiary Dividend Income	(10,000)	
Cost of Goods Sold	800,000	250,000
Other Expenses	259,400	108,000
Dividends Declared	60,000	12,500
Total	$ 0	$ 0

(d) Neither firm has provided for income tax. The firms qualify as an affiliated group and thus will file a consolidated tax return based on a 30% corporate tax rate. The original purchase was not a nontaxable exchange.

Required:
(1) Prepare a consolidated worksheet based on the trial balances. Include a provision for income tax and include the income distribution schedules.
(2) Record the provisions for tax on the books of the separate firms.

Problem 6-8. On January 1, 19X1, Palm Company acquired 70% of the common stock of Sand Company for $337,500. On this date, Sand had total owner's equity of $425,000, including retained earnings of $175,000. Any excess of cost over book value is attributable to goodwill, which is to be amortized over 15 years.

During 19X1 and 19X2, Sand Company reported the following information:

	19X1	19X2
Net income before taxes	$50,000	$90,000
Dividends	10,000	30,000

During 19X1 and 19X2, Palm has appropriately accounted for its investment in Sand using the simple equity method, including income tax effects.

On December 31, 19X1, Palm sold some equipment to Sand with a cost of $50,000 and a book value of $25,000. The sales price was $37,000. Sand is depreciating the equipment over a 4-year life, assuming no salvage value and using the straight-line method.

On January 1, 19X2, Palm held merchandise acquired from Sand for $15,000. During 19X2, Sand sold merchandise to Palm for $80,000, of which one-half is held by Palm on December 31, 19X2. Sand's usual gross profit on affiliated sales is 40%.

Palm and Sand do not qualify as an affiliated group for tax purposes and thus will file separate tax returns. Assume a 30% corporate tax rate and an 80% dividends-received deduction. The original purchase was a taxable exchange.

The following trial balances were prepared on December 31, 19X2:

	Palm Company	Sand Company
Inventory, December 31, 19X2.	$100,000	$105,000
Other Current Assets.	396,050	325,000
Investment in Sand Company.	378,100	
Land.	140,000	80,000
Buildings and Equipment.	315,000	340,000
Accumulated Depreciation.	(120,000)	(130,000)
Deferred Tax Asset/Liability.	(2,436)	
Income Taxes Payable.	(31,260)	(27,000)
Other Current Liabilities.	(150,000)	(70,000)
Long-Term Liabilities.	(200,000)	(140,000)
Common Stock—Palm.	(200,000)	
Other Paid-In Capital—Palm.	(100,000)	
Retained Earnings—Palm.	(474,000)	
Common Stock—Sand.		(150,000)
Other Paid-In Capital—Sand.		(100,000)
Retained Earnings—Sand.		(200,000)
Net Sales.	(600,000)	(380,000)
Cost of Goods Sold.	360,000	185,000
Operating Expenses.	140,000	105,000
Subsidiary Income.	(44,100)	
Provision for Income Taxes.	32,646	27,000
Dividends Declared.	60,000	30,000
Total.	$ 0	$ 0

Required:

Complete the worksheet for consolidated financial statements for the year ended December 31, 19X2. Round all computations to the nearest dollar.

Problem 6-9. Heinrich Company purchased an influential 25% interest in Fink Company on January 1, 19X6, for $320,000. At that time, Fink's stockholders' equity was $1,000,000.

Fink Company assets had market value similar to book value except for a building that was undervalued by $40,000. The building had an estimated remaining life of 20 years. Any remaining excess was attributed to goodwill with a 10-year life.

The following additional information is available:

(a) On July 1, 19X6, Heinrich sold a machine to Fink for $24,000. The cost of the machine to Heinrich was $16,000. The machine is being depreciated on a straight-line basis over 10 years.

(b) Heinrich provides management services to Fink at a billing rate of $15,000 per year. This arrangement started in 19X6.

(c) Fink has sold merchandise to Heinrich since 19X7. Sales were $10,000 in 19X7 and $25,000 in 19X8. The merchandise is sold to provide a gross profit rate of 25%. Heinrich had $2,000 of these goods in its December 31, 19X7 inventory and $3,000 of such goods in its December 31, 19X8 inventory.

(d) The income earned and dividends paid by Fink are as follows:

Year	Income	Dividends
19X6	$48,000	$10,000
19X7	50,000	10,000
19X8	65,000	10,000

Required:

Prepare all entries necessitated by Heinrich's investment in Fink Company for 19X6 through 19X8 using the equity method for an influential investment. Supporting schedules should be in good form. Ignore taxes.

Problem 6-10. On January 1, 19X6, Anton Company purchased a 30% interest in Champ Company for $180,000. Anton Company prepared the following determination and distribution of excess schedule:

Price paid...		$180,000
Less interest acquired:		
Common stock ($5 par)	$100,000	
Paid-in capital in excess of par	200,000	
Retained earnings	150,000	
Total stockholders' equity	$450,000	
Interest acquired	30%	135,000
Excess of cost over book value...........................		$ 45,000
Less excess attributable to equipment, 30% × $30,000		
(10-year life)		9,000
Goodwill (20-year life)...................................		$ 36,000

The following additional information is available:

(a) Champ Company sold a machine to Anton Company for $30,000 on July 1, 19X7. At this date, the machine had a book value of $25,000 and an estimated future life of 5 years. Straight-line depreciation (to the nearest month) is being used. For income tax purposes, the gain on the sale was taxable in the year of the sale.

(b) The following applies to Anton Company sales to Champ Company for 19X7 and 19X8:

	19X7	19X8
Intercompany merchandise in beginning inventory..............		$ 4,000
Sales for the year...	$10,000	15,000
Intercompany merchandise in ending inventory.................	4,000	5,000
Gross profit on sales......................................	40%	40%

(c) Internally generated net incomes (after taxes) for the two firms are as follows:

	19X6	19X7	19X8
Anton Company	$40,000	$50,000	$55,000
Champ Company	25,000	30,000	25,000

(d) Champ paid dividends of $5,000, $10,000, and $10,000, in 19X6, 19X7, and 19X8, respectively.

(e) The corporate income tax rate is 30%.

Required:

Prepare all adjustments to Anton Company's investment in Champ Company account, as required by APB Opinion No. 18, on December 31, 19X6, 19X7, and 19X8. Consider income tax implications. (Only the incremental taxes applicable to the intercompany investment needs to be considered.) Supporting calculations and schedules should be in good form.

Problem 6-11. Bastian Inc., a domestic corporation having a fiscal year ending June 30, has purchased common stock in several other domestic corporations. As of June 30, 19X8, the balance in Bastian's investment account was $870,600, the total cost of stock purchased less the cost of stock sold. Bastian Inc. wishes to restate the investment account to reflect the provisions of APB Opinion No. 18.

Data concerning the investments follow:

		Hupp Inc.	Geer Inc.	Cargo Inc.
Shares of common stock outstanding...............		3,000	32,000	100,000
Shares purchased by Bastian	(a)	300	8,000	30,000
	(b)	810		
Date of purchase	(a)	July 1, 19X5	June 30, 19X6	June 30, 19X7
	(b)	July 1, 19X7		
Cost of shares purchased	(a)	$49,400	$46,000	$670,000
	(b)	142,000		

Balance sheet at date indicated:

Assets	Hupp Inc. July 1, 19X7	Geer Inc. June 30, 19X6	Cargo Inc. June 30, 19X7
Current assets.....................	$ 362,000	$ 39,600	$ 994,500
Property, plant, and equipment			
(net of depreciation)	1,638,000	716,400	3,300,000
Patent (net of amortization)			148,500
Total assets	$2,000,000	$756,000	$4,443,000

Liabilities and Equity			
Liabilities	$1,500,000	$572,000	$2,494,500
Common stock...................	260,000	80,000	1,400,000
Retained earnings	240,000	104,000	548,500
Total liabilities and equity........	$2,000,000	$756,000	$4,443,000

Additional information:

	Hupp Inc.	Geer Inc.	Cargo Inc.
Changes in common stock since July 1, 19X5	None	None	None
Average remaining life of plant assets at date of			
balance sheet (above)	12 years	9 years	22 years
Analysis of retained earnings:			
Balance, July 1, 19X5....................................	$234,000		
Net income, July 1, 19X5, to June 30, 19X6	53,400		
Dividend paid—April 1, 19X6....................................	(51,000)		
Balance, June 30, 19X6	$236,400	$104,000	
Net income (loss), July 1, 19X6, to June 30, 19X7	55,600	(2,000)	
Dividend paid—April 1, 19X7....................................	(52,000)		
Balance, June 30, 19X7	$240,000	$102,000	$548,500
Net income, July 1, 19X7, to June 30, 19X8	25,000	18,000	330,000
Dividends paid:			
December 31, 19X7..			(150,000)
June 1, 19X8		(5,600)	
Balance, June 30, 19X8	$265,000	$114,400	$728,500

Bastian's first purchase of Hupp stock was made because of the high rate of return expected on the investment. All later purchases of stock were made to gain substantial influence over the operations of the various companies.

In December, 19X7, changing market conditions caused Bastian to reevaluate its relation to Geer. On December 31, 19X7, Bastian sold 6,400 shares of Geer for $54,400.

For Hupp and Geer, the fair market values of the net assets did not differ materially from the book values shown in the balance sheets. For Cargo, fair market values exceeded book values only with respect to the patent, which had a market value of $151,500 in excess of book value and a remaining life of 15 years as of June 30, 19X7.

At June 30, 19X8, Bastian's inventory included $48,600 of items purchased from Cargo during May and June at a 20% markup over Cargo's cost.

Required:

Prepare a worksheet to calculate the balance of Bastian's investment account as of June 30, 19X8, and its investment income by year for the three years then ended. Transactions should be listed in chronological order, and supporting computations and schedules should be in good form. Ignore income taxes. Amortization of goodwill, if any, is to be over a 40-year period. Use the following columnar headings for the worksheet:

Date	Description	Investments			Investment Income For Year Ended June 30			Other Accounts	
		Hupp Dr. (Cr.)	Geer Dr. (Cr.)	Cargo Dr. (Cr.)	19X6 Cr. (Dr.)	19X7 Cr. (Dr.)	19X8 Cr. (Dr.)	Name	Amount Dr. (Cr.)

(AICPA adapted)

WORKSHEET 6-1

Affiliates File Consolidated Income Tax Return
Company P and Subsidiary Company S
Worksheet for Consolidated Financial Statements
For Year Ended December 31, 19X3

	(Credit balance amounts are in parentheses.)	Trial Balance	
		Company P	Company S
1	Cash	205,000	380,000
2	Inventory, Dec. 31, 19X3	150,000	120,000
3	Plant and Equipment	900,000	1,100,000
4	Accumulated Depreciation	(440,000)	(150,000)
5			
6	Investment in Company S	1,115,000	
7			
8			
9	Goodwill		
10	Liabilities		(150,000)
11	Common Stock, Co. P	(800,000)	
12	Retained Earnings, Jan. 1, 19X3, Co. P	(900,000)	
13			
14			
15	Common Stock, Co. S		(500,000)
16	Retained Earnings, Jan. 1, 19X3, Co. S		(700,000)
17			
18	Sales	(600,000)	(400,000)
19	Cost of Goods Sold	350,000	200,000
20			
21	Expenses	100,000	100,000
22	Subsidiary Income	(80,000)	
23		0	0
24	**Combined Income Before Tax**		
25	**Provision for Income Tax**		
26	**Income Tax Payable**		
27			
28	**Combined Net Income**		
29	To Minority Interest (see distribution schedule)		
30	Balance to Controlling Interest (see distribution schedule)		
31	Total Minority Interest		
32	Retained Earnings, Controlling Interest, Dec. 31, 19X3		
33			

Worksheet 6-1 (see page 362)

Eliminations & Adjustments				Consolidated Income Statement	Minority Interest	Controlling Retained Earnings	Consolidated Balance Sheet	
Dr.		Cr.						
							585,000	1
		(9)	35,000				235,000	2
		(5)	20,000				1,980,000	3
(5)	4,000						(582,000)	4
(6)	4,000							5
		(1)	80,000					6
		(2)	960,000					7
		(3)	75,000					8
(3)	75,000	(4)	15,000				60,000	9
							(150,000)	10
							(800,000)	11
(4)	10,000					(854,000)		12
(5)	16,000							13
(8)	20,000							14
(2)	400,000				(100,000)			15
(2)	560,000				(135,000)			16
(8)	5,000							17
(7)	100,000			(900,000)				18
(9)	35,000	(7)	100,000	460,000				19
		(8)	25,000					20
(4)	5,000	(6)	4,000	201,000				21
(1)	80,000							22
								23
				(239,000)				24
(10)	71,700			71,700				25
		(10)	71,700				(71,700)	26
	1,385,700		1,385,700					27
				(167,300)				28
				12,600	(12,600)			29
				154,700		(154,700)		30
					(247,600)		(247,600)	31
						(1,008,700)	(1,008,700)	32
							0	33

(continued)

Eliminations and Adjustments:
 (1) Eliminate the parent's entry recording its share of the current year's subsidiary income. This step returns the investment account to its balance on January 1, 19X3.
 (2) Eliminate 80% of the January 1, 19X3 subsidiary equity balances against the investment in Company S.
 (3) Distribute the $75,000 excess of cost to the goodwill account.
 (4) Amortize the goodwill at an annual amount of $5,000 for each of the past two years and for the current year.
 (5) Remove from retained earnings the undepreciated gain at the beginning of the year on the sale of the equipment. Since the sale was by the parent, the entire adjustment is removed from the controlling interest in retained earnings.
 (6) Adjust accumulated depreciation and the current year's depreciation expense for the $4,000 overstatement of depreciation caused by the original $20,000 intercompany gain.
 (7) Eliminate intercompany merchandise sales of $100,000 to avoid double counting.
 (8) Reduce the cost of goods sold by the $25,000 of intercompany profit included in the beginning inventory. Since the sale was made by the subsidiary, the reduction to retained earnings is borne 80% by the controlling interest and 20% by the minority interest.
 (9) Reduce the ending inventory to its cost to the consolidated firm by decreasing it $35,000, and increase the cost of goods sold by $35,000.
(10) Record the provision for income tax, calculated as follows: $239,000 \times .3 = $71,700.

Subsidiary Company S Income Distribution

Gross profit on ending inventory (50% × $70,000)..................(9) $35,000	Internally generated income before tax ..	$100,000
	Gross profit on beginning inventory (50% × $50,000)..................(8)	25,000
	Adjusted income before tax	$ 90,000
	Company S share of taxes (30% × $90,000)..................(10)	**27,000**
	Company S net income	$ 63,000
	Minority share	20%
	Minority interest	$ 12,600

Parent Company P Income Distribution

Amortization of goodwill.............(4) $ 5,000	Internally generated income before tax ..	$150,000
	Realized profit on equipment ($20,000 × 20%)..................(6)	$ 4,000
	Adjusted income before tax	$149,000
	Company P share of taxes (30% × $149,000)................(10)	**44,700**
	Company P net income	$104,300
	Share of subsidiary net income (80% × $63,000)	50,400
	Controlling interest	$154,700

WORKSHEET 6-2

Nonaffiliated Group for Tax Purposes
Company P and Subsidiary Company S
Worksheet for Consolidated Financial Statements
For Year Ended December 31, 19X4

	(Credit balance amounts are in parentheses.)	Trial Balance	
		Company P	Company S
1	Cash	19,200	80,000
2	Inventory, Dec. 31, 19X4	170,000	150,000
3	Plant and Equipment	600,000	550,000
4	Accumulated Depreciation	(410,000)	(120,000)
5			
6	Investment in Company S	504,000	
7			
8			
9	Goodwill		
10	Common Stock, Co. P	(250,000)	
11	Retained Earnings, Jan. 1, 19X4, Co. P	(510,450)	
12			
13			
14	Common Stock, Co. S		(250,000)
15	Retained Earnings, Jan. 1, 19X4, Co. S		(350,000)
16			
17	Sales	(430,000)	(240,000)
18	Cost of Goods Sold	280,000	150,000
19			
20	Expenses	70,000	30,000
21	**Provision for Income Tax**	25,890	18,000
22	Subsidiary Income	(31,500)	
23	**Income Tax Payable**	(24,000)	(18,000)
24	**Deferred Tax (Liability) Asset**	(13,140)	
25		0	0
26	Combined Net Income		
27	To Minority Interest (see distribution schedule)		
28	Balance to Controlling Interest (see distribution schedule)		
29	Total Minority Interest		
30	Retained Earnings, Controlling Interest, Dec. 31, 19X4		
31			

Worksheet 6-2 (see page 366)

Eliminations & Adjustments				Consolidated Income Statement	Minority Interest	Controlling Retained Earnings	Consolidated Balance Sheet	
Dr.		Cr.						
							99,200	1
		(9)	16,000				304,000	2
		(5)	40,000				1,110,000	3
(5)	8,000						(514,000)	4
(6)	8,000							5
		(1)	31,500					6
		(2)	450,000					7
		(3)	22,500					8
(3)	22,500	(4)	6,000			•	16,500	9
							(250,000)	10
(4)	4,500					(474,708)		11
(5)	24,000							12
(8)	24,000	(10)	16,758					13
(2)	187,500				(62,500)			14
(2)	262,500				(81,900)			15
(5)	8,000	(10)	2,400					16
(7)	100,000			(570,000)				17
		(7)	100,000	322,000				18
(9)	16,000	(8)	24,000					19
(4)	1,500	(6)	8,000	93,500				20
(11)	4,602			48,492				21
(1)	31,500							22
							(42,000)	23
(10)	19,158	(11)	4,602				1,416	24
	721,760		721,760					25
				(106,008)				26
				11,900	(11,900)			27
				94,108		(94,108)		28
					(156,300)		(156,300)	29
						(568,816)	(568,816)	30
							0	31

(continued)

Eliminations and Adjustments:

(1) Eliminate the parent's entry recording its share of subsidiary income for the current year. This entry now includes the parent's share of the subsidiary income *after tax*, since the firms are taxed as separate entities.

(2) Eliminate 75% of the January 1, 19X4 subsidiary equity balances against the investment in Company S.

(3) Distribute the $22,500 excess of cost in the investment account to the goodwill account.

(4) Amortize the goodwill for the current year and the three previous years at $1,500 per year.

(5) Eliminate the unamortized intercompany profit on the equipment sale by Company S as of January 1, 19X4. This elimination includes a $40,000 reduction in the asset account, an $8,000 decrease in accumulated depreciation, and a $32,000 (*before-tax*) decrease in beginning retained earnings. Since the sale was by the subsidiary, the retained earnings adjustment is allocated 75% to the controlling interest and 25% to the minority interest.

(6) Adjust the current year's depreciation expense and accumulated depreciation by the $8,000 current year's portion of the intercompany profit on the equipment sale.

(7) Eliminate intercompany merchandise sales of $100,000 to avoid double counting.

(8) Remove the gross profit on intercompany sales recorded by Company P in 19X3 from its January 1, 19X4 retained earnings. The beginning inventory of Company S included $60,000 of goods sold by Company P with a gross profit of 40%, or $24,000. On a consolidated basis, the cost of goods sold is overstated, and this step removes $24,000 from the consolidated cost of goods sold.

(9) Remove the $16,000 gross profit from the ending inventory and increase the cost of goods sold by the same amount. The Company S ending inventory includes $40,000 of goods sold by Company P with a gross profit of 40%.

(10) Adjust the beginning retained earnings balances for the tax effects of previous adjustments, as follows:

		Retained Earnings Increase	
	Total	25% Minority Interest	75% Controlling Interest
Prepaid tax on $32,000 unamortized intercompany equipment gain of step (5), paid by Company S (30% × $32,000)...............................	$ 9,600	$2,400	$ 7,200
Prepaid tax on $32,000 unamortized intercompany gain of step (5), paid by Company P (30% tax on 20% **taxable portion** of 75% share of after-tax gain of $22,400*).......	1,008		1,008
Prepaid tax relating to Company P gross profit on goods in Company S beginning inventory, step (8) (30% × $24,000).....................................	7,200		7,200
Goodwill amortization (30% × $4,500)...................	1,350		1,350
Total increase in retained earnings......................	$19,158	$2,400	$16,758

*70% × $32,000 = $22,400

Step (10) increases the minority share of January 1, 19X4 retained earnings by $2,400 and increases the controlling share of January 1, 19X4 retained earnings by $16,758. The deferred tax liability is decreased by the total, $19,158.

(11) Adjust the current-year tax provision for the tax effects of previous adjustments to the current year's income, as follows:

	Increase in Provision for Income Tax		
	Total	25% Minority Interest	75% Controlling Interest
Expiration of prepaid tax on equipment gain of step (6), paid by Company S (30% × $8,000)............................	$2,400	$600	$1,800
Expiration of prepaid tax on equipment gain of step (6), paid by Company P (30% tax on 20% **taxable portion** of 75% share of the aftertax realized gain of $5,600*)	252		252
Expiration of prepaid tax relating to gross profit on Company P goods in Company S beginning inventory, step (8) (30% × $24,000)..	7,200		7,200
Prepaid tax originating on gross profit on Company P goods in Company S ending inventory, step (9) (30% × $16,000)...	(4,800)		(4,800)
Goodwill amortization (30% × $1,500)	(450)		(450)
Total increase in provision for income tax...................	$4,602	$600	$4,002

*70% × $8,000 = $5,600

No adjustment results from the amortization of goodwill since it is not tax deductible.

Subsidiary Company S Income Distribution

	Internally generated net income **after tax** (70% × $60,000)................	$42,000
	Realized gain on depreciable asset sale ($8,000 – $2,400 tax) ....(6) **(11)**	5,600
	Adjusted net income	$47,600
	Minority share	25%
	Minority interest	$11,900

Parent Company P Income Distribution

Ending inventory profit ($16,000 – $4,800 tax) ....(9) **(11)**	$11,200	Internally generated net income **after tax** (70% × $80,000)................	$56,000
Goodwill amortization ($1,500 – $450 tax) ....(4) **(11)**	1,050	Beginning inventory profit ($24,000 – $7,200 tax) ....(8) **(11)**	16,800
		75% of subsidiary adjusted income less tax [(75% × $47,600) – (30% tax × 20% **taxable portion** × 75% × $47,600)]........................	33,558
		Controlling interest.................	$94,108

CHAPTER 7

Special Issues in Accounting for an Investment in a Subsidiary

This chapter considers several issues concerning the acquisition and sale of a parent's interest in a subsidiary. The first concern is unique purchase situations. A parent may purchase its interest directly from the subsidiary at the time of original issue. This will require special consideration when consolidating. Procedures also are developed for ownership interests that are acquired in a series of separate purchases over time.

This chapter then will consider the issues involved when a parent company sells all or a portion of its controlling interest in a subsidiary. Not only must the sale be properly recorded, special care must be also taken in accounting for any portion of the investment retained.

The final equity concern of the chapter is the procedure needed in consolidation when the subsidiary has preferred stock in its equity structure. An apportionment of retained earnings may be needed in order to properly account for the parent's interest in common stock. If the parent owns any subsidiary preferred stock, it must be treated as retired in the consolidation process.

The chapter concludes with an appendix that provides the consolidation procedures needed when a worksheet is used to produce *only* a consolidated balance sheet. These procedures are really only of concern when preparing for the CPA Exam. The Exam uses this approach to save time and space. It is not a worksheet that is used in practice since the accountant must prepare a consolidated income statement, a consolidated statement of retained earnings, and a consolidated balance sheet. There would be no reason to use a worksheet for only one of the three statements.

PARENT ACQUISITION OF STOCK DIRECTLY FROM SUBSIDIARY

A parent firm may organize a new corporation and supply all of the common stock equity funds in exchange for all of the newly organized firm's common stock. Since the newly formed corporation receives the funds directly, there will be no difference between the price paid for the shares and the equity in assets acquired. Thus, the determination and distribution of excess schedule will show no excess of cost over book value or excess of book value over cost.

In other cases, the parent firm will allow the newly organized subsidiary to sell a portion of the shares to persons outside the consolidated group. If the shares are sold to outsiders at a price equal to the price paid by the parent, the cost and book value again will be equal. However, if a price greater or less than the price paid by the parent is charged to outside parties, an excess of cost or book value will result. This excess occurs because the total price paid by the parent will not equal its ownership interest multiplied by the total subsidiary common stockholders' equity. Normally, the excess of cost is recorded as goodwill, and an excess of book value is recorded as a deferred credit since the only asset held by a newly organized firm is cash, which is not subject to adjustment. If noncash assets are given in exchange for the subsidiary shares, these assets would be adjusted according to the normal distribution of excess procedures.

An existing corporation might sell a sufficient number of new shares to grant a controlling interest to the buying firm. For example, assume Company S had the following equity balances prior to a sale of shares to Company P:

Common stock, $10 par, 10,000 shares............	$100,000
Paid-in capital in excess of par..................	150,000
Retained earnings............................	220,000
Total stockholders' equity....................	$470,000

Assume Company S sells 30,000 additional shares directly to Company P at $50 per share, for a total of $1,500,000. Subsequent to the sale, the equity balances of Company S appear as follows:

Common stock, $10 par, 40,000 shares.........	$ 400,000
Paid-in capital in excess of par................	1,350,000
Retained earnings...........................	220,000
Total stockholders' equity...................	$1,970,000

A determination and distribution of excess schedule must be prepared for this investment as it would be for any acquisition of a controlling interest. There is no direct connection between the price paid and the interest in subsidiary equity received. The monies paid become a part of the subsidiary's total equity. The interest purchased is a 75% interest (30,000 of 40,000 shares) in the total equity after the sale of the new shares, not a 100% interest in the funds provided by the specific sale of the new shares purchased by the parent. The following determination and distribution of excess schedule would be prepared for the interest purchased by the parent:

Price paid		$1,500,000
Less interest acquired:		
Common stock ($10 par)	$ 400,000	
Paid-in capital in excess of par	1,350,000	
Retained earnings	220,000	
Total stockholders' equity	$1,970,000	
Interest acquired	75%	1,477,500
Excess of cost over book value		$ 22,500

The excess would be distributed using normal purchase rules. Any adjustment of existing identifiable accounts would be limited to 75% of the difference between book and market values since only a 75% interest has been purchased. Any remaining excess would be considered goodwill.

PIECEMEAL ACQUISITION OF INTEREST IN SUBSIDIARY

Past examples of combinations in this text have involved an acquisition of a controlling interest in a subsidiary through its single purchase of stock. A parent also may acquire a controlling interest as a result of a series of purchases of subsidiary stock. Current practice follows the *parent company concept*, which views each block as a separate ownership interest with a different excess of cost or book value for each block. Each block is seen as having separate causal factors for the difference between the price paid and the underlying book value. Thus, each block requires a separate determination and distribution of excess schedule and separate elimination steps. The *proportionate consolidation concept* would follow this same approach. The *economic unit concept* would follow alternative procedures. (The three concepts mentioned here are discussed further in the appendices for all of the consolidations chapters, which follow Chapter 8.)

CONTROL ACHIEVED UPON INITIAL INVESTMENT

When control is achieved with the initial investment, consolidation procedures already are in effect when subsequent blocks are purchased. Thus, no major change in accounting methods is required. Another determination and distribution of excess schedule must be prepared for each new investment, and additions to the existing consolidated worksheet procedures must be acknowledged.

Assume Company P purchases on the open market its original 60% interest in Company S on January 1, 19X1, for $126,000, when Company S has the following balance sheet:

Assets		Liabilities and Equity	
Current assets	$ 50,000	Liabilities	$ 40,000
Equipment (net)	150,000	Common stock ($10 par)	100,000
		Retained earnings.	60,000
Total assets	$200,000	Total liabilities and equity	$200,000

Further assume that the current assets require no adjustment, and the equipment has a net market value of $180,000 and a 5-year remaining life.

Goodwill resulting from the purchase of the stock will be amortized over a 10-year period. The following determination and distribution of excess schedule would be prepared on *January 1, 19X1*, for the first acquisition:

Price paid		$126,000
Less interest acquired:		
Common stock.	$100,000	
Retained earnings	60,000	
Total stockholders' equity	$160,000	
Interest acquired	**60%**	96,000
Excess of cost over book value (debit balance)		$ 30,000
Excess of cost attributable to equipment: **60%** ×		
$30,000 undervaluation (to be amortized over **5 years**) . . .		18,000 Dr
Goodwill (**10-year** amortization)		$ 12,000 Dr

On January 1, 19X3, Company P purchases on the open market an additional 20% interest in Company S by paying $50,000. The following balance sheet of Company S on January 1, 19X3, reflects two years of continued operations:

Assets		Liabilities and Equity	
Current assets.	$ 80,000	Liabilities	$ 50,000
Building (net).	80,000	Common stock ($10 par)	100,000
Equipment (net)	90,000	Retained earnings.	100,000
Total assets	$250,000	Total liabilities and equity	$250,000

Company P's analysis on January 1, 19X3, indicates that the equipment listed on Company S's balance sheet now is undervalued by $24,000 and has a 3-year remaining life. The current assets and the building appear to have market values equal to their book values. Goodwill is assumed to have a 10-year life. Based on this analysis, the following determination and distribution of excess schedule would be prepared for the *January 1, 19X3* investment:

Price paid		$50,000
Less interest acquired:		
Common stock.	$100,000	
Retained earnings	100,000	
Total stockholders' equity	$200,000	
Interest acquired	**20%**	40,000
Excess of cost over book value (debit balance).		$10,000
Excess of cost attributable to equipment: **20%** × **$24,000**		
undervaluation (to be amortized over **3 years**)		4,800 Dr
Goodwill (**10-year** amortization)		$ 5,200 Dr

Note that this determination and distribution of excess schedule is *free standing*; that is, it is completely independent of the appraisals made for the January 1, 19X1 schedule.

The additional worksheet procedures that arise from this piecemeal acquisition are shown in Worksheet 7-1 on pages 458–461. The trial balances of Companies P and S are shown as they would appear on December 31, 19X3. The investment in the Company S account is based on the use of the simple equity method during the current and previous years. The December 31, 19X3 balance was determined as follows:

Cost of **60%** investment (January 1, 19X1).		$126,000
Add equity share of change in Company S retained earnings as of January 1, 19X3:		
Balance, January 1, 19X3.	**$100,000**	
Balance, January 1, 19X1.	**60,000**	
Increase in retained earnings	**$ 40,000** × **60%** =	24,000
Cost of **20%** investment (January 1, 19X3).		50,000
Add equity share of Company S 19X3 net income:		
80% × $35,000.		28,000
Investment account balance, December 31, 19X3		**$228,000**

The combined net income of $78,080 is distributed to the controlling and minority interests as shown in the income distribution schedules that accompany Worksheet 7-1. *Since only the parent's share of excesses of cost or book value is recorded,* all amortizations of excess resulting from parent company purchases are deducted *only* from the controlling interest.

When investment blocks are carried *at cost,* each block must be converted separately to its simple equity balance as of the *beginning* of the year. For each block, the adjustment is based on the change in subsidiary retained earnings between the date of acquisition of the individual block and the beginning of the current year.

The determination and distribution of excess schedule for the second block should consider existing unrealized intercompany profits recorded by the subsidiary. Suppose the subsidiary of the previous example sold merchandise to the parent during 19X2, and a $2,000 subsidiary profit is included in the parent's ending inventory of merchandise and in the subsidiary retained earnings. *In theory,* the determination and distribution of excess schedule prepared for the 20% investment purchased on January 1, 19X3, should reflect the unrealized gross profit on sales applicable to the 20% interest purchased. Thus, the determination and distribution of excess schedule would be revised to distribute the excess as follows:

Excess of cost over book value.	$10,000
Deferred gross profit on inventory sale (**20%**).	400
Excess of cost attributable to equipment (3-year life)	(4,800)
Goodwill (10-year life).	$ 5,600

The deferred gross profit on the inventory sale means that the minority interest just acquired is overstated since the profit already is included in retained earnings. The decrease in the equity acquired increases the excess of cost over book value, thereby making more excess available to remaining assets.

The following entry would distribute the revised excess on the 19X3 worksheet:

Accumulated Depreciation—Equipment.	4,800	
Goodwill	5,600	
Deferred Gross Profit on Inventory Sale		400
Investment in Company S		10,000

The following elimination for the $2,000 profit in the beginning inventory then would be made:

Retained Earnings—Controlling Interest (**60%** interest at time of original sale)	1,200	
Retained Earnings—Minority Interest (20%)	400	
Deferred Gross Profit on Inventory Sale	400	
Cost of Goods Sold (beginning inventory).		2,000

In practice, the concept of materiality often will prevail, and the above procedure may not be followed. The determination and distribution of excess schedule may not recognize the deferred inventory profit which will result in less excess being available to other assets. In this case, goodwill will be down by $400; this also would reduce goodwill amortization in the years that follow. Under this practical approach, worksheets for periods subsequent to the second purchase will ignore the deferred profit existing on the purchase date and will distribute the retained earnings adjustment according to the ownership percentages existing at the time the worksheet is prepared. In this example, the 20% profit applicable to the inventory on the second purchase date would be allocated to the parent with the following adjustment on the worksheet:

Retained Earnings—Controlling Interest (**80%**)	1,600	
Retained Earnings—Minority Interest (20%)	400	
Cost of Goods Sold (beginning inventory).		2,000

Notice that the practical approach eventually leads to the same result on the distribution of retained earnings as the theoretically correct approach. Under the correct theoretical approach the parent retained earnings is reduced for 60% of the profit at the end of the first year. Eventually, it absorbs the other 20% interest through greater amortization of goodwill. Under the practical approach, the parent picks up the added 20% at the end of the first year. There is only a timing difference as to when the parent absorbs the 20% interest in the beginning inventory profit.

CONTROL NOT ACHIEVED UPON INITIAL INVESTMENT

Ordinarily it is improper to prepare consolidated statements when an initial investment in the stock of another firm represents less than a 50% interest. Such an investment is carried under the cost or the sophisticated equity method, depending upon the percentage of interest acquired. APB Opinion No. 18 generally requires the use of the sophisticated equity method when the interest equals or exceeds 20% of the outstanding common shares of an investee corporation.[1] If a second block of stock is purchased, resulting in an interest that exceeds 50%, consolidation becomes appropriate. Current practice is derived from the parent company concept, which views each block as a separate ownership interest with independent causes of excess cost or book value. Thus, each block will have a separate determination and distribution of excess schedule and will have separate elimination procedures on the consolidated worksheet. Added complications arise because the original investment must be subjected to the consolidation process retroactively. The complexities involved depend on whether the original investment was recorded under the sophisticated equity or the cost method. Alternative procedures, derived from the economic unit concept, will be addressed in the appendix following the consolidation chapters.

Original Interest Under the Equity Method.   The sophisticated equity method of APB Opinion No. 18 requires that the original excess of cost over book value be amortized as an adjustment of investment income in subsequent years. The amortization pattern depends on the underlying nature of the excess. The Opinion admits that it may be difficult to ascertain the nature of the excess; thus, goodwill may be assumed to be the inferred cause of the entire excess of cost over book value of an investment.

To illustrate the sophisticated equity method, assume Company P purchases on the open market a 20% interest in Company S on *January 1, 19X1*, for $48,000. The balance sheet of Company S on January 1, 19X1, is:

Assets			Liabilities and Equity		
Current assets		$ 50,000	Liabilities		$ 50,000
Building and			Common stock ($10 par). .		50,000
equipment (net)	$225,000		Retained earnings		100,000
Less accumulated					
depreciation	75,000	150,000			
Total assets.		$200,000	Total liabilities and equity. .		$200,000

Assuming the excess of cost is attributable to goodwill, the determination and distribution of excess schedule would be prepared as follows:

Price paid			$48,000
Less interest acquired:			
Common stock	$ 50,000		
Retained earnings	100,000		
Total stockholders' equity	$150,000		
Interest acquired	**20%**	30,000	
Goodwill (to be amortized over **20** years)		$18,000	

---

[1]Opinions of the Accounting Principles Board No. 18, *The Equity Method of Accounting for Investments in Common Stock* (New York: American Institute of Certified Public Accountants, 1971), par. 17.

This schedule requires that the investor reduce the investment account $900 ($18,000 ÷ 20) per year. Since goodwill cannot be recorded in the absence of consolidation and merely is buried in the investment account, the amortization required must be accomplished indirectly through the investment income account. If Company S reports income of $15,000 for 19X1, for example, Company P would record the following sophisticated equity adjustment to the $48,000 recorded investment cost:

```
Investment in Company S ....................................  2,100
    Investment Income.......................................          2,100
        To recognize 20% of Company S reported income less
        amortization of goodwill [(20% × $15,000) – $900].
```

Continuing this example, assume that on January 1, 19X2, Company P acquires an additional 60% interest in Company S on the open market for a price of $130,000. The balance sheet of Company S appears as follows on January 1, 19X2:

Assets			Liabilities and Equity	
Current assets		$ 70,000	Liabilities..............	$ 40,000
Building and equipment...	$225,000		Common stock ($10 par)..	50,000
Less accumulated			Retained earnings	115,000
depreciation	90,000	135,000		
Total assets.............		$205,000	Total liabilities and equity..	$205,000

If it is assumed that the current assets have book values equal to their market values and the equipment with a 9-year remaining life is undervalued by $9,000, the determination and distribution of excess schedule for the 60% acquisition on *January 1, 19X2*, would be prepared as follows:

Price paid		$130,000	
Less interest acquired:			
Common stock....................................	$ 50,000		
Retained earnings	115,000		
Total stockholders' equity	$165,000		
Interest acquired	60%	99,000	
Excess of cost over book value (debit balance)		$ 31,000	
Excess of cost attributable to equipment: **60%** × $9,000			
undervaluation (amortized over 9 years)		5,400	Dr
Goodwill (to be amortized over **20** years)		$ 25,600	Dr

Assuming Company S reports net income of $20,000 for 19X2, Company P would make the following *simple equity* adjustment for its entire investment:

```
Investment in Company S ....................................  16,000
    Subsidiary Income.......................................          16,000
        To adjust for 80% of Company S reported income of $20,000.
```

Since control now has been achieved, it is appropriate to use the simple equity method. It no longer is necessary to amortize the excess resulting from the

January 1, 19X1 and January 1, 19X2 investments through the investment account, since the amortizations will be recorded on the consolidated worksheet as shown in Worksheet 7-2 on pages 462–465. The balance in the investment account results from the investments and income adjustments, which are summarized as follows:

Cost of **20%** investment (January 1, 19X1)	$ 48,000
19X1 sophisticated equity adjustment	2,100
Cost of **60%** investment (January 1, 19X2)	130,000
19X2 simple equity adjustment for **80%** interest	16,000
Investment balance, December 31, 19X2.	**$196,100**

If the parent wished for consistency in the recording of the investment, it could elect to remove the previous year's amortization of excess adjustments from the investment account and restore them to the parent's retained earnings. This would mean that the worksheet could include all amortization adjustments, not just those subsequent to obtaining control.

Original Interest Under the Cost Method. When the investment acquired prior to obtaining control is recorded under the cost method, the easiest procedure is to convert the investment account to its simple equity balance if the later investment in the subsidiary is to be recorded under the simple equity method in future periods. Conversion to the simple equity method thus will make the prior investment compatible with the later investment made to secure control. The conversion preferably should be made directly *on the parent's books*.

Assume Company P in the previous illustration originally purchased only a 10% interest for $24,000 on January 1, 19X1, and used the cost method to record its investment in Company S. The following determination and distribution of excess schedule would be prepared as of *January 1, 19X1*:

Price paid		$24,000
Less interest acquired:		
Common stock	$ 50,000	
Retained earnings	100,000	
Total stockholders' equity	$150,000	
Interest acquired **10%**		15,000
Goodwill (to be amortized over 20 years)		$ 9,000

When Company P acquires controlling interest on January 1, 19X2, it would convert the 10% interest to the simple equity method *on its books* as follows:

Investment in Company S	1,500	
Retained Earnings		1,500
To adjust for **10%** of the $15,000 increase in the subsidiary		
retained earnings during 19X1.		

It would not be necessary to amortize the $450 ($9,000 ÷ 20 years) of goodwill through the investment account, since that amortization can be done in the normal manner on the 19X2 worksheet for consolidated statements. The conversion process simplifies eliminations and adjustments because the entire original excess of cost of $9,000 will appear on the worksheet.

If the parent does not make the conversion entry on its books, a cost conversion entry should be made on the worksheet. Worksheet 7-3, pages 466–469, is similar to Worksheet 7-2, except that Company P used the *cost* method on an original *10%* investment in Company S and did not convert to the simple equity method on January 1, 19X2. Note that the balance in the investment account would be:

Cost of **10%** investment (January 1, 19X1) . . . . $ 24,000
Cost of **60%** investment (January 1, 19X2)   130,000
19X2 simple equity adjustment (**70%** × Company S income of $20,000)   14,000
Investment balance, December 31, 19X2. . . . . $168,000

Alternative Procedure for Cost Method Investment.
When control is not achieved on the first purchase, ARB No. 51 permits a parent to use the date control is achieved as the date of acquisition for both blocks.[2] Thus, a parent is excused from analyzing the cause of excess for a prior-to-achieving-control investment and is allowed to let the original investment remain under the cost method up to the date control is achieved if the result of doing so is not material. In the previous case of Companies P and S, the original 10% interest purchased for $24,000 could be added to the $130,000 cost of the second investment to produce the following determination and distribution of excess schedule on *January 1, 19X2:*

Price paid (January 1, 19X1 plus January 1, 19X2		
investments, $24,000 + $130,000).	**$154,000**	
Less interest acquired:		
Common stock. . . . . $ 50,000		
Retained earnings 115,000		
Total stockholders' equity $165,000		
Interest acquired **70%**	115,500	
Excess of cost over book value (debit balance).	$ 38,500	
Excess of cost attributable to equipment: **70%** × $9,000		
undervaluation (amortized over 9 years)	6,300	Dr
Goodwill (to be amortized over 20 years)	$ 32,200	Dr

The procedure of lumping investments together *cannot* be recommended on theoretical grounds, since the facts surrounding the separate investments are ignored. Also, when the original investment meets or exceeds 20% of the shares

[2]Accounting Research Bulletin No. 51, *Consolidated Financial Statements* (New York: American Institute of Certified Public Accountants, 1959), par. 10.

of the subsidiary, this procedure would be a direct violation of APB Opinion No. 18.

The parent may use the cost method for blocks that are acquired prior to achieving control and continue to use it for blocks acquired after achieving control. In this situation, each block would be *independently converted* to the equity method as of the beginning of the year, prior to making any elimination entries. The cost-to-equity conversion technique was described in Chapter 3.

SALE OF PARENT'S INVESTMENT IN COMMON STOCK

A parent may sell all of its subsidiary interest or enough shares to fall below the greater-than-50% interest generally required for consolidated reporting. Such an action makes it unnecessary to continue consolidated reporting and requires that a gain or loss on the sale of the investment be recorded. There may be other situations in which a parent sells a part of its shares of subsidiary common stock but still retains a greater-than-50% interest after the sale. When such an event occurs, subsequent financial reports still would be prepared on a consolidated basis. In theory, the single-firm viewpoint derived from the *economic unit concept* could be applied to such a stock sale. This view holds that the consolidated firm has sold shares to the minority interest and no gain or loss should be reflected on the consolidated income statement as a result of the intercompany transaction.[3] It has become common practice, however, to record a gain or loss on such sales. This treatment is based on the *parent company concept* that views the transaction as a sale of a corporate asset (an investment) and the purchaser as an outside party (not an existing minority interest) at the time of the sale. The new owner-ship interest, of course, does become a minority shareholder subsequent to the purchase.

SALE OF ENTIRE INVESTMENT

The sale of the entire investment in a subsidiary terminates the need for consoli-dated financial statements. In fact, when a sale occurs during the parent's fiscal year, the results of the subsidiary operations prior to the sale date typically are not consolidated. In recording the sale of the investment in a subsidiary, the accountant's primary concern is to adjust the carrying value of the investment so that the correct gain or loss on the sale can be recorded. The results of the subsidiary's operations up to the date of sale must be reported in one of two ways: (1) the net results of operations as a separate line item in the determination of income from continuing operations or (2) as a disposal of a segment of a business.

---

[3]For additional coverage of the economic unit concept, see the appendices for all of the consolidations chapters, which follow Chapter 8.

The accountant also must determine if the sale of the investment in a subsidiary constitutes a disposal of a segment of a business as defined by APB Opinion No. 30. The Opinion states: ". . . the term *segment of a business* refers to a component of an entity whose activities represent a separate major line of business or class of customer."[4] The Opinion indicates that a segment can be in the form of a subsidiary. However, an interpretation of the Opinion makes it clear that not all subsidiaries qualify as segments of a business. For example, a parent may own several subsidiaries engaged in mining coal. If one subsidiary is sold, that would not constitute a sale of a major line of business since the parent still is involved in coal mining. When the sale of a subsidiary qualifies as a disposal of a business segment, both the gain or loss on the sale and the results of operations for the period are shown net of tax in a separate discontinued-segment section of the income statement. When the sale does not qualify as a disposal of a business segment, the gain or loss and the results of operations for the period usually are shown on the income statement as a part of the normal recurring operations.

The complexities of properly recording the sale of an entire subsidiary investment are shown in the following example. Suppose Company P purchased an 80% interest in Company S on January 1, 19X1, for $250,000, and the following determination and distribution of excess schedule was prepared:

Price paid		$250,000	
Less interest acquired:			
Common stock ($10 par).	$100,000		
Retained earnings, January 1, 19X1.	150,000		
Total stockholders' equity	$250,000		
Interest acquired	80%	200,000	
Excess of cost over book value (debit balance)		$ 50,000	
Excess of cost attributable to equipment (5-year life).		20,000	Dr
Goodwill (10-year life)		$ 30,000	Dr

Company S earned $40,000 in 19X1 and $25,000 in 19X2. Company P sells the entire 80% interest on January 1, 19X3, for $320,000. Assuming the use of the simple equity method, Company P's separate statements reflect the following:

Purchase price.	$250,000
Share of subsidiary income, 19X1, 80% × $40,000	32,000
Share of subsidiary income, 19X2, 80% × $25,000	20,000
Investment in Co. S, December 31, 19X2	$302,000

The investment account and the parent's January 1, 19X3 retained earnings balance reflect a $52,000 increase as a result of subsidiary operations in 19X1 and 19X2. On this basis, it appears that there is an $18,000 gain on the sale of the

---

[4]Opinions of the Accounting Principles Board No. 30, *Reporting the Results of Operations* (New York: American Institute of Certified Public Accountants, 1973), par. 13.

investment ($320,000 selling price less $302,000 simple-equity-adjusted cost). This result does not agree, however, with the consolidated financial statements prepared for 19X1 and 19X2, which included as expenses the amortizations of excess required by the determination and distribution of excess schedule. The parent's share of subsidiary income appeared as follows in the consolidated statements:

	19X1	19X2	Total
Share of subsidiary income to Company P (80%)	$32,000	$20,000	$52,000
Less amortization of excess of cost of investment over book value:			
Adjustment for depreciation on equipment:			
$20,000 ÷ 5 = $4,000 per year	(4,000)	(4,000)	(8,000)
Adjustment for amortization of goodwill:			
$30,000 ÷ 10 = $3,000 per year	(3,000)	(3,000)	(6,000)
Net increase in Company P income due to ownership of Company S investment	$25,000	$13,000	$38,000

Thus, while Company P's separate books show a $52,000 share of Company S income, the consolidated statements reflect only $38,000, the difference being caused by the $14,000 of amortizations indicated by the determination and distribution of excess schedule. Clearly, the recording of the sale of the parent's interest must be based on the $38,000 share of income, since that amount of income is shown on the prior income statements of the consolidated firm. Before recording the sale of the investment, Company P must adjust its books to be consistent with prior consolidated statements. The entry needed will adjust the January 1, 19X3 retained earnings account on the separate books of the parent to the December 31, 19X2 balance of the controlling interest in retained earnings shown on the consolidated statements. The adjusting entry on the books of Company P is:

Retained Earnings (January 1, 19X3).	14,000	
Investment in Company S		14,000
To adjust the investment account and Company P retained		
earnings account for amortizations made on past		
consolidated statements.		

If the sophisticated equity method was used, the amortizations would be reflected already in the investment account and no adjustment would be needed. Under either method, the entry to record the sale then would be:

Cash	320,000	
Investment in Company S ($302,000 – $14,000).		288,000
Gain on Disposal of Subsidiary		32,000
To record the gain on the sale of the 80% interest in		
Company S.		

Note that the $14,000 adjusting entry for the past years' amortizations of excess normally would have been made on the consolidated worksheet for 19X3.

However, since there will be no further consolidations, the adjustment must be made directly on Company P's books. The gain (net of tax) on the disposal of the subsidiary will appear as a separate item on the income statement for 19X3 if the sale of the subsidiary meets the criteria for a disposal of a business segment.

In this example, if Company P had used the cost method, the investment account still would be shown at the original cost of $250,000. It then would be necessary to update the investment and retained earnings accounts on the separate books of Company P to include its $38,000 (net of amortizations) share of subsidiary income for 19X1 and 19X2. This adjustment would allow the accounts of the parent on January 1, 19X3, to conform to past consolidated statements. The following entries would be made on the books of Company P to record the sale of the parent's 80% interest:

Investment in Company S	38,000	
Retained Earnings (January 1, 19X3)		38,000
To record the parent's share of subsidiary income as shown on prior years' consolidated statements.		
Cash	320,000	
Investment in Company S ($250,000 + $38,000)		288,000
Gain on Disposal of Subsidiary		32,000

It also is necessary to adjust the investment account for any unrealized intercompany gains and losses. These profits would have been deferred in the most recent consolidated statement, but under the cost or simple equity method they are not reflected in the investment account. Again, we must adjust the investment account to reflect the income reported in past consolidated statements. Suppose the parent had on hand at the sale date inventory on which the subsidiary recorded a $1,000 profit. Since the parent owns an 80% interest, the adjusting entry on the day the investment is sold would be:

Retained Earnings	800	
Investment in Company S		800

Assume the investment in the previous example was sold for $320,000 on July 1, 19X3, and Company S reported income of $12,000 for the first six months of 19X3. Since Company S will not be a part of the consolidated group at the end of the period, the results of its operations will not be consolidated with those of the parent. Therefore, the parent must record its share of subsidiary income for the current period to the date of disposal. The parent's net share of subsidiary income would be calculated on a basis consistent with past consolidated statements, as follows:

Share of subsidiary income for first six months to Company P (80%)	$9,600
Less amortizations of excess of cost over book value that would have been made on consolidated statements:	
Equipment depreciation adjustment, $4,000 per year × 1/2 year	(2,000)
Amortization of goodwill adjustment, $3,000 per year × 1/2 year	(1,500)
Net share of subsidiary income	$6,100

The parent would proceed to record the July 1, 19X3 sale of its subsidiary investment as follows:

1. Assuming the past use of the simple equity method, the parent's investment account on January 1, 19X3, is adjusted to reflect the amortizations made on past consolidated statements (as calculated on page 416).

Retained Earnings (January 1, 19X3)	14,000	
Investment in Company S		14,000

2. The parent's share of subsidiary income for the partial year is recorded. This amount is the $6,100 income net of amortizations (as calculated on page 417).

Investment in Company S	6,100	
Operating Income of Subsidiary Disposed of During Year . . .		6,100

3. The sale of the investment for $320,000 is recorded.

Cash	320,000	
Investment in Company S		294,100
Gain on Disposal of Subsidiary		25,900

The adjusted cost of the investment is determined as follows:

Original cost (January 1, 19X1)	$250,000
Simple equity income adjustments for 19X1 and 19X2	52,000
Amortization of excess (entry 1)	(14,000)
Share of Company S income for six months (entry 2)	6,100
Net cost, July 1, 19X3	$294,100

SALE OF PORTION OF INVESTMENT

The sale of a portion of an investment in a subsidiary requires unique treatment, depending on whether effective control is lost as a result of the sale. Special procedures also must be used when a sale of a partial interest occurs during a reporting period.

Loss of Control.   A parent may sell a portion of its investment in a subsidiary so that its remaining interest falls below 50%. This situation may occur for foreign subsidiaries when the foreign government passes a law forbidding control of its firms by nonresidents. Such a sale also may be made to avoid consolidating affiliated firms. FASB Statement No. 94 now requires the consolidation of nonhomogeneous subsidiaries that previously did not have to be consolidated.[5] Some sell-downs did occur after the issuance of that Statement to avoid adding the substantial debt of real estate and financing subsidiaries to the consolidated statements. If an interest is reduced below 50%, consolidation procedures no longer will apply. This situation would require that the parent

---

[5]Statement of Financial Accounting Standards No. 94, *Consolidation of All Majority-owned Subsidiaries* (Stamford: Financial Accounting Standards Board, 1987), Par 9.

company books be adjusted to make them consistent with prior consolidated statements. Exactly the same adjusting entries as in the immediately preceding section are needed to adjust the parent's investment account. Note that the adjustments are made for the *entire* interest previously owned, not just the portion sold. If in the preceding example Company P sells one-half instead of all of its 80% interest, the investment account should be adjusted for the entire 80% interest in past and current years' subsidiary income, net of amortizations. The 40% interest sold must be adjusted to record the sale properly, and the 40% interest retained also must be adjusted, since it no longer will be consolidated. Past adjustments that would be handled as part of the annual consolidation process now must be made directly to the investment account, so that the investment remaining conforms with APB Opinion No. 18. The sophisticated equity method described in that Opinion should be applied to remaining interests of 20% or more.[6]

If one-half of Company P's investment of the preceding section is sold for $160,000 on July 1, 19X3, the following entries would be recorded:

1. Assuming the past use of the simple equity method, the parent's investment account on January 1, 19X3, is adjusted to reflect the amortizations made on past consolidated statements.

Retained Earnings (January 1, 19X3)	14,000	
Investment in Company S		14,000

2. The parent's share of subsidiary income for the partial year is recorded. This amount is the $6,100 income net of amortizations.

Investment in Company S	6,100	
Subsidiary Income		6,100

Note that this income is no longer from a "disposed-of subsidiary."

3. The sale of one-half of the investment for $160,000 is recorded. The resulting gain is always ordinary income and never a gain from a "discontinued segment."

Cash	160,000	
Investment in Company S (**1/2** of $294,100 adjusted cost		
calculated on page 418)		147,050
Gain on Sale of Investment		12,950

Note that the sale of a partial interest will not qualify as a discontinued segment. Thus, the operating results on the investment to the sale date and the gain or loss on the sale would be shown as a part of ordinary income from continuing operations.

Control Retained.   A parent company may sell a portion of its investment in a subsidiary but still have an interest that exceeds 50% after the sale. For

---

[6]Opinions of the Accounting Principles Board No. 18, *The Equity Method of Accounting for Investments in Common Stock* (New York: American Institute of Certified Public Accountants, 1971), par. 17.

example, assume that on January 1, 19X1, a parent purchased from outside parties 8,000 of the total 10,000 shares of a subsidiary. On January 1, 19X3, the parent sold 2,000 shares and thereby lowered its percentage of ownership to 60%. Since the parent still had control, the 2,000 shares were sold, in essence, to minority shareholders. According to the *economic unit concept* of business combinations, which focuses on the position of the entire combined entity, this transaction should be viewed as a treasury stock transaction that occurred strictly between members of a consolidated group. Thus, any change in equity due to the resale of the stock should be treated as an adjustment to paid-in capital.

According to the *parent company concept*, which focuses on only the position of the controlling interest, the sale of a portion of an interest in a subsidiary should be viewed as producing a gain or loss to be reported on the income statement. This treatment is common in practice and is required by the SEC, unless the sale is part of a broader corporate reorganization. Therefore, this treatment will be used in this text.

To illustrate the recording of such a partial sale, return to the example for which a determination and distribution of excess schedule was prepared on page 415. Assume that on January 1, 19X3, Company P sells 2,000 subsidiary shares to lower its total interest to 60%. Only the portion of the investment account sold is to be adjusted to the sophisticated equity method to allow the proper recording of the sale. The 60% retained need not be adjusted on Company P's books, since all amortization adjustments on the 60% interest will be made on future consolidated statements. The adjustment of the 20% interest on the separate books of Company P must agree with the treatment of that interest in prior consolidated statements. Assuming the use of the simple equity method, the portion of the investment sold must be adjusted for its share of the past amortizations made on consolidated statements. Since the 19X1 and 19X2 amortizations on page 416 totaled $14,000 for an 80% interest, the amortizations for the 20% interest sold would be *one-fourth* of $14,000, or $3,500. The parent would make the following entry:

Retained Earnings (January 1, 19X3)	3,500	
Investment in Company S		3,500
To adjust for amortizations made on previous consolidated statements for the portion of the subsidiary investment sold.		

To record the sale of the investment, the parent would remove from its books *one-fourth* of the simple-equity-adjusted cost of January 1, 19X3 (calculated at $302,000 on page 415), which along with the previous $3,500 adjustment nets to $72,000. If the sale price is less than $72,000, a loss would be recorded. If the sale price is greater than $72,000, a gain would be recorded, as shown in the following entry to record the sale of the investment for $80,000:

Cash	80,000	
Investment in Company S [(**1/4** × $302,000) − $3,500 amortization adjustment]		72,000
Gain on Sale of Subsidiary Stock		8,000

If the parent in the previous example had used the cost method, only the portion of the investment sold would be adjusted to the sophisticated equity method on the parent's books. The analysis on page 416 shows that the parent's 80% share of income for 19X1 and 19X2 was $38,000 on a consolidated basis, net of amortizations. The 20% interest sold must be adjusted by *one-fourth* of $38,000, or $9,500. The remaining 60% will be adjusted in future worksheets. The entry to adjust the 20% interest would be:

```
Investment in Company S ....................................   9,500
     Retained Earnings (January 1, 19X3)..........................          9,500
          To adjust for the parent's share of past consolidated income
          pertaining to the interest sold.
```

The parent then would proceed to record the sale of the investment for $80,000 as follows:

```
Cash .....................................................  80,000
     Investment in Company S (1/4 of original $250,000 cost +
          $9,500 equity income) .................................         72,000
     Gain on Sale of Subsidiary Stock...........................          8,000
```

Intraperiod Sale of a Partial Interest.   When a sale of an interest during the reporting period does not result in loss of control, careful analysis is needed to insure that the worksheet adheres to consolidation theory. Referring to the situation on page 420, assume Company P sells one-fourth of its 80% interest for $80,000 on July 1, 19X3, and subsidiary income for the first half of the year is $12,000. Assuming the use of the simple equity method, the parent would adjust its own investment and the beginning-of-the-year retained earnings accounts for *one-fourth* of the amortizations of excess cost recorded on the prior years' consolidated worksheets. The adjustment would be recorded as follows:

```
Retained Earnings (January 1, 19X3)...........................   3,500
     Investment in Company S ..................................          3,500
          To record one-fourth of the $14,000 amortizations (shown on
          page 416) for 19X1 and 19X2.
```

A parent using the cost method would adjust the retained earnings for the subsidiary income, net of amortizations, for 19X1 and 19X2 (20% × $38,000 income on a consolidated basis).

Next, the parent would calculate its share of subsidiary income for the first half of 19X3 applicable to the 20% interest sold and adjusted for partial-year amortizations of excess relating to that portion of the investment as follows:

Income on 20% interest in Company S sold (20% × $12,000)	$2,400
Less amortizations of excess of cost over book value that would be necessary on consolidated statements:	
Equipment depreciation adjustment,	
$4,000 per year × 1/2 year × **1/4** interest sold	(500)
Amortization of goodwill adjustment,	
$3,000 per year × 1/2 year × **1/4** interest sold	(375)
Net share of income on interest sold	$1,525

The parent then would make a sophisticated equity method adjustment for this income and record the sale as follows:

```
Investment in Company S ...............................   1,525
   Subsidiary Income......................................            1,525
      To record share of first 6 months' subsidiary income
      applicable to the 20% interest sold and adjusted for partial-
      year amortizations of excess relating to that portion of the
      investment.
Cash ..................................................  80,000
   Investment in Company S [(1/4 × $302,000) – $3,500
      amortizations + $1,525 income] ........................            73,525
   Gain on Sale of Subsidiary Stock..........................            6,475
      To record sale of 20% interest in subsidiary.
```

The sale of a partial interest that does not result in loss of control requires special procedures on the consolidated worksheet for the period in which the sale occurs. Worksheets of later periods would not include any complications resulting from the sale. In Worksheet 7-4 on pages 470–473, the following should be noted:

1. The investment in Company S account reflects its simple equity balance on December 31, 19X3, for the remaining 60% interest held. The balance is computed as follows:

```
December 31, 19X2 balance applicable to remaining (60%) interest
   held at year end, 3/4 × $302,000 ...............................   $226,500
Add 60% of subsidiary reported income of $30,000....................     18,000
                                                                      ─────────
   Simple equity balance, December 31, 19X3 ........................   $244,500
                                                                      ═════════
```

2. The balance in Gain on Sale of Subsidiary Stock is the gain resulting from the 20% interest sold.
3. The balance in Subsidiary Income includes 60% of the subsidiary's $30,000 19X3 income, plus the $1,525 earned on the 20% interest prior to its sale.
4. The share of income applicable to the interest sold, $2,400 is transferred to the minority interest. The share of subsidiary income purchased by the minority interest is not reduced for the amortizations of excess cost applicable to the parent's purchase. These amortizations apply only to the income recorded by the controlling interest. The amortizations are recorded and allocated to the parent for the portion of the year prior to the sale. Step (1) on Worksheet 7-4 makes the transfer and records the partial year amortizations. In entry form, the procedure is:

```
Subsidiary Income (on 20% interest for first 6 months) ............  1,525
Expenses (amortizations of excess for the first 6 months)..........    875
   Income Sold to Minority (income for the first 6 months,
      no amortization).........................................            2,400
```

Carefully study the income distribution schedules for Worksheet 7-4. The minority interest receives its 40% interest in subsidiary income for the entire year, but there is a deduction for the income purchased from the parent for the first 6 months. The parent company income distribution schedule claims 60% of the subsidiary income for the entire year plus a 20% interest in the first 6 months' income.

If the parent, Company P, had used the cost method, there would be few changes in Worksheet 7-4. Step (1) would be unchanged; however, an entry would be needed to convert the remaining 60% interest to the simple equity method at the beginning of the year. Step (2) would not be applicable, since there would be no current-year equity adjustment to reverse. Steps (3) through (6) would remain the same.

Complications Resulting from Intercompany Transactions.   When a sale of subsidiary stock results in loss of control, the parent should adjust its investment account on the date of the sale for its share of unrealized subsidiary gains and losses resulting from intercompany transactions. When control is not lost as the result of a sale of subsidiary shares, the adjustment on the consolidated worksheet for unrealized gains and losses resulting from previous intercompany transactions need be recorded only as it applies to the interest sold. The remaining controlling interest's share of these gains and losses can be adjusted on subsequent consolidated worksheets. On these worksheets, retained earnings adjustments for unrealized gains and losses would be distributed according to the relative ownership interests existing on the dates the worksheets are prepared.

SUBSIDIARY PREFERRED STOCK

The existence of preferred stock in the capital structure of a subsidiary complicates the calculation of a parent's claim on subsidiary retained earnings, both at the time of acquisition and in the preparation of subsequent consolidated statements. In previous examples the subsidiary had only common stock outstanding, so that all retained earnings were associated with common stock, and the parent had a claim on subsidiary retained earnings in proportion to its ownership interest. When a subsidiary has preferred stock outstanding, however, the preferred stock also may have a claim on retained earnings. This claim may be caused by a liquidation value in excess of par value and/or by participation and cumulative dividend rights. When these conditions exist, the retained earnings must be divided between the preferred and common stockholder interests.

Once retained earnings are allocated between the common and preferred stockholders, the intercompany investments can be eliminated. The investment in subsidiary common stock account will be eliminated against the total equity claim of the common stockholders. If there is an investment in subsidiary preferred stock account, it will be eliminated against the preferred stockholders' total equity.

DETERMINATION OF PREFERRED SHAREHOLDERS' CLAIM ON RETAINED EARNINGS

The allocation of the retained earnings to the preferred and common stockholder interests is accomplished by employing the procedures used to calculate the book value of preferred and common stock. Although typically covered in intermediate accounting, the topic will be reviewed briefly in the following paragraphs.

The preferred shareholders' claim on retained earnings equals the claim they would have if the firm was dissolved. In addition to the par value of the preferred shares, there may be a stipulated liquidation value in excess of par and/or dividend preferences. In the rare case of a liquidation value in excess of par, an amount equal to the liquidation bonus (liquidation value less par value) must be segregated from retained earnings as a preferred shareholder claim. Liquidation values should not be confused with paid-in capital in excess of par which results from the sale of preferred shares. Such paid-in capital is not available to preferred shareholders in liquidation and is not part of the book value of preferred shares. Instead, it becomes part of the total paid-in capital that is available to common shareholders.

In addition to a liquidation bonus, there must be an analysis of any cumulative and/or participation clauses applicable to the preferred stock. Other than the effect of a liquidation bonus, if the preferred stock is noncumulative and nonparticipating, the preferred stockholders would have no claim, and all the retained earnings attach to the common stock. However, if there are preferred shareholder claims resulting from cumulative and/or participation clauses, these claims reduce the retained earnings applicable to the common stock. For example, if the preferred stock is noncumulative but fully participating, the retained earnings are allocated pro rata according to the total par or stated values of the preferred and common stock. If the preferred stock is cumulative but nonparticipating and, for example, has two years' dividends in arrears, a claim on retained earnings equal to the two years of dividends exists, although there is no liability to pay the preferred dividends until a dividend is declared.

When preferred stock is both cumulative and fully participating, the arrearage for prior periods is met first. The remaining retained earnings are allocated pro rata according to the total par values of the preferred and common stock. When preferred stock is cumulative and participating but no dividends are in arrears, the analysis is the same as if the preferred stock were noncumulative but participating.

When preferred stock is cumulative and limited in participation to a percentage of par value, the arrearage for prior periods is met first and is excluded from the limited participation. The lesser of a pro rata share of the remaining retained earnings or the limiting percentage of the preferred stock's par value is allocated to the preferred claim. Any retained earnings remaining after this allocation are assigned to the common stock.

APPORTIONMENT OF RETAINED EARNINGS

Additional procedures are required when a subsidiary with preferred stock that has liquidation and/or dividend preferences is consolidated, even if none of the preferred shares are owned by the parent. In this situation, allocation of retained earnings to the preferred and common stock is as follows:

1. The determination and distribution of excess schedule prepared as of the date of the parent's investment in common stock must include only that portion of retained earnings that is allocable to the common stock on the purchase date.
2. Periodic equity adjustments for the parent's investment in common stock are made only for the common shareholders' claim on income. The preferred shareholders' claim on the current year's income, including dividends paid or accumulated and any participation rights for the current year, must be deducted to arrive at income available to common shareholders. When the cost method is used, the worksheet simple equity conversion adjustment is made for the parent's share of change in the retained earnings applicable to common stock since the date of acquisition.
3. Subsidiary retained earnings must be allocated between preferred and common stockholders on consolidated worksheets. The parent's investment in common stock account then is eliminated against the parent's pro rata share of only the equity attaching to common stock.

To illustrate these procedures, assume Company S has the following stockholders' equity on January 1, 19X3, the date on which Company P purchases an 80% interest in the common stock for $150,000:

Preferred stock, $100 par, 6% cumulative.........	$100,000
Common stock, $10 par	100,000
Retained earnings............................	80,000
Total equity	$280,000

The preferred stock has a liquidation value equal to par value, and dividends are 2 years in arrears as of January 1, 19X3. Company S assets have a market value equal to book value. Any excess purchase price is attributable to goodwill with a 10-year life. The determination and distribution of excess schedule would be prepared as follows:

Price paid......................................			$150,000
Less interest acquired:			
Common stock ($10 par).......................		$100,000	
Retained earnings:			
Balance, Jan. 1, 19X3.........................	**$80,000**		
Less preferred dividends in arrears			
(2 years × $6,000)	**12,000**	**68,000**	
Total equity applicable to common stock............		$168,000	
Interest acquired................................		80%	134,400
Goodwill (10-year life)............................			$ 15,600

Assume that income is exactly $25,000 per year in future years and no dividends are paid. Each year, the following entry would be made by Company P using the simple equity method of accounting for its subsidiary investment:

Investment in Common Stock of Company S 15,200
   Subsidiary Income.   15,200
      To adjust for 80% of Company S income applicable to
      common stock ($25,000 reported income – $6,000
      cumulative claim of preferred stock).

Worksheet 7-5, pages 474–477, is a consolidated financial statements worksheet for the year ended *December 31, 19X5* (3 years subsequent to the purchase). The investment in common stock account includes the original cost of the investment plus 3 years (3 × $15,200 = $45,600) of simple equity adjustments for income and dividends. The worksheet is unique in that it subdivides the subsidiary retained earnings into two parts: one for the common portion and one for the preferred portion of retained earnings. Step (1) of Worksheet 7-5 accomplishes this apportionment. In entry form the procedure is:

Retained Earnings, Jan. 1, Co. S[7] 24,000
   Retained Earnings, allocated to preferred stock, Jan. 1, Co. S . . .   24,000

This division of retained earnings is only for worksheet purposes; the subsidiary will maintain only one retained earnings account.

After the eliminations and adjustments are completed, the resulting combined net income of $173,440 is allocated as shown in the income distribution schedules. Since none of the preferred stock is owned by controlling shareholders, the minority interest receives all applicable preferred income plus 20% of the income allocable to common stock. It should be observed that the Minority Interest column, as well as the minority interest shown on a formal balance sheet, includes the minority interest in both preferred and common shares.

The worksheet just analyzed can handle all types of subsidiary preferred stockholder claims. Once the claim is determined, with supporting calculations, it can be isolated in a separate worksheet account, *Retained Earnings Allocated to Preferred Stock.*

When a parent uses the cost method to record its investment in a subsidiary, slightly different worksheet procedures are used. In the previous illustration, if Company P had used the cost method, the investment account still would be at the $150,000 original cost. In addition, there would be no subsidiary income shown, and the January 1, 19X5 retained earnings of Company P would not reflect the 19X3 and 19X4 simple equity adjustments. As described earlier, a conversion to the simple equity method is made on the worksheet. Since the beginning-of-the-period investment balance is needed for elimination, the equity adjustment converts the investment account to the January 1, 19X5 balance, as follows:

---

[7]The remaining retained earnings reflects the common stockholders' interest.

Retained earnings, Company S, January 1, 19X5	$130,000	
Less 4 years' arrearage of preferred dividends.	24,000	
Retained earnings applicable to common stock, January 1, 19X5		**$106,000**
Retained earnings, Company S, January 1, 19X3	$ 80,000	
Less 2 years' arrearage of preferred dividends.	12,000	
Retained earnings applicable to common stock, January 1, 19X3		**68,000**
Increase in common stock portion of retained earnings		$ 38,000
Controlling interest (80%)		$ 30,400

The conversion entry for $30,400 would debit the investment account and credit the Company P retained earnings account. The investment account now would be stated at its simple-equity-adjusted, January 1, 19X5 balance. Worksheet steps (1), (3), (4), and (5) would be made just as in Worksheet 7-5. Only step (2) would be omitted, since it is not applicable to the cost method. The partial worksheet on page 428 includes the conversion and subsequent eliminations and adjustments under the cost method. All remaining procedures for this example would be identical to those used in Worksheet 7-5.

PARENT INVESTMENT IN SUBSIDIARY PREFERRED STOCK

A parent may purchase all or a portion of the preferred stock of a subsidiary. Normally, preferred stock is nonvoting; therefore, it is not considered in determining whether the parent owns a controlling interest in the subsidiary. Thus, a 100% ownership of nonvoting preferred stock and a 49% interest in voting common stock normally would not require the preparation of consolidated statements.

From a consolidated viewpoint, the parent's purchase of subsidiary preferred stock usually is viewed as a retirement of the stock.[8] The amount paid is compared to the sum of the original proceeds resulting from the issuance of the shares and any claim the shares have on retained earnings, and an increase or decrease in equity as a result of the retirement is calculated. When the price paid is less than the preferred equity retired, the resulting increase in equity is credited to the controlling paid-in capital account, not the retained earnings account, since it results from a transaction with the consolidated firm's shareholders. A decrease in equity, which occurs when the price paid exceeds the preferred equity, would offset against the paid-in capital applicable to the preferred stock. If not enough of the preferred stock paid-in capital exists, the remaining decrease would be taken from the controlling retained earnings and viewed as a retirement dividend.

---

[8]It also would be possible to view the investment as treasury shares, in which case they would appear as a contra-account to the preferred stock in the minority interest section of the consolidated balance sheet. This approach, however, does not have popular support. It could be justified only if there is an intent to reissue the shares.

Subsidiary Preferred Stock, None Owned by Parent
Cost Method Used for Investment in Common Stock

	Partial Trial Balance		Eliminations & Adjustments	
	Company P	Company S	Dr.	Cr.
Investment in Common Stock of Co. S.	150,000		**(C)** 30,400	(3) 164,800
				(4) 15,600
Goodwill			(4) 15,600	(5) 4,680
Retained Earnings, Jan. 1, 19X5, Co. P	(309,600)		(5) 3,120	**(C)** 30,400
Preferred Stock ($100 par), Co. S		(100,000)		
Retained Earnings Allocated to Preferred Stock, Jan. 1, 19X5, Co. S				(1) 24,000
Common Stock ($10 par), Co. S		(100,000)	(3) 80,000	
Retained Earnings, Jan. 1, 19X5, Co. S		(130,000)	(1) 24,000	
			(3) 84,800	
Expenses	100,000	25,000	(5) 1,560	

Eliminations and Adjustments:
(C)   The cost-to-equity conversion entry was explained prior to the partial worksheet.
(1)   Distribute the beginning-of-the-period subsidiary retained earnings into the portions allocable to common and preferred stock. The typical procedure would be to consider the stated subsidiary retained earnings as applicable to common and to remove the preferred portion. This distribution reflects 4 years of arrearage (as of January 1, 19X5) at $6,000 per year.
(3)   Eliminate the pro rata subsidiary common stockholders' equity at the beginning of the period against the investment account. This step includes elimination of the 80% of subsidiary retained earnings applicable to common stock.
(4)   Distribute the excess of cost according to the determination and distribution of excess schedule.
(5)   Amortize the goodwill for the past two years and the current year.

To illustrate this type of investment, assume Company P in the previous example purchased 600 shares (60%) of Company S preferred stock on January 1, 19X3, for $65,000. The increase or decrease in equity resulting from the retirement would be calculated as follows:

Price paid			$65,000
Less **preferred** interest acquired:			
Preferred stock ($100 par)	$100,000		
Claim on dividends (2 years in arrears × $6,000 per year)	12,000		
Total preferred interest	$112,000		
Interest acquired	60%	67,200	
Increase in equity (credit Paid-In Capital)			**$ 2,200**

Though viewed as retired, the preferred stock investment account will continue to exist on the books of the parent in subsequent periods. At the end of each period, the investment must be "retired" on the consolidated worksheet. The procedures used depend on whether the parent accounts for the investment in preferred stock under the equity method or the cost method. Under the equity method, the parent adjusts the investment in preferred stock account each period for any additional claim on the subsidiary retained earnings, including any continued arrearage or participation privilege. In this example, the arrearage of dividends would be recorded each year, 19X3 to 19X5, as follows:

Investment in Company S Preferred Stock...................... 3,600
   Subsidiary Income..   3,600
     To acknowledge 60% of the annual increase in the Company S
     preferred stock dividend arrearage.

Assuming the equity adjustments are made properly, any original discrepancy between the price paid for the preferred shares and their book value would be maintained. The equity method also acknowledges that, even though the shares are viewed as retired in consolidated reports, the controlling interest is entitled to its proportionate share of combined net income based on both its common and preferred stock holdings.

Worksheet 7-6, pages 478–481, displays the consolidation procedures that would be used for the ownership interest in preferred stock described above. This worksheet parallels Worksheet 7-5 except that the parent owns 60% of the subsidiary preferred stock. The investment is listed at its $65,000 cost plus three years of equity adjustments to reflect the increasing dividend arrearage.

Combined net income is distributed as shown in the income distribution schedules that accompany the worksheet. The distributions respect the controlling/minority ownership of both common and preferred shares. The common and preferred equity interests of the minority again are summarized on the worksheet and for presentation on the formal balance sheet.

If a parent uses the cost method for its investment in subsidiary preferred stock, the investment should be converted to its equity balance as of the beginning of the period. In this example, if the cost method is used for the investment in preferred stock, the following conversion adjustment would be made on the worksheet:

Investment in Company S Preferred Stock...................... 7,200
   Retained Earnings (January 1, 19X5, Co. P)   7,200

The adjustment reflects 2 years of arrearage at $6,000 per year times the 60% ownership interest. Eliminations and adjustments would proceed as in Worksheet 7-6, except that there would be no need for step (6).

This example contains only cumulative preferred stock. However, the same principles would apply to participating preferred stock, and the allocation procedures outlined earlier in this chapter would be used. Only the subdivision of the subsidiary retained earnings and the amounts of the equity adjustments would differ.

APPENDIX: WORKSHEET FOR A CONSOLIDATED BALANCE SHEET

Previous chapters displayed procedures applicable to worksheets that produced a consolidated income statement, retained earnings statement, and balance sheet. However, there may be occasions when only consolidated balance sheets are required, and the separate balance sheets of the affiliates form the starting point for consolidation procedures. Such occasions are rare in practice, but are of concern to students desiring to take the CPA Exam. Past examinations have used balance-sheet-only consolidation problems as an expedient method for testing purposes. This type of problem requires less time to solve while still testing the candidates' knowledge of consolidations.

A balance sheet worksheet requires only adjustments to balance sheet accounts. No adjustments for nominal accounts are required. Your past experience often will lead you to consider the impact of an elimination on the nominal accounts, but you must adjust your thinking to cover only the remaining impact of an elimination on the balance sheet. For example, intercompany merchandise sales no longer will require an elimination of the sales and cost of goods sold relative to the transaction. The following sections examine the simplified procedures that are used on a consolidated balance sheet worksheet.

INVESTMENT ACCOUNT

When the investment account is maintained under the simple equity method, it will reflect the same point in time as do the subsidiary equity balances. There is no need to eliminate the parent's entry for its share of subsidiary income. Instead, the pro rata share of subsidiary equity balances may be eliminated directly against the investment account.

Investments maintained under the sophisticated equity method are also at a common point in time and thus can be eliminated directly against the underlying subsidiary equity. The distributable excess, however, will be only that which remains net of the amortizations made in the current and previous periods.

Investments maintained at cost should be converted to the simple equity method as of the *end of the year* to agree in time with the subsidiary equity balances. The entire conversion adjustment is carried to the controlling retained earnings.

Excesses are distributed according to the determination and distribution of excess schedules. Once distributed, the excesses are amortized to the balance sheet date, and the entire amortization is carried to the controlling retained earnings.

MERCHANDISE SALES

Only the intercompany profit in the ending inventory needs adjustment. The profit is eliminated from the inventory and from retained earnings. The adjustment to retained earnings is allocated according to the minority/controlling ownership percentages in effect when the subsidiary made the intercompany sale. If the parent made the sale, the adjustment is made only to the controlling retained earnings. The intercompany profit in the beginning inventory either has been realized through the subsequent sale of the merchandise to an outside party, or if the units in the beginning inventory are still on hand at year end, they would be included in the adjustment for intercompany profit in the ending inventory.

PLANT ASSET SALES

The only matter for concern in the case of intercompany plant asset sales is the adjustment of the asset and retained earnings accounts for the undepreciated portion of the intercompany gain or loss as of year end. The asset account is adjusted to its cost to the consolidated firm; accumulated depreciation is adjusted for all periods to date; and retained earnings is adjusted for the undepreciated profit or loss that is to be deferred to future periods. If the subsidiary sold to the parent, the retained earnings adjustment is allocated to the minority and controlling interests that existed at the time of the sale.

INVESTMENT IN BONDS

The amortized balance in Investment in Company S Bonds is eliminated against the bonds payable and any related discount or premium balance. The net disparity in amounts is the net retirement gain or loss remaining at year end, which is carried to retained earnings. When the subsidiary is the issuer, the retained earnings adjustment is allocated to the minority and controlling interests.

LEASES

For operating leases, it is necessary only to reclassify the asset and accumulated depreciation as owned assets, rather than assets under operating leases. Where direct financing leases exist, the intercompany debt resulting from the capitalized lease must be eliminated. Also, it is necessary to reclassify the asset and accumulated depreciation as owned assets rather than assets under capital leases. An intercompany sales-type lease requires the same procedures as a direct-financing lease plus an additional adjustment to defer the remaining undepreciated intercompany profit on the lease. If the subsidiary leased the asset to the parent, the retained earnings adjustment is allocated to the minority and controlling interest that existed at the inception of the lease.

ILLUSTRATION

To illustrate the procedures used for the balance sheet worksheet, assume Company P purchased an 80% interest in Company S on January 1, 19X1. Company P uses the cost method to record its investment in Company S. The determination and distribution of excess schedule prepared for this purchase is as follows:

Price paid		$750,000
Less interest acquired:		
Common stock ($10 par).	$200,000	
Retained earnings, January 1, 19X1.	600,000	
Total stockholders' equity	$800,000	
Interest acquired	80%	640,000
Excess of cost over book value (debit balance)		$110,000
Excess of cost attributable to building (10-year remaining life)		30,000 Dr
Goodwill (20-year life)		$ 80,000 Dr

The facts pertaining to intercompany sales by Company S to Company P are as follows:

	19X3	19X4
Intercompany sales	$80,000	$100,000
Gross profit.	30%	40%
Intercompany sales in ending inventory	20,000	40,000
Unpaid balance, end of the year.	30,000	35,000

On January 1, 19X2, Company P sold a new piece of equipment that cost $10,000 to Company S for $15,000. Company S is depreciating the equipment over 5 years on a straight-line basis.

Company S has outstanding $100,000 of 20-year, 5% bonds due January 1, 19X9. Interest is payable on January 1 for the previous year. The bonds originally were sold to yield 6%. On January 1, 19X3, Company P purchased the bonds on the open market at a price to yield 8%.

Worksheet 7-7, pages 482–483, contains the balance sheets and eliminations and adjustments for Companies P and S on December 31, 19X4. After the worksheet steps are completed, the amounts are combined to produce the consolidated balance sheet. The time saving of the balance sheet worksheet results from the fact that there is no combined net income to calculate and distribute.

QUESTIONS

1. Under what circumstances is a determination and distribution of excess schedule needed when a parent acquires its controlling interest in stock directly from the subsidiary?
2. What is a piecemeal purchase? Describe the accounting consequences of such an acquisition as they affect the determination and distribution of excess schedules and worksheet procedures.
3. Is it possible that a piecemeal acquisition could include a transaction that qualifies as a pooling of interests? If so, explain the ramifications.
4. Explain how the equity method investment account balance generally can be recalculated to verify its correctness when an investment in a subsidiary has been acquired in more than one purchase.

5. What factors determine whether the sale of a parent's entire interest in a subsidiary qualifies as a disposal of a segment?

6. Parent Company sold its entire 75% interest in Subsidiary Company for $100,000. The interest originally was purchased at a price in excess of book value. May it be said that the parent realized a $20,000 gain on the sale (a) assuming a correct simple equity method investment account balance of $80,000? (b) assuming a correct cost method investment account balance of $80,000? Explain.

7. Describe the adjustments required when a parent sells enough of its ownership interest in a subsidiary to lose control. How do these adjustments differ when the parent sells part of its ownership interest, but not enough to lose control?

8. What special consolidation procedures are required when a subsidiary has preferred stock outstanding?

9. If a parent company owns 80% of the preferred stock and 45% of the common stock of a subsidiary, would the parent company normally have a controlling interest in the subsidiary? Explain.

10. What are the consolidation procedures required when a parent owns subsidiary preferred stock?

EXERCISES

Exercise 1. Prior to January 2, 19X4, Peter and Salem were separate corporations. Salem Corporation is contemplating a major expansion and sought to be purchased by a larger corporation with available cash. Peter Corporation issued $900,000 of bonds and used the proceeds to buy 30,000 newly issued Salem shares at $30 each. Just prior to the issue of the bonds and the issue and purchase of Salem stock, Peter and Salem had the following separate balance sheets:

Assets	Peter Corporation	Salem Corporation
Current assets	$ 600,000	$ 50,000
Land..	150,000	60,000
Property, plant, and equipment	700,000	400,000
Total assets....................................	$1,450,000	$510,000
Liabilities and Stockholders' Equity		
Current liabilities	$ 250,000	$100,000
Common stock ($5 par)	400,000	100,000
Retained earnings................................	800,000	310,000
Total liabilities and equity	$1,450,000	$510,000

Purchasing the 30,000 new shares gave Peter Corporation a 60% controlling interest (30,000 of a total 50,000 common shares). On the purchase date, Salem's property was undervalued by $100,000. Any remaining excess cost can be attributed only to goodwill.

Prepare a determination and distribution of excess schedule for Peter Corporation's investment in Salem. Prepare a consolidated balance sheet for the consolidated firm immediately after the purchase by Peter Corporation.

Exercise 2. Barker Corporation purchased a 60% interest in Hard Knock Company on January 1, 19X1, for $150,000. On that date, Hard Knock Company had the following stockholders' equity:

Common stock ($10 par)........................	$100,000
Retained earnings	20,000
	$120,000

Any excess of cost over market value was due to equipment with a 10-year life.

Barker Corporation purchased another 20% interest for $40,000 on January 1, 19X3, when Hard Knock Company had the following stockholders' equity:

Common stock ($10 par)........................	$100,000
Retained earnings	50,000
	$150,000

Any excess of cost over market value was due to goodwill with a 20-year life. On December 31, 19X5, Barker Corporation and Hard Knock Company had the following balance sheets:

Assets	Barker Corporation	Hard Knock Company
Current assets	$ 270,000	$ 80,000
Investment in Hard Knock Company.................	190,000	
Property, plant, and equipment	740,000	240,000
Total assets......................................	$1,200,000	$320,000

Liabilities and Stockholders' Equity		
Current liabilities	$ 400,000	$100,000
Stockholders' equity:		
Common stock ($10 par)	500,000	100,000
Retained earnings.............................	300,000	120,000
Total liabilities and stockholders' equity	$1,200,000	$320,000

Prepare the consolidated balance sheet of Barker Corporation and subsidiary Hard Knock Company on Dec. 31, 19X5, subsequent to the purchase of the additional 20% block by Barker.

Exercise 3. Gray Corporation purchased a 10% interest in Mirro Company on January 1, 19X1. The following determination and distribution of excess schedule was prepared on the purchase date:

Price paid...		$35,000
Less interest acquired:		
Common stock ($10 par)	$100,000	
Retained earnings	120,000	
Stockholders' equity	$220,000	
Interest acquired	10%	22,000
Excess of cost over book value..............................		$13,000
Attributed to equipment: 10% × $30,000 undervaluation		
(10-year life)		3,000
Goodwill (20-year life).......................................		$10,000

From January 1, 19X1, through December 31, 19X5, Mirro Company paid no dividends and reported the following net incomes:

19X1	$ 8,000	19X4	$20,000
19X2	10,000	19X5	22,000
19X3	20,000		

On January 1, 19X6, Gray Corporation purchased 7,000 additional shares of Mirro Company from existing shareholders for $250,000. This purchase raised Gray's interest to 80%. Mirro Company had the following balance sheet just prior to Gray's second purchase:

Assets		Liabilities and Equity	
Current assets	$125,000	Liabilities	$ 65,000
Buildings (net)	140,000	Common stock, $10 par	100,000
Equipment (net)	100,000	Retained earnings.	200,000
Total assets	$365,000	Total liabilities and equity	$365,000

At the time of the second purchase, Gray determined that Mirro's equipment was understated by $50,000 and had a 5-year remaining life. All other book values approximated market values. Any remaining excess is attributed to goodwill with a 20-year life.
  (1) Prepare a determination and distribution of excess schedule for the second purchase.
  (2) Record the investment made by Gray on January 1, 19X6.
  (3) Since control has now been achieved, Gray will use the simple equity method for its investment in Mirro. Assume that the cost method was used to account for the initial 10% interest. Convert the 10% interest to the simple equity method balance on January 1, 19X6.

Exercise 4. Cleft Company purchased a 20% interest in Key Industries on January 1, 19X2, for $100,000 and another 60% interest on January 1, 19X4, for $360,000. Key had the following stockholders' equity balances immediately prior to each purchase:

Stockholders' Equity	Jan. 1, 19X2	Jan. 1, 19X4
Common stock ($7 par)	$350,000	$350,000
Paid-in capital in excess of par	100,000	100,000
Retained earnings	20,000	100,000
Total equity	$470,000	$550,000

Cleft's analysis on the two purchase dates revealed the following: (1) On January 1, 19X2, Key's equipment was undervalued by $10,000 and had a remaining life of 5 years. (2) On January 1, 19X4, Key's equipment was undervalued by $9,000, with a 3-year remaining life. (3) Any excess attributable to goodwill is to be amortized over 10 years.
    Key had income of $30,000 in 19X4 and $50,000 in 19X5 and paid its first dividend, a $.20 per share dividend to common stock, on December 30, 19X5.
  (1) Prepare a determination and distribution of excess schedule for each investment.
  (2) Assuming the cost method is used for both investments, prepare the calculations necessary to convert the investment account to its simple-equity-adjusted balance on December 31, 19X5.

Exercise 5. Roy Company purchased a 90% interest in Van Company for $405,000 on January 1, 19X3. Any excess of cost over book value was attributed to goodwill, which is being amortized over 20 years. Both companies end their reporting periods on December 31. Since the investment in Van Company is consolidated, Roy Company has chosen to use the cost method to maintain its investment.

On December 31, 19X6, Roy Company sold 8,000 shares of Van Company for $650,000. The following stockholders' equity balances of Van Company are available:

	Jan. 1, 19X3	Jan. 1, 19X6
Common stock ($10 par)	$100,000	$100,000
Retained earnings	250,000	420,000
Total equity	$350,000	$520,000

Van Company earned $70,000 during 19X6. Prepare a determination and distribution of excess schedule. Record the sale of the shares of Van Company and any other adjustments needed to the investment account.

Exercise 6.   Doering Company has the following balance sheet on December 31, 19X5:

Assets		Liabilities and Equity		
Current assets	$160,000	Liabilities		$100,000
Investment in Brass		Equity:		
Company	150,000	Common stock		
Property, plant, and		($10 par)	$500,000	
equipment (net)	390,000	Retained earnings	100,000	600,000
		Total liabilities and		
Total assets	$700,000	equity		$700,000

The investment in Brass Company account reflects the original cost of an 80% interest (40,000 shares) purchased on January 1, 19X2. On the date of the purchase, Brass stockholders' equity had a book value of $150,000. Brass's other book values approximated market, except for a machine with a 5-year remaining life that was undervalued by $20,000. Any additional excess was attributed to goodwill and given a 10-year life.

A review of Brass's past financial statements reveals the following:

	Income	Dividends Paid
19X2	$ 10,000	$ 3,000
19X3	25,000	3,000
19X4	40,000	4,000
19X5	35,000	4,000
Total	$110,000	$14,000

Doering sold 2,000 shares of Brass common stock on January 1, 19X6, for $25,000.

Prepare the necessary entries on Doering's books to account accurately for the sale of the 2,000 Brass shares. Provide a determination and distribution of excess schedule along with all other necessary computations as support.

Exercise 7.   Dorn Inc. purchased 24,000 shares of Schmitt Corporation, which equated to an 80% interest, on January 1, 19X5. The following determination and distribution of excess schedule was prepared:

Determination and Distribution of Excess Schedule

Price paid for investment in Schmitt		$700,000
Less interest acquired:		
Common stock ($10 par)	$300,000	
Retained earnings	400,000	
Total stockholders' equity.	$700,000	
Interest acquired	80%	560,000
Excess of cost over book (debit balance)		$140,000
Building (80% × $50,000 undervaluation with		
10-year life, amortized = 4,000 per year)		40,000 Dr
Goodwill (40-year life = 2,500 per year).		$100,000 Dr

Schmitt Corporation reported net income of $35,000 for the six months ended July 1, 19X8. Dorn's simple-equity-adjusted investment balance was $764,000 as of December 31, 19X7.

Prepare all entries for the sale of the Schmitt Corporation shares for each of the following situations.
(a) 24,000 shares are sold for $850,000.
(b) 12,000 shares are sold for $400,000.
(c) 6,000 shares are sold for $200,000.

Exercise 8. On January 1, 19X2, Boelter Company purchased 80% of the outstanding common stock of Miller Corporation for $280,000. On this date, Miller Corporation stockholders' equity was as follows:

6% preferred stock (1,000 shares, $100 par)	$100,000
Common stock (20,000 shares, $10 par)	200,000
Retained earnings.	90,000
Total stockholders' equity	$390,000

Prepare a determination and distribution of excess schedule under each of the following situations (any excess of cost over book value is attributable to goodwill with a 10-year life):
(a) The preferred stock is cumulative, with dividends 1 year in arrears at January 1, 19X2, and has a liquidation value equal to par.
(b) The preferred stock is noncumulative, but fully participating.
(c) The preferred stock is cumulative, with dividends 2 years in arrears as of January 1, 19X2, has a liquidation value equal to par, and is 10% (limited) participating.

Exercise 9. Acme Construction Company had the following stockholders' equity on January 1, 19X1, the date on which Russel Company purchased an 80% interest in the common stock for $700,000:

8% cumulative preferred stock (5,000 shares, $100 par)	$ 500,000
Common stock (40,000 shares, $20 par)	800,000
Retained earnings	100,000
Total stockholders' equity.	$1,400,000

Acme Construction Company did not pay preferred dividends in 19X0.
(1) Prepare a determination and distribution of excess schedule. Assume that the preferred stock's liquidation value is equal to par and that any excess of cost is attributable to goodwill with a 20-year life.

(2) Assume Acme Construction has the following net income (loss) for 19X1 and 19X2 and does not pay any dividends:

19X1 .... $60,000
19X2 .... (10,000)

Prepare the entries necessary on Russel's books to adjust its investment account to the simple equity balance at the end of 19X1 and 19X2.

Exercise 10. On December 31, 19X4, Ziemer Corporation purchased an 80% interest in the common stock of Kirk Company for $400,000. The stockholders' equity of Kirk Company on December 31, 19X4, was as follows:

8% cumulative preferred stock (2,000 shares, $100 par)................... $200,000
Common stock ($10 stated value) 300,000
Retained earnings 160,000
                                                                     $660,000

Any excess of cost over book value was attributable to goodwill and had been given a 20-year life. The common stock investment is accounted for under the cost method.

Ziemer Corporation purchased 1,000 shares of the cumulative preferred stock of Kirk Company on January 1, 19X5, for $98,000. Kirk Company issued a total of 2,000 preferred shares on January 1, 19X1. Dividends on preferred stock were paid in 19X1 and 19X2, but not in subsequent years. Ziemer Corporation accounts for its investment using the cost method.

During 19X5 and 19X6, Kirk Company paid no dividends and its retained earnings balance on December 31, 19X6, was $210,000. Kirk Company income during 19X7 was $60,000.

(1) Calculate the preferred and common stockholders' equity claim on Kirk Company retained earnings balance at January 1, 19X7.
(2) Prepare the cost-to-simple-equity conversion and the elimination that would be made on the December 31, 19X7 consolidated trial balance worksheet for the investment in preferred stock.
(3) Prepare the cost-to-simple-equity conversion and the elimination that would be made on the December 31, 19X7 consolidated trial balance worksheet for the investment in common stock. Provide a determination and distribution of excess schedule as support.

PROBLEMS

Problem 7-1. The following determination and distribution of excess schedule was prepared on January 1, 19X2, the date on which Patti Company purchased a 60% interest in Sardon Company:

Price paid. $120,000
Less interest acquired:
  Common stock ($10 par) .... $ 75,000
  Retained earnings 60,000
    Total stockholders' equity $135,000
    Interest acquired 60%   81,000
Excess of cost over book value attributable to goodwill
  (20-year life) .... $ 39,000

On December 31, 19X3, Patti Company purchased an additional 20% interest in Sardon Company for $70,000. Sardon stockholders' equity was determined to be the following at that date:

Common stock	$ 75,000
Retained earnings	85,000
Total stockholders' equity	$160,000

Any excess of cost over book value was attributed to goodwill and given a 20-year life. On December 31, 19X5, the following trial balances are available:

	Patti Company	Sardon Company
Current Assets	220,000	65,000
Investment in Sardon Company	249,000	
Property, Plant, and Equipment (net)	450,000	170,000
Current Liabilities	(110,000)	(20,000)
Common Stock ($10 par)	(500,000)	(75,000)
Retained Earnings, Jan. 1, 19X5	(198,000)	(100,000)
Sales	(400,000)	(110,000)
Subsidiary Income	(36,000)	
Cost of Goods Sold	200,000	50,000
Other Expenses	100,000	15,000
Dividends Declared	25,000	5,000
Total	0	0

Required:
(1) Prepare the determination and distribution of excess schedule for the second purchase of Sardon stock by Patti Company.
(2) Prepare the worksheet necessary to produce the consolidated financial statements of Patti Company and its subsidiary as of December 31, 19X5. Include income distribution schedules.

Problem 7-2. On January 1, 19X1, James Company purchased 70% of the common stock of Chris Company for $244,000. On this date, Chris had common stock, other paid-in capital, and retained earnings of $50,000, $100,000, and $150,000, respectively.

On May 1, 19X2, James Company purchased an additional 20% of the common stock of Chris Company for $92,000.

Net income and dividends for 2 years for Chris Company were as follows:

	19X1	19X2
Net income for year	$60,000	$90,000
Dividends, declared in December	20,000	30,000

In 19X2, the net income of Chris from January 1 through April 30 was $30,000.

On January 1, 19X1, the only tangible asset of Chris that was undervalued was equipment, which was worth $20,000 more than book value. The equipment has a remaining life of 4 years and straight-line depreciation is used. Goodwill, if any, is to be amortized over 10 years.

On May 1, 19X2, any excess of cost over book value is due to goodwill, to be amortized over 10 years.

In the last quarter of 19X2, Chris sold $50,000 in goods to James, at a gross profit rate of 30%. On December 31, 19X2, $10,000 of these goods are in James's ending inventory.

The trial balances for the companies on December 31, 19X2, are as follows:

	James Company	Chris Company
Inventory, Dec. 31.	100,000	50,000
Other Current Assets.	127,000	180,000
Investment in Chris Company.	?	
Land	50,000	50,000
Buildings and Equipment.	350,000	320,000
Accumulated Depreciation.	(100,000)	(60,000)
Other Intangibles	20,000	
Current Liabilities.	(120,000)	(40,000)
Bonds Payable		(100,000)
Other Long-Term Liabilities	(200,000)	
Common Stock—James	(200,000)	
Other Paid-In Capital—James.	(100,000)	
Retained Earnings—James	(214,000)	
Common Stock—Chris.		(50,000)
Other Paid-In Capital—Chris		(100,000)
Retained Earnings—Chris		(190,000)
Net Sales	(520,000)	(450,000)
Cost of Goods Sold	300,000	260,000
Operating Expenses	120,000	100,000
Subsidiary Income.	?	
Dividends Declared	50,000	30,000
Total	0	0

Required:
(1) Using this information, prepare determination and distribution of excess schedules for the two purchases.
(2) James Company carries the Investment in Chris Company under the simple equity method. In general journal form, record the entries that would be made to apply the equity method in 19X1 and 19X2.
(3) Compute the balance that should appear in Investment in Chris Company and in Subsidiary Income on December 31, 19X2 (the second year). Fill in these amounts on James Company's trial balance on the worksheet for 19X2.
(4) Complete the worksheet for consolidated financial statements for 19X2.

Problem 7-3. On January 1, 19X4, Madden Company purchased a 20% interest in Clayton Company for $100,000. Two years subsequent to this purchase, Madden Company acquired an additional 45% interest in Clayton Company for $250,000.

Balance sheets of Clayton Company immediately prior to these purchases were as follows:

Assets	Jan. 1, 19X4	Jan. 1, 19X6
Current assets	$150,000	$120,000
Land.	150,000	150,000
Equipment (net).	200,000	300,000
Total assets.	$500,000	$570,000

Liabilities and Equity

Liabilities......................................	**$100,000**	**$110,000**
Equity:		
Common stock ($5 par).........................	$100,000	$100,000
Paid-in capital in excess of par...................	150,000	150,000
Retained earnings.............................	150,000	210,000
Total equity...................................	$400,000	$460,000
Total liabilities and equity	$500,000	$570,000

On January 1, 19X4, and January 1, 19X6, Clayton's book values approximated market values, except for the land, which was undervalued by $50,000. Any resulting goodwill is being amortized over 10 years.

The original 20% investment had been maintained under the sophisticated equity method. Since it now will be necessary to prepare consolidated statements, the simple equity method is in use for 19X6.

On December 31, 19X6, Madden's investment in Clayton Company was determined as follows:

Original cost of 20% investment	$100,000
19X4-X5 equity adjustment, net of excess amortization..................	10,000
Original cost of 45% investment	250,000
65% of income, January 1, 19X6—December 31, 19X6..................	26,000
Investment in Clayton Company	$386,000

The following trial balances were prepared on December 31, 19X6:

	Madden Company	Clayton Company
Current Assets	250,000	225,000
Investment in Clayton Company	386,000	
Land...	240,000	150,000
Building (net)	480,000	
Equipment (net).......................................	400,000	220,000
Other Assets..	20,000	5,000
Liabilities...	(340,000)	(100,000)
Common Stock ($10 par)...............................	(1,000,000)	
Common Stock ($5 par)................................		(100,000)
Paid-In Capital in Excess of Par........................		(150,000)
Retained Earnings, Jan. 1, 19X6........................	(350,000)	(210,000)
Sales	(900,000)	(350,000)
Subsidiary Income	(26,000)	
Cost of Goods Sold....................................	540,000	180,000
Other Expenses	250,000	130,000
Dividends Declared....................................	50,000	
Total	0	0

Required:

Prepare the worksheet necessary to produce the consolidated financial statements of Madden Company and its subsidiary as of December 31, 19X6. Include the determination and distribution of excess and income distribution schedules.

Problem 7-4. On January 1, 19X1, Parmida Company purchased 20% of the common stock of Slice Company for $80,000. On this date, Slice had common stock, other paid-in capital, and retained earnings of $50,000, $100,000, and $150,000, respectively. On this date, any excess of cost over book value is due to goodwill, to be amortized over 10 years.

On January 1, 19X2, Parmida Company purchased an additional 60% of the common stock of Slice Company for $264,000. On this date, the only tangible asset of Slice that was undervalued was land, which was worth $30,000 more than book value. Goodwill, if any, is to be amortized over 10 years.

Net income and dividends for 2 years for Slice Company were as follows:

	19X1	19X2
Net income for year	$60,000	$90,000
Dividends, declared in December......	20,000	30,000

For 19X1, Parmida accounted for its investment using the sophisticated equity method. For 19X2, Parmida accounted for all of its investment using the simple equity method.

On July 1, 19X2, Slice purchased equipment for $40,000 and immediately sold it to Parmida for $50,000. Parmida is using the equipment and depreciating it over 5 years, using the straight-line method and assuming no salvage value.

The trial balances for both firms on December 31, 19X2, are as follows:

	Parmida Company	Slice Company
Inventory, Dec. 31.......................................	100,000	50,000
Other Current Assets.....................................	177,000	180,000
Investment in Slice Company	398,000	
Land..	50,000	50,000
Buildings and Equipment.................................	350,000	320,000
Accumulated Depreciation................................	(100,000)	(60,000)
Other Intangibles	20,000	
Current Liabilities.......................................	(120,000)	(40,000)
Bonds Payable		(100,000)
Other Long-Term Liabilities	(200,000)	
Common Stock—Parmida...................................	(200,000)	
Other Paid-In Capital—Parmida	(100,000)	
Retained Earnings—Parmida	(253,000)	
Common Stock—Slice		(50,000)
Other Paid-In Capital—Slice		(100,000)
Retained Earnings—Slice.................................		(190,000)
Net Sales	(520,000)	(450,000)
Cost of Goods Sold	300,000	270,000
Operating Expenses	120,000	100,000
Gain on Sale of Equipment		(10,000)
Subsidiary Income.......................................	(72,000)	
Dividends Declared	50,000	30,000
Total	0	0

Required:
(1) Using this information, prepare determination and distribution of excess schedules for the two purchases.
(2) Prepare the worksheet necessary to produce the consolidated financial statements of Parmida and Slice as of December 31, 19X2. Include income distribution schedules.

Problem 7-5. On January 1, 19X1, Prug Company purchased an 80% interest (8,000 shares) directly from Bohr Company on the day Bohr was organized for $160,000.

On April 1, 19X5, Prug Company purchased 1,000 additional shares of Bohr Company for $38,900. Bohr had an exceptional first quarter with income of $9,000. No dividends had been paid. Any excess of cost is considered to be goodwill with a 10-year life. Unrealized gains and losses applicable to the 10% interest are ignored on the basis of materiality.

The subsidiary sells merchandise to the parent at cost plus 50%. Intercompany sales were $60,000 during 19X5; $20,000 was unpaid at year end. There were $9,000 of such goods in the beginning inventory of Prug Company and $15,000 of such goods in the ending inventory. However, the ending inventory had been adjusted down to its market value of $12,000.

The parent sold a machine with a book value of $10,000 to the subsidiary for $15,000 on January 1, 19X4. The machine had a 5-year life as of January 1, 19X4, and is being depreciated on a straight-line basis.

Bohr Company issued $100,000 of face value, 5-year, 6% bonds on January 1, 19X3. The bonds sold at a premium of $4,500 since the market rate of interest was 5%. On January 1, 19X4, when the market rate was 8%, Prug Company purchased all of these bonds for $93,400. Straight-line amortization is being used for the bonds.

Bohr Company paid a $1 per share cash dividend on December 31, 19X5.

The following trial balances were prepared as of December 31, 19X5:

	Prug Company	Bohr Company
Cash.	12,050	103,700
Accounts Receivable.	80,000	40,000
Inventory	43,100	63,000
Plant and Equipment.	400,000	300,000
Accumulated Depreciation.	(200,000)	(80,000)
Investment in Bohr Company Stock	198,900	
Investment in Bohr Company Bonds.	96,700	
Liabilities	(64,100)	(40,000)
6% Bonds Payable.		(100,000)
Premium on Bonds Payable		(1,800)
Common Stock ($10 par)	(200,000)	(100,000)
Paid-In Capital in Excess of Par.		(100,000)
Retained Earnings, Jan. 1, 19X5	(300,000)	(80,000)
Sales.	(250,000)	(120,000)
Cost of Goods Sold	150,000	80,000
Other Expenses	50,000	20,000
Subsidiary Income.	(9,000)	
Interest Income.	(7,650)	
Interest Expense.		5,100
Dividends Declared		10,000
Total	0	0

Required:

Prepare the worksheet necessary to produce the consolidated financial statements of Prug Company and its subsidiary as of December 31, 19X5. Include the determination and distribution of excess and income distribution schedules.

Suggestion: Determine what method Prug Company is using to maintain its investment in Bohr Company stock account (i.e., cost, simple equity, or sophisticated equity) before attempting the requirements of this problem.

Problem 7-6. During 19X7, Away Company acquired a controlling interest in Stallman Inc. Trial balances of the companies at December 31, 19X7, are as follows:

	Away Company	Stallman Inc.
Cash..	100,000	78,000
Notes Receivable	100,000	
Accounts Receivable	200,000	100,000
Interest Receivable......................................	3,000	
Dividends Receivable.....................................	4,500	
Inventories..	924,000	125,000
Investment in Stallman Inc.	470,500	
Property, Plant, and Equipment...........................	1,250,000	500,000
Accumulated Depreciation	(500,000)	(150,000)
Deferred Charges	25,000	
Patents and Licenses		50,000
Accounts Payable..	(425,000)	(80,000)
Notes Payable...		(75,000)
Dividends Payable		(5,000)
Capital Stock	(300,000)	(100,000)
Retained Earnings, Jan. 1, 19X7	(1,605,000)	(400,000)
Sales and Services.......................................	(1,800,000)	(750,000)
Subsidiary Income	(45,000)	
Interest Income	(3,000)	
Cost of Goods Sold	1,350,000	525,000
Administrative and Selling Expenses.......................	251,000	174,000
Interest Expense		3,000
Dividends Declared.......................................		5,000
Total...	0	0

The following information is available regarding the transactions and accounts of the two companies:

(a) An analysis of the investment in Stallman Inc. account follows:

	Description	Amount	Interest Acquired
January 1, 19X7	Investment	$325,000	70%
September 30, 19X7...............	Investment	105,000	20%
Total..........................		$430,000	90%
December 31, 19X7	90% of Stallman income for 19X7	45,000	
December 31, 19X7	90% of Stallman dividends for 19X7	(4,500)	
Total..........................		$470,500	

The net income of Stallman Inc. for the 9 months ended September 30, 19X7, was $25,000.

(b) The price paid by the parent on January 1, 19X7, to achieve control reflects uncertainty as to the future value of the patents. The remaining amortization is 10 years.

(c) On September 30, 19X7, Away Company loaned its subsidiary $100,000 on a 1-year, 12% note. Interest and principal are payable in quarterly installments beginning December 31, 19X7. The December 31, 19X7 payment was made by Stallman but was not received by Away. Away Company has no other notes receivable outstanding.

(d) Stallman Inc.'s sales principally are engineering services billed at cost plus 50%. During 19X7, Away Company was billed for $40,000, of which $16,500 was treated as a deferred charge at December 31, 19X7.

(e) During the year, parent company sales to the subsidiary totaled $60,000, of which $10,000 remained in the inventory of Stallman Inc. at December 31, 19X7.

(f) In 19X7, Away constructed certain tools at a cost of $15,000 and sold them to Stallman Inc. for $25,000. Stallman Inc. depreciates such tools using the straight-line method over a 5-year life. One-half year's depreciation is taken in the year of acquisition.

Required:

Prepare the worksheet necessary to produce the consolidated financial statements of Away Company and its subsidiary for the year ended December 31, 19X7. Include the determination and distribution of excess and income distribution schedules.

(AICPA adapted)

Problem 7-7. On January 1, 19X3, Horton Corporation purchased 90% (18,000 shares) of the outstanding common stock of Neff Company for $468,000. Just prior to Horton Corporation's purchase, Neff Company had the following stockholders' equity:

Common stock ($5 par).......................	$100,000
Paid-in capital in excess of par.................	300,000
Retained earnings............................	100,000
Total stockholders' equity	$500,000

At this time, Neff Company's book values approximated market values. Any excess of cost was attributed to goodwill and given a 20-year life.

On January 1, 19X7, Neff Company retained earnings balance amounted to $200,000. No changes had taken place in the paid-in capital accounts since the original sale of common stock on July 10, 19X0.

On July 1, 19X7, Horton Corporation sold 2,000 of its Neff Company shares to Welch Corporation for $75,000. At the time of this sale, Horton had no intention of selling the balance of its holding in Neff Company.

In an unexpected move on December 31, 19X7, Horton Corporation sold its remaining 80% interest in Neff Company to Welch Corporation for $500,000.

Neff Company reported income and dividends for 19X7 are as follows:

	Income	Dividends
January 1, 19X7–July 1, 19X7	$25,000	$.50/share
July 1, 19X7–December 31, 19X7	35,000	.50/share

Required:

Prepare the determination and distribution of excess schedule for Horton Corporation's purchase of Neff Company common stock on January 1, 19X3. Then prepare all the entries on Horton's books needed to reflect the changes in its investment account from January 1, 19X7, to December 31, 19X7. (Assume Horton uses the cost method to report its investment in Neff Company.)

Problem 7-8. The following information is available regarding the investments of Billings Corporation in Chassel Company for the years 19X1–19X5:

Date	Transaction	Interest	Price
1/1/X1	Purchased common	10%	$ 25,000
1/1/X2	Purchased preferred	60	30,000
1/1/X3	Purchased common	50	140,000
1/1/X5	Purchased common	20	60,000
1/1/X6	Sold common	10	35,000

The stockholders' equity section of Chassel Company's balance sheet has not changed since the January 1, 19X0 original sale of preferred stock to the public, except for the balance in the retained earnings account. The stockholders' equity as of January 1, 19X5, is as follows:

6% cumulative preferred stock
  ($50 par, liquidation value equals par value)......................... $ 50,000
Common stock ($10 par)... 100,000
Paid-in capital in excess of par.. 20,000
Retained earnings.. 150,000

    Total stockholders' equity $320,000

Other relevant facts are as follows:
(a) On January 1, 19X1, Chassel had a $60,000 retained earnings balance, and there were no dividends in arrears on the preferred stock.
(b) The excess of cost over book value on each investment in common stock was viewed as goodwill with a 10-year life.
(c) The 10% interest sold on January 1, 19X6, was the interest purchased on January 1, 19X1.
(d) Income and dividends were as follows for 19X1–19X5:

	Net Income	Preferred Dividends	Common Dividends
19X1	$25,000	$3,000	None
19X2	30,000	3,000	$6,000
19X3	30,000	3,000	5,000
19X4	25,000	None	None
19X5	20,000	None	None

Billings's investment account balances for its interests in Chassel Company were calculated as follows on December 31, 19X5:

Investment in preferred stock:
  Original cost.. $ 30,000
  Plus dividends in arrears for 19X4................................... 1,800

    Balance, December 31, 19X5 .... $ 31,800

Investment in common stock:
  January 1, 19X1 purchase.. $ 25,000
  January 1, 19X3 purchase... 140,000
  19X3 Chassel income, $30,000 × 60%................................ 18,000
  19X3 Chassel dividends, $5,000 × 60%.............................. (3,000)
  19X4 Chassel income, $25,000 × 60%................................ 15,000
  January 1, 19X5 purchase... 60,000
  19X5 Chassel income, $20,000 × 80%................................ 16,000
  December 31, 19X5 sale .... (35,000)

    Balance, December 31, 19X5 .... $236,000

Required:
Assume the investment accounts are to be maintained properly under the simple equity method. Prepare all necessary correcting entries on the books of Billings Corporation as of January 1, 19X6. (Assume nominal accounts are open.) All supporting computations and schedules should be in good form.

Problem 7-9. Marsha Corporation purchased an 80% interest in the common stock of Trans Corporation on December 31, 19X3, for $720,000, when Trans had the following condensed balance sheet:

Assets		Liabilities and Stockholders' Equity	
Current assets	$ 500,000	Liabilities..................	$ 600,000
Land......................	100,000	Preferred stock (8%	
		cumulative, $100 par).....	100,000
Building (net)	400,000	Common stock ($20 par)	750,000
Equipment (net)............	500,000	Retained earnings..........	50,000
Total assets...............	$1,500,000	Total liabilities and equity ...	$1,500,000

On the December 31, 19X3 purchase date, the dividends on the preferred stock were 2 years in arrears. Also on this date, the book values of Trans's assets approximated market values, except for the building which was undervalued by $28,000 and had a 20-year remaining life. Any resulting goodwill is being amortized over a 10-year life.

For 19X4–19X6, earnings and dividends for Trans Corporation were as follows:

	Income	Preferred Dividends	Common Dividends
19X4......................	$40,000		
19X5......................	50,000	$16,000	
19X6......................	80,000	24,000	$26,750

The following trial balances of the two firms were prepared on December 31, 19X6:

	Marsha Corporation	Trans Corporation
Current Assets......................................	806,400	463,250
Investment in Trans Corporation	720,000	
Land...	400,000	210,000
Building..	950,000	500,000
Accumulated Depreciation—Building	(200,000)	(160,000)
Equipment	1,500,000	740,000
Accumulated Depreciation—Equipment	(400,000)	(200,000)
Liabilities..	(800,000)	(550,000)
Preferred Stock, 8%		(100,000)
Common Stock ($20 par)............................	(2,000,000)	(750,000)
Retained Earnings, Jan. 1, 19X6	(860,000)	(124,000)
Sales..	(2,100,000)	(1,000,000)
Subsidiary Dividend Income	(21,400)	
Cost of Goods Sold	1,155,000	600,000
Other Expenses.....................................	650,000	320,000
Dividends Declared.................................	200,000	50,750
Total...	0	0

On January 1, 19X5, Marsha sold production equipment to Trans for $55,000 with a 5-year remaining life. Marsha's original cost was $80,000, and accumulated depreciation on the date sold was $50,000.

Required:

Prepare the worksheet necessary to produce the consolidated financial statements of Marsha Corporation and its subsidiary as of December 31, 19X6. Include the determination and distribution of excess and income distribution schedules.

Problem 7-10. The following information pertains to Titan Corporation and its two subsidiaries, Boat Corporation and Motor Corporation:

(a) The three corporations are all in the same industry and their operations are homogeneous. Titan Corporation exercises control over the boards of directors of Boat Corporation and Motor Corporation and has installed new principal officers in both.

(b) Boat Corporation had a retained earnings balance of $92,000 at January 1, 19X7, and had income of $15,000 for the first 3 months of 19X7 and $20,000 for the first 6 months of 19X8.

(c) Titan Corporation acquired 250 shares of fully participating Motor preferred stock for $7,000 and 14,000 shares of Motor common stock for $196,000 on January 2, 19X8. Motor Corporation had a net income of $20,000 in 19X8 and did not declare any dividends.

(d) Motor Corporation's inventory includes $22,400 of merchandise acquired from Boat Corporation subsequent to July, 19X8, for which no payment has been made. Boat Corporation marked up the merchandise 40% on cost.

(e) Titan Corporation acquired in the open market twenty-five $1,000, 6% bonds of Boat Corporation for $21,400 on January 1, 19X5. Boat Corporation bonds mature December 31, 19Y0. Interest is paid each June 30 and December 31. Straight-line amortization is allowed on the basis of materiality.

(f) The 19X8 year-end balance in the investment in Boat Corporation stock account is composed of the items shown in the following schedule:

Date	Description	Amount
4/1/X7	Cost of 5,000 shares of Boat Corp. stock.	$ 71,400
12/31/X7	20% of the dividends declared in December, 19X7, by Boat Corp.	(9,000)
12/31/X7	20% of the 19X7 annual net income of Boat Corp.	12,000
7/1/X8	Cost of 15,000 shares of Boat Corp.	226,200
12/31/X8	80% of the dividends declared in December, 19X8, by Boat Corp.	(24,000)
12/31/X8	80% of the 19X8 annual net income of Boat Corp.	32,000
12/31/X8	Total	$308,600

(g) The December 31, 19X8 trial balances for the three corporations appear as follows:

	Titan Corporation	Boat Corporation	Motor Corporation
Cash.	100,000	87,000	95,000
Accounts Receivable.	158,200	210,000	105,000
Inventories	290,000	90,000	115,000
Advance to Boat Corporation	17,000		
Dividends Receivable	24,000		
Property, Plant, and Equipment	777,600	325,000	470,000
Accumulated Depreciation	(180,000)	(55,000)	(160,000)
Investment in Boat Corporation:			
6% Bonds	23,800		
Common Stock	308,600		
Investment in Motor Corporation:			
Preferred Stock	7,400		
Common Stock	207,200		
Notes Payable	(45,000)	(14,000)	(44,000)
Accounts Payable	(170,000)	(96,000)	(86,000)
Bonds Payable.	(285,000)	(150,000)	(125,000)
Discount on Bonds Payable	8,000		
Dividends Payable.	(22,000)	(30,000)	
Preferred Stock ($20 par).	(400,000)		(50,000)
Common Stock ($10 par).	(600,000)	(250,000)	(200,000)
Retained Earnings, Jan. 1,19X8	(154,600)	(107,000)	(100,000)
Sales	(1,050,000)	(500,000)	(650,000)

	Titan Corporation	Boat Corporation	Motor Corporation
Other Revenue........................	(2,100)		
Subsidiary Income:			
Common Stock (Boat)	(32,000)		
Preferred Stock (Motor)	(400)		
Common Stock (Motor).............	(11,200)		
Cost of Goods Sold..................	650,000	300,000	400,000
Other Expenses	358,500	160,000	230,000
Dividends Declared..................	22,000	30,000	
Total.............................	0	0	0

Required:

Prepare the worksheet necessary to produce the consolidated financial statements of Titan Corporation and its subsidiaries as of December 31, 19X8. Consolidated retained earnings should be allocated to Titan Corporation, and the minority interests should be shown separately in the consolidated balance sheet column. The consolidation is to be accounted for as a purchase. All supporting computations and schedules should be in good form.

(AICPA adapted)

Problem 7-11. On January 1, 19X7, Black Jack Corporation purchased all of the preferred stock and 60% of the common stock of Zenon Company for $56,000 and $110,000, respectively. Immediately prior to the purchases, Zenon Company had the following stockholders' equity:

8% cumulative preferred stock ($100 par, 2 years in arrears)...............	$ 50,000
Common stock ($10 par)...	100,000
Paid-in capital in excess of par (common stock)........................	20,000
Retained earnings	30,000
Total stockholders' equity	$200,000

The December 31, 19X8 trial balances of the two firms are as follows:

	Black Jack Corporation	Zenon Company
Cash...	31,400	10,000
Accounts Receivable (net).............................	80,000	76,000
Inventories	230,000	44,000
Other Current Assets	20,000	8,000
Property, Plant, and Equipment	1,450,000	122,000
Accumulated Depreciation	(420,000)	(25,000)
Investment in Zenon Preferred Stock	56,000	
Investment in Zenon Common Stock	120,200	
Liabilities...	(350,000)	(18,000)
Common Stock—Black Jack............................	(1,000,000)	
Retained Earnings—Black Jack	(195,000)	
Preferred Stock—Zenon ($100 par).....................		(50,000)
Common Stock—Zenon		(100,000)
Paid-In Capital in Excess of Par—Zenon................		(20,000)
Retained Earnings—Zenon.............................		(41,000)
Sales	(420,000)	(96,000)
Cost of Goods Sold.....................................	300,000	60,000
Other Expenses	80,000	26,000

	Black Jack Corporation	Zenon Company
Dividends Declared..................................	25,000	4,000
Subsidiary Income—Preferred.......................	(4,000)	
Subsidiary Income—Common........................	(3,600)	
Paid-In Capital in Excess of Par—Black Jack.............		
Total...	0	0

Additional information:
(a) On January 1, 19X7, Zenon Company's only plant asset, equipment, had a market value of $200,000. All its other assets and liabilities had market values equal to their book values. The equipment had an estimated remaining life of 8 years and is being depreciated on a straight-line basis.
(b) On December 30, 19X7, and December 30, 19X8, Zenon Company paid preferred stock dividends of $8 per share.
(c) Zenon Company had a net income of $15,000 in 19X7 and $10,000 for 19X8.
(d) Zenon Company sold a piece of equipment with a book value of $8,000 to Black Jack Corporation for $13,000 on January 2, 19X7. The machine had an estimated future life of 5 years, and straight-line depreciation is being used.
(e) During 19X8, Black Jack sold $20,000 of goods to Zenon for cost plus 40%. Zenon had $2,800 of such purchases in its beginning inventory and $7,000 of such purchases in its ending inventory. Zenon owed Black Jack $2,000 for purchases at year end. During 19X8, Zenon sold $8,000 of goods to Black Jack at cost plus 60%. $1,200 of these goods were in Black Jack's beginning inventory and $1,600 of such goods were in its ending inventory. Black Jack owed Zenon $6,000 for purchases at year end.
(f) On January 1, 19X9, Black Jack Corporation sold its 60% interest in Zenon Company common stock for $130,000.

Required:
(1) Prepare the worksheet necessary to produce the consolidated financial statements of Black Jack Corporation and its subsidiary for the year ended December 31, 19X8. Include the determination and distribution of excess and income distribution schedules.
(2) Prepare the entries on Black Jack Corporation's books to reflect the sale of its investment in Zenon Company common stock on January 1, 19X9.

Problem 7-12. Condensed (unconsolidated) statements of income and retained earnings statements for the year ended December 31, 19X5, and the balance sheets as of December 31, 19X5, of Pace Company and its subsidiary, Smith Company, are as follows:

Condensed Statements of Income	Pace Company	Smith Company
Sales	$(4,000,000)	$(1,700,000)
Cost of goods sold	2,982,000	1,015,000
Operating expenses	400,000	377,200
Dividend income..................................	(75,000)	
Subsidiary income	(232,000)	
Interest expense		7,800
Net income......................................	$ (925,000)	$ (300,000)

	Pace Company	Smith Company
Retained Earnings Statements		
Balance, January 1, 19X5	$(2,100,000)	$ (640,000)
Net income......................................	(925,000)	(300,000)
Dividends declared...............................	170,000	100,000
Balance, December 31, 19X5	$(2,855,000)	$ (840,000)
Balance Sheets		
Cash..	$ 486,000	$ 249,600
Accounts receivable	235,000	185,000
Inventories	475,000	355,000
Machinery and equipment (net).....................	2,231,000	530,000
Investment in stock of Smith Company	954,000	
Investment in bonds of Smith Company	58,000	
Accounts payable	(384,000)	(62,000)
Bonds payable...................................		(120,000)
Unamortized discount on bonds payable		2,400
Common stock, Pace Company......................	(1,200,000)	
Common stock, Smith Company.....................		(250,000)
Paid-in capital in excess of par....................		(50,000)
Retained earnings (carried down)	(2,855,000)	(840,000)
Total...	0	0

Additional information:

(a) On January 3, 19X3, Pace acquired from the sole stockholder of Smith Company a patent valued at $40,000 and 80% of the outstanding common stock of Smith. Pace's total cost of the transaction was $440,000 in cash. The net book value of Smith stock on the date of acquisition was $500,000, and the book values of the individual assets and liabilities were equal to their fair market values. Pace charged the entire $440,000 to the account, Investment in Stock of Smith Company. The patent, for which no amortization had been charged, had a remaining legal life of 4 years as of January 3, 19X3.

(b) On July 1, 19X5, Pace reduced its interest in Smith Company stock to 75% by selling shares for $70,000 to an unaffiliated company at a profit of $16,000. Pace recorded the proceeds as a credit to its investment account.

(c) For the 6 months ended June 30, 19X5, Smith had a net income of $140,000. Pace recorded 80% of this amount on its books of account prior to the time of sale.

(d) During 19X4, Smith sold merchandise to Pace for $130,000, which was at a markup of 30% over Smith's cost. On January 1, 19X5, $52,000 of this merchandise remained in Pace's inventory. This merchandise subsequently was sold by Pace in February 19X5 at a profit of $8,000.

(e) In November 19X5, Pace sold merchandise to Smith for the first time. Pace's cost for this merchandise was $80,000, and the sale was made at 120% of cost. Smith's inventory at December 31, 19X5, contained $24,000 of the merchandise that was purchased from Pace.

(f) On December 31, 19X5, there was a $45,000 payment in transit from Smith Company to Pace Company. Accounts Receivable and Accounts Payable include intercompany receivables and payables.

(g) In December 19X5, Smith declared and paid cash dividends of $100,000 to its stockholders.

(h) On December 31, 19X5, Pace purchased, for $58,000, 50% of the outstanding bonds issued by Smith. The bonds mature on December 31, 19X9, and originally were issued at a discount. On December 31, 19X5, the balance in Smith's account, Unamortized Discount on Bonds Payable, was $2,400. It is the intention of the management of Pace to hold these bonds until their maturity.

Required:

Prepare the worksheet in vertical format for the consolidated financial statements of Pace Company and its subsidiary as of December 31, 19X5. Include the determination and distribution of excess and income distribution schedules.

(AICPA adapted)

APPENDIX PROBLEMS

Problem 7A-1. Prior to January 1, 19X7, the stockholders of East Company and West Company approved the merger of the two companies. On January 1, 19X7, 5,000 shares of East Company $10 par common stock were issued and recorded at par value to West Company stockholders in exchange for the 3,000 shares of West Company $20 par common stock outstanding. The transaction met the criteria for a pooling of interest.

The following December 31, 19X7 balance sheets have been prepared.

Assets	East Company	West Company
Cash	$ 36,400	$ 28,200
Notes receivable	22,000	9,000
Notes receivable discounted	(8,100)	
Accounts receivable	20,900	21,700
Interest receivable	13,000	3,300
Dividends receivable		
Inventories	81,200	49,600
Property, plant, and equipment	83,200	43,500
Accumulated depreciation	(12,800)	(9,300)
Investment in West Company	50,000	
Total assets	$285,800	$146,000

Liabilities and Stockholders' Equity		
Notes payable	$ 4,000	$ 12,000
Accounts payable	42,000	19,600
Dividends payable		4,500
Interest payable	2,600	2,100
Common stock—East	120,000	
Paid-in capital in excess of par—East	28,500	
Retained earnings—East	88,700	
Common stock—West		60,000
Paid-in capital in excess of par—West		20,000
Retained earnings—West		27,800
Total liabilities and stockholders' equity	$285,800	$146,000

The following additional information is available:

(a) Net income for 19X7 (disregard income taxes):

East Company................................ $21,700

West Company 10,200

(b) On December 31, 19X7, West Company owed East Company $16,000 on open account and $8,000 in interest-bearing notes. East Company discounted $3,000 on the notes received from West Company with the First State Bank.

(c) On December 31, 19X7, West Company accrued interest payable of $120 on the notes payable to East Company: $40 on the note of $3,000 discounted with the bank and $80 on the remaining note of $5,000. East Company did not accrue interest receivable from West Company.

(d) During 19X7, East Company sold merchandise, which cost $30,000, to West Company for $40,000. West Company's December 31 inventory included $10,000 of this merchandise priced at West Company's cost.

(e) On July 1, West Company sold equipment, which had a book value of $15,000, to East Company for $17,000. East Company recorded depreciation on the equipment in the amount of $850 for 19X7. The remaining life of the equipment at the date of sale was 10 years.

(f) West Company shipped merchandise to East Company on December 31, 19X7, and recorded an account receivable of $6,000 for the sale. West Company's cost for the merchandise was $4,800. Because the merchandise was in transit, East Company did not record the transaction. The terms of the sale were F.O.B. shipping point.

(g) West Company declared a dividend of $1.50 per share on December 30, 19X7, payable on January 1, 19X8. East Company made no entry for the declaration.

Required:

Using the balance-sheet-only method of consolidation, complete the December 31, 19X7 worksheet for East Company and its subsidiary.

Suggestion: The investment was improperly recorded at par value. The equity of West must be added to East following the equity transfer rules.

Problem 7A-2. The December 31, 19X9 post-closing trial balances of Encanto Corporation and its subsidiary, Norris Corporation, are as follows:

	Encanto Corporation	Norris Corporation
Cash...	167,250	101,000
Accounts Receivable	178,450	72,000
Notes Receivable	87,500	28,000
Dividends Receivable................................	36,000	
Inventories	122,000	68,000
Property, Plant, and Equipment......................	487,000	252,000
Accumulated Depreciation	(117,000)	(64,000)
Investment in Norris Corporation	240,800	
Accounts Payable....................................	(222,000)	(76,000)
Notes Payable	(79,000)	(89,000)
Dividends Payable		(40,000)
Common Stock ($10 par)..........................	(400,000)	(100,000)
Retained Earnings...................................	(501,000)	(152,000)
Total...	0	0

The following additional information is available:

(a) Encanto initially acquired 60% of the outstanding common stock of Norris in 19X7. There was no difference between the cost and book value of the net assets acquired. As of December 31, 19X9, the percentage owned is 90%. An analysis of the investment in Norris Corporation account is as follows:

	Description	Amount
December 31, 19X7	Acquired 6,000 shares	$ 70,800
December 31, 19X8	60% of 19X8 net income of $78,000	46,800
September 1, 19X9	Acquired 3,000 shares	92,000
December 31, 19X9	Subsidiary income for 19X9	67,200*
December 31, 19X9	90% of dividends declared	(36,000)
Investment balance, December 31, 19X9		$240,800

*Subsidiary income for 19X9:

60% × $96,000	$57,600
30% × $96,000 × 33-1/3%	9,600
Total	$67,200

Norris net income is earned ratably during the year. Amortization of the excess of cost over the net assets acquired is being recorded over 60 months.

(b) On December 15, 19X9, Norris declared a cash dividend of $4 per share of common stock, payable to shareholders on January 7, 19Y0.

(c) During 19X9, Encanto sold merchandise to Norris. Encanto's cost for this merchandise was $68,000, and the sale was made at 125% of cost. Norris's inventory at December 31, 19X9, included merchandise purchased from Encanto at a cost to Norris of $35,000.

(d) In December, 19X8, Norris sold merchandise to Encanto for $67,000, which was at a markup of 35% over Norris's cost. On January 1, 19X9, $54,000 of this merchandise remained in Encanto's inventory. This merchandise subsequently was sold by Encanto at a profit of $11,000 during 19X9.

(e) On October 1, 19X9, Encanto sold excess equipment to Norris for $42,000. Data relating to this equipment are as follows:

Book value on Encanto's records	$36,000
Method of depreciation	Straight-line
Estimated remaining life on October 1, 19X9	10 years

(f) Near the end of 19X9, Norris reduced the balance of its intercompany account payable to zero by transferring $8,000 to Encanto. This payment still was in transit on December 31, 19X9.

Required:

Prepare the worksheet necessary to produce the consolidated balance sheet of Encanto Corporation and its subsidiary as of December 31, 19X9. Include the determination and distribution of excess schedule for Encanto's purchase of Norris common stock on September 1, 19X9.

(AICPA Adapted)

Problem 7A-3.   Case Inc. acquired all of the outstanding $25 par common stock of Frey Inc. on June 30, 19X4, in exchange for 40,000 shares of its $25 par common stock. The business combination meets all the criteria for a pooling of interests. On June 30, 19X4,

Case Inc. common stock closed at $65 per share on a national stock exchange. Both corporations continued to operate as separate businesses, maintaining separate accounting records with years ending December 31.

Additional information is as follows:

(a) Case Inc. uses the simple equity method to account for its investment in Frey. The investment account has not been adjusted to reflect intercompany transactions.

(b) On June 30, 19X4, Frey's assets and liabilities had market values equal to book values, except for the land which had a market value of $550,000.

(c) On June 30, 19X4, Frey paid cash dividends of $4 per share on its common stock.

(d) On December 10, 19X4, Case paid a cash dividend totaling $256,000 on its common stock.

(e) On June 30, 19X4, immediately before the combination, the stockholders' equities were:

	Case Inc.	Frey Inc.
Common stock	$2,200,000	$1,000,000
Additional paid-in capital.	1,660,000	190,000
Retained earnings.	3,036,000	980,000
Total.	$6,896,000	$2,170,000

(f) Frey's long-term debt consisted of 10-year, 10% bonds issued at face value on March 31, 19W8. Interest is payable semiannually on March 31 and September 30. Case had purchased Frey's bonds at the face value of $320,000 in 19W8, and there has not been any change in ownership.

(g) During October, 19X4, Case sold merchandise to Frey at a total invoice price of $720,000, which included a profit of $180,000. At December 31, 19X4, one-half of the merchandise remained in Frey's inventory, and Frey had not paid Case for the merchandise purchased.

(h) The 19X4 net income amounts per the separate books of Case and Frey were $890,000 (exclusive of equity in Frey earnings) and $580,000, respectively.

(i) The retained earnings balances at December 31, 19X3, were $2,506,000 and $820,000 for Case and Frey, respectively.

(j) On December 31, 19X4, the companies had the folowing post-closing trial balances:

	Case Inc.	Frey Inc.
Cash.	825,000	330,000
Accounts and Other Current Receivables	2,140,000	835,000
Inventories	2,310,000	1,045,000
Land.	650,000	300,000
Depreciable Assets (net)	4,575,000	1,980,000
Investment in Frey Inc..	2,430,000	
Long-Term Investments and Other Assets.	865,000	385,000
Accounts Payable and Other Current Liabilities	(2,465,000)	(1,145,000)
Long-Term Debt	(1,900,000)	(1,300,000)
Common Stock ($25 par).	(3,200,000)	(1,000,000)
Additional Paid-In Capital	(1,850,000)	(190,000)
Retained Earnings.	(4,380,000)	(1,240,000)
Total.	0	0

Required:
(1) Prepare the worksheet necessary to produce the consolidated balance sheet of Case Inc. and its subsidiary for the year ended December 31, 19X4.
(2) Prepare the formal consolidated statement of retained earnings for December 31, 19X4.

Problem 7A-4. On January 1, 19X1, Press Company acquired 90% of the common stock of Solid Company for $317,000. On this date, Solid had total owner's equity of $270,000, including retained earnings of $100,000.

On January 1, 19X1, any excess of cost over book value is attributable to the undervaluation of land, building, and goodwill. Land is worth $20,000 more than cost. Building is worth $40,000 more than book value. It has a remaining useful life of 6 years and is depreciated using the straight-line method. Goodwill is to be amortized over 10 years.

During 19X1 and 19X2, Press has appropriately accounted for its investment in Solid using the simple equity method.

During 19X2, Solid sold merchandise to Press for $40,000, of which $15,000 is held by Press on December 31, 19X2. Solid's usual gross profit on affiliated sales is 40%. On December 31, 19X2, Press still owes Solid $8,000 for merchandise acquired in December.

On October 1, 19X0, Solid sold $100,000 par value of 10-year, 10% bonds for $102,000. The bonds pay interest semiannually on April 1 and October 1. Straight-line amortization is used. On October 2, 19X1, Press repurchased $60,000 par value of the bonds for $59,100. Straight-line amortization is used.

On January 1, 19X2, Press purchased equipment for $111,332 and immediately leased the equipment to Solid on a 3-year lease. The minimum lease payments of $40,000 are to be made annually on January 1, beginning immediately, for a total of three payments. The implicit interest rate is 8%. The useful life of the equipment is 3 years. The lease has been capitalized by both companies. Solid is depreciating the equipment using the straight-line method and assuming a salvage value of $6,332. A lease amortization schedule, applicable to both companies, follows:

Carrying Value on	Carrying Value	Interest Rate	Interest	Payment	Principal Reduction
1/1/19X1	111,332				
	−40,000				
1/1/19X2	71,332	8%	5,707	40,000	34,293
	−34,293				
1/1/19X3	37,039	8%	2,961*	40,000	37,039
	−37,039				
1/1/19X4	0				

* Adjusted for rounding error.

The balance sheet for the firms on December 31, 19X2, was as follows:

Assets	Press Company	Solid Company
Accounts receivable	72,000	50,000
Bond interest receivable................................	1,500	
Minimum lease payments receivable	80,000	
Unearned interest income	(2,961)	
Inventory...	86,000	80,000
Other current assets	60,236	183,668
Investment in Solid Company...........................	344,000	
Investment in Solid bonds..............................	59,225	
Land...	60,000	30,000
Buildings and equipment...............................	300,000	230,000
Accumulated depreciation..............................	(100,000)	(50,000)
Equipment under capital lease		111,332
Accumulated depreciated equipment under lease		(35,000)
Total	$960,000	$600,000

Liabilities and Equity

	Press Company	Solid Company
Accounts payable	$ 78,000	$ 70,000
Bond interest payable..................................		2,500
Lease interest payable		5,707
Other current liabilities................................	57,000	48,911
Lease obligation payable		71,332
Bonds payable	150,000	100,000
Premium on bonds		1,550
Common stock—Press..................................	200,000	
Other paid-in capital—Press	150,000	
Retained earnings—Press	325,000	
Common stock—Solid..................................		100,000
Other paid-in capital—Solid		70,000
Retained earnings—Solid		130,000
Total	$960,000	$600,000

Required:

Complete the worksheet for a consolidated balance sheet as of December 31, 19X2. Round all computations to the nearest dollar.

WORKSHEET 7-1

Investment Acquired in Blocks; Immediate Control
Company P and Subsidiary Company S
Worksheet for Consolidated Financial Statements
For Year Ended December 31, 19X3

	(Credit balance amounts are in parentheses.)	Trial Balance	
		Company P	Company S
1	Current Assets	60,000	130,000
2	Investment in Company S	228,000	
3			
4			
5			
6	Building	400,000	80,000
7	Accumulated Depreciation—Building	(100,000)	(5,000)
8	Equipment		150,000
9	**Accumulated Depreciation—Equipment**		**(90,000)**
10			
11	Goodwill		
12			
13	Liabilities	(100,000)	(30,000)
14	Common Stock, Co. P	(200,000)	
15	**Retained Earnings, Jan. 1, 19X3, Co. P**	**(210,000)**	
16			
17	Common Stock, Co. S		(100,000)
18	Retained Earnings, Jan. 1, 19X3, Co. S		(100,000)
19	Sales	(400,000)	(200,000)
20	Cost of Goods Sold	300,000	120,000
21	**Expenses**	**50,000**	**45,000**
22			
23			
24			
25	Subsidiary Income	(28,000)	
26		0	0
27	Combined Net Income		
28	To Minority Interest (see distribution schedule)		
29	Balance to Controlling Interest (see distribution schedule)		
30	Total Minority Interest		
31	Retained Earnings, Controlling Interest, Dec. 31, 19X3		
32			

Worksheet 7-1 (see page 408)

Eliminations & Adjustments				Consolidated Income Statement	Minority Interest	Controlling Retained Earnings	Consolidated Balance Sheet	
Dr.		Cr.						
							190,000	1
		(1)	28,000					2
		(2)	160,000					3
		(3a)	30,000					4
		(4a)	10,000					5
							480,000	6
							(105,000)	7
							150,000	8
(3a)	18,000	(3b)	10,800				(79,600)	9
(4a)	4,800	(4b)	1,600					10
(3a)	12,000	(3c)	3,600				13,080	11
(4a)	5,200	(4c)	520					12
							(130,000)	13
							(200,000)	14
(3b)	7,200					(200,400)		15
(3c)	2,400							16
(2)	80,000				(20,000)			17
(2)	80,000				(20,000)			18
				(600,000)				19
				420,000				20
(3b)	3,600			101,920				21
(3c)	1,200							22
(4b)	1,600							23
(4c)	520							24
(1)	28,000							25
	244,520		244,520					26
				(78,080)				27
				7,000*	(7,000)			28
				71,080*		(71,080)		29
					(47,000)		(47,000)	30
						(271,480)	(271,480)	31
							0	32

(continued)

Eliminations and Adjustments:

(1) Eliminate the parent's entry recognizing 80% of the subsidiary net income for the current year. This step restores the investment account to its balance at the beginning of the year, so that it can be eliminated against Company S beginning-of-the-year equity balances.

(2) Eliminate the 80% controlling interest in beginning-of-the-year subsidiary equity accounts against the investment account. The 60% and 20% investments could be eliminated separately if desired.

(3a) The $30,000 excess of cost on the original 60% investment is distributed to the accumulated depreciation and goodwill accounts according to the determination and distribution of excess schedule prepared on January 1, 19X1.

(b) Since the equipment has a 5-year remaining life on January 1, 19X1, the depreciation should be increased $3,600 per year for 3 years. This entry corrects the controlling retained earnings for the past 2 years by $7,200 and corrects the current depreciation expense by $3,600.

(c) The $12,000 original goodwill is to be amortized $1,200 per year for 3 years. The controlling retained earnings must be corrected for 2 past years ($2,400), and the current year's expenses are increased by $1,200.

(4a) The $10,000 excess of cost on the 20% block is distributed to the accumulated depreciation and goodwill accounts according to the determination and distribution of excess schedule prepared on January 1, 19X3.

(b) The $4,800 excess attributable to the equipment is to be depreciated over 3 years. Therefore, current expenses are increased by $1,600.

(c) The $5,200 increase to the goodwill account is to be amortized over 10 years, requiring current expenses to be increased by $520.

Subsidiary Company S Income Distribution

	Internally generated net income..........	$35,000
	Adjusted income	$35,000
	Minority share	20%
	Minority interest......................	$ 7,000*

Parent Company P Income Distribution

Equipment depreciation:			Internally generated net income..........	$50,000
Block 1, 60% ....(3b)	$3,600		80% × Company S adjusted income of	
Block 2, 20% ....(4b)	1,600		$35,000.............................	28,000
Goodwill amortization:				
Block 1, 60%.....................(3c)	1,200			
Block 2, 20%.....................(4c)	520			
			Controlling interest	$71,080*

WORKSHEET 7-2

Investment Acquired in Blocks; Control Achieved with Second Block
Company P and Subsidiary Company S
Worksheet for Consolidated Financial Statements
For Year Ended December 31, 19X2

		Trial Balance	
	(Credit balance amounts are in parentheses.)	Company P	Company S
1	Current Assets	69,900	85,000
2	Investment in Company S	196,100	
3			
4			
5			
6	Building and Equipment	300,000	150,000
7	**Accumulated Depreciation—Building and Equipment**	**(200,000)**	**(30,000)**
8	**Goodwill**		
9			
10	Liabilities		(20,000)
11	Common Stock, Co. P	(100,000)	
12	Retained Earnings, Jan. 1, 19X2, Co. P	(200,000)	
13	Common Stock, Co. S		(50,000)
14	Retained Earnings, Jan. 1, 19X2, Co. S		(115,000)
15	Sales	(300,000)	(100,000)
16	Cost of Goods Sold	200,000	60,000
17	**Expenses**	**50,000**	**20,000**
18			
19			
20	Subsidiary Income	(16,000)	
21		0	0
22	Combined Net Income		
23	To Minority Interest (see distribution schedule)		
24	Balance to Controlling Interest (see distribution schedule)		
25	Total Minority Interest		
26	Retained Earnings, Controlling Interest, Dec. 31, 19X2		
27			

Worksheet 7-2 (see page 412)

Eliminations & Adjustments				Consolidated Income Statement	Minority Interest	Controlling Retained Earnings	Consolidated Balance Sheet	
Dr.		Cr.						
							154,900	1
		(1)	16,000					2
		(2)	132,000					3
		(3a)	17,100					4
		(4a)	31,000					5
							450,000	6
(4a)	5,400	(4b)	600				(225,200)	7
(3a)	17,100	(3b)	900				40,520	8
(4a)	25,600	(4c)	1,280					9
							(20,000)	10
							(100,000)	11
						(200,000)		12
(2)	40,000				(10,000)			13
(2)	92,000				(23,000)			14
				(400,000)				15
				260,000				16
(3b)	900			72,780				17
(4b)	600							18
(4c)	1,280							19
(1)	16,000							20
	198,880		198,880					21
				(67,220)				22
				4,000*	(4,000)			23
				63,220*		(63,220)		24
					(37,000)		(37,000)	25
						(263,220)	(263,220)	26
							0	27

(continued)

Eliminations and Adjustments:

(1) Eliminate the parent's entry recognizing the 80% interest in subsidiary net income under the simple equity method. This step restores the investment account to its balance at the beginning of the year.

(2) Eliminate the 80% controlling interest in beginning-of-the-year subsidiary equity accounts against the investment account. If desired, the two investment blocks may be eliminated separately.

(3a) The remaining excess of cost over book value on the original 20% investment is $17,100 ($18,000 less 1 year of $900 amortization). It must be remembered that under the sophisticated equity method, amortization entries prior to securing control reduce the investment account. Always remember that *only the unamortized original excess remains*. The remaining $17,100 excess is carried to the goodwill account according to the determination and distribution of excess schedule prepared on January 1, 19X1.

(b) Goodwill amortization of $900 is recorded for the current year. Recall that no amortization is needed for periods prior to achieving control, since that amortization was recorded previously through the parent's investment account. Thus, the controlling retained earnings is reduced already.

(4a) The excess attributable to the January 1, 19X2 60% acquisition is distributed to the accumulated depreciation and goodwill accounts according to the determination and distribution of excess schedule for this second acquisition.

(b) Depreciation for the current year is increased $600 according to the January 1, 19X2 determination and distribution of excess schedule.

(c) Goodwill amortization of $1,280 increases expenses for the current year as required by the January 1, 19X2 determination and distribution of excess schedule.

Subsidiary Company S Income Distribution

	Internally generated net income..........	$20,000
	Adjusted income	$20,000
	Minority share	20%
	Minority interest.....................	$ 4,000*

Parent Company P Income Distribution

Equipment depreciation:			Internally generated net income..........	$50,000
Block 2, 60% ....(4b)	$	600	80% × Company S adjusted income of	
Goodwill amortization:			$20,000.............................	16,000
Block 1, 20% ....(3b)		900		
Block 2, 60%...................(4c)		1,280	Controlling interest	$63,220*

WORKSHEET 7-3

Investment Acquired in Blocks; Control Achieved with Second Purchase;
Cost Method on First Investment
Company P and Subsidiary Company S
Worksheet for Consolidated Financial Statements
For Year Ended December 31, 19X2

	(Credit balance amounts are in parentheses.)	Trial Balance	
		Company P	Company S
1	Current Assets	93,900	85,000
2	**Investment in Company S**	**168,000**	
3			
4			
5			
6	Building and Equipment	300,000	150,000
7	**Accumulated Depreciation—Building and Equipment**	**(200,000)**	**(30,000)**
8	**Goodwill**		
9			
10	Liabilities		(20,000)
11	Common Stock, Co. P	(100,000)	
12	**Retained Earnings, Jan. 1, 19X2, Co. P**	**(197,900)**	
13	Common Stock, Co. S		(50,000)
14	Retained Earnings, Jan. 1, 19X2, Co. S		(115,000)
15	Sales	(300,000)	(100,000)
16	Cost of Goods Sold	200,000	60,000
17	Expenses	50,000	20,000
18			
19			
20	Subsidiary Income	(14,000)	
21		0	0
22	Combined Net Income		
23	To Minority Interest (see distribution schedule)		
24	Balance to Controlling Interest (see distribution schedule)		
25	Total Minority Interest		
26	Retained Earnings, Controlling Interest, Dec. 31, 19X2		
27			

Worksheet 7-3 (see page 413)

Eliminations & Adjustments				Consolidated Income Statement	Minority Interest	Controlling Retained Earnings	Consolidated Balance Sheet	
Dr.		Cr.						
							178,900	1
(C)	1,500	(1)	14,000					2
		(2)	115,500					3
		(3a)	9,000					4
		(4a)	31,000					5
							450,000	6
(4a)	5,400	(4b)	600				(225,200)	7
(3a)	9,000	(3b)	900				32,420	8
(4a)	25,600	(4c)	1,280					9
							(20,000)	10
							(100,000)	11
(3b)	450	(C)	1,500			(198,950)		12
(2)	35,000				(15,000)			13
(2)	80,500				(34,500)			14
				(400,000)				15
				260,000				16
(3b)	450			72,330				17
(4b)	600							18
(4c)	1,280							19
(1)	14,000							20
	173,780		173,780					21
				(67,670)				22
				6,000*	(6,000)			23
				61,670*		(61,670)		24
					(55,500)		(55,500)	25
						(260,620)	(260,620)	26
							0	27

(continued)

Eliminations and Adjustments:

(C) Convert the original 10% investment to the simple equity method: 10% × $15,000 change in Company S Retained Earnings.

(1) Eliminate the parent's entry recognizing the 70% interest in subsidiary net income under the simple equity method. This step restores the investment account to its balance at the beginning of the year.

(2) The 70% controlling interest in the beginning-of-the-year subsidiary equity accounts is eliminated against the investment account.

(3a) The original excess of cost on the 10% investment ($9,000) still is contained in the investment account and now can be recognized as goodwill according to the January 1, 19X1 determination and distribution of excess schedule.

(b) Goodwill for the past year and current year is amortized at $450 per year. Note that the Company P beginning-of-the-year retained earnings is corrected for the prior year's goodwill amortization. Amortization was not recorded previously since the cost method was in use.

(4a) The excess attributable to the January 1, 19X2 60% acquisition is distributed to the accumulated depreciation and goodwill accounts according to the determination and distribution of excess schedule for the 60% block on January 1, 19X2.

(b) Depreciation for the current year is increased $600.

(c) Goodwill of $1,280 is amortized for the current year.

Subsidiary Company S Income Distribution

	Internally generated net income..........	$20,000
	Adjusted income	$20,000
	Minority share	30%
	Minority interest.......................	$ 6,000*

Parent Company P Income Distribution

Equipment depreciation:			Internally generated net income..........		$50,000
Block 2, 60% ....(4b)	$ 600		70% × Company S adjusted income of		
Goodwill amortization:			$20,000.............................		14,000
Block 1, 10% ....(3b)	450				
Block 2, 60%.....................(4c)	1,280				
			Controlling interest		$61,670*

WORKSHEET 7-4

Sale of Subsidiary Interest During Period; No Loss of Control
Company P and Subsidiary Company S
Worksheet for Consolidated Financial Statements
For Year Ended December 31, 19X3

	(Credit balance amounts are in parentheses.)	Trial Balance	
		Company P	Company S
1	Investment in Company S (60%)	244,500	
2			
3			
4	Equipment	600,000	100,000
5	Accumulated Depreciation—Equipment	(100,000)	(60,000)
6	Other Assets	581,500	305,000
7	Goodwill		
8	Common Stock, Co. P	(500,000)	
9	Retained Earnings, Jan. 1, 19X3, Co. P	(700,000)	
10			
11	Common Stock, Co. S		(100,000)
12	Retained Earnings, Jan. 1, 19X3, Co. S		(215,000)
13	Sales	(500,000)	(200,000)
14	Cost of Goods Sold	350,000	140,000
15	Expenses	50,000	30,000
16			
17			
18	**Gain on Sale of Subsidiary Stock, Co. P**	**(6,475)**	
19	Subsidiary Income	(19,525)	
20			
21	**Income Sold to Minority (second 20% block)**		
22		0	0
23	Combined Net Income		
24	To Minority Interest (see distribution schedule)		
25	Balance to Controlling Interest (see distribution schedule)		
26	Total Minority Interest		
27	Retained Earnings, Controlling Interest, Dec. 31, 19X3		
28			

Worksheet 7-4 (see page 422)

Eliminations & Adjustments				Consolidated Income Statement	Minority Interest	Controlling Retained Earnings	Consolidated Balance Sheet	
Dr.		Cr.						
		(2)	18,000					1
		(3)	189,000					2
		(4)	37,500					3
							700,000	4
(4)	15,000	(5)	9,000				(154,000)	5
							886,500	6
(4)	22,500	(6)	6,750				15,750	7
							(500,000)	8
(5)	6,000					(689,500)		9
(6)	4,500							10
(3)	60,000				(40,000)			11
(3)	129,000				(86,000)			12
				(700,000)				13
				490,000				14
(1)	875			86,125				15
(5)	3,000							16
(6)	2,250							17
				(6,475)				18
(1)	1,525							19
(2)	18,000							20
		(1)	2,400		(2,400)			21
	262,650		262,650					22
				(130,350)				23
				9,600*	(9,600)			24
				120,750*		(120,750)		25
					(138,000)		(138,000)	26
						(810,250)	(810,250)	27
							0	28

(continued)

Eliminations and Adjustments:

(1) The income earned by the parent on the 20% interest sold on July 1, though earned by the controlling interest, now belongs to the minority interest. The minority interest owns 20% of the reported subsidiary income for the half-year ($12,000), which is $2,400. The minority is unaffected by amortizations resulting from a previous price paid by the parent. Note that step (1) credits the account, Income Sold to Minority, to accomplish the transfer of the income to the minority interest. The offsetting debits are explained as follows:

20% of subsidiary income for the first six months, adjusted for one-fourth of the parent's half-year amortization of excess) or (20% × $12,000) − [1/4 × 1/2 × ($4,000 + $3,000)]	$1,525
Depreciation adjustment (1/4 × 1/2 × $4,000)	500
Goodwill amortization (1/4 × 1/2 × $3,000)	375
Total debits	$2,400

   Amortizations based on an 80% interest for the first half of the year are proper, since the consolidation involves an 80% controlling interest for the first half of the year and a 60% controlling interest for the second half of the year.

(2) Eliminate the parent's entry recording its 60% share of subsidiary net income of $30,000. This step restores the 60% interest to its simple-equity-adjusted cost at the beginning of the year, so that the investment can be eliminated against subsidiary equity balances at the beginning of the year.

(3) Eliminate 60% of the subsidiary equity balances at the beginning of the year against the investment account. An excess cost of $37,500 remains. This amount is three-fourths (60% ÷ 80%) of the original excess shown on page 415, since only a 60% interest is retained, as compared to an original investment of 80%.

(4) Since only three-fourths of the original investment remains, 75% of the excesses shown in the original determination and distribution of excess schedule on page 415 are recorded.

(5) 75% of the original $4,000 annual depreciation adjustments are recorded for the past two years and the current year. Note that the remaining depreciation adjustments applicable to the interest sold are recorded already.

(6) 75% of the original $3,000 annual goodwill amortization is recorded for the past two years and the current year. Again, amortizations of goodwill applicable to the interest sold have been recorded already.

Subsidiary Company S Income Distribution

	Internally generated net income, ...	$ 30,000
	Adjusted income	$ 30,000
	Minority share	40%
	Minority interest for full year	$ 12,000
	Less income purchased (20% × $12,000,	
	first 6 months)	**2,400**
	Minority interest	$ 9,600*

Parent Company P Income Distribution

Depreciation adjustment on 60% interest . . . . (5) $3,000	Internally generated net income	$100,000
Goodwill amortization on 60% interest . . . . (6) 2,250		
	Adjusted income	$ 94,750
	60% × Company S income of $30,000. . . .	18,000
	20% × Company S income for first 6	
	months (net of amortization)	**1,525**
	Gain on sale of subsidiary interest	**6,475**
	Controlling interest	$120,750*

WORKSHEET 7-5

Subsidiary Preferred Stock, None Owned by Parent
Company P and Subsidiary Company S
Worksheet for Consolidated Financial Statements
For Year Ended December 31, 19X5

	(Credit balance amounts are in parentheses.)	Trial Balance	
		Company P	Company S
1	Current Assets	259,600	150,000
2	Property, Plant, and Equipment (net)	400,000	250,000
3	Investment in Common Stock of Company S	195,600	
4			
5			
6	Goodwill		
7	Liabilities	(150,000)	(45,000)
8	Common Stock, Co. P	(200,000)	
9	Retained Earnings, Jan. 1, 19X5, Co. P	(340,000)	
10	Preferred Stock ($100 par), Co. S		(100,000)
11	**Retained Earnings Allocated to Preferred Stock, Jan. 1, 19X5, Co. S**		
12	Common Stock ($10 par), Co. S		(100,000)
13	Retained Earnings, Jan. 1, 19X5, Co. S		(130,000)
14			
15	Sales	(450,000)	(200,000)
16	Cost of Goods Sold	200,000	150,000
17	Expenses	100,000	25,000
18	Subsidiary Income	(15,200)	
19		0	0
20	Combined Net Income		
21	To Minority Interest (see distribution schedule)		
22	Balance to Controlling Interest (see distribution schedule)		
23	Total Minority Interest		
24	Retained Earnings, Controlling Interest, Dec. 31, 19X5		
25			

Eliminations and Adjustments:
(1) Distribute the beginning-of-the-period subsidiary retained earnings into the portions allocable to common and preferred stock. The typical procedure would be to consider the stated subsidiary retained earnings as applicable to common and to remove the preferred portion. This distribution reflects 4 years of arrearage (as of January 1, 19X5) at $6,000 per year.

Worksheet 7-5 (see page 426)

Eliminations & Adjustments		Consolidated Income Statement	Minority Interest	Controlling Retained Earnings	Consolidated Balance Sheet	
Dr.	Cr.					
					409,600	1
					650,000	2
	(2) 15,200					3
	(3) 164,800					4
	(4) 15,600					5
(4) 15,600	(5) 4,680				10,920	6
					(195,000)	7
					(200,000)	8
(5) 3,120				(336,880)		9
			(100,000)			10
	(1) 24,000		(24,000)			11
(3) 80,000			(20,000)			12
(1) 24,000			(21,200)			13
(3) 84,800						14
		(650,000)				15
		350,000				16
(5) 1,560		126,560				17
(2) 15,200						18
224,280	224,280					19
		(173,440)				20
		9,800	(9,800)			21
		163,640		(163,640)		22
			(175,000)		(175,000)	23
				(500,520)	(500,520)	24
					0	25

(2)   Eliminate the parent's entry recording its share of subsidiary current income.
(3)   Eliminate the pro rata subsidiary common stockholders' equity at the beginning of the period against the investment account. This step includes elimination of the 80% of subsidiary retained earnings applicable to common stock.
(4)   Distribute the excess of cost according to the determination and distribution of excess schedule.
(5)   Amortize the goodwill for the past 2 years and the current year.

(continued)

Subsidiary Company S Income Distribution

Internally generated net income, (no adjustments)	$25,000
Less preferred cumulative claim to minority	(6,000*)
Common stock income	**$19,000**
Minority share	20%
Minority interest in common income	$ 3,800
Total minority interest (**$6,000*** + $3,800) . .	$ 9,800

Parent Company P Income Distribution

Amortization of goodwill . . . .(5)	$1,560	Internally generated net income	$150,000
		80% × Company S adjusted income on common stock of $19,000.	15,200
		Controlling interest.	$163,640

WORKSHEET 7-6

Subsidiary Preferred Stock Owned by Parent
Company P and Subsidiary Company S
Worksheet for Consolidated Financial Statements
For Year Ended December 31, 19X5

	(Credit balance amounts are in parentheses.)	Trial Balance	
		Company P	Company S
1	Current Assets	194,600	150,000
2	Property, Plant, and Equipment (net)	400,000	250,000
3	Investment in Company S Common Stock	195,600	
4			
5			
6	**Investment in Company S Preferred Stock**	**75,800**	
7			
8	Goodwill		
9	Liabilities	(150,000)	(45,000)
10	Common Stock, Co. P	(200,000)	
11	**Paid-In Capital in Excess of Par, Co. P**		
12	Retained Earnings, Jan. 1, 19X5, Co. P	(347,200)	
13	Preferred Stock ($100 par), Co. S		(100,000)
14	Retained Earnings Allocated to Preferred Stock, Jan. 1, 19X5, Co. S		
15	Common Stock ($10 par), Co. S		(100,000)
16	Retained Earnings, Jan. 1, 19X5, Co. S		(130,000)
17			
18	Sales	(450,000)	(200,000)
19	Cost of Goods Sold	200,000	150,000
20	Expenses	100,000	25,000
21	Subsidiary Income—Common	(15,200)	
22	**Subsidiary Income—Preferred**	**(3,600)**	
23		0	0
24	Combined Net Income		
25	To Minority Interest (see distribution schedule)		
26	Balance to Controlling Interest (see distribution schedule)		
27	Total Minority Interest		
28	Retained Earnings, Controlling Interest, Dec. 31, 19X5		
29			

Eliminations and Adjustments:

(1–5)   Same as Worksheet 7-5; the common stock investment elimination procedures are unaffected by the investment in preferred stock.

(6)   Eliminate the entry recording the parent's share of income allocable to preferred stock. If declared, intercompany preferred dividends also would have been eliminated. This adjustment restores the investment account to its beginning-of-the-period equity balance.

Worksheet 7-6 (see page 429)

Eliminations & Adjustments			Consolidated Income Statement	Minority Interest	Controlling Retained Earnings	Consolidated Balance Sheet	
Dr.		Cr.					
						344,600	1
						650,000	2
	(2)	15,200					3
	(3)	164,800					4
	(4)	15,600					5
	(6)	3,600					6
	(7)	72,200					7
(4) 15,600	(5)	4,680				10,920	8
						(195,000)	9
						(200,000)	10
	(7)	2,200				(2,200)	11
(5) 3,120					(344,080)		12
(7) 60,000				(40,000)			13
(7) 14,400	(1)	24,000		(9,600)			14
(3) 80,000				(20,000)			15
(1) 24,000				(21,200)			16
(3) 84,800							17
			(650,000)				18
			350,000				19
(5) 1,560			126,560				20
(2) 15,200							21
(6) 3,600							22
302,280		302,280					23
			(173,440)				24
			6,200	(6,200)			25
			167,240		(167,240)		26
				(97,000)		(97,000)	27
					(511,320)	(511,320)	28
						0	29

(7) The parent's ownership portion of the par value and beginning-of-the-period retained earnings applicable to preferred stock is eliminated against the balance in the investment in preferred stock account. The difference in this case was an increase in equity, and it was carried to the controlling paid-in-capital.

(continued)

Subsidiary Company S Income Distribution

Internally generated net income, (no adjustments)	$25,000
Less preferred cumulative claim:	
to minority, 40% × $6,000..............	(2,400*)
to controlling, 60% × $6,000	**(3,600)**
Common stock income	$19,000
Minority share	20%
Minority interest in common income	$ 3,800
Total minority interest ($2,400* + $3,800)..	$ 6,200

Parent Company P Income Distribution

Amortization of goodwill . . . .(5) $1,560	Internally generated net income	$150,000
	60% × Co. S income attributable to	
	preferred stock	**3,600**
	80% × Co. S adjusted income on	
	common stock of $19,000	15,200
	Controlling interest	$167,240

WORKSHEET 7-7

Balance Sheet Only
Company P and Subsidiary Company S
Worksheet for Consolidated Balance Sheet
December 31, 19X4

	(Credit balance amounts are in parentheses.)	Balance Sheet	
		Company P	Company S
1	Cash	61,936	106,535
2	Accounts Receivable	80,000	200,000
3	Inventory, Dec. 31, 19X4	60,000	150,000
4	Land	300,000	250,000
5	Building	800,000	600,000
6	Accumulated Depreciation—Building	(400,000)	(100,000)
7	Equipment	120,000	95,000
8	Accumulated Depreciation—Equipment	(70,000)	(30,000)
9	Investment in Company S Bonds	90,064	
10	Investment in Company S Stock	750,000	
11			
12	Goodwill		
13	Accounts Payable	(92,000)	(75,000)
14	Bonds Payable		(100,000)
15	Discount on Bonds Payable		3,465
16	Common Stock, Co. P	(500,000)	
17	Retained Earnings, Dec. 31, 19X4, Co. P	(1,200,000)	
18			
19			
20			
21	Common Stock, Co. S		(200,000)
22	Retained Earnings, Dec. 31, 19X4, Co. S		(900,000)
23			
24		0	0
25	Total Minority Interest		
26			

Eliminations and Adjustments:
(C) Investment in Company S Stock is converted to the simple equity method *as of December 31, 19X4,* as follows:
80% × $300,000 increase in retained earnings = $240,000.
(1) 80% of the subsidiary equity balances are eliminated against the investment in stock account.
(2) The $110,000 excess of cost is distributed according to the determination and distribution of excess schedule.
(3) The excess attributable to the building is amortized for 4 years at $3,000 per year.
(4) The excess attributable to goodwill is amortized for 4 years at $4,000 per year.
(5) The intercompany trade balance is eliminated.

Worksheet 7-7 (see page 432)

Eliminations & Adjustments				Minority Interest	Consolidated Balance Sheet	
Dr.		Cr.				
					168,471	1
		(5)	35,000		245,000	2
		(6)	16,000		194,000	3
					550,000	4
					1,400,000	5
(2)	30,000	(3)	12,000		(482,000)	6
		(7)	5,000		210,000	7
(7)	3,000				(97,000)	8
		(8)	90,064			9
(C)	240,000	(1)	880,000			10
		(2)	110,000			11
(2)	80,000	(4)	16,000		64,000	12
(5)	35,000				(132,000)	13
(8)	100,000					14
		(8)	3,465			15
					(500,000)	16
(3)	12,000	(C)	240,000		(1,402,377)	17
(4)	16,000					18
(6)	12,800	(8)	5,177			19
(7)	2,000					20
(1)	160,000			(40,000)		21
(1)	720,000	(8)	1,294	(178,094)		22
(6)	3,200					23
	1,414,000		1,414,000			24
				(218,094)	(218,094)	25
					0	26

(6) The gross profit of $16,000 (40% × $40,000) recorded by Company S and applicable to merchandise in Company P's ending inventory is deferred by reducing the inventory and retained earnings. Since the sale was made by Company S, the adjustment is allocated to the minority and controlling retained earnings.

(7) As of December 31, 19X4, $2,000 (2/5) of the profit on the equipment sale still is to be deferred. Since the sale was made by Company P, the controlling retained earnings absorbs this adjustment, and the equipment and accumulated depreciation accounts are adjusted.

(8) Investment in Company S Bonds is eliminated against the net book value of the bonds. The net gain on the worksheet retirement is allocated to the minority and controlling retained earnings, since the subsidiary originally issued the bonds.

CHAPTER 8

Subsidiary Equity Transactions, Indirect and Mutual Holdings

This chapter is concerned with subsidiary equity transactions and complicated parent ownership arrangements that affect the recording and consolidations of the parent's investment in a subsidiary. First, we will consider the impact of subsidiary equity transactions on the investment of the parent company. The subsidiary may issue stock dividends, sell additional shares of stock, or repurchase outstanding shares. Each of these transactions has an effect on the procedures used by the parent to record and to consolidate its investment in the subsidiary.

Second, this chapter will deal with more complex ownership structures. Accounting procedures will be developed for indirect holdings and mutual holdings. Indirect holdings are situations where a parent holds a controlling interest in a subsidiary and the subsidiary is, in turn, a parent of another company. A mutual holding exists when the subsidiary owns voting common stock of the parent company.

SUBSIDIARY STOCK DIVIDENDS

A subsidiary may issue stock dividends to convert retained earnings into paid-in capital. The minimum amount to be removed from retained earnings is the par value or stated value of the shares distributed. However, according to accounting principles, when the distribution does not exceed 20% to 25% of the previously outstanding shares, an amount equal to the market value of the shares should be removed from retained earnings and transferred to paid-in capital. The recording of stock dividends at market value is defended by the following statement from ARB No. 43:

> . . . a stock dividend does not, in fact, give rise to any change whatsoever in either the corporation's assets or its respective shareholders' proportionate

interests therein. However, it cannot fail to be recognized that, merely as a consequence of the expressed purpose of the transaction and its characterization as a dividend *in related notices to shareholders and the public at large, many recipients of stock dividends look upon them as distributions of corporate earnings and usually in an amount equivalent to the fair value of the additional shares received.*[1]

Accounting theory, however, is not consistent when it comes to recording the receipt of dividends by an investor. Even though the false impression of the "typical" investor is sufficient reason to allow the issuing corporation to record the market value of the shares distributed, the investor is not permitted to do likewise. In fact, the investor must not record income when stock dividends are received but must acknowledge the true impact of the transaction, which is that nothing of substance has been given or received. Thus, the investor merely makes a memo entry indicating that the cost of the original investment now is allocated to a greater number of shares. The revised number of shares is important in computing cost per share if there is a subsequent partial sale of the investment.

To review the recording of a stock dividend and to provide a basis for worksheets, assume Company P acquired an 80% interest in Company S on January 1, 19X1, at which time the following determination and distribution of excess schedule was prepared:

Price paid		$200,000
Less interest acquired:		
Common stock ($10 par).	$100,000	
Retained earnings	80,000	
Total stockholders' equity	$180,000	
Interest acquired 80%		144,000
Goodwill (10-year life)		$ 56,000 Dr

On January 2, 19X3, Company S declared and distributed a 10% stock dividend. Prior to declaration of the dividend, its stockholders' equity appeared as follows:

Common stock ($10 par)	$100,000
Retained earnings.	120,000
Total stockholders' equity.	$220,000

In the following entry to record the stock dividend, Company S acknowledged the $25 market value of the 1,000 shares distributed:

---

[1]Accounting Research and Terminology Bulletin No. 43, *Restatement and Revision of Accounting Research Bulletins* (New York: American Institute of Certified Public Accountants, 1961), Ch. 7, Sec. B, par. 10.

Retained Earnings (or Stock Dividends Declared)	25,000	
($25 market value × 1,000 shares).		
Common Stock ($10 par × 1,000 shares)		10,000
Additional Paid-In Capital from Stock Dividend		
(1,000 shares × $15 excess over par)		15,000

PARENT USING THE SIMPLE EQUITY METHOD

Continuing the example, on January 1, 19X3, Company P has a simple-equity-adjusted balance of $232,000 in its investment in Company S account, derived as follows:

Original cost		$200,000
Share of undistributed income:		
Company S retained earnings, January 1, 19X3.	$120,000	
Company S retained earnings, January 1, 19X1.	80,000	
Increase in retained earnings	$ 40,000	
Ownership interest	80%	32,000
Simple-equity-adjusted balance, January 1, 19X3		$232,000

During 19X3, Company S earned $20,000 and made no other dividend declarations. Company P would make the following entries under the simple equity method:

Receipt of stock dividend:

Jan. 2, 19X3	Memo: Investment in Company S now includes 800 added shares for a total of 8,800 shares. The parent's interest remains at 80%.

Recording of equity income:

Dec. 31, 19X3	Investment in Company S	16,000	
	Subsidiary Income.		16,000
	To record the 80% interest in Company S $20,000 reported net income for 19X3.		

The partial worksheet on page 487 lists the investment in Company S account at the December 31, 19X3 simple-equity-adjusted cost of $248,000. Note that the partial worksheet includes the redistributed capital structure of Company S which results from the stock dividend. It should be clear that the complications arising from stock dividends pertain primarily to their recording by the separate affiliated firms. There is only a minimal effect on the consolidated worksheet.

PARENT USING THE SOPHISTICATED EQUITY METHOD

Using the sophisticated equity method, the parent would have a balance in its investment in Company S account of $220,800 derived as follows:

	Partial Trial Balance		Eliminations & Adjustments	
	Company P	Company S	Dr.	Cr.
Investment in Co. S	248,000			(1) 16,000
				(2) 176,000
				(3) 56,000
Goodwill			(3) 56,000	(4) 16,800
Common Stock, Co. P	(500,000)			
Retained Earnings, Co. P	(420,000)		(4) 11,200	
Common Stock ($10 par), Co. S		(110,000)	(2) 88,000	
Additional Paid-In Capital from Stock Dividend, Co. S		(15,000)	(2) 12,000	
Retained Earnings, Co. S (reduced $25,000 for stock dividend)		(95,000)	(2) 76,000	
Subsidiary Income	(16,000)		(1) 16,000	
Expenses	30,000	18,000	(4) 5,600	

Eliminations and Adjustments:
(1)   Eliminate the parent's entry recording its share of subsidiary income for the current year. There is no complication caused by the stock dividend, since it does not constitute income to Company P.
(2)   Eliminate 80% of Company S equity balances as restructured by the stock dividend. If the subsidiary recorded the stock dividend with a debit to Stock Dividends Declared, 80% of that account would be eliminated in this step.
(3)   Distribute the excess cost to the goodwill account as required by the determination and distribution of excess schedule.
(4)   Amortize the goodwill for 3 years. Amortization for the 2 prior years reduces the controlling interest in retained earnings, while the current-year amortization reduces current combined net income.

Original cost		$200,000
Share of undistributed income:		
Company S retained earnings, January 1, 19X3.	$120,000	
Company S retained earnings, January 1, 19X1.	80,000	
Increase in retained earnings	$ 40,000	
Ownership interest	80%	32,000
Goodwill amortization, 2 years × $5,600		(11,200)
Sophisticated equity-adjusted balance, January 1, 19X1		$220,800

During 19X3, Company P would make the same memo entry as under the simple equity method to record the stock dividend. The following entry would be made to record equity income for 19X3:

Dec. 31, 19X3   Investment in Company S   10,400
                   Subsidiary Income.....................   10,400
                   To record the 80% interest in Company S
                   reported income for 19X3 less $5,600
                   amortization of goodwill.

The partial worksheet that follows would apply to the investment maintained under the sophisticated equity method. Note the following special features:

1. The investment is at the sophisticated equity balance of $231,200 ($220,800 balance on January 1, 19X3, plus $10,400 equity income for 19X3.)
2. The retained earning of Company P is $408,800. This is $11,200 less than under the simple equity method since there is $5,600 per year of goodwill amortization subtracted for 19X1 and 19X2.
3. Subsidiary income is the sophisticated equity amount of $10,400.

	Partial Trial Balance		Eliminations & Adjustments	
	Company P	Company S	Dr.	Cr.
Investment in Co. S	231,200			(1) 10,400
				(2) 176,000
				(3) 44,800
Goodwill			(3) 44,800	(4) 5,600
Common Stock, Co. P	(500,000)			
Retained Earnings, Co. P	(408,800)			
Common Stock ($10 par), Co. S		(110,000)	(2) 88,000	
Additional Paid-In Capital from Stock Dividend, Co. S		(15,000)	(2) 12,000	
Retained Earnings, Co. S (reduced $25,000 for stock dividend)		(95,000)	(2) 76,000	
Subsidiary Income	(10,400)		(1) 10,400	
Expenses	30,000	18,000	(4) 5,600	

Eliminations and Adjustments:
(1) Eliminate the parent's entry recording its share of subsidiary income for the current year. There is no complication caused by the stock dividend, since it does not constitute income to Company P.
(2) Eliminate 80% of Company S equity balances as restructured by the stock dividend. If the subsidiary recorded the stock dividend with a debit to Stock Dividends Declared, 80% of that account would be eliminated in this step.
(3) Distribute the remaining (8 years) excess cost to the goodwill account as required by the determination and distribution of excess schedule.
(4) Amortize the goodwill for the current year.

4. Only the goodwill remaining on January 1, 19X3, is entered when distributing the excess in step (3). Recall that the prior years' amortizations have already reduced the investment account and the parent retained earnings. Note that only the current-year amortization is made in step (4).

PARENT USING THE COST METHOD

In the preceding example, if the parent, Company P, had used the cost method to record its investment in Company S, no adjustments would have been made to the investment account. The investment in Company S still would be carried at its original cost of $200,000 on the December 31, 19X3 worksheet.

The declaration of a stock dividend by a subsidiary requires a more difficult process for the conversion of the parent's investment account from a cost to a simple equity basis. The conversion must reflect all the changes in subsidiary retained earnings since acquisition, including the retained earnings transferred to paid-in capital as a result of a stock dividend. The correct simple equity conversion would be made as follows for the preceding example:

Retained earnings, January 2, 19X3 (after stock dividend)	$95,000
Retained earnings, January 1, 19X1	80,000
Change in retained earnings balance	$15,000
Retained earnings transferred to paid-in capital ($25 × 1,000 shares) as a result of stock dividend	25,000
Total change in retained earnings	$40,000
Ownership interest	80%
Simple equity conversion	$32,000

A faster approach to the simple equity conversion is to consider the change in total subsidiary stockholders' equity available to common stockholders as follows:

Subsidiary equity, January 1, 19X3	$220,000
Subsidiary equity, January 1, 19X1	180,000
Net change	$ 40,000
Ownership interest	80%
Simple equity conversion	$ 32,000

Normally, a parent will maintain a permanent file with the needed information for this adjustment. This faster method, however, could be useful in later years if facts surrounding the stock dividend were not readily available. The faster procedure will work well, provided in the interim periods there have been no other changes in subsidiary paid-in capital, such as a subsidiary sale or retirement of its shares.

The $32,000 simple equity conversion would be the first step on a worksheet when the cost method is used for the subsidiary investment. This step converts the investment in subsidiary account to its simple equity balance at the beginning of 19X3. The entry would be:

```
Investment in Company S ...............................  32,000
       Retained Earnings (January 1, 19X3)  ......................          32,000
```

The remaining worksheet procedures would not include the elimination of the current year's subsidiary income, but otherwise it would be identical to steps (2) through (4) of the partial worksheet on page 487.

SUBSIDIARY SALE OF ITS OWN COMMON STOCK

In virtually all cases where the subsidiary issues additional shares of stock, the transaction impacts the parent's investment in the subsidiary account. Even though the parent purchases none of the newly issued shares, its share of subsidiary equity has changed and consolidation procedures must acknowledge the change. When the parent purchases some of the newly issued shares, the adjustment needed depends on whether the ownership interest after the purchase is equal to, less than, or greater than the ownership interest prior to the purchase. The adjustments resulting from a subsidiary stock sale are made at the time of the sale when the equity method is used, or they are part of the cost-to-equity conversion process when the cost method is used.

SALE OF SUBSIDIARY STOCK TO MINORITY SHAREHOLDERS

A parent may allow a subsidiary to sell additional shares of stock in order to raise equity funds. A sale of stock by the subsidiary to new or existing minority shareholders results in an increase in the total stockholders' equity against which the controlling interest has a claim. However, the effect of increasing the number of subsidiary shares in the hands of minority stockholders is to lower the controlling interest ownership percentage. Thus, the controlling ownership receives a smaller portion of a larger subsidiary equity. The net effect on the value of the controlling interest depends on the price at which the shares are sold.

A subsidiary stock sale may appear to create a gain or a loss to the parent, since there is an effect on the value of the controlling interest. The *parent company concept* supports this position since it focuses on the ownership of the parent. The more commonly used procedure in practice is derived from the *economic unit concept*. From the viewpoint of the single entity, how the parent's interest changes is the result of a transaction between the consolidated firm and its shareholders. Essentially, new stock has been issued. Any increase in the parent's interest is viewed as generating additional paid-in capital. A decrease in the parent's interest reduces paid-in capital in excess of par if it exists; otherwise, parent retained earnings is reduced.

In 1980, the AICPA Accounting Standards Executive Committee released an issues paper supporting the recognition of gains and losses on some of these types of transactions, and in 1983 the SEC issued Staff Bulletin 51, which endorsed the gain or loss treatment if the stock is sold in a public offering and is not part of a broader reorganization that will involve other capital transactions. The recognition of a gain or loss is supported on the grounds that it should not matter whether the parent decreases its interest by selling shares (in which case a gain or loss is recognized) or whether the parent decreases its interest by directing the subsidiary to issue additional shares. The public offering requirement assures that a gain or loss is not created arbitrarily but instead relies on a well-defined market value. This text will use the gain/loss approach only for public offerings (to comply with SEC requirements) but will retain the use of the adjustment of paid-in capital for other sales.

Parent Using the Equity Method.   A parent company using either the simple or sophisticated equity method usually will need to make an adjustment to its investment account when its subsidiary sells additional shares of stock to minority shareholders. To illustrate, assume Company P has a 90% interest in Company S. The interest was purchased on January 1, 19X1, at which time the following determination and distribution of excess schedule was prepared:

Price paid		$140,000	
Less interest acquired:			
Common stock ($10 par).	$100,000		
Retained earnings, January 1, 19X1.	50,000		
Total stockholders' equity	$150,000		
Interest acquired	90%	135,000	
Goodwill (10-year life)		$ 5,000	Dr

On January 1, 19X4, 2,000 shares of previously unissued common stock are sold to the minority interest. As a result, the parent's interest is reduced to 75% (9,000 ÷ 12,000). An analysis of the controlling interest before and after the sale of 2,000 new subsidiary shares to minority shareholders follows. The analysis shows the three possibilities: shares sold at book value (Case 1), at more than book value (Case 2), and at less than book value (Case 3).

	Case 1	Case 2	Case 3
Sale price per share	$24	$30	$20
Company S shareholders' equity prior to sale	$240,000	$240,000	$ 240,000
Add to common stock, $10 par × 2,000 shares	20,000	20,000	20,000
Add to paid-in capital in excess of par	28,000	40,000	20,000
Company S shareholders' equity subsequent to sale. .	$288,000	$300,000	$ 280,000
Controlling interest subsequent to sale (75%)	$216,000	$225,000	$ 210,000
Prior controlling interest (90% × $240,000)	216,000	216,000	216,000
Net increase (decrease) in controlling interest.	$ 0	$ 9,000	($ 6,000)

Based on the results of the three cases within the above table, it should be noted that no change in controlling interest occurs when a subsidiary sells new stock to minority shareholders at book value. An increase occurs when the stock is sold above book value, and a decrease results when the stock is sold below book value.

Assuming the shares were not sold in a public offering, no gain or loss would be recognized. The parent would adjust its investment in subsidiary account to record the effect on controlling interest in each of the three cases as follows:

Case 1:	Memo entry only to record a change from a 90% to a 75% interest.		
Case 2:	Investment in Company S	9,000	
	Paid-In Capital in Excess of Par		9,000
	To record increase in ownership interest.		
Case 3:	Paid-In Capital in Excess of Par	6,000	
	Investment in Company S		6,000
	To record decrease in ownership interest. It is assumed that parent additional paid-in capital exists to offset the decrease.		

Note that when the equity method is used, these entries would be made directly on the books of the parent; they are not worksheet adjustments.

To illustrate the effect of Case 2 on consolidation, assume subsidiary income for 19X4 was $40,000 and no dividends were declared. The investment account balance under the simple equity method would be determined as follows:

Original cost.	$140,000
Simple equity income adjustments, 19X1 through 19X3, 90% × $90,000 increase in retained earnings	81,000
Increase from stock sale to minority on January 1, 19X4.	9,000
Simple equity adjustment for 19X4 subsidiary income, 75% × $40,000 income. .	30,000
Balance, December 31, 19X4	$260,000

In the partial worksheet (shown on page 493) for the year ended December 31, 19X4, the trial balances of Company P and Company S reflect the sale of 2,000 additional shares at $30 per share (Case 2).

If the shares were sold in a public offering, a gain or loss could be recognized based on the market value of the shares sold. The gain/loss approach takes the position that the parent has sold indirectly a portion of its interest. This means that the portion of any excess of cost or book value applicable to the interest sold should be adjusted for that interest sold, just as it would be if the parent sold a portion of its interest directly. In the preceding example, the parent's ownership interest decreased from 90% to 75% as a result of the subsidiary stock sale. Of the total original goodwill of $5,000, $833 (15% interest sold divided by 90% original interest times $5,000) is applicable to the interest sold and must be removed from the investment account. Goodwill has been amortized over three years of its 10-year life; thus, $250 [($833 ÷ 10) × 3] of the goodwill applicable to the interest sold already has been amortized on the consolidated worksheets. Since the 15% interest no longer will be consolidated, it is necessary to adjust the parent's

Company P and Subsidiary Company S
Partial Worksheet (Simple Equity Method, No Gain or Loss Recorded)
For Year Ended December 31, 19X4

	Trial Balance		Eliminations & Adjustments	
	Company P	Company S	Dr.	Cr.
Investment in Co. S (75%)	260,000			(1) 30,000
				(2) 225,000
				(3) 5,000
Goodwill			(3) 5,000	(4) 2,000
Common Stock, Co. P	(400,000)			
Paid-In Capital in Excess of Par, Co. P	(9,000)			
Retained Earnings, Co. P	(320,000)		(4) 1,500	
Common Stock, Co. S		(120,000)	(2) 90,000	
Paid-In Capital in Excess of Par, Co. S		(40,000)	(2) 30,000	
Retained Earnings, Co. S		(140,000)	(2) 105,000	
Subsidiary Income	(30,000)		(1) 30,000	
Expenses	40,000	27,000	(4) 500	

Eliminations and Adjustments:
(1) Eliminate the parent's entry recording subsidiary income for the current year. The parent's share is now **75%** of the subsidiary undistributed net income. If the sale had occurred *during the year,* the *old* percentage of ownership would be applied to income earned prior to the sale date.
(2) Eliminate the parent's **75%** share of subsidiary equity balances at the beginning of the year against the investment account.
(3) Distribute to the goodwill account the original excess of cost over book value as required by the January 1, 19X1 determination and distribution of excess schedule.
(4) Amortize the goodwill for the past 3 years and the current year.

retained earnings for the $250 of amortizations. The net or remaining goodwill applicable to the interest is $583 ($833 – $250) which should be deducted from the increase or added to the decrease in controlling interest resulting from the stock sale. The same procedure would be used for any other excesses of cost or book value applicable to identifiable assets. The net impact of the subsidiary stock sale at the three alternative prices is:

	Case 1	Case 2	Case 3
Sale price per share	$24	$30	$20
Net increase (decrease) in controlling interest	$ 0	$9,000	($6,000)
Adjustment for net goodwill applicable to interest sold	(583)	(583)	(583)
Gain (loss) on interest sold	($583)	$8,417	($6,583)

The parent would record the effect on the controlling interest in each case as follows:

Case 1:	Retained Earnings (three years' amortization on 1/6 of $5,000 goodwill)	250	
	Loss on Sale of Subsidiary Stock.	583	
	Investment in Company S (1/6 of $5,000 goodwill).		833
	To record loss on subsidiary stock sale.		
Case 2:	Investment in Company S ($9,000 − $833 goodwill)	8,167	
	Retained Earnings	250	
	Gain on Sale of Subsidiary Stock		8,417
	To record gain on subsidiary stock sale.		
Case 3:	Retained Earnings	250	
	Loss on Sale of Subsidiary Stock.	6,583	
	Investment in Company S ($6,000 + $833 goodwill). . . .		6,833
	To record loss on subsidiary stock sale.		

To illustrate the effect of Case 2 on consolidation, assume subsidiary income for 19X4 was $40,000 and no dividends were declared. The investment account balance under the simple equity method would be determined as follows:

Original cost.	$140,000
Simple equity income adjustments, 19X1 through 19X3, 90% × $90,000	
increase in retained earnings	81,000
Increase from stock sale to minority on January 1, 19X4.	8,167
Simple equity adjustment for 19X4 subsidiary income, 75% × $40,000 income. .	30,000
Balance, December 31, 19X4	$259,167

In the Case 2 partial worksheet (shown on page 495) for the year ended December 31, 19X4, the trial balances of Company P and Company S reflect the sale of 2,000 additional shares at $30 per share where the gain is to be recognized.

The consolidated worksheet may require the adjustment of both the controlling and minority interests in beginning retained earnings for intercompany transactions originating in previous periods. When such adjustments are necessary, the current, not the original, ownership interest percentages are used.

Parent Using the Cost Method.   A parent using the cost method records only dividends received from a subsidiary. Usually, no adjustment is made for any other changes in the subsidiary stockholders' equity, including changes caused by sales of subsidiary stock. As a result, the entry to convert from the cost method to the equity method on future worksheets must consider not only the equity adjustments for the subsidiary undistributed income but also adjustments in the parent's ownership interest caused by subsidiary stock sales. A parent using the cost method still would list the subsidiary investment at its original cost.

The partial worksheet on page 496 demonstrates the consolidation procedures needed for Case 2 when the cost method is used. This example further assumes the sale of subsidiary stock was a private offering and no gain needs to be recognized.

Company P and Subsidiary Company S
Partial Worksheet (Simple Equity Method, Gain or Loss Recorded)
For Year Ended December 31, 19X4

	Trial Balance		Eliminations & Adjustments	
	Company P	Company S	Dr.	Cr.
Investment in Co. S. (75%)	259,167			(1) 30,000
				(2) 225,000
				(3) 4,167
Goodwill			(3) 4,167	(4) 1,668
Common Stock, Co. P	(400,000)			
Paid-In Capital in Excess of Par, Co. P	(9,000)			
Retained Earnings, Co. P	(320,000)		(4) 1,251	
Common Stock, Co. S		(120,000)	(2) 90,000	
Paid-In Capital in Excess of Par, Co. S		(40,000)	(2) 30,000	
Retained Earnings, Co. S		(140,000)	(2) 105,000	
Subsidiary Income	(30,000)		(1) 30,000	
Gain on Sale of Subsidiary Stock	(8,417)			
Expenses	40,000	27,000	(4) 417	

Eliminations and Adjustments:
(1) Eliminate the parent's entry recording subsidiary income for the current year. The parent's share is now 75% of the subsidiary undistributed net income. If the sale had occurred *during the year*, the *old* percentage of ownership would be applied to income earned prior to the sale date.
(2) Eliminate the parent's 75% share of subsidiary equity balances at the beginning of the year against the investment account.
(3) Distribute to the goodwill account the remaining (5/6) excess of cost over book value that was shown on the original determination and distribution of excess schedule.
(4) Amortize the remaining goodwill for the past three years and the current year (5/6 × 500 per year = $417).

To review this process, the cost-to-simple-equity conversion amount for Case 2 is determined as it would apply to the December 31, 19X5 worksheet:

Undistributed income:
  90% of change in retained earnings of Company S from
    January 1, 19X1, to January 1, 19X4, 90% × $90,000 . . . . $ 81,000
  75% of change in retained earnings of Company S from
    January 1, 19X4, to January 1, 19X5, 75% × $40,000   30,000
    Increase in Company P retained earnings. $111,000
Adjustment to paid-in capital:
  Controlling interest in Company S equity subsequent to sale on
    January 1, 19X4, 75% × $300,000 . . . . $225,000
  Controlling interest in Company S equity prior to sale on
    January 1, 19X4, 90% × $240,000   216,000
    Net increase in paid-in capital.   9,000
Total increase in investment account. $120,000

Company P and Subsidiary Company S
Partial Worksheet (Cost Method, No Gain or Loss Recorded)
For Year Ended December 31, 19X4

	Trial Balance		Eliminations & Adjustments	
	Company P	Company S	Dr.	Cr.
Investment in Co. S. (75%)	140,000		(C) 90,000	(1) 225,000
				(2) 5,000
Goodwill			(2) 5,000	(3) 2,000
Common Stock, Co. P	(400,000)			
Paid-In Capital in Excess of Par, Co. P				(C) 9,000
Retained Earnings, Co. P ($81,000 less since no equity income was recorded)	(239,000)		(3) 1,500	(C) 81,000
Common Stock, Co. S		(120,000)	(1) 90,000	
Paid-In Capital in Excess of Par, Co. S		(40,000)	(1) 30,000	
Retained Earnings, Co. S		(140,000)	(1) 105,000	
Expenses	40,000	27,000	(3) 500	

Eliminations and Adjustments:
(C)   The simple equity conversion is recorded:

Undistributed income:
  90% of change in retained earnings of Company S from January 1, 19X1, to January 1,
  19X4, 90% × $90,000 . . . . $81,000
Adjustment to paid-in capital resulting from the subsidiary stock sale:
  Controlling interest in Company S equity subsequent to sale on January 1, 19X4, 75% ×
  $300,000 . . . . $225,000
  Controlling interest in Company S equity prior to sale on January 1, 19X4,
  90% × $240,000   216,000

      Net increase in paid-in capital   9,000
Total increase in the investment account $90,000

(1)   Eliminate 75% of the subsidiary equity balances at the beginning of the year against the investment account.
(2)   Distribute the excess of cost to the goodwill account as shown by the original determination and distribution
      of excess schedule.
(3)   Amortize the goodwill for the past 3 years and the current year.

A dangerous shortcut might be attempted, whereby the net change in the
controlling ownership interest is calculated by comparing 90% of the total
subsidiary equity on January 1, 19X1, to 75% of the total subsidiary equity on
January 1, 19X5. This shortcut will produce the correct adjustment to the investment in subsidiary account, but it will *not* provide the analysis needed to
distribute the adjustment to the parent's paid-in capital and retained earnings.

A unique situation arises for a firm using the cost method that wishes to record a gain or loss on a subsidiary stock sale. In order to record the gain or loss, the equity-adjusted cost must be calculated on the date of the transaction, and the investment account must be adjusted for the gain or loss. This means that, when consolidating, the investment account is adjusted for the impact of the subsidiary stock sale but not for the parent's share of subsidiary earned income. In the previous example, it would be necessary to do a cost-to-equity adjustment based on a 90% interest prior to the subsidiary stock sale and a 75% interest subsequent to the sale. This approach does have the advantage of making the adjustment only once on the parent's books rather than repeating it on each year's worksheet.

PARENT PURCHASE OF NEWLY ISSUED SUBSIDIARY STOCK

A parent may purchase all or a portion of the newly issued stock. The general approach in such cases is to compare the change in equity before and after the sale to the price paid for the additional interest. When the ownership interest remains the same, there will be no adjustment. When the ownership interest increases, any difference between the change in equity and the price paid is the excess of cost or book value attributable to the new block. When the ownership interest decreases, the difference between the change in equity and the price paid is viewed as a gain or a loss on the sale of an interest for a public offering or a change in paid-in capital or retained earnings for a private offering. Let us consider these three cases based on the previous example for which the determination and distribution of excess schedule was shown on page 491. Recall that the subsidiary is issuing 2,000 new shares of common stock for $30 per share.

		Maintain Interest		Increase Interest		Decrease Interest	
1	Shares purchased by parent	1,800		2,000		1,000	
2	Total shares owned by parent after purchase	10,800		11,000		10,000	
3	Total subsidiary shares outstanding after issue	12,000		12,000		12,000	
4	Subsidiary equity after the sale	$300,000		$300,000		$300,000	
5	Parent's ownership percent after purchase **(2 ÷ 3)**	90%		91.67%		83.33%	
6	Parent's new equity interest after purchase **(4 × 5)**		$270,000		$275,000		$250,000
7	Subsidiary equity prior to the sale	$240,000		$240,000		$240,000	
8	Parent's ownership percent prior to the purchase	90%		90%		90%	
9	Parent's equity interest prior to purchase **(7 × 8)**		$216,000		$216,000		$216,000
10	Change in parent's equity interest due to purchase **(6 − 9)**		$ 54,000		$ 59,000		$ 34,000
11	Price paid **($30 × 1)**		54,000		60,000		30,000
12	Increase (decrease) in parent's equity interest over price paid **(10 − 11)**	$ 0		$ (1,000)		$ 4,000	

In the first case, the parent maintains its ownership interest by purchasing 90% of the newly issued shares. Note that there is no difference between the price paid by the parent for the new shares and the dollar change in the parent's ownership interest due to the purchase. Thus, no entry is needed other than to record the purchase of the shares as follows:

```
Investment in Company S (1,800 shares × $30) ...............  54,000
   Cash .............................................              54,000
```

No new disparity between cost and underlying equity is created. As a result, *no additional equity adjustment is needed when the parent maintains its ownership interest, and the same price is paid by all buyers.*

In the second case, the parent has increased its ownership interest to 91.67%. The price paid in excess of the additional interest could be allocated to various assets and liabilities, based on differences between cost and market value. However, the adjustments would be limited to the size of the new interest, 1.67%, times the disparities between book and market values. Based on materiality, this new excess usually would be considered goodwill. No entry would be made at the time of the purchase other than to record the added purchase of the shares as follows:

```
Investment in Company S (2,000 shares × $30) ...............  60,000
   Cash .............................................              60,000
```

Future eliminations would be based on the 91.67% interest; the new $1,000 of excess would require separate distribution and amortization on future worksheets.

In the final case, the parent did not buy enough shares to maintain its ownership interest. This means that there will be a decrease in its interest, which is viewed as a decrease in its investment. If the shares are sold in a public offering, a gain or loss on the decrease in interest is recorded. If there is not a public offering, the increase would be an addition to paid-in capital. A decrease would be a debit to existing paid-in capital. If there is no existing paid-in capital on the parent's books, retained earnings would be reduced. In the third example, the investment account increased $34,000, and the price paid was only $30,000. In addition to recording the purchase of the shares, an entry should be made to record the $4,000 increase in the parent's ownership interest. The entries for the transactions discussed would be:

```
Investment in Company S (1,000 shares × $30) ...............  30,000
   Cash .............................................              30,000

Investment in Company S ..................................   4,000
   Paid-In Capital in Excess of Par ...........................       4,000
```

The above entry to record the increase assumes that the sale was not a public offering since no gain or loss was recorded. This entry is made at the time of the purchase and assumes the use of the equity method. If the cost method were used, it would be made as part of the cost-to-equity conversion process. Had the subsidiary sale been a public offering, a gain would have been recorded at the time of the issuance. Also, it would have been necessary to adjust the investment account for the amortization of goodwill applicable to the interest sold. However, it would not be a material amount since only 7.41% [(90% − 83.33%) ÷ 90%] of the original interest was sold.

SUBSIDIARY PURCHASE OF ITS OWN COMMON STOCK

When a subsidiary acquires some of its own shares from the minority interest, the resulting reduction of shares outstanding effectively increases the parent's ownership percentage. Thus, such an acquisition is considered to be an indirect purchase of an additional interest in the subsidiary by its parent company.[2] From a consolidated viewpoint, the subsidiary is acting as an agent of the parent which desires the additional interest in the subsidiary. This means that another block of stock has been purchased that will require a determination and distribution of excess schedule. Typically, the subsidiary would record the purchase of the shares as treasury stock at cost. On subsequent consolidated worksheets, the treasury stock account would be eliminated against the underlying equity it represents.

Some consolidated firms still may practice what could be termed the *retirement method*. This method has the subsidiary retire the minority shares purchased. The parent company then adjusts its subsidiary investment account for the impact of the retirement on its interest in the subsidiary.[3] The continued use of this method can be defended only on the basis of materiality.

PURCHASE OF SHARES AS TREASURY STOCK

To illustrate a subsidiary treasury stock purchase, assume the parent, Company P, owned a 70% interest in Company S. On January 1, 19X1, Company S had the following stockholders' equity:

---

[2]*Accounting Interpretations of APB Opinion No. 16* (New York: American Institute of Certified Public Accountants, 1972), par. 26.

[3]To illustrate the retirement method, consider this example. A subsidiary has 10,000 shares outstanding and has a total stockholders' equity of $240,000. The parent company owns 7,000 shares prior to the purchase of 2,000 minority shares by the subsidiary for $52,000. The purchase changes the parent's interest to 87.5%. However, as the calculation below shows, the dollar amount of the parent's interest has been reduced due to the large amount paid by the subsidiary for the minority shares. The parent's change in equity would be calculated as follows:

Parent interest prior to retirement,	
70% × $240,000 equity	$168,000
Parent interest after retirement,	
87.5% × ($240,000 − $52,000)	164,500
Adjustment	$ 3,500

The adjustment in the investment is accompanied by an adjustment in the parent company paid-in capital in excess of par since the decrease in interest results from a stock transaction in which the parent did not actively participate.

Capital stock ($10 par)	$100,000
Paid-in capital in excess of par.	50,000
Retained earnings.	90,000
Total stockholders' equity.	$240,000

On this date, the subsidiary purchased 2,000 of its 10,000 outstanding shares. The following entry then was recorded by Company S as a result of this purchase from minority shareholders at a cost of $26 each:

Treasury Stock (at cost).	52,000	
Cash		52,000

As a result of the purchase, Company S had the following stockholders' equity:

Capital stock ($10 par)	$100,000
Paid-in capital in excess of par.	50,000
Retained earnings.	90,000
Total	$240,000
Less treasury stock (at cost)	52,000
Total stockholders' equity.	$188,000

Although the subsidiary views the investment as treasury stock, the consolidated viewpoint treats the investment as an additional interest purchased by the parent. This is the first time an investment on the books of the subsidiary should be eliminated against subsidiary equity. Assuming no assets or liabilities had market values different from book values, the parent's determination and distribution of excess schedule would be prepared as follows:

Price paid.		$52,000
Less interest acquired in Company S:		
Common stock ($10 par).	$100,000	
Paid-in capital in excess of par	50,000	
Retained earnings, January 1, 19X1.	90,000	
Total stockholders' equity	$240,000	
Interest acquired	**20%**	48,000
Excess of cost over book value attributed to goodwill		
(with a 40-year life).		$ 4,000 Dr

The parent's additional 20% investment caused by the subsidiary treasury stock purchase will have the following ramifications on subsequent worksheets:

1. The subsidiary will maintain the investment in treasury stock at cost and would have no reason to make equity adjustments to the cost. This means that a cost-to-equity conversion entry will be required for the investment on the worksheet. The adjustment to the investment account will require an adjustment to the controlling retained earnings.

2. The treasury stock account, which is treated as an additional investment in the subsidiary on the worksheet, will be eliminated against the *subsidiary equity accounts* like any other investment in subsidiary account. The excess will be distributed and amortized. All previous years' amortizations are, as always, adjustments to controlling retained earnings only.

3. All adjustments of intercompany profits will be based on a 90% (original 70% plus new 20%) interest as of January 1, 19X1.

4. The adjusted internally reported income of the subsidiary now will be distributed 90% to the controlling interest and 10% to the minority interest.

The above procedures, which treat the subsidiary acquisition of shares as a new block, are a strict interpretation of the *parent company concept*, which focuses on the parent's interest including the isolation of the excess of cost over book value on each block. An alternative approach that is consistent with the treatment of this transaction under the *economic unit concept* is contained in the Discussion Memorandum. Additional information is covered in the appendix to the consolidated chapters that follows this chapter.

RESALE OF SHARES HELD IN TREASURY

The purchase and resale of treasury stock by a subsidiary would be handled as two separate events using the previously described methods. There may be alternative procedures which could be used if there is the intent to resell the treasury shares in the near future. When, for example, the treasury stock is purchased and resold within the consolidated firm's fiscal period, a shortcut is possible. Since there would be no change in the parent's percentage of ownership by the end of the period, the parent only needs to make an adjustment equal to its ownership interest multiplied by the subsidiary's increase or decrease in equity as a result of the treasury stock transaction. This adjustment should be carried to the additional paid-in capital of the parent and is not viewed as an operating gain or loss since it results from dealings with the firm's own shareholders. Using the same reasoning, a decrease in equity reduces parent retained earnings only when no additional paid-in capital is available.

This procedure also might be justified for treasury stock transactions crossing over fiscal periods. It is necessary only that the subsidiary treasury stock account be left on the consolidated worksheet at cost and eliminations be made according to the parent's ownership percentage, unadjusted for the number of treasury shares. When the treasury shares are resold, the parent would adjust its accounts in the same manner as was done for a treasury stock purchase and resale within a fiscal period.

If a parent is using the cost method and did not adjust for subsidiary treasury stock transactions, an adjustment can be made as part of the cost-to-equity conversion process.

INDIRECT HOLDINGS

A parent company may own a controlling interest in a subsidiary which, in turn, owns a controlling interest in another firm. For example, Company A may own a

75% interest in Company B which, in turn, owns an 80% interest in Company C. Thus, A has indirect holdings in C. This situation could be diagrammed as follows:

The treatment of the *level one* investment in B and the *level two* investment in C can be mastered with the theory that has been discussed, but the procedures must be applied carefully. The procedures are applied easily to indirect holdings when the level one investment already exists at the time of the level two purchase. Complications arise in preparing the determination and distribution of excess schedule for the new investment when the level two investment exists prior to the time that the parent achieves control over the subsidiary (level one investment). These complications result because the level two investment held by the subsidiary represents one of the subsidiary's assets that may require adjustment to market value on the determination and distribution of excess schedule prepared at the time of the parent's level one acquisition. The use of separate and distinct determination and distribution of excess schedules for each level of investment should facilitate the maintaining of proper accounting when two or more levels are involved.

LEVEL ONE HOLDING ACQUIRED FIRST

Assume Company A purchased a 75% interest in Company B on January 1, 19X1, at which time the following determination and distribution of excess schedule was prepared:

Price paid		$400,000	
Less interest acquired in Company B:			
Common stock ($10 par).............................	$200,000		
Retained earnings, January 1, 19X1....................	100,000		
Total stockholders' equity	$300,000		
Interest acquired	75%	225,000	
Excess of cost over book value attributed to building and			
equipment (10-year life).............................		$175,000	Dr

On January 1, 19X2, the subsidiary, Company B, purchased an 80% interest in Company C, and the following schedule was prepared:

Price paid		$270,000	
Less Company B's interest acquired in Company C:			
Common stock ($10 par).............................	$100,000		
Retained earnings, January 1, 19X2....................	120,000		
Total stockholders' equity	$220,000		
Interest acquired	80%	176,000	
Excess of cost over book value attributed to goodwill			
(20-year life)		$ 94,000	Dr

Equity adjustments must be made carefully. Company A must be sure that Company B has included its equity income from Company C in its net income before Company A records its percentage share of Company B income.

Assume the following internally generated net incomes:

	Company A	Company B	Company C
19X1................................	$100,000	$100,000	$20,000
19X2................................	70,000	76,000	30,000
19X3................................	90,000	100,000	30,000

On this basis, the following simple equity adjustments would be required:

Date	Company B's Books			Company A's Books		
19X1 Dec. 31	None (interest in Company C not yet acquired).			Investment in Company B .... Subsidiary Income................ To adjust for 75% of Company B reported income.	75,000	75,000
19X2 Dec. 31	Investment in Company C .... Subsidiary Income................ To adjust for 80% of Company C reported income.	24,000	24,000	Investment in Company B .... Subsidiary Income................ To adjust for 75% of Company B total income ($76,000 plus $24,000 subsidiary income).	75,000	75,000
19X3 Dec. 31	Investment in Company C .... Subsidiary Income................ To adjust for 80% of Company C reported income.	24,000	24,000	Investment in Company B .... Subsidiary Income................ To adjust for 75% of Company B total income ($100,000 plus $24,000 subsidiary income).	93,000	93,000

Worksheet 8-1, pages 530–533, is based on the trial balances of the three separate firms on December 31, 19X3. The investment account balances reflect the equity adjustments previously shown. The following additional information for 19X3 is assumed:

	Intercompany Sales by B to A	Intercompany Sales by C to B
Selling company goods in buyer's January 1, 19X3 inventory..............	$ 8,000	$ 6,000
Sales during 19X3......................	50,000	40,000
Selling company goods in buyer's December 31, 19X3 inventory	10,000	10,000
Gross profit on all sales	25%	30%

The investment accounts must be handled carefully when any eliminations are made in order to ensure that the minority interest accounts are available to receive amortizations of excesses. It is suggested that the level one investment be eliminated first, thereby reducing Company B retained earnings to the minority interest. Then it will be possible to allocate the amortizations of excess resulting from the level two (Company C) holding to the controlling interest (Company A) and the Company B minority interest. Since Company B owns the interest in Company C, the Company B minority interest must share in the amortizations of excess resulting from the investment in Company C.

In Worksheet 8-1, the combined net income is $196,100, which must be distributed to the two minority interests and to the controlling interest. Distribution must proceed from the *lowest* level (level two) to ensure proper distribution. Company B adjusted income includes 80% of Company C adjusted income. Thus, the Company C income distribution schedule must be completed first, followed by the distribution schedules for Companies B and A. These schedules accompany Worksheet 8-1.

If the cost method was used in the previous example, the investment account balances still would contain the January 1, 19X1, $400,000 cost of the Company B investment and the January 1, 19X2, $270,000 cost of the Company C investment. Conversion entries would be made on the consolidated worksheet to update both investment accounts to their January 1, 19X3 simple equity balances. It is advisable to make equity adjustments at the *lowest* level of investment first, because the retained earnings of the midlevel firm must be adjusted for its share of investment income before the parent can adjust for the change in its subsidiary's retained earnings. The following simple equity conversion entry would be made first for Company B's investment in Company C:

Investment in Company C	24,000	
Retained Earnings (Company B)		24,000
80% of $30,000 increase in Company C retained earnings		
between January 1, 19X2, and January 1, 19X3.		

The following conversion entry then would be made for Company A's investment in Company B:

Investment in Company B	150,000	
Retained Earnings (Company A)		150,000
75% of $200,000 increase in Company B retained earnings		
(including previous equity adjustment for Company B)		
between January 1, 19X1, and January 1, 19X3.		

Eliminations and adjustments would be made as on Worksheet 8-1, except that there would be no need to eliminate the current year's equity adjustment.

LEVEL TWO HOLDING EXISTS AT TIME OF PARENT'S PURCHASE

When a parent acquires a controlling interest in another parent company, the determination and distribution of excess schedule must be based on the acquired firm's *consolidated* balance sheet. For example, assume Company Y purchased an 80% interest in Company Z on January 1, 19X1, and Company X purchased a 70% interest in Company Y on January 1, 19X3. Also assume that on January 1, 19X3, Company Y owns equipment which is undervalued by $40,000 and Company Z (the subsidiary) has equipment which is undervalued by $100,000. Company X would prepare the determination and distribution of excess schedule on page 505 based on the controlling interest in Company Y.

Note the following features of the schedule:
1. Company Y consolidated equity is multiplied by the parent's (Company X) ownership interest to arrive at the excess of cost over book value.

2. When a Company Y (level one investment) asset is to be adjusted, it should be adjusted for the parent's ownership portion (70%) of the value discrepancy.
3. When a Company Z (level two investment) asset is to be adjusted, it should be adjusted for only the Company X ownership share of the Company Y share (70% × 80%, or 56%) of the value discrepancy.
4. Resulting goodwill is based on the consolidated asset values for Companies Y and Z.

Price paid		$700,000
Less interest acquired:		
Company Y common stock	$400,000	
Company Y controlling interest in consolidated retained earnings	320,000	
Total Company Y stockholders' equity...............	$720,000	
Interest acquired	70%	504,000
Excess of cost over book value (debit balance)		$196,000
Excess of cost attributable to Company Y equipment:		
70% × $40,000 undervaluation		**28,000** Dr
Excess of cost attributable to Company Z equipment:		
70% × 80% × $100,000 undervaluation		**56,000** Dr
Goodwill (20-year life)		$112,000 Dr

When the simple equity method is used for the investments, the procedures illustrated in Worksheet 8-1 apply without modification. When the cost method is used, simple equity conversion adjustments again proceed from the lowest level. Be sure to note, however, that in this example Company X would convert to the equity basis for the change in Company Y retained earnings after January 1, 19X3.

CONNECTING AFFILIATES

A business combination involving connecting affiliates exists when a parent firm has a direct (level one) investment in a company and an indirect (level two) investment in the same company sufficient to result in control. For example, the following diagram illustrates a connecting affiliate structure:

Not only does Company P have a 90% interest in Company S-1, but it also has, in effect, a 67% interest in Company S-2, calculated as follows:

Direct 40%
Indirect (90% × 30%) 27%
Total. 67%

This type of structure is consolidated more readily once the determination and distribution of excess schedule has been prepared. Caution must be used in the schedule preparation because of differing dates for each investment. Referring to the diagram, the special concerns in consolidating connecting affiliates are as follows:

1. Company S-2 generally is not included in the consolidation process until the total percentage of S-2 shares held by the parent and its subsidiaries (70% in this example) exceeds 50%. Prior to that time, an investment of 20% or more is treated according to APB Opinion No. 18, and a less than 20% investment is accounted for under the cost method.

2. Any amortizations of excess resulting from the 30% investment of Company S-1 in Company S-2 are distributed to the controlling and S-1 minority interests in retained earnings on a 90/10 basis.

3. Any adjustments to retained earnings caused by Company S-2–generated transactions are distributed 30% to minority S-2, 3% (10% × 30%) to minority S-1, and 67% [40% + (90% × 30%)] to the controlling interest.

4. Income distributions would begin with Company S-2: 30% of its income would go to minority S-2, 30% would flow to the Company S-1 distribution schedule, and 40% would flow to the Company P schedule. Company P will receive 90% of the Company S-1 adjusted income (including the 30% share of Company S-2).

5. When either equity method is used, Companies P and S-1 each must adjust for its interest in Company S-2, even though neither firm's interest by itself would merit consolidation techniques.

6. When the cost method is used, each investment is converted to the simple equity method from the purchase date forward. Again, equity conversions must begin at the lowest level. For example, the Company S-1 investment in Company S-2 must be converted first, so that Company S-1 retained earnings is updated before the Company P investment in Company S-1 is converted to the simple equity method.

MUTUAL HOLDINGS

A mutual holding structure exists when the subsidiary owns any percentage of the parent company common stock. Such an investment must be eliminated in the consolidation process. There are two methods through which such holdings may be consolidated. The first and more popular method is called the *treasury stock method*. From a consolidated viewpoint, the subsidiary acquisition of parent shares is viewed as a retirement of the shares or as a temporary treasury stock purchase where there is an intent to resell the shares. Under both approaches to the treasury stock method, the shares are *off the market* and have *no claim to income*. The other method is termed the *reciprocal method*, which allocates to the minority interest a percentage of the parent income. This method requires simultaneous equations and becomes even more complicated when there are excesses of cost or book value applicable to each set of investments and/or intercompany profit transactions. The method will be explained in its simplest state, but it is considered to be obsolete and theoretically unsound in that it views parent shares held by the subsidiary as being alive and entitled to a share of combined net income.

TREASURY STOCK METHOD

The treasury stock method does not view parent shares held by the subsidiary as outstanding. When it is intended that the shares are to be reissued, they are viewed as treasury shares and are recorded at cost. When resold, an excess received over cost is carried to additional paid-in capital. If cost exceeds proceeds on resale, the difference is offset against existing paid-in capital. If there is no paid-in capital, retained earnings is reduced. When it is not intended that the shares be reissued, the stock is retired on the worksheet using the original investment cost as the retirement price. Regardless of the approach used, the resulting capital account adjustments fall entirely upon the parent. The subsidiary is viewed as an agent accomplishing the transaction. An important requirement of either of the treasury stock approaches is that the subsidiary investment in the parent be *maintained at its original cost*. Since the stock is not to be viewed as outstanding, it has no claim on income. If equity adjustments have been made by error, they must be reversed on the consolidated worksheet.

To illustrate the treasury stock method, consider the following example. Suppose Company P acquired an 80% interest in Company S on January 1, 19X1, at which time the following determination and distribution of excess schedule was prepared:

Price paid		$200,000
Less interest acquired:		
Common stock ($10 par)	$100,000	
Retained earnings	50,000	
Total stockholders' equity	$150,000	
Interest acquired	80%	120,000
Excess of cost over book value attributed to equipment		
(20-year remaining life)		$ 80,000 Dr

Further assume that on January 1, 19X3, Company S purchases a 10% interest in the parent for $80,000. There would be no need for a determination and distribution of excess schedule for the subsidiary investment, since no excess of cost or book value is acknowledged or distributed. For 19X3, the parent will make the normal simple equity adjustment to acknowledge its 80% interest in subsidiary income of $20,000:

Investment in Company S 16,000
    Subsidiary Income.......................................   16,000
        To record 80% of subsidiary reported income of $20,000.

There is no equity adjustment for the Company S investment in the parent since it must remain at cost.

    The trial balances of the two firms on December 31, 19X3, are contained in the first two columns of Worksheet 8-2 on pages 534–537. The investment in Company S account on Worksheet 8-2 is computed as follows:

Original cost.	$200,000
80% × 19X1 and 19X2 undistributed income of $40,000	32,000
19X3 simple equity adjustment	16,000
Balance, December 31, 19X3	$248,000

    Examination of the formal statements of the consolidated firm reveals that the treasury shares are held by the consolidated firm and no income accrues to them. These statements, based on Worksheet 8-2, are as follows:

Company P and Subsidiary Company S Consolidated Income Statement For Year Ended December 31, 19X3	
Sales.	$500,000
Less cost of goods sold	300,000
Gross profit.	$200,000
Less expenses	144,000
Combined net income	$ 56,000
Minority interest of Company S	4,000
Consolidated net income.	$ 52,000

Company P and Subsidiary Company S Retained Earnings Statement For Year Ended December 31, 19X3	Minority Interest	Controlling Interest
Balance, January 1, 19X3	$18,000	$192,000
Net income	4,000	52,000
Balance, December 31, 19X3	$22,000	$244,000

Company P and Subsidiary Company S			
Consolidated Balance Sheet			
December 31, 19X3			
Assets		**Stockholders' Equity**	
Equipment...... $868,000		Minority interest...........	$ 42,000
Less accumulated		Controlling interest:	
depreciation... 162,000		Common stock......... $500,000	
		Retained earnings 244,000	744,000
		Total	$786,000
		Less treasury stock (at cost)..	80,000
Total assets	$706,000	Net stockholders' equity.....	$706,000

RECIPROCAL METHOD

To understand the objections to the reciprocal method, it is necessary to examine the procedures required by the method. This will be done using the same example as was used for the treasury stock method. The same determination and distribution of excess schedule would be prepared for the parent company investment in the subsidiary. But, unlike the treasury stock method, a separate determination and distribution of excess schedule must be prepared for the subsidiary investment in the parent firm.

On January 1, 19X3, Company S purchases a 10% interest in Company P. The determination and distribution of excess schedule for this investment is prepared as follows:

Price paid..		$80,000	
Less interest acquired:			
Common stock....................................	$500,000		
Retained earnings.................................	200,000		
Total stockholders' equity	$700,000		
Ownership interest	**10%**	70,000	
Excess of cost over book value attributed to goodwill			
(10-year life).......................................		$10,000	Dr

Typically, the determination and distribution of excess schedule will be based only on Company P equity and not on the total controlling interest. The excess could be distributed to the separate assets of Company P (including the investment in Company S), but based on materiality, it usually would be distributed only to goodwill. The parent and the subsidiary may use either the cost method or the equity method to account for intercompany investments. In Worksheet 8-3 on pages 538–541, both firms are assumed to be using the simple equity method. Company P has recorded subsidiary income of $16,000 (80% × Company S reported income of $20,000), and Company S has recorded investment income of $4,000 (10% × Company P internal income of $40,000).

In Worksheet 8-3, the combined net income is distributed to Company P and Company S by solving simultaneously the following equations which are based on each company's *adjusted internally generated income:*

Let P = Company P income
Let S = Company S income

$$P = \$36,000 + .8S$$
$$S = \$19,000 + .1P$$

Solution:
$$P - .8S = \$36,000$$
$$-.1\,P + S = \$19,000$$

Multiply the first solution equation by .1 and then add the equations:

$$.1\,P - .08S = \$3,600$$
$$+ (-.1\,P + 1.00S = \$19,000)$$
$$.92S = \$22,600$$
$$S = \$24,565$$

Substitute for S in the first equation:

$$P = \$36,000 + .8(\$24,565)$$
$$P = \$55,652$$

To minority interest: 20% × Company S income of $24,565 = $4,913
To controlling interest: 90% × Company P income of $55,652 = $50,087

The treasury stock method usually is more practical to use than the reciprocal method and is supported by ARB No. 51, which states, "Shares of the parent held by a subsidiary should not be treated as outstanding stock in the consolidated balance sheet."[4] Further support comes from an American Accounting Association publication, which states:

> *Shares of the controlling company's capital stock owned by a subsidiary before the date of acquisition of control should be treated in consolidation as treasury stock. Any subsequent acquisition or sale by a subsidiary should likewise be treated in the consolidated statements as though it had been the act of the controlling company.*[5]

QUESTIONS

1. What effect does a subsidiary stock dividend have on consolidation procedures (a) when the equity method is used? (b) when the cost method is used?
2. Indicate how one calculates the dollar impact on the parent company's investment account of a sale of additional common stock by a subsidiary to minority shareholders only.

---

[4]Accounting Research Bulletin No. 51, *Consolidated Financial Statements* (New York: American Institute of Certified Public Accountants, 1959), par. 13.
[5]*Accounting and Reporting Standards for Corporate Financial Statements and Preceding Statements and Supplements* (Columbus, OH: American Accounting Association, 1957), 44.

3. Assume a subsidiary issues additional shares of common stock, but the parent buys none of these shares. Further assume the parent's interest (in dollars) increases as a result of the transaction. What are the alternative theories of dealing with the increase and under what circumstances might each be appropriate?

4. Assume the parent company owns an 80% interest in a subsidiary just prior to the issuance of additional shares by the subsidiary. Indicate the type of adjustment you would make to the investment account if:
    a. The parent purchased 80% of the new shares.
    b. The parent purchased all the newly issued shares.
    c. The parent purchased 50% of the new shares.

5. What is the applicable general accounting theory for the purchase of treasury shares by a subsidiary? How should the investment be recorded on the subsidiary's books, and what are the consolidated worksheet procedures for the treasury stock?

6. What special procedures are necessary when making equity adjustments to record subsidiary income when an indirect holding situation exists?

7. What new procedures are needed on the determination and distribution of excess schedule when a parent acquires a controlling interest in a subsidiary company which, at the time of the acquisition, also owns a controlling interest in another firm?

8. What is a connecting affiliate, and how is income distributed to the parent calculated?

9. Describe a mutual holding and the alternative methods used to consolidate such holdings.

10. Why might the reciprocal method of accounting for mutual holdings be considered theoretically unsound?

11. Under the treasury stock method of accounting for mutual holdings, intent determines the exact treatment of the parent shares owned by the subsidiary. Explain the different treatments available under the treasury stock method.

EXERCISES

Exercise 1. On January 1, 19X7, Pate Industries purchased 90% of the outstanding stock of Band Controls for $700,000. At the time of the acquisition, Band Controls had the following stockholders' equity:

Common stock ($10 par).....................	$300,000
Paid-in capital in excess of par.................	150,000
Retained earnings............................	200,000
Total stockholders' equity	$650,000

It was determined that Band Controls' book values approximated market as of the purchase date. Any excess of cost over book value was attributed to goodwill and given a 20-year life.

On July 1, 19X7, Band Controls distributed a 10% stock dividend when the market value of its common stock was $25 per share. A cash dividend of $.50 per share was distributed on December 31, 19X7. Band Controls' net income for 19X7 amounted to $120,000 and was earned evenly throughout the year.

(1) Prepare the entry required on Band Controls' books to reflect the stock dividend distributed on July 1, 19X7. Prepare the stockholders' equity section of Band Controls' balance sheet as of December 31, 19X7.

(2) Prepare the simple equity method entries that Pate Industries would make during 19X7 to record its investment in Band Controls.

(3) Prepare the eliminations that would be made on the December 31, 19X7 consolidated worksheet. (Assume the use of the simple equity method.)

Exercise 2. Pluto Company owned a 90% interest in Saturn Company on January 1, 19X6, when Saturn had the following stockholders' equity:

Common stock ($10 par).....................	$100,000
Paid-in capital in excess of par.................	250,000
Retained earnings...........................	200,000
Total stockholders' equity..................	$550,000

On July 1, 19X6, Saturn sold 2,000 additional shares to minority shareholders in a public offering for $48 per share. Saturn's net income for 19X6 was $50,000, and the income was earned evenly during the year.

Pluto uses the simple equity method to record the investment in Saturn. Summary entries are made each December 31 to record the year's activity.

Prepare Pluto's equity adjustments for 19X6 that result from the above activities of Saturn Company during 19X6. Assume Pluto has $500,000 of paid-in capital in excess of par.

Exercise 3. On January 1, 19X8, Tom Company purchased an 80% interest in Car Company for $400,000. On the purchase date, Car Company had the following stockholders' equity:

Common stock ($10 par).....................	$200,000
Paid-in capital in excess of par.................	100,000
Retained earnings...........................	150,000
Total stockholders' equity.................	$450,000

Assets and liabilities have market values equal to book values. Any excess is due to goodwill and is to be amortized over a 20-year life.

Car Company had net income of $50,000 for 19X8. No dividends were paid or declared during 19X8.

On January 1, 19X9, Car Company sold 10,000 shares of common stock at $40 per share in a public offering.

Assuming the parent uses the simple equity method, prepare all parent company entries required for the issuance of the shares. Also prepare a new determination and distribution of excess schedule for the investment if it is needed. Assume the following alternative situations:

(1) Tom Company purchased 8,000 shares.
(2) Tom Company purchased 9,000 shares.
(3) Tom Company purchased 5,000 shares.

Suggestion: It is helpful to use a three-column table which, for each case, organizes the changes in ownership interest. See the schedule on page 497.

Exercise 4. The following comparative statements of stockholders' equity were prepared for Nolte Corporation:

	Jan. 1, 19X3	Jan. 1, 19X5	Jan. 1, 19X8
Common stock ($10 par)	$300,000	$300,000	$300,000
Paid-in capital in excess of par	60,000	60,000	60,000
Retained earnings		42,000	120,000
Total	$360,000	$402,000	$480,000
Less treasury stock (at cost)		(75,000)	(75,000)
Total stockholders' equity	$360,000	$327,000	$405,000

Tarman Corporation purchased 60% of Nolte Corporation common stock for $12 per share on January 1, 19X3, when the latter corporation was formed.

On December 31, 19X4, Nolte Corporation purchased 5,000 shares of its own common stock from minority interests for $15 per share. These shares were accounted for as treasury stock at cost.

Nolte had $50,000 of net income in 19X8 and never has declared a cash dividend.

Assuming Tarman Corporation uses the cost method to record its investment in Nolte Corporation, prepare the necessary cost-to-simple-equity conversion and the eliminations and adjustments required on the consolidated worksheet as of December 31, 19X8. Include all pertinent supporting calculations in good form. Any excess of cost over book value is considered to be goodwill with a 10-year life.

Exercise 5. You have secured the following information for Companies A, B, and C concerning their internally generated net incomes (excluding subsidiary income) and dividends paid:

	A	B	C
19X5 Internally generated net income	$30,000	$20,000	$10,000
Dividends declared and paid	10,000	5,000	
19X6 Internally generated net income	50,000	30,000	25,000
Dividends declared and paid	10,000	5,000	5,000
19X7 Internally generated net income	40,000	40,000	30,000
Dividends declared and paid	10,000	5,000	5,000

(1) Assume Company A purchased an 80% interest in Company B on January 1, 19X5, and Company B purchased a 60% interest in Company C on January 1, 19X6. Prepare the simple equity method adjusting entries made by Companies A and B for subsidiary investments for the years 19X5 through 19X7.

(2) Assume Company B acquired a 70% interest in Company C on January 1, 19X5, and Company A acquired a 90% interest in Company B on January 1, 19X7. Prepare the simple equity method adjusting entries made by Companies A and B for subsidiary investments for the years 19X5 through 19X7.

Exercise 6. Company B purchased an 80% interest in the common stock of Company C for $580,000 on January 1, 19X1. Any excess of cost is attributable to goodwill with a 20-year life. Company B maintains its investment in Company C under the cost method.

Company A purchased a 60% interest in the common stock of Company B on January 1, 19X5, for $2,500,000. Any excess of cost is attributable to Company C equipment, which is understated by $80,000, and a Company B building, which is understated by $200,000. Any remaining excess is considered goodwill. Relevant stockholders' equities are as follows:

	Company B	Company C	
	1/1/X5	1/1/X1	1/1/X5
Common stock	$ 400,000	$100,000	$100,000
Paid-in capital in excess of par.................	1,100,000	150,000	150,000
Retained earnings...........................	2,000,000	300,000	450,000

(1) Prepare a determination and distribution of excess schedule for the investment in Company B.

(2) On January 1, 19X6, Company C sold a machine with a net book value of $35,000 to Company A for $50,000. The machine has a 5-year life. Prepare the eliminations and adjustments needed on the December 31, 19X7 trial balance worksheet that relate to this intercompany sale.

Exercise 7. Companies A, B, and C produced the following separate internally gen-erated net incomes during 19X9:

	A	B	C
Sales...	$300,000	$400,000	$100,000
Less cost of goods sold.........................	200,000	300,000	60,000
Gross profit	$100,000	$100,000	$ 40,000
Expenses	60,000	30,000	10,000
Internally generated net income	$ 40,000	$ 70,000	$ 30,000

Company A purchased an 80% interest in Company B on January 1, 19X6, and Company B purchased a 60% interest in Company C on January 1, 19X7. Each investment was acquired at a price equal to the book value of the stock purchased.

Additional information:

(a) Company A purchased goods billed at $30,000 from Company C during 19X9. The price includes a 66-2/3% markup on cost. One-half of the goods are held in Company A's year-end inventory.

(b) Company B purchased goods billed at $30,000 from Company A during 19X9. Company A always bills Company B for cost plus 50%. Company B had $6,000 of Company A goods in its beginning inventory and $2,400 of Company A goods in its ending inventory.

(c) Company C purchased goods billed at $15,000 from Company B during 19X9. Company B bills Company C at cost plus 25%. At year end, $7,500 of the goods remain unsold. The goods were inventoried at $5,000, under the lower-of-cost-or-market procedure.

(d) Company B sold a machine to Company C on January 1, 19X8, for $50,000. Company B's cost was $70,000, and accumulated depreciation on the date of sale was $40,000. The machine is being depreciated on a straight-line basis over 5 years.

Prepare the consolidated income statement for 19X9, including the distribution of combined net income supported by distribution schedules.

Exercise 8. On January 1, 19X6, Hinsdale Company purchased an 80% interest in Kork Company for $110,000. The purchase price represented a $10,000 excess over book value, which was attributed to goodwill and given a 10-year life. The investment is recorded under the simple equity method.

On January 1, 19X8, Going Company purchased a 60% interest in Hinsdale Company for $350,000. Going Company believes that the goodwill remaining on the investment by

Hinsdale in Kork is stated correctly. Comparative equities of Hinsdale Company and Kork Company immediately prior to the purchase revealed:

Stockholders' Equity	Hinsdale Company	Kork Company
Common stock ($5 par)	$200,000	
Common stock ($10 par)		$100,000
Paid-in capital in excess of par	100,000	20,000
Retained earnings	150,000	80,000
Total stockholders' equity	$450,000	$200,000

An analysis of the separate accounts of Hinsdale and Kork on January 1, 19X8, revealed that Kork's inventory was undervalued by $20,000 and that Hinsdale's equipment with a 5-year future life was undervalued by $30,000. All other book values approximated market values for Hinsdale and Kork.

Prepare the determination and distribution of excess schedule for Goning's purchase of Hinsdale Company on January 1, 19X8.

Exercise 9. The following diagram depicts the investment affiliations between Companies M, `N` and O:

The following facts apply to 19X3 operations:

	M	N	O
Internally generated net income	$200,000	$90,000	$40,000
Dividends declared and paid	40,000	10,000	5,000

All investments were made at a price equal to book value.
(1) Prepare the simple equity method adjustments that would be made for the investments owned by Companies M and N during the year 19X3.
(2) Intercompany inventory transactions affecting 19X3 were as follows:

	Sold by N to O	Sold by O to M
Profit on sales	25%	30%
Beginning inventory of intercompany goods	$10,000	$15,000
19X3 sales	50,000	75,000
Ending inventory of intercompany goods	12,000	20,000

Using the facts given, determine the combined income of the consolidated firm, the minority interest, and the consolidated net income. Income distribution schedules may be used for support.

Exercise 10. Myles Corporation and its subsidiary, Dowling Corporation, had the following trial balances as of December 31, 19X8:

	Myles Corporation	Dowling Corporation
Current Assets.....................................	400,000	182,000
Investment in Dowling Corporation	398,000	
Investment in Myles Corporation		150,000
Property, Plant, and Equipment (net)	850,000	400,000
Liabilities.......................................	(200,000)	(100,000)
Common Stock ($10 par)...........................	(1,000,000)	(500,000)
Retained Earnings, Jan. 1, 19X8	(400,000)	(100,000)
Sales	(800,000)	(350,000)
Dividend Income..................................		(2,000)
Subsidiary Income	(18,000)	
Cost of Goods Sold	600,000	240,000
Expenses	150,000	80,000
Dividends Declared................................	20,000	
Total...	0	0

Myles Corporation purchased its 60% interest in Dowling Corporation for $350,000 on January 1, 19X6. At that time, Dowling's retained earnings balance was $50,000. Any excess of cost over book value was attributed to goodwill and given a 20-year life.

Dowling Corporation purchased a 10% interest in Myles Corporation on January 1, 19X8, for $150,000. Myles's book values approximated market values at the time of the purchase. Any resulting goodwill is being amortized over 20 years.

No intercompany transactions occurred during 19X8.

(1) Prepare determination and distribution of excess schedules for the intercompany investments.
(2) Prepare the 19X8 consolidated income statement, including the combined net income distribution, using the reciprocal method for mutual holdings.
(3) Prepare the 19X8 consolidated income statement, including the combined net income distribution, using the treasury stock method for mutual holdings. Prepare the supporting income distribution schedules.
(4) State how the investment in Myles stock will appear on the consolidated balance sheet under the two alternative methods of accounting for mutual holdings.

PROBLEMS

Problem 8-1. On January 1, 19X7, Zak Corporation purchased 8,000 shares of Tarman Company stock and 18,000 shares of Sarge Company stock for $180,000 and $270,000, respectively. The excess of cost over book value on each investment was attributed to goodwill and given a 10-year life.

Tarman Company and Sarge Company had the following stockholders' equities immediately prior to Zak's purchases:

	Tarman Company	Sarge Company
Common stock ($5 par)	$ 50,000	
Common stock ($10 par)		$300,000
Paid-in capital in excess of par	100,000	
Retained earnings	70,000	100,000
Total stockholders' equity.............................	$220,000	$400,000

Additional information:

(a) Net income for Tarman Company and Sarge Company for 19X7 and 19X8 follows (income is assumed to be earned evenly throughout the year):

	19X7	19X8
Tarman Company	$25,000	$30,000
Sarge Company	30,000	40,000

(b) No cash dividends were paid or declared by Tarman or Sarge during 19X7 and 19X8.

(c) Tarman Company distributed a 10% stock dividend on December 31, 19X7. Tarman stock was selling at $25 per share when the stock dividend was declared.

(d) On July 1, 19X8, Tarman Company sold 2,750 shares of stock at $32 per share in a private offering. Zak Corporation purchased none of these shares. The sale was not a public offering; therefore, no gain or loss is recognized.

(e) Sarge Company sold 5,000 shares of stock on July 1, 19X7, in a private offering at $20 per share. Zak Corporation purchased 3,700 of these shares.

(f) On January 1, 19X8, Sarge Company purchased 5,000 shares of its common stock from minority interests at $14 per share.

Required:

Assume Zak Corporation uses the simple equity method. For 19X7 and 19X8 record each of the adjustments to the investment accounts. Provide all supporting calculations in good form.

Problem 8-2. On January 1, 19X6, Barstow Corporation acquired a 60% interest in Kantor Company and an 80% interest in Saeger Company. The purchase prices were $200,000 and $250,000 respectively. The excess of cost over book value for each investment was considered to be goodwill with a 10-year life. Neither subsidiary is trading its stock publicly.

Immediately prior to the purchases, Kantor Company and Saeger Company had the following stockholders' equities:

	Kantor Company	Saeger Company
Common stock ($10 par)	$200,000	
Common stock ($20 par)		$200,000
Paid-in capital in excess of par	50,000	
Retained earnings	100,000	100,000
Total stockholders' equity.............................	$350,000	$300,000

Additional information:

(a) Kantor Company and Saeger Company had the following net incomes for 19X6 through 19X8 (incomes were earned evenly throughout the year):

	19X6	19X7	19X8
Kantor Company.................................	$50,000	$60,000	$60,000
Saeger Company	40,000	30,000	55,000

(b) Kantor Company had the following equity-related transactions for the first three years after it became a subsidiary of Barstow Corporation:

July 1, 19X6	Sold 5,000 shares of its own stock at $20 per share. Barstow purchased 3,000 of these shares.
December 31, 19X7	Paid a cash dividend of $1 per share.
July 1, 19X8	Purchased 5,000 shares of minority-owned stock as treasury shares at $25 per share.

(c) Saeger Company had the following equity-related transactions for the first three years after it became a subsidiary of Barstow Corporation:

December 31, 19X6	Issued a 10% stock dividend. The estimated market value of Saeger common stock was $30 per share on the declaration date.
October 1, 19X7	Sold 4,000 shares of its own stock at $25 per share. Of these shares, 200 were purchased by Barstow.

(d) Barstow Corporation has $200,000 of additional paid-in capital on December 31, 19X8.

Required:

Barstow Corporation uses the cost method to account for its investments in subsidiaries. Convert its investments to the simple equity method as of December 31, 19X8, and provide adequate support for the entries. Assume that the 19X8 nominal accounts are closed.

Suggestion: Since the stock sales were not public offerings, no gain or loss is recognized; instead, the adjustment is to the paid-in capital of the parent company.

Problem 8-3. On January 1, 19X6, Parson Company purchased 80% of the outstanding common stock of Schell Company for $650,000.

On January 1, 19X8, Schell Company sold 25,000 shares of common stock to the public at $9 per share. Parson Company did not purchase any of these shares. It is considered appropriate for the parent to record a gain or loss on the subsidiary stock sale; however, no entry has been made by the parent. Schell Company had the following stockholders' equity at the end of 19X5 and 19X7:

	December 31	
	19X5	19X7
Common stock ($2 par)	$200,000	$200,000
Paid-in capital in excess of par	400,000	400,000
Retained earnings	100,000	180,000
Total stockholders' equity	$700,000	$780,000

On the January 1, 19X6 acquisition date, Schell Company's book values approximated market values, except for a building that was undervalued by $60,000. The building had an estimated future life of 20 years. Any additional excess was attributed to goodwill and given a 10-year life.

Trial balances of the two firms as of December 31, 19X8, are as follows:

	Parson Company	Schell Company
Cash	229,040	30,000
Accounts Receivable (net)	280,000	190,000
Inventory	325,000	175,000
Investment in Schell Company	650,000	
Property, Plant, and Equipment	2,450,000	1,400,000
Accumulated Depreciation.	(1,256,000)	(536,000)
Liabilities	(750,000)	(210,000)
Common Stock ($10 par)	(1,500,000)	
Common Stock ($2 par)		(250,000)
Paid-In Capital in Excess of Par.		(575,000)
Retained Earnings, Jan. 1, 19X8	(375,000)	(180,000)
Sales.	(1,600,000)	(750,000)
Subsidiary Dividend Income	(23,040)	
Cost of Goods Sold	1,120,000	450,000
Other Expenses	405,000	220,000
Dividends Declared	45,000	36,000
Total	0	0

During 19X8, Schell Company sold $200,000 of merchandise to Parson Company at cost plus 25%. This was the first intercompany sale between the two firms. $50,000 of the goods remain in Parson's ending inventory.

Required:

Prepare the worksheet necessary to produce the consolidated financial statements of Parson Company and its subsidiary as of December 31, 19X8. Include the determination and distribution of excess and income distribution schedules.

Problem 8-4. On January 1, 19X7, Mitta Corporation purchased a 60% interest (12,000 shares) in Trainer Company for $158,000. Trainer stockholders' equity on the purchase date was as follows:

Common stock ($5 par)	$100,000
Paid-in capital in excess of par.	50,000
Retained earnings.	80,000
Total stockholders' equity	$230,000

At the purchase date, Trainer's book values for assets and liabilities closely approximate market values. Any excess of cost over book value is attributed to goodwill with a 10-year life.

On January 1, 19X8, Trainer Company sold 5,000 shares of common stock in a public offering at $20 per share. Mitta Corporation purchased 4,000 shares. Any excess of cost over book value on the additional interest was attributed to goodwill and given a 10-year life.

During 19X8, Mitta sold $30,000 of goods to Trainer at a gross profit of 25%. There were $6,000 of Mitta goods in Trainer's beginning inventory, and $8,000 of Mitta goods in Trainer's ending inventory.

Merchandise sales by Trainer to Mitta were $20,000 during 19X8 at a gross profit of 30%. There were $6,000 of Trainer goods in Mitta's beginning inventory and $2,000 of Trainer goods in Mitta's ending inventory.

Intercompany gross profit rates have been constant for many years. There are no intercompany payables/receivables.

Mitta's investment in Trainer Company balance was determined as follows:

Original cost..	$158,000
60% of Trainer 19X7 income ($40,000 × 60%)...........................	24,000
Subtotal	$182,000
Less 60% of Trainer dividends declared in 19X7 (60% × $8,000)............	(4,800)
Subtotal	$177,200
Cost to acquire additional shares (new issue).........................	80,000
64% of Trainer 19X8 income ($50,000 × 64%).........................	32,000
Subtotal	$289,200
Less 64% of Trainer dividends declared in 19X8 (64% × $10,000)...........	(6,400)
Investment balance, December 31, 19X8............................	$282,800

Trainer has paid a quarterly $.10 dividend per outstanding common share since the second quarter of 19X6.

The trial balances of the two firms as of December 31, 19X8, are as follows:

	Mitta	Trainer
Cash	104,200	63,500
Accounts Receivable	113,600	60,000
Inventory	350,000	80,000
Investment in Trainer Company	282,800	
Property, Plant, and Equipment............................	1,800,000	360,000
Accumulated Depreciation.................................	(600,000)	(89,500)
Accounts Payable..	(180,000)	(64,000)
Other Current Liabilities	(26,000)	(8,000)
Bonds Payable	(500,000)	
Common Stock ($10 par)	(1,000,000)	
Common Stock ($5 par)		(125,000)
Paid-In Capital in Excess of Par		(125,000)
Retained Earnings, Jan. 1, 19X8	(212,600)	(112,000)
Sales...	(1,950,000)	(600,000)
Subsidiary Income.......................................	(32,000)	
Cost of Goods Sold	1,170,000	420,000
Other Expenses	630,000	130,000
Dividends Declared	50,000	10,000
Total	0	0

Required:

Prepare the worksheet necessary to produce the consolidated financial statements of Mitta Corporation and its subsidiary as of December 31, 19X8. Include the determination and distribution of excess and income distribution schedules.

Problem 8-5. The audit of Barns Company and its subsidiaries for the year ended December 31, 19X2, was completed. The working papers contain the following information:

(a) Barns Company acquired 4,000 shares of Webb Company common stock for $320,000 on January 1, 19X1. Webb Company purchased 500 shares of its own stock as treasury shares for $48,000 on January 1, 19X2.

(b) Barns Company acquired all 8,000 outstanding shares of Elcho Company stock on January 1, 19X1, for $600,000. On January 1, 19X2, Elcho Company issued through a private sale 2,000 additional shares to new minority shareholders at $85 per share. Barns has no investments other than the stock of Webb and Elcho.

(c) Elcho Company originally issued $200,000 of 10-year, 8% mortgage bonds at 98, due on January 1, 19X5. On January 1, 19X2, Webb Company purchased $150,000 of these bonds in the open market at 98. Interest on the bonds is paid each June 30 and December 31.

(d) Condensed balance sheets of Webb and Elcho on January 1, 19X1, and January 1, 19X2, are as follows:

	Webb Company		Elcho Company	
	1/1/X1	1/1/X2	1/1/X1	1/1/X2
Current assets	$195,000	$225,000	$280,400	$205,000
Property, plant, and equipment	305,000	350,000	613,000	623,800
Unamortized bond discount...........			1,600	1,200
Total.............................	$500,000	$575,000	$895,000	$830,000
Current liabilities....................	$100,000	$125,000	$ 95,000	$105,000
Bonds payable.......................			200,000	200,000
Capital stock ($50 par)	250,000	250,000	400,000	400,000
Retained earnings...................	150,000	200,000	200,000	125,000
Total.............................	$500,000	$575,000	$895,000	$830,000

(e) Total dividends declared and paid during 19X2 were as follows:

Barns Company	....	$24,000
Webb Company	....	25,000
Elcho Company	....	10,000

In addition to the dividend payments, Barns Company and Webb Company each had declared dividends of $1 per share payable in January 19X3.

(f) On June 30, 19X2, Barns sold equipment with a book value of $8,000 to Webb for $10,000. Webb depreciates equipment by the straight-line method based on a 10-year life.

(g) Barns Company consistently sells to its subsidiaries at prices that realize a gross profit of 25% on sales. Webb and Elcho Companies sell to each other and to Barns Company at cost. Prior to 19X2, intercompany sales were negligible, but the following sales were made during 19X2:

	Total Sales	Included in Purchaser's Inventory at December 31, 19X2
Barns Company to Webb Company	$172,000	$ 20,000
Barns Company to Elcho Company..............	160,000	40,000
Webb Company to Elcho Company	25,000	5,000
Webb Company to Barns Company	28,000	8,000
	$385,000	$ 73,000

(h) At December 31, 19X2:

Barns Company owed Webb Company...................................	$24,000
Webb Company owed Elcho Company	16,000
Elcho Company owed Barns Company	12,000
Total..	$52,000

(i) The following trial balances as of December 31, 19X2, were prepared:

	Barns	Webb	Elcho
Cash.......................................	110,000	23,500	165,200
Accounts Receivable.........................	85,000	73,500	105,000
Inventories	138,000	163,000	150,000
Investment in Webb Company Stock	320,000		
Investment in Elcho Company Stock...........	600,000		
Investment in Elcho Company Bonds..........		148,000	
Property, Plant, and Equipment	700,000	525,000	834,000
Accumulated Depreciation....................	(402,000)	(325,000)	(240,000)
Accounts Payable	(202,000)	(150,500)	(86,900)
Dividends Payable...........................	(12,000)	(5,000)	
Bonds Payable..............................	(400,000)		(200,000)
Unamortized Bond Discount..................			800
Capital Stock ($50 par)	(600,000)	(250,000)	(500,000)
Paid-In Capital in Excess of Par...............			(70,000)
Retained Earnings, Jan. 1, 19X2*.............	(278,200)	(170,000)	(115,000)
Treasury Stock (at cost)		48,000	
Gain on Sale of Equipment	(2,000)		
Sales.......................................	(2,950,000)	(1,550,000)	(1,750,000)
Interest Income on Bonds		(13,000)	
Dividend Income	(28,000)		
Cost of Goods Sold..........................	2,500,000	1,200,000	1,400,000
Operating Expenses	405,000	280,000	290,500
Interest Expense	16,200	2,500	16,400
Total	0	0	0

*Reduced directly for dividends declared.

Required:

Prepare the worksheet necessary to produce the consolidated financial statements of Barns Company and its subsidiaries for the year ended December 31, 19X2. Include the determination and distribution of excess and income distribution schedules. Any excess of cost over book value is attributable to goodwill with a 10-year life. All bond discounts are assumed to be amortized on a straight-line basis.

(AICPA adapted)

Suggestion: The treasury stock represents a separate block of stock to be eliminated. The impact of the subsidiary sale of shares should not be reflected as an income statement gain or loss.

Problem 8-6. The following diagram depicts the relationships between Mary Company, Jack Company, and Jill Company on December 31, 19X8:

Mary Company purchased its interest in Jack Company on January 1, 19X6, for $200,000. Jack Company purchased its interest in Jill Company on January 1, 19X7, for $75,000. Mary Company purchased its interest in Jill Company on January 1, 19X8, for $72,000.

The following stockholders' equities are available:

	Jack Company December 31, 19X5	Jill Company December 31,	
		19X6	19X7
Common stock ($10 par)	$150,000		
Common stock ($20 par)		$100,000	$100,000
Paid-in capital in excess of par	75,000		
Retained earnings	75,000	50,000	80,000
Total equity	$300,000	$150,000	$180,000

On January 2, 19X8, Jill Company sold a machine to Mary Company for $20,000. The machine had a book value of $10,000, with an estimated life of 5 years and is being depreciated on a straight-line basis.

Jack Company sold $20,000 of merchandise to Jill Company during 19X8 to realize a gross profit of 30%. Of this merchandise, $5,000 remained in Jill Company's December 31, 19X8 inventory. Jill owes Jack $3,000 on December 31, 19X8, for merchandise delivered during 19X8.

Trial balances of the three firms prepared from general ledger account balances on December 31, 19X8, are as follows:

	Mary Company	Jack Company	Jill Company
Cash	66,500	60,000	30,000
Accounts Receivable	200,000	55,000	30,000
Inventory	360,000	80,000	50,000
Investment in Jack Company	266,000		
Investment in Jill Company	86,000	107,500	
Property, Plant, and Equipment	2,250,000	850,000	350,000
Accumulated Depreciation	(938,000)	(377,500)	(121,800)
Intangibles	15,000		
Accounts Payable	(215,500)	(61,000)	(22,000)
Accrued Expenses	(12,000)	(4,000)	(1,200)
Bonds Payable	(500,000)	(300,000)	(100,000)
Common Stock ($5 par)	(500,000)		
Common Stock ($10 par)		(150,000)	
Common Stock ($20 par)			(100,000)
Paid-In Capital in Excess of Par	(700,000)	(75,000)	
Retained Earnings, Jan. 1, 19X8	(290,000)	(130,000)	(80,000)
Sales	(1,800,000)	(500,000)	(300,000)
Gain on Sale of Equipment			(10,000)
Subsidiary Income	(58,000)	(20,000)	
Cost of Goods Sold	1,170,000	350,000	180,000
Other Expenses	525,000	100,000	90,000
Dividends Declared	75,000	15,000	5,000
Total	0	0	0

Required:

Prepare the worksheet necessary to produce the consolidated financial statements of Mary Company and its subsidiaries as of December 31, 19X8. Include the determination and distribution of excess and income distribution schedules. Any excess of cost is assumed to be attributable to goodwill with a 20-year life.

Problem 8-7. Shelby Corporation purchased 90% of the outstanding stock of Boehm Company on January 1, 19X4, for $600,000 cash. At that time, Boehm Company had the following stockholders' equity balances. Common Stock: $200,000; Paid-In Capital: $80,000; and Retained Earnings: $300,000.

All book values approximated market values except for the plant assets (undervalued by $50,000 and with an estimated remaining life of 10 years). Any goodwill was amortized over 20 years.

DeNoma Company acquired a 60% interest in Shelby on January 1, 19X6, for $750,000. At this time, Shelby had consolidated shareholders' equity of Common Stock: $500,000; Paid-In Capital: $150,000; and Controlling Retained Earnings: $500,000 *(not including amortization of excess price applicable to investment in Boehm).*

At that time, it was also determined that Shelby's plant assets were undervalued by $50,000 and had a 10-year remaining life. Boehm's plant assets were undervalued by $18,519. Any goodwill is to be amortized over 20 years.

Intercompany merchandise sales from Boehm to Shelby for 19X7 were (1) seller's goods in buyer's beginning inventory ($7,500); (2) sales during 19X7 ($125,000); (3) seller's goods in buyer's ending inventory ($10,000); and (4) gross profit on intercompany sales (80%).

On July 1, 19X6, Shelby sold plant assets with a cost of $80,000 and accumulated depreciation of $45,000 to DeNoma for $50,000. Remaining life on the date of sale was estimated to be 5 years.

Shelby and DeNoma use the simple equity method to account for their investments.

The trial balances on December 31, 19X7 were as follows:

	DeNoma Company	Shelby Corporation	Boehm Company
Inventory	75,000	60,000	40,000
Other Current Assets	900,000	5,000	390,000
Plant Assets	1,200,000	800,000	600,000
Accumulated Depreciation	(450,000)	(300,000)	(200,000)
Investment in Shelby Corporation	894,000		
Investment in Boehm Company		825,000	
Common Stock	(1,500,000)	(500,000)	(200,000)
Paid-In Capital in Excess of Par		(150,000)	(80,000)
Retained Earnings	(922,000)	(620,000)	(500,000)
Sales	(900,000)	(700,000)	(600,000)
Cost of Goods Sold	570,000	425,000	400,000
Expenses	205,000	200,000	150,000
Subsidiary Income	(72,000)	(45,000)	
Total	0	0	0

Required:

Prepare the determination and distribution of excess schedule for Shelby's investment in Boehm and DeNoma's investment in Shelby. Prepare the December 31, 19X7 consolidated worksheet and income distribution schedules.

Suggestion: The determination and distribution of excess schedule must show an adjustment to Shelby's retained earnings for the amortization of excess applicable to Shelby's investment in Boehm. (Hint for consolidated balance sheet: The reduced retained earnings in the determination and distribution of excess schedule must be adjusted before eliminating the pro rata share of equity balances.)

Problem 8-8. The following diagram depicts the relationships between Ackley Company, Biernat Company, and Cromwell Company on December 31, 19X7:

Information regarding the preceding investments follows:

(a) Ackley Company purchased its 40% interest in Cromwell Company on December 31, 19X3, for $50,000. On that date, Cromwell Company's book values approximated market values. Cromwell's plant assets consisted of several pieces of equipment that were being depreciated on a straight-line basis with estimated future lives of 10 years.

(b) On January 1, 19X6, Ackley Company purchased a 75% interest in Biernat Company for $400,000. The following determination and distribution of excess schedule was prepared at that time:

Price paid.		$400,000
Less interest acquired:		
Common stock ($5 par)	$300,000	
Paid-in capital in excess of par	100,000	
Retained earnings	30,000	
Total stockholders' equity	$430,000	
Interest acquired	75%	322,500
Excess of cost over book value.		$ 77,500
Excess of cost attributable to building (20-year life),		30,000
75% × $40,000.		
Goodwill (10-year life).		$ 47,500

(c) On January 1, 19X7, Biernat Company acquired a 40% interest in Cromwell Company for $92,000. Cromwell's book values approximated market values at this date.

(d) The following stockholders' equities have been made available:

	Cromwell Company December 31 19X3	Cromwell Company December 31 19X6	Biernat Company December 31 19X5
Noncumulative $6 preferred stock			
($100 par and liquidating value)			$ 50,000
Common stock ($5 par).			300,000
Common stock ($10 par)	$200,000	$200,000	
Paid-in capital in excess of par			100,000
Retained earnings (deficit)	(50,000)	30,000	30,000
Total equity	$150,000	$230,000	$480,000

(e) The following is information regarding intercompany merchandise sales in 19X7:

	Ackley to Cromwell	Cromwell to Biernat
Seller's merchandise in buyer's December 31, 19X6 inventory...	$ 2,000	
19X7 sales..	16,000	$5,000
Seller's merchandise in buyer's December 31, 19X7 inventory...	1,000	1,000
Intercompany receivable/payable on December 31, 19X7...	3,000	500
Gross profit on sales..................................	30%	40%

Trial balances of the three firms as of December 31, 19X7, are as follows:

	Ackley Company	Biernat Company	Cromwell Company
Cash	117,800	49,300	20,000
Accounts Receivable (net)	200,000	100,000	44,000
Inventory	277,000	206,000	58,000
Investment in Cromwell Company.............	50,000	92,000	
Investment in Biernat Company	400,000		
Property, Plant, and Equipment................	2,800,000	1,500,000	220,000
Accumulated Depreciation....................	(1,120,000)	(593,000)	(90,000)
Accounts Payable............................	(206,000)	(112,000)	(4,000)
Bonds Payable	(1,000,000)	(700,000)	
Preferred Stock.............................		(50,000)	
Common Stock ($5 par)	(500,000)	(300,000)	
Common Stock ($10 par)			(200,000)
Paid-In Capital in Excess of Par	(700,000)	(100,000)	
Retained Earnings, Jan. 1, 19X7	(270,000)	(61,000)	(30,000)
Sales.......................................	(1,500,000)	(850,000)	(400,000)
Subsidiary Dividend Income	(18,800)	(800)	
Cost of Goods Sold	1,050,000	552,500	240,000
Other Expenses	350,000	240,000	140,000
Preferred Dividends Declared		3,000	
Common Dividends Declared	70,000	24,000	2,000
Total	0	0	0

Required:

Prepare the worksheet necessary to produce the consolidated financial statements of Ackley Company and its subsidiaries as of December 31, 19X7. Include the determination and distribution of excess and income distribution schedules.

Problem 8-9. On January 1, 19X1, Paro Company purchased 80% of the common stock of Salger Company for $368,000. On this date, Salger had common stock, other paid-in capital, and retained earnings of $50,000, $140,000, and $220,000, respectively.

Any excess of cost over book value is due to goodwill, to be amortized over the maximum period permitted.

In both 19X1 and 19X2, Paro has accounted for the investment in Salger using the cost method.

On January 1, 19X2, Salger purchased 500 shares (5%) of the common stock of Paro Company from outside investors for $37,500. It is expected that the shares may be resold later. Salger uses the cost method in accounting for the investment. Any excess is attributed to goodwill with a 5-year life.

During the last quarter of 19X2, Paro sold merchandise to Salger for $40,000, one-fourth of which is still held by Salger on December 31, 19X2. Paro's usual gross profit on intercompany sales is 40%.

The trial balances for Paro and Salger on December 31, 19X2, are as follows:

	Paro Company	Salger Company
Inventory	170,000	120,000
Other Current Assets	248,000	258,500
Investment in Salger Company	368,000	
Investment in Paro Company		37,500
Land	80,000	70,000
Buildings and Equipment	400,000	280,000
Accumulated Depreciation	(180,000)	(90,000)
Current Liabilities	(98,000)	(74,000)
Long-Term Liabilities	(250,000)	(100,000)
Common Stock—Paro Company	(100,000)	
Other Paid-In Capital—Paro Company	(200,000)	
Retained Earnings—Paro Company	(350,000)	
Common Stock—Salger Company		(50,000)
Other Paid-In Capital—Salger Company		(140,000)
Retained Earnings—Salger Company		(260,000)
Net Sales	(640,000)	(350,000)
Cost of Goods Sold	360,000	200,000
Operating Expenses	160,000	90,000
Dividend Income	(8,000)	(2,000)
Dividends Declared	40,000	10,000
Total	0	0

Required:

Complete the worksheet for consolidated financial statements for the year ended December 31, 19X2. Use the treasury stock method for the investment in Paro Company. Round all computations to the nearest dollar. Include a determination and distribution of excess schedule and income distribution schedules.

Problem 8-10. Using the data of Problem 8-9, prepare the 19X2 consolidated worksheet of Paro Company and its subsidiary using the reciprocal method. The distribution of combined net income should be determined by solving simultaneous equations. Include a determination and distribution of excess schedule and income distribution schedule.

Problem 8-11. On January 1, 19X6, Heckert Company purchased a controlling interest in Allen Company. The following information is available:

(a) Heckert Company purchased 1,600 shares of Allen Company outstanding stock on January 1, 19X5, for $48,000 and purchased an additional 1,400 shares on January 1, 19X6, for $52,000.

(b) An analysis of the stockholders' equity accounts at December 31, 19X5, and 19X4, follows:

	Heckert Company December 31		Allen Company December 31	
	19X5	19X4	19X5	19X4
Common stock ($10 par).............	$150,000	$150,000		
Common stock ($5 par)...............			$ 20,000	$ 20,000
Paid-in capital in excess of par.........	36,000	36,000	10,000	10,000
Retained earnings....................	378,000	285,000	112,000	82,000
Total...........................	$564,000	$471,000	$142,000	$112,000

(c) Allen Company's marketable securities consist of 1,500 shares of Heckert Company stock purchased on June 15, 19X6, in the open market for $18,000. The securities were purchased as a temporary investment and were sold on January 15, 19X7, for $25,000.

(d) On December 10, 19X6, Heckert Company declared a cash dividend of $.50 per share, payable January 10, 19X7, to stockholders of record on December 20, 19X6. Allen Company paid a cash dividend of $1 per share on June 30, 19X6, and distributed a 10% stock dividend on September 30, 19X6. The stock was selling for $15 per share ex-dividend on September 30, 19X6. Allen Company paid no dividends in 19X5.

(e) Allen Company sold machinery, with a book value of $4,000 and a remaining life of 5 years, to Heckert Company for $4,800 on December 31, 19X6. The gain on the sale was credited to the other income account.

(f) Allen Company includes all intercompany receivables and payables in its trade accounts receivable and trade accounts payable accounts.

(g) During 19X6, the following intercompany sales were made:

	Net Sales	Included in Purchaser's Inventory at December 31, 19X6
Heckert Company to Allen Company...............	$ 78,000	$24,300
Allen Company to Heckert Company..............	104,000	18,000
	$182,000	$42,300

Heckert Company sells merchandise to Allen Company at cost. Allen Company sells merchandise to Heckert at the regular selling price to make a normal profit margin of 30%. There were no intercompany sales in prior years.

The trial balances of the two firms at December 31, 19X6, are as follows:

	Heckert Company	Allen Company
Cash...	37,900	29,050
Marketable Securities......................................	33,000	18,000
Trade Accounts Receivable	210,000	88,000
Allowance for Doubtful Accounts...........................	(6,800)	(2,300)
Intercompany Receivables.................................	24,000	
Inventories..	275,000	135,000
Machinery and Equipment	514,000	279,000
Accumulated Depreciation.................................	(298,200)	(196,700)
Investment in Allen Company (at cost)	100,000	
Patents...	35,000	
Dividends Payable...	(7,500)	

	Heckert Company	Allen Company
Trade Accounts Payable	(195,500)	(174,050)
Intercompany Payables	(8,000)	
Common Stock ($10 par)	(150,000)	
Common Stock ($5 par)		(22,000)
Paid-In Capital in Excess of Par	(36,000)	(14,000)
Retained Earnings	(370,500)	(102,000)
Sales and Services	(850,000)	(530,000)
Dividend Income	(3,000)	
Other Income	(9,000)	(3,700)
Cost of Goods Sold	510,000	374,000
Depreciation Expense	65,600	11,200
Administrative and Selling Expenses	130,000	110,500
Total	0	0

Required:

Prepare the worksheet necessary to produce the consolidated financial statements of Heckert Company and its subsidiary for the year ended December 31, 19X6. Include the determination and distribution of excess and income distribution schedules. Assume any excess of cost over book value is attributable to goodwill with a 20-year life. For any mutual holdings, use the treasury stock method.

(AICPA adapted)

WORKSHEET 8-1

Indirect Holdings; Intercompany Sales
Company A and Subsidiary Companies B and C
Worksheet for Consolidated Financial Statements
For Year Ended December 31, 19X3

	(Credit balance amounts are in parentheses.)	Trial Balance		
		Company A	Company B	Company C
1	Inventory, Dec. 31, 19X3	80,000	20,000	30,000
2				
3	Other Assets	60,000	146,000	130,000
4	Building and Equipment	300,000	200,000	150,000
5	Accumulated Depreciation	(100,000)	(60,000)	(30,000)
6	Investment in Company B	643,000		
7				
8				
9	Investment in Company C		318,000	
10				
11				
12	Goodwill			
13	Common Stock ($10 par), Co. A	(300,000)		
14	**Retained Earnings, Jan. 1, 19X3, Co. A**	**(500,000)**		
15				
16				
17				
18	Common Stock ($10 par), Co. B		(200,000)	
19	**Retained Earnings, Jan. 1, 19X3, Co. B**		**(300,000)**	
20				
21				
22				
23	Common Stock ($10 par), Co. C			(100,000)
24	**Retained Earnings, Jan. 1, 19X3, Co. C**			**(150,000)**
25				
26	Sales	(400,000)	(300,000)	(150,000)
27	Cost of Goods Sold	250,000	160,000	80,000
28				
29				
30	Expenses	60,000	40,000	40,000
31				
32	Subsidiary Income	(93,000)	(24,000)	
33				
34		0	0	0
35	Combined Net Income			
36	To Minority Interest, Company C (see distribution schedule)			
37	To Minority Interest, Company B (see distribution schedule)			
38	To Controlling Interest (see distribution schedule)			
39	Total Minority Interest			
40	Retained Earnings, Controlling Interest, Dec. 31, 19X3			
41				

Worksheet 8-1 (see page 503)

Eliminations & Adjustments				Consolidated Income Statement	Minority Interest	Controlling Retained Earnings	Consolidated Balance Sheet	
Dr.		Cr.						
		(11)	2,500				124,500	1
		(13)	3,000					2
							336,000	3
(3)	175,000						825,000	4
		(4)	52,500				(242,500)	5
		(1)	93,000					6
		(2)	375,000					7
		(3)	175,000					8
		(5)	24,000					9
		(6)	200,000					10
		(7)	94,000					11
(7)	94,000	(8)	9,400				84,600	12
							(300,000)	13
(4)	35,000					(458,895)		14
(8)	3,525							15
(10)	1,500							16
(12)	1,080							17
(2)	150,000				(50,000)			18
(2)	225,000				(72,965)			19
(8)	1,175							20
(10)	500							21
(12)	360							22
(6)	80,000				(20,000)			23
(6)	120,000				(29,640)			24
(12)	360							25
(9)	90,000			(760,000)				26
(11)	2,500	(9)	90,000	401,700				27
(13)	3,000	(10)	2,000					28
		(12)	1,800					29
(4)	17,500			162,200				30
(8)	4,700							31
(1)	93,000							32
(5)	24,000							33
	1,122,200		1,122,200					34
				(196,100)				35
				5,760*	(5,760)			36
				29,460*	(29,460)			37
				160,880*		(160,880)		38
					(207,825)		(207,825)	39
						(619,775)	(619,775)	40
							0	41

(continued)

Eliminations and Adjustments:

(1) Eliminate the entry made by Company A to record its share of Company B income. This step returns the investment in Company B account to its January 1, 19X3 balance to aid the elimination process.

(2) Eliminate 75% of the January 1, 19X3 Company B equity balances against the investment in Company B.

(3) Distribute the $175,000 excess of cost to the building and equipment account according to the determination and distribution of excess schedule applicable to the level one investment.

(4) Amortize the excess (added depreciation) according to the determination and distribution of excess schedule. This step requires adjustment of Company A retained earnings for 19X1 and 19X2, plus adjustment of 19X3 expenses.

(5) Eliminate the entry made by Company B to record its share of Company C income. This returns the investment in Company C account to its January 1, 19X3 balance to aid elimination.

(6) Eliminate 80% of the January 1, 19X3 Company C equity balances against the investment in Company C.

(7) Distribute the $94,000 excess of cost to goodwill according to the determination and distribution of excess schedule applicable to the level two investment.

(8) Amortize the excess (goodwill amortization) according to the determination and distribution of excess schedule. Since created by actions of subsidiary Company B, the 19X2 amortization must be prorated 25% ($1,175) to the Company B minority interest and 75% ($3,525) to the controlling interest. Note that the Company B minority interest appears on the worksheet only after the first-level investment has been eliminated, again pointing to the need to eliminate the level one investment first.

(9) Eliminate intercompany sales to prevent double counting in the consolidated sales and cost of goods sold.

(10) Eliminate the Company B profit contained in the beginning inventory. Since Company B generated the sale, the correction of beginning retained earnings is split 75% to the controlling interest and 25% to the minority interest. The cost of goods sold is decreased since the beginning inventory was overstated.

(11) The cost of goods sold is adjusted and the ending inventory is reduced by the $2,500 of Company B profit contained in the ending inventory.

(12) Eliminate the Company C profit contained in the beginning inventory. Since Company C generated the retained earnings adjustment, it is apportioned as follows:

To minority interest in Company C (20%)	$ 360
To minority interest in Company B (25% of 80%)	360
To controlling interest (75% of 80%)	1,080
Total	$1,800

(13) The cost of goods sold is adjusted and the ending inventory is reduced by the $3,000 of Company C profit contained in the ending inventory.

Company C Income Distribution

Ending inventory profit . . . .(13)	$ 3,000	Internally generated income	$ 30,000
		Beginning inventory profit. . . . .(12)	1,800
		Adjusted income	$ 28,800
		Company B share, 80%.	23,040
		Company C minority interest, 20%.	$ 5,760*

Company B Income Distribution

Ending inventory profit . . . .(11)	$ 2,500	Internally generated income	$100,000
Amortization of goodwill resulting from purchase of investment in Company C. . . . .(8)	4,700	Beginning inventory profit. . . . .(10)	2,000
		80% of Company C adjusted income. . . .	23,040
		Adjusted income	$117,840
		Company A share, 75%	88,380
		Company B minority interest, 25%.	$ 29,460*

Company A Income Distribution

Building and equipment depreciation resulting from investment in Company B. . . . .(4)	$17,500	Internally generated income	$ 90,000
		75% of Company B adjusted income. . . .	88,380
		Controlling interest	$160,880*

WORKSHEET 8-2

Mutual Holdings, Treasury Stock Method
Company P and Subsidiary Company S
Worksheet for Consolidated Financial Statements
For Year Ended December 31, 19X3

	(Credit balance amounts are in parentheses.)	Trial Balance	
		Company P	Company S
1	Investment in Company S (80%)	248,000	
2			
3			
4	**Investment in Company P (10%), at cost**		**80,000**
5	Equipment	608,000	180,000
6	Accumulated Depreciation	(100,000)	(50,000)
7	Common Stock, Co. P	(500,000)	
8	Retained Earnings, Jan. 1, 19X3, Co. P	(200,000)	
9	Common Stock, Co. S		(100,000)
10	Retained Earnings, Jan. 1, 19X3, Co. S		(90,000)
11	Sales	(300,000)	(200,000)
12	Cost of Goods Sold	180,000	120,000
13	Expenses	80,000	60,000
14	Subsidiary Income	(16,000)	
15	**Treasury Stock (at cost)**		
16		0	0
17	Combined Net Income		
18	To Minority Interest (see distribution schedule)		
19	Balance to Controlling Interest (see distribution schedule)		
20	Total Minority Interest		
21	Retained Earnings, Controlling Interest, Dec. 31, 19X3		
22			

Eliminations and Adjustments:
(1) Eliminate the entry made by the parent during the current year to record its share of Company S income.
(2) Eliminate 80% of the January 1, 19X3 subsidiary equity balances against the investment in Company S account.
(3) Distribute the excess of cost over book value to the equipment account as specified by the determination and distribution of excess schedule.
(4) Amortize the excess of $80,000 for the past two years and the current year.
(5) The investment in Company P must be at cost. If any equity adjustments have been made, they must be reversed and the investment in the parent returned to cost. If the shares are to be reissued, as is the case in this example, the investment then is transferred to the treasury stock account, a contra-account to total consolidated stockholders' equity.

Worksheet 8-2 (see page 508)

| Eliminations & Adjustments | | Consolidated Income Statement | Minority Interest | Controlling Retained Earnings | Consolidated Balance Sheet | |
Dr.	Cr.					
	(1) 16,000					1
	(2) 152,000					2
	(3) 80,000					3
	(5) 80,000					4
(3) 80,000					868,000	5
	(4) 12,000				(162,000)	6
					(500,000)	7
(4) 8,000				(192,000)		8
(2) 80,000			(20,000)			9
(2) 72,000			(18,000)			10
		(500,000)				11
		300,000				12
(4) 4,000		144,000				13
(1) 16,000						14
(5) 80,000					80,000	15
340,000	340,000					16
		(56,000)				17
		4,000*	(4,000)			18
		52,000*		(52,000)		19
			(42,000)		(42,000)	21
				(244,000)	(244,000)	21
					0	22

As an alternative to step (5), the cost of the treasury shares could be used to retire them on the worksheet as follows:

Common Stock, Company P..	50,000	
Retained Earnings, Company P	30,000	
Investment in Company P...		80,000

(continued)

Subsidiary Company S Income Distribution

Internally generated net income..........	$20,000
Adjusted income	$20,000
Minority share	20%
Minority interest......................	$ 4,000*

Parent Company P Income Distribution

Amortization of excess cost— depreciation . . . .(4) $4,000		Internally generated net income . . . . $40,000 80% × Company S adjusted income of $20,000. 16,000	
		Controlling interest $52,000*	

WORKSHEET 8-3

Mutual Holdings, Reciprocal Method
Company P and Subsidiary Company S
Worksheet for Consolidated Financial Statements
For Year Ended December 31, 19X3

	(Credit balance amounts are in parentheses.)	Trial Balance	
		Company P	Company S
1	Investment in Company S (80%)	248,000	
2			
3			
4	**Investment in Company P (10%)**		**84,000**
5			
6			
7	Equipment	608,000	180,000
8	Accumulated Depreciation	(100,000)	(50,000)
9	Goodwill		
10	**Common Stock, Co. P**	**(500,000)**	
11	**Retained Earnings, Jan. 1, 19X3, Co. P**	**(200,000)**	
12			
13	Common Stock, Co. S		(100,000)
14	Retained Earnings, Jan. 1, 19X3, Co. S		(90,000)
15	Sales	(300,000)	(200,000)
16	Cost of Goods Sold	180,000	120,000
17	Expenses	80,000	60,000
18			
19	**Subsidiary (or Investment) Income**	**(16,000)**	**(4,000)**
20			
21		0	0
22	Combined Net Income		
23	**To Minority Interest (see solution to simultaneous equations, page 510)**		
24	**Balance to Controlling Interest (see solution to simultaneous equations)**		
25	Total Minority Interest		
26	Retained Earnings, Controlling Interest, Dec. 31, 19X3		
27			

Eliminations and Adjustments:
(1–4) Same as entries 1–4 of Worksheet 8-2.
   (5) Eliminate the entry made by Company S to record its share of Company P income.
   (6) Eliminate 10% of the January 1, 19X3 parent equity balances against the investment in Company P account. Note that 10% of the original January 1, 19X3 Company P retained earnings is eliminated without regard to the $8,000 amortization of excess adjustment, since this adjustment was not included in the original determination and distribution of excess schedule.

Worksheet 8-3 (see page 509)

Eliminations & Adjustments				Consolidated Income Statement	Minority Interest	Controlling Retained Earnings	Consolidated Balance Sheet	
Dr.		Cr.						
		(1)	16,000					1
		(2)	152,000					2
		(3)	80,000					3
		(5)	4,000					4
		(6)	70,000					5
		(7)	10,000					6
(3)	80,000						868,000	7
		(4)	12,000				(162,000)	8
(7)	10,000	(8)	1,000				9,000	9
(6)	50,000						(450,000)	10
(4)	8,000					(172,000)		11
(6)	20,000							12
(2)	80,000				(20,000)			13
(2)	72,000				(18,000)			14
				(500,000)				15
				300,000				16
(4)	4,000			145,000				17
(8)	1,000							18
(1)	16,000							19
(5)	4,000							20
	345,000		345,000					21
				(55,000)				22
				4,913	(4,913)			23
				50,087		(50,087)		24
					(42,913)		(42,913)	25
						(222,087)	(222,087)	26
							0	27

(7) Distribute the excess of cost over book value to the goodwill account as specified by the determination and distribution of excess schedule.

(8) Amortize the excess for the current year.

(continued)

Company S Adjusted Internally Generated Income (see page 510)

Amortization of excess cost—goodwill amortization....................(8) $1,000	Unadjusted internally generated income . .	$20,000
	Adjusted	$19,000

Company P Adjusted Internally Generated Income (see page 510)

Amortization of excess cost— depreciation.........................(4) $4,000	Unadjusted internally generated income .. $40,000
	Adjusted $36,000

Note: If intercompany profit adjustments existed, they would be entered in the income distribution schedule.

Appendices to the Consolidations Chapters

APPENDIX A: ALTERNATIVE CONSOLIDATION CONCEPTS

The 1991 FASB Discussion Memorandum *Consolidation Policy and Procedure* identified three basic consolidation concepts, each of which has an impact on consolidated financial statements where there is a minority interest. The three concepts have been referenced in Chapters 2 through 8 to indicate the theoretical basis for the methods used in this text. This appendix will review these concepts, indicate where appropriate the impact of the alternative concepts on each chapter using a summary matrix, and show the detailed application of the major alternative concepts to each chapter that is impacted. The three concepts can be identified as follows:

Economic Unit Concept.   This concept often was termed the "entity theory" in accounting literature. It focuses on the statements of the consolidated firm as those of a single economic entity. The statements and the procedures used to prepare them are not dependent on the size of the minority interest. The balance sheet includes all of the subsidiary's assets (with a possible exception for goodwill) and liabilities at 100% of market value on the date control is achieved. The total stockholders' equity simply is divided between the controlling and minority interests. The consolidated income statement shows consolidated net income as the amount available for both the controlling and minority interests. All intercompany transactions and unrealized profits are 100% eliminated regardless of the size of the minority interest.

Parent Company Concept.   This concept has been referred to as the "proprietary theory." It focuses on the equity interest of the parent firm. The balance sheet includes the parent's interest in subsidiary assets at market value on the date the parent purchases its interest, but the minority share of subsidiary assets remains at book value. The minority equity interest is shown either as a liability or between liabilities and stockholders' equity. The consolidated income statement subtracts the minority interest in income from the combined income of the two firms to arrive at consolidated net income, which is only the controlling interest. The income statement, however, includes all of the subsidiary's transactions. Under the strictest interpretation of the parent company concept, only the controlling ownership percentage of intercompany transactions and unrealized profits would be eliminated. In practice, however, it is common to eliminate 100% of these transactions and profits.

Proportionate Consolidation.   This method is similar to the parent company concept in that it focuses on the controlling interest's equity and income. The unusual nature of the method is its inclusion of only the parent's ownership percentage of subsidiary income statement transactions. Also, it includes only the parent's ownership share of assets and liabilities in the consolidated balance sheet. The parent's ownership share of assets and liabilities is recorded at market value as of the purchase date. The minority share of income and the minority share of equity never appear in the consolidated statements.

You will notice that current practice, which is presented in Chapters 2 through 8 of this text, is not totally consistent with any one consolidation theory. Rather, current practice is a mixture of the economic unit and parent company concepts. This text and current practice are grounded in conservatism. This means that the parent company concept is used for recording the purchase of an interest in a subsidiary. Conservatism is reflected here through the write-up to market value of only the interest purchased; no adjustment is made to the minority interest, which has not sold. The economic unit concept is applied to intercompany transactions. Conservatism is apparent here in the elimination of 100% of intercompany transactions and 100% of unrealized profits. No profit may be recorded, even on the minority interest, until there has been a transaction with a party outside the consolidated firm. The FASB Discussion Memorandum states that a hybrid concept is not unreasonable and may best serve financial reporting objectives. Thus, one should not conclude that in the future all procedures will conform to one concept.

SUMMARY COMPARISON OF THE CONCEPTS WITH CHAPTER REFERENCE

The major issues that differ among the methods are compared in the following chart. Each segment is labeled by the chapter in which the issue is contained, and in each segment the most common current practice is shown in bold print. The chart is followed by a detailed explanation of each major issue.

Conditions for Consolidations *Chapter 2*	Economic Unit Ability to control another entity	**Parent Company** **Majority ownership**	Proportionate Majority ownership
Adjustment of Subsidiary Accounts to Market Value *Chapter 2*	Economic Unit 100% market One variation of the concept records only the parent % of goodwill	**Parent Company** **Parent ownership % to market value** **Minority interest remains at book value**	Proportionate Parent ownership % to market value Minority interest is not recorded
Presentation of Minority Interest in Equity *Chapter 2*	**Economic Unit** **Subdivision of total stockholders' equity**	Parent Company Separate section between liabilities and equity or as a liability	Proportionate Does not appear in consolidated balance sheet
Adjustments for Amortization of Excess at Purchase *Chapter 3*	Economic Unit Based on 100% of market and shared by minority and controlling interest	**Parent Company** **Based on parent % and charged only to controlling interest**	Proportionate Based on parent % and charged only to controlling interest
Presentation of Minority Share of Consolidated Income *Chapter 3*	Economic Unit Consolidated income is for both groups Allocation of consolidated income is made to minority and controlling interest	**Parent Company** **Deducted (like an expense) to arrive at consolidated income which is parent-only interest**	Proportionate Only parent share of transactions is included Only income shown is parent's interest Minority interest is not present
Elimination of Intercompany Transactions *Chapters 4 and 5*	**Economic Unit** **Eliminate 100%**	Parent Company Two alternatives: eliminate 100% or only parent's ownership %	Proportionate Eliminate only parent's ownership %
Elimination of Unrealized Intercompany Profits *Chapter 4*	**Economic Unit** **Defer 100%**	Parent Company Only parent's ownership % is deferred	Proportionate Only parent's ownership % is deferred
Elimination of Intercompany Bonds *Chapter 5*	**Economic Unit** **Retire on worksheet** **100% of gain or loss borne by issuer**	Parent Company Retire on worksheet: difference between cost and par to buyer; difference between par and book value to issuer	Proportionate Retire on worksheet: difference between cost and par to buyer; difference between par and book value to issuer

	Economic Unit	Parent Company	Proportionate
Piecemeal Acquisition, Control Upon Later Acquisition *Chapter 7*	Initial block adjusted to market value on date control is achieved Full market value of subsidiary assets and liabilities recorded	**Only parent's ownership % of market value on each block is recorded based on market values on each purchase date**	Only parent's ownership % of market value on each block is recorded based on market values on each purchase date

	Economic Unit	Parent Company	Proportionate
Piecemeal Acquisition, Control Upon Initial Acquisition *Chapter 7*	Purchase and sale of interests by parent treated as treasury stock transaction with no gain or loss	**Each block is a separate investment with parent's ownership % of market value on each block recorded based on market values on each purchase date**	Each block is a separate investment with parent's ownership % of market value on each block recorded based on market values on each purchase date

	Economic Unit	Parent Company	Proportionate
Change in Parent Ownership Percentage as a Result of Subsidiary Purchase or Sale of Its Shares *Chapter 8*	Purchase and sale of subsidiary shares treated as treasury stock transaction with no gain or loss	**Decrease in interest caused by the transaction creates gain or loss** **Increase in interest is treated as if it were the purchase of an additional block**	Decrease in interest caused by the transaction creates gain or loss Increase in interest is treated as if it were the purchase of an additional block

CONSOLIDATION PROCEDURES ON THE DATE OF PURCHASE (CHAPTER 2)

Alternative consolidation theories impact the determination and distribution schedule, the consolidated worksheet, and the consolidated balance sheets discussed in Chapter 2. Let us return to the example of a purchase of an 80% interest on page 83 of Chapter 2. The price paid for the 80% interest was $800,000 plus $10,000 of direct acquisition cost. The following entry was made to record the purchase:

Investment in Subsidiary S (16,000 shares × $50 market value + $10,000 direct acquisition costs)	810,000	
Common Stock (16,000 shares × $10 par)		160,000
Paid-In Capital in Excess of Par		640,000
Cash (for acquisition costs)		10,000

The trial balance for each company immediately after the purchase was as follows:

	Company P		Company S	
Cash.	200,000		150,000	
Accounts Receivable	300,000		250,000	
Inventory	500,000		300,000	
Land	100,000			
Buildings (net)	900,000			
Equipment (net).	650,000		400,000	
Investment in Subsidiary S	810,000			
Current Liabilities.		300,000		100,000
Bonds Payable.		500,000		300,000
Common Stock ($10 par)		660,000		
Common Stock ($5 par)				50,000
Paid-In Capital in Excess of Par		1,140,000		350,000
Retained Earnings.		860,000		300,000
Total	3,460,000	3,460,000	1,100,000	1,100,000

Now, we will consider the effect of alternative consolidation concepts on consolidation procedures on the date of acquisition.

PARENT COMPANY CONCEPT

The parent company concept is used throughout the text and was applied to this example in Chapter 2 (which is repeated here.) The determination and distribution of excess schedule considered only the excess of cost over book value on the parent company's interest and adjusts only the parent's ownership interest in the subsidiary's assets and liabilities. The schedule was prepared as follows:

Company P and Subsidiary Company S Determination and Distribution of Excess Schedule Parent Company Concept (also Proportionate Concept) December 31, 19X1			
Price paid for investment in Company S including direct acquisition costs		$810,000	
Less interest acquired:			
Common stock ($5 par).	$ 50,000		
Paid-in capital in excess of par.	350,000		
Retained earnings	300,000		
Total stockholders' equity.	$700,000		
Interest acquired.	80%	560,000	
Excess of cost over book value (debit balance)		$250,000	
Less undervaluation of interest in current assets:			
Inventory ($50,000 total × 80%)		40,000	Dr
Less undervaluation of interest in identifiable long-lived assets:			
Equipment ($150,000 total × 80%).		120,000	Dr
Goodwill.		$ 90,000	Dr

Refer to Worksheet 2-6 on page 118, and notice the following features that result from the determination and distribution of excess schedule:

- Only the parent ownership percentage of the subsidiary equity accounts is eliminated. The remaining portion of the minority equity interest is extended to the consolidated balance sheet as the minority equity interest.
- On the formal balance sheet, the minority equity will be shown in the aggregate as either a liability or a separate item between liabilities and stockholders' equity.
- Subsidiary asset accounts are adjusted only for the parent ownership percentage of the difference between market and book value. The minority interest in these assets remains at book value. Likewise, if there were liabilities with a market value different from book value, they also would be adjusted for only 80% of the disparity. This means, for example, the inventory is listed on the balance sheet at the sum of 80% of market value and 20% of book value. It is the lack of consistency in valuation that subjects the parent company concept to controversy.

PROPORTIONATE CONCEPT

The proportionate concept is really a narrower interpretation of the parent company concept. It excludes the minority interest entirely from the consolidated statements. The determination and distribution of excess schedule would be the same as that prepared under the parent company concept. Only the parent ownership percentage of the differences between market and book values is acknowledged.

The difference comes in the consolidated worksheet, which for our example is Worksheet A-1 on pages 564–565. Notice these unique features of the worksheet:

- The entire minority interest is eliminated. The parent ownership percentage is eliminated against the parent's investment account. The minority interest in equity is used to eliminate the minority ownership interest in the book value of all subsidiary assets and liabilities. This means that only the parent ownership percentage of the market value of subsidiary assets and liabilities is extended to the consolidated balance sheet.
- There is no minority equity interest to extend to the consolidated balance sheet.

ECONOMIC UNIT CONCEPT

There are two variations of this concept. The first version is referred to by the FASB Discussion Memorandum as the economic unit concept—*full goodwill*. This concept acknowledges 100% of the market value of all assets and liabilities including goodwill. In our example, that means that each identifiable asset and liability is adjusted 100% to market value. The minority interest in retained earnings is increased for the minority percentage of these adjustments. Since in our example, $90,000 was available for an 80% interest in goodwill, it is assumed that $90,000 ÷ 80%, or $112,500, would be the value of total goodwill.

The determination and distribution of excess schedule must be modified to allow for the adjustment of the minority interest percentage of the differences between book and market values.

Company P and Subsidiary Company S
Determination and Distribution of Excess Schedule
Economic Unit Concept—Full Goodwill
December 31, 19X1

		Controlling Interest	Minority Interest	Total
Price paid for investment in Company S including direct acquisition costs....................................		$810,000		
Less interest acquired:				
Common stock ($5 par)	$ 50,000			
Paid-in capital in excess of par	350,000			
Retained earnings	300,000			
Total stockholders' equity.......................	$700,000			
Interest acquired	80%	560,000		
Excess of cost over book value (debit balance)		$250,000		
Less undervaluation of interest in current assets:				
Inventory ($50,000 total, allocate 80/20)		40,000	$10,000	$ 50,000 Dr
Less undervaluation of interest in identifiable long-lived assets:				
Equipment ($150,000 total, allocate 80/20)		120,000	30,000	150,000 Dr
Goodwill ($112,500 total, allocate 80/20)		$ 90,000	22,500	112,500 Dr
Minority interest in adjustments....................			$62,500	

This determination and distribution of excess schedule would be the foundation of the procedures in Worksheet A-2 on pages 566–567. Note the following features of this worksheet:

- Only the parent ownership percentage of the minority stockholders' equity is eliminated.
- The excess of cost over book value on the parent's investment of $250,000 is supplemented by the excess of market value over cost of all assets and liabilities, including goodwill, of $62,500. Assets, including goodwill, then are adjusted to 100% of market value.
- The minority interest is increased for the minority's share of market value adjustments. This is done by increasing minority retained earnings. Also, it could be done by issuing an appraisal capital account. This issue is moot,

however, since the components of the minority equity usually are not shown in the consolidated balance sheet.

- The minority interest, including the adjustment for market values, will appear on the consolidated balance sheet as a subdivision of stockholders' equity.

The second version of the economic unit concept is termed the economic unit concept—*purchased goodwill*. It differs only in the adjustment made to recognize goodwill. Only the parent company's purchased portion of goodwill is acknowledged. The argument is that the price applicable to goodwill is really the price paid to secure control of the subsidiary, and the premium paid for control is not a function of the size of the interest purchased. All identifiable assets and liabilities are adjusted to market value. The determination and distribution of excess schedule would be prepared as follows:

Company P and Subsidiary Company S
Determination and Distribution of Excess Schedule
Economic Unit Concept—Purchased Goodwill
December 31, 19X1

		Controlling Interest	Minority Interest	Total
Price paid for investment in Company S including direct acquisition costs...........................		$810,000		
Less interest acquired:				
Common stock ($5 par)	$ 50,000			
Paid-in capital in excess of par	350,000			
Retained earnings	300,000			
Total stockholders' equity.......................	$700,000			
Interest acquired	80%	560,000		
Excess of cost over book value (debit balance)		$250,000		
Less undervaluation of interest in current assets:				
Inventory ($50,000 total, allocate 80/20)		40,000	$10,000	$ 50,000 Dr
Less undervaluation of interest in identifiable long-lived assets:				
Equipment ($150,000 total, allocate 80/20).........		120,000	30,000	150,000 Dr
Goodwill (only that paid for by parent)		$ 90,000		90,000 Dr
Minority interest in adjustments....................			$40,000	

This schedule leads to the procedures found in Worksheet A-3 on pages 568–569. The procedures are identical to those in Worksheet A-2 except that the minority equity interest is increased only for the minority's percentage of adjustments to identifiable assets. No adjustment to the minority interest is made for goodwill.

CONSOLIDATION PROCEDURES IN SUBSEQUENT PERIODS (CHAPTER 3)

The determination and distribution of excess schedules prepared under the alternative concepts impact worksheet procedures in subsequent periods. The amount of market value recorded with respect to subsidiary assets affects amortization procedures in later periods.

PARENT COMPANY CONCEPT

This concept adjusts the subsidiary assets and liabilities for only the parent's ownership percentage times the difference between market and book values on the acquisition date. This means that in later periods only the amortization of excesses applicable to the parent's interest are recorded on the consolidated worksheet. This is the method used in all worksheets in this text. To review this procedure, refer to Worksheets 3-5 and 3-6 on pages 190 and 194. You will see that in Worksheet 3-6 prior years' amortizations are carried only to the controlling retained earnings and the current year amortization is removed only from the parent company's income distribution schedule. Also, the parent company concept views consolidated net income as only that which accrues to the controlling interest. Notice at the bottom of the income statement column in Worksheet 3-5, the combined net income of $108,708 is allocated $12,000 to the minority interest and $96,708 to the controlling interest. On the formal income statement, the minority interest is viewed as an expense and is deducted from combined net income to arrive at consolidated net income.

PROPORTIONATE CONCEPT

This concept prepares the same determination and distribution of excess schedule as the parent company concept. Only that portion of the excess attributable to the parent's interest is acknowledged. Since only the excess applicable to the controlling interest is recorded on the worksheet, only the parent's interest is amortized, as is true under the parent company concept.

The only difference in worksheet procedure is that the minority interest in all accounts, including the nominal accounts, is eliminated. This can be accomplished by eliminating the minority interests in all accounts, as was done in Worksheet A-2 or by carrying only the controlling interests in all accounts to the worksheet subsidiary trial balance. In either case, the minority interest in all nominal accounts is absent from the consolidated income columns, and the only income shown is that applicable to the controlling interest. There would be no minority interest column on the worksheet. The final balance sheet would have no minority interest, and the minority interest in all balance sheet accounts would be absent.

ECONOMIC UNIT CONCEPT—FULL GOODWILL

This concept increases all identifiable assets and liabilities to full market value and records estimated goodwill so that it applies to the entire subsidiary. It adjusts the minority retained earnings for the minority share of market value adjustments. Worksheet A-4 on pages 570–572 is the economic unit concept with full goodwill applied to the worksheet example found in Worksheet 3-5. The determination and distribution of excess schedule prepared on page 138 would be revised as follows to allow for the adjustment of the minority interest:

Paulos Company and Subsidiary Carlos Company Determination and Distribution of Excess Schedule Economic Unit Concept—Full Goodwill January 1, 19X1			Controlling Interest	Minority Interest	Total	
Price paid (including $10,000 direct acquisition costs)			$800,000			
Less interest acquired:						
Capital stock ($10 par).............................		$100,000				
Paid-in capital in excess of par		150,000				
Retained earnings		250,000				
Total stockholders' equity.........................		$500,000				
Interest acquired.................................		80%	400,000			
Excess of cost over book value of subsidiary interest (debit balance)			$400,000			
Less adjustments to current assets and debt:						
Inventory undervalued $5,000, allocate 80/20			4,000	$ 1,000	$ 5,000	Dr
Bonds payable (4-year life) overstated by $13,248; record discount, allocate 80/20			10,598	2,650	13,248	Dr
Land understated $50,000; increase land			40,000	10,000	50,000	Dr
Building (20-year life) understated $200,000; decrease accumulated depreciation, allocate 80/20...........			160,000	40,000	200,000	Dr
Equipment (5-year life) overstated $20,000; reduce equipment, allocate 80/20			(16,000)	(4,000)	(20,000)	Cr
Balance of excess reflecting additional goodwill **(10-year life) ($201,402 ÷ 8), allocate 80/20...........**			$201,402	50,350*	251,752	Dr
Increase in minority interest.........................				$100,000		

*$201,402 ÷ 80% × 20% = $50,350 estimated minority goodwill.

Worksheet A-4, elimination 3 combines the $400,000 excess applicable to the controlling interest with the $100,000 increased minority retained earnings. This requires that all adjustments to market value on the worksheet be for 100% of the difference between book and market values. Under the full goodwill version of this concept, this includes the recognition of the entire estimated value of goodwill, not just the portion purchased by the parent firm. Likewise, the amortizations of excess in eliminations 4b, c, d, and f are applicable to a 100% adjustment. Note that if amortizations were for prior periods, the amortizations would be allocated 80/20 between controlling and minority retained earnings. In our example, notice that the amortizations of excess adjustments flow through the subsidiary income distribution schedule so that they, like subsidiary income, are allocated 20% to the minority interest and 80% to the controlling interest. This is in contrast to the examples in the text where the entire amortization is applicable only to the controlling interest and thus flows directly through the parent income distribution schedule. Notice also the bottom of the consolidated income column. True to the economic unit concept, the term (consolidated net income) applies to the combined income of the two firms. The consolidated net income is allocated to the two ownership groups.

ECONOMIC UNIT CONCEPT—PURCHASED GOODWILL

The procedures are identical to the full goodwill version of the concept except that only the interest in goodwill purchased by the parent is acknowledged in the determination and distribution of excess schedule. This means that in Worksheet A-4, elimination 3f would record only the $201,402 of goodwill applicable to the controlling interest. The $50,350 of goodwill that is estimated to apply to the minority interest is not recorded; thus, the increase to the minority retained earnings would be less by $50,350. The amortization of goodwill would be only that applicable to the controlling interest; $20,140 would replace the $25,175 in elimination 4f. This means that since only the controlling interest in goodwill is amortized, the adjustment would flow directly through the parent's income distribution schedule. In subsequent periods, only the controlling retained earnings would be reduced for the parent's share of goodwill amortizations.

INTERCOMPANY INVENTORY AND FIXED ASSET SALES (CHAPTER 4)

Current practices for intercompany transactions, which are reflected in Chapter 4, can be summarized as follows:

- 100% of all intercompany transactions are eliminated regardless of which of the affiliates makes the intercompany sale.
- 100% of all unrealized intercompany profits are deferred. The adjustment is allocated 100% to the controlling interest when the parent is the seller. The deferred profit is allocated between the controlling and minority interest when the subsidiary is the seller.

These procedures are derived from the economic unit concept which suggests that from the standpoint of a single economic entity, there has been no sale to outside interests, and there is no cause to recognize a profit. Where there is a minority interest and the seller is the subsidiary, there is no cause for even the minority shareholders to profit from a "nontransaction." Most accounting literature dealing with the parent company concept also recommends the above procedures, though there are limited cases where the entire adjustment for subsidiary-generated unrealized profits are allocated only to the controlling interest even when a minority interest exists.

There are some parent company theorists who would eliminate only the parent company percentage of intercompany transactions and unrealized profits regardless of who the seller was. The theory is that when the subsidiary sells to the parent, the minority interest should be allowed to realize any profit to which the parent company agreed. When the parent sells to the subsidiary, it is felt that the profit made selling to the minority interest should be realized. These procedures are in keeping with the belief that the minority interest is a separate entity on which profits may be made. The proportionate consolidation concept would eliminate only the parent company percentage of intercompany transactions and unrealized profits. Keep in mind that for subsidiary-generated sales, only the parent ownership percentage of the sales is included in the subsidiary accounts. Either the trial balance includes the parent company percentage of all subsidiary accounts or the minority interest in all subsidiary accounts is eliminated as the first step in the worksheet.

Let us consider the impact that elimination of only the parent company percentage of intercompany transactions and unrealized profits would have on the consolidated worksheet. We will revisit Worksheet 4-3 on page 264 and list those eliminations that would be impacted for intercompany merchandise sales.

(3) Only the parent company percentage of beginning inventory profit is eliminated.

Retained Earnings, Jan. 1, 19X2, Co. P.	6,400	
Cost of Goods Sold		6,400

(4) Only the parent company percentage of intercompany sales is eliminated.

Sales	96,000	
Cost of Goods Sold		96,000

(5) Only the parent company percentage of intercompany ending inventory profit is eliminated.

Cost of Goods Sold	4,800	
Inventory, December 31, 19X2		4,800

(6) Only the parent company percentage of intercompany debt is eliminated.

Accounts Payable	48,000	
Accounts Receivable		48,000

The subsidiary income distribution schedule would not be adjusted for any intercompany profits since the minority share of such profits is allowed to remain. The parent's share of subsidiary-generated intercompany profits would be adjusted for only in the parent's income distribution schedule. For parent company–generated profits, only the parent company percentage of intercompany profits would be adjusted for in the parent's income distribution schedule.

The effect of eliminating only the parent company percentage of intercompany fixed asset sales can be considered by referring to Worksheet 4-5 on page 272. The following eliminations would change:

(3)   Only 80% of the gain is eliminated. The parent company ownership percentage of the asset is restored to its original cost and accumulated depreciation on the date of sale.

Machinery	1,600	
Gain on Sale of Machine	8,000	
Accumulated Depreciation—Machinery		9,600

(4)   Depreciation for the current year would be reduced for only the parent company share of the realized intercompany profit.

Accumulated Depreciation—Machinery	1,600	
Depreciation Expense		1,600

The parent company income distribution schedule would be debited for $8,000 of unrealized gain and credited for $1,600 of gain realized through use. This is exactly the same adjustment that would be made if the seller was the subsidiary company.

INTERCOMPANY BONDS AND LEASES (CHAPTER 5)

The methods used in practice and in this text are consistent with the economic unit concept. This is true because 100% of the intercompany transactions are eliminated, and any resulting adjustment to income is shared by the controlling and minority interest whenever the transaction is subsidiary generated.

INTERCOMPANY BONDS

There is little support for eliminating only the parent portion of intercompany bonds although that is an inevitable result of the proportionate consolidation concept. This concept would make available on the trial balance only the parent company percentage of subsidiary bonds and related premium or discount. Also, it would include only the parent's percentage of interest expense.

There is an alternative procedure used by some writers to eliminate intercompany bonds. They would calculate the difference between the book value of the bonds and par as a gain or loss attributed to the issuer of the bonds. The difference between the purchase price of the bonds and the par value would be recorded as a gain or loss to the purchasing affiliate. Assuming the parent was the purchaser, the "purchase" gain or loss would be allocated only to the controlling interest. The "issuer" gain or loss would be allocated between the controlling and minority interest. This procedure is viewed as a manifestation of the parent company and the proportionate consolidation concept of business combinations by the FASB Discussion Memorandum. The method would appear to have little theoretical tie to any concept and is viewed by this text as only an alternative mechanical procedure.

INTERCOMPANY LEASES

The text eliminates 100% of the accounts resulting from operating leases and reclassifies 100% of the leased asset as an owned productive asset. This approach is consistent with the economic unit concept and the version of the parent company concept that eliminates 100% of intercompany transactions. There would be little justification for eliminating only the parent share of a lease or to reclassify only the parent's share of the leased asset. This would, however, be a natural result of the proportionate consolidation concept, since only the parent company percentage of all subsidiary transactions is available for elimination.

To date, the accounting literature dealing with intercompany leasing is too sparse to allow one to identify the impact of alternative consolidation concepts. Clearly, the methods used to eliminate intercompany capital leases in this text are consistent with the economic unit concept and that version of the parent company concept which eliminates 100% of intercompany transactions. There seems little merit in eliminating only the parent percentage of intercompany capital leases. Perhaps the elimination of the intercompany profit on sales-type capital leases is debatable because the conceptual differences would be the same as those applicable to intercompany fixed asset sales. One version of the parent company concept and the proportionate consolidation concept would hold that only the parent company portion of the intercompany gain should be deferred and recognized over time as the asset is used.

PIECEMEAL ACQUISITION OF INTEREST IN SUBSIDIARY (CHAPTER 7)

Chapter 7 dealt with piecemeal acquisitions by developing a separate determination and distribution of excess schedule for each investment block. Then, each block was separately eliminated and adjustments to assets and liabilities were separately amortized. As is true for all equity transactions in the text, the parent company concept was in use. This concept focuses on the ownership of each individual block and compares the price paid with the underlying equity on each purchase date. The same methods would be used under the proportionate concept.

The economic unit concept prepares only one determination and distribution of excess schedule, and adjusts the subsidiary assets to market value only once, the day control is achieved. Any block purchased after control is achieved is treated as a treasury stock transaction. Any prior interest owned on the date control is achieved is adjusted to market value and combined with the later purchase into a single determination and distribution of excess schedule.

CONTROL ACHIEVED UPON INITIAL INVESTMENT

The economic unit concept holds that the date control is achieved is the date to adjust all assets and liabilities to their full market value. This means that the minority interest in the subsidiary also is adjusted to market value on the date control is achieved, as was demonstrated in Chapter 2. There are no further adjustments to market value if the parent later purchases a portion of the minority interest. Later purchases of an additional interest by the parent are considered to be retirements of the subsidiary's shares. The example of the 60% original interest followed by the purchase of a 20% interest analyzed on page 407 of Chapter 7 now will be reconsidered under the economic unit concept. At the time of the original 60% interest, the following determination and distribution of excess schedule would be prepared under the variant of the economic unit concept that recognizes full goodwill:

Company P and Subsidiary Company S
Determination and Distribution of Excess Schedule
Economic Unit Concept—Full Goodwill
January 1, 19X1

		Parent	Minority	Total
Price paid		$126,000		
Less interest acquired:				
Common stock	$100,000			
Retained earnings.....................................	60,000			
Total stockholders' equity...........................	$160,000			
Interest acquired.....................................	60%	96,000		
Excess of cost over book value (debit balance)		$ 30,000		
Excess of cost attributable to equipment, $30,000,				
allocate 60/40, 5-year amortization.....................		18,000	$12,000	$30,000 Dr
Goodwill, implied $20,000, allocate 60/40,				
10-year amortization		$ 12,000	8,000	20,000 Dr
Increase in minority interest.............................			$20,000	

Since goodwill on the 60% interest was $12,000, it was implied that total goodwill would be $20,000 ($12,000 ÷ .6). Under the variant of the economic unit concept that records only purchased goodwill, just the $12,000 adjustment applicable to the minority interest in the equipment would be recorded on the worksheet.

Since assets and liabilities are adjusted to full market value on the date control is achieved, there is no further adjustment of assets and liabilities on the date of a later purchase of a portion of the minority interest. Instead, the parent is viewed as retiring the block of subsidiary stock it acquires. In our example, the later purchase of an additional 20% interest, $50,000, is paid to retire the shares, and the determination and distribution of excess schedule on page 557 is prepared.

The above schedule could include an adjustment for material amounts of unrealized intercompany profits on assets sold by the subsidiary to the parent.

The excess that results when eliminating the 20% interest is not used to adjust assets or liabilities, but is used to record a decrease in the controlling

> **Company P and Subsidiary Company S**
> **Determination and Distribution of Excess Schedule**
> **Economic Unit Concept—Full Goodwill**
> **January 1, 19X3**
>
> | | | | |
> |---|---|---|---|
> | Price paid .... | | | $50,000 |
> | Less interest acquired: | | | |
> | Common stock .... | | $100,000 | |
> | Retained earnings......................... | $100,000 | | |
> | Prior adjustment to market value.............. | 50,000 | | |
> | Equipment amortization, 1 year.............. | (6,000) | | |
> | Goodwill amortization, 1 year .... | (2,000) | 142,000 | |
> | Total shareholder equity .... | | $242,000 | |
> | Interest acquired........................... | | 20% | 48,400 |
> | Excess cost viewed as retirement premium ...... | | | $ 1,600 |

interest as a result of the retirement premium. If the parent has paid-in capital in excess of par, it would be reduced for the retirement premium. In this case, the parent had no paid-in capital in excess of par which necessitated debiting the parent's retained earnings. The worksheet elimination of the later 20% interest would be as follows:

```
Common stock, Company S (20% × $100,000)................  20,000
Retained earnings, Company S (20% of adjusted balance of
    $142,000)..........................................  28,400
Retained earnings, Company P (retirement premium) ...........   1,600
    Investment in Company S ...............................            50,000
```

In subsequent periods, the 20% interest either would be maintained under the simple equity method or would be converted from cost to equity to ease elimination and to maintain the original $1,600 excess cost on the date of the 20% purchase.

CONTROL NOT ACHIEVED UPON INITIAL PURCHASE

The economic unit concept adjusts subsidiary assets and liabilities to 100% of market value on the date control is achieved. It is a one-time adjustment and is not recalculated for separate blocks. All adjustments are based on the price paid for the interest that establishes control. The previous interest is adjusted to reflect the price paid for the later interest and a holding gain or loss is recorded when consolidating. Let us return to the example found on page 410 of Chapter 7. The initial 20% interest is accounted for under the sophisticated equity method. At the time of acquiring the 60% interest on January 1, 19X2, the determination and distribution of excess schedule would be revised to adjust the prior 20% interest and the remaining 20% minority interest to market value as follows:

Company P and Subsidiary Company S
Determination and Distribution of Excess Schedule
Economic Unit Concept—Full Goodwill
January 1, 19X2

	New 60% Interest		Prior Interest	Minority Interest	Total
Price paid......................................		$130,000			
Less interest acquired:					
Common stock............................	$ 50,000				
Retained earnings	115,000				
Total stockholders' equity..................	$165,000				
Interest acquired	60%	99,000			
Excess of cost over book value (debit balance)....		$ 31,000			
Excess attributed to equipment, $9,000,					
9-year life, allocate 60/20/20		5,400	$ 1,800	$ 1,800	$ 9,000 Dr
Goodwill, $42,666, 20-year life, allocate 60/20/20 ..		$ 25,600	8,533	8,533	42,666 Dr
Increase in interest			$10,333	$10,333	

This example follows the version of the economic unit concept that records the goodwill applicable to the entire firm. It was inferred from the price paid for a 60% interest that the total goodwill was worth $42,666 ($25,600 ÷ .6). The variant of the economic unit concept that recognizes only purchased goodwill would record just the $25,600 goodwill applicable to the 60% interest.

The consolidated worksheet would adjust the minority interest to reflect its undervaluation on the control date. There also would have to be an adjustment to record a holding gain or loss on the prior 20% interest owned by the parent. In this case, the loss is calculated as follows:

Carrying value of the investment on January 1, 19X2:
    Original cost $48,000
    19X1 equity adjustment 2,100
    Balance $50,100
Adjusted value on date control is achieved:
    Book value of subsidiary interest, 20% × $165,000.............. $33,000
    Adjustment to market value per determination and
      distribution of excess schedule 10,333
        43,333
Parent company loss on 20% interest........................... $ 6,767

This adjustment would result in the following elimination entries on the consolidated worksheet on the date control is achieved:

Common Stock, Company S (20% of $50,000)...............	10,000	
Retained Earnings, Company S (20% of $115,000).............	23,000	
Investment in Company S (20% interest)...................		33,000
Equipment (per determination and distribution schedule)........	1,800	
Goodwill (per determination and distribution schedule)...........	8,533	
Loss on Investment in Company S..........................	6,767	
Investment in Company S		17,100

In later periods, the loss would be a debit to controlling retained earnings.

APPENDIX A QUESTIONS

1. A parent company purchased an 80% interest in a subsidiary company. There is a sufficient excess of cost over book value to increase the carrying value of a fixed asset and to record goodwill. How would the amount of these adjustments differ depending on the alternative consolidation concepts?

2. A parent company purchased an 80% interest in a subsidiary for a price that was $80,000 in excess of the underlying book value of the interest purchased. The entire excess was attributed to goodwill with a 10-year life. How would the amount of goodwill recorded and the amount of goodwill amortization be affected by the use of alternative consolidation concepts?

3. Alternative consolidation concepts lead to differing methods of disclosing the minority share of income and the minority interest in total equity on the balance sheet. Indicate the disclosure of both the minority share of income and the total minority interest in equity under the alternative consolidation concepts.

4. Suppose that an 80%-owned subsidiary company sold a machine to the parent at the end of 19X3 at an intercompany profit of $10,000 and that the asset has a 10-year life. How would the worksheet adjustments for the intercompany profits in 19X3 and 19X4 be affected by the choice of alternative consolidation concepts?

5. A parent company purchased a 70% interest in a subsidiary in 19X3. In 19X6, the parent company purchased an additional 10% interest in the subsidiary. How would the procedures differ for consolidating the 10% interest according to the economic unit concept versus the parent company concept?

APPENDIX A EXERCISES

Exercise A-1. Patrick Company purchased an 80% interest in Arnold Company for $680,000 on December 31, 19X3. At the time of the purchase, Arnold had the following balance sheet:

Assets		Liabilities and Equity	
Current assets...............	$ 80,000	Current liabilities.............	$120,000
Land	140,000	Common stock, $10 par	100,000
Building	300,000	Paid-in excess of par	200,000
Equipment..................	200,000	Retained earnings............	300,000
Total.....................	$720,000	Total.....................	$720,000

At the time of the purchase, all accounts had market values similar to the existing book values except for the building which was appraised at $450,000. The building has a 20-year remaining life. Goodwill, if recorded, would be amortized over 10 years.

(1) Prepare a determination and distribution of excess schedule for the investment in Arnold Company using:
  (a) The proportionate consolidation concept.
  (b) The economic unit concept—full goodwill.
(2) Prepare the elimination entries that would be made to prepare a consolidated balance sheet on December 31, 19X1, using:
  (a) The proportionate consolidation concept.
  (b) The economic unit concept—full goodwill.

Exercise A-2. Hilton Company purchased an 80% interest in Neal Company on January 1, 19X3, for a price $80,000 in excess of book value. The entire excess was attributed to goodwill with a life of 10 years. The two firms prepared the following separate income statements for 19X3:

	Hilton Company	Neal Company
Sales.	$600,000	$200,000
Cost of goods sold.	400,000	80,000
Selling and administrative expenses.	110,000	40,000
Net income	$ 90,000	$ 80,000

Hilton Company uses the cost method to record its investment in Neal. Neal paid no dividends in 19X3. There were no intercompany transactions during 19X3.

Prepare income statements for 19X3 using:
(1) The parent company concept.
(2) The proportionate consolidation concept.
(3) The economic unit concept—full goodwill.

Exercise A-3. Pankow Company owns a 60% interest in Schwartz Company. On January 1, 19X1, Schwartz sold a machine to Pankow for $100,000. The net book value of the machine on Schwartz's books was $70,000 at the time of the sale. The machine has a 5-year life and no salvage value.

Prepare the elimination entry that would be made on a consolidated trial balance worksheet prepared on December 31, 19X2, using:
(1) The parent company concept.
(2) The proportionate consolidation concept.
(3) The economic unit concept.

APPENDIX A PROBLEMS

Problem A-1. (*This is Problem 3-7 using the economic unit concept.*) Sauer Company prepared the following balance sheet on January 1, 19X1:

Assets		Liabilities and Equity	
Current assets...............	$ 50,000	Liabilities	$140,000
Land	75,000	Common stock ($10 par)	100,000
Buildings	350,000	Paid-in capital	
Accumulated depreciation—		in excess of par............	120,000
buildings	(140,000)	Retained earnings (deficit)	(25,000)
Total assets	$335,000	Total liabilities and equity.....	$335,000

On this date, Roland Company purchased 8,000 shares of Sauer Company's outstanding stock for a total price of $270,000. Also on this date, the buildings were understated by $40,000 and were felt to have a 10-year remaining life. Any remaining discrepancy between the price paid and book value was attributed to goodwill and estimated to have a 20-year life. Since the purchase, Roland Company has used the cost method to record the investment and its related income.

Roland Company and Sauer Company have prepared the following separate trial balances on December 31, 19X2:

	Roland Company	Sauer Company
Current Assets..	180,000	115,000
Land	150,000	75,000
Buildings	590,000	350,000
Accumulated Depreciation—Buildings	(265,000)	(182,000)
Investment in Sauer Company	270,000	
Liabilities	(175,000)	(133,000)
Common Stock ($10 par)	(200,000)	(100,000)
Paid-In Capital in Excess of Par		(120,000)
Retained Earnings, January 1, 19X2......................	(495,000)	15,000
Sales...	(360,000)	(120,000)
Dividend Income (from Sauer Company)	(4,000)	
Cost of Goods Sold	179,000	50,000
Expenses	120,000	45,000
Dividends Declared	10,000	5,000
Total	0	0

The economic unit concept—full goodwill is to be used for consolidated statements.

Required:
(1) Prepare a determination and distribution of excess schedule for the investment.
(2) Prepare the 19X2 consolidated worksheet. Include columns for eliminations and adjustments, the consolidated income statement, the minority interest, the controlling retained earnings, and the consolidated balance sheet. Prepare supporting income distribution schedules.
(3) Prepare the 19X2 consolidated statements including the income statement, retained earnings statement, and the balance sheet.

Problem A-2. (*This is Problem 4-9 under the economic unit concept.*) On January 1, 19X1, Pepper Company acquired 80% of the common stock of Salt Company for $220,000. On this date, Salt had total owners' equity of $200,000. During 19X1 and 19X2, Pepper has appropriately accounted for its investment in Salt using the simple equity method.

Any excess of cost over book value is attributable to inventory (worth $12,500 more than cost), to equipment (worth $25,000 more than book value), and to goodwill. FIFO is used for inventories. The equipment has a remaining life of 4 years, and straight-line depreciation is used. Goodwill is to be amortized over 10 years.On January 1, 19X2, Pepper held merchandise acquired from Salt for $20,000. During 19X2, Salt sold merchandise to Pepper for $40,000, $10,000 of which is still held by Pepper on December 31, 19X2. Salt's usual gross profit is 50%.

On December 31, 19X1, Pepper sold equipment to Salt at a gain of $15,000. During 19X2, the equipment was used by Salt. Depreciation is being computed using the straight-line method, a 5-year life, and no salvage value.

The following trial balances were prepared for the Pepper and Salt companies for December 31, 19X2.

	Pepper Company	Salt Company
Inventory, December 31	110,000	50,000
Other Current Assets	241,000	235,000
Investment in Salt Company	328,000	
Other Long-Term Investments	20,000	
Land	140,000	80,000
Buildings and Equipment	375,000	200,000
Accumulated Depreciation	(120,000)	(30,000)
Other Intangibles		20,000
Current Liabilities	(150,000)	(70,000)
Bonds Payable		(100,000)
Other Long-Term Liabilities	(200,000)	(50,000)
Common Stock—Pepper Company	(200,000)	
Other Paid-In Capital—Pepper Company	(100,000)	
Retained Earnings—Pepper Company	(320,000)	
Common Stock—Salt Company		(50,000)
Other Paid-In Capital—Salt Company		(50,000)
Retained Earnings—Salt Company		(150,000)
Net Sales	(600,000)	(315,000)
Cost of Goods Sold	350,000	150,000
Operating Expenses	150,000	60,000
Subsidiary Income—Pepper Company	(84,000)	
Dividends Declared—Pepper Company	60,000	
Dividends Declared—Salt Company		20,000
Total	0	0

Required:

Complete the worksheet for consolidated financial statements for the year ended December 31, 19X2. Use the economic unit concept—full goodwill.

Problem A-3. (*This is Problem 4-9 under the proportionate concept.*) On January 1, 19X1, Pepper Company acquired 80% of the common stock of Salt Company for $220,000. On this date, Salt had total owner's equity of $200,000. During 19X1 and 19X2, Pepper has appropriately accounted for its investment in Salt using the simple equity method.

Any excess of cost over book value is attributable to inventory (worth $12,500 more than cost), to equipment (worth $25,000 more than book value), and to goodwill. FIFO is used for inventories. The equipment has a remaining life of 4 years, and straight-line depreciation is used. Goodwill is to be amortized over 10 years.On January 1, 19X2, Pepper held merchandise acquired from Salt for $20,000. During 19X2, Salt sold merchandise to Pepper for $40,000, $10,000 of which is still held by Pepper on December 31, 19X2. Salt's usual gross profit is 50%.

On December 31, 19X1, Pepper sold equipment to Salt at a gain of $15,000. During 19X2, the equipment was used by Salt. Depreciation is being computed using the straight-line method, a 5-year life, and no salvage value.

The following trial balances were prepared for the Pepper and Salt companies for December 31, 19X2.

	Pepper Company	Salt Company
Inventory, December 31	110,000	50,000
Other Current Assets	241,000	235,000
Investment in Salt Company	328,000	
Other Long-Term Investments	20,000	
Land	140,000	80,000
Buildings and Equipment	375,000	200,000
Accumulated Depreciation	(120,000)	(30,000)
Other Intangibles		20,000
Current Liabilities	(150,000)	(70,000)
Bonds Payable		(100,000)
Other Long-Term Liabilities	(200,000)	(50,000)
Common Stock—Pepper Company	(200,000)	
Other Paid-In Capital—Pepper Company	(100,000)	
Retained Earnings—Pepper Company	(320,000)	
Common Stock—Salt Company		(50,000)
Other Paid-In Capital—Salt Company		(50,000)
Retained Earnings—Salt Company		(150,000)
Net Sales	(600,000)	(315,000)
Cost of Goods Sold	350,000	150,000
Operating Expenses	150,000	60,000
Subsidiary Income—Pepper Company	(84,000)	
Dividends Declared—Pepper Company	60,000	
Dividends Declared—Salt Company		20,000
Total	0	0

Required:

Complete the worksheet for consolidated financial statements for the year ended December 31, 19X2. Use the proportionate concept.

WORKSHEET A-1

80% Interest; Proportionate Concept
Company P and Subsidiary Company S
Worksheet for Consolidated Balance Sheet
December 31, 19X1

		Trial Balance	
		Company P	Company S
1	Debits:		
2	Cash	200,000	150,000
3	Accounts Receivable	300,000	250,000
4	Inventory	500,000	300,000
5	Land	100,000	
6	Buildings (net)	900,000	
7	Equipment (net)	650,000	400,000
8	**Investment in Subsidiary S**	810,000	
9			
10	**Goodwill**		
11	Total	3,460,000	1,100,000
12	Credits:		
13	Current Liabilities	300,000	100,000
14	Bonds Payable	500,000	300,000
15	Common Stock ($10 par), Co. P	660,000	
16	Paid-In Capital in Excess of Par, Co. P	1,140,000	
17	Retained Earnings, Co. P	860,000	
18	**Common Stock ($5 par), Co. S**		50,000
19	**Paid-In Capital in Excess of Par, Co. S**		350,000
20	**Retained Earnings, Co. S**		300,000
21			
22	Total	3,460,000	1,100,000

Worksheet A-1 (see page 547)

Eliminations & Adjustments				Consolidated Balance Sheet			
Dr.		Cr.		Dr.		Cr.	
							1
		(1)	**30,000**	320,000			2
		(1)	**50,000**	500,000			3
(2)	**40,000**	**(1)**	**60,000**	780,000			4
				100,000			5
				900,000			6
(2)	**120,000**	**(1)**	**80,000**	1,090,000			7
		(1)	**560,000**				8
		(2)	**250,000**				9
(2)	**90,000**			90,000			10
							11
(1)	**20,000**						12
(1)	**60,000**					380,000	13
						740,000	14
						660,000	15
						1,140,000	16
						860,000	17
(1)	**50,000**						18
(1)	**350,000**						19
(1)	**300,000**						20
							21
	1,030,000		1,030,000	3,780,000		3,780,000	22

Eliminations and Adjustments:
(1) Eliminate 100% of the subsidiary equity accounts. 80% is eliminated against investment amount, 20% against all subsidiary assets and liabilities.
(2) Distribute the balance of the investment account, $250,000, to the specific subsidiary accounts according to the determination and distribution of excess schedule:

Excess of cost over book value............................		$250,000
Distribute to:		
Inventory..	$ 40,000	
Equipment	120,000	
Goodwill	90,000	250,000
		$ 0

WORKSHEET A-2

80% Interest; Economic Unit Concept—Full Goodwill
Company P and Subsidiary Company S
Worksheet for Consolidated Balance Sheet
December 31, 19X1

		Trial Balance	
		Company P	Company S
1	Debits:		
2	Cash	200,000	150,000
3	Accounts Receivable	300,000	250,000
4	**Inventory**	500,000	**300,000**
5	Land	100,000	
6	Buildings (net)	900,000	
7	**Equipment (net)**	650,000	**400,000**
8	**Investment in Subsidiary S**	**810,000**	
9			
10	**Goodwill**		
11	Total	3,460,000	1,100,000
12	Credits:		
13	Current Liabilities	300,000	100,000
14	Bonds Payable	500,000	300,000
15	Common Stock ($10 par), Co. P	660,000	
16	Paid-In Capital in Excess of Par, Co. P	1,140,000	
17	Retained Earnings, Co. P	860,000	
18	**Common Stock ($5 par), Co. S**		50,000
19	**Paid-In Capital in Excess of Par, Co. S**		350,000
20	**Retained Earnings, Co. S**		300,000
21	**Minority Interest**		
22	Total	3,460,000	1,100,000

Worksheet A-2 (see page 548)

Eliminations & Adjustments			Consolidated Balance Sheet		
Dr.	Cr.	Minority Interest	Dr.	Cr.	
					1
			350,000		2
			550,000		3
(2) 50,000			850,000		4
			100,000		5
			900,000		6
(2) 150,000			1,200,000		7
	(1) 560,000				8
	(2) 250,000				9
(2) 112,500			112,500		10
					11
					12
				400,000	13
				800,000	14
				660,000	15
				1,140,000	16
				860,000	17
(1) 40,000		10,000			18
(1) 280,000		70,000			19
(1) 240,000	(2) 62,500	122,500			20
		202,500		202,500	21
872,500	872,500		4,062,500	4,062,500	22

Eliminations and Adjustments:
(1) Eliminate 80% of the subsidiary equity accounts against the investment account.
(2) Distribute the balance of the investment account, $250,000, plus the $62,500 increase in the minority interest, to the specific subsidiary accounts according to the determination and distribution of excess schedule:

Excess of cost over book value............................		$312,500
Distribute to:		
Inventory...	$ 50,000	
Equipment	150,000	
Goodwill...	112,500	312,500
		$ 0

WORKSHEET A-3

80% Interest; Economic Unit Concept—Purchased Goodwill
Company P and Subsidiary Company S
Worksheet for Consolidated Balance Sheet
December 31, 19X1

		Trial Balance	
		Company P	Company S
1	Debits:		
2	Cash	200,000	150,000
3	Accounts Receivable	300,000	250,000
4	**Inventory**	500,000	**300,000**
5	Land	100,000	
6	Buildings (net)	900,000	
7	**Equipment (net)**	650,000	**400,000**
8	**Investment in Subsidiary S**	**810,000**	
9			
10	**Goodwill**		
11	Total	3,460,000	1,100,000
12	Credits:		
13	Current Liabilities	300,000	100,000
14	Bonds Payable	500,000	300,000
15	Common Stock ($10 par), Co. P	660,000	
16	Paid-In Capital in Excess of Par, Co. P	1,140,000	
17	Retained Earnings, Co. P	860,000	
18	**Common Stock ($5 par), Co. S**		50,000
19	**Paid-In Capital in Excess of Par, Co. S**		350,000
20	**Retained Earnings, Co. S**		300,000
21	**Minority Interest**		
22	Total	3,460,000	1,100,000

Worksheet A-3 (see page 549)

Eliminations & Adjustments			Minority Interest	Consolidated Balance Sheet		
Dr.		Cr.		Dr.	Cr.	
						1
				350,000		2
				550,000		3
(2)	50,000			850,000		4
				100,000		5
				900,000		6
(2)	150,000			1,200,000		7
		(1) 560,000				8
		(2) 250,000				9
(2)	90,000			90,000		10
						11
						12
					400,000	13
					800,000	14
					660,000	15
					1,140,000	16
					860,000	17
(1)	40,000		10,000			18
(1)	280,000		70,000			19
(1)	240,000	(2) 40,000	100,000			20
			180,000		180,000	21
	850,000	850,000		4,040,000	4,040,000	22

Eliminations and Adjustments:
(1)   Eliminate 80% of the subsidiary equity accounts against the investment account.
(2)   Distribute the balance of the investment account, $250,000, plus the $40,000 increase in the minority interest, to the specific subsidiary accounts according to the determination and distribution of excess schedule:

Excess of cost over book value.............................		$290,000
Distribute to:		
Inventory..	**$ 50,000**	
Equipment	**150,000**	
Goodwill	**90,000**	290,000
		$ 0

WORKSHEET A-4

Simple Equity Method, First Year
Paulos Company and Subsidiary Carlos Company
Worksheet for Consolidated Financial Statements
For Year Ended December 31, 19X1

	(Credit balance amounts are in parentheses.)	Trial Balance	
		Paulos	Carlos
1	Cash	100,000	50,000
2	Inventory	226,000	62,500
3	Land	200,000	150,000
4	Building	800,000	600,000
5	**Accumulated Depreciation—Building**	(80,000)	(315,000)
6	**Equipment**	400,000	150,000
7	**Accumulated Depreciation—Equipment**	(50,000)	(70,000)
8	**Investment in Carlos Company**	832,000	
9			
10			
11	**Goodwill**		112,500
12	Current Liabilities	(100,000)	
13	Bonds Payable		(200,000)
14	**Discount on Bonds**		
15	Common Stock, Paulos	(1,500,000)	
16	Retained Earnings, Jan. 1, 19X1, Paulos	(700,000)	
17	Common Stock ($10 par), Carlos		(100,000)
18	Paid-In Capital in Excess of Par, Carlos		(150,000)
19	**Retained Earnings, Jan. 1, 19X1, Carlos**		(250,000)
20	Sales	(350,000)	(200,000)
21	**Cost of Goods Sold**	150,000	80,000
22	**Expenses**	120,000	60,000
23			
24			
25	Subsidiary Income	(48,000)	
26	Dividends Declared		20,000
27		0	0
28	Consolidated Net Income		
29	To Minority Interest (see distribution schedule)		
30	Balance to Controlling Interest (see distribution schedule)		
31	Total Minority Interest		
32	Retained Earnings, Controlling Interest, Dec. 31, 19X1		
33			

Eliminations & Adjustments				Consolidated Income Statement	Minority Interest	Controlling Retained Earnings	Consolidated Balance Sheet	
Dr.		Cr.						
							150,000	1
							288,500	2
(3e)	50,000						400,000	3
							1,400,000	4
(3d)	200,000	(4d)	10,000				(205,000)	5
		(3c)	20,000				530,000	6
(4c)	4,000						(116,000)	7
(1)	16,000	(1)	48,000					8
		(2)	400,000					9
		(3)	400,000					10
(3f)	251,752	(4f)	25,175				339,077	11
							(100,000)	12
							(200,000)	13
(3b)	13,248	(4b)	2,940				10,308	14
							(1,500,000)	15
						(700,000)		16
(2)	80,000				(20,000)			17
(2)	120,000				(30,000)			18
(2)	200,000	(3)	100,000		(150,000)			19
				(550,000)				20
(3a)	5,000			235,000				21
(4b)	2,940	(4c)	4,000	214,115				22
(4d)	10,000							23
(4f)	25,175							24
(1)	48,000							25
		(1)	16,000		4,000			26
	1,026,115		1,026,115					27
				(100,885)				28
				(4,177)	(4,177)			29
				(96,708)		(96,708)		30
					(200,177)		(200,177)	31
						(796,708)	(796,708)	32
							0	33

(continued)

Eliminations and Adjustments:
(1) Eliminate the current-year entries made in the investment in Carlos Company account and in the subsidiary income account. The investment account now is adjusted to its January 1, 19X1 balance so that it may be eliminated.
(2) Eliminate the 80% ownership portion of the subsidiary equity accounts against the investment. A $400,000 excess cost remains.
(3) Distribute the $400,000 excess cost plus the $100,000 increase in the minority interest as follows, in accordance with the determination and distribution of excess schedule:
   (a) Increase the beginning inventory by $5,000. However, the beginning inventory has been closed to the cost of goods sold; thus, the cost of goods sold is increased by $5,000. If the inventory had not been sold, the inventory account would be adjusted. The cost of goods sold in the later period of sale then would be adjusted on a subsequent worksheet.
   (b) Record discount of $13,248 on the bonds payable.
   (c) Reduce the equipment by $20,000 by reducing the asset account directly.
   (d) Increase the building by $200,000 by decreasing its accumulated depreciation account.
   (e) Increase the land by $50,000.
   (f) Increase the goodwill by $251,752.
(4) Record amortizations resulting from the asset and liability revaluations of step (3). The adjustments are lettered (a) through (f) to correspond with the revaluations in step (3):
   (a) No amortization required; adjustment already charged to the cost of goods sold.
   (b) Amortize the discount as follows:
        Net present value of controlling interest in Carlos bonds, January 1, 19X1:

Face	$200,000	
Discount.	13,248	$186,752
Multiply by 8% effective interest rate.		.08
Effective interest expense		$ 14,940
Nominal interest, 6% × $200,000		12,000
Discount amortization.		$ 2,940

   (c) Record annual decrease in equipment depreciation expense; $20,000 net decrease in the equipment divided by 5-year life equals $4,000.
   (d) Record annual increase in building depreciation expense; $200,000 net increase in the building divided by 20-year life equals $10,000.
   (e) No amortization results from adjustment of the land.
   (f) Record additional annual amortization of the goodwill; $251,752 net increase in the goodwill divided by 10-year life equals $25,175. It is assumed that the previously recorded goodwill of $125,000 on January 1, 19X1, also is being amortized over 10 years.

Subsidiary Carlos Company Income Distribution

Inventory adjustment. . . . .(3a)	$ 5,000	Internally generated net income	$60,000
Discount amortization . . . .(4b)	2,940	**Equipment Depreciation (4c)**	**4,000**
Building depreciation . . . .(4d)	10,000		
Goodwill amortization . . . .(4f)	25,175		
		Adjusted income.	$20,885
		Minority share.	20%
		Minority interest	$ 4,177

Parent Paulos Company Income Distribution

Internally generated net income	$80,000
80% × Carlos Company adjusted income	
of $20,885.	16,708
Controlling interest.	**$96,708**

APPENDIX B: LEVERAGED BUYOUTS

It has become a common occurrence to form a skeleton corporation for the sole purpose of acquiring a controlling interest in an existing corporation. Frequently, the management of the corporation to be acquired are the instigators of the acquisition. Some leveraged buyouts are financed in part by funds supplied by investment partnerships. Investors are expected to have supplied over 10 billion dollars to these partnerships in 1994, which would equal investments made in these funds in the record year of 1987. It is anticipated that the increased funds coupled with rising prices paid in leveraged buyouts will lead to lower returns on these investments than have existed in the past.[1] A successful example of a leveraged buyout is offered by Harley Davidson Corporation, the only American manufacturer of motorcycles. Once a separate corporation, Harley Davidson was acquired by AMF Corporation. After several years of being a subsidiary, the Harley Davidson division was purchased by new investors, including employees, and again became a separate corporation.

When structured properly, a leveraged buyout follows purchase accounting principles. With only minor exceptions, the market values of the assets and liabilities of the firm subject to the leveraged buyout are recorded. In order to record assets and liabilities at market value, there must be a change in control. The new control group does not have to be a single individual; it is sufficient to have a group of investors with a common interest act as a control group. The requirements for what constitutes a control group were issued by the Emerging Issues Task Force of the FASB in 1989.[2]

The most difficult accounting task in a leveraged buyout is to determine the total value available for assignment to the firm's assets and liabilities. The total value is the sum of the value assigned to outstanding shares of common stock. Where there may be three blocks of stock, the three blocks are the market value block, the equity-adjusted cost block, and the book value block. The number of shares included in each block are determined as follows.

MARKET VALUE BLOCK

This block includes the shares owned by shareholders of the new control group *who were not owners* of the shares of the prior company. This block also may include the shares of some shareholders who owned shares of the prior company. In order to include a former shareholder's shares in the market value block, one of two conditions must be met:

1. The shareholder's new residual ownership interest must be greater than the *residual ownership interest* in the prior firm. The shareholder's new residual ownership interest cannot, however, exceed 5%. The residual ownership interest includes all outstanding common and preferred shares except those

---

[1]Greg Steinmetz, "LBO Funds Lure Investors, But Returns Worry Some," *Wall Street Journal*, 29 June 1994.

[2]Highlights of Financial Reporting Issues, *Leveraged Buyouts: Emerging Issues Task Force Consensus Issue No. 88-16* (Norwalk: Financial Accounting Standards Board, May 1989).

shares that have liquidation or redemption features. This is different from the definition of ownership interest that includes only common shares.

2.   If the former shareholder's residual interest percentage decreased, *all* of the following requirements must be met to record the shares at market value:

   a.   The shareholder's voting interest in common stock must be under 20%.

   b.   The individual must have supplied less than 20% of the new firm's total capital including debt.[3]

   c.   The shareholder's new residual ownership interest must be less than 5% and all former owners whose residual ownership interest decreased must have a new residual interest of less than 20%.

There is a limitation on the number of shares included in the market value block; it is based on the amount of monetary consideration given to owners of the former firm. Monetary consideration includes cash, debt, and debt-type securities such as mandatory redeemable preferred stock. If at least 80% of the consideration given to all shareholders (including continuing shareholders) is monetary, there is no limitation on the market value block. If monetary consideration is under 80% of the total, the market value block is limited to the monetary consideration percentage times the total common shares outstanding. Thus, for example, if the percentage of shares that would otherwise qualify was 90%, but monetary consideration given for common shares was 70%, the market value block would be limited to 70% of the outstanding shares. The nonqualifying 20% interest would be assigned book value.

EQUITY-ADJUSTED COST BLOCK

Shares of continuing shareholders who owned shares of the former firm are recorded at their simple-equity-adjusted cost unless they meet the above requirements to be included in the market value block. The shareholders whose interests do not qualify for inclusion in the market value block are termed "continuing shareholders."

BOOK VALUE BLOCK

These are the shares that would otherwise be included in the market value block but are excluded because of the 80% monetary consideration test. Recall the prior example where 90% of the shares otherwise qualified for the market value block, but only 70% of the consideration was monetary. The excluded 20% of the shares would be valued at current book value.

ACQUISITION MEETING THE 80% MONETARY CONSIDERATION TEST

As an example of a leveraged buyout's meeting the 80% monetary consideration test, assume Former Company had the following balance sheet on the date it is acquired by a new ownership group, New Company:

---

[3]This test is applied in steps starting with common stock and proceeding to each lesser risk security. The test may be passed at any level. See Highlights of Financial Reporting Issues, *Leveraged Buyouts: Emerging Issues Task Force Consensus Issue No. 88-16.*

Assets		Liabilities and Equity	
Current assets.	$100,000	Liabilities	$ 80,000
Land and buildings (net). . . .	200,000	Common stock (10,000 shares,	
		$2 par)	20,000
Equipment (net)	50,000	Paid-in capital in excess of par.	70,000
		Retained earnings.	180,000
Total assets	$350,000	Total liabilities and equity	$350,000

The market values of Former Company's assets and liabilities equal book value, except for the land and buildings which have a fair market value of $300,000. New Company was formed initially by selling 2,000 shares of no par stock for $20 each and borrowing $300,000. The market value of Former Company shares is $40 each. 10,000 shares of Former Company are acquired as follows:

1. 2,000 New Company shares are exchanged for 1,000 Former Company shares. These 1,000 shares are owned by continuing shareholders who are members of the new control group. These shares do not meet the tests required to be included in the market value block and must be recorded at simple-equity-adjusted cost. Their equity-adjusted cost for Former Company shares is $38. The shares originally were purchased for $30 when the retained earnings of Former Company was $100,000.
2. 500 Former Company shares are received in exchange for 1,000 New Company shares from parties that are former owners but that are not members of the new control group. The shares do meet the criteria to be included in the market value block.
3. The remaining 8,500 Former Company shares are purchased for $340,000 cash from shareholders that are not owners of the new firm.

Monetary consideration was used to acquire 85% of Former Company shares. Since this exceeds the required 80% level, the entire interest acquired from shareholders that are not considered continuing members is recorded at market value. The value to be assigned to the net assets is calculated as follows:

Market Value Block:	
8,500 shares acquired for cash at $40 market value.	$340,000
500 shares acquired in exchange for 1,000 New Company shares from	
parties that are not continuing members at $40 market value	20,000
Total Market Value	$360,000
Equity-Adjusted Cost Block:	
1,000 shares acquired in exchange for 2,000 New Company shares from	
continuing shareholders at $38 simple-equity-adjusted cost	38,000
Total	$398,000

The determination and distribution of excess schedule would be prepared as follows for the 90% interest acquired from former shareholders that are not continuing members:

Price paid, 9,000 × $40		$360,000
Interest acquired:		
Stockholders' equity	$270,000	
Percentage	90%	243,000
Excess of cost over book value		$117,000
Land and buildings, 90% × $100,000		90,000
Goodwill		$ 27,000

The determination and distribution of excess schedule would be prepared as follows for the 10% interest acquired from continuing shareholders:

Simple equity-adjusted cost, 1,000 × $38		$38,000
Interest acquired:		
Stockholders' equity	$270,000	
Percentage	10%	27,000
Excess of cost over book value		$11,000
Land and buildings, 10% × $100,000		10,000
Goodwill		$ 1,000

Separate determination and distribution of excess schedules are recommended for each block since it is possible to have one of the schedules indicate a bargain purchase that would not allow full recognition of market values for long-term fixed assets. If the two blocks were combined into a single determination and distribution of excess schedule, goodwill from one block could offset a bargain on another.

The entries to record the formation of New Company and to acquire Former Company are as follows:

Formation of New Company

Cash	40,000	
Common Stock, No Par (2,000 shares × $20)		40,000

Borrowing of $300,000

Cash	300,000	
Long-Term Debt		300,000

Acquisition of Former Company

Current Assets	100,000	
Land and Buildings ($200,000 + $90,000 + $10,000)	300,000	
Equipment	50,000	
Goodwill ($27,000 + $1,000)	28,000	
Liabilities		80,000
Cash		340,000
Common Stock, No Par (3,000 shares in exchange for 500		
Former shares × $40 and 1,000 Former shares × $38)		58,000

ACQUISITION NOT MEETING THE 80% MONETARY CONSIDERATION TEST

Let us revise the previous example slightly:

1. Instead of borrowing $300,000, only $240,000 is borrowed.
2. Instead of acquiring 8,500 shares for cash from parties that are not members of the new control group, assume 6,500 shares are acquired for cash at $40 each and a total of 2,500 shares are acquired by exchanging 5,000 shares of New Company common stock. 2,000 New Company shares are still being issued to former shareholders that are part of the new control group in exchange for 1,000 Former Company shares.

Now only 65% (6,500 for cash ÷ 10,000 total shares acquired) of the shares are acquired in exchange for cash and can be recorded at market value. The remaining 2,000 shares acquired from parties that were not continuing members of Former Company are recorded at book value. The value assigned to the net assets is calculated as follows:

Market Value Block:

6,500	shares acquired for cash at $40 market value.....................	$260,000

Equity-Adjusted Cost Block:

1,000	shares acquired in exchange for 2,000 New Company shares from continuing members of Former Company; at $38 simple equity-adjusted cost	38,000

Book Value Block:

2,500	shares acquired in exchange for 5,000 New Company shares from Former Company shareholders who are not a part of the new control group at book value of $27 per share ($270,000 total equity ÷ 10,000 shares)...	67,500
	Total...	$365,500

A determination and distribution of excess schedule would be prepared for the 65% interest acquired for cash as follows:

Price paid, 6,500 × $40		$260,000
Interest acquired:		
Stockholders' equity	$270,000	
Percentage...	65%	175,500
Excess of cost over book value		$ 84,500
Land and buildings, 65% × $100,000		65,000
Goodwill..		$ 19,500

The determination and distribution of excess schedule for the 1,000 shares acquired from continuing shareholders is unchanged.

Simple-equity-adjusted cost, 1,000 × $38			$38,000
Interest acquired:			
Stockholders' equity	$270,000		
Percentage	10%	27,000	
Excess of cost over book value		11,000	
Land and buildings, 10% × $100,000		10,000	
Goodwill		1,000	

There would be no adjustment to market value for the 2,000 shares acquired from noncontinuing shareholders in exchange for New Company shares.

The entries to record the formation of New Company and acquire Former Company are as follows:

Formation of New Company

Cash	40,000	
Common Stock, No Par (2,000 shares).		40,000

Borrowing of $240,000

Cash	240,000	
Long-Term Debt		240,000

Acquisition of Former Company

Current Assets	100,000	
Land and Buildings ($200,000 + $65,000 + $10,000)	275,000	
Equipment	50,000	
Goodwill ($19,500 + $1,000)	20,500	
Liabilities		80,000
Cash (6,500 × 40)		260,000
Common Stock, No Par (7,000 shares in exchange for 2,500		
Former shares × $27 and 1,000 Former shares × $38)		105,500

APPENDIX B QUESTIONS

1. A leveraged buyout that meets the 80% monetary consideration test may not allow the recognition of market values for the interest acquired from shareholders of the predecessor firm. Under what conditions is the interest of former company shareholders recorded at market value? If market value is not allowed, at what value are the shares recorded?

2. Some of the interest acquired in a leveraged buyout may have to be recorded at the underlying book value of the former firm. Under what conditions does this occur?

3. Lever Company was formed to purchase all of the outstanding shares of Ancient Company in a leveraged buyout. 85% of the outstanding Ancient shares were purchased for cash from persons not part of the new control group. The remaining shares were purchased from individuals that would qualify as continuing shareholders who are members of the new control group. What procedures would you follow to assign values to the assets of Ancient Company?

APPENDIX B EXERCISES

Exercise B-1. Modum Corporation was formed on January 1, 19X1, by issuing 4,000 shares of $10 par stock for $20 per share. Modum Corporation is going to engage in a leveraged buyout of Antique Company. Antique Company had the following stockholders' equity on January 1, 19X1:

Common stock ($10 par, 10,000 shares outstanding)	$100,000
Paid-in capital in excess of par	150,000
Retained earnings	80,000
Total equity	$330,000

The market value of Antique Company shares is $40 each. 1,000 Antique shares will be acquired from continuing members of Antique Company's control group in exchange for 2,000 Modum Corporation shares. The equity-adjusted cost of the control group's shares is $25 per share. Calculate the total cost of Antique Company under each of the following assumptions:

(1) Modum Corporation borrows $280,000 and purchases for $40 each the remaining 9,000 shares held by parties outside the control group of Antique Company.

(2) Modum Corporation borrows $240,000 and purchases 8,000 noncontrol group shares for $40 each. Modum issues 2,000 of its shares in exchange for 1,000 Antique Company shares held by noncontrol group members.

(3) Modum Corporation borrows $200,000 and purchases 7,000 noncontrol group shares for $40 each. Modum issues 4,000 of its shares in exchange for 2,000 Antique Company shares held by noncontrol group members.

Exercise B-2. Old Time Company has the following balance sheet on January 1, 19X1, when it is the target of a leveraged buyout by Hercules Corporation:

Assets		Stockholders' Equity	
Cash	$ 50,000	Common stock ($5 par, 10,000 shares)	$ 50,000
Inventory	100,000	Paid-in capital in excess of par	160,000
Property and plant	200,000	Retained earnings	140,000
Total assets	$350,000	Total equity	$350,000

The property and plant have a market value of $230,000.

Hercules Corporation incorporated by issuing 3,000 shares of $10 par common stock for $40 each. The company also borrowed $160,000 from long-term lenders. The leveraged buyout was accomplished as follows:

1,000 shares exchanged on a 1-to-1 basis with continuing members of the old control group. The equity-adjusted cost per share for these shares was $38. These shares do not need the criteria to be included in the market value block.

2,000 shares exchanged on a 1-to-1 basis with noncontrol group members.

7,000 shares of Old Time purchased from noncontrol group members for $40 per share.

Prepare the balance sheet of Hercules Corporation immediately after the leveraged buyout. Provide supporting calculations in good form.

APPENDIX B PROBLEM

Problem B-1. Newtone Company was formed on January 1, 19X5. The shareholder group issued 4,000 shares of $10 par common stock for $25 per share. The company was formed by an employee group to purchase Oldtime (a subsidiary of Gigantic Corporation) which had the following balance sheet on the January 3, 19X5 acquisition date:

Assets		Liabilities and Stockholders' Equity	
Cash	$ 60,000	Bonds payable	$150,000
Inventory	130,000	Common stock ($10 par)......	100,000
Accounts receivable..........	40,000	Paid-in capital in excess	
Equipment..................	75,000	of par	120,000
Building (net)................	120,000	Retained earnings............	85,000
Land	30,000	Total liabilities and	
Total assets	$455,000	stockholders' equity........	$455,000

The market values differed from book values in the case of the inventory, equipment, and building which were appraised at $150,000, $100,000, and $200,000, respectively.

The market value of Newtone stock is $25 per share. 2,000 Newtone shares were exchanged for 1,000 Oldtime shares with parties who were continuing members of the control group of Oldtime. These shares do not qualify for inclusion in the market value block. The equity-adjusted cost of the shares held by Oldtime's control group was $45 per share. These individuals also will be part of the control group of Newtone. The 9,000 remaining shares of Oldtime were acquired from parties that are not part of Newtone's control group.

Required:
(1) Assume Newtone borrowed $250,000 on a long-term note. Newtone then paid $50 per share for 7,000 shares of Oldtime and issued 4,000 of its shares in exchange for 2,000 Oldtime shares. Prepare all entries to record the formation of Newtone Corporation, the borrowing, and the buyout of Oldtime. Include a support schedule for the values assigned to the accounts.
(2) Assume Newtone borrowed $300,000 on a long-term note. Newtone then paid $50 per share for 8,000 shares of Oldtime and issued 2,000 of its shares in exchange for 1,000 Oldtime shares. Prepare all entries to record the formation of Newtone Corporation, the borrowing, and the buyout of Oldtime. Include a support schedule for the values assigned to the accounts.

Suggestion: Be sure to determine if the 80% test is met in each case before proceeding to assign values to the accounts.

PART 2

Multinational Accounting

Every day our world seems to get a little smaller and new relationships are established between countries and their people. This is evident in today's business environment which is clearly global in nature. As more and more business is conducted between entities in different countries there is a greater need for reliable and comparable financial information. However, there are a great number of differences which exist between accounting and professional standards employed in different countries. Significant efforts are under way to address these differences and harmonize accounting standards. Many domestic companies are transacting business with foreign entities. If these transactions are settled in other than the domestic currency, exchange rate changes between the domestic and foreign currency may expose the domestic entity to potential gain or loss. Special accounting principles have been developed to account for such foreign currency transactions. A growing number of U.S. companies are acquiring financial interests in foreign entities. These investments must be accounted for, in dollars, on the financial statements of the U.S. investor. The foreign entity's financial statements must be remeasured and/or translated into dollars and then those balances must be reflected in the financial statements of the U.S. company. Specialized accounting principles must be followed in the remeasurement/translation process.

CHAPTER 9

The International Accounting Environment

Local economies have developed into national economies and today more than ever these national economies are developing into a single world economy. Trade between different nations certainly is not new for it has existed since biblical times and has provided the means by which certain nations have evolved into world powers. England and the Netherlands are just two examples of countries that have been active in international trade for centuries. However, it has been since World War II that international trade has increased significantly, and many more goods and services are becoming part of a global economy.

Already, the 1990s have seen amazing changes that will certainly make a global economy a reality for an increasing number of business entities. Dramatic changes in Eastern Europe and the former Soviet Union have acknowledged the capitalistic system of business and are presenting opportunities for international trade. The dismantling of the Berlin Wall represented a humanitarian action of major importance and is symbolic of the elimination of barriers to the freer movement of not only people and ideas but also goods and services between nations. The European Union[1] (EU) forms a single market that unites twelve member countries (Belgium, Denmark, France, Germany, Greece, Ireland, Italy, Luxembourg, The Netherlands, Portugal, Spain, and the United Kingdom). In terms of the number of consumers, this single market could be as large as the United States and Japan combined. The majority of U.S. businesses see the European Union as an opportunity that cannot be ignored. Today's business executives realize that, in order to remain competitive, they must be aware of how increasingly global economics will affect their businesses and begin to develop business plans which are responsive.

---

[1]In 1992 the Maastricht Treaty changed the name of the European Community to the European Union. The European Community was formed in 1978 by the merger of the European Economic Community (Common Market), the European Coal and Steel Community, and Euratom.

In late 1993 the United States, Canada, and Mexico agreed to a comprehensive free trade agreement affecting these North American countries. The agreement, known as the North American Free Trade Agreement (NAFTA), will bring together into one market an estimated 370 million consumers and create the world's largest trading block. NAFTA will phase out a number of existing trade tariffs, reduce ownership restrictions, and ease certain immigration requirements. Although many businesses were in favor of the agreement, certain U.S. interests expressed concerns that businesses would relocate to Mexico in order to take advantage of lower labor costs and less stringent environmental regulations.

Another major factor affecting international business is the General Agreement on Tariffs and Trade (GATT) which is designed to reduce barriers to world trade through multilateral agreements. GATT was organized in the late 1940s and today there are 111 member nations. GATT's main features are a schedule of tariff concessions, a code of principles and rules governing imports and exports, and periodic meetings to provide a forum for trade discussions.

Not only are goods and services trading in international markets but also the securities of the companies involved. International securities trading has increased rapidly due to a number of forces. As companies expand into different international markets, they need to acquire the factors of production in those markets and, thus, need to raise additional capital. For example, the construction of a new manufacturing facility in France requires French francs to pay for the construction and other operating costs. International securities trading also offers investors the opportunity to diversify their portfolios against loss from currency fluctuations, political instabilities, and economic downturns. The financing of a government's deficit spending and the private financing (privatization) of an industry that was previously owned by the government are additional instances that require international securities trading. Capital demands in these instances are so great that domestic security markets alone are unable to satisfy them.

As our global economy develops, it becomes apparent that goods and services, financial capital, and technology are being traded among a growing number of parties worldwide. Common economic, political, and cultural goals also are being exchanged as evidenced by the single-market concept of the EU and recent developments in Eastern Europe. It is only logical that financial information must be exchanged on an international scale. Accounting must develop internationally in order to meet the needs of multinational companies, international capital markets, and international investors.

Multinational companies need comparable accounting standards which may be used to measure the effectiveness and efficiency of their various international subsidiaries, branches, and/or other equity investments. In order to efficiently allocate and regulate the exchange of capital, international capital markets need to evaluate the adequacy of financial statements and disclosures made by those companies seeking to raise capital. Comparable standards of accounting and financial disclosure for companies competing for capital on an international scale are critical to the functioning of such markets. Finally, individual investors are exposed to opportunities on an international scale and need comparable financial information upon which to base their decisions. Evaluating the profitability or financial position of two competing investment opportunities will have meaning only if comparable accounting standards are in place. The international growth of business and investing naturally creates a need for the international development of accounting. The development of international accounting standards must be based on an understanding of international business and markets and the factors that affect accounting in various countries.

FORMS OF INTERNATIONAL BUSINESS INVOLVEMENT

International business may take many different forms. However, in all instances, it involves a commercial activity that transcends national boundaries or borders. Modern businesses are learning that the factors of production are mobile and can be found in or transferred to nations around the world. Amazing numbers of companies are making this discovery and successfully adapting to our global economy. Coca-Cola and Levi's jeans can be found around the world along with an ever more surprising list of goods and services. We should no longer be surprised to learn that small manufacturing firms in our hometowns sell their products in several nations.

As previously mentioned, international business can take many forms ranging from casual international involvement to the large multinational enterprise. Normally, a company's international involvement begins with buying from or selling to a party in another nation. Such activity may be rather infrequent or it may develop into a major component of the business. Exhibit 9-1 highlights a company in the footwear industry. This industry was once centered in the eastern United States and served primarily U.S. consumers. The company demonstrates how global economies have changed an industry and how such changes may represent excellent opportunities.

At the extreme end of international business is the multinational enterprise. Such a company generally has numerous manufacturing or distribution facilities in a variety of nations. Factors of production are acquired from around the world and its markets are worldwide. Management is international in scale, and its capital needs are secured on an international level. Exhibit 9-2, on page 586, highlights a multinational company that manufactures and distributes around the world.

THE FOCUS OF INTERNATIONAL ACCOUNTING

With all of the economic developments in the world occurring at such a rapid rate, it is not surprising that international accounting is also rapidly developing. Professional organizations have special interest groups focusing on the area, and a number of organizations concerned with the process of establishing international accounting standards have emerged.

Exhibit 9-1
Allen-Edmonds Shoe Corporation

Allen-Edmonds is a closely held manufacturer of fine quality footwear for both men and women. The company's primary manufacturing facility and headquarters are in Port Washington, Wisconsin. Building a strong competitive future is not new to the company. In 1984, the company's plant was destroyed by fire, but within weeks the company was back in production.

Then, in 1987, the Allen-Edmonds' request to participate in the Tokyo Shoe Fair was turned down by the Japanese government. Feeling that U.S. companies were being singled out since European manufacturers were invited to attend, John Stollenwerk, Allen-Edmonds' dynamic president and principal owner, "crashed" the fair. With fifty pairs of shoes in hand, Stollenwerk set up a booth outside the exhibit hall, was invited to join the fair inside, and became the first U.S. manufacturer of men's dress shoes to sell in Japan.

Allen-Edmonds currently advertises in more than a dozen foreign languages, and its export sales have grown from less than one percent in 1984 to in excess of ten percent in less than ten years. Export markets include over 35 countries with Italy, Canada, and Japan being the three largest. The company hopes to increase export sales to 25% of its more than $40 million of annual sales. (International trade is not limited to sales. The company imports high-quality calfskin from Germany.) In 1991, the company was awarded the U.S. Commerce Department's "E" Award for exporting excellence. Clearly, the company has translated the need and desire for international trade into a positive opportunity.

In many instances, there are no special differences in accounting that result from international trade as compared to domestic trade. For example, methods of transfer pricing and overhead allocation are not significantly affected by the fact that international activity is involved. However, there are some areas where accounting principles and practices are uniquely different due to the presence of international activity. International accounting generally is said to consist of several specialized areas of technical involvement. The primary areas are as follows:

1. The identification and understanding of accounting principles used in different nations, especially as to how they differ from nation to nation.
2. The identification of the various organizations and interests involved in the process of establishing international accounting and auditing principles and standards.
3. The special accounting valuation and recognition principles associated with accounting for transactions that are recorded in one nation's currency and settled in another nation's currency. These transactions are referred to as *foreign currency transactions*.
4. The translation of financial statements that are measured in one nation's currency into another nation's currency.

Exhibit 9-2
Johnson Controls, Incorporated

Johnson Controls, Inc. is a Fortune 500 company headquartered in the Midwest with worldwide sales in excess of $4.5 billion. The company operates from more than 450 locations worldwide, and its operations are concentrated in four primary industries: facility control systems (energy management, temperature and ventilation control, security, etc.), automotive seating, automotive batteries, and plastic containers.

All of the industry groups are involved in international operations, and the company has realized significant growth in international markets. For example, the temperature control system in the first McDonald's to open in Russia is manufactured by Johnson Controls. A Johnson Controls subsidiary in Italy is the largest manufacturer of P.E.T. (polyethylene terephthalate) plastic bottles in Europe. Approximately one-half of the soft drinks sold in Europe are sold in glass containers, compared to 20% in the U.S. As European bottlers convert to P.E.T., Johnson Controls will experience new opportunities.

The international nature of this company can be gleaned from studying just one of its industry segments. The controls segment of the company has manufacturing facilities in the U.S., Italy, Mexico, The Netherlands, and Germany. The facility control systems segment has marketing operations in the U.S., Canada, Italy, Mexico, The Netherlands, and Germany. Through a network of subsidiaries and branches, fully staffed sales offices exist in the U.S., Canada, Australia, Austria, Belgium, France, Hong Kong, Italy, Malaysia, Mexico, The Netherlands, Norway, Saudi Arabia, Singapore, Spain, Switzerland, the United Kingdom, and Germany. Joint ventures also have been established with Japanese and other foreign companies. Marketing of the control systems involves distributors represented in approximately 40 countries. Johnson Controls is truly a multinational company and recognizes the opportunities presented by a global economy.

Due to the expanding nature of international trade and capital markets, today's accounting professional must have some knowledge of international accounting. The balance of this chapter will focus on the various accounting principles used in certain nations and the establishment of international accounting principles and standards.

The development of accounting principles and standards is an extremely complex process involving various special interest groups and varying degrees of due process. By studying the standard-setting process in the United States, one realizes how complex the process can be. This complexity holds true in the development of accounting principles and standards in other nations, too. However, it is the factors influencing the process that vary from nation to nation.

FACTORS INFLUENCING THE DEVELOPMENT OF ACCOUNTING

Accounting standards are not defined by nature but, rather, are man-made and therefore differ from nation to nation. A major factor influencing the development of accounting principles has been the political environment in which a nation has developed. For example, nations that previously were ruled or colonized by another country tend to have developed principles similar to those of the ruling nation. Nations such as the United States, Canada, and the Bahamas have accounting principles that historically were patterned after those found in the United Kingdom. Those nations that have more democratic political environments tend to develop principles more through private standard-setting groups than through government decree or regulation. Tax laws and legal requirements of a country also may influence the development of accounting. For example, a country's methods of measuring taxable income must be used for financial accounting or book purposes.

The type and pace of economic development also have influenced the development of accounting. Economies which are more agrarian usually are made up of smaller family business entities and have not experienced the need for accounting sophistication, such as consolidated financial statements and capitalized lease accounting. On the other hand, those nations which have experienced more rapid economic growth have realized the need for higher-level systems of accounting. Furthermore, as businesses have grown, in most instances in a corporate form, widening investor bases and greater capital needs have led to more emphasis on financial disclosure and the need for audited financial statements.

Other factors, such as the religious, cultural, and educational backgrounds of a nation's people, also affect the development of business and, therefore, accounting. Thus, the development of accounting in each nation is influenced by a variety of factors, whose significance varies from nation to nation. For example, almost every nation has experienced inflation on a long-term basis. In those nations where inflation has been extreme, such as Brazil and Argentina, inflation-adjusted financial statements are required. Yet in the United States the interest in inflation-adjusted financial statements has waned due to the moderation of inflation rates. In order to better understand the various factors influencing accounting, selected accounting principles in several nations will be highlighted in the following sections.

ACCOUNTING PRINCIPLES IN FRANCE

France first became a republic in 1792 after the French Revolution and currently is a democratic republic with an elected president and an appointed prime minister. The parliament consists of the National Assembly and the Senate. The nation is a founding member of the European Community, now the European Union, and is a strong trading partner with much of Western Europe. Approximately one-half of France's gross national product is accounted for by industry, and well over two-thirds of its exports are manufactured goods. France is a net importer with oil products representing the major import.

The main forms of business organization in France are corporations called Société Anonyme (SA), some of which may be traded on a French stock exchange, and private limited companies called Société à Responsabilité Limitée (SARL). At a minimum, all businesses must produce at least monthly journals and ledgers prepared in accordance with the General Chart of Accounts, or Plan Comptable. The Plan Comptable is much more than a chart of accounts; it contains accounting definitions, forms of financial statements, and valuation and measurement rules.

Accounting in France is heavily regulated by the government; thus, it is more macro based than firm, or micro, based. However, the accounting profession in France is well developed and consists of several organizations which issue recommendations on accounting and auditing. The Ordre des Experts Comptables et des Comptables Agréés (OECCA) is the main professional organization, and its members are independent accountants who serve primarily as business advisors. The members are not auditors nor are they accountants working in industry. The other major professional group is the Compagnie Nationale des Commissaires aux Comptes (CNCC), or Institute of Statutory Auditors. In addition to these organizations, the Conseil National de la Comptabilité (CNC), or National Accounting Board, is composed of accountants and representatives of industry, banking, and the securities industry. The CNC advises the French government on accounting principles and studies various accounting and disclosure alternatives. Within the French government, the Tax Authority, which is a branch of the Ministry of Finance, makes recommendations on accounting. Also, the Commission des Opérations de Bourse (COB), which is similar to the SEC in the United States, is an important governmental body influencing accounting and auditing.

Most businesses, with small businesses being the exception, must have audited financial statements. The company must designate an independent statutory auditor (commissaire aux comptes) and an alternate (suppléant), both of which serve for a six-year term. The auditing standards are similar to those in the U.S., and the audit report in substance expresses an opinion that the financial statements present fairly. In addition to this report, the auditor opines that the financial statements are in conformity with principles established by law and that management has applied the rules in good faith. A special report also is presented that relates to transactions between the company and its directors that are not related to normal business and/or are not at arm's length.

The accounting principles in France are promulgated by the government and are consistent with the applicable directives of the EU. These principles are influenced heavily by tax policy. The basic financial statements consist of a balance sheet and an income statement along with explanatory notes. The form of the statement differs from that of U.S. companies and no statement of changes or of cash flows is required.

Some major differences exist between accounting principles in France and the United States. The inventory of French companies normally is determined using the weighted average method and lower-of-cost-or-market. It is interesting to note that the LIFO method, which is so popular in the United States, is not allowed in France for either book or tax purposes. Fixed assets normally are stated at historical cost, although revaluations to fair market value may be recorded in certain instances. The depreciation of fixed assets generally is based on the straight-line method. Accelerated methods may be used for tax purposes; however, the amounts in excess of straight-line are not included in accumulated depreciation but, rather, are recorded as a component of owners' equity. There are few differences between principles used for book and tax purposes. Principles of tax allocation are not applied to these differences except in the case of consolidated financial statements.

Corporate income in France is taxed at 39% plus an additional 3% tax if the income is distributed. Long-term capital gains are taxed at 15% plus an additional 3% if distributed. Net operating losses may be carried back three years and forward five years. Dividends received are taxable unless the dividend is from a company in which the taxpayer owns more than 10%. Profits and losses from foreign sources generally are not included in the calculation of taxable income.

ACCOUNTING PRINCIPLES IN BRAZIL

Brazil was colonized by the Portuguese and gained its independence in 1822. It is a federal republic headed by a president and a two-chamber legislature. Brazil is one of the largest nations in the world in terms of physical size and is in the top ten nations in the world in terms of population and industrial production. The nation historically has been a major exporter of agricultural goods. However, it has developed into a major industrial power and is exporting significant amounts of manufactured products, thus enabling itself to be a net exporter of goods. The industrial development has not come without cost to the nation, the environment, and its people. Key to Brazil's problems has been the huge amounts of foreign debt incurred that cannot be serviced. This debt burden has led to an increased money supply and hyperinflation.

Business entities are governed by commercial and civil codes. Common corporate forms of organization include the sociedade por acoes (the corporation) and the sociedade por quotas de responsabilidade limitada (the private limited liability company). A variety of partnership forms also are available, including one that is a mixture of a partnership and a corporation. The Brazilian government has specific requirements with respect to the records and journals that must be kept.

The accounting profession is organized according to the educational levels of its members. Contadores are accounting graduates. They are allowed to provide a variety of professional services including audits. Technicos de contabilidade are accounting technicians who are restricted to practicing in specific areas. A controlling force in the profession is the Federal Accounting Council which is a quasi-official organization whose membership is elected by the Regional Accounting Council. The Institute of Brazilian Accountants, a private organization of accountants, and the Securities Commission also are forces influencing the accounting profession.

Independent audits performed by auditors registered with the Securities Commission are required of public companies, financial institutions, stock exchanges, and certain other types of companies. The demand for independent audits, though not required by law, is extending to other companies.

The most significant area of difference in accounting principles between Brazil and the United States deals with accounting for inflation. The extreme rates of inflation experienced in Brazil have rendered financial statements based on historical cost of questionable utility. In response, a system of monetary correction or inflation accounting is required by law. Certain assets and owners' equity are required to be adjusted or "indexed" for inflation. Even though this is not a complete adjustment of the statement accounts, it does address the major categories of nonmonetary items affected by price level changes. A category of assets referred to as permanent assets and owners' equity is adjusted for inflation. Permanent assets include net property, plant and equipment, long-term investments, and deferred charges. Depreciation expense also is adjusted for inflation. Although not comprehensive, this adjustment approximates the inflationary gain or loss on net monetary items or, if you will, the extent to which the equity of the company is not protected from inflation. This adjustment is then classified as a component of income for both book and tax purposes. From time to time in the U.S., the accounting profession and the Securities and Exchange Commission have encouraged and/or required inflation-adjusted financial statements on a supplementary basis. However, in Brazil such adjusted statements are primary, not supplementary.

There are several other areas in which accounting principles differ between Brazil and the United States. LIFO is not an acceptable inventory method and straight-line depreciation is most common. Leases are accounted for as operating leases in all instances, and research and development costs are more often deferred rather than expensed. Consolidated financial statements are required if the investment in the subsidiary is more than 30% of the investor's net worth. Differences between book and taxable income are few and are accounted for by tax allocation.

Income of Brazilian corporations and branches of foreign corporations is generally taxed at a flat rate of 30%. Capital gains do not receive any special tax treatment, and net operating losses may only be carried forward subject to certain limitations. Certain "tax holidays" and incentives exist in order to encourage development in specific industries and geographic areas.

ACCOUNTING PRINCIPLES IN HUNGARY

The Republic of Hungary in Central Europe has been affected by a number of nations including Poland, Austria, and Russia. In the 1940s it began a program of industrialization based on the Soviet system. Influenced by perestroika and glastnost in the late 1980s, Hungary began a number of reforms affecting business. New company laws, the privatization of state-owned industries, and new legislation dealing with private industry and the securities market have marked a period of economic and political reform. Hungary is an independent republic with a president and parliament. The government is attempting to develop a more market-oriented economy through the privatization of businesses and the termination of subsidies. The economy is heavily dependent on foreign trade and is encouraging the formation of private capital whether from domestic or foreign sources. Although not a member of the European Union, Hungary offers excellent trading opportunities in a number of areas.

Business entities are regulated by the Companies Act and may be organized in several forms including a public limited company (Rt) and a limited company (Kft). Several partnership forms also are available along with trade associations, joint ventures, and sole proprietorships.

The accounting profession in Hungary is controlled primarily by the Ministry of Finance. The Ministry has established a National Chart of Accounts which defines accounting statements, practices, and principles. There are various classes of accountants in Hungary categorized by educational and experiential background. The Ministry of Finance recognizes official auditors and regulates corporate controllers. The Hungarian Auditors' Association is a professional body that is developing auditing standards. All Rts and certain Kfts are required to have an annual audit by an auditor who is registered with the Ministry of Finance.

Accounting principles are established by regulation or tax law. Currently, there are major differences between accounting principles in Hungary and the U.S. For example, in Hungary there are no differences between book and tax income of a temporary nature; therefore, there is no tax allocation. Companies can have only a calendar year end, and consolidated financial statements are not required. All leases are deemed to be of an operating nature, and the legal ownership of assets is the primary focus. Tangible assets are depreciated primarily by the straight-line method with the rates being prescribed by law. However, modest accelerated methods may be used for certain assets primarily affected by rapid technological change. Long-term intangible assets, unlike in the U.S., are not subject to amortization. Interestingly, no general provisions are allowed for inventory obsolescence or uncollectible receivables. Only specific write-downs are allowed based on verifiable evidence. Certain exceptional/nonrecurring expenditures, as defined by law, may be amortized over the current year and the next two years.

Compared to the nations highlighted in the previous pages, Hungary represents the least developed in terms of accounting principles and professional independence. However, the Ministry of Finance is developing a new accounting system which will be modeled after the European Union directives and international accounting standards.

HARMONIZATION OF ACCOUNTING STANDARDS

The differences in accounting and auditing practices among nations quickly become apparent. Although a common list of environmental or influencing factors may emerge, they apply to nations in differing degrees. However, one might ask why identical transactions occurring in different nations should not receive identical accounting treatment. For example, consider a lease that transfers substantially all of the utility value of an asset to a lessee. Shouldn't the same lease in Canada, France, Brazil, or Poland be accounted for the same way? Should different currencies, languages, or political parties make a difference? The fact is that there are major differences among national accounting standards. This results in financial statements that do not report reality or effectively meet the needs of international user groups. The resulting confusion can be quite significant as illustrated in Exhibit 9-3.

This exhibit illustrates how differences among national accounting standards can have a very significant impact on financial statements. In the instant case, the differences arise primarily with respect to accounting for a merger between a British and American firm that resulted in the creation of SmithKline Beecham. The 1989 annual report for the company provides additional information for U.S. investors which reconciles GAAP in the United Kingdom to GAAP in the U.S. Excerpts from the 1989 annual report of SmithKline Beecham dealing with this reconciliation are contained in the Student Companion Enrichment Manual to this text and are the focus of Exercise 6 at the end of this chapter.

The development of a global economy increases the demand for capital and the need for reliable and comparable financial information to support investment decisions. Furthermore, the privatization of business in certain countries is creating an additional demand for capital. The Securities and Exchange Commission (SEC) requires foreign entities that wish to sell securities on U.S. stock exchanges to meet special requirements. These companies must either present their financial statements in accordance with U.S. GAAP or reconcile them to U.S. GAAP. For many companies, this process is a major effort because their own accounting standards are less rigorous than those of the U.S. It is possible that the filing requirements of the SEC and the requirement to conform to GAAP have made the U.S. capital markets less competitive. U.S. investors also have difficulty in analyzing the financial statements of foreign investment opportunities because they are often not comparable to GAAP statements. Certainly, companies seeking capital through international sources should not be advantaged or disadvantaged as a result of the accounting principles and disclosures that they may or may not employ. The development of comparable accounting and auditing standards would be in the best interest of a properly functioning global economy. It is to this end that the harmonization of accounting standards is directed.

The harmonization of accounting standards may take several approaches and is a combination of an evolutionary process and a standard-setting process. One approach to harmonization involves bilateral agreements between two countries. This is often a more expedient and efficient method of reducing differences in standards. Although differences are reduced, differences on a more global scale will continue to exist. This approach has been employed between the U.S. and Canada. In some instances a more regional approach to standard setting has been employed. For example, the European Union has established legally binding accounting directives to be used among its member nations. Of particular importance is the fourth directive which is concerned with the form and content of annual reports and financial statements as well as the need for audits. Consolidated financial statements are addressed by the seventh directive which emphasizes economic versus legal aspects of control. Although the directives have a long due process and implementation period, they represent an important step toward the harmonization of accounting standards as well as other economic issues. It is important to note that these directives also apply to U.S. companies that operate in the member nations of the EU.

A final approach to the harmonization of accounting standards involves an international standard-setting process. The goal is to involve a number of professional accounting organizations in order to develop accounting standards that will be accepted by all countries. This obviously represents a monumental task which must be sensitive to the variety of cultural, ethical, and economic differences that exist between countries. This approach to the harmonization is becoming dominant, and a major force behind the effort has been the International Accounting Standards Committee (IASC).

Exhibit 9-3
Condemned to Confusion

What is it that worries us in the international business community as preparers and users of accounts and why? Let me demonstrate by referring to my own company, SmithKline Beecham, which was formed in 1989 by a merger between the British company Beecham and the American firm SmithKline. It was, in business terms—as most of the financial markets seemed to agree—a marriage made in heaven. It is also a marriage where the partners and investors are currently condemned to live in confusion from the rival demands of British and American accounting standards.

Let me explain. You might hesitate to invest in a company if you read in its accounts that it had net negative shareholders' funds of £330m; that would not sound like a very good bet. On the other hand, you might well invest in one with three and a half billion pounds of shareholders' funds. Let me tell you that these are not two different companies but two portraits of one and the same company, SmithKline Beecham—the first according to UK GAAP, the second according to US GAAP. Both figures are drawn from our 1989 accounts. And the craziness doesn't end there: our net income last year, according to US standards, was £90m; according to British standards it was almost 50% higher, at £130m.

I could produce a number of such examples drawn from SmithKline Beecham. Suffice it to say that you could be forgiven for thinking that you were looking at two different companies, depending on which standards you used. These absurdities arose because of a merger between a British and an American company which was based, as I have already said, on sound business sense.

Such wild variation in figures conspire to make our company suspect, not to say downright fishy, in the eyes of the international investment community. You will appreciate this when I tell you that our US held shares are currently trading at a discount of around 17% on our London shares; and principally because of market perceptions informed—or should I say misinformed—by contradictory accounting standards. All of which makes my life difficult.

In case you should think this is a particular problem related to one particular company, let me pick another example at random out of the press recently. Many of you will have watched Mr. Rupert Murdoch's recent efforts to refinance News Corp. He recently revalued News Corp's intangible assets—newspaper titles and the like—by £1.8 bn, thereby enabling him to comply with the debt ratios permitted by his banks. He was allowed to do that by Australian accounting standards. In the UK or the US, this would have been prohibited and News Corp could now be fighting for survival.

Source: *IASC News*, April, 1991, Vol. 20, No. 1. Excerpts from a paper presented by Hugh Collum, Finance Director and Chief Financial Officer of SmithKline Beecham.

The International Accounting Standards Committee. The International Accounting Standards Committee (IASC) was formed as an independent private organization in 1973 and has the following major objectives: (1) to formulate and publish accounting standards to be observed in the presentation of financial statements and to promote their worldwide acceptance and (2) to work for the harmonization of accounting standards and procedures relating to the presentation of financial statements. Because of the organization's private nature, standards issued by the IASC are not legally enforceable; rather, compliance is voluntary. Membership in the IASC consists of over 100 accounting bodies representing more than 70 countries. Business of the IASC is carried on by a board consisting of representatives from developed and developing nations and organizations having an interest in financial reporting. In 1982, an important mutual commitment was reached with the International Federation of Accountants (IFAC)[2] whereby the IFAC recognizes the IASC as the sole body having the authority to promulgate accounting standards and to negotiate for their acceptance. Furthermore, the IFAC nominates all the members of the IASC's board. These cooperative efforts and the initiatives by the IASC have led to the recognition of the IASC as the leader in establishing accounting standards on a worldwide basis, including developing and newly industrialized nations. In 1990, the IASC approved a statement of intent designed to set forth how the comparability of financial statements and principles will be implemented.

Within the structure of the IASC is the Consultative Group which advises the board of the IASC as to policies and practical/conceptual issues affecting the acceptance of international accounting standards. The Consultative Group is comprised of representatives from a range of users, preparers of financial statements, and standard-setting bodies. Included, among others, are representatives from the World Bank, International Association of Financial Executives' Institute, and the International Federation of Stock Exchanges. In 1990, the European Community (now the European Union) also committed itself to taking a more involved role in the activities of the IASC.

The IASC is a dominant force in the process of harmonizing accounting standards throughout the world. There is an increase in the number of nations whose accounting systems are being developed in conformity with IASC standards. An increasing number of financial statements disclose either their conformity with IASC standards or how they differ from such standards. The IASC has issued thirty-one International Accounting Standards (IASs), of which twenty-nine are still operative, for financial statements for periods beginning on or after January 1, 1991. In addition, the IASC has published the *Framework for the Preparation and Presentation of Financial Statements* and a Statement of Intent entitled the *Comparability of Financial Statements*. Exhibit 9-4 briefly summarizes several of the IASs, which represent an important effort to harmonize accounting standards.

A major project of the IASC has dealt with the comparability of financial statements. Initially the project, in the form of Exposure Draft 32, was aimed at

---

[2]See pages 596–597 for a discussion of the IFAC.

**Exhibit 9-4
Highlights of Selected IASs**

IAS No. 9, *Accounting for Research and Development Activities*

Generally research and development (R&D) costs should be charged to expense in the period in which costs are incurred. Certain R&D costs may be deferred if they meet specific criteria which link such costs to a clearly defined product or process. Deferred costs are subject to amortization over the expected period of sale for the product or service.

IAS No. 12, *Accounting for Taxes on Income*

Tax expense is to be included in the calculation of net income and should be determined using either the deferral or liability method. Certain timing (temporary) differences may be excluded from the calculation of deferred taxes if reversal of the differences is not indicated. Deferred tax assets should not be recognized unless there is a reasonable expectation that they will be realized. The tax benefit associated with a net operating loss carryforward should not be recognized unless realization is assured beyond a reasonable doubt.

IAS No. 17, *Accounting for Leases*

The substance of leases should be evaluated to determine if substantially all of the risks and rewards of ownership have been transferred to the lessee. Leases are classified as either finance (capitalized) leases or operating leases. Accounting for sale and leaseback transactions provides for more recognition of the gain or loss on sale than does GAAP in the U.S.

IAS No. 22, *Accounting for Business Combinations*

Business combinations should be accounted for as a purchase, except that the pooling of interests method may be appropriate in certain circumstances. The criteria for a pooling are less specific than those in the U.S. Goodwill should be recognized and generally is amortized over its useful life.

IAS No. 24, *Related Party Disclosures*

Related party relationships involving control should be disclosed even if no transactions occurred between the parties. Related party transactions require disclosure of the nature of the relationship, the type of transaction involved, and elements of the transaction necessary for a proper understanding of the financial statements.

---

reducing the options found in the IAS; however, the project has expanded to strengthen the focus of harmonization of accounting standards. The IASC is strongly encouraging standard setters in separate countries to establish principles that are consistent with IASC standards. Exposure Draft 32 was widely circulated by the IASC and comments were received from over thirty countries. After reviewing the comments, the IASC issued the Statement of Intent entitled *Comparability of Financial Statements.* The Statement of Intent calls for the revision of certain existing IASs so that they enhance comparability, establish adequate disclosure, and provide guidance regarding their implementation. It is expected that the IASC will eliminate from acceptability over twenty current alternatives found in IASs. In those instances where alternatives are allowed for like transactions, one method will be identified as the "benchmark" (preferable) alternative. Companies adopting an alternative other than the benchmark are encouraged to reconcile to what the results would have been had the benchmark method been employed. The IASC also will expose again their proposals regarding LIFO accounting, capitalization of research and development, and capitalization of interest. Certain proposals dealing with investments and financial instruments are being temporarily deferred. The comparability project is a major undertaking toward the harmonization of accounting. In establishing comparability, many standard setters, government/regulatory bodies, reporting companies, and users of financial information will be asked to make some major adjustments and sacrifices in the name of harmonization. For example, the IASC is proposing the elimination or "blacklisting" of principles such as LIFO and pooling of interests. These are major areas whose proposed elimination will generate a tremendous reaction.

The IASC's accomplishments to date are impressive; yet there certainly will be new challenges facing it in the future. Professional bodies that are members of the IASC have pledged their support to bring domestic accounting standards into conformity with IASC standards. In the U.S., the AICPA and several other professional bodies as members of the IASC will be affected by this cooperative movement. Although the FASB is not a member of the IASC, it undoubtedly will have to be responsive to these pressures.

The International Federation of Accountants.   Organized in 1977, the International Federation of Accountants (IFAC) is a private standard-setting body whose membership consists of the same professional bodies as those belonging to the IASC. The IFAC primarily is concerned with harmonizing accounting and auditing practices throughout the world. It is involved, not with establishing principles per se, but, rather, with becoming the spokesperson for the international accounting profession. Therefore, the IFAC is more appropriately compared to the AICPA than the FASB, which is more akin to the IASC.

The IFAC is organized into six committees: planning, education, ethics, financial and management accounting, international auditing practices, and public sector. International Auditing Guidelines have been issued dealing with a variety of auditing topics similar to those dealt with by the Auditing Standards Board in the U.S. The Education Committee and the Ethics Committee have both issued a number of guidelines regarding the competence and ethical qualities of international accountants. The other committees of the IFAC also have issued a number of statements and guidelines.

The success of the organizations discussed above is dependent on a variety of factors. Harmonization of accounting standards may be flawed until greater attention is focused on a conceptual framework of accounting from which to build. Certainly, the experiences of the U.S. accounting environment suggest the importance and struggles associated with such a framework. Standards generally cannot be imposed; rather, they must be acceptable after appropriate due process. This process must recognize the environmental similarities and, perhaps more important, the dissimilarities between nations. A bridging of the factors separating nations must be accomplished subject to significant time and funding constraints. However, as national economies develop into global economies, the harmonization of accounting standards will become more of a natural process.

QUESTIONS

1. What is meant by the privatization of industry and how does it affect international security markets?
2. In what way do capital markets influence the harmonization of accounting standards?
3. How has the rate of inflation in Brazil affected accounting principles in that country?
4. What is the accounting measurement issue that results from a U.S. company's acquiring inventory on account from a foreign vendor and having to settle or pay for the transaction with foreign currency?
5. Identify several factors that may explain why accounting principles differ between countries.
6. What are the primary areas of international accounting that a multinational corporation should be aware of?
7. How might the independence and autonomy of accounting professionals in a country influence accounting standard setting?
8. How would a U.S. company have to adjust its inventory balances in order to have them comparable to inventory balances contained in financial statements of a French company?
9. How does accounting for depreciable assets differ between Brazil and France?
10. Describe the major differences between the U.S. and Hungary regarding the accounting for tangible and intangible assets.
11. What are the major objectives of the International Accounting Standards Committee?
12. What are the two primary approaches to the harmonization of accounting standards?

EXERCISES

Exercise 1. The single market created by the European Community (EC)—now the European Union (EU)—will eliminate trade barriers among its member nations. Most U.S. businesses see the EU as an opportunity for growth.
(1) Discuss some of the apparent opportunities presented by the EU.
(2) Discuss why harmonization of accounting standards among members of the EU is important to the success of the EU.

Exercise 2. The level of a country's technological development is a factor influencing the development of accounting principles. A small agrarian economy is interested in developing a presence as an exporter of high technology products. Discuss how this new focus may affect the development of accounting.

Exercise 3. In the U.S., accounting for income taxes requires the recognition of deferred taxes which result from differences between accounting and tax bases of assets and liabilities. Discuss how accounting principles in France and Hungary affect the recognition of deferred taxes in those countries and whether these differences penalize U.S. companies.

Exercise 4. Identify and discuss the major differences you might expect to find when comparing the income statement of a Brazilian auto manufacturer to that of a U.S. auto manufacturer.

Exercise 5. Harmonization of accounting standards through a private standard-setting process will have both advantages and disadvantages to American investors and businesses.
(1) Discuss the advantages of harmonization to American investors.
(2) Discuss why differences in accounting principles and disclosure requirements may place American businesses at a competitive disadvantage.
(3) Discuss how the U.S. accounting profession can influence the process of harmonization.

Exercise 6. In 1989, Beecham, a British company, merged with SmithKline, an American firm, to create SmithKline Beecham. The newly created company is a British company which prepares its financial statements according to generally accepted accounting principles (GAAP) in the United Kingdom. As discussed in Exhibit 9-3, the use of U.K. GAAP results in financial statements that are significantly different from the financial statements that would have resulted if U.S. GAAP were employed. In order to better understand these differences, the 1989 annual report identifies the applicable differences between U.K. and U.S. GAAP. Using the excerpts from the annual report appearing in the Student Companion Enrichment Manual which accompanies this text, identify the nature and amounts of the primary differences in accounting principles affecting net income and shareholders' equity for the year 1989.

CHAPTER 10

Foreign Currency Transactions

As discussed in the previous chapter, modern businesses often find themselves affected by a global economy that presents a variety of challenges and opportunities. Companies in the U.S. realize the importance of international trade and are expanding their market share into a number of foreign nations. In turn, other nations are expanding their market share into the U.S. as more companies acquire factors of production on an international scale. This exporting and importing activity has increased significantly in recent years as evidenced by the following measures, in billions of dollars, of activity:

U.S. Exports and Imports of Merchandise

	1975	1980	1985	1990	1991	1992	1993
Exports	107.652	220.626	213.133	394.030	421.730	448.164	464.767
Imports	98.503	244.871	345.276	495.042	485.453	532.665	580.543

Source: Department of Commerce.

When two parties from different nations transact business, each normally would like to carry out the transaction by using its own national currency. However, it is only possible to use one currency as the medium of exchange in the transaction. Therefore, a decision must be made as to which currency to use, and rates of exchange must be established between the two competing currencies.

For example, if an American manufacturer of footwear purchases leather from a German supplier, a decision must be made as to whether the transaction will be settled in U.S. dollars or German marks. If German marks are used as the medium of exchange, a rate of exchange between the U.S. dollar and the German mark must be established. Given that rates of exchange vary over time, the number of U.S. dollars needed to acquire the necessary German marks also could change over time. As time passes, if more dollars are needed to acquire the necessary marks to pay for the leather, the U.S. purchaser is exposed to an additional business risk. The more volatility there is in exchange rates, the more risk the party is exposed to. Similarly, if the dollar is used as the medium of exchange, this risk would be transferred to the German vendor.

It becomes readily apparent that the decision as to which currency will be used for settlement purposes becomes an important factor in negotiating such transactions. Due to the volatility of currency exchange rates, companies transacting business in foreign markets must aggressively control and measure exchange risk. Management must develop a model that enables them to forecast the direction, magnitude, and timing of exchange rate changes. This model, in turn, can be used to develop a strategy to minimize foreign exchange losses and maximize foreign exchange gains.

Business transactions that are settled in a currency other than that of the domestic currency are referred to in this text as *foreign currency transactions*. The currency used to settle the transaction is referred to as the *denominated currency*. The denominated amount of a foreign currency transaction must be measured in the domestic currency for reporting purposes. This process involves the use of exchange rates and is referred to as *foreign currency translation*.

THE INTERNATIONAL MONETARY SYSTEM

Denominating a transaction in a currency other than the entity's domestic currency requires the establishment of a *rate of exchange* between the currencies. The international monetary system establishes rates of exchanges between currencies through the use of a variety of systems. The selection of a particular monetary system and the resulting exchange rates have a significant effect on international business and the risk associated with such business.

ALTERNATIVE INTERNATIONAL MONETARY SYSTEMS

Several major international monetary systems have been employed over time, and occasionally there are suggestions that previous systems be reestablished. Prior to 1933 the monetary system was the *gold system* which provided a strict apolitical system based on gold. The currencies of nations were backed by or equivalent to some physical measure of gold. For example, Nation A has 1 million currency units backed by 1,000 ounces of gold, and Nation B has 2 million currency units also backed by 1,000 ounces of gold. With gold as the common denominator, exchange rates between currencies could be established. In the above example, 1 unit of Nation A's currency could be exchanged for 2 units of Nation B's currency. A nation's supply of gold, therefore, influences its money supply, rates of exchange, prices, and international trading levels (imports and exports).

In 1944 the *Bretton Woods Agreement*, which created the International Monetary Fund (IMF) and a *fixed rate exchange system*, was signed. The fixed rate system was a gold/U.S. dollar system which required each nation to set a par value for its currency in terms of gold or the U.S. dollar. In turn, the U.S. dollar's value was defined in terms of gold. Modest variations from a currency's par value were allowed and each nation could adjust its money supply in order to maintain its par value. The IMF could provide support to a nation in order to maintain its par value. Changes in a currency's par value were referred to as *devaluations* and *revaluations*.

As pressures to maintain the par values established by the fixed rate system increased, pressure was placed on the U.S. dollar. The ability of the dollar to support the system became questionable, and there were fears that countries with dollar surpluses might seek to convert these dollars into gold. In 1971, the U.S. government, for all practical purposes, terminated the Bretton Woods Agreement by suspending the convertibility of the dollar into gold.

Currencies temporarily became part of a *floating system* where rates of exchange were in response to the supply and demand factors affecting a currency. Shortly thereafter, the *Smithsonian Agreement* was accepted by the IMF. This agreement devaluated the U.S. dollar and did not allow for the convertibility of the dollar into gold. Par values of currencies were established along with a wider margin of acceptable values around the par value. The Smithsonian Agreement was short-lived, and in response to increasing pressures on the U.S. dollar, the fixed rate system was abandoned in 1973.

Today, the international monetary system is a floating system whereby the factors of supply and demand primarily define currency exchange rates. Each nation's central bank may intervene in order to move its currency toward a target rate of exchange. This intervention results in a managed or "dirty" float versus a "clean" float. Supply and demand factors along with possible central bank intervention result in an exchange system with much more uncertainty and risk than experienced in a fixed rate system. Unfortunately, a myriad of factors beyond supply and demand affect exchange rates in a floating system. Some of these factors are[1]:

- The speed of recovery from a recession.
- A nation's vulnerability to an energy crisis.
- A nation's trade and payment balances.
- The supply of and growth in the domestic money supply.
- Stability in the national economy, including a stable inflation rate, political stability, national prosperity, labor costs, and unemployment rates.
- A currency's vulnerability to rumors.
- Domestic interest rates and changes in these rates. (If interest rates are relatively high, others will want to obtain that currency and invest it in the securities of that nation and earn high yields.)
- The strength or weakness of the domestic GNP as a major gauge of a nation's underlying economic strength.
- Confidence and expectations, especially during uncertainty and crisis.
- In a dirty float, the amount of governmental intervention in the market.

Although the present international monetary system is best described as a floating system, there are a number of special variations within the system. Some nations still maintain a fixed system whereby the rate of exchange is established

---

[1]Thomas G. Evans, Martin E. Taylor, and Oscar Holzmann, *International Accounting and Reporting* (Boston: PWS-Kent Publishing Company, 1988), pp. 134–135.

by the central bank as in the case of Brazil. However, because these fixed rates are changed frequently, sometimes daily, they may be viewed as a controlled or "dirty" float. A currency that is frequently adjusted downward, such as those in less developed nations, is referred to as a "crawling peg" currency. Tiered systems also exist whereby special rates are established for certain types of transactions, such as import and export sales and dividend payments, to accomplish desired political and economic objectives. For example, to encourage exports and to discourage capital withdrawal, a foreign government may establish favorable official rates for export sales and less favorable exchange rates for the payment of dividends to investors in other countries. The forces of supply and demand, however, occasionally make it difficult for a government to maintain an official exchange rate. In response, the government either devalues or revalues its currency. The European Union (EU) also has created a combined currency called the *European Currency Unit* (ECU). Although not in a physical form, the ECU is made up of proportional amounts of the currencies EU members. The ECU will be subject to less volatility than any single currency, and there are proposals to make the ECU the single physical currency of Europe.

THE MECHANICS OF EXCHANGE RATES

An exchange rate is a measure of how much of one currency may be exchanged for another currency. These rates may be in the form of either *direct* or *indirect* *quotes* made by a foreign currency trader who usually is employed by a large commercial bank. A direct quote measures how much of the domestic currency must be exchanged to receive 1 unit of the foreign currency (1 FC). This method is used in the U.S., and direct quotes are published daily in financial papers such as the *Wall Street Journal*. Indirect quotes measure how many units of foreign currency will be received for 1 unit of the domestic currency. To illustrate these methods, if the direct quote for French francs (FF) is $0.25, this means that 1 FF would cost $0.25. The indirect quote would be the reciprocal of the direct quote, or 4 FF per dollar ($1.00 divided by $0.25).

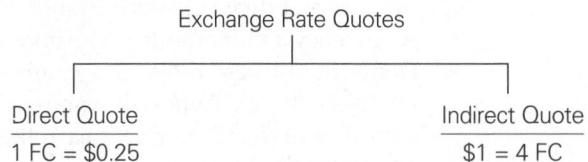

Exchange Rate Quotes

Direct Quote
1 FC = $0.25

Indirect Quote
$1 = 4 FC

The business news often reports that a currency has strengthened (gained) or weakened (lost) relative to another currency. Assuming a direct quote system, such changes measure the difference between the new rate and the old rate as a percentage of the old rate. For example, if the dollar strengthened or gained 20% against the French franc from its previous rate of $0.25, the dollar would now command more francs. To be exact, the new exchange rate would be $0.20. Therefore, the strengthening currency would be evidenced by a reduction in the directly quoted amount and an increase in the indirectly quoted amount. The opposite would be true for a weakening of the domestic currency. The reaction to a strengthening or weakening of a currency depends on what type of transaction is contemplated. For example, an American exporter would want a weaker dollar because the foreign importer would need fewer of its currency units to acquire a dollar's worth of U.S. goods. If the dollar strengthened so that you could acquire more foreign currency units for a dollar, importers would benefit.

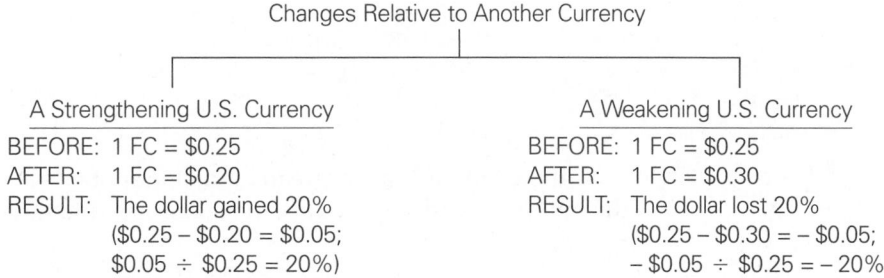

Exchange rates often are quoted in terms of a *buying rate* and a *selling rate*. The buying and selling rates represent what the currency broker is willing to pay to acquire or sell a currency. The difference or spread between these two rates represents the broker's commission. For example, assume a currency broker agrees to pay $0.20 to a holder of a foreign currency and agrees to sell that currency to a buyer of foreign currency for $0.22. In this case, the broker will receive a commission of $0.02 ($0.22 – $0.20).

In addition to all of the above exchange rate terms, there are two primary types of exchange rates. A *spot rate* is the rate of exchange for a currency with delivery, selling, or buying of the currency normally occurring within 2 business days. In addition to exchange rates governing the immediate delivery of currency, *forward rates* apply to the exchange of different currencies at a future point in time, such as in 30 or 180 days.

The agreement to exchange currencies at a future date is contained in a *forward exchange contract* which is designed to protect against future changes in spot rates. The forward exchange contract specifies the future exchange date and the forward rate of exchange. Although future exchange dates typically are quoted in 30-day intervals, contracts can be written covering any number of days. To illustrate a forward contract, assume the forward rate on a British pound (£) to be delivered in 90 days is $1.6501. This means that after the specified time from the inception of the contract date (90 days), £1 will be exchanged for $1.6501 regardless of what the spot rate is at that time.

If the forward rate is greater than the spot rate at inception of the contract, the contract is said to be at a *premium*. The opposite situation results in a *discount*.

The difference between the forward and spot rates represents a contract expense or income to the purchaser of the forward contract that normally is amortized over the life of the contract. There are a number of factors that influence forward rates and thus account for the difference between a forward rate and a spot rate. A primary factor is the interest rate differentials between holding an investment in foreign currency and holding an investment in domestic currency. For example, if a broker sold a contract to deliver foreign currency in 30 days, the interest differential would be the difference between:

1. The interest earned on investing foreign currency for the 30 days prior to delivery date, and
2. The 30 days of interest lost on the domestic currency that was not invested but was used to acquire the foreign currency needed for delivery.

Other factors accounting for the difference between forward and spot rates include: movements in spot rates, the time period covered by the contract, expectations of future exchange rate movements, and the political and economic environments for a given country.

It is important that the student of international accounting have an understanding of the international monetary system and exchange rates. As previously mentioned, changes in exchange rates represent an additional business risk when transactions are denominated in a foreign currency. The accounting for foreign currency transactions demonstrates the importance of both spot and forward rates.

ACCOUNTING FOR FOREIGN CURRENCY TRANSACTIONS

Assume a U.S. company sells mining equipment to a British company and the equipment must be paid for in 30 days with U.S. dollars. This transaction is denominated in dollars and will be measured by the U.S. company in dollars. Changes in the exchange rate between the U.S. dollar and the British pound from the transaction date to the settlement date will not expose the U.S. company to any risk or gain. Now assume that the same transaction occurs except that the transaction is to be settled in British pounds. Because this transaction is denominated in pounds and will be measured by the U.S. company in dollars, changes in the exchange rate subsequent to the transaction date could expose the U.S. company to risk or gain. For example, if the U.S. dollar strengthens relative to the pound (one receives more pounds per dollar), settlement of the receivable will result in collecting a fixed amount of British pounds which are worth fewer dollars, and the U.S. company will experience a loss due to exchange rate changes. If the dollar weakens, the opposite effect would be experienced, as the U.S. company would receive a gain due to exchange rate changes. To summarize, *changes in exchange rates do not affect transactions that are both denominated and measured in the reporting entity's currency.* Therefore, these transactions require no special accounting treatment. However, *if a transaction is denominated in a foreign currency and measured in the reporting entity's currency, changes in the exchange rate result in a gain or loss to the reporting entity.* These gains or losses are referred to as *exchange gains or losses,* and their recognition requires special accounting treatment.

Originally, two methods were proposed for the treatment of exchange gains or losses arising from foreign currency transactions. After considering the merits of these two methods, the FASB adopted what is referred to as the "two-transaction method." This method views the initial foreign currency transaction as a separate transaction. The effect of any subsequent changes in the exchange rates and the resulting exchange gain or loss is viewed as a separate transaction. Therefore, the initial transaction is recorded independently of the settlement transaction. This method is consistent with accepted accounting techniques, which normally account for the financing of a transaction as a separate and distinct event. (The required two-transaction method is used in all instances with one exception. The exception relates to a hedge on a foreign currency commitment that is discussed later in this chapter. Therefore, unless otherwise stated, the two-transaction method will be used throughout the chapter.)

In order to illustrate the two-transaction method, assume that a U.S. company sells mining equipment on June 1, 19X9, with the corresponding receivable to be paid or settled on July 1, 19X9. The equipment has a selling price of $306,000 and a cost of $250,000. On June 1, 19X9, the British pound is worth $1.70 and on July 1, 19X9, the pound is worth $1.60. Illustrations 10-1 and 10-2 present the entries to record the sale of the mining equipment assuming that the transaction is denominated in dollars and then in pounds. It is important to note from Illustration 10-1 that when the transaction is denominated in dollars, the U.S. company does not experience an exchange gain or loss. However, because the British company measures the transaction in pounds but denominates the transaction in

---

Illustration 10-1
Transaction Denominated in **Dollars**: *Two-Transaction Method*

U.S. Company (dollars)			British Company (pounds)		
June 1, 19X9					
Accounts Receivable	306,000		Equipment	180,000*	
Sales Revenue		306,000	Accounts Payable		180,000
Cost of Goods Sold	250,000				
Inventory		250,000			
July 1, 19X9					
Cash	306,000		Accounts Payable	180,000	
Accounts Receivable		306,000	**Exchange Loss**	**11,250**	
			Cash		191,250**

Note: The U.S. company experienced no exchange gain or loss because its transaction was *both* denominated and measured in dollars. However, under the two-transaction method, the British company did experience an exchange loss since its transaction was measured in pounds and denominated in dollars.

*($306,000 ÷ $1.70 = 180,000)
**($306,000 ÷ $1.60 = 191,250)

Illustration 10-2
Transaction Denominated in **Pounds**: *Two-Transaction Method*

U.S. Company (dollars)			British Company (pounds)		
June 1, 19X9					
Accounts Receivable	306,000		Equipment	180,000	
Sales Revenue		306,000	Accounts Payable		180,000
Cost of Goods Sold	250,000				
Inventory		250,000			
July 1, 19X9					
Cash	288,000		Accounts Payable	180,000	
Exchange Loss	**18,000***		Cash		180,000
Accounts Receivable		306,000			

Note: The loss is considered to be part of a separate financing decision and unrelated to the original sales transaction.

*The *decrease* in the value of the British pound from $1.70 to $1.60 results in an *exchange loss* to the U.S. firm since the pounds it *received* are less valuable than they were at the transaction date. [180,000 × ($1.60 − $1.70) = −$18,000]

dollars, it experiences an exchange loss. When the transaction is denominated in pounds, as in Illustration 10-2, the U.S. company experiences an exchange loss (or gain). The exchange loss (or gain) is accounted for separately from the sales transaction and does not affect the U.S. company's gross profit on the sale. This separately recognized exchange gain or loss is not viewed as an extraordinary item, but should be included in determining net income from operations for the period and should be disclosed in the financial statements or in a note to the statements.[2] Finally, it is important to note in Illustration 10-2 that the British company does not experience an exchange gain or loss. This is because the British company both measured and denominated the transaction in pounds.

UNSETTLED FOREIGN CURRENCY TRANSACTIONS

If a foreign currency transaction is unsettled at year end, a gain or loss should be recognized to reflect the change in the exchange rate occurring between the transaction date and year end. This treatment focuses on accrual accounting and the fact that exchange gains and losses occur over time rather than only at the date of settlement or payment.

To illustrate the accounting for unsettled transactions, assume a U.S. company purchases goods from a foreign firm on November 1, 19X1. The purchase in the amount of 1,000 foreign currencies (FC) is to be paid for on February 1, 19X2. To record or measure the transaction, the domestic company would make the following entry, assuming an exchange rate of 1 FC = $0.50:

Inventory. 500
    Accounts Payable.   500
        Purchase of inventory for 1,000 FC when the exchange rate is
        1 FC = $0.50.

Assuming the exchange rate on the December 31, 19X1 year end is 1 FC = $0.52, the following entry would be necessary:

Exchange Loss* [1,000 × ($0.52 − $0.50)]. 20
    Accounts Payable   20
        To accrue the exchange loss on the unperformed portion of the
        foreign currency transaction when 1 FC = $0.52.

*The *increase* in the value of each FC from $0.50 to $0.52 results in a *loss* to the domestic firm since, as of year end, the firm would have to *pay out* more dollars than originally recorded in order to eliminate the liability.

Assuming an exchange rate of 1 FC = $0.55 on the settlement date (February 1, 19X2), the domestic entity would make the following entry to record the settlement:

Accounts Payable ($500 + $20) 520
Exchange Loss [1,000 × ($0.55 − $0.52)]. 30
    Cash   550
        To record payment of liability for 1,000 FC when 1 FC = $0.55.

The December 31 entry implies that if the transaction had been settled at year end, the domestic firm would have had to expend $520 to acquire 1,000 FC.

---

[2]FASB Statement No. 52, *Foreign Currency Translation* (Stamford: Financial Accounting Standards Board, 1981), par. 30.

Therefore, a loss of $20 is traceable to the unperformed portion of the transaction. Some theorists have suggested that an exchange gain or loss should not be recognized prior to settlement because the gain or loss has not been "realized" through settlement. This position fails to recognize the merits of accrual accounting and is in conflict with the position of the FASB.

HEDGING WITH FORWARD EXCHANGE CONTRACTS

Whenever the value of an asset or liability denominated in a foreign currency would be adversely affected due to fluctuating exchange rates, management would prefer to eliminate or reduce such adverse effects. Amounts adversely affected may be a receivable from a foreign customer, a liability to a foreign vendor, a foreign bank loan, or even a net investment position in a foreign subsidiary. Management may be able to control this business risk by engaging in a variety of hedging-type transactions. Hedging in connection with foreign currency transactions is discussed in this chapter. The following chapter discusses hedging in connection with a net investment position in a foreign subsidiary.

Hedging is a form of risk reduction management in response to fluctuating currency exchange rates. To avoid exposure to changes in future exchange rates when a foreign transaction is denominated in a foreign currency, it is possible to agree currently to buy or sell the foreign currency at a preestablished, rather than an uncertain, rate of exchange. This would be accomplished through the use of a *forward exchange contract*. The forward contract allows one to hedge against any exchange losses that may arise since the contract fixes the future rate of exchange. In the preceding example of a foreign currency transaction, the U.S. company experienced a $50 exchange loss because it had to settle a liability denominated in 1,000 FC at a settlement date exchange rate of 1 FC = $0.55, rather than at the original transaction date exchange rate of 1 FC = $0.50. However, if a forward contract had provided for the delivery of the needed foreign currency at a forward rate of 1 FC = $0.52, the exchange loss would have been reduced to $20 since the transaction could have been settled with currency acquired at a rate of 1 FC = $0.52 rather than 1 FC = $0.55.

Forward exchange contracts are used in foreign currency transactions in one of two ways. First, a forward contract may be used to hedge against either the exposed position created by a single transaction or the net exposed position created by several transactions. An *exposed net asset position* exists when a foreign currency transaction, or a series of such transactions, results in foreign-currency-denominated assets exceeding foreign-currency-denominated liabilities.

A second use of a forward contract with respect to foreign currency transactions is in response to an *identifiable foreign currency commitment*. In this instance, the forward contract is acquired as a hedge because there is an existing commitment that will result in a future transaction denominated in a foreign currency. This hedge is in response to an exposed position that will arise via the commitment rather than an exposed position that has arisen already via existing foreign currency transactions.

Hedge on Exposed Position.   Forward exchange contracts are similar to purchase commitments in that both are forms of executory contracts in which future exchange rates have been established. Typically, executory contracts are not recorded until at least partial performance has taken place by one of the parties to the contract. The fact that forward contracts may be sold after inception indicates that they are economic resources and is the basis for suggestions that unperformed forward contracts should be recorded as assets stated at market price. The FASB views an unperformed forward exchange contract as an asset for which changes in value due to exchange rate fluctuations should be recognized as a component of current operating income. The FASB states that:

> *A gain or loss (whether or not deferred) on a forward contract . . . shall be computed by multiplying the foreign currency amount of the forward contract by the difference between the spot rate at the balance sheet date and the spot rate at the date of inception of the forward contract (or the spot rate last used to measure a gain or loss on that contract for an earlier period).*[3]

If a forward contract represents a hedge on an exposed position resulting from an existing foreign currency transaction, the gain or loss on the contract is recognized currently rather than deferred. To illustrate, assume the following:

1. On November 1, 19X1, a U.S. firm buys inventory from a foreign company, payable on February 1, 19X2, in the amount of 1,000 FC.
2. On November 1, 19X1, the U.S. firm purchases a 90-day forward contract to buy 1,000 FC at a forward rate of 1 FC = $0.506.
3. Spot rates on selected dates are as follows:

Date	Spot Rate	Forward Rate
November 1, 19X1	1 FC = $0.50	.506
December 31, 19X1	1 FC = 0.52	
February 1, 19X2	1 FC = 0.55	

Illustration 10-3 presents the following entries on the books of the U.S. firm that reflect the proper accounting for these facts. The entries have been separated between those relating to the purchase of inventory and those relating to the forward contract. This emphasizes that the firm is entering into two separate but related transactions. One relates to a transaction with a foreign party that is denominated in foreign currency. This transaction presents exposure to risk resulting from exchange rate changes. The other transaction accounts for a forward contract between the company and a broker and is designed to hedge against exchange risk. Accounting for a forward contract requires that the value of the foreign currency due to or from the broker be periodically adjusted to its market value based on currency spot rates.

Changes in the spot exchange rate affecting the hedging transaction are reflected in the account Foreign Currency Due from [to] Broker only. Notice that the account representing dollars due to (from) the broker is fixed in amount and

---

[3]*Ibid.*, par. 18.

Illustration 10-3

Hedging an Exposed Liability

Relating to Purchase of Inventory[1]	Relating to Purchase of Forward Contract

November 1, 19X1

Inventory.............................	500*		Foreign Currency Due from Broker	500	
Accounts Payable		500	Deferred Contract Premiums	6*	
Purchase of inventory for 1,000			Dollars Due to Broker..............		506*
FC when 1 FC = $0.50.			Purchase of 1,000 FC to be		
*Not affected by change in			delivered in 90 days when forward		
exchange rate.			rate is 1 FC = $0.506.[2]		
			*Not affected by change in		
			exchange rate.		

December 31, 19X1

Exchange Loss......................	20		Foreign Currency Due from Broker	20	
Accounts Payable		20	Exchange Gain.....................		20
To accrue the exchange loss on the			To record the gain on the forward		
unperformed portion of the foreign			contract when the year-end spot		
currency transaction when 1 FC =			rate is 1 FC = $0.52. At year end,		
$0.52.			the 1,000 FC is worth $520 versus		
			the $500 recorded initially.[3]		
			Contract Expense	4*	
			Deferred Contract Premium		4
			To amortize the forward contract		
			premium ($6 × 2/3).		
			*Not affected by change in		
			exchange rate.		

February 1, 19X2

			Dollars Due to Broker................	506	
			Cash..............................		506*
			To record payment of cash due to		
			broker.		
			*Not affected by change in		
			exchange rate.		
Accounts Payable	520		Investment in Foreign Currency........	550	
Exchange Loss......................	30		Foreign Currency Due from Broker ...		520
Investment in Foreign Currency......		550	Exchange Gain.....................		30
To record settlement of the liability			To record receipt of foreign		
when 1 FC = $0.55.			currency from broker when		
			1 FC = $0.55.		
			Contract Expense	2	
			Deferred Contract Premium		2
			To amortize the balance of the		
			forward contract premium.		

[1]Note that the first two entries are identical to those on page 607 when *no* forward exchange contract was purchased.

[2]An alternative for this entry would be a memo entry to describe the commitment resulting from the contract. Such treatment emphasizes the executory nature of the contract.

[3]If the contract is not recorded initially, exchange gains or losses would be recognized and an allowance for exchange gains or losses would be employed. For example, in the illustration the entry would be:

Allowance for Exchange Gains or Losses	20	
Exchange Gain		20

does not change given exchange rate fluctuations. The entries shown in Illustration 10-3 reflect the objective of a forward contract, which is to hedge against exchange losses. The exchange loss that would have been experienced without the hedge was offset effectively as illustrated below:

	Without the Hedge	With the Hedge
Exchange gain (loss) on foreign currency transaction [1,000 FC × ($0.55 – $0.50)]	$(50)	$(50)
Exchange gain (loss) on hedge [1,000 FC × ($0.55 – $0.50)]		50
Contract income (expense) [1,000 FC × ($0.506 – $0.50)]		(6)
Effect on net income	$(50)	$ (6)

Unfortunately, not all hedging transactions are as effective in reducing foreign currency transaction exchange losses. For instance, when a forward contract establishes a forward rate, it is possible that changes in the spot rate may not move in the same direction. Considering the previous transactions, assume the same facts except that the spot rates are as follows:

Date	Rate
November 1, 19X1	1 FC = $0.50
December 31, 19X1	1 FC = 0.49
February 1, 19X2	1 FC = 0.48

In effect, the hedge eliminated potential exchange gains as follows:

	Without the Hedge	With the Hedge
Exchange gain (loss) on foreign currency transaction [1,000 FC × ($0.48 – $0.50)]	$20	$ 20
Exchange gain (loss) on hedge [1,000 FC × ($0.48 – $0.50)]		(20)
Contract income (expense) [1,000 FC × ($0.506 – $0.50)]		(6)
Effect on net income	$20	$ (6)

It is important to note that forward contracts also may be used to sell foreign currencies at a more favorable rate than the spot rate existing at the settlement date. To illustrate, assume a domestic company sells goods to a foreign purchaser for 1,000 FC when the spot rate is 1 FC = $0.50, and assume the receivable is to be paid in 60 days in foreign currency. If the spot rate at the settlement date was 1 FC = $0.475, the domestic company would have an exchange loss of $25 [1,000 FC × ($0.475 – $0.50)]. A forward exchange contract to sell the 1,000 FC at a forward rate of 1 FC = $0.49, or $490 (1,000 FC × $0.49), would have reduced the exchange loss to a net amount of $10 [1,000 FC × ($0.49 – $0.50)].

The previous examples assumed that a forward contract covered the same period of time as the settlement period, which is defined as the period of time between the transaction date and the settlement date. However, it is possible that a forward contract could cover a period of time different from the settlement period. The previous examples also assumed that the forward contract was for the same number of foreign currency units as required by the foreign currency transaction. It also is possible that a forward contract could be for a number of foreign currency units different from the number of units required by the transaction.

If a forward contract expires before the settlement date, the gain or loss on the hedge or contract is given the same accounting treatment as previously discussed; the gain or loss on the hedge will partially offset the gain or loss on the foreign currency transaction. If a forward contract expires after the settlement date, the gain or loss on the hedge accruing after the settlement date is recognized as a component of current operating income. Regardless of when the contract expires, the contract premium or discount should be amortized over the life of the contract.

If a forward contract is for a fewer number of foreign currency units than the foreign currency transaction, the contract gain or loss is still recognized as a partial hedge on the exposed position. However, if the forward contract is for a greater number of foreign currency units than the exposed asset or liability position, special treatment is required. The gain or loss on that portion of the contract which exceeds the exposed position is accounted for as a *speculative hedge*. Accounting for speculative hedges is discussed in a later section of this chapter.

Hedge on Identifiable Foreign Currency Commitment.   In Illustration 10-3 the company purchased inventory for 1,000 FC which was recorded at $500 when the exchange rate was 1 FC = $0.50. This inventory basis will subsequently be used to determine the cost of sales and subsequent gross profit arising from the sale of inventory. Assuming the company would sell the inventory for $800, it would experience a gross profit of $300 ($800 − $500). To change the example slightly, assume that the company entered into a contract to purchase this inventory with delivery in two months followed by a subsequent sale to a customer for $800. At the time of the purchase commitment the exchange rate is 1 FC = $0.46 and at delivery date the exchange rate remains at $0.50. If the company could have recorded the inventory at a basis of $460 (1,000 FC × $0.46) by using the spot exchange rate at the commitment date, the gross profit on the subsequent sale would have been $340 ($800 − $460) rather than the previous $300. In other words, it may be desirable for a company to establish the dollar basis of an item at the commitment date rather than the later transaction date. This would be the case if the company anticipates exchange rate changes between the commitment date and the transaction date, which would adversely affect the company.

Fortunately, there is a solution to this dilemma. A company could fix or establish the basis of an item at the commitment date by hedging, at that date, the subsequent transaction. For example, the company discussed above could hedge the commitment by acquiring a forward exchange contract. If the contract has a forward rate of 1 FC = $0.48 when the spot exchange rate is 1 FC = $0.46 at commitment date, the basis of the inventory being purchased will be established using the spot exchange rate at the commitment date. In order to fix the basis of the item using the spot rate at the commitment date, any exchange gains or losses on the forward exchange contract (hedge) that occur from the commitment date to the transaction date are deferred. At the transaction date the deferred gains or losses on the forward exchange contract are recognized as part of the basis for the item in question.

In order to qualify for this special treatment of deferring the gains or losses, the hedge on the identifiable foreign currency commitment must meet the following two conditions[4]:

1. The forward contract must be designated as and be effective as a hedge of the commitment.
2. The foreign currency commitment must be firm.

The first condition is a function of management intent in that it must couple the hedge with the foreign currency commitment. Technically, determining whether the transaction is effective as a hedge is possible only after it is known whether the hedge offsets the transaction gain or loss. However, a hedge in the same currency as the transaction would be effective. A commitment that is noncancelable or cancelable upon remote conditions or payment of significant penalties would appear to satisfy the second condition. Even if the two conditions for deferral are satisfied, certain losses on the hedge may not be deferred. If a loss on the hedge occurs between the commitment date and the transaction date, it should not be deferred if such deferral would result in recognizing losses in later periods. For example, if the deferral of a loss causes the basis of acquired inventory to increase to the point where a profit cannot be recognized on its subsequent sale, then the loss should not be deferred but, rather, be recognized currently.

Foreign currency commitments are frequently hedged through the use of forward exchange contracts. However, it is important to note that other forms of hedging that meet the two conditions for deferral are also acceptable. For example, in the case of purchasing inventory and trying to fix the basis at the commitment date, a loan could have been used to hedge the commitment. If the company had made a loan to another party and required repayment in foreign currency, this could effectively hedge the commitment and provide the necessary foreign currency to pay for the inventory. In conclusion, it is possible to hedge an identifiable foreign currency commitment in several ways. In any case, the goal is to fix or establish the basis of an item. Although the previous examples have focused on fixing the basis of inventory and the resulting cost of sales in order to preserve a desired gross profit, a company may also want to fix the basis of sales. For example, if a customer commits to buy a product for delivery in two months, the company may want to fix the basis of sales at the commitment date rather than wait until the transaction date. This would be true if the company expects to experience exchange losses due to the dollar's strengthening relative to the foreign currency.

---

[4]*Ibid.*, par. 21.

Although the two conditions previously discussed may be satisfied, the hedging transaction may exceed the amount of the related foreign currency commitment or extend beyond the time at which the transaction date of the commitment occurs. This transaction date is when the event that was committed to is recorded. In these situations, the gain or loss on the transaction should be accounted for as follows:

1. The gain or loss traceable to the portion of the hedging transaction in excess of the commitment should be deferred to the extent that the transaction provides an after-tax hedge. The gain or loss so deferred should be included as an offset to the related tax effects in the period such tax effects are recognized.
2. That portion of a gain or loss on a hedging transaction in excess of the amount that provides a hedge on an after-tax basis should not be deferred.
3. The gain or loss traceable to the time period after the transaction date of the commitment should not be deferred.[5]

It is important to note that *the deferral of gains or losses on a hedge of a foreign currency commitment never are deferred beyond the transaction date of the commitment.* Once the transaction date has occurred, there is no longer a hedge on a commitment but, rather, a hedge on an exposed position. Subsequent to this point, all gains or losses on the hedge are recognized as a component of operating income.

If a hedge on an identifiable foreign currency commitment is terminated before the transaction date of the commitment, any deferred gain or loss as of the termination date should continue to be deferred until the transaction date of the commitment.

 To illustrate a hedge on an identifiable foreign currency commitment, assume the following:

1. The conditions necessary for the deferral of exchange gains or losses prior to the transaction date have been satisfied.
2. On January 1, 19X1, a domestic firm agrees to sell goods to a foreign customer, with delivery to be made on March 1, 19X1. The goods, valued at 1,000 FC and having a cost of $400, are to be paid for 90 days after delivery.
3. On January 1, 19X1, the domestic firm purchased a 150-day forward contract to sell 1,000 FC at a forward rate of 1 FC = $0.495.
4. Spot rates on selected dates are as follows:

January 1, 19X1	1 FC = $0.50
March 1, 19X1	1 FC = 0.49
June 1, 19X1	1 FC = 0.485

In Illustration 10-4 the entries on the books of the U.S. company reflect the proper accounting for these facts.

At the commitment date, the seller wanted to fix the basis of sales because of an expected strengthening of the dollar relative to the foreign currency. This

---

[5]*Ibid.*

Illustration 10-4
Hedging on an Identifiable Foreign Currency Commitment

Relating to Sale of Goods	Relating to Purchase of Forward Contract

January 1, 19X1

Dollars Due from Broker 495*
Deferred Contract Discount. 5*
    Foreign Currency Due to Broker. 500
    Purchase of contract to sell 1,000
    FC in 150 days at the forward rate
    of 1 FC = $0.495.
    *Not affected by change in
    exchange rate.

March 1, 19X1

Accounts Receivable 490
Deferred Exchange Gain 10
    Sales 500*
    To record the sale when the spot
    rate is 1 FC = $0.49 and to
    recognize the deferred gain on the
    forward contract as an adjustment
    to sales.
    *Not affected by change in
    exchange rate.

Foreign Currency Due to Broker. 10
    Deferred Exchange Gain 10
    To record the deferred gain on the
    forward contract when the spot
    rate is 1 FC = $0.49.

Cost of Goods Sold. 400*
    Inventory. 400*
    To record the cost of goods sold.
    *Not affected by change in
    exchange rate.

Contract Expense 2*
    Deferred Contract Discount. 2
    To amortize the forward contract
    discount ($5 × 60 ÷ 150).[1]
    *Not affected by change in
    exchange rate.

June 1, 19X1

Foreign Currency. 485
Exchange Loss. 5
    Accounts Receivable 490
    To record collection of receivable
    when the spot rate is 1 FC = $0.485.

Foreign Currency Due to Broker. 490
    Exchange Gain. 5
    Foreign Currency. 485
    To record the transfer of FC to the
    broker when the spot rate is
    1 FC = $0.485.

Cash. 495
    Dollars Due from Broker 495
    To record receipt of cash at the
    established forward rate of
    1 FC = $0.495.

Contract Expense 3
    Deferred Contract Discount. 3
    To amortize the balance of the
    contract discount.

[1]As an alternative, the premium or discount amortization may be included in the determination of the dollar basis of the transaction, which would have been achieved by debiting sales rather than contract expense.

would allow the seller to achieve the anticipated gross profit of $100, which is the difference between the $400 inventory cost and the sales value of $500 (1,000 FC × spot rate of 1 FC = $0.50 at the commitment date). The hedge on the commitment was employed to preserve this anticipated gross profit on the sale. Extending the hedge past the transaction date was done to reduce the risk of exchange fluctuations' affecting the collection value of the account receivable. The effect of the hedge on the foreign currency commitment and the exposed asset position is illustrated below:

	Desired Position	Without Hedge	With Hedge
Sales price	$500	$490*	$500
Cost of goods sold	(400)	(400)	(400)
Gross profit	$100	$ 90	$100
Exchange gain (loss) on foreign currency transaction		(5)**	(5)
Exchange gain (loss) on hedge			5
Contract income (expense) [1,000 FC × ($0.495 − $0.50)]			(5)
Net income effect	$100	$ 85	$ 95

*This represents the 1,000 FC at the March 1, 19X1 exchange rate of 1 FC = $0.49.
**This represents the 1,000 FC receivable originally recorded at $490 but collected for $485 when the exchange rate was 1 FC = $0.485.

If the risk of adverse exchange rate changes during the commitment period had not been hedged, the actual gross profit on the sale would have been reduced to $90 ($490 − $400) because sales would have been recorded at the spot exchange rate on March 1 (1,000 FC × $0.49 = $490 of sales). However, the hedge was effective in maintaining the original anticipated dollar basis of the transaction and allowed for the recognition of a $100 gross profit. This was accomplished by hedging the commitment and fixing the sales at the spot exchange rate that existed on the commitment date (1,000 FC × $0.50 = $500 of sales). Furthermore, extending the hedge beyond the transaction date resulted in offsetting the subsequent exchange rate loss. Once again, the direct cost to manage these risks was the contract expense of $5, which represented the difference between the original spot rate and the forward rate.

Although the illustration ignored the tax impact of the transactions, the FASB, as previously stated, provides for hedging on an after-tax basis. A hedge on an after-tax basis recognizes that there may be a tax impact associated with the foreign currency commitment itself and a separate tax impact associated with the gain or loss on the forward contract. In the illustration, for example, there is a tax impact associated with the sale of inventory and a tax impact associated with the gain on the forward contract to hedge the foreign currency commitment. The desired objective is for the gain (loss) on such a hedge less the net related tax impact to equal the exchange loss (gain) associated with the settlement of the foreign currency commitment.

Companies engaged in material hedging transactions frequently disclose the extent of this activity in the notes to their financial statements. The hedging on foreign currency commitments and transactions is disclosed by two companies as shown in Exhibits 10-1 and 10-2.

Forward Contracts as Means of Speculation.   In addition to employing forward contracts as a means of hedging an exposed position or a foreign currency commitment, they may be employed as a means of speculating in foreign currencies. Foreign currencies are traded actively as commodities, thus providing opportunities for speculation. For example, a U.S. investor might purchase a forward contract to sell foreign currency at a given forward rate. The investor may not even possess the foreign currency, but subsequently will attempt to sell the contract at a gain. The investment in the speculative contract is initially recorded at the forward rate with no separate recognition of the contract premium or discount. A gain or loss on a contract held in speculation should be determined by:

> . . . *multiplying the foreign currency amount of the forward contract by the difference between the forward rate available for the remaining maturity of the contract and the contracted forward rate (or the forward rate last used to measure a gain or loss on that contract for an earlier period).*[6]

The initial accounting treatment for speculative contracts is similar to that used for other investments. First, upon acquisition, the investment is initially recorded at its fair market value. For a speculative contract its initial fair market value is the forward rate for the contract. Furthermore, no separate accounting is given to the premium or discount because these in substance are the broker's fee or commission. Like other investments, such fees are included in the basis of the investment. The subsequent accounting for gains or losses on the speculative contract results in the basis of the investment being adjusted to fair market value. This process is consistent with current requirements to measure investments at fair value.

Exhibit 10-1
Advanced Micro Devices, Incorporated

NOTES TO CONSOLIDATED FINANCIAL STATEMENTS

Gains and losses associated with currency rate change on forward contracts are recorded currently in income unless the contract hedges a firm commitment, in which case any gains or losses are deferred and included as a component of the related transaction. Generally, the interest element of the forward contract is recognized over the life of the contract. As of December 27, 1992, the company had approximately $27 million in net forward contracts.

Source: Advanced Micro Devices, Incorporated, 1992 financial report.

---

[6]*Ibid.*, par. 19.

Exhibit 10-2
Xerox Corporation

NOTES TO CONSOLIDATED FINANCIAL STATEMENTS
   1 (In Part): Financial Instruments
   The company enters into foreign exchange contracts and foreign currency option contracts to manage its exposure to foreign currency rates. At December 31, 1992 and 1991, the company held approximately $674 million and $1.5 billion, respectively, of such instruments maturing through early 1994, primarily in European and Japanese currencies. Realized and unrealized gains and losses on contracts that qualify as hedges of foreign subsidiaries are recognized in the same period that the foreign currency exposure is recognized. At December 31, 1992 and 1991, approximately 1.0 million and 7.4 million, respectively, of net losses had been deferred. Gains and losses on contracts that do not qualify for hedge accounting are recognized in income as foreign currency exchange rate changes.

Source: Xerox Corporation financial reports.

   In order to illustrate the accounting for a speculative contract, assume the following:

1.   On November 1, 19X2, a calendar-year investor purchased a 90-day forward contract to buy 1,000 FC at a forward rate of 1 FC = $0.505, when the spot rate was 1 FC = $0.50.
2.   On December 31, 19X2, the forward rate for a 30-day forward contract was 1 FC = $0.51.
3.   On February 1, 19X3, the investor paid the broker and received the foreign currency. The spot rate was 1 FC = $0.515.

   The following entries reflect the proper accounting for these facts:

19X2			
Nov. 1	Foreign Currency Due from Broker	505	
	Dollars Due to Broker		505
	To record the purchase of the forward contract when the forward rate is 1 FC = $0.505.		
Dec. 31	Foreign Currency Due from Broker	5	
	Exchange Gain		5
	To recognize the speculation gain based on the difference between the forward rate available for the remaining maturity and the original forward rate [1,000 FC × ($0.51 − $0.505)].		
19X3			
Feb. 1	Dollars Due to Broker	505	
	Cash		505
	To record the payment to the broker at the agreed rate of 1 FC = $0.505.		
	Foreign Currency	515	
	Foreign Currency Due from Broker		510
	Exchange Gain		5
	To record the receipt of 1,000 FC when the spot rate was 1 FC = $0.515.		

Note that the investor's exchange gain prior to maturity was measured by the difference between forward rates and that no separate recognition was given to the contract premium. The total exchange gain of $10 is based on the difference between the spot rate at the maturity of the contract and the original forward rate [1,000 FC × ($0.515 – $0.505)].

Although the illustration assumed the investor took delivery of the foreign currency, in a more typical situation an investor would not hold a forward contract to maturity but would sell the contract to another party. Assuming the same facts except that the investor sold the contract for $5 on December 31, 19X2, the following entry would have been made on December 31, in addition to the other November 1 and December 31 entries:

```
19X2
Dec. 31   Cash. . . . . . . . . . . . . . . . . . . . . . . . . . . . . . . . . . . . . . . . . .        5
          Dollars Due to Broker . . . . . . . . . . . . . . . . . . . . . . . . . . . . . . .      505
              Foreign Currency Due from Broker . . . . . . . . . . . . . . . . . .            510
```

As mentioned previously, the special treatment given forward contracts held for speculation also is required for other forward contracts to the extent they exceed:

1. That amount required to cover an exposed net asset or liability position, and/or
2. That amount needed to hedge on an after-tax basis an identifiable foreign currency commitment.

Summary.   The presence of free or floating exchange rates and the accompanying volatility in such rates have affected significantly how domestic companies do business abroad. In addition, foreign currencies are viewed as commodities to be traded actively. This chapter has discussed the accounting for foreign currency transactions and several of the risk management actions that may be taken in response to exchange rate fluctuations. The various hedging transactions discussed are summarized as follows:

	Hedge on an Exposed Position	Hedge on an Identifiable Commitment	Speculative Hedge
Basic Purpose of Forward Contract	Reduce exchange rate risk between the transaction and settlement dates.	Maintain the anticipated dollar basis of the transaction by reducing exchange rate risk between the commitment and transaction dates.	Speculate on the changing value of the currencies.
Recognition of Gain or Loss on Forward Contract	Recognize on an accrual basis as a component of net income.	Defer gain or loss experienced between the commitment and transaction dates. Adjust the dollar basis of the transaction by the deferred amount. Gains or losses subsequent to the transaction date are recognized on an accrual basis as a component of net income.	Recognize on an accrual basis as a component of net income.

continued

	Hedge on an Exposed Position	Hedge on an Identifiable Commitment	Speculative Hedge
Measurement Basis for Gain or Loss on Forward Contract	Difference between the spot rates over the life of the contract.	Difference between the spot rates on the commitment and transaction dates for the deferred amount. Difference between the spot rates on the transaction and settlement dates for the amount included as a component of net income.	Difference between the forward rates over the life of the contract.
Accounting for Contract Premium or Discount	Recognize over the life of the contract as a financing expense.	Recognize over the life of the contract as a financing expense. As an alternative, adjust the dollar basis of the transaction for the premium or discount amortization between the commitment and transaction dates.	No separate recognition but, rather, becomes part of the investment basis.

DISCLOSURE OF OFF-BALANCE-SHEET RISK

There has been an explosive increase in the number of financial instruments that are designed to protect companies against the financial risks associated with volatile markets. In 1986, the FASB added a project to its agenda that focused on innovative financial instruments and their associated off-balance-sheet (OBS) risk. Statement of Financial Accounting Standards No. 105 was issued in 1990.[7] The Statement addresses disclosure requirements for financial instruments and is part of a larger project. Standards regarding how financial instruments and transactions should be recognized and measured will be developed in the future. The disclosure requirements in FASB Statement No. 105 are relevant to foreign currency because several types of financial instruments have been developed to address the risk associated with the volatility of exchange rate changes.

The FASB defines a financial instrument as cash, evidence of an ownership interest in an entity, or a contract that both[8]:

1. Imposes on one entity a contractual obligation (a) to deliver cash or another financial instrument to a second entity, or (b) to exchange financial instruments on potentially unfavorable terms with the second entity.
2. Conveys to that second entity a contractual right (a) to receive cash or another financial instrument from the first entity, or (b) to exchange other financial instruments on potentially favorable terms with the first entity.

Given a financial instrument, the risk of accounting loss versus economic loss must be evaluated. Accounting loss represents the maximum loss that could be recorded on an instrument. For example, if an instrument has a cost basis of $40,000 and a market value of $60,000, the maximum accounting loss would be $40,000 even though the maximum decline in market or economic value could be $60,000. Accounting loss is a combination of three risks:

[7]FASB Statement No. 105, *Disclosure of Information about Financial Instruments with Off-Balance-Sheet Risk and Financial Instruments with Concentrations of Credit Risk* (Norwalk, CT: Financial Accounting Standards Board, 1990).
[8]*Ibid.*, par. 6.

1. Credit risk: the risk that a party to the contract may fail to perform according to the terms of the contract.
2. Market risk: the risk that changes in market prices may make an instrument less valuable or more onerous.
3. Physical risk: the risk that an instrument may be stolen or lost.

The first two risks are evaluated by the FASB as the basis for OBS risk.

The FASB defines OBS risk as the possible accounting loss traceable to credit risk and/or market risk that is not recognized because either: (a) the loss has not yet occurred, or (b) the financial instrument is not recognized on the financial statements as an asset or liability. Financial instruments with OBS risk include: loan commitments written; standby and commercial letters of credit written; options written; interest rate caps, floors, and swaps written; future contracts; forward contracts and foreign currency swaps. In many instances, these instruments are not given accounting recognition; therefore, financial statement disclosure becomes necessary in order to provide users of financial statements a basis for assessing risks and possible accounting losses.

The FASB extends financial disclosure for OBS risk by requiring the following information by class of financial instrument[9]:

1. The face or contract amount (or notional principal amount if there is no face or contract amount).
2. The nature and terms, including, at a minimum, a discussion of (a) the credit and market risk of those instruments, (b) the cash requirements of those instruments, and (c) the related accounting policy pursuant to the requirements of APB Opinion No. 22, *Disclosure of Accounting Policies*.

For financial instruments with OBS credit risk, the following additional disclosures must be presented[10]:

1. The amount of accounting loss the entity would incur if the party to the financial instrument failed completely to perform according to the terms of the contract and the collateral or other security, if any, for the amount due proved to be of no value to the entity.
2. The entity's policy of requiring collateral or other security to support financial instruments subject to credit risk, information about the entity's access to that collateral or other security, and the nature and a brief description of the collateral or other security supporting those financial instruments.

Furthermore, FASB Statement No. 105 requires companies to disclose all significant concentrations of credit risk arising from all financial instruments, whether from an individual counterparty or groups of counterparties. A concentration of credit risk exists when a counterparty or counterparties, due to economic or other conditions, may be hampered from performing according to the terms of the contract and associated collateral or other security proved to be of no value.

---

[9]*Ibid.*, par. 17.
[10]*Ibid.*, par. 18.

With respect to foreign currencies, OBS risk will be encountered when foreign currency swaps, forward contracts, or call options on foreign currency exist. With respect to these items, the disclosures required for OBS risk must be presented. In order to illustrate the disclosures associated with foreign currency instruments, Exhibit 10-3 presents excerpts from a financial report.

Exhibit 10-3
Disclosure of OBS Risk
The Quaker Oats Company and Subsidiaries

Note 1

Summary of Significant Accounting Policies

Futures, Swaps, Options and Forward Contracts. *The Company enters into a variety of futures, swaps, options and forward contracts in its management of foreign currency and commodity price exposures. Realized and unrealized gains and losses on foreign currency options and forward contracts are recognized currently in other income and expense. Realized and unrealized gains and losses on foreign currency options that hedge exchange rate exposure on future raw material purchases are deferred and recorded in inventory in the period in which purchases occur. Realized and unrealized gains and losses on foreign currency options, currency swaps and forward contracts that are effective as net investment hedges are recognized in a component of share-holders' equity. Realized and unrealized gains and losses on commodity futures contracts and options are deferred and recorded in inventory in the period in which purchases occur.*

Note 18

Financial Instruments

Foreign Currency Forward Contracts. *As of June 30, 1993, the Company had forward contracts for the purchase and sale of European, Canadian and other currencies, with purchases totaling $2.3 million and sales totaling $237.4 million. These contracts hedge balance sheet and operating income currency exposures. While the contracts generally mature in less than 12 months, total sales include obligations to sell $8.2 million in British pounds in fiscal 1998.*

Deutsche Mark Swap. *In fiscal 1988, the Company swapped $25.0 million for deutsche marks in two separate transactions. In August 1992, the Company repaid 18.5 million deutsche marks for $12.6 million. The Company is required to exchange 27.9 million deutsche marks for $15.0 million in August 1997 and to make semi-annual interest payments of 0.9 million deutsche marks through August 1997.*

Source: Quaker Oats Company, 1993 financial report.

QUESTIONS

1. Explain how the gold standard differs from the floating international monetary system.
2. Explain how the direct and indirect exchange rates are affected when the U.S. dollar strengthens against the Japanese yen.

3. If the dollar was expected to strengthen relative to a foreign currency, what effect might this have on a U.S. exporter and an investor who has a speculative hedge to sell foreign currency?

4. Identify some of the factors that might explain the difference between a spot rate and a forward rate.

5. A U.S. company imports foreign goods from France and Japan and all transactions are denominated in the respective foreign currencies. The dollar is expected to strengthen relative to the French currency and weaken relative to the Japanese currency. Explain how hedging might be employed in these circumstances.

6. How would interest differentials explain a situation where the spot rate is greater than the forward rate?

7. Under what conditions would a hedge on an exposed asset position result in offsetting exchange gains?

8. Why would a U.S. exporter hedge a foreign sale at the date of the commitment rather than at the transaction date?

9. Explain how an exporter's gross profit can be maintained if the dollar begins to strengthen relative to the currency used to settle the transaction.

10. A U.S. company has a forward contract to buy 1,000 foreign currency units as a hedge against a payable of 800 foreign currency units. Explain the accounting for the excess hedge.

11. A U.S. company has sold inventory to a French customer and the transaction is denominated in German marks. Explain how taking out a loan from a German bank might serve as a hedge against the sale.

12. Financial instruments may expose a company to off-balance-sheet (OBS) risk. Explain what is meant by OBS risk.

EXERCISES

Exercise 1. Booker, Inc. manufactures printing presses and acquires some of its component parts from a German fabricator. On December 15, 19X4, when 1 mark (M) = $0.60, it purchased components costing 300,000 M from a German company. The resulting account payable is due in 30 days when 1 M = $0.59. Booker has a calendar year end, and the spot rate at that time was 1 M = $0.58. *lost purchasing power.*

(1) Prepare the journal entries to record the above transactions.

(2) How might borrowing the necessary funds to pay the vendor affect net income assuming a German bank loan is employed?

Exercise 2. Given the facts of Exercise 1, assume Booker, Inc. secured a loan from a German bank on December 31, 19X4. The principal amount of the loan is 300,000 M, bears interest at 12%, and is payable in 30 days when 1 M = $0.56. Calculate the effect on net income from the original transaction described in Exercise 1 and the bank loan for the years 19X4 and 19X5.

Exercise 3. Ward Manufacturing builds large commercial ovens for curing painted parts and acquires certain control devices from foreign vendors. On June 1, 19X8, the company received, f.o.b. destination, materials from a foreign vendor. Payment of 50,000 foreign currency units (FC) is due in 90 days. At the same time the company acquired a forward contract to buy 60,000 FC in 90 days. Critical 19X8 spot rates are as follows:

June 1	1 FC = $1.10
June 30	1 FC = 1.15
July 31	1 FC = 1.09
August 31	1 FC = 1.12

Critical 19X8 forward rates are as follows:

June 1, 90-day rate	1 FC = $1.13
June 30, 60-day rate	1 FC = 1.14
July 31, 30-day rate	1 FC = 1.11

Prepare a schedule to show the monthly effect on net income of these events for the months of June, July, and August.

Exercise 4. Cortez Electronics buys subassemblies from a foreign vendor. On June 1, 19X9, the company committed to acquire subassemblies costing 400,000 foreign currency units (FC). The parts will be shipped, f.o.b. shipping point, on June 15, 19X9, with payment due on July 31, 19X9. Cortez is considering two alternative forms of hedging their exposed liability position. One alternative would involve acquiring a forward contract on June 1 to buy 400,000 FC for delivery on July 31, 19X9. The forward rate would be 1 FC = $0.62 and the spot rate on June 1 is 1 FC = $0.60. As an alternative, the company has an opportunity to lend $240,000 to another party with payment due in FC and interest at the rate of 8%. The loan would be dated June 1, 19X9, and would be due on July 31, 19X9.

Determine under what conditions the company would favor one alternative over the other.

Exercise 5. Mineco is a manufacturer of heavy equipment and is expanding its export sales. On June 15, 19X7, the company contracted to deliver equipment to a foreign customer on July 15, 19X7. The sales price of 850,000 FC was to be paid 60 days after delivery. The equipment has a cost to manufacture of $530,000. On June 15, 19X7, the company acquired a forward contract to sell 850,000 FC on September 15, 19X7. The following table details various aspects of these transactions.

Event	Date	Spot Rate	Forward Rate to 9/15/X7
Contract to sell	6/15/X7	1 FC = $0.82	1 FC = $0.83
Deliver equipment	7/15/X7	1 FC = 0.80	1 FC = 0.81
Year end	7/31/X7	1 FC = 0.78	1 FC = 0.80
Collect payment	9/15/X7	1 FC = 0.79	

Prepare the journal entries necessary to record the above transactions for Mineco.

Exercise 6. Maxwell Enterprises purchases forward exchange contracts for a variety of reasons. Determine the effect on 19X8 net income of each of the following hedging transactions.

(1) Forward Contract A was purchased on November 1, 19X8, for speculative purposes at a forward rate of 1 FC = $1.45 when the spot rate was $1.50. This 90-day contract to buy 100,000 FC has a forward rate of $1.43 on December 31, 19X8.

(2) Forward Contract B was purchased on September 1, 19X8, as a hedge against a commitment to take delivery of equipment on December 1, 19X8. The equipment will be used by Maxwell in its manufacturing division and has a cost of 100,000 FC. Maxwell must settle the transaction in foreign currency on February 1, 19X9. The 150-day forward contract to buy 80,000 FC had a forward rate of $1.47. The spot rates on September 1, 19X8, December 1, 19X8, and December 31, 19X8, were $1.49, $1.48, and $1.475, respectively.

(3) Forward Contract C was purchased on October 1, 19X8, to cover an exposed asset position when the spot and forward rates were $1.48 and $1.49, respectively. The contract to sell 30,000 FC expired on December 1, 19X8, when the spot rate was $1.48.

(4) Forward Contract D was purchased for speculation and had terms identical to Contract C. Maxwell sold the contract on November 1, 19X8, for $250 net of commissions.

Exercise 7. AVC Manufacturing purchases subassemblies from a Canadian vendor. The company anticipates purchasing a two-month supply of subassemblies from Canada with the following terms: 200,000 subassemblies, 2,000,000 Canadian dollars (CD) due in 30 days. AVC anticipates that 1 CD will equal $0.88 at the date of purchase and $0.91 in 30 days. At present, AVC has recorded a receivable from a European customer that is due at approximately the same time the Canadian vendor will have to be paid. The receivable is recorded at $2,350,000 and is to be paid in foreign currency (FC). When the receivable comes due, it is expected that the 1,000,000 FC to be received will have a value of $2,200,000.

These transactions expose AVC to a significant amount of foreign currency exchange risk. In order to hedge against this risk, management is considering a contract to sell foreign currency units for Canadian dollars. The forward contract calls for the payment of 830,000 FC in exchange for 2,000,000 CD along with a contract fee of $15,000. AVC's management wants to maximize cash flows and minimize exchange losses.

Determine whether AVC is better off to accept this forward contract or proceed without hedging.

Exercise 8. Stratco Manufacturing engages in a number of foreign currency transactions which have resulted in the following current balances:

Cash	400,000	Canadian dollars
Cash	300,000	French francs
Accounts receivable	1,200,000	French francs
Accounts receivable	850,000	Canadian dollars
Accounts payable	500,000	French francs
Accounts payable	700,000	German marks
Notes payable—line of credit	300,000	French francs

Management anticipates that the following exchange rate changes will occur in the near future:

The French franc will weaken against the dollar by 10%.
The Canadian dollar will strengthen relative to the dollar by 5%.
The German mark will strengthen against the dollar by 15%.

Develop a strategy that will minimize Stratco's foreign currency exchange loss.

Exercise 9. Financial instruments may expose a company to off-balance sheet (OBS) risk.

(1) Identify the sources of risk that may result in an accounting loss.
(2) Explain why a forward contract to sell foreign currency is a financial instrument.
(3) Given the disclosure excerpts contained in Exhibit 3, explain why Quaker Oats Company is at risk with respect to the deutsche mark swap.

PROBLEMS

Problem 10-1. People Power, Inc. (PPI) is an international temporary service that provides contract help throughout the world. Selected transactions occurring during its calendar business year 19X5 are as follows:

Transaction A: On October 1, 19X5, PPI paid a European advertising agency 200,000 foreign currency units (FC) for an advertising campaign. In anticipation of this transaction, on September 1, 19X5, PPI purchased a 30-day contract to buy 200,000 FC at a forward rate of $1.26.

Transaction B: On December 20, 19X5, a European customer contracted for a temporary work force to begin working on March 1, 19X6, for a three-week project. The contract fee is 100,000 FC and, at the commitment date, PPI purchased a 60-day forward contract to sell 120,000 FC at a forward rate of $1.285. At December 31, 19X5, a 49-day contract to sell FC had a forward rate of $1.31.

Transaction C: On December 15, 19X5, PPI purchased supplies from a European vendor. The 100,000 FC invoice is due in 30 days. At the same time, the company purchased a 30-day forward contract to buy 100,000 FC at a forward rate of $1.29.

Transaction D: PPI purchased three speculative forward contracts during 19X5. One contract was purchased on October 1, 19X5, and was a 90-day contract to buy 50,000 FC at a forward rate of $1.31. Sixty days later, the contract was sold at a forward rate of $1.32. Another contract to sell 40,000 FC in 60 days was acquired on December 1, 19X5, when the forward rate was $1.29. The contract is still held at year end. The forward rate for a 30-day contract to sell is $1.30 on December 31, 19X5.

A final contract to sell 100,000 FC in 180 days was acquired on November 1, 19X5, at a forward rate of $1.33. On December 1, 19X5, this contract was designated as a hedge on a firm foreign currency commitment when the forward rate for the remaining 150 days was $1.34.

Relevant spot exchange rates are as follows:

Date	1 FC =
September 1, 19X5	$1.25
October 1, 19X5	1.30
December 1, 19X5	1.31
December 15, 19X5	1.30
December 20, 19X5	1.29
December 31, 19X5	1.28
March 1, 19X6	1.32

Required:
(1) With respect to transaction A, calculate the effect of the transaction on net income and what the effect would have been had a forward contract not been employed.
(2) With respect to transaction B, calculate the deferred and recognized gain or loss on the forward contract as of December 31, 19X5.
(3) With respect to transaction C, calculate the net income effect of the transaction as of December 31, 19X5.
(4) With respect to transaction D, calculate the 19X5 income effect of the various speculative hedges.

Problem 10-2. Austin Engineering Corporation assembles small pocket calculators, which it sells primarily in domestic markets. However, Austin has been developing sales markets in France and has been purchasing subassemblies from a Japanese manufacturer. Selected transactions for 19X8 are as follows:
(a) On March 1, Austin purchased 6,000 calculator subassemblies from the Japanese manufacturer for a total price of $9,600, to be paid in dollars on April 20, 19X8. On March 1, the exchange rate was 1 yen (¥) = $0.37.

(b) On May 5, Austin sold 22,000 calculators to a French importer for a total selling price of 1,350,000 francs (FF). At the time of the sale, the exchange rate was 1 FF = $0.18; however, when payment was received in francs on May 26, 19X8, the exchange rate was 1 FF = $0.22.

(c) On July 2, 19X8, Austin purchased more subassemblies from the Japanese manufacturer; however, due to changing economic conditions, the entire purchase price of $36,900 was to be paid in yen on September 1. The relevant exchange rates were:

July 2	1 ¥ = $0.41
September 1	1 ¥ = $0.44

On July 2, to hedge against future currency devaluations, Austin purchased a 60-day forward contract to buy yen at a forward rate of 1 ¥ = $0.416.

(d) Another major sale for 1,000,000 FF was made to the French importer on September 8, 19X8, when the exchange rate was 1 FF = $0.23. On September 25, when the exchange rate was 1 FF = $0.22, Austin purchased a 30-day forward contract to sell 1,000,000 FF at a forward rate of 1 F = $0.19. When payment in francs was received from the importer on October 25, 19X8, the exchange rate was 1 FF = $0.18.

(e) A final 19X8 purchase of subassemblies took place on December 16 when the exchange rate was 1 ¥ = $0.40. The purchase price of 200,000 ¥ was to be paid on January 25, 19X9. At the time of the purchase, Austin acquired a 30-day forward contract to buy the yen at a forward rate of 1 ¥ = $0.404.

(f) To plan properly for a noncancelable commitment to purchase subassemblies for delivery on March 25, 19X9, Austin acquired on December 26, 19X8, a 90-day forward exchange contract to buy yen at a forward rate of 1 ¥ = $0.415. On December 26, the exchange rate was 1 ¥ = $0.41. The forward exchange contract was for 210,000 ¥, all of which will be used to cover the noncancelable commitment.

(g) The following exchange rates are in effect on December 31, 19X8:

$$1 ¥ = \$0.42$$
$$1 FF = \$0.17$$

Required:

Assuming Austin's year end is December 31, prepare the 19X8 journal entries to account for all of Austin's transactions.

Problem 10-3. Bakerite Industries manufactures industrial ovens used for curing painted parts. The ovens are manufactured in Ohio from parts purchased in the United States and Germany. Selected transactions involving foreign currency risk are described below. On November 1, 19X6, Bakerite received an order for two large ovens from a Japanese manufacturer. The ovens will be sold for 67,500,000 yen (¥). Because of concerns over the strengthening of the dollar relative to the yen, on December 1, 19X6, Bakerite purchased a 90-day forward contract to sell 67,500,000 ¥ at $0.0067. On December 15, 19X6, necessary component parts were received from a German vendor. Terms of the purchase require payment in 30 days and an amount due of 100,000 German marks (M). At December 15, 19X6, Bakerite is uncertain as to how the dollar will change in value against the mark. In keeping with this uncertainty, management has decided to purchase on December 15, 19X6, a forward contract to purchase 50,000 M in 30 days at a forward rate of $0.68. The ovens purchased by the Japanese manufacturer were shipped f.o.b. shipping point on December 31, 19X6, with terms of net 30 days. The cost to manufacture the ovens was $330,000. The Japanese customer paid their invoice on January 15, 19X7, at which time Bakerite sold the yen at the spot rate. On January 31, 19X7, the forward contract to sell yen was sold at a forward rate of $0.0068.

Bakerite has a December 31 year end, and selected rates of exchange are as follows:

Date	1 ¥ =	1 M =
November 1, 19X6	$0.00680	
December 1, 19X6	0.00685	
December 15, 19X6		$0.690
December 20, 19X6	0.00670	
December 31, 19X6	0.00674	0.685
January 15, 19X7	0.00672	0.670
January 31, 19X7	0.00675	

Required:

(1) Prepare the journal entries necessary to record all of the transactions relating to the above facts through the year end December 31, 19X6.
(2) Determine whether management's decision to hedge the invoice payable in marks was a good decision.
(3) Determine whether management's decision to hedge the receivable in yen was a good decision.

Problem 10-4. Jenner Corporation recently has begun to expand its international markets and has engaged in several foreign currency transactions. In one particular series of transactions, the company purchased components from a French manufacturer on October 1, 19X8. The components cost 800,000 French francs (FF), and Jenner anticipated that the components could be assembled at its Kentucky plant for an additional cost of $40,000. Upon receipt of the goods on October 20, 19X8, Jenner entered into an agreement with a British company to purchase the finished goods for $224,900, to be settled in British pounds (£). The goods will be shipped on November 30, 19X8, with payment to be received on January 20, 19X9.

Required:

(1) Assuming the liability to the French vendor becomes due before the payment from the British company is received, how can Jenner protect itself against fluctuations in the respective foreign currencies?
(2) Assuming the payment to the French vendor is due subsequent to the receipt of pounds from the British company, how can Jenner guard against foreign currency fluctuations relative to the dollar?
(3) Assume that on October 20, 19X8, Jenner purchases a forward contract to sell British pounds for 800,000 French francs (FF) on January 20, 19X9. Assume that the payment to the French vendor may be paid on or after January 20, 19X9. Given the following rates, calculate the contract premium or discount on the forward contract.

Spot rates as of October 20, 19X8:

$$£1 = \$1.73$$
$$£1 = 17.3\ FF$$
$$1\ FF = £0.058$$
$$1\ FF = \$0.10$$

Forward rate as of October 20, 19X8, for delivery on January 20, 19X9:

$$£1 = 16\ FF$$

(4) Assume the same spot and forward rates as given in (3) and that the following additional forward rates are available:

Forward rates as of October 20, 19X8, for delivery on January 20, 19X9:

$$£1 = \$1.72$$
$$\$1 = 9.5\ FF$$

Calculate whether Jenner is better off (a) using one forward contract of £50,000 for 800,000 FF to settle the amount due the French vendor or (b) buying two contracts: one to sell £50,000 for dollars and the other to sell dollars for 800,000 FF.

Problem 10-5. Wagner Corporation transacts business in a number of foreign currrencies. On July 1, 19X8, the company signed a 60-day, 400,000 foreign currency A (FC-A) note with a foreign bank. The note is to be repaid in FC-A and bears simple interest at the rate of 7.2%. The company used the proceeds of the note to purchase manufacturing equipment. The equipment will be depreciated by the straight-line method over a useful life of 15 years (salvage value is to be ignored).

On July 15, 19X8, the company committed to purchase inventory from a foreign vendor with a delivery date of August 15, 19X8. Payment of 250,000 foreign currency B (FC-B) is due on October 15, 19X8. In order to limit their exposure on this transaction, the company hedged the commitment by acquiring a contract to buy 250,000 FC-B for delivery on October 15, 19X8. At that time the forward rate was 1 FC-B = $1.06.

On August 1, 19X8, the company acquired a forward contract to buy 404,800 FC-A on August 31, 19X8, in order to repay the loan taken out on July 1. The contract was at the forward rate of 1 FC-A = $0.66.

On September 1, 19X8, the company shipped (f.o.b. shipping point) finished goods to a foreign vendor with payment due on October 15, 19X8. These items were the inventory that the company ordered on July 15 as discussed above. The sales price was 600,000 foreign currency C (FC-C).

Selected spot rates are as follows:

19X8	1 FC-A =	1 FC-B =	1 FC-C =
July 1	$0.62		
July 15		$1.04	
July 31	0.66	1.05	
August 1................	0.65		
August 15..............		1.08	
August 31..............	0.64	1.06	
September 1			$0.56
September 30	0.67	1.07	0.62

Required:

Prepare a schedule by month that details the effect on net income of the above transactions for the months of July, August, and September, 19X8.

Problem 10-6. Boyd Enterprises has begun to purchase certain component parts from a foreign vendor. These purchases will be denominated in foreign currency units (FC) and the company is trying to evaluate various alternative methods of paying for the purchases. The company does not expect to order from the foreign vendor more than twice a year and with the following terms:

Commitment (order date)...............	30 days before delivery
Delivery.............................	f.o.b. destination
Payment date........................	60 days after receipt
Late payments.......................	Charged interest at the rate of 1/2% per month.

Various alternative methods of payment are as follows:

Option A	Do not hedge the exposed liability position.
Option B	Hedge the commitment with a forward contract due on payment date.

Option C   Hedge the commitment with a forward contract due 30 days after payment date.

Option D   Hedge the transaction at delivery date versus commitment date.

Option E   Borrow foreign currency on the payment date with repayment of the note in 30 days. The note bears interest at 6% and is denominated in foreign currency units.

The company wants to evaluate the options under two alternative assumptions regarding spot and forward rates. The assumptions are as follows:

	Assumption 1	Assumption 2
Spot rate at commitment date	$1.200	$1.20
Spot rate at delivery date.........................	1.224	1.17
Spot rate on payment date	1.289	1.12
Spot rate 30 days after payment date	1.320	1.10
90-day forward rate at commitment date...........	1.250	1.14
120-day forward rate at commitment date..........	1.280	1.11
60-day forward rate at delivery date	1.270	1.10

Required:

Prepare a schedule that shows the effect on net income for each of the payment options given the assumptions regarding exchange rates. Assume that the average purchase is for 100,000 FC.

Problem 10-7. Trico Manufacturing, Inc. has been a client of yours for the past five years and has continued to increase its international activities. At present, the company has major vendors in Germany, Brazil, and Mexico. It distributes its products throughout Canada, the United Kingdom, and Europe. Prior to this time, the company has not engaged in hedging but realizes that the volume of foreign currency activity now may warrant the use of hedging. The following situations are typical of Trico's international involvement which requires your consulting expertise.

Situation A: Management signed a contract with a German vendor to manufacture 100,000 finished units at a per unit cost of 1,360 German marks (M). The finished goods will then be shipped directly to a French wholesaler who will pay for the goods in German marks. Each of the units will be sold for 1,700 M. Through a special agreement, the German vendor will defer payment for the goods until the time the French customer pays this invoice. However, the German vendor will charge an additional 5% for the privilege.

Situation B: Management is considering constructing a warehouse in Germany at an estimated cost of 620,000 M. Construction is expected to take 90 days at which time payment is due in full.

Situation C: Because of the volatility of the Brazilian cruzeiro, management's purchases from Brazilian vendors are settled in U.S. dollars. However, the cruzeiro provides an investor with some interesting speculative opportunities. Trico's investment policy is to invest short-term funds in U.S. treasury bills which have an average yield of 8.25%.

Required:

(1) With respect to Situation A, describe the methodology or construct a decision model that could be used to determine whether the special agreement provision should be utilized.

(2) With respect to Situation B, assume that at the beginning of construction, the spot rate is 1 M = $1.74. At completion of the warehouse, it is expected that the dollar will lose 10% versus the German mark. In order to minimize exchange risk, Trico is proposing to lend dollars to a British company payable in marks. Define the terms of the loan, including the interest rate, so that it serves as an effective hedge against the exchange risks associated with the warehouse construction.

(3) With respect to Situation C, assume that as an alternative to investing $200,000 in treasury bills for 30 days, management purchases a 90-day forward contract for 55 million cruzeiros (Cr). The current spot rate is 1 CR = $0.0040 and the 90-day forward rates are $0.0042 to sell currency and $0.00412 to buy currency. Calculate what the forward rates would have to be for both selling and buying in 30 days (a 60-day forward contract price) so that the speculative hedge would double the treasury bill return in dollars.

CHAPTER 11

Translation of Foreign Financial Statements

The magnitude of U.S. investment abroad has increased significantly in response to a more global economy, reduction in trade barriers, and the growth of international capital markets. Similarly, these same factors have encouraged an increase in foreign investment in the U.S. The size and growth of these investment patterns are suggested by the following statistics:

U.S. Investment Position Abroad

	1988	1989	1990	1991	1992
In millions of dollars	499,500	535,870	424,096	460,955	486,670

U.S. Business Acquired or Established by Foreign Direct Investors

	1988	1989	1990	1991	1992 (Preliminary)
Number of investments	1,424	1,580	1,617	1,091	690
Investment outlays in millions of dollars.	72,692	71,163	65,932	25,538	13,469

Source: Department of Commerce.

The previous chapter identified a variety of transactions that may occur between a domestic (U.S.) company and a foreign entity. These transactions were not dependent on the domestic company's having any type of ownership interest in the foreign entity. However, as the above statistics suggest, many domestic companies do have an ownership interest in or control of foreign companies, and accounting for these interests presents special problems. The accounting treatments of domestic and foreign entity relationships that involve some degree of control are summarized as follows:

Domestic Entity	Foreign Entity	Accounting Treatment
Home Office	Branch	Branch accounting
Parent	Subsidiary	Consolidated financial statements or separate financial statements
Investor	Investee	Investment in foreign entity at cost or equity

The above relationships suggest the need to combine or consolidate the foreign entity's financial statements with those of the domestic entity. The financial statements of a foreign entity typically are measured in the currency of that foreign country. This currency usually is different from the reporting currency of the domestic entity. Therefore, a methodology must be developed to express the foreign entity's financial statements in the reporting currency of the domestic entity. The process of expressing amounts denominated or measured in foreign currencies into amounts measured in the reporting currency (dollars) of the domestic entity (U.S.) is referred to as *foreign currency translation*.

In addition to establishing a methodology for translation, the process is complicated by the reality that the foreign financial statements may have been prepared using accounting principles that are different from those of the domestic reporting entity. As discussed in Chapter 9, there are a number of differences between generally accepted accounting principles (GAAP) employed in the United States and principles employed in financial statements of certain foreign entities. Therefore, prior to translation, the statements of a foreign entity must be adjusted to reflect the principles (GAAP) employed by the domestic reporting entity. For example, a foreign subsidiary may not be required to capitalize leases although the lease would be capitalized if GAAP followed by the parent company were employed. Before proceeding with translation, the accounting for these leases must be adjusted to conform with the principles employed by the reporting activity. The international efforts to harmonize accounting principles are slowly eliminating the need for such adjustments.

PREVIOUS TRANSLATION METHODOLOGIES

Although it is necessary to translate foreign financial statements, the development of a rational and acceptable method has been difficult. Several issues have dominated the development of an acceptable methodology. The objectives of translation have changed over time as the profession has struggled with the need to generate translated financial statements that reflect economic reality. In addition, a decision must be made as to which exchange rates, current or historical, should be used to translate accounts into the reporting currency. If different accounts are translated using differing exchange rates, the basic balance sheet equation will not balance. In order to balance, a translation adjustment is necessary. Translation methodologies have had to deal with the question of how to account for and interpret this translation adjustment.

EARLY STANDARDS ESTABLISHED BY THE FASB

Since the Financial Accounting Standards Board (FASB) began in 1973, three standards have been established. The first two are covered briefly here as background for the Statement of Financial Accounting Standards No. 52, which is in force currently.

Statement of Financial Accounting Standards No. 1.   Prior to 1973, domestic firms could employ any number of translation methods. This situation prompted the FASB in 1973 to issue Statement of Financial Accounting Standards No. 1, *Disclosure of Foreign Currency Translation Information*. The Statement did not express a preference for any particular translation method, but it did require disclosure of certain information regarding translation policies and the accounting for translation adjustments.

Statement of Financial Accounting Standards No. 8.   As a result of expanding activities of U.S. firms in foreign markets, changes in the international monetary system, and the existence of alternative translation methods, the FASB began in 1973 an extensive study of foreign currency translation. This effort produced Statement of Financial Accounting Standards No. 8, *Accounting for the Translation of Foreign Currency Transactions and Foreign Currency Financial Statements*, which superseded sections of previous pronouncements dealing with foreign operations and translation (ARB No. 43, APB Opinion No. 6, and FASB Statement No. 1). The Statement emphasized that the translation process should change the unit of measure from foreign currency to dollars without changing the accounting principles. Therefore, the foreign entity's measurement bases and principles of revenue/expense recognition that conform to generally accepted accounting principles should not be affected by the translation process. The Statement evaluated alternative translation methods and recognized the temporal method as being most compatible with its objectives.

Under the *temporal method*, translation is a function of whether a balance sheet account measures current values or historical costs. Accounts measured by the foreign entity at current values will be translated using the current spot rate at the date of the financial statement. The objective is to measure the amount of domestic currency (dollars) that could be exchanged for the foreign currencies represented by an account's current value. For example, if accounts receivable have a current value of 10,000 foreign currencies (FC), the translated value should reflect the equivalent number of dollars that would be received in exchange for the receivables.

Balance sheet accounts that are measured by the foreign entity at historical cost are to be translated at the spot rates that existed at the date of the original transaction. Therefore, if a foreign entity acquired equipment by paying 100,000 FC on July 1, 19X7, the equipment would be translated into dollars using the spot rate that existed on July 1, 19X7. Equity account balances also represent historical costs and are to be translated at the historical spot rates that existed at the date of the equity transaction.

Income statement accounts that do not represent the amortization of historical costs should be translated at the spot rate that existed at the date of the revenue or expense transaction. The use of such specific spot rates produces a practical dilemma which is resolved through the use of weighted average exchange rates for the period covered by the income statement. Some revenues and expenses result from the amortization of assets or liabilities measured at historical costs. Such revenues and expenses should be translated at the historical spot rates used to translate the underlying historical costs being amortized. Thus, if the 19X8 depreciation expense relates to the equipment acquired on July 1, 19X7, depreciation expense in foreign currency should be translated using the historical spot rate that existed on July 1, 19X7.

The translation of trial balance accounts (assets, liabilities, equities, revenues, and expenses) at different spot rates (current, historical, and weighted average) results in an inequality which represents the translation exchange gain or loss. Under the temporal method, this gain or loss is included as a component of net income.

The use of various spot rates to translate a foreign entity's trial balance under the temporal method is summarized as follows:

Trial Balance Account	Spot Rate Used for the Temporal Method
Assets and liabilities:	
Measured at current values	Current rates
Measured at historical cost	Historical rates
Equity accounts:	
Other than retained earnings	Historical rates
Retained earnings	Translated beginning balance plus translated net income less dividends translated at historical rates
Revenues and expenses:	
Representing amortization of historical amounts	Historical rates
Not representing amortization of historical amounts	Weighted average rates
Translation gain or loss	A balancing amount included as a component of current net income

STATEMENT OF FINANCIAL ACCOUNTING STANDARDS NO. 52

Following its promulgation in 1975, FASB Statement No. 8 became the subject of considerable controversy. When the Statement was applied, multinational corporations reported significant fluctuations in profits as a result of foreign currency exchange rate variations and the presentation of translation losses as a component of reported income. FASB Statement No. 8 was criticized for its failure to reflect the underlying economic realities of foreign operations and rate changes and for its reporting requirements that resulted in data being volatile due to rate changes rather than operating factors. Suppose a U.S. company has a British subsidiary whose only asset is an investment in securities of various British companies. The securities are valued at current values and have been acquired only through the use of equity capital. Assuming that the dollar weakens relative to the pound, translation into dollars under the temporal method would have resulted in the recognition of a translation loss. However, because the securities ultimately will be liquidated into pounds, the exchange rate between the pound and dollar has no bearing on the profitability of the British company.

In late 1981, after considering two exposure drafts in response to these criticisms, the FASB issued Statement of Financial Accounting Standards No. 52, *Foreign Currency Translation*. FASB Statement No. 52 adopted a *functional currency* approach which focuses on whether the domestic reporting entity's cash flows will be indirectly or directly affected by changes in the exchange rates of the foreign entity's currency. Assume a foreign entity operates exclusively in its own country using only its currency. It is questionable whether changes in the exchange rate between its currency and that of the parent entity would directly affect the parent's cash flows. After all, how could changes in the rate of exchange between the German mark and the dollar affect you if your transactions were primarily denominated in marks? However, if a foreign entity operates in a currency other than its own currency, exchange rate changes between these currencies presumably will affect directly cash flows of the parent. In this instance, the resulting effect should be the same as if transactions were denominated in a foreign currency.

FUNCTIONAL CURRENCY IDENTIFICATION

In order to achieve the objectives of the translation process, it is critical to identify the foreign entity's functional currency. The functional currency is the currency of the primary economic environment in which the entity generates and expends cash. For example, assume a French company that is a subsidiary of a U.S. company purchases labor and materials from French sources and pays for these items with French francs. The finished product of the company is sold to French customers and payment is received in francs. In this situation, changes in the exchange rate between the French franc and the dollar of the U.S. parent do not generally have an economic impact on the French company or its U.S. parent. Because of this, the French company's day-to-day operations are not dependent on the economic environment of the U.S. parent's currency (dollars). Therefore, the French franc would be considered the functional currency of the French company.

The identification of the functional currency is not always easily arrived at. Assume the French company discussed above received most of its debt capital in the form of dollars from an American bank and that its products were sold primarily in the U.S. with payment being received in dollars. In this case, changes in the exchange rate between the franc and the dollar would affect the parent company's cash flows. The French company's day-to-day operations are dependent on the economic environment of the U.S. parent's currency (dollars). Changes in the foreign entity's assets and liabilities will, or have the potential to, impact immediately on the cash flows of the U.S. parent. It is important to note that a foreign entity may have a functional currency which is not its domestic currency or that of the parent entity. Thus, the French company could have the German mark as its functional currency, rather than the franc or the dollar, if the mark is the currency that primarily influences the company's cash flows. This might be the case if the French company's financing, sales, and purchases of goods and services are denominated in marks.

Identification of the functional currency is not subject to definitive criteria. However, certain basic economic factors should be considered in making this identification.[1] Some of these factors are summarized as follows:

Factors Suggesting the Functional Currency

Indicator	Foreign Subsidiary's Currency as Functional Currency	Parent's Currency as Functional Currency
Cash flows	Cash flows are primarily in the foreign currency. Such flows do not impact the parent's cash flows.	Cash flows directly impact the parent's cash flows and are readily available to the parent.
Sales price	Sales prices are influenced by local factors rather than exchange rates.	Sales prices are influenced by international factors and exchange rate changes.
Sales market	There is an active and primarily local market.	The sales market is primarily in the parent's country.
Expenses	Goods and services are acquired locally and denominated in local currencies.	Goods and services are acquired from the parent's country.
Financing	Financing is secured locally and denominated in local currencies. Debt is serviced through local operations.	Financing is secured primarily from the parent or is denominated in the parent's currency.
Intercompany transactions and arrangements	Intercompany transaction volume is low. Major interrelationships between foreign and parent operations do not exist.	Intercompany transaction volume is high. There are major interrelationships between entities. Foreign entity holds major assets and obligations of the parent.

Although these factors focus on the parent's currency as a possible functional currency, it is important to remember that the functional currency may be one other than that of the foreign entity or the parent.

These factors should be considered both individually and collectively in order to identify the functional currency. The selection of a functional currency should be applied consistently over time, unless significant changes suggest that the functional currency has changed. Changes should not be accounted for on a retroactive basis or as a cumulative effect.

OBJECTIVES OF THE TRANSLATION PROCESS

The focus of FASB Statement No. 52 is critical to achieving the objectives of translation. The compatibility resulting from translating various financial statements into a common reporting currency is a practical necessity. However, this process should not alter the significance of the results and relationships experienced by the individual entities comprising the unified whole. Consistent with this underlying concern, the translation process should accomplish the following objectives:

   a. *Provide information that is generally compatible with the expected economic effects of a rate change on an enterprise's cash flows and equity.*

---

[1]Statement of Financial Accounting Standards No. 52, *Foreign Currency Translation* (Stamford: Financial Accounting Standards Board, 1981), par. 42.

  b. *Reflect in consolidated statements the financial results and relationships of the individual consolidated entities as measured in their functional currencies in conformity with U.S. generally accepted accounting principles.*[2]

The first objective recognizes that exchange rate changes may or may not have any substantial or direct effect on the cash flows and economic well-being of the constituent entities. The effect of exchange rate changes is dependent on the parent company's proper identification of the functional currency. If changes in exchange rates are not expected to have an immediate or potentially immediate effect on the cash flows, the current period income should not be affected. However, if exchange rate changes are expected to immediately, or have the potential to immediately, affect the parent company's cash flows, the effect of such changes should be included in current income.

The expected economic effects of rate changes must be reflected properly in financial statements and may be analyzed as follows:

Expected Economic Effect of Rate Changes	Accounting Response to Effect of Rate Changes
Cash inflows increase and/or cash outflows decrease.	Translation gains should be included in net income.
Cash inflows decrease and/or cash outflows increase.	Translation losses should be included in net income.
Cash inflows and/or outflows are not affected.	No translation gain or loss should be included in net income. The effect of rate changes will not be realized until the parent's investment in the foreign entity is disposed of or liquidated. Therefore, the effect of translation does not affect current income and is shown as a separate component of equity.

Expected Economic Effects of Rate Changes When the Functional Currency Is Not the Foreign Currency.   The first objective of translation seeks to provide accounting information that is consistent or compatible with the expected economic effects of rate changes. This objective is satisfied by focusing on the functional currency and may be demonstrated by consideration of the following example. Assume that a foreign subsidiary is formed on January 1, 19X9, when the rate of exchange is 1 foreign currency (FC) = $1.50. At the date of formation, the subsidiary:

1. Received a $30,000 equity investment in dollars from the parent company's sale of stock.
2. Received a $120,000 loan in dollars from a U.S. bank.
3. Purchased a parcel of land for $150,000 payable in dollars.

---

[2]*Ibid.*, par. 4.

At the end of 19X9 when the rate of exchange is 1 FC = $2.00, the parcel of land is sold for $200,000.

When evaluating the factors used to identify the functional currency, it would appear that the dollar is the functional currency because: financing is denominated in dollars, acquisitions of goods and services are paid for in dollars, and sales are receivable in dollars. Furthermore, the substance of these transactions suggests that the foreign subsidiary is merely a conduit through which the U.S. parent conducts business and experiences dollar cash flows. Therefore, if the translation process is sound, it should provide information that is compatible with the expected economic effects of rate changes. In this particular example, the translated dollar amounts for the subsidiary should be identical to the dollar balances that would have resulted had the U.S. parent engaged in these transactions without the foreign subsidiary serving as a conduit.

If the U.S. parent had engaged in these transactions without the foreign subsidiary as a conduit, the following analysis would have been appropriate:

Parent's entries to record the transactions—measured in U.S. dollars:

1/1/X9	Cash	150,000	
	Owners' Equity		30,000
	Loans Payable		120,000
	To record receipt of $30,000 from stock sale and $120,000 from loan proceeds.		
	Land	150,000	
	Cash		150,000
	To record purchase of land.		
12/31/X9	Cash	200,000	
	Land		150,000
	Gain on Sale		50,000
	To record sale of land.		

Resulting financial statements at year end—measured in U.S. dollars:

Balance Sheet

Cash......................................	200,000
Loan Payable..............................	120,000
Owners' Equity:	
Original Amount	30,000
Net Income................................	50,000
	200,000

Income Statement

Gain on Sale	50,000

If the U.S. parent engaged in the transactions through a foreign subsidiary, the following analysis would be appropriate:

Foreign subsidiary's entries to record the transactions—measured in FC:

```
1/1/X9      Cash ...................................   100,000
               Owners' Equity ..........................            20,000
               Loans Payable ...........................            80,000
               To record receipt of $30,000 equity
               investment and $120,000 loan, both of which
               are measured in U.S. dollars.

            Land ...................................   100,000
               Cash ...................................           100,000
               To record purchase of land for $150,000.

12/31/X9    Loan Payable ............................   20,000
            Exchange Gain on Loan ...................            20,000
               To adjust $120,000 loan payable, which is
               denominated in dollars, to an equivalent
               amount of FC due to change in rate from 1 FC
               = $1.50 to 1 FC = $2.00.

            Cash ...................................   100,000
               Land ...................................           100,000
               To record sale of land for $200,000.
```

Resulting financial statements at year end—measured in FC and translated into U.S. dollars (using the temporal method):

Balance Sheet

	FC	Relevant Exchange Rate	$
Cash....................................	100,000	2.00	200,000
Loan Payable...............................	60,000	2.00	120,000
Owners' Equity:			
Original Amount	20,000	1.50	30,000
Net Income	20,000	see below	50,000
	100,000		200,000

Income Statement

	FC	Relevant Exchange Rate	$
Exchange Gain on Loan	20,000	2.00	40,000
Translated Adjustment		**to balance**	**10,000**
	20,000		50,000

When comparing the above resulting financial statements to those presented earlier, assuming the transactions occurred without the foreign subsidiary, it is important to note that the statements are identical. The first objective of the translation process has been satisfied and the results confirm that:

1. The foreign subsidiary merely acted as a conduit through which the U.S. parent operated.

2. The transactions of the foreign entity had an immediate or potentially immediate impact on the dollar cash flows and, therefore, the impact was included in net income.
3. If the dollar is the functional currency, the foreign subsidiary's translated financial statements are identical to those statements that would have resulted had the transactions been originally recorded in the dollar functional currency.

Expected Economic Effects of Rate Changes When the Functional Currency Is the Foreign Currency. If the foreign currency (FC) is the functional currency, rate changes are not expected to have an immediate impact on the parent's cash flows. Therefore, in response to rate changes, the accounting information should not include any translation adjustment in the determination of current net income. Instead, translation adjustments should be classified as a separate component of owners' equity. This component of owners' equity would be recognized as a component of net income when realized through the liquidation or disposition of the foreign entity. In order to demonstrate these concepts, consider the following example.

Assume a foreign subsidiary is formed on January 1, 19X9, when the rate of exchange is 1 FC = $1.50. At the date of formation the subsidiary:

1. Received 20,000 FC from the U.S. parent.
2. Received an 80,000 FC loan from a local bank.
3. Purchased a parcel of land from a local party for 100,000 FC.

At the end of 19X9 when the rate of exchange is 1 FC = $2.00, the parcel of land is sold to a local party for 100,000 FC.

When evaluating the factors used to identify a functional currency, it would appear that the FC is the functional currency because: financing is denominated in FC, acquisitions of goods and services are paid for in FC, and sales prices are based on local economics and are collected in FC. Furthermore, the substance of these transactions suggests that the foreign subsidiary operates independently of the U.S. parent, and its day-to-day operations are not dependent on the economic environment of the U.S. parent's currency but on that of the foreign country. An analysis of the foreign entity's activities is as follows:

Foreign subsidiary's entries to record the transactions—measured in FC:

1/1/X9	Cash	100,000	
	Owners' Equity		20,000
	Loans Payable		80,000
	To record receipt of 20,000 FC from equity investment and 80,000 FC from loan proceeds.		
	Land	100,000	
	Cash		100,000
	To record purchase of land for 100,000 FC.		
12/31/X9	Cash	100,000	
	Land		100,000
	To record sale of land for 100,000 FC.		

Resulting financial statements at year end—measured in FC and translated into
U.S. dollars (using the functional method):

Balance Sheet

	FC	Relevant Exchange Rate	$
Cash	100,000	2.00	200,000
Loan Payable	80,000	2.00	160,000
Owners' Equity:			
Original Amount	20,000	1.50	30,000
Net Income	N/A		N/A
Translation Adjustment		**to balance**	**10,000**
	100,000		200,000

In comparing the results of the above example to that of the prior example,
where the foreign entity was merely a conduit and the functional currency was
the dollar, several important differences surface. Notice that the exchange rate
change required an adjustment to the loan payable when the dollar was the
functional currency but did not require this adjustment when the foreign currency was the functional currency. When the FC is the functional currency,
changes in the exchange rate did not produce a gain with respect to the loan
because the loan is denominated in FC and rate changes have no impact on the
settlement value of the loan. There is no indication that the exchange rate
changes will impact immediately the parent's cash flows. Therefore, to include
the translation adjustment as a component of income would not be compatible
with the economic effects of the rate change. It is quite likely that the foreign
entity will redeploy available cash by buying more goods and services and/or by
repaying the loan. In either case, cash flows are not being remitted to the parent.
Because the impact on the parent's cash flows is unclear, the translation adjustment is included as a separate component of owners' equity.

The potential impact on cash flows will become apparent if the parent
liquidates or disposes of its investment in the foreign subsidiary. At that time, the
separate component of equity may be transferred to the income statement and be
recognized as a separate component of income. To illustrate, assume that in the
above example the foreign subsidiary is liquidated after having sold the land.
Keeping in mind that the FC is the functional currency, 80,000 FC of cash would
be used to repay the loan (ignoring interest for purposes of discussion), and this
would leave 20,000 FC of cash. In the final liquidation transaction, the 20,000 FC
of cash is remitted to the parent in exchange for its equity investment. The 20,000
FC received by the parent has a value of $40,000 (assuming the exchange rate
remains at 1 FC = $2.00). When compared to the historical basis of the parent's
$30,000, equity in the subsidiary represents a $10,000 realized gain which may
now be recognized in income.

In reviewing the subsidiary's balance sheet presented above, it becomes
apparent that another objective of the translation process has been satisfied. The
FASB stated that the translation process should produce (consolidated) financial

statements that reflect the financial results and relationships of the individual entities as measured in their functional currency. This objective can be achieved when the foreign entity's currency is the functional currency and when the same exchange rates are employed to translate accounts. In our example where the FC was the functional currency, the current exchange rate was used to translate all assets and liabilities. Therefore, this preserved the relationship between these accounts which existed prior to translation. Prior to translation, the FC statements reflected that 80% of assets were financed by debt capital, the debt to equity ratio was 4:1, and the current ratio was 1.25:1 (assuming that the loan is a current liability). After the FC statements have been translated into dollars, the above results and relationships are retained. The current ratio is still 1.25:1, and debt capital is still four times greater than equity capital.

The above illustrations emphasize the importance of properly identifying the functional currency. The expected economic effects of rate changes vary and the foreign subsidiary's financial statements differ significantly depending upon the identification of the functional currency. The translation process set forth by the FASB does achieve its objectives when the functional currency is properly identified.

Adoption of a translation method that fails to reflect properly the economic effects of rate changes may produce misleading results. FASB Statement No. 8 was subject to the major criticism that it resulted in the recognition of major translation losses that distorted earnings and had no effect on cash flows. The functional currency approach does not remeasure foreign operations as though they originally had been conducted in the domestic reporting currency. Rather, this approach retains the financial results and relationships that were influenced by the economic environment in which the foreign entity operates.

BASIC TRANSLATION PROCESS: FUNCTIONAL CURRENCY TO REPORTING CURRENCY

Before beginning the translation process, the financial statements of the foreign entity must be adjusted to conform with generally accepted accounting principles. This is an important step in light of the differences in accounting principles that currently exist among nations. The next step in the translation process is to identify the functional currency. The discussion that follows assumes that the foreign entity's currency is the functional currency.

Once a foreign entity's functional currency has been identified, it must be translated into the domestic entity's reporting currency (dollars for U.S. companies) using an appropriate exchange rate. In studying the problems associated with foreign currency translation, the FASB concluded that the results and relationships presented in functional currency financial statements would be retained if the translation is based exclusively on the current rate of exchange between the functional currency and the reporting currency. Generally, this *current rate* method is governed by the following procedures:

1. All assets and liabilities are translated at the current exchange rate at the date of translation.

2. Elements of income are translated at the current exchange rates that existed at the time that the revenues and expense were recognized. As a practical consideration, income elements normally are translated at a weighted average exchange rate for the period.

3. Equity accounts other than retained earnings are translated at historical exchange rates. If the domestic parent's investment in a foreign company has been acquired as a purchase (versus pooling of interests), the historical rate on the date of acquisition is used to translate equity accounts. If a pooling of interests has occurred, the original historical rate in effect when the foreign company experienced the equity transaction is used for translation purposes.

4. Translated retained earnings generally is equal to:
   a. The translated retained earnings at the end of the prior period, plus
   b. The translated income (see item 2), less
   c. The value of dividends translated at the appropriate historical exchange rates at the date of declaration.

   If the domestic company has acquired an interest in a foreign company during the current period, the retained earnings balance at the date of acquisition should be translated using the rate at that time. Only after the year of acquisition will retained earnings be translated as the sum of items (a) through (c).

5. Components of the statement of cash flows are translated at the exchange rates in effect at the time of the cash flows. Operations are translated at the rate used for income elements. The reconciliation of the change in cash and cash equivalents during the period should include the effect of exchange rate changes on cash balances.

In all translations that follow, it will be assumed that purchase accounting, rather than pooling of interests accounting, is appropriate unless otherwise stated.

DEMONSTRATING THE TRANSLATION PROCESS

The basic translation process just discussed is applicable to the preparation of consolidated financial statements, home and branch combined statements, and investments accounted for under the equity method.

With respect to consolidated financial statements, one of the primary criteria to determine if consolidation is appropriate deals with the extent of control the parent entity exercises over the subsidiary. For foreign subsidiaries, effective control is determined, in part, by currency restrictions and the possibility of nationalization of the operations by foreign governments. Assuming consolidation is appropriate, the financial statements of the foreign entity must be translated into dollars according to the principles expressed in FASB Statement No. 52. Then intercompany eliminations are made, and the statements are consolidated according to the principles of consolidation discussed earlier in this text.

Illustration 11-1
Fori Corporation
Trial Balance Translation
December 31, 19X1

Account	Balance in Functional Currency	Relevant Exchange Rate ($/FC)	Balance in Dollars
Cash	10,000 FC	1.05	$ 10,500
Accounts Receivable	20,000	1.05	21,000
Due from Dome	15,000	1.05	15,750
Inventory (at cost)	30,000	1.05	31,500
Prepaid Insurance	3,000	1.05	3,150
Land (acquired March 1, 19X1)	25,000	1.05	26,250
Depreciable Assets	120,000	1.05	126,000
Cost of Goods Sold	180,000	1.03	185,400
Depreciation Expense	13,000	1.03	13,390
Income Tax Expense	30,000	1.03	30,900
Other Expenses (including interest)	20,000	1.03	20,600
Total debits	466,000 FC		$484,440
Accounts Payable	20,000 FC	1.05	$ 21,000
Taxes Payable	30,000	1.05	31,500
Accrued Interest Payable	1,000	1.05	1,050
Mortgage Payable—Land	20,000	1.05	21,000
Common Stock	80,000	1.00	80,000
Retained Earnings	20,000	Note A	20,000
Sales—Dome	80,000	1.03	82,400
Sales—Other	200,000	1.03	206,000
Gain on Sale of Depreciable Assets	2,000	1.03	2,060
Allowance for Doubtful Accounts	1,000	1.05	1,050
Accumulated Depreciation	12,000	1.05	12,600
Cumulative Translation Adjustment (to balance)			5,780
Total credits	466,000 FC		$484,440

Note A—The beginning balance of retained earnings normally is equal to the translated value of the previous period's ending retained earnings. However, since 19X1 is the first year Dome has owned Fori, the beginning balance is set equal to the January 1, 19X1 (acquisition date) balance of retained earnings in foreign currency translated at the January 1, 19X1 spot rate. The balance sheet for 19X1 would show a translated value for retained earnings equal to the translated beginning balance of retained earnings plus the translated value of net income less dividends translated at the rate existing on the declaration date.

Illustration 11-1 demonstrates the translation of a subsidiary's financial statements for the purpose of preparing consolidated financial statements and is based on the following facts:

1. Fori Corporation began operations on January 1, 19X0. On January 1, 19X1, when net assets totaled 100,000 foreign currency units (FC), 90% of Fori stock

was acquired by Dome Corporation. Fori's functional currency is the foreign currency, and it maintains its records in the functional currency.

2. Sales to Dome are billed in the foreign currency, and all receivables from Dome have been collected, except for the amount shown in the account Due from Dome. All other sales are billed in the foreign currency as well. The level of sales and purchases was constant over the year.

3. Selected exchange rates between the functional currency and the dollar are as follows:

Date	Rate
January 1, 19X0	1 FC = $0.98
January 1, 19X1	1 FC = 1.00
March 1, 19X1	1 FC = 1.015
December 31, 19X1	1 FC = 1.05
19X1 average	1 FC = 1.03

ACCOUNTING FOR TRANSLATION ADJUSTMENTS

Translation adjustments result from the process of translating foreign financial statements *from their functional currency into the domestic entity's reporting currency*. Because various exchange rates (current, historical, and weighted average) are used in the translation process, the basic equality of the balance sheet equation is not preserved. Therefore, from a mechanical viewpoint, the translation adjustment is an amount necessary to balance a translated entity's trial balance. Translation adjustments do not exist in terms of the functional currency and have no immediate effect on the cash flows of the foreign or domestic entity. At the time of the translation, the effect that exchange rate fluctuations may have on the reporting (parent) entity is uncertain and remote. Therefore, it would be improper to include the translation adjustment in current reported earnings. However, the translation adjustment must be reported somewhere. Rather than being included as a component of reported earnings, the translation should be included as a component of equity.

Although translation adjustments have no immediate effect on reported earnings, they may ultimately affect income when there is a *partial or complete sale or complete or substantially complete liquidation of the investment in the foreign entity*.[3] Unfortunately, the FASB has not defined what constitutes a substantially complete liquidation. Given such a sale or liquidation, some or all of the accumulated translation adjustment included in equity would be removed and included as part of the gain or loss on disposition of the investment. For example, assume a company owns 100% of a foreign entity and their investment account has a balance of $4,200,000 and their owners' equity includes a debit of $320,000 representing the accumulated translation adjustment. If the entire investment in

---

[3]See FASB Interpretation No. 37, *Accounting for Translation Adjustments upon Sale of Part of an Investment in a Foreign Entity* (Norwalk, CT: Financial Accounting Standards Board, 1983) and Statement of Financial Accounting Standards No. 52, *op. cit.*, pars. 110 and 119.

the subsidiary is sold for $4,750,000, the translation adjustment does affect the gain on sale as follows:

Proceeds from sale of investment	$4,750,000
Basis of investment account	(4,200,000)
	550,000
Balance in accumulated translation adjustment	(320,000)
Gain on sale of investment	$ 230,000

It is important to note that if only a portion of the investment in the subsidiary were sold, then only a pro rata portion of the translation adjustment would have been allocated to the sale.

Although the translation adjustment is a balancing amount necessary to satisfy the balance sheet equation, the current period's adjustment may be calculated directly as follows:

1. The change in exchange rates during the period multiplied by the amount of net assets (i.e., owners' equity) held by the domestic investor at the beginning of the period, plus
2. The difference between the weighted average exchange rate used in translating income elements and the end-of-period exchange rate multiplied by the increase or decrease in net assets for the period, excluding capital transactions, plus (minus)
3. The increase (decrease) in net assets as a result of capital transactions, including investments by the domestic investor during the period (e.g., stock issuances and retirements and dividends), multiplied by the difference between the end-of-period exchange rate and the exchange rate at the time of the transaction.

Based on the information given in Illustration 11-1, the direct calculation of the translation adjustment is as follows:

Recomputation of Annual Translation Adjustment

Net assets owned by the investor at beginning of period multiplied by the change in exchange rates during the period [0* × ($1.05 – $1.00)]	$ 0
Increase in net assets (excluding capital transactions) multiplied by the difference between the current rate and the average rate used to translate income [39,000 FC × ($1.05 – $1.03)]	780
Increase in net assets due to capital transactions (including investments by the domestic investor) multiplied by the difference between the current rate and the rate at the time of the capital transaction [100,000 FC × ($1.05 – $1.00)]	5,000
Translation adjustment	$5,780

*Although Fori Corporation began operations in 19X0, the parent company, Dome Corporation, had not acquired an interest until 19X1. Therefore, Dome had no investment in Fori as of the beginning of 19X1.

Note that the recomputation measures only the $5,780 translation adjustment traceable to 19X1. After the first year of operation, the annual translation adjustments will be accumulated and presented as a component of equity. For example, if Fori Corporation has a translation adjustment of $4,400 traceable to 19X2, the equity section of the balance sheet at the end of 19X2 will show a cumulative adjustment of $10,180 ($5,780 + $4,400).

The translation demonstrated in Illustration 11-1 has accomplished the objectives of translation as presented in FASB Statement No. 52. The economic effect of the exchange rate change (i.e., translation adjustment) has been presented as an increase in stockholders' equity. The spot rate had increased from a beginning-of-the-year rate of 1 FC = $1.00 to an end-of-period rate of 1 FC = $1.05. This change indicates that the foreign currency strengthened relative to the dollar. Therefore, the domestic company's investment in the net assets of the foreign subsidiary has increased in accounting value as evidenced by the increase in stockholders' equity. In addition, the translated financial statements reflect the same financial results and relationships of the foreign company as originally measured in its functional currency. For instance, the following ratios indicate that the original relationships have been preserved after translation.

Ratio	Before Translation	After Translation
Current	1.53 (78,000 ÷ 51,000)	1.53 (81,900 ÷ 53,550)
Debt-to-equity	0.51 (71,000 ÷ 139,000)	0.51 (74,550 ÷ 145,950)
Gross profit %	36% (100,000 ÷ 280,000)	36% (103,000 ÷ 288,400)

GAINS AND LOSSES EXCLUDED FROM INCOME

The separate component of equity in which cumulative translation adjustments are reported also should include gains and losses attributable to:

1. Foreign currency transactions that are designated and effective as economic hedges of a net investment in a foreign entity, commencing as of the designation date.
2. Intercompany foreign currency transactions that are of a long-term investment nature (i.e., settlement is not planned or anticipated in the foreseeable future) when the entities to the transaction are consolidated, combined, or accounted for by the equity method in the reporting enterprise's financial statements.[4]

In order to illustrate a foreign currency translation that is a hedge on a net investment in a foreign entity, assume a U.S. company has a wholly owned French company in which the French franc is the functional currency. If the franc weakens relative to the dollar, a translation adjustment with a debit balance will be included as a separate reduction of equity due to the effect of the rate change on the net investment. The U.S. parent can hedge against this decline in owners' equity by securing a loan payable in francs and identifying the transaction as a hedge on the net investment in the French subsidiary. As the franc weakens, the basis of the franc-denominated liability will decrease (it will take fewer dollars to settle the debt), and an exchange gain will occur. Because the foreign currency transaction (securing a loan payable in francs) has been designated and is

---

[4]Statement of Financial Accounting Standards No. 52, *op. cit.,* par. 20.

effective as a hedge of the net investment, the exchange gain or loss should be recognized as an offset to the translation adjustment associated with the net investment. In substance, the effect of the exchange rate changes on the net investment and the related hedge (foreign currency transaction) is viewed as one combined effect rather than two separate and distinct effects. If, after-tax effects, the gain (loss) on the hedge is greater than the corresponding translation loss (gain), the excess transaction gain (loss) must be included in the determination of the period's net income.

The second example of an exchange gain or loss that may be excluded from income and be included as a component of equity relates to certain long-term investment transactions between a domestic company and its foreign subsidiary. For example, assume a U.S. parent borrows funds from a French subsidiary with the loan being denominated in francs. If the settlement of the loan is not planned or anticipated in the foreseeable future, the effect of rate changes on the loan also would not have a foreseeable effect on the income of the U.S. parent. Therefore, the effect of rate changes on long-term investment transactions should be reflected in owners' equity, not current net income.

CONSOLIDATING THE FOREIGN SUBSIDIARY

Once a foreign entity's financial statements have been translated into the reporting currency, certain eliminations and adjustments due to intercompany transactions generally will be required. With regard to the exchange rate that should be used to translate such transactions, the FASB concluded that all intercompany balances, except for intercompany profits and losses, should be translated at the rates used for all other accounts. Intercompany profits and losses should be translated using the exchange rate that existed at the date of the sale or transfer. As a practical matter, however, average rates or approximations may be used to translate such profits and losses.

In order to demonstrate the consolidation process, the facts of Illustration 11-1 will be discussed further. Assume Dome Corporation paid 105,000 FC for its 90% interest in Fori Corporation, and recall that at the time of acquisition (January 1, 19X1) Fori equity consisted of 80,000 FC of common stock and 20,000 FC of retained earnings. Upon acquisition of Fori, Dome recorded its investment as follows:

Investment in Fori.	105,000	
Cash (105,000 × $1.00).		105,000

The acquisition cost of 105,000 FC exceeds by 15,000 FC the 90,000 FC [90% × (80,000 FC + 20,000 FC)] book value of the net assets acquired. This excess of cost over book value is assumed to be traceable to undervalued equipment which is depreciated by the straight-line method and has a 10-year useful life. The initial difference between cost and book values should be calculated in the foreign currency and then translated into dollars using the rate of exchange at the date of acquisition.

Because the foreign subsidiary is to be consolidated, the cost or simple equity method would be used by the parent. Assuming the simple equity method is used, the parent would record its interest in the current-period income and declared dividends of the foreign subsidiary. However, Dome would not recognize the current-period amortization of the excess of cost over book value component of its investment. The 19X1 income for Fori and Dome's equity share is calculated as follows:

Account	Balance in Functional Currency	Relevant Exchange Rate ($/FC)	Balance in Dollars
Sales—Dome	80,000	1.03	$ 82,400
Sales—Other.........................	200,000	1.03	206,000
Gain on Sale of Depreciable Assets	2,000	1.03	2,060
Cost of Goods Sold........................	(180,000)	1.03	(185,400)
Depreciation Expense.......................	(13,000)	1.03	(13,390)
Income Tax Expense........................	(30,000)	1.03	(30,900)
Other Expenses (including interest)	(20,000)	1.03	(20,600)
Net Income	39,000		$ 40,170
Dome's share...........................			90%
Dome's interest in Fori net income (in dollars)			$ 36,153

The parent's entry to record its interest in the foreign subsidiary's undistributed income would be as follows:

Investment in Fori..	36,153	
Subsidiary Income......................................		36,153

Worksheet 11-1, pages 652–654, shows the consolidated financial statements of the Dome and Fori corporations. The trial balance amounts for Dome are assumed and Fori's balances are based on Illustration 11-1. Steps (1) and (2) of the worksheet follow the usual procedures of eliminating the current-period entry recording the parent's share of the subsidiary net income and its share of the subsidiary equity accounts as of the beginning of the period. Steps (5) and (6) follow the usual worksheet eliminations and adjustments for intercompany transactions. Step (3) allocates 90% of Fori's cumulative adjustment to the controlling interest.

Step (4) recognizes that the excess of cost over book value of 15,000 FC must be translated at the exchange rate existing at year end. However, the amortization of this excess must be translated at the average exchange rate for the period. These rates result in the following translated amounts for the worksheet entry:

Depreciable assets (15,000 FC × $1.05).....................................	$15,750
Accumulated depreciation (15,000 FC ÷ 10 × $1.05)........................	1,575
Depreciation expense (15,000 FC ÷ 10 × $1.03)	1,545

The cumulative adjustment included in step (3) results from changes in exchange rates which have occurred:

1. Since the excess at the beginning of the period was translated ($750 credit adjustment),

2. Since the accumulated amortization at the beginning of the period was translated ($75 debit adjustment), and
3. Since the current period's amortization of the excess was translated ($45 credit adjustment).

Because the excess of cost over book value is not recorded by the foreign subsidiary (assuming push-down accounting is not applied), the effect of such rate changes on this excess has not been included previously in the cumulative translation adjustment. The $720 additional cumulative adjustment traceable to the excess of cost over book value is determined as follows:

	Exchange Rate Used		
	Beginning or Average	End of Period	Difference
1. Excess at beginning of period...............	$15,000	$15,750	$750
2. Less accumulated amortization at beginning of period.....................			
3. Less current amortization expense...........	(1,545)	(1,575)	(30)
Net balance...............................	$13,455	$14,175	$720

The consolidation procedures just discussed also are applicable to periods subsequent to the first year of acquisition. Although the methodology is the same, the following should be noted:

1. The parent must continue to recognize its interest in the amortization of any original excess of cost over book value.
2. Any additional cumulative adjustment traceable to the excess of cost over book value should continue to be recognized.

TRANSLATION FOR THE COST OR EQUITY METHOD: UNCONSOLIDATED INVESTMENTS

Unconsolidated foreign investments are accounted for by either the cost method or the sophisticated equity method. Under the cost method, a complete translation of the foreign financial statements is not necessary. The parent company must record the cost basis of its investment in dollars. If the cost is incurred in foreign currency, the exchange rate at the date of acquisition should be used. Investment income is translated at the exchange rate at the date dividends are declared. If factors existing in the foreign environment suggest a permanent impairment in the value of the investment, the basis of the investment should be reduced appropriately.

If the parent's interest in the foreign subsidiary is between 20% and 50%, the subsidiary will not be consolidated and the sophisticated equity method should be employed. This method requires the adjustment of subsidiary income or loss for the amortization of differences between book and market values of the investment and any intercompany profits or losses. Application of this method to an investment in a foreign entity will be demonstrated using the facts of Illustration 11-1.

WORKSHEET 11-1

Consolidating the Foreign Subsidiary
Dome Corporation and Subsidiary Fori Corporation
Worksheet for Consolidated Financial Statements (in dollars)
For Year Ended December 31, 19X1

	(Credit balance amounts are in parentheses.)	Trial Balance	
		Dome Corp.	Fori Corp.
1	Cash	56,800	10,500
2	Accounts Receivable	112,000	21,000
3	Allowance for Doubtful Accounts	(5,600)	(1,050)
4	Due from Dome		15,750
5	Inventory, Dec. 31, 19X1	154,700	31,500
6	Prepaid Insurance	9,050	3,150
7	Investment in Fori Corporation	141,153	
8			
9			
10	Land	125,000	26,250
11	Depreciable Assets	500,000	126,000
12	Accumulated Depreciation	(100,000)	(12,600)
13	Accounts Payable	(112,000)	(21,000)
14	Taxes Payable	(150,000)	(31,500)
15	Accrued Interest Payable	(16,000)	(1,050)
16	Mortgage Payable—Land	(105,000)	(21,000)
17	Common Stock	(350,000)	(80,000)
18	Paid-In Capital in Excess of Par	(100,000)	
19	Retained Earnings, Jan. 1, 19X1	(116,000)	(20,000)
20	**Cumulative Translation Adjustment—Fori**		(5,780)
21	**Cumulative Translation Adjustment—Dome**		
22			
23	Sales—Dome		(82,400)
24	Sales—Other	(908,600)	(206,000)
25	Gain on Sale of Depreciable Assets	(8,600)	(2,060)
26	Cost of Goods Sold	703,850	185,400
27	Depreciation Expense	45,600	13,390
28	Income Tax Expense	108,000	30,900
29	Other Expenses (including interest)	51,800	20,600
30	Subsidiary Income	(36,153)	
31		0	0
32	Combined Net Income		
33	To Minority Interest		
34	Balance to Controlling Interest		
35	Total Minority Interest		
36	Retained Earnings, Controlling Interest, Dec. 31, 19X1		
37			

Eliminations & Adjustments				Consolidated Income Statement	Minority Interest	Controlling Retained Earnings	Consolidated Balance Sheet	
Dr.		Cr.						
							67,300	1
							133,000	2
							(6,650)	3
		(5)	15,750					4
							186,200	5
							12,200	6
		(1)	36,153					7
		(2)	90,000					8
		(4)	**15,000**					9
							151,250	10
(4)	**15,750**						641,750	11
		(4)	**1,575**				(114,175)	12
(5)	15,750						(117,250)	13
							(181,500)	14
							(17,050)	15
							(126,000)	16
(2)	72,000				(8,000)		(350,000)	17
							(100,000)	18
(2)	18,000				(2,000)	(116,000)		19
(3)	**5,202**				(578)			20
		(3)	5,202				(5,922)	21
		(4)	720					22
(6)	82,400							23
				(1,114,600)				24
				(10,660)				25
		(6)	82,400	806,850				26
(4)	**1,545**			60,535				27
				138,900				28
				72,400				29
(1)	36,153							30
	246,800		246,800					31
				(46,575)				32
				4,017	(4,017)			33
				42,558		(42,558)		34
					(14,595)		(14,595)	35
						(158,558)	(158,558)	36
							0	37

Eliminations and Adjustments:
(1) Eliminate the entries in the subsidiary income account against the investment in Fori account to record the parent's 90% controlling interest in the subsidiary.
(2) Eliminate 90% of the subsidiary's January 1, 19X1 equity balances against the balance of the investment account.
(3) Distribute the cumulative translation adjustment between controlling and minority interest.
(4) Distribute the excess of cost over book value of 15,000 FC and record appropriate amortization.
(5) Eliminate the intercompany trade balances.
(6) Eliminate the intercompany sales assuming that none of the goods purchased from Fori remain in Dome's ending inventory.

Subsidiary Fori Corp. Income Distribution

	Internally generated net income........	$40,170
	Adjusted income	$40,170
	Minority share	10%
	Minority interest.....................	$ 4,017

Parent Dome Corp. Income Distribution

Equipment depreciation...............	$1,545	Internally generated net income........	$ 7,950
		Share of subsidiary income	
		(90% × $40,170)	36,153
		Controlling interest	$42,558

Assume Dome Corporation paid 35,000 FC ($35,000) for a 30% interest in Fori Corporation on January 1, 19X1, when Fori's equity was 100,000 FC. Any excess of cost is considered traceable to undervalued equipment which is depreciated by the straight-line method and has a 10-year remaining useful life. Dome's interest in the adjusted net income of Fori is calculated as follows:

Fori net income translated into dollars....................................	$40,170
Dome's share...	30%
Dome's interest in Fori net income	$12,051
Amortization of excess related to the equipment	
[(35,000 FC – (30% × 100,000 FC) ÷ 10 years × $1.03 average rate]	(515)
Dome's equity share of Fori net income adjusted for amortization of excess.....	$11,536

The investor also must recognize its interest in the cumulative translation adjustment for 19X1, calculated as follows:

Cumulative translation adjustment (from Illustration 11-1)	$5,780
Dome's share	30%
Dome's interest in the cumulative translation adjustment	$1,734

The following entries are to record Dome's interest in the foreign entity under the sophisticated equity method:

```
19X1
Jan. 1    Investment in Fori Corporation . . . . . . . . . . . . . . . . . . . .   35,000
              Cash. . . . . . . . . . . . . . . . . . . . . . . . . . . . . . . . . . . . . . . .            35,000
                  To record the initial investment of 35,000 FC when
                  the spot rate was 1 FC = $1.00.

Dec. 31   Investment in Fori Corporation . . . . . . . . . . . . . . . . . . . .   13,270
              Subsidiary Income . . . . . . . . . . . . . . . . . . . . . . . . . . .            11,536
              Cumulative Translation Adjustment. . . . . . . . . . . . . . .             1,734
                  To record share of net income adjusted for the
                  amortization of excess and share of cumulative
                  translation adjustment.
```

Notice that under the sophisticated equity method the investor recorded both the amortization of the excess of cost over book value and its share of the current year's translation adjustment.

REMEASURED FINANCIAL STATEMENTS

The previous illustrations of the translation process assumed that the currency of the foreign entity was the functional currency. However, there are certain instances when the functional currency is not the currency of the foreign entity. In these instances the financial statements of the foreign entity must be remeasured into the functional currency before the financial statements can be translated. The remeasurement process is intended to produce financial statements that are the same as if the entity's transactions had been originally recorded in the functional currency. Generally speaking, the remeasurement process is based on the same temporal method originally adopted by FASB Statement No. 8. In essence, the historical exchange rates between the functional currency and the foreign currency are used to remeasure certain accounts. The adjustment resulting from the remeasurement process is referred to as a remeasurement gain or loss and is included as a component of net income. The remeasurement process is encountered in two situations. One situation arises when the entity's financial statements are prepared in a currency that is not the functional currency. Another situation arises when the foreign entity is in a highly inflationary economy.

Books of Record Not Maintained in Functional Currency.   It is possible that a foreign entity may maintain its records in a currency that is not its functional currency. For instance, assume a French subsidiary of an American company purchases materials from British vendors with amounts due payable in British pounds. The materials are assembled in France and then returned to England for resale. Sales revenues are collected in pounds. Considering the factors used to identify the functional currency, the pound would be the French company's functional currency. However, the French company maintains its books of record (accounting records) in French francs although its functional currency is the British pound. In this example the financial statements prepared in francs would have to be remeasured into pounds before they could be translated into dollars.

Now assume a French subsidiary of an American company purchased its materials in the U.S., payable in dollars, and then sold the finished goods in the

U.S., collectible in dollars. The French company's functional currency would be the dollar although it maintained its books of record in francs. In this example, the financial statements prepared in francs would have to be remeasured into dollars. Since the remeasurement process results in dollar financial statements, there is no further need for any translation.

The remeasurement process requires that both current and historical exchange rates be used. These exchange rates represent the relationship between the books of record currency and the functional currency. Examples of accounts that should be remeasured at historical rates include the following:

Marketable securities carried at cost:
   Equity securities
   Debt securities not intended to be held until maturity
Inventories carried at cost
Prepaid expenses such as insurance, advertising, and rent
Property, plant, and equipment
Accumulated depreciation on property, plant, and equipment
Patents, trademarks, licenses, and formulas
Goodwill
Other intangible assets
Deferred charges and credits, except deferred income taxes and policy acqui-
   sition costs for life insurance companies
Deferred income
Common stock
Preferred stock carried at issuance price
Examples of revenues and expenses related to nonmonetary items:
   Cost of goods sold
   Depreciation of property, plant, and equipment
   Amortization of intangible items such as goodwill, patents, licenses, etc.
   Amortization of deferred charges or credits except deferred income taxes
      and policy acquisition costs for life insurance companies[5]

A special remeasurement rule is necessary for inventory (and other assets, such as marketable securities) when the rule of cost or market, whichever is lower, is applied. Before the rule is applied, the inventory cost and market amounts must be expressed in the functional currency. A possible result is for an inventory write-down to occur in the functional currency, even if no write-down is suggested in the books of record currency. It also is possible for a write-down in the books of record currency to be no longer appropriate in the functional currency.

The remeasurement into a functional currency is demonstrated in Illustration 11-2, pages 658–659, which is based on the following facts:

1. Clancy Corporation began operations on January 1, 19X1, as a wholly owned foreign subsidiary of Drake Inc., a U.S. company.
2. Inventory in the books of record currency (BR) is carried at market, even though its historical cost is 16,000 BR. Inventory was acquired uniformly

----

[5]*Ibid.*, par. 48.

throughout the year. The weighted average cost method is used to determine the cost of sales.

3. Depreciable assets were acquired (sold) on the following dates:

Date	Cost
January 1, 19X1	100,000 BR
May 1, 19X1	30,000 BR
July, 1, 19X1	(10,000) BR

The asset sold was acquired on January 1, 19X1. The selling price of this asset was 11,000 BR.

4. Depreciation is based on the straight-line method and a 10-year useful life.
5. Relevant direct exchange rates are as follows:

Date	FC/BR	$/FC
January 1, 19X1	1 BR = 2.0 FC	1 FC = $1.40
May 1, 19X1	1 BR = 2.1 FC	1 FC = 1.30
July 1, 19X1	1 BR = 2.4 FC	1 FC = 1.10
December 31, 19X1	1 BR = 2.8 FC	1 FC = 1.00
19X1 average	1 BR = 2.5 FC	1 FC = 1.25

Highly Inflationary Economies.   When an entity's financial statements are expressed in the functional currency, the statements are translated directly into the parent's reporting currency. However, this procedure is not followed for a foreign entity with a functional currency of a country that has a highly inflationary economy. The FASB defines such an economy as one that has a cumulative inflation rate of approximately 100% or more over a 3-year period. Other factors, such as the trend of inflation, also may suggest a highly inflationary economy.[6] Currently, a number of third world nations have economies that meet the definition of highly inflationary.

If a foreign entity's currency has lost its utility as a measure of a store of value and lacks stability, it probably would not serve as a useful functional currency. To ignore this situation in subsequent translations might produce misleading results. The translation of noncurrent assets of a foreign company in a highly inflationary economy at current rates of exchange produces curious results. The translated amounts may not represent reasonable dollar-equivalent measures of such assets' historical costs. Suppose a foreign company acquires a fixed asset for a cost of 100,000 FC when the exchange rate is 1 FC = $1.00. Since that time, the foreign country has experienced a cumulative rate of inflation of 270%, and the current rate of exchange is 1 FC = $0.40. If the fixed asset was translated using the current-rate method, the translated value of the asset would be $40,000 versus its original translated cost of $100,000. One proposed solution to this curious result would be to adjust the foreign financial statements for inflation rates since acquisition and then apply the current-rate method. The

---

[6]*Ibid.,* par. 11.

Illustration 11-2
Clancy Corporation
Trial Balance Translation
December 31, 19X1

Account	Balance in BR	Relevant Exchange Rate (FC/BR)	Balance in FC	Relevant Exchange Rate ($/FC)	Balance in Dollars
Cash..................	10,000 BR	2.80	28,000 FC	1.00	$ 28,000
Accounts Receivable....	28,000	2.80	78,400	1.00	78,400
Inventory (at market)* ..	15,000	Note A	40,000	1.00	40,000
Prepaid Expenses	5,000	2.50	12,500	1.00	12,500
Depreciable Assets	120,000	Sch. A	239,000	1.00	239,000
Cost of Goods Sold.....	145,000	2.50	362,500	1.25	453,125
Depreciation Expense...	11,500	Sch. A	23,200	1.25	29,000
Other Expenses	27,000	2.50	67,500	1.25	84,375
Income Tax Expense....	16,500	2.50	41,250	1.25	51,562
Remeasurement Loss...			62,650	1.25	78,313
Total debits..........	378,000 BR		955,000 FC		$1,094,275
Accounts Payable	7,500 BR	2.80	21,000 FC	1.00	$ 21,000
Accrued Expenses......	12,000	2.80	33,600	1.00	33,600
Notes Payable	84,000	2.80	235,200	1.00	235,200
Common Stock	40,000	2.00	80,000	1.40	112,000
Cumulative Translation					
Adjustment.........	0		0		(32,075)
Retained Earnings......	0	Note B	0		0
Sales	220,000	2.50	550,000	1.25	687,500
Gain on Sale of					
Depreciable Asset	1,500	Note C	7,400	1.25	9,250
Allowance for Doubtful					
Accounts............	2,000	2.80	5,600	1.00	5,600
Accumulated					
Depreciation.........	11,000	Sch. A	22,200	1.00	22,200
Total credits	378,000 BR		955,000 FC		$1,094,275

*In more complex instances, the remeasurement of ending inventory and cost of sales will depend on the inventory valuation method used. LIFO ending inventory will consist of the (1) beginning inventory multiplied by the applicable exchange rate(s) plus (2) unsold current purchases multiplied by the applicable exchange rate(s).

inflation-adjusted value of the fixed asset would be 270,000 FC (100,000 FC × 270%), and its translated value at current rates would be $108,000 (270,000 FC × $0.40). This translated amount is more meaningful than the $40,000 value previously determined. The FASB decided against adjusting foreign amounts for inflationary effects and instead decided that the domestic currency (dollars) should serve as the foreign entity's functional currency. Thus, the foreign entity's statements should be remeasured into the functional currency (U.S. dollars). Applying this to the fixed asset example would require the use of the original

Note A—The historical cost and market value of the ending inventory must be remeasured into the functional currency before the rule of cost or market, whichever is lower, may be applied.

Historical cost (16,000 × 2.50) 40,000
Market value (15,000 × 2.80) 42,000

Because the historical cost in functional currency is less than the market value in functional currency, historical cost will be the carrying basis.

Note B—The remeasured value of zero for retained earnings represents the beginning-of-the-period value. The balance sheet for 19X1 would show a remeasured value for retained earnings equal to the remeasured value of undistributed net income. This value also would represent the remeasured value for beginning retained earnings in the 19X2 trial balance.

Note C— The remeasured value of the gain must be inferred, based on the following entry to record the sale of the asset:

Cash (11,000 × 2.40) 26,400
Accumulated Depreciation (500 × 2.00) 1,000
Depreciable Assets (10,000 × 2.00)   20,000
Gain on Sale of Depreciable Asset   7,400

Schedule A
Remeasurement of Depreciable Assets, Depreciation Expense, and Accumulated Depreciation

	Balance in BR	Exchange Rate FC/BR	Balance in FC
Depreciable assets:			
January 1, 19X1 acquisition	100,000 BR	2.00	200,000 FC
May 1, 19X1 acquisition	30,000	2.10	63,000
July 1, 19X1 disposition	(10,000)	2.40	(24,000)
	120,000 BR		239,000 FC
Depreciation expense:			
January 1, 19X1 acquisition	9,000 BR	2.00	18,000 FC
	500	2.00	1,000
May 1, 19X1 acquisition	2,000	2.10	4,200
	11,500 BR		23,200 FC
Accumulated depreciation:			
Annual expense	11,500 BR	see above	23,200 FC
Asset disposed	(500)	2.00	(1,000)
	11,000 BR		22,200 FC

historical rate of exchange and results in a remeasured value of $100,000 (100,000 FC × $1.00). This value is more meaningful than the $40,000 value previously determined, and it does not commingle historical and inflation-adjusted values into the same set of financial statements. It is important to note that (1) this will result in the remeasurement of the statements into dollars, making any further translation unnecessary, and (2) the remeasurement gain or loss should be included in the income for the period.

Special Consolidation Procedures for Remeasured Financial Statements. The example of consolidation procedures in Worksheet 11-1 is based on foreign financial statements which have been translated using the current-rate method. In those instances where a foreign entity's financial statements are remeasured rather than initially translated, it is important to recognize the following special features:

1. The remeasurement gain or loss is recognized as a component of net income rather than a component of stockholders' equity.
2. Remeasurement gains or losses from prior years would be included in the remeasured amount of retained earnings at the beginning of the current year.
3. When remeasuring balances that are traceable to transactions occurring prior to the parent's date of acquisition, the historical exchange rate existing at the date of the acquisition should be used. This assumes that the acquisition is accounted for as a purchase.
4. If the investor is using the equity method of accounting for its investment in the investee, income from the investment should include the investor's share of the remeasurement gain or loss. Therefore, the investment account must be adjusted to reflect the investor's interest in the remeasurement gain or loss. For example, if an investor has a 60% interest in an investee and there is a current remeasurement gain of $50,000, the following entry would be made under the equity method:

Investment in Investee.................................	30,000	
Investment Income.................................		30,000

SUMMARY OF TRANSLATION AND REMEASUREMENT METHODOLOGIES

This chapter has discussed the translation and/or remeasurement of foreign financial statements into the reporting currency (dollars) of the domestic parent/investor entity. Translation of foreign financial statements is employed when a foreign entity's financial statements are measured in their functional currency and then expressed in the reporting currency of the domestic parent/investor entity. The remeasurement of foreign financial statements is appropriate when:

1. A foreign entity's books of record are not maintained in the functional currency, and/or
2. A foreign entity's functional currency is that of a highly inflationary economy.

It is important to note that a domestic parent/investor entity may have a number of subsidiary/investee entities that require translation and/or remeasurement. For example, a U.S. parent may have:

1. A subsidiary whose financial statements are measured in their functional currency and then are *translated* into dollars, and
2. Another subsidiary whose financial statements are measured in a currency other than the *foreign* functional currency, in which case the statements must be *remeasured* into the foreign functional currency and then translated into dollars, and

3.   Another subsidiary whose financial statements are measured in a currency other than the *dollar* functional currency, in which case the statements must be *remeasured* into dollars, and
4.   Another subsidiary whose financial statements are measured in a functional currency of a country that has a *highly inflationary economy*, in which case the statements must be remeasured into dollars.

The accounting policies footnote (Exhibit 11-1) to the financial statements of Tecumseh Products Company illustrates how both translation and remeasurement are applied to the foreign subsidiaries of the company.

The situations requiring the use of a particular translation and/or remeasurement methodology are summarized in a flowchart presented in the Student Companion Enrichment Manual.

TAX ALLOCATION AND DISCLOSURE REQUIREMENTS

Interperiod tax allocation is appropriate when temporary differences exist due to differences in the timing or recognition of items for financial statement purposes and for tax purposes. To the extent that remeasurement gains or losses and/or translation adjustments are recognized in different periods for financial

---

Exhibit 11-1
Tecumseh Products Company (DEC)
Notes to Consolidated Financial Statements

Note 2:
   Foreign Currency Translation

The assets and liabilities of the Company's Canadian and European subsidiaries are translated into U.S. dollars at current exchange rates, and revenues and expenses are translated at average monthly exchange rates. The resulting translation adjustments are recorded in a separate component of stockholders' equity:

(Dollars in millions)	1993	1992
Balance at January 1	$11.0	$23.8
Effect of balance sheet translations:		
Amount	(12.0)	(15.1)
Tax effect	2.8	2.3
Balance at December 31	$ 1.8	$11.0

For the Company's Brazilian subsidiary, which operates in a highly inflationary economy, inventory and plant and equipment and related income statement items are translated at historical exchange rates while other assets and liabilities are translated at current exchange rates. The resulting translation adjustment is included in other expense and was $2.0 million, $2.1 million, and $6.6 million in 1993, 1992, and 1991, respectively.

Source: Tecumseh Products Company 1993 annual report.

and tax purposes, tax allocation is required. In addition, the principles of intra-period tax allocation require that the income taxes related to items recorded as components of equity should also be allocated to equity. Therefore, this would be applicable to translation adjustments and certain gains or losses excluded from income that are recorded as components of equity.

FASB Statement No. 52 requires that foreign currency transaction and hedging gains or losses included in the determination of net income be disclosed in the financial statements or the accompanying notes. An analysis of the separate component of equity affected by certain foreign currency transactions and hedges and translation adjustments should be presented. The analysis may be in a separate statement, in a note to the financial statements, or as part of the statement of changes in equity. At a minimum, the analysis should disclose:

1. Beginning and ending amount of cumulative translation adjustments.
2. The aggregate adjustment for the period resulting from translation adjustments and gains and losses from certain hedges and intercompany balances.
3. The amount of income taxes for the period allocated to translation adjustments.
4. The amounts transferred from cumulative translation adjustments and included in determining net income for the period as a result of the sale or complete or substantially complete liquidation of an investment in a foreign entity.[7]

Although the various effects of rate changes subsequent to the end of the period normally are not disclosed, their effects on unsettled balances arising from foreign currency transactions should be disclosed if significant.

QUESTIONS

1. A foreign corporation maintains its books and records in the British pound. What types of cash outflows might suggest that the pound is not the corporation's functional currency?
2. Specify the basic objectives in translating foreign currency financial statements.
3. Define the term "functional currency" and describe several instances in which a foreign entity's currency may not be the functional currency.
4. Discuss how manufacturing equipment and the related depreciation expense measured in a foreign company's functional currency would be translated under the temporal method assuming:
   (a) purchase accounting was used.
   (b) pooling of interests accounting was used.
5. In some instances a foreign entity's financial statements must be remeasured prior to translation or in lieu of translation. Identify those instances in which remeasurement is necessary.
6. A U.S. company acquired an 80% interest in a French company whose functional currency is the French franc. The transaction was accounted for as a purchase and the price paid exceeded the underlying book value due to appreciated equipment.

---

[7]*Op. cit.*, par. 31.

Explain why the recognition and amortization of this excess results in a translation adjustment.

7. Discuss why the current-rate method may not be applied to a foreign entity whose functional currency is that of a country whose economy is highly inflationary.

8. Prior to disposition or liquidation of a foreign investee, cumulative translation adjustments are reflected as a separate component of owners' equity. Identify those foreign currency transactions that are given similar treatment.

9. What rates should be used to translate and eliminate the balances resulting from a sale of inventory to a foreign subsidiary by a domestic parent?

10. Under what circumstances might the cumulative translation adjustment be removed from stockholders' equity?

EXERCISES

Exercise 1. Items (1) through (8) are based on the following information:

Johnson Incorporated, a U.S. company, has a wholly owned foreign subsidiary with the following December 31, 19X3 trial balance in foreign currency:

	Debit	Credit
Current Assets	1,000,000	
Building and Equipment	5,800,000	
Land	1,500,000	
Cost of Sales	4,000,000	
Selling, General, and Administrative Expenses	375,000	
Current Liabilities		500,000
Mortgage Payable		3,000,000
Common Stock		800,000
Paid-In Capital in Excess of Par		1,000,000
Retained Earnings		1,800,000
Sales Revenue		5,500,000
Accumulated Depreciation		75,000
	12,675,000	12,675,000

When Johnson acquired the subsidiary 1 FC was equal to $0.58. Other exchange rates are as follows:

Date	Rate
June 1, 19X2	1 FC = $0.62
January 1, 19X3	1 FC = 0.60
February 1, 19X3	1 FC = 0.61
Weighted average, 19X3	1 FC = 0.70
December 31, 19X3	1 FC = 0.75

(1) Assuming the foreign currency is the functional currency, the December 31, 19X3 translated value of current liabilities is:

(a) $350,000   (c) $300,000

(b) $500,000   (d) $375,000

(2) Land costing 900,000 FC was acquired on June 1, 19X2, and 600,000 FC was acquired on February 1, 19X3. Assuming the functional currency is the dollar, the December 31, 19X3 translated value of land is:

    (a) $1,500,000   (c) $924,000

    (b) $1,125,000   (d) $870,000

(3) Assuming the foreign currency is the functional currency, the December 31, 19X3 translated value of sales revenue is:

    (a) $4,125,000   (c) $5,500,000

    (b) $3,300,000   (d) $3,850,000

(4) Assuming no additional common stock has been issued since acquisition of the subsidiary, the translated value of common stock:

    (a) Is the same regardless of whether the dollar or the foreign currency is the functional currency.

    (b) Is always translated at the beginning of the year exchange rate.

    (c) Is translated at the current exchange rate.

    (d) Is translated at the rate of exchange when the stock was originally issued rather than at the time the shares were acquired by the parent.

(5) If the foreign currency was not the functional currency, accumulated depreciation would be remeasured into the functional currency through the use of the:

    (a) Current exchange rate.

    (b) Exchange rate at the date the subsidiary was acquired.

    (c) Exchange rates existing when the depreciable assets were acquired.

    (d) Weighted exchange rate.

(6) Assume the foreign currency is not the functional currency and the mortgage was secured on February 1, 19X3, when 1 FC equaled 2 functional currency units. One functional currency unit equaled $1.45 on February 1, 19X3, and $1.50 on December 31, 19X3. The translated value of the mortgage payable on December 31, 19X3, is:

    (a) $6,000,000   (c) $9,000,000

    (b) $1,830,000   (d) $4,500,000

(7) If the foreign currency were that of a highly inflationary economy:

    (a) The dollar would be considered the functional currency.

    (b) Land would be remeasured at the current exchange rate.

    (c) The mortgage payable would be remeasured at the historical exchange rate.

    (d) Net income would not be affected by the remeasurement process.

(8) If retained earnings reflected the declaration of a 200,000 FC dividend on February 1, 19X3, which was paid on June 1, 19X3, the translated value of the dividend would be:

    (a) $122,000   (c) $150,000

    (b) $140,000   (d) $120,000

Exercise 2. Hughes Consulting formed a French company to market its climate control devices in Western Europe. Hughes contributed $200,000 of cash and $320,000 of inventory upon formation of the company. The French company paid in dollars general and administrative expenses of $110,000 at the end of the first three months of operation. Sales on account and cost of sales for the first three months were $440,000 and $280,000, respectively, and were denominated in U.S. dollars. The sales occurred uniformly throughout the three-month period. Spot exchange rates between the French franc (FF) and the dollar during the first three months were as follows: beginning, 1 FF = $0.20; average, 1 FF = $0.22; and ending, 1 FF = $0.24.

    Prepare the French company's trial balance at the end of the first three months both in French francs and U.S. dollars. Discuss how the objectives of the translation process have been achieved in this example.

Exercise 3. Grant Company is a German subsidiary of Tri-Coast, a U.S.-based manufacturer. The majority of Grant's cash flows are in the British pound, which has been determined to be the functional currency. Grant's condensed trial balance in German marks (M) as of December 31, 19X5, is as follows:

	Debit	Credit
Cash and Receivables.....................................	1,100,000	
Inventory..	1,500,000	
Property, Plant, and Equipment (net).....................	1,985,000	
Accounts Payable		900,000
Long-Term Debt..		1,300,000
Dividends Payable...		100,000
Stockholders' Equity..		1,200,000
Sales Revenue		7,500,000
Expenses...	6,415,000	
	11,000,000	11,000,000

The company employs the FIFO inventory method. The most recent purchase of inventory occurred on August 1, 19X5, and November 1, 19X5, in the amounts of 800,000 M and 1,100,000 M, respectively. Depreciable assets consist of the following acquisitions:

Acquisition Date	Cost Measured in Marks
February 1, 19X3	1,800,000
October 5, 19X4	300,000
April 1, 19X5	400,000

Depreciation is based on the straight-line method with a 10-year useful life and no salvage value. One-half year of depreciation is taken in the year of acquisition and the year of disposition.

The long-term debt was incurred to finance the February 1, 19X3 acquisition of equipment. The current-year dividend was declared on November 1, payable on January 10, 19X6, to shareholders of record on December 15, 19X5.

The following exchange rates existed:

Date	1 Mark =	1 £ =
February 1, 19X3	£0.27	$1.50
October 5, 19X4	0.30	1.55
March 1, 19X5	0.32	1.53
April 1, 19X5	0.31	1.52
August 1, 19X5	0.33	1.54
November 1, 19X5	0.34	1.57
December 15, 19X5	0.35	1.58
December 31, 19X5	0.36	1.60
19X5 Average	0.33	1.55
January 10, 19X6	0.37	1.61

(1) Calculate the dollar value of the following accounts as of December 31, 19X5:
   (a) Inventory
   (b) Depreciation Expense
   (c) Accounts Payable
   (d) Long-Term Debt
   (e) Dividends Payable
(2) Discuss how the effect of remeasuring the trial balance into the functional currency would be accounted for.

(3) Discuss whether a hedge on the net investment would have been beneficial and what form it might have taken.

Exercise 4. Grandey Corporation acquired a 25% interest in a foreign entity on January 1, 19X9, for $2,900,000. The book value of the entity on that date was 20,800,000 foreign currency units (FC) and any excess cost over book value is allocated to depreciable assets with a 10-year life and no salvage value. The straight-line method of depreciation is used. A dividend of 1,800,000 FC was declared on November 1, 19X9, and paid on December 1, 19X9. There were no intercompany transactions between the two entities during 19X9, and the foreign entity had the following condensed trial balance on December 31, 19X9.

Condensed Trial Balance (in FC)
December 31, 19X9

Assets	138,000,000	Liabilities.	110,000,000
Expenses.	59,000,000	Sales	68,000,000
		Owners' Equity	19,000,000
Total Debits.	197,000,000	Total Credits	197,000,000

The foreign entity's functional currency is the foreign currency and various 19X9 spot exchange rates are as follows:

January 1 . . . . .1 FC = $0.50
November 1 . . . . .1 FC =   0.58
December 1. . . . . .1 FC =   0.59
December 31. . . . . .1 FC =   0.62
Average . . . . .1 FC =   0.54

Determine the December 31, 19X9 balance in Grandey's investment in foreign entity account.

Exercise 5. Shaid Corporation is a wholly owned subsidiary of Hawkes Inc. Shaid, a South American company, was organized on July 1, 19X5, when the general price level index in its country was 400. The price level index is 1,000 at December 31, 19X6. The general price level index in the U.S., where Hawkes is incorporated, has gone from 110 to 121 during the same time period.

Shaid's accounting records contain the following information:

(a) Inventory is accounted for by the LIFO inventory method on a periodic basis. The 19X6 beginning inventory is composed entirely of purchases made on July 1, 19X5. Inventory information for 19X6 is as follows:

Date	Account	Amount in Foreign Currency
January 1, 19X6	Beginning Inventory	30,000 FC
April 1, 19X6	Purchases	18,000
June 1, 19X6	Purchases	25,000
October 1, 19X6	Purchases	40,000
November 1, 19X6	Purchases	20,000
December 31, 19X6	Ending Inventory	52,000

(b) Equipment was acquired and sold as detailed in the following schedule. There were no intercompany equipment transactions.

Date	Cost Acquired (Sold)
July 1, 19X5	120,000 FC
April 1, 19X6	50,000
October 1, 19X6	(16,000)

The selling price of the equipment sold was 13,200 FC. This equipment was acquired on July 1, 19X5.

(c) Depreciation is computed using the straight-line method over an 8-year life. Salvage value is ignored. A half-year of depreciation is taken in the years of acquisition and disposition.

(d) The November 1 inventory purchase in part (a) was acquired from Hawkes Inc., with payment due in foreign currency in 90 days. On November 1, Hawkes purchased a 90-day forward contract to sell the 20,000 FC to a broker at a forward rate of 1 FC = $1.27.

(e) Relevant exchange rates are as follows:

Date	Rate
July 1, 19X5	1 FC = $1.19
April 1, 19X6	1 FC = 1.23
June 1, 19X6	1 FC = 1.22
October 1, 19X6	1 FC = 1.25
November 1, 19X6	1 FC = 1.26
December 31, 19X6	1 FC = 1.28
19X6 average	1 FC = 1.24

Calculate the translated value of the following accounts:

(1) Cost of goods sold for 19X6.

(2) Gain or loss on the October 1, 19X6 equipment sale.

(3) Hawkes' liability to broker associated with the forward contract, as of December 31, 19X6.

Exercise 6. For each of the following independent cases, determine the translated value of the relevant accounts.

Case A: A foreign subsidiary has inventory accounted for by the lower-of-cost-or-market rule. The 19X7 ending inventory, with a cost of 180,000 FC, was written down to a market value of 176,000 FC. The cost of the inventory is traceable to an October 1, 19X7 purchase of 150,000 FC and a December 15, 19X7 purchase of 30,000 FC. The foreign company's functional currency is the U.S. dollar. Relevant exchange rates on October 1, 19X7, December 15, 19X7, and December 31, 19X7, are 1 FC = $1.76, 1 FC = $1.72, and 1 FC = $1.82, respectively. Calculate the translated value of the December 31, 19X7 ending inventory.

Case B: A foreign subsidiary purchased inventory for 380,000 FC from its U.S. parent on November 1, 19X7. The parent's cost of the inventory sold was $500,000. As of December 31, 19X7, the subsidiary has 60% of the inventory on hand. The subsidiary's functional currency is the foreign currency. Relevant exchange rates on November 1, 19X7, and December 31, 19X7, are 1 FC = $2.00 and 1 FC = $2.10, respectively. Calculate the translated value of the subsidiary's December 31, 19X7 inventory after eliminating the intercompany profit.

Case C: A foreign subsidiary acquired depreciable assets measured in foreign currency A (FCA) over several years. The subsidiary's functional currency is foreign currency B

(FCB). All assets are depreciable on a straight-line basis over a 10-year useful life. Relevant asset costs and exchange rates are as follows:

	Asset Cost	1 FCA =	1 FCB =
January 1, 19X6	380,000	2.10 FCB	$1.10
March 1, 19X6	710,000	1.98	1.08
July 1, 19X6	216,000	1.92	1.06
December 1, 19X6	30,000	2.01	1.04
19X6 average		2.03	1.05

Calculate the translated value of the 19X6 depreciation expense.

Exercise 7. Rengate Electronics, Inc. has an 80% interest in Tuturro, a foreign manufacturer of electronic control devices. The foreign currency (FC) is Tuturro's functional currency. Tuturro's net assets at the beginning of the current year 19X3 are 2,500,000 FC. The following events occurred during the current year:
(a) Net income of 1,000,000 FC was recognized. Included in this amount was 200,000 FC of rental expense resulting from leases. These same leases should be capitalized according to U.S. GAAP. Capitalization would have resulted in depreciation expense and interest expense of 130,000 FC and 140,000 FC, respectively. Furthermore, net assets at the beginning of the year would have decreased by 100,000 FC.
(b) Common stock was issued on July 1, 19X3, for 200,000 FC.
(c) Dividends of 50,000 FC were declared on both March 1 and September 1. In both instances the dividends were actually paid on the first day of the month following the date of declaration.
(d) Treasury stock was acquired on October 1, 19X3, at a cost of 100,000 FC.
(e) In the case of all of the stock transactions, Rengate continued to maintain an 80% interest in the subsidiary.
Relevant exchange rates are as follows:

Date	1 FC =
January 1, 19X3	$1.020
March 1, 19X3	1.022
April 1, 19X3	1.018
July 1, 19X3	1.015
September 1, 19X3	1.011
October 1, 19X3	1.008
December 31, 19X3	1.005
19X3 Average	1.012

(1) Calculate the translation adjustment for the year 19X3.
(2) Discuss how a bank loan or a forward contract could have been employed to hedge against the translation adjustment.

Exercise 8. Fuente Enterprises is a foreign company that was acquired by a U.S. firm on January 1, 19X7. At that time Fuente had 2,000,000 units of inventory at a cost of 800,000 foreign currency units (FC) and acquired additional inventory during the year as follows:

	Units	Cost in FC
February 15 purchase............	1,200,000	600,000
July 1 purchase	2,150,000	1,840,000
September 20 purchase..........	1,650,000	2,940,000

During the year Fuente sold 5,900,000 units. Fuente's currency is that of a highly inflationary economy and spot exchange rates during the year were as follows:

January 1 . . . . .1 FC = $5.10	September 20. . . . . .1 FC = $2.80
February 15. . . . . .1 FC = 4.20	December 31 . . . . .1 FC = 2.10
July 1 .1 FC = 3.15	19X7 average . . . . .1 FC = 3.58

The ending inventory had a market value of 2,200,000 FC.

Assuming Fuente uses the FIFO inventory method and applies lower of cost or market, calculate the 19X7 cost of sales and ending inventory.

PROBLEMS

Problem 11-1. On October 1, 19X5, Codensco acquired a 100% interest in the net assets of Fabrico, a foreign company, for $10,000,000. At that time, the net assets of Fabrico were 8,300,000 foreign currency (FC) units as measured in conformity with GAAP. A condensed trial balance for Fabrico as of December 31, 19X7, is as follows:

	Debit		Credit	
Working Capital	2,840,000	FC		
Property, Plant, and Equipment (net).	15,690,000			
Other Assets.	1,340,000			
Long-Term Debt.			7,800,000	FC
Common Stock (issued on 1/1/X4).			2,000,000	
Paid-In Capital in Excess of Par.			5,000,000	
Retained Earnings			3,420,000	
19X7 Net Income.			1,650,000	
	19,870,000	FC	19,870,000	FC

The trial balance is based, in part, on certain national accounting principles that are accepted in the country in which Fabrico operates. However, these principles do not conform to U.S. GAAP. These differences are summarized as follows:

Tax allocation—The trial balance includes a tax expense equal to the current year's tax liability. If tax allocation were employed, the tax expense and deferred tax liability would increase by 300,000 FC and 1,200,000 FC, respectively.

Land appreciation—Appreciation on a parcel of land was recognized in 19X7 as resulting in an increase in land and retained earnings of 200,000 FC.

Building appreciation—Appreciation was also recognized on certain buildings. The effect is that buildings and accumulated depreciation at the beginning of the year are overstated by 1,200,000 FC and 160,000 FC, respectively. The current depreciation is overstated by 50,000 FC. Because such appreciation is not recognized for tax purposes, the tax provision and liability are not affected by the item.

A dividend of 200,000 FC was declared on February 1, 19X7, and was paid on March 1, 19X7.

The long-term debt of Fabrico includes a loan from Codensco which was made on July 1, 19X7. The loan bears interest at the rate of 10% and has a principal amount payable in dollars of $670,000. Both Fabrico and Codensco have made all 19X7 adjusting entries applicable to the loan including recognition of appropriate transaction gains or losses.

Relevant exchange rates are as follows:

January 1, 19X4	$1.05	March 1, 19X7	$1.31
October 1, 19X5	1.12	July 1, 19X7	1.34
January 1, 19X7	1.28	December 31, 19X7	1.37
February 1, 19X7	1.30	19X7 Average	1.33

Required:

(1) Calculate the 19X7 translation adjustment assuming the foreign currency is the functional currency.

(2) Prepare all the necessary eliminating and adjusting entries upon consolidation for the year 19X7 assuming use of the cost method. Any excess of cost over book value is traceable to goodwill with a 10-year useful life.

Problem 11-2. On January 1, 19X7, Reno Investments acquired an interest in Gruber Manufacturing which is a German firm that builds medical equipment. The purchase price of $17,600,000 was for an 80% interest in Gruber's net book value of $20,000,000. The net book value included $12,000,000 of retained earnings on January 1, 19X7, when the spot rate was 1 German mark (M) = $0.50. Gruber recognized net income and declared dividends, measured in German marks, during the years 19X7 and 19X8 as follows:

	Net Income		Dividends Declared	
	Amount	Average Spot Rate	Amount	Relevant Spot Rate
19X7	4,200,000	1 M = $0.52	800,000	1 M = $0.58
19X8	5,600,000	1 M = 0.50	900,000	1 M = 0.53

On December 31, 19X8, when the spot rate was 1 M = $0.52, Gruber had net equity of 28,100,000 M. During 19X9 Gruber recognized income of 3,900,000 M when the average exchange rate was 1 M = $0.48. On October 1, 19X9, Gruber declared a dividend of 400,000 M when the spot rate was 1 M = $0.51. The dividend was paid on November 1, 19X9, when the spot rate was 1 M = $0.52. The spot rate on December 31, 19X9, was 1 M = $0.53.

Required:

Calculate the translated amounts for the following items:

(1) Retained earnings as of December 31, 19X9.

(2) The 19X9 translation adjustment.

(3) The 19X9 translation adjustment traceable to the original cost in excess of book value. Assume that the excess is to be amortized over 10 years using a straight-line method.

Problem 11-3. Divall is a French company whose functional currency is the French franc (FF). The company was founded on July 1, 19X7, with the sale of stock for 11,880,000 FF, of which 10,000,000 FF represented par value. On January 1, 19X9, a U. S. company purchased for cash all of the stock of Divall for 14,000,000 FF when the retained earnings balance of Divall was 1,200,000 FF. The excess paid over book value is attributable to undervalued depreciable property which had a remaining useful life of 12 years at the date of acquisition.

Divall's unadjusted trial balance in FF on December 31, 19X9, is as follows:

	Debit	Credit
Cash and Receivables	2,210,000	
Inventory	5,700,000	
Prepaid Assets	122,000	
Property, Plant, and Equipment	7,533,000	

	Debit	Credit
Accumulated Depreciation		817,000
Other Assets...	1,200,000	
Accounts and Notes Payable		2,984,000
Dividends Payable (declared on December 1, 19X9)		320,000
Common Stock		10,000,000
Paid-In Capital in Excess of Par.........................		1,880,000
Dividends Declared....................................	320,000	
Retained Earnings, 1/1/X9		1,200,000
Sales Revenue		8,954,000
Cost of Goods Sold....................................	6,060,000	
Selling, General, and Administrative Expenses.............	3,010,000	
	26,155,000	26,155,000

The trial balance has not been adjusted to reflect gains and losses on the following transactions:

(a) Inventory includes materials purchased from a German company in the amount of 230,000 FF. At the date of purchase, 1 FF = 0.35 M (German Marks) and at December 31, 19X9, 1 FF = 0.38 M. The purchase which is denominated in M is payable in early January of the next year.

(b) Notes payable includes a loan from a U.S. bank in the amount of 700,000 FF. The loan was received on August 1, 19X9, and is denominated in dollars.

The December 31, 19X9 ending inventory includes 430,000 FF of goods, which is a portion of the amount purchased from the U.S. parent on October 1, 19X9. The original purchase, which was denominated in FF, had a value of $130,000 and a cost to the parent of $104,000.

Relevant direct exchange rates ($/FF) are as follows:

July 1, 19X7	$0.140
January 1, 19X9	0.170
August 1, 19X9	0.173
October 1, 19X9................................	0.180
December 1, 19X9..............................	0.179
December 31, 19X9	0.178
19X9 Average..................................	0.174

Required:

(1) Prepare for Divall the December 31, 19X9 adjusted trial balance in FF and the translated value of the account balances in dollars. Supporting schedules should be in good form.

(2) Prepare the parent's journal entries related to the investment in the foreign subsidiary and all necessary eliminating and adjusting entries upon consolidation assuming use of the simple equity method. Supporting schedules should be in good form.

Problem 11-4. Portland and Associates is a U.S.-based company that develops and manages resort hotels. On June 1, 19X3, the company paid $2,819,200 for a 30% interest in Britco, which is a British company. The net assets of Britco were £6,000,000 at the date of Portland's acquisition. Britco also develops and manages hotels located primarily in France. The French franc is Britco's functional currency even though the company raises capital for its projects primarily in the United Kingdom. Britco's condensed trial balance in pounds as of December 31, 19X5, is as follows:

	Debit	Credit
Working Capital...	2,400,000	
Real Estate	23,000,000	
Accumulated Depreciation		3,700,000
Long-Term Debt.......................................		16,000,000
Common Stock		2,000,000
Retained Earnings....................................		4,300,000
19X5 Net Loss	600,000	
	26,000,000	26,000,000

The common stock was issued at par on January 1, 19X2. Workpapers for the year ended December 31, 19X4, indicate that retained earnings had a remeasured basis of 49,400,000 FF and a dollar equivalent of $5,280,000.

Real estate measured in pounds, along with related depreciation information, is analyzed as follows:

Acquisition Date	Cost	12/31/X4 Accumulated Depreciation	19X5 Depreciation Expense
March 1, 19X2	6,200,000	1,400,000	340,000
January 1, 19X3	12,000,000	1,200,000	600,000
June 1, 19X5	4,800,000		160,000
	23,000,000	2,600,000	1,100,000

The long-term debt represents a major refinancing which occurred on March 1, 19X4. Relevant exchange rates are as follows:

Date	1 £ =	1 FF =
January 1, 19X2	10.0 FF	$0.13
March 1, 19X2	10.3	0.13
January 1, 19X3	10.9	0.14
June 1, 19X3	11.2	0.12
March 1, 19X4	12.5	0.13
May 1, 19X5	12.4	0.12
June 1, 19X5	12.3	0.11
December 31, 19X5	11.8	0.10
19X5 Average	12.0	0.11

Required:
(1) Calculate the remeasurement gain or loss and the translation adjustment.
(2) Discuss the accounting treatment given the items calculated in (1) above.
(3) Calculate the December 31, 19X5 carrying value of Portland's investment in Britco assuming:
  (a) The carrying value as of December 31, 19X4, was $3,600,00 excluding any cumulative remeasurement and translation amounts.
  (b) A dividend of £400,000 was declared on May 1, 19X5, and paid on June 1, 19X5.
  (c) The sophisticated equity method is employed, and any goodwill is to be amortized over 20 years.

Problem 11-5. Reslin Corporation is a New York–based manufacturer of photographic supplies. On August 1, 19X3, Reslin expanded its network of operations by opening a branch office in Great Britain. The following information is available regarding accounts of the home office and branch for the year ended December 31, 19X5:

(a) On December 22, 19X5, the home office shipped merchandise billed at $12,600 to the branch office. The merchandise was received in January, 19X6.

(b) The branch office received all of its beginning inventory and 40% of its ending inventory from the home office. The home office bills the goods at cost plus a markup of 12% of cost. Purchases are made uniformly throughout the year, and branch inventory is accounted for by the FIFO method. The 19X5 beginning inventory of the branch office is £86,000. The current cost of ending inventories at December 31, 19X5, excludes the shipment in transit.

(c) A photographer on location in Great Britain purchased film on account from the branch office. Upon returning to the U.S., however, the photographer erroneously paid the account to the New York office on December 30, 19X5. The bookkeeper recorded the $1,300 payment on the books of the home office but did not notify the branch office.

(d) On December 30, the branch office authorized a remittance of £4,400 to be made to the home office. Payment was received by the home office on January 2, 19X6.

(e) On December 31, the branch office recorded the December allocated general and administrative expense from the home office as £570 instead of £750.

(f) The annual insurance premium is paid by the branch office on March 31 of each year.

(g) As of May 1, 19X5, the rate of exchange is £1 = $1.60. The previous rate, which had been in effect since 19X2, was £1 = $1.75. The average annual rate of exchange was £1 = $1.65.

Trial balances at December 31, 19X5, for the home office and its branch are as follows. No adjustments required by home office accounting procedures have been recorded.

	Branch Office Trial Balance (£)	Home Office Trial Balance ($)
Cash	65,000	140,000
Accounts Receivable	100,000	205,000
Inventory, Dec. 31, 19X5	131,250	650,000
Prepaid Insurance	1,500	
Customer Deposits (refundable)	680	2,300
Property, Plant, and Equipment	950,000	2,710,000
Investment in Branch		23,940
Cost of Goods Sold	1,424,750	3,780,000
Selling Expenses	41,000	113,000
General and Administrative Expense.	92,500	366,000
Depreciation Expense	120,000	250,000
Accounts Payable.	(130,000)	(290,000)
Customer Deposits (refundable)	(680)	(2,300)
Mortgage Payable on Building	(203,000)	(512,000)
Accumulated Depreciation.	(380,000)	(995,000)
Home Office Equity	(3,320)	
Capital Stock ($2 par)		(320,000)
Retained Earnings, Jan. 1, 19X5		(510,000)
Sales.	(2,209,680)	(4,750,940)
Shipments to Branch (at retail)		(860,000)
Total	0	0

Required:

Prepare a columnar worksheet to present the combined income statement and combined balance sheet of Reslin Corporation and its foreign branch office with all amounts stated in U.S. dollars. Key and explain worksheet eliminations and adjustments, and show supporting computations in good form. Ignore income taxes.

Problem 11-6. Brazilco is a wholly owned subsidiary of Stabco, Inc., a U.S. clothing company. The foreign country in which Brazilco operates has experienced inflation of approximately 40% per year for the past four years. The December 31, 19X6 trial balance for Brazilco is as follows:

	Debit	Credit
Cash and Receivables.............................	950,000 FC	
Inventory...	245,000	
Leasehold Improvements...........................	870,000	
Furniture and Fixtures............................	320,000	
Accumulated Amortization—Leaseholds...........		174,000 FC
Accumulated Depreciation—Furniture and Fixtures...		80,000
Accounts Payable.................................		525,000
Notes Payable....................................		710,000
Common Stock....................................		400,000
Retained Earnings................................		320,000
Sales Revenue...................................		2,860,000
Cost of Sales....................................	1,840,000	
Amortization/Depreciation Expense................	119,000	
Other Expenses..................................	725,000	
	5,069,000 FC	5,069,000 FC

Brazilco began operations on July 1, 19X4, by issuing 300,000 FC of common stock to Stabco. An additional 100,000 FC of common stock were issued on March 1, 19X6. The leasehold improvements were completed on January 1, 19X5, and are amortized on a straight-line basis over 10 years. The note payable was incurred to finance the leasehold improvements. The furniture and fixtures were acquired when operations began in 19X4 and are depreciated on a straight-line basis over 10 years.

The inventory has a year-end cost of 255,000 FC and is accounted for at the lower of cost or market. The write-down of year-end inventory is included in cost of sales. Included in the inventory is a purchase of goods from the parent company on September 1, 19X6. The inventory had a cost to the parent of $120,000 and was sold to the subsidiary for 200,000 FC. One-half of the inventory remains in Brazilco's year-end inventory. Other purchases of inventory experience an average turnover of twelve times and are acquired uniformly throughout the year.

The retained earnings consists of the following items:

19X4 net income..	140,000 FC
19X5 net income..	210,000
19X6 dividends declared on 2/1/19X6	(30,000)
	320,000 FC

It is important to note that the above net income figures include the effect of amortization and depreciation.

Relevant exchange rates are as follows:

Date	Rate
July 1, 19X4	$1.55
19X4 Average	1.50
January 1, 19X5	1.40
19X5 Average	1.35
February 1, 19X6	1.28
March 1, 19X6	1.25
September 1, 19X6	1.10
December 31, 19X6	0.92
19X6 Average	0.70

Required:
(1) Prepare a remeasured trial balance in dollars as of December 31, 19X6.
(2) Prepare the elimination entry necessary to account for the intercompany sale of inventory.

Problem 11-7. On January 1, 19X8, Hadley Corporation paid 34,000,000 FC to acquire an 80% interest in Greco Manufacturing, a foreign company. At that time Greco's owners' equity, in foreign currency (FC), was as follows:

Common Stock	17,000,000 FC
Paid-In Capital in Excess of Par	8,000,000
Retained Earnings	12,480,000

During 19X8 Greco purchased inventory from local suppliers with the exception of the following amounts which were purchased from the parent company Hadley:

June 15 purchase	$5,400,000
December 1 purchase	2,380,000

Hadley's cost on the above sales is 70% of the sales value. Invoice amounts were due the parent, payable in dollars, 45 days after receipt. Of the December 1 purchase, 40% remains unsold as of year end.

Sales during the year were all denominated in FC with the exception of the following sales which were denominated in U.S. dollars:

July 31 (payment due 8/31/X8)	$12,450,000
December 15 (payment due 1/15/X9)	4,800,000

The sales proceeds were immediately converted into FC.

On December 1, Greco secured financing for a planned addition to their manufacturing facility. The total amount borrowed of 30,000,000 FC was loaned by the following sources:

A German bank	20,000,000 FC
The parent company	10,000,000

The loan from the German bank bears interest at the rate of 12% and the principal amount of 8,000,0000 M is to be repaid in German marks in 36 months. Relevant rates of exchange between FC and the German mark are as follows: December 1, 1 FC = 0.40 M and December 31, 1 FC = 0.41 M. The $15,400,000 loan from the parent bears interest at the rate of 7% and is payable in dollars on December 1, 19X9.

On December 31, 19X8, Greco's condensed trial balance in FC was as follows:

	Debit	Credit
Current Assets	34,200,000	
Depreciable Assets	121,320,000	
Accumulated Depreciation		24,570,000
Other Assets	20,670,000	
Cost of Sales	125,850,000	
Selling, General, and Administrative Expenses	32,340,000	
Income Tax Expense	12,740,000	
Current Liabilities		15,880,000
Noncurrent Liabilities		72,000,000
Common Stock		17,000,000
Paid-In Capital in Excess of Par		8,000,000
Retained Earnings		12,480,000
Sales		197,190,000
	347,120,000	347,120,000

Relevant spot exchange rates for the year 19X8 are as follows:

January 1	1 FC = $1.50	December 1	1 FC = $1.54
June 15	1 FC = 1.46	December 15	1 FC = 1.56
July 31	1 FC = 1.48	December 31	1 FC = 1.58
August 31	1 FC = 1.45	Average	1 FC = 1.53

Required:
(1) Prepare an analysis of Greco's exchange gains or losses, in FC, that resulted from the foreign currency transactions detailed above.
(2) Calculate the total translation adjustment including that which is traceable to the excess of cost over book value. Assume the excess is amortized over 10 years on a straight-line basis.
(3) Prepare all of the eliminating and adjusting entries that would be necessary in order to prepare consolidated financial statements.
(4) Prepare a schedule to calculate the minority interest amount that would appear on the consolidated balance sheet.

Problem 11-8. Mirronics Corporation has been the original owner of LeBec, a French company that manufactures alternative energy systems for a number of German customers. Although LeBec maintains its books and records in French francs (FF), its functional currency is the German mark (M). LeBec's forecasted trial balance, in francs, as of December 31, 19X8, is expected to be as follows:

	Debit	Credit
Cash and Receivables.......................................	1,388,000	
Inventory...	2,230,000	
Depreciable Assets	2,470,000	
Accumulated Depreciation		1,235,000
Other Assets...	300,000	
Cost of Sales	3,980,000	
Depreciation Expense.....................................	247,000	
Other Expenses..	1,280,000	
Current Liabilities		1,870,000
Noncurrent Liabilities.....................................		1,300,000
Common Stock		1,200,000
Retained Earnings..		860,000
Sales		5,430,000
Totals..	11,895,000	11,895,000

The inventory represents costs that were incurred evenly over the last quarter of 19X8 and the cost of sales represents costs that were incurred evenly over the first six months of 19X8. The depreciable assets were acquired during the first quarter of 19X3. The other assets represent deposits and prepaid items that were incurred during the last quarter of 19X8. Other expenses and sales occurred evenly throughout the year. The common stock was issued on January 1, 19X3, and February 1, 19X8, in the amounts of 1,100,000 FF and 100,000 FF, respectively. The remeasured value of retained earnings as of January 1, 19X8, was 560,000 M.

Mirronics has experienced a weakening U.S. market and is under extreme pressure to maximize reported earnings. In response, Mirronics wants to hedge against remeasurement losses and current year translation adjustments. It is anticipated that the necessary hedges will require Mirronics to secure a long-term loan from a German bank. Such a loan could be taken out at the beginning of the fourth quarter of 19X8 and would bear interest at the rate of 9%.

Various actual and expected exchange rates are as follows:

	1 FF =	1 M =
January 1, 19X3	0.50 M	$0.40
1st quarter average, 19X3...............	0.50	0.41
January 1, 19X8	0.46	0.55
February 1, 19X8	0.43	0.57
1st six months average, 19X8	0.41	0.56
19X8 average	0.39	0.53
October 1, 19X8	0.37	0.54
4th quarter average, 19X8	0.36	0.52
December 31, 19X8	0.35	0.51

Required:
(1) Prepare a remeasured forecasted trial balance for LeBec as of December 31, 19X8.
(2) Prepare a schedule to calculate the expected translation adjustment traceable to 19X8.
(3) Identify the amount of a German bank loan that would be necessary to minimize the adverse effects of remeasurement and translation on Mirronics' equity.

Problem 11-9. Balfour Corporation acquired 100% of Tobac, Incorporated, a foreign corporation, for 33,000,000 foreign currency units (FC). The acquisition, which was accounted for as a purchase, occurred on July 1, 19X5, when Tobac's equity, in foreign currency units, was as follows:

Common Stock	19,000,000　FC
Paid-In Capital in Excess of Par...........	8,480,000
Retained Earnings	2,520,000

Any excess of cost over book value is traceable to goodwill which is to be amortized over 10 years. Balfour uses the simple equity method to account for its investment in Tobac.

On April 1, 19X7, Tobac acquired additional equipment costing 4,000,000 FC. Equipment is depreciated by the straight-line method over 10 years. No other equipment had been acquired or disposed of since 19X4. Tobac employes the LIFO inventory method. Ending inventory on December 31, 19X7, consists of:

Acquired in the 1st quarter of 19X4........	1,000,000　FC
Acquired in the 1st quarter of 19X5........	500,000
Acquired in the 1st quarter of 19X7........	6,500,000

The cost of sales is traceable to goods purchased during 19X7 as follows:

Acquired uniformly over the last 9 months	23,400,000
Acquired in the 1st quarter	4,200,000

Other expenses were incurred evenly over the year.

On April 1, 19X7, Tobac borrowed $1,280,000 from the parent company in order to help finance the purchase of equipment. The note is due in 1 year and bears interest at the rate of 8%. Principal and interest amounts are due to the parent in dollars.

Various spot rates are as follows:

	1 FC =		1 FC =
1st quarter, 19X4 Average........	$0.46	December 31, 19X6	$0.60
19X4 Average..................	0.49	1st quarter, 19X7 Average........	0.62
January 1, 19X5	0.51	April 1, 19X7....................	0.64
1st quarter, 19X5 Average........	0.53	19X7 Average...................	0.67
July 1, 19X5....................	0.55	Last 9 months, 19X7 Average.....	0.66
December 31, 19X5	0.58	December 31, 19X7	0.65
Last 6 months, 19X5 Average.....	0.57		
19X6 Average..................	0.58		

The December 31, 19X7 trial balances for Tobac and Balfour are as follows:

	Tobac	Balfour
Cash	3,087,385　FC	$ 4,463,200
Net Accounts Receivable	12,000,000	15,350,000
Inventory	8,000,000	16,300,000
Due from Tobac		1,356,800
Investment in Tobac—See Note A		23,712,363

	Tobac	Balfour
Depreciable Assets	34,000,000	68,000,000
Accumulated Depreciation	(12,300,000)	(42,000,000)
Due to Balfour	(2,087,385)	
Other Liabilities	(3,700,000)	(27,000,000)
Common Stock	(19,000,000)	(35,000,000)
Paid-In Capital in Excess of Par	(8,480,000)	(2,000,000)
Retained Earnings, 1/1/X7	(7,520,000)	(4,500,000)
Sales	(40,000,000)	(98,000,000)
Cost of Sales	27,600,000	64,000,000
Depreciation Expense	3,300,000	8,076,800
Interest Expense on Balfour Loan (accrued on 12/31/X7)—See Note B	118,154	
Exchange Gain on Balfour Loan—See Note B	(30,769)	
Other Expenses	5,012,615	10,000,000
Interest Income		(76,800)
Subsidiary Income		(2,682,363)
Totals	0	0

Note A: Balfour's Investment in Tobac consists of the following:

Initial investment (33,000,000 FC × 0.55)	$18,150,000
Last 6 months, 19X5 income (2,000,000 FC × 0.57)	1,140,000
19X6 income (3,000,000 FC × 0.58)	1,740,000
19X7 income	2,682,363
Balance	$23,712,363

Note B: The original loan from Balfour was 2,000,000 FC or $1,280,000 (2,000,000 FC × 0.64). On December 31, 19X7, it would require 1,969,231 FC ($1,280,000 divided by 0.65) to settle the loan. This represents an exchange gain of 30,769 FC (2,000,000 FC − 1,969,231 FC).

The year-end balance due to Balfour is determined as follows:

Principal balance	1,969,231	FC
Accrued interest ($1,280,000 × 8% × 9/12 divided by 0.65)	118,154	
Balance	2,087,385	FC

The interest is accrued at year end and, therefore, interest expense should be translated at the year-end rate.

Required:

Assuming the FC is Tobac's functional currency, translate Tobac's trial balance and prepare a consolidating worksheet using the format of Worksheet 11-1.

Problem 11-10. Assume the same facts as Problem 11-9 with the following exceptions:
(a) Tobac's functional currency is the U.S. dollar.
(b) Balfour's Investment in Tobac consists of the following:

Initial investment (33,000,000 FC × 0.55)	$18,150,000
Last 6 months, 19X5 income (including the remeasurement gain or loss)	1,610,000
19X6 income (including the remeasurement gain or loss)	1,860,000
19X7 income (excluding the remeasurement gain or loss)	3,495,363
Balance	$25,115,363

Note that the balance has not yet been adjusted for the 19X7 remeasurement gain or loss.

(c) The trial balances for Tobac and Balfour are the same as in Problem 11-9 with the following exceptions:

	Balfour
Investment in Tobac	$25,115,363
Retained Earnings, 1/1/X7	(5,090,000)
Subsidiary Income	(3,495,363)

Required:

Remembering that Tobac's functional currency is the U.S. dollar, translate Tobac's trial balance and prepare a consolidating worksheet using the format of Worksheet 11-1.

Remember that transactions traceable to pre-7/1/X5 should be remeasured at the rate in effect on 7/1/X5. This is because on 7/1/X5 Balfour acquired its interest in Tobac and established the dollar basis of net assets existing at that time.

PART 3

Special Reporting Concerns

Publicly traded companies are subject to numerous financial reporting and disclosure requirements which are set forth by the Securities and Exchange Commission (SEC). Such companies are required to file interim (quarterly) financial statements with the SEC and report such information to their shareholders. Interim periods are viewed as an integral part of a larger annual period and are affected by a number of special accounting principles. These companies also are required to disclose certain segmental information relating to major product groups and foreign operations. The various types of income must be reported on a per share basis. Two major per share amounts are Primary Earnings per Share and Fully Diluted Earnings per Share. These per share amounts attempt to show the effect on earnings per common share resulting from complex capital structures.

CHAPTER 12

Interim Reporting and Segmental Data

This chapter focuses on two areas of significance to most large, publicly held companies: interim reporting and segmental disclosure. The relevance of financial information is enhanced if the information is provided on a timely basis. Interim financial reporting addresses the need for timely information and provides users with relevant data which may be used to evaluate the present and help to project future results. The division of an annual reporting period into shorter interim periods results in some unique accounting problems which are addressed in this chapter. Segmental data also are concerned with providing relevant information that enhances interfirm comparability. Many companies consist of operating units that differ significantly from each other in terms of products, markets served, and manufacturing methods. Therefore, it becomes difficult to compare these diverse entities to other entities that may not have such diversity. In order to resolve this apparent lack of comparability, diverse companies are divided into segments that reflect the unique components of the company's business. Not only does segmental data improve comparability, but it also allows users to better understand how economic conditions may affect various segments of a business. The criteria for segmental disclosures are discussed in this chapter along with the specific content of such disclosures.

INTERIM REPORTING

To satisfy the need for timely financial information, many business entities have developed interim reporting models that provide financial information on a monthly or quarterly basis or at other defined intervals. These interim data may consist of statements of financial position and retained earnings, income statements, and statements of cash flows. However, primary emphasis is placed on the public disclosure of interim income data.

A substantial amount of empirical research has been devoted to an examination of the utility of publicly disclosed interim financial reports. This research has identified significant stock market reaction to the issuance of interim reports and has noted the influence of interim reports on actual investment decisions. Interim reports provide such an important basis for the prediction of annual income that the demand for these reports nearly parallels the demand for annual reports.

The established utility of interim data emphasizes the importance of applying generally accepted accounting principles, including the principle of adequate disclosure, to interim reports. Therefore, the American Institute of Certified Public Accountants, the National Association of Accountants, the Financial Executives Institute, the Financial Analysts Federation, the Securities and Exchange Commission, and the principal stock exchanges have directed efforts toward the development and improvement of interim financial reporting.

APPROACHES TO REPORTING INTERIM DATA

Earlier forms of interim reporting provided the user of such data with various disclosures other than the computation of net income. However, as the importance of interim income statements became more apparent, different views of the interim period developed. One view of the interim period is that it represents a distinct, independent accounting period, separate from the annual accounting period. Therefore, interim net income should be determined by using the same principles and estimations as would be used if the interim period were an annual accounting period. For example, annual research and development incurred during the interim period should be expensed in that period, rather than deferred to future interim periods.

Another view of the interim period is that it is an integral part of the annual period and does not stand as a distinct, independent period. Therefore, interim data should include appropriate adjustments and estimates so that they can be used to predict annual amounts. For example, assume annual income normally includes a year-end accrual for executive bonuses in the amount of $120,000. If the interim statements are to serve as a predictor of annual values, it would seem appropriate that quarterly income statements should include a proportionate amount of this year-end adjustment. Including a $30,000 adjustment for bonuses in the quarterly income statement would allow one to predict annual bonuses in the amount of $120,000. If this interim adjustment were not made, bonuses would be reflected only in the fourth quarter, and previous quarters would not have provided the user with a basis for predicting this annual amount. From this example, one can see that an interim period is viewed as an integral part of a larger annual period. This view of the interim period has been adopted as the underlying theory used to formulate interim accounting principles and practices.

ACCOUNTING PRINCIPLES BOARD OPINION NO. 28

In 1973, the Accounting Principles Board issued APB Opinion No. 28, *Interim Financial Reporting*, which applies to both internally and externally issued reports. This Opinion was in response to the growing interest in the credibility of interim data and to the apparent need for an authoritative statement from the accounting profession regarding generally accepted accounting principles for such data. The Opinion also may have been influenced by the interim reporting requirements of the SEC.

APB Opinion No. 28 is based on the conclusion that an interim period should be viewed as *an integral part of the annual period,* not as a distinct, independent period. The Opinion reflects the APB's concern for the consistent application of principles by stating that financial statements for each interim period should be based on the *same accounting principles and practices* that are used for the preparation of annual financial statements. However, certain modifications of these principles and practices that relate to costs and expenses may be necessary so that the reported results of an interim period are more indicative of anticipated annual income statement amounts. Modifications of accounting principles and practices also are necessary in order to provide timely information.

Modifications for Costs and Expenses.   Those costs that are directly related or allocated to products sold or to services rendered for annual reporting purposes should be given similar treatment for interim reporting purposes. However, the following modifications are acceptable in the area of inventory costing:

1. The gross profit method or other estimation methods that are not acceptable for annual purposes may be used for interim purposes in those instances where taking an interim physical inventory would be too costly or where perpetual inventory records are lacking or unreliable. Furthermore, use of the gross profit method provides a timely measurement which may not be the case if other methods of inventory accounting were employed. The inventory method used for interim purposes should be disclosed. Significant differences between estimates of the perpetual annual inventory and the annual physical inventory also should be recorded in interim statements on a proportionate basis.
2. Use of the LIFO method for interim purposes may result in inventory liquidations that will be replaced by year end. To compensate for these interim liquidations, the interim cost of goods sold should include the *replacement cost* of temporarily liquidated inventory rather than its historical cost.
3. The use of lower of cost or market may suggest inventory losses for the interim period. Recoveries of these losses in subsequent periods should be recognized as gains to the extent of the losses previously recognized in interim periods within the same fiscal year. An exception to this rule is that temporary market declines that can reasonably be expected to be restored in the fiscal year need not be recognized for the interim period.
4. The use of standard costs for determining inventory generally should be applied on the same basis as is required for annual purposes. Price variances and volume variances that are planned and expected to be absorbed by year

end should be deferred at interim reporting dates.[1] However, unplanned or unanticipated variances should be reported at the end of an interim period.

Illustration of an Interim Liquidation of Inventory.   In order to illustrate the special treatment given interim liquidations, assume a company's LIFO inventory available for sale during the third quarter consisted of beginning inventory of 1,200 units at a cost of $20 each and current purchases of 2,000 units at a cost of $30 each. Assume 2,500 units were sold during the quarter with the expectation that they would be replaced for $32 a unit. Management anticipates that the annual ending inventory will be 1,100 units. Therefore, although the beginning inventory has been liquidated by 500 units, management expects to replenish 400 of these units by year end. Assuming the company anticipates paying $32 each to replenish the inventory, the third quarter cost of sales would be calculated as follows:

Current purchases (2,000 units @ $30).	$60,000
Prior inventory (500 units @ $20 original cost).	10,000
Excess replacement cost (400 units @ $12)	4,800
	$74,800

The entry to record the third quarter cost of sales would be as follows:

Cost of Sales	74,800	
Inventory		70,000
Excess of Replacement Cost for Temporary Liquidation.		4,800
To record cost of sales with a historical cost of $70,000 and an excess of additional replacement cost equal to $4,800 ($12 × 400 units).		

The Excess of Replacement Cost for Temporary Liquidation is classified as a current liability on the interim financial statements. When the 400 units are replenished in the fourth quarter at an assumed cost of $32, the following entry is made:

Inventory	8,000	
Excess of Replacement Cost for Temporary Liquidation.	4,800	
Accounts Payable (Cash)		12,800
To record replenishment of inventory previously liquidated.		

Notice that the 400 units replenish the inventory account at a cost of $20 each as though no liquidation had occurred. That is, the inventory now consists of 1,100 units (700 at the end of the third quarter plus the 400 replenished) at a cost of $20 each.

Illustration of Cost or Market for Interim Inventory.   Assume at the end of the second quarter, ending inventory has a cost of $380,000 and a market value of $350,000. The use of lower of cost or market would require a $30,000 loss due to market declines to be recognized in the second quarter. At the end of the third quarter, the company has ending inventory with a cost of $520,000 and a market value of $560,000. Of the $40,000 excess of market value over cost, the

---

[1]Accounting Priniciples Board Opinion No. 28, *Interim Financial Reporting* (New York: American Institute of Certified Public Accountants, 1973), par. 14.

company can recognize $30,000 of this amount as a recovery of the second quarter loss. Therefore, the third quarter financial statements would include a $30,000 gain due to market recoveries.

Reporting of Costs Unrelated to Inventory. In reporting costs and expenses that are not allocated to products sold or to services rendered but are charged against income in the interim period, the following standards apply:

(a) *Costs and expenses other than product costs should be charged to income in interim periods as incurred, or be allocated among interim periods based on an estimate of time expired, benefit received, or activity associated with the periods. Procedures adopted for assigning specific cost and expense items to an interim period should be consistent with the bases followed by the company in reporting results of operations at annual reporting dates. However, when a specific cost or expense item charged to expense for annual reporting purposes benefits more than one interim period, the cost or expense item may be allocated to those interim periods.*

(b) *Some costs and expenses incurred in an interim period, however, cannot be readily identified with the activities or benefits of other interim periods and should be charged to the interim period in which incurred. Disclosure should be made as to the nature and amount of such costs unless items of a comparable nature are included in both the current interim period and in the corresponding interim period of the preceding year.*

(c) *Arbitrary assignment of the amount of such costs to an interim period should not be made.*

(d) *Gains and losses that arise in any interim period similar to those that would not be deferred at year end should not be deferred to later interim periods within the same fiscal year.*[2]

To illustrate the above concepts, assume the following expenditures have occurred at the beginning of the second quarter:

1. A 12-month insurance premium was paid in the amount of $1,200.
2. Research costs in the amount of $18,000 were paid and are expected to benefit the company over the next 18 months.
3. A contribution in the amount of $1,000 was made, although the benefits to subsequent quarters are uncertain.

The expenses to be recognized in the second quarter are as follows:

Insurance expense ($1,200 ÷ 12 × 3 months) . . . . $ 300
Research costs ($18,000 ÷ 3 quarters—not to be deferred beyond year end)   6,000
Contribution expense   1,000
                                                                                                                  $7,300

---

[2]*Ibid.*, par. 15.

Certain costs and expenses of an entity are subject to year-end adjustments, such as inventory shrinkage, allowance for uncollectible accounts, and year-end bonuses. These adjustments should not be recognized totally in the final interim period if they relate to activities of other interim periods. Therefore, to generate interim financial reports that contain a reasonable portion of annual expenses, a portion of estimated year-end adjustments should be allocated to each interim period on the basis of a revenue or a cost relationship. For example, a company that estimates an expected material year-end adjustment to its perpetual inventory, based on a physical inventory, should allocate a portion of that estimated adjustment to each interim period. In this case, a portion of the annual estimated inventory shrinkage could be allocated to the quarter using a ratio of current quarter cost of sales to annual estimated cost of sales. Changes in earlier quarters' estimates should be accounted for in the current quarter.

The costs and expenses as well as revenues of some businesses are subject to seasonal variations. Since interim reports for such businesses must be considered as representative of the annual period, APB Opinion No. 28 states that:

> . . . such businesses should disclose the seasonal nature of their activities, and consider supplementing their interim reports with information for twelve-month periods ended at the interim date for the current and preceding years.[3]

Adjustments Related to Prior Interim Periods.   By the definitions set forth in FASB Statement No. 16, *Prior Period Adjustments*, many items that were viewed previously as prior period adjustments became elements of current operating income. However, certain items are treated as adjustments related to prior interim periods of the current fiscal year. These items include an adjustment or settlement of: litigation or similar claims, income taxes, renegotiation proceedings, or utility revenue under rate-making processes. Treating these items as prior period adjustments is appropriate if all of the following criteria are met:

(a) *The effect of the adjustment or settlement is material in relation to income from continuing operations of the current fiscal year or in relation to the trend of income from continuing operations or is material by other appropriate criteria, and*

(b) *All or part of the adjustment or settlement can be specifically identified with and is directly related to business activities of specific prior interim periods of the current fiscal year, and*

(c) *The amount of the adjustment or settlement could not be reasonably estimated prior to the current interim period but becomes reasonably estimable in the current interim period.*[4]

If such an item occurs in other than the first interim period of the current fiscal year and if all or part of the item is an adjustment related to prior interim periods of the current fiscal year, it should be reported as follows:

---

[3]*Ibid.*, par. 13.
[4]Statement of Financial Accounting Standards No. 16, *Prior Period Adjustments* (Stamford: Financial Accounting Standards Board, 1977), par. 13.

(a) *The portion of the item that is directly related to business activities of the enterprise during the current interim period, if any, shall be included in the determination of net income for that period.*

(b) *Prior interim periods of the current fiscal year shall be restated to include the portion of the item that is directly related to business activities of the enterprise during each prior interim period in the determination of net income for that period.*

(c) *The portion of the item that is directly related to business activities of the enterprise during prior fiscal years, if any, shall be included in the determination of net income of the first interim period of the current fiscal year.*[5]

Disclosure also is required regarding adjustments related to prior interim periods of the current year in the period in which the adjustment occurs. Disclosures should be made for each prior period of the current year setting forth both the effect on and actual adjusted amount of income from continuing operations, net income, and related per share amounts.

Finally, it is important to note that those adjustments that are related to prior interim periods do not include normal recurring corrections and adjustments that result from the use of estimates. For example, in the current interim period, the revision of estimates used to measure uncollectible accounts is not accounted for as an adjustment related to prior interim periods. Instead, this correction is accounted for in the current interim period and prospectively, as is the case with other changes in estimates.

ACCOUNTING FOR INCOME TAXES IN INTERIM STATEMENTS

Keeping in mind that the interim period is viewed as an integral part of a larger annual period, interim financial statements should reflect a proportionate amount of the estimated annual income taxes. Each interim period will not be viewed as a separate tax period; therefore, estimates of annual tax amounts and rates become critical. The basic objective of accounting for income taxes in interim periods is to estimate the annual effective tax rate and apply that rate to the interim periods' pretax net incomes.

Accounting for income taxes in interim financial statements is based on the application of principles established in APB Opinion Nos. 23 and 24, FASB Interpretation No. 18, and FASB Statement No. 109. In addition, the following guidelines are applicable to the determination of an effective tax rate for interim purposes that is representative of the estimated annual effective tax rate:

1. The effective tax rate for the annual fiscal period must be estimated at the end of each interim period and applied to year-to-date interim income. The current interim period's tax expense or benefit is the difference between (a) the year-to-date tax expense or benefit and (b) the amounts of tax reported in previous interim periods of the current year.

2. The estimated effective tax rate should reflect tax planning alternatives, such as capital gains rates, permanent differences, and tax credits.

---

[5]*Ibid.*, par. 14.

3. Nonordinary items of income or loss (unusual *or* infrequently occurring items, extraordinary items, discontinued operations, and the cumulative effect of changes in accounting principles) are *not* included in the computation of the estimated annual effective tax rate, nor are these items prorated over the balance of the fiscal period. The tax effect on these items is determined incrementally.

4. Changes in tax legislation are to be accounted for in interim periods subsequent to the effective date of the legislation.[6]

The first guideline is designed to insure that the interim income tax rate is representative of the tax rate applicable to the entire fiscal period. For example, if income from continuing operations during the first interim period is $25,000, under a graduated taxing system the effective tax rate at this level of income might be 15%. However, if the annual ordinary income is expected to be $335,000, the effective annual tax rate might be approximately 34%. Therefore, the latter rate should be used as the interim tax rate. If this estimated annual effective tax rate were not used, a reader of the first interim period's financial statements might conclude that income is taxed at only 15%.

Mechanically speaking, the first guideline also provides an effective way of accounting for changes in the estimated annual effective tax rate. As mentioned earlier, normal recurring corrections and adjustments that result from the use of estimates are accounted for in the current interim period. Applying the estimated annual effective tax rate to the year-to-date income and then subtracting (adding) the tax expenses (benefits) traceable to prior interim periods of the current year results in a difference that represents:

1. The tax on the current interim period's pretax income at the present estimated annual effective tax rate and

2. Corrections of previous interim periods' tax expenses or benefits resulting from a change in the estimated annual effective tax rate.

To illustrate, assume that the first quarter's pretax income of $40,000 was taxed at a tax rate of 30% resulting in a $12,000 tax expense. At the end of the second quarter, the estimated annual effective tax rate is 32% and the second quarter's pretax income is $50,000. The tax on the year-to-date pretax income of $90,000 ($40,000 + $50,000) is $28,800 (32% × $90,000). Subtracting from this year-to-date amount the first quarter tax expense of $12,000 results in a current second quarter tax expense of $16,800. The $16,800 consists of:

1. The tax on the second quarter's pretax income at the present estimated annual effective tax rate (50,000 × 32%) $16,000

2. Corrections of prior interim period's tax expense resulting from a change in the estimated annual effective tax rate [$40,000 × (32% − 30%)]........... 800

$16,800

As stated in the second guideline, the estimated effective tax rate also should reflect tax-planning alternatives. If necessary, the rate should be revised

---

[6]Accounting Principles Board Opinion No. 28, *op. cit.*, pars. 19–20.

each interim period in order to reflect changed expectations. Both the first and fourth guidelines indirectly emphasize that changes in the estimated annual effective tax rate should be accounted for as a change in estimate. Therefore, such changes in the tax rate from period to period should be reflected in the tax expense or benefit of the current period in which the change occurs.

The third guideline recognizes that nonordinary items of income or loss may have a distortive effect on estimated annual effective tax rates; therefore, they are excluded from such calculations. This guideline also recognizes that such items are not allocated to other interim periods of the current year. Thus, such items are accounted for entirely in the interim period in which they occur, and the resulting tax impact must be separately determined. The separate determination of the tax employs an incremental approach which is demonstrated in a later section of this chapter.

The fourth guideline echoes the underlying theory of the second guideline in that changes in estimated tax rates are to be accounted for currently and prospectively. Changes in tax legislation are just one possible explanation for a change in estimated annual effective tax rates.

The computation of the estimated effective tax rate is presented in Cases A and B of Illustration 12-1. Case C demonstrates the determination of the tax expense traceable to interim income and the handling of a change in the estimated effective tax rate.

Year-to-Date Operating Losses.   In some instances, an interim year-to-date (YTD) operating loss may be present. Given this loss, a question arises as to the potential tax benefit associated with the loss. The potential tax benefit is a function of several factors.

The YTD loss first must be combined with the projected income or loss for the remaining interim periods of the *current* fiscal year. If the YTD loss is offset by the projected income, a tax benefit traceable to the YTD loss may be recognized. However, if it is more likely than not that some portion of the projected income will not be recognized, that portion of the projected income is not available to be offset by the YTD losses. The concept of "more likely than not" means a level of likelihood at least more than 50% and requires the consideration of many sources of evidence both positive and negative.[7] For example, a backlog of unfilled orders and/or a strong earnings history exclusive of the YTD loss would suggest that more likely than not losses may be offset by projected income. A history of operating losses or unsettled circumstances or economic conditions may suggest that more likely than not losses will not be offset totally by projected income.

After considering the projected income or loss for the balance of the current year, an estimated annual operating loss may exist. The potential tax benefit traceable to this estimated annual operating loss is a function of the following factors:

1.   The extent to which the operating loss may be offset by income of prior fiscal years included in the carryback period and/or

---

[7]Further discussion of the phrase "more likely than not" can be found in Statement of Financial Accounting Standards No. 109, *Accounting for Income Taxes* (Norwalk, CT: Financial Accounting Standards Board, 1992).

Illustration 12-1

Case A
Income in All Interim Periods—Tax Credit; No Permanent Differences

Year-to-date (YTD) income is $170,000, and projected income for the balance of the fiscal year is $30,000. No permanent differences exist, and it is anticipated that an annual tax credit of $13,250 will be available. Corporate income is taxed as follows: first $50,000 at 15%, next $25,000 at 25%, over $75,000 at 34%. A surtax of 5% is imposed on income over $100,000 up to $335,000. The effective tax rate is computed as follows:

	Income (Loss)
YTD income	$170,000
Projected income.	30,000
Annual income.	$200,000
Permanent differences	-0-
Adjusted income	$200,000
Tax on adjusted income	$ 61,250*
Tax credits.	(13,250)
Net tax.	$ 48,000
Effective tax rate	24% (48,000 ÷ 200,000)

*[($50,000 × 15%) + ($25,000 × 25%) + ($125,000 × 34%) + ($100,000 × 5%)]

Case B
Income in All Interim Periods—Permanent Difference; No Tax Credit

Year-to-date (YTD) income is $30,000 and projected income for the balance of the fiscal year is $90,000. Annual income includes $10,000 of expense which is never deductible for tax purposes (i.e., a permanent difference). Assume the tax rate is 40%. The effective tax rate is computed as follows:

	Income (Loss)
YTD income	$ 30,000
Projected income.	90,000
Annual income.	$120,000
Permanent differences	10,000
Adjusted income	$130,000
Tax on adjusted income	$ 52,000
Tax credits.	-0-
Net tax.	$ 52,000
Effective tax rate	43% (52,000 ÷ 120,000)**

**Note that the rate always is based on estimated annual income versus adjusted income.

Case C
Income in All Interim Periods—Change in Effective Tax Rate

Interim Period (Quarter)	Ordinary Income Loss		Effective Tax Rate	Tax Expense (Benefit)		
	Current Period	Year-to-Date		Year-to-Date	Previously Reported	Current Period
First	$30,000	$ 30,000	40%	$12,000		$12,000
Second	40,000	70,000	40	28,000	$12,000	16,000
Third	20,000	90,000	45	40,500	28,000	12,500
Fourth	50,000	140,000	45	63,000	40,500	22,500

2.   The extent to which the operating loss may be offset by future annual income which is more likely than not to be recognized in the carryforward period.

The basic concern addressed by these factors is whether the operating loss is able to be offset against operating income and therefore result in a tax benefit. If the facts suggest that such a benefit is more likely than not, the benefit should be recognized in the calculation of the effective annual tax rate.

Offsetting YTD Operating Losses Against Subsequent Interim Income.
The benefit associated with a YTD operating loss should be recognized if the loss will be offset against income in later interim periods of the fiscal year. This offset against income may be recognized if it is more likely than not that such income will be recognized. It is important to note that only the probability of income in subsequent interim periods of the *current* fiscal year is to be evaluated. Whether subsequent fiscal years will generate income is totally irrelevant to this evaluation. Although "more likely than not" is a subjective concept, knowledge of a company's past performance, existing commitments relating to the future, and seasonal patterns must be considered. APB Opinion No. 28 states that:

> *An established seasonal pattern of loss in early interim periods offset by income in later interim periods should constitute evidence that realization is assured beyond reasonable doubt, unless other evidence indicates the established seasonal pattern will not prevail. The tax effects of losses incurred in early interim periods may be recognized in a later interim period of a fiscal year if their realization, although initially uncertain, later becomes assured beyond reasonable doubt. When the tax effects of losses that arise in the early portions of a fiscal year are not recognized in that interim period, no tax provision should be made for income that arises in later interim periods until the tax effects of the previous interim losses are utilized.[8]*

The offset of an established seasonal loss by subsequent interim income is demonstrated in Case A of Illustration 12-2 on page 694. Case B of this illustration demonstrates a YTD loss whose tax benefit is not certain initially but later becomes recognizable.

Offsetting YTD or Annual Operating Losses Against Income of Prior Fiscal Years.
In certain instances, a current YTD interim loss may not be offset entirely by income in later interim periods. However, as suggested by the first factor discussed above, the tax benefit of the YTD should be recognized to the extent that the loss may be carried back against the prior three years of income. Loss carrybacks must begin with the earliest of the prior three years and then proceed to the next earliest year. The tax benefit traceable to the loss, therefore, is a function of the tax rate applied to a prior year's income. Case C of Illustration 12-2 involves the carryback of a YTD loss. Note that in this case the loss is not offset completely against prior income. However, the tax benefit is recognized to whatever extent possible.

---

[8]Accounting Principles Board Opinion No. 28, *op. cit.,* par. 20.

The same carryback principles apply if an annual loss is anticipated. For example, if a company has a YTD loss of $40,000 and an anticipated annual loss of $100,000, the amount of tax benefit would be dependent upon the extent to which the $100,000 loss may be carried back. If a company has a year-to-date income of $60,000 and an anticipated annual loss of $20,000, the estimated annual effective tax rate would be dependent upon the tax benefit associated with the annual loss of $20,000. These principles are demonstrated in Case D of Illustration 12-2.

Offsetting Annual Operating Losses Against Future Annual Income.

To the extent that losses are not absorbed by income in later interim periods and/or the prior three years of income, tax benefits still may be recognized currently. Losses not offset already may be carried forward against future annual income which more likely than not will be recognized in the 15-year carryforward period. Estimating whether future annual income will more likely than not be recognized is one of the most difficult aspects of determining the estimated annual effective tax rate associated with operating losses. Certain amounts of future annual income may have a low level of likelihood that they will be recognized. For example, if an entity has a history of operating losses and is in an industry experiencing a significant number of bankruptcies, a low level of likelihood would seem reasonable. Alternatively, certain amounts of future annual income have a high level of likelihood. For example, the future taxable amounts represented by deferred tax liabilities are considered to have a very high level of likelihood. Therefore, such future taxable amounts will more likely than not be recognized and serve as a basis for offsetting a current annual operating loss. The principles of offsetting current annual operating losses against likely future annual income are demonstrated in Case E of Illustration 12-2 on page 695.

Operating Losses That Are Not Offset.

If present net operating losses cannot be offset totally by any of the options discussed (subsequent interim income, carrybacks, or carryforwards), the potential tax benefit is reduced accordingly. However, those losses that are not offset may be offset subsequently against future years' recognized income or additional deferred tax liabilities which may arise in the carryforward period. When the tax benefit associated with these remaining losses is recognized, it is classified the same as the item against which the losses were offset. For example, if the remaining losses were offset against subsequent income from continuing operations, the benefit would become a component of income from continuing operations. However, if the remaining losses were offset against a subsequent extraordinary item, the tax benefit would be classified as extraordinary. To demonstrate these principles, consider the facts of Case E in Illustration 12-2. In this instance, the annual anticipated loss of $80,000 was used to offset $10,000 of prior years' income and $50,000 of likely future income in the carryforward period taxed at 40%. Therefore, the equivalent of $60,000 ($10,000 + $50,000) of the loss was offset in order to generate the $24,000 tax benefit. The remaining loss of $20,000 (original $80,000 − $60,000 offset) may offset future income or deferred tax liabilities arising in the 15-year carryforward period. Assuming the subsequent year has a recognized

Illustration 12-2

Case A

Seasonal YTD Loss Offset by Subsequent Interim Income Which Is "More Likely Than Not"

Interim Period (Quarter)	Ordinary Income		Effective Tax Rate	Tax Expense (Benefit)		
	Current Period	Year-to-Date		Year-to-Date	Previously Reported	Current Period
First	$(30,000)	$(30,000)	40%	$(12,000)		$(12,000)
Second	20,000	(10,000)	40	(4,000)	$(12,000)	8,000
Third	40,000	30,000	40	12,000	(4,000)	16,000
Fourth	40,000	70,000	40	28,000	12,000	16,000

Case B

YTD Loss Where Tax Benefit Is Uncertain Initially

Interim Period (Quarter)	Ordinary Income		Effective Tax Rate	Tax Expense (Benefit)		
	Current Period	Year-to-Date		Year-to-Date	Previously Reported	Current Period
First	$(30,000)	$(30,000)	0%			
Second	20,000	(10,000)	0			
Third	40,000	30,000	40	$12,000		$12,000
Fourth	40,000	70,000	40	28,000	$12,000	16,000

Case C

YTD Loss with No Assurance of Subsequent Interim Income; $30,000 of Prior Three Years' Income Taxed at 50%

Interim Period (Quarter)	Ordinary Income		Effective Tax Rate	Tax Expense (Benefit)		
	Current Period	Year-to-Date		Year-to-Date	Previously Reported	Current Period
First	$(40,000)	$(40,000)	38%	$(15,000)[a]		$(15,000)
Second	10,000	(30,000)	50	(15,000)	$(15,000)	
Third	35,000	5,000	40[b]	2,000	(15,000)	17,000
Fourth	30,000	35,000	40	14,000	2,000	12,000

[a]Only $30,000 of the $40,000 loss can be offset against the prior years' income, resulting in a tax benefit of $15,000.
[b]The current-year statutory tax rate is 40%.

Case D

YTD and Anticipated Annual Loss with $60,000 of Prior Three Years' Income Taxed at 50%

Interim Period (Quarter)	Ordinary Income		Effective Tax Rate	Tax Expense (Benefit)		
	Current Period	Year-to-Date		Year-to-Date	Previously Reported	Current Period
First	$(40,000)	$ (40,000)	30%[c]	$(12,000)		$(12,000)
Second	(30,000)	(70,000)	30	(21,000)	$(12,000)	(9,000)
Third	5,000	(65,000)	30	(19,500)	(21,000)	1,500
Fourth	(35,000)	(100,000)	30	(30,000)	(19,500)	(10,500)

[c]The effective tax rate of 30% is based on a $30,000 tax benefit ($60,000 × 50%) expressed as a percentage of the $100,000 anticipated annual loss.

Case E
YTD and Anticipated Annual Loss with Carrybacks and Carryforwards Available

Interim Period (Quarter)	Ordinary Income		Effective Tax Rate	Tax Expense (Benefit)		
	Current Period	Year-to-Date		Year-to-Date	Previously Reported	Current Period
First	$(20,000)	$(20,000)	30%[d]	$ (6,000)		$ (6,000)
Second	15,000	(5,000)	30	(1,500)	$ (6,000)	4,500
Third	(35,000)	(40,000)	30	(12,000)	(1,500)	(10,500)
Fourth	(40,000)	(80,000)	30	(24,000)	(12,000)	(12,000)

[d]The calculation of the effective tax rate is based on the following:

Prior 3 years of income of $10,000 taxed at a prior rate of 40%	$ 4,000
Deferred tax liability reversing in the next 15 years based on the current tax rate of 40% ($50,000 of temporary differences)	20,000
Total tax benefit	$24,000

$24,000 ÷ $80,000 anticipated annual loss = 30%

Note: If likely future income in the carryforward period had been at least $70,000, then a tax benefit would have been recognized on the entire current operating loss of $80,000. The $80,000 of loss would have been carried back in the amount of $10,000 and carried forward in the amount of $70,000.

Case F
YTD and Anticipated Annual Loss with a $40,000 Carryback at 30% Available

Interim Period (Quarter)	Ordinary Income		Effective Tax Rate	Tax Expense (Benefit)		
	Current Period	Year-to-Date		Year-to-Date	Previously Reported	Current Period
First	$(10,000)	$(10,000)	25%[e]	$ (2,500)		$(2,500)
Second	(20,000)	(30,000)	25	(7,500)	$ (2,500)	(5,000)
Third	(30,000)	(60,000)	Note	(12,000)	(7,500)	(4,500)
Fourth	12,000	(48,000)	25	(12,000)	(12,000)	

[e]The calculation of the effective tax rate is based on the following:

Prior 3 years of income of $40,000 taxed at a prior rate of 30%	$12,000

The effective tax rate of 25% is based on the $12,000 total tax benefit expressed as a percentage of the $48,000 anticipated annual loss.

Note: If the rate of 25% were used, a YTD tax benefit of $15,000 would be suggested. However, a YTD loss of $60,000 could receive a benefit of only $12,000 (30% × $40,000 prior year's income). Therefore, the YTD benefit is limited to $12,000. This special rule arises when a YTD operating loss exceeds the annual operating loss. Notice that both YTD and annual amounts must be losses. In this case the YTD tax benefit is based on the YTD operating loss.

pretax income from continuing operations of $25,000 which would be taxed at 40%, a tax benefit of $8,000 ($20,000 × 40%), representing the offsetting of the remaining $20,000 loss against the income from continuing operations, would be recognized. The subsequent year's net tax expense on the continuing income would be $2,000, for an effective tax rate of 8% ($2,000 ÷ $25,000). The net tax expense results from the tax expense of $10,000 on the $25,000 of income reduced by the $8,000 tax benefit.

Case F of Illustration 12-2 demonstrates a special limitation of the tax benefits associated with operating losses. This special limitation arises when a YTD operating loss exceeds the annual operating loss.

Nonordinary Items of Income or Loss.   Certain elements making up an entity's net income are reported separately and/or shown net of tax. These elements include unusual or infrequently occurring items, discontinued operations, extraordinary items, and cumulative effects of changes in accounting principles.

There also are interim gains or losses that are accounted for directly as a component of owners' equity. The tax impact on these items should be determined by the same methodology as is used for nonordinary items. As previously stated, these items are not included in the determination of the estimated effective tax rate applied to ordinary income. Therefore, the tax effect of these nonordinary items must be determined independently on an incremental basis. If *one* nonordinary item exists, the incremental income tax is the *difference* between:

1.   The income tax expense (benefit) traceable to the estimated annual *ordinary* income, and
2.   The income tax expense (benefit) traceable to the *total income* [the estimated annual ordinary income plus (less) the incremental nonordinary gain (loss)].

When several nonordinary items exist, the calculation of their individual tax impact becomes more complex. This complexity usually occurs because of differences in tax rates for nonordinary items, surtax charges, and tax credit limitations. If several nonordinary items exist, the incremental tax traceable to each nonordinary item or category is determined as follows:

1.   The incremental income tax expense (benefit) traceable to *all* nonordinary categories is the difference between:
    (a)   The income tax expense (benefit) traceable to the estimated annual ordinary income and
    (b)   The income tax expense (benefit) traceable to the *total* income (the estimated annual ordinary income and *all* nonordinary gains and losses).
2.   The incremental income tax benefit traceable to *all* nonordinary *loss* categories is the difference between:
    (a)   The income tax (benefit) traceable to the *total* income (step 1b) and
    (b)   The income tax expense (benefit) traceable to the *total* income *plus all* nonordinary *loss* categories.
3.   The incremental income tax expense traceable to *all* nonordinary *gain* categories is the difference between:
    (a)   The incremental income tax expense (benefit) traceable to *all* nonordinary items (step 1) and
    (b)   The incremental income tax benefit traceable to *all* nonordinary *loss* categories (step 2).
4.   Next, the incremental income tax benefit traceable to each *individual* nonordinary *loss* category is the difference between:

(a)   The income tax expense (benefit) traceable to the *total* income (step 1b) and

(b)   The income tax expense (benefit) traceable to total income *plus* the *individual* nonordinary *loss* category.

5.   Then, the incremental income tax benefit traceable to *all* nonordinary *loss* categories (step 2) is *apportioned ratably* to each individual loss category based on the incremental income tax benefit of each *individual* nonordinary *loss* category (step 4).

6.   The incremental income tax expense traceable to each *individual* nonordinary *gain* category is the difference between:

(a)   The income tax expense (benefit) traceable to the *total* income (step 1b) and

(b)   The income tax expense (benefit) traceable to total income *less* the *individual* nonordinary gain category.

7.   Finally, the incremental income tax expense traceable to *all* nonordinary *gain* categories (step 3) is *apportioned ratably* to each individual gain category based on the incremental income tax expense traceable to each *individual* nonordinary *gain* category (step 6).

The tax impact of nonordinary gains and losses based on the above steps is demonstrated in Illustration 12-3. It is important to remember that the principles discussed earlier regarding offsetting YTD losses also are applicable to nonordinary loss categories.

If there is a nonordinary loss, the tax benefit of the loss should be recognized if it can be offset by other existing YTD elements of income and projected income for the balance of the year, which is likely. If the nonordinary loss category cannot be offset by elements of income in the current fiscal year, the principles discussed previously regarding carrybacks against prior years' income and carryforwards against likely future income would be applicable. Illustration 12-4, pages 701–702, demonstrates the offsetting of a nonordinary (an extraordinary item) loss under various situations.

ACCOUNTING FOR DISCONTINUED OPERATIONS

The accounting effects of a discontinued operation should be reflected in an income statement as two distinct components: (1) income or loss from operations of the discontinued operation prior to the measurement date and (2) income or loss on disposal of the discontinued operation. Both of these items should be presented net of tax. When interim statements are prepared, a problem arises in that income or loss from operations of the discontinued operation, recognized in an interim period prior to the measurement date, will have been included in ordinary income of the prior period(s) and in the determination of the effective tax rate of the prior period(s). Once the measurement date has been established, the total taxes of the prior periods must be allocated between ordinary income (loss) traceable to continuing operations and ordinary income (loss) traceable to the now-discontinued operations. This allocation of the previously reported tax involves the following steps:

Illustration 12-3

Tax Impact on Nonordinary Gains and Losses

Facts:

Ordinary income of		$180,000
Nonordinary losses consist of:		
Loss (Category #1)	$(30,000)	
Loss (Category #2)	(20,000)	(50,000)
Nonordinary gains consist of:		
Gain (Category #3)	$ 20,000	
Gain (Category #4)	10,000	30,000
Total income of		$160,000

Tax information:

Tax rate on income	30%
Surtax on income between $100,000 and $170,000	5%
Tax credit	10,000
Tax rate on Gain (Category #3) which is also exempt	
from the surtax	20%

Calculation of Total Incremental Tax Impact:

	Ordinary Income	Total Income	Total Income **plus** Nonordinary Losses	Total Income **less** Nonordinary Gains
Pretax income	$180,000	$160,000	$210,000 ($160,000 + $50,000)	$130,000 ($160,000 – $30,000)
Tax expense (benefit)*	**A** $47,500	**B** $38,000	**C** $54,500	$ 31,000**

*Tax on income: $180,000 × 30% = $54,000	$160,000 { $140,000 × 30% = $42,000	$210,000 { $190,000 × 30% = $57,000	
	20,000 × 20% = 4,000	20,000 × 20% = 4,000	
Surtax: $ 70,000 × 5% = 3,500	$ 40,000 × 5% = 2,000	$ 70,000 × 5% = 3,500	
Tax credit: (10,000)	(10,000)	(10,000)	
Tax expense: **A** $47,500	**B** $38,000	**C** $54,500	

Incremental tax expense (benefit) traceable to:

D	All nonordinary items	($38,000 – $47,500) . . . . (step 1: **B – A**)	$ (9,500)
E	All nonordinary losses	($38,000 – $54,500) . . . . (step 2: **B – C**)	$(16,500)
F	All nonordinary gains	[$(9,500) – $(16,500)] . . . . (step 3: **D – E**)	$ 7,000

**In order for there to be a $7,000 incremental tax expense, the tax on total net income less all nonordinary losses must be $31,000 ($38,000 tax expense on all items less the $7,000 incremental tax impact). The tax on total income less nonordinary gains is *always* calculated in this manner.

Calculation of Incremental Tax Benefit Traceable to Each Individual Loss Category:

	Total Income	Total Income plus Nonordinary Losses	Total Income plus Loss (Category 1)	Total Income plus Loss (Category 2)
Pretax income....................	$160,000	$210,000	$190,000	$180,000
Tax expense (benefit)***	B $38,000	C $54,500	G $48,500	H $45,000

***Tax on income:	$190,000 $\left\{\begin{array}{l}\end{array}\right.$ $\begin{array}{l}\$170,000 \times 30\% = \$51,000 \\ 20,000 \times 20\% = 4,000\end{array}$	$180,000 $\left\{\begin{array}{l}\end{array}\right.$ $\begin{array}{l}\$160,000 \times 30\% = \$48,000 \\ 20,000 \times 20\% = 4,000\end{array}$	
Surtax:	$\$ 70,000 \times 5\% = 3,500$	$\$ 60,000 \times 5\% = 3,000$	
Tax credit:	(10,000)	(10,000)	
Tax expense:	G $48,500	H $45,000	

Incremental tax expense (benefit) traceable to:

  E All nonordinary losses ($38,000 – $54,500) .... $(16,500)
             (step 1: **B** – **C**)
  I   Nonordinary loss (Category #1) ($38,000 – $48,500) .... $(10,500)
             (step 4, first loss category: **B** – **G**)
  J   Nonordinary loss (Category #2) ($38,000 – $45,000) .... $ (7,000)****
             (step 4, second loss category: **B** – **H**)

  ****Notice that the sum of the incremental tax benefit on categories 1 and 2 of $17,500
       [($10,500) + ($7,000)] does not equal the incremental tax benefit of $16,500 on all
       losses. It is for this very reason that an apportionment of the tax impact of individual
       categories is necessary.

Apportionment of Tax Benefit Traceable to Nonordinary Losses:

The $16,500 incremental tax benefit traceable to all nonordinary losses is ratably apportioned to each individual loss category as follows:

		Each Loss Category		
		Incremental Benefit	Percent	Apportioned Amount
Loss (Category #1)	**I**	$(10,500)	60%	$ (9,900) = (60% × $16,500)
Loss (Category #2)	**J**	(7,000)	40	(6,600) = (40% × $16,500)
		$(17,500)	100%	**E** $(16,500)****

(continued)

Calculation of Incremental Tax Expense Traceable to Each Individual Gain Category:

	Total Income	Total Income less Nonordinary Gains	Total Income less Gain (Category #3)	Total Income less Gain (Category #4)
Pretax income	$160,000	$130,000	$140,000	$150,000
Tax expense (benefit)*****	**B** $38,000	**B − F** $31,000	**K** $34,000	**L** $34,500

*****Tax on income:	$140,000 × 30% = $42,000	$150,000 {	$130,000 × 30% = $39,000
			20,000 × 20% = 4,000
Surtax:	$ 40,000 × 5% = 2,000		$ 30,000 × 5% = 1,500
Tax credit:	(10,000)		(10,000)
Tax expense:	**K** $34,000		**L** $34,500

Incremental tax expense (benefit) traceable to:

F All nonordinary gains [$(9,500) − $(16,500)] $7,000
        (step 3: **D − E**)
M Nonordinary gain (Category #3) ($38,000 − $34,000)   4,000
        (step 6, first gain category: **B − K**)
N Nonordinary gain (Category #4) ($38,000 − $34,500)   3,500
        (step 6, second gain category: **B − L**)

Apportionment of Tax Expense Traceable to Nonordinary Gains:

The $7,000 incremental tax expense traceable to all nonordinary gains is ratably apportioned to each individual gain category as follows:

		Each Gain Category		
		Incremental Benefit	Percent	Apportioned Amount
Gain (Category #3)	**M**	$4,000	53%	$3,710 = (53% × $7,000)
Gain (Category #4)	**N**	3,500	47	3,290 = (47% × $7,000)
		$7,500	100%	**F** $7,000

Summary of Tax Impact Associated with Ordinary and Nonordinary Items:

	Pretax Income (Loss)	Tax Expense (Benefit)
Ordinary Income.	$180,000	**A** $47,500
Loss (Category #1)	(30,000)	(9,900)
Loss (Category #2)	(20,000)	(6,600)
Gain (Category #3)	20,000	3,710
Gain (Category #4)	10,000	3,290
Totals.	$160,000	**B** $38,000

Illustration 12-4

Case A
Offsetting a Nonordinary Loss Against Ordinary Income

Interim Period (Quarter)	Type of Income	Income (Loss) Current Period	Income (Loss) Year-to-Date	Effective Tax Rate	Tax Expense (Benefit) Year-to-Date	Tax Expense (Benefit) Previously Reported	Tax Expense (Benefit) Current Period
First	Continuing Op.	$ 40,000	$ 40,000	26%	$10,400		$10,400
Second	Continuing Op.	30,000	70,000	28	19,600	$10,400	9,200
Third	Continuing Op.	20,000	90,000	28	25,200	19,600	5,600
Third	Extraordinary	(50,000)	(50,000)	Note A	(14,000)		(14,000)
Fourth	Continuing Op.	40,000	130,000	30	39,000	25,200	13,800
Fourth	Extraordinary		(50,000)	Note B	(15,000)	(14,000)	(1,000)

Note A: The entire extraordinary loss can be offset against ordinary income which has an effective tax rate of 28%.

Note B: Due to a change in the estimated effective tax rate, the benefit associated with the extraordinary loss has increased.

Case B
Offsetting a Nonordinary Loss Assuming: Future Interim Income
Is Not "More Likely Than Not," and
Carrybacks and Carryforwards Are Not Available

Interim Period (Quarter)	Type of Income	Income (Loss) Current Period	Income (Loss) Year-to-Date	Effective Tax Rate	Tax Expense (Benefit) Year-to-Date	Tax Expense (Benefit) Previously Reported	Tax Expense (Benefit) Current Period
First	Continuing Op.	$ 40,000	$ 40,000	26%	$10,400		$10,400
Second	Continuing Op.	30,000	70,000	28	19,600	$10,400	9,200
Third	Continuing Op.	20,000	90,000	28	25,200	19,600	5,600
Third	Extraordinary	(110,000)	(110,000)	Note C	(25,200)		(25,200)
Fourth	Continuing Op.	40,000	130,000	30	39,000	25,200	13,800
Fourth	Extraordinary		(110,000)	Note D	(33,000)	(25,200)	(7,800)

Note C: Because future income is not "more likely than not," the extraordinary loss can be offset only against YTD income.

Note D: Because additional income is available in the fourth quarter, an additional amount of tax benefit traceable to the extraordinary loss can be realized. Additional benefit also is recognized because of the change in the effective tax rate.

(continued)

Case C
Offsetting a Nonordinary Loss Assuming: Future Interim Income Is "More Likely Than Not," and a Carryback Is Available Against Prior Income of $30,000 Taxed at 30%

Interim Period (Quarter)	Type of Income	Income (Loss)			Tax Expense (Benefit)		
		Current Period	Year-to-Date	Effective Tax Rate	Year-to-Date	Previously Reported	Current Period
First	Continuing Op.	$ 40,000	$ 40,000	26%	$10,400		$10,400
Second	Continuing Op.	30,000	70,000	28	19,600	$10,400	9,200
Third	Continuing Op.	20,000	90,000	28	25,200	19,600	5,600
Third	Extraordinary	(180,000)	(180,000)	Note E	(45,400)		(45,400)
Fourth	Continuing Op.	40,000	130,000	28	36,400	25,200	11,200
Fourth	Extraordinary		(180,000)	Note F	(45,400)	(45,400)	

Note E: Because future interim income of $40,000 is assured, the extraordinary loss can be offset against $130,000 of current year income at an estimated effective tax rate of 28%. This results in a tax benefit of $36,400. In addition, another $30,000 of the extraordinary loss can be offset against prior income of $30,000. This results in an additional tax benefit of $9,000 for a total benefit of $45,400 ($36,400 + $9,000). If future interim income had not been more likely than not, the total benefit would have consisted of $25,200 resulting from an offset of YTD income plus the $9,000 resulting from the carryback against prior years' income.

Note F: Of the $180,000 extraordinary loss, $160,000 has been offset ($130,000 against current income and $30,000 against prior years). The tax benefit on the remaining $20,000 of loss not offset may be recognized in the future, as subsequent annual income becomes recognized. If $20,000 of future income was more likely than not to be recognized in the carryforward period, the tax benefit on the entire extraordinary loss could have been recognized in the current year.

1. The original YTD and balance-of-the-year projections used to calculate the estimated effective tax rate are allocated between the continuing and discontinued operations.
2. The original tax-planning alternatives, permanent differences, and tax credits used to calculate the tax rate are allocated between the continuing and discontinued operations.
3. The projected items being allocated in (1) and (2) are the originally reported amounts. That is, the projections relating to the balance of the year are not changed or revised but remain the same as in the prior interim periods. To permit the revision of an earlier projection would have the effect of accounting for a change in estimate on a retroactive basis, which is not acceptable.
4. The amounts now allocated to continuing operations are used to calculate a new effective tax rate traceable to continuing operations. The tax on the continuing operations of the prior interim period(s) also is recalculated.
5. The new tax on the continuing operations of the prior interim period(s) is compared to the originally reported tax (which included both the continuing and discontinued operations), with the difference representing the tax traceable to the discontinued operations.

From the measurement date forward, the discontinued operations will not be commingled with the continuing operations. Thus, the tax effect of the discontinued operations is calculated, on an incremental basis as is the case with other nonordinary items of income. The interim effect of a discontinued operation is demonstrated in Illustration 12-5.

ACCOUNTING FOR A CHANGE IN ACCOUNTING PRINCIPLE

APB Opinion No. 28 indicates that, in general, a change in accounting principle during an interim period should be accounted for in accordance with APB

Illustration 12-5
Discontinued Operation

Facts:

After issuing first-quarter interim data, the company adopted in the second quarter a formal plan calling for the disposal of one of its operations. Ordinary income reported in the first quarter included a $10,000 loss traceable to the operation being discontinued. It is assumed that any loss traceable to the discontinued operation will have tax benefits and that the estimated effective tax rate of 40% on income from continuing operations, used in the first quarter, is to be revised to 45% and applied to the remaining continuing operations.

Analysis:

The following schedule illustrates the retroactive restatement of previously issued interim data in order to disclose separately both continuing and discontinued operations.

Interim Period (Quarter)	Type of Income	Income (Loss)		Effective Tax Rate	Tax Expense (Benefit)		
		Current Period	Year-to-Date		Year-to-Date	Previously Reported	Current Period
First	Continuing Op.	$ 40,000	$ 40,000	40%	$16,000		$16,000
First—Restated	Continuing Op.	50,000	50,000	45	22,500		22,500
First—Restated	Discontinued— Operating Inc. (D-OI)	(10,000)		Note A	(6,500)		(6,500)
First—Restated	Discontinued Loss on Disposal (D-LD)						
Second	Continuing Op.	30,000	80,000	45	36,000	$22,500	13,500
Second	D-OI	5,000	(5,000)	Note B	(2,250)	(6,500)	4,250
Second	D-LD	(60,000)	(60,000)	Note B	(27,000)		(27,000)
Third	Continuing Op.	50,000	130,000	45	58,500	36,000	22,500
Third	D-OI		(5,000)	Note B	(2,250)	(2,250)	
Third	D-LD		(60,000)	Note B	(27,000)	(27,000)	
Fourth	Continuing Op.	55,000	185,000	45	83,250	58,500	24,750
Fourth	D-OI		(5,000)	Note B	(2,250)	(2,250)	
Fourth	D-LD		(60,000)	Note B	(27,000)	(27,000)	

Note A—The $6,500 tax benefit traceable to the discontinued operation is the result of comparing the tax of $22,500 traceable to continuing operations with the $16,000 of tax previously recognized on the continuing operations. Therefore, the difference between the two tax amounts relates to the exclusion and inclusion, respectively, of the results traceable to the discontinued operation. Notice that the total tax expense presented for the first period, restated, totals $16,000, which is the tax originally reported for the first quarter.

Note B—These amounts represent the incremental tax traceable to the discontinued operation less amounts reported in previous interim periods. For example, the $4,250 represents the difference between (1) the tax benefit on the loss to date traceable to the discontinued operations (45% × $5,000) and (2) the tax benefit of $6,500 traceable to the discontinued segment's operating loss recognized in prior periods. The ($27,000) represents the loss on disposal of $60,000 multiplied by the 45% tax rate.

Opinion No. 20, *Accounting Changes*. To simplify the accounting for such changes, the APB encouraged management to adopt accounting changes in the first interim period of the current fiscal year. Nevertheless, the APB recognized that changes would continue to be made in other than the first interim period and, therefore, prescribed special procedures. However, these procedures were amended in 1974 by FASB Statement No. 3, *Reporting Accounting Changes in Interim Financial Statements*. When interim reports are prepared, the proper accounting for a change in an accounting principle depends on (1) whether the change requires the determination of a cumulative effect or retroactive restatement and (2) whether the change takes place in the first interim period of the fiscal year.

A Change Requiring Retroactive Restatement.   A change requiring retroactive restatement of previously issued annual financial statements, rather than the determination of the cumulative effect, will require the restatement of previously issued interim financial information. If such a change occurs in other than the first interim period, such restatement also will involve the restatement of taxes to reflect the estimated effective tax rate, which is based on annual ordinary income (or loss) as determined in accordance with the newly adopted accounting principle. The restatement of the previous tax rate is affected only by the change in principle and, therefore, does not allow for any revisions of projected data that were used to calculate the earlier tax rate. This treatment is consistent with the principle that changes in estimates should not be accounted for on a retroactive basis.

A Change Requiring a Cumulative Effect.   If a cumulative-effect-type change takes place in the first interim period of the fiscal year, the cumulative effect of the change on retained earnings as of the beginning of the year should be included in net income of the first interim period. However, if the cumulative-effect-type change is made in other than the first interim period, it is assumed for accounting purposes that it took place in the first interim period. Therefore, the change should be accounted for as follows:

1. Financial statements for all interim periods in the current fiscal year should be restated to reflect the adoption of the new principle, and
2. The cumulative effect of the change on retained earnings as of the beginning of the current fiscal year should be included in the restated net income of the first interim period rather than in the interim period in which the change was adopted.[9]

   Accounting for the cumulative effect of a change in principle may result in a restated tax rate for the interim periods prior to the change. As is the case with all other restatements of earlier tax rates, only the effect of the *nonordinary* income items should be considered. Therefore, the tax on the cumulative effect should be computed on an *incremental* basis, as previously illustrated for nonordinary

---

[9]Statement of Financial Accounting Standards No. 3, *Reporting Accounting Changes in Interim Financial Statements* (Norwalk, CT: Financial Accounting Standards Board, 1974), par. 10.

Illustration 12-6
Change in Accounting Principle: Cumulative Effect

Facts:

During the third quarter, management decided to change depreciation methods. The effect of the change is to decrease the pretax income of quarters one and two by $30,000 and $20,000, respectively. The effect on prior years is to decrease pretax income by $40,000.

Analysis:

The following schedule illustrates the restatement of previously issued interim data in order to reflect the cumulative effect of the change.

Interim Period (Quarter)	Type of Income	Income (Loss) Current Period	Income (Loss) Year-to-Date	Effective Tax Rate	Tax Expense (Benefit) Year-to-Date	Tax Expense (Benefit) Previously Reported	Tax Expense (Benefit) Current Period
First	Continuing Op.	$80,000	$ 80,000	40%	$32,000		$32,000
Second	Continuing Op.	50,000	130,000	40	52,000	$32,000	20,000
First—Restated	Continuing Op.	50,000	50,000	42*	21,000		21,000
First—Restated	Cum. Effect	(40,000)	(40,000)	Note A	(16,800)		(16,800)
Second—Restated	Continuing Op.	30,000	80,000	42	33,600	21,000	12,600
Second—Restated	Cum. Effect		(40,000)	Note A	(16,800)	(16,800)	
Third & Fourth	Continuing Op.	70,000	150,000	42	63,000	33,600	29,400
Third & Fourth	Cum. Effect		(40,000)	Note A	(16,800)	(16,800)	

*Note that a new effective tax rate of 42% has been calculated as a result of modifications relating only to the change in accounting principle.

Note A: It is assumed that the cumulative effect of a $40,000 loss will offset annual income taxed at an effective rate of 42%. This results in a tax benefit of $16,800 (40,000 × 42%).

items of income or loss, and the tax previously reported for ordinary income of the pre-change interim periods should be restated as follows:

> *The restated tax (or benefit) shall reflect the year-to-date amounts and annual estimates originally used for the pre-change interim periods, modified only for the effect of the change in accounting principle on those year-to-date and estimated annual amounts.*[10]

The principle described above for a cumulative-effect-type change is demonstrated in Illustration 12-6.

A cumulative-effect-type change in principle also requires the following disclosures:

1. *For the interim period in which the new accounting principle is adopted:*
    (a) *Income from continuing operations, net income, and related per share amounts computed on a pro forma basis for (i) the interim*

---

[10]FASB Interpretation No. 18, *Accounting for Income Taxes in Interim Periods* (Stamford: Financial Accounting Standards Board, 1977), par. 64.

period in which the change is made and (ii) any interim periods of
prior fiscal years for which financial information is being presented;

(b) The nature of and justification for the change and the effect of the
change on income from continuing operations, net income, and
related per share amounts for that interim period;

(c) When that period occurs after the first period: (i) the effect of the
change on income from continuing operations, net income, and
related per share amounts for each current fiscal year interim period
prior to the change and (ii) income from continuing operations, net
income, and related per share amounts for each restated current
fiscal year interim period prior to the change.

2. In the period of change, if no financial information for interim periods of
prior fiscal years is being presented:

(a) the actual and pro forma amounts of income from continuing
operations, net income, and related per share amounts for the
interim period of the immediately preceding fiscal year that corresponds to the interim period of change.

3. For year-to-date and last-twelve-months-to-date financial reports
through the interim period of the adoption:

(a) the effect of the change on income from continuing operations, net
income, and related per share amounts and their pro forma bases.

4. For a subsequent (post-change) interim period of the fiscal year in which
the new accounting principle is adopted:

(a) the effect of the change on income from continuing operations, net
income, and related per share amounts for that post-change interim
period.[11]

In a change to the LIFO inventory method, the disclosures for a
cumulative-effect-type change are required except that the cumulative effect of
the change on retained earnings and pro forma amounts should not be determined. If the change is made in other than the first interim period, all pre-change
interim statements must be restated to reflect the adoption of the new accounting
principle. The beginning inventory computed by the previous inventory method
is assumed to be the beginning measure of base stock for purposes of applying LIFO.

DISCLOSURES OF SUMMARIZED INTERIM DATA

To maintain the timeliness of interim data, companies frequently report summarized interim data rather than complete financial statements. When publicly
traded companies report summarized interim data, the following disclosures are
required at a minimum:

(1) Sales or gross revenues, provision for income taxes, extraordinary items
(including related income tax effects), cumulative effect of a change in
accounting principles or practices, and net income.

---

[11]Statement of Financial Accounting Standards No. 3, *op. cit.*, par. 11.

(2) Primary and fully diluted earnings per share data for each period presented, determined in accordance with the provisions of APB Opinion No. 15, *Earnings per Share.*

(3) Seasonal revenue, costs or expenses.

(4) Significant changes in estimates or provisions for income taxes.

(5) Disposal of a segment of a business and extraordinary, unusual, or infrequently occurring items.

(6) Contingent items.

(7) Changes in accounting principles or estimates.

(8) Significant changes in financial position.[12]

In addition to providing this data for the current quarter, such data should be provided for the current year-to-date or the last twelve months-to-date, plus comparable data for the preceding year. The second-quarter condensed statements of consolidated income and reinvested earnings for the Quaker Oats Company are presented in Exhibit 12-1.

Frequently, companies do not issue separate fourth-quarter reports or provide fourth-quarter disclosure of summarized data because annual audited statements will be forthcoming. In such cases, a note to the annual financial statements should disclose the effect of the following items for the fourth quarter: disposals of a segment, extraordinary items, unusual or infrequently occurring items, and changes in accounting principles. Disclosure in the annual financial statements also should include the aggregate effect of year-end adjustments that are material to the fourth-quarter results.

REPORTING FOR BUSINESS SEGMENTS OF AN ENTERPRISE

The significance of reporting for segments is related closely to the corporate merger activity that took place during the 1960s. Prior to this time, merger activity could be characterized as either horizontal or vertical integration. *Horizontal integration* refers to the acquisition of companies in similar or closely related businesses, while *vertical integration* refers to acquisitions that would improve the production and/or marketing efforts of the acquiring company. However, due to increased legal and governmental pressure, the merger activity of the 1960s departed from earlier patterns and was characterized by the acquisition of companies with activities that primarily were unrelated to the activities of the acquiring company. These mergers resulted in what generally are referred to as *conglomerates* or diversified companies. To adapt to the competitive pressures of these companies, many other firms began to diversify internally rather than through business acquisitions. Many of today's businesses are characterized as diversified companies. For example, Sears Roebuck is involved in retail merchandising, automobile rentals, insurance, real estate sales, and securities brokerage.

It soon became apparent that disclosure of the aggregate activities of diversified companies in the form of consolidated financial statements no longer

---

[12]Accounting Principles Board Opinion No. 28, *op. cit.*, par. 30.

Exhibit 12-1
The Quaker Oats Company and Subsidiaries

Condensed Consolidated Statements of Income and Reinvested Earnings (Unaudited)

Dollars in Millions (Except Per Share Data)

	Three Months Ended December 31		Six Months Ended December 31	
	1993	1992	1993	1992
Net Sales	$1,353.9	$1,332.7	$2,888.2	$2,826.9
Cost of goods sold	672.0	677.5	1,421.6	1,418.0
Gross profit	681.9	655.2	1,466.6	1,408.9
Selling, general and administrative expenses	576.6	553.8	1,176.6	1,136.5
Interest expense—net	22.4	15.3	36.7	33.2
Other expense (income)—net	12.5	(5.9)	30.0	43.3
Income before income taxes and cumulative effect of accounting changes	70.4	92.0	223.3	195.9
Provision for income taxes	27.6	35.8	89.1	79.5
Income before cumulative effect of accounting changes	42.8	56.2	134.2	116.4
Cumulative effect of accounting changes—net of tax				(115.5)
Net income	42.8	56.2	134.2	0.9
Preferred dividends—net of tax	1.0	1.0	2.0	2.1
Net Income Available for Common	$ 41.8	$ 55.2	$ 132.2	$ (1.2)
Per Common Share:				
Income before cumulative effect of accounting changes	$ 0.63	$ 0.77	$ 1.94	$ 1.58
Cumulative effect of accounting changes				(1.59)
Net income	$ 0.63	$ 0.77	$ 1.94	$ (0.01)
Dividends declared	$ 0.53	$ 0.48	$ 1.06	$ 0.96
Average Number of Common Shares Outstanding (in thousands)	67,409	72,028	68,216	72,418
Reinvested Earnings:				
Balance beginning of period	$1,244.8	$1,071.2	$1,190.1	$1,162.3
Net income	42.8	56.2	134.2	0.9
Dividends	(36.0)	(34.7)	(72.5)	(70.5)
Common stock issued for stock purchase and incentive plans	(1.3)	(1.5)	(1.5)	(1.5)
Balance end of period	$1,250.3	$1,091.2	$1,250.3	$1,091.2

See accompanying notes to the condensed consolidated financial statements.

would satisfy the informational needs of various parties. For example, in the case of Sears Roebuck, consolidated financial statements would not reveal how each industry group or segment contributed to sales or earnings. Furthermore, it would be difficult to compare the financial statements of a company purely in retail merchandising to Sears' financial statements because of their diversified nature. In the mid 1960s, professional business groups, governmental agencies, and investors began to emphasize the importance of disclosing the business activities of the unrelated segments that composed a diversified company. While differing on the means and extent of implementing the desire for additional information, the concept of segmental reporting has been endorsed by the American Institute of Certified Public Accountants, the Financial Executives Institute, the Financial Analysts Federation, the National Association of Accountants, the Securities and Exchange Commission, and the Federal Trade Commission.

Although total-enterprise financial statements provide users with a basis for evaluating the performance of an enterprise as a whole, total performance is a function of the performance of the various segments that constitute the enterprise. Therefore, an analysis of a segment's investment opportunities, risks indicated by its profitability, its growth potential, and its production and marketing processes provides interested parties with an excellent basis for evaluating present and future performance of the segment and the enterprise as a whole. Segmental information also may provide users with an improved basis for making interenterprise comparisons between companies that have a single industry or product affiliation and segments of a similar nature within diversified companies.

There is a strong body of empirical research that supports the position that segmental data have utility. This research and the prominence of diversified companies effectively have established the importance of segmental data for maintaining an efficient capital market. For example, studies have suggested that segmental data can lead to more accurate predictions of enterprise earnings and changes in earnings levels. In addition, surveys have shown that sophisticated users, such as financial analysts, find the use of segmental data to be a significant factor in the area of security valuation.

STATEMENT OF FINANCIAL ACCOUNTING STANDARDS NO. 14

Prior to 1976, diversified companies were free to determine the extent of segmental information to be disclosed in their financial reports to the public. These disclosures frequently concentrated on information concerning segmental revenues and profit contributions. In 1976, the Financial Accounting Standards Board issued FASB Statement No. 14, *Financial Reporting for Segments of a Business Enterprise*, which deals with the following topics:

1. The qualifications of a reportable segment.
2. The specific segmental data that must be disclosed and how such data should be disclosed.
3. The additional data that must be disclosed concerning foreign operations, export sales, and sales to major customers.

The Statement sets forth minimum disclosure requirements for all public companies composed of reportable segments. Reporting companies also are encouraged to provide additional disclosures when relevant. However, the minimum disclosures need to be presented only when a public enterprise issues a complete set of annual financial statements that presents financial position, results of operations, and cash flows in conformity with generally accepted accounting principles.[13]

Definition of a Segment.   A major issue involved in segmental reporting is the determination of a business segment. Theoretically, a segment should be defined in response to the informational needs of user groups. For example, an equity investor may find the definition of segments in terms of product lines to be most useful, while the needs of another user may suggest that segments be defined in terms of broad geographical areas served by the company. Approaches to the definition of a segment have focused on such variables as geographical markets, product lines, broad industry groups, and/or profit centers employed for internal planning and control. Established classification systems for segmental reporting, such as the Standard Industrial Classification and the Enterprise Standard Industrial Classification, have been used in certain instances. However, research has suggested that such systems may not be the most appropriate means of defining business segments.

The FASB elected to define a segment as:

> . . . a component of an enterprise engaged in providing a product or service
> or a group of related products and services primarily to unaffiliated cus-
> tomers (i.e., customers outside the enterprise) for a profit.[14]

Although more decisive guidelines for the definition of a segment could have been established, the FASB recognized that no single set of segment criteria would be applicable to all companies. Therefore, the FASB concluded that the definition of a segment should be left to the discretion of management. However, the following factors should be considered when determining segments:

(a) The nature of the product. *Related products or services have similar purposes or end uses. Thus, they may be expected to have similar rates of profitability, similar degrees of risk, and similar opportunities for growth.*

(b) The nature of the production process. *Sharing of common or inter-changeable production or sales facilities, equipment, labor force, or service group or use of the same or similar basic raw materials may suggest that products or services are related. Likewise, similar degrees of labor intensiveness or similar degrees of capital intensiveness may indicate a relationship among products or services.*

(c) Markets and marketing methods. *Similarity of geographic market-ing areas, types of customers, or marketing methods may indicate a relationship among products or services. . . . The sensitivity of the market to price changes and to changes in general economic conditions*

---

[13]*FASB Statement No. 18,* "Financial Reporting for Segments of a Business Enterprise—Interim Financial Statements," removed the former requirement that interim financial statements include segmental information.

[14]Statement of Financial Accounting Standards No. 14, *Financial Reporting for Segments of a Business Enterprise* (Stamford: Financial Accounting Standards Board, 1977).

may also indicate whether products or services are related or unrelated.[15]

If practicable, these factors should be applied on a worldwide basis. If not practicable, foreign operations may be viewed as a single segment.

Given a defined industry segment, segmental data do not need to be disclosed unless the segment qualifies as a reportable segment by satisfying *one or more* of the following criteria:

(a) *Its revenue (including both sales to unaffiliated customers and interseg-ment sales or transfers) is 10 percent or more of the combined revenue (sales to unaffiliated customers and intersegment sales or transfers) of all of the enterprise's industry segments.*

(b) *The absolute amount of its operating profit or operating loss is 10 percent or more of the greater, in absolute amount, of:*

   (i) *The combined operating profit of all industry segments that did not incur an operating loss, or*

   (ii) *The combined operating loss of all industry segments that did incur an operating loss.*

(c) *Its identifiable assets are 10 percent or more of the combined identifiable assets of all industry segments.*[16]

Certain exceptions to these criteria are permitted. For example, if a segment currently fails to satisfy one or more of the criteria, but has done so in the past or is expected to do so in the future, segmental disclosures should be presented so that the comparability of past and future reporting periods is preserved. Alter-natively, if a segment currently happens to satisfy one or more of the criteria, but normally does not, it may be best to view the segment as nonreportable. How-ever, in this situation, appropriate reasons for not reporting segmental activities should be disclosed. Illustration 12-7 demonstrates the application of the criteria for determining whether a segment is reportable.

Other practical limitations concerning the number of reportable segments are identified as follows:

1. As the number of reportable segments increases above ten, serious consider-ation should be given as to whether the volume of segmental data begins to diminish the utility of segmental reporting.

2. The reportable segments in the aggregate should represent a substantial portion of the total enterprise's activities. The substantial portion test is satisfied if the combined revenue from *sales to unaffiliated customers* of all *reportable* segments is at least 75 percent of the combined revenue from *sales to unaffiliated customers* of all *industry* segments. If this test is not satisfied, additional segments should be classified as reportable until the test is satis-fied, subject to the practical limitation discussed in item (1).

3. If a single reportable segment accounts for a "dominant portion" of the total enterprise's activities, segmental reporting is not required, although the

---

[15]*Ibid.*, par. 100.
[16]*Ibid.*, par. 15.

Illustration 12-7

Reportable Segments: Demonstration of Criteria

Facts:

Whalen Corporation has classified its operations into industry segments and has provided the following data for each segment:

		Revenues			
Segment	Unaffiliated Customers	Intersegment Sales	Total	Operating Profit (Loss)	Identifiable Assets
A..........................	$100,000	$15,000	$115,000	$ 45,000	$ 280,000
B..........................	20,000		20,000	(10,000)	80,000
C..........................	230,000	40,000	270,000	130,000	1,100,000
D..........................	45,000	5,000	50,000	(60,000)	320,000
E..........................	37,000	8,000	45,000	25,000	295,000
F..........................	140,000	14,000	154,000	85,000	760,000
	$572,000	$82,000	$654,000	$215,000	$2,835,000
Corporate level..............	60,000		60,000	20,000	705,000
Total.....................	$632,000	$82,000	$714,000	$235,000	$3,540,000

Analysis:

The determination of which segments are reportable requires the following evaluation, in which only combined data relating to the segments (not including corporate-level activity) are employed:

1. Total sales to unaffiliated customers $572,000
    Total intersegment sales.. 82,000
    Combined revenue... $654,000

nature of this dominant segment should be disclosed. A dominant segment is one whose "revenue, operating profit or loss, and identifiable assets each constitute more than 90 percent of related combined totals for all industry segments, and no other industry segment meets any of the 10-percent tests. . ."[17]

Based on the basic facts presented in Illustration 12-7, the practical limitations regarding the number of reportable segments have been satisfied. There are no more than ten reportable segments, no segment is dominant, and the reportable segments represent a substantial portion of the enterprise's activities, determined as follows:

Sales to unaffiliated customers of all reportable segments (all segments except Segment B):

---

[17]*Ibid.*, par. 20.

Segment revenue required to satisfy criterion (a):

$$\$654,000 \times 10\% = \$65,400$$

2. Segment	Operating Profit	Operating Loss
A	$ 45,000
B		$10,000
C	130,000
D		60,000
E	25,000
F	85,000
Total	$285,000	$70,000

Portion of absolute amount of the greater of the operating profit or the operating loss to satisfy criterion (b):

$$\$285,000 \times 10\% = \$28,500$$

3. Segment identifiable assets required to satisfy criterion (c):

$$\$2,835,000 \times 10\% = \$283,500$$

Whether the criteria are satisfied is summarized as follows:

Segment	Revenue		Criterion Satisfied Operating Profit (Loss)		Identifiable Assets		Segment Reportable
A	Yes	($115,000 > $65,400)	Yes	($ 45,000 > $28,500)	No	($ 280,000 < $283,500)	Yes
B	No	($ 20,000 < $65,400)	No	($ 10,000 < $28,500)	No	($ 80,000 < $283,500)	No
C	Yes	($270,000 > $65,400)	Yes	($130,000 > $28,500)	Yes	($1,100,000 > $283,500)	Yes
D	No	($ 50,000 < $65,400)	Yes	($ 60,000 > $28,500)	Yes	($ 320,000 > $283,500)	Yes
E	No	($ 45,000 < $65,400)	No	($ 25,000 < $28,500)	Yes	($ 295,000 > $283,500)	Yes
F	Yes	($154,000 > $65,400)	Yes	($ 85,000 > $28,500)	Yes	($ 760,000 > $283,500)	Yes

All of the segments are reportable except for Segment B.

$$\$572,000 - \$20,000 = \$552,000$$

Minimum level of sales to unaffiliated customers of all industry segments:

$$\$572,000 \times 75\% = \$429,000$$

The sales to unaffiliated customers of all reportable segments exceed the minimum level needed to satisfy the substantial portion limitation.

Content of Segment Disclosure.   For each segment that has been determined to be reportable, the nature of the segment's products and services and its respective revenue, operating profit or loss, and identifiable assets must be disclosed. In addition, certain other disclosures are required.

Disclosure of Segmental Revenues.   The revenue to be disclosed by each of the reporting segments should include an amount for sales to unaffiliated customers and a separate amount for sales to other segments (intersegment sales). With respect to intersegment sales, the method of pricing these sales (transfer pricing) should be disclosed, and any change in methods should be discussed fully in terms of the nature and effect of the change.

Although a specific transfer pricing method is not required by FASB Statement No. 14, several methods are available. Alternative methods range from pricing based on incremental costs incurred to pricing based on negotiations that are intended to simulate actual market conditions. In the opinion of the authors, the objectives and utility of segmental reporting are best served by a transfer pricing method that, when possible, approximates the actual selling price that would have been experienced if the sale had involved an unaffiliated customer.

The reported revenue of each segment also should include interest earned from outside sources and interest earned on intersegment trade receivables. However, interest earned on advances or loans to other segments should not be included in revenues unless the lending segment's principal operations are of a financial nature.

Disclosure of Segmental Operating Profit.   Since operating profit is of primary interest to users of segmental data, each reportable segment must disclose its operating profit or loss, which represents the revenues discussed previously, including intersegment sales, less the operating expenses traceable to the revenues. Operating expenses that are not directly traceable to one segment but are common or traceable to several segments should be allocated among the benefiting segments on a reasonable basis. The allocation method selected should be disclosed as well as the nature and effect of any changes in methods.

A variety of expense allocation methods have been used, ranging from sophisticated modeling techniques to arbitrary methods that have not captured the true relationship between cost incurrence and segment performance. Theoretically, the allocation of common costs should be based on a cause-and-effect approach, since the costs would not be incurred if ultimately they did not benefit the segments. However, a controversy has focused on whether allocation is practical and whether it produces comparability among companies. As a result, an acceptable alternative approach avoids allocation altogether by disclosing only directly traceable costs. This alternative, however, presents the problem of having to distinguish clearly between directly traceable costs and allocable costs.

The operating profit or loss of each reportable segment should not include the effects of any of the following:

- General corporate expenses.
- Interest expense on nontrade advances or loans from other segments (except in the case of a segment that has borrowed from another segment whose operations are mainly financial in nature).
- Domestic and foreign income taxes.
- Equity in the profits or losses of unconsolidated subsidiaries and investees.
- Gains or losses on discontinued operations.
- Extraordinary items.
- The cumulative effect of changes in accounting principles.
- Minority interests.

The nature of the items excluded from the operating profit or loss should be disclosed, and an analysis of how the items relate to each segment should be provided. In addition to the disclosure of operating profit or loss, management may disclose other measures of segmental profit, such as profit contribution (segment revenue less directly traceable costs), if the nature of the profit measure is disclosed adequately.

Disclosure of Segmental Identifiable Assets.   To evaluate segmental profitability more fully, FASB Statement No. 14 requires disclosure of each reportable segment's identifiable assets that were employed to generate the revenue and operating profit or loss of that segment. Therefore, the tangible and intangible assets used exclusively by the segment and the allocated portion of shared assets are presented net of their related valuation allowances, such as accumulated depreciation and allowances for uncollectible accounts. Excluded from the measure of identifiable assets are those assets not used in the operations of a segment, such as corporate-level assets. Advances or loans to other segments should be excluded as well, unless the lending segment's operations are primarily financial in nature.

The various information presented for reportable segments normally will not equal the corresponding amounts for the consolidated whole. For example, the total of identifiable assets for the reportable segments will not equal the total assets of the consolidated whole. This difference in the totals is explained by noting that reportable amounts:

1. Do not include amounts traceable to those segments that are nonreportable.
2. Include intersegment transactions that are eliminated from consolidated amounts.
3. Do not include amounts traceable to corporate-level activities.

In order to reconcile to the consolidated amounts, several additional steps are necessary. First, the type of information to be disclosed by reportable segments also must be disclosed for all nonreportable segments as though they were one reportable segment. Second, intersegment activity must be separately disclosed. For example, if a segment includes an intersegment sale, this amount must be eliminated in order to reconcile it to consolidated sales. Finally, amounts traceable to corporate-level activities must be disclosed so that they agree with consolidated amounts.

The standard on segmental reporting also requires that the following additional disclosures be made:

1. For each reportable segment:
    (a) *the aggregate amount of depreciation, depletion, and amortization expense;*
    (b) *the amount of capital expenditures (i.e., additions to its property, plant, and equipment);*
    (c) *the enterprise's equity in the net income from and investment in the net assets of unconsolidated subsidiaries and other equity method investees whose operations are vertically integrated with that seg-*

*ment's operations and the geographic areas in which those vertically
integrated equity method investees operate;*

*(d)   the effect of a change in accounting principle on the operating profit
       in the period in which this change is made.*[18]

The segmental disclosures required by FASB Statement No. 14 must be
presented within the body of the financial statements, entirely in the footnotes to
the financial statements, or in separate schedules that are included as an integral
part of the financial statements. An example of the disclosure format appears in
Illustration 12-8.

Disclosure of Foreign Operations.   As discussed in the earlier chapters
dealing with foreign operations, international trading activity is a significant
part of today's business environment. Therefore, it is important for the user of
financial statements to be able to identify the extent to which such foreign
activity affects a multinational entity's performance. Certainly economic, political, and social differences between nations in which a company operates may
have a bearing on how financial information for a multinational company is

Illustration 12-8
Segmental Report
For Year Ended December 31, 19X8

	Reportable Segments		All Nonreportable Segments	Adjustments and Eliminations*	Consolidated
	A	B			
Revenues:					
From unaffiliated customers........	$10,000	$12,000	$5,000		$27,000
From intersegment sales..........	3,000		2,000	$(5,000)	
Total........................	$13,000	$12,000	$7,000	$(5,000)	$27,000
Operating profit....................	$ 3,000	$ 1,000	$ 500	$ (400)	$ 4,100
Equity in income of Co. X...........					300
General corporate expenses.........					(600)
Interest expense					(200)
Income from continuing operations before income taxes.............					$ 3,600
Identifiable assets at 12/31/X8	$20,000	$17,000	$8,000	($ 350)	$44,650
Investment in net assets of Co. X					6,350
Corporate assets....................					5,000
Total assets at 12/31/X8............					$56,000

*The nature of these adjustments and eliminations would be discussed in the notes accompanying this segmental report.

---

[18]*Ibid.*, par. 27.

evaluated. Recognizing the importance of international activity, the FASB also requires public companies to disclose key financial data for significant foreign operations.

An enterprise's foreign operations are defined as:

> . . . those revenue-producing operations (except for unconsolidated subsidiaries and other unconsolidated investees) that (a) are located outside of the enterprise's home country and (b) are generating revenue either from sales to unaffiliated customers or from intraenterprise sales or transfers between geographic areas.[19]

Information about a company's foreign operations and domestic operations must be disclosed if one or both of the following criteria are satisfied:

> (a) Revenue generated by the enterprise's foreign operations from sales to unaffiliated customers is 10 percent or more of consolidated revenue as reported in the enterprise's income statement.
> (b) Identifiable assets of the enterprise's foreign operations are 10 percent or more of consolidated total assets as reported in the enterprise's balance sheet.[20]

If an entity's foreign operations are conducted in two or more geographical areas, the required information should be presented separately for each significant foreign geographical area and in the aggregate for those foreign geographical areas not deemed to be significant. The groupings of foreign operations into geographical areas should reflect those factors that are most important to an entity's particular situation. Factors to be considered include geographical proximity, economic similarities, and similarities in business practices. For example, a geographical area may include all Latin American countries or all European Union countries. Once the geographical areas have been defined, those areas that are significant must be identified. A significant geographical area is one whose sales to unaffiliated customers or identifiable assets are 10% or more of the corresponding consolidated amount.

When the foreign operations of an enterprise satisfy the necessary criteria, the enterprise must disclose the following information for domestic operations and foreign operations, or if appropriate, for each significant foreign geographical area, and for the aggregate of foreign geographical areas deemed not to be significant:

1. Revenue as defined for segment disclosure, including sales between geographical areas,
2. Operating profit or loss as defined for segment disclosure, or net income or some other measure of profitability, and
3. Identifiable assets as defined for segment disclosure.

---

[19]*Ibid.*, par. 31.
[20]*Ibid.*, par. 32.

This information should be reconciled to the respective consolidated totals in a manner similar to that demonstrated in Illustration 12-8.

Export Sales and Sales to Major Customers.   The previous discussion regarding the disclosures for foreign operations does not focus on the domestic operation. However, it is important to note that a domestic operation may have foreign involvement in the form of import or export activity. In order to better understand the extent and effect of such involvement, the FASB requires the disclosure of export sales by public companies. When an entity's domestic operations contain sales to *unaffiliated* foreign customers, these export sales must be disclosed if they account for 10% or more of total entity sales to unaffiliated customers.

When an enterprise has sales to major customers or governmental agencies, sales to any single customer should be disclosed if these sales account for 10% or more of total enterprise revenue. For purposes of this disclosure, a group of entities under common control is considered to be a single customer. Federal, state, local, and foreign governments or agencies each should be considered a single customer.

When disclosure about major customers is appropriate, the nature and amount of the major sales and the identity of the segments making the sales should be disclosed. However, the names of the customers do not need to be disclosed.[21]

In order to illustrate the reporting for business segments, a portion of PepsiCo, Inc.'s 1993 annual report is presented in Exhibit 12-2.

Exhibit 12-2
Business Segments

This information constitutes Notes 2 and 3 to the Consolidated Financial Statements. (dollars in millions)

PepsiCo operates on a worldwide basis within three industry segments: beverages, snack foods and restaurants. The beverage segment primarily markets its Pepsi, Diet Pepsi, Mountain Dew and other brands worldwide and 7UP internationally, and manufactures concentrates for its brands for sale to franchised bottlers worldwide. The segment also operates bottling plants and distribution facilities located in the U.S. and key international markets, and distributes ready-to-drink Lipton tea products under a joint venture agreement. In addition, under separate distribution and joint venture agreements, the segment distributes certain previously existing as well as jointly-developed Ocean Spray juice products. The snack food segment manufactures, distributes and markets chips and other snacks worldwide, with Frito-Lay representing the domestic business. The international snack food business includes major operations in Mexico, the United Kingdom (U.K.) and Canada. The restaurant segment consists primarily of the operations of the worldwide Pizza Hut, Taco Bell and KFC chains. PFS, PepsiCo's restaurant distribution operation, supplies company-owned and franchised restaurants principally in the U.S. For purposes of this presentation, the net sales and operating profits of PFS' franchisee operations have been allocated to each restaurant chain.

---

[21]Statement of Financial Accounting Standards, No. 30, *Disclosure of Information about Major Customers* (Stamford: Financial Accounting Standards Board, 1979), par. 6.

"Unallocated Expenses, net" includes the corporate headquarters expenses, equity in net income of affiliates, minority interests—primarily in the Gamesa (Mexico) and Wedel (Poland) snack food businesses, foreign exchange translation and transaction gains and losses and other corporate items not allocated to the business segments. "Corporate Assets" consist principally of short-term investments held outside the U.S. and investments in affiliates.

PepsiCo has invested in about 70 joint ventures, principally international and all within PepsiCo's three industry segments, in which it exercises significant influence but not control. Equity in net income of these affiliates, which includes the 1992 unusual charge noted below, was $30.1, $40.1, and $32.2 in 1993, 1992 and 1991, respectively. The decline in 1993 primarily reflects expansion costs in the beverage affiliate in India and lower margins at Snack Ventures Europe (SVE). International snack food affiliates, which represented the largest component of equity in net income of affiliates, contributed $24.1, $23.2 and $20.5 in 1993, 1992 and 1991, respectively. Dividends received from affiliates totaled $16.4, $29.6 and $32.6 in 1993, 1992 and 1991, respectively.

PepsiCo's year-end investments in affiliates totaled $1.1 billion in 1993, $904.9 in 1992 and $1.1 billion in 1991. The increase in 1993 reflects investments in certain franchised bottling operations in Argentina and Mexico totaling $179.0 and smaller investments in 15 new international joint ventures, partially offset by partner buyouts, and resulting consolidation, of franchised bottling affiliates in Spain and the Northwestern U.S. as well as the KFC U.K. joint venture. The decline in 1992 reflected consolidation of two international snack food affiliates, due to the securing of a controlling interest in the Gamesa cookie joint venture (Mexico) and the partner buyout of Hostess Frito-Lay (Canada), partially offset by investments in the California Pizza Kitchen (CPK) domestic casual dining restaurant chain and SVE. Significant investments in affiliates at year-end 1993 included $223.4 in a Midwestern U.S. franchised bottler, $156.7 in the KFC Japan joint venture, $95.2 in a franchised bottler with operations in Argentina, Chile and Uruguay, $86.8 in CPK and $73.9 in SVE.

Unusual Items

Unusual charges in 1992 and 1991, principally for restructurings, totaled $193.5 in 1992 and $170.0 in 1991 as follows:

Beverages—1992 includes $145.0 in charges consisting of $115.4 to reorganize and streamline domestic operations, and $29.6 to streamline an acquired franchised bottling business in Spain and other international field operations.

Snack Foods—1992 includes a $40.3 charge principally to consolidate the Smiths and Walkers businesses in the U.K. 1991 includes $127.0 in charges consisting of $91.4 to streamline domestic operations, $23.6 to streamline operations in the U.K. and $12.0 to dispose of or reduce ownership in a small unprofitable business in Japan.

Restaurants—1991 includes $43.0 in charges at KFC consisting of $34.0 to streamline operations and $9.0 related to a delay in the U.S. rollout of a new product.

Unallocated Expenses, net—1992 includes an $8.2 charge to streamline operations of the SVE joint venture.

Impact of Accounting Changes on Comparability of 1992 to Prior Years

In 1992, PepsiCo adopted Statements of Financial Accounting Standards, "Employers' Accounting for Postretirement Benefits Other Than Pensions" (SFAS 106) and "Accounting for Income Taxes" (SFAS 109). As compared to the previous accounting method, the adoption of SFAS 106 reduced 1992 operating profit by $52.1, decreasing beverage, snack food and restaurant profits by $16.1, $28.2 and $6.1 (almost all domestic), respectively, and increasing 1992 unallocated expenses, net by $1.7. As compared to the previous accounting method, the adoption of SFAS 109 reduced 1992 operating profit by $20.7, decreasing beverage, snack food and restaurant profits by $6.3, $2.6 and $9.3, respectively, and increasing 1992 unallocated expenses, net by $2.5. (See Notes 10 and 13.)

Unusual items in 1990 and 1989 resulted in a total charge of $83.0 in 1990 and a net credit of $4.4 in 1989.

Included in operating profits for 1990 were charges for trade receivables exposures of $10.5 in domestic beverages and $10.6 in domestic snack foods, a $17.6 charge for closure of certain underperforming restaurants (Pizza Hut—$9.0, Taco Bell—$4.0 and KFC—$4.6) and reorganization charges of $10.4 for Pizza Hut. Included in unallocated expenses, net was an $18.0 charge for accelerated contributions to the PepsiCo Foundation and a $15.9 charge to reduce the carrying value of an international Pizza Hut affiliate.

(continued)

The net credit in 1989 consisted of a credit of $32.5 in international beverages resulting from a decision to retain an operation previously held for sale, reorganization charges of $12.3 in international beverages, $8.0 at KFC and $5.5 at Taco Bell and a $2.3 net charge in domestic snack foods.

Industry Segments:	Net Sales					Operating Profits				
	1993	1992	1991	1990	1989	1993	1992	1991	1990	1989
Beverages:										
Domestic	$ 5,918.1	$ 5,485.2	$ 5,171.5	$ 5,034.5	$ 4,623.3	$ 936.9	$ 686.3	$ 746.2	$ 673.8	$ 577.6
International	2,720.1	2,120.4	1,743.7	1,488.5	1,153.4	172.1	112.3	117.1	93.8	98.6
	8,638.2	7,605.6	6,915.2	6,523.0	5,776.7	1,109.0	798.6	863.3	767.6	676.2
Snack Foods:										
Domestic	4,365.3	3,950.4	3,737.9	3,471.5	3,211.3	900.7	775.5	616.6	732.3	667.8
International	2,661.5	2,181.7	1,512.2	1,295.3	810.5	288.9	209.2	140.1	160.3	105.9
	7,026.8	6,132.1	5,250.1	4,766.8	4,021.8	1,189.6	984.7	756.7	892.6	773.7
Restaurants:										
Domestic	8,025.7	7,115.4	6,258.4	5,540.9	4,684.8	685.1	597.8	479.4	447.2	356.5
International	1,330.0	1,116.9	868.5	684.8	565.9	92.9	120.7	96.2	75.2	57.8
	9,355.7	8,232.3	7,126.9	6,225.7	5,250.7	778.0	718.5	575.6	522.4	414.3
Combined Segments:										
Domestic	18,309.1	16,551.0	15,167.8	14,046.9	12,519.4	2,522.7	2,059.6	1,842.2	1,853.3	1,601.9
International	6,711.6	5,419.0	4,124.4	3,468.6	2,529.8	553.9	442.2	353.4	329.3	262.3
	$25,020.7	$21,970.0	$19,292.2	$17,515.5	$15,049.2	$3,076.6	$2,501.8	$2,195.6	$2,182.6	$1,864.2
Unallocated Expenses, net						(170.1)	(130.6)	(83.8)	(140.5)	(91.6)
Operating Profit						$2,906.5	$2,371.2	$2,111.8	$2,042.1	$1,772.6
Results by Restaurant Chain:										
Pizza Hut	$ 4,128.7	$ 3,603.5	$ 3,258.3	$ 2,949.9	$ 2,453.5	$ 372.1	$ 335.4	$ 314.5	$ 245.9	$ 205.5
Taco Bell	2,901.3	2,460.0	2,038.1	1,745.5	1,465.9	253.1	214.3	180.6	149.6	109.4
KFC	2,325.7	2,168.8	1,830.5	1,530.3	1,331.3	152.8	168.8	80.5	126.9	99.4
	$ 9,355.7	$ 8,232.3	$ 7,126.9	$ 6,225.7	$ 5,250.7	$ 778.0	$ 718.5	$ 575.6	$ 522.4	$ 414.3

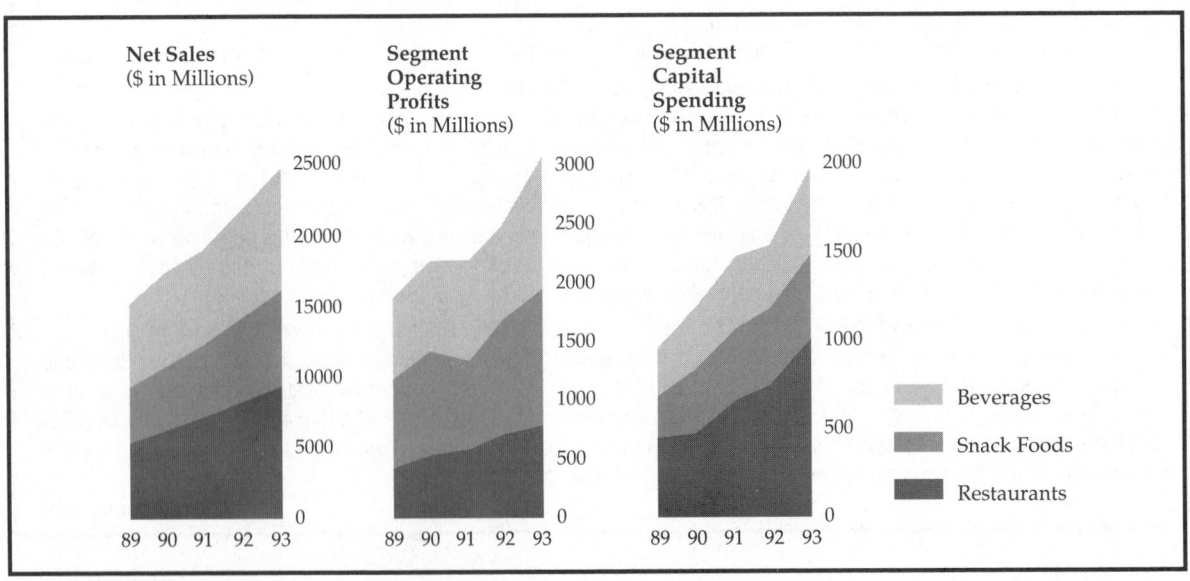

Net Sales ($ in Millions)

Segment Operating Profits ($ in Millions)

Segment Capital Spending ($ in Millions)

Beverages
Snack Foods
Restaurants

Geographic Areas[a]:	Net Sales			Segment Operating Profits			Identifiable Assets		
	1993	1992	1991	1993	1992	1991	1993	1992	1991
United States	$18,309.1	$16,551.0	$15,167.8	$2,522.7	$2,059.6	$1,842.2	$13,589.5	$11,957.0	$10,777.8
Canada and Mexico	2,819.5	2,214.2	1,434.7	324.8	251.0	198.7	2,581.1	2,395.2	917.3
Europe	1,819.0	1,349.0	1,170.3	47.4	52.6	30.9	2,666.1	1,948.4	2,367.3
Other	2,073.1	1,855.8	1,519.4	181.7	138.6	123.8	1,675.1	1,282.0	1,138.7
Total	$25,020.7	$21,970.0	$19,292.2	$3,076.6	$2,501.8	$2,195.6	$20,511.8	$17,582.6	$15,201.1

Industry Segments:				Identifiable Assets					
	1993	1992	1991				1993	1992	1991
Beverages	$ 9,105.2	$ 7,857.5	$ 6,832.6	By Restaurant Chain:					
Snack Foods	4,994.5	4,628.0	4,114.3	Pizza Hut			$2,232.9	$1,676.8	$1,454.3
Restaurants	6,412.1	5,097.1	4,254.2	Taco Bell			2,075.9	1,523.7	1,157.1
Corporate	3,194.0	3,368.6	3,574.0	KFC			2,103.3	1,896.6	1,642.8
Total	$23,705.8	$20,951.2	$18,775.1				$6,412.1	$5,097.1	$4,254.2

				Capital Spending[b]					
	1993	1992	1991				1993	1992	1991
Beverages	$ 491.3	$ 343.7	$ 425.8	By Restaurant Chain:					
Snack Foods	491.4	446.2	406.0	Pizza Hut			$ 295.0	$ 212.8	$ 214.7
Restaurants	1,004.4	757.2	648.4	Taco Bell			459.4	339.0	230.5
Corporate	20.8	18.0	4.1	KFC			250.0	205.4	203.2
Total	$ 2,007.9	$ 1,565.1	$ 1,484.3				$1,004.4	$ 757.2	$ 648.4
Domestic	$ 1,388.0	$ 1,069.0	$ 1,036.9						
International	619.9	496.1	447.4						
Total	$ 2,007.9	$ 1,565.1	$ 1,484.3						

				Acquisitions and Investments in Affiliates[c]					
	1993	1992	1991				1993	1992	1991
Beverages	$ 711.5	$ 717.5	$ 285.2	By Restaurant Chain:					
Snack Foods	75.5	201.3	47.7	Pizza Hut			$ 312.9	$ 247.7	$ 103.1
Restaurants	588.7	480.4	470.7	Taco Bell			186.8	72.4	52.3
				KFC			89.0	160.3	315.3
Total	$ 1,375.7	$ 1,399.2	$ 803.6				$ 588.7	$ 480.4	$ 470.7
Domestic	$ 757.3	$ 549.5	$ 608.3						
International	618.4	849.7	195.3						
Total	$ 1,375.7	$ 1,399.2	$ 803.6						

(a) The results of centralized concentrate manufacturing operations in Puerto Rico and Ireland have been allocated based upon sales to the respective areas.

(b) Includes noncash amounts related to capital leases, largely in the restaurant segment, of $26.3 in 1993, $15.5 in 1992 and $26.5 in 1991.

(c) Includes noncash amounts related to treasury stock and debt issued in domestic transactions of $364.5 in 1993, $189.5 in 1992 and $162.7 in 1991. Of these noncash amounts, 65%, 58% and 8%, respectively, related to the beverage segment and the balance related to the restaurant segment.

(continued)

	Amortization of Intangible Assets						
	1993	1992	1991		**1993**	1992	1991
Beverages	$ 157.4	$ 137.6	$ 118.3	By Restaurant Chain:			
Snack Foods	40.9	40.5	35.9	Pizza Hut	$ 44.7	$ 33.3	$ 25.6
Restaurants	105.4	87.8	54.1	Taco Bell	23.0	16.4	11.4
				KFC	37.7	38.1	17.1
Total	$ 303.7	$ 265.9	$ 208.3		$ 105.4	$ 87.8	$ 54.1

	Depreciation Expense						
	1993	1992	1991		**1993**	1992	1991
Beverages	$ 358.5	$ 290.6	$ 251.7	By Restaurant Chain:			
Snack Foods	279.2	251.2	215.8	Pizza Hut	$ 193.4	$ 150.5	$ 136.6
Restaurants	457.2	374.3	324.4	Taco Bell	124.6	101.5	82.5
Corporate	6.6	6.9	8.1	KFC	139.2	122.3	105.3
Total	$ 1,101.5	$ 923.0	$ 800.0		$ 457.2	$ 374.3	324.4

Source: Courtesy, Pepsico, Inc. © 1993.

QUESTIONS

1. Explain why interim statements may be more useful if an interim period is viewed as an integral part of a larger annual period.
2. If a company expensed annual promotional fees, how would it account for such fees if they were incurred in the first quarter of the year?
3. Explain how a temporary liquidation of LIFO inventory is accounted for in an interim period.
4. If a change in accounting principle occurs in the third quarter of the year, how should it be disclosed in the interim statement?
5. If the estimated annual effective tax rate is different from an earlier interim estimate, how is the change in rate accounted for?
6. If a company typically accrues bonuses for officers at year end, how should such bonuses be reflected in interim statements?
7. Assume a company has a year-to-date (YTD) operating loss and that income in subsequent interim periods is not "more likely than not." If the YTD operating loss exceeds income in the carryback period, how is the YTD tax benefit determined?
8. If a decision to discontinue an operation is made in the third quarter, how does the decision affect previously reported interim data?
9. Why does segmental data improve interfirm comparability?
10. What factors should be considered in the determination of what constitutes a segment?
11. What criteria must be satisfied in order for an identified segment to be considered a reportable segment?
12. A reportable segment is a manufacturer and has interest income traceable to sales on account to other segments and working capital loans to other segments. In determining the reportable segments' operating profits, how should the interest income be included?
13. Identify the factors that may explain why the sum of revenues traceable to reportable segments does not equal consolidated revenues.

14. A U.S. public company has engaged in sales to foreign companies and governments. Some of the foreign companies are affiliates of the U.S. company. Under what conditions must these sales be separately disclosed?

EXERCISES

Exercise 1. The following data represent the accounting results and projections of four separate cases for the year ended September 30, 19X9, with YTD totals as of May 31, 19X9.

	Case A	Case B	Case C	Case D
Statutory tax rate.................	34%	34%	28%	28%
Year-to-date realized pretax income (loss).........................	$100,000	$(260,000)	$(120,000)	$160,000
Pretax income (loss) projected for the remainder of the year........	85,000	(320,000)	180,000	(245,000)
Annual tax credit available.........	6,000	21,000	3,000	3,000

The following additional information is available:

Case B: Pretax income was $145,000 in 19X6, $190,000 in 19X7, and $110,000 in 19X8. The effective tax rate was 30% in each of these years.

Case C: A total deduction of $15,000 is included in the 19X9 figures. Such deduction is not allowed for income tax purposes. Established seasonal patterns assure the realization of the tax benefit associated with the YTD loss and the $3,000 available tax credit.

Case D: YTD income includes interest income of $18,000 on tax-free municipal bonds. Pretax income (loss) was $80,000 in 19X6, ($20,000) in 19X7, and $60,000 in 19X8. The effective tax rate was 35% in each of these years.

Calculate the effective annual tax rate for each case.

Exercise 2. Dreyfus Corporation has second-quarter revenues of $730,000. In addition, the following expense information is available:
(a) During the quarter, 4,000 units of inventory were sold even though only 3,400 units were purchased at an average price of $150 each. The first quarter ending inventory consisted of 2,000 units with a cost of $120 each. The company anticipates additional purchases will cost $170 each, and its inventory at year end will consist of 3,000 units. Cost of sales is determined by the LIFO inventory method.
(b) An outside research organization was paid $120,000 during the quarter for new technology which should benefit the company for three years.
(c) The company allows employees to carry over to future years, vacation time which has not been previously used. At year end, the company typically accrues a vacation liability which averages about $80,000. Vacation time is assumed to be both earned and taken uniformly throughout the year.
(d) The company has a statutory tax rate of 30% on the first $100,000 of pretax income and 32% on all additional amounts. Tax credits of $8,000 have been earned to date, although $15,000 of credits are anticipated for the entire year. The company had pretax income in quarter one of $40,000 and an effective tax rate of 25%. The company is projecting third and fourth quarter pretax income to be $70,000.
Calculate the second-quarter after-tax net income from operations.

Exercise 3. The statutory tax rate for 19X7 is 30%. For each of the following cases, determine the YTD tax benefit traceable to the YTD operating loss.

	Case A	Case B	Case C	Case D
YTD operating (loss)	$(80,000)	$(80,000)	$(80,000)	$(20,000)
Projected interim income (loss) for balance of year:				
More likely than not	120,000		50,000	(40,000)
Not more likely than not		30,000		
Carryback income (tax rate):				
Third prior year (30%)				30,000
Second prior year (25%)		20,000	40,000	4,000
First prior year (25%)		10,000	10,000	24,000
Likely future income in carryforward period				30,000

Exercise 4. Wert Company has sought assistance in preparing its second-quarter income statement for 19X2. Figures for sales revenue, selling expenses, and general and administrative expenses are $860,000, $68,000, and $117,000, respectively.

For each of the following situations, determine the cost of goods sold and prepare an interim income statement in good form for the three months ended June 30, 19X2.

(1) Wert uses a standard cost accounting system for inventory and product costs. Net unfavorable cost variances for the second quarter total $2,600 and represent the difference between actual and standard production costs. Management considers such variances as a manufacturing cost and includes them in the income statement above the gross profit line. It is expected that an unfavorable purchase price variance of $900 will be absorbed by December 31, 19X2. Production for the second quarter at standard cost was $600,000. Beginning and ending finished goods inventories (standard cost) were $71,000 and $98,000, respectively.

(2) The LIFO cost of goods sold was $596,000 and includes sales of 15,000 units costed out at their 19X1 base layer cost of $7 per unit. The current replacement cost of these units is $11 per unit. It is expected that the 19X2 year-end inventory will be 2,000 units less than the 19X1 year-end inventory.

(3) Beginning inventory of $52,000 reflects a first-quarter write-down of $2,200 due to the application of the lower-of-cost-or-market rule. Through a market price recovery in the second quarter, inventory increased in value by $3,750. Wert purchased 18,000 units of inventory ($28 per unit) in the second quarter. Ending inventory (FIFO basis) was $60,500.

Exercise 5. Weiss Corporation reported $65,000 of pretax income from continuing operations during the first quarter of 19X9. Projected income for the remainder of 19X9 was $140,000, of which $110,000 was traceable to continuing operations. Estimated annual tax credits were $5,000. The statutory tax rate is 34%. Second-quarter pretax income from continuing operations was $42,000, with anticipated income from continuing operations for the remainder of 19X9 of $60,000.

During the second quarter, Weiss Corporation decided to discontinue an operation. Prior to the measurement date, amounts traceable to the discontinued operation included a $4,000 income for the first quarter and a $5,500 loss for the second quarter. The discontinued operation had a second-quarter, postmeasurement date loss of $8,000. The operation estimated additional losses prior to disposition to be $30,000 plus an estimated gain on the disposal of the assets of $10,000. The company revised its estimated tax credits traceable to annual continuing operations to $8,000.

Prepare in good form the calculation of the original and restated interim income (loss) and tax expense (benefit) for Weiss Corporation's first two quarters of 19X9. Include a supporting schedule showing the calculation of the estimated effective tax rates.

Exercise 6. Tripper Industries, Inc. decided to change accounting principles in the third quarter of the current year. Originally, the first six months had a YTD pretax income of $40,000, a projected pretax income for the balance of the year of $60,000, and an estimated annual effective tax rate of 20%. The rate is based on statutory rates of 15% on the first $50,000 of income, 25% on the next $50,000 of income, and 35% on amounts in excess of $100,000. Had the new principle been adopted at the beginning of the year, the first six months' pretax income would have been $30,000 and projected pretax income for the balance of the year would have been $30,000. The effect of the change in principle on prior years is to decrease net income by $50,000.

The third-quarter pretax income, based on the new accounting principle, is $50,000, and the projected pretax income for the balance of the year is $40,000.

Calculate the pretax income and related tax expense (benefit) for the first three quarters of the current year.

Exercise 7. Williams Incorporated is in its fifth year of operations and has had prior pretax income and taxes as follows:

	Pretax Income	Effective Tax Rate	Tax Expense
19X1	$30,000	26%	$ 7,800
19X2	40,000	28%	11,200
19X3	30,000	25%	7,500
19X4	20,000	25%	5,000

In the first quarter of 19X5, the company experienced a pretax loss of $50,000 and projected income for the balance of the year was zero.

In the second quarter of 19X5, the company once again incurred a pretax loss of $20,000. However, income of $30,000 was projected for the balance of the year and is more likely than not to be recognized. In the third quarter, the company recognized an extraordinary gain of $50,000 and reported a modest pretax operating income of $20,000. Income of $25,000 was projected for the balance of the year and is more likely than not to be recognized. A pretax income of $15,000 was recognized in the final quarter along with $2,000 of tax credits. The final quarter included a penalty expense of $4,000 which is not deductible for tax purposes.

Calculate the tax expense (benefit) for each quarter of the current year assuming the 19X5 statutory tax rate is 25%. Tax credits are subject to the same carryback and carryforward rules as net operating losses.

Exercise 8. Selected information is available for Segments A, B, C, and D and a corporate level as follows:

| | Segment | | | | |
	A	B	C	D	Corporate
Sales:					
To unaffiliated customers	$ 800,000	$ 700,000		$100,000	
To affiliated customers.....................	50,000	100,000		10,000	
Cost of sales...............................	600,000	400,000		120,000	
Interest expense:					
On trade receivables.......................	30,000	20,000		5,000	
On loans from B	10,000				
On outside loans..........................	20,000	10,000		2,000	$ 60,000

	Segment				
	A	B	C	D	Corporate
Net interest income:					
On trade receivables.....................	30,000	30,000		2,000	
On loans to A............................		10,000	$ 40,000		
On outside loans.........................			350,000		
On investments..........................					120,000
Cumulative effect of change in accounting principle.....................		40,000			
Identifiable assets excluding loans receivable from A..................................	2,400,000	3,000,000	2,200,000	100,000	1,300,000
Loans receivable from A		120,000	400,000		

Assuming Segment C is a financial institution and all other segments are manufacturers, determine which segments are reportable.

Exercise 9. The following information is given for the seven segments of Staven Supplies:

Segment	Revenues	Operating Profit (Loss)	Identifiable Assets
1.................................	$1,540,000	$ 602,000	$1,600,000
2.................................	805,000	(208,000)	870,000
3.................................	1,948,000	530,000	1,250,000
4.................................	1,070,000	375,000	1,800,000
5.................................	760,000	220,000	965,000
6.................................	980,000	402,000	1,400,000
7.................................	1,071,000	(106,000)	1,380,000
Corporate-level items...................	820,000	170,000	560,000
	$8,994,000	$1,985,000	$9,825,000
Intercompany adjustments and eliminations.........................	(278,300)	(75,000)	(305,000)
Consolidated total......................	$8,715,700	$1,910,000	$9,520,000

10% of the revenues of segments 2, 4, and 5 are traceable to intersegment sales.
(1) Determine which segments are reportable.
(2) Determine whether a substantial portion of Staven's total operations is represented by reportable segments.
(3) Determine which segments would qualify as significant geographical areas, assuming the following geographical classifications:

Location	Segment
Central America	1, 2, 3
Middle East	4, 5
Western Europe	6, 7

Exercise 10. Badger Industries is a large international company with extremely diversified activities. These activities include:
(a) Food-processing operations in Chicago, Tulsa, and Louisville. Processed foods under several labels are sold to independent grocers throughout the Midwest and Southwest. Cans used in the operation are manufactured by Krystal Can Company, a wholly owned subsidiary.
(b) Seven citrus groves in central Florida. Approximately 70% of a harvest is trucked to the company's Louisville food-processing operation; the balance of the harvest is processed, on location, into frozen juice concentrates.

(c) A Cleveland operation that manufactures packaging for perishable food products and cardboard packaging for transporting equipment components, such as engines and transmissions.

(d) Four large resort hotels, three of which are located along the eastern seaboard, and one of which is located in the Bahamas.

(e) A chain of travel agencies in the New York and Boston areas.

(f) A paper products division that manufactures napkins, paper plates, paper towels, and greeting cards. These products are sold to grocery stores and variety stores.

Determine how the activities of Badger should be classified into segments for external reporting purposes.

PROBLEMS

Problem 12-1. Prior to the second quarter of 19X9, Portico, Inc. had depreciated its assets by the straight-line method. However, during the second quarter of 19X9, the company changed to an accelerated method of depreciation. The effect of the change on the first quarter of 19X9 was an increase in pretax income of $5,000. The effect of the change in prior years was to decrease pretax income by $84,000. The first quarter of 19X9 had originally reported a pretax income of $30,000 and a tax expense of $5,832. The projected income for the balance of the year was originally estimated to be $60,000 at the end of the first quarter. However, due to the change in depreciation methods, the projection should have been $75,000. Pretax income, based on the new depreciation method for the second quarter of 19X9 and the balance of the year, is $25,000 and $80,000, respectively. At this time, anticipated annual tax credits were $4,000.

During the third quarter of 19X9, the company experienced a pretax income of $40,000 and projected $20,000 of pretax income for the balance of the year. Annual tax credits were anticipated to be $3,000. Also during the quarter, the company experienced an extraordinary gain of $20,000, which is taxed at 20%.

The statutory tax rate is 15% on the first $50,000 of income, 25% on the next $50,000, and 35% on all additional income.

Required:

Calculate the pretax income and related tax expense for the first three quarters of 19X9.

Problem 12-2. Paxton Company has sought assistance in preparing its third-quarter income statement for 19X8. Pertinent data for the third quarter are as follows:

(a) The estimated effective tax rate has been revised in the third quarter to 40% as compared to management's earlier estimate of 30%. This new rate also is to be used to restate prior periods due to the decision to discontinue operations.

(b) Income before taxes from all operations was $1,420,000.

(c) The cost of goods sold from all operations was determined by the LIFO inventory method as follows:

	Total	Average Cost Per Unit
Beginning inventory	$ 500,000	$50
Purchases	1,800,000	60
Goods available	$2,300,000	
Ending inventory	100,000	
	$2,200,000	

It is expected that the annual 19X8 ending inventory will be $400,000 and the replacement cost of inventory will be $65 per unit during the fourth quarter of 19X8.

(d) Included in the revenues is a rather unusual, first-time sale of marketable securities that were acquired in an earlier year as part of an investment portfolio. The securities sold during the third quarter had a basis of $210,000 and were sold for $185,000.

(e) During the third quarter, management adopted a plan calling for the discontinuation of its engineering consulting division. The performance of this division, excluding disposals of assets, is as follows:

	Quarter			
	1	2	3	4 (Expected)
Revenue	$800,000	$ 400,000	$ 200,000	$ 300,000
Depreciation.................	(25,000)	(20,000)	(18,000)	(18,000)
Other operating expenses.....	(700,000)	(1,100,000)	(622,000)	(632,000)
Income before taxes.........	$ 75,000	$ (720,000)	$(440,000)	$(350,000)

Approximately 90% of all third-quarter revenue and expenses relate to the period prior to the measurement date. It is expected that the operations of the division during 19X9 prior to final disposal will result in a pretax loss of $100,000.

Some of the assets of the discontinued division were sold prior to the measurement date for a loss of $50,000. The balance of the division's assets will be disposed of in 19X9 for an estimated gain of $500,000.

(f) Revenue for the third quarter also includes $160,000 of revenue resulting from the settlement of a rate dispute traceable to the first quarter of 19X8. The amount of the settlement could not be estimated previously.

Previously issued interim income statements reported pretax net losses of $950,000 for the first two quarters of 19X8. At that time, only $400,000 of the losses were carried back to prior years (at a prior-year rate of 30%), with no assurance that the balance of the losses had tax benefits (i.e., could be carried forward).

Required:

Prepare in good form a partial income statement for the third quarter of 19X8 and all necessary supporting schedules.

Problem 12-3. Mikelson Company, a California corporation listed on the Pacific Coast Stock Exchange, budgeted activities for 19X5 as follows:

	Amount	Units
Net sales	$6,000,000	1,000,000
Cost of goods sold	3,600,000	1,000,000
Gross profit.......................................	$2,400,000	
Selling, general, and administrative expenses	1,400,000	
Operating income	$1,000,000	
Nonoperating revenue and expenses......................		
Income before income taxes............................	$1,000,000	
Estimated income taxes (current and deferred)	550,000	
Net income..	$ 450,000	
Earnings per share of common stock	$4.50	

Mikelson has operated profitably for many years and has experienced a seasonal pattern of sales volume and production. For 19X5, sales volume is expected to follow a quarterly pattern of 10%, 20%, 35%, and 35%, respectively, because of the seasonality of the industry. Also, due to production and storage capacity limitations, it is expected that production will follow a pattern of 20%, 25%, 30%, and 25% per quarter, respectively.

At the end of the first quarter of 19X5, the controller of Mikelson prepared and issued the following interim report for public release:

	Amount	Units
Net sales	$ 600,000	100,000
Cost of goods sold	360,000	100,000
Gross profit	$ 240,000	
Selling, general, and administrative expenses	275,000	
Operating loss	$ (35,000)	
Loss from warehouse fire	(175,000)	
Loss before income taxes	$(210,000)	
Estimated income taxes		
Net loss	$(210,000)	
Loss per share of common stock	$(2.10)	

The following additional information is available for the first quarter, but was not included in the public information released:

(a) The company uses a standard cost system in which standards are set at currently attainable levels on an annual basis. At the end of the first quarter, there was an underapplied fixed factory overhead (volume variance) of $50,000 that was treated as an asset at the end of the quarter. Production during the quarter was 200,000 units, of which 100,000 were sold.

(b) The selling, general, and administrative expenses were budgeted on a basis of $900,000 fixed expenses for the year plus $0.50 variable expenses per unit of sales.

(c) Assume the warehouse fire loss met the conditions of an extraordinary loss. The warehouse had an undepreciated cost of $320,000; $145,000 was recovered from insurance on the warehouse. No other gains or losses are anticipated this year from similar events or transactions, nor has Mikelson had any similar losses in preceding years; thus, the full loss will be deductible as an ordinary loss for income tax purposes.

(d) The effective income tax rate, for federal and state taxes combined, is expected to average 55% of income before income taxes during 19X5. There are no permanent differences between pretax accounting income and taxable income.

Required:

(1) Without reference to the specific situations described in this problem, what are the standards of disclosure for interim financial data (published interim financial reports) for publicly traded companies? Explain.

(2) Identify the weaknesses in form and content of Mikelson's interim report without reference to the additional information.

(3) For each of the four items of additional information, indicate the preferable treatment for interim reporting purposes and explain why that treatment is preferable.

(AICPA adapted)

Problem 12-4. During 19X8, Midway Corporation reported first six months' pretax income of $120,000 from continuing operations and a year-to-date tax expense of $37,668. The tax expense reflects projected pretax income for the balance of the year of $100,000 and the following statutory tax rates:

Tax on first $50,000.............................. 15%
Tax on next $25,000 .... 25%
Tax on next $25,000 .... 34%
Tax on next $235,000 .... 39%
Tax on remaining income 34%

The first six months also included the following nonordinary items:

A. Extraordinary gain........................ $10,000
B. Loss on discontinued operations .... (80,000)
C. Loss on noncurrent marketable securities
   recorded as a component of owners'
   equity .... (85,000)

Required:
Calculate the incremental tax impact traceable to each of the nonordinary items directly affecting income or owners' equity.

Problem 12-5.　Miretni Corporation had pretax income in prior years as follows:

	Pretax Income	Effective Tax Rate
19X5	$20,000	25%
19X6	10,000	22%
19X7	15,000	25%
19X8	5,000	30%

Future likely income in the carryforward period is estimated to be $30,000, and the future enacted tax rate is 22%.

During the first quarter of 19X9, the company reported pretax income of $30,000 and projected a loss for the balance of the year of $70,000. The statutory tax rate for 19X9 is 30%, and the company anticipates annual tax credits of $2,000. The tax credits may be carried back against taxes in the prior three years and/or against taxes on future likely income in the carryforward period.

During the second quarter of 19X9 management decided to discontinue one of its operations. Data relating to this operation are as follows:

Premeasurement date income (loss):
　Quarter 1, 19X9 .... $(20,000)
　Quarter 2, 19X9 .... $(30,000)
Postmeasurement date income (loss):
　Quarter 2, 19X9 .... $ (8,000)
　Subsequent quarters .... $(40,000)

The first quarter's 19X9 projection of a $70,000 loss for the balance of the year would have been a projected income of $40,000 had the discontinued operation not been included. Furthermore, the projected annual tax credit would have been only $1,200, excluding the discontinued operation.

During the second quarter of 19X9, the company reported a pretax income from continuing operations of $36,000. The company projected income from continuing operations for the balance of the year to be $54,000 and an annual tax credit to be $3,000.

Required:

Prepare in good form the calculation of the income (loss) and tax expense (benefit) for the first two quarters of 19X9.

Problem 12-6. Niemoth Inc. has retained you to prepare interim data. The following information is available.

(a) During the third quarter of 19X4, it was discovered that the second quarter contained the effect of a LIFO liquidation, which was expected to be offset by year end. The liquidation of 2,000 units was recorded at their base cost of $12 per unit even though the year-end liquidation was estimated to be only 500 units. Units purchased during the last half of 19X4 are expected to have an average cost of $16 per unit. Prior to the detection of this error, the income for the first six months of 19X4 was $38,000.

(b) During the third quarter of 19X4, the company decided to change its method of accounting for depreciable assets. The effect of the change was to decrease prior years' income by $65,000, increase the first six months' income by $7,000, and increase the third-quarter income to $32,000.

(c) During the fourth quarter of 19X4, the company decided to discontinue an operation with the following realized and unrealized income (loss):

> Premeasurement date:
> Prior years (19X3 and 19X2) . . . . $(27,000)
> First six months of 19X4 0
> Third quarter of 19X4 . . . . (8,000)
> Fourth quarter of 19X4 . . . . (7,000)
> Postmeasurement date:
> Fourth quarter of 19X4 . . . . (6,000)
> 19X5 operations . . . . (22,000)
> 19X5 disposal of assets 26,000

Fourth-quarter income from continuing operations was $16,000, and annual tax credits were actually $2,000.

(d) During the first quarter of 19X5, the continuing operations generated income of $28,000. The discontinued operation reported operating losses of $24,000 with projected gains on disposal of assets of $20,000. These latter amounts are in lieu of the earlier postmeasurement date estimates for 19X5 generated in the fourth quarter of 19X4.

(e) The statutory tax rate is 30%, and income and tax credit projections were as follows:

Quarter	Balance of Year Projected Income (Loss)	Projected Annual Tax Credits
First six months, 19X4:		
Originally	$(70,000)	$4,000
After change in depreciation	$(52,000)	$4,000
After eliminating disc. operations	$(52,000)	$4,000
Third quarter, 19X4:		
Originally	$(30,000)	$1,000
After eliminating disc. operations	$ 11,000	$1,000
First quarter of 19X5	$ 82,000	$6,000

(f) Income as originally reported in the prior three years was $34,000 in total and was taxed at a rate of 25%. Future income in the carryforward period is not considered likely.

Required:

Calculate the interim income and tax expense for all the quarters of 19X4 and the first quarter of 19X5.

Problem 12-7. At the end of the first quarter of 19X9, Interco reported pretax income from continuing operations of $30,000 and projected another $60,000 of income for the balance of the year. It was estimated that certain tax credits totaling $6,000 would be available during the year.

Midway through the second quarter, the company decided to change its method of computing depreciation. The change had the following effects:

	Incremental Impact on Pretax Income
Prior years	$25,000
First quarter	7,000
First half of second quarter.........	4,000
First-quarter projection for the balance of the year	22,000

The second quarter resulted in a pretax loss of $80,000 which was based on the newly adopted depreciation method. Unfortunately, a loss of $2,000 was projected for the balance of the year. The estimated amount of annual tax credits was reduced to zero.

Due to the poor results in the first half of the year, a decision was made in the third quarter to discontinue an operation. The discontinued operation had the following profits and losses:

	Income/ (Loss)
Premeasurement date realized effects traceable to the discontinued operation:	
First quarter	$(20,000)
Second quarter	(60,000)
Third quarter	(10,000)
Portion of earlier projections traceable to the discontinued operation:	
First-quarter projection	(15,000)
Second-quarter projection	(62,000)
Postmeasurement date effects traceable to the discontinued operation:	
Third quarter	(8,000)
Fourth-quarter estimate	(50,000)
Subsequent-year estimate	70,000

The third-quarter pretax income from continuing operations was $30,000, with a projected income of $20,000 for the balance of the year. It was estimated that annual tax credits of $2,000 would be available to the company in the fourth quarter.

Pretax income from continuing operations in the prior three years totaled $10,000 as originally reported. The statutory tax rate for the prior and current years is 30%. The likely income estimated for next year is $100,000 from continuing operations.

Required:

Prepare in good form the calculation of the income (loss) and tax expense (benefit) for the first three quarters of 19X9. Include restated quarters as needed, and prepare a schedule showing the calculation of the effective tax rates.

Problem 12-8. Tress Corp. is a rapidly growing company that has diversified into a number of different segments. The following partial trial balance, which includes the effect of intercompany transactions, is for the year ended December 31, 19X9:

Net Sales	$(14,332,250)
Cost of Goods Sold	7,180,000
General and Administrative Expenses.	1,620,000
Gain on Sale of Fixed Asset.	(100,000)
Investment Income	(315,000)
Interest Income.	(162,000)
Extraordinary Loss.	230,000
Discontinued Operations:	
Loss from Operations	781,000
Loss from Disposal of Assets.	481,000
Income Tax Expense	940,000

Tress Corp. has five distinct segments (A–E) in addition to corporate operations. Net sales are allocated to the segments as follows:

Segment	Net Sales
A.	$ 4,023,500
B.	2,749,000
C.	574,500
D.	6,185,250
E	800,000
Total	$14,332,250

Ten percent of D's sales are made to A, and 7% of B's sales are made to C. The cost of the goods sold to A by D is $200,000, and the cost of the goods sold to C by B is $144,000. The total cost of goods sold is allocated to the segments by the following percentages: A 30%, B 29%, C 6%, D 24%, and E 11%. Of the items C purchased from B, 25% are included in C's ending inventory.

Of general and administrative expenses, 20% are traceable to corporate operations. The balance is allocated in proportion to the segment revenues, including interest income and the gain on the sale of the fixed asset.

Investment income is traceable to corporate operations.

Interest income is traceable directly to the segments and the corporate level as follows:

Segment A.	$48,000
Segment B	19,000
Segment C	
Segment D.	60,000
Segment E	12,000
Corporate level	23,000

Segment B's (a manufacturing segment) interest income includes $9,000 traceable to a short-term $100,000 loan to C.

Unconsolidated assets are identifiable as follows:

	A	B	C	D	E	Corporate
Current assets.	$ 912,000	$ 681,000	$ 305,000	$ 309,000	$ 389,000	$ 115,000
Property, plant, and equipment (net)	7,136,000	4,643,000	1,480,000	4,181,000	1,543,000	1,737,000

Included in B's property, plant, and equipment is a machine that B purchased at the beginning of the year from A for $300,000. Segment A originally purchased the machine for $250,000, two years prior to the sale. Accumulated depreciation (straight-line method) on the machine was $50,000 at the time of the sale. Segment B recorded $30,000 of depreciation on the machine for the year based on the straight-line method. The gain on the sale of equipment is included in A's revenue.

Required:

Develop a schedule that will report the revenues, operating profits, and identifiable assets of the reportable segments and other segments and will reconcile these items to the December 31, 19X9 consolidated amounts.

Problem 12-9. The following data pertain to segmental and corporate-level activity of Justice Corporation for 19X9.

Segment	Net Revenue	Cost of Sales	General and Administrative Expenses	Assets
A	$ 400,000	$ 250,000	$ 50,000	$ 450,000
B	250,000	100,000	90,000	370,000
C	1,000,000	700,000	150,000	960,000
D	500,000	450,000	100,000	650,000
E	1,100,000	600,000	250,000	1,000,000
F	150,000	100,000	100,000	300,000
Corporate	40,000	N/A	50,000	280,000
	$3,440,000	$2,200,000	$790,000	$4,010,000

During the year, Segment A sold inventory with a cost of $140,000 to Segment D for $200,000. Of this purchase from Segment A, one-fourth of the inventory remains in Segment D's ending inventory. Segment A also lent Segment B $50,000 during the year of which $30,000 remains unpaid. Interest income of $4,000 is included in Segment A's net revenues. Segment E, a lending institution, made various loans to Segment F during the year. The annual interest income was $28,000, and Segment E has a year-end loan receivable from Segment F of $80,000. On July 1, 19X9, Segment B sold equipment with a book value of $270,000 to Segment C for $300,000. The equipment will be depreciated by Segment C over 10 years by the straight-line method.

Required:

(1) Determine which of the segments are reportable.
(2) Determine if the practical limitations concerning the number of reportable segments have been satisfied.
(3) Identify and calculate the various eliminations that are necessary to reconcile the segmental data to the corresponding consolidated amounts.

Problem 12-10. Agri-Tech Company is composed of six segments. The revenues, operating profit, and identifiable assets of each segment for the year ended December 31, 19X3, are as follows:

Segment	Revenues	Operating Profit (Loss)	Identifiable Assets
A	$ 20,000	$ 5,000	$ 25,000
B	280,000	90,000	210,000
C	15,000	(7,000)	30,000
D	175,000	20,000	70,000
E	35,000	12,000	60,000
F	45,000	15,000	45,000
Corporate level			20,000
	$570,000	$135,000	$460,000

Segments A through C are domestic segments; Segments D through F are foreign geographical areas.

The cost of goods sold for domestic segments is equal to 30% of revenues, including interest income. The cost of goods sold for foreign operations is 25% of the sales price.

Corporate expenses account for $23,250 of the general, administrative, and selling expenses, which total $300,000.

The provision for income tax for 19X3 is $25,500. Interest expense on corporate-level debt is $12,000. All revenues are to unaffiliated customers except:

(a) A sale of goods from domestic Segment C to foreign Segment D. The goods were transferred at a price of $3,000. As of year end, 20% of these goods remain in D's inventory.

(b) At midyear, domestic Segment B advanced to foreign Segment D the sum of $5,000, which is to be repaid with interest in one year at an annual interest rate of 10%. Domestic Segment B is a financial institution.

(c) A sale identical to that described in (a) was made by Segment B to Segment C.

Required:

Develop a segmental report for Agri-Tech Company based on geographical areas. Be sure to include support for the determination of reportable foreign operations by geographical area.

CHAPTER 13

The Disclosure of Earnings Per Share Data

The determination of earnings per share (EPS) of common stock has received considerable attention from the accounting and financial communities because EPS is significant with respect to the evaluation of an entity's past and future operations. The importance of EPS also has been demonstrated by both theoretical analysis and empirical research dealing with security valuation and dividend policy.

THE SUBSTANCE OF APB OPINION NO. 15

Accounting Principles Board Opinion No. 15, *Earnings per Share*, requires on the face of the income statement the disclosure of EPS data that are consistent with the income statement presentation. Therefore, per share data normally are presented for each of the following levels of income: income from continuing operations, discontinued operations, extraordinary items, the cumulative effect of changes in principles, and net income.[1] The purpose of this per share disclosure is to show the potential or prospective effect that certain securities will have on EPS. These securities include common and preferred stocks, bonds, warrants, stock options, stock purchase contracts, stock subscriptions, and other agreements to issue stock.

---

[1]Mutual enterprises, registered investment enterprises, government-owned enterprises, and not-for-profit enterprises are not subject to this requirement. Per share data also need not be prepared for parent company statements accompanying consolidated statements, for statements of wholly owned subsidiaries, and for special purpose statements. Statement of Financial Accounting Standards No. 21 has amended APB Opinion No. 15 to the extent that EPS disclosure for nonpublic enterprises no longer is required.

Rather than focusing on EPS of outstanding stock, the per share calculation emphasizes a statistic that will have maximum predictive value. Therefore, attention is placed on determining what EPS would be if certain securities were converted into common stock and if the conversion effect would be dilutive (i.e., cause a decrease in EPS). This approach is conservative, since, in most cases, the disclosure of antidilutive effects on EPS (i.e., potential increases in EPS) is not permitted.

The extent of the EPS disclosure also is dependent upon whether the capital structure of an entity is viewed as simple or complex. A *simple* capital structure has no securities outstanding (or agreements to issue such securities) that, in the aggregate, could dilute earnings per outstanding common share. If there are securities outstanding that, in the aggregate, could dilute earnings per outstanding common share, but such dilution is less than 3%, this capital structure also is considered to be simple. A capital structure is *complex* if various securities outstanding could have a dilutive effect of at least 3%.

For simple capital structures, per share data should be labeled as *earnings per common share*. Corporations whose capital structures are complex are required to present two measures of EPS (dual presentation): primary earnings per share and fully diluted earnings per share.

Primary earnings per share (PEPS) is the amount of net income attributable to each share of common stock plus other securities that are in substance equivalent to common stock and are referred to as *common stock equivalents*. The PEPS disclosure reflects the prospective viewpoint of APB Opinion No. 15. For example, a user of financial statements may be concerned with the following question: Given a constant level of income, if changes occur in the entity's capital structure, what would future EPS be? Such a question is significant particularly when agreements that could increase outstanding shares already exist. If EPS data are to serve predictive purposes, then the possible effect of common stock equivalents, which eventually may or may not increase the number of outstanding shares of common stock, must be disclosed. If EPS data were to serve only as an indicator of past operations, however, then the effect of common stock equivalents would be of little value.

Fully diluted earnings per share (FDEPS) is the amount of net income attributable to each share of common stock, common stock equivalent, and *other dilutive securities*. For the most part, the other dilutive securities influencing FDEPS will consist of securities that failed to meet the conditions established for common stock equivalents, and of common stock equivalents whose effect on FDEPS and PEPS is computed differently. The intent of disclosing FDEPS is to provide per share data that reflect the maximum potential dilution arising from securities that, upon conversion or exercise, would increase the number of common shares outstanding. PEPS may be described as a conservative measure, while FDEPS is an ultraconservative measure.

The basic starting point for the calculation of PEPS and FDEPS is determining earnings per common share. This latter per share statistic is computed as follows:

$$\text{Earnings per Common Share} = \frac{\text{Adjusted Net Income (ANI)}}{\text{Weighted Average Number of Shares Outstanding During the Period (S)}}$$

The *adjusted net income* (ANI) represents reported net income reduced by the amount of noncumulative preferred stock dividends declared this period or the current period dividends in arrears on cumulative preferred stock. In those capital structures where two or more classes of common stock exist, per share data are computed for the "ordinary" class of common stock. Therefore, net income must be adjusted also for the dividends declared or currently in arrears on other classes of common stock.

The computation of PEPS and FDEPS is a repetitive process for assessing the prospective effect of potentially dilutive securities on per share data. Each potentially dilutive security will have an assumed effect on the number of shares used to compute EPS and may have an assumed effect on the net income used in the computation. As each security is considered, a *share adjustment* (SA), representing the change in shares traceable to the security, and an *income adjustment* (IA), representing the change in income traceable to the security, must be determined. Again, all securities will have a share adjustment, but not all securities will have an income adjustment. For example, if a convertible preferred stock were considered the equivalent of common stock, the number of shares used to compute EPS would be increased by a share adjustment equal to the number of common shares that would have been issued upon conversion of the preferred stock. In addition, the earnings used to compute EPS would be increased by an income adjustment equal to the current dividends on preferred stock that would not have been declared if the preferred stock had been converted into common stock.

The basic methodology for computing EPS, which is demonstrated in Illustration 13-1, involves the following steps:

1. For each security, calculate $\text{EPS}_i = \dfrac{\text{ANI}_{i-1} + \text{IA}_i}{S_{i-1} + \text{SA}_i} = \dfrac{\text{ANI}_i}{S_i}$

   where: ANI_{i-1} = the adjusted net income before considering security i.
   IA_i = income adjustment traceable to security i.
   S_{i-1} = the shares assumed to be outstanding before considering security i.
   SA_i = the share adjustment traceable to security i.
   ANI_i = the adjusted net income considering security i.
   S_i = the shares assumed outstanding considering security i.

2. Determine the change in EPS, as follows: $\Delta\text{EPS}_i = \text{EPS}_i - \text{EPS}_{i-1}$
   where: ΔEPS_i = the change in EPS resulting from the evaluation of security i.

3. Consider whether security i is dilutive, as follows:

   If ΔEPS_i is negative, then security i has a dilutive effect and should be considered.

   If ΔEPS_i is positive, then security i has an antidilutive effect and usually should be ignored.

Illustration 13-1

Basic Methodology for Computing EPS

Assume that EPS of common stock is $2 $\left(\dfrac{ANI}{S} = \dfrac{\$2,000,000}{100,000} \right)$.

Assume that there are two common stock equivalents ($i = 1, 2$) with income adjustments (IA) and share adjustments (SA) as indicated in the following analysis:

Earnings per common share	ANI_{i-1}	IA_i	ANI_i	S_{i-1}	SA_i	S_i	EPS_i
	$200,000		$200,000	100,000		100,000	$2.00
$i = 1$	200,000	$20,000	220,000	100,000	20,000	120,000	1.83
$i = 2$	220,000		220,000	120,000	10,000	130,000	1.69*

*This amount will be reported as the EPS.

Although the sign of EPS will indicate whether or not a security is dilutive, other procedures can be used to identify antidilutive securities before the change in EPS actually is measured. These procedures are discussed in later sections of the chapter.

The earnings per common share (ANI ÷ S) is the basis upon which the potential dilutive effect of the first security is determined. It also may be necessary to compare EPS_{i-1} with the EPS for another level of income because a security may have a dilutive effect on one level of income (e.g., income from continuing operations) and an antidilutive effect on another level of income (e.g., an extraordinary loss). Since a security that has a dilutive effect on *any* level of income should be included in the computation of per share data for all other levels, the base EPS against which the dilutive effects of other securities is assessed should be the *highest* income figure (e.g., income from continuing operations or perhaps income after extraordinary gains).

To demonstrate this concept of assessing the dilutive effect of a common stock equivalent, assume the following:

Income from continuing operations	$100,000
Extraordinary loss	(20,000)
Net income	$ 80,000
Weighted average number of common shares outstanding	40,000

The earnings per common share is as follows:

Income from continuing operations per common share	$2.50
Extraordinary loss per common share	(.50)
Net income per common share	$2.00

Assuming that a common stock equivalent will result in a share adjustment of 10,000 shares and an income adjustment of $22,500 on income from continuing operations, the EPS considering the common stock equivalent is as follows:

Income from continuing operations per share
  [($100,000 + $22,500) ÷ (40,000 + 10,000)] $2.45
Extraordinary loss per share [$20,000 ÷ (40,000 + 10,000)]. (.40)
Net income per share $2.05

In this example, if net income is the base for evaluating potential dilution, the common stock equivalent would be ignored because it is antidilutive ($2.05 versus $2.00). However, if the base against which dilution is evaluated is the highest income figure, or income from continuing operations in this example, the common stock equivalent would be considered as dilutive ($2.45 versus $2.50). Therefore, in order to assess properly the dilutive nature of a common stock equivalent, its effect on the highest level of income should be the determining factor.

PRIMARY EARNINGS PER SHARE

As mentioned previously, primary earnings per share represents the earnings per share of common stock and common stock equivalents. The initial problem in calculating PEPS is to determine which securities are common stock equivalents. As defined in APB Opinion No. 15, a common stock equivalent is:

> . . . *a security which is not, in form, a common stock but which usually contains provisions to enable its holder to become a common stockholder and which, because of its terms and the circumstances under which it was issued, is in substance equivalent to a common stock.*[2]

The designation of a security as a common stock equivalent is based on an evaluation of the security's substance rather than its form. Changes in the economic value of a common stock equivalent are largely a function of changing values resulting from earnings and earnings potential of the common stock to which they are equivalent. This functional relationship exists even if the common stock equivalent is not converted into the common stock or such conversion is not imminent. The various types of common stock equivalents are discussed in the following paragraphs.

OPTIONS AND WARRANTS

Options and warrants represent rights to acquire shares of common stock in exchange for cash (exercise price) in accordance with underlying agreements.

---

[2]Accounting Principles Board Opinion No. 15, *Earnings per Share* (New York: American Institute of Certified Public Accountants, 1969), par. 25.

The following securities also are considered to be the equivalent of options and warrants: stock purchase contracts, stock subscriptions not yet fully paid, deferred compensation plans requiring the issuance of common stock,[3] and convertible securities allowing or requiring the payment of cash at conversion (regardless of yield). These securities derive their entire value from the right to acquire common stock and, therefore, are viewed automatically as common stock equivalents at all times. However, as a practical matter, a security will not be included in the calculations of PEPS unless the following criteria are satisfied:

1. The security must be exercisable within five years from the end of the current period.

2. The market price of the common stock obtainable upon exercise must be greater than the exercise price for substantially all of three consecutive months ending with the last month of any past or present period for which per share data are being presented. Once the three-month test is satisfied in any period, past or present, the security will be considered a common stock equivalent from that period on (assuming that the first criterion is satisfied as well).

The second criterion is established as a practical matter rather than as an absolute necessity. It prevents securities from being in and out of the EPS computation because of market price fluctuations above and below the exercise price.

Assuming that the two criteria have been met, the option or warrant will not enter into the calculation of PEPS unless the effect is dilutive. Such an effect will be experienced if, during the reporting period, the average market price of the common stock obtainable upon exercise is greater than the exercise price. The reporting period typically is three months; however, if a longer period is involved, a quarterly averaging technique may be employed.

Outstanding options or warrants that qualify as common stock equivalents are assumed to be exercised at the beginning of the period or at the issuance date, if later. The assumed exercise of these securities would result in the generation of funds in an amount equal to the *earliest* effective exercise price during the five-year period multiplied by the assumed number of shares to be obtained. These hypothetical funds could be employed in a variety of ways. For example, the funds could be used to reduce debt and, thereby, reduce interest expense, to purchase short-term government securities as an investment, or to expand the business and, thereby, earn the corporation's normal return on invested capital.

The APB recognized that some use of the funds had to be assumed, even though there was no certainty that the assumed use would approximate the actual use of funds received when options or warrants actually were exercised. Therefore, to achieve consistency, the APB recommended the use of the *treasury stock method*, which assumes that the generated funds are used to acquire common stock at the average market price for the period. This assumption is

---

[3]For a detailed discussion of the treatment of stock compensation plans in EPS computations, see FASB Interpretation No. 31, *Treatment of Stock Compensation Plans in EPS Computations* (Stamford: Financial Accounting Standards Board, 1980).

advantageous because the purchase of common stock does not result in an income adjustment. However, if a warrant allows or requires the tendering or retirement of debt, or if a convertible security requires the payment of cash upon conversion, an income adjustment would be necessary. This adjustment would be equal to the net-of-tax interest on debt or the dividend on convertible preferred stock.

For each option or warrant, the share adjustment under the treasury stock method is determined by using the following formula:

$$\text{Share Adjustment (SA)} = \begin{array}{c}\text{Total Shares Obtainable}\\\text{upon Exercise of Security}\end{array} - \begin{array}{c}\text{Exercise Proceeds}\\\hline\text{Average Market}\\\text{Price of Shares}\end{array}$$

The share adjustment always will be a positive number because options or warrants cannot influence PEPS unless the effect is dilutive, i.e., unless the average market price is greater than the exercise price. The share adjustment must be converted into a weighted average in those instances where the security was not outstanding during the entire period. If a security is exercised during the period, the number of treasury shares assumed to be acquired also is based on the average market price of the shares prior to exercise.

To demonstrate the treasury stock method, assume that options to acquire 4,000 shares of common stock were granted on January 1, 19X2, and still are outstanding as of December 31, 19X2. The options expire two years from the date of the grant and can be exercised at a price of $12 per share. EPS prior to considering the options is $2, based on 25,000 shares. Assuming an average annual market price of $13.25, EPS would be computed as follows:

Income adjustment (IA): Not applicable
Share adjustment (SA):

$$(SA) = \begin{array}{c}\text{Total Shares Obtainable}\\\text{upon Exercise of Security}\end{array} - \left[\begin{array}{c}\text{Exercise Proceeds}\\\hline\text{Average Market}\\\text{Price of Shares}\end{array}\right]*$$

$$= 4,000 - \frac{(\$12 \times 4,000 \text{ shares})}{\$13.25} = 4,000 - 3,623$$

$$= 377 \text{ shares}$$

*The maximum number of treasury shares that could be acquired assuming all options are exercised and all treasury shares are purchased at the average market price.

EPS considering option (EPS_i):

$$EPS_i = \frac{ANI_{i-1} + IA_i}{S_{i-1} + SA_i}$$

$$= \frac{\$50,000 + 0}{25,000 + 377} = \$1.97$$

When the reporting period is no longer than three months, a *quarterly averaging technique* should be used in applying the treasury stock method. However, if market prices are relatively stable during the year, the treasury stock method may be applied on an annual basis using the annual average market price, as was done in the previous example. The quarterly averaging technique as well as the concepts affecting the application of the treasury stock method for options and warrants to be considered in the computation of PEPS are demonstrated in Illustration 13-2.

Illustration 13-2

PEPS Computations: Options and Warrants

1. At the beginning of 19X6, 250,000 shares of common stock were outstanding. The net income for 19X6 was $400,000.
2. During 19X6 the following stock warrants existed:
   Warrant X—10,000 warrants issued in 19X2, giving the holder of each warrant the right to purchase 1 share of common stock for $40. 1,000 warrants were exercised on June 30, 19X6.
   Warrant Y—5,000 warrants issued in 19X4, giving the holder of each warrant the right to purchase 1 share of common stock for $50 anytime after December 31, 19Y2.
3. Both warrants X and Y previously had met the three-month test.
4. Relevant market price information for 19X6 was as follows:

Quarter	Average Market Price
1	$41
2	43
3	49
4	53

Calculation of Income and Share Adjustments for PEPS

Stock Warrant X

This warrant is considered in the calculation of PEPS because it meets both the five-year and three-month tests.

9,000 Warrants Not Exercised

Income adjustment: Not applicable
Share adjustment:

Using the Quarterly Averaging Technique

Quarter	Shares Obtainable	Treasury Shares Acquired	SA
1	9,000	$\dfrac{\$360,000}{\$41} = 8,780$	220
2	9,000	$\dfrac{\$360,000}{\$43} = 8,372$	628
3	9,000	$\dfrac{\$360,000}{\$49} = 7,347$	1,653
4	9,000	$\dfrac{\$360,000}{\$53} = 6,792$	2,208
			4,709

Weighted average SA: 4,709 ÷ 4 = 1,177 shares

(continued)

1,000 Warrants Exercised

Income adjustment: Not applicable
Share adjustment:

Using the Quarterly Averaging Technique

Quarter	Shares Obtainable	Treasury Shares Acquired	SA
1	1,000	$\dfrac{\$40,000}{\$41^*} = 976$	24
2	1,000	$\dfrac{\$40,000}{\$43^*} = 930$	70
3	Not applicable		—
4	Not applicable		—
			94

Weighted average SA: 94 ÷ 4 = 24 shares

*Average market price during the period prior to exercise.

Stock Warrant Y

This warrant is not considered in the calculation of PEPS because it fails to meet the five-year test.

Calculation of PEPS

	ANI_{i-1}	IA_i	ANI_i	S_{i-1}	SA_i	S_i	EPS_i
Earnings per common share............	$400,000		$400,000	250,500*		250,500	$1.5968
X (not exercised)	400,000		400,000	250,500	1,177	251,677	1.5893
X (exercised).........................	400,000		400,000	251,677	24	251,701	1.5892
Y	Not a common stock equivalent—fails 5-year test						

*Weighted average of shares outstanding during the year: 250,000 shares + 1/2 of 1,000 shares issued on June 30 = 250,500.

THE SPECIAL 20% RULE

The treasury stock method is complicated further when the potential exercise of all options and warrants, whether dilutive or not, would result in the actual issuance of additional shares that, in the aggregate, exceed 20% of the outstanding shares of common stock at the end of the period. In this case, all options and warrants that meet the five-year and three-month criteria are assumed to be exercised, whether dilutive or not, and the aggregate exercise proceeds are applied as follows:

   a. *As if the funds obtained were first applied to the repurchase of outstanding common shares at the average market price during the period (treasury stock method) but not to exceed 20% of the outstanding shares; and then*

   b. *As if the balance of funds were applied first to reduce any short-term or long-term borrowings and any remaining funds were invested in U.S.*

> *government securities or commercial paper, with appropriate recogni-*
> *tion of any income tax effect.*[4]

The results of these two steps are aggregated for all options and warrants, and if the net effect is dilutive, all options and warrants should enter into the determination of PEPS. With the 20% rule in effect, an income adjustment may result as well.

To demonstrate the 20% rule, assume that options to acquire 15,000 shares of common stock were granted on November 1, 19X0, and are outstanding at the end of 19X2. The options expire on December 31, 19X4, and may be exercised at $20 per share. In addition, on April 30, 19X1, warrants to acquire 10,000 shares of common stock were issued. These warrants are outstanding as of December 31, 19X2, expire on December 31, 19X6, and may be exercised at $25 per share. For the year 19X2, 100,000 shares of common stock were outstanding, net income was $450,000, and the only outstanding debt of the company was $200,000 in 5% bonds. The tax rate is 40%, and the average market price of common stock in all quarters was $22 per share. Because the total number of shares (15,000 + 10,000, or 25,000) obtainable by the options and warrants is greater than 20% of the outstanding common stock (20% × 100,000, or 20,000 shares), the 20% rule is applicable and would be applied to 19X2 as follows:

Total proceeds [(15,000 × $20) + (10,000 × $25)] $550,000
Less proceeds used to purchase up to 20,000 shares at $22 each 440,000
Proceeds available to retire debt and interest $110,000

Share adjustment:
  SA = 25,000 shares – 20,000 shares = 5,000 shares
Income adjustment:
  IA = $110,000 × 5% interest rate × (1 – 40% tax rate) = $3,300

The PEPs is calculated as follows: $EPS_i = \dfrac{\$450,000 + \$3,300}{100,000 + 5,000} = \$4.32$

If the market value of the common stock had been higher, it is possible that 20,000 shares of treasury stock would not have been acquired. For example, using the same assumptions, except that the average market price was $30 per share, the share and income adjustments would be as follows:

Share adjustment:
  SA = 25,000 shares – 18,333 shares ($550,000 ÷ $30) = 6,667 shares
Income adjustment:
  Not applicable because all available proceeds were used to acquire treasury stock in an amount not exceeding 20% of the outstanding common stock.

CONTINGENT SHARE AGREEMENTS

Contingent share agreements involve the issuance of common shares when certain conditions are met. Generally, such agreements outline conditions involving one or more of the following:

---

[4]Accounting Principles Board Opinion No. 15, *op. cit.*, par. 38.

1. The passage of time along with other conditions.
2. The maintenance of some level of earnings.
3. The attainment of some level of earnings.
4. Changes in the market price of shares that require the issuance of additional shares.

The calculation of PEPS generally will include shares called for by a contingent share agreement subject to the following guidelines:

1. Shares will be included if the contingency has been satisfied.
2. The share adjustment will include the shares since the beginning of the period or the date of inception of the agreement if later.
3. Although a share adjustment will be required, an income adjustment will not be necessary since the conditions of the agreement have been achieved or are assumed to be achieved.
4. If subsequently the contingency is no longer satisfied, previous EPS calculations will be retroactively restated to remove the contingent shares.

Current-period PEPS calculations always will include contingent shares that are issuable solely upon the passage of time. If the necessary condition is the attainment in the current period of a level of earnings that has been achieved, the necessary shares will be included in the calculation of PEPS. For those contingent share agreements that call for the maintenance or attainment of the present level of earnings in a subsequent period, the necessary shares will be included in current period PEPS. However, if in the subsequent period the earnings level has not been maintained, the shares will be excluded from the calculation of PEPS, and earlier calculations that included the shares will be retroactively restated. To illustrate, assume that Reynolds, Inc. has 500,000 shares of common stock outstanding during 19X7, net income of $750,000, and two contingent share agreements. Contingent share agreement A became binding at the beginning of 19X7 and calls for the issuance of 20,000 common shares if 19X7 net income is at least $700,000. Contingent share agreement B became binding on July 1, 19X7, and calls for the issuance of 60,000 common shares if 19X8 net income is at least equal to the 19X7 level. The calculation of PEPS would be as follows:

$$PEPS = \frac{\$750,000 + 0}{500,000 + 20,000 + 30,000} = \$1.36$$

Notice that the share adjustment for agreement B is 30,000 shares, which reflects the fact that the agreement became binding on July 1, 19X7. If the 19X8 net income is only $720,000, the 19X7 PEPS would be restated so that the previously included share adjustment of 30,000 shares would be removed as follows:

$$PEPS = \frac{\$750,000 + 0}{500,000 + 20,000} = \$1.44$$

If a contingent share agreement calls for the attainment of a higher level of earnings in the future, PEPS would not include the contingent shares because the condition has not yet been satisfied. If the condition is satisfied in a subsequent period, the EPS calculations for earlier periods should not be restated.

Those agreements that call for the issuance of additional shares if certain market price changes occur present a special situation. If market prices at the end of the current period would result in the issuance of additional shares, the calculation of PEPS will include a share adjustment. Assume that a company issued 100,000 shares to a party on January 1, 19X7 when the market price of a common share was $10 for a total market value of $1,000,000 (100,000 × $10). A contingent share agreement exists that states that if the market value for these shares is less than $1,000,000 at the end of 19X8, additional shares will be issued so that a total market value of $1,000,000 is achieved. If the market value per share at the end of 19X7 is $9.50, it would require a total of 105,263 shares ($1,000,000/$9.50) to equal the required total value. Therefore, the 19X7 calculation of PEPS would include a share adjustment for the additional 5,263 shares to be issued per the contingent share agreement. Earlier reported EPS would be retroactively restated if the number of shares ultimately required by the agreement changes. For example, if in the above situation the final market value at the end of 19X8 is $9.70, then only 103,093 shares ($1,000,000/$9.70) would be required to produce the required market value. Therefore, only 3,093 additional shares would have to be issued, and the earlier reported EPS would be restated to reflect a share adjustment of 3,093 rather than the previous 5,263 shares.

CONVERTIBLE SECURITIES

A convertible security is one that can be converted into common stock at the option of the holder. Therefore, a portion of the security's value may be traceable to the value of the related common stock. At the time of original issuance, if a significant portion of the convertible security's value is traceable to this conversion feature, the security should be considered a common stock equivalent.

Effective Yield Test.   The effective yield test is used for determining whether a convertible security is a common stock equivalent. According to this test, if the convertible security's effective yield, based on the market price at the time of issuance, is less than two-thirds of the then current average Aa corporate bond yield, the security should be considered a common stock equivalent. Satisfaction of the yield test suggests that the holder of convertible securities is willing to accept less than the current rate of return (as indicated by the average Aa corporate bond yield) because of the intrinsic value associated with the convertible securities' being equivalent to common stock.

In applying the effective yield test, it should be noted that:

1. It is a one-time test, applied at original issuance, and the security either is or is not classified as a common stock equivalent at that time. However, if another convertible security, with the same terms (excluding market price or issue price) as the security failing the yield test, exists or is issued later and is considered a common stock equivalent, then the security initially failing the test should be reclassified as a common stock equivalent.

2. The yield test using the Aa corporate bond yield is applicable to securities issued after February 28, 1982.[5] Securities issued prior to that date should use the bank prime interest rate rather than the bond yield for purposes of the test.

3. If the dividend or interest rate on the convertible security is scheduled to change over the next five-year period, the lowest scheduled rate during that period should be used for the yield test.

In addition to meeting the effective yield test, a convertible security must be convertible within five years from the end of the current reporting period if the security is to be considered a common stock equivalent.

The "If Converted" Method.   For each outstanding convertible security that is determined to be a common stock equivalent, it is assumed that the security was converted into common stock as of the beginning of the period or the issuance date, if later.[6] Therefore, both a share adjustment and an income adjustment are necessary. The share adjustment is determined by calculating the weighted average number of common shares that would have been outstanding if conversion had taken place. If various conversion rates exist over the five-year period, the conversion rate in effect during the current period (or if not immediately convertible, the earliest effective conversion rate) should be used. The income adjustment is equal to the net-of-tax interest expense or the preferred stock dividend that would not have been paid or accumulated if the conversion had taken place. Furthermore, the after-tax effect of a premium or discount amortization must be eliminated from income. In the case of convertible bonds, the income adjustment should include *nondiscretionary* adjustments that were based on some measure of net income, e.g., bonus expense or royalty expense.

To illustrate, assume that $100,000, 4%, 20-year bonds were issued on July 1, 19X2, at a price of 98. Each $1,000 bond is convertible into 10 shares of common stock, beginning July 1, 19X3. Assuming that the effective yield test is satisfied and that the effective tax rate is 40%, the income adjustment and share adjustment for 19X2 would be computed as follows:

Income adjustment:
    Interest = [(4% × $100,000) + ($2,000 discount ÷ 20 years)] × 1/2 year
            = $2,050
    Interest after tax = $2,050 × (1 − 40% tax rate) = $1,230
Share adjustment:
    Number of shares = 100 bonds × 10 shares = 1,000 shares
    Weighted average shares = 1,000 × 1/2 year = 500 shares

Dilutive Effect.   When a convertible security is considered a common stock equivalent, it will be included in the PEPS calculation only if its effect is dilutive.

[5]Statement of Financial Accounting Standards No. 55, *Determining Whether a Convertible Security Is a Common Stock Equivalent* (Stamford: Financial Accounting Standards Board, 1982), pars. 7–8.
[6]When a common stock equivalent convertible security actually has been converted during a period, the "if converted" method is applied in the prior period. However, the results of applying this method are included in EPS calculations only if the effect is dilutive.

To determine whether a convertible security is dilutive, an *incremental impact per share* test can be applied as follows:

1. Divide the income adjustment traceable to the convertible security by the share adjustment traceable to the convertible security. This amount is the incremental impact per share.
2. If the incremental impact per share is greater than EPS_{i-1}, then the new EPS_i will be greater than EPS_{i-1}. Therefore, if the incremental impact per share is greater than EPS_{i-1}, ignore the security because it is antidilutive.
3. If the incremental impact per share is less than EPS_{i-1}, the new EPS_i will be lower than EPS_{i-1}. Therefore, if the incremental impact per share is less than EPS_{i-1}, include the security because it is dilutive.

To ensure that only the dilutive securities enter the per share computations, the following guidelines should be followed:

1. All other primary EPS dilution adjustments must be deducted first, i.e., consider convertibles last.
2. Each convertible security must be considered individually in the order of increasing incremental impacts per share, starting with the lowest. (This ensures that no security is considered dilutive initially only to find that, due to the presence of more dilutive securities, it has a greater incremental impact than the final adjusted primary EPS.[7])

To demonstrate these guidelines for determining whether securities are dilutive, assume the following information regarding convertible securities A and B:

1.

	Yield	Income Adjustment	Share Adjustment	Incremental Impact per Share
Security A	8%	$9,700	1,000	$9.70
Security B	4	4,000	1,500	2.67

2. EPS before considering the convertible securities is $10, based on 10,000 shares.

If the convertible securities are considered in the order presented, EPS would be as follows:

	ANI_i	S_i	EPS_i
EPS before convertibles	$100,000	10,000	$10.00
Security A	109,700	11,000	9.97
Security B	113,700	12,500	9.10

However, if the convertible securities are considered individually in the order of increasing incremental impacts, as suggested by the guideline, EPS would be as follows:

---

[7]Paul M. Fischer and Martin J. Gregorcich, "Calculating Earnings per Share," *The Journal of Accountancy* (May 1973): p. 64.

	ANI_i	S_i	EPS_i
EPS before convertibles	$100,000	10,000	$10.00
Security B	104,000	11,500	9.04
Security A	113,700	12,500	9.10

In this case, security A is antidilutive. Therefore, the EPS should be reported as $9.04, rather than the $9.10 from the previous analysis.

FULLY DILUTED EARNINGS PER SHARE

 The actual calculation of fully diluted earnings per share (FDEPS) generally is based on the weighted average of shares used to calculate PEPS, adjusted in certain instances, plus the effect of other dilutive securities. Recall that FDEPS reflects the maximum dilution of EPS that would have resulted if all conversions, exercises of options and warrants, and issuances of contingent shares had taken place at the beginning of the period (or issuance date, if later). However, FDEPS sometimes may include the antidilutive effects of actual conversions and/or exercises.

OPTIONS AND WARRANTS

The impact that options and warrants may have on FDEPS is determined by: (1) reconsidering options and warrants that were viewed as common stock equivalents for purposes of calculating PEPS and (2) considering for the first time options and warrants that did not qualify for purposes of calculating PEPS. The three-month test and the 20% test, which were discussed previously, are applicable to the calculation of FDEPS.

The reconsideration of options and warrants that were viewed as common stock equivalents for PEPS is necessary because of certain modifications governing the calculation of FDEPS. For options and warrants that have not been exercised, the share adjustment is based on the use of the market price at the end of the period or the average market price, whichever is greater. Unlike PEPS, the exercise proceeds are based on the lowest exercise price during the next ten years. Therefore, the share adjustment is determined as follows:

$$\text{Share Adjustment (SA)} = \frac{\text{Total Shares Obtainable}}{\text{upon Exercise of Security}} - \frac{\text{Exercise Proceeds}}{\substack{\text{Ending Market Price of Shares or} \\ \text{Average Market Price,} \\ \text{Whichever Is Greater}}}$$

If options and/or warrants have been exercised during the period, the share adjustment for the time prior to exercise always is based on the market price at the date of exercise.

Certain options and warrants that did not qualify for purposes of calculating PEPS must be considered for purposes of calculating FDEPS. These options and warrants include those that:

1. Were not exercisable within five years from the end of the current period or
2. Met the five-year and three month tests but would have had an antidilutive effect on PEPS.

Options and warrants that fail the five-year criterion for common stock equivalency will enter the calculation of FDEPS if the security is exercisable within ten years from the end of the period and if the higher of the average market price or the ending market price exceeds the *lowest* exercise price during the ten-year period. This rule will produce the maximum dilutive effect possible.

Another unique aspect of the fully diluted computation involves those securities that are omitted from the calculation of PEPS only because the average market price is less than the exercise price. If the ending market price is higher than the exercise price, even though the average market price is not, the security is included in the computation of FDEPS.

Although financially unattractive and antidilutive, options and/or warrants that were exercised during the period when the market price was less than the exercise price are included in the computation of FDEPS for that part of the period prior to exercise. For this calculation, it is assumed that the securities are exercised at the beginning of the period or at the date of issuance, if later, and the market price at the exercise date is used in the calculation of the share adjustment.

When the reporting period is longer than three months, a quarterly averaging technique should be used when the share adjustment is computed for FDEPS. After each quarter is considered in the weighted average, using the higher of the quarter's average or the ending market price, the weighted average share adjustment is compared to the share adjustment calculated by using the actual market price at the end of the period or at the date of exercise, if earlier. The share adjustment used for FDEPS will be the *larger* of (1) the share adjustment derived by the quarterly averaging technique or (2) the share adjustment derived by use of the end-of-period market price.

For example, assume that EPS on a year-to-date basis is desired and that the following information is available:

| | | Quarter | | |
	1	2	3	4
(1) SA based on the higher of the quarter's average or ending market price	1,250	1,320	1,690	2,000
(2) Weighted average of year-to-date quarters	1,250	1,285[a]	1,420[b]	1,565[c]
(3) SA at end of period, using the end-of-period market price	1,100	1,320	1,580	2,100
(4) SA used for the year-to-date presentation (higher of 2 or 3)	1,250	1,320	1,580	2,100

[a] $(1,250 + 1,320) \div 2$
[b] $(1,250 + 1,320 + 1,690) \div 3$
[c] $(1,250 + 1,320 + 1,690 + 2,000) \div 4$

Special features affecting options and warrants in the calculation of FDEPS are summarized as follows:

1. The SA is based on the greater of the ending market price or the average market price.
2. The exercise proceeds are based on the lowest exercise price during the next ten years.
3. For options exercised during the year:
   a. The SA prior to exercise is based on the market price at date of exercise, and
   b. The security is included in FDEPS prior to exercise, even if the effect is antidilutive.

The quarterly averaging technique as well as the concepts affecting the application of the treasury stock method for options and warrants to be considered in the computation of FDEPS is demonstrated in Illustration 13-3. This illustration is based on the same facts as in Illustration 13-2, which was concerned with options and warrants in the calculation of PEPS. Illustrations 13-2 and 13-3 should be compared in order to note the differing treatment given options and warrants in the PEPS and FDEPS computations.

Illustration 13-3
FDEPS Computations: Options and Warrants

In addition to the facts given in Illustration 13-2, relevant market price information for 19X6 was as follows:

	Market Price	
Quarter	Average	Ending
1	$41	$42
2	43	44
3	49	52
4	53	51

Calculation of Income and Share Adjustments for FDEPS

Stock Warrant X

This warrant was considered in the calculation of PEPS because it met both the five-year and three-month tests. However, 9,000 shares must be reconsidered for purposes of calculating FDEPS, using the market prices at the end of the period. The adjustments for the 1,000 shares exercised must be recalculated, using the market price on the exercise date.

9,000 Warrants Not Exercised

Income adjustment: Not applicable
Share adjustment: The greater number of shares according to the following calculations:

Using the Quarterly Averaging Technique

Quarter	Shares Obtainable	Treasury Shares Acquired	SA
1	9,000	$\dfrac{\$360,000}{\$42} = 8,571$	429
2	9,000	$\dfrac{\$360,000}{\$44} = 8,182$	818
3	9,000	$\dfrac{\$360,000}{\$52} = 6,923$	2,077
4	9,000	$\dfrac{\$360,000}{\$53} = 6,792$	2,208
			5,532

Weighted average SA: 5,532 ÷ 4 = 1,383 shares

Using the Year-End Market Price

Shares Obtainable	Treasury Shares Acquired	SA
9,000	$\dfrac{\$360,000}{\$51} = 7,059$	1,941 shares

1,000 Warrants Exercised

Income adjustment: Not applicable
Share adjustment:

Quarter	Shares Obtainable	Treasury Shares Acquired	SA
1	1,000	$\dfrac{\$40,000}{\$44^*} = 909$	91
2	1,000	$\dfrac{\$40,000}{\$44} = 909$	91
3	Not applicable		—
4	Not applicable		—
			182

Weighted average SA: 182 ÷ 4 = 46 shares

*Market price at date exercised.

Stock Warrant Y

This warrant was excluded from the calculation of PEPS because it failed the five-year test; however, it is considered for FDEPS because it satisfies the ten-year test.

Income adjustment: Not applicable
Share adjustment: The greater number of shares according to the following calculations:

(continued)

Using the Quarterly Averaging Technique

Quarter	Shares Obtainable	Treasury Shares Acquired	SA
1	Not applicable—antidilutive		—
2	Not applicable—antidilutive		—
3	5,000	$\dfrac{\$250,000}{\$52} = 4,808$	192
4	5,000	$\dfrac{\$250,000}{\$53} = 4,717$	283
			475

Weighted average SA: $475 \div 4 = 119$ shares

Using the Year-End Market Price

Shares Obtainable	Treasury Shares Acquired	SA
5,000	$\dfrac{\$250,000}{\$51} = 4,902$	98 shares

Calculation of FDEPS

	ANI_{i-1}	IA_i	ANI_i	S_{i-1}	SA_i	S_i	EPS_i
Earnings per common share............	$400,000	—	$400,000	250,500*	—	250,500	$1.5968
X (not exercised)	400,000	—	400,000	250,500	1,941	252,441	1.5845
X (exercised)........................	400,000	—	400,000	252,441	46	252,487	1.5842
Y	400,000	—	400,000	252,487	119	252,606	1.5835

*Weighted average of shares outstanding during the year: 250,000 shares + 1/2 of 1,000 shares issued on June 30 = 250,500.

CONTINGENT SHARE AGREEMENTS

Those contingent share agreements that were included in the calculation of PEPS will be included in the calculation of FDEPS. Those contingent shares that were based on the attainment of a higher level of future earnings were not included in PEPS. However, these shares will be included in the calculation of FDEPS if the effect is dilutive even though the specified conditions have not been attained.

To illustrate, assume that Reynolds, Inc. had 19X7 net income of $750,000, 500,000 shares of common stock outstanding, and a contingent share agreement which became binding at the beginning of 19X7. The agreement called for the issuance of 80,000 shares of common stock in 19X8 if net income in that year reached at least $792,000. The calculation of 19X7 FDEPS would be as follows:

$$PEPS = \frac{\$750,000 + \$42,000}{500,000 + 80,000} = \$1.37$$

If in 19X8 the required net income level were not achieved, the 19X7 calculation of FDEPS would be retroactively restated to remove the share adjustment traceable to the contingent share agreement.

CONVERTIBLE SECURITIES

Convertible securities that satisfied the effective yield test for common stock equivalency will be considered in FDEPS. In addition, convertible securities that failed this test and/or the five-year test may be included in the calculation of FDEPS if both of the following conditions are satisfied:

1. The security must be convertible within ten years from the end of the current period. If the conversion rate varies during this time, the conversion rate most favorable to the holder of the security (i.e., the rate giving the holder the greatest number of common shares per convertible security) should be used.
2. The effect of the convertible security must be dilutive, as determined in calculating PEPS.

It is important to note that there is no effective yield test required for FDEPS.

The "if converted" method also is used in the calculation of FDEPS. Therefore, the income adjustment and share adjustment are determined in the same manner as for PEPS. However, if a security was converted during the period, conversion is assumed to have occurred at the beginning of the period, and when the "if converted" method is employed, the conversion rate that existed at the date of the actual conversion is used, regardless of whether the effect is dilutive or antidilutive.

To illustrate the proper treatment of a conversion during the period, assume that on July 1, 19X2, $1,000,000 of 6% bonds were converted into 5,000 shares of common stock. The bonds originally were issued at par and the effective tax rate is 40%. The FDEPS prior to considering this security is $6.50.

The income and share adjustments for this security are as follows:

Income adjustment:
$$IA = 6\% \times \$1,000,000 \times (1 - 40\% \text{ tax rate}) \times 1/2 \text{ year} = \$18,000$$
Share adjustment:
$$SA = 5,000 \text{ shares} \times 1/2 \text{ year} = 2,500 \text{ shares}$$

The effect of the income and share adjustments is antidilutive ($18,000 ÷ 2,500 shares = $7.20 per share) when compared to the preconversion FDEPS of $6.50. However, both the income and share adjustments would be included in the calculation of FDEPS because the security actually was converted during the period.

DISCLOSURE REQUIREMENTS

In addition to presenting both primary and fully diluted earnings per share on the face of the income statement, entities with complex capital structures are required to provide the following disclosures:

> . . . a description, in summary form, sufficient to explain the pertinent rights and privileges of the various securities outstanding. Examples of information which should be disclosed are dividend and liquidation preferences, participation rights, call prices and dates, conversion or exercise

prices or rates and pertinent dates, sinking fund requirements, usual voting rights, etc.

A schedule or note relating to the earnings per share data should explain the bases upon which both primary and fully diluted earnings per share are calculated. This information should include identification of any issues regarded as common stock equivalents in the computation of primary earnings per share and the securities included in the computation of fully diluted earnings per share. It should describe all assumptions and any resulting adjustments used in deriving the earnings per share data. There should also be disclosed the number of shares issued upon conversion, exercise or satisfaction of required conditions, etc., during at least the most recent annual fiscal period and any subsequent interim period presented.[8]

In addition to this disclosure, it may be desirable to provide computations that indicate how the various EPS amounts were determined.

APB Opinion No. 15 also requires disclosure of the following supplementary EPS data:

1. EPS data based on the assumption that all significant conversions that occurred during the period took place at the beginning of the period. This disclosure would be provided regardless of whether or not the effect was dilutive.
2. EPS data reflecting subsequent period conversions that took place prior to the completion of the financial report.
3. EPS data reflecting the assumption that preferred stock or debt is retired at the beginning of the period (or date of issuance, if later) when the proceeds from an actual sale of common stock or equivalent occurring during the current period or shortly thereafter are used, or are intended to be used, to retire the preferred stock or debt.[9]

It is important to note that the supplementary disclosures are in addition to the normal disclosures required by APB Opinion No. 15 and that the supplementary disclosures are not to appear on the face of the income statement, but rather in its related notes.

GENERAL GUIDELINES

The following general guidelines summarize the basic aspects of computing and disclosing PEPS and FDEPS. Many of these aspects are demonstrated in Illustration 13-4, which is a comprehensive problem demonstrating both the PEPS and FDEPS computations.

1. Per share data should reflect only the potential dilution of EPS. Normally, securities whose conversion or exercise would increase EPS are not included

---

[8]*Ibid.*, pars. 19–20.
[9]*Ibid.*, pars. 22–23.

in the computation of per share data. However, an antidilutive effect may result from options, warrants, and/or convertible securities that have been exercised during the year. For FDEPS, the SA calculation is based on the market price at date of actual exercise for options and warrants and the actual conversion rate at date of conversion for convertible securities. The SA for these securities is included in FDEPS, even if the effect is antidilutive.

2. Securities whose conversion or exercise would decrease a reported loss per share are not included in the computation of per share data if all levels of the income statement (e.g., net loss from continuing operations, extraordinary items, etc.) are losses. However, if at least one level of the income statement is not a loss, dilutive securities must be included in the computation of per share data for all levels of the income statement.

3. Except in certain instances involving contingent issuances, previously reported EPS are not to be restated retroactively when estimates that influence the calculation of per share data subsequently are revised. However, EPS data are restated retroactively for stock dividends, stock splits, and pooling agreements. When stock dividends and/or splits have taken place after the end of the period but before completion of the financial statements, EPS data for the period should give effect to the stock dividend and/or split.

4. The computation of the number of shares to be used as the denominator in the EPS statistic is based on a weighted average of shares rather than the number of shares outstanding at the end of the period. This refinement gives recognition to the fact that capital provided by equity investors may have been available for only a portion of the period. The weighted average number of shares also is considered to be representative of the future number of shares to which earnings are traceable; therefore, the prospective nature of the per share calculation is emphasized. It is important to note that when a security is converted into common shares, it is included in the weighted average number of outstanding common shares automatically. For example, if a bond was converted at midyear into 1,000 shares of common stock, the shares of common stock would not be considered as outstanding in the first six months of the year but would be included as outstanding common stock for the last six months. Therefore, the 1,000 shares traceable to the convertible bond should not be added to outstanding shares in the last six months because the 1,000 shares are included already.

5. If either PEPS or FDEPS represent dilution that is at least 3% of simple earnings per common share, disclosure of both PEPS and FDEPS is required. Otherwise, only earnings per common share would be disclosed. However, if the current period is to be included in comparative financial statements, the disclosure of both PEPS and FDEPS always is recommended. This way the cumulative change in PEPS and FDEPS can be traced to specific years, even if the yearly change is less than 3%.

6. It is not common to consider options and warrants in either the PEPS or FDEPS computations until they meet the three-month test, although it is permissible to do so. All options and warrants in the illustrations, exercises, and problems in this text are assumed to have satisfied this test, unless data with which to apply the test are given.

Illustration 13-4

Demonstration of PEPS and FDEPS Computations

1. Manchester Corporation's 19X2 income statement reflects the following:

Income from continuing operations before cumulative effect of
   changes in accounting principles............................... $88,100
Cumulative effect on prior years of changes in accounting
   principles.. (7,300)
Net income.. $80,800

2. As of January 1, 19X2, 20,000 shares of common stock were issued and outstanding. On May 1, 19X2, 10,000 shares of common stock were sold for $15 per share.
3. An analysis of securities relevant to the computation of earnings per share is as follows:

   Security A—consisting of 2,000 stock options granted in 19X1. Each option is exchangeable for one share of common stock at an option price of $13 per share up to October 1, 19X2, and $14 per share thereafter. The options expire on October 1, 19X6. One-half of the options were exercised on July 1, 19X2. The market price exceeded the exercise price for substantially all of the last three months in 19X1.

   Security B—consisting of 1,000 warrants, each exchangeable for one share of common stock at a price of $13 beginning after December 31, 19X9.

   Security C—consisting of a contingent share agreement (adopted on June 30, 19X2), whereby 4,000 shares of common stock will be issued to key personnel if pretax income increases by $3,000 in 19X3 and again in 19X4.

   Security D—consisting of 5%, $100,000 convertible bonds, issued on April 1, 19X2, at a price of 100. The average Aa corporate bond yield was 9% on April 1, 19X2. Each $1,000 bond is convertible into 20 shares of common stock beginning April 1, 19X4.

   Security E—consisting of 2,000 shares of 6% cumulative, convertible preferred stock, which was issued in 19X1 at par when the average Aa corporate bond yield was 8%. Each share of the preferred stock (par value, $10) is convertible into one share of common stock until the end of 19X5, after which time two shares of common stock would have been received. However, all of the preferred stock was converted on September 1, 19X2. During 19X2, dividends were paid on the preferred stock up to the date of conversion.

4. The corporate tax rate is 40%.
5. Daily market prices per share of common stock were as follows:

Date	Price	Date	Price
1/1/X2.....................	$11.00	7/1/X2.....................	14.50
3/31/X2	14.00	9/30/X2	14.00
5/1/X2.....................	15.00	12/31/X2	16.00
6/30/X2	$14.00		

6. Average market prices per share of common stock during 19X2 were as follows:

First quarter $12.00
Second quarter 15.00
Third quarter 14.50
Fourth quarter 15.50

7. Since the illustration involves a complex capital structure, earnings per common share would not be presented in the financial statements; however, it must be computed as the basis for the computations of PEPS and FDEPS.

Calculation of Earnings per Common Share

An analysis of the common stock account reveals the following changes in the number of shares outstanding:

Date	Item	No. of Shares
1/1/X2	Beginning balance	20,000
5/1/X2	Additional sale..............	10,000
7/1/X2	Exercise of Security A	1,000
9/1/X2	Conversion of Security E.....	2,000

The weighted average of shares outstanding is as follows:

Time Span	No. of Shares	Weight (in Months)	Share-Months
1/1/X2–4/30/X2	20,000	4	80,000
5/1/X2–6/30/X2	30,000	2	60,000
7/1/X2–8/31/X2	31,000	2	62,000
9/1/X2–12/31/X2	33,000	4	132,000
Total		12	334,000

Weighted average SA: 334,000 ÷ 12 = 27,833 shares

Earnings per common share would be as follows:

Income from continuing operations before cumulative effect of changes in accounting principles .... $3.14[a]
Cumulative effect on prior years of changes in accounting principles ...... (0.26)
Net income $2.88

[a]Before computing EPS, the reported income has been appropriately reduced by the 19X2 preferred stock dividend of $800 (6% × $20,000 × 2/3 year). Therefore, the EPS before the cumulative effect of changes in principles is based on income of $87,300.

Calculation of PEPS

The basic methodology presented in Illustration 13-1 is used to compute the PEPS as follows:

(continued)

	ANI_{i-1}	IA_i	ANI_i	S_{i-1}	SA_i	S_i	EPS_i
Earnings per common share..........	$87,300	—	$87,300	27,833	—	27,833	$3.14[b]
Security A..........................	87,300	—	87,300	27,833	117[c]	27,950	3.12
Security B.........................	Not a common stock equivalent—fails 5-year test						
Security C.........................	Not a common stock equivalent—specified conditions not attained						
Security D.........................	87,300	$2,250[d]	89,550	27,950	1,500[e]	29,450	3.04
Security E.........................	Not a common stock equivalent—fails effective yield test						

[b] To insure that antidilutive securities would be identified properly, earnings per common share of $3.14 was used instead of the final per share figure of $2.88.

[c] Weighted average of quarters for Security A:

Quarter	Dilutive*	Shares Obtainable	Treasury Shares Acquired	SA
1	No	—	—	—
2	Yes	2,000	$\dfrac{\$26,000}{\$15} = 1,733$	267
3	Yes	1,000	$\dfrac{\$13,000}{\$14.50} = 897$	103
4	Yes	1,000	$\dfrac{\$14,000}{\$15.50} = 903$	97
				467

Weighted average SA: 467 ÷ 4 = 117 shares

*Dilutive if average market price is greater than exercise price.

[d] 5% × $100,000 × 9/12 year = $3,750. After-tax effect: 60% × $3,750 = $2,250.

[e] 100 bonds × 20 shares = 2,000 shares assumed outstanding as of April 1, 19X2. Therefore, weighted average = 2,000 × 3/4 year = 1,500 shares.

Primary earnings per share would be presented as follows:

Earnings per common share and common equivalent share:
Income from continuing operations before cumulative effect
of changes in accounting principles...................... $3.04
Cumulative effect on prior years of changes in
accounting principles................................ (0.25)*

Net income $2.79

*The $7,300 cumulative effect divided by the final S_i of 29,450.

Calculation of FDEPS

	ANI_{i-1}	IA_i	ANI_i	S_{i-1}	SA_i	S_i	EPS_i
Earnings per common share..........	$87,300	—	$87,300	27,833	—	27,833	$3.14
Security A (not exercised)	87,300	—	87,300	27,833	125[f]	27,958	3.12
Security A (exercised).................	87,300	—	87,300	27,958	52[g]	28,010	3.12
Security B..........................	87,300	—	87,300	28,010	187[h]	28,197	3.10
Security C..........................	87,300	$3,600[i]	90,900	28,197	2,000[i]	30,197	3.01
Security E[j]........................	90,900	800[k]	91,700	30,197	1,333[l]	31,530	2.91
Security D..........................	91,700	2,250[m]	93,950	31,530	1,500[m]	33,030	2.84

[f] The year-end market price is used for the entire period when it produces greater dilution than the quarterly average. Thus, the share adjustment is the 125 incremental shares resulting from use of the year-end market price, rather than the quarterly average of 108 shares. These amounts are computed as follows:

Quarter	Dilutive*	Shares Obtainable	Treasury Shares Acquired	SA
1	Yes	1,000	$\dfrac{\$13{,}000}{\$14} = 929$	71
2	Yes	1,000	$\dfrac{\$13{,}000}{\$15} = 867$	133
3	Yes	1,000	$\dfrac{\$13{,}000}{\$14.50} = 897$	103
4	Yes	1,000	$\dfrac{\$14{,}000}{\$16} = 875$	__125__
				432

Weighted average SA: 432 ÷ 4 = 108 shares

*Dilutive if the greater of the average or the end-of-period market price exceeds the exercise price.

gWeighted average of quarters for Security A—Exercised:

Quarter	Dilutive*	Shares Obtainable	Treasury Shares Acquired	SA
1	Yes	1,000	$\dfrac{\$13{,}000}{\$14.50} = 897$	103
2	Yes	1,000	$\dfrac{\$13{,}000}{\$14.50} = 897$	103
3	Not applicable			—
4	Not applicable			—
				206

Weighted average SA: 206 ÷ 4 = 52 shares

*Dilutive if the market price at the date of exercise is greater than the exercise price. The share adjustment for the time prior to exercise always is based on the market price at the exercise date, regardless of whether or not the result is dilutive. Note that securities exercised when the market price is less than the exercise price always are included in FDEPS, even if the effect is antidilutive.

hThe year-end market price is used for the entire period when it produces greater dilution than the quarterly average. Thus, the share adjustment is the 187 incremental shares resulting from use of the year-end market price, rather than the quarterly average of 124 shares. These amounts are computed as follows:

Quarter	Dilutive*	Shares Obtainable	Treasury Shares Acquired	SA
1	Yes	1,000	$\dfrac{\$13{,}000}{\$14} = 929$	71
2	Yes	1,000	$\dfrac{\$13{,}000}{\$15} = 867$	133
3	Yes	1,000	$\dfrac{\$13{,}000}{\$14.50} = 897$	103
4	Yes	1,000	$\dfrac{\$13{,}000}{\$16} = 813$	__187__
				494

Weighted average SA: 494 ÷ 4 = 124 shares

*Dilutive if the greater of the average or the ending market price exceeds the exercise price.

i For purposes of computing FDEPS, it is assumed that the net-of-tax increases in 19X3 and 19X4 income [($3,000 + $3,000) × 60% = $3,600] have been realized. The weighted average number of shares would be 2,000 (4,000 × 1/2 year).

(continued)

ⁱ Security E has a lower incremental impact than Security D and should be considered first.

ᵏThe preferred stock dividend is $800, computed as follows: 6% × $20,000 × 2/3 year = $800.

ˡWhen actual conversion of a security takes place during the period, conversion is assumed at the beginning of the period or at issuance, if later, for purposes of calculating FDEPS. Since the shares issued upon conversion already have been considered as outstanding, the SA is based on the period prior to conversion (2,000 × 8/12 = 1,333).

ᵐThe income and share adjustments for the convertible bonds are the same as they were in the PEPS computation.

Fully diluted earnings per share would be presented as follows:

Earnings per common share—assuming full dilution:
Income from continuing operations before cumulative effect of changes in accounting principles ... $2.84
Cumulative effect on prior years of changes in accounting principles .... (0.22)*
Net income $2.62

*The $7,300 cumulative effect divided by the final S_i of 33,030.

QUESTIONS

1. Why do EPS calculations assume conversions of securities that in fact were not converted during the year? Is this valid? Why or why not?
2. Explain why FDEPS is considered an ultraconservative measure of EPS.
3. When is the disclosure of PEPS and/or FDEPS required to be presented within financial statements?
4. When would the assumed exercise of options and/or warrants result in an income adjustment?
5. How do income taxes and an unamortized discount on convertible bonds affect the income adjustment when calculating EPS?
6. When is the quarterly averaging technique appropriate? Is the quarterly average always used for FDEPS?
7. How are contingent share agreements analyzed for purposes of computing primary EPS? Fully diluted EPS?
8. If a convertible security has various conversion rates, which rate should be used for the computation of the share adjustment?
9. If a security has actually been exercised or converted into common shares during the reporting period, is the security included in per share computations if the effect is antidilutive?
10. A contingent share agreement called for the issuance of additional shares of common stock if the pretax earnings next period increased over the current pretax earnings level by 10%. How would the current income adjustment be determined for both PEPS and FDEPS?
11. Explain when an option would be considered antidilutive for purposes of computing PEPS.
12. If an option has several exercise prices available in the future, why is the lowest exercise price used for purposes of calculating FDEPS?

EXERCISES

Exercise 1. Sharp Products has various convertible securities which are summarized as follows:

Security A: 10,000, 10% convertible 10-year bonds, issued on June 1, 19X4, at 97. Each of the $100 bonds may be converted into 3 shares of common stock after June 1, 19X7. The Aa corporate bond yield was 12% at the date of issuance.

Security B: 2,000, 7% convertible 15-year bonds with a $100 face value. These bonds were issued on January 1, 19X3, at 102 and are convertible into common stock as follows:

> 4 shares per bond after January 1, 19X4
> 5 shares per bond after January 1, 19X5
> 6 shares per bond after January 1, 19X7

The Aa corporate bond yield at the date of issuance was 11%. On August 1, 19X6, 40% of the bonds were converted.

Security C: 5,000 shares of $2.50 preferred stock, $50 par, each convertible into 2 shares of common stock after January 1, 19Y4. The Aa corporate bond yield was 10% on January 1, 19X5, when the stock was issued.

Calculate the annual income and share adjustments for each convertible security for both PEPS and FDEPS. Assume all premiums and discounts are amortized by the straight-line method. The effective tax rate is 40%.

Exercise 2. Westcor Corporation had the following stock transactions during the year 19X7:

January 1, 19X7	Beginning balance 1,800,000 shares of common stock.
February 1, 19X7	The corporation purchased 150,000 shares of treasury stock.
April 1, 19X7	The corporation issued a 20% stock dividend.
July 1, 19X7	Preferred stock was converted into 55,000 shares of common stock.
November 1, 19X7	An additional 700,000 shares of common stock were issued.

Calculate the weighted average number of shares for 19X7.

Exercise 3. At the beginning of 19X5, Webco Company had 200,000 shares of common stock outstanding. During the year, the company also had outstanding debt as follows:

> $100,000 notes payable bearing interest at 8%
> $20,000 notes payable bearing interest at 7%

In 19X3, the company issued 25,000 options exercisable into 25,000 shares of common stock with an exercise price of $38 beginning January 1, 19X4. On July 1, 19X5, 4,000 options were exercised when the market price was $44.

Webco reported $95,000 of net income for the year ended December 31, 19X5. The applicable tax rate is 30%. Common stock market price data are given as follows:

	Average Market Price	Ending Market Price
First quarter	$36	$37
Second quarter	44	44
Third quarter	36	37
Fourth quarter	41	39
Average for the year	38	

Calculate the 19X5 annual income and share adjustments for FDEPS. Assume that the options met the "3-month test" in the second quarter of 19X5.

Exercise 4. Assume the same facts as in Exercise 3 except that only 106,000 shares of common stock were outstanding at the beginning of 19X5.

Calculate the 19X5 annual income and share adjustments for FDEPS.

Exercise 5. Chaplin Industries had net income of $1,950,000 for the year ended December 31, 19X8. As of January 1, 19X8, Chaplin had 550,000 shares of outstanding common stock. An additional 15,000 shares were issued on April 1, 19X8. Chaplin also had 200, 7%, 10-year, $1,000 convertible bonds outstanding which were issued on March 1, 19X7, to be converted after September 1, 19X7. On July 1, 19X8, 75 of these bonds were converted into 1,500 shares of common stock. The average Aa corporate bond yield was 12% on March 1, 19X7.

On September 15, 19X8, the board of directors declared a 2:1 stock split to be effective October 1, 19X8. The corporate tax rate is 34%.

Calculate PEPS for the year ended December 31, 19X8.

Exercise 6. Throughout the last four years, Rough and Ready Wear Inc. has offered several different options and warrants to shareholders and employees. All are exercisable within five years of the current year end, 19X6, and have passed the three-month test in prior years. It has been determined that if all options and warrants had been exercised at the beginning of 19X6, 50,000 shares of stock would have been issued. However, none of the options or warrants were exercised in 19X6. The total proceeds from the options and warrants would have been $1,500,000 for PEPS and $1,450,000 for FDEPS. There were 200,000 shares of common stock outstanding on December 31, 19X6.

On January 1, 19X6, the company had outstanding 15% interest-bearing bonds with a $100,000 face value and annual premium amortization of $300. Government securities earned an average return of 12% throughout 19X6. The tax rate is 25%, and current-year average and ending market prices for the common stock are $33 and $34, respectively. No other outstanding securities existed in 19X6.

(1) Compute the income and share adjustments for both PEPS and FDEPS for 19X6.
(2) What may be the reason for the lower total proceeds for FDEPS?
(3) Assuming that the income and share adjustments for PEPS are $11,000 and 10,000 shares, respectively, and that the weighted number of shares outstanding in 19X6 is 200,000, determine the minimum adjusted net income needed in order for dual disclosure to be required.

Exercise 7. Craig Manufacturing has various stock options outstanding during 19X9. All of the options were issued on January 1, 19X9, and are summarized as follows:

Option	Number of Options	Number of Shares per Option	Exercise Price per Option	Earliest Exercise Date
W	2,000	1	$39	19X9
X	4,000	1	34	19X9
Y	2,000	2	74	19Y6

At the beginning of 19X9, there were 50,000 common shares outstanding. However, on May 1, 19X9, one-half of the X options were exercised when the market price per share was $36. For 19X9, the average market price per share was $37, and the year-end market price per share is $38. Net income for 19X9 is $250,000.

Calculate the 19X9 PEPS and FDEPS. Ignore the quarterly averaging technique.

Exercise 8. Dunphry Co. had net income of $775,000 after dividends for the fiscal year ending March 31, 19X9. Dunphry had 200,000 shares of common stock outstanding as of

April 1, 19X8. The company issued 500, $200, 7%, 10-year convertible bonds on January 1, 19X7, at 103. The premium is being amortized by the straight-line method over a 10-year period. Each bond is convertible into 2 shares of common stock. Dunphry also had 10,000 convertible preferred shares outstanding on April 1, 19X8. Each preferred share has a quarterly dividend of $1.00 per share and is convertible into 1 share of common stock. However, after March 31, 19Y2, each preferred share may be converted into 1-1/2 shares. At the date of issue, the market price of the preferred stock was $58. The average Aa corporate bond yield was 12% when the convertible bonds and preferred stocks were issued. In addition, the company has a contingent share agreement with its officers to issue 25,000 shares of common stock if the earnings in any given year exceed $900,000. The market price of the common stock was $102 at year end and the average market price for the year was $80. The applicable tax rate is 38%.

Calculate the PEPS and FDEPS for the year ended March 31, 19X9.

Exercise 9. In 19X4, Cosmos Corporation purchased some Luna Corporation voting common stock from Luna's stockholders. As part of the agreement, Cosmos promised to issue 2,000 additional shares of its voting common stock to the Luna stockholders as soon as Cosmos realizes an annual net income of $40,000. The contingency consideration expires in 19X8. Net income in 19X4 and 19X5 was $15,000 and $6,000, respectively.

On March 1, 19X5, 400 options, each exercisable into 40 shares of Cosmos voting common stock, were issued. The exercise price is $36 per option. No options were exercised during 19X5. The market prices during the year were as follows:

Quarter	Average	Ending
1	$10	$10
2	7	7
3	10	12
4	11	10

The market price on March 1, 19X5, was $9.50. The tax rate is 40%. There were 20,000 weighted average shares outstanding in 19X5.

Calculate the 19X5 PEPS and FDEPS.

Exercise 10. Earth Corporation has net income of $900,000 for the fiscal year ending September 30, 19X9. The common stock account on October 1, 19X8, showed 240,000 shares outstanding. The company issued $2,000,000 of 6%, 10-year convertible bonds on June 1, 19X9, at 98. The bonds were dated June 1, 19X9, with interest payable on June 1 and December 1. The bond discount is amortized semiannually on a straight-line basis. Each $100 bond is convertible into 1 share of common stock. On August 1, 19X9, $500,000 of these bonds were converted. The remaining bonds should be considered common stock equivalents. The only other securities that the company had outstanding on October 1, 19X8, were 14,000 shares of convertible preferred stock, which returns a yearly dividend of $2.25 per share and is convertible into 1 share of common stock for each share of preferred. At date of issue, the market price of the preferred stock was $40, and the average Aa corporate bond yield was 9%. On December 1, 19X8, an additional 6,000 shares of the same convertible preferred stock were issued at a price of $60 per share when the average Aa corporate bond yield was 9.5%. All shares of preferred stock outstanding during the year received the full cash dividend. The tax rate applicable to Earth Corporation is 48%.

Present all EPS data required for Earth Corporation. Show all schedules and computations in good form.

PROBLEMS

Problem 13-1. Young Industries reported $985,000 of net income before dividends for 19X8. Young had 205,000 shares of common stock outstanding as of January 1, 19X8, purchased 10,000 shares of treasury stock on June 1, 19X8, and declared a 10% stock dividend on August 1, 19X8. In addition, Young had the following securities:

(a) Class A options with a 1:1 common stock conversion and an exercise price of $30. 40,000 options were issued on January 1, 19X6, and could be exercised after January 1, 19X7.

(b) Class B options issued on January 1, 19X5, with an exercise price of $26. Each option is convertible into 1 share of common stock after January 1, 19X8. 30,000 options were issued and all options were exercised on March 1, 19X8, when the market price was $32.

(c) 25,000, 9%, 15-year, $100 convertible bonds issued on January 1, 19X2, at a price of $2,550,000 when the average Aa corporate bond yield was 12%. Each bond is convertible into 3 shares of common stock. The premium is being amortized using the straight-line method.

(d) 8%, 10-year, $100 convertible bonds, 10,000 issued on January 1, 19X6, at 103 when the Aa corporate bond rate was 12%. Each of the bonds is convertible into 2 shares of common stock beginning in 19X9. The premium is being amortized using the straight-line method.

(e) 40,000 shares of cumulative 5% preferred stock, $50 par value. Dividends are in arrears for both 19X7 and 19X8.

Common stock market price data are given as follows:

	Average Market Price	Ending Market Price
First quarter	$31	$33
Second quarter	36	37
Third quarter	34	32
Fourth quarter	34	27

The effective tax rate for Young is 25%.

Required:

Calculate PEPS for 19X8.

Problem 13-2. Boyd Manufacturing Company reported net income for the year 19X5 in the amount of $1,140,000 after recognizing income tax expense of $760,000. The company's weighted average number of common shares outstanding for the year 19X5 was 560,000. In addition to common shares, the following securities or agreements exist:

Convertible preferred stock: 20,000 shares of preferred stock were issued on June 1, 19X4. Each share has a par value of $50, is convertible into 2 shares of common stock beginning in 19X5, and has a cumulative dividend of $2.

Stock option A: 5,000 options were issued on March 1, 19X5, for a price of $2 per option. Each option has an exercise price of $23 per option and may be exchanged for common stock as follows:

1 share per option beginning in 19X5

1.5 shares per option beginning in 19X7

On September 30, 19X5, 2,000 options were exercised.

5,000, 8% convertible bonds: These 10-year bonds were issued on June 1, 19X5, at a price of 98. Each bond has a face value of $100, pays interest semiannually, and is convertible into 4.5 shares of common stock beginning in 19X6.

12,000, 7% convertible bonds: These 15-year bonds were issued on March 1, 19X3, at a price of 103. Each bond has a face value of $100, pays interest semiannually, and is convertible into common stock as follows:

  4 shares per bond beginning in 19X5
  5 shares per bond beginning in 19X7
  6 shares per bond beginning in 19X9

On November 1, 19X5, 2,000 bonds were converted into common stock.

On June 1, 19X5, the company established a contingent share agreement that would entitle certain employees of the company to receive 55,000 shares of common stock if 19X6 net income before taxes increased 10% over the 19X5 level.

Other relevant information is as follows:

Date	Aa Bond Rate	Market Price per Share	
		Average	Ending
3/1/X3	10.5		
6/1/X4	9.0%		
6/1/X5	10.0		
19X5:			
First quarter		$24	$23
Second quarter		25	26
Third quarter		26	27
Fourth quarter		23	22

Required:
Compute the primary and fully diluted earnings per share for the year 19X5.

Problem 13-3. Tall Tales Publications Inc. is considering several contingent share agreements as part of its purchase of Real Romance Books Corporation. Tall Tales is concerned about the impact on its EPS for 19X5 and 19X6. As chief accountant, you must determine the expected income and share adjustments for PEPS and FDEPS for each agreement for both years and report to the board of directors. The agreement to puchase Real Romance is expected to go into effect on April 1, 19X5. Net incomes for the consolidated companies for 19X5 and 19X6 are expected to be $4,600,000 and $4,800,000, respectively. The contingent share agreements are as follows:

(a) Stockholders of Real Romance will receive 40,000 shares of Tall Tales voting common stock on May 1, 19X8.

(b) Tall Tales will issue 500 shares of its voting common stock to Real Romance shareholders for every $10,000 of net income over $4,250,000 in 19X5 and net income over $4,500,000 in 19X6.

(c) Tall Tales will issue 1,000 shares of its voting common stock to Real Romance shareholders for every $10,000 of net income between $4,500,000 and $5,000,000 for each of the next three years, 19X5, 19X6, and 19X7.

(d) When net income reaches $4,750,000, Real Romance shareholders will receive 40,000 shares of Tall Tales voting common stock. This agreement expires December 31, 19X8.

(e) When net income reaches $5,000,000, Real Romance shareholders will receive 40,000 shares of Tall Tales voting common stock. This agreement expires December 31, 19X8.

(f) The market value of Tall Tales stock on April 1, 19X5, is expected to be $35 per share. Tall Tales will issue 24,000 shares at that time and guarantees the original total stock value ($35 × 24,000) on December 31 of every year through 19X8. If the total value is not maintained, additional shares will be issued as necessary. The market value is $30 and $28 at the end of 19X5 and 19X6, respectively.

Required:

Present the effect on PEPS and FDEPS for each of the above agreements.

Problem 13-4. EPS is the single most featured financial statistic about modern corporations. Daily published quotations of stock prices for many securites recently have been expanded to include a times earnings figure that is based on EPS. Often the focus of analysts' discussions will be on the EPS of the corporation receiving their attention.

Required:

(1) Explain how dividends or dividend requirements on any class of preferred stock that may be outstanding affect the computation of EPS.

(2) One of the technical procedures applicable in EPS computations is the treasury stock method.

  (a) Briefly describe the circumstances under which it might be appropriate to apply the treasury stock method.

  (b) There is a limit to the extent to which the treasury stock method is applicable. Indicate what this limit is, and give a succinct indication of the procedures that should be followed beyond the treasury stock limits.

(3) Under some circumstances, convertible debentures would be considered common stock equivalents, while under other circumstances they would not.

  (a) When is it proper to treat convertible debentures as common stock equivalents? What is the effect on the computation of EPS in such cases?

  (b) If convertible debentures are not considered as common stock equivalents, explain how they are handled for purposes of EPS computations.

(AICPA adapted)

Problem 13-5. Stopkin Inc. reported net income before dividends of $2,010,000 for 19X9. Stopkin had 900,000 shares of common stock outstanding as of January 1, 19X9, along with the following securities:

(a) 6% convertible bonds issued on March 15, 19X8, at 99. Each $150 bond is convertible into 3 shares of common stock. The discount is amortized over 5 years using the straight-line method. The 1,000 convertible bonds originally were issued when the Aa corporate bond rate was 10%.

(b) 7% convertible bonds issued on June 1, 19X6, at par. Each $45 bond is convertible into 1 share of common stock. The 5,000 bonds were issued when the Aa corporate bond rate was 12%.

(c) 9% convertible bonds, $100 par, issued on January 1, 19X7, at 103 when the Aa corporate bond rate was 10%. Each of the 2,000 bonds has a 1:2 conversion ratio. The premium is being amortized over 5 years using the straight-line method.

(d) $2.50 cumulative preferred stock, $50 par, each convertible into 1 share of common stock. The 8,000 preferred shares were issued in 19X7 at par when the Aa corporate bond yield was 8%. Dividends are in arrears for 19X8 and 19X9.

(e) 5,000 shares of $3 preferred stock, $45 par, each convertible into 1 share of common stock. The Aa corporate bond yield was 8% in 19X6 when the stock was issued.

On July 1, 19X9, 75% of the 7% convertible bonds were converted. The statutory tax rate for Stopkin is 34%.

Required:
Calculate PEPS for 19X9.

Problem 13-6. The following financial statements and additional information relate to Quin Industries:

Quin Industries
Partial Balance Sheet
June 30, 19X8

Current liabilities:
Accounts payable	....	$ 70,000
15% note payable	....	75,000
Total current liabilities	....	$ 145,000

Long-term debt:
15% note payable, net of current portion	....	$ 150,000
12% convertible $100 bonds, net of $4,800 premium, due 6/30/Y8 (in 10 years)	....	84,800
Total long-term debt	....	$ 234,800

Stockholders' equity:
$4 cumulative preferred stock, $100 par, 25,000 shares authorized, 10,000 shares issued and outstanding	....	$1,000,000
Additional paid-in capital—preferred	....	100,000
Common stock, $10 par, 150,000 shares authorized, 50,000 shares issued and outstanding	....	500,000
Additional paid-in capital—common	....	30,000
Total paid-in capital	....	$1,630,000
Retained earnings	....	4,000,000
Total stockholders' equity	....	$5,630,000
Total liabilities and stockholders' equity	....	$6,009,800

Quin Industries
Partial Income Statement
For Year Ended June 30, 19X8

Income from continuing operations before extraordinary loss	....	$1,000,000
Extraordinary loss, net of $50,000 tax benefit	....	(50,000)
Net income	....	$ 950,000

The following additional information applies:
(a) The 19X8 weighted average number of shares of common stock is 49,000.
(b) On January 1, 19X8, 200 of the $100 bonds were converted into common stock.
(c) The bond conversion schedule is:

Year of Conversion	Number of Shares per $100 Bond
19X8	10
19X9	12
19Y0	15

On the day the bonds were issued, the average Aa corporate bond yield was 15%. All bonds and notes were issued prior to July 1, 19X7. The premium on the 15-year bonds is being amortized on a straight-line basis.
(d) On May 1, 19X8, dividends of $1.25 per share were paid to common stockholders.

(e) Options and warrants: At the 19X8 year end, the following were outstanding:
   Option #1:   Issued January 1, 19X6; exercise price, $25; 2,000 options exercisable into
                2,000 shares of common stock.
   Option #2:   Issued July 1, 19X6; exercise price, $30; 8,000 options exercisable into
                8,000 shares of common stock.
   Warrant A: Issued July 1, 19X7; exercise price, $50; 1,000 warrants exercisable as 2
                common stock shares per warrant.
   Warrant B: Issued December 31, 19X7; exercise price, $86; 300 warrants exercisable
                as 2 common stock shares per warrant.
   All options and warrants currently are exercisable. None were exercised in the
   current year.
(f) Quin Industries invests in corporate bonds yielding an annual return of 13%. Because
   of the costly interest rate related to the notes payable, Quin is anxious to retire that
   debt as quickly as possible.
(g) The market prices of the common stock were:

	Year Ended	
	6/30/X8	6/30/X7
Average common stock prices:		
First quarter	$26	$35
Second quarter	27	30
Third quarter	30	32
Fourth quarter	35	24
End-of-quarter prices:		
First quarter	30	35
Second quarter	25	33
Third quarter	33	29
Fourth quarter	40	21
Annual average	29	30

   For the treasury stock method, Quin uses quarterly averaging. For the 20% rule, Quin
   uses the annual average where appropriate.
(h) The tax rate is 50%

Required:
(1) Using the above information, calculate PEPS and FDEPS for the year ending June 30,
   19X8.
(2) Does Quin Industries have to disclose PEPS and FDEPS for the current fiscal year?
   Why or why not?

Problem 13-7. Nexton Industries has the following securities outstanding as of June
30, 19X9:

Option A: Issued November 1, 19X6; exercise price is $32. The 2,500 options are exercisable
         into 2,500 shares of common stock beginning September 1, 19X8.
Option B: Issued January 30, 19X7; exercise price of $32 through March 31, 19X9, then $34.
         The 4,000 options are exercisable into 4,000 shares of common stock. On January 1,
         19X9, 2,000 options were exercised when the market price was $35.
7% convertible preferred stock: $38 par, 5,000 shares issued and outstanding for the entire
         year. The shares were issued when the Aa corporate bond yield was 11%. Each
         preferred share is convertible into 1 common share.
8% convertible bonds: Issued on May 1, 19X6, at par. Each of the 2,000, $100 bonds was
         issued with a 1:3 conversion ratio, to be convertible after May 1, 19Y6. The Aa
         corporate bond yield at date of issue was 12.5%.

Contingent share agreement: Nexton has agreed to issue its officers 10,000 shares of common stock if net earnings exceed $600,000 in a year and will issue an additional 15,000 shares if net earnings exceed $700,000.

Nexton reported $650,000 of net income for the year ended June 30, 19X9. Common shares outstanding as of July 1, 19X8, were 250,000. The applicable tax rate is 35%. Common stock market price data are given as follows:

	Average Market Price	Ending Market Price
First quarter	$33	$33
Second quarter	34	35
Third quarter	37	36
Fourth quarter	37	38
Average for the year	35	

Required:
Calculate PEPS and FDEPS for the year ended June 30, 19X9.

Problem 13-8. The controller of Midar Corporation has requested assistance in determining PEPS and FDEPS figures for the company for the fiscal year ending on September 30, 19X1.

Working papers disclose the following beginning balances and transactions in the company's capital stock accounts during the 19X0–19X1 fiscal year:

(a) Common stock (at October 1, 19X0, stated value $10, authorized 300,000 shares; effective December 1, 19X0, stated value $5, authorized 600,000 shares):
   Balance, October 1, 19X0—60,000 shares issued and outstanding.
   December 1, 19X0—60,000 shares issued in a 2-for-1 stock split.
   December 1, 19X0—280,000 shares (stated value $5) issued at $39 per share.

(b) Treasury stock—common:
   March 1, 19X1—purchased 40,000 shares at $38 per share.
   April 1, 19X1—sold 40,000 shares at $40 per share.

(c) Stock purchase warrants, Series A (initially, each warrant, along with $60, was exchangeable for 1 common share; effective December 1, 19X0, each warrant became exchangeable for 2 common shares at $30 per share):
   October 1, 19X0—25,000 warrants issued at $6 each.

(d) Stock purchase warrants, Series B (each warrant, along with $40, is exchangeable for 1 common share):
   April 1, 19X1—20,000 warrants authorized and issued at $10 each.

(e) First mortgage bonds, 5-1/2%, due 19Y5 (nonconvertible; priced to yield 5% when issued):
   Balance, October 1, 19X0—authorized, issued, and outstanding—the face value of $1,400,000.

(f) Convertible debentures, 7%, due 19Y9 (initially, each $1,000 bond was convertible at any time until maturity into 12-1/2 common shares; effective December 1, 19X0, the conversion rate became 25 shares for each bond):
   October 1, 19X0—authorized and issued at their face value (no premium or discount) of $2,400,000.

The following table shows market prices for the company's securities and the assumed average Aa corporate bond yield during 19X0–19X1:

	Price (or Rate) at			Average for Year Ended September 30, 19X1
	October 1, 19X0	April 1, 19X1	September 30, 19X1	
Common stock	66	40	36-1/4	37-1/2*
First morgage bonds	88-1/2	87	86	87
Convertible debentures.	100	120	119	115
Series A warrants.	6	22	19-1/2	15
Series B warrants.		10	9	9-1/2
Average Aa corporate bond yield	8%	7-3/4%	7-1/2%	7-3/4%

*Adjusted for stock split

Required:

Compute the EPS data that the controller has requested, assuming that net income for the year is $540,000. Show all supporting schedules in good form. (Because of the relative stability of the market price for Midar Corporation common stock, the annual average market price may be used where appropriate in the calculations. Assume an income tax rate of 48%.)

(AICPA adapted)

Problem 13-9. The following information relates to PQB Corporation:

PQB Corporation
Partial Balance Sheets
December 31, 19X3 and 19X4

	19X4	19X3
Current liabilities:		
Accounts payable	$ 200,000	$ 200,000
Notes payable:		
8%, 3-month, due 2/1/X4.		100,000
10%, 6-month, due 3/1/X5.	100,000	
Long-term liabilities:		
Bonds payable:		
10% stated rate, 20-year bonds, due 12/31/Y4	4,000,000	5,000,000
8% stated rate, 15-year convertible bonds,		
due 12/31/Y6, net of discount.	4,820,000	9,610,000
Total liabilities	$ 9,120,000	$14,910,000
Stockholders' equity:		
Preferred stock:		
6% cumulative, $100 par, 30,000 shares authorized;		
8,000 shares outstanding in 19X3		$ 800,000
10,000 shares outstanding in 19X4	$ 1,000,000	
4% cumulative, convertible, $100 par, 50,000 shares		
authorized;		
30,000 shares outstanding in 19X3		3,000,000
20,000 shares outstanding in 19X4	2,000,000	
Common stock:		
$20 par, 5,000,000 shares authorized;		
1,000,000 shares issued, of which 800,000 are		
outstanding in 19X3		20,000,000
1,306,000 shares issued, of which		
1,106,000 are outstanding in 19X4*	26,120,000	
Total paid-in capital.	$29,120,000	$23,800,000

*Note that 200,000 shares are held in treasury.

PQB Corporation
Partial Income Statement
For Year Ended December 31, 19X4

Income from continuing operations	$15,202,667
Extraordinary gain from early extinguishment of debt	
(net of $96,000 tax expense)	104,000
Net income	$15,306,667

Additional information:

(a) The average Aa corporate bond yields on selected dates were:

    1/1/W1—10%   1/1/W5—14%   1/1/W9—5.75%
    1/1/X2—12%   1/1/X3—8%   12/31/X3—9%
    12/31/X4—10%

(b) All preferred stock was issued at par on these dates:

6%	4%
1/1/W1—8,000 shares	1/1/W9—10,000 shares
1/1/X4—2,000 shares	1/1/X3—20,000 shares

(c) A 15% common stock dividend was issued to shares outstanding as of 5/1/X4.

(d) 4% preferred stock is convertible into 3 shares of common until 19X8, then into 5 shares of common. On August 31, 19X4, 10,000 shares of preferred stock were converted.

(e) The 8% bonds with an original face value of $10,000,000 were issued at 95-1/2 on January 1, 19X2. Each $1,000 bond is convertible into 30 shares of common stock. On June 30, 19X4, half of the bonds were converted. The discount is being amortized on a straight-line basis.

(f) The current tax rate is 48%.

(g) Common stock market price data:

	19X4	
	Average Market Price	Ending Market Price
First quarter	$46	$47
Second quarter	42	43
Third quarter	45	48
Fourth quarter	50	47
Average for the year	46	

(h) Option A consists of 3,000 options, each of which may be used to acquire 4 shares of common stock at an exercise price of $180. Half of the options were exercised on June 30, 19X4. The balance of the options may be exercised within the next six years. The quarterly averaging technique is to be used.

Required:

Calculate PEPS for 19X4.

PART 4

Partnerships

Businesses with more than one owner usually are organized as either a partnership or a corporation. It is important that the differences between these types of organizations be understood. Partnerships are significantly influenced by the agreements reached among their partners and the *Uniform Partnership Act*. Furthermore, partnerships employ special accounting principles and present special considerations for tax purposes. The admission or withdrawal of partners may be accounted for in several ways which are unique to this form of organization. Changes in the ownership structure of a partnership results in the dissolution of the prior partnership and the creation of a new partnership. Partners also may find it necessary to terminate or liquidate the partnership entity. Liquidation procedures must comply with certain legal requirements and need special care so that the rights of those with claims against partnership assets are respected.

CHAPTER 14

Partnerships: Characteristics, Formation, and Accounting for Activities

A partnership is an association of two or more people for the purpose of carrying on a trade or business as co-owners. Partnerships continue to be a popular form of organization for many smaller businesses as well as certain larger businesses. Common examples of partnerships include professional services, such as the practice of accounting or law, real estate investment/development companies, and a variety of smaller manufacturing concerns.

In a majority of states, the legal nature and functioning of a partnership is governed by the Uniform Partnership Act (UPA). The UPA deals with such topics as the rights of partners, relations with persons dealing with the partnership, and the dissolution and termination of a partnership.

CHARACTERISTICS OF A PARTNERSHIP

Practicing accountants frequently are asked to advise clients regarding the formation of a business and the accounting for the business activities. Often a choice must be made between a partnership and a corporate form of organization. Therefore, it is important for accounting students to understand the basic characteristics of a partnership and the related accounting implications.

RELATIONSHIP OF PARTNERS

A partnership represents a voluntary association of individuals carrying out a business purpose. In this association, a *fiduciary relationship* exists among the partners, requiring them to exercise good faith, loyalty to the firm, and sound business judgment in conducting the firm's business. An individual partner is viewed as a co-owner of partnership property, creating a *tenancy in partnership*. When specific assets are contributed by a partner, they lose their identity as to source and become the shared property of the partnership. Without the consent of all partners, such property cannot be utilized by any partner for personal purposes.

The relationship between partners also is characterized as one of *mutual agency,* which means that each partner is an agent for the other partners and the partnership when transacting partnership business. Therefore, in carrying on the business of the partnership, the acts of every partner bind the partnership itself, even when a partner commits a wrongful act or a breach of trust. However, if a partner has no authority to act for the partnership and the party with whom the partner is dealing knows this, the partnership is not bound by the partner's actions.

LEGAL LIABILITY OF A PARTNERSHIP

Partnerships are classified as either general or limited regarding liability of the partners. In a *general partnership,* the partners act publicly on behalf of the partnership and are personally liable, jointly and severally, for the unsatisfied obligations of the partnership. This unlimited liability is in sharp contrast to the limited liability of a corporation and its shareholders. Thus, if a partnership were insolvent, the unsatisfied creditors could seek to recover against the net personal assets of individual partners. Newly admitted partners, who are personally liable for partnership debts incurred subsequent to this admission, are liable for debts of the previous partnership only to the extent of their capital interest in the partnership.

In contrast, a *limited partnership* consists of one or more general partners and one or more limited partners who contribute capital but do not participate in the management of the company. The one or more general partners have unlimited liability as in the case of a general partnership. However, the limited partners' liability for partnership obligations is restricted to a stated amount, usually equal to their capital interest in the partnership.

UNDERLYING EQUITY THEORIES

Equity theories relate to how an entity is viewed from an accounting and legal viewpoint. These theories deal with the question of who is the entity. For example, an entity may be viewed as all providers of capital, individual owners (partners/shareholders), management, or a separate, distinct legal entity. Partnerships have been primarily affected by the *proprietary theory,* which looks at the entity through the eyes of the owners. Characteristics of a partnership that emphasize that the entity is viewed as the individual owners include the following:

- Salaries to partners are viewed as distributions of income rather than a component of income.
- Unlimited liability of general partners extends beyond the entity to the individual partners.
- Income of the partnership is not taxed at the partnership level but, rather, is included as part of the partners' individual taxable income.
- An original partnership is dissolved upon the admission or withdrawal of a partner.

Partnerships also have been influenced by the *entity theory* which views the business unit as a separate and distinct entity possessing its own existence apart from the individual partners. This theory is characteristic of corporations; yet, it is the basis for certain partnership characteristics. For example, a partnership may enter into contracts in its own name. Also, property contributed to a partnership by individual partners becomes the property of the partnership, and the contributing partner no longer retains a claim to the specific assets contributed.

FORMATION AND AGREEMENTS

A partnership may come into existence without having to receive formal, legal, or state approval, and may result simply from the actions of the parties involved. This lack of formality may be viewed as an advantage of a partnership. However, it is still necessary to carefully plan and evaluate various factors affecting the partnership. Forward thinking when organizing a partnership will benefit both the business and its partners.

In order to properly capture the intent of the partners involved, it is advisable to develop a written partnership agreement. Critical issues that must be addressed include: admission of partners, withdrawal of partners, and the allocation of profits and losses. Such an agreement is referred to as the *articles of partnership* and, at minimum, should include the following provisions:

1. Partnership name and address.
2. Partners' names and addresses.
3. Effective date of partnership.
4. A description of the general business purpose and the limited duration of such purpose, if applicable.
5. Powers and duties of partners.
6. Procedures governing the valuation of assets invested.
7. Procedures governing the admission of a new partner(s).
8. Procedures governing the distribution of profits and losses.
9. Procedures governing the payment or receipt of interest on loans (versus capital contributions) with partners.
10. Salaries to be paid to partners.
11. Withdrawals of capital to be allowed each partner and the determination of what constitutes excess withdrawals.
12. Procedures governing the death of a partner and the determination of the decedent's equity in the partnership.
13. Procedures governing the retirement of a partner and the determination of the partner's equity in the partnership.
14. Matters requiring the consent of all partners.
15. The date when the profits and losses are divided and the partnership books are closed.
16. The basis of accounting (e.g., accrual or cash).

As the accounting for a partnership is developed more fully in this text, it will become apparent that the articles of partnership provide crucial guidance.

Even though the UPA covers certain topics found in the articles of partnership, it is important to note that many sections of the UPA are applicable only in the absence of a partnership agreement. Legal and accounting issues affecting a partnership are resolved best by evaluating the intent of the partners as set forth in a partnership agreement, rather than looking to the UPA.

ACCEPTABLE ACCOUNTING PRINCIPLES

There is a general presumption that an entity's financial position and results of operations should be accounted for in conformity with generally accepted accounting principles (GAAP). As GAAP has developed and become more complex, many have questioned the applicability of such principles to smaller business organizations, a large number of which are organized as partnerships. In response to this concern, it is recognized that in some circumstances a basis or method of accounting other than GAAP may be appropriate and not adversely affect the fairness of the financial statements.

The Auditing Standards Board recognizes several comprehensive bases of accounting (OCBOA) other than GAAP including:

- The cash (receipts and disbursements) basis of accounting and modifications of the basis such as a modified accrual basis.
- The tax basis of accounting based on taxation principles that are used to file an income tax return.

Tax basis accounting generally consists of a cash basis or accrual basis format with certain exceptions which primarily result from tax regulations differing from GAAP. The tax basis of accounting is a frequent choice of many partnerships. Depreciation accounting can be used to illustrate the focus of tax basis accounting. Assume a depreciable asset has an economic useful life of six years and is consumed uniformly over its life. If accrual accounting were used, it would seem that the asset should be depreciated over six years using the straight-line method of depreciation. However, adoption of the tax basis of accounting could involve the use of a shorter life and an accelerated depreciation method. Furthermore, in some instances tax basis accounting would allow the immediate expensing of depreciable assets even though such treatment would not be justified by accrual accounting.

The recognition of these other comprehensive bases provides many smaller and specialized entities, many of which may be partnerships, with an acceptable alternative to GAAP. The use of OCBOA will not impair the fairness of their financial statements as evaluated by outside independent accountants. In practice, it is very common to find partnerships using a comprehensive basis of accounting other than GAAP. Due to the special tax aspects of a partnership, many such entities use the tax basis of accounting rather than GAAP.

PARTNERSHIP DISSOLUTION

Although a partnership is formed easily and does not need state approval, its life is limited, and it may be dissolved much more easily than a corporation. *Dissolution* is defined in Section 29 of the UPA as "the change in the relation of the partners caused by any partner ceasing to be associated in the carrying on as distinguished from the winding up of the business." Generally, a partnership is dissolved upon the death, withdrawal, or bankruptcy of an individual partner (owner). The admission of a new partner also results in the dissolution of the former partnership. Thus, any change in the association of the individual partners is termed dissolution.

Although dissolution occurs when there is a change in a partner's association with the other partners, it does not result necessarily in the termination of the basic business function. Therefore, a change in the ownership structure dissolves the former partnership, but often, this change results in the formation of a new partnership to carry on the business purpose of the original partnership. The dissolution of a partnership resulting from the admission or withdrawal of a partner is more fully discussed in Chapter 15 of this text.

TAX CONSIDERATIONS

Unlike corporations, a partnership is not a separate taxable entity but a conduit through which taxable income or operating losses pass to the tax returns of the individual partners. The partnership must file an information return (Federal Form 1065) with the partnership revenues and expenses, which pass through to the individual partners.

Even though a partnership is not a taxable entity, accounting for partnerships for tax-reporting purposes can become extremely complex. The tax code does not view a partnership as a separate distinct entity but focuses, rather, on the individual partners. Therefore, activities of the partnership must be evaluated from a tax standpoint based on their impact on individual partners. This viewpoint results in special rules which must be understood by practicing accountants. Furthermore, the unique tax-related aspects of a partnership must be understood in order to advise clients as to whether or not the partnership form of organization is appropriate. The appendix to this chapter discusses in greater detail the tax-related aspects of a partnership.

ACCOUNTING FOR PARTNERSHIP ACTIVITIES

The activities of a partnership consist of several phases, including the initial contribution of capital to the partnership. This initial phase provides the capital necessary to begin operating activities. The remainder of this chapter discusses accounting for the partners' capital investments and the allocation of operating profits and losses among the partners. Although partners' capital investments may be subsequently influenced by partners entering or exiting the partnership and the liquidation of a partnership, these topics are discussed in the next chapter.

CONTRIBUTIONS AND DISTRIBUTIONS OF CAPITAL

The capital contributed by shareholders to a corporation is accounted for in several accounts including capital stock, paid-in capital in excess of par, and retained earnings. Unlike a corporation, the capital investment in a partnership generally is accounted for through two accounts for each partner, a temporary account referred to as the drawing account and a permanent account referred to as the capital account.

It is not unusual for a partner to withdraw available assets (typically cash) from a partnership throughout the year. Preferably the amount and timing of a partner's withdrawal of assets should be addressed in the articles of partnership. However, practically speaking, withdrawals are often informal and are not easily projected due to cash flow constraints. In some instances, withdrawals in excess of some amount are considered to be direct reductions of a partner's capital account rather than a withdrawal. Some partnerships view any withdrawal as a direct reduction of a capital account. However, in some partnerships a separate account referred to as a drawing account is used to record a partner's withdrawal of capital. Withdrawals of assets, regardless of how accounted for, reduce the overall capital of individual partners and the partnership.

A partner's withdrawals also include payments that are made by the partnership on behalf of an individual partner. For example, if a partnership pays off an individual partner's automobile loan, this is no different than if the partner had withdrawn the cash from the partnership and then paid off the loan personally.

The drawing account is a temporary account and is periodically closed to the partner's capital accounts. The balance sheet of a partnership therefore will present only the capital account balances of the partners. To summarize, the drawing account established for each partner is debited and credited for the following transactions:

Drawing Account

Debit	Credit
Periodic withdrawals of partnership assets up to a specified amount	Closing of balance to partner's capital account

Each partner's interest in the net assets of the partnership is measured at book value in the capital account established for that partner. This account indicates the destination of capital (claims to net assets) upon dissolution of the partnership. It is important to note that the capital balance does not normally reflect the fair market value or tax basis of the partner's interest in the net assets of the partnership.

To summarize, the partner's capital account is debited and credited for the following transactions:

Capital Account

Debit	Credit
Withdrawals in excess of a specified amount	Initial and subsequent investments of capital
Closing of a net debit balance in the partner's drawing account	Partner's share of partnership profits
Partner's share of partnership losses	

As is the case with all entities, the investment of capital in a partnership should be measured at the fair market value of all tangible and intangible assets contributed. An individual partner's liabilities that have been assumed by the partnership also should be recorded at fair market value.

The exception to this would be in the case where a partnership has adopted the tax basis of accounting. The appendix to this chapter discusses how a partner's interest in capital is measured for tax purposes. The proper valuation of each partner's net investment of capital is extremely important. For example, if an asset invested by a partner is undervalued by the partnership and is sold immediately for a gain, all the partners share in the realized gain, which properly should have accrued to the original investing partner.

The postclosing balances in the capital accounts of the various partners represent each partner's interest in the net assets of the partnership at a point in time. A partner's interest in the partnership is different from the partner's interest in the profits and losses of the partnership. To illustrate, assume partners A and B have capital balances of $8,000 and $32,000, respectively.

Also assume that profits and losses are allocated to partners A and B in the amount of 40% and 60%, respectively. These profit and loss ratios would not be confused with the partners' capital ratios which are 20% ($8,000 divided by $40,000) and 80% ($32,000 divided by $40,000) for A and B, respectively.

Occasionally, partners will loan assets to the partnership, or the partnership will loan assets to partners. It is important from a legal standpoint to differentiate between a loan and an additional investment of capital, especially when the liquidation of a partnership occurs. The nature of such transactions should be made clear by examining the intent of the individual partner or the partnership. If the contribution by a partner is really an additional investment of capital, it should be accounted for in the partner's capital account. However, if the transaction is truly a loan, it should be accounted for in a separate loan account for the partner, and provision for the payment of interest on the loan should be made.

Illustration 14-1 demonstrates the use of various partnership accounts in order to record partnership activity.

DIVISION OF PROFITS AND LOSSES

An important process to be outlined in the articles of partnership is the manner in which profits and losses are to be divided among the partners. There are several alternative methods of allocating profits and losses. However, if the articles of partnership are silent on this point, Section 18 of the UPA states that profits and losses are to be divided equally among the partners.

The division of partnership income should be based on an analysis of the correlation between the capital and labor committed to the firm by individual partners and the income that subsequently is generated. As a result, profits might be divided in one or more of the following ways:

1. According to a ratio,
2. According to the capital investments of the partners, and/or
3. According to the labor (or service) rendered by the partners.

Illustration 14-1

Examples of Accounting for Partnership Activity

Event	Entry		
Partner A contributes cash to the partnership. Partner B contributes inventory and office equipment, and the partnership assumes the liability associated with the equipment. The equipment was recorded by B at a book value of $6,000. However, the equipment's fair market value is $4,000.	Cash...................... Inventory................. Office Equipment........... Note Payable .... Partner A, Capital .... Partner B, Capital.........	10,000 5,000 4,000	2,000 10,000 7,000
Partner B loans the partnership $3,000 to be repaid in one year at a stated annual interest rate of 6%.	Cash...................... Partner B, Loan	3,000	3,000
A personal debt owed by Partner A is paid by the partnership.	Partner A, Drawing .... Cash...................	500	500
Partners A and B withdraw cash of $500 and $1,200, respectively. Drawings in excess of $1,000 are viewed as excessive withdrawals and are charged against capital.	Partner A, Drawing .... Partner B, Drawing .... Partner B, Capital........... Cash..................	500 1,000 200	1,700
The net income of the partnership is divided equally between the partners.	Income Summary .... Partner A, Capital .... Partner B, Capital.........	10,000	5,000 5,000
The partners' drawing accounts are closed to their respective capital accounts.	Partner A, Capital .... Partner B, Capital........... Partner A, Drawing .... Partner B, Drawing	1,000 1,000	1,000 1,000

Profit and Loss Ratios.   Partnership agreements frequently call for the division of profits and losses according to some ratio. Normally, the ratio designed for the division of profits also is used for the division of losses, unless a specific provision to the contrary exists. This method obviously provides a simplified way of dividing profits and, if approached properly, may provide an equitable division as well. Theoretically, the ratio should attempt to combine into one base the capital and service contributions made by the respective partners. Again, it is important to note that a partner's interest in profits and losses is often different from the partner's interest in total partnership capital (net assets).

To illustrate this method, assume the articles of partnership state that partnership profits and losses should be divided between partners A and B in the ratio of 60:40. Partnership income of $20,000 would be divided as follows:

	Partner A	Partner B
Income to partners:		
A: $20,000 × 60%	$12,000	
B: $20,000 × 40%		$8,000

Capital Investments of Partners.   The capital investments of the partners, represented by the balances in their respective capital accounts, may be employed as a basis for dividing a portion of the profits. The division is accomplished by imputing interest on the invested capital at some specified rate. This interest is not viewed as a partnership expense, but rather as a means of allocating profits and losses among the partners. Typically, the balance of profits not allocated on the basis of invested capital is allocated according to some profit and loss ratio.

When the partners' capital investments are to be used as the basis for allocating profits, the partnership agreement should specify:

1. Whether the respective partners' capital balances are to be determined before or after the partners' year-to-date withdrawals recorded in their drawing accounts are offset against their capital accounts.
2. Whether the amount of capital investment for allocation purposes is to be:
   a. capital at the beginning of the accounting period,
   b. capital at the end of the accounting period, or
   c. weighted average capital during the accounting period.
3. The rate of interest to be imputed on the invested capital.

With respect to the first point, it is important that the partnership agreement clearly establish how invested capital is to be determined. Since each partner's equity is a combination of capital and drawing account balances, partners' drawings may be offset against the balances in their respective capital accounts for purposes of allocating income based on invested capital. However, a partnership agreement may state that only withdrawals above a certain limit are to be viewed as offsets against capital balances. It is possible for a partnership agreement to call for interest to be imputed only if the amount of invested capital exceeds some prescribed limit or average amount.

To illustrate the use of invested capital as a basis for allocating partnership profits, assume:

1. Partnership profit is $20,000.
2. Interest on invested capital is to be imputed at the rate of 10%.
3. Profits not allocated on the basis of invested capital are to be allocated equally among the partners.
4. The capital accounts of partners A and B, just prior to the closing of their drawing accounts, are as follows:

Partner A, Capital			
10/1/X1	30,000	1/1/X1	100,000
		7/1/X1	10,000

Partner B, Capital			
4/1/X1	10,000	1/1/X1	60,000

If interest is to be imputed on the partners' invested capital at the beginning of the period (1/1/X1), the partnership profit of $20,000 would be allocated as follows:

	Partner A	Partner B	Total
Interest on beginning capital:			
A: 10% × $100,000	$10,000		$10,000
B: 10% × $ 60,000		$6,000	6,000
			$16,000
Balance per ratio (equally)	2,000	2,000	4,000
Allocation of profit	$12,000	$8,000	$20,000

If interest is to be imputed on the partners' invested capital at the end of the period, the partnership profit of $20,000 would be allocated as follows:

	Partner A	Partner B	Total
Interest on ending capital:			
A: 10% × $80,000	$ 8,000		$ 8,000
B: 10% × $50,000		$5,000	5,000
			$13,000
Balance per ratio (equally)	3,500	3,500	7,000
Allocation of profit	$11,500	$8,500	$20,000

If interest is to be imputed on the partners' weighted average invested capital during the period, the partnership profit of $20,000 would be allocated as follows:

	Partner A	Partner B	Total
Interest on weighted average capital:			
A: 10% × $97,500 (Schedule A)	$ 9,750		$ 9,750
B: 10% × $52,500 (Schedule B)		$5,250	5,250
			$15,000
Balance per ratio (equally)	2,500	2,500	5,000
Allocation of profit	$12,250	$7,750	$20,000

Schedule A
Weighted Average Capital of Partner A

(1) Amount Invested	(2) Number of Months Invested	(1) × (2) Weighted Dollars
$100,000	6	$ 600,000
110,000	3	330,000
80,000	3	240,000
	12	$1,170,000

Weighted average capital: $1,170,000 ÷ 12 = $ 97,500

Schedule B
Weighted Average Capital of Partner B

(1) Amount Invested	(2) Number of Months Invested	(1) × (2) Weighted Dollars
$ 60,000	3	$180,000
50,000	9	450,000
	12	$630,000

Weighted average capital: $630,000 ÷ 12 = $ 52,500

Services Rendered by Partners.   A partner's labor or service to the firm may be a primary force in the generation of revenue. Normally, the profit and loss agreement recognizes variations in effort by calling for a portion of income to be allocated to partners as salary. Such salaries, like interest on capital investments, are viewed as a means of allocating income rather than as an expense. It is important to note that this treatment of partners' salaries differs from the treatment of employee/shareholder salaries in a corporation, and the difference should be considered when the performance of a partnership is compared with that of a competing corporation.

When dealing with a profit and loss agreement that employs salaries as a means of allocating income, it is important not to confuse such salaries with partners' drawings. For example, a partner's withdrawing $1,000 a month from the partnership may suggest that $12,000 of partnership income is being distributed to the partner as an annual salary or that these withdrawals may be ignored for purposes of dividing profits. Generally, a partner's drawing is not viewed as a salary but as a withdrawal of assets that reduces the partner's equity. For clarification purposes, the partnership agreement should state whether regular withdrawals of specific amounts should be viewed as salary for purposes of allocating income among the partners.

Bonuses to partners also may be used as a means of recognizing a partner's service to the firm. Such bonuses usually are figured as a percentage of partnership income either before or after certain other components of the allocation process. In its most simple form, the bonus is a percentage of net income. However, if the bonus is to reward service beyond that already recognized by salaries and/or interest, the bonus may be expressed as a percentage of partnership net income after salaries and interest. In some instances the bonus may be expressed as a percentage of net income after the bonus. To illustrate the calculation of a bonus, assume a partnership has net income of $120,000 of which $60,000 and $5,000 have already been allocated as salaries and interest, respectively. The bonus is defined in the partnership agreement as 10% of partnership net income after salaries and interest. The bonus is calculated as follows:

$$\text{Bonus} = X\% \text{ (Net Income} - \text{Salaries} - \text{Interest)}$$
$$\text{Bonus} = 10\% \text{ ($120,000} - \$60,000 - \$5,000)$$
$$\text{Bonus} = 10\% \text{ ($55,000)}$$
$$\text{Bonus} = \$5,500$$

If the agreement had stated that the bonus would be calculated based on net income after salaries, interest, and bonus, the calculation would be as follows:

$$Bonus = X\% \text{ (Net Income – Salaries – Interest – Bonus)}$$
$$Bonus = 10\% \text{ (\$120,000 – \$60,000 – \$5,000 – Bonus)}$$
$$110\% \text{ Bonus} = 10\% \text{ (\$120,000 – \$60,000 – \$5,000)}$$
$$110\% \text{ Bonus} = 10\% \text{ (\$55,000)}$$
$$110\% \text{ Bonus} = \$5,500$$
$$Bonus = \$5,000$$

Multiple Bases of Allocation.   In many cases, income is allocated to the respective partners by combining several allocation techniques. To illustrate, assume a profit and loss agreement of the ABC partnership contains the following provisions:

1. Interest of 6% is to be paid on that portion of a partner's ending capital balance in excess of $100,000.
2. Partner C is to receive a bonus equal to 10% of partnership income after the bonus.
3. Salaries of $13,000 and $12,000 are to be paid to partners A and C, respectively.
4. The balance of income is to be distributed in the ratio of 2:1:1 to A, B, and C, respectively.

Assuming a partnership income of $33,000 and ending capital balances of $80,000, $150,000, and $110,000 for partners A, B, and C, respectively, income is distributed to the partners as shown in Illustration 14-2.

Illustration 14-2
Profit Allocation: Multiple Bases

	Partner A	Partner B	Partner C	Total
Interest on excess capital balance...		$3,000	$ 600	$ 3,600
Bonus..............................			3,000*	3,000
Salaries...........................	$13,000		12,000	25,000
Subtotal	$13,000	$3,000	$15,600	$31,600
Remaining profit...................	700	350	350	1,400
Income allocation..................	$13,700	$3,350	$15,950	$33,000

*Bonus = 10% (Net income – Bonus)
Bonus = 10% ($33,000 – Bonus)
(110%) Bonus = $3,300
Bonus = $3,000

Allocation of Profit Deficiencies and Losses.   In the previous examples of profit allocations, the partnership income was large enough to satisfy all of the provisions of the profit and loss agreement. However, if the income is not sufficient or an operating loss exists, one of the two following alternatives may be employed:

1. Completely satisfy all provisions of the profit and loss agreement and use the profit and loss ratios to absorb any deficiency or additional loss caused by such action.
2. Satisfy each of the provisions to whatever extent is possible. For example, the allocation of salaries would be satisfied to whatever extent possible before the allocation of interest is begun.

To illustrate these alternatives, assume the same information used in Illustration 14-2 for the ABC partnership, except that the partnership income is $22,000. In Illustration 14-3, the income of $22,000 is divided by using the first alternative. When studying Illustration 14-3, it is important to note that the allocation of interest, bonus, and salaries results in an excessive allocation or deficiency of $8,600 (subtotal of $30,600 less the income of $22,000), which must be subtracted from the partners' previous allocated amounts. This deficiency is allocated among the partners according to their profit and loss ratios just like a remaining profit except that it is subtracted rather than added.

Illustration 14-3
Profit Allocation: Deficiency Allocated in Profit and Loss Ratio

	Partner A	Partner B	Partner C	Total
Interest on excess capital balance...		$3,000	$ 600	$ 3,600
Bonus..........................			2,000*	2,000
Salaries........................	$13,000		12,000	25,000
Subtotal	$13,000	$3,000	$14,600	$30,600
Deficiency	(4,300)	(2,150)	(2,150)	(8,600)
Income allocation..............	$ 8,700	$ 850	$12,450	$22,000

*Bonus = 10% (Net income − Bonus)
 Bonus = 10% ($22,000 − Bonus)
(110%) Bonus = $2,200
 Bonus = $2,000

Normally, the first method also is used when the partnership has an overall loss. For example, given a partnership loss of $2,400, the methodology in Illustration 14-3 would be employed, except that a bonus would not be recognized.

The allocation of the assumed loss of $2,400 is shown in Illustration 14-4. In this case the allocation of the interest and salaries results in allocating $28,600 of income even though there is a loss of $2,400. This results in a deficiency of $31,000 (subtotal of $28,600 plus the loss of $2,400) which must be allocated among the partners according to their profit and loss ratios.

The second alternative, which is used less frequently, requires that the provisions of the profit and loss agreement be ranked by order of priority. Assuming the components listed in Illustration 14-3 are already in order of priority, a partnership income of $22,000 would be distributed as shown in Illustration 14-5.

Illustration 14-4

Loss Allocation: Deficiency Allocated in Profit and Loss Ratio

	Partner A	Partner B	Partner C	Total
Interest on excess capital balance...		$3,000	$ 600	$ 3,600
Bonus (not applicable).............				
Salaries.........................	$13,000		12,000	25,000
Subtotal	$13,000	$3,000	$12,600	$28,600
Deficiency	(15,500)	(7,750)	(7,750)	(31,000)
Loss allocation	$ (2,500)	$(4,750)	$ 4,850	$ (2,400)

The salaries of $16,400 would be allocated to partners A and C according to the ratio suggested by their normal salaries of $13,000 and $12,000, respectively. Therefore, A would receive 13/25 of the $16,400, or $8,528, while C would receive 12/25, or $7,872.

Special Allocation Procedures.   A partnership profit and loss agreement may include special provisions for handling items that represent (1) corrections of prior years' income or (2) current period, nonoperating gains or losses. Even though a correction of prior years' income may not satisfy the criteria for a prior-period adjustment, as defined by the Financial Accounting Standards Board, it may be more equitable to allocate the item among the partners according to the profit and loss agreement for the relevant prior period rather than the current period. For example, assume that partners A, B, and C, who previously shared profits equally, currently share profits in the ratio of 2:2:1. Also assume that in the current year, the partnership incurs a loss of $10,000 due to the settlement of litigation involving a matter arising in a prior period. Rather than allocating the loss according to the current profit ratios, it may be more equitable to base the allocation on the prior ratios.

Illustration 14-5

Profit Allocation: Deficiency Allocated by Order of Priority

	Partner A	Partner B	Partner C	Total
Interest on excess capital balance...		$3,000	$ 600	$ 3,600
Bonus...........................			2,000*	2,000
Salaries.........................	$8,528		7,872	16,400
Income allocation.................	$8,528	$3,000	$10,472	$22,000

*Bonus = 10% (Net income – Bonus)
   Bonus = 10% ($22,000 – Bonus)
(110%) Bonus = $2,200
   Bonus = $2,000

A similar procedure may be adopted for the current period realization of nonoperating gains or losses. Rather than allocating a gain on the sale of a plant asset according to the partners' current profit-sharing ratios, it may be more equitable to use the ratios that existed during the period when unrealized appreciation actually took place. To illustrate, assume that land with a basis of $40,000 has been held for three years and is sold for $60,000 in the current period. Based on the assumed profit-sharing ratios of prior periods and amounts of annual appreciation, the $20,000 gain would be allocated to partners A, B, and C as follows:

Year	Profit Ratios	Appreciation	Profit Allocation		
			A	B	C
1	1:1:2	$ 4,000	$1,000	$1,000	$2,000
2	2:1:2	10,000	4,000	2,000	4,000
3	2:2:2	6,000	2,000	2,000	2,000
		$20,000	$7,000	$5,000	$8,000

If the partnership had not established special provisions for handling such items, the gain of $20,000 would have been allocated equally among the partners according to their current profit ratio of 2:2:2.

APPENDIX: TAX-RELATED ASPECTS OF A PARTNERSHIP

As pointed out in the chapter, a partnership is not a separate taxable entity. However, the tax impact of partnership activities must be allocated to the partners and reported by them on their individual tax returns. This process is referred to as the *flowthrough of tax items*. Because the partnership is a conduit for tax purposes, certain elements of revenue and expense maintain their identity on the individual partner's tax return. For example, a partner's share of partnership investment income also will be classified as investment income on the individual return. It is important that certain items maintain their identity on the individual return because they are subject to special limitations and rules. Therefore, accounting for partnership income requires that certain items of revenue and expense be separately reported on the partnership informational tax return.

TAX BASIS OF A PARTNER'S INTEREST

Because the partnership is not viewed for tax purposes as a separate distinct entity but rather as consisting of separate distinct individuals, the individual partner's interest in the partnership must be measured for tax purposes. This individual interest is referred to as the partner's tax basis. The tax basis is primarily used to measure the tax gain or loss resulting from a partner's sale of his/her interest in the partnership.

In the most simple of cases, the partner's tax basis is equal to cash contributed plus his/her personal tax basis in other property transferred to the partnership. This personal tax basis would represent the tax basis of the asset before transfer to the partnership. To illustrate, assume a partner contributes $10,000 cash and equipment with a fair market value of $70,000. The original cost of the equipment less depreciation taken for tax purposes resulted in a personal tax basis of $50,000. The tax and GAAP (book) basis of the partner's interest is calculated as follows:

	Tax Basis	GAAP (Book) Basis
Cash contributed................	$10,000	$10,000
Equipment......................	50,000	70,000
Basis of partner's interest.........	$60,000	$80,000

Notice that the partner's tax basis in assets prior to transfer is not changed subsequent to transfer. In other words, the individual partner receives no increase (step-up) or decrease (step-down) in basis.

The calculation of a partner's tax basis becomes more complex when personal liabilities are transferred to and assumed by the partnership.

A partner's tax basis is decreased by the value of the liabilities assumed by other partners. When the other partners assume a portion of the debt, it is as though that amount of debt has been forgiven. Forgiveness of debt represents income to a taxpayer. This income is eventually recognized upon the sale of a partnership interest because the tax basis has been reduced by this amount; therefore, the gain on the sale is increased by this amount. Alternatively, a partner's tax basis is increased by the value of other partners' liabilities assumed by them. The allocation among partners of liabilities transferred to a partnership is based on the partners' respective profit and loss ratios.

To illustrate, assume partners A and B contribute assets with personal tax bases of $80,000 and $110,000, respectively. Liabilities associated with these assets are $30,000 and $60,000, respectively for A and B. Profits and losses are allocated 40% to partner A and 60% to partner B. The tax basis of the partners is determined as follows:

	Partner A	Partner B
Tax basis of assets contributed.............................	$80,000	$110,000
Tax basis of other partner's liabilities assumed (40% of $60,000 for A and 60% of $30,000 for B)............................	24,000	18,000
Tax basis of liabilities assumed by other partners (60% of $30,000 for A and 40% of $60,000 for B)..........................	(18,000)	(24,000)
Tax basis of partner's interest..............................	$86,000	$104,000

It is important to note that the sum of the tax bases of partners' interests ($86,000 plus $104,000 in the above example) must always equal the sum of the tax basis of assets contributed by the partners ($80,000 plus $110,000 in the above example).

The initial tax basis of a partner subsequently changes due to the ongoing activities of the partnership. The basis will be increased by the following:

1. Additional contributions of individual assets.
2. The partner's share (based on profit and loss ratios) of increases in partnership liabilities resulting from:
   a. Assuming partners' personal liabilities.
   b. Direct liabilities of the partnership.
3. The partner's share of partnership taxable income.
4. The partner's share of separately identified items of income not included in tax income (loss).

A partner's basis will be decreased by the following:

1. Distributions of partnership assets.
2. The portion of the partner's additional personal liabilities assumed by the partnership.
3. The partner's share of partnership tax losses.
4. The partner's share of separately identified items of loss not included in taxable income (loss).

A partner's tax basis may not be decreased below zero. If operating losses would decrease the basis below zero, they are carried forward by the partners and used to offset subsequent increases in basis.

AVOIDANCE OF DOUBLE TAXATION

Major differences exist between partnerships and corporations in the area of taxation. These differences result from the fact that corporations, unlike partnerships, are viewed as separate and distinct taxable entities. The primary result of this difference is that a corporation is taxed when the income is earned, and the individual shareholders are taxed when the income is distributed as dividends. This characteristic is referred to as *double taxation*, and its significance depends on the extent to which dividends are distributed and on the tax rates to which the owners are subject. The effect of double taxation may be minimized if employee-shareholders do not receive dividends, but are rewarded in the form of salaries, which are deductible expenses. However, the Internal Revenue Service must be satisfied that the amount of such salaries is reasonable. A corporation also may attempt to avoid double taxation by accumulating earnings or by electing to be taxed as a partnership through a Subchapter S election.

Rather than distributing taxable dividends, the corporation may retain income so that the shareholders are not taxed on that income. However, if the shareholders sell their stock in the corporation and if the stock sells at a price that exceeds its tax basis, the gain on the sale would be taxed at the rate applied to capital gain. In effect, the accumulated earnings then become taxed.

It should be noted, however, that the retention of income may not be practical because of the accumulated earnings tax. This tax is a penalty imposed on a corporation that accumulates its earnings to avoid the income tax that would have been incurred by the shareholders if dividends had been distributed. The intent to avoid taxes may be established by demonstrating that the corporation has accumulated earnings in excess of the reasonable needs of the business. Reasonable needs of the business would include such items as plant expansion, asset replacement, debt retirement, stock retirement, customer-supplier loans, and working capital.

The disadvantage associated with double taxation may be eliminated if a corporation elects to be taxed as a Subchapter S corporation. Under this election, the corporation is treated as a partnership for tax purposes. The corporate entity itself pays no tax, and the shareholders pay tax on their share of corporate income, whether or not it is distributed to them. This special treatment is based on the view that certain corporations, in substance, are the same as a partnership. This analogy is appropriate for nonpublic corporations, in which major shareholders act in the same capacity as partners in a partnership.

The corporation electing to be taxed as a Subchapter S corporation must meet certain requirements. For example, the corporation must have only one class of stock owned by thirty-five or fewer stockholders. Certain technical procedures also are employed with respect to the determination and classification of taxable income.

Some of the more significant tax-related differences between a partnership and a corporation are summarized in Exhibit 14-1.

Exhibit 14-1
Significant Tax-Related Differences
Between a Partnership and a Corporation

	Partnership	Corporation
Level(s) of Taxation	Not a separate taxable entity but, rather, a conduit through which taxable items are passed on to the owners (partners). The individual partners are taxed on their shares of partnership income, whether distributed or not, at the progressive tax rates applicable to individuals.	A separate, distinct taxable entity apart from the shareholder. Therefore, income is taxed once at the corporate level and again at the shareholder level when such income is distributed, i.e., double taxation. The corporation is taxed at progressive rates ranging from 15% to 39%.
Maintaining the Identity of Various Elements of Taxable Income	Elements making up a partnership's income maintain their special tax status on the returns of the individual partners; e.g., if a partnership has tax-exempt income, it retains its identity in the preparation of the individual partners' tax returns as tax-exempt income.	Elements making up corporate income do not maintain their special status when distributed to shareholders in the form of a dividend; e.g., if corporate income includes some tax-exempt income, that income will be taxed to the shareholders when distributed in the form of a dividend.
Other Tax	The tax advantages associated with certain fringe benefits are much greater for employee-shareholders than they would be if the employees were partners in a firm. Such fringe benefits may involve profit-sharing plans, pension plans, medical reimbursement and insurance plans, group life insurance, and death benefits.	

QUESTIONS

1. Assuming a business is insolvent (liabilities exceed assets), compare the legal liability of the owners if the business is a partnership rather than a corporation.
2. With respect to the allocation of profits among partners, what is the significance of classifying cash received from a partner as a loan rather than contributed capital?
3. Discuss how partners' salaries are viewed in a partnership and how the proprietary theory explains this viewpoint.
4. What is the concept of double taxation and why isn't it characteristic of a partnership?
5. What adjustments are necessary in order to compare the income of a business organized as a partnership to that of a similar business organized as a corporation?
6. Discuss what special allocation procedures might be addressed in a partnership's profit and loss agreement.
7. Under what circumstances might a salary or bonus be more appropriate than interest on capital balances as a means of allocating profits?
8. With respect to the allocation of profits among partners, what is the logic underlying the accounting for "withdrawals in excess of a specified amount" as a direct reduction of the capital account?
9. A partner receives $1,000 a month from the partnership. What is the significance of viewing the payment as a withdrawal versus a salary?
10. When employing a bonus as a means of allocating profits, why is net income after the bonus, rather than before the bonus, generally used to calculate the bonus?
11. When assets are contributed to a partnership by an individual partner, the partnership's tax basis of the assets is generally not the fair market value at date of transfer. What is the logic underlying this treatment?

EXERCISES

Exercise 1. In 19X1, a new partnership purchased land on the edge of the town of Otisville. The partners erected a building and opened a furniture and appliance store under the name of Otisville Furniture Fair. The partnership agreement specified that profits or losses should be shared equally after the allocation of partners' salary allowances and interest on average capital balances.

Otisville has grown considerably, and the store is now one of the most prominent stores in a fashionable suburban area. Good management, imaginative merchandising, and the general growth in the economy have made Otisville Furniture Fair the leading and most profitable firm of its type in the Otisville trade area.

Now the partners wish to admit another investor and incorporate the business. The original partners will purchase at par an amount of preferred stock equal to the book value of their interest in the partnership and common stock equal to that portion of fair market value that exceeds their book value. The new investor will purchase, at a 10% premium over par value, common and preferred stock equal to one-third of the total number of shares purchased by the original partners. The corporation then will purchase the Otisville Furniture Fair partnership at its fair market value from the partners. After the consummation of the partners' plan, the corporation will acquire the partnership assets, assume the liabilities, and employ the partners to manage the corporation.

(1) List and explain the differences in terms and valuations that would be expected in comparing the assets that appear on the balance sheet of the proposed corporation and the assets that appear on the partnership balance sheet.

(2) List and explain the differences that would be expected in a comparison of an income statement prepared for the proposed corporation and an income statement prepared for the partnership.

(AICPA adapted)

Exercise 2. Hanyard, Robertson, Turman, and Kelly own a publishing company that they operate as a partnership. The partnership agreement includes the following:

(a) Hanyard receives a salary of $20,000 and a bonus of 3% of income after all bonuses.

(b) Robertson receives a salary of $10,000 and a bonus of 2% of income after all bonuses.

(c) All partners are to receive 10% interest on their average capital balances.

The average capital balances are as follows:

Hanyard	$50,000
Robertson	45,000
Turman	20,000
Kelly	47,000

(d) Any remaining profits are to be divided equally among the partners.

(1) Determine how a profit of $105,000 would be allocated among the partners.

(2) Determine how a loss of $40,000 would be allocated among the partners.

(3) Determine how a profit of $40,000 would be allocated among the partners assuming the following priority system: Income should be allocated by first giving priority to interest on invested capital, then bonuses, then salary, and then according to the profit and loss percentages.

Exercise 3. You are asked to provide guidance as to how to allocate profits and losses for the following two partnerships:

(1) Riley, Scott, and Thompson are partners in a law firm that practices in several different areas of law including patent law, family law, and corporate law. Each of the partners practices in a different area of law.

(2) Norman and Manning is a partnership specializing in tool and die making. The partnership has several major contracts, and the partners work closely with each other on each contract.

   Discuss what combinations of bonus, salary, and interest on capital would provide for the most equitable allocation of profit and losses for each of the partnerships described above.

Exercise 4. Medina, Harris, and Anderson are partners in Entertainment Systems. The partnership earned a modest profit of $30,000 in 19X3. The partnership agreement includes the following regarding the allocation of profits or losses:

(a) Interest of 8% is to be paid on the portion of a partner's ending capital balance in excess of $75,000.

(b) Medina and Harris receive salaries of $20,000 and $30,000, respectively. Both individuals are actively involved with day-to-day operations.

(c) The balance of income is to be distributed in the ratio of 2:1:1 to Medina, Harris, and Anderson, respectively.

Assume ending capital balances of $60,000, $80,000, and $100,000 for partners Medina, Harris, and Anderson, respectively.

(1) Allocate the profit among the partners assuming:
 (a) The profit and loss ratios are used to absorb any deficiency or additional loss.
 (b) Each of the provisions of the profit and loss agreement are satisfied to whatever extent possible. The priority order is interest, salaries, and then remaining amounts per the profit and loss ratios.
(2) Discuss which method would be best suited for this partnership.

Exercise 5. Jackson, Karner, and Lawson are partners in a lumber company. Their partnership agreement provides for the following profit and loss distributions:
 (a) Jackson, Karner, and Lawson are to receive salaries of $20,000, $18,000, and $6,825, respectively. Jackson is to receive a bonus equal to 10% of income before the bonus.
 (b) Each partner is to receive 10% interest on the weighted average capital balance.
 (c) Withdrawals are considered to be reductions of capital for purposes of interest calculations.
 (d) Any remaining profits or losses are to be divided equally among the partners.
     Capital balance information for 19X9 is as follows:

	Jackson	Karner	Lawson
Beginning capital balance, January 1, 19X9	$5,000	$3,000	$20,000
Withdrawal of capital, April 1, 19X9	(500)		(1,000)
Capital investment, July 1, 19X9	1,000	2,000	7,500
Withdrawal of capital, October 1, 19X9	(500)	(1,000)	

Assume Jackson's share of the allocated profits is to be withdrawn. Determine how much profit the partnership must earn to allow Jackson to withdraw exactly $30,500 excluding previous withdrawals. Supporting schedules should be in good form.

Exercise 6. Hurley and Anderson are partners in a bar and grill. Included in their partnership agreement is a provision that any monthly withdrawals over $2,000 would be considered a reduction of capital. Hurley's withdrawal and investment information for the year 19X3 is as follows:

Date	Investment	Withdrawals Greater than $2,000	Allocation of Profits
January 1 (beg. balance)	$100,000		
April 1			$5,000
June 1		$2,500	
July 1			5,000
July 31	1,500		
October 1			5,000
December 1		3,000	
December 31			5,000

Determine Hurley's:
(1) Ending capital balance
(2) Simple average capital balance
(3) Weighted average capital balance

Exercise 7. Xavier, Yates, and Zale are partners in a dry cleaning business. Their partnership agreement provides that the partners shall receive interest on their respective average yearly capital balances at the rate of 8%. Any residual profits or losses shall be divided equally among the partners.
The following information is available for the second year of operations:

(a) Partners' capital balances as of January 1, 19X2:

> Xavier $24,000
> Yates 17,500
> Zale 13,000

(b) Additional investments were made during the year as follows:

> Xavier . . . . $4,500 on April 1, 19X2
> Zale . . . . $2,000 on July 1, 19X2, and
> $15,000 on September 1, 19X2

(c) The drawing accounts of the partners have the following debit balances at the end of 19X2:

> Xavier . . . . $ 1,000
> Yates   1,000
> Zale   500

(d) Partnership income for the year is $21,100.

(1) Discuss the advantages and disadvantages of using the weighted average capital balance as the base for determining interest on capital contributed.

(2) Determine the interest on weighted average capital balances that partners Xavier, Yates, and Zale should receive for the year 19X2. Assume that the partners' withdrawals are not to influence the capital balances for purposes of computing interest.

(3) Determine the capital account balances for Xavier, Yates, and Zale after all closing entries have been journalized and posted at the end of 19X2. Supporting schedules should be in good form.

Exercise 8. Powers, Scott, and Riley intend to start a business together that will be organized as a partnership. The partners are considering adopting one of the following two alternative profit-sharing agreements.

		Agreement #1	Agreement #2
Salaries:	Powers	$ 70,000	$ 29,200
	Scott	30,000	30,000
	Riley		
Bonus to Powers as a percentage of profit.		5%	15%
Interest on average capital.		8%	10%
Estimated average capital balances:			
	Powers	$ 50,000	$ 50,000
	Scott	100,000	100,000
	Riley	150,000	150,000
Remaining profit percentage:			
	Powers	40%	50%
	Scott	40	35
	Riley	20	15

Powers seeks your advice as to which agreement would be best for them to accept.

(1) Discuss the issues involved in determining the correct choice.

(2) Calculate the level of income at which Powers is indifferent between the choices.

APPENDIX EXERCISES

Exercise A-1. Thomas is considering joining Baker and Nap in a partnership. Baker and Nap will each contribute cash of $39,000 to the new partnership. The partners will share profits and losses equally and all partners have individual tax rates of 30%. Thomas is considering contributing a parcel of land to the partnership that has a fair market value of $99,000 and an individual tax basis of $39,000. If the parcel is contributed to the partnership, the partnership would sell the parcel and distribute $6,000 to each partner in order to pay the resulting individual taxes on the sale. Thomas wants to know if they would be better off to personally sell the parcel and contribute the after-tax proceeds to the partnership. How would you advise Thomas?

Exercise A-2. Berkshire Investments is a partnership consisting of three partners: Pearson, Ellis, and Parker. Pearson and Ellis each have a 40% interest in capital prior to withdrawals and the allocation of profits. Ellis and Parker are considering selling their interest in the partnership and want to estimate the personal tax impact of this sale. The activity of the partnership is summarized as follows:

	Fair Market Value/GAAP Basis	Tax Basis
Contributions of cash:		
Pearson	$ 80,000	$80,000
Ellis	25,000	25,000
Contributions of noncash assets:		
Ellis	100,000	70,000
Parker	60,000	68,000
Liabilities transferred to the partnership:		
Ellis	45,000	45,000
Parker	20,000	20,000
Withdrawals of cash:		
Pearson	30,000	30,000
Ellis	20,000	20,000
Parker	15,000	15,000
Allocation of Profits:		
Pearson	30,000	28,000
Ellis	30,000	28,000
Parker	30,000	28,000

(1) Calculate the book and tax basis of Ellis's and Parker's interest in the partnership.
(2) Discuss why a partner's percentage interest in capital may change over time.

PROBLEMS

Problem 14-1. Metco Company is a partnership owned by Sloan, Robinson, and Malone. Their partnership agreement contains the following provisions regarding the allocation of profits and losses:
(a) Sloan and Robinson are to receive salaries of $10,500 and $16,100, respectively.
(b) Malone is to receive a bonus of 10% of partnership income after the bonus.
(c) All partners are to receive interest of 5% on their weighted average capital balances. Withdrawals are to be considered reductions in capital for the purpose of calculating the interest amounts.
Investment and withdrawal information for each partner is as follows:

	Sloan	Robinson	Malone
Beginning capital balance 1/1/X8 ...	$20,000	$30,000	$40,000
Withdrawal of capital 4/1/X8 ...	(4,000)	(6,000)	
Withdrawal of capital 5/1/X8 ...			(10,000)
Capital investment 7/1/X8. ...	2,000		8,000
Withdrawal of capital 10/1/X8 ...	(1,000)	(2,000)	

Required:
(1) Prepare a schedule to allocate an $88,000 profit among the partners.
(2) Sloan has an opportunity to take a position at McMichaels, Inc. McMichaels has offered Sloan a total compensation package worth $38,000. In addition, if Sloan sold his interest in the partnership, they could earn $2,000 per year on the proceeds from the sale of the partnership interest. Therefore, Sloan has the opportunity to have annual income of $40,000.

Sloan would like to know how much partnership income would have to be in order to receive a profit allocation equal to this new alternative opportunity.

Problem 14-2. Nichols, James, and Wilson are environmental consultants who agree to consolidate their individual practices into a partnership as of January 1, 19X4. Each partner is contributing the following assets and related liabilities:

Fair Value	Nichols	James	Wilson
Cash. ...	$20,000	$ 5,000	$20,000
Accounts receivable ...	24,000	15,000	35,000
Supplies ...	5,000	2,000	3,000
Equipment ...	28,000	24,200	34,000
Equipment notes payable ...	(18,000)	(10,000)	(24,000)
	$59,000	$36,200	$68,000
Tax basis of equipment ...	$20,000	$24,000	$22,000

The partnership agreement provides for the allocation of profits as follows:

(a) All partners will receive 6% interest on their weighted average capital balances as defined. Capital balances will be reduced by amounts withdrawn in excess of partners' salaries. The resulting weighted average will then be reduced by salaries. Partners with deficit balances will have their profits reduced by the interest on such amounts.
(b) Salaries for Nichols, James, and Wilson are $40,000, $32,000, and $50,000, respectively. All salaries are withdrawn during the year.
(c) Each partner will receive a bonus equal to 20% of individual gross billings in excess of $100,000.
(d) James will receive an extra 10% bonus of net income reduced by the value of items (a) to (c) above.
(e) Remaining profits will be allocated among partners equally.

During the year 19X4 the partnership recognized the following net income components:

Gross billings:	
Nichols ...	$120,000
James ...	80,000
Wilson. ...	180,000

Depreciation expenses:
    Book amount.............................   6,120
    Tax return amount   20,144
    Other operating expenses....................   203,880

During the year the partners had the following drawings in excess of their salaries:

	Nichols	James	Wilson
March 1..	$10,000		
June 1...		$ 4,000	
September 1		12,000	$20,000

Required:
(1) Determine how the 19X4 accounting income of $170,000 would be allocated among the partners.
(2) Determine the net capital balances for each partner as of December 31, 19X4.
(3) Perform the same requirements as for items (1) and (2) but assume the calculations are being made for tax purposes.

Problem 14-3. A client is seeking your advice on how to organize a new business. The client is proposing to acquire several single-story residences and convert them into group homes for the elderly. Each home would house eight elderly individuals, and the home would be staffed 24 hours a day. Residents would receive housing, food, and daily planned activities for a monthly fee. Group homes are licensed by the state and are closely monitored. Such homes do not provide any direct health care to the residents.

The client plans to have an active role in the organization and management of the homes and is seeking another individual or two to provide necessary capital as passive investors. It is anticipated that the homes will operate at a loss for the first twelve to eighteen months. The client hopes to open two group homes for each of the next four years and then sell this interest in the business.

Your client is interested in organizing the company as a partnership and is interested in how that might affect them and other potential partners.

Required:
Identify and discuss some of the characteristics of a partnership which your client should be aware of.

Problem 14-4. Anderson, Brown, and Avery are business partners who share profits and losses 60%, 20%, and 20%, respectively. In addition, the profit and loss agreement includes the following provisions:

(a) Interest of 9% is to be paid on that portion of average capital that exceeds $100,000. Capital is defined as net of withdrawals.
(b) Anderson, Brown, and Avery receive salaries of $40,000, $30,000, and $30,000, respectively.
(c) Avery will receive a bonus equal to 10% of the partnership income after the bonus.

In addition to the above facts, the following errors/adjustments relate to the current year:

(a) A contribution of $25,000 by Anderson should have been classified as a loan as of the beginning of the year. The loan had a 6% interest factor.
(b) Uniformly throughout the year Brown withdrew a total of $20,000 in excess of his salary. The partners may now agree to consider this extra salary.
(c) The bonus was calculated as a percentage of net income before the bonus.

The partners are trying to decide whether these errors/adjustments significantly damage the previous conclusion regarding the allocation of profits. Original net income for the year was $210,000. Anderson, Brown, and Avery have average capital balances of $125,000, $150,000, and $175,000, respectively before considering the errors/adjustments.

Required:

(1) Calculate the allocation of profits before the errors/adjustments.

(2) Calculate the effect of the errors/adjustments on the allocation of profits.

Problem 14-5. Bryant-Domer Company is a partnership that sells appliances to the retail trade and also sells wholesale to builders and contractors. The partnership agreement provides for a 14% imputed interest rate on invested capital, salaries of $12,000 and $16,000 for Bryant and Domer, respectively, and a 10% bonus for Domer. Changes in the 19X8 capital accounts of both partners, excluding normal withdrawals, were as follows:

Bryant, Capital				Domer, Capital			
12/1/X8	5,500	1/1/X8	85,000	4/1/X8	3,000	1/1/X8	96,800
		2/1/X8	2,000			7/1/X8	6,500
		9/1/X8	1,500			10/1/X8	4,500

Required:

For each of the following independent situations, prepare the profit allocation schedule for Bryant-Domer Company. Supporting calculations should be in good form.

(1) Interest on invested capital is based on ending capital balances per above less year-to-date normal withdrawals of $8,000 for Bryant and $6,300 for Domer. The bonus is a percentage of partnership income before the bonus; 19X8 income was $39,942. The provisions of the partnership agreement are to be satisfied to whatever extent possible in the following order: interest, salaries, and bonus. Any remaining partnership income is to be allocated 60% to Bryant and 40% to Domer.

(2) Interest on invested capital is based on weighted average capital balances. The bonus is a percentage of partnership income after the bonus; 19X8 income was $66,000. All provisions of the partnership agreement are to be satisfied completely, and any remaining income or deficiency created is to be allocated 75% to Bryant and 25% to Domer.

(3) Interest is based on ending capital balances in excess of $62,000. The bonus is a percentage of partnership income after the bonus; 19X8 income after salaries and bonus was $8,000. All provisions of the partnership agreement are to be satisfied completely. The articles of partnership are silent on the matter of profit and loss division between the partners.

Problem 14-6. Carson, Dowman, and Evans own an office automation and consulting business organized as a partnership. Evans is considering retirement from the partnership. In order to more fairly measure Evans's interest in capital, an audit of the company's first two years of operations was performed in early 19X9. The original partnership agreement called for Carson to receive a 10% bonus on income after the bonus, with the remaining profits or losses to be divided as follows: Carson, 30%; Dowman, 30%; and Evans, 40%. Reported income for 19X7 was $44,000.

In the second year of operations, the agreement was modified to reflect Evans's decision to become less involved in the business. The new agreement called for Carson still to receive a 10% bonus on income after the bonus, but altered the allocation of remaining amounts as follows: Carson, 35%, Dowman, 35%, and Evans, 30%. Reported income for 19X8 was $42,000.

The partners always had agreed that any adjustment to reported amounts would be allocated based on the profit and loss agreement in effect during the period to which the adjustment relates. The audit indicated that the following items were not accounted for properly:

(a) 19X7:

   (i) Failed to amortize the business name contributed by Carson. The fair market value of the intangible was $50,000 and should have been amortized over a ten-year life using straight-line amortization.

   (ii) Failed to defer prepaid insurance premiums of $3,000.

   (iii) A capital withdrawal of $5,000 made by Carson on July 1, 19X7, was classified incorrectly as a Note Receivable.

   (iv) Failed to accrue $2,000 of employee wages on December 31, 19X7.

   (v) Failed to record consulting fees of $8,400 earned in 19X7 but billed in 19X8.

(b) 19X8:

   (i) Purchases of inventory included a computer invoiced on December 31, 19X8, for $4,000 but not yet received. Terms were f.o.b. destination. The item was not included in the year-end physical inventory.

   (ii) Failed to accrue $8,600 of rent expense on December 31, 19X8.

   (iii) Failed to reverse $3,000 of interest income properly accrued at the end of 19X7, resulting in income recognition in both years.

Required:

Assume the following unadjusted December 31, 19X8 capital account balances: Carson, $25,000; Dowman, $30,000; and Evans, $28,000. Prepare a schedule to reflect the adjusted capital balances as of December 31, 19X8. Supporting calculations should be in good form.

APPENDIX PROBLEMS

Problem 14A-1. Fandek and Franklin formed a partnership on January 1, 19X7, and contributed assets and liabilities to the partnership as follows:

	Fandek		Franklin	
	Market Value	Tax Basis	Market Value	Tax Basis
Net assets contributed:				
Cash.....................	$60,000	$60,000	$10,000	$10,000
Securities................			15,000	10,000
Goodwill	12,000	0		
Equipment			65,000	40,000
Equipment loan...........			(42,000)	(42,000)

Fandek and Franklin will have initial interests in capital of 60% and 40%, respectively, and will share profits and losses equally. The partners also agreed that they would receive monthly withdrawals in the amounts of $2,000 and $3,000, respectively, for Fandek and Franklin.

During the year, the company recognized sales of $240,000 and a corresponding cost of sales equal to $144,000 (60% of sales). Of the total sales, $60,000 is uncollected at year end. These sales are being recognized for tax purposes by the installment method.

For accounting purposes only, the goodwill is being amortized over a 3-year period on a straight-line basis. Equipment also is being amortized on a straight-line basis assuming a 10-year useful life and a $5,000 residual value. For tax purposes, the equipment is depreciated by the Modified Accelerated Cost Recovery System (MACRS) and has a 19X7 depreciation rate of 25%.

Of the original securities contributed, securities with a book and tax basis of $6,000 and $2,000, respectively, were sold for $8,000. The remaining securities have a fair market value of $5,000.

Required:

(1) Assuming the partnership reports 19X7 net income of $54,000 in conformity with GAAP, prepare a schedule to reconcile this amount to the tax basis measure of net income.

(2) Calculate the tax basis for each of the partners at the end of 19X7.

CHAPTER 15

Partnerships: Ownership Changes and Liquidation

In theory, a partnership may be viewed as a conduit or entity through which individual partners carry on a common business purpose. It is natural that the circumstances surrounding the individual partners' lives may change and affect their involvement in the partnership. Individual partners may increase or decrease their interest in the partnership or withdraw entirely from the partnership. In turn, new partners may become involved in the partnership. Such ownership changes are common in a partnership just as they are in other forms of organizations, such as a corporation. However, unlike a corporation which is recognized as a separate and distinct entity having an infinite life, changes in the ownership structure of a partnership result in the dissolution of the previous partnership.

The Uniform Partnership Act (UPA) defines *dissolution* as "the change in the relation of the partners caused by any partner ceasing to be associated in the carrying on as distinguished from the winding up of the business." Sections 31 and 32 of the UPA identify the various causes of dissolution and suggest that the admission or withdrawal of a partner results in dissolution. Although dissolution ends the association of partners for their original purpose, it does not result necessarily in the termination of the partnership's basic business function. The remaining partners may continue to operate the business, or they may decide to terminate, or *liquidate*, the business.

The previous chapter stressed the importance of a well-conceived partnership agreement. Changes in the ownership structure of a partnership are one of the most important areas that should be addressed. Often the initial concerns of a new partnership are such that the partners overlook the certain reality that someday there will be a change in the ownership. Accountants can be of significant help to their clients in advising them in the structuring of buy/sell agreements for the partnership. Proper planning for such changes will help to ensure smooth and equitable transitions.

In certain instances, a partnership may elect not to continue but, rather, liquidate and distribute its net assets to the partners. For example, a partnership may be organized to develop and manage a real estate investment for a designated period of time. At the end of the designated period of time, the partnership will be liquidated. It is important to note that, unlike a dissolution where the partnership purpose continues, a liquidation results in the termination or winding up of the business purpose.

OWNERSHIP CHANGES

Changes in the ownership structure of a corporation are everyday occurrences, as evidenced by the activity of security exchanges. These changes typically involve transactions between existing and prospective shareholders and, therefore, create no special accounting problems for the corporate entity, other than updating its listings of stockholders. In the case of a partnership, however, changes in ownership structure are events that require special accounting treatment.

Accounting for changes in the ownership of a partnership is influenced heavily by the legal concept of dissolution. When there is a change in the ownership structure, the original partnership is dissolved and most often a new partnership is created. This dissolution and subsequent creation of a partnership indicate that a new legal entity has been created and accounting should measure properly the initial contributions of capital being made to the new partnership.

Accounting for a partnership is influenced by the propriety theory, which views a partnership not as a distinct entity but rather as a group of individual investors. Measuring changes in the equity of the individual partners is a major aspect of partnership accounting. Because ownership changes result in the dissolution of the partnership, this provides an excellent opportunity for accounting to measure the current wealth or equity of the partners. Changes in the ownership structure of the partnership are presumed to be arm's-length transactions which reflect the current value of the partnership. Therefore, such changes may indicate that:

1. The existing assets of the original partnership should be revalued,
2. Previously unrecorded intangible assets exist that are traceable to the original partnership, *and/or*
3. Intangible assets, such as goodwill, exist that are traceable to a new partner.

In practice, a change in ownership normally suggests the need to both revalue net assets and recognize intangible assets.

ADMISSION OF A NEW PARTNER

The admission of a new partner requires the approval of the existing partners, although a partner's interest may be assigned to someone outside the partnership without the consent of the other partners. However, assigning an interest does not dissolve the partnership, and it does not allow the assignee to participate in the management of the partnership or to review transactions and records of the partnership. The assignee receives only the agreed-upon portion of the assigning partner's profit or loss.

Assuming a new partner has been approved by the existing partners, the new partner normally will experience the same general risks and rights of ownership as do the other existing partners. However, creditors presenting claims against the partnership that were incurred prior to admission of the new partner cannot attach the personal assets of the new partner for settlement of their claims. Therefore, the level of liability of a new partner is less than that of an existing partner. Section 17 of the UPA states that:

> *A person admitted as a partner into an existing partnership is liable for all the obligations of the partnership arising before his admission as though he had been a partner when such obligations were incurred, except that this liability shall be satisfied only out of partnership property.*

 Contribution of Assets to Existing Partnership.   One method of gaining admission to an existing partnership involves contributing assets directly to the partnership entity itself. In this case, the exchange represents an arm's-length transaction between the entity and the incoming partner. If the book value of the original partnership's net assets approximates fair market value, the incoming partner's contribution would be expected to be equal to the portion of the equity that the new partner is acquiring. For example, if an incoming partner is to acquire a one-fourth interest in a partnership that has a book value and a fair market value of $60,000, the original $60,000 now would represent a three-fourths interest in the new partnership. Therefore, the total partnership capital must be $80,000, of which $60,000 is traceable to the old partners and $20,000 is traceable to the assets contributed by the new partner.

An incoming partner may acquire an interest in the partnership for a price *in excess of* that indicated by the book value of the original partnership's net assets. This situation would suggest the existence of:

1. Unrecognized appreciation on the recorded net assets of the original partnership, *and/or*
2. Unrecognized goodwill that also is traceable to the original partnership.

However, it is possible that an incoming partner may acquire an interest in the partnership at a price *less than* that indicated by the book value. This situation would suggest the existence of:

1. Unrecognized depreciation or write-downs on the recorded net assets of the original partnership, *and/or*
2. A contribution by the incoming partner of some intangible asset (goodwill) in addition to a measured contribution.

When an incoming partner's contribution is different from that indicated by the book values of the original partnership, the admission of the partner typically is recorded by either the *bonus method* or the *goodwill method*. These two methods are mutually exclusive of each other. Both methods permit the assumption that there is unrecorded goodwill to be recognized. However, the use of either method does not prevent the recognition of differences between the book value and fair market value of recorded net assets.

H. storia Cost

Bonus Method.

The bonus method strictly follows the principle that net assets should be recorded at historical cost. Furthermore, increases in the value of net assets should not be recognized until they are realized through an actual exchange transaction. Decreases or write-downs in the value of net assets, which are suggested by market value, may be recognized even though they are not realized by an actual exchange transaction. Therefore, when a new partner is admitted to an existing partnership, the total capital of the new partnership consists of the following:

1. The book value of the previous partnership *less*
2. Any write-downs in the value of the previous partnership's net assets *plus*
3. The value of the consideration paid to the partnership by the incoming partner.

The book-value-based approach of the bonus method does not recognize increases in net asset values suggested by the consideration that the incoming partner pays. However, the method does indirectly recognize such increases by reallocating or adjusting the capital balances of the partners. For example, if increases in net asset values are suggested as being traceable to the original partners, this suggests that their equity or capital has increased. This increase in capital, or bonus, is accomplished by increasing their capital balances. If increases in net asset values are not recognized, this increase in capital, or bonus, must be offset by decreasing the capital of the incoming partner. Therefore, the incoming partner's new capital balance is equal to the value of the consideration paid by the new partner less the bonus or increase in capital recorded for the original partners. These adjustments result in the new incoming partner's capital balance *always* being equal to:

1. The book value of the new partnership (book value of the previous partnership plus the value of consideration received from the incoming partner)
2. Times the interest in capital being acquired by the incoming partner.

$$
\left[
\begin{array}{c}
\text{BV of old partnership} \\
+ \\
\text{MV of new partnership} \\
\text{contribution}
\end{array}
\right]
\times \text{new partner's interest \%} =
\begin{array}{c}
\text{new partner's} \\
\text{capital} \\
\text{balance}
\end{array}
$$

The previous partners' capital balances then will be adjusted to the extent of the bonus using the profit and loss ratios in existence prior to the new partner's admission.

Bonus to the Old Partners.   When an incoming partner's contribution indicates the existence of unrecorded net asset appreciation and/or unrecorded goodwill, the bonus method does not record these previously unrecorded items, but rather grants a "bonus" to the old partners. The bonus, which increases the capital accounts of the old partners, is made possible by recording in the new partner's capital account only a portion of the actual contribution to the partnership.

To illustrate this method, assume the following:

Existing Partners	Capital Balance	Percentage Interest in Capital	Percentage Interest in Profit
Partner A	$30,000	40%	50%
Partner B	45,000	60	50

Then assume that C invests $27,000 in the partnership in exchange for a 20% interest in capital and a 30% interest in profits. Partners A and B will have a 20% and a 50% interest, respectively, in the profits of the new partnership. Since the total capital of the new partnership equals $102,000 ($30,000 + $45,000 + $27,000) and the new partner is acquiring a 20% interest in capital, it seems reasonable that the incoming partner's capital account initially should reflect 20% of the total capital, or $20,400. The $6,600 difference between C's contribution and the interest recorded for C indicates the existence of unrecorded intangibles (goodwill) or unrecorded appreciation on existing assets. Regardless of the identity of the $6,600, the value must be allocated to the appropriate parties. If the unrecorded value had been realized through a sale, the resulting profit would have been divided between the old partners in accordance with their profit and loss agreement. Therefore, assuming the $6,600 is identified as a bonus to the old partners and is divided between them according to their profit and loss ratio prior to admission of the new partner, the entry to record C's investment is as follows:

Assets.	27,000	
A, Capital		3,300
B, Capital		3,300
C, Capital		20,400

Bonus to the New Partner.   When the new partner invests some intangible asset, such as business acumen or an established clientele, it is possible to have a bonus credited to the new partner. For example, given the same basic facts as in the previous illustration, assume that C invests $10,000 for a 20% interest in capital and a one-third interest in profits. Total capital of the partnership would be $85,000 ($30,000 + $45,000 + $10,000) and C's share of the total capital would be 20%, or $17,000. Partner C is acquiring a $17,000 interest in capital in exchange for an investment of $10,000, and the old partners are transferring $7,000 of their capital to C in exchange for unrecorded intangible assets invested by C. Partner C's admission is recorded by the following entry:

Assets.	10,000	
A, Capital	3,500	
B, Capital	3,500	
C, Capital		17,000

Partner C's bonus may be viewed as a cost incurred to acquire C's goodwill. Since all costs to acquire assets eventually affect income and are allocated among the partners, C's bonus is allocated to A and B according to their profit and loss ratio.

Overvaluation of the Old Partnership.   The recording of a bonus traceable to the incoming partner was based on the assumption that the new partner was contributing an intangible asset in addition to other assets valued at $10,000. However, the substance of the transaction may indicate that no intangibles are being contributed and the existing assets of the old partnership are overvalued. For example, in the previous illustration, C invested $10,000 in return for a 20% interest in the new partnership's total capital. Therefore, the total capital of the new partnership may be interpreted from C's investment to be equal to $50,000 ($10,000 ÷ 20%). Of this total, $10,000 is traceable to the new partner, and the balance of $40,000 represents the fair market value of the old partners' capital. Assuming this is a proper interpretation of the substance of the transaction between the new partner and the partnership, C's admission to the partnership is recorded as follows:

A, Capital	17,500	
B, Capital	17,500	
Assets		35,000

     To record the write-down of the original partners' capital from
     a book value of $75,000 ($30,000 + $45,000) to its implied
     fair market value of $40,000.

Assets	10,000	
C, Capital		10,000

     To record C's contribution of assets to the partnership.

After these entries are posted, the total capital of the new partnership is $50,000 ($30,000 + $45,000 − $35,000 + $10,000), of which C's share is $10,000 (20% × $50,000), as initially represented by the balance in C's capital account.

Goodwill Method.   The goodwill method emphasizes the legal significance of a change in the ownership structure of a partnership. From a legal viewpoint, the entrance of a new partner results in the dissolution of the previous partnership and the creation of a new legal entity. Since a new entity has resulted, the assets transferred to this entity should be recorded at their current fair market value. After a complete analysis, both tangible and intangible assets acquired by the new entity, including goodwill created by the previous partnership, should be recorded.

Therefore, the total capital of the new partnership will consist of the following values:

1. The book value of the net assets of the previous partnership *plus*
2. Unrecognized appreciation or less unrecognized depreciation on the recorded net assets of the previous partnership *plus*
3. Unrecognized goodwill traceable to the previous partnership *plus*
4. The value of the consideration, both tangible and intangible, received from the new incoming partner.

BV of old partnership	+	unrecognized appreciation (or – unrecognized depreciation)	+	unrecognized GW of old partnership	+	MV of new partners' contribution, including GW	=	total capital of new partnership

When the bonus method is used to account for the admission of a new partner, the total capital of the new entity equals the book value of the previous partners' capital adjusted for asset write-downs, if appropriate, plus the incoming partner's investment. When the goodwill method is employed, however, the total capital of the new partnership must approximate the fair market value of the entity.

To illustrate the goodwill method, assume the following:

Existing Partners	Capital Balance	Percentage Interest in	
		Capital	Profit
Partner A	$30,000	40%	50%
Partner B	45,000	60	50

If C invests $27,000 in the partnership in exchange for a 20% interest in capital and a one-third interest in profit, such an investment implies that the entity has a fair market value of $135,000 ($27,000 ÷ 20%). However, the book value of the new partnership equals only $102,000 when the former partners' capital balances of $75,000 are added to C's $27,000 investment. Thus, $33,000 must be added to the existing book value.

Another interpretation of the transaction would be that, given the $102,000 book value of the new partnership, a 20% interest should have cost $20,400 ($102,000 × 20%). The new partner paid an extra $6,600 ($27,000 – $20,400) for a 20% interest in the difference between the implied fair market value and the book value of the new entity. Therefore, the total difference must be $33,000 ($6,600 ÷ 20%).

 Asset Appreciation.   The difference between the higher fair market value and the book value of the new entity, as previously discussed, may be traceable to unrecognized appreciation and/or unrecognized goodwill. Each of these possible explanations should be analyzed thoroughly to account properly for a change in the ownership structure of a partnership. If differences between the fair market value and the book value of recorded assets are identifiable, appropriate adjustments to asset balances should be considered. Since a change in ownership structure creates a new, distinct legal entity, every attempt should be made to identify differences between fair market and book values. However, the absence of objective and independent valuations often prevents such an analysis. For example, fair market values are not readily available for certain specialized assets, and the alternative of engaging an independent appraiser could become an expensive option. Furthermore, estimating fair market values with the use of specific price-level indexes is often difficult because of the absence of relevant indexes. Another reason for not recording changes in market values is that the resulting differences between the bases for tax purposes and the bases for book purposes would require more complex records.

Assuming objective measures of unrecorded appreciation are available, the appreciation would be recognized and allocated to the previous partners according to their old profit and loss ratios. To illustrate, assume that the $33,000 difference in values from our previous example is entirely traceable to the unrecognized appreciation of the recorded net assets of the previous partnership. This appreciation and the investment by C would be recorded as follows:

Assets (from C)	27,000	
Specific Assets	33,000	
A, Capital		16,500
B, Capital		16,500
C, Capital		27,000

 Goodwill Traceable to the Old Partners.   Unrecorded goodwill also may be identifiable. In the previous example, assuming there are no differences between the fair market value and book value of recorded assets, the new partner's willingness to pay more than the proportionate book value of the new entity indicates that goodwill existed prior to the new partner's admission. If this intangible asset could have been sold prior to the admission of the partner, the realized profit would have been allocated to the old partners. Therefore, the goodwill is recorded and allocated to the old partners according to their profit and loss ratio. The investment by C is recorded under the goodwill method as follows:

Assets	27,000	
Goodwill	33,000	
A, Capital		16,500
B, Capital		16,500
C, Capital		27,000

It is important to note that the new partner's capital account balance represents a 20% interest in the total capital of the new partnership, as verified by the following computation:

Original capital	$ 75,000
C's investment	27,000
Goodwill	33,000
	$135,000
C's interest	× 20%
C's capital balance	$ 27,000

In comparing the assumption that the $33,000 difference was traceable to asset appreciation versus goodwill, it should be noted that:

1. In one case, the debit is to the specific appreciated assets versus goodwill, yet the amount is the same.
2. Some combination of appreciated assets and goodwill could account for the $33,000 difference.

3. The adjusted capital balances of the partners are the same regardless of whether asset appreciation and/or goodwill is recognized.

The recognition of goodwill traceable to the previous partners is criticized by some accountants. If the concept of a new legal entity is cast aside, some would argue that the goodwill is self-created and, therefore, should not be recognized. APB Opinion No. 17, *Intangible Assets*, prohibits the recognition of goodwill unless it has been purchased from another entity. To argue that the new partnership is in substance a continuation of the previous partnership would prevent the recognition of goodwill traceable to the old partnership. Furthermore, viewing the new partnership as a continuation of the previous partnership also would prevent the recognition of appreciation on other assets as well.

It also may be argued that the difficulties associated with the measurement of the fair market value of existing assets unjustifiably forces the recognition of goodwill for lack of a more precise analysis. However, the argument that the fair market value of a new partnership, as indicated by the new partner's investment, is not objectively or independently determined overlooks the basic nature of the transaction. Negotiations between previous partners and a new partner would be described as arm's length, since both parties involved are seeking independently a fair price.

Asset Write-downs.   Given the same basic facts as in the previous illustrations, assume that C invests $10,000 to acquire a 20% interest in the partnership of A and B. C's investment implies a fair market value of the new entity equal to $50,000 ($10,000 ÷ 20%). However, the book value of the new partnership equals $85,000, consisting of the old partners' capital balances of $75,000 plus C's investment of $10,000. This difference between the fair market value and the higher book value indicates the existence of unrecorded write-downs and/or goodwill contributed by the incoming partner.

If objective evidence supports the write-down of existing assets, the previous partners' capital balances would be reduced accordingly in proportion to their profit and loss ratios. The amount of the suggested write-down is calculated by comparing the implied market value of $50,000 to the $85,000 representing the book value of the previous partnership plus the new partner's investment. Therefore, the difference of $35,000 is equal to the necessary write-down which would be recorded as follows:

A, Capital	17,500	
B, Capital	17,500	
Assets		35,000

This reduces the net assets of the previous partnership to $40,000 and the new partner's investment of $10,000 then would represent 20% of the new partnership's total capital of $50,000 ($40,000 + $10,000).

Goodwill Traceable to the New Partner.   Assuming net assets should not be written down, the amount of the unrecorded goodwill may be computed as the difference between:

1. The amount that should have been paid by the new partner, as indicated by the book value of the previous partnership (calculated by dividing the

original book value of the partnership by the total percentage interest of the original partners in the new partnership, and subtracting the original book value),

$$\left[\begin{array}{c} \text{book value} \\ \text{of old} \\ \text{partnership} \end{array} \div \begin{array}{c} \text{old partners'} \\ \text{interest in} \\ \text{new partnership} \end{array}\right] - \begin{array}{c} \text{book value} \\ \text{of old} \\ \text{partnership} \end{array} = \begin{array}{c} \text{new} \\ \text{partner's} \\ \text{capital} \end{array}$$

and
2. The amount actually paid by the new partner.

In this example, the $75,000 original book value would represent 80% of the new partnership capital, or $93,750 ($75,000 ÷ 80%). Therefore, it appears that the new partner should have paid $18,750 ($93,750 less the original $75,000 book value) for a 20% interest in the partnership; however, the partner actually paid only $10,000. The difference between what should have been paid ($18,750) and the amount actually paid ($10,000) represents the goodwill traceable to the incoming partner. The investment by C would be recorded under the goodwill method as follows:

Assets.	10,000	
Goodwill.	8,750	
C, Capital		18,750

Note that the new partner's capital account balance represents a 20% interest in the total capital of the new partnership, as shown by the following computation:

Original capital.	$75,000
C's investment	10,000
Goodwill.	8,750
	$93,750
C's interest	× 20%
C's capital balance.	$18,750

The fact that a new legal entity is created supports the recognition of goodwill and other contributed assets at their fair market value. If the concept of a new entity is set aside, the goodwill may be viewed as being purchased by the previous partnership in exchange for partnership equity. Accounting theory and current practice support the recording of goodwill acquired or purchased from other entities.

 Revaluation of Assets and Goodwill.   The previous examples of accounting for a new partner's investment assumed that either asset write-downs or invested goodwill were appropriate as mutually exclusive choices. In reality, some combination of the two may be appropriate. Continuing with the previous example, assume that the $75,000 book value of the previous partnership has a market value of $64,000, and new partner C's investment remains at $10,000.

The first step to be taken is to recognize the write-down of the previous partnership's net assets as follows:

A, Capital	. . . .	5,500	
B, Capital	. . . .	5,500	
Assets.	. . . .		11,000

The adjusted value of the previous partnership then is used to determine the goodwill traceable to the new partner. In this example, the $64,000 market value of the previous partnership would represent 80% of the new partnership capital, or $80,000 ($64,000 ÷ 80%). Therefore, it appears that the new partner should have paid $16,000 ($80,000 less the market value of the previous partnership) for a 20% interest in the partnership. The difference between what should have been paid ($16,000) and the amount actually paid ($10,000) represents the goodwill traceable to the incoming partner. The entry to record C's investment is as follows:

Assets.	. . . .	10,000	
Goodwill	. . . .	6,000	
C, Capital	. . . .		16,000

Methodology for Determining Goodwill.   An analysis of the previous examples reveals that goodwill may be traceable to either the original partners or the incoming partner. To apply the goodwill method properly, the following methodology may be helpful in identifying the origin of the goodwill and its amount:

1. Determine the entity's fair market value, as indicated by the new partner's investment (new partner's investment divided by the percentage interest acquired in the partnership).
2. If the fair market value determined is:
    (a) Greater than the book value of the new partnership adjusted for net asset appreciation or write-downs, implied goodwill is traceable to the old partners and is allocated among them according to their old profit ratios. The amount of goodwill is equal to the difference between (1) the fair market value indicated by the new partner's investment and (2) the adjusted book value of the new partnership.
    (b) Less than the adjusted book value of the new partnership, implied goodwill is traceable to the new partner. The amount of goodwill is equal to the difference between (1) the amount that should have been paid by the new partner to acquire an interest in the adjusted book value of the previous partnership and (2) the actual amount paid.
3. The initial capital balance of the new partner always is equal to the new partner's interest in the total capital of the new partnership after goodwill is recognized.

Comparison of Bonus and Goodwill Methods.   The bonus method adheres to the historical cost concept and often is used in accounting practice. It is objective in that it establishes total capital of the new partnership at an amount based on actual consideration received from the new partner. The bonus method indirectly acknowledges the existence of goodwill by giving a bonus to either old or new partners.

The goodwill method results in the recognition of an asset implied by a transaction rather than recognizing an asset actually purchased. Historically, goodwill has been recognized only when purchased so that a more objective measure of its value is established. Therefore, opponents of the goodwill method contend that goodwill is not determined objectively and other factors may have influenced the amount of investment required from the new partner. Also, certain recipients of partnership financial statements may question the valuation of goodwill, since increasing total assets may result in an understatement of the return on total assets or equity.

Use of the goodwill method also could produce inequitable results if either of the following conditions exist:

1. The new partner's interest in profits does not equal the new partner's initial interest in capital.
2. Former partners do not share profits and losses in the same relationship to each other as they did before the admission of a new partner.

The importance of these concepts can be illustrated using the following facts:

	Old Partners		New Partner
	A	B	C
Original capital	$30,000	$45,000	
Original profit and loss percentage	50%	50%	
New partner's capital			$27,000
New profit and loss percentage	33¹/₃%	33¹/₃%	33¹/₃%
New partner's interest in capital			20%

The new capital balances that result from using the goodwill method and the bonus method are as follows:

	Old Partners		New Partner
	A	B	C
Goodwill method:			
Goodwill allocation	$16,500	$16,500	
New capital balances	46,500	61,500	$27,000
Bonus method:			
Bonus allocation	3,300	3,300	
New capital balances	33,300	48,300	20,400

Assuming the recorded goodwill proves to be worthless (or assuming that goodwill is amortized in total), the decline in asset value would reduce the partners' capital balances according to their profit and loss ratio as follows:

	Partners			
	A	B	C	Total
Capital balances if goodwill method used	$46,500	$61,500	$27,000	$135,000
Goodwill write-off (amortization)	(11,000)	(11,000)	(11,000)	(33,000)
Capital balances after write-off	$35,500	$50,500	$16,000	$102,000
Capital balances if bonus method used	33,300	48,300	20,400	102,000
Differences	$ 2,200	$ 2,200	$ (4,400)	0

The capital balances that result from using the two methods are different because the new partner's interest in profits and interest in capital are not equal. In this illustration, C acquired a 20% capital interest and a 33⅓% interest in profits. Therefore, C paid for 20% of the implied goodwill but had to absorb 33⅓% of the goodwill amortization.

To further illustrate the concepts, assume the same facts, except that the new profit and loss percentages are 50%, 30%, and 20% for partners A, B, and C, respectively. If the recorded goodwill proves to be worthless, the decline in asset value would affect the partners' capital balances as follows:

	Partners			
	A	B	C	Total
Capital balances if goodwill method used.....	$46,500	$61,500	$27,000	$135,000
Goodwill write-off (amortization)	(16,500)	(9,900)	(6,600)	(33,000)
Capital balances after write-off..............	$30,000	$51,600	$20,400	$102,000
Capital balances if bonus method used.......	33,300	48,300	20,400	102,000
Differences..............................	$ (3,300)	$ 3,300	0	0

In this case, partners A and B shared equally in the initial recording of goodwill, but unequally in the subsequent amortization of goodwill.

Now assume the same facts, except that the new profit and loss percentages are 40%, 40%, and 20% for partners A, B, and C, respectively. After the amortization of goodwill, the capital balances would be identical to those achieved under the bonus method, as indicated in the following table:

	Partners			
	A	B	C	Total
Capital balances if goodwill method used.....	$46,500	$61,500	$27,000	$135,000
Goodwill write-off (amortization)	(13,200)	(13,200)	(6,600)	(33,000)
Capital balances after write-off..............	$33,300	$48,300	$20,400	$102,000
Capital balances if bonus method used.......	$33,300	$48,300	$20,400	$102,000

The equality between the capital balances is achieved because neither of the two conditions that produce inequities exists. If these conditions do exist, preference is given typically to the bonus method because of the possible inequities that may result from the write-off of goodwill.

Contribution of Assets to Existing Partners.   A new partner also may be admitted to the partnership by acquiring all or part of the capital interest of one or more existing partners in exchange for some consideration (assets). In this case, the new partner deals directly with an existing partner or partners rather than with the partnership entity. Therefore, the acquisition price is paid to the selling partner(s) and not to the partnership itself. The partnership records the redistribution of capital interests by transferring all or a portion of the seller's capital to the new partner's capital account but does not record the transfer of any assets.

To illustrate, assume the following facts:

| | | Percentage Interest in | |
Existing Partners	Capital Balance	Capital	Profit
Partner A	$30,000	40%	50%
Partner B	45,000	60	50

Now assume new partner C purchased 50% of A's interest in capital and 50% of B's interest in capital in exchange for $50,000. This purchase resulted in C's having a 50% interest in the total partnership capital.

There are several alternative ways of recording the contribution of assets by C to the existing partners. If the consideration paid by the incoming partner is not used to impute the fair market value of the partnership, the transaction would be recorded by the partnership entity as follows:

```
A, Capital (50% × $30,000). . . . . . . . . . . . . . . . . . . . . . . . . . . . . . . . . .   15,000
B, Capital (50% × $45,000). . . . . . . . . . . . . . . . . . . . . . . . . . . . . . . . . .   22,500
   C, Capital . . . . . . . . . . . . . . . . . . . . . . . . . . . . . . . . . . . . . . . . . . . . .              37,500
```

The $50,000 actually paid by C was not used as a basis for the entry because it represents consideration paid to the individual partners personally rather than to the partnership entity. This accounting treatment frequently is compared to that of a corporation when a stockholder sells shares or an interest in corporate capital to another investor in the corporation. The corporation does not record the transaction or use it as a basis for revaluing corporate assets but merely acknowledges the changing identity of its shareholders. The above entry also is appropriate if the existing partners sold their interests for less than book value. Even though depreciation of existing assets is suggested, such depreciation is not recorded because the transaction did not involve the partnership entry itself.

An alternative but less frequently used method of recording this transaction would be to impute the fair market value of the partnership entity from the consideration paid by the new partner. For example, if C paid $50,000 to acquire a 50% interest in the capital of the partnership vis-à-vis the individual partners, the total implied current value of the partnership would be $100,000 ($50,000 ÷ 50%). The difference between the imputed value of $100,000 and the partnership's previous book value of $75,000 ($30,000 + $45,000) is interpreted to represent undervalued existing assets and/or goodwill traceable to the old partnership. This alternative interpretation would result in recording the transaction as follows:

Assets and/or Goodwill..................................	25,000	
A, Capital		12,500
B, Capital		12,500
To record the previously unrecognized increase in value of the partnership.		

A, Capital [50% × ($30,000 + $12,500)]	21,250	
B, Capital [50% × ($45,000 + $12,500)]	28,750	
C, Capital		50,000
To record the transfer of the original partners' adjusted capital to incoming partner C.		

Normally, this alternative method is not employed because (1) the transaction was not between the partnership and the incoming partner but rather between individual partners, and (2) the consideration paid by the incoming partner may not provide a reliable indicator of the partnership entity's current value. However, the method may provide useful information for deciding how to allocate the acquisition price between the selling partners. The selling partners' original capital plus their share of any imputed value increments may indicate the current values for which the incoming partner was paying. For example, the purchase price of $50,000 may be allocated to partners A and B as follows:

| | Partners | | |
	A	B	Total
Original capital.....................................	$30,000	$45,000	$ 75,000
Share of value increment...........................	12,500	12,500	25,000
Total imputed value	$42,500	$57,500	$100,000
Percentage acquired by new partner.................	50%	50%	50%
Total purchase price	$21,250	$28,750	$ 50,000

WITHDRAWAL OF A PARTNER

When a partner withdraws, the partnership agreement should be consulted to determine if any guidelines have been established that would influence the procedure. The withdrawal of a partner requires a determination of the fair market value of the partnership entity and a measurement of partnership income to the date of withdrawal. Also, in many cases, the equity of the retiring partner may not be equal to the partner's capital balance as a result of (1) the existence of accounting errors, (2) differences between the fair market value and the recorded book value of assets, and/or (3) unrecorded assets such as goodwill.

If accounting errors are discovered, they should be treated as prior-period adjustments and corrected by adjusting the capital balances of the partners. Theoretically, an error should be allocated to partners' capital balances according to the profit and loss ratio that existed when the error was committed. Therefore, it is necessary to identify the period to which the error is traceable. This practice can become complicated, and a well-designed partnership agreement should include procedures for dealing with the correction of errors.

Recognizing differences between book value and fair market value may be as appropriate when an individual withdraws from the partnership as when an individual is admitted. If accounting recognition of such differences is not desired, however, these differences nevertheless should influence the amount to be paid to the withdrawing partner.

The Selling of an Interest to Existing Partners.   As is the case with the admission of a partner, the withdrawal of a partner may involve (1) a transaction with existing partners or a new partner, or (2) a transaction with the partnership entity itself. In the first case, the equity of the withdrawing partner will be purchased with the personal assets of existing or new partners rather than with the assets of the partnership.

To illustrate, assume the following:

	Partners		
	A	B	C
Capital balance	$30,000	$50,000	$20,000
Profit and loss percentage	40%	40%	20%
Percentage interest in capital	30%	50%	20%

Now assume partner A withdraws from the partnership and C uses personal funds to purchase A's interest at its current value of $36,000. If the price paid by C is not used to impute the value of the entity, the transaction would be recorded as follows:

A, Capital	30,000	
C, Capital		30,000

The above entry also is appropriate if the existing partners sold their interests for less than book value. Even though depreciation of existing assets is suggested, such depreciation is not recorded because the transaction did not involve the partnership entity itself. As previously discussed, an alternative treatment would be to recognize any value increment indicated by the transaction and then transfer the adjusted capital balances.

The Selling of an Interest to the Partnership.   When a withdrawing partner sells an interest to the partnership rather than to an individual partner, the bonus or goodwill methods may be employed. The bonus method is used most frequently, but the choice between methods should be based on a thorough analysis of the transaction.

Using the same facts as in the previous illustration and assuming the use of the bonus method, the purchase of A's equity by the partnership would be recorded as follows:

A, Capital	30,000	
B, Capital	4,000	
C, Capital	2,000	
Cash		36,000

The entry indicates that the remaining partners granted a bonus to A, measured by the difference between the recorded capital and the fair market value of A's equity. The bonus is charged to the remaining partners according to their proportionate profit and loss ratio.

The goodwill method focuses on the payment to the withdrawing partner as an indication of the fair market value of the partnership. If the imputed goodwill or undervalued assets were disposed of, the partners would divide the gain according to their profit and loss ratio. Assuming existing assets are properly valued, the $36,000 payment to A consists of A's capital balance of $30,000 plus a $6,000 share of the unrecorded goodwill. Therefore, the $6,000 represents A's 40% interest in total goodwill of $15,000 ($6,000 ÷ 40%).

Two alternatives are now available: (1) recognize only the goodwill that is traceable to the retiring partner or (2) recognize the amount of goodwill traceable to the entire entity. The first alternative stresses the importance of recognizing only the amount of goodwill that actually is purchased from the withdrawing partner. Using this alternative, A's withdrawal would be recorded as follows:

Goodwill	6,000	
A, Capital		6,000
A, Capital	36,000	
Cash		36,000

If the amount of goodwill traceable to the entire entity is recognized, the goodwill would be allocated to the partners according to their profit and loss ratio, as reflected in the following entries to record A's withdrawal:

Goodwill	15,000	
A, Capital		6,000
B, Capital		6,000
C, Capital		3,000
A, Capital	36,000	
Cash		36,000

Whether part or all of the goodwill is recognized, opponents of this procedure contend that transactions between partners should not be viewed as arm's length; therefore, the measure of goodwill may not be determined objectively. Also, inequitable results may be produced if the remaining partners subsequently change their profit and loss ratio.

It is important to note that a withdrawing partner could sell his/her interest in a partnership for less than book value. If that interest is sold to the partnership, the following recognition would take place depending on whether the bonus or goodwill method is employed:

1. Bonus method: A bonus traceable to the remaining partners would be recognized. The bonus would be measured as the difference between the withdrawing partner's capital balance (book value) and the consideration paid for the partner's interest.
2. Goodwill method: Paying less than the withholding partner's capital balance (book value) would suggest that existing assets are overvalued. A write-down of existing assets would be recognized as the difference between the withdrawing partner's capital balance and the consideration paid for the

partner's interest. As an alternative, the asset write-down traceable to the entire entity could be recognized based on the amount suggested by the transaction with the withholding partner. The write-down traceable to the withdrawing partner represents the percentage interest (based on profit and loss ratios) in the asset write-down traceable to the entire entity.

Effects of a Partner's Withdrawal.

When the interest of a withdrawing partner is acquired by the remaining partners or the partnership, serious demands upon the liquidity of the partners and the partnership may result. If withdrawal is due to the death of the partner, funds may be provided from the proceeds of life insurance policies taken out by the partnership itself or by individual partners. For example, if partner A takes out a life insurance policy on partner B and B subsequently dies, the proceeds payable to A may be used to acquire B's interest.

The UPA, in Section 42, states that a retiring or deceased partner's estate may receive interest as an ordinary creditor on that portion of the withdrawing partner's capital interest that remains in the partnership (i.e., has not been disbursed yet). In lieu of interest, the UPA states that the profits attributable to the use of the withdrawing partner's capital still retained in the partnership may be received. Once again, a partnership agreement that addresses the valuation of a withdrawing partner's interest and the means of payment is a valuable aid in properly accounting for the withdrawal of a partner.

PARTNERSHIP LIQUIDATION

Unlike a dissolution where the partnership continues its business purpose, a liquidation results in the partnership's ending or terminating its business. The process of liquidation consists of the conversion of partnership assets into a distributable form and the distribution of these assets to creditors and owners. To achieve an orderly and legally sound liquidation, some fundamental guidelines need to be identified.

LIQUIDATION GUIDELINES

The underlying theme in accounting for partnership liquidation is the equitable distribution of the assets. To be equitable, a distribution should recognize the legal rights of the partnership creditors and individual partners. All liquidation expenses and gains or losses from conversion of partnership assets also must be allocated to the partners before assets actually are distributed to the individual partners. Failure to consider these factors may result in the premature or incorrect distribution of assets to a partner. If a premature or incorrect distribution of assets cannot be recovered, the partnership fiduciary who authorized the distribution may be held liable.

The Ranking of Partnership Liabilities.

The UPA establishes rules governing the priority in which partnership assets are distributed to creditors and partners. Subject to any agreement to the contrary, the following sequence of payments should be observed:

1. Amounts owed to creditors other than partners.
2. Amounts owed to partners other than for capital and profits, i.e., partners' loans to the partnership.
3. Amounts owed to partners as capital.
4. Amounts owed to partners as profits not currently closed to partners' capital accounts.

Although loans from partners have a higher legal priority than amounts owed as capital and profits, the doctrine of *right of offset* sets aside this ranking in favor of procedural and economic considerations that facilitate the actual liquidation process. The effect of this doctrine is that loans due to partners, which have a credit balance, are combined with the respective partners' capital balances. Without the right of offset it would be possible to distribute assets to a partner in payment of the loan balance while at the same time the partner has a debit capital account balance. In order to eliminate the debit capital balance, the partnership would have to recover personal assets from the partner. Therefore, it is possible for the partnership to distribute assets to the partner and then try to recover assets from the partner, hoping that such assets are still available. The doctrine of right of offset eliminates this problem by combining the loan and capital balances.

Amounts owed to partners as capital and profits are viewed typically as one element rather than two separate priority levels. Therefore, items 2, 3, and 4 may be combined without destroying the fairness of a distribution.

Liability for Debit Capital Balances.   The UPA, in Section 40, states that partners should contribute assets to the partnership to the extent of their debit balances. However, if such a contribution is not possible because of special personal or legal considerations, the debit balance will be viewed as a realization loss and allocated according to the remaining partners' profit and loss ratio. For example, assume partners A, B, and C share in profits and losses in the ratio of 1:2:1, respectively. If C is unable to contribute any asset to eliminate a debit capital balance, that balance would be allocated to A and B in the ratio of 1:2. Partners who absorb other partners' debit capital balances have a legal claim against the deficient partner. However, the collectibility of such a claim depends on the personal wealth of the deficient partner.

The Marshaling of Assets.   The provisions that call for the contribution of personal assets to a liquidating partnership illustrate the characteristics of unlimited liability discussed in the previous chapter. However, such personal liability depends on the legal doctrine of *marshaling of assets*. This doctrine, which is applied when the partnership and/or one or more of the partners are insolvent, states that:

1. Partnership assets are first available for the payment of partnership debts. Any excess assets are available for payment of the individual partner's debts, but only to the extent of the partner's interest in the capital of the partnership.
2. Personal assets of a partner are applied against personal debts, ranked in order of priority as follows:
   (a) Amounts owed to personal creditors.
   (b) Amounts owed to partnership creditors.
   (c) Amounts owed to partners by way of contribution.

"Amounts owed to partners by way of contribution" refers to amounts owed the partnership as represented by the partner's debit capital balance. This amount is viewed by the UPA as separate from the amounts owed to personal creditors. For example, if a partner has personal assets of $12,000, personal liabilities of $8,000, and a debit capital balance of $16,000, personal assets would be distributed as follows:

Payable to personal creditors.	$ 8,000
Payable to partnership for debit capital balance.	4,000
Total personal assets	$12,000

Under common law and federal bankruptcy law, which may be applicable when the UPA has not been adopted, amounts owed to partners by way of contribution are on an equal basis *(pari passu)* with personal creditors of the partner. According to this rule, the $12,000 of personal assets would be distributed as follows:

Payable to personal liabilities [($8,000 $\div$ $24,000) $\times$ $12,000].	$ 4,000
Payable to partnership for debit capital balance [($16,000 $\div$ $24,000) $\times$ $12,000]	8,000
Total personal assets	$12,000

The legal doctrine of marshaling of assets is demonstrated by the following cases:

Case A—Insolvent Partners

The partnership is solvent, with total assets of $16,000 and total liabilities of $9,000. Information relating to the individual partners is as follows:

	Partner A	Partner B
Total personal assets	$10,000	$15,000
Total personal liabilities.	13,000	18,000
Partnership capital balances	5,000	2,000

Analysis: Unsatisfied personal creditors may attach a partner's interest in the solvent partnership, but only to the extent of the partner's capital balance. Thus, unsatisfied personal creditors could seek recourse as follows:

	Partner A	Partner B
Unsatisfied personal creditors	$3,000	$3,000
Interest in partnership capital available to personal creditors	(3,000)	(2,000)
Personal liabilities not satisfied	0	$1,000

Case B—Insolvent Partnership

The partnership is insolvent, with total assets of $23,000 and total liabilities of $25,000. Information relating to individual partners is as follows:

	Partner A	Partner B
Total personal assets	$10,000	$8,000
Total personal liabilities	6,000	7,000
Partnership capital balances	500	(2,500)

Analysis: Unsatisfied partnership creditors may seek recourse from the individual partners in accordance with a proper marshaling of assets, as reflected in Illustration 15-1.

Illustration 15-1
Distribution of Assets—Insolvent Partnership

	Partner A		Partner B		AB Partnership			
	Assets	Liab.	Assets	Liab.	Assets	Liab.	A, Capital	B, Capital
Beginning balances[1]	$10,000	$6,000	$8,000	$7,000	$23,000	$25,000	$ 500	$(2,500)
Payment of liabilities	(6,000)	(6,000)	(7,000)	(7,000)	(23,000)	(23,000)		
	$ 4,000	0	$1,000	0	0	$ 2,000	$ 500	$(2,500)
Payment of partnership creditors[2]	(2,000)					(2,000)	2,000	
	$ 2,000	0	$1,000	0	0	0	$2,500	$(2,500)
Payment toward debit capital balance[3]			(1,000)		$ 1,000			1,000
	$ 2,000	0	0	0	$ 1,000	0	$2,500	$(1,500)
Capital distribution to A . . .	1,000				(1,000)		(1,000)	
Balances[4]	$ 3,000	0	0	0	0	0	$1,500	$(1,500)

[1]Beginning asset balances represent realizable values.

[2]Unsatisfied partnership creditors may claim the net personal assets of any solvent partner, regardless of the amount of the partner's interest in the capital of the partnership. A's capital interest is increased by the payment of partnership liabilities.

[3]If the payment toward the debit capital balance had preceded B's payment of personal liabilities, a proper marshaling of assets would not have been achieved and B's personal creditors would not have been satisfied.

[4]If B later pays the debit capital balance, the funds would be distributed to A. However, if B cannot pay, the loss will be borne by A.

Case C—Insolvent Partner and Partnership

The partnership is insolvent, with total assets of $20,000 and total liabilities of $25,000. Information relating to individual partners is as follows:

	Partner A	Partner B
Total personal assets	$13,000	$2,000
Total personal liabilities....................................	10,000	15,000
Partnership capital balances	(7,000)	2,000

Analysis: Partner B is solvent, and the recourse B's personal creditors have against the partnership depends upon A's future contribution to the partnership. Illustration 15-2 reflects the distribution of assets in accordance with the marshaling concept.

Illustration 15-2
Distribution of Assets—Insolvent Partner and Partnership

	Partner A		Partner B		AB Partnership			
	Assets	Liab.	Assets	Liab.	Assets	Liab.	A, Capital	B, Capital
Beginning balances[1] ...	$13,000	$10,000	$12,000	$15,000	$20,000	$25,000	$(7,000)	$2,000
Payment of liabilities ...	(10,000)	(10,000)	(12,000)	(12,000)	(20,000)	(20,000)		
	$ 3,000	0	0	$ 3,000	0	$ 5,000	$(7,000)	$2,000
Payment of partnership creditors	(3,000)					(3,000)	3,000	
Balances[2]	0	0	0	$ 3,000[3]	0	$ 2,000	$(4,000)	$2,000

[1]Beginning asset balances represent realizable values.

[2]A later pays $4,000 to the partnership to eliminate the debit capital balance; the payment will be allocated first to the partnership liabilities and then to B. However, if A is not able to make a payment, claims against the partnership by the creditors and B will be totally uncollectible.

[3]The unsatisfied personal creditors of B are unable to seek recovery against the credit capital balance of B because the partnership itself is not solvent.

LUMP SUM LIQUIDATIONS

The guidelines discussed in the preceding section are important factors influencing the procedural and legal aspects of a partnership liquidation. Upon liquidation of a partnership, the amount of assets ultimately to be distributed to the individual partners is determined through the use of either a lump sum liquidation schedule or an installment liquidation schedule.

A lump sum liquidation requires that all assets be realized before a distribution is made to partners, thus avoiding the possibility of a premature distribution. To illustrate a lump sum liquidation, assume the following:

1. Asset, liability, loan, and capital balances are as shown in Illustration 15-3, after books for the final operational period are closed.
2. Profit and loss percentages for partners A, B, and C are 40%, 40%, and 20%, respectively.

Illustration 15-3
Lump Sum Liquidation Statement

	Cash	Noncash Assets	Liabilities	Loan from A	Capital Balances A	B	C
Beginning balances........	$10,000	$120,000	$80,000	$9,000	$25,000	$10,000	$6,000
February 15, sale of assets at a gain...............	60,000	(50,000)			4,000	4,000	2,000
March 2, sale of assets at a loss...............	10,000	(30,000)			(8,000)	(8,000)	(4,000)
Payment of liquidation expenses..............	(2,000)				(800)	(800)	(400)
March 7, sale of assets at a loss...............	20,000	(40,000)			(8,000)	(8,000)	(4,000)
Balances	$98,000	0	$80,000	$9,000	$12,200	$ (2,800)	$ (400)
Payment of liabilities.......	(80,000)		(80,000)				
Balances	$18,000	0	0	$9,000	$12,200	$ (2,800)	$ (400)
B's contribution	2,800					2,800	
Balances	$20,800	0	0	$9,000	$12,200	0	$ (400)
Absorption of C's balance ..					(400)		400
Balances	$20,800	0	0	$9,000	$11,800	0	0
Payment to A.............	(20,800)			(9,000)	(11,800)		
Final balances............	0	0	0	0	0	0	0

3. Personal assets and debts of the partners are as follows:

	A	B	C
Total personal assets	$30,000	$40,000	$20,000
Total personal liabilities............................	10,000	37,200	24,000

4. Sales of assets are as follows:

Date	Book Value	Selling Price	Gain (Loss)
February 15	$50,000	$60,000	$10,000
March 2	30,000	10,000	(20,000)
March 7	40,000	20,000	(20,000)

5. Total liquidation expenses of $2,000 are paid on March 4.

Illustration 15-3 presents the lump sum distribution and demonstrates the following concepts that were discussed previously:

1. Gains and losses on realization are allocated according to the partners' profit and loss ratio.
2. Claims against the partnership are paid in the proper order.
3. The marshaling of assets doctrine is followed to determine the disposition of B's and C's debit balances in their capital accounts. That is, a partner's personal assets first are used to satisfy personal liabilities. Then, to the extent possible, remaining assets are contributed to the partnership to eliminate debit capital balances.

4. C's debit capital balance is charged against A, the only personally solvent partner.
5. Partner A will have a claim against C's personal assets for the debit balance that was absorbed.

INSTALLMENT LIQUIDATIONS

The complete liquidation process easily might extend over several months or longer, and it may not be possible to postpone payments to creditors and partners until all assets have been realized. Therefore, payments may be made on an installment basis to creditors and partners during the liquidation process. To avoid the problem associated with premature payments, installment payments may be made to partners only after anticipating all liabilities, possible losses, and liquidation expenses. To provide a proper solution to installment liquidations, either a schedule of safe payments is prepared as amounts become available for distribution or a predistribution plan is used to direct the distribution of any available sum.

Schedule of Safe Payments.   The possibility of premature payments to partners is reduced by using a schedule of safe payments, which reflects a conservative approach to liquidation. The schedule indicates how available funds should be distributed to partners. It is based on the anticipation of all possible liabilities and expenses, including those expected to be incurred in the process of liquidation. The effect of these items on partnership capital is allocated among the partners according to their profit and loss agreement.

In keeping with the conservative approach, the schedule also is based on the assumption that all noncash assets will be worthless; therefore, the assumed loss is allocated among the partners according to their profit and loss ratio. The allocation of the assumed loss could produce debit balances in partners' capital accounts, and these balances are treated as being uncollectible. Therefore, the assumed debit capital balances are allocated to those partners with credit balances according to their profit and loss ratio. When the allocation of estimated liabilities, expenses, liquidation losses, and debit balances is completed, assets may be distributed safely to the partners in amounts equal to the resulting credit capital balances.

A new schedule of safe payments is prepared each time a distribution to partners is scheduled. These schedules support an installment liquidation statement, which summarizes changes in real account balances as the liquidation proceeds. When the partners' capital balances are in the profit and loss ratio, all partners will share in a given distribution. All future distributions to partners will be allocated automatically according to their profit ratio, thus eliminating the need for another schedule of safe payments.

To illustrate the use of schedules of safe payments in conjunction with an installment liquidation, assume the following:

1. Asset, liability, loan, and capital balances are shown in Illustration 15-4 after books for the final operational period are closed.
2. Profit and loss percentages for partners A, B, and C are 40%, 40%, and 20%, respectively.

3.   Sales of assets are as follows:

Date	Book Value	Selling Price	Gain (Loss)
February 15	$60,000	$40,000	$(20,000)
March 2	30,000	15,000	(15,000)
March 17	10,000	20,000	10,000
April 1	20,000	24,000	4,000

4.   Liquidation expenses are estimated to be $10,000. Cash is to be restricted in that amount until expenses are paid.
5.   Installment distributions of unrestricted cash are made on February 17, March 5, March 18, and April 2.
6.   Total liquidation expenses of $8,000 are paid on March 4.

   Illustration 15-4 is based on these facts and demonstrates the following concepts:

1.   Gains and losses on realization are allocated according to the partners' profit and loss ratio.
2.   Unsold noncash assets are assumed to be worthless for purposes of determining the safe payments to partners.
3.   Loan balances are combined with capital balances according to the right of offset doctrine. This offset can result in partners receiving distributions of capital before other partners' loan accounts have been paid (as in the February 17 distribution in Illustration 15-4). However, such distributions may be placed in escrow until it is certain that debit balances will not develop in these partners' capital accounts.
4.   Distributions are applied to a partner's loan balance before they are applied to the partner's capital balance.
5.   Typically, the doctrine of marshaling of assets is ignored until all assets have been realized, at which time debit balances in partners' capital accounts may be satisfied through contributions of personal assets.
6.   A schedule of safe payments is an iterative process that will cease when the schedule indicates that a given distribution will be shared among all partners. Further distributions will be allocated among the partners according to their profit and loss ratio. For example, when the March 5 distribution in Schedule A indicates that all partners will receive a portion of the distribution, the distribution on March 18 would be made in the profit and loss ratio, with results identical to those that would be indicated by continuing the schedule of safe payments:

Partner	(1) Total Distribution to All Partners	(2) Partner's Profit and Loss Percentage	(1) × (2) Amount to Be Distributed	Amount to Be Distributed per Schedule of Safe Payments
A	$20,000	40%	$ 8,000	$ 8,000
B	20,000	40	8,000	8,000
C	20,000	20	4,000	4,000
			$20,000	$20,000

Illustration 15-4
Installment Liquidation Statement

	Cash	Noncash Assets	Liabilities	Loan from A	Capital Balances A	B	C
Beginning balances.............	$10,000	$120,000	$30,000	$5,000	$25,000	$55,000	$15,000
February 15, sale of assets.......	40,000	(60,000)			(8,000)	(8,000)	(4,000)
Balances	$50,000	$ 60,000	$30,000	$5,000	$17,000	$47,000	$11,000
Payment of liabilities............	(30,000)		(30,000)				
February 17, distribution (Schedule A)................	(10,000)					(10,000)	
Balances	$10,000	$ 60,000	0	$5,000	$17,000	$37,000	$11,000
March 2, sale of assets	15,000	(30,000)			(6,000)	(6,000)	(3,000)
Payment of liquidation expenses	(8,000)				(3,200)	(3,200)	(1,600)
Balances	$17,000	$ 30,000	0	$5,000	$ 7,800	$27,800	$ 6,400
March 5, distribution (Schedule A)................	(17,000)			(800)		(15,800)	(400)
Balances	0	$ 30,000	0	$4,200	$ 7,800	$12,000	$ 6,000
March 17, sale of assets	$20,000	(10,000)			4,000	4,000	2,000
Balances	$20,000	$ 20,000	0	$4,200	$11,800	$16,000	$ 8,000
March 18, distribution (Schedule A)................	(20,000)			(4,200)	(3,800)	(8,000)	(4,000)
Balances	0	$ 20,000	0	0	$ 8,000	$ 8,000	$ 4,000
April 1, sale of assets	$24,000	(20,000)	0	0	1,600	1,600	800
Balances	$24,000	0			$ 9,600	$ 9,600	$ 4,800
Final distribution	(24,000)				(9,600)	(9,600)	(4,800)
Balances	0	0	0	0	0	0	0

Schedule A—Schedule of Safe Payments

	A	B	C	Total
Profit and loss percentage.........................	40%	40%	20%	100%
February 17 Distribution				
Combined capital and loan balances before distribution	$22,000	$47,000	$11,000	$80,000
Estimated liquidation expenses.....................................	(4,000)	(4,000)	(2,000)	(10,000)
Balances..	$18,000	$43,000	$ 9,000	$70,000
Maximum loss possible..	(24,000)	(24,000)	(12,000)	(60,000)
Balances..	$ (6,000)	$19,000	$ (3,000)	$10,000
Allocation of debit capital balances.................................	6,000	(9,000)	3,000	0
Safe payment	0	$10,000	0	$10,000
March 5 Distribution				
Combined capital and loan balances before distribution	$12,800	$27,800	$ 6,400	$47,000
Maximum loss possible..	(12,000)	(12,000)	(6,000)	(30,000)
Safe payments..	$ 800	$15,800	$ 400	$17,000
March 18 Distribution (schedule not required)				
Combined capital and loan balances before distribution	$16,000	$16,000	$ 8,000	$40,000
Maximum loss possible..	(8,000)	(8,000)	(4,000)	(20,000)
Safe payments..	$ 8,000	$ 8,000	$ 4,000	$20,000

7. The partner with the greatest ability to absorb anticipated losses (i.e., preserves a credit capital balance after allocating anticipated losses) will be the first to receive a safe payment.

Predistribution Plan.   Schedules of safe payments provide a means of guaranteeing the propriety of installment distributions to partners, especially in complex situations. However, a predistribution plan provides a less tedious means of determining distributions to partners. The predistribution plan is prepared in advance of actual distributions and provides the user with information regarding the order and amount of all future distributions. As was the case with schedules of safe payments, the predistribution plan (1) combines partners' loan balances with their capital balances; (2) anticipates all possible liabilities, losses on realization, and liquidation expenses; and (3) recognizes that the partner with the greatest ability to absorb anticipated losses will be the first partner to receive safe payments.

To prepare the predistribution plan, all anticipated but unrecorded liabilities and liquidation expenses are allocated to the various partners' capital balances according to their profit and loss ratio. The resulting capital balances then are evaluated to determine the maximum loss from realization that could be absorbed by the partners before a debit balance is created in each of their capital accounts. As suggested by the schedule of safe payments, the partner who maintains a credit capital balance after assuming that all noncash assets are worthless is the partner with the greatest ability to absorb realization losses. Therefore, that partner will be the first to receive an actual distribution of assets.

The maximum loss a partner could absorb (*maximum loss absorbable*), before a debit balance in the partner's capital account is created, is determined by the following calculation:

$$\text{Maximum Loss Absorbable (MLA)} = \frac{\text{Partner's Capital Balance}}{\text{Partner's Profit and Loss Percentage}}$$

Since the partner with the largest MLA will be the first to receive an actual distribution, the MLAs are used to indicate the order in which partners will receive distributions. However, it should be noted that the MLAs do not indicate the amounts of the distributions. To illustrate, assume a partnership consists of three partners (A, B, and C) who have capital balances, before the realization of noncash assets, of $70,000, $60,000, and $40,000, respectively, and profit and loss percentages of 35%, 25%, and 40%, respectively. The maximum losses absorbable by partners A, B, and C are determined as follows:

Partner	(1) Capital Balance	(2) Profit and Loss Percentage	(1) ÷ (2) Maximum Loss Absorbable	Rank
A	$70,000	35%	$200,000	Second
B	60,000	25	240,000	First
C	40,000	40	100,000	Third

If all partners had identical MLAs, all partners would share in any given distribution. Therefore, the amount of any distribution to be paid to a particular partner can be determined by calculating the distributions needed ultimately to give all partners the same MLA. In the present example, Partner B should receive distributions first until his/her MLA is equal to the next highest MLA of $200,000. If B's capital balance was reduced to $50,000 (next highest MLA multiplied by the partner's profit and loss percentage, $200,000 × 25%) as the result of an actual distribution of $10,000, B's new MLA would be equal to A's original MLA as follows:

Partner	(1) Capital Balance	(2) Profit and Loss Percentage	(1) ÷ (2) Maximum Loss Absorbable
A	$70,000	35%	$200,000
B	50,000	25	200,000
C	40,000	40	100,000

Therefore, the first $10,000, or any portion thereof, that is available for distribution to partners should be paid entirely to partner B.

Partners A and B should now receive distributions until their MLAs of $200,000 are reduced to the next highest MLA of $100,000, traceable to Partner C. If A's capital balance was reduced to $35,000 ($100,000 × 35%) and B's capital balance was reduced to $25,000 ($100,000 × 25%) as the result of actual distributions of $35,000 and $25,000, respectively, to these partners, all partners then would have equivalent MLAs. Thus, the predistribution plan suggests that the next $60,000 ($35,000 + $25,000), or any portion thereof, that is available for distribution to partners should be paid to partners A and B according to the profit ratio of 35:25 and all further distributions should be divided among all partners according to their respective profit ratio.

The process of preparing the predistribution plan is summarized as follows:

1. Calculate each partner's MLA.
2. Rank partners in descending order according to the amounts of their MLAs.
3. Determine what amount must be paid to the partner ranked first to achieve equality between the MLAs of that partner and the second-ranked partner. This amount represents the safe payment that can be paid to the first-ranked partner.
4. Determine what amount must be paid in total to those partners having equivalent MLAs so that their new MLAs would be equal to those of the next-highest-ranked partner. This amount would be divided among the partners receiving the distribution according to the relationship that their profit percentages have to each other.
5. Continue step 4 until all partners have equivalent MLAs.
6. When all partners have equal MLAs, distributions would be allocated according to the partners' profit ratio.

To demonstrate this entire process, the following facts are used as the basis for the predistribution plan in Illustration 15-5.

	Partners		
	A	B	C
Profit and loss percentage.	30%	50%	20%
Combined capital and loan balance.	$33,000	$45,000	$14,000

Total liabilities of the partnership equal $20,000.
Total liquidation expenses are expected to be $10,000.

To relate the predistribution plan in Illustration 15-5 to an actual distribution, assume that distributions are made as follows:

Date	Amount	Purpose
February 15	$20,000	Pay liabilities
March 1	5,000	Pay partners
March 15	8,000	Pay liquidation expenses
March 27	9,000	Pay partners
April 4	30,000	Pay partners

Rather than constructing numerous schedules of safe payments to determine the recipients of these distributions, the predistribution plan indicates the following distribution:

				Payable to			
Date	Amount	Liabilities	Liquidation Expenses	A	B	C	Level per Plan (Illus. 15-5)
February 15	$20,000	$20,000					I
March 1	5,000			$ 5,000			III
March 15	8,000		$8,000				II
March 27	9,000			1,000			III
				3,000	$ 5,000		IV
April 4	30,000			3,000	5,000		IV
				6,600	11,000	$4,400	V
	$72,000	$20,000	$8,000	$18,600	$21,000	$4,400	

Several aspects of this distribution need to be emphasized. First of all, notice that actual payments to partners precede the payment of the liquidation expenses. This action is acceptable because the computations in Illustration 15-5 already had allowed for liquidation expenses of $10,000. However, if liquidation expenses exceed the estimated amount of $10,000, previous payments to partners could prove to be premature and ultimately could require repayments from partners to the partnership. Another important feature is that all payments required by a specific level of the plan shown in Illustration 15-5 must be satisfied before another level of the plan is entered. Finally, when a particular distribution is divided among several partners, the amount is allocated to the sharing partners according to their respective profit ratio.

Illustration 15-5

Predistribution Plan
Computation of Payments to Partners

		Capital Balances			Maximum Loss Absorbable		
		A	B	C	A	B	C
(1)	Profit and loss percentage............	30%	50%	20%			
	Capital and loan balance..............	$33,000	$45,000	$14,000			
	Allocate expected liquidation						
	expenses.........................	(3,000)	(5,000)	(2,000)			
(2)	Balances..........................	$30,000	$40,000	$12,000			
	Maximum loss absorbable (MLA)						
	[(2) ÷ (1)].......................				$100,000	$80,000	$60,000
(3)	Amount needed to reduce highest-						
	ranked MLA to next-highest-ranked						
	MLA..............................				$ (20,000)		
	New MLAs.........................				$ 80,000	$80,000	$60,000
(4)	Reduction in capital (payment)						
	needed to achieve reduction in MLA						
	[(3) × (1)]........................	(6,000)					
(5)	New capital balance [(2) – (4)].........	$24,000	$40,000	$12,000			
(6)	Amount needed to reduce highest-						
	ranked MLAs to next-highest-ranked						
	MLA..............................				(20,000)	(20,000)	
	New MLAs.........................				$ 60,000	$60,000	$60,000
(7)	Reduction in capital (payment) needed						
	to achieve reduction in MLA						
	[(6) × (1)]........................	(6,000)	(10,000)				
(8)	New capital balance [(5) – (7)].........	$18,000	$30,000	$12,000			

When MLAs are equal, future distributions are allocated to all partners according to their profit and loss percentages.

			Payable to			
Level	Amount	Liabilities	Estimated Liquidation Expenses	A	B	C
I	First $20,000	$20,000				
II	Next $10,000		$10,000			
III	Next $6,000			100%		
IV	Next $16,000			37.5% (3/8)	62.5% (5/8)	
V	Any additional payments			30%	50%	20%

QUESTIONS

1. How does one measure the amount of goodwill traceable to the admission of a new partner?
2. Identify several reasons why an incoming partner may pay the partnership more consideration for a capital interest than is suggested by the book value of the previous partnership.
3. When an incoming partner's investment suggests the need to revalue existing recorded assets and recognize goodwill traceable to the previous partners, how is the amount of these adjustments determined?
4. Assume a CPA is acquiring a capital interest in an existing partnership of CPAs. Identify several examples of intangibles which the incoming partner is contributing that may suggest goodwill traceable to that partner. *Client base, business network, personal motivation, specialized knowledge*
5. Why is the bonus method of accounting for ownership changes more widely used in practice?
6. Discuss how the admission of a new partner is accounted for if the partner acquires an interest from an existing partner rather than the partnership.
7. Under what conditions might the use of the goodwill method prove to be inequitable as compared to the bonus method?
8. If goodwill is suggested by the withdrawal of a partner, what arguments support recognizing only that portion of the goodwill traceable to the withdrawing partner?
9. If an individual partner is insolvent, discuss the rights its unsatisfied creditors have against the partnership assuming that the Uniform Partnership Act is applicable.
10. If a partnership is insolvent, discuss the procedures that govern how unsatisfied partnership creditors may recover from individual partners.
11. What is the impact on partnership creditors of applying common law, rather than the Uniform Partnership Act, in the marshaling of assets?
12. What assumption is made in a schedule of safe payments regarding the marshaling of assets doctrine?
13. Given a partnership liquidation, what circumstances would explain a partner's contributing personal assets even though he/she does not have a deficit capital balance?

EXERCISES

Exercise 1. Riley and Smith are partners with present capital balances (book values) of $500,000 and $400,000, respectively. The partners share profits and losses according to the following percentages: 60% for Riley and 40% for Smith. Tyler is to join the original partnership upon contribution of $250,000 to the partnership in exchange for a 20% interest in capital and a 15% interest in profits and losses. Tyler's contribution consists of $170,000 of cash and equipment having a fair market value of $80,000 (the tax basis of equipment is $42,000). The assets of the original partnership have a book value equal to their fair market value except that land has a book value of $15,000 and a market value of $55,000. The tax basis for Riley and Smith's capital balances before Tyler's entry is $425,000 and $330,000, respectively.

(1) Calculate the capital balances for each individual in the new partnership, assuming use of both the bonus and goodwill methods. All implied goodwill is traceable to the original partners. *allocated*

(2) Calculate the tax basis of the partners' capital balances after admitting the new partner.

Exercise 2. Rainbow Properties is a partnership consisting of three partners: Ross, Gilmore, and Bates. The partnership's primary business is the acquisition and development of land into homesites. Projects require a significant amount of capital, which often is borrowed from area banks. The three partners share profits and losses equally and have the following capital balances: $160,000 for Ross, $120,000 for Gilmore, and $200,000 for Bates. Recently, Ross was approached to sell her personal interest in the partnership to William Lane for $210,000.

(1) What advantages would there be to the partnership if Lane acquired an interest directly from the partnership rather than directly from Ross?
(2) What amount would Lane have to contribute to the partnership in order to have the same interest in capital as would have been acquired had Lane purchased an interest directly from Ross?
(3) Assume Lane purchased a one-fourth interest in the partnership by contributing $210,000 to the partnership. Prepare the entry to record the contribution noting that existing land has a fair market value of $330,000 and a book value of $300,000 and goodwill is recognized.

Exercise 3. Anderson, Garner, Mason, and Sanders are business partners who have capital balances of $27,000, $36,000, $45,000, and $32,000, respectively. Their partnership agreement calls for the allocation of profits and losses at the rates of 20%, 30%, 30%, and 20%, respectively. Sanders is withdrawing from the partnership.

(1) Assuming Sanders' interest in the partnership is sold for $37,000, calculate the remaining partners' capital balances under both the bonus and goodwill methods.
(2) Assuming Sanders' interest in the partnership is sold for $25,000, calculate the remaining partners' capital balances under both the bonus and goodwill methods.

Exercise 4. Marcus and Wellington are partners with capital balances of $32,000 and $68,000, respectively, as of July 1, 19X7. Marcus has a 30% interest in profits and losses. All assets of the partnership are at fair market value except as follows:

	Book Value	Market Value
Equipment	$150,000	$142,000
Inventory	43,000	50,000
Building	274,000	250,000
Land	60,000	105,000
	$527,000	$547,000

The partnership has decided to admit Kelly and Springer as new partners. Kelly contributes cash of $55,000 for a 20% interest in capital and a 30% interest in profits and losses. Springer contributes cash of $10,000 and equipment with a fair market value of $50,000 for a 25% interest in capital and a 35% interest in profits and losses. Springer is also bringing special expertise and client contacts to the new partnership.

Prepare entries to record the admission of Kelly and Springer assuming the use of:
(1) Bonus method
(2) Goodwill method

Exercise 5. The following information relates to Pfarr and Williams, who are partners in a business being liquidated:

	Pfarr	Williams
Partnership balances:		
Loan payable—Williams...............................		$ 5,000
Capital balance (deficit).................................	$20,000	$(14,000)
Profit and loss percentage	70%	30%
Personal assets (including partnership loan payable)...........	$30,000	$ 22,000
Personal liabilities......................................	$15,000	$ 21,000

(1) After applying the right of offset doctrine, indicate how each partner's personal assets would be distributed assuming the Uniform Partnership Act is applicable.

(2) Determine the effect on the calculations in (1) if the right of offset doctrine was ignored.

(3) After applying the right of offset doctrine, indicate how each partner's personal assets would be distributed assuming common law is applicable.

Exercise 6. JKL Construction Company, a partnership, has total assets of $149,000 and total liabilities of $165,000. The following information relates to the individual partners:

	Jason	Kelly	Linden
Total personal assets..............................	$52,000	$41,500	$28,000
Total personal liabilities	47,000	33,500	34,000
Partnership capital balance (deficit).................	7,000	3,000	(26,000)
Profit and loss percentage..........................	50%	30%	20%

If Linden inherits $16,000 after liquidation of the JKL partnership, what will be the priority and amount of claims existing against the $16,000? What claims (who and how much) will remain unsatisfied?

Exercise 7. Cooper, Clancy, and Clayton are partners in a construction company that develops multifamily housing. Their business has been unstable, and they are considering liquidating the partnership.

Clancy believes that the business should be liquidated, and on October 31, 19X2, the company's net book value of $270,000 would be disposed of at a loss of $15,000.

Clayton thinks that the company should develop another project, which would generate a profit of $40,000, and then liquidate. Furthermore, Clayton feels that the net book value, which then would be $310,000, could be disposed of for $260,000.

Cooper is seeking your advice regarding which alternative would be best for them. The following information has been provided to you by Clayton:

	Cooper	Clancy	Clayton
Partnership capital balance (deficit)	$170,000	$ (20,000)	$120,000
Profit and loss percentage	30%	50%	20%
Personal assets.................................	$110,000	$110,000	$ 60,000
Personal liabilities	$ 80,000	$105,000	$ 56,000

Assuming the Uniform Partnership Act is applicable, prepare an analysis of the two alternatives for Cooper.

Exercise 8. Coleman, Moore, and Ramsey are partners in a business being liquidated. The partnership has cash of $8,000, noncash assets with a book value of $96,000, and liabilities of $63,000. The following information relates to the individual partners as of June 1, 19X7.

	Coleman	Moore	Ramsey
Loan payable to partners		$ 5,000	
Capital balance (deficit).....................	$47,000	$(14,000)	$ 3,000
Profit and loss percentage	60%	20%	20%
Personal assets...........................	$10,000	$ 15,000	$25,000
Personal liabilities	$ 5,000	$ 6,000	$15,000

On June 15, 19X7, assets with a book value of $30,000 were sold for $20,000 cash. The proceeds were used to pay off liabilities of the partnership. During the balance of June, no additional assets were liquidated and outside creditors began to pressure the partnership for payment. On July 1, the partners agreed to contribute personal assets, to whatever extent possible, in order to eliminate their respective capital deficits. Shortly thereafter, assets with a book value of $20,000 and a market value of $23,000 were distributed to Coleman.

Assuming additional noncash assets with a book value of $40,000 are sold in July for $54,000, determine how available cash would be distributed.

Exercise 9. Delaney, Gray, and Sullivan are considering the liquidation of their partnership, which has assets of $110,000 and liabilities, including a $10,000 loan from Sullivan, of $30,000. Delaney and Gray each have capital balances of $33,000. Profits and losses are shared 30%, 30%, and 40% for Delaney, Gray, and Sullivan, respectively.

Prepare a predistribution plan to govern the possible liquidation, assuming liquidation expenses of $10,000.

PROBLEMS

Problem 15-1. Buckner and Pressey are partners in a dry cleaning business in which profits and losses are shared equally. Buckner and Pressey have capital balances of $40,000 and $60,000, respectively.

Required:
For each of the six situations presented, prepare the necessary journal entries for the partnership records.

	Situations		
	(1)	(2)	(3)
Admission of new partner:			
Entering partner...................	Nelson	Nelson	Nelson
Purchase price	$60,000	$30,000	$40,000
Interest in capital acquired..........	30%	20%	30%
Paid to	Partnership	Partnership	Pressey
Method used	Bonus	Goodwill	N/A

	Situations		
	(4)	(5)	(6)
Withdrawal of previous partner:			
Exiting partner....................	Buckner	Buckner	Buckner
Selling price	$48,000	$25,000	$39,000
Interest in capital sold..............	40%	20%	30%
Paid by.........................	Partnership	Partnership	Partnership
Method used	Bonus	Goodwill traceable to exiting partner	Goodwill traceable to all partners

Problem 15-2. Burns, Flint, and Levy are partners in a business that has the following capital balances as of December 31, 19X7:

Burns, capital................................	$45,000
Flint, capital	75,000
Levy, capital	60,000

Profits during the year 19X8 are to be allocated among the partners according to the following agreement:

(a) Burns, Flint, and Levy are to be allocated semiannual salaries of $30,000, $42,000, and $50,000, respectively.

(b) Burns is to receive a bonus of 10% of net income after the bonus.

(c) The partners have profit and loss percentages of 50%, 20%, and 30% for Burns, Flint, and Levy, respectively.

Profits for the first half of 19X8 were $140,000.

On July 1, 19X8, Berger acquired a 25% interest in capital from the partnership for $130,000. Certain assets of the original partnership have a fair market value in excess of book value in the amount of $30,000. Berger's investment in the partnership is to be accounted for according to the goodwill method. Upon the admission of Berger, the profit-sharing agreement of the partnership was revised to provide for a semiannual salary to Berger of $50,000. Burns would receive a bonus according to the prior agreement and the profit and loss percentages for Burns, Flint, Levy, and Berger were as follows: 40%, 20%, 20%, and 20%, respectively.

After allocating the profit of $192,000 for the second half of 19X8, Burns elected to sell his interest to Flint for $200,000. At that time, Levy also elected to sell her interest to the partnership for $210,000. The sale will be recorded according to the goodwill method.

Required:
Develop a schedule that details the activity in the partners' capital accounts during the year 19X8.

Problem 15-3. Andrews and Block are partners in an engineering consulting firm sharing profits and losses 40% and 60%, respectively, and their capital balances are $110,000 and $150,000, respectively. The recorded net assets of the firm are as follows:

	Book Value	Market Value
Working capital.....................................	$110,000	$100,000
Net property and equipment.........................	90,000	108,000
Noncurrent liabilities	60,000	60,000

In addition to the recorded assets, the partners feel that the firm has goodwill which has been valued at $40,000 because the firm enjoys a strong client base and has earnings that are consistently above industry averages.

Carver is interested in merging his environmental consulting firm with Andrews and Block. Carver's net assets to be conveyed to the partnership include the following:

	Book Value	Market Value
Working capital....................................	$50,000	$40,000
Net equipment	60,000	50,000

In addition to the above-recorded net assets, Carver feels that his business contacts and expertise will add value to the existing partnership. Carver has valued these intangibles at $20,000.

Required:
(1) If Carver were to acquire a 30% interest in the new partnership, how much additional cash would Carver have to contribute to the partnership?
(2) If Carver were admitted to the partnership, all partners would share equally in profits and losses. All parties are somewhat uncertain about the values placed on intangible assets. Andrews and Block favor using the goodwill method to record Carver's investment in the partnership. Calculate the amount of risk to all partners this method would entail should the intangible assets not have value.
(3) Discuss how a profit and loss agreement might be used to reward a new partner for intangible assets, and yet not record the intangibles on the financial statements.

Problem 15-4. The balance sheet of Alamo Trucking as of December 31, 19X8, is as follows:

Assets		Liabilities and Capital	
Cash	$ 15,000	Accounts payable............	$ 32,000
Accounts receivable, net......	85,000	Loans payable...............	240,000
Equipment, net	210,000	Duke, capital	16,000
Land	60,000	Johnson, capital	22,000
Securities, at cost	20,000	Olsen, capital................	80,000
Total assets	$390,000	Total liabilities and capital.....	$390,000

Earnings for the first quarter of 19X9 were $32,000. The partnership agreement calls for a monthly salary of $2,000 each for Duke and Johnson. Olsen is to receive interest of 20% on her quarterly beginning capital balance. Remaining profits or losses are to be allocated equally among the partners.

At the beginning of the second quarter, Meyers acquired a one-fourth interest in the partnership for $45,000. The partnership agreed to record the investment by the goodwill method and to modify the profit and loss agreement as follows:

	Duke	Johnson	Olsen	Meyers
Monthly salary..............................	$2,000	$2,000		$1,000
Bonus as a percentage of earnings after the bonus....................................				10%
Interest on beginning quarterly capital........			20%	
Profit and loss percentage....................	30%	20%	40%	10%

Second-quarter earnings were $22,000.

At the beginning of the third quarter, Olsen's interest in capital and profits was sold to Zeller for $92,000. The third quarter had reported earnings of $44,000.

At the beginning of the fourth quarter, Duke's interest in capital and profits was sold to the partnership for $30,000. This transaction was to be recorded by the goodwill method, recognizing goodwill traceable to the exiting partner only. The remaining partners retained their proportionate profit and loss ratio.

After Duke's retirement, Mitchell agreed to purchase a 50% interest in the partnership for $225,000. The recording of this investment was to be made using the goodwill method and was to reflect the differences between the book value and market value of certain assets as of the transaction date. Their values as of October 1, 19X9, were as follows:

	Book Value	Market Value
Accounts receivable (net)	$92,000	$73,000
Land	60,000	72,000

Required:

Prepare a schedule analyzing the changes in partners' capital balances since December 31, 19X8. Supporting calculations should be in good form.

Problem 15-5. Book value and market value information for the public accounting firm of Davis, Baker, and Winslow as of December 31, 19X9, is as follows:

	Book Value	Market Value
Cash	$ 78,000	$ 78,000
Receivables, net	43,000	32,000
Furniture and fixtures, net	22,000	18,000
Technical library, net	14,000	17,000
Securities, at cost	16,000	21,000
Other assets	2,000	
Total	$175,000	$166,000
Accounts payable	$ 4,500	
Wages and salaries payable	5,400	
Notes payable	20,100	
Loans payable, Davis	12,000	
Davis, capital	64,000	
Baker, capital	80,000	
Winslow, capital	(11,000)	
Total	$175,000	

In recent years, the partnership experienced serious disagreement over a variety of business issues. Liquidating the partnership has become a very real but rather lengthy alternative. Baker is impatient with the process of liquidation and offers to sell his interest in the partnership to Davis and Winslow for $70,000. The remaining partners would use the bonus method to record the transaction and then proceed with the liquidation. Winslow is anxious to proceed with the liquidation because her personal assets of $80,000 barely cover personal liabilities of $72,000.

Required:

Assuming liquidation expenses are estimated to be $6,000, would Davis and Winslow be well advised to accept Baker's offer or to just proceed directly with the liquidation of the firm? Supporting calculations should be in good form.

Problem 15-6. Tuttle, Lumas, and Sullivan are partners who share profits and losses 40%, 25%, and 35%, respectively. Unfortunately, their partnership has experienced financial hardships and they have decided to liquidate the partnership. On July 1, 19X7, the partnership has the following capital and loan balances:

	Tuttle	Lumas	Sullivan
Capital balances.	$(18,000)	$(10,000)	$47,000
Loan balances.		4,000	8,000

On July 1, 19X7, the partnership has cash of $8,000, noncash assets of $210,000, and liabilities of $187,000. It is anticipated that costs to liquidate the partnership will be approximately $12,000.

On July 15, 19X7, assets with a book value of $10,000 and a market value of $18,000 were distributed to Lumas. Also at this time, assets with a book value of $20,000 were sold for $16,000. The partners decided that individuals with deficit balances should contribute available personal net assets to the partnership. The partners' personal assets and liabilities at this time are as follows:

	Tuttle	Lumas	Sullivan
Personal assets.	$20,000	$35,000	$83,000
Personal liabilities.	14,000	13,000	34,000

On August 1, 19X7, assets with a book value of $170,000 were sold for $160,000 and available cash was distributed to the partners. The balance of the assets was sold on August 10, 19X7, for $18,000 and actual liquidation expenses of $14,000 were paid.

The Uniform Partnership Act is governing in cases of insolvency.

Required:

Prepare an installment liquidation schedule with all the necessary supporting schedules.

Problem 15-7. Baker, Tubbs, and Knapp have decided to liquidate their partnership due to competitive pressures. At this time the partnership has cash of $21,000, noncash assets of $140,000, and liabilities of $130,000. The partners' capital balances, loan balances, and profit/loss percentages are as follows:

	Baker	Tubbs	Knapp
Capital balances	$12,000		$10,000
Loan balances.	$ 2,000	$3,000	$ 4,000
Profit/loss percentage	60%	20%	20%

Liquidation expenses are estimated to be $4,000.

Required:

(1) Prepare a predistribution plan that may be used to determine how liquidation proceeds would be distributed to the partners.
(2) Given the predistribution plan, indicate the order in which the following alternative distributions would be allocated:

Distribution A: Cash of $175,000.

Distribution B: Cash of $156,500 and equipment with a value of $17,000 given to Baker.

(3) Assume that the noncash assets of the partnership are liquidated as follows:

	Book Value	Proceeds
First sale	$40,000	$60,000
Second sale	70,000	82,000
Third sale	30,000	12,000

Determine how the cash available after each sale would be distributed using an installment liquidation schedule.

(4) Compare the result of required part (2) Distribution A to required part (3) and comment on the comparison.

Problem 15-8. In light of major downturns in the economy, Barker Manufacturing experienced declining profits and defaults on several loans. In a recent meeting, the three partners in the business agreed to continue operations another six months if the partners would make personal loans to the company. These loans were made; yet no significant favorable changes occurred, and the partners agreed to liquidate the partnership. The trial balance prior to liquidation is as follows:

	Debit	Credit
Cash..........................		$ 2,000
Other Assets...................	$141,000	
Loans from Barker..............		50,000
Loans from Dunton.............		24,000
Other Liabilities		82,000
Capital, Barker		16,000
Capital, Dunton	18,000	
Capital, Jacoby................	15,000	
	$174,000	$174,000

Following the decison to liquidate, the partners agreed that available funds will be distributed at the end of each month. Furthermore, if necessary, the partners will contribute available personal assets to satisfy capital deficits. However, they agreed that the right of offset with respect to partnership loans would be observed.

During the first month of liquidation, assets with a book value of $32,000 were sold for $26,000. Actual liquidation expenses of $4,000 occurred, and future liquidation expenses of $3,000 were estimated. Personal assets and liabilities were as follows:

	Barker	Dunton	Jacoby
Personal assets (including loans to partnership)	$160,000	$48,000	$50,000
Personal liabilities...............................	100,000	30,000	21,000

During the second month of liquidation, assets with a book value of $68,000 were sold for $30,000. Actual liquidation expenses of $5,000 were incurred during the month, and no future liquidation expenses were anticipated. Personal assets and liabilities were as follows:

	Barker	Dunton	Jacoby
Personal assets (including loans to partnership)	$130,000	$40,000	$28,000
Personal liabilities...............................	110,000	20,000	24,000

During the third and final month of liquidation, the balance of the other assets were sold for $11,000. Personal assets and liabilities were as follows:

	Barker	Dunton	Jacoby
Personal assets (including loans to partnership)	$108,000	$36,000	$20,000
Personal liabilities...............................	90,000	18,000	26,000

Required:

Assume the profit and loss percentages are 50%, 30%, and 20% for Barker, Dunton, and Jacoby, respectively. Prepare a schedule that details monthly cash distributions for the liquidation.

Problem 15-9. McCoy, Roper, and Hahn have decided to liquidate their real estate partnership. Liquidation expenses are estimated to be $21,000. Liabilities to outside creditors equal $20,000. The partners' profit and loss percentages, partnership loans (payable to the partners), and capital balances are as follows:

	Profit & Loss %	Loan Payable	Capital (Deficit)
McCoy	40%	$25,000	$20,000
Roper	40		(12,000)
Hahn......................	20	15,000	15,000

Required:
(1) Prepare a schedule for a predistribution plan showing how available cash would be distributed.
(2) Indicate how $70,000 cash would be distributed noting that McCoy also received a parcel of land from the partnership valued at $27,000.

Problem 15-10. **Part I:** The partnership of Aikens, Barnes, and Clinton is winding up its affairs. The following information has been gathered:
(a) The trial balance of the partnership at June 30, 19X7, is as follows:

Cash	6,000	
Accounts Receivable......................................	22,000	
Inventory...	14,000	
Property, Plant, and Equipment (net)......................	99,000	
Aikens, Loan	12,000	
Clinton, Loan...	7,500	
Accounts Payable...		17,000
Aikens, Capital		67,000
Barnes, Capital		45,000
Clinton, Capital..		31,500
Total	160,500	160,500

(b) The partners share profits and losses as follows: Aikens, 50%; Barnes, 30%; and Clinton, 20%.
(c) The partners are considering an offer of $100,000 for the accounts receivable, inventory, and plant assets as of June 30. The $100,000 would be paid to the partners in installments, but the number and amounts are to be negotiated.

Required:
Prepare a predistribution plan schedule as of June 30, 19X7, showing how the $100,000 would be distributed as it becomes available.

Part II: Assume the same facts as in Part I, except that the partners have decided to liquidate their partnership instead of accepting the offer of $100,000. Cash is distributed to the partners at the end of each month.

A summary of liquidation transactions follows:

July:
 $16,500—collected on accounts receivable; balance is uncollectible
 $10,000—received from sale of entire inventory
 $ 1,000—liquidation expenses paid
 $ 8,000—cash retained in the business at the end of month

August:
 $ 1,500—liquidation expenses paid
    —Clinton's capital was reduced when Clinton accepted a piece of special equipment that had a book value of $4,000. The partners agreed that a value of $10,000 should be placed on the machine for liquidation purposes.

$ 2,500—cash retained in the business at the end of the month
September:
   $75,000—received on sale of remaining plant assets
   $ 1,000—liquidation expenses paid
   No cash was retained in the business.

Required:

Prepare a schedule of cash payments as of September 30, 19X7, showing how the cash actually was distributed. Supporting calculations should be in good form.

(AICPA adapted)

Problem 15-11. The partnership agreement of Smith, Bailey, Davis, Williams, and Perry contained a buy-and-sell agreement, among numerous other provisions, which would become operative in case of the death of any partner. Some provisions contained in the buy-and-sell agreement were as follows:

1. Purposes of the buy-and-sell agreement:
   - (a) The partners mutually desire that the business shall be continued by the survivors without interruption or liquidation upon the death of one of the partners.
   - (b) The partners also mutually desire that the deceased partner's estate shall receive the full value of the partner's interest in the partnership, and the estate shall share in the earnings of the partnership until the deceased partner's interest is fully purchased by the surviving partners.
2. Purchase and sale of deceased partner's interest:
   - (a) Upon the death of a partner, the partnership shall continue to operate.
   - (b) Upon the partner's death, the survivors shall purchase, and the executor or administrator of the deceased partner's estate shall sell to the surviving partners, the deceased partner's interest in the partnership for the price and upon the terms and conditions hereinafter set forth.
   - (c) The deceased partner's estate shall retain the deceased partner's interest until the amount specified in the next paragraph is paid in full by the surviving partners.
   - (d) The partners agree that the purchase price for the partnership interest shall be an amount equal to the deceased partner's capital account at the date of death. Said amount shall be paid to the legal representative of decedent as follows:
     - (1) The first installment of 30% of said capital account shall be paid within 60 days from the date of death of the partner, or within 30 days from the date on which the personal representative of decedent becomes qualified by law, whichever date is later, and
     - (2) The balance shall be due in four equal installments, which shall be payable annually on the anniversary date of said death.
3. Deceased partner's estate's share of the earnings:
   - (a) The partners mutually desire that the deceased partner's estate shall be guaranteed a share in the earnings of the partnership over the period said estate retains an interest in the partnership. Said estate shall not be deemed to have an interest in the partnership after the final installment for the deceased partner's capital account is paid, even though a portion of the guaranteed payments specified below may be unpaid and may be due and owing.
   - (b) The deceased partner's estate's guaranteed share of the earnings of the partnership shall be determined from two items and shall be paid at different times as follows:
     - (1) First, interest shall be paid on the unpaid balance of the deceased partner's capital account at the same date that the installment on the purchase price is paid. The amount to be paid shall be an amount equal to accrued interest at

the rate of 6% per annum on the unpaid balance of the purchase price for the deceased partner's capital account.

(2) Second, the partners agree that the balance of the guaranteed payment from the partnership earnings shall be an amount equal to 25% of the deceased partner's share of the aggregate gross receipts of the partnership for the full 36 months preceding the month of the partner's death. Said amount shall be payable in 48 equal monthly installments without interest, and the first payment shall be made within 60 days following the death of the partner or within 30 days from the date on which the personal representative of the deceased becomes qualified, whichever date is later, provided, however, that the payment so made under this provision during any 12-month period shall not exceed the highest annual salary on a calendar-year basis received by the partner for the three calendar years immediately preceding the date of the partner's death. In the event that said payment would exceed said salary, then an amount per month shall be paid that does not so exceed said highest monthly salary, and the term over which payment shall be paid to the beneficiary shall be lengthened beyond the said 48 months in order to complete said payment.

Smith and Perry were killed simultaneously in an automobile accident on January 10, 19X7. The surviving partners notified the executors of both estates that the first payment due under the buy-and-sell agreement would be paid on March 10, 19X7, and subsequent payments would be paid on the tenth day of each month as due.

The following information was determined from the partnership records:

| Partner | Profit and Loss Percentage | Capital Accounts on 1/10/X7 | Annual Salaries to Partners | | |
			19X4	19X5	19X6
Smith	30%	$25,140	$16,500	$17,000	$17,400
Bailey	25	21,970	15,000	15,750	16,500
Davis	20	4,780	12,000	13,000	14,000
Williams	15	5,860	9,600	10,800	12,000
Perry	10	2,540	8,400	9,600	10,800

The partnership gross receipts for the three prior years were:

19X4	$296,470
19X5	325,310
19X6	363,220

Required:

Prepare a schedule of the amount to be paid to the Smith Estate and to the Perry Estate in March, 19X7; December, 19X7; and January, 19X8. The schedule should identify the amounts attributable to earnings, to interest in the guaranteed payments, and to capital. Supporting calculations should be in good form.

(AICPA adapted)

PART 5

Governmental and Not-for-Profit Accounting

Whereas management in the private sector devotes its energy and talent to maximize profits, governmental units and not-for-profit organizations focus on service. The recipients often do not pay in proportion to services received. For example, the costs of fire or police protection, education, park systems, environmental conservation, welfare, and other governmental or not-for-profit services are borne by the general population.

The primary objective of external financial reporting for governmental units and not-for-profit organizations is accountability. However, there is no "bottom-line" amount or earnings per share figure to judge success. Instead, there is the elusive factor of service. To control activities and measure service, variations in the accounting and reporting process are introduced. Budgets have far greater power for control, particularly when they are entered formally into the accounting records in order to provide close comparisons with actual results. With financial resources being derived from many different sources, some with specific restrictions as to their consumption, fund accounting has traditionally been used to display proper use for intended purposes. More recently, standard setters have moved away from fund accounting for private not-for-profit organizations to an organization-wide reporting of unrestricted and donor-restricted assets and liabilities.

CHAPTER 16

Governmental Accounting: The General Fund and the Account Groups

This chapter, the first of two that address accounting procedures used by governmental bodies, deals with the general fund. This fund accounts for most of the ordinary transactions of a governmental body. Also explained are the unique methods used to record fixed assets and long-term debt in separate accounting records called "groups." The presentation is applicable to state and local governments. The governmental accounting procedures of this and the following chapter provide a general understanding of "fund" accounting, which is expanded upon in Chapters 18 and 19 to cover universities, hospitals, and voluntary health and welfare organizations.

Accounting and financial reporting for governmental and not-for-profit (also called nonprofit) entities has become more important because of the increasing portion of our national economy devoted to this sector. Decision makers, such as legislators, citizens, managers, and contributors, need better information about governmental and not-for-profit organizations if they are to make optimal resource allocations to those entities and manage them efficiently and effectively. In addition, many accounting students will hold governmental and not-for-profit accounting jobs, perform audits on such organizations, and take the CPA examination, which contains questions on governmental and not-for-profit accounting.

COMMERCIAL AND GOVERNMENTAL ACCOUNTING: A COMPARISON

Illustration 16-1A is a summary of the flow of resources in a profit-seeking business enterprise. *Demand for goods and services* made by customers in the commercial sector of the economy is satisfied by business enterprises. *Assets* of a business enterprise are supplied voluntarily by *proprietors, stockholders, bond-*

holders, and other creditors. The assets are consumed during *operating processes* which produce *goods and services* sold to customers who choose to deal with the firm. The sales generate *revenue* for the company. The objective of the entity is to generate net income. The income statement measures the attainment of this goal by matching revenues earned with expenses incurred using accrual accounting.

Illustration 16-1A

Flows of Resources Through a Business Enterprise

Expenses (outflows of economic resources) are incurred for the purpose of generating revenue. Owners share the resulting income or loss.

A separate cash flow statement is prepared to show the cash consequences of the period's operating, financing, and investing activities.

Illustration 16-1B is a summary of the flow of resources for a governmental entity. Residents and businesses within a government's jurisdiction *demand goods and services* from the governmental unit. *Assets* of a government are supplied primarily through the involuntary payment of *taxes* by taxpayers. Typical taxes are those levied on property, income, and sales of goods and services. There also may be some financing provided by *creditors.* The assets are consumed during *operating processes*, which produce *goods and services* dispensed to those who are

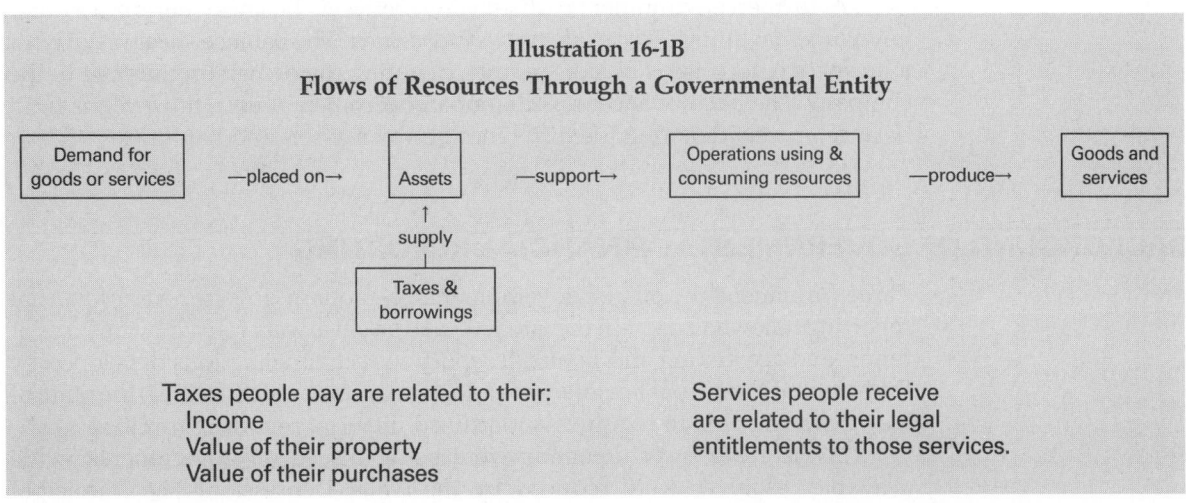

Illustration 16-1B

Flows of Resources Through a Governmental Entity

Taxes people pay are related to their:
Income
Value of their property
Value of their purchases

Services people receive
are related to their legal
entitlements to those services.

legally entitled to receive them. The operations performed to provide services are not intended to generate a profit. Leftover resources at the end of a fiscal period merely lessen the need for revenue in the next period. The results of operations for an accounting period are summarized in a statement called the Statement of Revenues, Expenditures, and Changes in the Fund Balance.

To finance general governmental activities, revenues are raised according to laws and are increases in financial resources that flow from outside the governmental unit—for example, taxes based on incomes or property values. Expenditures, such as salary payments, debt principal and interest payments, and fixed assets purchases, are incurred according to budget appropriations and are decreases in financial resources that flow to entities outside the governmental unit. The expenditures usually are not related to the amounts of taxes people pay. For example, a 7-year-old child who pays no taxes may receive a public education. Other increases in financial resources for general governmental purposes are termed "other financing sources." These include transfers from other funds within the same governmental unit and resources from several other sources including proceeds from bond issues and resources from the sale of fixed assets. Other decreases in financial resources for general governmental activities come from "other financing uses," which are typified by a transfer of financial resources to another fund within the same governmental unit. In addition, many governments engage in business activities that provide goods or services to users and finance these activities through user charges.

An important focus of governmental financial reporting is demonstrating *fiscal compliance*. Operating statements report whether or not financial resources received during a period are sufficient to cover expenditures of a period. Furthermore, in addition to total expenditures, whether or not spending in particular areas was in compliance with approved budgets is reported. Consequently, division of resources into *funds*, each of which is a self-balancing set of accounts, is used to keep track of the flows of financial resources dedicated to specific activities. Financial reporting on fund activities should reveal whether uses of financial resources were within restrictions imposed by law or by third parties.

A further environmental distinction between business enterprises and governmental units is *ownership versus jurisdiction*. The balance sheet residual of a business enterprise is owners' equity, denoting the ownership interest in the company. The balance sheet residual of a governmental unit, however, is fund balance, merely denoting the difference between assets and liabilities.

BACKGROUND OF GOVERNMENTAL FINANCIAL REPORTING

Three prominent periods of developments in modern governmental financial reporting followed crises. In the late 1800s, large cities were rocked by misuses of funds, and accounting and financial reporting recommendations developed by the National Municipal League were adopted by some cities. In 1904, the State of New York was first to require standardized financial reporting by cities.

In the 1930s, new demands were being placed on governments while available resources were reduced by the Great Depression. The Municipal

Finance Officers of America (MFOA)[1] formed its National Committee on Municipal Accounting (NCMA)[2] to promulgate accounting and financial reporting standards. The NCMA Bulletin No. 1, *Principles of Municipal Accounting*, was issued in 1934. Governmental accounting standards evolved through the actions of the NCMA and its successors. The National Committee on Governmental Accounting issued *Governmental Accounting, Auditing and Financial Reporting* (GAAFR), also called the "Blue Book," in 1968. The National Council on Governmental Accounting (NCGA) was organized in 1974, independent of the MFOA. Consequently, subsequent revisions of GAAFR codified and explained governmental financial reporting principles, but they did not have the status of "authoritative pronouncements."

In the 1970s, many cities faced fiscal stress and near-bankruptcy. Many people believed that governmental accounting and financial reporting methods were responsible in part for those problems and believed those problems were not being addressed adequately by the NCGA. Lack of confidence in the ability of the NCGA to address financial reporting issues effectively led to the formation of the Governmental Accounting Standards Board (GASB) in 1984.

Financial reporting standard setting for governmental units has a long history and has been a focus of numerous standard-setting boards. Illustration 16-2 presents an abridged history of financial reporting standards applicable to governments issued by major standard setters.

ORGANIZATION AND PROCESSES OF THE FASB AND THE GASB

The GASB is a sister board to the Financial Accounting Standards Board (FASB). The Financial Accounting Foundation (FAF), which appoints both boards, is responsible for their funding and the determination of their respective jurisdictions and resolves disputes which may arise between the boards.

Both the FASB and the GASB subscribe to a due process of standard setting to ensure that preparers, attestors, and users of financial statements affected by standards have a voice in the establishment of those standards. Due process includes: (1) issuing discussion memoranda setting forth financial reporting issues and arguments for and against possible alternative standards; (2) issuing exposure drafts proposing financial reporting standards regarding issues; (3) issuing standards after considering written comments, testimony from public hearings, and research conducted by FASB and GASB staff and others throughout the due process period.

JURISDICTIONS OF THE FASB AND THE GASB

The authority to set external financial reporting standards for business and nonbusiness organizations rests with several standard-setting bodies. The iden-

---

[1]Now the Government Finance Officers Association (GFOA).
[2]Renamed National Committee on Governmental Accounting in 1951 and reorganized as the National Council on Governmental Accounting (NCGA) in 1974. The NCGA was superseded by the GASB in 1984.

Illustration 16-2
Major Contributions of Governmental Accounting Standard Setters

Year	MFOA/GFOA Committees	AICPA	GASB
1934 to 1941	NCMA—*Principles of Municipal Accounting* and twelve later standards		
1951 to 1968	NCGA—four publications including 1968 *Governmental Accounting, Auditing and Financial Reporting* (GAAFR)		
1974		*Audits of State and Local Governmental Units*	
1979 to 1982	NCGA—Four statements including the 1980 GAAFR, six interpretations, and one Concepts Statement, *Objectives of Accounting and Financial Reporting for Governmental Units*		
1980		Statement of Position 80-2 declared that financial statements presented in accordance with NCGA Statement No. 1 are in conformity with generally accepted accounting principles	
1984 to 1994			GASB, organized in 1984, has issued 24 standards and two concepts statements, *Objectives of Financial Reporting* and *Accounting for Service Efforts and Accomplishment Reporting*. Numerous projects are under way. *Codification of Governmental Accounting and Financial Reporting Standards* contains generally accepted accounting principles for governmental units and is issued annually.

tity of an entity's primary standard setter depends upon the nature of the operating activities of the entity issuing financial reports. Illustration 16-3 shows the primary standard setters for commercial, governmental, and not-for-profit entities.

Accountants and auditors of a reporting entity often rely on financial reporting standards issued by bodies of expert accountants, such as AICPA committees, that are not the entity's primary financial reporting standard setter. In addition, accountants sometimes rely on widely recognized industry practices and other relevant accounting literature, such as accounting textbooks and AICPA issues papers, in preparing financial reports in accordance with generally

Illustration 16-3

Authorities for Commercial, Governmental, and Not-for-Profit Accounting Reporting Standards

Type of Entity	Primary Financial Reporting Standard Setter(s)
Business enterprises	Financial Accounting Standards Board (FASB) and Securities and Exchange Commission (SEC)
Federal government	General Accounting Office (GAO), Comptroller General, Department of the Treasury, Office of Management and Budget (OMB), and Federal Accounting Standards Advisory Board (FASAB)
State/local governments	Governmental Accounting Standards Board (GASB)
Colleges and universities	Public—GASB Private—FASB
Hospitals	Public—GASB Private—FASB
Voluntary health and welfare organizations	FASB
Certain not-for-profit organizations	FASB

accepted accounting principles (GAAP). In order for accountants to know which financial reporting standards have primacy when there are multiple possibilities, the AICPA has published a hierarchy of applicable accounting principles referred to as the "GAAP hierarchy."[3] The GAAP hierarchy is directed at nongovernmental entities that look primarily to the FASB for financial reporting standards and at governmental entities that look primarily to the GASB for financial reporting standards. Generally, nongovernmental entities follow FASB pronouncements, APB Opinions, and AICPA Accounting Research Bulletins, while state and local governments follow GASB pronouncements and AICPA and FASB pronouncements if they are made applicable to state and local governments by GASB action.

GASB OBJECTIVES OF FINANCIAL REPORTING

We have seen differences in environments and purposes of financial reporting between business enterprises and governmental entities. These differences have led to the creation of separate financial reporting standard-setting boards for business enterprises and governments, and each board has examined and defined the objectives of financial reporting by its respective constituency. *Objectives of Financial Reporting by Business Enterprises*, Concept Statement No. 1, was

---

[3]Statement on Auditing Standards No. 69, *The Meaning of "Present Fairly in Conformity with Generally Accepted Accounting Principles" in the Independent Auditor's Report* (New York: American Institute of Certified Public Accountants, Jan. 1992).

issued by the FASB in 1978. *Objectives of Financial Reporting*, Concept Statement No. 1, was issued by the GASB in 1987.

In its Concept Statement No. 1, the GASB stated that "accountability is the cornerstone of all financial reporting in government."[4] A closely related concept referred to by the GASB in the concept statement is interperiod equity. Both concepts are described below.

The GASB believes that financial reporting helps a government fulfill its duty to be publicly accountable to its citizenry. They believe that taxpayers have a "right to know"; that is, a right to receive information about government activities that may lead to public debates. At a minimum, accountability through financial reporting means "providing information to assist in evaluating whether the government was operated within the legal constraints imposed by the citizenry."[5]

A significant part of accountability is interperiod equity, which may be demonstrated by showing "whether current-year revenues are sufficient to pay for current-year services or whether future taxpayers will be required to assume burdens for services previously provided."[6] State and local government financial reports should possess the characteristics of understandability, reliability, relevance, timeliness, consistency, and comparability.

MEASUREMENT FOCUS AND BASIS OF ACCOUNTING

Measurement focus refers to which resources are being measured. *Basis of accounting* refers to when the effects of transactions or events should be recognized for financial reporting purposes. In May 1990, the GASB issued a standard, GASB Statement No. 11, *Measurement Focus and Basis of Accounting—Governmental Fund Operating Statements*, which changed some basic recognition and measurement guidance for governments.[7] This new measurement focus is called the "flow of financial resources." The GASB also chose the accrual basis of accounting to accompany the flow of financial resources. The application of Statement No. 11 is, however, prohibited until its effective date—which the GASB has recently moved to delay. The originally scheduled effective date for Statement No. 11 was for fiscal years ending on or after June 15, 1995. In August 1993, the GASB issued Statement No. 17 which delays the effective date of Statement No. 11 indefinitely. Also, governments are prohibited from implementing Statement No. 11 before the effective date. Reasons for this delay center on several related GASB agenda projects, the financial reporting model, capital reporting, pension accounting, and other projects, which need to be completed to avoid piecemeal implementation of Statement No. 11.

It is conceivable that the GASB conclusions on the reporting project and on related issues will necessitate some Statement No. 11 provisions being modified

---

[4]GASB Concept Statement No. 1, *Objectives of Financial Reporting* (Norwalk, CT: Governmental Accounting Standards Board, 1987), par. 58.

[5]*Ibid.*

[6]*Ibid.*, par. 61.

[7]GASB Statement No. 11, *Measurement Focus and Basis of Accounting—Governmental Fund Operating Statements* (Norwalk, CT: Governmental Accounting Standards Board, May 1990).

and therefore never being applicable in practice. Hence, this chapter emphasizes the currently effective accounting and reporting model of state and local governments. A comparison of generally accepted definitions for financial resources, revenues, other financing sources, expenditures, other financing uses, and general long-term debt currently used and proposed in GASB Statement No. 11 are shown in the appendix to this chapter.

GOVERNMENTAL ACCOUNTING STRUCTURE OF FUNDS

Governmental units use individual funds to account for financial resources used for specific purposes. Each fund is an accounting entity containing a self-balancing set of accounts for which financial statements can be prepared. Business enterprises, on the other hand, report all of their profit-making activity on a single income statement and summarize their financial position on a single balance sheet.

General purpose financial statements for governments aggregate financial information by fund type as shown in the combined balance sheet on page 942. The combined balance sheet is not subjected to the rules of consolidation to eliminate the effects of interfund transactions and interfund balances. Consolidated financial statements restricted to summarizing the effects of transactions between a governmental unit and external parties are not presented. Governmental activity does not reduce well to a single statement about profit or loss. Rather, demonstrating accountability (i.e., compliance with laws governing numerous activities) is the purpose of governmental financial reporting.

Three fund types and two account groups are used in government financial reporting:

1. *Governmental funds* account for activities that provide citizens with services financed primarily by taxes and intergovernmental grants. These funds have a "working capital" focus and include only current assets and current liabilities.
2. *Proprietary funds* account for business-type activities that derive their revenue from charges to users for goods or services. They follow the commercial accounting model in measuring net income. An example would be a publicly owned utility.
3. *Fiduciary funds* account for resources for which the governmental unit acts as a trustee or agent.
4. *Account groups* account for and serve as a record of general fixed assets and general long-term liabilities. Financial resources and current amounts do not appear in account groups.

The GASB specifies different methods of applying the accrual concept in accounting for governmental funds and proprietary funds. The modified accrual basis, a hybrid system that includes some aspects of accrual accounting and some aspects of cash-basis accounting, is used for recognition of revenues and expenditures of governmental funds and similar (governmental-type) fiduciary funds. The accrual basis refers to recognition of revenues and expenses of proprietary funds and similar (proprietary-type) fiduciary funds as in business accounting.

GOVERNMENTAL FUNDS

All governments have a general fund and may have other governmental funds as well, depending on the types of activities of the government. The four governmental funds are:

1. *The general fund* that accounts for resources that have no specific restrictions and are available for operational expenditures not relegated to one of the other governmental funds. Since it accounts for general operations, it is the most essential fund. Every governmental unit has a general fund.
2. *Special revenue funds* that account for resources that legally are restricted to expenditure for specific operational purposes, such as a toll tax levied to be used for road maintenance.
3. *Capital projects funds* that account for resources to be used for the construction or acquisition of major capital facilities.
4. *Debt service funds* that account for resources to be used for payment of general long-term debt and interest.

The remainder of this chapter will discuss the basic categories of transactions affecting governmental funds followed by accounting for the general fund and the account groups. The next chapter will deal with the remaining governmental funds, the proprietary funds, and the fiduciary funds.

ACCOUNTING FOR TRANSACTIONS OF GOVERNMENTAL FUNDS

The modified accrual method of accounting is used for governmental funds to measure the flow of working capital. Under the modified accrual method of accounting, *revenue* is recorded in the accounting period in which it is both measurable and available to finance expenditures made during the current fiscal period (this includes resources expected to be available within 60 days of year end). *Expenditures* are recognized in the period in which the liabilities are both measurable and incurred.

Revenues.   These are increases in financial resources from transactions with external parties that do not have to be repaid. Revenues may come from nonexchange or exchange transactions. Nonexchange transactions are those in which people and companies pay amounts to governments but governments give nothing directly to the payors in return. Exchange transactions are those in which the government provides goods or services for fees. Under modified accrual, some revenues are recognized on the accrual basis, and some revenues are recognized on the cash basis. Revenue from property taxes, intergovernmental grants, entitlements, and shared revenues, interest on investments and delinquent taxes, and billed charges for services are normally recognized under the accrual basis if funds will be available for use in a current period or within 60 days of year end.

Property taxes are recorded as revenue at the time taxes are levied on property owners provided the taxes will be available to spend during the current period. Taxes levied in one year, but not available until the following year, are recognized as deferred revenue. Governments are conservative in recognizing property tax revenue. Only the net amount estimated to be collected is recognized.

Resources to be received from federal, state, or local governmental units (intergovernmental grants, entitlements, and shared revenues for operational purposes) should be recognized as revenue in the year for which the resources are available to finance expenditures. If resources are received prior to the period they may be used, or if the receivable is not expected to be collected soon enough to be used for the current fiscal period, Deferred Revenues is credited. Some grants to a governmental unit may carry strong restrictions on their use. For example, the federal government may be willing to give a locality a grant providing it builds a bridge over a river and connects its main road to the federal highway. In this case, the restricted grant should be recognized as revenue only to the extent that expenditures have been made, with the remainder of the grant revenue recorded as deferred. This type of restricted grant sometimes is called an *expenditure-driven* grant.

Revenues from donations of fiscal resources should be recognized in governmental funds when the assets are received. Donations of capital assets are not recognized in the governmental funds. Rather, donations of capital assets are recognized in the general fixed assets account group discussed later in this chapter.

Revenue for charges for services should be recognized when billed and expected to be received within 60 days of year end. Such revenues may be from goods or services provided for fees, such as golf course fees, garbage removal fees, inspection fees, and sales of maps and other publications.

Interest and dividend revenue from investments should be recognized when earned. Investment gains and losses should be recognized when an investment is sold.

Revenues normally recognized under the cash basis method include fees for licenses and permits, fines and forfeits, and parking meter receipts. These resources are recognized when received in cash because the amount is usually not known prior to collection. In addition, these items are often not an important source of a governmental unit's income.

Taxes levied directly on taxpayers usually are accounted for on a cash basis because the return and remittance ordinarily are received at the same time. Examples are taxes on income, inheritance, gasoline, general sales, and tobacco. The GASB notes that it is "neither necessary nor practical to attempt to accrue taxpayer-assessed income and gross receipts [including sales] taxes unless taxpayer liability and collectibility have been established." For these taxes, the taxpayer is expected to compute the amount of the tax liability and submit payment with the return. The due date for taxpayer-assessed taxes applicable to the reporting period, such as income taxes, also may be extended 60 days past the end of the fiscal period.

Other Financing Sources.   These inflows of financial resources arise from issuing general long-term debt, recording the present value of capital lease obligations, selling capital assets, and receiving interfund operating transfers in. Use of the other financing sources classification avoids multiple countings of inflows as revenues. Proceeds from issuing general long-term debt represent inflows of financial resources that must be repaid to lenders from later tax revenues. Tax revenue recorded in the general fund would be counted as revenue twice if amounts transferred to another governmental fund were recorded in the second fund as revenue rather than as other financing sources. The same is true for proceeds from the sale of a fixed asset. Financial resources raised by tax revenues are used to purchase fixed assets. Their sale later is a conversion of fixed assets into financial resources, not a raising of new financial resources from entities outside the governmental unit.

Expenditures.   Most *expenditures* are decreases in financial resources as a result of transactions with external parties. Some expenditures, however, result from consumption of previously purchased financial resources, such as inventories and prepaid items. In certain situations, transactions with external parties that result in decreases in financial resources are classified as other financing uses. Expenditures are recognized in the period the fund liability is both measurable and incurred. This usually means that an expenditure is recognized if the related liability is expected to be liquidated through the use of expendable available financial resources. Expenditures result from operating activities, acquiring capital assets, and servicing debt. In many cases, expenditures will be recorded simultaneously with cash payments. Consider the following examples:

Expenditures (Control)	50,000	
Cash		50,000
The payment of current maintenance expenses.		
Expenditures (Control)	100,000	
Cash		100,000
Acquisition of a new capital asset for cash.		

Accounting for interest on general long-term debt is an exception to the accrual basis approach. Such expenditures are recorded on a cash basis to match them with the tax revenue raised for the interest payment.

Expenditures (Control)	42,000	
Cash		42,000
Payment of $12,000 of interest and $30,000 principal on existing general obligation debt.		

Other expenditures will be recorded if the amount is to be paid with existing resources. Consider the following entries to record wages:

General Fund:		
Expenditures (Control)	16,500	
Cash		10,500
Liability for State and Federal Withholdings		6,000

While the liability for withholdings is current, the liability for future payment of compensated absences (such as for vacations and holidays) are considered to be long-term liabilities. Under the modified accrual basis of governmental accounting, such long-term liabilities would not be recorded in the general fund. Rather, they will be recorded in the general long-term debt account group as follows:

```
Amount to be Provided in Future Periods. . . . . . . . . . . . . . . . . . . . . . . 1,500
     Liability for Compensated Absences . . . . . . . . . . . . . . . . . . . . . . . . .          1,500
```

The compensated absences liability to be included in the fund is the amount reasonably expected to be paid from the existing governmental fund financial resources. The noncurrent liability is recognized in the general long-term debt account group. Interest on long-term debt is recorded when due.

The GASB requires that a liability for claims and judgments outstanding be recognized in the accounts if it is probable that the liability has been incurred and the amount can be reasonably estimated. During the year, the government will record the amounts paid or vouchered as payable as expenditures in the fund. The noncurrent liability for claims and judgments is recorded directly in the general long-term debt account group.

In many cases, cash will be paid or a liability recorded to purchase goods and services in advance of their use. These items are recorded as financial resources (assets) as follows:

```
Prepaid Rent . . . . . . . . . . . . . . . . . . . . . . . . . . . . . . . . . . . . . . . . . . 12,000
Prepaid Insurance . . . . . . . . . . . . . . . . . . . . . . . . . . . . . . . . . . . . . . 18,000
Supplies Inventory. . . . . . . . . . . . . . . . . . . . . . . . . . . . . . . . . . . . . . 40,000
     Cash . . . . . . . . . . . . . . . . . . . . . . . . . . . . . . . . . . . . . . . . . . . . . .           70,000
     Acquiring goods and services to be consumed in the future.
```

Under the *consumption method*, expenditures are recorded when the financial resources are consumed:

```
Expenditures (Control). . . . . . . . . . . . . . . . . . . . . . . . . . . . . . . . . . . 45,000
     Prepaid Rent . . . . . . . . . . . . . . . . . . . . . . . . . . . . . . . . . . . . . . . .          10,000
     Prepaid Insurance . . . . . . . . . . . . . . . . . . . . . . . . . . . . . . . . . . .          15,000
     Supplies Inventory. . . . . . . . . . . . . . . . . . . . . . . . . . . . . . . . . . .          20,000
          Receiving services and consuming supplies acquired
          previously.
```

Notice that expenditures show the consumption of only those assets defined as financial resources. This is a narrower definition than that used in the private sector for expenses where the measurement focus is flows of economic resources. Expenses are the expirations of economic resources which include not only the use of current assets but also the amortization of long-term assets such as buildings and equipment. Examples of the differences between recording expenditures and expenses are as follows:

A Governmental Fund Using the Flows of Financial Resources Measurement Focus		A Business Entity Using the Flows of Economic Resources Measurement Focus	
Expenditures 10,000		Salary Expense 10,000	
Cash	10,000	Cash	10,000
Payment of salaries; expiration of financial resource.		Payment of salaries; expiration of economic resource.	
Expenditures 90,000		Equipment 90,000	
Cash	90,000	Cash	90,000
Purchase of truck; expiration of financial resource.		Purchase of truck.	
		Depreciation Expense. 15,000	
		Accumulated Depreciation	15,000
		Expiration of economic resource.	

An alternative method of accounting for prepaid items and supplies is the *purchases method*, which results in recording an expenditure upon acquisition, regardless of when actually consumed. Under this method, prepaid items are not recorded on the balance sheet. Significant amounts of inventory at year end are recorded by a debit to Supplies Inventory and a credit to the Fund Balance—Reserved for Supplies. Unlike the consumption method, however, no adjustments are made to the expenditures account or the unreserved fund balance. Although both the consumption and purchase methods are recognized as acceptable alternatives, the purchases method is outdated and will no longer be acceptable under GASB Statement No. 11.

Other Financing Uses.   The greatest use of this account classification is for operating transfers-out to other governmental funds. Using this classification for such funds outflows prevents double counting of expenditures. For example, if an amount transferred from the general fund to the debt service fund were debited to expenditures and then debited to expenditures again in the debt service fund when interest and long-term debt principal were liquidated, a double counting of expenditures would occur. Also classified as Other Financing Uses are claims incurred against financial resources from refunding general long-term debt (using proceeds from issuing new debt to pay old debt).

The following summary shows the debit and credit effects of flows of financial resources through a governmental fund. Notice that governmental funds operating statements report expenditures rather than expenses.

Governmental Funds Actual Transactions

Debits	Credits
Expenditures	Revenues
Other Financing Uses	Other Financing Sources

Operating Debt.   Governments may issue short- and long-term debt to finance their operating activities. The financing is treated as *operating debt* when the debt is not incurred to acquire capital assets or other long-term economic benefits for the government. Examples of short-term operating debt include accounts payable to vendors and tax anticipation notes. Examples of long-term operating debt include compensated absences, long-term vendor financing, and debt incurred to pay claims and judgments.

Proper recording of operating debt by government accountants is to classify the debt as short term or long term. Reporting of short-term debt is in the fund as a liability. Reporting of long-term debt is in the fund as an "other financing source" with an additional entry to record the liability in the general long-term debt account group.

Tax anticipation notes are an example of short-term operating debt. Cash inflows from property tax or income tax collections peak near the due dates for payment. Prior to their receipt, a governmental unit may have obligations that must be paid. Local banks usually provide short-term financing, using as security the taxing power of the government, which is required to sign an instrument referred to as a tax anticipation note. Receipt of cash from such notes would be recorded in the general fund with the following entry:

Cash	150,000	
Tax Anticipation Notes Payable		150,000

Later, as cash inflows from taxes provide resources, the following entry would record the payment of the notes and the interest:

Tax Anticipation Notes Payable	150,000	
Expenditures (Control) (for interest)	1,875	
Cash		151,875

Interest costs associated with short-term and long-term operating debt are recognized when due. Interest is not accrued.

General Long-Term Capital Debt.   Debt financing incurred to acquire capital assets or other long-term economic benefits through governmental funds is termed *general long-term capital debt*. The majority of the proceeds acquired from issuing this debt is accounted for in capital projects funds, as an other financing source, which are discussed in Chapter 17. The face amount of capital debt is accounted for in the general long-term debt account group discussed later in this chapter. Debt service (principal and interest payments) on all general long-term debt is accounted for in the debt service funds discussed in Chapter 17.

USE OF BUDGETARY ACCOUNTING

Generally, finance personnel work with operating department personnel to develop a proposed expenditures budget for a fiscal year. The governmental unit's legislative body deliberates and acts on the budget which authorizes a certain level of expenditures for operating activities, capital acquisitions, and debt service. Authorized expenditures are termed *appropriations*. An authorization to raise revenue and, perhaps, long-term debt is approved. Estimates for other financing sources, and other financing uses also are budgeted. An executive head, such as a governor or mayor, may be responsible for approving the budget or sending it back to the legislative body for further action. The budget, as finally approved, is recorded in the general ledger in summarized control accounts, and in the subsidiary ledgers in detail accounts.

GENERAL LEDGER ENTRIES

Budgetary totals for appropriations (which are authorized expenditures), estimated revenues, other financing sources, and other financing uses are recorded in the general ledger as control accounts over more detailed budgetary entries in subsidiary ledgers. The following summary shows the debit and credit effects of budgetary entries:

Governmental Fund Budgetary Entries

Debit	Credit
Estimated Revenues (Control)	Appropriations (Control)
Estimated Other Financing	Estimated Other Financing
Sources (Control)	Uses (Control)

If estimated inflows do not equal estimated outflows, the difference is either a debit or credit to the budgetary fund balance—unreserved. A budgetary entry is made to the appropriate fund as follows:

Estimated Revenues (Control)......................	10,000,000	
Estimated Other Financing Sources (Control)	1,000,000	
Appropriations (Control)		9,300,000
Estimated Other Financing Uses (Control)............		1,500,000
Budgetary Fund Balance—Unreserved		200,000
To *record* an approved annual budget.		

Actual transactions occurring during the budget year are recorded in separate general ledger accounts. This simplifies the closing process. To close the budgetary accounts, merely reverse the entry made to record the budget. Amounts may include amendments to the original budget recorded during the year. The closing entry must be entered in the same fund:

Appropriations (Control)	9,300,000	
Estimated Other Financing Uses (Control).............	1,500,000	
Budgetary Fund Balance—Unreserved	200,000	
Estimated Revenues (Control).....................		10,000,000
Estimated Other Financing Sources (Control)		1,000,000
To *close* an annual budget as amended.		

SUBSIDIARY LEDGER ENTRIES

Illustration 16-4, on pages 862–863, will be used to show the relationship between the general ledger control accounts and the subsidiary ledgers detail accounts. Usually, budgets are prepared according to object of expenditure. These are, for example, salaries, employee benefits, utilities, and supplies. Each object of expenditure is a line item in the budget or a classification of authorized spending by a department. The appropriation for each line item is recorded in an expenditures subsidiary ledger account as a credit. During the accounting period, such credits will be offset by debits recording actual expenditure transactions. The credit balance in the subsidiary ledger account tells managers how much money they have remaining to spend for that line item purpose. Budgetary amounts of estimated other financing uses and actual other financing uses are recorded in the same manner. The detailed information recorded in the subsidiary ledgers is recorded at least at the level of budgetary control. That is, the accounting records should show whether authorized spending for a line item was exceeded.

A subsidiary ledger for revenues also is maintained. The budgetary amount of each revenue source is recorded in a revenues subsidiary ledger account as a debit. During the accounting period, such debits will be offset by credits recording actual revenue recognition. Budgetary amounts of estimated other financing sources and actual other financing sources are recorded in the same manner.

To emphasize accounting techniques and conserve space, this book will use only general ledger control accounts in its examples for budgetary and actual accounts.

OVERVIEW OF GENERAL FUND PROCEDURES

Illustration 16-4, on pages 862–863, is designed to be a simple example of general fund procedures that is not burdened by the complexities that follow in this chapter. It is meant to acquaint you with the mechanics of governmental accounting. There are three important features of this example you should understand:

1. There are three types of accounts in the general ledger. *Permanent balance sheet accounts* contain financial resources, liabilities, and fund balances. *Budgetary accounts* are used to record the budget. Budget amounts are entered at the start of the period, possibly amended during the period, and closed at the end of the period. There are no actual transactions recorded in these accounts during the period. *Operating accounts* record the expenditures, other financing uses, revenues, and other financing sources that occur during the period.
2. There are three types of journal entries made during the accounting period. The *budgetary entry* enters the budget into the accounting records. The *operating entries* record actual events. The *closing entries* close the budgetary accounts in one entry and the actual accounts in a second closing entry.
3. For every entry in the general ledger, there are detailed entries in the subsidiary ledgers.

Let us now follow these summary entries in Illustration 16-4. Each entry is explained as follows:

1. The budget is entered into the general ledger budgetary accounts. An excess of estimated revenues and estimated other financing sources over appropriations and estimated other financing uses would create a credit to the budgetary fund balance. In this case, appropriations (there are no estimated other financing uses) exceed revenues and estimated other financing sources; thus, there is a debit to the budgetary fund balance. The debit entry to the budgetary fund balance anticipates a decrease in the fund balance during the period. Budgetary amounts may be amended during the year by legislative action, but are otherwise left unchanged during the period and are reversed at the end of the period as part of the closing procedure. The budgetary entry is:

Estimated Revenues (Control)...............................	97,000	
Estimated Other Financing Sources (Control)	5,000	
Budgetary Fund Balance	3,000	
Appropriations (Control)		105,000

This entry is supported by detailed entries in subsidiary ledger revenue accounts, other financing sources accounts, and expenditure accounts. See entries marked "1" in the subsidiary ledger accounts. The real control feature of the budget entry is found in the subsidiary ledgers. Consider the subsidiary ledger revenue and other financing sources accounts. Budgeted amounts are entered in the accounts as debits so that they can be compared to the actual credits as they actually occur. At any time during the year, a fast comparison of budget versus year-to-date actual is possible. At the end of the year, actual amounts are compared to budgeted to arrive at a variance. Appropriations (budgeted expenditures) are entered as credits so that they can be compared to actual debits as they occur. Again, there can be a comparison of budget versus year-to-date actual for variance analysis at the end of the period.

2. Property taxes are recorded as receivables at the time taxes are levied on property owners. Revenue is credited in the period for which the taxes are levied (that is, in the period the money will be spent) provided the taxes are

---

Illustration 16-4

Simple Example of Governmental Accounts—General Ledger and Subsidiary Ledger Entries

GENERAL LEDGER ACCOUNTS:

Permanent Balance Sheet Accounts:

Cash

1/1/X2 Balance	8,000	(7) Pay vouchers	110,000
(5) Tax collection	90,500		
(3) Cash revenues	14,500		
(4) Asset sale	4,800		
12/31/X2 Balance	7,800		

Property Tax Receivable

1/1/X2 Balance	12,000	(5) Tax collection	90,500
(2) Tax Levy	85,000		
12/31/X2 Balance	6,500		

Vouchers Payable

(7) Vouchers paid	110,000	1/1/X2 Balance	13,000
		(6) Expenditures	106,800
		12/31/X2 Balance	9,800

Fund Balance

(9) Close 19X2	2,500	1/1/X2 Balance	7,000
		12/31/X2 Balance	4,500

Budgetary Accounts:

Estimated Revenues (Control)

(1) Budget entry	97,000	(8) Close budget	97,000

Estimated Other Financing Sources (Control)

(1) Budget entry	5,000	(8) Close budget	5,000

Appropriations (Control)

(8) Close budget	105,000	(1) Budget entry	105,000

Budgetary Fund Balance

(1) Budget entry	3,000	(8) Close budget	3,000

Operating Accounts:

Revenues (Control)

(9) Close actual	99,500	(2) Tax levy	85,000
		(3) Cash revenues	14,500

Other Financing Sources (Control)

(9) Close actual	4,800	(4) Asset sale	4,800

Expenditures (Control)

(6) Expenditures	106,800	(9) Close actual	106,800

SUBSIDIARY LEDGER ACCOUNTS:

Expenditures—Salary

(6) Expenditures	57,000	(1) Enter budget	55,000
Balance	2,000		

Expenditures—Supplies

(6) Expenditures	22,000	(1) Enter budget	23,000
		Balance	1,000

Expenditures—Repairs

(6) Expenditures	9,600	(1) Enter budget	9,000
Balance	600		

Expenditures—Capital

(6) Expenditures	11,500	(1) Enter budget	11,000
Balance	500		

Expenditures—Miscellaneous

(6) Expenditures	6,700	(1) Enter budget	7,000
Balance	300		

Revenues—Property Tax

(1) Enter budget	82,000	(2) Tax Levy	85,000
		Balance	3,000

Revenues—Fines

(1) Enter budget	12,000	(3) Cash collected	11,500
Balance	500		

Revenues—Licenses

(1) Enter budget	3,000	(3) Cash collected	3,000

Other Financing Sources—Asset Sale

(1) Enter budget	5,000	(4) Cash collected	4,800
Balance	200		

due by the end of the period. Not shown are the individual receivables for each property recorded in a receivables subsidiary ledger.

Property Taxes Receivable............................	85,000	
Revenues (Control)...................................		85,000

3. Revenues from fines and licenses are recorded when cash is received because these amounts cannot be predicted accurately. The detailed source of each revenue is recorded in the subsidiary ledger.

Cash...	14,500	
Revenues (Control)...................................		14,500

4. Proceeds from the sale of used fixed assets are recorded in the general and subsidiary ledgers.

Cash...	4,800	
Other Financing Sources (Control)		4,800

5. Property taxes are collected, including amounts from previous periods.

Cash...	90,500	
Property Taxes Receivables...........................		90,500

6. Expenditures are recorded when the liability is incurred and formal vouchers are prepared. Vouchers are documents attached to vendor invoices that contain information about the payables. They must be signed to authorize payments of the liabilities. Details of the expenditures are recorded in the subsidiary ledger.

| Expenditures (Control) . . . . | 106,800 | |
| Vouchers Payable . . . . | | 106,800 |

7. Vouchers are paid.

| Vouchers Payable . . . . | 110,000 | |
| Cash. . . . . | | 110,000 |

8. The budgetary entry is closed by reversing the original budgetary entry. This "zeros out" the budgetary accounts.

Appropriations (Control)	105,000	
Estimated Revenues (Control).		97,000
Estimated Other Financing Sources (Control)		5,000
Budgetary Fund Balance		3,000

This entry is made only in the general ledger. The amounts in the subsidiary ledgers are not removed, but remain so that they can be compared to actual amounts.

9. Actual revenues and actual other financing sources are closed against actual expenditures to arrive at the change in the actual fund balance for the year. Again, this entry is made only in the general ledger. Detailed amounts are left in the subsidiary ledger so that variance analysis may be performed.

Revenues (Control).	99,500	
Other Financing Sources (Control)	4,800	
Fund Balance.	2,500	
Expenditures (Control)		106,800

Each subsidiary ledger revenue, other financing sources, and expenditures account now may be analyzed as to the cause of variances. Finally, the balances are closed to allow for the recording of the next period's activity.

ACCOUNTING FOR THE GENERAL FUND— AN EXPANDED EXAMPLE

To visualize the accounting process of the general fund and the flow of information that produces the financial reports, the activities of the city of Middletown will be examined for the fiscal year ended September 30, 19X4. The general fund trial balance on September 30, 19X3, is as follows:

City of Middletown General Fund Trial Balance September 30, 19X3		
Cash	$235,000	
Taxes Receivable—Delinquent	30,000	
Allowance for Uncollectible Delinquent Taxes.		$ 20,000
Tax Liens Receivable	24,000	
Allowance for Uncollectible Tax Liens		8,000
Supplies Inventory.	10,000	
Vouchers Payable.		170,000
Fund Balance—Reserved for Inventory.		10,000
Fund Balance—Unreserved, Designated for Public Safety . . .		16,000
Fund Balance—Unreserved, Undesignated		75,000
Totals	$299,000	$299,000

The city has $271,000 in financial resources (cash, net receivables, and inventory). The liability Vouchers Payable offsets $170,000 of the resources with the fund balances offsetting the remaining $101,000. The fund balance may be *reserved* to show obligations of a fund or legal restrictions on financial resources. The fund balance also may be reserved if amounts are committed and not available as cash, such as outstanding purchase orders or supplies inventory. The reserves are adjusted at year end.

The second classification of fund balances is *unreserved*, which may be divided between *designated* and *undesignated*. The $16,000 designated for equipment may show the city council's intent to purchase a new police car. Only the $75,000 is unreserved and undesignated and, thus, available for unrestricted use in 19X4.

Uncollected property taxes may appear in three accounts. Taxes Receivable—Current is debited when property taxes are levied and Revenue is credited. When uncollected property taxes are past due and interest revenue begins to accrue, the account balance is transferred to Taxes Receivable—Delinquent. When tax liens (a claim to take property for unpaid taxes) are placed on properties for uncollected taxes, the remaining amount of uncollected property taxes is transferred to Tax Liens Receivable. In the Middletown September 30, 19X3 general fund trial balance, all property taxes receivable are past due. An allowance account for estimated uncollectibles is established for each receivable.

Recording the Budget.   The city council and the mayor have approved the budget for the following fiscal year, with estimated revenues of $1,350,000, appropriations of $1,300,000, and an estimated transfer of $30,000 to be made during the year to the debt service fund. Again, transfers to other funds are not expenditures and are segregated in the budgetary entry into a budgetary account labeled Estimated Other Financing Uses (Control). The October 1, 19X3 entry to record Middletown's fiscal year 19X4 budget for its general fund is:

1.	Estimated Revenues (Control).	1,350,000	
	Appropriations (Control)		1,300,000
	Estimated Other Financing Uses (Control)		30,000
	Budgetary Fund Balance—Unreserved		20,000

To support total estimated revenues of $1,350,000, a breakdown of sources should be provided in the explanation of the budget entry or in a separate schedule. In practice, there could be as many as one hundred or more revenue items. For purposes of illustration, however, the number of revenue items is condensed, as shown in the following schedule of estimated revenues:

City of Middletown General Fund Estimated Revenues For Year Ending September 30, 19X4	
General property taxes	$ 882,500
Fines	75,500
Licenses and permits	50,000
Revenue from federal grants	200,000
Other revenues	142,000
Total estimated revenues	$1,350,000

Just as the total projected income is debited to Estimated Revenues (Control) in the general ledger, so each of the detailed estimated sources is debited to its own account in the subsidiary revenue ledger. The following subsidiary account for general property taxes illustrates the procedure of posting to subsidiary records:

Revenue Ledger

ACCOUNT General Property Taxes					ACCOUNT NO.
DATE	ITEM	DEBIT (Estimate)	CREDIT (Actual)		BALANCE (DR.) CR.
Oct. 1	Budget estimate	882,500			(882,500)

Not only must the accounting system provide for control of revenues, but it also must accommodate expenditures. To provide a basis for comparison between expected and actual expenditures, budgetary as well as actual expenditures accounts are an integral part of the accounting system. In the entry to record Middletown's budget for its general fund, the credit to Appropriations (Control) represents the estimate of the expenditures of $1,300,000 for the coming year. In support of the appropriations total, a summary of approved estimated expenditures by departments or activities might appear as follows:

City of Middletown
Department or Activity Appropriations
For Year Ending September 30, 19X4

General government: legislative, judicial, and executive	$ 129,000
Public safety	277,300
Education	591,450
Highways and streets	94,500
Sanitation and health	97,750
Welfare	51,000
Culture and recreation	59,000
Total appropriations	$1,300,000

Each of these departments or activities must submit detailed appropriation requests on the basis of subfunctions and object of expenditure. The Education Division, for example, might present the following estimate of expenditures:

Middletown City
Education Division
Request for Appropriation
For Year Ending September 30, 19X4

Supplies	$160,000
Salaries	350,000
Equipment	60,000
Professional fees	21,450
Total	$591,450

A further modification to controlling expenditures is to establish subsidiary accounts by division or department. If this approach is followed by Middletown City, each of the expenditure items for the Education Division would have its own subsidiary account, such as the one that follows for supplies. Each expenditure account would be designed to show the original appropriation, the encumbrances (amounts committed), the expenditures (amounts spent), and the remaining unobligated (i.e., neither encumbered nor expended) balance.

Education Division Expenditure Ledger

ACCOUNT Supplies							ACCOUNT NO.
		ENCUMBRANCES			EXPENDITURES		UNOBLIGATED
DATE	ITEM	DEBIT	CREDIT	BALANCE	ITEM	TOTAL	BALANCE
Oct. 1	Budget appropriation						**160,000**

Recording Actual Revenues and Transfers. Property taxes are a major source of revenue for Middletown's general fund and should be recognized in the fiscal period for which the taxes are levied. The property tax roll provides information about property owners, legal descriptions, and amounts of gross tax levies. The following journal entry shows that the total tax levy against property owners is debited to Taxes Receivable—Current in a general ledger entry. The amount of allowance for uncollectible taxes is credited in the same journal entry, and the net amount (the amount the government expects to receive) is credited to Revenues (Control):

2. Taxes Receivable—Current 919,000
    Revenues (Control)   881,300
    Allowance for Uncollectible Current Taxes   37,700

Recording the revenue for the expected amount to be received is different from the accounting we would see for a business enterprise. A business enterprise would credit revenue for the entire amount of sales. In a separate entry, bad debt expense would be debited for the amount of receivables expected to be uncollectible. In a business enterprise, bad debt expense is viewed as a cost of doing business. The costs of doing business for a period (expenses) are matched on the income statement with revenues for the same period to determine net income. In governmental funds, however, property tax revenues are generated by levying taxes rather than by earning them through the production and sale of goods and services. Consequently, uncollected taxes are viewed as reductions of revenue, not as costs of doing business. If allowance amounts prove eventually to be overstated, they are written down with an offsetting credit entry to revenue. If understated, they are increased with an offsetting debit to revenue.

The general property taxes account in the subsidiary revenue ledger is credited for the actual revenue. After the preceding entry is posted, General Property Taxes appears as follows:

Revenue Ledger

ACCOUNT General Property Taxes				ACCOUNT NO.
DATE	ITEM	DEBIT (Estimate)	CREDIT (Actual)	BALANCE (DR.) CR.
Oct. 1	Budget estimate	882,500		(882,500)
1	Tax levy		**881,300**	(1,200)

During the fiscal period, a debit balance in a subsidiary revenue account usually represents additional revenue expected in the future. At the end of the fiscal period, a debit balance indicates a deficiency of actual revenue as compared to estimated revenue, while a credit balance shows an excess of actual over estimated revenues.

During the year, the following additional events related to revenue are recorded in the general fund of Middletown, whose beginning trial balance is shown on page 864.

Event	Entry in the General Fund		
Of the total delinquent taxes of $30,000 carried over from the prior period, $14,000 is collected. The balance is uncollectible.	3. Cash .... Allowance for Uncollectible Delinquent Taxes.. Taxes Receivable—Delinquent	14,000 16,000	 30,000
The excess allowance for uncollectible delinquent taxes is transferred to Revenues (Control). This transaction is viewed as a change in an accounting estimate made in a prior period.	4. Allowance for Uncollectible Delinquent Taxes.. Revenues (Control)	4,000	 4,000
Of $24,000 total tax liens carried over from the prior period, $11,000 is collected. The balance is uncollectible.	5. Cash .... Allowance for Uncollectible Tax Liens......... Tax Liens Receivable....................	11,000 8,000	 19,000
The remaining Tax Liens Receivable are charged against Revenues (Control). This transaction is viewed as a change in an accounting estimate made in a prior period.	6. Revenues (Control) .... Tax Liens Receivable....................	5,000	 5,000
Of current taxes receivable (due on or before the end of the fiscal period), $850,000 is collected during the year and $12,700 is written off as uncollectible.	7. Cash .... Allowance for Uncollectible Current Taxes..... Taxes Receivable—Current	850,000 12,700	 862,700
A 1% sales tax on restaurant food and beverages beginning on the first day of the last quarter is adopted by Middletown. The annual budget is amended to reflect the impact of this new legislation.	8. Estimated Revenues (Control)............... Budgetary Fund Balance	9,000	 9,000
Restaurant food and beverage sales for the last quarter of the year is estimated at $950,000.	9. Sales Tax Receivable....................... Revenues (Control)	9,500	 9,500
Police fines of $79,000 are imposed and collected during the year.	10. Cash .... Revenues (Control)	79,000	 79,000

Pet licenses are sold for two-year periods. Half of the pet license fees collected during the current year apply to the current year. The other half apply to next year. None of the fees are refundable.	11. Cash ....
	  Revenues (Control) ....
	  Deferred Revenues......................
		12,000	
			 6,000
			 6,000

Event	Entry in the General Fund		
Revenues from other licenses and permits apply only to the current period and are not refundable.	12. Cash .... Revenues (Control)	35,000	35,000
Interest revenue earned on investment of idle cash during the year.	13. Cash .... Revenues (Control)	17,000	17,000
A contribution by a business to entice the city to extend a storm sewer to its property along a city street.	14. Cash .... Revenues (Control)	130,000	130,000
City Council decided that the city's Fund Balance—Unreserved, Undesignated was too lean and rescinded its plan to buy a new police car.	15. Fund Balance—Unreserved, Designated for Public Safety .... Fund Balance—Unreserved, Undesignated.....................	16,000	16,000
At year end, property taxes not collected are classified as delinquent, as are the estimated uncollectible allowances.	16. Taxes Receivable—Delinquent .... Taxes Receivable—Current ($919,000 − $862,700)	56,300	56,300
	17. Allowance for Uncollectible Current Taxes..... Allowance for Uncollectible Delinquent Taxes ($37,700 − $12,700)	25,000	25,000
Middletown receives a $150,000 check from the federal government for the current fiscal year to assist in the operation of its child-care program and documentation promising an additional $50,000, half of which is for the current fiscal year and half for the next fiscal year.	18. Cash .... Due from Federal Government .... Revenues (Control) .... Deferred Revenue.......................	150,000 50,000	175,000 25,000

As indicated in the second and fourth entries, a revision of the estimated amount of uncollectible current and delinquent taxes and tax liens is treated as a change in accounting estimate through Revenues (Control). Only adjustments of confirmed errors of prior periods are recorded directly in the account Fund Balance—Unreserved, Undesignated.

Recording Encumbrances and Actual Expenditures. To prevent over-expenditure, the Middletown general fund uses an encumbrance system. An encumbrance can be viewed as an "expected expenditure" and assists the administration to avoid overspending and to plan for payment of the "expected liability" on a timely basis. It can also be viewed as a contra-account to the fund balance to reflect the ultimate decrease that will occur. Under this system, whenever a purchase order or other commitment is approved, an entry is made to record the estimated cost of the commitment. For example, an approved purchase order for school supplies, estimated to cost $10,000, is recorded as follows:

19.	Encumbrances (Control)................................. Fund Balance—Reserved for Encumbrances	10,000	10,000

The entry is posted to the general ledger, where Encumbrances (Control) is a quasi-expenditure account and where Fund Balance—Reserved for Encumbrances is a form of restriction of the fund balance. The entry also is entered in the encumbrances section of the supplies account of the subsidiary expenditure ledger for the Education Division, reducing the unobligated balance, as follows:

Education Division Expenditure Ledger

ACCOUNT Supplies							ACCOUNT NO.
		ENCUMBRANCES			EXPENDITURES		UNOBLIGATED
DATE	ITEM	DEBIT	CREDIT	BALANCE	ITEM	TOTAL	BALANCE
Oct. 1	Budget appropriation						160,000
4	Purchase order	**10,000**		10,000			150,000

When the invoice is received for the purchase of items or services, the encumbrance entry is reversed, and the encumbrance is lifted to permit the deduction of the actual amount. The contra-account to the fund balance is no longer needed since the expenditure recorded will directly reduce the fund balance in the closing procedure. Note that it is always the amount of the original estimate and not the actual cost that is used in the reversing entry. Assuming that the invoice for supplies amounts to $10,200, the two entries to record the invoice are:

20. Fund Balance—Reserved for Encumbrances   10,000
        Encumbrances (Control)   10,000
            To reverse entry for encumbrance at estimated cost.

21. Expenditures (Control)   10,200
        Vouchers Payable   10,200
            To record invoice at actual cost.

The supplies account in the subsidiary expenditure ledger appears as follows:

Education Division Expenditure Ledger

ACCOUNT Supplies							ACCOUNT NO.
		ENCUMBRANCES			EXPENDITURES		UNOBLIGATED
DATE	ITEM	DEBIT	CREDIT	BALANCE	ITEM	TOTAL	BALANCE
Oct. 1	Budget appropriation						160,000
4	Purchase order	10,000		10,000			150,000
Nov. 7	Invoice received		**10,000**	-0-	**10,200**	10,200	149,800

When the encumbrance and the actual amount are identical, the unobligated balance is not changed. However, when the amounts are not identical, the net effect is an adjustment of the unobligated balance to reflect the amount of the actual expenditure. Thus, at any time, the subsidiary ledgers provide a continuing record of the unobligated balances and of how closely the actual expenditures match encumbrances. The following equation is derived from an examination of the supplies account:

Unobligated balance
= Appropriations – Expenditures total – Encumbrances balance

The encumbrances account can appear as a contra to the Fund Balance—Unreserved, Undesignated at year end as shown in the following example:

Fund balances:		
Reserved for Encumbrances		XXX
Unreserved, Undesignated	XXX	
—Encumbrances	XXX	XXX
Total Fund Balance		XXX

It is, however, preferable to close it against the fund balance at year end to make it clear what amount of the fund balance is available for the future. At year end, the remaining balance in the encumbrance account may be closed against the Fund Balance—Unreserved, Undesignated.

Fund Balance—Unreserved, Undesignated	XXX	
Encumbrances		XXX

This will leave the amount of the outstanding encumbrances in the Fund Balance—Reserved for Encumbrances, which is reported in the fund balances section of the balance sheet. Such treatment demonstrates the commitment of the government to provide for outstanding purchase orders and serves to reduce the amount of expendable available financial resources for new expenditures indicated in the Fund Balance—Unreserved, Undesignated. Encumbrances are *not* reported in the Statement of Revenues, Expenditures, and Changes in Fund Balances since the actual transaction with outside parties has not yet occurred.

For expenditures such as salaries, which are subject to little variation and to additional internal controls, it is not customary to involve the encumbrance accounts. When salaries are paid, they are recorded directly as expenditures and reduce the unobligated balance of the salaries account in the subsidiary expenditure ledger.

Encumbrances of a Prior Period.   When encumbrances are carried over from the prior year to the current year, the encumbrance closing entry of the prior year is reversed in order to reinstate the past commitments that will be honored in the current year.

Encumbrances	XXX	
Fund Balance—Unreserved, Undesignated		XXX

Included in the current year budgetary entry for appropriations should be an amount equal to that prior year-end encumbrance. The encumbrances will be disposed of in the manner described earlier. The unreserved fund balance will ultimately be reduced by the current year's actual expenditures.

The following events relate to Middletown's expenditures and transfers during the year.

Event	Entry in the General Fund
Throughout the year, encumbrances totaling $738,000 were recorded; there were no prior year encumbrances.	22. Encumbrances (Control) .... 738,000 Fund Balance—Reserved for Encumbrances 738,000

Event	Entry in the General Fund

Vouchers were approved, liquidating $700,000 of encumbrances for:

Supplies............................	$300,000
Building	200,000*
Other expenditures	272,000
Total	$772,000

*This also requires an entry in the general fixed asset account group.

Vouchers were approved for the following nonencumbered items:

Salaries	$490,000
Other expenditures	28,000
Total	$518,000

Vouchers totaling $1,300,000 were paid.

Transfer of $30,000 is made to the debt service fund.

Supplies totaling $260,000 were consumed.

Adjust Fund Balance—Reserved for Inventory of Supplies to equal inventory. (See following discussion.)

23. Fund Balance—Reserved for
     Encumbrances......................   700,000
       Encumbrances (Control)..............   700,000

24. Inventory of Supplies   300,000
    Expenditures (Control)   472,000
      Vouchers Payable   772,000

25. Expenditures (Control)   518,000
      Vouchers Payable   518,000

26. Vouchers Payable   1,300,000
      Cash   1,300,000

27. Other Financing Uses (Control)   30,000
      Cash   30,000

28. Expenditures (Control)   260,000
      Inventory of Supplies   260,000

29. Fund Balance—Unreserved,
     Undesignated......................   40,000
      Fund Balance—Reserved for
        Inventory of Supplies   40,000

Fund Balance Reserves.

The amount of unreserved fund balance represents expendable, available financial resources. Any resources not available to finance expenditures of the current or future years must be removed from the unreserved fund balance. The reserve for encumbrances has already been discussed. Another asset for Middletown is the inventory of supplies, which will not be converted into cash and will not be available to meet future commitments. Therefore, the unreserved fund balance must be restricted by an amount equal to the inventory on the financial statement date. In this case, the amount of the inventory at year end is $50,000 ($10,000 + $300,000 − $260,000). The account Fund Balance—Reserved for Inventory of Supplies is kept equal to the inventory amount by periodic adjustment through the unreserved fund balance account.

Corrections of Prior Year's Errors.

Corrections of previous years' errors in nominal accounts are made directly through the account Fund Balance—Unreserved, Undesignated. For example, Middletown failed to record invoiced expenditures for last year of $30,600 that were not encumbered. Of this amount, $10,100 was paid this year and incorrectly debited to Expenditures (Control). The unpaid portion of $20,500 was to be vouchered. The entry would be:

30. Fund Balance—Unreserved, Undesignated 30,600
    Expenditures (Control)   10,100
    Vouchers Payable   20,500
      To correct error for failure to record expenditures
      chargeable to last year.

The preclosing year-end trial balance for Middletown is as follows:

City of Middletown General Fund Trial Balance September 30, 19X4		
Cash	$ 203,000	
Property Taxes Receivable—Delinquent.	56,300	
Allowance for Uncollectible Delinquent Taxes.		$ 25,000
Deferred Revenue		31,000
Inventory of Supplies	50,000	
Vouchers Payable.		190,700
Sales Taxes Receivable.	9,500	
Due from Federal Government.	50,000	
Fund Balance—Reserved for Inventory of Supplies.		50,000
Fund Balance—Unreserved, Undesignated.		20,400
Revenues (Control)		1,331,800
Expenditures (Control)	1,250,100	
Other Financing Uses (Control).	30,000	
Encumbrances (Control).	38,000	
Fund Balance—Reserved for Encumbrances.		38,000
Estimated Revenues (Control).	1,359,000	
Appropriations (Control).		1,300,000
Estimated Other Financing Uses (Control)		30,000
Budgetary Fund Balance—Unreserved.		29,000
	$3,045,900	$3,045,900

CLOSING THE GENERAL FUND

The simplest closing process is first to reverse the budgetary entries and then to close the actual revenue and expenditure accounts, including the other financing sources and uses accounts, into the Fund Balance—Unreserved, Undesignated account. The outstanding balance in the encumbrances account is also temporarily closed. Closing entries for Middletown would appear as follows:

31. Appropriations (Control).	1,300,000	
Estimated Other Financing Uses (Control)	30,000	
Budgetary Fund Balance—Unreserved.	29,000	
Estimated Revenues (Control)		1,359,000
To reverse entry recording budget (including amendment).		

The final closing entry would be:

32. Revenues (Control)	1,331,800	
Expenditures (Control).		1,250,100
Other Financing Uses (Control).		30,000
Fund Balance—Unreserved, Undesignated . .		51,700
Fund Balance—Unreserved, Undesignated	38,000	
Encumbrances (Control)		38,000

FINANCIAL REPORTS OF THE GENERAL FUND

Financial statements of state and local governments are presented in columnar form for all fund types and account groups, with a combined total column, permitting an overview of the total governmental unit's operation. Existing standards require a governmental unit to issue annual combined financial statements covering all of its funds and account groups as its minimum general purpose financial statements for compliance with generally accepted accounting principles. Greater detail, including comparative data, may be provided by supplemental reports for individual funds and account groups. Both combined and individual fund and account group reports will be illustrated when appropriate.

To illustrate the recommended form of the financial statements, the year-end reports of Middletown's general fund are developed from the year-end trial balance shown on page 873. These reports consist of a balance sheet and a statement of revenues, expenditures, and changes in fund balances.

BALANCE SHEET

The general fund year-end balance sheet for Middletown City, shown in Illustration 16-5, differs substantially from its private business counterpart. First, it deals primarily with current assets and current liabilities, and the difference between these two amounts appears as the fund balance—either reserved (committed) or unreserved. Second, the long-term classifications of assets and liabilities are excluded, since the general fixed assets are included in the general fixed assets account group, and the general long-term debt is carried in the general long-term debt account group.

STATEMENT OF REVENUES, EXPENDITURES, AND CHANGES IN FUND BALANCES

The Statement of Revenues, Expenditures, and Changes in Fund Balances is to be interpreted as an operating statement and is prepared on an all-inclusive basis, disclosing all elements that contributed to the change in fund balances. The statement contains details on the major revenue sources and on expenditures by function or program. Other financing sources or uses and any corrections that altered the fund balance also are presented. The detailed source of each revenue and purpose for each expenditure is obtained from the subsidiary ledger, not the control entries of the previous example.

For governmental funds for which an annual budget legally is adopted, a separate Statement of Revenues, Expenditures, and Changes in Fund Balances—Budget and Actual is required. This statement must show both budgeted and actual amounts in order to be in compliance with generally accepted accounting principles. A variance column showing the difference between budgeted and actual amounts is advisable.

The Statement of Revenues, Expenditures, and Changes in Fund Balances—Budget and Actual for Middletown, shown in Illustration 16-6, omits the

Illustration 16-5

City of Middletown
General Fund Balance Sheet
September 30, 19X4

Assets

Cash		$203,000
Property taxes receivable—delinquent	$ 56,300	
Less allowance for uncollectible delinquent taxes.........	25,000	31,300
Sales tax receivable......................................		9,500
Due from federal government............................		50,000
Inventory of supplies....................................		50,000
Total assets		$343,800

Liabilities and Fund Equity

Liabilities:		
Vouchers payable...................................	$190,700	
Deferred revenue	31,000	
Total liabilities.....................................		221,700
Fund balances:		
Reserved for encumbrances	$ 38,000	
Reserved for inventory of supplies....................	50,000	
Unreserved, undesignated...........................	34,100	
Total fund equity.....................................		122,100
Total liabilities and fund equity		$343,800

comparative figures for the preceding period, although normally they would be useful in a financial evaluation. The statement reflects estimated and actual amounts of revenues, expenditures, and other changes that relate to this year. The beginning fund balance and ending fund balance amounts are the total of unreserved and reserved fund balances. The final actual fund balances amount ($122,100) must agree with the total fund equity shown on the balance sheet.

INTRODUCTION TO THE ACCOUNT GROUPS

Accounting control over general fixed assets and general long-term capital debt is maintained in the general fixed assets account group (GFAAG) and the general long-term debt account group (GLTDAG). Notice that the titles of these self-balancing sets of accounts end with the term "account group" rather than "fund." This difference in terminology from other funds removes any implication of accounting for monies. No current amounts are contained in the account

Illustration 16-6

City of Middletown General Fund
Statement of Revenues, Expenditures, and Changes in Fund Balances—
Budget and Actual
For the Fiscal Year Ended September 30, 19X4

	Budget	Actual	Variance Favorable (Unfavorable)
Revenues:			
General property taxes.............	$ 882,500	$ 880,300	$ (2,200)
Fines............................	75,500	79,000	3,500
Licenses and permits	50,000	41,000	(9,000)
Intergovernmental revenues.........	200,000	175,000	(25,000)
Sales tax	9,000	9,500	500
Other revenues....................	142,000	147,000	5,000
Total revenues	$1,359,000	$1,331,800	$(27,200)
Expenditures:			
General government...............	$ 129,000	$ 120,305	$ 8,695
Public safety	277,300	252,795	24,505
Highways and streets	94,500	86,100	8,400
Sanitation and health	97,750	87,750	10,000
Welfare	51,000	46,000	5,000
Culture and recreation	59,000	53,400	5,600
Education	591,450	603,750	(12,300)
Total expenditures...............	$1,300,000	$1,250,100	$ 49,900
Excess of revenues over expenditures ..	$ 59,000	$ 81,700	$ 22,700
Other financing sources (uses)	(30,000)	(30,000)	-0-
Excess of revenues and other sources over expenditures and other uses	$ 29,000	$ 51,700	$ 22,700
Fund balances, October 1, 19X3........	101,000	101,000	-0-
Correction of prior year's expenditures..	-0-	(30,600)	(30,600)
Fund balances, September 30, 19X4....	$ 130,000	$ 122,100	$ (7,900)

groups.[8] They are used only to keep accounting control of general fixed assets and general long-term debt of the governmental unit.

ACCOUNTING AND FINANCIAL REPORTING FOR GENERAL FIXED ASSETS

Fixed assets of a proprietary fund or a fiduciary fund are accounted for within those funds and often are referred to as *fund capital assets*. All other fixed assets are considered *general fixed assets* and are accounted for in the general fixed assets

---

[8]General long-term debt will be shown as a governmental fund liability "when due." Also, a portion should be shown as a governmental fund liability if it is expected to be paid with expendable available financial resources. These portions are removed from the GLTDAG. Examples of reclassification of long-term debt to current debt are included in the next chapter.

account group. This account group, which was created to control fixed assets that are not resources of any specific fund, may be thought of as an inventory record of fixed assets for the purpose of assigning responsibility for custody and proper use. Five fixed asset categories are recommended: land, buildings, improvements other than buildings, machinery and equipment, and construction in progress. Each category should have a control account in the ledger and should be substantiated by supporting detailed records.

There is one class of fixed assets that governmental units may omit from their general fixed assets account group. These assets are the public domain or *infrastructure* fixed assets, such as sidewalks, streets, curbs, and bridges. Their inclusion in formal reports is recommended but not required. Whatever policy is adopted, however, must be consistently applied and disclosed in the notes to the financial statements. If infrastructure assets are formally included in the general fixed assets account group, they should be recorded as Improvements Other than Buildings. Most governmental units do not record infrastructure assets, but maintain separate descriptive records on costs and financing sources.

The acquisition of a general fixed asset is recorded in the general fixed assets account group by a debit to one of the five specific asset accounts. The credit indicates the original funding source of the asset, selected from the following recommended titles:

> Investment in General Fixed Assets
> —Capital Projects Funds
> —General Fund Revenues
> —Special Revenue Funds
> —Donations

To illustrate this procedure, a building acquired with general fund revenues would require the following entries:

Fund or Group in Which Entry Is Recorded	Entry		
General fund	33. Expenditures (Control)............................	200,000	
	Vouchers Payable.............................		200,000
	(This entry is part of the entry on page 872, which records vouchers of $772,000.)		
General fixed assets account group	34. Buildings......................................	200,000	
	Investment in General Fixed Assets—		
	General Fund Revenues.....................		200,000

The basis of a fixed asset is cost or, if the asset is donated, estimated fair market value at time of receipt. Subsequent to the acquisition of a fixed asset, capital outlay and maintenance expenditures must be accounted for separately, as they are in commercial accounting, since maintenance expenditures should not increase the book values of fixed assets.

When a governmental unit disposes of a general fixed asset, the original cost of the asset is removed from the general fixed assets account group. In the general fund, proceeds from the sale are recorded with a credit to Other Financing Sources (Control). For example, if a governmental unit sells equipment for

$110,000, carried in the general fixed assets account group at $100,000, the following entries would be made:

Fund or Group in Which Entry Is Recorded	Entry		
General fund	35. Cash......................................	110,000	
	Other Financing Sources (Control)..............		110,000
General fixed assets account group	36. Investment in General Fixed Assets—		
	General Fund Revenues....................	100,000	
	Machinery and Equipment....................		100,000

Instead of selling the equipment, assume the governmental unit traded it for a larger model costing $235,000, with an allowance of $110,000 for the smaller unit. Record the new asset at its total cost, with the trade-in value merely functioning as a reduction in the amount to be paid. The entries then would be:

Fund or Group in Which Entry Is Recorded	Entry		
General fund	37. Expenditures (Control).........................	125,000	
	Vouchers Payable...........................		125,000
General fixed assets account group	38. Investment in General Fixed Assets—		
	General Fund Revenues....................	100,000	
	Machinery and Equipment....................		100,000
	39. Machinery and Equipment......................	235,000	
	Investment in General Fixed Assets—		
	General Fund Revenues....................		235,000

Notice that there is no accumulated depreciation involved in the typical recording of the sale or exchange of a general fixed asset. When net income is determined, as in proprietary funds (or when capital maintenance is important, as in some fiduciary funds), depreciation expense must be recognized in operating statements. But governmental funds are not concerned with either of these elements.

> To record depreciation expense in governmental funds would inappropriately mix two fundamentally different measurements, expenses and expenditures. General fixed asset acquisitions require the use of governmental fund financial resources and are recorded as expenditures. General fixed asset sale proceeds provide governmental fund financial resources. Depreciation expense is neither a source nor a use of governmental fund financial resources, and thus is not properly recorded in the accounts of such funds.[9]

If a government chooses to record accumulated depreciation (not a common practice), the entry is made in the general fixed assets account group by debiting the appropriate investment in the general fixed asset account and crediting the accumulated depreciation account. Entries for the disposition of a general fixed asset would remove the related accumulated depreciation.

---

[9]Statement 1, *Governmental Accounting and Financial Reporting Principles* (Chicago: Municipal Finance Officers Association of the United States and Canada, March 1979), p. 10.

The general fixed asset account group is included in the combined balance sheet. A listing of general fixed assets balanced by the source of funds for the assets is a required presentation. A Statement of Changes in General Fixed Assets should be a part of the financial section of a comprehensive annual financial report (CAFR), which is discussed in Chapter 17, if that information is not included in the notes. Typical presentations include: (1) a Schedule of Changes in Fixed Assets by Major Class (such as Land, Buildings) in the notes to the financial statements; (2) a Schedule of Changes in General Fixed Assets by Function and Activity (such as General Government, Public Safety, Highways) in the financial section of the CAFR; and (3) a Comparative Statement of General Fixed Assets by Source in the financial section of the CAFR. The latter statements for Middletown are shown as follows. The statements include the transactions used as examples in this section.

City of Middletown
Comparative Statement of General Fixed Assets by Source
September 30, 19X4 and 19X3

	19X4	19X3
General fixed assets:		
Land...	$12,595,000	$12,595,000
Buildings....................................	28,555,000	28,355,000
Improvements other than buildings...............	10,367,500	10,367,500
Machinery and equipment......................	4,525,000	4,390,000
Construction in progress......................	17,222,500	17,222,500
Total general fixed assets....................	$73,265,000	$72,930,000
Investment in general fixed assets by source:		
Capital projects funds..........................	$58,791,000	$58,791,000
General fund revenues..........................	5,624,000	5,289,000
Special revenue funds	3,095,000	3,095,000
Donations	5,755,000	5,755,000
Total investment in general fixed assets..........	$73,265,000	$72,930,000

Governmental units generally comply with legal regulations in accounting for fixed assets. However, supporting records in a governmental unit often are incomplete and fail to provide the data that should be the output of a properly functioning system of asset control. The GASB has projects under way that are examining whether accounting for and financial reporting of capital assets can be changed to improve the quality of information provided to managers, citizens, legislators, and other users of governmental financial reporting.

ACCOUNTING AND FINANCIAL REPORTING
FOR GENERAL LONG-TERM DEBT

When long-term debt is related to and will be paid from proprietary or fiduciary funds, it is accounted for in those funds and is termed a *specific fund liability*.

When long-term debt is related to and will be paid from governmental funds, the balance sheet reporting is in the general long-term debt account group.

The general long-term debt account group, which was designed to monitor long-term debt that is not the responsibility of any particular fund, furnishes a record of the unmatured principal of all general long-term obligations of the governmental unit. Referring to a long-term obligation as "general" indicates that the community can use its taxing power to pay debt principal and interest. General long-term debt is classified as term bonds, serial bonds, and other general long-term liabilities. Balancing debits are to Amounts Available in Debt Service Fund or to Amounts to Be Provided. The general long-term debt account group is not limited to liabilities arising from debt issuance and may include numerous types of unmatured general government liabilities, for example, claims and judgments, accumulated sick leave and other compensated absences, underfunded pension contributions, and capital lease obligations, as well as un-matured bonds and notes. Interest is not accounted for in the general long-term debt account group. To maintain the self-balancing nature of the account group, the incurrence of long-term obligations is recorded by debiting Amount to Be Provided for Payment of [properly identified] Debt and crediting a liability account.

To illustrate the entries for the general long-term debt account group, assume that a unit incurs a general long-term obligation in the form of term bonds of $1,000,000 to acquire property.[10] Regardless of whether the bonds are issued at a premium or discount, the bond issue is recorded at its face amount in the general long-term debt account group. As shown in the following entry, the bonds are recorded in the general long-term debt account group at the face value to be redeemed at maturity.

40. Amount to Be Provided for Payment of Term Bonds . . . 1,000,000
     Term Bonds Payable.   1,000,000

Payment of both principal and interest is handled by the debt service fund, where "service" is synonymous with "payment," but the general long-term debt account group records only amounts that become available in the debt service fund for retirement of general long-term debt principal. Assuming the debt service fund receives an annual appropriation of $80,000 to provide for the eventual retirement of the term bonds, the following entry is recorded in the general long-term debt account group.

41. Amount Available in Debt Service Funds—Term Bonds. . . . 80,000
     Amount to Be Provided for Payment of Term Bonds   80,000

In the combined balance sheet of a governmental unit, balances in the accounts, Amount Available and Amount to Be Provided, are shown as debits.

If sound actuarial practices have been employed, the debt service fund will retire the obligation at the appropriate time, and the general long-term debt account group will make the following entry:

---

[10]A term bond is one in which the entire principal is due on one date. A serial bond issue is redeemed in periodic payments. Term bonds are rare, but better illustrate entries in the general long-term debt account group.

42. Term Bonds Payable. 1,000,000
     Amount Available in Debt Service Funds—
        Term Bonds.   1,000,000

A comparative Statement of General Long-Term Debt for Middletown is shown below. The statement includes the transactions used as examples in this section to issue term bonds and to adjust the Amount Available in Debt Service Funds—Term Bonds and Amounts to Be Provided for Payment of Term Bonds accounts. Retirement of the term bonds would occur in a later period.

The general long-term debt account group is part of the combined balance sheet; additional information about long-term debt may appear in the notes and later in the financial section of the CAFR. Information about significant contingent liabilities, pension plan obligations, accumulated sick leave and other compensated absences, debt service requirements to maturity, commitments under noncapitalized leases, and changes in general long-term debt are required disclosures. A Statement of Changes in General Long-Term Debt is required in the CAFR unless such information is disclosed in the notes.

City of Middletown
General Long-Term Debt Account Group
Statement of General Long-Term Debt
For the Year Ended December 31, 19X4
(with comparative totals for 19X3)

	19X4	19X3
Amounts available and to be provided for the retirement of general long-term debt:		
Amount available in debt service fund	$ 2,102,100	$ 2,022,100
Amount to be provided for:		
Retirement of general obligation debt.	20,859,950	19,939,950
Retirement of special assessment debt.	2,000,000	2,000,000
Pension contribution payable from subsequent year's budget	141,123	139,000
Capital lease purchases	135,894	99,950
Unfunded compensated absences.	163,758	160,325
Unfunded claims and judgments.	592,145	412,222
Total amounts available and to be provided	$25,994,970	$24,773,547
General long-term debt payable:		
General obligation debt	$22,962,050	$21,962,050
Special assessment debt with governmental commitment	2,000,000	2,000,000
Unfunded pension costs.	141,123	139,000
Capital lease payable	135,894	99,950
Unfunded compensated absences.	163,758	160,325
Unfunded claims and judgments.	592,145	412,222
Total general long-term debt payable	$25,994,970	$24,773,547

REVIEW OF ENTRIES FOR THE GENERAL FUND AND ACCOUNT GROUPS

The following example will provide a comprehensive review of the general fund, the general fixed assets account group, and the general long-term debt account group. The general fund balance sheet for Junction City, as of December 31, 19X2, is as follows:

Junction City
General Fund Balance Sheet
December 31, 19X2

Assets

Cash		$100,000
Taxes receivable, delinquent, 19X2.......................	$50,000	
Less allowance for uncollectible delinquent taxes—19X2...	20,000	30,000
Tax liens receivable, 19X1.................................	$25,000	
Less allowance for uncollectible tax liens, 19X1	5,000	20,000
Inventory of supplies.....................................		20,000
Total assets		$170,000

Liabilities and Fund Equity

Liabilities:		
Vouchers payable.....................................		$ 30,000
Fund balances:		
Reserved for encumbrances	$40,000	
Reserved for inventory of supplies.....................	20,000	
Unreserved, undesignated.............................	80,000	
Total fund equity.....................................		140,000
Total liabilities and fund equity		$170,000

During 19X3, the following entries are recorded in the general fund of Junction City. If an event also requires that an entry be made in one of the account groups, the necessary entry is indicated as part of the event.

Event	Entry in the General Fund		
The budget is approved.	Estimated Revenues (Control)	600,000	
Estimated inflows are from:	Estimated Other Financing Sources (Control)......	284,000	
Revenues $600,000	Budgetary Fund Balance—Unreserved...........	26,000	
General long-term debt issuance 200,000	Appropriations (Control).......................		860,000
Transfers from other funds 60,000	Estimated Other Financing Uses (Control)		50,000
Sales of fixed assets carried at			
$100,000 24,000			
Estimated outflows are for:			
Expenditures [Includes 19X2 hold-			
over encumbrances ($40,000) and			
use of supplies ($20,000)]........ 860,000			
Transfers to other funds 50,000			
The amount of the Fund Balance—Reserved for	Encumbrances (Control)	40,000	
Encumbrances was reinstated in Encumbrances.	Fund Balance—Unreserved, Undesignated		40,000
Property taxes of $500,000 are levied, of which	Taxes Receivable—Current....................	500,000	
$30,000 is estimated to be uncollectible.	Allowance for Uncollectible Current Taxes		30,000
	Revenues (Control)..........................		470,000

Event	Entry in the General Fund		
Cash obtained from local banks to finance government operations in advance of collection of first property tax installment.	Cash....................................... Tax Anticipation Note Payable................	200,000	200,000

Collection of taxes and related interest for the year:

Current taxes	$450,000
Delinquent taxes, 19X2.............	32,000
Interest on delinquent taxes........	2,000
Tax liens, 19X1	10,000
Interest on tax liens, 19X1	1,000
Total	$495,000

Cash.......................................	495,000	
Taxes Receivable—Current..................		450,000
Taxes Receivable—Delinquent, 19X2		32,000
Tax Liens Receivable, 19X1..................		10,000
Revenues (Control)..........................		3,000

Event	Entry in the General Fund		
Repayment of tax anticipation note payable plus interest upon collection of property taxes.	Tax Anticipation Notes Payable................. Expenditures (Control)........................ Cash.......................................	200,000 3,000	203,000
Property against which there are unpaid tax liens for 19X1 is sold for $7,000. (The loss is an adjustment of current revenue, since it represents a change in estimate.)	Cash....................................... Allowance for Uncollectible Tax Liens, 19X1 ...... Revenues (Control)........................... Tax Liens Receivable, 19X1..................	7,000 5,000 3,000	15,000
Tax liens totaling $18,000 are issued against 19X2 delinquent taxpayers.	Tax Liens Receivable, 19X2.................... Taxes Receivable—Delinquent, 19X2	18,000	18,000
Allowance for Uncollectible Delinquent Taxes is reclassified and is reduced, so as not to exceed the related receivable of $18,000. As a change in estimate, the credit is made to Revenues (Control).	Allowance for Uncollectible Delinquent Taxes, 19X2....................................... Allowance for Uncollectible Tax Liens, 19X2 .. Revenues (Control).......................	20,000	18,000 2,000
Uncollected current taxes are declared delinquent and the related allowance is reclassified.	Taxes Receivable—Delinquent, 19X3 .... Taxes Receivable—Current.................. Allowance for Uncollectible Current Taxes .... Allowance for Uncollectible Delinquent Taxes, 19X3.......................................	50,000 30,000	50,000 30,000
Revenue for licenses, fees, and fines is recognized.	Fines Receivable............................. Cash....................................... Revenues (Control).........................	3,000 67,000	70,000
To acquire land, a general long-term $200,000 serial bond issue is sold for 102. The premium is transferred to the debt service fund.	Cash....................................... Other Financing Sources (Control)	204,000	204,000

This event requires an entry in the general long-term debt account group:	Other Financing Uses (Control)................. Cash.......................................	4,000	4,000
Amount to Be Provided for Payment of Serial Bonds.................. 200,000 Serial Bonds Payable ... 200,000			

Other funds transfer $60,000 to the general fund.	Cash....................................... Other Financing Sources (Control)	60,000	60,000
Additional amount encumbered for approved purchase orders was $600,000.	Encumbrances (Control) .... Fund Balance—Reserved for Encumbrances....	600,000	600,000

Event	Entry in the General Fund

The following vouchers were approved:

General expenditures...............	$760,000
Purchase of equipment..............	40,000
Purchase of supplies (a perpetual inventory system is used).........	70,000
Total	$870,000

Expenditures (Control).........................	800,000	
Inventory of Supplies..........................	70,000	
Vouchers Payable............................		870,000

Of this total, $630,000 was encumbered.

The following entry is required in the general fixed assets account group:

Machinery and Equipment...	40,000	
Investment in General Fixed Assets—General Fund ..		40,000

Fund Balance—Reserved for Encumbrances......	630,000	
Encumbrances (Control)		630,000

$50,000 was transferred from the general fund to other funds.

Other Financing Uses (Control)..................	50,000	
Cash......................................		50,000

Vouchers totaling $880,000 were paid.

Vouchers Payable............................	880,000	
Cash......................................		880,000

The year-end supplies inventory amounted to $26,000.

Expenditures (Control).........................	64,000	
Inventory of Supplies ($20,000 + $70,000 – $26,000).................................		64,000

Fund Balance—Reserved for Inventory of Supplies is adjusted to agree with the inventory of supplies.

Fund Balance—Unreserved, Undesignated	6,000	
Fund Balance—Reserved for Inventory of Supplies ($26,000 – $20,000)		6,000

Equipment carried at $100,000 in the general fixed assets account group is sold for $24,000.

The following entry is required in the general fixed assets account group:

Investment in General Fixed Assets—General Fund ..	100,000	
Machinery and Equipment		100,000

Cash.......................................	24,000	
Other Financing Sources (Control)		24,000

Closing entries.

Appropriations (Control).........................	860,000	
Estimated Other Financing Uses (Control)	50,000	
Estimated Revenues (Control)		600,000
Estimated Other Financing Sources (Control)....		284,000
Budgetary Fund Balance—Unreserved.........		26,000

Revenues (Control)............................	542,000	
Other Financing Sources (Control)	288,000	
Fund Balance—Unreserved, Undesignated	91,000	
Expenditures (Control)		867,000
Other Financing Uses (Control)...............		54,000
Fund Balance—Unreserved, Undesignated	10,000	
Encumbrances (Control)		10,000

APPENDIX

In May 1990, the GASB issued a standard that changed recognition and measurement guidance for governmental and expendable trust fund operating statement elements. GASB Statement No. 11 states that financial reporting for governmental and expendable trust funds should focus on demonstrating interperiod equity, that is, whether current-year revenues are sufficient to pay for current-year services.[11] To achieve this measure of interperiod equity, Statement No. 11 expands the measurement focus from current financial resources to include all financial resources. It requires the adoption of the full accrual basis of accounting.

One major change in GASB Statement No. 11 is the reporting of expenditures in the operating statement in the year in which the liability is incurred. Expenditures for such items as compensated absences, unfunded pension benefits, claims, and judgments previously were not recognized until the liability was due. Statement No. 11 gives no guidance to the reporting of the related long-term liabilities in the balance sheet.

In addition, operating debt borrowings and repayments will be excluded from the operating statement under GASB Statement No. 11 so as to prevent government units from appearing to achieve interperiod equity merely by borrowing money to finance current operations. Under Statement No. 11, these borrowings, whether short term or long term, will be reported as liabilities, not other financing sources.

The significant changes in revenue and expenditure recognition under GASB Statement No. 11 will have a pervasive impact on state and local governmental financial reporting. As a result, Statement No. 11 is indefinitely postponed until several related GASB projects—the financial reporting model, capital reporting, and accounting for pensions—are completed. Generally accepted definitions of terms in the current governmental model are compared with definitions from Statement No. 11 in the table below:

Generally accepted definitions of terms prior to and after GASB Statement No. 11 implementation:

Current GAAP	GASB Statement No. 11
Financial Resources: Cash and other assets that in the normal course of operations will become cash.	**Financial Resources:** Cash, claims to cash (e.g., debt securities of another entity and accounts and taxes receivable), claims to goods or services (e.g., prepaid items), consumable goods (such as supplies inventories), and equity securities of another entity obtained or controlled as a result of past transactions or events.
Revenues: Increases in net current assets from transactions other than expenditure refunds, residual equity transfers, and other financing sources.	**Revenues:** Increases in financial resources from transactions other than residual equity transfers, and other financing sources.

---

[11]GASB Statement No. 11, *Measurement Focus and Basis of Accounting—Governmental Fund Operating Statements* (Norwalk, CT: Governmental Accounting Standards Board, May, 1990), par. 8.

Other Financing Sources: General long-term debt proceeds, amounts equal to the present value of minimum lease payments arising from capital leases, proceeds from the sale of general fixed assets, and amounts of operating transfers-in.

Expenditures: Decreases in net financial resources. Expenditures include current operating expenses requiring the present or future use of net current assets, debt service and capital outlays, and intergovernmental grants, entitlements, and shared revenues.

Other Financing Uses: Transfers to other funds.

Modified Accrual Accounting: Revenues and other financing sources are recognized when they are measurable and available to finance expenditures of the current period. Expenditures are recognized when the fund liability is incurred except for (a) inventories that may be considered expenditures when purchased or used, and (b) prepaid items that may be considered expenditures when paid or consumed.

General Long-Term Debt: Long-term debt expected to be repaid from governmental funds.

Other Financing Sources: Financial resources obtained from issuing general long-term capital debt, recording the present value of capital leases, selling capital assets, and recording interfund operating transfers-in.

Expenditures: Transactions or events that result in claims against financial resources, regardless of when cash is paid. Expenditures may result from operating activity, capital acquisitions, and debt service.

Other Financing Uses: Claims incurred against financial resources from the refunding of general long-term capital debt (using proceeds from issuing new debt to pay old debt) and operating transfers-out, and the issuance discounts on general long-term capital debt.

Accrual Accounting: A basis of accounting that recognizes the effects of transactions or events on the resources of an entity when they take place, regardless of when cash is received or paid. Inventories and prepaid items should be recorded as financial resources when acquired and reported as expenditures in the period they are consumed.

General Long-Term Capital Debt: Those liabilities that are expected to be paid from the financial resources of governmental funds and provide long-term financing (a) to acquire capital assets, including infrastructure, or (b) for certain nonrecurring projects or activities that have long-term economic benefit.

Operating Debt: Debt that provides financial resources to and is expected to be repaid from the financial resources of governmental funds and is not general long-term capital debt. Examples of operating debt are: tax anticipation notes, compensated absences, and debt incurred to pay claims and judgments.

QUESTIONS

1. The objective of a business enterprise is to generate _____. The objective of a government is to produce _____ _____ _____. What entitles a recipient to receive what is produced by a government?

2. Describe four environmental differences between governmental activities of a government and the activities of a business enterprise.

3. What is the oversight body, or parent organization, of the Financial Accounting Standards Board (FASB) and the Governmental Accounting Standards Board (GASB)? Over which entities does each board have primary financial reporting standard-setting authority?

4. When the FASB and GASB have not issued financial reporting standards covering matters within their respective standard-setting jurisdictions, where else in the "GAAP hierarchy" may an accountant or auditor look for authoritative guidance?

5. What is meant by the measurement focus in accounting? What is the measurement focus for governmental funds?

6. Why is interperiod equity measurement important in governmental fund accounting?

7. Define a fund as the term is used in governmental accounting in contrast to how the term is used in commercial accounting.

8. The use of four governmental funds has been recommended. Identify the fund described in each of the following cases:

   (a) The fund that accounts for charges levied against properties directly benefited by a major capital improvement.

   (b) The fund that accounts for revenues from a city sales tax legally restricted to finance new construction.

   (c) The fund that accounts for payment of principal and interest on general long-term debt.

   (d) The fund that accounts for proceeds from a bond issue to be used to construct a central library.

   (e) Every governmental unit should have this fund to account for day-to-day operations.

9. Define revenues and expenditures as the terms apply to governmental funds.

10. Distinguish between operating debt and capital debt.

11. List the advantages of introducing budgetary accounts into the accounting system.

12. Discuss the significance of the encumbrance system.

13. For what purpose does the general fixed assets account group exist?

14. Discuss the purpose of the general long-term debt account group.

15. Why does the GASB consider the recording of depreciation inappropriate in the general fund?

EXERCISES

Exercise 1. Select the best answer for each of the following multiple-choice questions. (Nos. 3, 5, 8, and 9 are AICPA adapted.)

(1) In a governmental fund, which one of the following constitutes revenue?
   (a) Cash received from another fund of the same unit.
   (b) Bond proceeds.
   (c) Property taxes.
   (d) Refund on an invoice for fuel.

(2) In a governmental fund, which of the following is considered an expenditure?
   (a) The purchase of a capital asset.
   (b) The consumption of supplies.
   (c) Salaries earned by employees.
   (d) All of the above.

(3) Fixed assets donated to a governmental unit should be recorded:
   (a) At estimated fair value when received.
   (b) At the lower of donor's carrying amount or estimated fair value when received.
   (c) At the donor's carrying amount.
   (d) As a memorandum entry only.

(4) In the recording of a city's budget, which one of the following accounts is debited?
   (a) Appropriations (Control).
   (b) Estimated Revenues (Control).
   (c) Estimated Other Financing Uses (Control).
   (d) Encumbrances (Control).

(5) Which of the following accounts of a governmental unit is credited when taxpayers are billed for property taxes?
   (a) Appropriations.
   (b) Taxes Receivable—Current.
   (c) Estimated Revenues.
   (d) Revenues.

(6) When a portion of property tax proceeds recorded in the general fund is transferred to another fund, the account to be debited in the general fund is:
   (a) Expenditures (Control).
   (b) Revenues (Control).
   (c) Estimated Revenues (Control).
   (d) Other Financing Uses (Control).

(7) The general long-term debt account group includes:
   (a) All long-term debt of a governmental unit.
   (b) General long-term capital debt applicable to governmental funds.
   (c) Long-term capital debt and all long-term operating debt applicable to governmental funds.
   (d) All general long-term capital debt plus accrued interest thereon.

(8) When equipment was purchased with general fund resources, an appropriate entry was made in the general fixed asset account group. What accounts would have been increased in the general fund?
   (a) Due from the general fixed asset account group.
   (b) Expenditures.
   (c) Appropriations.
   (d) No entry should be made in the general fund.

(9) Which of the following accounts should Moon City close at the end of its fiscal year?
   (a) Vouchers Payable.
   (b) Expenditures.
   (c) Fund Balance.
   (d) Fund Balance—Reserved for Encumbrances.

(10) The following entry appears in the general long-term debt account group records:

Amount Available in Debt Service Funds   XXX
   Amount to Be Provided for Payment of Bonds   XXX

An acceptable explanation for this entry would be that it records the:
   (a) Issuance of bonds.
   (b) Receipt of resources by the debt service fund to cover bond redemption.
   (c) Maturing of a bond issue.
   (d) Redemption of a bond issue.

Exercise 2. Given the following information, you have been asked to record the budget for the general fund of the city of Cedarfield:

(1) Inflows for 1994 are expected to total $525,000 and include property tax revenue of $350,000, fines of $5,000, state grants of $70,000, and bond issue proceeds of $100,000.

(2) Expenditures for general operations and equipment purchases for the year are estimated to be $475,000.

(3) Authorized transfers include $30,000 to the debt service fund to pay interest on bond indebtedness and $15,000 to the capital projects fund to pay for cost overruns on construction of a new civic center.

(4) Additional estimated receipts include $15,000 operating transfer from the special revenue fund and a $50,000 payment from the Electric Utility Enterprise Fund for property taxes.

Exercise 3. The following information concerns tax revenues for the city of Orange. The balances concerning property taxes on January 1, 19X3 were:

Delinquent property taxes receivable..........	$135,000
Allowance for uncollectible delinquent taxes	(45,000)
Tax liens receivable	45,000
Allowance for uncollectible tax liens	(23,000)

Prepare entries in the general fund for the following 19X3 events:

Jan.   Since current property taxes would not be collected for several months, $275,000 was borrowed using tax anticipation notes.

Feb.   Tax liens of $12,000 were collected; in addition $2,000 of interest was collected that had not been accrued. The balance of tax liens was settled by receiving $16,000 for the property subject to the tax liens.

Apr.   Collections on delinquent property taxes were $100,000, and interest of $4,500 was collected. The interest had not been accrued. The balance of the account was converted into tax liens.

July   Current property taxes were levied for $420,000 with a 5% allowance for uncollectible amounts.

Sept. Collection of current property taxes totaled $375,000. The tax anticipation notes were paid off with interest of $18,000.

Exercise 4. Prepare journal entries in the general fund for the following 19X4 transactions that represent inflows of financial resources to Red City:

(1) To pay the wages of part-time city maintenance employees, the Cemetery Expendable Trust Fund transfers $40,000 to the general fund.

(2) A resident donates land worth $50,000 for a park.

(3) The city is notified by the state that it will receive $25,000 in road assistance grants this year.

(4) A fire truck with an original cost of $36,000 is sold for $7,000.

(5) License stickers for park use are sold for $5,000. The fees cover this year and next year. Patrolmen are paid from these fees to check for cars in the park without stickers.

Exercise 5. Prepare entries in the general fund for the following transactions that represent outflows of financial resources to the city of Blue in 19X4:

(1) Vouchers are prepared for the following items and amounts:

Salaries......................................	$120,000
Repairs and maintenance.....................	60,000
Inventory of supplies........................	35,000
Capital equipment	125,000
Tax anticipation notes:	
Principal	200,000
Interest	13,000

(2) A transfer for $53,000 is made to the debt service fund.

(3) There was no inventory of supplies at the start of the year. The inventory of supplies at year end is $2,500.

Exercise 6. Foster City had the following balance sheet accounts and amounts as of January 1, 19X4:

Inventory of supplies........................	$ 22,000
Fund balance, reserved for inventory...........	(22,000)
Fund balance, reserved for encumbrances......	(15,000)
Fund balance, unreserved, undesignated	(40,000)

Prepare general fund journal entries for the following 19X4 transactions:

(1) Prior-period supplies encumbrances are reinstated in 19X4. These are included in the 19X4 budget.

(2) Orders are placed for supplies inventory at an estimated cost of $70,000.

(3) All inventory ordered (including amounts encumbered last year) is received; actual invoices are for $86,000.

(4) The physical inventory of supplies at year end is $26,000.

Exercise 7. You are maintaining a subsidiary ledger account for Police Training Expenditures for 19X3. The following columns are used:

Date	Item	Encumbrances Dr.	Cr.	Bal.	Expenditures	Unobligated Balance

Inventory purchases are initially recorded as expenditures.

Record the following 19X3 transactions in the Police Training Expenditures subsidiary ledger account:

Jan. 1   The budget includes $23,000 for police-training expenditures.

Jan. 15   Equipment and supplies, estimated at $14,000 cost, are ordered.

Feb. 1   Vouchers for $5,000 are approved for items not encumbered.

Feb. 15   Items encumbered for $12,000 on January 15 are received with invoices totaling $12,300. Supplies are expended when purchased; however, an inventory is taken at year end, and expenditures are adjusted at that time.

June 3   The remaining encumbered expenditures arrive. The invoice totals $4,300 including items not included in the encumbered amount.

Dec. 31   An inventory of training supplies is taken and recorded at $1,500.

Exercise 8. Prepare the entries to record the following general fund transactions for the village of Vail for the year ended September 30, 19X4:

(a) Revenues are estimated at $350,000; expenditures are estimated at $340,000.

(b) A tax levy is set at $350,000, of which 1% will likely be uncollectible.

(c) Purchase orders amounting to $240,000 are authorized.

(d) Tax receipts total $280,000.

(e) Invoices totaling $225,000 are received and vouchered for orders originally estimated at $223,000.

(f) Salaries amounting to $103,000 are approved for payment.

(g) A state grant-in-aid of $100,000 is received.

(h) Fines and penalties of $10,000 are collected.

(i) Property for a village park is purchased, costing $90,000. No encumbrance had been made for this item.

(j) Additional recreational property valued at $88,000 is donated.

(k) Amounts of $12,000 due to other village funds are approved for payment. (Note: To establish the liability to other funds, credit Due to Other Funds.)

(l) The village's share of sales tax due from the state is $30,000. Payment will be received in 30 days.

(m) Vouchers totaling $175,000 are paid.

(n) Accounts are closed at year end.

Exercise 9. The preclosing trial balance of the general fund of Marsh Village for fiscal year ended June 30, 19X5, is as follows:

	Debit	Credit
Cash	$ 210,000	
Receivables (net)	134,000	
Vouchers Payable		$ 125,000
Fund Balance—Reserved for Encumbrances		60,000
Fund Balance—Unreserved, Undesignated		92,000
Budgetary Fund Balance		50,000
Estimated Revenues (Control)	600,000	
Estimated Other Financing Sources (Control)	150,000	
Appropriations (Control)		650,000
Estimated Other Financing Uses (Control)		50,000
Expenditures (Control)	593,000	
Encumbrances (Control)	60,000	
Revenue (Control)		620,000
Other Financing Sources (Control)		151,500
Other Financing Uses (Control)	51,500	
Total	$1,798,500	$1,798,500

(1) Prepare closing entries.

(2) Prepare a Statement of Revenues, Expenditures, and Changes in Fund Balance—Budget and Actual for the fiscal year ended June 30, 19X5. (Include amounts with variances and the total fund equity.)

(3) Prepare a balance sheet as of June 30, 19X5.

Exercise 10. A city purchased land costing $50,000 for park development. The amount had been encumbered at $55,000. Ten years later, because of a population shift, the park is no longer practical. The city sells the land for $117,000. Prepare journal entries to record the purchase and subsequent sale of the land, indicating in what fund or group each entry would be made. Use this format:

Event	Fund or Group	Entry

Exercise 11. For the following transactions, prepare the entries that would be recorded in the general fixed assets account group for the city of Evert:

(a) From special revenue funds resources, the city purchased property costing $1,200,000, with three-fourths of the cost allocated to a building.

(b) A mansion belonging to the great-granddaughter of the city's founder was donated to the city. The land cost the original owner $600, and the house was built for an additional $50,000. At the time of donation, the property had an estimated market value of $550,000, of which $330,000 was allocable to the land. The property was accepted and is to be used as a park and as a museum.

(c) A central fire station, financed by general obligation bonds, was two-thirds complete at year end with costs to date of $900,000 that were recorded in the capital project fund.

(d) A new fire engine was purchased for $151,000. The city traded a used fire engine originally purchased for $100,000. The trade-in value was $21,000. Both engines were purchased from general property tax revenues.

(e) A new street was completed at a cost of $250,000, which is to be charged, through the capital projects fund's special assessments, against property owners in the vicinity. The city follows GASB recommendations relative to recording infrastructures.

Exercise 12. Prepare the entries that would be made in the general long-term debt account group for the following events:

(a) To finance the construction of an art center, $13,000,000 of general obligation term bonds were sold for $12,500,000.

(b) The general fund allocated $1,300,000 to a debt service fund to begin to provide for retirement of the bonds in (1) at maturity.

(c) To help finance an addition to the community health center, $6,000,000 of 6%, 10-year serial bonds were sold at 101. $960,000 was transferred from the general fund to the debt service fund to cover the annual interest and the first serial redemption.

(d) Serial bonds of $600,000 matured and were retired through the debt service fund.

PROBLEMS

Problem 16-1. Select the best answer for each of the following multiple-choice questions. (Nos. 5 and 6 are AICPA adapted.)

(1) The measurement focus for governmental funds is the:
   (a) Flow of cash.
   (b) Flow of financial resources.
   (c) Amount of gross revenue.
   (d) Matching of revenues and expenditures.

(2) Interperiod equity measurement for governmental funds determines whether:
   (a) There is a positive cash flow.
   (b) There is a profit.
   (c) Current-year revenues are sufficient to pay for current-year services.
   (d) Actual amounts exceed budgeted amounts.

(3) The proceeds of a long-term bond issue were used by a county to acquire general fixed assets. The long-term liability is recorded:
   (a) Only in the general long-term debt account group.
   (b) Only in the general fund.
   (c) Both in the general fund and in the general long-term debt account group.
   (d) In the appropriate governmental fund, depending on the nature of the asset involved.

(4) What is the underlying reason a governmental unit uses separate funds to account for its transactions?
   (a) Governmental units are so large that it would be unduly cumbersome to account for all transactions as a single unit.
   (b) Because of the diverse nature of the services offered and legal provisions regarding activities of a governmental unit, it is necessary to segregate activities by functional nature.

(c) Generally accepted accounting principles require that not-for-profit entities report on a funds basis.

(d) Many activities carried on by governmental units are short-lived and their inclusion in a general set of accounts could cause undue probability of error and omission.

(5) The primary authoritative body for determining the measurement focus and basis of accounting standards for governmental fund operating statements is the:
   (a) Governmental Accounting Standards Board (GASB).
   (b) National Council on Governmental Accounting (NCGA).
   (c) Government Accounting and Auditing Committee of the AICPA (GAAC).
   (d) Financial Accounting Standards Board (FASB).

(6) Encumbrances outstanding at year end in a state's general fund should be reported as a:
   (a) Liability in the general fund.
   (b) Fund balance reserve in the general fund.
   (c) Liability in the general long-term debt account group.
   (d) Fund balance designation in the general fund.

Problem 16-2. Select the best answer for each of the following multiple-choice questions. (Nos. 3, 6–10 are AICPA adapted.)

(1) Lacking sufficient cash for operations, a city borrows money from a bank, using as collateral the expected receipts from levied property taxes. Upon receipt of cash from the bank, the general fund would credit:
   (a) Revenues (Control).
   (b) Other Financing Sources (Control).
   (c) Tax Anticipation Notes Payable.
   (d) Taxes Receivable—Delinquent.

(2) The recorded amount for uncollectible taxes was overstated. To revise the estimate during the same fiscal period, the journal entry would credit:
   (a) Expenditures (Control).
   (b) Revenues (Control).
   (c) Allowance for Uncollectible Delinquent Taxes.
   (d) Fund Balance—Unreserved, Undesignated.

(3) The encumbrances control account of a governmental unit is increased when:

	A voucher payable is recorded	The budgetary accounts are closed
(a)	no	no
(b)	no	yes
(c)	yes	yes
(d)	yes	no

(4) If not expenditure-driven, a grant approved by the federal government to assist in a city's welfare program during the current year should be credited to:
   (a) Revenues (Control).
   (b) Fund Balance—Reserved for Welfare Programs.
   (c) Fund Balance—Unreserved, Undesignated.
   (d) Other Financing Sources (Control).

(5) Which one of the following equations will yield the appropriations available balance in an expenditure subsidiary ledger account?

(a) Appropriations – expenditures total.

(b) Appropriations – encumbrances balance.

(c) Appropriations – expenditures total – encumbrances balance.

(d) Appropriations – expenditures total + encumbrances balance.

(6) Elm City issued a purchase order for supplies with an estimated cost of $5,000. When the supplies were received, the accompanying invoice indicated an actual price of $4,950. What amount should Elm debit (credit) to the reserve for encumbrances after the supplies and invoice were received?

(a) $ (50)

(b) $ 50

(c) $ 4,950

(d) $ 5,000

(7) The following are Boa City's fixed assets:

Fixed assets used in proprietary fund activities....................	$1,000,000
Fixed assets used in expendable trust funds	1,800,000
All other fixed assets...	9,000,000

What aggregate amount should Boa account for in the general fixed assets account group?

(a) $ 9,000,000

(b) $10,000,000

(c) $10,800,000

(d) $11,800,000

(8) Pine City's year end is June 30. Pine levies property taxes in January of each year for the calendar year. One-half of the levy is due in May and one-half is due in October. Property tax revenue is budgeted for the period in which payment is due. The following information pertains to Pine's property taxes for the period from July 1, 1990, to June 30, 1991:

	Calendar Year	
	1990	1991
Levy	$2,000,000	$2,400,000
Collected in:		
May....................	950,000	1,100,000
July...................	50,000	60,000
October	920,000	
December	80,000	

The $40,000 balance due for the May 1991 installments was expected to be collected in August 1991. What amount should Pine recognize for property tax revenue for the year ended June 30, 1991?

(a) $2,160,000

(b)   2,200,000

(c)   2,360,000

(d)   2,400,000

(9) Dodd Village received a gift of a new fire engine from a local civic group. The fair value of this fire engine was $400,000. The entry to be made in the general fixed assets account group for this gift is:

		Debit	Credit
(a)	Memorandum entry only		
(b)	General fund assets	$400,000	
	Private gifts		$400,000
(c)	Investment in general fixed assets	$400,000	
	Gift revenue		$400,000
(d)	Machinery and equipment	$400,000	
	Investment in general fixed assets from private gifts		$400,000

(10) The following information pertains to Spruce City's liability for claims and judgments:

Current liability at January 1, 1992	$100,000
Claims paid during 1992	800,000
Current liability at December 31, 1992	140,000
Noncurrent liability at December 31, 1992........................	200,000

What amount should Spruce report for 1992 claims and judgment expenditures?
   (a) $1,040,000
   (b)   940,000
   (c)   840,000
   (d)   800,000

Problem 16-3. Omitting amounts, prepare journal entries in the general fund to record the following selected events:
   (a) The budget is approved. The city will float a bond issue to finance fixed assets. Inflows of resources are expected to exceed outflows.
   (b) Property taxes are levied, of which some percentage will be uncollectible.
   (c) Some of the delinquent property taxes from last year are collected. Others are written off as uncollectible, using the available allowance account.
   (d) Purchase orders are approved.
   (e) Payroll for the month is vouchered. Ignore payroll deductions.
   (f) An invoice is vouchered for an amount less than its encumbrance.
   (g) Bonds are sold at face value to finance the acquisition of new fixed assets.
   (h) Fixed assets are purchased.
   (i) Short-term tax anticipation notes are issued.

Problem 16-4. On July 1, 19X0, the beginning of its fiscal year, the trial balance of the general fund of the city of St. Pauli was as follows:

	Debit	Credit
Cash...	$ 20,000	
Tax Receivable—Delinquent	120,000	
Allowances for Uncollectible Delinquent Taxes.................		$ 12,000
Interest and Penalties Receivable on Taxes	8,000	
Allowance for Uncollectible Interest and Penalties.............		800
Due from Other Funds	28,000	
Vouchers Payable		87,200
Fund Balance Reserved for Encumbrances		16,000
Fund Balance—Unreserved, Undesignated....................		60,000
	$176,000	$176,000

The following events occurred:
   (a) The budget shows estimated general fund revenues of $450,000 and estimated expenditures (including $16,000 encumbered in the prior year) of $392,000.

(b) In July, the item ordered in the previous year was received at an invoice cost of $16,400. A voucher is prepared.

(c) Property taxes amounting to $300,000 were levied, with 4% estimated to be uncollectible.

(d) Cash collections during the year were as follows:

Current taxes	$270,000
Delinquent taxes (in full settlement)	104,000
Interest and penalties on last year's taxes (in full settlement)	7,600
Due from other funds	28,000
	$409,600

The controller wishes variations in estimates to be recorded in the appropriate revenue or expenditure account.

(e) Purchase orders totaling $276,000 were placed. Later, invoices for $260,000 were received and vouchered; supplies inventory purchases were $16,000 of the total. The purchase covered $254,000 of the encumbrances.

(f) Payrolls of $50,000 were paid. (Ignore payroll taxes and other deductions.) In addition, vouchers totaling $280,000 were paid. (Supplies inventory purchases were $16,000 of the total.)

(g) An automobile was purchased for the fire department. It cost $16,000 and was not previously encumbered. The invoice is vouchered.

(h) At year end, $6,000 in supplies were on hand. There were no supplies on hand a year ago. The city wishes to show the inventory and to establish a proper reserve.

Required:
(1) Prepare journal entries that would be made in the general fund for the following events.
(2) Prepare closing entries.
(3) Prepare a Statement of Revenues, Expenditures, and Changes in Fund.

Problem 16-5. A summary of the general fund transactions for the city of Clear Lake for the year ended December 31, 19X7, is as follows:

(a) A budget was approved, showing estimated revenues of $800,000, appropriations of $775,000, transfers-in of $27,000 from other funds, and required transfers of $20,000 to other funds.

(b) The reserve for encumbrance at the end of 19X6 was $25,000. Amounts encumbered in the prior period are included in appropriations for 19X7.

(c) Property taxes for $550,000 were levied. In past years, 1% of the property taxes levied proved uncollectible.

(d) Encumbrances for $25,000 had not been liquidated by the end of 19X6. Invoices for all these items were received in 19X7 and totaled $24,000.

(e) Collections from property taxes totaled $544,000, of which $20,000 represented collections on delinquent taxes. Delinquent taxes of $8,000 remain uncollected, on which a $3,000 allowance is carried. Remaining taxes receivable—current and taxes receivable—delinquent were converted into taxes receivable—delinquent and tax liens receivable, respectively.

(f) Purchase orders totaling $600,000 were issued. Subsequently, invoices were received amounting to $585,000 for items estimated to cost $580,000. Included were supplies for $10,000.

(g) An ending inventory of supplies amounted to $2,000, for which the fund balance should be reserved.

(h) A tract of land was purchased for $250,000. Payment was made from the general fund, in whose appropriations the item had been included. The amount had not been encumbered. The purchase was made with the intent of reselling the land to a suitable developer.

(i) Clear Lake received $300,000 as its part of federal revenue-sharing programs. Grants-in-aid of $60,000 due from the state government are recorded. None of the grants is expenditure-driven.

(j) Required transfers of $20,000 are made to other funds.

(k) A $50,000 payment is made on a mortgage payable. The payment includes $21,000 of interest and a principal payment of $29,000.

(l) An offer was received from a land developer who will pay $380,000 for the land acquired by the city in (h). The sale is approved. The developer remits $100,000 with a note due in 90 days, bearing 8% interest. Any gain is to be considered revenue.

(m) Transfers received from other funds amount to $23,000.

(n) The developer in (l) remits payment for the note plus interest.

Required:

(1) Prepare journal entries to record the general fund transactions.

(2) Prepare closing entries for the general fund.

(3) Prepare a Statement of Revenues, Expenditures, and Changes in Fund Balances—Budget and Actual. On January 1, 19X7, the unreserved fund balance showed a debit balance (deficit) of $180,000.

Problem 16-6. The general fund trial balance of the city of Oakwood at December 31, 19X3, was as follows:

	Debit	Credit
Cash	$ 62,000	
Taxes Receivable—Delinquent	46,000	
Allowance for Uncollectible Delinquent Taxes		$ 8,000
Stores Inventory	18,000	
Vouchers Payable		28,000
Fund Balance—Reserved for Stores		18,000
Fund Balance—Reserved for Encumbrances		12,000
Fund Balance—Unreserved, Undesignated		60,000
	$126,000	$126,000

The following data pertain to 19X4 general fund operations:

(a) Budget adopted:

Revenues and other financing sources:

Taxes	$220,000
Fines, forfeits, and penalties	80,000
Miscellaneous revenues	100,000
Share of bond issue proceeds	200,000
	$600,000

Expenditures and other financing uses:

Program operations	$300,000
General administration	120,000
Stores	60,000
Capital outlay	80,000
Transfer to debt service fund	20,000
	$580,000

Encumbrances from 19X3 are included in the budget.

(b) Taxes were assessed at an amount that would result in revenues of $220,800, after deduction of 4% of the tax levy as uncollectible.

(c) Orders placed for:

Program operations	$176,000
General administration	80,000
Capital outlay	60,000
	$316,000

(d) The city council designated $20,000 of the unreserved fund balance for possible appropriation for capital outlay.

(e) Cash collections and transfer:

Delinquent taxes (balance is uncollectible)	$ 38,000
Current taxes	226,000
Refund of overpayment on equipment invoice in 19X3	4,000
Fines, forfeits, and penalties	88,000
Miscellaneous revenues	90,000
Share of bond issue proceeds	200,000
Operating transfer from capital projects fund	18,000
	$664,000

(f) Vouchers approved for payment (all previously encumbered):

	Estimated	Actual
Applicable to prior year but rebudgeted	$ 12,000	$ 12,000
Program operations	144,000	154,000
General administration	84,000	80,000
Capital outlay	62,000	62,000
	$302,000	$308,000

(g) Additional vouchers approved, not previously encumbered:

Program operations	$148,000
Store supplies	40,000
General administration	38,000
Capital outlay	18,000
Transfer to debt service fund	20,000
	$264,000

(h) A taxpayer overpaid 19X4 taxes by $2,000. (The taxes were credited to miscellaneous revenue upon receipt.) The taxpayer applied for a $2,000 credit against 19X5 taxes. The city council granted the request. The council instructed the city controller to adjust the estimated uncollectible current taxes to cover the remaining uncollected balance.

(i) Vouchers paid amounted to $580,000.

(j) Stores inventory on December 31, 19X4, amounted to $12,000.

Required:

Using control accounts, prepare journal entries to record the foregoing data. Omit explanations.   (AICPA adapted)

Problem 16-7. Prepare journal entries to record the following events using the general fund and the general fixed assets account group:

(a) The general fund vouchered the purchase of trucks for $65,000. The purchase had been encumbered earlier in the year at $60,000.

(b) Several years ago, equipment costing $15,000 was acquired with general fund revenues. It was sold for $5,000, with proceeds belonging to the general fund.

(c) Early in the year, a citizen donated land appraised at $100,000 to the city. She submitted plans for a new library and agreed to cover the total cost of construction, paying the company directly as work proceeds. At year end, the building was two-thirds finished, with costs to date of $300,000. The expenditures are recorded in a capital projects fund.

(d) A snow plow was purchased with general fund cash for $48,000, which represented a cost of $61,000 less trade-in of $13,000 for an old snow plow originally purchased for $35,000 from special revenue funds. As an emergency purchase, the acquisition of the new snow plow had not been encumbered.

Problem 16-8. Prepare the necessary journal entries to record the following transaction for the city of Maineville during 19X4, in the general fund and account groups, and specify the account group used. Entries in the Debt Service Fund and Capital Projects Funds should be ignored.

(a) General obligation term bonds with a face value of $2,500,000 were sold for $2,550,000. The proceeds from the bond issue were to be used to construct a new library and were received by the capital projects fund.

(b) $200,000 was transferred from the general fund to the debt service fund to begin saving for the retirement of the bonds in transaction (a) at maturity.

(c) $150,000 was transferred from the general fund to the debt service fund to retire a portion of a serial bond due in 19X1.

(d) A police car was purchased for $18,000 plus the trade-in of an old police car with a market value of $3,000 originally purchased for $15,000 from the general fund.

(e) The serial bonds funded in transaction (c) were retired on their maturity date.

(f) By year end, $450,000 of the work had been completed on the new library.

Problem 16-9. The following schedule of general fixed assets was obtained from the records of the city of Elm:

City of Elm
Schedule of General Fixed Assets
December 31, 19X3

General fixed assets:

Land	$1,000,000
Buildings	2,150,000
Improvements other than buildings	1,400,000
Machinery and equipment	800,000
Construction in progress	250,000
Total general fixed assets	$5,600,000

Investments in general fixed assets from:
Capital projects funds:

Serial bonds	$1,900,000
Federal grants	800,000
State grants	450,000
General fund	1,250,000
Special revenue funds	1,200,000
Total investment in general fixed assets	$5,600,000

A summary of fixed asset transactions for 19X4 follows:

(a) Construction on the new school, a capital project started during 19X3, was completed at a total cost of $850,000, which was financed by a serial bond issue. No other construction was in progress at the beginning of 19X4.

(b) A citizen donated 400 acres of land to the city to be used as a park. The land had a fair market value of $140,000 when donated.

(c) The municipal waterworks constructed a new pumping plant at a cost of $120,000. The plant was financed from the water utility revenues. The water utility is accounted for in a proprietary fund.

(d) The fire department traded in an old fire engine and $105,000 cash for a new model. The old equipment originally had cost $65,000, and $15,000 was allowed on the trade-in.

(e) The city hall was refurbished at a cost of $40,000, which was paid from general fund revenues. The refurbishing constituted a capital improvement.

(f) Road use taxes of $30,000 were collected by a special revenue fund, of which $20,000 has been used for improvements other than buildings.

Required:

(1) Prepare journal entries only for those transactions that are to be accounted for in the general fixed assets account group. Use the city's account titles.

(2) Prepare a schedule of general fixed assets as of December 31, 19X4.

Problem 16-10. The city of Chester was incorporated on January 1, 19X2. On December 31, 19X7, a careful study of the city's records revealed the following information regarding long-term debt:

(a) General obligation bonds in the amount of $1,500,000 were authorized and issued at face value on July 1, 19X2, to finance the construction of a school. The 6% bonds pay interest semiannually on January 1 and July 1 and mature 10 years from the issuance date.

(b) Serial bonds of $1,000,000 were sold at 99 on January 1, 19X4, to help finance a new city hall and cultural center. An additional $750,000 was received from an anonymous benefactor. The 5% serial bonds were to be redeemed in annual amounts of $100,000, beginning on January 1, 19X7. A sinking fund was established on January 2, 19X4, to provide for the retirement of the serial bonds. Deposits of $70,000 were to be made on January 2 of each year, beginning in 19X4. All amounts deposited were invested immediately at a net yield of 8%.

(c) Property owners were assessed $750,000, to be paid in five equal annual installments, to finance construction of a storm sewer system and repaving of the affected roadways. To have cash when needed to pay for the construction, $600,000 of 5%, 5-year bonds were issued at face value by the Storm Sewer Proprietary Fund.

(d) Term bonds totaling $400,000 were sold at face value on January 1, 19X5, to finance construction. The 5%, 10-year bonds pay interest semiannually on January 1 and July 1. Each year, starting with January 1, 19X5, $40,000 was to be set aside in a sinking fund to provide for retirement of the bonds at maturity. Any income earned by the sinking fund was to be applied to the semiannual interest payments.

Required:

(1) Prepare only the journal entries for the transactions that would be recorded in the general long-term debt account group through December 31, 19X7.

(2) Prepare a schedule of general long-term debt for the city of Chester as of December 31, 19X7.

Problem 16-11. The January 2, 19X8, trial balance of Dawn Township follows:

	Dr.	Cr.
Cash	$45,000	
Taxes Receivable—Delinquent	20,000	
Allowance for Uncollectible Delinquent Taxes.		$ 2,000
Tax Liens Receivable.	4,000	
Allowance for Uncollectible Tax Liens.		1,000
Due from Parks Fund	12,000	
Inventory of Supplies	5,000	
Vouchers Payable.		43,000
Due to Utility Fund.		4,000
Fund Balance—Reserved for Supplies Inventory		5,000
Fund Balance—Unreserved, Undesignated.		31,000
	$86,000	$86,000

The following events occurred during the first six months of 19X8:
(a) The adopted budget showed:

Estimated expenditures.	$620,000
Transfers to other funds	27,000
Estimated revenues	655,000

(b) Six-month tax anticipation notes were issued in the amount of $120,000.
(c) Property taxes of $430,000 were levied, with 2% of the gross levy considered uncollectible.
(d) Tax liens proved uncollectible. The property was foreclosed and sold for $4,000.
(e) Amounts encumbered totaled $250,000.
(f) Cash collected:

All delinquent property taxes.	$ 20,000
Current taxes.	290,000
Due from Parks Fund.	11,000
Fines and penalties.	23,000
	$344,000

(g) Items vouchered totaled $186,000, representing $183,000 of encumbrances. Included in both were $26,000 for supplies, for which a perpetual inventory system is maintained.
(h) Cash payments:

Vouchered items.	$151,000
Nonvouchered items that were	
not encumbered	49,000
Due to Utility Fund	4,000
	$204,000

(i) Supplies inventory on June 30 was $21,000.

Required:
(1) Using the format below, complete the general fund worksheet for the six months ended June 30, 19X8. Ignore entries for any other fund or group. Label entries on the

worksheet according to their corresponding events. Formal journal entries are not required.

(2) Prepare a balance sheet as of June 30, 19X8.

Accounts	Trial Balance Dr.	Trial Balance Cr.	Operating Entries Dr.	Operating Entries Cr.	Revenue and Expenditures Dr.	Revenue and Expenditures Cr.	Balance Sheet Dr.	Balance Sheet Cr.

Problem 16-12. You have been engaged by the town of Rock Elm to examine its June 30, 19X8 balance sheet. You are the first CPA to be engaged by the town, and you find that acceptable methods of municipal accounting have not been employed. The town clerk stated that the books had not been closed and presented the following trial balance of the general fund as of June 30, 19X8:

	Dr.	Cr.
Cash	$150,000	
Taxes Receivable—Current Year	59,200	
Allowance for Uncollectible Current Taxes		$ 18,000
Taxes Receivable—Delinquent	8,000	
Allowance for Uncollectible Delinquent Taxes		10,200
Estimated Revenues	310,000	
Appropriations		348,000
Donated Land	27,000	
Expenditures—Building Addition Constructed	50,000	
Expenditures—Serial Bonds Paid	16,000	
Other Expenditures	280,000	
Revenues		354,000
Accounts Payable		126,000
Fund Balance—Unreserved, Undesignated		82,000
Budgetary Fund Balance	38,000	
	$938,200	$938,200

Additional information:

(a) The estimated uncollectible taxes of $18,000 for Taxes Receivable—Current Year were determined to be reasonably estimated, but for the prior year they should not exceed 100% of Taxes Receivable Delinquent.

(b) Included in the revenues account is a credit of $27,000 representing the value of land donated by the state for construction of a municipal park.

(c) The Expenditures—Building Addition Constructed balance is the cost of an addition to the town hall building. This addition was constructed and completed in June, 19X8. The general fund recorded the payment as authorized.

(d) The Expenditures—Serial Bonds Paid balance reflects the transfer to the debt service fund for serial bond retirement. A transfer of $7,000 for interest payments on this bond issue is included in Other Expenditures.

(e) Operating supplies ordered in the prior fiscal year and chargeable to that year were received and consumed in June, 19X7. The vendors' invoices amounting to $8,800 for these supplies were incorrectly charged to Other Expenditures when paid in July of 19X7.

(f) Outstanding purchase orders at June 30, 19X8, for operating supplies totaled $2,100. These purchase orders were not recorded on the books.

(g) The balance in Revenues includes credits for $20,000 for a note issued to a bank to obtain cash in anticipation of tax collections and for $1,000 for the sale of scrap iron from the town's water plant. The note was still outstanding at June 30, 19X8. Opera-

tions of the water plant are accounted for in the Water Fund (a proprietary fund), which is to receive the proceeds from the scrap sale.
(h) At year end, current taxes are to be reclassified as delinquent.

Required:
(1) Prepare the adjusting entries for the general fund for the fiscal year ended June 30, 19X8. Account titles should be respected if acceptable, even though different. Closing entries are not required.
(2) Prepare formal adjusting journal entries for the general fixed assets account group and for the general long-term debt account group.

(AICPA adapted)

CHAPTER 17

Governmental Accounting: Other Governmental Funds, Proprietary Funds, and Fiduciary Funds

A variety of funds may be used to record events and to exhibit results for a specific area of responsibility. In a small town, there may not be enough activity to warrant more than a general fund, but the larger the governmental unit and the more diverse the activities with which it is involved, the greater the necessity to introduce special funds. While the Governmental Accounting Standards Board (GASB) recognizes the need for funds to manage and demonstrate accountability, they caution against too many funds that unnecessarily fragment financial reporting. GASB Statement No. 1 suggests that a governmental unit establish only the *minimum* number of funds consistent with legal and operating requirements.

SPECIAL REVENUE FUNDS

When revenue obtained from specified sources is restricted by law or donor for a specified current operating purpose or to the acquisition of a relatively minor fixed asset, accounting is accomplished through a *special revenue fund*. Although the government will have only one general fund, it could have many special revenue funds, or none at all. Examples of activities that are accounted for in special revenue funds are non-exchange transactions such as the levy of a hotel room tax to pay for expenditures that promote tourism, federal and state grant proceeds restricted to financing community development expenditures, gasoline tax revenues for highway maintenance, specific federal and/or state funds for education, and exchange transactions such as golf fees charged at a city golf course to cover a portion of the cost of course maintenance. These revenues are recognized under the modified accrual method of accounting.[1] The following are examples of revenues recorded in the special revenue funds.

---

[1]When revenue raised for activities are on a fee basis for goods or services provided and the operations are intended to be self-supporting, the flows of resources are accounted for in proprietary funds discussed later in this chapter.

Event	Entry in the Special Revenue Funds

During the year, local hotels/motels paid to the city a room tax totaling $98,000. The remittance included $6,000 payable from last year and $92,000 expected to be available in the current year.

Cash.........................	98,000	
Taxes Receivable		6,000
Revenues (Control)..........		92,000
To record the current year's receipt of hotel/motel room fees including $6,000 accrued in the prior year.		

In addition, the city estimates a $9,000 receivable from December rentals. In this city, the hotels/motels are allowed a one-month administrative lead time and are not required to pay the December tax until January 31 of the following year.

Taxes Receivable	9,000	
Revenues (Control)..........		9,000
To recognize hotel/motel room fees applicable to December.		

Charges for services from exchange transactions for the year are as follows:

Cash.........................	370,000	
Accounts Receivable	10,000	
Revenues (Control)..........		360,000
Deferred Revenue		20,000
To record current year's revenues earned and deferred that arose from exchange transactions.		

	Earned	Collected
Golf fees (collected at time of use)	$ 35,000	$ 35,000
Garbage fees (collected in advance of providing service)	240,000	260,000
Snow removal fees (collected after service is provided)	85,000	75,000
Total	$360,000	$370,000

A federal grant is received for economic development. An additional $50,000 is due prior to year end. Revenue is recognized when expenditures are incurred for the grant program.

Cash.........................	100,000	
Due from Federal Government....	50,000	
Deferred Revenue		150,000

In a special revenue fund, the accounting must be designed to permit close scrutiny of activities. If resources are greater than anticipated, the project is not permitted to expand beyond the original authorization, nor is money permitted to accumulate beyond reasonable needs. However, sufficient resources should be generated to permit the activity. The desired control may be accomplished by using the same accounting procedures as those used by the general fund. Annual budgets are prepared for each special revenue fund and are required to be integrated into the accounting system by using the appropriate budgetary control accounts and their related subsidiary records. Commitments are recorded by using an encumbrance and expenditure system. Since both the accounting procedures and the financial statements for special revenue funds parallel so closely those of the general fund, they will not be illustrated beyond the revenue recognition examples shown above.

When a governmental unit has more than one special revenue fund, generally accepted accounting principles require that these funds be presented in *combining* balance sheets, revenue and expenditure statements, and budget and actual statements. Combining statements provide information on each special revenue fund plus a total column of all the special revenue funds. Illustration 17-1 presents a Combining Balance Sheet and Illustration 17-2 presents a Combining Statement of Revenues, Expenditures, and Changes in Fund Balances. In addition, a Combining Statement of Revenues, Expenditures, and Changes in Fund Balances—Budget and Actual would also be required.

Along with the other fund types, the total of the special revenue funds is included in the Combined Balance Sheet and the Combined Statement of Revenues, Expenditures, and Changes in Fund Balances. In addition, a government having both a general fund and special revenue funds prepares a Combined Statement of Revenues, Expenditures, and Changes in Fund Balances—Budget and Actual for the two fund types. The columnar format is similar to that illustrated below and includes the general fund and totals of the special revenue funds.

General Fund			Special Revenue Funds			Total		
Budget	Actual	Variance- Favorable (Unfavorable)	Budget	Actual	Variance- Favorable (Unfavorable)	Budget	Actual	Variance- Favorable (Unfavorable)

Illustration 17-1

City of Berryville—Special Revenue Funds
Combining Balance Sheet
December 31, 19X3

Assets	Community Development Block Grant	Tourism Promotion Projects	Charges for City Golf Course	Total
Cash	$100,000	$ 98,000	$370,000	$568,000
Taxes receivable		9,000	10,000	19,000
Due from other governmental agencies	50,000	40,000		90,000
Total assets	$150,000	$147,000	$380,000	$677,000

Liabilities and Fund Balances				
Liabilities:				
Vouchers payable		$ 15,000	$105,000	$120,000
Due to other funds		10,000	55,000	65,000
Deferred revenue	$150,000	35,000	20,000	205,000
Total liabilities	$150,000	$ 25,000	$180,000	$355,000
Fund balances:				
Reserved for encumbrances		$ 95,000	$175,000	$270,000
Unreserved, designated		27,000	25,000	52,000
Total fund balances	0	$122,000	$200,000	$322,000
Total liabilities and fund balances	$150,000	$147,000	$380,000	$677,000

Illustration 17-2

City of Berryville

Special Revenue Funds

Combining Statement of Revenues, Expenditures, and

Changes in Fund Balances

For Year Ended December 31, 19X3

	Community Development Block Grant	Tourism Promotion Projects	Charges for City Golf Course	Total
Revenues....................................	$40,000	$101,000	$360,000	$501,000
Expenditures................................	40,000	40,000	200.000	280,000
Excess of revenues over (under) expenditures		$ 61,000	$160,000	$221,000
Other financing sources (uses):				
Operating transfers-out......................		$ 10,000	$ 55,000	$ 65,000
Total other financing sources (uses)............	0	$ 10,000	$ 55,000	$ 65,000
Excess of revenues and other financing sources over (under) expenditures and other financing uses................................		$ 51,000	$105,000	$156,000
Fund balances—January 1		$ 71,000	$ 95,000	$166,000
Fund balances—December 31	0	$122,000	$200,000	$322,000

CAPITAL PROJECTS FUNDS

Capital projects funds account for the purchase, construction, or capital lease of major *general* fixed assets, which excludes construction of capital facilities by proprietary funds that account for their own construction activities. Each project should be accounted for separately in subsidiary records to demonstrate compliance with legal and contractual provisions.

Resources for capital projects result from transfers received from the general fund or some other fund, proceeds of general obligation bonds, grants from another governmental unit, or special assessments levied against property owners who benefit from the project. Grants from another governmental unit and special assessments levied are recorded as revenues. Bond proceeds (because they must be repaid) and transfers from other funds (because they previously were recognized as revenue) are accounted for as other financing sources.

NCGA Statement 1, *Governmental Accounting and Financial Reporting Principles,* coordinated the accounting and financial reporting treatments for all governmental funds. As a result, it shifted emphasis for capital projects funds from a project-reporting basis to an annual or other budget-period basis. When the capital projects are expected to take several years to complete and will involve large amounts of money, budgetary control is advisable. The operating budget is prepared on an *annual* basis; therefore, it includes the expected revenues, estimated other financing sources, and estimated expenditures for only the current fiscal year. The following entry records the annual budget:

Estimated Other Financing Sources (Control)* XXX
Estimated Revenues (Control)** XXX
    Appropriations (Control)***   XXX
    Budgetary Fund Balance—Unreserved (either debited or credited) ...   XXX

* Resources from the general fund or other funds and the sale of general obligation bonds.
** Resources from county, state, or federal grants, interest income on temporary investments, and from special assessments.
*** Estimated expenditures for current year.

The full amount of the bond issue proceeds, including the premium and net of any discount and issuance costs incurred, is recorded as an Other Financing Source in the fund that will use the resources. Since bond premiums and discounts arise because of adjustments to the interest rate, the premium and any payment received for accrued interest are transferred to the debt service fund to cover future *interest* payments. If bonds are sold at a discount, a project authorization must be reduced by the bond discount amount and/or issuance costs unless additional resources are transferred from the general fund or other funds.

Proceeds of bond issues not immediately needed for project expenditures are often temporarily invested to earn interest. These temporary investments are limited to securities whose yield does not exceed that of the new debt. Interest earned on temporary investments is recognized as revenue in the capital projects fund. It is often required to be transferred to the debt service fund to help finance bond interest expenditures.

Adopting the annual reporting period permits the accounting for many events to be the same as for the general fund and the special revenue funds.[2]

Capital projects funds have the authority through annually approved budgets to continue expenditures within prescribed limits until a project is completed. Although a project may not be completed at the end of a fiscal period, typical closing entries are recorded. Annual closing permits the actual activity to be compared with the legally adopted annual operating budget. Also, in the closing process, the credit to Expenditures (Control) provides the amount of capitalizable expenditures to be recorded in the general fixed assets account group for Construction in Progress.

The actual cost of a capital project probably will differ from its estimated cost. A deficiency usually is covered by a transfer from the general fund. If an excess of resources exists upon completion of the project, it generally is returned to the general fund or to the debt service fund. Such a transfer is called a *residual equity transfer* and, because it is nonrecurring and nonroutine, it is reported as an adjustment to the beginning fund balances of both governmental funds involved. Upon completion of the project, it is customary to withhold part of the

[2]Authoritative literature endorses the use of an encumbrance system for those funds. Many governments also use an encumbrance system in their capital projects funds.

payment until final inspection and approval. The liability is recorded in Contracts Payable—Retained Percentage.

To illustrate accounting for capital projects funds, assume the city of Berryville plans to build a $300,000 addition to its municipal auditorium. The project will begin in 19X3 and is to be completed in 19X4. The following entries record the events that occur during construction:

Event	Entry in the Capital Projects Fund		
The project budget is $300,000, to be financed by a general bond issue. The 19X3 operating budget is based on 1/3 of the work's being completed that year. The city uses an other financing sources (control) account.	Estimated Other Financing Sources (Control).....................	300,000	
	Appropriations (Control)..........		100,000
	Budgetary Fund Balance— Unreserved..................		200,000
A $300,000, 8% general obligation bond issue is floated in at 101...............................	Cash	303,000	
	Other Financing Sources (Control) ..		303,000
An entry also is made in the general long-term debt account group: Amount to Be Provided ...... 300,000 Serial Bonds Payable 300,000			
The bond premium is transferred to the debt service fund to be used for interest.	Other Financing Uses (Control).......	3,000	
	Cash		3,000
An entry also is made in the debt service fund: Cash..................... 3,000 Other Financing Sources ... 3,000 (Note: Since bond premium is assumed to be used for interest payments, no entry is made in the GLTDAG.)			
A contract is signed for the auditorium construction at an estimated cost of $270,000.	Encumbrances (Control)	270,000	
	Fund Balance—Reserved for Encumbrances		270,000
The architect's bill for $10,650 is received, of which $7,650 is paid. Upon final building approval the balance is due. The item was not encumbered.	Expenditures (Control)	10,650	
	Cash		7,650
	Contracts Payable—Retained Percentage		3,000
A partial billing is received from the contractor for $60,000, equal to the amount encumbered for these items. Contracts Payable is credited for the liability to the principal contractor. (If the amount of equivalent encumbrance is not specified, the encumbrance entry is reversed for the amount of the billing.)	Fund Balance—Reserved for Encumbrances	60,000	
	Encumbrances (Control)		60,000
	Expenditures (Control)	60,000	
	Contracts Payable...............		60,000
The contractor is paid $60,000.	Contracts Payable..................	60,000	
	Cash		60,000

Event	Entry in the Capital Projects Fund		

Event	Entry in the Capital Projects Fund		
Books for 19X3 are closed.	Budgetary Fund Balance—		
	Unreserved...................	200,000	
	Appropriations (Control)............	100,000	
	Estimated Other Financing Sources		
	(Control)....................		300,000

Event	Entry in the Capital Projects Fund		

The credit to Expenditures (Control) is the basis for the following entry in the general fixed assets account group:
 	
Construction in Progress 70,650
  Investment in General
    Fixed Assets—Capital
    Project Funds   70,650
	Other Financing Sources (Control)	303,000	

	Expenditures (Control)...........		70,650
	Other Financing Uses (Control).....		3,000
	Fund Balance—Unreserved,		
	Undesignated		229,350

Event	Entry in the Capital Projects Fund		
Encumbrances are closed at year end.	Fund Balance—Unreserved,		
	Undesignated	210,000	
	Encumbrances (Control)		210,000

Event	Entry in the Capital Projects Fund		

19X4
The operating budget for 19X4 is recorded; completion is estimated to cost an additional $215,000, including the amount encumbered in the previous year.
	Budgetary Fund Balance—
	  Unreserved.................
	    Appropriations (Control)..........
		215,000	215,000

The encumbrances are reinstated at the beginning of 19X4.	Encumbrances (Control) ....
	  Fund Balance—Unreserved,
	    Undesignated ....
		210,000	210,000

The contract is completed in 19X4. Additional cost is $227,000, of which $10,000 is withheld in a separate account until final inspection and approval.	Expenditures (Control) ....
	  Contracts Payable...............
	  Contracts Payable—
	    Retained Percentage ....
		227,000	217,000
			
			10,000

	Fund Balance—Reserved for
	  Encumbrances ....
	    Encumbrances (Control) ....
		210,000	210,000

The construction is accepted and the contractor and architect are paid.	Contracts Payable.................
	Contracts Payable—Retained
	  Percentage ....
	  Cash........................
		217,000
		
		13,000
			230,000

Books for 19X4 are closed.	Appropriations (Control)............
	  Budgetary Fund Balance—
	    Unreserved.................
		215,000	215,000

Event	Entry in the Capital Projects Fund	
The credit to Expenditures (Control) is the basis for the following entry in the general fixed assets account group:	Fund Balance—Unreserved, Undesignated . . . . 227,000 Expenditures (Control)	227,000

Buildings 297,650
    Construction in
        Progress   70,650
    Investment in General Fixed
        Assets—Capital Projects
        Funds   227,000

Event	Entry in the Capital Projects Fund	
The residual balance is transferred to debt service fund.	Residual Equity Transfer-Out . . . . 2,350 Cash.	2,350

An entry also is made in the debt service fund:
Cash.   2,350
    Residual Equity Transfer-In. . . .   2,350
Residual Equity Transfer-In.   2,350
    Fund Balance—Reserved for
        Debt Service   2,350
(Note: Since the project was financed with general obligation debt, an additional entry in the GLTDAG indicating availability of funds to repay the debt is required.)
Amount Available in the
    Debt Service Fund   2,350
    Amount to Be Provided   2,350

Event	Entry in the Capital Projects Fund	
The Municipal Auditorium Capital Fund Project Fund is closed.	Fund Balance—Unreserved, Undesignated . . . . 2,350 Residual Equity Transfer-Out	2,350

When a governmental unit has more than one capital project in progress during the year, generally accepted accounting principles require that combining financial statements be presented. Illustration 17-3 presents a combining balance sheet for the city of Berryville's capital projects funds. The 19X3 year-end balance sheet for the auditorium project, for which the accounting entries were shown, and the 19X3 year-end balance sheet for a bridge construction capital project, for which the accounting entries are *not* shown, are included in the combining balance sheet. The total column also is reported in a Capital Projects Fund column in the combined balance sheet. Cities often have many more than two capital projects in progress during a year, and each project is reported in the combining financial statements.

The combining statement of revenues, expenditures, and changes in fund balances will show as revenues those resources obtained by special assessment, by grant, or from some other governmental unit. Transfers from other funds within the same governmental unit or proceeds of a bond issue are presented as other financing sources. The form used in Illustration 17-4 on page 913 is the one currently preferred, with the final amount representing the total of both reserved and unreserved fund balances.

Illustration 17-3

City of Berryville
Capital Projects Funds
Combining Balance Sheet
December 31, 19X3

Assets	Municipal Auditorium	Bridge Construction Project	Total
Cash	$232,350	$102,000	$334,350
Special assessments receivable..........		160,000	160,000
Investments		40,000	40,000
Total assets	$232,350	$302,000	$534,350
Liabilities and Fund Balance			
Vouchers payable.......................		$157,000	$157,000
Contracts payable—retained percentage..	$ 3,000	50,000	53,000
Total liabilities	$ 3,000	$207,000	$210,000
Fund balances:			
Reserved for encumbrances...........	$210,000	$ 90,000	$300,000
Unreserved, undesignated	19,350	5,000	24,350
Total fund balances	$229,350	$ 95,000	$324,350
Total liabilities and fund balances	$232,350	$302,000	$534,350

DEBT SERVICE FUNDS

As discussed in Chapter 16, the function of the general long-term debt account group is to provide a record of the unredeemed principal of long-term liabilities incurred to acquire general fixed assets. Closely related to this account group are *debt service funds*, whose primary function is to account for financial resources accumulated to cover the payment of principal and interest on those obligations shown in the general long-term debt account group.

As in other governmental funds, the modified accrual basis is used for recognizing revenues, other financing sources, and expenditures in debt service funds. Interest on general long-term debt is an item for which the accrual basis is modified. For example, assume a governmental unit has a fiscal year ending June 30, with interest on long-term debt to be paid on July 31. Since expenditures are authorized by appropriations, it is essential that expenditures be recorded in the same period as the appropriations. Thus, the interest will not be accrued on June 30, because the appropriation to cover the interest will not be provided until the budget for the next period is recorded on July 1. This method recognizes expenditures for interest when they are "due."

The most popular method of raising long-term resources is by the issuance of serial bonds, which are redeemed in a series of installments. Term bonds, whose total face value becomes due at one time, are now extremely rare. When

Illustration 17-4

City of Berryville

Capital Projects Funds

Combining Statement of Revenues, Expenditures, and

Changes in Fund Balances

For Year Ended December 31, 19X3

	Municipal Auditorium	Bridge Construction Project	Total
Revenues...........................		$118,000	$ 118,000
Expenditures........................	$ 70,650	157,000	227,650
Excess (deficiency) of revenues over expenditures......................	$ (70,650)	$ (39,000)	$(109,650)
Other financing sources (uses):			
Proceeds of bonds................	$303,000	$196,000	$ 499,000
Payments to Debt Service	(3,000)	(62,000)	(65,000)
Total other financing sources (uses) ..	$300,000	$134,000	$ 434,000
Excess (deficiency) of revenues and other sources over expenditures and other uses.......................	$229,350	$ 95,000	$ 324,350
Fund balances at beginning of year.....			
Fund balances at end of year	$229,350	$ 95,000	$ 324,350

serial bonds are issued, there is no substantial accumulation of cash in a sinking fund for redemption of the principal, unless the first series will not mature for several fiscal periods and contributions for retirement are to begin immediately. Instead, the budget for the year of payment provides for interest and principal redemption. In debt service funds, an entry to record the budget seldom is used because expenditures for principal and interest are known and there is no need to compare them with budgetary amounts.

Resources to cover expenditures may come from several sources. A portion of a property tax levy may be authorized to be recorded directly in a debt service fund. The entries would be similar to those made in the general fund to record a tax levy. The net amount of taxes estimated to be collected is credited to Revenues (Control), since the resources are received from outsiders. Transfers received by the debt service fund from funds that already have recorded the resources as revenues are credited to Other Financing Sources (Control). As discussed in Chapter 16, this procedure prevents Revenues (Control) from being credited in two funds for the same resources—once in the originating fund (in this case, the general fund) and again in the recipient fund (in this case, a debt service fund).

Prior to redemption, the bond liability for unmatured general obligation debt is not recorded in a debt service fund, but is entered in the general long-term debt account group. However, when a serial bond matures and payment of interest is due, the following entry is recorded in a debt service fund:

```
Expenditures (Control) ........................................ XXX
    Matured Bonds Payable...................................      XXX
    Matured Interest Payable..................................      XXX
```

An entry to record payment of these matured items then would be made. Simultaneously, an entry to record reduction of the bond principal is made in the general long-term debt account group. Many governmental units employ the services of financial institutions to conduct actual payments for interest and serial redemptions. When cash is released to such a fiscal agent, the account debited is Cash with Fiscal Agent. Upon notification by the agent that actual payments have been made, the debt service fund entry is:

```
Matured Bonds Payable....................................... XXX
Matured Interest Payable.................................... XXX
    Cash with Fiscal Agent...................................      XXX
```

The following entries would be made in a debt service fund for the indicated events that relate to a serial bond issue. As demonstrated by these entries, the interaction between funds and groups is especially prevalent in accounting for general obligation bond issues.

Event

An 8%, $300,000 general obligation serial bond issue for bridge construction is sold at 101. The premium is transferred from the capital projects fund to the debt service fund.

Entries are also made in the capital project fund:
```
Cash.......................... 303,000
    Other Financing Sources........        303,000
Other Financing Uses ............. 3,000
    Cash.........................          3,000
```
and in the general long-term debt account group:
```
Amount to Be Provided............ 300,000
    Serial Bonds Payable............        300,000
```

Of the property taxes, $50,000 is levied specifically to cover debt service on these bonds; the levy, less 1% of the taxes estimated to be uncollectible, is recorded in the debt service fund.

All property taxes are collected, except for $400 that is written off. The difference between estimated and actual uncollectible taxes is recorded in Revenues (Control).

Assuming $30,000 is to be used toward the first installment on the principal payment:
```
Amount Available in the Debt
    Service Fund ................... 30,000
    Amount to Be Provided ...........        30,000
```

Entry in the Debt Service Fund

```
Cash................................ 3,000
    Other Financing Sources (Control) ....        3,000
```

```
Taxes Receivable—Current............ 50,000
    Allowance for Uncollectible Current
        Taxes .........................              500
    Revenues (Control).................           49,500
```

```
Cash................................ 49,600
Allowance for Uncollectible Current
    Taxes .......................... 400
    Taxes Receivable—Current..........           50,000
```

```
Allowance for Uncollectible Current
    Taxes .......................... 100
    Revenues (Control)................              100
```

Event	Entry in the Debt Service Fund		
The fund receives $7,000 of its $9,000 share of state gasoline taxes. The city is not entitled to the balance until the next fiscal period.	Cash.............................. Due from State..................... Revenues (Control)................ Deferred Revenues	7,000 2,000	 7,000 2,000
A transfer of $30,000 is received from the general fund.	Cash.............................. Other Financing Sources (Control)	30,000	 30,000

Since the $30,000 is for payment of principal, an additional entry is made in the GLTDAG:
 Amount Available in the Debt
     Service Fund 30,000
     Amount to Be Provided 30,000			

Cash is transmitted to a fiscal agent for payment of the first $60,000 of maturing bonds and $24,000 of interest due on the last day of the fiscal period.	Cash with Fiscal Agent .... Cash..........................	84,000	 84,000
The matured bonds and interest are recorded.	Expenditures (Control)............... Matured Bonds Payable .... Matured Interest Payable	84,000	 60,000 24,000

$60,000 of principal is matured and no longer long term. The entry to reclassify the debt in the GLTDAG:
 Serial Bonds Payable 60,000
     Amount Available in the Debt
     Service Fund 60,000			

The fiscal agent reports that all payments have been made, except for $1,000 of interest.	Matured Bonds Payable .... Matured Interest Payable .... Cash with Fiscal Agent	60,000 23,000	 83,000
Books are closed at year end.	Revenues (Control)................... Other Financing Sources (Control) ...... Expenditures (Control) .... Fund Balance—Reserved for Debt Service	56,600 33,000	 84,000 5,600

Assets transferred to a debt service fund must be used to redeem bonds or to pay interest. There are no unreserved assets. Any excess of assets over liabilities is reserved for debt service. Therefore, at year end, the accounts are closed to Fund Balance—Reserved for Debt Service, rather than to an unreserved fund balance.

In addition to term bonds and serial bonds, debt service funds may be used to service debt arising from notes or warrants having a maturity of more than one year after date of issue, and to make periodic payments on capital leases. Although each issue of long-term debt is a separate obligation with unique legal restrictions and servicing requirements, GASB standards provide that, if legally permissible, a single debt service fund may be used to account for the service of all issues of tax-supported and special-assessment debt. If legal restrictions do not allow the servicing of all issues to be accounted for by a single debt service fund, the number of debt service funds should be held to a minimum.

Debt service funds employ two financial statements for reporting purposes: a balance sheet and a statement of revenues, expenditures, and changes in fund balances. If two or more debt service funds are used, they are presented in *combining* statements. Illustration 17-5 is a combining balance sheet for Vernon Town. This balance sheet has a column for general obligation debt, for which the

Illustration 17-5

Vernon Town
Debt Service Funds
Combining Balance Sheet
December 31, 19X3

Assets	General Obligation Debt	Special Assessment Debt	Total
Cash....................................	$5,600	$ 20,000	$ 25,600
Cash with fiscal agents...................	1,000		1,000
Due from state........................	2,000		2,000
Special assessment receivable............		20,000	20,000
Special assessment receivable—deferred ..		160,000	160,000
Total assets..........................	$8,600	$200,000	$208,600

Liabilities and Fund Balance			
Liabilities:			
Matured interest payable...............	$1,000		$ 1,000
Deferred revenue.....................	2,000	$160,000	162,000
Fund balance:			
Reserved for debt service	5,600	40,000	45,600
Total liabilities and fund balance	$8,600	$200,000	$208,600

entries were shown, and a column for special assessment debt, for which the entries were *not* shown.

The notes to the financial statements would explain that the money to cover the final matured bonds and interest for the Health Center Debt Service Fund has been forwarded to a fiscal agent. Once word is received that these payments have been made, that fund will be closed.

The combining statement of revenues, expenditures, and changes in fund balances for Vernon Town's debt service funds is shown in Illustration 17-6 on page 917. This statement itemizes revenues by source and expenditures by nature, and it summarizes the causes of changes in fund balances during the period.

SPECIAL ASSESSMENTS

Local governments may provide capital improvements and services for the primary benefit of particular groups of property owners, which will be paid partially or totally by the same property owners. Such arrangements are called *special assessment projects* and are accounted for through the local government.

Service-type special assessments cover operating activities, such as snow plowing, that do not result in increases in fixed assets. Payment for service special assessments seldom is arranged on an installment basis. A single charge is added to the property tax bill. Service assessments are accounted for in the fund type (usually the general fund, a special revenue fund, or an enterprise fund) that best reflects the nature of the transaction.

Capital-improvement special assessments result in additions or improvements to a government's fixed assets. If an improvement provides capital assets that become part of an enterprise activity, such as water main construction for a utility, accounting would be done in an enterprise fund. If the improvement results in a general fixed asset, such as streets, gutters, or sidewalks, the asset would be recorded in the general fixed asset account group (if the government records infrastructure assets), in which case the accounting is divided into two phases.

The *first phase* consists of financing and constructing the project and usually will be accounted for through a capital projects fund. The initiative for such projects often is taken by the property owners who request the improvement. However, authorization must be approved through appropriate channels. Special assessment projects typically are financed through issues of long-term debt, but may be financed with existing government resources. Once the project is approved, the estimates for the budget period (not the total project budget) are recorded in a capital projects fund.

Illustration 17-6
Vernon Town
Debt Service Funds
Combining Statement of Revenues, Expenditures, and
Changes in Fund Balances
For Year Ended December 31, 19X3

	General Obligation Debt	Special Assessment Debt	Total
Revenues:			
Taxes..............................	$ 49,600	$20,000	$69,600
Intergovernmental....................	7,000		7,000
Total revenues......................	$ 56,600	$20,000	$76,600
Expenditures:			
Principal retirement	$ 60,000		$60,000
Interest charges.......................	24,000		24,000
Total expenditures..................	$ 84,000	0	$84,000
Excess (deficiency) of revenues over expenditures	$(27,400)	$20,000	$ (7,400)
Other financing sources (uses):			
Operating transfers in.................	33,000		33,000
Excess (deficiency) of revenues and other financing sources over expenditures	$ 5,600	$20,000	$25,600
Fund balances at beginning of year		20,000	20,000
Fund balances at end of year	$ 5,600	$40,000	$45,600

Proper recordings of inflows of financial resources into the capital projects fund depend upon the source of financing. Illustration 17-7 presents proper recording of inflows under three possible sources of financing. When the capital improvements are financed by special-assessment-related debt for which the government is obligated in some manner, such as accounting for resources raised and for the expenditure of funds during construction, accounting procedures are the same as for other capital projects assuming secondary liability in the event of default by property owners.

When the capital improvements are financed by debt for which the government is not obligated in any manner, proceeds from issuing the debt are credited by the governmental unit to Contributions from Property Owners, in the capital projects fund.

When the capital improvements are financed by existing governmental resources and debt is not issued, transfers from other funds are credited to Other Financing Sources, in the capital projects fund.

Expenditures are recorded in the capital projects fund as costs are incurred for the special assessment project. At year end, the capitalizable costs of an unfinished special assessment project are entered in the general fixed assets account group.

Illustration 17-7   Accounting for Special Assessment Projects under Three Methods of Financing*

Debt Issued	Flows of Financial Resources through the Capital Projects Fund	
Government obligated in some manner	Cash............................... 200,000 Other Financing Sources— Bond Proceeds	200,000
Government not obligated in any manner	Cash............................... 200,000 Contributions from Property Owners ..	200,000
Debt not issued	Cash............................... 200,000 Other Financing Sources—Transfers from Other Funds.................	200,000
	Expenditures incurred during construction are recorded in the same manner as expenditures recorded for other capital projects.	

*Note that budgetary entries have been omitted from this illustration.

Capital Projects Fund

Expenditures (Control).   80,000
   Cash.   80,000

General Fixed Assets Account Group

Construction in Progress.   80,000
   Investment in General Fixed
     Assets—Capital Projects Funds
     (Special Assessments).   80,000

Completion of the special assessment project in the second year is recorded with the following entries:

Capital Projects Fund

Expenditures (Control).   120,000
   Cash.   120,000

General Fixed Assets Account Group
(This entry also is shown in Illustration 17-7.)

(Proper Fixed Asset Account)   200,000
   Construction in Progress.   80,000
   Investment in General Fixed
     Assets—Capital Projects Funds
     (Special Assessments).   120,000

The *second phase* of accounting for special assessment projects consists of collecting the special assessments on an installment basis from benefited property owners and repaying the cost of financing the project. When the government

Eventual Recording of Constructed Asset in the General Fixed Assets Account Group	Recording of Special Assessment Debt in the General Long-Term Debt Account Group

Fixed Asset Account. 200,000
  Construction in Progress. . . .   80,000
  Investment in General Fixed
    Assets   120,000
	Amounts to Be Provided for
	  Payment of Special
	  Assessment Debt 200,000
	  Special Assessment Bonds
	    Payable 200,000

Fixed Asset Account. 200,000
  Construction in Progress. . . .   80,000
  Investment in General Fixed
    Assets   120,000
	Long-term debt is not recorded because the government is not obligated for the debt. Debt service is accounted for through an agency fund.

Fixed Asset Account. 200,000
  Construction in Progress. . . .   80,000
  Investment in General Fixed
    Assets   120,000
	Long-term debt is not issued.

	Liquidation of the special assessment debt is described in the text.

is obligated in some manner for the special assessment debt, the liability should be recorded in the general long-term debt account group, as shown in this entry:

```
Amount to Be Provided for Payment of
     Special Assessment Debt .......................... 200,000
     Special Assessment Debt with Governmental Commitment. .     200,000
```

In some cases, the governmental unit has the primary responsibility for repayment of the bonds. In these situations, they are recorded, as follows, in the general long-term debt account group with the same type of entry used to record any other general obligation debt.

```
Amount to Be Provided for Payment of
     Special Assessment Debt .......................... 200,000
     Special Assessment Bonds Payable.....................     200,000
```

(This entry also is used as an example in Illustration 17-7.)

The Special Assessment Receivable and Special Assessment Revenue are divided between current and deferred portions in the debt service fund. Amounts levied and demanded to service related debt in the current period are credited to Revenues (Control) as shown below. The remainder to be collected and used for debt service in future periods is credited to Deferred Revenues.

```
Special Assessments Receivable—Current..................  20,000
Special Assessments Receivable—Deferred................ 180,000
     Revenues (Control).....................................      20,000
     Deferred Revenues.....................................     180,000
```

Through the term of the debt, the amount to be collected from property owners for a period is levied and demanded by the governmental unit; consequently, that portion of deferred revenue should be recognized as revenue in that period. Recognition of the receivable from the levy and the revenue is shown below. Details of the assessments are entered in a subsidiary ledger, where the levy against each property owner and collections from the owner are indicated.

```
Special Assessments Receivable—Current..................  20,000
     Special Assessments Receivable—Deferred..............      20,000

Deferred Revenues.....................................  20,000
     Revenues (Control).....................................      20,000
```

The general long-term debt account group is updated to reflect the amount available in the debt service fund. The debt is liquidated in the same manner as other governmental-fund debt.

When the government is not obligated in any manner, collection of the special assessment and debt service payments should be accounted for through an agency fund (discussed on pages 936–938 in the Agency Funds section) since the government is acting merely as an agent for the property owners and bondholders. In that case, the debt is not shown in the general long-term debt account group; it should appear, however, in the notes to the financial statements.

When no debt is issued, Revenues (Control) is credited in the recipient fund for the current levy of the special assessment. Amounts to be levied and collected in future periods are credited to Deferred Revenues.

PROPRIETARY FUNDS

The funds discussed to this point have been governmental funds. The second category of funds—*proprietary funds*—now will be discussed. By definition, the term "proprietary" means pertaining to a proprietor and implies that users of goods or services will be charged on the basis of consumption, similar to the practice in private industries. Usually charges are set to recover as much as possible of the total cost, including depreciation. Whatever is not recovered must be subsidized.

All proprietary funds are involved with providing goods or services. If they serve the general public, their activities are accounted for in *enterprise funds*. If they serve other departments of the same governmental unit or a different governmental unit, their activities are accounted for in *internal service funds*.

Proprietary funds focus on capital maintenance to measure whether revenues were sufficient to cover expenses (including the amortization of noncurrent items) of the fiscal period. This is consistent with a flows of economic resources measurement focus coupled with the accrual basis of accounting. Financial reporting for proprietary funds is similar to financial reporting for business enterprises in that income statements show revenues, expenses, and net income for a fiscal period, and balance sheets include both current and noncurrent assets and liabilities of the entity. The proprietary fund balance sheet residual is comprised of contributed capital and retained earnings.

In a recent pronouncement, the GASB concluded that proprietary funds *must* follow all accounting standards set forth by the FASB prior to November 30, 1989, unless they specifically conflict with a GASB pronouncement. In addition, a proprietary activity may apply all FASB pronouncements issued after that date unless they conflict with or contradict GASB standards.[3]

One of the rare times that amounts transferred from another fund are treated as revenue is in the case of proprietary funds furnishing goods or services to other funds. For example, a computer center accounted for in an internal service fund may provide service to the general fund. This transaction is *quasi-external*, because the item would have been treated as revenue if it had been billed to an outsider. Therefore, the billing represents revenue to the internal service fund and an expenditure to the general fund. Entries in each fund are as follows:

Internal Service Fund	Due from the General Fund............. XXX	
	Revenue	XXX
General Fund	Expenditure........................... XXX	
	Due to the Internal Service Fund	XXX

Conversely, if a proprietary fund pays the general fund for services, the proprietary fund records expenses and the general fund records revenue. For example,

---

[3]GASB Statement No. 20, *Accounting and Financial Reporting for Proprietary Funds and Other Governmental Entities That Use Proprietary Fund Accounting* (Norwalk, CT: Governmental Accounting Standards Board, Sept. 1993).

the general government may bill an enterprise fund for payments in lieu of property taxes. Entries in each fund are:

General Fund	Due from the Enterprise Fund................ XXX	
	Revenue.................................	XXX
Enterprise Fund	Expenses................................... XXX	
	Due to the General Fund...................	XXX

Such treatment is necessary for the proper determination of a proprietary fund's operation and for rate setting.

ENTERPRISE FUNDS

Enterprise funds account for goods or services provided by a governmental unit to the general public. The user is charged for these goods or services, based on consumption. For example, the operations of utilities, public housing, public parking, municipal solid waste landfills, economic development corporations, cultural activities, and airports would be covered by enterprise funds. These funds continue indefinitely and are self-supporting, depending upon the amounts charged to cover part or all of the costs of operation, debt service, and maintenance of capital facilities. Net income is accumulated in an account labeled Unreserved Retained Earnings. To remain self-sustaining, the fund must deduct depreciation expense in the determination of net income. Losses eventually would require either an increase in charges or a contribution from some other source.

At the inception of an enterprise fund (or internal service fund), capital must be provided either by issuance of long-term debt or by transfer from some other source, such as a municipality's general fund. In the latter case, the amount received is credited to an account labeled *Residual Equity Transfer* from the general fund. At the end of the year, the residual equity transfer is closed into Contributed Capital—from Municipality. Note the similarity of this account to the paid-in capital account of a corporation. As a measure of original asset sources, the contribution remains in the fund indefinitely or until the fund is terminated. If operations are profitable and arrangements specify that profits shall be shared with the general fund, an amount analogous to a dividend is charged against Unreserved Retained Earnings. Financing may also be provided from loans or advanced by the municipality. In such cases, the loans or advances are recorded as payables in the proprietary funds and receivables in the general fund.

Contributed capital also is increased when capital assets financed by special assessments are acquired by an enterprise fund. When special assessments are levied, instead of crediting Revenues (Control) as is done in governmental funds, Contributed Capital from Special Assessments is credited. Upon acquisition or completion of the capital asset, its cost is capitalized in the enterprise fund.

An enterprise fund's operational efficiency may be monitored in part by the net income or net loss figure. As in commercial operations, budgets are prepared. However, budgets are not recorded formally in the accounts, perhaps because the fund's self-supporting nature requires a high degree of operational freedom, but more likely because fixed budgetary amounts would be of much less value when there is a variable demand by the public for goods and services.

Control accounts for revenues and expenses commonly are used, with details in supporting records. In accounting for revenues, two control accounts are used: Operating Revenues (Control) for charges for services and Nonoperating Revenues (Control) for grants received, interest and rent earned, or other miscellaneous financial revenues. A similar breakdown is used to account for expenses: Operating Expenses (Control) for expenses directly related to goods or services produced, such as salaries, depreciation, heat, light, materials, and taxes, and Nonoperating Expenses (Control) for financial expenses, such as bond interest. Except for the use of these four nominal control accounts, journal entries for revenues and expenses, including adjustments, are much the same as in private enterprise accounting.

One of the unusual features of accounting for enterprise funds is the introduction of restricted assets and the current liabilities to be paid therewith. *Restricted assets* are assets (cash and investments) upon which some limitation has been imposed that makes them available only for designated purposes. Examples of restricted assets are amounts of customer deposits subject to refund, proceeds from long-term debt for construction, and monies set aside for bond interest or principal redemption.

Restricted assets and their related current liabilities must be recorded in specially designated accounts so that the segregation of these items is ensured. For example, if a water utility receives deposits covering meter installations for customers and these deposits are refundable, they would be recorded as follows:

Restricted Assets—Customers' Deposits Cash XXX
    Customers' Deposits Payable from Restricted Assets   XXX

If the deposits are invested, the entry to record the investment would be:

Restricted Assets—Customers' Deposits Investments XXX
    Restricted Assets—Customers' Deposits Cash   XXX

The existence of restricted assets and their related current liabilities is especially common when an enterprise fund is used to account for a public utility. A major source of funding for utilities is the sale of revenue bonds, which are floated to permit the construction of, or an addition to, a facility. Since payments for these bonds depend on the existence of operating income, the bond indenture usually includes several restrictions. For example, it may require that the bond proceeds be expended only for construction, making the proceeds a restricted asset. The following entry would be required:

Restricted Assets—Revenue Bond Construction Cash XXX
    Revenue Bonds Payable   XXX

As amounts are committed, the liability would be identified as payable from a restricted asset.

Construction in Process XXX
    Construction Contracts Payable from Restricted Assets   XXX

Payment of the liability would be recorded with the following entry:

Construction Contracts Payable from Restricted Assets   XXX
    Restricted Assets—Revenue Bond Construction Cash   XXX

If a municipality received approval to expand its utility facilities by issuing a combination of special assessment bonds and revenue bonds, the following entry would be required in an enterprise fund:

Restricted Assets—Construction Cash   XXX
    Special Assessment Bonds Payable.   XXX
    Revenue Bonds Payable   XXX

Note that the redemption and servicing of both the revenue bonds and the special assessment bonds are the financial responsibility of the utility enterprise

---

Illustration 17-8

Clermont County
Water and Sewer Fund
Balance Sheet
December 31, 19X3

Assets

Current assets:		
Cash	$ 257,036	
Receivables (net)	33,480	
Inventories and prepaid expenses	24,230	
Total current assets		$ 314,746
Restricted assets:		
Cash with fiscal agent for bond service	$ 80,444	
Revenue bond construction cash	17,760	
Revenue bond debt service cash	5,000	
Revenue bond fund:		
Cash	$ 10,355	
Investments	113,800	124,155
Customers' deposits:		
Investments	$ 63,000	
Interest receivable on investments.	650	63,650
Total restricted assets		291,009
Property, plant, and equipment:		
Land	$ 211,100	
Buildings	$ 447,700	
Less accumulated depreciation.	90,718	356,982
Improvements other than buildings.	$3,887,901	
Less accumulated depreciation.	348,944	3,538,957
Machinery and equipment.	$1,841,145	
Less accumulated depreciation.	201,138	1,640,007
Construction in process	22,713	
Total property, plant, and equipment.		5,769,759
Total assets		$6,375,514

fund. Therefore, the liability appears in the enterprise fund balance sheet rather than the general long-term debt account group.

The balance sheet of a commercial utility may begin with its fixed assets because they are extremely important. However, the combining of the balance sheet of a government-owned utility with the balance sheets of other governmental funds is simplified if the conventional sequence is followed. The balance sheet for the Clermont County Water and Sewer Fund, in Illustration 17-8 on pages 924 and 925, adheres to such a presentation, with restricted assets following the regular current assets and preceding the fixed assets. Note also that current liabilities are segregated to show amounts payable from regular current assets and amounts payable from restricted assets.

Liabilities and Fund Equity		
Liabilities:		
Current liabilities (payable from current assets):		
Vouchers payable	$ 195,071	
Accrued wages and taxes payable.	2,870	
Construction contracts payable	8,347	$ 206,288
Current liabilities (payable from restricted assets):		
Construction contracts payable	$ 17,760	
Accrued revenue bond interest payable.	32,444	
Matured revenue bonds payable.	48,000	
Customer deposits	63,000	161,204
Total current liabilities.		$ 367,492
Long-term liabilities:		
Revenue bonds payable.		2,448,000
Total liabilities.		$2,815,492
Fund equity:		
Contributed capital:		
Contribution from municipality.		$1,392,666
Retained earnings:		
Reserved for bond debt service	$ 5,000	
Reserved for bond retirement.	124,155	
Total reserved.	$ 129,155	
Unreserved.	2,038,201	
Total retained earnings.		2,167,356
Total fund equity		$3,560,022
Total liabilities and fund equity.		$6,375,514

Most revenue bonds for enterprise funds are serial bonds that require the earmarking of monies for the payment of interest and for the establishment of a fund for principal redemption. These resources are labeled restricted assets. The current interest and serial installment payables are recorded as current liabilities payable from restricted assets. To further protect the bondholder, at least psychologically, many serial revenue bonds require that unreserved retained earnings be restricted in an amount equal to the excess of restricted assets related to debt service of the bond issue over the current liability for interest and principal. If the amounts in the Water and Sewer Fund balance sheet (Illustration 17-8) are compared with assumed amounts at the end of the previous year, the additional amount to be reserved would be determined as follows:

	Dec. 31 19X3	Dec. 31 19X2 (assumed)
Restricted assets related to revenue bonds:		
Cash with fiscal agent for bond service	$ 80,444	$ 87,200
Revenue bond debt service cash	5,000	3,000
Revenue bond fund	124,155	93,975
Total	$209,599	$184,175
Current liabilities related to revenue bonds:		
Accrued revenue bond interest payable	$ 32,444	$ 37,200
Matured revenue bonds payable	48,000	50,000
Total	$ 80,444	$ 87,200
Excess of bond-related restricted assets over bond-related current liabilities	$129,155	$ 96,975

If the bond indenture requires that the reserves be increased to equal the bond-related restricted assets that are not offset by bond-related current liabilities, the following entry becomes necessary:

Retained Earnings—Unreserved ($129,155 − $96,975)	32,180	
Retained Earnings—Reserved for Bond Debt Service		
($5,000 − $3,000)		2,000
Retained Earnings—Reserved for Bond Retirement		
($124,155 − $93,975)		30,180

The statement of revenues, expenses (not expenditures), and changes in retained earnings for an enterprise fund, as shown in the *GASB Codification of Governmental Accounting and Financial Reporting,* focuses on total retained earnings, both reserved and unreserved. Such a statement for the Clermont County Water and Sewer Fund is shown in Illustration 17-9.

In 1989, the GASB issued Statement No. 9, *Reporting Cash Flows of Proprietary and Nonexpendable Trust Funds and Governmental Entities That Use Proprietary Fund Accounting.* It stipulated that a statement of cash flows for such funds should show movements of combined unrestricted and restricted cash and cash equivalents for the reported period, segregated into four categories:

1. Cash flows from *operating* activities, which would include cash received from sales of goods or services and cash paid to suppliers, employees, and providers of services.
2. Cash flows from *noncapital financing activities*, which would include proceeds from borrowings not related to capital asset acquisition and repayments thereon, as well as operating grants or transfers not related to capital asset acquisition.
3. Cash flows from *capital and related financing activities* to acquire or dispose of capital assets, which would include grants or transfers related to capital asset acquisition.
4. Cash flows from *investing* activities.

The statement of cash flows should report net cash provided or used for each of the four categories. This objective can be accomplished by using the direct method, as shown in Illustration 17-10A for a hypothetical electric utility. The GASB recommends the use of this method. In addition, a reconciliation of net *operating* income to net cash flow from operating activities (Category 1) must be provided in a separate schedule to accompany the cash flows statement or in the

---

Illustration 17-9
Enterprise Fund

Clermont County
Water and Sewer Fund
Statement of Revenues, Expenses, and Changes in Retained Earnings
For Year Ended December 31, 19X3

Operating revenues:		
Charges for services		$ 727,150
Operating expenses:		
Personnel services (salaries and fees)	$306,100	
Materials and supplies	106,580	
Depreciation	103,600	
Heat, light, power, and taxes	47,900	
Total operating expenses		564,180
Operating income		$ 162,970
Nonoperating revenues (expenses):		
Operating grants	$ 5,000	
Interest revenue	2,830	
Rental income	1,000	
Interest expense	(92,988)	
Total nonoperating revenues (expenses)		(84,158)
Net income		$ 78,812
Retained earnings at beginning of year (reserved and		
unreserved)		2,088,544
Retained earnings at end of year (reserved and		
unreserved)		$2,167,356

Illustration 17-10A

Zenith City

Electric Utility Fund

Statement of Cash Flows

Increase (Decrease) in Cash and Cash Equivalents

For Year Ended June 30, 19X3

Cash flows from operating activities:		
Cash received from customers	$456,000	
Cash paid to suppliers and employees	(400,300)	
Other operating revenues.	7,500	
Net cash provided by operating activities		$ 63,200
Cash flows from noncapital financing activities:		
Net repayments under revolving loan arrangement.	$ (10,700)	
Operating grants received	50,000	
Operating transfers-out to other funds	(37,500)	
Net cash provided by noncapital financing activities . . .		1,800
Cash flows from capital and related financing activities:		
Proceeds from sale of capital bonds.	$125,000	
Principal and interest paid on capital bonds.	(100,000)	
Acquisition and construction of capital assets	(75,000)	
Proceeds from sale of equipment.	70,000	
Net cash provided by capital and related financing activities.		20,000
Cash flows from investing activities:		
Purchases of investment securities.	$ (62,500)	
Proceeds from sale and maturities of securities.	36,500	
Interest and dividends received on investments	3,000	
Net cash used in investing activities.		(23,000)
Net increase in cash and cash equivalents		$ 62,000
Cash and cash equivalents at beginning of year		100,000
Cash and cash equivalents at end of year.		$162,000

notes to the financial statements. Such a reconciliation is presented in Illustration 17-10B on page 929.

If a municipality operates more than one enterprise fund, combining statements are required in order to disclose the detail of each fund. GASB standards also require that segment information for major nonhomogeneous enterprise funds be presented to prevent misleading financial statements. Presentation of segment information in the notes to the financial statements is preferable, but some information may be in the combining statements. Examples of segments include utility operations, parking operations, cultural activities, and economic developments. Disclosures include material operating subsidies and material enterprise fund tax revenues, operating income (loss), and net income (loss).

Illustration 17-10B		
Zenith City		
Electric Utility Fund		
Reconciliation of Net Operating Income to Net Cash Provided by		
Operating Activities		
For Year Ended June 30, 19X3		
Net operating income (loss)............................		($ 49,800)
Adjustments to reconcile net operating income to		
net cash provided by operating activities:		
Depreciation	$122,000	
Provision for uncollectible accounts..................	1,000	
Changes in assets and liabilities:		
Increase in accounts receivable....................	(15,000)	
Decrease in inventory	2,000	
Decrease in prepaid expenses......................	500	
Increase in accounts payable......................	2,500	
Total adjustments..............................		113,000
Net cash provided by operating activities.................		$ 63,200

INTERNAL SERVICE FUNDS

Internal service funds are similar to enterprise funds in that they are self-sustaining, depend on amounts charged for services rendered, and receive start-up resources. The difference is that users of their services are other departments of the same governmental unit or other governmental units. A computer center, a printing department, a central purchasing department, a central garage, and risk financing and self-insurance activities are accounted for in internal service funds.

Since internal service funds do not deal with the general public and usually do not issue bonds that result in restrictions, they do not have restricted assets. Their accounting procedures resemble those for a commercial business. Internal service funds must recover their costs, including depreciation, or be subsidized. Therefore, they maintain records of fixed assets and use the accrual basis of accounting. Budgetary accounts are not used, although budget forecasts facilitate the calculation of overhead rates to be applied in determining charges.

As discussed for enterprise funds, the establishment of an internal service fund may be by a contribution or an advance from the municipality. Charges to customer departments are considered quasi-external transactions and appear as expenditures in the governmental funds, expenses in the other proprietary funds, and revenue to the internal service fund.

The financial statements of internal service funds consist of the balance sheet, the statement of revenues, expenses, and changes in retained earnings, and the statement of cash flows. When more than one internal service fund exists, combining statements are prepared. These statements closely resemble commercial financial statements and will not be illustrated.

FIDUCIARY FUNDS: TRUST AND AGENCY FUNDS

As mentioned in Chapter 16, fiduciary funds account for resources for which a governmental unit is acting as a trustee or agent. This category of funds includes expendable trust funds, nonexpendable trust funds, pension trust funds, and agency funds.

TRUST FUNDS

Assets held by a governmental unit that functions as a trustee may be donated by a corporation or by an individual for the educational or cultural benefit of the community. The accounting for these assets and the operation of the trust fund depend on the document that created the fund. If both the assets contributed (the principal) and the earnings may be expended, the fund is an *expendable trust fund*, which is accounted for on a modified accrual basis, in much the same manner as a governmental fund. Budgetary accounts are essential for monitoring expenditures of the principal and income. Since they are similar to governmental funds, expendable trust funds will not be reviewed.

If earnings but not principal may be expended, the fund is a *nonexpendable trust fund*. These funds are accounted for in much the same manner as proprietary funds. Nonexpendable trust funds result from the acceptance of assets that are invested to produce earnings for a designated purpose. For example, a donor might contribute real property and investments, designating that earnings be used to enhance a city's art collection. Depreciation on real property included in the principal of the trust would be recognized in order to protect that principal. It also would be essential to differentiate between principal items and revenue items. The most complete segregation will result if two endowment funds are established—one to record principal items and another to account for the earnings. The procedure becomes especially useful if bonds are purchased at a premium as part of the trust fund. Cash flows and available revenue are not identical because of the amortization of the premium. The segregation process protects the principal.

When donors establish a nonexpendable trust, the assets donated are credited to Fund Balance in the endowment principal trust fund. Later, revenues earned are credited to Revenues (Control). A liability to the endowment earnings fund for the period's interest earnings is established and a debit is made to recognize the operating transfer.

The only source of assets for the endowment earnings fund is the net earnings transferred from the endowment principal fund. These earnings are credited to Other Financing Sources (Control). Distributions of such revenues are recorded as expenditures. In the year-end closing process of the endowment earnings fund, any difference between the amounts received from the principal fund and total expenditures is closed to Fund Balance—Reserved for Endowments, which indicates that the undistributed assets are restricted.

The procedures for both the endowment principal trust fund and the endowment earnings fund for Cedar City are illustrated by the events and entries shown on pages 932–933.

The financial statements for the endowment principle trust fund (a nonexpendable trust fund) are a balance sheet, a statement of revenues, expenses, and changes in fund balances, and a statement of cash flows. The financial statements of the endowment earnings trust fund (an expendable trust) are a balance sheet, and a statement of revenues, expenditures, and changes in fund balances. These statements isolate principal and earnings components. Balance sheets for Cedar City's Governmental Accounting Scholarship Fund are shown in Illustration 17-11.

PENSION TRUST FUNDS

Public employees retirement system funds are accounted for in *pension trust funds.* In no other area of accounting is actuarial assistance so vital. Abiding by the requirements of the retirement plan and considering the employee popula-

---

Illustration 17-11
Cedar City
Endowment Principal Trust Fund
Balance Sheet
For Period Ended December 31, 19X3

Assets

Cash	$10,640
Investments	40,000
Unamortized premiums on investments	360
	$51,000

Liabilities and Fund Balance

Due to Endowment Earnings Fund	$ 1,000
Fund Balance—Nonexpendable	50,000
	$51,000

Cedar City
Endowment Earnings Trust Fund
Balance Sheet
For Period Ended December 31, 19X3

Assets

Cash	$ 500
Due from Endowment Principal Fund	1,000
	$ 1,500

Fund Balance

Fund Balance—Reserved for Endowments	$ 1,500

tion as to age, gender, marital status, and the myriad of other variables that affect working lives and retirement, actuaries must estimate the amount of resources necessary as of a given date to meet retirement commitments. To protect the employees' interests, pension trust funds should use a full accrual basis of accounting.

Contributions to a retirement plan may be from both employer and employees (a contributory plan) or from employer only (a noncontributory plan). Employees who resign usually have the option to withdraw their own contributions (but not the employer's contributions) or to leave them in the plan as vested amounts, providing certain requirements are met. The amounts belong to the employee, who will have access to them upon meeting prescribed retirement conditions.

Increases in the resources of pension trust funds result from employee and employer contributions and investment earnings and are recorded as operating revenues. Decreases in resources result from payments to retired employees and from refunds and are treated as operating expenses.

All assets of a pension trust belong to the employees, and claims against these assets are reflected in either the liabilities or the restricted fund balance reserves. To indicate that there is a restriction against all resources, journal entries record reservations of the pension trust fund balance. The reserved fund balances represent resources associated with specific employee groups supporting the various stages of the retirement plan. There are four reserves commonly used in pension trust funds:

1. *Fund Balance—Reserve for Employee Contributions* represents the amount of accumulated contributions made by nonretired participating employees, plus earnings on these contributions.

Event
Cedar City receives an endowment of $50,000 to establish a nonexpendable trust fund whose revenue is to be used to encourage students to study governmental accounting.
9% bonds with a face value of $40,000 are purchased at 101, maturing in 10 years. The premium will be amortized using the straight-line method.
Bond interest of $3,600 is received.
The liability to endowment revenues fund for net revenue is recorded.
Cash due is remitted.
A grant of $3,000 is given to a student.
Books are closed at year end.

2. *Fund Balance—Reserve for Employer Contributions* represents the amount of accumulated contributions made by the employer pertaining to nonretired participating employees, plus earnings on these contributions. This account is increased for any unfunded liability resulting from actuarial valuation.

3. *Fund Balance—Benefit and Disability Reserve* represents amounts transferred from the first two reserves upon the retirement or disability of an employee, plus earnings on amounts transferred.

4. *Fund Balance—Undistributed Investment Earnings Reserve* represents amounts earned on assets attributable to the first three reserves, but not yet allocated to them.

In addition to the reserved fund balances, there is the account Fund Balance—Unreserved, Undesignated that typically has a debit balance representing the shortage of net assets (the actuarial deficiency) to cover the total amount reserved for the retirement system.

To demonstrate the accounting process for a pension trust fund, the journal entries recording each event and its effect on the reserves for Desert City's pension trust fund for employees' retirement are shown on pages 934 and 935. All entries illustrated are made in one trust fund and represent amounts for the entire year. The journal entries for the original events record asset inflows and outflows and are similar to entries shown previously for other funds. The revenue and expense accounts are closed to the unreserved fund balance, and the reserve accounts are adjusted for the amounts of revenue and expense that ultimately affect them. The entries in the reserve accounts, shown on page 935, are made periodically, usually at year end, in order to update the status of the reserves that represent the assets.

Entries in Endowment Principal Trust Fund (Nonexpendable Trust)			Entries in Endowment Earnings Trust Fund (Expendable Trust)		
Cash............................	50,000		No entry.		
Fund Balance		50,000			
Investments	40,000		No entry.		
Unamortized Premium................	400				
Cash............................		40,400			
Cash............................	3,600		No entry.		
Unamortized Premium.............		40			
Revenues (Control).................		3,560			
Operating Transfer Out (Control).........	3,560		Due from Endowment Principal Fund	3,560	
Due to Endowment Earnings Fund		3,560	Other Financing Sources (Control)		3,560
Due to Endowment Revenues Fund	3,560		Cash............................	3,560	
Cash............................		3,560	Due from Endowment Principal Fund ..		3,560
No entry.			Expenditures (Control)................	3,000	
			Cash............................		3,000
Revenues (Control)...................	3,560		Other Financing Sources (Control)	3,560	
Operating Transfer Out		3,560	Expenditures (Control)..............		3,000
			Fund Balance—Reserved for		
			Endowments....................		560

The two entries for reinstatement to the unreserved fund balance of $20,500 and $9,000, respectively, need further explanation. Payments to retired employees or payments to employees who resign and withdraw their contributions are debited to Operating Expenses (Control). Amounts equal to these payments no longer need to be reserved from the fund balance. They are returned to the unreserved fund balance by reversing the entry that created them, using the amount of the payment and the appropriate reserve.

The balance sheet for Desert City's pension trust fund as of December 31, 19X3, is shown in Illustration 17-12 on page 936. The fund has been operating for several years. A feature of the balance sheet is the presence of four reserve accounts, which is understandable because all assets are reserved for the benefit of specific employee groups.

Event	Entry for Original Event		
Cash contributions are received from:	Cash	150,000	
Employees .... $ 60,000	Operating Revenues (Control)......		150,000
Employer............................... 90,000			
Total................................ $150,000			
Earnings of $84,000 on investments are received and $1,200 is accrued.	Cash	84,000	
	Interest Receivable on Investments...	1,200	
	Operating Revenues (Control)......		85,200
Payments of $19,000 are made to retired employees and $1,500 is payable.	Operating Expenses (Control)	20,500	
	Cash		19,000
	Benefits Payable		1,500
Refunds of $6,300 were made and $2,700 is due to employees who resigned and withdrew their contributions.	Operating Expenses (Control)	9,000	
	Cash		6,300
	Due to Resigned Employees........		2,700
Books are closed at year end.	Operating Revenues (Control)........	235,200	
	Operating Expenses (Control)		29,500
	Fund Balance—Unreserved,		
	Undesignated		205,700

Changes in the retirement reserves of a pension trust are so revealing that an analysis of changes in each of the reserves for the year should be prepared. It should be structured with a column for each reserve and a total, showing beginning balances, additions, deductions, and final balances.

The statement of revenues, expenses, and changes in fund balances adheres to the all-inclusive approach, whereby the net income is added to the total of all fund balances at the beginning of the period to yield their total at the end of the period. A statement of cash flows is not required.

The GASB is in the process of developing new guidance for accounting and financial reporting for pension plans. GASB Statement No. 5, issued in 1986, requires extensive footnote disclosure for governmental pension plans as well as ten-year trend data. A recently issued Exposure Draft (March 1994) requires

Closing Entries to Adjust the Reserve Accounts		Closing Entries		
Amounts are reserved, based on contributions.		Fund Balance—Unreserved, Undesignated................	150,000	
		Fund Balance—Member Contributions		60,000
		Fund Balance—Employer Contributions		90,000
Amounts are reserved, based on allocated investment earnings:		Fund Balance—Unreserved, Undesignated................	85,200	
Employees' contributions	$23,000	Fund Balance—Member Contributions		23,000
Employer's contributions...................	37,000	Fund Balance—Employer Contributions		37,000
Benefit and disability	22,000	Fund Balance—Benefit and Disability Reserve		22,000
Undistributed earnings....................	3,200	Fund Balance—Undistributed Investment Earnings Reserve ..		3,200
Total	$85,200			
For retiring employees, transfer from contribution reserves to benefit reserve:		Fund Balance—Member Contributions	6,000	
Of employees...........................	$ 6,000	Fund Balance—Employer Contributions	10,000	
Of employers	10,000	Fund Balance—Benefit and Disability Reserve		16,000
Total	$16,000			
Reinstatement to the unreserved fund balance of amount equal to payments and related liability. (See discussion of this entry on page 934.)		Fund Balance—Benefit and Disability Reserve	20,500	
		Fund Balance—Unreserved, Undesignated..............		20,500
Reinstatement to the unreserved fund balance of amount equal to refunds and related liability. (See discussion of this entry on page 934.)		Fund Balance—Member Contributions	9,000	
		Fund Balance—Unreserved, Undesignated..............		9,000
Adjust balance of employer contribution reserve to reflect revised unfunded liability of $3,000 per periodic actuarial valuation.		Fund Balance—Unreserved, Undesignated................	3,000	
		Fund Balance—Employer Contributions		3,000

Illustration 17-12
Desert City
Employees' Retirement Trust Fund
Balance Sheet
December 31, 19X3

Assets

Cash	$ 76,152
Investments	1,109,549
Interest receivable on investments	1,200
Total assets	$1,186,901

Liabilities and Fund Balances

Liabilities:		
Due to resigned employees	$	2,700
Benefits payable		1,500
Total liabilities	$	4,200
Fund balances:		
Reserved for:		
Employee contributions	$	338,564
Employer contributions		763,155
Benefits and disability		320,782
Undistributed investment earnings		3,200
Total reserved for employees' retirement system		$1,425,701
Unreserved, undesignated		(243,000)
Total fund balances		$1,182,701
Total liabilities and fund balances		$1,186,901

pension expense (or expenditure) for defined benefit plans to be determined on an actuarial basis and recognizes a liability for the portion of the expense that is not funded.

Accounting for postretirement benefits other than pensions (GASB Statement No. 12) also provides disclosure, not accounting guidance, for state and local government employers who provide these benefits. Accounting guidance for postretirement benefits is forthcoming from the GASB.

AGENCY FUNDS

An *agency fund* is required when money collected or withheld, such as deductions from government employees' salaries for social security or for hospitalization premiums, must be forwarded to the proper destination. Agency funds frequently have no end-of-period balances because money is transferred prior to the end of the period. When the money has not been forwarded, a liability to the ultimate recipient is shown. There is no fund balance, and the only financial statement would be a balance sheet listing the assets held and the related liabilities, supported by a statement of changes in assets and liabilities. The latter statement shows for each asset and liability its beginning balance, any additions or deletions, and the final balance. If the agency fund is to receive a fee for its services, the amount usually is recorded as a liability to the general fund of the governmental unit. The general fund records a receivable and revenue if the amount is to be collected within the current period. For example, state law may give a county the responsibility for collecting property taxes levied within its boundaries, with the county receiving a fee to cover its administration of the plan. The county, as well as each political subdivision, would record its share of taxes receivable in its general fund. The tax agency fund of Zee County would make the following series of entries for the events described:

Event	Entry in Tax Agency Fund		

Gross taxes receivable to be collected for all units are as follows:

		Taxes Receivable for All Units	1,000,000	
Zee County	$ 300,000	Due to Other Governmental Units		1,000,000
X City	600,000			
T Town	100,000			
Total	$1,000,000			

Entry in Zee County general fund:
Taxes Receivable	300,000	
Revenue		300,000

Taxes are collected.

Cash	1,000,000	
Taxes Receivable for All Units		1,000,000

The liability to each unit is recorded, net of 2% fee earned by the county for collection and processing for other units. (The county would not charge itself a fee.) The fee is to be remitted to the county general fund.

Due to Other Governmental Units	1,000,000	
Due to Zee County General Fund		314,000
Due to X City		588,000
Due to T Town		98,000

Entry in Zee County general fund:
Due from Agency Fund	314,000	
Taxes Receivable		300,000
Revenue		14,000

Cash is released to each governmental unit.

Due to Zee County General Fund	314,000	
Due to X City	588,000	
Due to T Town	98,000	
Cash		1,000,000

Entry in Zee County general fund:
Cash	314,000	
Due from Agency Fund		314,000

The general fund of X City records the receipt of cash from the tax agency fund, net of the fee, as follows:

Cash (for net proceeds)	588,000	
Expenditures (Control) (for fee charged)	12,000	
Taxes Receivable—Current		600,000

Agency funds also are used in the case of a capital project undertaken by a governmental unit in which special assessment bonds were issued, but for which the unit has no financial responsibility in case of nonpayment. The unit functions as an agent, a financial conduit between the bondholders and the owners of the assessed property. When property owners are assessed, an entry is recorded in the agency fund:

Special Assessments Receivable—Current...................... XXX
Special Assessments Receivable—Deferred XXX
    Due to Special Assessment Bond Creditors XXX

When collections from assessed property owners are received by the agency fund, this entry is made:

Cash.. XXX
    Special Assessments Receivable—Current...................... XXX
    Due to Special Assessment Bond Creditors (Interest) XXX

Upon payment to the bondholders, the entry is:

Due to Special Assessment Bond Creditors XXX
Due to Special Assessment Bond Creditors (interest) XXX
    Cash.. XXX

Neither the liability for principal repayment nor the debt service expenditures are recorded in any other fund or group because the governmental unit was not obligated in any manner.

GOVERNMENTAL ACCOUNTING—INTERACTIONS AMONG FUNDS

In governmental accounting, each fund or group is a separate accounting entity, entrusted to record only a limited phase of an event. Complete recording, as shown in Chapters 16 and 17, often involves more than one fund or group. In addition, transactions among funds are frequent. Throughout this and the previous chapter, interfund transactions have been defined. They include (1) operating transfers, (2) residual equity transfers, and (3) quasi-external transactions. Another interfund transaction is a reimbursement. One fund may reimburse another for supplies, or other items paid on its behalf. For example, the general fund might pay the entire rental of a facility even though the facility is to be used for both the general government and activities of a special revenue fund. When the expenditure is made by the general fund, the entry is:

Expenditures.. XXX
    Cash.. XXX

When the reimbursement is received from the special revenue fund for its share of the rent, the entries in each fund are:

General fund: Cash................................. XXX
                           Expenditures........................ XXX
Special revenue fund: Expenditures........................ XXX
                           Cash............................. XXX

To serve as a reference and to review governmental accounting, Illustration 17-13 on pages 940 and 941 is a matrix of selected events that are recorded in more than one fund or group. Used in the matrix are the four governmental funds (general, special revenue, debt service, and capital projects), the two types of proprietary funds (enterprise and internal service), a trust and agency fund, and the two account groups for general fixed assets and general long-term debt.

The entries to record the events related to the fourteen events in the matrix are as follows:

Journal Entries for Transactions Affecting More than One Fund

	Funds	Accounts		
1.	General Fund	Expenditures (Control)	40,000	
		Vouchers Payable		40,000
	General Fixed Assets Account Group	Equipment	40,000	
		Investment in General Fixed Assets—General Fund Revenues		40,000
2.	Capital Projects Fund	Cash	508,000	
		Other Financing Sources (Control)		508,000
		Other Financing Uses (Control)	8,000	
		Cash		8,000
	Debt Service Fund	Cash	8,000	
		Other Financing Sources (Control)		8,000
	General Long-Term Debt Account Group	Amount to Be Provided for Payment of Serial Bonds	500,000	
		Serial Bonds Payable		500,000
3.	General Fund	Other Financing Uses (Control)	150,000	
		Cash		150,000
	Debt Service Fund	Cash	150,000	
		Other Financing Sources (Control)		150,000
	General Long-Term Debt Account Group	Amount Available in Debt Service Fund—Serial Bonds	100,000	
		Amount to Be Provided for Payment of Serial Bonds		100,000
4.	Debt Service Fund	Expenditures (Control)	150,000	
		Matured Bonds Payable		100,000
		Matured Interest Payable		50,000
		Cash with Fiscal Agent	150,000	
		Cash		150,000
		Matured Bonds Payable	100,000	
		Matured Interest Payable	50,000	
		Cash with Fiscal Agent		150,000
	General Long-Term Debt Account Group	Serial Bonds Payable	100,000	
		Amount Available in Debt Service Fund—Serial Bonds		100,000
5.	Capital Projects Fund	Expenditures (Control)	50,000	
		Cash		50,000
	General Fixed Assets Account Group	Improvements Other than Buildings	200,000	
		Construction in Progress		150,000
		Investments in General Fixed Assets—Capital Projects Funds (Special Assessments)		50,000
6.	General Fund	Due from Enterprise Fund	5,000	
		Revenues (Control)		5,000
	Enterprise Fund	Property Tax Expense	5,000	
		Due to General Fund		5,000
7.	Internal Service Fund	Due from General Fund	12,000	
		Due from Special Revenue Fund	20,000	
		Revenues (Control)		32,000

(continued)

Funds	Accounts		
General Fund	Expenditures (Control)	12,000	
	Due to Internal Service Fund		12,000
Special Revenue Fund	Expenditures (Control)	20,000	
	Due to Internal Service Fund		20,000
8. General Fund	Residual Equity Transfer to Nonexpendable Trust Fund..........	98,500	
	Cash..		98,500
Nonexpendable Trust Fund	Cash..	98,500	
	Residual Equity Transfer from General Fund (Contributed Capital)..		98,500
9. General Fund	Expenditures (Control)	16,000	
	Cash..		16,000
Nonexpendable Pension Trust Fund	Cash..	16,000	
	Revenues (Control)......................................		16,000
10. Special Revenue Fund	Expenditures (Control)	15,000	
	Cash..		15,000
General Fund	Cash..	15,000	
	Expenditures (Control)		15,000

(continued)

Illustration 17-13

Matrix of Selected Events Requiring Entry in More than One Fund or Account Group

Events to Be Recorded

1. Purchase of equipment with general fund resources for $40,000.
2. Issuance of $500,000 of general obligation serial bonds at an $8,000 premium for city hall construction.
3. Transfer by general fund to meet $100,000 matured serial bonds and $50,000 interest payments.

4. Payment of $50,000 bond interest and $100,000 matured serial bonds. Fiscal agent is used for payment.
5. Completion of special assessment construction project. $150,000 paid to date, $50,000 final payment.
6. Levy of $5,000 property taxes by general fund against city's utility (quasi-external).

7. Billing of general and special revenue funds for central computer service ($12,000 and $20,000) (quasi-external).
8. Contribution made by city to establish a nonexpendable trust fund of $98,500.
9. Remittance of the city's $16,000 share of pension fund costs for current period.

10. Reimbursement of $15,000 by the special revenue fund to the general fund for general government supplies expenditures initially made in the general fund properly charged to a community development project.
11. Recording of depreciation, $6,000 enterprise fund, $13,000 internal service fund.
12. Redemption of final $100,000 serial of general obligation bonds, with $3,000 deficiency covered by general fund. Fiscal agent is used for payment.

13. Closing entry for capital projects fund involving a partially completed project. Cost to date is $130,000; revenues during the period are $300,000.
14. Payroll expenditures totaled $5,000 and included $1,000 payroll withholdings for taxes and insurance plus employer's share of these costs. $1,000 is transferred to an agency fund for remittance as follows: Private insurance company, $200; federal government, $600; and state government, $150. The agency fund makes the remittances.

Funds	Accounts		
11. Enterprise Fund	Depreciation Expense	6,000	
	Accumulated Depreciation		6,000
Internal Service Fund	Depreciation Expense	13,000	
	Accumulated Depreciation		13,000
12. General Fund	Other Financing Uses (Control).	3,000	
	Cash.		3,000
Debt Service Fund	Cash.	3,000	
	Other Financing Sources (Control)		3,000
	Cash with Fiscal Agent	100,000	
	Cash.		100,000
	Expenditures (Control)	100,000	
	Matured Bonds Payable.		100,000
	Matured Bonds Payable.	100,000	
	Cash with Fiscal Agent		100,000
General Long-Term Debt Account Group	Amounts Available in Debt Service Fund	100,000	
	Amount to Be Provided for Payment of Serial Bonds		100,000
	Serial Bonds Payable	100,000	
	Amounts Available in Debt Service Fund		100,000

(continued)

	Governmental Funds				Proprietary Funds		Fiduciary Fund	Account Groups		
General	Special Revenue	Debt Service	Capital Projects	Enter-prise	Internal Service	Trust and Agency	General Fixed Assets	General Long-Term Debt	
X	—	—	—	—	—	—	X	—	1.
—	—	X	X	—	—	—	—	X	2.
X	—	X	—	—	—	—	—	X	3.
—	—	X	—	—	—	—	—	X	4.
—	—	—	X	—	—	—	X	—	5.
X	—	—	—	X	—	—	—	—	6.
X	X	—	—	—	X	—	—	—	7.
X	—	—	—	—	—	X	—	—	8.
X	—	—	—	—	—	X	—	—	9.
X	X	—	—	—	—	—	—	—	10.
—	—	—	—	X	X	—	—	—	11.
X	—	X	—	—	—	—	—	X	12.
—	—	—	X	—	—	—	X	—	13.
X	—	—	—	—	—	X	—	—	14.

Funds	Accounts		
13. Capital Projects Fund	Revenues (Control)...	300,000	
	Expenditure (Control)......................................		130,000
	Fund Balance—Unreserved, Undesignated		170,000
General Fixed Assets Account Group	Construction in Progress....................................	130,000	
	Investment in General Fixed Assets—Capital Projects Fund		130,000
14. General Fund	Expenditures (Control)	5,000	
	Due to Agency Fund		1,000
	Cash...		4,000
Agency Fund	Due from General Fund.....................................	1,000	
	Due to Insurance Company................................		200
	Due to Federal Government		650
	Due to State		150
General Fund	Due to Agency Fund	1,000	
	Cash...		1,000
Agency Fund	Cash..	1,000	
	Due from General Fund....................................		1,000
	Due to Insurance Company................................	200	
	Due to Federal Government	650	
	Due to State	150	
	Cash...		1,000

Illustration 17-15 on page 946 provides a summary of governmental accounting and financial reporting principles.

ANNUAL FINANCIAL REPORTING

The principal role of financial reporting is to provide information. A Comprehensive Annual Financial Report should be prepared by every governmental unit in order to demonstrate that it has complied with the provisions of the law. The comprehensive annual financial report includes at least two sets of financial statements, along with their notes and any additional data that may be considered necessary. These two sets are (1) the general purpose combined financial statements and (2) combining statements by fund type. General purpose com-

Combined Balance Sheet—All Fund Types and Account Groups
December 31, 19X4

	Governmental Funds				Proprietary Funds		Fiduciary Funds	Account Groups		Totals (Memorandum Only)	
	General	Special Revenue	Debt Service	Capital Projects	Enter-prise	Internal Service	Trust and Agency	General Fixed Assets	Long-Term Debt	December 31, 19X4	December 31, 19X3
Assets:											
Cash	$258,500	$101,385	$ 43,834	$431,600	$257,036	$ 29,700	$ 216,701			$1,338,756	$1,258,909
Cash with fiscal agent			102,000							102,000	
Investments at cost or amortized cost	65,000	37,200	160,990				1,239,260			1,502,450	1,974,354

Combined Statement of Revenues, Expenditures, and Changes in Fund Balances
All Governmental Funds and Expendable Trust Funds
For Fiscal Year Ended December 31, 19X4

| | Governmental Funds | | | | Fiduciary Funds | Totals (Memorandum Only) Year Ended | |
	General	Special Revenue	Debt Service	Capital Projects	Expendable Trust	December 31, 19X4	December 31, 19X3
Revenues:							
Taxes	$881,300	$189,300	$79,177			$1,149,777	$1,137,900
Special assessments levied				$240,000		240,000	250,400
Licenses and permits	103,000					103,000	96,500

bined financial statements furnish in columnar form an overview of the financial position of all funds and account groups and the operating results of all funds. The headings of a combined balance sheet and combined statement of revenues, expenditures, and changes in fund balances follow:

A complete set of general purpose combined financial statements would include a:

1. Combined balance sheet for all fund types and account groups.
2. Combined statement of revenues, expenditures, and changes in fund balances for all governmental funds and expendable trust funds.
3. Combined statement of revenues, expenditures, and changes in fund balances—budget and actual for the general and special revenue funds.
4. Combined statement of revenues, expenditures or expenses, and changes in retained earnings or fund balances for all proprietary funds, nonexpendable trust funds, and pension trust funds.
5. Combined statement of cash flows for all proprietary funds and nonexpendable trust funds.
6. Notes to the financial statements including segment information for major nonhomogeneous enterprise funds, schedules of long-term debt, and significant policies.
7. Required supplementary information (e.g., possibly some pension-related information and risk-financing and self-insurance activity).

The general purpose financial statements (GPFS) constitute the minimum financial reporting necessary for a fair presentation in accordance with generally accepted accounting principles. The GPFS are part of the *financial section* of a Comprehensive Annual Financial Report (CAFR) along with the auditor's report and combining, individual fund, and account group statements and/or schedules, which provide more detailed financial information than the combined statements. For example, the combined balance sheet shows that capital projects funds have a cash balance of $431,600. A breakdown of this amount is shown in the following combining balance sheet for all capital projects funds:

	City Hall Project	Gas Pipeline Project	Stadium Project	Totals 19X7	19X6
Capital Projects Funds **Combining Balance Sheets** **December 31, 19X4**					
Assets:					
Cash	$240,000	$108,000	$83,600	$431,600	$237,000

Two sections of the CAFR, which are in addition to the financial section, are the *introductory section* and the *statistical section*. The introductory section of the CAFR includes a table of contents, a letter of transmittal from the chief executive or finance officer to the mayor (or the mayor and legislative body), and other information. The letter of transmittal tells about the contents of the CAFR, management's view of the economic condition of the governmental unit, and the community and management's summary of governmental operating activity. The statistical section reports numerous statistics about the governmental unit and the community, such as general governmental expenditures by function and community demographic statistics.

The GASB Codification of Governmental Accounting and Financial Reporting provides an excellent pyramid of financial reporting, as shown in Illustration 17-14. The top of the pyramid represents highly aggregated consolidated financial statements while the bottom represents details of transactions. Current government financial reporting is in the mid-levels of the pyramid. As GASB continues to deliberate its financial reporting model, the level of detail provided on the financial statements will be discussed. Indeed, the GASB recently sponsored a popular reporting (condensed summary reporting) research project directed at the top of the pyramid financial reporting.

REPORTING ENTITY

GASB Statement No. 14, issued in June 1991, defines the criteria a government must use to determine whether its reporting entity should be limited to the primary government or whether one or more of the associated organizations (referred to as component units) are also part of the government's reporting entity. The criteria are financial accountability as measured by (1) fiscal dependence or (2) the ability of a primary government to impose its will on the potential component unit or (3) the potential to receive specific financial benefit or burden. Typical component units may include authorities, commissions, boards, pension plans, development corporations, hospitals, and school districts.

AUDITS OF STATE AND LOCAL GOVERNMENTS

In order for users of the financial statements to have assurance that the statements are prepared in conformity with accounting and reporting standards set

Illustration 17-14   THE FINANCIAL REPORTING "PYRAMID"

Source: GASB Codification, Section 1900.114.

forth by the GASB, the statements are accompanied by an audit report. Most governments are audited annually because of state or federal requirements or because long-term creditors demand audited statements as part of the debt agreements. The audits of governmental units are broader than audits of a business. The financial audit, which is the primary audit, deals with compliance with fiscal requirements including applicable accounting standards and federal and state laws. Special performance audits of economy and efficiency and program results emphasize managerial effectiveness. Government auditing standards have been developed by the American Institute of Certified Public Accountants (AICPA) and are published in the AICPA audit guide, *Audits of State and Local Governmental Units*.[4]

In 1984, the federal government passed the Single Audit Act requiring audits of all entities receiving federal grants and contracts. The Single Audit Act requires state and local governments that receive $100,000 or more of *federal financial assistance* to have a single audit for that fiscal year, and state and local governments receiving between $25,000 and $100,000 to have either a single audit or a series of separate grant program audits. The act exempts governments receiving less than $25,000 of federal assistance. Audit reports prepared under

---

[4]American Institute of Certified Public Accountants, *Audits of State and Local Governmental Units*, rev. ed. (New York: AICPA, 1986), p. 29.

Illustration 17-15
Summary of Governmental Accounting

	Governmental Funds				Expendable Trust Funds	Nonexpendable Trust Funds		Proprietary Funds		Account Groups	
	General Fund	Special Revenue Funds	Capital Project Funds	Debt Service Funds	Expendable Trust and Agency Funds	Pension Trust Funds	Endowment Principal Funds	Internal Service Funds	Enterprise Funds	General Long-Term Debt Account Group	General Fixed Asset Account Group
Basis of accounting	Modified Accrual	Modified Accrual	Modified Accrual	Modified Accrual	Modified Accrual	Accrual	Accrual	Accrual	Accrual	n/a	n/a
Measurement focus	Flow of Resources	Flow of Resources	Flow of Resources	Flow of Resources	Flow of Resources	Economic Resources	Economic Resources	Economic Resources	Economic Resources	n/a	n/a
Formal recording of budget	Yes	Yes	Optional	No	No	No	No	No	No	n/a	n/a
Encumbrance accounting	Yes	Yes	Yes	No	Optional	No	No	No	No	n/a	n/a
Maintains records of fixed assets	No	No	No	No	No	Yes	Yes	Yes	Yes	n/a	Yes
Maintains records of long-term debt	No	No	No	No	No	Yes	Yes	Yes	Yes	Yes	n/a
Balance Sheet	Yes	Yes	Yes	Yes	Yes	Yes	Yes	Yes	Yes	Yes	Yes
Statement of Revenues, Expenditures, and Changes in Fund Balance	Yes	Yes	Yes	Yes	Yes	No	No	No	No	No	No
Statement of Revenues, Expenditures, and Changes in Fund Balance—Budget and Actual	Yes	Yes	No	No	No	No	No	No	No	No	No
Statement of Revenues, Expenses, and Changes in Retained Earnings	No	No	No	No	No	Yes	Yes	Yes	Yes	No	No
Statement of Cash Flows	No	No	No	No	No	Yes	Yes	Yes	Yes	No	No

the Single Audit Act include (1) an opinion on the fairness of financial statement presentation, (2) a report on the study and evaluation of internal control systems' ability to provide reasonable assurance that federal programs are being managed in compliance with laws and regulations, and (3) a report on compliance with laws and regulations that may have a material effect on specific programs.

QUESTIONS

1. Discuss the similarities between a special revenue fund and a general fund.
2. Why are fixed assets, acquired with proceeds from general obligation bond issues, not permanently accounted for in a capital projects fund?
3. If a capital projects fund has authority to continue operations over several fiscal periods, why is it desirable to close its records at the end of each period?
4. Explain the necessity to introduce a deferred revenues account in the levy of capital special assessments.
5. Give the entry in the general long-term debt account group to record the issuance of bonds related to construction of general fixed assets from special assessments where the governmental unit has assumed responsibility for payment in case of default. Explain the purpose of the entry.
6. The debt service fund does not use budgetary accounts. What is the logic for not doing so?
7. When a debt service fund receives resources, it might credit Revenues (Control) or Other Financing Sources (Control). Under what circumstances would each of these credits be used?
8. What is the characteristic that determines whether an activity should be accounted for in a special revenue fund or in an enterprise fund?
9. What is the appropriate measurement focus applied to enterprise funds, and how does this cause accounting for an enterprise fund to closely resemble accounting for a business enterprise?
10. Describe two major types of interfund transfers. Under what circumstances are each used?
11. What is the difference between an agency fund and a trust fund?
12. What is the difference between an enterprise fund and an internal service fund?
13. Explain the difference between expenses and expenditures in a state and local government.
14. Describe the difference between accounting for governmental funds and proprietary funds.
15. List and describe the nature of the four reserves in the accounting for employees pension trust funds.

EXERCISES

Exercise 1. Select the best answer for each of the following multiple-choice items. (Nos. 2, 3, 5, and 7–10 are AICPA adapted.)

(1) Accounting for special revenue funds closely resembles the accounting for:
    (a) General funds.
    (b) Capital projects funds.
    (c) Enterprise funds.
    (d) Agency funds.

(2) In which of the following fund types of a city government are revenues and expenditures recognized on the same basis of accounting as the general fund?
   (a) Nonexpendable trust.
   (b) Internal service.
   (c) Enterprise.
   (d) Debt service.

(3) Revenues that are legally restricted to expenditures for specified purposes should be accounted for in special revenue funds, including:
   (a) Accumulation of resources for payment of general long-term debt principal and interest.
   (b) Pension trust fund revenues.
   (c) Gasoline taxes to finance road repairs.
   (d) Proprietary fund revenues.

(4) Bonds are issued at a premium by a capital projects fund. The premium should be:
   (a) Retained in the capital projects fund.
   (b) Credited directly to the unreserved fund balance of the capital projects fund.
   (c) Transferred to the debt service funds.
   (d) Used to reduce the net cost of the project involved.

(5) Which of the following funds of a governmental unit recognizes revenues in the accounting period in which they become available and measurable?

	General Fund	Enterprise Fund
(a)	Yes	No
(b)	No	Yes
(c)	Yes	Yes
(d)	No	No

(6) At the beginning of a fiscal period, encumbrances that remained at the previous year end relating to an incomplete project in the capital projects funds generally are reinstated by crediting:
   (a) Fund Balance—Unreserved, Undesignated.
   (b) Fund Balance—Reserved for Encumbrances.
   (c) Encumbrances (Control).
   (d) Expenditures (Control).

(7) On June 28, 19X1, Gold City's debt service fund received funds for the future repayment of bond principal. As a consequence, the general long-term debt account group reported:
   (a) An increase in the amount available in debt service funds and an increase in the fund balance.
   (b) An increase in the amount available in debt service funds and an increase in the amount to be provided for bonds.
   (c) An increase in the amount available in debt service funds and a decrease in the amount to be provided for bonds.
   (d) No changes in any amount until the bond principal is actually paid.

(8) Which of the following statements is correct concerning a governmental entity's combined statement of cash flows?
   (a) Cash flows from capital financing activities are reported separately from cash flows from noncapital financing activities.
   (b) The statement format is the same as that of a business enterprise's statement of cash flows.
   (c) Cash flows from operating activities may not be reported using the indirect method.
   (d) The statement format includes columns for the general, governmental, and proprietary fund types.

(9) In a government's comprehensive annual financial report (CAFR), proprietary fund types are included in which of the following combined financial statements?

	Statement of Revenues, Expenditures, and Changes in Fund Balances	Balance Sheet
(a)	Yes	Yes
(b)	No	No
(c)	No	Yes
(d)	Yes	No

(10) The billings for transportation services provided to other governmental units are recorded by the internal service fund as:
   (a) Interfund exchanges.
   (b) Intergovernmental transfers.
   (c) Transportation appropriations.
   (d) Operating revenues.

Exercise 2. Select the best answer for each of the following multiple-choice items. (Nos. 3, 4, 6, and 7–9 are AICPA adapted.)
(1) Resources for a capital improvement are provided by special assessments. At the start of the second year of the project, a reclassification entry in the debt service fund that debits Deferred Revenues would credit:
   (a) Special Assessments Receivable—Deferred.
   (b) Revenues (Control).
   (c) Unreserved Fund Balance.
   (d) Fund Balance Reserved for Special Assessments.

(2) If a governmental unit makes no guarantees regarding repayment of a capital improvement special assessment bond issue, the liability for the bonds would:
   (a) Not appear in the financial statements or in their notes.
   (b) Not appear in the financial statements, but would appear in the notes to the financial statements.
   (c) Appear in the capital projects funds.
   (d) Appear in the general long-term debt account group.

(3) Gaffney City's serial bonds are serviced through a debt service fund with cash provided by the general fund. In a debt service fund's statements, how are cash receipts and cash payments reported?

	Cash Receipts	Cash Payments
(a)	Revenues	Expenditures
(b)	Revenues	Operating transfers
(c)	Operating transfers	Expenditures
(d)	Operating transfers	Operating transfers

(4) Taxes collected and held by Dunne County for a school district would be accounted for in which of the following funds?
   (a) Trust.
   (b) Agency.
   (c) Special revenue.
   (d) Internal service.

(5) The following is a correct entry:

    Construction in Progress XXX
          Investment in General Fixed Assets—Capital Projects Funds ..   XXX

   The entry would be found in the:
   (a) Capital projects funds.
   (b) Enterprise funds.
   (c) General fund.
   (d) General fixed assets account group.

(6) In a government's comprehensive annual financial report (CAFR), account groups are included in which of the following combined financial statements?

	Balance Sheet	Statement of Revenues, Expenditures, and Changes in Fund Balances
(a)	Yes	No
(b)	No	Yes
(c)	Yes	Yes
(d)	No	No

(7) Clover City's comprehensive annual financial report contains both combining and combined financial statements. Total columns are:
   (a) Required for both combining and combined financial statements.
   (b) Optional, but commonly shown, for combining financial statements and required for combined financial statements.
   (c) Required for combining financial statements and optional, but commonly shown, for combined financial statements.
   (d) Optional, but commonly shown, for both combining and combined financial statements.

(8) In what fund type should the proceeds from special assessment bonds issued to finance construction of sidewalks in a new subdivision be reported?
   (a) Agency fund.
   (b) Special revenue fund.
   (c) Enterprise fund.
   (d) Capital projects fund.

(9) Eureka City should issue a statement of cash flows for which of the following funds?

	Eureka City Hall Capital Projects Fund	Eureka Water Enterprise Fund
(a)	No	Yes
(b)	No	No
(c)	Yes	No
(d)	Yes	Yes

Exercise 3. Select the best response for each of the following multiple-choice questions which refer to the transactions of Finch City. (No. 4 is AICPA adapted.)

On March 2, 19X1, Finch City issued 10-year general obligation bonds at face amount, with interest payable March 1 and September 1. The proceeds were to be used to finance the construction of a civic center over the period April 1, 19X1, to March 31, 19X2. During the fiscal year ended June 30, 19X1, no resources had been provided to the debt service fund for the payment of principal and interest.

(1) On June 30, 19X1, Finch's debt service fund should include interest payable on the general obligation bonds for:

(a) 0 months.   (b) 3 months.   (c) 4 months.   (d) 6 months.

(2) Proceeds from the general obligation bonds should be recorded in the:
(a) General fund.
(b) Capital projects fund.
(c) General long-term debt account group.
(d) Debt service fund.

(3) The liability for the general obligation bonds should be recorded in the:
(a) General fund.
(b) Capital projects fund.
(c) General long-term debt account group.
(d) Debt service fund.

(4) On June 30, 19X1, Finch's combined balance sheet should report the construction in progress for the civic center in the:

	Capital Projects Fund	General Fixed Assets Account Group
(a)	Yes	Yes
(b)	Yes	No
(c)	No	No
(d)	No	Yes

Exercise 4. Prepare journal entries to record the following events. Identify every fund(s) or group of accounts in which an entry is made.
(a) The city authorized the construction of a city hall to be financed by a $400,000 contribution of the general fund and the proceeds of a $2,000,000 general obligation serial bond issue. Both amounts are budgeted to be received in the current year. Expenditures during the current year are estimated to be $850,000. Budgetary accounts are used.
(b) The general fund remits the $400,000.
(c) The bonds are sold for 101; the premium is transferred to the debt service fund. The premium is to be used for interest payments.

(d) A contract is signed with Rollins Construction Company for the construction of the city hall for an estimated contract cost of $2,300,000.

(e) By year end, $1,000,000 is paid against the contract with Rollins Construction Company.

Exercise 5. In 19X3, the town of Waterview authorized the construction of two concrete roadways. The public works department estimates the project cost at $400,000, $40,000 of which is transferred from the general fund to the capital projects fund. The balance will be paid for through a special assessments levy on benefiting property owners. $360,000, 4-year, 10% special assessment bonds are issued at face value, on January 1, 19X3, to finance the property owners' portion. Payments of $45,000 plus interest are made each June 30 and December 31. The bonds were issued. The town guarantees payment of the debt.

Purchase orders totaling $80,000 are issued and a contract is signed for the estimated $320,000 additional cost of the project. Invoices for all purchase orders total $74,000. The actual contract cost is $325,000. Liabilities for these amounts are entered. Except for $30,000 withheld on the contract until final approval, all liabilities related to the completed construction are paid. Waterview does not use budgetary accounts for these projects. Prepare entries in the capital projects fund for these events.

Exercise 6. This exercise is based on the facts of Exercise 5 for the town of Waterview's special assessment project. Assume special assessment property owners make the required payments to the debt service fund and the debt service fund, in turn, makes the payments required by the serial bonds. Record all entries in the debt service fund and in the long-term capital debt group of accounts for 19X3.

Exercise 7. Prepare journal entries required by a debt service fund to record the following transactions:
(a) On January 2, a $5,000,000, 6%, 10-year general obligation serial bond issue is sold at 99. Interest is payable annually on December 31, along with one-tenth of the original principal.
(b) At year end, the first serial of bonds matures, along with interest on the bond issue.
(c) The general fund transfers cash to meet the matured items.
(d) A check for the matured items is sent to First Bank, the agent handling the payments.
(e) Later, the bank reports that the first serial has been redeemed. One check for interest of $9,000 was returned by the post office because the bond owner had moved. The bank will search for the new address.

Exercise 8. Prepare journal entries to record the following events in the city of Rosewood's Water Commission enterprise fund:
(a) From its general fund revenues, the city transferred $300,000, which is restricted for the drilling of additional wells.
(b) Billings for water consumption for the month totaled $287,000, including $67,000 billed to other funds within the city.
(c) The Water Commission collected $42,000 from other funds and $190,000 from other users on billings in (b).
(d) To raise additional funds, the utility issued $700,000 of 5%, 10-year revenue bonds at face value. Proceeds are restricted to the development of wells.
(e) The contract with the well driller showed an estimated cost of $930,000.
(f) The well driller bills its cost plus normal profit amount of $360,000 at year end.
(g) The utility pays a $300,000 billing from the well driller.

Exercise 9. On January 1, 19X4, Jack Kinn donated $100,000 to the city of Larkin to be set aside as a trust fund for water quality improvements made by the city. The funds were fully invested in bonds purchased at a premium with a face value of $94,000. During the year, cash received on investments was $7,500. Premiums on the bonds purchased were amortized at $600 per year. All income earned is transferred to the endowment revenue fund. A total of $6,000 was transferred to a special revenue fund to carry out the purpose of the trust. The city uses an endowment principal fund and an endowment earnings fund. Prepare the journal entries to record these transactions. Prepare the balance sheet of both funds as of December 31, 19X4.

Exercise 10. Indicate into which fund a city would record each of the following transactions. (You need not make any entries.)
(a) Fixed assets are purchased with general fund cash.
(b) Long-term serial bonds are issued to finance the construction of a new art museum. The bonds are sold at a premium.
(c) The general fund transfers a sufficient amount of money to cover principal and interest requirements of a debt issue.
(d) The fund receiving the payment in (c) makes the scheduled payment of principal and interest.
(e) A special assessment project is half-completed at year end.
(f) Income is earned by the endowment principal fund and is transferred to a recipient fund, which is restricted as to its expenditures by a trust agreement.
(g) Possible depreciation entries on assets are recorded.
(h) The government-owned water utility issues debt to purchase new equipment.
(i) The new city prison is completed, and there are funds left over that are transferred to the fund responsible for repaying the debt used to finance the project.
Use the following symbols and funds for your responses:

GF	General	E-P	Endowment—Principal
SRF	Special Revenue	E-E	Endowment—Earnings
DSF	Debt Service	GFAAG	General Fixed Assets Account
CPF	Capital Projects		Group
ENT	Enterprise	GLTDAG	General Long-Term Debt
INT	Internal Service Fund		Account Group

Exercise 11. Match the appropriate letter indicating the recording of the following transactions:
(1) General obligation bonds were issues at par. _____
(2) Approved purchase orders were issued for supplies. _____
(3) The above-mentioned supplies were received and the related invoices were approved. _____
(4) General fund salaries and wages were incurred. _____
(5) The internal service fund had interfund billings. _____
(6) Revenues were earned from a previously awarded grant. _____
(7) Property taxes were collected in advance. _____
(8) Appropriations were recorded on adoption of the budget. _____
(9) Short-term financing was received from a bank, secured by the city's taxing power. _____
(10) There was an excess of estimated inflows over estimated outflows. _____

Recording of transactions:
A. Credit appropriations control.
B. Credit budgetary fund balance—unreserved.

C. Credit expenditures control.
D. Credit deferred revenues.
E. Credit interfund revenues.
F. Credit tax anticipation notes payable.
G. Credit other financing sources.
H. Credit other financing uses.
I. Debit appropriations control.
J. Debit deferred revenues.
K. Debit encumbrances control.
L. Debit expenditures control.   (AICPA adapted)

Exercise 12. Identify the letter that best describes the accounting and reporting by the following funds and account groups.

(1) Enterprise fund fixed assets.   _____
(2) Capital projects fund.   _____
(3) General fixed assets.   _____
(4) Infrastructure fixed assets.   _____
(5) Enterprise fund cash.   _____
(6) General fund.   _____
(7) Agency fund cash.   _____
(8) General long-term debt.   _____
(9) Special revenue fund.   _____
(10) Debt services fund.   _____

A. Accounted for in a fiduciary fund.
B. Accounted for in a proprietary fund.
C. Accounted for in a quasi-endowment fund.
D. Accounted for in a self-balancing account group.
E. Accounted for in a special assessment fund.
F. Accounts for major construction activities.
G. Accounts for property tax revenues.
H. Accounts for payment of interest and principal on tax supported debt.
I. Accounts for revenues from earmarked sources to finance designated activities.
J. Reporting is optional.
                                                                (AICPA adapted)

PROBLEMS

Problem 17-1. Select the best response for each of the following multiple-choice questions. (Nos. 1–8 are AICPA adapted.)

(1) Maple Township issued the following bonds during the year ended June 30, 19X3:

Bonds issued for the Garbage Collection Enterprise Fund that will
   service the debt $500,000
Revenue bonds to be repaid from admission fees collected by the
   Township Zoo Enterprise Fund.................................. 350,000

What amount of these bonds should be accounted for in Maple's general long-term debt account group?

(a) 0   (b) $350,000   (c) $500,000   (d) $850,000

(2) On December 31, 19X9, Elm Village paid a contractor $4,500,000 for the total cost of a new Village Hall built in 19X9 on Elm-owned land. Financing for the capital project was provided by a $3,000,000 general obligation bond issue sold at face amount on December 31, 19X9, with the remaining $1,500,000 transferred from the general fund. What account and amount should be reported in Elm's 19X9 financial statements for the general fund?

(a) Other Financing Sources (Control) $4,500,000
(b) Expenditures (Control) $4,500,000
(c) Other Financing Sources (Control) $3,000,000
(d) Other Financing Uses (Control) $1,500,000

(3) During 19X9, Spruce City reported the following receipts from self-sustaining activities paid for by users of the services rendered:

> Operation of water supply plant.............. $5,000,000
> Operation of bus system   900,000

What amount should be accounted for in Spruce's enterprise funds?

(a) 0   (b) $900,000   (c) $5,000,000   (d) $5,900,000

(4) Through an internal service fund, Wood County operates a centralized data-processing center to provide services to Wood's other governmental units. In 19X9, this internal service fund billed Wood's Parks and Recreation Fund $75,000 for data-processing services. What account should Wood's internal service fund credit to record this $75,000 billing to the Parks and Recreation Fund?
(a) Operating Revenues (Control)
(b) Interfund Exchanges
(c) Intergovernmental Transfers
(d) Data-Processing Department Expenses

(5) The following information pertains to Pine City's special revenue fund in 19X9:

> Appropriations............................ $6,500,000
> Expenditures.............................. 5,000,000
> Other financing sources................... 1,500,000
> Other financing uses...................... 2,000,000
> Revenues.................................. 8,000,000

After Pine's general fund accounts were closed at the end of 19X9, the fund balance increased by:

(a) $3,000,000   (b) $2,500,000   (c) $1,500,000   (d) $1,000,000

(6) Kew City received a $15,000,000 federal grant to finance the construction of a center for rehabilitation of drug addicts. The proceeds of this grant should be accounted for in the:
(a) Special revenue funds.
(b) General fund.
(c) Capital projects funds.
(d) Trust funds.

(7) Lisa County issued $5,000,000 of general obligation bonds at 101 to finance a capital project. The $50,000 premium was to be used for payment of interest. The transactions involving premium should be accounted for in the:
(a) Capital projects funds, debt service funds, and the general long-term debt account group.

(b) Capital projects funds and debt service funds only.

(c) Debt service funds and the general long-term debt account group only.

(d) Debt service funds only.

(8) In 19X9, a state government collected income taxes of $8,000,000 for the benefit of one of its cities that imposes an income tax on its residents. The state remitted these collections periodically to the city. The state should account for the $8,000,000 in the:

(a) General fund.

(b) Agency funds.

(c) Internal service funds.

(d) Special assessment funds.

Problem 17-2. (Nos. 1 and 5–8 are AICPA adapted.)

(1) The following revenues were among those reported by Ariba Township in 19X9:

Net rental revenue (after depreciation) from a parking garage owned by Ariba	$ 40,000
Interest earned on investments held for employees' retirement benefits.	100,000
Property taxes.	6,000,000

What amount of the foregoing revenues should be accounted for in Ariba's governmental funds?

(a) $6,140,000   (b) $6,100,000   (c) $6,040,000   (d) $6,000,000

Items (2) / (3) are based on the following information:

The events relating to the city of Albury's debt service funds that occurred during the year ended December 31, 19X1, are as follows:

Debt principal matured	$2,000,000
Unmatured (accrued) interest on outstanding debt at January 1, 19X1	50,000
Interest on matured debt	900,000
Unmatured (accrued) interest on outstanding debt at December 31, 19X1	100,000
Interest revenue from investments.	600,000
Cash transferred from the general fund for retirement of debt principal	1,000,000
Cash transferred from the general fund for payment of matured interest	900,000

All principal and interest due in 19X1 were paid on time.

(2) What is the total amount of expenditures that Albury's debt service funds should record for the year ended December 31, 19X1?

(a) $900,000   (b) $950,000   (c) $2,900,000   (d) $2,500,000

(3) How much revenue should Albury's debt service funds record for the year ended December 31, 19X1?

(a) $600,000   (b) $1,600,000   .(c) $1,900,000   (d) $2,500,000

(4) The following assets are among those owned by the city of Foster:

Apartment building (part of the principal of a nonexpendable trust
  fund) . . . . $ 200,000
City hall.   800,000
Three fire stations.   1,000,000
City streets and sidewalks   5,000,000

How much should be included in Foster's general fixed assets account group?
(a) Either $1,800,000 or $6,800,000.
(b) Either $2,000,000 or $7,000,000.
(c) $6,800,000.
(d) $7,000,000.

(5) The following information pertains to Grove City's interfund receivables and payables at December 31, 19X2:

Due to special revenue fund from general fund . . . . $ 10,000
Due to agency fund from special revenue fund   4,000

In Grove's special revenue fund balance sheet at December 31, 19X2, how should
these interfund amounts be reported?
(a) As an asset of $6,000.
(b) As a liability of $6,000.
(c) As an asset of $4,000 and a liability of $10,000.
(d) As an asset of $10,000 and a liability of $4,000.

(6) Financing for the renovation of Fir City's municipal park, begun and completed
during 19X2, came from the following sources:

Grant from state government . . . . $ 400,000
Proceeds from general obligation bond issue   500,000
Transfer from Fir's general fund   100,000

	Revenues	Other financing sources
(a)	$1,000,000	$ 0
(b)	$ 900,000	$ 100,000
(c)	$ 400,000	$ 600,000
(d)	$ 0	$1,000,000

(7) On April 1, 19X2, Oak County incurred the following expenditures in issuing long-
term bonds:

Issue costs . . . . $ 400,000
Debt insurance.   90,000

When Oak establishes the accounting for operating debt service, what amount should
be deferred and amortized over the life of the bonds?

(a) $0 .   (b) $900,000   (c) $400,000   (d) $490,000

(8) Lake County received the following proceeds that are legally restricted to expenditure for specified purposes:

Levies on affected property owners to install sidewalks............. $ 500,000
Gasoline taxes to finance road repairs   900,000

What amount would be accounted for in Lake's special revenue funds?
  (a) $1,400,000
  (b) $ 900,000
  (c) $ 500,000
  (d) $ 0

Problem 17-3. The following information pertains to Arnold Township's construction and financing of a new administration center:

Estimated total cost of project $9,000,000
Project financing:
  State entitlement grant   3,000,000
  General obligation bonds:
    Face amount   6,000,000
    Stated interest rate 6%
    Issue date .... December 1, 19X0
    Maturity date .... November 30, 19Y0

Arnold's fiscal year ended on June 30, 19X1. The following events occurred that affected the capital projects fund established to account for this project:

July 1, 19X0—The capital projects fund borrowed $300,000 from the general fund for preliminary expenses.
July 9, 19X0—Engineering and planning costs of $200,000, for which no encumbrance had been recorded, were paid to Krew Associates.
December 1, 19X0—The bonds were sold at 101. The premium is transferred to the debt service fund.
December 1, 19X0—The entitlement grant was formally approved by the state.
April 30, 19X1—A $7,000,000 contract was executed with Kimmel Construction Corp., the general contractors for the major portion of the project. The contract provides that Arnold will withhold 4% of all billings pending satisfactory completion of the project.
May 9, 19X1—$1,000,000 of the state grant was received.
June 10, 19X1—The $300,000 borrowed from the general fund was repaid.
June 30, 19X1—Progress billing of $1,200,000 was received from Kimmel.

Arnold uses encumbrance accounting for budgetary control. Unencumbered appropriations lapse at the end of the year.

Required:
(1) Prepare journal entries in the administration center capital projects fund to record the foregoing transactions.
(2) Prepare the June 30, 19X1 closing entries for the administration center capital projects fund.
(3) Prepare the Administration Center Capital Projects Fund balance sheet at June 30, 19X1.
(4) Prepare entries needed in other funds and groups.

(AICPA adapted)

Problem 17-4. During 1991, Krona City issued bonds for financing the construction of a civic center, and bonds for financing improvements in the environmental controls for its water and sewer enterprise. The latter bonds require a sinking fund for their retirement. Items (1)–(4) represent items Krona should report in its 1991 financial statements. For each item, determine whether it would be included in each of the funds and account groups listed below.

A. General fund.
B. Enterprise funds.
C. Capital projects funds.
D. Debt service funds.
E. General fixed assets account group.
F. General long-term debt account group.

(1) Bonds payable.   _____
(2) Accumulated depreciation.   _____
(3) Amounts identified for the repayment of the two bond issues.   _____
(4) Reserve for encumbrances.   _____

(AICPA adapted)

Problem 17-5. You are given the following postclosing trial balance for the Special Assessment Capital Projects Fund of the city of Stone Bank as of January 1, 19X2. The project was started last year and should be completed in June of 19X2.

	Dr	Cr
Cash	$290,000	
Contracts Payable—Retained Percentage		$ 60,000
Fund Balance—Reserved for Encumbrances		80,000
Fund Balance—Unreserved, Undesignated		150,000
	$290,000	$290,000

The special assessments are collected by the debt service fund, which also makes payments of principal and interest. The city has guaranteed payment of the debt in the event of nonpayment by the special assessment property owners. The debt service fund has the following balances on January 1, 19X2:

	Dr	Cr
Cash	$ 20,000	
Special Assessments Receivable—Current	250,000	
Special Assessments Receivable—Deferred	250,000	
Revenue		$250,000
Deferred Revenue		250,000
Fund Balance—Reserved for Debt Service		20,000
	$520,000	$520,000

The following events occurred during 19X2:

January 2—The city adopted an operating budget for 19X2 construction activities. Expenditures are estimated at $223,400 including amounts encumbered in the prior year. Budgetary accounts are used.

January 5—Prior-year encumbrances are restored, and new encumbrances of $138,000 are recorded.

February 1—$220,000 of special assessments are collected, along with interest of $17,600. Interest of $2,400 was billed on the uncollected current assessments, which were classified as delinquent.

February 28—$115,000 was paid on outstanding special assessment bonds, including interest of $15,000.

March 14—Delinquent special assessments and interest thereon of $2,650 were collected.

May 1—Expenditures of $220,000 were vouchered to Contracts Payable. The usual 10% retained percentage was entered. The project is now complete at a total cost of $896,000.

May 10—A check for $100,000 was issued to the contractor.

Required:

Prepare journal entries to record each of the preceding events in the proper funds and groups of accounts using the following format:

Date	Fund or Account Group	Entry

Problem 17-6. The preclosing, year-end trial balance for a capital projects fund of the city of Craig as of December 31, 19X1, follows:

	Dr	Cr
Cash..	$ 90,000	
Investments	200,000	
Contracts Payable—Retained Percentage		$ 60,000
Revenues (Control).....................................		16,600
Other Financing Sources (Control)......................		900,000
Expenditures (Control).................................	676,600	
Other Financing Uses (Control)	10,000	
Encumbrances (Control).................................	80,000	
Fund Balance—Reserved for Encumbrances		80,000
Estimated Revenues (Control)	15,000	
Estimated Other Financing Sources (Control)	950,000	
Appropriations (Control)		630,000
Estimated Other Financing Uses (Control)...............		15,000
Budgetary Fund Balance—Unreserved		320,000
	$2,021,600	$2,021,600

Required:

(1) Prepare closing entries as of December 31, 19X1.

(2) Prepare the year-end statement of revenues, expenditures, and changes in fund balances for this project that began on January 2, 19X1.

(3) Prepare the balance sheet as of December 31, 19X1.

Problem 17-7. In response to a petition signed by the property owners of River Hills Subdivision, the city of Pierce will oversee the installation of sidewalks, curbs, and gutters in the subdivision, to be accounted for in the city's capital projects fund. Pierce reports on a calendar-year basis. Construction is estimated to cost $900,000 and will be financed by a $100,000 county grant, a $50,000 transfer from the city's general fund, and special assessments of $750,000 to be levied against subdivision property owners. One-third of the levy is to be due on February 1 of each year, starting with 19X1. The first $250,000 installment will be received by the capital projects fund directly. The remaining installments will be collected by the debt service fund and will be used to service the related bond debt. The project is to begin on January 15, 19X1, and is to take 18 months to complete. It is estimated that 70% of the work will be completed during 19X1.

To cover construction costs, a 6%, $500,000 special assessment serial bond issue will be floated on March 1, 19X1. Interest is to be paid semiannually on September 1 and March 1 by the debt service fund. One-fifth of the principal will be redeemed on March 1 of each year, starting with 19X2. Since interest earned on special assessments will offset bond interest cost, the city will not accrue interest.

Although the special assessments will provide cash to redeem the bond principal and pay the bond interest, Pierce has pledged its full faith and credit as security for the bond obligation.

The following events happen during 19X1:

January 2—The city council adopted the annual budget for the River Hills project in the capital projects fund.

January 2—The receivables from the general fund and the county were recorded.

January 5—Special assessments were levied in accordance with the plan, with one-third due on February 1.

January 9—Amounts due from the general fund and the county were received.

January 10—Encumbrances for the year were recorded at $675,000.

February 1—The first special assessment installment was collected.

March 1—Bonds with a $500,000 face value were sold at 101. Except for the price, other conditions remained in accordance with the bond plan. The premium was to be transferred to the debt service fund for interest payments.

March 1—$600,000 was invested in a 5% money market account by the capital projects fund.

August 31—$10,000 for interest payment was transferred by the capital projects fund to the debt service fund.

September 1—The semiannual bond interest was paid by the debt service fund.

December 15—The contractor submitted an invoice for $600,000 that was approved for payment, except for a 10% amount to be paid on completion and acceptance of the project. Related encumbrances totaled $595,000.

December 29—$400,000 was withdrawn from the money market investment. Interest of $16,600 was received.

December 30—The contractor was mailed a check for $540,000. In addition, vouchers for $76,600 were prepared and paid for items on the project that were not encumbered.

In addition—The next assessment installment was reclassified upon special direction of the city council, and an amount equal to project expenditures-to-date was capitalized.

Required:

For each of the preceding events, prepare the journal entries for all of the funds and groups of accounts involved, using the following format:

Date   Fund or Account Group   Entry

Problem 17-8. In compliance with a newly enacted state law, Hayward County assumed the responsibility of collecting all property taxes levied within its boundaries as of July 1, 19X3. The following composite property tax rate per $100 of net assessed valuation was developed for the fiscal year ending June 30, 19X4:

Hayward County General Fund	$ 6.00
Reed City General Fund	3.00
Newbury Township General Fund	1.00
	$10.00

All property taxes are due in quarterly installments and, after being collected, are distributed to the governmental units represented in the composite rate. To administer the collection and distribution of such taxes, Hayward County has established a tax agency fund.

Additional information:
(a) To reimburse itself for estimated administrative expenses of operating the tax agency fund, the county is to deduct 2% from the tax collections for Reed City and Newbury Township. The total amount deducted is to be remitted to the Hayward County general fund.
(b) Current-year tax levies to be collected by the tax agency fund are as follows:

	Gross Levy	Estimated Amount to be Collected
Hayward County..........................	$3,600,000	$3,500,000
Reed City	1,800,000	1,740,000
Newbury Township	600,000	560,000
	$6,000,000	$5,800,000

(c) In its original computation of the gross levy, Newbury Township made an error that will reduce both the gross and estimated amounts to be collected by $10,000.
(d) As of September 30, 19X3, the tax agency fund has received $1,440,000 in first quarter payments. On October 1, the agency fund made a distribution to the three governmental units on the basis of the composite property tax rate.

Required:
For the period July 1, 19X3, through October 1, 19X3, prepare journal entries to record the preceding transactions, using the following format:

Accounts	Hayward County Tax Agency Fund		Hayward County General Fund		Reed City General Fund		Newbury Township General Fund	
	Debit	Credit	Debit	Credit	Debit	Credit	Debit	Credit

(AICPA adapted)

Problem 17-9. The following trial balance of the Employees' Retirement System Fund for Redford City was prepared by a clerk who used only balance sheet accounts in recording the events for the fiscal year ended December 31, 19X2:

	Dr	Cr
Cash...	$ 28,000	
Investments	496,000	
Due to Resigned Employees.................................		$ 2,000
Annuities Payable		3,000
Surplus		519,000
	$524,000	$524,000

An investigation uncovered the following activity in the surplus account:

	Contributions		Retired Employees' Annuities	Total
	Employee	Employer		
Balances on January 1, 19X2	$100,000	$200,000	$159,000	$459,000
Events during 19X2:				
Amounts received (city still owes $4,000 at year end).....	16,000	32,000		48,000
Payments to retired employees			(13,000)	(13,000)
Annuities payable at year end			(3,000)	(3,000)
Annuities established for current retirees...............	(12,000)	(17,000)	29,000	
Investment earnings received (accrued earnings of $5,000 have not been recorded at year end)	8,000	13,000	9,000	30,000
Due to resigned employees for their contributions	(2,000)			(2,000)
Balances on December 31, 19X2	$110,000	$228,000	$181,000	$519,000

An actuarial report indicates that as of January 1, 19X2, there was an actuarially computed deficiency of $117,000 to fund plan requirements. As of December 31, 19X2, the deficiency is $104,000.

Required:

(1) Prepare journal entries to correct the balance sheet accounts as of January 1, 19X2, including the recording of the computed deficiency.

(2) Prepare journal entries to record the events transpiring during 19X2 as they should have been recorded originally. Prepare journal entries to update fund balances.

(3) Prepare a balance sheet of the Employees' Retirement System Fund as of December 31, 19X2.

Problem 17-10. The city of Danbury operates a central computer center through an internal service fund. The Computer Internal Service Fund was established by a contribution of $1,000,000 from the general fund on July 1, 19X2, at which time a building was acquired at a cost of $300,000 cash. A used computer was purchased for $600,000. The postclosing trial balance of the fund at June 30, 19X3, was as follows:

Cash...	$ 120,000	
Due from General Fund................................	140,000	
Inventory of Materials and Supplies	80,000	
Land..	60,000	
Building...	300,000	
Allowance for Depreciation—Building		$ 15,000
Computer Equipment.................................	660,000	
Allowance for Depreciation—Computer Equipment		264,000
Vouchers Payable (to Outsiders)		41,000
Contributions from General Fund		1,000,000
Retained Earnings—Unreserved		40,000
	$1,360,000	$1,360,000

The following information applies to the year ended June 30, 19X4:

(a) Materials and supplies were purchased on account for $74,000.

(b) The inventory of materials and supplies at June 30, 19X4, was $60,000.

(c) Salaries paid totaled $230,000, including related costs.

(d) A billing from the Utility Enterprise Fund for $40,000 was received and paid.

(e) Depreciation on the building and on the equipment was $7,500 and $132,000, respectively.

(f) Billings to other departments for service were as follows:

General Fund.............................. $392,000
Water and Sewer Fund 84,000
Special Revenue Fund....................... 42,000

(g) Unpaid interfund receivable balances at June 30, 19X4, were:

General Fund.............................. $136,000
Special Revenue Funds...................... 16,000

(h) Vouchers payable at June 30, 19X4, were $14,000.

Required:
(1) For the period July 1, 19X3, through June 30, 19X4, prepare journal entries to record the transactions in the Computer Internal Service Fund. The city uses control accounts for revenues and expenses.
(2) Prepare closing entries at June 30, 19X4.

Problem 17-11. A selected list of transactions for the city of Baylor for the fiscal year ending June 30, 19X8, follows:
(a) The city government authorized a budget with estimated revenues of $2,500,000 and appropriations of $2,450,000.
(b) The city's share of state gasoline taxes is estimated to be $264,500. These taxes are to be used only for highway maintenance. Appropriations are authorized in the amount of $250,000.
(c) Property taxes of $1,400,000 are levied by the city. In the past, uncollectible taxes have averaged 2% of the gross levy.
(d) A $1,000,000 term bond issue for construction of a school is authorized and sold at 102. The bond premium is transferred to the debt service fund to be used for payment of interest.
(e) Contracts are signed for the construction of the school at an estimated cost of $1,000,000.
(f) The school is constructed at a cost of $990,000.
(g) The debt service fund will need $150,000 from the general fund for estimated interest and principal payments for the year.
(h) A transfer of $100,000 is made by the general fund to the debt service fund.
(i) Earnings of the debt service fund amount to $3,050. Interest of $45,000 is paid.
(j) Land with a fair market value of $100,000 is donated to the city.
(k) The city received $205,000 in partial payment of its share of state gasoline taxes, with an additional $60,000 due from the state government in 60 days.
(l) Vouchers totaling $210,000, which represent highway labor maintenance costs, are approved for payment by the special revenue fund.

Required:
For each of the events described, prepare the journal entries for all of the funds and groups of accounts involved, using the following format:

Fund or Account Group   Journal Entry

Problem 17-12. The village of Dexter was recently incorporated and began financial operations on July 1, 19X8, the beginning of its fiscal year.

The following transactions occurred during this first fiscal year, July 1, 19X8, to June 30, 19X9:
(1) The village council adopted a budget for general operations during the fiscal year ending June 30, 19X9. Revenues were estimated at $400,000. Legal authorizations for expenditures were $394,000.

(2) Property taxes were levied for $390,000. It was estimated that 2% of this amount would prove to be uncollectible. These taxes were available on the date of the levy to finance current expenditures.

(3) During the year a resident of the village donated marketable securities, valued at $50,000, to the village under the terms of a trust agreement. The agreement stipulated that the principal is to be kept intact. The use of revenue generated by the securities is to be restricted to financing college scholarships for needy students. Revenue earned and received on these marketable securities amounted to $5,500 through June 30, 19X9.

(4) A general fund transfer of $5,000 was made to establish an Intragovernmental Service Fund to provide for a permanent investment in inventory.

(5) The village decided to install lighting in the village park. A special assessment project was authorized to install the lighting at a cost of $75,000. The appropriation was formally recorded. To finance the project, $3,000 is to be transferred from the general fund and the balance is from special assessments.

(6) Assessments were levied for $72,000, with the village contributing $3,000 from the general fund. All assessments and the village contributions were collected during the year.

(7) A contract for $75,000 was let for the installation of lighting. At June 30, 19X9, the contract was completed for $75,000. The contractor was paid all but 5%, which was retained to insure compliance with the terms of the contract. Encumbrances and other budgetary accounts are maintained.

(8) During the year, the internal service fund purchased various supplies at a cost of $1,900.

(9) Cash collections recorded by the general fund during the year were as follows:

Property taxes	$386,000
Licenses and permits	7,000

(10) The village council decided to build a village hall, at an estimated cost of $500,000, to replace space occupied in rented facilities. The village does not record project authorizations. It was decided that general obligation bonds bearing interest at 6% would be issued. On June 30, 19X9, the bonds were issued at their face value of $500,000, payable in 20 years. No contracts have been signed for this project, and no expenditures have been made.

(11) A fire truck was purchased for $15,000, and the voucher was approved. Payment was made through the general fund. This expenditure was previously encumbered for $14,500.

Required:

Prepare journal entries to properly record each of the preceding transactions in the appropriate fund(s) or group of accounts of Dexter for the fiscal year ended June 30, 19X9. Use the following funds and groups of accounts:

- General fund
- Capital projects fund
- Internal service fund
- Endowment principal fund
- Endowment earnings fund
- General long-term debt account group
- General fixed assets account group

Journal entries should be numbered to correspond with the appropriate transactions. Do not prepare closing entries for any fund.

Your answer sheet should be organized as follows:

Transaction No.	Fund or Group of Accounts	Account Title and Explanation	Amounts	
			Debit	Credit

(AICPA adapted)

Problem 17-13. Port Washington's citizens authorized the construction of a new library. As a result of this project, the city had the following transactions during 19X3:

(a) On January 3, 19X3, a $600,000 serial bond issue having a stated interest rate of 8% was authorized for the acquisition of land and the construction of a library building. The bonds are to be redeemed in 10 equal annual installments beginning February 1, 19X4.

(b) On January 10, 19X3, the city made a $50,000 down payment deposit on the purchase of land, which is to be the site of the library. The contracted price for the land is $150,000, which is $40,000 below what the city estimated it would have to spend to acquire a site.

(c) On March 1, 19X3, the city issued serial bonds having a $450,000 face value at 102. The bond indenture requires any premium to be set aside for servicing bond interest.

(d) On March 10, 19X3, the city paid the remaining amount on the land contract and took title to the land.

(e) On March 17, 19X3, the city signed a $400,000 construction contract with Rower Construction Company.

(f) On July 10, 19X3, the contractor was paid $200,000 based on work completed to date.

(g) On September 1, 19X3, a semiannual interest payment was made on the outstanding bonds. (The general fund transferred funds to supplement the cash received from the premium in part c.)

(h) On December 1, 19X3, the city issued serial bonds having a $100,000 face value at par.

(i) On December 2, 19X3, the contractor completed the library and submitted a final billing of $210,000, which includes $10,000 of additional work authorized by the city in October 19X3. The $210,000 was paid to the contractor on December 12, 19X3.

(j) Through December 10, 19X3, the city had invested excess cash (from the bond offering) in short-term certificates of deposit. The amount collected on these investments totaled $12,000.

Required:
(1) Prepare the journal entries in all fund/account groups.
(2) Prepare any appropriate year-end adjusting and closing entries for the capital projects fund and the general fixed asset account group.
(3) Prepare a statement of revenues, expenditures, and changes in fund balance for 19X3 for the capital project fund.

Problem 17-14. Albury City was incorporated as a municipality and began operations on January 1, 19X1. The budget approved by the city council was recorded, but the cash basis was used in Albury's books for all 19X1 transactions. Albury has decided to use encumbrance accounting. Albury's cash basis general fund trial balance at December 31, 19X1, is presented as follows in the preprinted worksheet found in the Text Companion section of your Student Companion Enrichment Manual.

Debits

Cash..	$499,800
Expenditures (Control)..................................	145,000
Estimated revenues (Control)............................	228,200
Total...	$873,000

Credits

Appropriations (Control)................................	$204,000
Revenues (Control).....................................	216,800
Bonds Payable...	400,000
Premium on Bonds Payable	6,000
Budgetary Fund Balance	24,200
Fund Balance—Unreserved, Undesignated.................	22,000
Total...	$873,000

Additional information:

Revenues	Budgeted	Actual
Property taxes	$205,200	$192,000
Licenses...	14,800	15,800
Fines..	8,200	9,000
Totals	$228,200	$216,800

Expenditures		
Services..	$ 90,000	$ 77,000
Supplies..	38,000	22,000
Equipment..	76,000	46,000
Totals	$204,000	$145,000

It was estimated that 5% of the property taxes would not be collected. Accordingly, property taxes were levied to yield the budgeted amount of $205,200. Taxes of $192,000 had been collected by December 31, 19X1, and it was expected that all remaining collectible taxes would be received by February 28, 19X2.

Supplies of $8,000 and equipment of $20,000 were received, but the vouchers were not yet recorded at December 31, 19X1. Purchase orders were still outstanding for supplies and equipment not yet received, in the amounts of $2,400 and $7,600, respectively. Supplies on hand at December 31, 19X1 totaled $3,400.

On November 1, 19X1, Albury issued 4%, 10-year obligation term bonds of $400,000 at 101½. Interest is payable each May 1 and November 1 until the maturity date. Cash from the bond premium is to be set aside and restricted for payment of interest. The bonds were issued to finance the construction of a firehouse, but no contracts had been executed by December 31, 19X1.

Required:

(1) Create your own worksheet using the following format or complete the printed one found in the Text Companion section of your Student Companion Enrichment Manual. On the worksheet be sure to show adjustments and distributions to the proper funds or account groups, before closing entries, in conformity with generally accepted accounting principles applicable to governmental entities. Formal adjusting entries are *not* required.

Suggestion: You may extend existing balances to proper columns without an entry. For example, Bonds Payable can be extended directly to the General Long-Term Debt column.

Albury City
Worksheet to Correct Trial Balance
December 31, 19X1

Accounts	Trial Balance	Adjustments		General Fund	Debt Service Fund	Capital Projects Fund	General Fixed Assets	General Long-Term Debt
		Debit	Credit					

(2) Prepare a Statement of Revenues, Expenditures, and Charges in Fund Balance—Budget and Actual for 19X1 for the general fund.

(AICPA adapted)

CHAPTER 18

Accounting for Not-for-Profit Organizations: Public and Private Universities

This chapter and the next detail accounting for the four major not-for-profit organizations. These organizations include (1) colleges and universities, (2) hospitals, (3) voluntary health and welfare organizations, and (4) other organizations such as museums, country clubs, and religious organizations. In this chapter, the unique characteristics of not-for-profit organizations and the accounting and reporting standard-setting activity in this sector are discussed. The new accounting and reporting guidance for private not-for-profit organizations is presented, followed by separate sections on accounting and financial reporting for public versus private colleges and universities. The next chapter is concerned with accounting and financial reporting for health care organizations, voluntary health and welfare organizations, and other not-for-profit organizations.

GENERAL CHARACTERISTICS OF NOT-FOR-PROFITS

Not-for-profit activities are a significant portion of the economy of the United States. All not-for-profit organizations provide services without the intention of realizing a profit. Such organizations are generally financed by contributions, earnings from endowments or other investments, charges for services, and government grants. External users of financial statements have common interests in assessing (1) the services an organization provides and its ability to continue those services, (2), its creditworthiness, and (3) how managers discharge their stewardship responsibilities and other aspects of their performance.[1]

---

[1]FASB Statement No. 117, *Financial Statements of Not-for-Profit Organizations* (Norwalk, CT: Financial Accounting Standards Board, 1993), par. 4.

FUND ACCOUNTING

To satisfy the requirement of accounting for a diversity of resources and their use, fund accounting has traditionally been used. Fund accounting has been used to organize and manage resources for various purposes in accordance with regulations, restrictions, or limitations imposed by parties outside the institution, or with directions issued by the governing board. A clear distinction of funds that are externally restricted and those that are internally designated by action of the governing board has been maintained in the accounts and disclosed in the financial reports.

THE BUDGET

Budgets are also prepared in not-for-profit organizations. As in a commercial enterprise, the budgeting process should involve the establishment of goals, the measurement of actual performance, and the comparison of actual with projected performance to evaluate results. This process requires the input of persons who can determine what resources will become available, what the group desires to achieve with those resources, and how the resources should be applied to yield the greatest benefit. If the organization or program is well established, a useful starting point is the previous year's budget and its variances, adjusted for any changes in objectives. If the group or program is new, the preparation of an effective operating budget requires careful research to produce realistic estimates of both revenues and expenditures.

Expenditures should be planned to maximize service output without producing either a surplus or a deficit. A sizable excess of revenues over expenditures implies that more or better service could be provided. A deficit may indicate the need to curtail future services, since future funds may have to be committed to cover past deficits.

In accounting for not-for-profit organizations, it is not as common to find budgetary amounts formally entered into principal ledger accounts as it is in governmental accounting. Often, detailed budgetary amounts are entered directly in appropriate subsidiary records, and encumbrances representing outstanding purchase orders and other commitments for materials and supplies are entered directly in an encumbrance column in the subsidiary expenditures record. Although subsidiary records are not supported by principal ledger control accounts when this procedure is followed, some degree of control is achieved by comparing the subsidiary records with actual revenues and expenditures.

If a budgetary entry is recorded, it would be similar to the one used in governmental accounting, and it would be reversed at year end. Assuming estimated revenues exceed estimated expenditures and allocations, the budgetary entry would be:

Estimated Revenues	XXX	
Estimated Expenditures (or Budget Allocations for Expenditures)		XXX
Unallocated Balance		XXX

BASIS OF ACCOUNTING

All not-for-profit organizations use the accrual basis of accounting. There are some modifications in governmental not-for-profit organizations that record expenditures for capital outlays and do not recognize depreciation. The operating statements of public colleges and universities do not report the total revenue and expenditure activity of the institution, but only that related to current funds. The private not-for-profit organizations, particularly with the new Financial Accounting Standards Board (FASB) guidance, use full accrual accounting. Organizationwide operating statements are expense oriented, including depreciation expense.

DEVELOPMENT OF ACCOUNTING PRINCIPLES

Early development of accounting principles for nonprofit organizations was largely the responsibility of not-for-profit industry groups, including the National Association of College and University Business Officers (NACUBO), the Health Care Financial Management Association (HFMA), and the National Health Council. These industry groups, representing colleges and universities, hospitals, voluntary health and welfare organizations, and other organizations such as museums, country clubs, and religious organizations, developed manuals with accounting guidance. In response to an increasing awareness of the not-for-profit sector, the American Institute of Certified Public Accountants (AICPA) worked in conjunction with these industry groups to develop and issue four audit guides in the early 1970s. These guides have been updated and amended over the years and constitute generally accepted accounting principles (GAAP) for not-for-profits.

1. Audits of Colleges and Universities (May 1, 1993)
2. Audits of Providers of Health Care Services (May 1, 1993)
3. Audit Guide for Voluntary Health and Welfare Organizations (May 1, 1993)
4. Audits of Certain Nonprofit Organizations (SOP 78-10)

As a result of the separate evolution of standards by each nonprofit industry group, significant differences exist for the four types of not-for-profits in terms of fund classifications, measurement criteria, account classifications, and financial statement disclosures.

JURISDICTION FOR ACCOUNTING AND FINANCIAL REPORTING

Jurisdiction for accounting and financial reporting for not-for-profit organizations is shared by the FASB and the Government Accounting Standards Board (GASB). The GASB has jurisdiction over accounting and financial reporting of governmental not-for-profits (public colleges and universities and government hospitals). The FASB has jurisdiction over accounting and financial reporting of all private not-for-profit organizations including private colleges and universities, private health care providers, voluntary health and welfare organizations, and other private not-for-profits.

NEW FASB STANDARDS

Recently, the FASB issued Statement No. 116: *Accounting for Contributions Received and Contributions Made,* and Statement No. 117: *Financial Statements of Not-for-Profit Organizations.* The issuance of these standards represents the culmination of almost 15 years of work by the FASB which began with the issuance of Concepts Statement No. 4: *Objectives of Financial Reporting by Nonbusiness Organizations* (1980). These statements make drastic changes in measurement and reporting for private not-for-profits and are effective for fiscal years beginning after December 15, 1994. (Small not-for-profits with less than $5 million in total assets and $1 million in total expenses have one more year to change standards.) Early adoption is encouraged.

These standards replace *certain sections* of the existing AICPA guidance for *private* not-for-profits, eliminate the inconsistent reporting practices that have existed for the various types of nonprofit organizations, and simplify the current manner of reporting. The AICPA's Not-for-Profit Organizations Committee is working diligently on the new audit guide (the combined version of the now separate college and university, voluntary health and welfare, and other nonprofit organizations) to consider additional guidance for Statement Nos. 116 and 117. Similarly, the AICPA's Health Care Committee is revising its guidance to conform to the new FASB Statements. Exposure drafts of the new audit guides are due in early 1995.

Under the jurisdictional agreement of the Financial Accounting Foundation with the FASB and GASB, the new FASB standards will apply only to *private not-for-profit* organizations—unless the GASB specifies that it is to apply to governmental not-for-profit organizations as well. The issuance of Statement Nos. 116 and 117 creates a divergence in accounting and financial reporting for private versus public organizations. This divergence is most pronounced for public versus private universities and is expected to continue for some time. Although the GASB currently has a project in the early stages of development that addresses the financial statements to be used for public colleges and universities, a final standard is not expected to be issued for several years. Therefore, the AICPA Audit Guide remains the authoritative guidance for public colleges and universities. For organizations other than colleges and universities, especially hospitals, GASB standards are similar to FASB standards, as those organizations are reported in governmental enterprise funds, which generally follow FASB standards. Therefore, this text will provide a comparison of public and private college and university accounting and will present all other not-for-profit organizations using the new private sector FASB guidance.

ACCOUNTING FOR NOT-FOR-PROFIT UNIVERSITIES

The responsibilities of a not-for-profit university may be classified as academic, financial, student services, and public relations. Academic functions include instruction, research, and public service. The financial sphere covers the management and reporting of business and financial affairs as well as auxiliary enterprises, such as housing, food service, and student union operation. Student services includes all student activities not directly classified as academic or financial, such as admissions, records, health, counseling, and publications. Public relations involves the communication and establishment of goodwill with academic and administrative staff, alumni, and the community.

The effectiveness with which a university accomplishes its objectives in these four areas depends in part upon the resources at its disposal. A university levies tuition fees, but these fees do not cover total operational costs. Therefore, other sources of revenue are essential. These sources include gifts, income from endowment funds, and grants from governmental units or foundations, and for public universities, appropriations from state legislatures.

As a result of the great differences in accounting and financial reporting between public and private sector colleges and universities, this chapter will first make a presentation of accounting and financial statements for *public* colleges and universities following the guidance set forth in the AICPA *Audits of Colleges and Universities* (1993),[2] and next, a presentation for *private* colleges and universities following pronouncements set forth by the FASB that supersede sections of the Audit Guide.[3]

ACCOUNTING FOR PUBLIC UNIVERSITIES

Traditional accounting procedures for public universities emphasize the flow of financial resources and fund accounting. College and university funds include three broad categories: current funds, plant funds, and trust and agency funds. The day-to-day activities of a public university are recorded in its current funds, which consist of two self-balancing subfunds. The *unrestricted current fund* represents amounts that are available for any current activity commensurate with the university's objectives. The *restricted current fund* accounts for those resources available only for an externally specified purpose. The segregation of unrestricted current funds from restricted current funds substantiates that the limitations placed on restricted funds by outside sources have been observed. *Plant funds* account for capital assets and for resources to be used to acquire additional capital assets or to retire indebtedness related to capital assets. Plant funds consist of several subgroups, each of which is designed to record a certain phase of activity related to fixed assets. *Endowment and similar funds* account for endowments received. In addition, a university may employ *loan funds*, *annuity funds*, and *agency funds*. Each fund may have its own accounting records, or if the university is large, all funds may be integrated into one record system. In this

---

[2]The GASB asserts that public colleges and universities may use either the governmental model as outlined in Chapter 16 or the AICPA audit guide model which will be described in this chapter.

[3]The divergence arising in financial accounting and reporting standards under the current two-board structure is most pronounced in colleges and universities. Recent GASB Statement No. 8 issued in 1988 (no requirement for depreciation by governmental universities), Statement No. 15 issued in 1991 (governmental college and university accounting and financial reporting may follow either the governmental model or the AICPA audit guide), and Statement No. 19 issued in 1993 (governmental colleges and universities must account for federally sponsored student financial aid in a current restricted fund) suggest sharp differences of opinion between the two boards on many issues.

situation, electronic data processing equipment probably would be used to produce reports for each fund.

The accrual basis is used in public university accounting. Operating or current funds record revenues and expenditues in nominal accounts. In the other funds, Fund Balance may be credited directly for resources received and debited directly for resource outflows. As a result, only the current funds present a statement of revenues and expenditures. The three principal financial statements for a public university are:

1. The statement of current funds revenues, expenditures, and other changes, which provides detail on revenues, expenditures, transfers to/from other funds, and other changes in fund balances for the period.
2. The balance sheet, which is a stacked presentation of individual fund balance sheets indicating the financial position of each fund.
3. The statement of changes in fund balances, which provides a summary of activities for the period in each fund and their impact on each fund balance account.

Each of these statements is explained and illustrated at appropriate points in the discussion that follows.

UNIVERSITY CURRENT FUNDS—UNRESTRICTED

The unrestricted current fund of a public university is similar to the general fund of a state or local government in that it accounts for current assets available to cover current operational costs and resulting current liabilities. No outside limitations apply to its resources.

A public university might establish one master control account for unrestricted revenues, with details as to major sources recorded in subsidiary records. More commonly, separate revenue accounts are established, using the following three major groups of revenues:

> Educational and general revenues group, with accounts for:
> > Student tuition and fees (recognized when due or billed, net of an appropriate allowance for uncollectibles)
> > Governmental appropriations (detailed as to federal, state, and local)
> > Governmental grants and contracts (detailed as to federal, state, and local)
> > Gifts and private grants
> > Endowment income
> > Other sources
>
> Auxiliary enterprises revenues
>
> Expired term endowment revenues

In the interest of full disclosure, operating revenues are recorded in these accounts. Auxiliary enterprises revenues are segregated to permit the evaluation of performance and the degree of self-support. Expired term endowment income represents dollar amounts of term endowments on which the restriction has lapsed, freeing them to become unrestricted resources.

Unrestricted current fund expenditures are the costs incurred to conduct the university's daily operations using unrestricted resources. Expenditures may be classified in a number of ways, depending on the purpose. In financial reports, the audit guide recommends classification by function for two major groupings, which are the same as the first two used to classify revenues.

Educational and general expenditures group, with accounts for:
  Instruction (expenditures for credit and noncredit courses)
  Research (expenditures to produce research results)
  Public support (expenditures for noninstructional services, including conferences, seminars, and consulting)
  Academic support (expenditures supporting instruction and public services, such as libraries, galleries, audiovisual services, and academic deans)
  Student services (expenditures for student admission and registration and cultural and athletic activities)
  Institutional support (expenditures for central administration)
  Operation and maintenance of plant
  Student aid (expenditures for scholarships, fellowships, tuition remissions, and outright grants)

Auxiliary enterprises expenditures

In addition to expenditures, the unrestricted current fund balance is affected by transfers. *Discretionary* or *nonmandatory transfers,* such as transfers to a loan fund or a plant fund, are transfers of unrestricted resources to other funds at the discretion of the university's governing authority. *Mandatory transfers* are required transfers of resources to other funds. Some mandatory transfers, such as amounts set aside for debt retirement and interest payment, result from binding legal contracts. Other mandatory transfers arise from the acceptance of a grant or donation that requires the university to match some or all of the amounts received. Although the source of mandatory transfers may be either unrestricted or restricted current funds, it is more commonly unrestricted funds.

Discretionary transfers are recorded by debiting either unrestricted current fund balance or a temporary equity account, such as Transfer to Loan Fund. The temporary equity account would be closed to unrestricted current fund balance at year end. Mandatory transfers, however, must be recorded by debiting the account Mandatory Transfers. These transfers, which may relate to either educational and general activities or to auxiliary enterprises, are segregated on financial reports of public universities.

To illustrate the accounting process in the unrestricted current fund, assume Rogers State University (a public institution) maintains separate records for each of its funds. It uses detailed revenue and expenditure accounts recommended by the audit guide, rather than broad control accounts, and the budget is recorded formally. Encumbrance items are entered directly into subsidiary records, but no formal entries for them are made. The summarized events affecting only the unrestricted current fund are described and recorded as follows. Events affecting more than one fund are described and recorded in the multicolumn interaction matrix in Illustration 18-4 beginning on page 992.

Event		Entry		

The following budget is approved:

Estimated revenues $3,300,000
Estimated expenditures 3,000,000

Unallocated balance . . . . $ 300,000

Estimated Revenues	3,300,000	
Estimated Expenditures		3,000,000
Unallocated Balance		300,000

(this is an optional entry)

Educational and general revenue is earned or billed:

Student tuition and fees (of which $20,000 is considered uncollectible) $1,700,000
Governmental appropriations. 750,000
Private gifts and grants. 250,000
Endowment income. 50,000
Other income 250,000

Total $3,000,000

Accounts Receivable	3,000,000	
Revenues—Student Tuition and Fees		1,680,000
Allowance for Uncollectibles		20,000
Revenues—Governmental Appropriations.		750,000
Revenues—Private Gifts and Grants.		250,000
Revenues—Endowment Income . .		50,000
Revenues—Other Income		250,000

Of the total revenues, $2,800,000 is collected.

| Cash. . . . . | 2,800,000 | |
| Accounts Receivable . . . . | | 2,800,000 |

Revenue billed for dormitories (an auxiliary enterprise) is $400,000, of which $20,000 is not yet received.

Cash.	380,000	
Accounts Receivable	20,000	
Revenues—Auxiliary Enterprises . .		400,000

Purchases of materials and supplies total $400,000, of which $25,000 is not yet paid.

Inventory of Materials	400,000	
Cash.		375,000
Accounts Payable		25,000

Expenditures are paid and assigned to:

Instruction $1,050,000
Research 100,000
Academic support. 150,000
Student services. 200,000
Institutional support 200,000
Operation and maintenance of plant. 400,000
Student aid 40,000
Auxiliary enterprises. 260,000

Total $2,400,000

Expenditures—Instruction	1,050,000	
Expenditures—Research	100,000	
Expenditures—Academic Support . . .	150,000	
Expenditures—Student Services	200,000	
Expenditures—Institutional Support	200,000	
Expenditures—Operation and Maintenance of Plant	400,000	
Expenditures—Student Aid	40,000	
Expenditures—Auxiliary Enterprises	260,000	
Cash.		2,400,000

Materials and supplies used:

Instruction . . . . $ 268,000
Student services. 22,000
Auxiliary enterprises 90,000

Total . . . . $ 380,000

Expenditures—Instruction	268,000	
Expenditures—Student Services	22,000	
Expenditures—Auxiliary Enterprises	90,000	
Inventory of Materials		380,000

(continued)

Event	Entry

Event		Entry		
Aid is granted to students:		Expenditures—Student Aid.........	175,000	
Remission of tuition	$ 140,000	Accounts Receivable		140,000
Cash scholarships..............	35,000	Cash........................		35,000
Total	$ 175,000			
The budgetary entry is reversed. (If optional budgetary entry has been made.)		Unallocated Balance..............	300,000	
		Estimated Expenditures...........	3,000,000	
		Estimated Revenues		3,300,000
The books are closed, with a separate closing entry for Auxiliary Enterprises to demonstrate the degree of success.		Revenues—Student Tuition and Fees......................	1,680,000	
		Revenues—Governmental Appropriations................	750,000	
		Revenues—Private Gifts and Grants	250,000	
		Revenues—Endowment Income	50,000	
		Revenues—Other Income	250,000	
		Expenditures—Instruction........		1,318,000
		Expenditures—Research.........		100,000
		Expenditures—Academic Support		150,000
		Expenditures—Student Services....................		222,000
		Expenditures—Institutional Support		200,000
		Expenditures—Operation and Maintenance of Plant..........		400,000
		Expenditures—Student Aid.......		215,000
		Fund Balance..................		375,000
		Revenues—Auxiliary Enterprises	400,000	
		Expenditures—Auxiliary Enterprises		350,000
		Fund Balance..................		50,000

UNIVERSITY CURRENT FUNDS—RESTRICTED

For an activity to enter the restricted current fund of a public university, some limitation must exist on the resources received from an external entity. The same revenue and expenditure accounts used in the unrestricted current fund are available, but restricted current fund revenues arise primarily from governmental grants and contracts, private gifts, and endowment income. Expenditures generally are relegated to instruction, research, and student aid.

Unless the restriction placed upon contributed resources or governmental grants is respected, these resources may have to be returned to the donor. Until they are expended properly, they should not be considered as revenue. As a consequence, expenditures govern the recognition of revenue. These resources are expenditure driven, similar to such items in governmental accounting. This situation requires the following entries in a restricted current fund:

Event	Entry		
Resources are contributed by a corporation for scholarships to minorities.	Assets Contributed . . . . XXX Fund Balance		XXX
Expenditures are made in compliance with restrictions; revenue is recognized.	Expenditures—Student Aid . . . . XXX Cash		XXX
	Fund Balance . . . . XXX Revenues—Private Gifts and Grants		XXX

Fund Balance is increased at the time of the receipt of the resources. Revenue is not recognized until resources are expended and then in the exact amount of the expenditures. As a result, revenues always will equal expenditures in the restricted current fund.

The following events affected the restricted current fund of Rogers State University. Only one fund balance account is maintained. Data on sources, purposes, and applications of restricted resources are recorded in subsidiary records.

Event	Entry		
A restricted gift of $70,000 is received to assist in library operations.	Cash . . . . Fund Balance	70,000	70,000
Endowment income of $8,000 is restricted to student aid activities.	Cash . . . . Fund Balance	8,000	8,000

Of the following expenditures, all but $4,000 are paid:
 For library operations $67,000
 For student aid 6,000
   Total $73,000
	Expenditures—Academic Support . . . .
	Expenditures—Student Aid . . . .
	  Cash . . . .
	  Accounts Payable . . . .
		67,000
		6,000
			69,000
			4,000

Revenues are recorded to the extent of expenditures.	Fund Balance . . . .
	  Revenues—Private Gifts and Grants . . . . .
	  Revenues—Endowment Income . . . .
		73,000	67,000
			6,000

The books are closed. Since revenues equal expenditures, Fund Balance is not involved.	Revenues—Private Gifts and Grants . . . .
	Revenues—Endowment Income . . . .
	  Expenditures—Academic Support . . . . . .
	  Expenditures—Student Aid . . . .
		67,000
		6,000
			67,000
			6,000

STATEMENT OF REVENUES, EXPENDITURES, AND OTHER CHANGES; THE BALANCE SHEET; STATEMENT OF CHANGES IN FUND BALANCES

The statement of revenues, expenditures, and other changes is provided by only the current funds of a public college or university, since the other funds record changes in resources directly through their fund balances. This statement shows the current funds revenues by source, expenditures by function, and other changes, such as mandatory and discretionary transfers. In the design recommended by the audit guide, the statement does not attempt to show net income or net loss, since this amount is not of primary concern to a not-for-profit unit. Instead, the final amount is the net increase or decrease in the unrestricted and restricted fund balances, which also is shown in the statement of changes in fund balances. The recommended form, presented in Illustration 18-1, shows columns for the unrestricted current fund, the restricted current fund, and the total.

Note that in the restricted current fund column the total revenues equal the total expenditures. Also note in this column the amount labeled "Excess of restricted receipts over transfers to revenues." Reviewing the entries in the restricted current fund on page 978, a total of $78,000 in restricted resources was

Illustration 18-1
Rogers State University
Statement of Current Funds, Revenues, Expenditures, and Other Changes
For Year Ended June 30, 19X5

	Unrestricted	Restricted	Total
Revenues:			
Educational and general:			
Student tuition and fees.....................................	$1,680,000		$1,680,000
Governmental appropriations...............................	750,000		750,000
Private gifts and grants	250,000	$67,000	317,000
Endowment income	70,000*	6,000	76,000
Other income..	250,000		250,000
Total educational and general revenues....................	$3,000,000	$73,000	$3,073,000
Auxiliary enterprises...	400,000		400,000
Expired term endowments	20,000*		20,000
Total revenues	$3,420,000	$73,000	$3,493,000
Expenditures and mandatory transfers:			
Educational and general:			
Instruction...	$1,318,000		$1,318,000
Research...	100,000		100,000
Academic support...	150,000	$67,000	217,000
Student services	222,000		222,000
Institutional support	200,000		200,000
Operation and maintenance of plant.........................	400,000		400,000
Student aid..	215,000	6,000	221,000
Total educational and general expenditures	$2,605,000	$73,000	$2,678,000
Mandatory transfers for principal payment....................	20,000*		20,000
Total..	$2,625,000	$73,000	$2,698,000
Auxiliary enterprises expenditures	350,000		350,000
Total expenditures and mandatory transfers................	$2,975,000	$73,000	$3,048,000
Other transfers and additions (deductions):			
Excess of restricted receipts over transfers to revenues		$25,000*	$ 25,000
Transfers to other funds..	$ (300,000)*		(300,000)
Net increase in fund balances..................................	$ 145,000	$25,000	$ 170,000

*Includes amounts from interaction matrix on pages 992–995.

received this period, but only $73,000 was expended, producing $5,000 of resources received and not expended. This item must be introduced on the statement of revenues, expenditures, and other changes in order to produce the correct net increase in Fund Balance.

An exceptionally high degree of accounting sophistication is required to interpret the statement of revenues, expenditures, and other changes in its present form. Its primary value is the detail it provides for revenues, expenditures, and transfers. However, if the primary emphasis is on resources made available (revenues) and resources applied (expenditures), a useful figure would be their difference, which is not furnished. The difference between total revenues and the sum of expenditures and mandatory transfers also is not provided, but it would have managerial value. The only net figure is the final amount of change in the fund balances. A superficial glance at the change of $145,000 in the unrestricted current fund could lead the unwary to conclude incorrectly that the fund grew by only this amount. In reality, the increase in the fund is $445,000, which is the excess of total revenues ($3,420,000) over total expenditures and mandatory transfers ($2,975,000). The discretionary transfers of $300,000 to various other funds reduced the change to $145,000.

A balance sheet for all funds, with separate, self-balancing totals for each fund is shown in Illustration 18-2 on pages 981 and 982. A statement of changes in fund balances for all funds is presented in Illustration 18-3 on pages 984 and 985. The balance sheet and statement of changes in fund balance will be referenced in the following discussion of other funds.

LOAN FUNDS

Loan funds are established to account for resources that are available for loans primarily to students and possibly to faculty and staff. Loan funds are revolving (self-perpetuating), with repayments of principal and the excess of interest collected over costs incurred becoming the base for additional loans. Both principal and earnings must be available for loan purposes. If only the income from a gift or grant may be used for loan purposes, the principal should not be in the loan fund but in the endowment fund.

The resources of loan funds consist mainly of gifts restricted for loan purposes and unrestricted current fund resources transferred by authorization of the governing board. Although assets are not segregated by restriction, the fund balance must reveal its restricted and unrestricted portions. In a public university, no revenue or expenditure accounts are used. Additions to the loan fund are recorded directly in the restricted or unrestricted fund balance, while expenditures and losses are deducted directly from the fund balance.

The following entries are recorded in the loan fund of Rogers State University. The loan funds are included in the balance sheet (Illustration 18-2) on pages 981 and 982 and the statement of changes in fund balances on pages 984–985 (Illustration 18-3).

Event	Entry		
A donation of $25,000 is received from an alumnus for student loan purposes.	Cash . . . . 　　Fund Balance—Restricted	25,000	25,000
Investments costing $5,000 are sold for $5,500. Gain is restricted.	Cash . . . . 　　Investments. . . . . 　　Fund Balance—Restricted	5,500	5,000 500
Loans totaling $24,000 are made to students.	Loans Receivable . . . . 　　Cash	24,000	24,000
Collections from other loans of restricted funds total $20,000 plus $1,000 of interest.	Cash . . . . 　　Loans Receivable . . . . 　　Fund Balance—Restricted	21,000	20,000 1,000
A $500 student loan made from restricted funds is uncollectible.	Fund Balance—Restricted . . . . 　　Loans Receivable	500	500

Illustration 18-2
Rogers State University
Balance Sheet
June 30, 19X5

Assets		Liabilities and Fund Balances	
Current funds:		**Current funds:**	
Unrestricted:		Unrestricted:	
Cash	$ 260,000	Notes and accounts payable	$ 230,000
Due from other funds	20,000	Due to other funds.	3,000
Investments.	255,000	Fund balances.	746,000
Receivables (net)	306,000		
Inventories of materials	110,000		
Prepaid expenses.	28,000		
Total unrestricted	$ 979,000	Total unrestricted	$ 979,000
Restricted:		Restricted:	
Cash	$ 153,000	Notes and accounts payable	$ 18,000
Due from other funds	20,000	Fund balances.	470,000
Investments.	247,000		
Receivables (net)	68,000		
Total restricted	$ 488,000	Total restricted	$ 488,000
Total current funds.	$ 1,467,000	Total current funds.	$ 1,467,000
Loan funds:		**Loan funds:**	
Cash	$ 29,500	Unrestricted.	$ 13,500
Due from other funds	3,000	Restricted.	82,500
Investments.	5,000		
Receivables (net)	58,500		
Total loan funds	$ 96,000	Total loan funds	$ 96,000

continued

Assets		Liabilities and Fund Balances	
Endowment and similar funds:		**Endowment and similar funds:**	
Cash	$ 460,000	Due to other funds	$ 40,000
Investments	1,270,000	Fund balances:	
		Unrestricted	440,000
		Restricted	1,250,000
Total endowment and similar funds	$ 1,730,000	Total endowment and similar funds	$ 1,730,000
Annuity and life income funds:		**Annuity and life income funds:**	
Cash	$ 137,000	Due to other funds	$ 195,000
Investments	530,500	Life income payable	1,500
		Annuities payable	256,221
		Fund balances:	
		Unrestricted	214,779
Total annuity and life income funds	$ 667,500	Total annuity and life income funds	$ 667,500
Plant funds:		**Plant funds:**	
Unexpended:		Unexpended:	
Cash	$ 275,000	Notes and accounts payable	$ 110,000
Due from other funds	195,000	Bonds payable	400,000
Investments	1,240,000	Fund balances:	
		Unrestricted	200,000
		Restricted	1,000,000
Total unexpended	$ 1,710,000	Total unexpended	$ 1,710,000
Renewals and replacements:		Renewals and replacements:	
Cash	$ 10,000	Fund balances:	
Deposits	100,000	Unrestricted	$ 235,000
Investments	150,000	Restricted	25,000
Total renewals and replacements	$ 260,000	Total renewals and replacements	$ 260,000
Retirement of indebtedness:		Retirement of indebtedness:	
Cash	$ 50,000	Fund balances:	
Deposits	250,000	Unrestricted	$ 115,000
		Restricted	185,000
Total retirement of indebtedness	$ 300,000	Total retirement of indebtedness	$ 300,000
Investment in plant:		Investment in plant:	
Land	$ 500,000	Bonds payable	$ 2,190,000
Land improvements	1,000,000	Mortgages payable	1,200,000
Buildings	20,000,000	Net investment in plant	$38,210,000
Equipment	15,000,000		
Library books	5,100,000		
Total investment in plant	$41,600,000	Total investment in plant	$41,600,000
Total plant funds	$43,870,000	Total plant funds	$43,870,000
Agency funds:		**Agency funds:**	
Cash	$ 50,000	Deposits held for others	$ 110,000
Investments	60,000		
Total agency funds	$ 110,000	Total agency funds	$ 110,000

ENDOWMENT AND SIMILAR FUNDS

The following types of endowment funds, each having its own fund balance account, are included in the category of Endowment and Similar Funds for a public university:

1. *Regular or pure endowments* are funds whose principal has been specified by the donor as nonexpendable. The resources are invested, and the earnings are available for expenditure, usually by the unrestricted current fund.
2. *Term endowments* are funds whose principal is expendable after a specified time period or after a designated event, at which point the resources are added to the unrestricted current fund, unless the original donor has specified some other application.
3. *Quasi-endowments* are funds set aside by the board or controlling body, usually from unrestricted current funds. Restricted current funds also may be set aside if the donor's limitations are not violated. Since these funds are discretionary, technically they do not belong to the endowment category, hence the addition to the title of "and Similar Funds."

Accounting should be detailed sufficiently in subsidiary records to demonstrate compliance with the restrictions of each endowment fund. In the balance sheet section for these funds (see Illustration 18-2), the assets are not segregated, but the fund balance section shows the endowment, term endowment, and quasi-endowment components for which separate accounts are established.

As gifts and bequests are received, either the account Fund Balance—Endowment or Fund Balance—Term Endowment is credited. Assets received as discretionary transfers result in a credit to Fund Balance—Quasi-Endowment. Gains or losses on the disposition of endowment assets are recorded directly in the appropriate fund balance account. Note that gains or losses are considered changes in principal and not as income or expense, unless otherwise specified by the donor.

The resources for endowment funds often are pooled for investment purposes, with the various fund balances sharing proportionately in the outcome based on the market values of investments at the time of pooling or at specified future dates. Procedures for investment pooling are discussed in Chapter 19. Income earned on restricted endowment resources should be transferred immediately to and recorded directly in the fund balance of the restricted current fund, the loan fund, the endowment fund, or a plant fund, depending upon which fund the donor has specified should reap the benefits. Income on which there is no restriction should be transferred to and recorded directly in the unrestricted current fund, where it is credited to Endowment Income. If, for some reason, there is a delay in making the transfer, the income received should be recorded in the endowment fund, with a credit to a liability to the proper fund. The costs of managing endowment funds should be borne by the university's unrestricted current fund.

Illustration 18-3

Rogers State University

Statement of Changes in Fund Balances

For Year Ended June 30, 19X5

	Current Funds	
	Unrestricted	Restricted
Revenues and other additions:		
Educational and general revenues..................................	$ 3,000,000	
Auxiliary enterprises revenues.......................................	400,000	
Expired term endowment revenues	20,000	
Gifts and bequests—restricted.......................................		$ 70,000
Investment income—restricted		28,000
Gain on sale of investments—restricted...........................		
Gain on sale of investments—unrestricted		
Retirement of indebtedness		
Expended on plant facilities		
Total revenues and other additions	$ 3,420,000	$ 98,000
Expenditures and other deductions:		
Educational and general expenditures	$ 2,605,000	$ 73,000
Auxiliary enterprises expenditures	350,000	
Loan cancellations and write-offs..................................		
Expired term endowments		
Adjustment of actuarial liability		
Retirement of indebtedness		
Expenditures for plant facilities.....................................		
Expenditures for plant maintenance		
Total expenditures and other deductions	$ 2,955,000	$ 73,000
Transfers among funds—additions (deductions):		
Mandatory principal payment..	$ (20,000)	
Other transfers...	(300,000)	
Total transfers..	$ (320,000)	0
Net increase (decrease) for the year	$ 145,000	$ 25,000
Fund balance—beginning of the year...............................	601,000	445,000
Fund balance—end of the year	$ 746,000	$470,000

To illustrate some of the accounting techniques, recording of transactions relating to endowment and similar funds is shown in the multicolumn presentation in Illustration 18-4.

Although most universities report their investments on a cost basis, the audit guide permits the use of market value, provided this basis is used for all investments of all funds. Under the market value method, unrealized gains and losses are recognized and are accounted for as if realized.

Loan Funds	Endowment and Similar Funds	Annuity and Life Income Funds	Plant Funds			
			Unexpended	Renewals and Replacements	Retirement of Indebtedness	Investment in Plant
$25,000	$ 120,000	$ 56,000	$ 90,000			$ 190,000
1,000		18,000	40,000	$ 5,000		
500						
	60,000	9,500				
						100,000
						40,000
$26,500	$ 180,000	$ 83,500	$ 130,000	$ 5,000	0	$ 330,000
$ 500						
	$ 20,000					
		$ 3,221				
					$100,000	
			$ 40,000			
				$ 50,000		
$ 500	$ 20,000	$ 3,221	$ 40,000	$ 50,000	$100,000	0
					$ 20,000	
$ 3,000	$ 150,000		$ 147,000			
$ 3,000	$ 150,000	0	$ 147,000	0	20,000	0
$29,000	$ 310,000	$ 80,279	$ 237,000	$ (45,000)	$ (80,000)	$ 330,000
67,000	1,380,000	134,500	963,000	305,000	380,000	37,880,000
$96,000	$1,690,000	$214,779	$1,200,000	$260,000	$300,000	$38,210,000

ANNUITY AND LIFE INCOME FUNDS

Resources may be accepted by a public university under the stipulation that periodic payments are to continue as an annuity to the donor or other designated beneficiary for an indicated time period. These resources should be accounted for in an *annuity fund* at their market value on the date of receipt. A liability for the actuarially computed present value of expected total annuity payments is recorded, with the excess credited to Annuity Fund Balance. As each payment is made, a debit is charged directly to the Annuity Payable each period and the liability is adjusted to bring it to an amount equal to the present value. For example, assume a retired administrator donated $50,000 to a university. The administrator is to receive annuity payments of $3,000 per year for life; thereafter, the principal is to be used for student aid. Assuming an estimated life of 15 years and an 8% interest rate, the present value of the annuity is actuarially computed to be $25,678. The entry to record receipt of the donation is:

Cash—Annuity	50,000	
Annuities Payable		25,678
Annuity Fund Balance		24,332

During the year, interest earned on annuity investments is added to the fund balance. At the end of the first year, the present value of the liability is adjusted by adding interest of $2,054 (8% × $25,678). The administrator is mailed a check for $3,000. Entries to record the adjustment of the liability to present value and payment to the annuitant are:

Annuity Fund Balance	2,054	
Annuities Payable		2,054
Annuities Payable	3,000	
Cash		3,000

A *life income fund* is used if all income received on contributed assets is to be paid to the donor or other specified recipient for life. When the original contributed assets are recorded at market value, the corresponding credit is to Life Income Fund Balance. As income is received, a liability for its payment is established immediately.

When the annuity payments or the life income payments cease, the principal is transferred to the donor-specified fund group or to the unrestricted current fund revenue if no principal restriction exists. Also, unless otherwise specified, gains or losses on the sale of investments are treated as changes in principal and are recorded directly in the appropriate fund balance account.

Events that affected the ongoing annuity and life income funds of Rogers State University are described and recorded as follows. The balance sheet section for these funds appears in Illustration 18-2.

Event	Entry		
Cash of $12,000 from life income fund investments and $18,000 from annuity fund investments is received. (Separate accounts are maintained for life income cash and annuity cash.)	Cash—Life Income	12,000	
	Life Income Payable		12,000
	Cash—Annuity	18,000	
	Annuity Fund Balance		18,000
A retired professor donated $100,000. The professor is to receive $6,000 per year for an estimated life of 10 years. Thereafter, the principal is to be used for student aid. The present value of the annuity is actuarially computed to be $40,260.	Cash—Annuity	100,000	
	Annuities Payable		40,260
	Annuity Fund Balance		59,740

Event	Entry		
Interest for the year on the annuity liability is recorded, 8% × $40,260.	Annuity Fund Balance	3,221	
	Annuities Payable.		3,221
Payments are made to:	Annuities Payable.	6,000	
Annuitant. $6,000	Cash—Annuity.		6,000
Life income beneficiaries 12,000	Life Income Payable.	12,000	
	Cash—Life Income		12,000
Annuity fund investments with a book value of $50,000 are sold for $59,500.	Cash—Annuity.	59,500	
	Investments—Annuity		50,000
	Annuity Fund Balance		9,500

If a university has a substantial amount of annuity and life income funds, two separate funds could be established, removing the necessity to identify each component of an entry. The typical financial reports of these funds would display only the financial condition (balance sheet) and the changes in fund balances (see Illustrations 18-2 and 18-3).

PLANT FUNDS

Plant funds of public universities include four separate, self-balancing subgroups:

1. *Unexpended plant fund* accounts for resources that are to be used to acquire properties. Such resources may be received as a gift or grant restricted to plant acquisition, in which case Fund Balance—Restricted is credited. Assets may be transferred by university authorities from the current funds or other funds, requiring a credit to Fund Balance—Unrestricted to record their receipt. When cash is expended to acquire existing capital assets, the appropriate fund balance account is debited as Cash is credited. The assets acquired are recorded in the Investment in Plant subgroup, discussed on page 988, with a credit to Net Investment in Plant. For a major construction project, a bond issue usually is floated. The proceeds and bond liability are recorded in the unexpended plant fund, preferably until the construction is completed. As work is begun, costs are debited to a construction in progress account. Upon completion, the total cost is transferred to the Investment in Plant subgroup, along with the related bond liability, with any difference between the two amounts recorded in Fund Balance—Unrestricted. If financing was achieved with a mortgage, the accounting procedure would be the same except for the designation of the liability as a mortgage payable.
2. *Plant fund for renewals and replacements* accounts for resources that are available to keep the physical plant in operating condition. Such expenditures seldom lead to capitalization. Resources transferred to this subgroup as a result of discretionary action by the governing board are recorded by crediting the account Fund Balance—Unrestricted. Resources received from

outside sources that specified that the amounts must be used for renewals and replacements are credited to Fund Balance—Restricted. When expenditures are made, the proper fund balance is debited, and the cash or a liability account is credited. The amount remaining in the two fund balance accounts represents the unexpended resources available for renewals and replacements.

3. *Plant fund for retirement of indebtedness* corresponds to the debt service fund of a governmental unit. This fund accounts for the resources accumulated for the payment of interest and principal of plant fund indebtedness. Since the liabilities are included in the investment in plant subgroup, payments of either interest or principal are recorded as direct reductions of the retirement of indebtedness fund balance.

4. The *investment in plant* subgroup controls all plant assets except those found in the endowment fund. This subgroup is similar to a combination of the general fixed assets and general long-term debt account groups of a governmental unit. Assets are acquired as a result of transfers from the unexpended plant fund subgroup, donations, and expenditures of the current funds. For a university, the costs of books and other library items are considered major outlays and are classified as plant assets. Liabilities related to the Investment in Plant also are shown in this subgroup. When principal is paid by the plant fund for retirement of indebtedness subgroup, the liability is reduced in the investment in plant subgroup, with a corresponding increase in Net Investment in Plant. Upon completion of a construction project whose costs were accumulated in the unexpended plant fund, the investment in plant subgroup debits the asset completed, credits any remaining related liability, such as Bonds Payable or Mortgage Payable, and credits the difference to the account Net Investment in Plant.

Public colleges and universities are not required to report a provision for *depreciation* of plant fund assets, but may elect to do so. The fact that depreciation need not be reported in its external financial statements does not prevent its computation and use in independent determinations of the total cost of operating the university. Such cost computations are useful in establishing charges for auxiliary enterprise services, which include dormitories, bookstores, cafeterias and restaurants, medical service, and the student union. Especially for services provided to the general public, amounts charged should include depreciation considerations, even though depreciation is not recorded formally. A part of the amount that a university receives from grants reimburses it for overhead, which should include depreciation. The only university fund in which a provision for depreciation must be entered is in the unusual case that fixed assets are part of a nonexpendable endowment fund, which must protect its principal.

Entries unique to the plant funds of Rogers State University are presented in the matrix on pages 990 and 991, with an indication of which of the four subgroups is recording the event. Additional events, each affecting more than one plant subgroup are presented in Illustration 18-4. The plant funds section of the balance sheet is shown in Illustration 18-2.

AGENCY FUNDS

Agency funds account for resources that are not the property of the university but that are held in the university's custody. An example of such resources is assets belonging to student organizations. The total amount of these resources represents a liability. As a result, there is no fund balance, and agency funds would not appear in the analysis of changes in fund balances. The balance sheet of Rogers State University, shown in Illustration 18-2, includes a section for agency funds.

BALANCE SHEET

The composite balance sheet in Illustration 18-2 is criticized for not giving the reader a conception of the university's total financial position. For example, Rogers State University's cash appears in nine different places and its investments in eight, and there are fifteen various fund balances. Alternative balance sheet presentations are permitted and one would be to present a combined balance sheet with a column for each fund and perhaps the total. The audit guide cautions, however, that "in the balance sheet, columnar fund group figures should not be crossfooted in a total column, to reflect an overall financial position of the institution, unless all necessary disclosures are made."[4] It further states that combining such items as cash into one total could be misleading since all cash is not available for discretionary spending but is, in part, restricted.

STATEMENT OF CHANGES IN FUND BALANCES

The most revealing financial report for a public university is the statement of changes in fund balances. It is a statement of the university's total activities for the period. In condensed form, it reveals for each fund (except agency funds) the revenues and other additions to fund balances, expenditures and other deductions from fund balances, and transfers between funds, both mandatory and discretionary. It concludes with the net increase or decrease in each fund balance, which is combined with the beginning balance to produce the ending fund balance as shown in the balance sheet. The agency funds are excluded since they have no fund balances.

The columnar format is illustrated in the audit guide, but with the customary warning that columns should not be crossfooted unless care is taken to provide full disclosure about the restricted nature of some items. A columnar statement of changes in fund balances for Rogers State University is shown in Illustration 18-3 on pages 984–985.

Although most items in the statement of changes in fund balances are straightforward, a few should be noted. When the retirement of indebtedness subgroup is reduced by principal payments on plant obligations, the investment in plant subgroup is increased correspondingly. Similarly, the unexpended plant fund subgroup's expenditures for plant assets increase the investment in plant

---

[4]*Audits of Colleges and Universities* (New York: American Institute of Certified Public Accountants, rev. ed., 1975), p. 57.

Event

Stock with a market value of $90,000 is received from an art patron to finance an art gallery addition.

A collection of first editions, appraised at $30,000, is donated to the university.

An $800,000 bond issue is sold at face value to finance a business school wing.

Construction of the wing is one-fourth completed.

Contract is completed at additional cost of $640,000 and is paid in full.

Land valued at $160,000 is donated by an alumnus.

Building repairs constituting a renewal of $50,000 are paid, of which $5,000 is from restricted resources.

Restricted earnings received on investments of:
Unexpended Fund $40,000
Renewals and Replacements Fund.   5,000

subgroup. As mentioned previously, most of the resources for payment come from the unrestricted current fund, whose fund balance was reduced when amounts were transferred to one of the plant subgroups. When payments actually are made, there is a shifting of amounts within the subgroups, but no additional net reduction. The other noteworthy item is that the section relating to transfers between funds is self-balancing—what increases one fund balance through mandatory or discretionary transfers reduces some other fund by the same amount.

MULTIPLE EFFECTS OF TRANSACTIONS OF A PUBLIC COLLEGE OR UNIVERSITY—THE INTERACTION MATRIX

The unrestricted current and restricted current funds of a college or university are operating funds in which operating activity is recorded in revenue and expenditure accounts. Other funds are nonoperating funds in which transactions normally affecting nominal accounts are entered directly into fund balances. As in governmental accounting, transactions frequently affect more than a single fund. The matrix in Illustration 18-4 shows effects of some transactions on more than one fund.

ACCOUNTING FOR PRIVATE COLLEGES AND UNIVERSITIES

As discussed in the previous section, FASB Statement Nos. 116 and 117 provide a major shift in accounting and financial reporting for private colleges and univer-

Plant Fund Subgroup	Entry		
Unexpended	Investments...	90,000	
	Fund Balance—Restricted..............................		90,000
Investment in Plant	Library Books.......................................	30,000	
	Net Investment in Plant..............................		30,000
Unexpended	Cash...	800,000	
	Bonds Payable......................................		800,000
Unexpended	Construction in Progress	200,000	
	Contracts Payable..................................		200,000
Unexpended	Construction in Progress	640,000	
	Contracts Payable..................................	200,000	
	Cash..		840,000
Investment in Plant	Land..	160,000	
	Net Investment in Plant..............................		160,000
Renewals and Replacements	Fund Balance—Restricted..............................	5,000	
	Fund Balance—Unrestricted............................	45,000	
	Cash..		50,000
Unexpended	Cash...	40,000	
	Fund Balance—Restricted..............................		40,000
Renewals and Replacements	Cash...	5,000	
	Fund Balance—Restricted..............................		5,000

sities from the audit guidance. The focus in financial reporting for private colleges and universities now emphasizes the organization as a whole. The financial statements present organization-wide totals of assets, liabilities, and net assets as well as information concerning organization-wide changes in net assets and organization-wide cash flows. Because of a shift away from a fund group focus to an organization-wide focus, there is no requirement for external financial statements to include fund group reporting. Three net asset classes—unrestricted, temporarily restricted, and permanently restricted—are used instead of fund balances. Events that were previously recorded as changes in fund balance will now be recorded as contributions, exchange transactions, capital acquisitions, or expenses. Contributions are distinguished from exchange transactions or agency relationships. Only contributions with donor-imposed restrictions affect the restricted assets. All other transactions, such as government and other awards funding research, are now considered exchange transactions and affect unrestricted net assets. Federally sponsored flow-through awards to students are accounted for as agency transactions rather than restricted asset activity.

ACCOUNTING FOR CONTRIBUTIONS

FASB Statement No. 116 provides guidance for recognition of contributions received and unconditional promises to give as revenues or gains *in the period received*. The standards set forth by FASB Statement No. 116 represent a signifi-

Illustration 18-4   Interaction Matrix for Public College and University Accounting

Event	Current Unrestricted		Current Restricted	
1. Cash transferred to plant fund for:				
Addition to plant (discretionary) . . . \$147,000 Payment of mortgage (mandatory) . . . . . 20,000 ⎯⎯⎯⎯⎯ Total \$167,000	Fund Balance (or Transfer to Plant Fund). . . . . . . 147,000 Mandatory Transfer for Principal Payment 20,000 Cash	167,000		
2. The board of trustees has agreed to transfer \$3,000 to the loan fund on the first day of the next fiscal year.	Fund Balance (or Transfer to Loan Fund). . . . . 3,000 Due to Other Funds	3,000		
3. The Board of Trustees has authorized an immediate transfer of \$150,000 to the endowment fund.	Fund Balance (or Transfer to Endowment Fund). . . 150,000 Cash	150,000		
4. Term endowments expired, making \$20,000 cash available.	Cash . . . . 20,000 Revenues— Expired Term Endowments	20,000		
5. Endowment fund investments carried at \$200,000 are sold for \$260,000 and investment earnings of \$40,000 are received and shared equally by the current funds.	Due from Other Funds . . . . 20,000 Revenue— Endowment Income	20,000	Due from Other Funds. . . . . . 20,000 Fund Balance	20,000
6. Common stock with a market value of \$120,000 is received as a pure endowment donation.				
7. Payment of \$100,000 is made on mortage related to completed plant.				
8. Completed building costs are transferred to investment in Plant subgroup.				
9. The books are closed.	Fund Balance. . . . . 20,000 Mandatory Transfer for Principal Pmt . . Revenue—Expired Term Endowments . . . . . 20,000 Revenue—Endowment Income . . . . 20,000 Fund Balance.	20,000 40,000		
If separate transfer accounts were used to record discretionary transfers, they would be closed at this point.	Fund Balance. . . . . 300,000 Transfer to Plant Fund . . . . Transfer to Loan Fund . . . . Transfer to Endowment Fund	147,000 3,000 150,000		

Loan		Endowment		

| Due from Unrestricted Current Funds .... | 3,000 | | | |
| Fund Balance—Unrestricted.... | | 3,000 | | |

| Cash .... | 150,000 |
| Fund Balance—Quasi-Endowment....... | | 150,000 |

| Fund Balance—Endowment....... | 20,000 |
| Cash .... | | 20,000 |

Cash	300,000
Investments.........		200,000
Fund Balance—Endowment.......		60,000
Due to Other Funds..		40,000

| Investments.......... | 120,000 |
| Fund Balance—Endowment ...... | | 120,000 |

(continued)

Event	Unexpended Plant		Plant Renewals and Replacements
1. Cash transferred to plant fund for: Addition to plant (discretionary) .... $147,000 Payment of mortgage (mandatory) ...... 20,000 Total.............. $167,000	Cash .... 147,000 Fund Balance— Unrestricted	147,000	
2. The board of trustees has agreed to transfer $3,000 to the loan fund on the first day of the next fiscal year.			
3. The board of trustees has authorized an immediate transfer of $150,000 to the endowment fund.			
4. Term endowments expired, making $20,000 cash available.			
5. Endowment fund investments carried at $200,000 are sold for $260,000 and investment earnings of $40,000 are received and shared equally by the current funds.			
6. Common stock with a market value of $120,000 is received as a pure endowment donation.			
7. Payment of $100,000 is made on mortgage related to completed plant.			

8. Completed building costs are transferred to investment in plant subgroup.	Bonds Payable 800,000
	 Fund Balance—
	   Unrestricted 40,000
	 Construction in
	   Progress..........
		840,000	

9. The books are closed. If separate transfer accounts were used to record discretionary transfers, they would be closed at this point.			

Plant Retirement of Indebtedness

Cash   20,000
   Fund Balance—
     Unrestricted . . .   20,000

Investment in Plant

Fund Balance—
  Unrestricted   100,000
  Cash   100,000

Mortgage Payable   100,000
  Net Investment in
   Plant   100,000
Building   840,000
  Bonds Payable   800,000
  Net Investment in
   Plant   40,000

cant departure from the AICPA audit guidance which deferred revenue recognition until the period expenditure or expenses were incurred for the restricted purposes.

Contributions are defined by FASB Statement No. 116 as "unconditional transfers of cash or other assets to an entity or a settlement or cancellation of its liabilities in a voluntary nonreciprocal transfer. . . ."[5] Other assets include securities, land, buildings, use of facilities or utilities, materials and supplies, intangible assets, services, and unconditional promises to give those items in the future. Exceptions to the general recognition provision of Statement No. 116 are made for contributions of services and works of art. Contributions other than services are recognized in the period received and are measured at their fair market value. Services would be recognized only if they (a) create or enhance nonfinancial assets; or (b) require specialized skills, are provided by individuals possessing those abilities, and typically would have to be purchased if not provided by donation. Not-for-profit organizations are not required to recognize contributions of works of art, historical treasures, and similar assets if the donated items are added to collections, held for public exhibition, and preserved, cared for, and protected.

Pledges (promise to give) are divided into unconditional pledges and conditional pledges. Unconditional pledges depend only on the passage of time or the demand by the university to be collected and are recognized as a receivable and revenue in the period made. Conditional pledges depend on the occurrence of uncertain future events and should be recognized as revenue when the conditions are substantially met (i.e., the pledge becomes unconditional). An example of a conditional pledge might be a donation restricted for construction of a new building given *only if* the organization can raise the remaining funds through additional contributions. Pledges or other assets received subject to such conditions are recorded as refundable advances until the conditions have been substantially met, at which time revenue is recorded.

FASB Statement No. 116 states that the "present value of estimated future cash flows using a discount rate commensurate with the risks involved is an appropriate measure of the fair value of unconditional promises to give cash." Promises receivable within one year need not be discounted. An allowance for doubtful contributions should be established based on historical experience and other factors to cover any uncertainties concerning collectibility. An unconditional pledge with no donor restriction is recognized as follows:

```
Contributions Receivable . . . . . . . . . . . . . . . . . . . . . . . . . . . . . . . . . . . . . . . .   XXX
        Revenues—Unrestricted Contributions . . . . . . . . . . . . . . . . . . . . . . . . .          XXX
Provision for uncollectible contributions . . . . . . . . . . . . . . . . . . . . . . . . . . . .   XXX
        Allowance for uncollectible contributions . . . . . . . . . . . . . . . . . . . . . . .          XXX
```

[5]FASB Statement No. 116, *Accounting for Contributions Received and Contributions Made* (Norwalk, CT: Financial Accounting Standards Board, 1993), para. 5. The FASB defines a nonreciprocal transfer as a transaction in which an organization receives an asset or cancellations of a liability without directly gaining value in exchange.

DONOR-IMPOSED RESTRICTIONS AND RECLASSIFICATIONS

In a major shift from existing practice, FASB Statement No. 116 states that donor-imposed restrictions have no bearing on the period in which contributions are recognized as revenue. Rather, these restrictions affect the manner of reporting contributions and related assets. All contributions received (or unconditional promises to give) are classified into one of three categories: unrestricted, temporarily restricted, or permanently restricted resources. A temporary restriction expires when the stipulated time has elapsed, when the stipulated purpose has been fulfilled, or over the useful life of donated asset. Expenditure or time restrictions require a *reclassification* entry to release the restriction. Gifts of long-lived assets (or long-lived assets acquired with restricted gifts of cash) with donor stipulations specifying the use of the donated asset are initially reported as temporarily restricted. The expiration (or release) of the time restriction is recorded over the useful life of the asset. Gifts of assets with no donor restrictions are classified as unrestricted. Organizations have an option to record long-lived assets acquired with donor-restricted cash as either temporarily restricted or unrestricted. If the asset is recorded as temporarily restricted, the university reclassifies a portion of the temporarily restricted amount each year as depreciation is recorded. This releasing of donor-imposed restrictions (reclassification) simultaneously decreases temporarily restricted net assets and increases unrestricted net assets in order to "match" the expenses they support (operating expenses, depreciation, etc. which decrease unrestricted net assets).

Universities also have the option to record contributions whose restrictions are met in the same reporting period as increases in unrestricted net assets, instead of increases in temporarily restricted net assets with subsequent reclassifications from temporarily restricted net assets to unrestricted net assets.

Further, SFAS No. 116 notes that if an expense is incurred for a purpose for which both unrestricted and temporarily restricted net assets are available, a donor-imposed restriction is fulfilled to the extent of the expense incurred unless the expense is for a purpose that is directly attributable to another specific external source of revenue. This provision to *use restricted resources* first to fund expenses is a significant change from the audit guides which allow institutions to choose the source of funding—either restricted or unrestricted.

A cash contribution restricted by the donor for a specific expenditure is recorded when received.	Cash......................................	XXX	
	Revenues—Temporarily Restricted Contributions............................		XXX
Expenses made in compliance with donor restrictions are funded by the restricted resources. Temporarily restricted net assets are released with a reclassification entry.	Expense..................................	XXX	
	Cash....................................		XXX
	Reclassification Out—Temporarily Restricted— satisfaction of donor restrictions...........	XXX	
	Reclassification In—Unrestricted—satisfaction of donor restrictions....................		XXX

An important point for the reader to understand about the provisions of FASB Statement No. 116 is the document's exclusion of certain transactions from the scope of contributions. Exchange transactions, that is, reciprocal transfers in which each party receives and sacrifices approximately equal value, are not considered restricted. Many transactions that have been accounted for in much the same way as contributions, for example, grants, awards, sponsorships, and appropriations, will be categorized as *exchange transactions* rather than contributions under FASB Statement No. 116 and accounted for as increases in unrestricted assets. Government grants which require performance by the not-for-profit organization will be accounted for as refundable deposits (liabilities) until earned. Unrestricted revenue will be earned when expenses are made in conjunction with the provisions of the grant. Other government grants, which are essentially pass-through financial aid to students, will now be accounted for as agency transactions.

Grant monies received.	Cash...................................... XXX	
	U.S. Government Grants Refundable.........	XXX
Expenses incurred in conjunction with provisions of grant.	Expenses.................................. XXX	
	Cash......................................	XXX
Revenue is recognized up the amount earned by incurring above expenses.	U.S. Government Grants Refundable.......... XXX	
	Revenues—Unrestricted...................	XXX

Permanently restricted contributions are termed endowments. Earnings on endowment investments may be recorded as a credit to unrestricted revenue or temporarily restricted revenue depending on donor specification as to the use of the earnings. Realized and unrealized gains and losses on endowment investments are reported as increases or decreases in unrestricted net assets unless their use is temporarily or permanently restricted by explicit donor stipulations or by law.

FINANCIAL STATEMENTS

Financial statements prepared in accordance with FASB Statement No. 117 represent a shift away from fund reporting to an emphasis on the organization as a whole. The equity account, fund balance, has been replaced with the term *net assets*. FASB Statement No. 117 requires classification of the organization's net assets based on the existence or absence of donor-imposed restrictions. The financial statements must display three classes of net assets: unrestricted, temporarily restricted, and permanently restricted. Changes in each of these three classes of net assets must also be reported. Reclassifications that simultaneously decrease temporarily restricted net assets and increase unrestricted net assets are reported separately.

External financial statements required are:

1. *Statement of Financial Position* (balance sheet) which will report organization-wide totals for assets, liabilities, and net assets, and net assets identified as unrestricted, temporarily restricted, and permanently restricted,
2. *Statement of Activities* which reports revenues, expenses, gains, losses, and reclassifications (between classes of net assets). Minimum requirements are

organization-wide totals, changes in net assets for each class of assets, and all expenses recognized only in the unrestricted classification. A display of a measure of operations in the statement of activities is permitted.

3. *Statement of Cash Flows* with categories (operating, financing, investing) similar to business organizations.

Private college and university financial statements report expenses rather than expenditures. Further, all expenses are reported as changes in unrestricted net assets. Whereas expenditures denote outlays of resources, expenses denote "using up" of resources. Therefore, flows of resources involving outlays of cash to purchase other assets are not presented in the statement of activities but instead in the statement of cash flows. Depreciation is also recorded as an expense.

In 1987 the FASB issued Statement No. 93, *Recognition of Depreciation by Not-for-Profit Organizations*, which required such organizations to disclose "depreciation expense for the period"[6] as well as several other disclosures that parallel requirements of APB Opinion No. 12 issued in 1967. Land and individual works of art or historical treasures that have an extraordinarily long life were excluded from these reporting requirements. Depreciation accounting was previously required for providers of health care organizations and voluntary health and welfare organizations. FASB Statement No. 93 primarily affected universities and organizations that would normally apply standards of SOP 78-10[7] that did not use depreciation accounting.

The FASB believes that disclosure of depreciation expense and accumulated depreciation provides useful information about how a not-for-profit organization's tangible assets are wearing out. The statement requires all not-for-profit organizations to recognize the cost of using up such assets in the general-purpose financial statements.

In addition, information about liquidity must be provided. This may be accomplished by sequencing assets and liabilities according to nearness of conversion to or use of cash on the statement of financial position. Such sequencing requires cash and contributions receivable restricted by donors to investment in land, building, and equipment to be included in "assets restricted to investment in land, building, and equipment" rather than cash and contributions. Cash and equivalents of permanent endowment funds held temporarily until suitable long-term investment opportunities are identified must be included in the classification "long-term investments."

Financial statements based on net asset classification is a much different concept from fund group reporting. Many not-for-profit organizations that have chosen to adopt FASB No. 117 early are choosing a single-column statement of financial position with assets and liabilities reported in an aggregated basis and a multicolumn statement of activities with separate columns displaying changes in each net asset class and a total column. These formats are displayed in this chapter and the next.

---

[6]FASB Statement No. 93, *Recognition of Depreciation by Not-for-Profit Organizations* (Norwalk, CT: Financial Accounting Standards Board, 1987) par. 5.
[7]Statement of Position 78-10 is discussed in Chapter 19.

Although most not-for-profit organizations are expected to continue with some type of fund structure for internal management, it is unclear if external reports will continue to include fund information. The illustrations in the body of the text in this chapter and the next assume fund accounting is no longer used. Accounting for events within existing fund groups and financial statements with disaggregated disclosure by fund group are illustrated in the appendix to each chapter. We have provided both alternatives because SFAS No. 117 does not prescribe any one format of the financial statements so long as the minimum disclosure requirements, listed above, are met. Therefore, fund accounting is still permitted.

Required note disclosures include a desciption of the fund accounting groups and their relationship to the classes of net assets, classification of revenues, expenses, gains, losses, classification and valuation of contributions, description of accounting policies for release of donor restrictions, anticipated collection period of contributions receivables, description of collections, and detail on contributed services not meeting the reporting criteria. Note that disclosure of expenses by natural classification is suggested, but not required.

Recording of both reciprocal exchange transactions and nonreciprocal contributions will change in order to provide organization-wide financial statements of assets, liabilities, net assets, changes in net assets, and cash flows. College and university administrators will have to carefully analyze the nature of each transaction to properly identify contributions and exchange transactions.

In addition, the following decisions must be made by universities in implementing the new standards:

1) Adopting a policy to release restrictions for donated long-lived assets, or long-lived assets acquired with restricted gifts of cash either a) immediately or b) over the useful life of the asset.

2) Reviewing endowment funds to determine which funds meet the definitions of temporarily or permanently restricted.

3) Reviewing all funds that are presently classified as restricted to determine if expenses have been incurred that meet the restrictions.

4) Choosing a display format and deciding on the degree of aggregation in the financial statements.

5) Deciding on a method for providing information on liquidity.

6) Deciding on the level of detail to provide regarding the three classes of net assets including whether to supply detail on the statement or in footnote disclosures.

7) Adopting *prospectively* recording revenues for all inflows—unrestricted, temporarily restricted, permanently restricted—and recording a cumulative effect in the year of adoption based on retroactive computation, or

8) Adopting *retroactively* restating opening balances of each of the three categories of net assets for the earliest year presented. Statement No. 117 does not require comparative annual financial statements, but does require retroactive restatement of prior financial statements if comparative statements are presented in the year the Statement is first applied.

To highlight the dramatic changes in accounting and financial reporting for private universities, the transactions from the public college and university example described in the previous section are recorded below following the new FASB guidance. Note that these illustrations assume no fund structure. (The same transactions are recorded in the appendix to the chapter within the fund structure as outlined in the AICPA college and university audit guide.)

Event	Entry		
Educational and general revenue is earned or billed:	Accounts Receivable	2,750,000	
Student tuition and fees (of which $20,000	Revenues—Student Tuition and Fees . . .		1,700,000
is considered uncollectible) $1,700,000	Revenues—Governmental Appropriations		750,000
Government appropriations 750,000	Revenues—Unrestricted Endowment		
Endowment income 50,000	Income		50,000
Other investment income 250,000	Revenues—Unrestricted Other Investment Income		250,000
The provision for uncollectible student accounts receivable is considered an expense and is allocated to institutional support.	Expenses—Institutional Support (Provision for Uncollectible Student Accounts Receivable	20,000	
	Allowance for Uncollectible Student Accounts Receivable		20,000
Unrestricted unconditional promises to give (pledges) total $250,000. 10% of these pledges are assumed uncollectible.	Contributions Receivable	250,000	
	Revenues—Unrestricted Contributions. .		250,000
	Expenses—Institutional Support (Provision for Uncollectible Contributions)	25,000	
	Allowance for Uncollectible Contributions		25,000
Of the total revenues, $2,800,000 is collected, including $200,000 of pledges.	Cash	2,800,000	
	Accounts Receivable		2,600,000
	Contributions Receivable		200,000
Revenue billed for dormitories (an auxiliary enterprise) is $400,000, of which $20,000 is not yet received.	Cash	380,000	
	Accounts Receivable	20,000	
	Revenues—Sales and Services of Auxiliary Enterprises		400,000
Purchase of materials and supplies totaling $400,000, of which $25,000 is not yet paid.	Inventory of Supplies	400,000	
	Cash		375,000
	Accounts Payable		25,000
Expenses are paid and assigned to:			
Instruction $1,050,000	Expenses—Instruction	1,050,000	
Research 100,000	Expenses—Research	100,000	
Academic support 150,000	Expenses—Academic Support	150,000	
Student services 200,000	Expenses—Student Services	200,000	
Institutional support 200,000	Expenses—Institutional Support	200,000	
Operation and maintenance of plant 400,000	Expenses—Operation and Maintenance of		
Scholarships and fellowships 40,000	Plant	400,000	
Sales and services of auxiliary	Expenses—Student Aid	40,000	
enterprises 260,000	Expenses—Sales and Services of Auxiliary Enterprises	260,000	
	Cash		2,400,000

(continued)

Event		Entry		
Materials and supplies used:				
Instruction	268,000	Expenses—Instruction	268,000	
Student services	22,000	Expenses—Student Services	22,000	
Auxiliary enterprises	90,000	Expenses—Sales and Services of Auxiliary		
		Enterprises	90,000	
		Inventory of Supplies		380,000
Aid is granted to students:		Expenses—Student Aid	175,000	
Remission of tuition	140,000	Accounts Receivable		140,000
Cash scholarships	35,000	Cash		35,000
Services that meet the criteria of (1) creating or enhancing nonfinancial assets or (2) requiring specialized skills and provided by individuals possessing those abilities and typically purchased if not donated. The fair market value of the services is $35,000.		Expenses—Instruction	35,000	
		Revenues—Unrestricted Contributions		35,000
Cash contributions are given without donor restriction.		Cash	100,000	
		Revenues—Unrestricted Contributions		100,000
A donor-restricted cash contribution is received to assist in library operations.		Cash		
		Revenues—Temporarily Restricted Contributions	70,000	70,000
Endowment income of $8,000 is restricted to student aid activities.		Cash	8,000	
		Revenues—Temporarily Restricted Endowment Income		8,000
Of the following expenses all but $4,000 are paid:		Expenses—Academic Support	67,000	
		Expenses—Student Aid	6,000	
For library operations	67,000	Accounts Payable		4,000
For student aid	6,000	Cash		69,000
Temporarily restricted revenues of $73,000 are reclassified as unrestricted when donor specifications are met.		Reclassification Out—Temporarily Restricted—Satisfaction of Program Restrictions	73,000	
		Reclassification In—Unrestricted—Satisfaction of Program Restrictions		73,000
A federal grant was awarded for future research.		Cash	100,000	
		U.S. Government Grants Refundable		100,000
Expenses for the research project totaled $45,000 to date. All expenses have been paid.		Expenses—Research	45,000	
		Cash		45,000
Revenue is recognized to the extent that resources have been properly spent.		U.S. Government Grants Refundable	45,000	
		Revenues—Unrestricted Government Grants and Contracts		45,000
Federal grants for student awards through the Pell Grant Program are received in the amount of $75,000.		Cash	75,000	
		Amounts Held on Behalf of Others		75,000
A contribution of $25,000 is received from an alumnus for student loan purposes.		Cash	25,000	
		Revenues—Temporarily Restricted Contributions		25,000

Event	Entry		
Investments costing $5,000 are sold for $5,500. Gain is restricted.	Cash................................ Investments .... Revenues—Temporarily Restricted— Net Realized Gains on Investments...	5,500	5,000 500
Loans totaling $24,000 are made to students. (FASB No. 116 assumes that restricted resources are used first.)	Loans Receivable .... Cash................................	24,000	24,000
	Reclassification Out—Temporarily Restricted—Satisfaction of Program Restrictions .... Reclassification In—Unrestricted Satisfaction of Program Restrictions ..	24,000	24,000
Collections from other loans made to students total $20,000 plus $1,000 of interest.	Cash................................ Loans Receivable .... Revenues—Unrestricted Other Investment Income	21,000	20,000 1,000
Federal government monies of $30,000 restricted for student loans are received.	Cash................................ U.S. Government Grants Refundable ...	30,000	30,000
A $500 student loan is uncollectible. Loss is allocated to student services expense.	Expenses—Institutional Support—(Loan Cancellations/Write-Offs)............ Loans Receivable	500	500
Common stock with a market value of $60,000 and $60,000 cash are received as pure endowment contribution.	Cash................................ Endowment Investments .... Revenues—Permanently Restricted Contributions.....................	60,000 60,000	120,000
Term Endowments expire, making $20,000 cash available. A reclassification entry is made to release the time restriction.	Reclassification Out—Temporarily Restricted—Expiration of Time Restrictions (Endowments).......... Reclassification In—Unrestricted— Expiration of Time Restrictions (Endowments)....................	20,000	20,000
Endowment fund investments carried at $200,000 are sold for $260,000 and investment earnings are $40,000 of which $20,000 is temporarily restricted for research and $20,000 is unrestricted. The gain is unrestricted.	Cash................................ Endowment Investments .... Revenues—Unrestricted Net Realized Gains on Endowment .... Revenues—Temporarily Restricted Endowment Income............... Revenues—Unrestricted Endowment Income..........................	300,000	200,000 60,000 20,000 20,000
Endowment investments are purchased with permanently restricted endowment cash.	Endowment Investments .... Cash...............................	360,000	360,000
The board of trustees has designated $150,000 to be used as a quasi-endowment.	Cash—Board-Designated Assets Limited to Long-Term Investment .... Cash...............................	150,000	150,000

(continued)

Event	Entry		
Cash of $12,000 from life income fund investments and $18,000 from annuity fund investments is received.	Cash..................................	12,000	
	Revenues—Temporarily Restricted Income on Life and Annuity Investments		12,000
	Cash..................................	18,000	
	Revenues—Temporarily Restricted Income on Life and Annuity Investments		18,000
A retired professor donated $100,000. The professor is to receive $6,000 per year for an estimated life of 10 years. Thereafter, the principal is to be used for student aid. The present value of the annuity at 8% is actuarially computed to be $40,260.	Cash..................................	100,000	
	Annuities Payable.....................		40,260
	Revenues—Temporarily Restricted Contributions......................		59,740
Interest on the annuity payable is recorded for the year (8% × $40,260 = $3,221).	Actuarial Adjustment of Annuities Payable..........................	3,221	
	Annuities Payable.....................		3,221
Payments are made to:			
Annuitant.......................... 6,000	Annuities Payable......................	6,000	
Life income beneficiaries.............. 12,000	Cash................................		6,000
	Payment to Life Income Beneficiaries.....	12,000	
	Cash................................		12,000
Annuity fund investments with a book value of $50,000 are sold for $59,500.	Cash..................................	59,500	
	Annuity Investments		50,000
	Revenues—Temporarily Restricted Net Realized Gains on Investments		9,500
Stock with a market value of $90,000 is donated by an art patron with the stipulation that it be used to help finance an art gallery addition.	Investments	90,000	
	Revenue—Temporarily Restricted Contributions......................		90,000
A collection of first editions, appraised at $30,000 is donated to the university. The university adopts a policy of recording contributed collections.	Library Books	30,000	
	Revenue—Unrestricted Contributions...		30,000
An $800,000 bond issue is sold at face value to finance a business school wing.	Cash..................................	800,000	
	Bonds Payable		800,000
Earnings received on investments are restricted for the art gallery addition.	Cash..................................	45,000	
	Revenues—Temporarily Restricted Investment Income		45,000
Construction of the wing is one-fourth completed.	Construction in Progress	200,000	
	Contracts Payable....................		200,000
Contract is completed at additional cost of $640,000 and is paid in full.	Construction in Progress	640,000	
	Contracts Payable.....................	200,000	
	Cash................................		840,000
	Building	840,000	
	Construction in Progress		840,000
Payment of $100,000 is made on mortgage related to the completed project.	Bonds Payable	100,000	
	Cash................................		100,000

Event	Entry		
Construction is completed on art gallery additions. Total costs are $250,000 financed with donor-restricted cash. University policy is to release restrictions when assets are placed in service.	Building . . . . Cash	250,000	250,000
	Reclassification Out—Temporarily Restricted—Satisfaction of Plant Acquisition Restrictions . . . . Reclassifications In—Unrestricted— Satisfaction of Plant Acquisition Restrictions	250,000	250,000
Land valued at $160,000 is donated by an alumnus.	Land . . . . Revenues—Unrestricted Property Contribution	160,000	160,000
Building repairs of $50,000 are paid, of which $10,000 is from restricted resources.	Expenses—Operation and Maintenance of Plant . . . . Cash	50,000	50,000
	Reclassification Out—Temporarily Restricted—Satisfaction of Program Restrictions . . . . Reclassifications In—Unrestricted— Satisfaction of Program Restrictions . .	10,000	10,000
Depreciation expense for the current period is $150,000. Depreciation expense is allocated to operation and maintenance of plant expenses.	Expenses—Operation and Maintenance of Plant (Provision for Depreciation) . . . . . Accumulated Depreciation	150,000	150,000
Closing entries are prepared. Each asset class is closed separately.	Revenues—Student Tuition and Fees . . . . . Revenues—Governmental Appropriations. Revenues—Unrestricted Contributions. . . . Revenues—Unrestricted Endowment Income. . . . . Revenues—Unrestricted Other Investment Income . . . . Revenues—Unrestricted Government Grants and Contracts . . . . Revenues—Unrestricted Net Realized Gains on Endowment . . . . Reclassifications In—Unrestricted— Satisfaction of Program Restrictions . . Reclassifications In—Unrestricted— Satisfaction of Plant Acquisition Restrictions . . . . Reclassification In—Unrestricted— Expiration of Time Restrictions. . . . . . . Expenses—Research . . . . Expenses—Instructional . . . . Expenses—Academic Support. . . . . Expenses—Student Services . . . . Expenses—Institutional Support . . . . Expenses—Operations and Maintenance of Plant. . . . . Expenses—Student Aid . . . . **Unrestricted Net Assets**	1,700,000 750,000 575,000 70,000 251,000 45,000 60,000 107,000 250,000 20,000	145,000 1,353,000 217,000 222,000 245,500 600,000 221,000 **824,500**
	Revenues—Sales and Services of Auxiliary Enterprises. . . . . Expenses—Sales and Services of Auxiliary Enterprises. . . . . **Unrestricted Net Assets**	400,000	350,000 **50,000**

Event	Entry		
	Revenues—Temporarily Restricted		
	Contributions......................	244,740	
	Revenues—Temporarily Restricted		
	Endowment Income...............	28,000	
	Revenues—Temporarily Restricted Net		
	Realized Gains on Investments	10,000	
	Revenues—Temporarily Restricted Income		
	on Annuity and Life Income		
	Investments	30,000	
	Revenues—Temporarily Restricted		
	Investment Income	45,000	
	Temporarily Restricted Net Assets........	34,481	
	Reclassifications Out—Temporarily		
	Restricted—Satisfaction of Program		
	Restrictons		107,000
	Reclassifications Out—Temporarily		
	Restricted—Expiration of Time		
	Restrictions		20,000
	Reclassifications Out—Temporarily		
	Restricted—Satisfaction of Plant		
	Acquisition Restrictions		250,000
	Payment to Life Income Beneficiaries...		12,000
	Loss on Actuarial Adjustment of Annuity		
	Payable.........................		3,221
	Revenues—Permanently Restricted		
	Endowment Contributions	120,000	
	Permanently Restricted Net Assets........		120,000

Institutions have been encouraged to develop a format for their financial statements that is most meaningful to their users. As a result, financial statement formats are expected to evolve over the next few years. Industry officials anticipate the need to monitor this development in order to determine whether limits should be placed on the flexibility allowed by FASB Statement No. 117.

Models suggested by the FASB, and included in this chapter, are (1) a single column, "corporate" format and (2) disaggregation by net asset class. Early adopters of Statement No. 117 seem to prefer the former model for the statement of financial position and the latter for the statement of activities. Illustration 18-5 presents the statement of activities. Illustration 18-6 presents the statement of financial position. A cash flow statement is included in Illustration 18-7.

Illustration 18-5
Private University
Statement of Activities
For Period Ended June 30, 19X5

	Unrestricted	Temporarily Restricted	Permanently Restricted	Total
Changes in net assets:				
Revenues and gains:				
Tuition and fees	$ 1,700,000			$ 1,700,000
Contributions	575,000	$ 244,740	$120,000	937,740
Government appropriations, grants, and contracts	795,000			795,000
Investment income on endowment	70,000	28,000		98,000
Other investment income	251,000	45,000		296,000
Sales and services of auxiliary enterprises . .	400,000			400,000
Investment income on life income and annuity agreements		30,000		30,000
Net realized gains on other investments		10,000		10,000
Net realized gains on endowment	60,000			60,000
Total revenues and gains	$ 3,851,000	$ 357,740	$120,000	$ 4,328,740
Net assets released from restrictions				
Satisfaction of program restrictions	107,000	(107,000)		0
Satisfaction of plant acquisition restrictions . .	250,000	(250,000)		0
Satisfaction of time restrictions	20,000	(20,000)		0
Total net assets released from restriction	$ 377,000	$ (377,000)		0
Total revenues and gains and other support	$ 4,228,000	$ (19,260)	$120,000	$ 4,328,740
Expenses and losses:				
Educational and general:				
Instruction	$ 1,353,000			$ 1,353,000
Research	145,000			145,000
Academic support	217,000			217,000
Student services	222,000			222,000
Institutional support	245,500			245,500
Operation and maintenance of plant	600,000			600,000
Student aid	221,000			221,000
Total educational and general expenses	3,003,500			3,003,500
Auxiliary enterprises	350,000			350,000
Total expenses	$ 3,353,500	$ 0	$ 0	$ 3,353,500
Actuarial adjustment on annuity obligatons		3,221		3,221
Payments to life income beneficiaries		12,000		12,000
Total expenses and losses	$ 3,353,500	$ 15,221	$ 0	$ 3,368,721
Increase (decrease) in net assets	$ 874,500	$ (34,481)	$120,000	$ 960,019
Net assets at beginning of year	$39,294,000	$2,047,981	$834,000	$42,175,981
Net assets at end of year	$40,168,500	$2,013,500	$954,000	$43,136,000

Illustration 18-6
Private University
Statement of Financial Position
For Period Ended June 30, 19X5

Assets:

Cash	$ 1,057,500
Short-term investments	717,000
Accounts receivable (net of 20,000 allowance)	344,000
Contributions receivable (net of 25,000 allowance)	50,000
Inventories of supplies	110,000
Prepaid expenses	28,000
Student loans receivable	58,500
Assets restricted to investment in land, building and equipment	1,350,000
Land, buildings, and equipment (net of accumulated depreciation of $150,000)	41,645,000
Long-term investments	1,422,721
Endowment investments	954,000
Total assets	$47,736,721

Liabilities and net assets:

Accounts payable and accrued liabilities	1,148,000
Other liabilities	1,500
Amounts held on behalf of others	110,000
Annuities payable	256,221
Long-term debt	3,000,000
U.S. government grants refundable	85,000
Total liabilities	4,600,721
Net assets:	
Unrestricted	40,168,500
Temporarily restricted	2,013,500
Permanently restricted	954,000
Total net assets	43,136,000
Total liabilities and net assets	47,736,721

Illustration 18-7
Private University
Statement of Cash Flows
For Period Ended June 30, 19X5

Cash flows from operating activities:	
Student tuition and auxiliary fees	$2,030,000
Governmental appropriations.	650,000
Research activities receipts	100,000
Interest and dividends received	308,000
Contributions received	395,000
Other receipts.	75,000
Salaries and wages paid to faculty and staff	(1,935,000)
Payments to vendors for goods and services	(958,000)
Disbursements to students for financial aid.	(81,000)
Payments to life income beneficiaries.	(12,000)
Net cash provided by (used for) operating activities	$ 572,000
Cash flows from investing activities:	
Proceeds from sales and maturities of investments.	325,000
Purchases of investments	(360,000)
Purchases of land, building, and equipment	(840,000)
Disbursements of loans to students and faculty.	(24,000)
Repayments of loans from students and faculty.	20,000
Net cash provided by (used for) investing activities.	$ (879,000)
Cash flows from financing activities:	
Proceeds from issuance of notes payable	$ 800,000
Payments on long-term debt	(100,000)
Receipts of interest and dividends restricted for reinvestment	75,000
Contributions received restricted for long-term investment.	200,000
Payments to annuitants.	(6,000)
Receipts of refundable governmental loan funds.	30,000
Net cash provided by (used for) financing activities.	$ 999,000
Net increase (decrease) in cash and cash equivalents.	692,000
Cash and cash equivalents at beginning of year.	365,500
Cash and cash equivalents at end of year	1,057,500

APPENDIX: PRIVATE UNIVERSITY ACCOUNTING AND FINANCIAL REPORTING WITHIN EXISTING FUND STRUCTURE

Most authorities expect private colleges and universities to continue to use a fund structure for internal management. Outside resource providers, debt markets, contributors, and federal and state agencies also will continue to require funds-based information. These may be thought of as "subsidiary" accounts of the university. An important change for private universities will be the recording of revenues and expenses in *all* funds, not just the current funds.

A first step in implementing the new FASB standards is to determine which assets in each of the funds to include in the three net asset classes. The following matrix may be helpful in comparing the fund groups and net assets classifications. Many of the funds will have more than one net asset class. This is because some transactions that traditionally have been recorded as restricted will now be considered unrestricted per the new FASB guidance. Under FASB No. 116, only donor-restricted resources resulting from non-reciprocal transactions will continue to be restricted. All other resources will be classified as unrestricted.

Fund Group	Net Asset Class
Current unrestricted funds	Unrestricted net assets
Current restricted funds	Unrestricted net assets
	Temporarily restricted net assets
Loan funds	Unrestricted net assets
	Temporarily restricted net assets
Endowment and similar funds	Unrestricted net assets
	Temporarily restricted net assets
	Permanently restricted net assets
Plant funds	Unrestricted net assets
	Temporarily restricted net assets

In this appendix, exhange transactions and contributions are recorded for a private college within the existing AICPA audit guide fund structure. In order to compare the information presented with the illustrations in the text that assumed no funds, the same transactions are recorded. The financial statements are presented with the AICPA audit guide fund groups in Illustrations 18A-1 and 18A-2 (pages 1019–1020). Minimum requirements of FASB Statement No. 117 are highlighted. The fund group model is included as an alternative in the materials sent by the National Association of College and University Business Officers (NACUBO) to college and university controllers in March 1994.[1] This model is closest to the existing model of financial statements for colleges and universities. Consequently, it may be the most understandable to those users who are familiar with the current financial statements. It may also, in certain circumstances, involve the fewest number of changes in systems and procedures to implement. If a statement of financial position and a statement of activities are presented on a fund group basis, interfund items must be identified and *eliminated* from the display of total assets, liabilities, and net assets.

---

[1]NACUBO Financial Accounting and Reporting Manual (NACUBO: October 1993).

Current Unrestricted Funds.   The transactions from the public college and university example described in the previous section are recorded below following FASB guidance for private universities. Most exchange transactions that affect the unrestricted net asset class will be recorded in this operating fund. Unrestricted contributions will also be recorded in this fund. Note that private colleges and universities record expenses instead of expenditures. Outflows of resources for capital asset acquisitions will not be recorded as expenditures, but as an exchange of one asset for another. In addition, depreciation will be recorded in the current unrestricted funds or in the plant funds and may be allocated to the functional areas.

Event		Entry		
Educational and general revenue is earned or billed:		Accounts Receivable	2,750,000	
Student tuition and fees (of which $20,000 is considered uncollectible)	$1,700,000	Revenues—Student Tuition and Fees . . . Revenues—Governmental Appropriations		1,700,000 750,000
Government appropriations.	750,000	Revenues—Unrestricted Endowment Income		50,000
Endowment income.	50,000			
Other investment income	250,000	Revenues—Unrestricted Other Investment Income		250,000
The provision for uncollectible student accounts receivable is considered an expense and is allocated to institutional support.		Expenses—Institutional Support (Provision for Uncollectible Student Accounts Receivable) . . . . Allowance for Uncollectible Student Accounts Receivable	20,000	20,000
Unrestricted contributions are pledged in the amount of $250,000. 10% of these pledges are assumed uncollectible.		Contributions Receivable. . . . . Revenues—Unrestricted Contributions. . Expenses—Institutional Support (Provision for Uncollectible Contributions) . . . . Allowance for Uncollectible Contributions	250,000 25,000	250,000 25,000
Of the total revenues, $2,800,000 is collected, including $200,000 of pledges.		Cash . . . . Accounts Receivable . . . . Contributions Receivable	2,800,000	2,600,000 200,000
Revenue billed for dormitories (an auxiliary enterprise) is $400,000, of which $20,000 is not yet received.		Cash . . . . Accounts Receivable . . . . Revenues—Sales and Services of Auxiliary Enterprises.	380,000 20,000	400,000
Purchase of materials and supplies totaling $400,000, of which $25,000 is not yet paid.		Inventory of Supplies . . . . Cash . . . . Accounts Payable	400,000	375,000 25,000
Expenses are paid and assigned to:				
Instruction	$1,050,000	Expenses—Instruction	1,050,000	
Research	100,000	Expenses—Research	100,000	
Academic support	150,000	Expenses—Academic Support.	150,000	
Student services.	200,000	Expenses—Student Services.	200,000	
Institutional support	200,000	Expenses—Institutional Support	200,000	
Operation and maintenance of plant.	400,000	Expenses—Operation and Maintenance of Plant.	400,000	
Scholarships and fellowships	40,000	Expenses—Student Aid	40,000	
Sales and services of auxiliary enterprises		Expenses—Sales and Services of Auxiliary Enterprises	260,000	
	260,000	Cash		2,400,000

(continued)

Event		Entry		
Materials and supplies used:				
Instruction	268,000	Expenses—Instruction	268,000	
Student services	22,000	Expenses—Student Services	22,000	
Auxiliary enterprises	90,000	Expenses—Sales and Services of Auxiliary		
		Enterprises	90,000	
		Inventory of Supplies		380,000
Aid is granted to students:		Expenses—Student Aid	175,000	
Remission of tuition	140,000	Accounts Receivable		140,000
Cash scholarships	35,000	Cash		35,000
Services that meet the criteria of (1) creating or enhancing nonfinancial assets or (2) requiring specialized skills, and provided by individuals possessing those abilities and typically purchased if not donated. The fair market value of the services is $35,000.		Expenses—Instruction	35,000	
		Revenues—Unrestricted Contributions		35,000
Cash contributions are given without donor restriction.		Cash	100,000	
		Revenues—Unrestricted Contributions		100,000
Closing entries are prepared for the unrestricted net assets.		Revenues—Student Tuition and Fees	1,700,000	
		Revenues—Governmental		
		Appropriations	750,000	
		Revenues—Unrestricted Contributions	385,000	
		Revenues—Unrestricted Endowment		
		Income	50,000	
		Revenues—Unrestricted Other		
		Investment Income	250,000	
		Expenses—Instructional		1,353,000
		Expenses—Research		100,000
		Expenses—Academic Support		150,000
		Expenses—Student Services		222,000
		Expenses—Institutional Support		245,000
		Expenses—Operations and		
		Maintenance of Plant		400,000
		Expenses—Student Aid		215,000
		Unrestricted Net Assets		**450,500**
		Revenues—Sales and Services of		
		Auxiliary Enterprises	400,000	
		Expenses—Sales and Services of		
		Auxiliary Enterprises		350,000
		Unrestricted Net Assets		**50,000**

Current Restricted Funds.   This fund will have both donor-restricted contributions and resources from exchange transactoins, including government grants, A difficult decision for many universities will be to differentiate donor-restricted contributions as defined by FASB No. 116 from exchange transactions.

Event		Entry		
A donor-restricted cash contribution is received to assist in library operations.		Cash	70,000	
		Revenues—Temporarily Restricted		
		Contributions		70,000
Endowment income of $8,000 is restricted to student aid activities.		Cash	8,000	
		Revenues—Temporarily Restricted		
		Endowment Income		8,000

Event	Entry		
Of the following expenses all but $4,000 are paid. For library operations . . . . $ 67,000 For student aid. 6,000	Expenses—Academic Support	67,000	
	Expenses—Student Aid.	6,000	
	Accounts Payable		4,000
	Cash		69,000

Temporarily restricted revenues of $73,000
are reclassified as unrestricted when donor
specifications are met.
	Reclassification Out—Temporarily
	  Restricted—Satisfaction of Program
	  Restrictions . . . .
		73,000	

	Reclassification In—Unrestricted— Satisfaction of Program Restrictions.		73,000
A federal grant was awarded for research.	Cash	100,000	
	U.S. Government Grants Refundable		100,000
Expenses for the research project totaled $45,000 to date. All expenses have been paid.	Expenses—Research	45,000	
	Cash		45,000
Revenue is recognized to the extent that resources have been properly spent.	U.S. Government Grants Refundable	45,000	
	Revenues—Government Grants and Contracts		45,000
Closing entries are prepared for the unrestricted net assets.	Revenues—Unrestricted Government Grants and Contracts.	45,000	
	Reclassifications In—Unrestricted— Satisfaction of Program Restrictions.	73,000	
	Expenses—Academic Support		67,000
	Expenses—Student Aid.		6,000
	Expenses—Research		45,000
	Unrestricted Net Assets		**0**
Closing entries are prepared for the temporarily restricted net assets.	Revenues—Temporarily Restricted Contributions	70,000	
	Revenues—Temporarily Restricted Endowment Income	8,000	

	Reclassifications Out—Temporarily
	  Restricted—Satisfaction of Program
	  Restrictons. . . . .
			73,000

	Temporarily Restricted Net Assets		**5,000**

Loan Funds.   Universities account for resources designated for student loan activity in a separate fund. This practice is expected to continue because of the large amounts of federal and state resources made available to universities for student loans. In addition, donor-restricted contributions may also specify use of the contributed resources for student loan purposes.

Event	Entry		
A contribution of $25,000 is received from an alumnus for student loan purposes.	Cash	25,000	
	Revenues—Temporarily Restricted Contributions		25,000
Investments costing $5,000 are sold for $5,500. Gain is restricted.	Cash	5,500	
	Investments.		5,000
	Revenues—Temporarily Restricted—Net Realized Gains on Investments		500
Loans totaling $24,000 are made to students. Collections from other loans made to students total $20,000 plus $1,000 of interest. (FASB No. 116 assumes that restricted resources are used first.)	Loans Receivable	24,000	
	Cash		24,000

	Reclassification Out—Temporarily
	  Restricted—Satisfaction of Program
	  Restrictions . . . .
		24,000	

	Reclassification In—Unrestricted— Satisfaction of Program Restrictions.		24,000

Event	Entry		
	Cash	21,000	
	Loans Receivable		20,000
	Revenues—Unrestricted Other Investment		
	Income		1,000
Federal government monies of $30,000 restricted for student loans are received.	Cash	30,000	
	U.S. Government Grants Refundable		30,000
A $500 student loan is uncollectible.	Expenses—Institutional Support (Loan		
	Cancellations/Write-Offs)	500	
	Loans Receivable		500
Closing entries are prepared for the unrestricted net assets.	Revenues—Unrestricted Interest Income	1,000	
	Reclassifications In—Unrestricted—		
	Satisfaction of Program Restrictions.	24,000	
	Expenses—Institutional Support.		500
	Unrestricted Net Assets		**24,500**
Closing entries are prepared for the temporarily restricted net assets.	Revenues—Temporarily Restricted		
	Contributions	25,000	
	Revenues—Temporarily Restricted Net		
	Realized Gains on Investments	500	
	Reclassifications Out—Temporarily		
	Restricted—Satisfaction of Program		
	Restrictons		24,000
	Temporarily Restricted Net Assets		**1,500**

Endowment and Similar Funds.

Colleges and universities traditionally account for permanent endowments, term endowments, and board-designat4ed (quasi-) endowment resources in separate funds. This practice is expected to continue because external users of financial data, for example, the debt market, consider all three categories of endowments important in the lending decision.

Event	Entry		
Common stock with a market value of $60,000 and $60,000 cash are received as pure endowment contribution.	Cash	60,000	
	Endowment Investments	60,000	
	Revenues—Permanently Restricted		
	Contributions.		120,000
Term endowments expire, making $20,000 cash available.	Reclassification Out—Temporarily Restricted		
	—Expiration of Time Restrictions.	20,000	
	Reclassification In—Unrestricted—		
	Expiration of Time Restrictions		20,000
Endowment fund investments carried at $200,000 are sold for $260,000 and investment earnings are $40,000, of which $20,000 is temporarily restricted for research projects and $20,000 is unrestricted.	Cash	300,000	
	Endowment Investments		200,000
	Revenues—Unrestricted Net Realized		
	Gains on Endowment		60,000
	Revenues—Temporarily Restricted		
	Endowment Income		20,000
	Revenues—Unrestricted Endowment		
	Income.		20,000
Investments are purchased with fund cash.	Endowment Investments	360,000	
	Cash.		360,000

Event	Entry		
Closing entries are prepared for the unrestricted net assets.	Reclassification In—Unrestricted—Expiration of Time Restrictions	20,000	
	Revenues—Unrestricted Income on Endowments.	28,000	
	Revenues—Unrestricted Net Realized Gains on Endowment	60,000	
	Unrestricted Net Assets		**100,000**
Closing entries are prepared for the temporarily restricted net assets.	Revenues—Temporarily Restricted Endowment Income	20,000	
	Reclassifications Out—Temporarily Restricted—Expiration of Time Restriction		20,000
	Temporarily Restricted Net Assets		**0**
Closing entries are prepared for the permanently restricted net assets.	Revenues—Permanently Restricted Endowment Contributions	120,000	
	Permanently Restricted Net Assets		**120,000**

Annuity and Life Income Funds.   As in the example of public colleges and universities, these funds account for resources available to the college or university upon the death of the donor. Periodic payments are made to the donors for an indicated time period.

Event		Entry		
Cash of $12,000 from life income fund investments and $18,000 from annuity fund investments is received.		Cash	12,000	
		Revenues—Temporarily Restricted Income on Investments		12,000
		Cash	18,000	
		Revenues—Temporarily Restricted Income on Investments		18,000
A retired professor donated $100,000. The professor is to receive $6,000 per year for an estimated life of 10 years. Thereafter, the principal is to be used for student aid. The present value of the annuity at 8% is actuarially computed to be $40,260.		Cash	100,000	
		Annuities Payable		40,260
		Revenues—Temporarily Restricted Contributions		59,740
Interest on the annuity is recorded for the year (8% × $40,260 = $3,221).		Actuarial Adjustment of Annuities Payable	3,221	
		Annuities Payable		3,221
Payments are made to:				
Annuitant	6,000	Annuities Payable	6,000	
Life income beneficiaries	12,000	Cash		6,000
		Payment to Life Income Beneficiaries	12,000	
		Cash		12,000
Annuity fund investments with a book value of $50,000 are sold for $59,500.		Cash	59,500	
		Annuity Investments		50,000
		Revenues—Temporarily Restricted Net Realized Gains on Investments		9,500

Event	Entry		
Closing entries are prepared for temporarily restricted net assets.	Revenues—Temporarily Restricted Contributions........................	59,740	
	Revenues—Temporarily Restricted Net Realized Gains on Investments...........	9,500	
	Revenues—Temporarily Restricted Income on Annuity and Life Income Investments.....	30,000	
	Payment to Life Income Beneficiaries.......		12,000
	Loss on Actuarial Adjustment of Annuities— Payable		3,221
	Temporarily Restricted Net Assets........		**84,019**

Plant Funds.   The plant funds are one area where accounting and reporting may be simplified in colleges and universities. The entries below assume one plant fund, although the subgroups described for a public university could be retained.

Event	Entry		
Stock with a market value of $90,000 is received from an art patron to finance an art gallery addition.	Investments .... Revenue—Temporarily Restricted Contributions.....................	90,000	90,000
A collection of first editions appraised at $30,000 is donated to the university. The university adopts a policy of recording contributed collections.	Library Books .... Revenue—Unrestricted Contributions...	30,000	30,000
An $800,000 bond issue is sold at face value to finance a business school wing.	Cash................................ Bonds Payable	800,000	800,000
Earnings received on investments are restricted for building acquisition.	Cash................................ Revenues—Temporarily Restricted Other Investment Income...........	45,000	45,000
Construction of the wing is one-forth completed.	Construction in Progress................ Contracts Payable...................	200,000	200,000
Contract is completed at additional cost of $640,000 and is paid in full.	Construction in Progress................ Contracts Payable.................... Cash...............................	640,000 200,000	840,000
	Building .... Construction in Progress..............	840,000	840,000
Payment of $100,000 is made on mortgage related to the completed project.	Bonds Payable .... Cash...............................	100,000	100,000
The cost of constructing an art gallery addition totals $250,000 financed with donor-restricted cash. University policy is to release restrictions when assets are placed in service.	Building .... Cash...............................	250,000	250,000
	Reclassification Out—Temporarily Restricted—Satisfaction of Plant Restrictions....................... Reclassifications In—Unrestricted— Satisfaction of Plant Acquisition Restrictions......................	250,000	250,000
Land valued at $160,000 is dontaed by an alumnus.	Land................................ Revenues—Unrestricted Property Contribution......................	160,000	160,000

Event	Entry		
Building repairs of $50,000 are paid, of which $10,000 is from restricted resources.	Expenses.............................	50,000	
	Cash.................................		50,000
	Reclassification Out—Temporarily Restricted—Satisfaction of Program Restrictions......................	10,000	
	Reclassifications In—Unrestricted— Satisfaction of Program Restrictions ..		10,000
Depreciation expense for the current period is $150,000. Depreciation expenses are allocated to operation and maintenance of plant expenses.	Expenses—Operation and Maintenance of Plant (Provision for Depreciation)	150,000	
	Accumulated Depreciation		150,000
Closing entries are prepared for the unrestricted net assets.	Reclassifications In—Unrestricted— Satisfaction of Plant Acquisition Restrictions.......................	250,000	
	Reclassifications In—Unrestricted— Satisfaction of Program Restrictions ..	10,000	
	Revenues—Unrestricted Property Contributions.....................	190,000	
	Expenses—Operation and Maintenance of Plant..........................		200,000
	Unrestricted Net Assets		**250,000**
Closing entries are prepared for the temporarily restricted net assets.	Revenues—Temporarily Restricted Contributions.....................	90,000	
	Revenues—Temporarily Restricted Other Investment Income	45,000	
	Temporarily Restricted Net Assets......	**125,000**	
	Reclassification Out—Temporarily Restricted—Satisfaction of Plant Acquisition........................		250,000
	Reclassification Out—Temporarily Restricted—Satisfaction of Program Restrictons		10,000

Agency Funds.   These funds account for resources held by the university on behalf of others. The new standards specifically include federal monies that pass through the university to student recipients (Pell grants) as agency transactions.

Event	Entry		
Federal grants for student awards through the Pell Grant Program are received in the amount of $75,000.	Cash	75,000	
	Amounts Held on Behalf of Others........		75,000

Interfund Transactions.   The following are examples of interfund transactions that may be found in a private college or university. Interfund activity must be clearly marked on the financial statements and eliminated in preparing the organization-wide totals of net assets and changes in net assets.

	Current Unrestricted Fund			Plant Funds		

Cash transferred to plant fund for:

Addition to plant (discretionary). Payment of mortgage (mandatory).

	Unrestricted Net Assets—			Cash	167,000	
	Mandatory Transfer . .	20,000		Unrestricted Net		
	Unrestricted Net Assets—			Assets—Mandatory		
	Discretionary			Transfer.		20,000
	Transfer.	147,000		Unrestricted Net		
	Cash		167,000	Assets—		
				Discretionary Transfer		147,000

	Current Unrestricted Fund			Loan Funds		

The board of trustees has agreed to transfer $3,000 to the loan fund on the first day of the next fiscal year as matching money for Federal Grants.

	Unrestricted Net Assets—			Cash	3,000	
	Mandatory Transfer . .	3,000		Unrestricted Net		
	Cash		3,000	Assets—Mandatory		
				Transfer.		3,000

	Current Unrestricted Fund			Endowment Funds		

The board of trustees has authorized an immediate transfer of $150,000 to the endowment fund.

	Unrestricted Net Assets—			Cash—Assets Limited to		
	Discretionary			Long-Term		
	Transfer.	150,000		Investment.	150,000	
	Cash		150,000	Unrestricted Net		
				Assets—		
				Discretionary Transfer		150,000

	Current Unrestricted Fund			Endowment Fund		

The $20,000 unrestricted endowment income and the $60,000 net realized gain on the endowment is transferred to the unrestricted current fund.

	Cash	80,000		Unrestricted Net Assets—		
	Unrestricted Net			Mandatory Transfer		
	Assets—Mandatory			Out	80,000	
	Transfer In		80,000	Cash		80,000

	Current Restricted Fund			Endowment Fund		

The $20,000 restricted endowment income is transferred to the current restricted fund. The restriction will be released when research expenses are incurred.

	Cash	20,000		Temporarily Restricted Net		
	Temporarily Restricted			Assets—Mandatory		
	Net Assets—			Transfer Out.	20,000	
	Mandatory			Cash		20,000
	Transfer In		20,000			

Illustration 18A-1
Private University
Statement of Activity
For Period Ended June 30, 19X5

	Current Funds	Loan Funds	Endowment and Similar Funds	Plant Funds	Total
Changes in unrestricted net assets:					
Revenues and gains:					
Tuition and fees	$1,700,000				$ 1,700,000
Contributions	385,000			$ 190,000	575,000
Government appropriations, grants, and contracts	795,000				795,000
Investment income on endowment	50,000		$ 20,000		70,000
Other investment income	250,000	$ 1,000			251,000
Net realized gains on endowment			60,000		60,000
Sales and services of auxiliary enterprises	400,000				400,000
Total unrestricted revenues and gains	$3,580,000	$ 1,000	$ 80,000	$ 190,000	$ 3,851,000
Net assets released from restrictions:					
Satisfaction of program restrictions	$ 73,000	24,000		10,000	107,000
Satisfaction of plant acquisition restrictions				250,000	250,000
Satisfaction of time restrictions			20,000		20,000
Total net assets released from restriction	73,000	24,000	20,000	260,000	377,000
Total unrestricted revenues and gains and other support	$3,653,000	$25,000	$ 100,000	$ 450,000	$ 4,228,000
Expenses and losses:					
Educational and general:					
Instruction	$1,353,000				$ 1,353,000
Research	145,000				145,000
Academic support	217,000				217,000
Student services	222,000				222,000
Institutional support	245,000	500			245,500
Operation and maintenance of plant	400,000			200,000	600,000
Student aid	221,000				221,000
Total educational and general expenses	2,803,000	500	0	200,000	3,003,500
Auxiliary enterprises	$ 350,000				350,000
Total expenses	$3,153,000	$ 500	$ 0	$ 200,000	$ 3,353,500
Increase (decrease) in unrestricted net assets	500,000	24,500	100,000	250,000	**874,500**
Transfers among funds—additions (deductions)					
Mandatory principal payment	(23,000)	3,000		20,000	
Mandatory transfer—endowment income	100,000		(100,000)		
Other transfers	(297,000)		150,000	147,000	
Total transfers	$ (220,000)	$ 3,000	$ 50,000	$ 167,000	$ 0
Changes in temporarily restricted net asset					
Contributions	$ 70,000	$25,000	$ 59,740	$ 90,000	$ 244,740
Income on life income and annuity investments			30,000		30,000
Endowment income	8,000		20,000		28,000
Other investment income				45,000	45,000
Net realized gains on other investments		500	9,500		10,000
Net assets released from restrictions	(73,000)	(24,000)	(20,000)	(260,000)	(377,000)
Payments to life income beneficiaries			(12,000)		(12,000)
Loss on actuarial adjustment on annuity payables			(3,221)		(3,221)
Increase (decrease) in temporarily restricted net assets	$ 5,000	$ 1,500	$ 84,019	$ (125,000)	**$ (34,481)**
Changes in permanently restricted net assets:					
Contributions			120,000		120,000
Increase (decrease) in permanently restricted net assets	0	0	120,000		**120,000**
Net assets at beginning of year	$1,071,000	$67,000	$1,509,981	$39,528,000	$42,175,981
Net assets at end of year	$1,356,000	$96,000	$1,864,000	$39,820,000	**$43,136,000**

Illustration 18A-2
Private University
Statement of Financial Position
For Period Ended June 30 19X5

Assets	Current Funds	Loan Funds	Endowment and Similar Funds	Plant Funds	Total
Cash	$ 625,000	$ 62,500	$ 35,000	$ 335,000	$ 1,057,500
Short-term investments	502,000	5,000	60,000	150,000	717,000
Accounts receivable	344,000				344,000
Contributions receivable	50,000				50,000
Inventories of materials	110,000				110,000
Prepaid expenses	28,000				28,000
Loans to students		58,500			58,500
Assets restricted to investment in land, buildings, and equipment				1,350,000	1,350,000
Land, buildings, and equipment				41,645,000	41,645,000
Long-term investments			1,182,721	240,000	1,422,721
Endowment investments			954,000		954,000
Total assets	**$1,659,000**	**$126,000**	**$2,231,721**	**$43,720,000**	**$47,736,721**

Liabilities and Net Assets	Current Funds	Loan Funds	Endowment and Similar Funds	Plant Funds	Total
Accounts payable and accrued liabilities	$ 248,000			$ 900,000	$ 1,148,000
Other liabilities			$ 1,500		1,500
Amounts held on behalf of others			110,000		110,000
Annuities payable			256,221		256,221
Long-term debt				3,000,000	3,000,000
U.S. government grants refundable	55,000	$ 30,000			$ 85,000
Total liabilities	**$ 303,000**	**$ 30,000**	**$ 367,721**	**$ 3,900,000**	**$ 4,600,721**
Net Assets:					
Unrestricted	$1,111,000	$ 13,500	$ 574,000	$38,470,000	**40,168,500**
Temporarily restricted	245,000	82,500	336,000	1,350,000	**2,013,500**
Permanently restricted			954,000		**954,000**
Total net assets	**$1,356,000**	**$ 96,000**	**$1,864,000**	**$39,820,000**	**$43,136,000**
Total liabilities and net assets	$1,659,000	$126,000	$2,231,721	$43,720,000	$47,736,721

QUESTIONS

1. Explain the difference between a contribution and an exchange transaction. How is each recorded under the new FASB guidance?
2. Describe the three classes of net assets required to be reported under FASB Statement No. 117.
3. How might a donor-imposed restriction expire?
4. Give an example of a contribution in each of the net asset classes.
5. Distinguish between a donor restriction and a condition.
6. When must not-for-profit organizations recognize contributed services and contributed collection items as revenue?

7. Under what circumstances is a government grant a contribution versus an exchange transaction?

8. What choices do not-for-profit organizations have as to display format for their financial statements?

9. What are the measurement focuses (identifying which resources are being measured) and bases of accounting (identifying when the effects of transactions or events should be recognized) used by public universities and private universities? How might the use of two measurement focuses benefit financial reporting for universities?

10. Depict the accounting for contributions (of cash, pledges, or investments that may be converted into cash) for a private university.

11. Interpret the following closing entry for a public university:

Revenues—Auxiliary Enterprises 500,000		
Expenditures—Auxiliary Enterprises.................		480,000
Fund Balance....................................		20,000

12. Of the various funds traditionally used in public university accounting, indicate which is probably the most complex and explain why.

13. What is included in the statement of activities?

14. Explain how FASB and GASB financial reporting standards regarding reporting of depreciation differ from one another.

15. Explain the major differences in accounting and financial reporting of public and private universities.

EXERCISES

Exercise 1. Indicate how the following events are recorded in a private university:

(1) Receipt of an unconditional promise to give. _____

(2) Receipt of a fixed asset with donor-specified use for an outreach program. _____

(3) Receipt of an unconditional cash contribution. _____

(4) Receipt of cash to be used for a specific purpose. _____

(5) Receipt of free accounting services. _____

(6) Receipt of time of volunteers who helped with fund-raising mailings. _____

(7) Receipt of an unconditional promise to give over a five-year period. _____

(8) Receipt of investments that are to be used to set up an endowment with earnings available for operations. _____

(9) Receipt of a conditional promise to give. _____

(10) Receipt of a fixed asset with no donor restriction. _____

(11) Receipt of a cash contribution to be used for a research project next year. _____

(12) Receipt of a cash contribution to be used for general operations next year at the discretion of management. _____

(13) Receipt of cash as part of a government grant funding a cancer research project. A report with research results will be prepared for the government funding agency. _____

(14) Receipt of a cash contribution to be used for acquisition of fixed assets. _____

(15) Receipt of a permanent collection of geography maps which will be displayed to the public. _____

(a) Credit Contributions—Unrestricted   (d) Credit Refundable Deposits
(b) Credit Contributions—Temporarily Restricted   (e) Credit Fund Balance
(c) Credit Contributions—Permanently Restricted   (f) No entry

Exercise 2. Indicate which of the following accounts would be used for the listed transactions in (1) a public university and (2) a private university.

Revenues   Auxiliary Expenses
Revenues—Unrestricted   Expenditures
Revenues—Temporarily Restricted   Expenses
Revenues—Permanently Restricted   Deferred Revenue
Auxiliary Revenues   Refundable Deposits (a liability)
Transfers (or Fund Balance)   Current Assets
Mandatory Transfers

The transactions to be classified are as follows:
(a) Pledges are received for a fund drive that is restricted for research expenditures.
(b) An allowance for uncollectible pledges for the above fund is established.
(c) Fees are collected for a seminar to be presented in the next fiscal period.
(d) Tuition for the current period is billed.
(e) An allowance for uncollectible tuition is recorded.
(f) Tuition remissions are granted to out-of-state students.
(g) Dormitory fees are billed.
(h) Salaries for union food service workers are paid.
(i) Supplies to be used during the period are purchased.
(j) A required transfer is made to the Plant Replacement Fund.
(k) The regents meet and transfer money to the endowment fund for a stated period of time.

Exercise 3. Record the following events that affect the unrestricted current fund of public University, which uses the typical control accounts for its revenues and expenditures. Omit explanations.
(a) Student fees of $400,000 were assessed, of which $375,000 have been collected and $4,000 are estimated to be uncollectible.
(b) The book store operates in rented space and is run on a break-even basis. Revenues totaled $80,000, of which 80% was collected to date. Salaries of $25,000 and rent of $10,000 are paid. Other operating expenses amount to $40,000, of which $5,000 has not been paid.
(c) A mandatory transfer of $75,000 was made for a payment due on the gymnasium building mortgage.
(d) The Student Aid Committee report showed:

Cash scholarships issued $5,000
Remission of tuition   2,000

(e) A check for $10,000 and a pledge for $4,500 are received from the local medical society to cover part of the cost of research on drug effects, one of the university's educational programs. The educational programs will be conducted and paid for in the next fiscal period.
(f) The endowment fund received a check for $6,000 of interest on investments. The premium amortization on the investment is $120. The unrestricted current fund is the recipient of the income.

Exercise 4. Record the following events that affect the restricted current fund of public University. Omit explanations.
- (a) A private grant of $50,000 was received, to be used exclusively for defraying costs of holding conferences on the topic of genes.
- (b) By year end, $45,000 of the grant mentioned in (a) had been applied to the purpose stipulated.
- (c) The grant provided that amounts not awarded by year end are to be transferred to the endowment fund. The liability to that fund is recorded.
- (d) An alumnus, a former athlete, contributed $20,000 to assist in the search for a basketball coach.

Exercise 5. Record the following events that affect the loan fund of Public University. Omit explanations.
- (a) An alumnus donates $220,000 to establish the student loan fund. Students are charged a 5% annual interest rate.
- (b) Loans of $180,000 are made to students.
- (c) The remaining $40,000 is deposited in the university credit union, which pays a current interest rate of 7%.
- (d) Loans of $20,000 are repaid, plus $800 of interest.
- (e) Interest of $1,400 is received from the university credit union.
- (f) A student who had borrowed $1,000 was in a serious bike accident and withdrew from school. The university wrote off the loan as uncollectible.

Exercise 6. Record the following events that affect Public University's endowment fund:
- (a) An alumnus donates $150,000 to the endowment fund. The cash is fully invested in bonds with a face value of $146,000 which are purchased at a $4,000 premium. The income earned is to be available for the Current Restricted Fund for curriculum improvement.
- (b) A check for interest is received for $16,000. The premium amortization is $320.
- (c) The income is transferred to the restricted current fund.
- (d) The bonds are sold for $160,500.

Exercise 7. Record the following events that affect Public University's annuity and life income funds.
- (a) On July 1, 19X0, J. H. March, Emeritus Professor of Accounting, moved out of the state. March donated to the university common stock with a cost basis of $50,000 and a market value of $90,000. March is to receive an annuity of $5,000 a year for life; at death, the securities are to be sold and the remaining cash balance is to be transferred to the student loan fund. At a 10% annual rate and a life expectancy of 12 years, the present value of the annuity payments is $34,068.
- (b) The stock paid $5,400 in dividends each 12-month period.
- (c) The annuities payable is adjusted to its present value. At year end, a payment of $5,000 is made to Professor March.
- (d) The annuities payable is adjusted to the present value. A second payment was made a year later.
- (e) A month later, Professor March died, eliminating the liability for future annuity payments.
- (f) The common stock was sold for $97,000. The cash balance was transferred to the student loan fund.

Exercise 8. Public University maintains the following active plant funds:

> Unexpended
> Renewals and Replacements
> Retirement of Indebtedness

Indicate in which fund each of the following transactions is recorded and make the appropriate entry:

(a) A transfer of $50,000 is received from the current unrestricted fund for the purpose of funding the payment of existing debt principal.

(b) The restricted current fund transfers $30,000 to be used for major repairs of university buildings. The $30,000 is spent on appropriate repairs.

(c) A transfer of $200,000 is made from the unrestricted current fund to the unexpended plant fund to finance an addition to the Fine Arts Building.

(d) Work on the Fine Arts addition is in progress. At year end, costs of construction total $80,000, of which $20,000 is unpaid. The university vice-president for finance prefers that transfers to the investment in plant subgroup be made only upon completion of any project.

(e) The project is completed during the next year at an additional cost of $140,000, of which $125,000 is paid.

(f) Unpaid contract costs of $35,000 are paid.

(g) Transfer of the Fine Arts addition is made to the investment in plant subgroup.

Exercise 9. Record the following events that affect public University's investment in plant subgroup.

(a) A partial payment of $50,000 is made from the unrestricted current fund on the gymnasium building mortgage, which is carried as a liability in the investment in plant subgroup.

(b) New gymnasium equipment costing $30,000 is purchased from the portion of the unexpended plant fund donated by a former Olympic medal winner for that purpose.

(c) The Fine Arts Building addition is completed at a total cost of $220,000. The contractor is paid.

(d) During a celebration after a basketball victory, $2,000 of gym equipment disappeared.

Exercise 10. Prepare journal entries to record the events below for Private University. Assume that fund accounting is not used.

(a) Student tuition assessed during the year was $400,000, of which $375,000 has been collected and 3% is estimated to be uncollectible.

(b) Student aid included $5,000 in cash scholarships and $2,000 in tuition remission.

(c) Salary and wages during the year included $25,000 for instruction, $10,000 for academic support, and $40,000 for institutional support, of which $5,000 has not been paid.

(d) A grant received of $50,000 in cash was restricted to use for laser technology research. A report of the research findings will be submitted to the grantor.

(e) An alumnus pledges $30,000 to be paid $10,000 per year over a 3-year period beginning at the end of this year. A 5% interest rate is used to discount this contribution to its present value.

(f) As a result of a pledge drive, $40,000 is pledged to be paid by the end of the accounting year. All pledges are restricted for research on genetics. Ten percent of pledges in the past have been shown to be uncollectible.

(g) By year end, $45,000 of the grant mentioned in (d) has been applied to the purpose stipulated. The grant provided that the amount not awarded by year end be reclassified as an endowment.

Exercise 11. Prepare journal entries to record the events below for Private University. Assume that fund accounting is not used.

(a) A cash gift of $75,000 was received from a local manufacturing firm to aid in the university's research project on the development of distance learning.

(b) Endowment income of $32,000 was received to provide scholarships to Management Information Systems students.

(c) By the close of the fiscal year, all but $5,000 in gifts for the distance learning project mentioned in (a) has been expensed, and of that expensed, all but $3,000 has been paid. All of the endowment income has been awarded in cash.

Exercise 12. Prepare journal entries to record the events below for Private University. Assume that fund accounting is not used.

(a) To establish the Herbon Student Loan Fund, two brothers donated $4,000 cash and securities that cost $8,000. Market value of the securities at time of donation was $16,000.

(b) The securities were later sold for $19,000. The original agreement stipulated that any gain on the sale or income received from securities be added to the loan fund.

(c) The board of trustees designated $3,000 of the unrestricted net assets cash for student loans.

(d) Loans of $24,000 were made to students at 6%.

(e) Collections on Herbon loans amounted to $20,000 plus $600 in interest.

(f) The board of trustees agreed that loans to students in the amounts of $900 were uncollectible. At year end, the board took action to write off the uncollectible loans outstanding of $900 against the existing allowance.

Exercise 13. Prepare journal entries to record the events below for Private University. Assume that fund accounting is not used.

(a) Upon her death, June Frost, a local businessperson, donated a portfolio of stock with a cost basis of $100,000 and a market value of $125,000. June's husband is to receive an annuity of $8,000 per year for life. His life expectancy is 10 years. An estimated rate of return of 8% yields a present value of $53,681 for the annuity.

(b) Dividends of $7,500 are received from life income investments.

(c) Annuity investments with a book value of $6,000 are sold for $6,500.

(d) The beneficiaries of the life income investments described in part (b) are paid.

(e) The annuity payable is updated to its present value at year end.

(f) The first annuity payment to June Forst's husband is made from part (a).

Exercise 14. Prepare journal entries to record the events below for Private University. Assume that fund accounting is not used.

(a) A $100,000, 10% serial bond issue, paying interest semiannually, was sold at 103 on an interest payment date. Proceeds equal to the face value of the bond issue are to be used to add a wing to the library.

(b) A lot valued at $30,000 was donated by a former librarian to permit building of the proposed library wing. The land is restricted for use as a library site only and can never be sold by the university.

(c) An architect was paid $20,000 for building plans. A contract for $900,000 was signed for construction of the library wing.

(d) Tuckpointing and other repairs to the library amounting to $35,000 were paid from resources previously provided specifically for that purpose by a retired faculty member.

(e) A donation of a collection of books on accounting, dating back to the 16th and 17th centuries, was made by a public accounting firm. The collection value was $15,000. No restrictions were placed on this gift.

APPENDIX EXERCISES

Exercise 18A-1. Record the following events that affect the current unrestricted funds of Private University, which has adopted the new FASB guidance on accounting for contributions and financial statement display. Assume fund accounting is used.

(a) Student fees of $400,000 were assessed, of which $375,000 have been collected and $4,000 are estimated to be uncollectible.

(b) The book store operates in rented space and is run on a break-even basis. Revenues totaled $80,000, of which 80% was collected to date. Salaries of $25,000 and rent of $10,000 are paid. Other operating expenses amount to $40,000, of which $5,000 has not been paid.

(c) A mandatory transfer of $75,000 was made for a payment due on the gymnasium building mortgage.

(c) The Student Aid Committee report showed:

Cash scholarships issued $5,000
Remission of tuition   2,000

(e) A check for $10,000 and a pledge for $4,500 are received from the local medical society to cover part of the cost of research on drug effects, one of the university's educational programs. The educational programs will be conducted and paid for in the next fiscal period.

(f) The endowment fund received a check for $6,000 of interest on investments. The premium amortization on the investment is $120. The unrestricted current fund is the recipient of the income.

Exercise 18A-2. Record the following events that affect the current restricted funds of Private University, which has adopted the new FASB guidance on accounting for contributions and financial statement display. Assume fund accounting is used.

(a) A private grant of $50,000 was received, to be used exclusively for defraying costs of holding conferences on the topic of genes.

(b) By year end, $45,000 of the grant mentioned in (a) had been applied to the purpose stipulated.

(c) The grant provided that amounts not awarded by year end are permanently restricted and are to be transferred to the endowment fund. The liability to that fund is recorded.

(d) An alumnus, a former athlete, contributed $20,000 to assist in the search for a basketball coach.

Exercise 18A-3. Record the following events that affect the loan fund of Private University, which has adopted the new FASB guidance on accounting for contributions and financial statement display. Assume fund accounting is used.

(a) An alumnus donates $220,000 to establish the student loan fund. Students are charged a 5% annual interest rate.

(b) Loans of $180,000 are made to students.

(c) The remaining $40,000 is deposited in the university credit union, which pays a current interest rate of 7%.

(d) Loans of $20,000 are repaid, plus $800 of interest.

(e) Interest of $1,400 is received from the university credit union.

(f) A student who had borrowed $1,000 was in a serious bike accident and withdrew from school. The university wrote off the loan as uncollectible.

Exercise 18A-4. Record the following events that affect Private University's endowment fund. Private University has adopted the new FASB guidance on accounting for contributions and financial statement display. Assume fund accounting is used.

(a) An alumnus donates $150,000 to the endowment fund. The cash is fully invested in bonds that are purchased at a premium. The income earned is to be available for the current restricted fund for curriculum improvement.

(b) A check for interest is received for $16,000. The premium amortization is $320.

(c) The income is transferred to the restricted current fund.

(d) The bonds are sold for $160,500.

Exercise 18A-5. Record the following events that affect Private University's annuity and life income funds. Private University has adopted the new FASB guidance on accounting for contributions and financial statement display. Assume fund accounting is used.

(a) On July 1, 19X0, J. H. March, Emeritus Professor of Accounting, moved out of the state. March donated to the university common stock with a cost basis of $50,000 and a market value of $90,000. March is to receive an annuity of $5,000 a year for life; at death, the securities are to be sold, and the remaining cash balance is to be transferred to the student loan fund. At a 10% annual rate and a life expectancy of 12 years, the present value of the annuity payments is $34,000.

(b) The stock paid $5,400 in dividends each 12-month period.

(c) A payment of $5,000 is made to Professor March. The annuities payable is adjusted to its present value.

(d) The annuities payable is adjusted to the present value. A second payment was made a year later.

(e) A month later, Professor March died, eliminating the liability for future annuity payments.

(f) The common stock was sold for $97,000. The cash balance was transferred to the student loan fund.

Exercise 18A-6. Record the following capital-related transactions for Private University plant funds. Private University has adopted the FASB accounting and financial reporting guidance. Assume fund accounting is used.

(a) Transfers of $250,000 are received from the current unrestricted fund for the purpose of funding the payment of existing debt principle ($50,000) and building an addition to the Fine Arts Building ($200,000).

(b) Contributions of $30,000 restricted for major repairs of university buildings are received. $20,000 is spent for appropriate repairs.

(c) A partial payment of $50,000 is made on the debt principal.

(d) Work on the Fine Arts addition is completed with a total cost of $220,000. Unpaid contract costs total $35,000.

(e) New gymnasium equipment costing $30,000 is purchased from funds previously donated by a former Olympic medal winner for that purpose.

(f) A building with a fair market value of $300,000 was conated to the university by an alumnus.

(g) Depreciation on all assets totaled $75,000.

(h) During a celebration after a basketball victory, $2,000 of gym equipment disappeared.

PROBLEMS

Problem 18-1. Select the best answer for each of the following multiple-choice items dealing with universities:

1. For the 19X7 fall semester, Brook Public University assessed its students $4,000,000 (net of refunds), covering tuition and fees for educational and general purposes. However, only $3,700,000 was expected to be realized because tuition remissions of $80,000 were allowed to faculty members' children attending Brook, and scholarships totaling $220,000 were granted to students. What amount should Brook include in educational and general current funds revenues from student tuition and fees?

   (a) $4,000,000   (b) $3,920,000   (c) $3,780,000   (d) $3,700,000

2. Private College is sponsored by a religious group. Volunteers from this religious group regularly contribute their skilled services to Private and are paid nominal amounts to cover their commuting costs. If Private does receive these services, it would have to purchase similar services. During 19X6, the total amount paid to these volunteers was $12,000. The gross value of services performed by them, as determined by reference to lay-equivalent salaries, amounted to $300,000. What amount should Private record as expenses in 19X6 for these volunteers' services?

   (a) $312,000   (b) $300,000   (c) $12,000   (d) 0

3. Abbott Public University's unrestricted current fund comprised the following:

Assets...	**$5,000,000**
Liabilities (including deferred revenues of $100,000)	3,000,000

   The fund balance of Abbott's unrestricted current fund was:

   (a) $1,900,000   (b) $2,000,000   (c) $2,100,000   (d) $5,000,000

4. The following receipts are among those recorded by Curry Private College during 19X9:

Unrestricted gifts...	**$500,000**
Restricted gifts (expended for current operating purposes).............	200,000
Restricted gifts (not yet expended)	100,000

   The amount that should be included in revenues is:

   (a) $800,000   (b) $700,000   (c) $600,000   (d) $500,000

5. In 19X7, the board of trustees of Burr Private University designated $100,000 from its current funds for college scholarships. Also in 19X7, the university received a bequest of $200,000 from an estate of a benefactor who specified that the bequest was to be used for hiring teachers to tutor handicapped students. None of the bequest has been spent. What amount should be accounted for as restricted net assets?

   (a) 0   (b) $100,000   (c) $200,000   (d) $300,000

6. The following information pertains to interest received by Beech Public University from endowment fund investments for the year ended June 30, 19X8:

	Received	Expended for Current Operations
Unrestricted.	$300,000	$100,000
Restricted.	500,000	75,000

What amount should be credited to endowment income for the year ended June 30, 19X8?

(a) $800,000   (b) $375,000   (c) $175,000   (d) $100,000

7. On July 31, 19X8, Sabio Public College showed the following amounts to be used for:

Renewal and replacement of college properties.	$200,000
Retirement of indebtedness on college properties.	300,000
Purchase of physical properties for college purposes, but unexpended at 7/31/X8 .	400,000

What total amount should be included in Sabio's plant funds at July 31, 19X8?

(a) $900,000   (b) $600,000   (c) $400,000   (d) $200,000

8. The following expenditures were among those incurred by Cheviot Public University during 19X7:

Administrative data processing	$ 50,000
Scholarships and fellowships.	100,000
Operation and maintenance of physical plant	200,000

The amount to be included in the functional classification "Institutional Support" expenditures account is:

(a) $50,000   (b) $150,000   (c) $250,000   (d) $350,000

(AICPA adapted)

Problem 18-2.   Record the following transactions. Identify each as a contribution or an exchange transaction and prepare any appropriate entries.

1. Private University coordinated its annual special event with the opening of the alumni weekend. Tickets to the special event were $200, and included a buffet (cost $30), admission to the university symphony (cost $30), and a reception (cost $35). A total of 1,000 tickets were sold.
2. A local manufacturing company gave $2,000,000 to Private University to commission a study on the relationship of worker stress to chronic disease. The results of the study will be used to educate the general public.
3. Allen Corporation gave a contribution of $850,000 to Private University. Allen Corporation specifies that the gift is to be invested in perpetuity, and that the income may be used by Private University to pay operating costs.
4. Local Corporation donated a building to Private College for use as new office space. The cost to Local was $75,000. The building was appraised by a professional real estate appraiser at $100,000, while another appraiser valued it at $110,000.
5. An alumna of XYZ Private College has notified the school that she will donate to the school any net proceeds in excess of $50,000 from her next novel. She stipulates that the college use her gift to buy new equipment for the writing lab.
6. Cheryl Debit, an accountant, spent Sunday afternoon at Private University sending out a mailing to members seeking more contributions for the building fund.

7. A very famous artist notified the local private university that she has included in her will her plans to donate all of her paintings for exhibit at the university art gallery. A copy of her will is included with her letter.

8. A grant in the amount of $400,000 from the U.S. Department of Labor and Economics was received by Private University to fund research on the impact of accounting standards. A report of research findings is to be submitted to the grantor.

9. $50,000 of U.S. government funds flow to Private University to be held for students qualifying for financial aid.

Problem 18-3. A partial balance sheet of Rapapo State University, a public university, as of the end of its fiscal year, July 31, 19X5, is as follows:

Rapapo State University
Current Funds Balance Sheet
July 31, 19X5

Assets		Liabilities and Fund Balances	
Unrestricted:		**Unrestricted:**	
Cash	$200,000	Accounts payable.	$100,000
Accounts receivable (net		Due to other fund.	40,000
of $15,000 allowance) . . .	360,000	Deferred revenue—tuition	
Prepaid expenses.	40,000	and fees	25,000
		Fund balance	435,000
Total unrestricted	$600,000	Total unrestricted	$600,000
Restricted:		**Restricted:**	
Cash	$ 10,000	Accounts payable.	$ 5,000
Investments.	210,000	Fund balance	215,000
Total restricted	$220,000	Total restricted	$220,000
Total current funds.	$820,000	Total current funds.	$820,000

The following information pertains to the year ended July 31, 19X6:

(a) Cash collected from students' tuition totaled $3,000,000. Of this amount, $362,000 represented accounts receivable outstanding at July 31, 19X5; $2,500,000 was for current-year tuition; and $138,000 was for tuition applicable to the semester beginning in August 19X6.

(b) Deferred revenue at July 31, 19X5, was earned during the year ended July 31, 19X6.

(c) Accounts receivable at July 31, 19X5, that were not collected during the year ended July 31, 19X6, were determined to be uncollectible and were written off against the allowance account. At July 31, 19X6, the allowance account was estimated at $10,000.

(d) During the year, an unrestricted appropriation of $60,000 was made by the state, to be paid to Rapapo sometime in August 19X6.

(e) During the year, unrestricted cash gifts of $80,000 were received from alumni. Rapapo's board of trustees allocated $30,000 of these gifts to the student loan fund.

(f) During the year, restricted fund investments costing $25,000 were sold for $31,000. Restricted fund investments were purchased at a cost of $40,000. Restricted fund investment income of $18,000 was earned and collected during the year. This income is restricted for an ongoing research project.

(g) Unrestricted general expenses of $2,500,000 were recorded in the voucher system. At July 31, 19X6, the unrestricted accounts payable balance was $75,000.

(h) The restricted accounts payable balance at July 31, 19X5, was paid. The restricted fund paid $10,000 from its investment income for costs of an ongoing research project.

(i) The $40,000 due to other funds at July 31, 19X5, was paid to the plant fund as required.

(j) One-quarter of the prepaid expenses at July 31, 19X5, expired during the current year and pertained to general education expense. There was no addition to prepaid expenses during the year.

Required:

(1) Prepare journal entries in summary form to record the foregoing transactions for the year ended July 31, 19X6. Letter each entry to correspond with the letter indicated in the description of its respective transaction, and omit explanations. Use the following format:

		Current Funds			
		Unrestricted		Restricted	
Entry Letter	Accounts	Debit	Credit	Debit	Credit

(2) Prepare a statement of current funds revenues, expenditures, and other changes, including a total column, for the year ended July 31, 19X6, and conclude with the fund balances at year end.

(AICPA adapted)

Problem 18-4. The following events occurred as part of the operations of Craig State University, a public university:

(a) To construct a new computer complex, the university floated at par a $22,000,000, 7% serial bond issue on October 1, paying interest on June 30 and December 31. Accrued interest is to be transferred to the retirement of indebtedness plant fund when construction begins. Construction costs are to be accumulated in the unexpended plant fund until the unit is completed.

(b) Since construction has begun, the accrued interest, which must be used to assist in meeting bond interest payments, is transferred. Payments for construction to date total $5,000,000.

(c) On December 31, a mandatory transfer of $385,000 is made from the unrestricted current fund to cover the remainder of the interest due on December 31 on the bond issue.

(d) The bond interest due on December 31 is paid.

(e) Construction of the complex is completed at an additional cost of $17,000,000. Payment is made for $16,000,000; the balance will be paid in one year under a retained percentage agreement.

(f) The cost of the complex is transferred.

(g) A required transfer of $2,770,000 is made from the unrestricted current fund to cover redemption of the first serial bond of $2,000,000 plus interest.

(h) Payments are made for the item in (g).

(i) A gift of land and a building was received, appraised at $200,000 and $350,000, respectively. The state's leading industrialist made the gift on condition that the university would assume a $90,000 mortgage on the property.

(j) Pledges of $100,000 to be paid in one year were received with the understanding that the funds would be used to remodel the building received in (i). It is estimated that $5,000 of the pledges will not be collected.

(k) A donor contributed $100,000 in cash for the acquisition of rare first editions for the university library. The director of the library located a collection of the first editions that was available for $160,000. The university board transferred $60,000 from the unrestricted current fund to cover the difference.

(l) The first edition collection is purchased and payment is made.

Required:

Prepare journal entries to record the events, indicating in which funds the entries are made.

Problem 18-5. The balance sheet of Washburn Private University as of the end of its fiscal year, June 30, 19X7, is as follows:

Washburn Private University
Statement of Financial Position
For Year Ended June 30, 19X7

Assets		Liabilities and Fund Balances	
Cash	$257,000	Accounts payable	$ 40,000
Accounts receivable—student tuition and fees less allowance for doubtful accounts of $9,000	311,000	Deferred revenue	66,000
		Long-term debt	100,000
State appropriations receivable	75,000	Total liabilities	206,000
Endowment investments	50,000	Net Assets:	
Property, plant, and equipment (net)	90,000	Unrestricted	$487,000
		Temporarily restricted	40,000
Total assets	$783,000	Permanently restricted	50,000
		Total net assets	577,000
		Total net assets and liabilities	$783,000

The following transactions occurred during the fiscal year ended June 30, 19X8:

(a) On July 7, 19X7, a gift of $90,000 was received from an alumnus. The alumnus requested that one-half of the gift be used for the purchase of equipment for the university athletic department and the remainder be used for the establishment of a premanently restricted endowment. The alumnus further requested that the income generated by the endowment be used annually to award a scholarship to a qualified disadvantaged student. On July 20, 19X7, the board of trustees resolved that the funds of the newly established endowment would be invested in savings certificates. On July 21, 19X7, the savings certificates were purchased.

(b) Revenue from student tuition and fees applicable to the year ended June 30, 19X8, amounted to $1,900,000. Of this amount, $66,000 was collected in the prior year and $1,686,000 was collected during the year ended June 30, 19X8. In addition, at June 30, 19X8, the university had received cash of $158,000 representing fees for the session beginning July 1, 19X8.

(c) During the year ended June 30, 19X8, the university had collected $308,000 of the outstanding accounts receivable at the beginning of the year. The remainder was determined to be uncollectible and was written off against the allowance account. At June 30, 19X8, the allowance account was adjusted to $6,000.

(d) During the year, interest charges of $6,000 were earned and collected on late student fee payments.

(e) During the year, the state appropriation was received. An additional unrestricted appropriation of $40,000 was made by the state, but it had not been paid to the university as of June 30, 19X8.

(f) A gift of $30,000 cash was received from alumni of the university restricted for economic research expenses.

(g) During the year, endowment investments that cost $21,000 were sold for $24,000. This includes accrued investment income amounting to $1,900. All income was restricted for improvement in classroom teaching.

(h) During the year, unrestricted operating expenses of $1,800,000 were recorded. They include:

Instruction...............................	500,000
Research.................................	400,000
Institutional support	100,000
Student aid...............................	100,000
Student services	200,000
Operation and maintenance of plant..........	500,000
	$1,800,000

At June 30, 19X8, $60,000 of these expenses remained unpaid.

(i) Temporarily Restricted funds of $13,000 were spent for specified economic research described in (f).

(j) The accounts payable at June 30, 19X7, were paid during the year.

(k) During the year, $7,000 interest was earned and received on the savings certificates purchased in (a).

(l) In honor of its 25th anniversary, Washburn Private University conducted a fund drive. Contributions of $16,000 were received. Additional unconditional pledges of $14,000 were promised for payment in December 19X8. It is anticipated that $2,000 of the pledges will be uncollectible.

Required:

(1) Prepare journal entries to record the transactions. Assumed fund accounting is not used.

(2) Prepare a statement of activities for the year ended June 30, 19X8, using a column for each of the three net asset classifications and a total column.

Problem 18-6. The following events occurred as part of the operations of Crush Private University.

(a) To construct a new business building, the university floated at par a $20,000,000, 8% serial bond issue on July 1. Interest is to be paid on December 31 and June 30. In addition, contributions from the community specifically for the new building totaled $5,000,000.

(b) Payments for construction to date total $7,000,000.

(c) Interest payments are made on December 31.

(d) Construction of the building is completed at an additional cost of $18,000,000. Payment is made for $16,000,000; the balance will be paid in one year under a retained percentage agreement. Institutional policy is to release donor restrictions when assets are placed in service.

(e) The first bond serial of $2,000,000 plus interest is paid.

(f) A gift of land and a building was received, appraised at $200,000 and $350,000, respectively. The gift was made on the condition that the university assume a $90,000 mortgage on the property. The university assumed the mortgage.

(g) Pledges with a present value of $200,000 to be paid over the next five years were received. The funds will be restricted for remodeling the building received in (f). It is estimated that $20,000 of the pledges will not be collected.

(h) A donation of $500,000 of stock was made by a wealthy citizen. The stock cannot be sold for five years. After the five-year period, the stock can be sold, and any proceeds are to be used to finance campus construction projects.

(i) Dividends of $10,000 on the stock in (h) were received and were also restricted for construction projects.

(j) Depreciation on the building received in (f) totaled $25,000.

Required:

(1) Prepare journal entries to record these events for Private University. Assume that fund accounting is not used.

(2) Prepare a statement of activities.

Problem 18-7. The preclosing trial balance of Park Private College has the following balances:

	Dr.	Cr.
Expenses—Instruction	1,230,000	
Expenses—Research	840,000	
Expenses—Academic Support	250,000	
Expenses—Student Services	200,000	
Expenses—Institutional Support	225,000	
Expenses—Operation and Maintenance of Plant	400,000	
Expenses—Student Aid	350,000	
Expenses—Auxiliary Enterprises Expenses	475,000	
Reclassifications Out—Temporarily Restricted—Satisfaction of Program Restrictions	75,000	
Reclassifications Out—Temporarily Restricted—Satisfaction of Equipment Acquisitions Restrictions	250,000	
Reclassifications Out—Temporarily Restricted—Expiration of Time Restrictions	50,000	
Tuition and Fees		1,500,000
Contributions—Unrestricted		265,000
Government Appropriations, Grants, and Contracts		800,000
Other Investment Income—Unrestricted		250,000
Sales and Services of Auxiliary Enterprises		500,000
Reclassifications In—Unrestricted—Satisfaction of Program Restrictions		75,000
Reclassifications In—Unrestricted—Satisfaction of Equipment Acquisition Restrictions		250,000
Reclassifications In—Unrestricted—Expiration of Time Restrictions		50,000
Contributions—Temporarily Restricted		200,000
Endowment Income—Temporarily Restricted		15,000
Contributions—Permanently Restricted		500,000
Net Realized Gains on Endowment—Temporarily Restricted		25,000
Unrestricted Net Assets, 1/1/X5		675,000
Temporarily Restricted Net Assets, 1/1/X5		975,000
Permanently Restricted Net Assets, 1/1/X5		2,500,000

Required:

(1) Prepare closing entries for the three net asset classifications.

(2) Prepare a statement of activities for the year ended December 31, 19X5, using a column for each of the net asset classifications.

Problem 18-8. Using the data in Problem 18-7 and the following additional information, prepare a statement of financial position for Park Private College.

	Dr.	Cr.
Cash...	275,000	
Accounts Receivable (net)..............................	625,000	
Contributions Receivable................................	85,000	
Inventory of Supplies....................................	55,000	
Student Loans Receivable...............................	300,000	
Land, Building, and Equipment (net).....................	1,000,000	
Long-term Investments..................................	3,025,000	
Accounts Payable.......................................		220,000
Amounts Held on Behalf of Others.......................		250,000
Long-term Debt...		560,000
U.S. Government Grants Refundable......................		100,000

APPENDIX PROBLEMS

Problem 18A-1. Select the best answer for each of the following multiple choice items. (Nos. 1–11 are AICPA adapted.)

1. An alumnus donates securites to Rex Private College and stipulates that the principal be held in perpetuity and revenues be used for faculty travel. Dividends received from the securities should be recognized as revenues in:
    (a) Endowment funds
    (b) Quasi-endowment funds
    (c) Restricted current funds
    (d) Unrestricted current funds

2. A private college's plant funds group includes which of the following subgroups?
    (1)   Renewals and replacement funds
    (2)   Retirement of indebtedness funds
    (3)   Restricted current funds

    (a) 1 and 2
    (b) 1 and 3
    (c) 2 and 3
    (d) none of the above

3. Funds received by a private college from donors who have stipulated that the principal is nonexpendable but that the income generated may be expanded for current operating needs would be accounted for as:
    (a) Contributions—Permanently Restricted
    (b) Contributions—Temporarily Restricted
    (c) Contributions—Unrestricted
    (d) Fund Balance Increases

4. The following funds were among those held by State College at December 31, 19X1:

Principal specified by the donor as nonexpendable.....................	$500,000
Principal expendable after the year 2000...............................	300,000
Principal designated from unrestricted net assets.......................	100,000

What amount should State College classify as permanently restricted endowments?

(a) $100,000
(b) $300,000
(c) $500,000
(d) $900,000

5. Is the recognition of depreciation expense required for public colleges and private not-for-profit colleges?

	Public	Private
(a)	No	Yes
(b)	No	No
(c)	Yes	Yes
(d)	Yes	No

6. In the loan fund of a private or public college, each of the following types of loans would be found *except*:
   (a) Faculty
   (b) Computer
   (c) Staff
   (d) Student

7. In 19X2, State University's board of trustees established a $100,000 fund to be retained and invested for scholarship grants. In 19X2, the fund earned $6,000 which had not been disbursed at December 31, 19X2. What amount should State report as unrestricted investment earnings at December 31, 19X2?
   (a) $0
   (b) $6,000
   (c) $100,000
   (d) $106,000

8. On January 2, 19X2, a graduate of Oak Private College established a permanent trust fund and appointed Security Bank as the trustee. The income from the trust fund is to be paid to Oak and used only by the School of Business to support student scholarships. What entry is required on Oak's books to record the receipt of cash from the interest on the trust fund?
   (a) Debit cash and credit deferred revenue
   (b) Debit cash and credit temporarily restricted endowment revenue
   (c) Debit cash and credit temporarily restricted contributions
   (d) Debit cash and credit unrestricted endowment revenue

9. At the end of the year, Cramer Private University's balance sheet comprised $15,000,000 of assets and $9,000,000 of liabilities (including deferred revenues of $300,000). What is the balance of Cramer's net assets?
   (a) $5,700,000
   (b) $6,000,000
   (c) $6,300,000
   (d) $15,000,000

10. Financial resources of a college or university that are currently expendable at the discretion of the governing board and that have *not* been restricted externally nor designated by the board for a specific purpose should be reported in the balance sheet as:
    (a) Board-designated current funds
    (b) Permanently restricted net assets
    (c) Unrestricted net assets
    (d) Temporarily restricted net assets

11. Which of the following accounts would appear in the plant fund of a not-for-profit private college?

	Fuel Inventory for Power Plant	Equipment
(a)	Yes	Yes
(b)	No	Yes
(c)	No	No
(d)	Yes	No

Problem 18A-2. Trial balance information for Foxbay Private University is as follows for the fiscal year beginning 7/1/X5:

	Current Funds Unrestricted	Current Funds Restricted	Plant Funds	Loan Funds	Endowment Funds	Total
Cash	23,000	2,000	1,000	300		26,300
Accounts receivable..........	950					950
Allowance for uncollectible student tuition receivable ...	(75)					(75)
Contributions receivable......	6,000	17,500	3,000	1,000		27,500
Allowance for uncollectible contributions..............	(60)	(75)	(30)	(10)		(175)
Short-term investments	15,000	15,000				30,000
Land, buildings, and equipment			400,000			400,000
Accumulated depreciation			(150,000)			(150,000)
Long-term investments			100,000	10,000		110,000
Endowment investments					90,000	90,000
Accounts payable............	(3,500)					(3,500)
Long-term debt..............			(150,000)			(150,000)
Unrestricted net assets	(41,315)		(103,970)	(2,290)		(147,575)
Temporarily restricted net assets:						
Accounting research study..		(31,425)				(31,425)
Student loans				(9,000)		(9,000)
Purchase of buildings and equipment			(100,000)			(100,000)
Periods after June 30, 19X5		(3,000)				(3,000)
Permanently restricted net assets					(90,000)	(90,000)
	0	0	0	0	0	0

The following information pertains to the year ended June 30, 19X6:

(a) Students were billed for tuition and fees of $250,000. Of this amount 3,000 were estimated to be uncollectible.

(b) A federal grant of $25,000 was received for an economic outlook study of the area. The research findings are to be summarized in a report to the government granting agency upon completion of the study.

(c) Foxbay Private University received cash gifts for the following purposes:

Unrestricted as to purpose	75,000
For use in future periods	20,000
For student loans	15,000
For acquisition of plant	150,000
Term endowment	5,000
Endowment in perpetuity, income restricted to use for molecular research. . .	30,000

(d) $225,000 cash was received on collection of student fees in (a).

(e) The cash gifts for the term endowment and the endowment were placed in long-term investments.

(f) Foxbay Private University received unconditional promises to give. The payments on unconditional promises to give are due as follows:

	Currently	In Future (Present Value)	Total
Unrestricted as to purpose.	4,500	2,000	6,500
For use in future periods		600	600
For accounting research.	3,750	3,250	7,000
For acquisition of plant.		750	750
Total	8,250	6,600	14,850

(g) 1% of the unrestricted and program-restricted promises to give were estimated to be uncollectible. No allowance was considered necessary on the contributions for plant.

(h) A donor gave investments having a fair value of $2,000 to create an annuity trust; the related present value of the annuity obligation is $900. Upon the death of the beneficiary the remaining trust assets are expendable for art gallery operations.

(i) A local lawyer provided five hours of service to draw up the annuity trust agreement mentioned in (h). She did not charge for her services. She normally would charge a client $750 for consultation on a similar type of agreement. If the lawyer's services were not donated, Foxbay would have hired a lawyer to draft an agreement.

(j) The university received $5,000 from an individual who restricted its use to research on global warming. If the research project is not initiated within six months, the individual requested that the money be returned. The unversity has notyet under-taken the research project. Two months remain in the time period specified by the donor.

(k) Investment income was received:

Yield from operating cash investments	750
Yield on endowment, unrestricted as to use.	4,000
Yield on endowment, restricted as to purpose	2,000
Yield on annuity trust created this year	250

(l) Payments became due on unconditional promises to give of $3,500 releasing the time restrictions. These promises, received in prior years, were not restricted.

(m) Equipment was purchased with $10,000 donor-restricted cash contributed in prior periods. University policy is to release restrictions over the useful life of the assets.

(n) Expenses, excluding depreciation and contributed goods and services, were incurred during the year:

Instruction.	100,000
Research—economic outlook study described in (2).	20,000
Research—accounting study described in (6).	15,000
Institutional support	54,000

Student aid.	....	25,000
Academic support.	....	22,000
Student services	....	18,000

(o) Included in the expenses reported in (n) were $20,000 spent on an economic outlook research project financed by a grant and $15,000 for accounting research financed with private gifts.

(p) Depreciation of $20,000 was recorded this year. All depreciation charges were related to plant assets qcquired by donor-restricted contributions.

(q) The actuarial adjustment of the present value of the annuity payable was $30 credit. An annuity payment of $150 was made.

Required:

(1) Prepare the journal entries to record the above transactions for the year ended June 30, 19X6. Assume fund accounting is used by Foxbay Private University. Use the following format:

Entry Letter	Fund	Debit (Dr.)	Credit (Cr.)

(2) Prepare a statement of activities for the year ended June 30, 19X6.

Problem 18A-3. From the information in 18A-2, prepare a statement of financial position for Foxbay Private University for the year ended June 30, 19X6. Assume fund accounting is used.

Problem 18A-4. The pre-closing trial balance of Augustus Private University is as follows:

	Current Funds	Loan Funds	Endowment and Similar Funds	Plant Funds	Total
Cash	52,500	11,550	11,000	33,500	108,550
Short-term investments	50,200	500	6,000	15,000	71,700
Accounts receivable	34,400				34,400
Contributions receivable.	5,000				5,000
Inventories of materials	11,000				11,000
Prepaid expenses.	28,000				28,000
Loans to students.		5,850			5,850
Assets restricted to investment in land, buildings, and equipment.				35,000	35,000
Land, buildings, and equipment.				4,180,000	4,180,000
Long-term investments.			159,210	124,000	283,210
Endowment investments.			9,540		9,540
Instruction expenses	135,300				135,300
Research expenses	14,500				14,500
Academic support expenses	21,700				21,700
Student services expenses.	22,200	50			22,250
Institutional support expenses	20,000				20,000
Operation and maintenance of plant expenses	40,000			20,000	60,000
Student aid expenses	24,100				24,100
Auxiliary enterprises expenses	35,000				35,000
Reclassification Out—temporarily restricted— satisfaction of program restrictions	7,300	2,400		1,000	10,700

(continued)

	Current Funds	Loan Funds	Endowment and Similar Funds	Plant Funds	Total
Reclassification Out—temporarily restricted— satisfaction of plant acquisition restrictions				15,000	15,000
Reclassification Out—temporarily restricted— satisfaction of time restrictions...................			2,000		2,000
Mandatory transfers out—principal payments	2,000				2,000
Discretionary transfers out........................	30,000				30,000
Total debits	533,200	20,350	187,750	4,423,500	5,164,800
Accounts payable...............................	24,800			90,000	114,800
Other liabilities			150		150
Amounts held on behalf of others			11,000		11,000
Annuities payable			23,200		23,200
Long-term debt.................................				300,000	300,000
U.S. government grants refundable.................	5,500	3,000			8,500
Tuition and fees	170,000				170,000
Unrestricted contributions	38,500				38,500
Government appropriations, grants, and contracts ...	79,500				79,500
Investment income on endowment.................	5,000		2,000		7,000
Other investment income.........................	25,000	100			25,100
Sales and services of auxiliary enterprises...........	40,000				40,000
Contributions—temporarily restricted...............	7,000	2,500	5,600	9,000	24,100
Investment income on life income and annuity agreements—temporarily restricted			3,000		3,000
Endowment Income—temporarily restricted.........	800		2,000		2,800
Other investment income—temporarily restricted				4,500	4,500
Net realized gains on other investments— temporarily restricted		50	950		1,000
Contributions—permanently restricted..............			12,000	19,000	31,000
Net realized gains on endowment— temporarily restricted			6,000		6,000
Reclassification In—unrestricted—satisfaction of program restrictions........................	7,300	2,400		1,000	10,700
Reclassification In—unrestricted—satisfaction of plant acquisition restrictions...................				15,000	15,000
Reclassification In—unrestricted—satisfaction of time restrictions...............................			2,000		2,000
Mandatory transfers in...........................				2,000	2,000
Discretionary transfers in........................		300	15,000	14,700	30,000
Unrestricted net assets—7/1/X6...................	107,800	3,900	1,400	260,000	373,100
Temporarily restricted net assets—7/1/X6	22,000	8,100	26,050	3,167,300	3,223,450
Permanently restricted net assets—7/1/X6..........			77,400	541,000	618,400
Total Credits	533,200	20,350	187,750	4,423,500	5,164,800

Required:

(1) Prepare closing entries for each fund.

(2) Prepare a statement of activities for the year ended June 30, 19X7 following a columnar format for each fund.

CHAPTER 19

Accounting for Not-for-Profit Organizations: Health Care Providers and Voluntary Health and Welfare Organizations

This chapter discusses accounting and financial reporting for health care entities, voluntary health and welfare organizations, and other not-for-profit organizations including museums, country clubs, and religious organizations. The accounting and financial reporting presentation for all not-for-profit entities has been updated to include the recent standards for contributions and for reporting certain basic information in the general-purpose external financial statements.

ACCOUNTING FOR PROVIDERS OF HEALTH CARE SERVICES— GOVERNMENTAL AND PRIVATE

Advancements in medical practice and increased demand for access to health care services have led to significant growth in the health care industry. Expenditures for medical care now equal more than 10% of the gross national product. Health care entities include hospitals, clinics, continuing care retirement communities, health maintenance organizations, home health agencies, and nursing homes. Classified by sponsorship or equity structure, health care units fall into three categories:

1. Investor-owned health care entities (or proprietary entities), which are privately owned and operated for a profit.
2. Governmental health care entities (or public entities), which are operated by a governmental unit and accounted for as an enterprise fund, such as a veterans' hospital.
3. Voluntary not-for-profit health care entities, including those with a religious affiliation, which are organized and sustained by members of a community.

Generally accepted accounting principles (GAAP) for hospitals and other health care organizations have evolved through the efforts of two industry professional associations, the American Hospital Association (AHA) and the

Health Care Financial Management Association (HFMA) and the American Institute of Certified Public Accountants (AICPA). The AICPA Health Care Audit Guide, issued in May 1993, is currently the principal source of accounting guidelines for health care entities, except where superseded by Financial Accounting Standards Board (FASB) or Governmental Accounting Standards Board (GASB) pronouncements. FASB Statement Nos. 116 and 117, described in the previous chapter, supersede sections of the audit guide for private health care entities and governmental health care entities that choose to follow FASB standards.[1]

A modern health care provider may be a complex entity with medical, surgical, research, teaching, and public service aspects. One very unusual element about health care operations is the manner of payment for services. A significant portion of the fees for health care service is paid by a third party, such as Medicare, Medicaid, Blue Cross, or some other insurance provider. Health care entities are reimbursed not on the basis of listed prices, but on the basis of the cost of providing services, as that cost is defined by the third-party payor. A cost determination must be made according to formulas agreed upon in the law (Medicare and Medicaid) or in the contract (other insurance providers). Cost determination requires allocation of overhead, including depreciation. Thus, not-for-profit health care organizations follow the accrual basis of accounting, permitting comparison of results with profit-oriented health care units.

With the many restrictions resulting from donations, endowments, insurance company contracts, and government regulations for reimbursement, the activities of a health care provider have traditionally been accounted for using fund accounting.[2] Health care entities employ two classes of funds:

1. *General Funds,* which account for resources available for general operations, with no restrictions placed upon those resources by an outsider, and other exchange transactions including resources from government grants and subsidies, tax support, and reimbursements from insurance contracts.
2. *Donor-restricted funds,* which account for temporarily restricted and permanently restricted resources. This class is subdivided into:
   a. *Specific purpose funds,* which account for donor-restricted resources temporarily restricted for current but specified operations.
   b. *Plant replacement and expansion funds,* which account for resources temporarily restricted by the donor for the acquisition, construction, or improvement of property, plant, and equipment.
   c. *Endowment funds,* which account for resources that are received to create permanently restricted endowments (whose income only may be expended) and temporarily restricted term endowments (whose principal eventually will become available for expenditure).

---

[1]FASB Statement Nos. 116 and 117 are applicable under GASB Statement No. 20, *Accounting and Financial Reporting for Proprietary Funds and Other Governmental Entities That Use Proprietary Fund Accounting* (Norwalk, CT: Governmental Accounting Standards Board, 1993), par. 7.

[2]Most hospitals use the fund structure described in this chapter. However, other health care entities, such as health maintenance organizations, nursing homes, and home health care agencies may find it unnecessary to use fund accounting.

    d. Other donor-restricted funds such as *annuities* or *life income funds*, or *loan funds*.

Each fund consists of a set of self-balancing accounts designed to reflect activities within its domain. Although the new FASB guidance on accounting and financial reporting represents a shift away from fund accounting to an organization-wide perspective, health care organizations are expected to continue some form of fund accounting for internal management and reporting. Some may even choose to continue to include information on funds in the external financial reports. To demonstrate the organization-wide emphasis on accounting and financial reporting, the following discussion assumes no fund structure. The appendix to this chapter illustrates accounting and financial reporting within the existing funds structure of a health care organization.

CLASSIFICATION OF ASSETS AND LIABILITIES

Assets of a health care provider comprise three distinct segments: current assets, assets whose use is limited, and property and equipment. Assets and liabilities are sequenced by liquidity and are classified as current or noncurrent according to GAAP.

Assets whose use is limited include assets set aside by the governing board for a specific purpose, sometimes referred to as *board-designated assets*. For example, the board may authorize that $10,000 be set aside for capital improvements, which would be recorded as follows:

```
Cash—Limited in Use for Capital Expansion . . . . . . . . . . . . . . . . . .  10,000
   Cash . . . . . . . . . . . . . . . . . . . . . . . . . . . . . . . . . . . . . . . . . . . . . . .            10,000
```

The limitation is internal and, therefore, assets remain unrestricted since "restrictions" can only be created by outside sources. This segment also includes assets resulting from an operational agreement entered into by the board, such as the proceeds of a bond issue limited in use as stipulated by the bond indenture. Assets set aside to provide for self-insurance or to meet depreciation fund requirements with third-party payors belong to this segment as well.

Property and equipment include the physical properties used in operations, along with their accumulated depreciation. Current liabilities may include accounts and notes payable, deposits from patients, and advances from and amounts payable to third-party payors. Long-term liabilities may include notes, mortgages, capital leases, bond payables, and estimated malpractice costs. The net assets of the entire health care organization (which represents the difference between assets and liabilities) are divided into three classes—permanently restricted net assets, temporarily restricted net assets, and unrestricted net assets—based on the existence or absence of donor-imposed restrictions.

Classification of Revenues, Expenses, Gains, and Losses.   Revenues, expenses, gains, and losses increase or decrease the net assets of a health care entity. Other events, such as expirations of donor-imposed restrictions, that simultaneously increase one class of net assets and decrease another (reclassifications) are reported as separate items. Revenues and gains may increase unrestricted net assets, temporarily restricted net assets, or permanently restricted net assets. Expenses reduce unrestricted net assets.

Revenues and expenses are considered *operating* if they relate to the principal activity of providing health care services. Revenues, expenses, gains, or losses from activities that are incidental to the providing of health care services or from events beyond the entity's control are classified as *nonoperating*.

With the desired detail incorporated in subsidiary support records, the following operating revenue control accounts are available:

1. *Patient Service Revenue*, the major revenue account for a hospital, in which the gross revenues earned are recorded on an accrual basis at established rates for:
   a. Routine services (room and board, general nursing, and home health care).
   b. Other nursing services (in operating, recovery, and delivery rooms).
   c. Professional services (physician's care, lab work, pharmacy, blood bank, radiology, dialysis, and physical therapy).
2. *Resident Service Revenue*, the major revenue account for a nursing home or continuing care retirement community. It records rental fees earned from residents or amortization of their advance payment of fees.
3. *Other Operating Revenue*, which records revenue from services other than health care provided to patients and residents. Also recorded is revenue from sales or services to persons other than patients. Thus, Other Operating Revenue would include:
   a. Revenue from educational programs, such as nursing school tuition.
   b. Revenue from specific-purpose contributions.
   c. Revenue from government grants to the extent that the related expenditures are included in operations. Grants that may be refundable if provisions are not met are recorded as a liability. As expenses are incurred, a matching portion of the grant is recorded from liabilities and recognized as current period revenue.
   d. Revenue from sales of medical or pharmacy supplies to employees or physicians.
   e. Revenue from sale of cafeteria meals to employees, medical staff, and visitors.
   f. Revenue from snack bars, gift shops, parking lots, and other service facilities.

The control account *Nonoperating Revenue* records revenue not related directly to an entity's principal operations. These items are primarily financial in nature and include unrestricted and donor-restricted pledges, gifts, or grants, unrestricted income from endowment funds, maturing of term endowment funds, income and gains from investments, and gains on sales of hospital property.

Patient Service Revenue is recorded on a gross charge basis. A third-party payor, such as Blue Cross, may reimburse a hospital on the basis of predetermined amounts that are less than the original gross charges for described services. The difference between the gross revenue and the amount expected to be collected from the third party is referred to as the *contractual adjustment*. It is deducted from the gross patient service revenue prior to preparing the financial statements. A credit is made to an allowance account in order to reduce the receivables to net expected. Also deducted from gross revenue are adjustments for charitable services to indigent patients from whom collection will not be possible and courtesy allowances granted to hospital employees. The AICPA audit guide states that the Provision for Bad Debts is to be reported as an expense. The objective of grouping these items is to be able to show the net patient service revenue, an expense for uncollectibles, and net receivables on the financial statements.

Payments made to a health care unit by third parties include reimbursement for depreciation. Often this portion of the payment is limited in use to replacing or adding to property, plant, or equipment. Total billings are included in revenue of the general funds to permit matching of total revenues and expenses. When collected, the specified portion is transferred to a special account with the entry:

Cash—Assets Whose Use Is Limited by Agreement with
    Third-Party Payors for Funded Depreciation.................... XXX
    Cash.. XXX

Titles given to operating expenses of a health care facility may differ, depending upon the nature of its activities. With supporting details in subsidiary records, the following control accounts are common to many health care organizations:

1. *Nursing Services Expense*, for the cost of nursing services directly related to the patient or resident.
2. *Other Professional Services Expense*, for professional services indirectly related to the patient or resident, such as lab fees or pharmacy costs. Note that some hospitals combine the two accounts Nursing Services Expense and Other Professional Services Expense into one account labeled Professional Care of Patients Expense.
3. *General Services Expense*, for costs of the cafeteria, food service, and housekeeping. Where food services constitute a major cost, some hospitals prefer to segregate them into the account Dietary Services Expense.
4. *Fiscal Services Expense*, for admitting, cashiering, and accounting costs.
5. *Administrative Services Expense*, for insurance, taxes, and personnel costs.
6. *Depreciation Expense*, if not already allocated.
7. *Interest Expense*, if not already allocated.
8. *Provision for Bad Debts*, if not already allocated.

For example, to record salaries earned, a debit would be made to each of the first five control accounts, with subsidiary records indicating that the charge was for salaries. The statement of activities (operating statement) would show the total for each service, such as Nursing Services Expense, but not the nature of that total (salaries, supplies, etc.). The footnotes to the financial statements provide detail on the nature of the expense, such as salaries, supplies, etc.

Accounting for Contributions Received. Health care entities may receive gifts or donations that meet the definition of an unconditional contribution. These contributions may be unrestricted as to use or may be limited to a specific use. Unrestricted contributions are recognized at fair market value with a credit to Other Operating Revenue—Unrestricted or Nonoperating Revenue—Unrestricted depending on whether these contributions are deemed to be ongoing major or central activities, or peripheral or incidental transactions.

Bequests and gifts restricted by the donor as to use for (1) specific operating purposes, (2) additions to plant, (3) endowments, or (4) annuities or life incomes are recorded *when received* at their fair market value with a credit to Revenues (other operating or nonoperating)—Temporarily Restricted or Revenues (other operating or nonoperating)—Permanently Restricted.[3] When expenditures are made consistent with the donors' stipulation, or when term endowments become available, a reclassification is made from the temporarily restricted net asset category to an unrestricted net asset category. Should resources from expired term endowments be restricted further, for example, to purchase equipment, they will remain in the temporarily restricted net asset category. Resources temporarily restricted for the purchase or construction of property, plant, and equipment may be released from restriction either in the period the asset is placed into service or over its useful life. Donor-restricted contributions in which the restriction will be met in the current period may be classified as unrestricted revenues. Some promises to give are conditional and will not be recognized until the condition is met.

Activities of health care providers are enhanced by volunteers who donate their time and abilities. Donated services must be recognized if the services received (1) create or enhance nonfinancial assets or (2) require specialized skills, are provided by individuals possessing those skills who are scheduled and supervised in much the same way as employees, and would typically need to be purchased if not provided by donation. Services provided by doctors, nurses, and other professionals in a health care entity may meet the above criteria. Incidental services provided by other volunteers for such things as fundraising or other activities that would not otherwise be staffed by employees would not meet the criteria. For example, most voluntary service by senior citizens, candy stripers, and others is not recorded. When an institution is operated by a religious group whose members receive token payment or no payment at all, the value of donated services should be charged to the proper expense account and credited to other operating revenue or nonoperating revenue depending on the nature of the donated services.

Donated items may also be unrestricted or restricted. Examples of donated items in a health care entity are laboratory and pharmaceutical supplies donated

---

[3]Prior to FASB Statement No. 116, health care organizations credited the appropriate temporarily restricted or permanently restricted fund balance account. When the donor-restricted assets were used for their intended purpose, they were recorded as a transfer or, more commonly, as a direct debit to the appropriate fund balance. The transfer was recorded in the general fund as a credit to Other Operating Revenue or Nonoperating Revenue as appropriate. Revenue recognition was delayed until expenditures were incurred. Transfers for capital purchases were not recorded as revenue, but as increases in the fund balance account of the general funds.

by drug companies or associations of doctors; donated property, plant, and equipment; and contributed use of facilities. Donated items are recognized at fair market value with a credit to Other Operating Revenue—Unrestricted or Nonoperating Revenue—Unrestricted depending on whether the donations constitute the entity's ongoing major or central operations or are peripheral or incidental transactions. If donated items have a donor-specified use, they may be temporarily restricted until they are used for their intended purpose. Unrestricted donations of property are recognized as Nonoperating Revenue—Unrestricted. If donations of property are donor restricted, the same entry is made but with a credit to temporarily or permanently restricted revenues.

Malpractice Claims.   The current environment in relation to medical malpractice claims has caused insurance companies to raise premiums to health care providers dramatically or to limit the amount of risk they are willing to insure. To find a health care provider that is fully insured against medical malpractice losses is a rarity. Many have dropped their malpractice insurance or have adopted other approaches for protection. Some pay losses as they occur. Others establish trust funds with a trustee.

The accounting issue is to determine when the costs of malpractice claims should be recognized. An AICPA statement stipulates that:

> *The ultimate costs of malpractice claims, which include costs associated with litigating or settling claims, should be accrued when the incidents occur that give rise to the claims, if it can be determined that it is probable that liabilities have been incurred and if the amounts of the losses can be reasonably estimated.*[4]

If the health care provider is covered by insurance, the premiums applicable to the reporting period are expensed, plus an amount for estimated claim costs for the reporting period not covered by the insurance arrangement. The entry to record claim costs is:

Medical Malpractice Costs (or Administrative Services Expense)	XXX	
Cash (or Unexpired Premiums)		XXX
Estimated Additional Malpractice Liability		XXX

Although hospitals report expenses on a functional basis by major program area, the medical malpractice costs are sometimes segregated from the other administrative services costs to emphasize their critical nature.

As a result of the large settlements granted in malpractice cases, some health care organizations became self-insured, establishing a trust account with an outside trustee who determines funding requirements. Two entries are necessary. The first establishes the estimated claim costs and liability:

Medical Malpractice Costs (or Administrative Services Expense)	XXX	
Estimated Malpractice Liability		XXX

---

[4]Statement of Position 87-1, *Accounting for Asserted and Unasserted Medical Malpractice Claims of Health Care Providers and Related Issues* (New York: American Institute of Certified Public Accountants, March 16, 1987), par. 21.

The second entry records the contribution to the trustee:

Cash—Limited in Use Under Malpractice Funding Arrangement XXX
    Cash   XXX

The amount in the trust account is reported in the balance sheet as an asset whose use is limited. Claims expected to be paid during the next operating cycle are classified as current liabilities, while the remainder of the liability balance is shown as noncurrent.

Whether the health care provider is covered by insurance, pays losses as they occur, or has a trust fund arrangement, the amount of the expense should reflect the best estimate of ultimate costs of malpractice claims related to incidents that occurred during the reporting period.

Illustrative Entries for General Funds.   To illustrate the recording of events for a hospital, the year's affairs of Fitale Hospital are summarized next. The illustrative entries employ broad categories of control accounts and natural expense classification.

Event		Entry		
Gross charges to patients are for:		Accounts Receivable	5,200,000	
		Patient Service Revenue		5,000,000
		Other Operating Revenue—		
Daily patient services	$3,200,000	Unrestricted		200,000
Other nursing services	500,000			
Professional services	1,300,000			
Other nonmedical services	200,000			
Total	$5,200,000			
Estimates are made for:		Provision for Bad Debts	22,000	
		Contractual Adjustments	380,000	
Contractual adjustments	$ 380,000	Allowance for Uncollectible		
Uncollectibles	22,000	Receivables and Third-Party		
Total	$ 402,000	Contractual Adjustments		402,000
An analysis of accounts receivable shows:		Cash	3,800,000	
		Allowance for Uncollectible		
Cash collected	$3,800,000	Receivables and Third-Party		
Contractual adjustments with		Contractual Adjustments	290,000	
third-party payors	200,000	Accounts Receivable		4,090,000
Uncollectible	90,000			
Total	$4,090,000			
The hospital determined that $200,000 of the services were to patients who met hospital criteria for charity care.		Charity Services	200,000	
		Accounts Receivable		200,000
Inventory purchases amounted to $700,000; payments totaled $690,000.		Inventories	700,000	
		Cash		690,000
		Accounts Payable		10,000
Drugs and supplies costing $720,000 are requisitioned.		Drugs and Supplies Used	720,000	
		Inventories		720,000
Salaries earned (ignore payroll deductions) amounted to $3,000,000, of which $2,950,000 is paid.		Wages, Salaries, and Benefits	3,000,000	
		Cash		2,950,000
		Accrued Expenses		50,000

Event	Entry		
Outside professional fees of $300,000 are paid.	Purchased Services . . . . Cash		
Jacob Pharmaceutical Co. donated $2,000 of medicines to Fitale Hospital. Such contributions constitute a major ongoing activity of the hospital. If not donated, these medicines would have to be purchased.	Inventories . . . . Other Operating Revenues— Unrestricted (Contributions)		
Unrestricted earnings from endowment funds totaled $540,000.	Cash . . . . Nonoperating Revenues—Unrestricted (Investment Earnings)	540,000	540,000
Payments are made on:	Current Installment of Long-Term Debt . . . . Notes Payable . . . . Interest Expense . . . . Cash	80,000 200,000 66,000	346,000
Current installment of long-term debt . . $ 80,000 Notes payable . . . . 200,000 Interest expense . . . . 66,000 Total . . . . $ 346,000			
A donor promised to give Fitale $50,000 annually for each of the next four years (recorded at present value).	Contributions Receivable . . . . Nonoperating Revenues—Unrestricted (Contributions)	165,606	165,606
The hospital was recently served with a malpractice lawsuit. A prominent local trial attorney decided to assist in the defense of the hospital. Normal fees are $150 per hour. 100 total hours were devoted to the case.	Purchased Services . . . . Nonoperating Revenues—Unrestricted (Contributions)	15,000	15,000
Equipment costing $110,000 is purchased for cash.	Property and Equipment . . . . Cash	110,000	110,000
Depreciation expense provision for the year is $400,000.	Depreciation Expense . . . . Accumulated Depreciation	400,000	400,000
The current portion of long-term debt is reclassified as current from:	Bonds Payable . . . . Mortgage Note Payable . . . . Current Installment of Long- Term Debt	50,000 30,000	80,000
Bonds payable . . . . $ 50,000 Mortgage note payable . . . . 30,000 Total . . . . $ 80,000			
Professional services donated to the hospital were recognized: Nursing services . . . . $ 17,000 Other professional medical services . . . 3,000	Wages, Salaries, and Benefits . . . . Other Operating Revenue— Unrestricted (Contributions)	20,000	20,000
A provision for medical malpractice costs of $450,000 is recorded. The hospital is self-insured.	Medical Malpractice Costs . . . . Estimated Malpractice Liability	450,000	450,000
A malpractice self-insurance trust at Third Bank is increased by $230,000.	Cash—Limited in Use Under Malpractice Funding Arrangement . . . . Cash	230,000	230,000
Third-party payor reimbursements of $250,000 are to be set aside for plant replacement.	Cash—Limited in Use by Agreement with Third-Party Payors for Plant . . . . Cash	250,000	250,000
Fitale received $50,000 cash from a donor to cover operating costs of the student nursing unit.	Cash . . . . Other Operating Revenue—Temporar- ily Restricted (Contributions)	50,000	50,000

(continued)

Event	Entry		
˹ment earnings are received in the amount of ,000 restricted for cancer research.	Cash............................... Nonoperating Revenues—Temporarily Restricted (Investment Earnings)....	75,000	75,000
$500,000 was donated to Fitale Hospital for investments in long-term securities as a pure endowment	Cash............................... Nonoperating Revenues—Permanently Restricted (Endowment Contributions)...................	500,000	500,000
Securities were purchased.	Endowment Investments............. Cash..............................	500,000	500,000
A term endowment expired. The $150,000 principal is now available for use by the hospital administration.	Reclassification Out—Temporarily Restricted—Satisfaction of Time Restriction...................... Reclassification In—Unrestricted— Satisfaction of Time Restriction.....	150,000	150,000
Receipts of $200,000 and an unconditional promise to give $100,000 were recorded. Gifts were to be used for operating room equipment.	Contributions Receivable.............. Cash.............................. Other Operating Revenues— Temporarily Restricted (Contributions)...................	100,000 200,000	300,000
Operating room equipment was purchased. The hospital elects to release the donor restriction over the useful life of the asset.	Equipment.......................... Cash..............................	200,000	200,000
The first year depreciation on the above operating equipment was recorded.	Depreciation Expense................. Accumulated Depreciation...........	40,000	40,000
The expiration of the donor restriction on the fixed asset is recognized by reclassifying from temporarily restricted to unrestricted. This reclassification "matches" the depreciation expense.	Reclassification Out—Temporarily Restricted—Satisfaction of Plant Acquisition Restriction............. Reclassification In—Unrestricted— Satisfaction of Plant Acquisition Restrictions......................	40,000	40,000
A $400,000 grant from a local manufacturer to be used for a patient nutritional study was received. Results of the study will be used to educate the public, not for the benefit of the donor.	Cash............................... Other Operating Revenues— Temporarily Restricted (Contributions)...................	400,000	400,000
Expenses were incurred for the patient nutritional study. Donor restrictions are expired to match specified expenses. A reclassification entry records the expiration of donor restrictions.	Wages, Salaries, and Benefits.......... Drugs and Supplies Used.............. Purchased Services................... Cash..............................	25,000 10,000 15,000	50,000
	Reclassification Out—Temporarily Restricted—Satisfaction of Program Restrictions...................... Reclassification In—Unrestricted— Satisfaction of Program Restriction..	50,000	50,000

At year end, the following closing entries are prepared. The closing entries allocate the natural expenses to the functional areas and update the three classes of net assets.

Event	Entry	
Fitale allocates natural expenses to the functional areas based upon which program they benefited when incurred.	Nursing Services.............................. Other Professional Services.................... General Services..............................	1,774,000 1,240,000 995,000

Event	Entry

	Fiscal Services...............................	283,000	
	Administrative Services	791,000	
	Wages, Salaries, and Benefits.................		3,045,000
	Drugs and Supplies Used.....................		730,000
	Purchased Services		330,000
	Medical Malpractice Costs....................		450,000
	Depreciation Expense........................		440,000
	Interest......................................		66,000
	Provision for Bad Debts		22,000
Unrestricted Net Assets closing entry.	Patient Service Revenue—Unrestricted	5,000,000	
	Other Operating Revenue—Unrestricted	222,000	
	Nonoperating Revenue—Unrestricted...........	720,606	
	Reclassifications In—Unrestricted—Satisfaction of Equipment Acquisition Restrictions	40,000	
	Reclassifications In—Unrestricted—Satisfaction of Time Restrictions	150,000	
	Reclassifications In—Unrestricted—Satisfaction of Program Restrictions	50,000	
	Charity Care................................		200,000
	Contractual Adjustments		380,000
	Nursing Services............................		1,774,000
	Other Professional Services		1,240,000
	General Services............................		995,000
	Fiscal Services..............................		283,000
	Administrative Services		791,000
	Unrestricted Net Assets		**519,606**
Temporarily Restricted Net Assets closing entry.	Other Operating Revenue—Temporarily Restricted...............................	750,000	
	Nonoperating Revenue—Temporarily Restricted ...	75,000	
	Reclassifications Out—Temporarily Restricted— Satisfaction of Equipment Acquisition Restrictions		40,000
	Reclassifications Out—Temporarily Restricted— Satisfaction of Time Restrictions		150,000
	Reclassifications Out—Temporarily Restricted— Satisfaction of Program Restrictions		50,000
	Temporarily Restricted Net Assets		**585,000**
Permanently Restricted Net Assets closing entry.	Nonoperating Revenue—Permanently Restricted Endowment Contributions..................	500,000	
	Permanently Restricted Net Assets		**500,000**

FINANCIAL STATEMENTS OF A HEALTH CARE PROVIDER

The financial statements of a health care provider include a statement of activities which presents organization-wide totals for changes in unrestricted net assets, temporarily restricted net assets, and permanently restricted net assets. The form is straightforward, showing operating revenues minus operating expenses as an increase (decrease) in net assets from operations. The nonoperating revenue is added to this amount. Expenses are reported using functional classifications. Further information on natural classifications of expenses is suggested footnote disclosure. In practice, comparative financial statements would be presented. To conserve space, the results of only one year's activities are shown in Illustration 19-1.

In addition to the statement of activities, a health care organization provides a statement of financial position and a statement of cash flows. The

Illustration 19-1
Fitale Hospital
Statement of Activities
For Year Ended December 31, 19X5

	Unrestricted	Temporarily Restricted	Permanently Restricted	Total
Revenues, gains, and other support:				
Patient services revenue (net of adjustments).............................	$4,420,000			$ 4,420,000
Other operating revenue	222,000	$ 750,000		972,000
Net assets released from restrictions:				
Satisfaction of program restrictions........	50,000	(50,000)		0
Satisfaction of equipment acquisition restrictions............................	40,000	(40,000)		0
Expiration of time restrictions	150,000	(150,000)		0
Total operating revenues, and other support	$4,882,000	$ 510,000		$ 5,392,000
Expenses and losses:				
Nursing services	$1,774,000			$ 1,774,000
Other professional services.................	1,240,000			1,240,000
General services..........................	995,000			995,000
Fiscal services............................	283,000			283,000
Administrative services	791,000			791,000
Total expenses and losses	$5,083,000			$ 5,083,000
Increase (decrease) in net assets from operations	$ (201,000)	510,000		$ 309,000
Nonoperating revenue	$ 720,606	$ 75,000	$ 500,000	$ 1,295,606
Increase (decrease) in net assets	$ 519,606	$ 585,000	$ 500,000	$ 1,604,606
Net assets at beginning of year	4,698,000	719,000	3,560,000	8,977,000
Net assets at end of year.....................	$5,217,606	$1,304,000	$4,060,000	$10,581,606

statement of financial position, shown in Illustration 19-2, includes assets and liabilities of all funds. The sequence begins with current assets, assets whose use is limited, property and equipment, and possibly other assets. Also shown are the current and other liabilities of the organization and the three classes of net assets, which represents the equity of the hospital.

The statement of cash flows, in Illustration 19-3, follows FASB Statement No. 95 guidance which encourages the use of the direct method to present cash flows, although it does accept the indirect method. FASB Statement No. 117 states that the provisions of FASB Statement No. 95 also should be applied to not-for-profit health care entities amended to include among the list of cash inflows from financing activities receipts from contributions and investment income that by donor stipulation are restricted for the purpose of acquisition, construction, improving property, plant, and equipment, or other long-lived assets, or establishing or increasing a permanent endowment or term endowment.

Illustration 19-2
Fitale Hospital
Statement of Financial Position
As of December 31, 19X5

Assets:	
Cash and cash equivalents	$ 735,000
Accounts and interest receivable	908,000
Inventories	81,000
Contributions receivable	265,606
Short-term investments	400,000
Assets restricted to investment in land, building, and equipment	445,000
Assets limited in use under malpractice funding agreement	440,000
Property, plant and equipment (net of depreciation)	5,250,000
Long-term investments	540,000
Endowment investments	4,060,000
Total assets	**$13,124,606**
Liabilities and net assets:	
Accounts payable	$ 53,000
Current installments of long-term debt	80,000
Accrued expenses	100,000
Notes payable	500,000
Estimated malpractice costs	640,000
Long-term debt	1,170,000
Total liabilities	**$ 2,543,000**
Net assets:	
Unrestricted	**$ 5,217,606**
Temporarily restricted	**1,304,000**
Permanently restricted	**4,060,000**
Total net assets	**$10,581,606**
Total liabilities and net assets	**$13,124,606**

ACCOUNTING FOR VOLUNTARY HEALTH AND WELFARE ORGANIZATIONS

To qualify as a voluntary health and welfare organization (VHWO), two criteria must be met. First, a primary source of revenue should be contributions from donors who do not themselves directly benefit from the organization's programs. A community symphony orchestra, for instance, would not qualify because it derives a large share of its revenue from box office receipts. Second, the program must be in the area of health, welfare, or community service, such as care for the elderly, the indigent, or the handicapped, or projects to protect the environment.

FUNDS

Although most contributions are made with no restrictions attached, some donations specify the purpose for which they must be expended. To segregate resources and demonstrate compliance with external restrictions, new guidance

Illustration 19-3
Fitale Hospital
Statement of Cash Flows
For Year Ended December 31, 19X5

Cash flows from operating activities:

Cash received from patients and third-party payors	$3,800,000
Cash received from contributions	450,000
Interest and dividends received	615,000
Cash paid to employees and suppliers	(3,990,000)
Interest paid	(66,000)
Net cash provided by (used for) operating activities	**$ 809,000**

Cash flows from investing activities:

Purchases of investments	$ (500,000)
Purchases of land, building, and equipment	(310,000)
Net cash provided by (used for) investing activities	**$ (810,000)**

Cash flows from financing activities:

Payments on notes payable	$ (200,000)
Payments on long-term debt	(80,000)
Contributions received restricted for endowment	500,000
Contributions received restricted for property, plant, and equipment	200,000
Net cash provided by (used for) financing activities	**$ 420,000**

Net increase (decrease) in cash and cash equivalents	**$ 419,000**
Cash and cash equivalents at beginning of year	**316,000**
Cash and cash equivalents at end of year	**$ 735,000**

Reconciliation of change in net assets to net cash provided by (used for) operating activities:

Change in net assets	$1,604,606

Adjustments to reconcile change in net assets to net cash provided by (used for) operating activities:

Depreciation	440,000
Increase in accounts receivable	(798,000)
Increase in contributions receivable	(265,606)
Decrease in inventories	18,000
Increase in accounts payable and accrued liabilities	60,000
Contributions received restricted for endowment	(500,000)
Contributions received restricted for property, plant, and equipment	(200,000)
Increase in liability for estimated malpractice costs	450,000
Net cash provided by (used for) operating activities	**$ 809,000**

for all not-for-profit organizations, outlined in Chapter 18, requires financial reports to include information on three classes of net assets: unrestricted, temporarily restricted, and permanently restricted. Many organizations will continue to further segregate resources with the use of fund accounting for internal management reporting. The external financial statements will report on the organization as a whole as required by FASB Statement No. 117. The appendix to this chapter illustrates accounting and financial reporting for voluntary health and welfare organizations assuming the following funds structure:

1. *Current unrestricted fund*, which accounts for resources that have no external restrictions and are available for current operations at the discretion of the governing board.
2. *Current restricted fund*, which accounts for assets received from outside sources for a current operating purpose specified by the donor.
3. *Land, building, and equipment fund*, which accounts for the activity related to fixed assets.
4. *Endowment fund*, which accounts for permanently restricted endowment principal and temporarily restricted term endowments.
5. *Agency (custodian) fund*, which accounts for assets that do not belong to the organization holding them.

ACCOUNTING PRINCIPLES AND PROCEDURES

The full accrual basis of accounting should be used in accounting and reporting for VHWOs if the reports are to be considered as prepared in accordance with GAAP.

The dependence upon public support for the majority of its resources influences the accounting for a VHWO. Two major categories are used to record and communicate inflows of resources: public support and revenues. *Public support* is the inflow of resources from voluntary donors who receive no direct, personal benefit from the organization's usual programs in exchange for their contributions. *Revenues* are inflows of resources resulting from a charge for service from financial activities or from other exchange transactions.

A significant aspect of accounting and reporting for VHWOs is that financial reports must show expenses on a program basis. As a result of this requirement, the costs of each program and supporting service are available, and the effectiveness with which the organization's resources have been managed can be measured.

PUBLIC SUPPORT

The following accounts are used to record receipts of assets in the public support category:

1. Contributions
2. Special Events Support

3. Legacies and Bequests
4. Received from Federated and Nonfederated Campaigns

Contributions. Contributions received are recognized as public support in the period received and as assets, decreases of liabilities, or expenses depending on the form of the benefits received.[5] Contributions are measured at their fair market value and reported as either unrestricted, temporarily restricted, or permanently restricted depending on donor stipulations. Contributions also include unconditional promises to give (pledges). Therefore, unconditional promises to give must also be recognized as support in the period received. Contributions may be unrestricted or restricted for a specific purpose. Contributions that have no donor-imposed restrictions attached to them are reported as unrestricted. Contributions that have donor-imposed restrictions attached to them must be classified as temporarily or permanently restricted based on the nature of the restriction.

Cash collections that do not involve a previous promise to give are credited to the account Contributions. VHWOs also receive pledges for contributions, which are recorded at the gross amount as Contributions Receivable, with a credit to Contributions. A provision and an allowance for estimated uncollectible pledges are established, based on historical collection experience. The provision for uncollectible pledges is an expense account, while the allowance is a contra-account to Pledges Receivable.

Expiration of donor-restrictions must be recognized in the period in which the restriction expires. The expiration of a restriction may be based on the lapse of time or the fulfillment of a stipulated purpose, or both. Recognition of an expiration of donor restrictions is done with a reclassification entry. Reclassifications result in an increase in the unrestricted class of net assets and a decrease in temporarily restricted net assets class. Such a reclassification increases unrestricted net assets to "match" the decrease resulting from the stipulated expense.

Temporarily restricted unconditional promises to give (pledges) are reclassified to unrestricted in the period in which the unconditional promise is received or the restriction lapses. A gift or promise to give that involves a condition is not considered a contribution until the condition is met and is therefore not recognized as an increase in net assets in the period in which it is received, but is disclosed in the footnotes.

Securities and other property received should be recorded at fair market value at the time of receipt. These assets are most likely to be received as temporarily or permanently restricted contributions. The donor may restrict not only the purpose but also the timing of use. If the donation is not available for use until some future fiscal period, it is recorded as Contributions—Temporarily Restricted. The amount is released from restriction (unclassified) in the period when it becomes available.

---

[5] A contribution is defined as an "unconditional transfer of cash or other assets to an entity or a settlement or cancellation of its liabilities in a voluntary nonreciprocal transfer by another entity acting other than as an owner" (FASB Statement No. 116, par. 5).

Contributed works of art, historical treasures, and similar assets need not be recognized as contributions "if the donated items are added to collections that (a) are held for public exhibition, education, or research rather than financial gain, (b) are protected and preserved, (c) are subject to an organization policy that requires the proceeds from sales of collection items to be used to acquire other items for collections."[6]

Although organizations can choose whether or not to capitalize their collections, the choice must be applied to all collections. Capitalization may be done retroactively or prospectively.

Common to VHWOs is the donation of materials to be used in providing service or to be processed for subsequent sale. These materials should be recorded as inventory, with a credit to Unrestricted Contributions at their market value when received, provided that they are substantial in amount and a measurable value for them can be established, either by sale shortly thereafter or by appraisal. An example would be the donation of clothing or household goods to Goodwill Industries.

Occasionally, a VHWO will be permitted to use building facilities rent free. In this situation, both the contribution and the rent expense should be recorded at fair rental value, usually equivalent to the amount that normally would be charged for rent. Donated fixed assets for which title is received, such as equipment or land and building, should be entered as an unrestricted, temporarily restricted, or permanently restricted contribution at market value depending upon the donor's stipulations. Expiration of donor restrictions will occur either at the time the asset is placed in service or over the asset's useful life. Permanent restrictions do not expire.

Although the range of personal services that volunteers donate varies between organizations, these services should be recorded if they are significant and if the following criteria are met:

1. The services received create or enhance nonfinancial assets, or
2. The services received require specialized skills, are provided by individuals possessing those skills, and would typically need to be purchased if not provided by donation. (Usually the individuals performing such services are treated in a similar fashion to employees; they have schedules, assigned duties, are supervised, etc.)

Promises to give services are also included. Recognizing contributed services that are specialized and would need to be purchased indicates to readers of the financial statements the impact these contributions have on the organization. It also indicates the need for future cash outflows in the event these services are no longer contributed.

If the criteria are met, donated services are recorded with a debit to an expense account, such as Salary Expense, and a credit to Contributions. Contributed services received that are not required to be recognized as revenues are disclosed at their fair value in the footnotes to the financial statements.

---

[6]Ibid., par. 11.

Special Events Support.   Another subdivision of the public support category covers an organization's special fund-raising events, in which the participant has the opportunity to receive something of value in exchange for a contribution. Raffles, dinners, bingo games, and bake sales are examples of special events. The gross inflow of resources is credited to Special Events Support in the fund that it is to benefit. Direct costs of the event, excluding promotional costs, are charged to Cost of Special Events. Comparing these two balances permits one to judge the effectiveness of the event. It also determines that portion of the proceeds that are contributions to the organization. FASB No. 117 states that if such "special events" are peripheral or incidental, they may be disclosed net of costs (which used to be the general practice) but if they are ongoing and major activities, then gross revenue is recorded and direct costs of those activities, are considered fund-raising expenses. Promotional costs, such as advertising or the salaries of employees involved in the event, are charged against fund-raising expense. The portion of the budget consumed by fund-raising expenses must also be revealed.

Legacies and Bequests.   Every VHWO hopes that its programs will be so deserving that they will encourage donors to make major contributions of personal property or real property through their wills. Since these items tend to be more substantial in amount, the audit guide recommends that such contributions be shown as a separate item of public support under Legacies and Bequests. They are entered as a credit to that account when the organization is reasonably certain of the amount to be received. Such contributions are classified as unrestricted, temporarily restricted, or permanently restricted based on donor stipulations.

Received from Federated and Nonfederated Campaigns.   The final item considered as public support is the amount received from federated (associated) and nonfederated organizations. This amount is credited to Received from Federated and Nonfederated Campaigns. An amount allocated by United Way to a health and welfare organization would be an example of support received from a federated organization. An amount raised by independent, professional fund-raising groups would be an illustration of resources received from nonfederated campaigns. Usually contributions received from federated and nonfederated campaigns are unrestricted.

REVENUES

In addition to public support, resources may be received from exchange transactions that are classified as unrestricted revenue. These resources would include the following accounts:

1. Membership Dues Revenue for dues charged members to join and use facilities or receive publications.
2. Program Services Fees for amounts charged clients for services of the organization, such as consulting, testing, or advising.
3. Sales of Publications and Supplies for proceeds from the sales of these items.

Investment transaction revenue classified as unrestricted or restricted, could include the following accounts:

1. Investment Revenue for interest, dividends, and other earnings.
2. Realized Gain on Investment Transactions for gains from the sale or exchange of investments.
3. Net Increase (or Decrease) in Carrying Value of Investments for the unrealized appreciation (or depreciation) of investments if they are carried at market value.

Each of the items of investment transactions revenue would be recorded as unrestricted or restricted depending on donor stipulations. Thus, the unrestricted revenue from an endowment would be recorded with a credit to Investment Revenue—Unrestricted. Restricted investment revenue is reported as temporarily or permanently restricted in compliance with the donor's wishes.

The audit guide permits VHWOs to carry their investments either at cost or at market value, but the same basis must be applied to all the investments. Cost includes not only the total cost of purchased investments but also the market value at the date of receipt of donated investments. When there is a relatively permanent reduction in market value, the impairment to cost should be recorded. If all investments are reflected at market value, the unrealized appreciation (or depreciation) is shown separately in Net Increase (or Decrease) in Carrying Value of Investments. Realized and Unrealized gains and losses on all investments are considered increases or decreases in unrestricted net assets unless restricted by donor or law.

PROGRAM AND SUPPORTING SERVICES COSTS

VHWOs exist to render service or to conduct programs. Their operating statements will not show typical expenses, such as salaries or rent, but will show the cost of each program or service the organization provides—the costs in which the general public, the contributors, and the controlling agencies primarily are interested. For example, the operating statement of an environmental protection association might show the cost of conducting a program to reduce river pollution or to provide an animal and bird sanctuary. These projects fall in an expense grouping called *Program Services*. The other expense grouping shown on an operating statement is referred to as *Supporting Services*, which includes fundraising costs, management and general costs, and membership development activities for the overall direction of the organization. Management and general activities include all management, financing, and administrative activities, except for direct activities of programs or fund raising. Fund-raising activities include publicizing and conducting fund-raising campaigns; maintaining donor mailing lists; conducting special fund-raising events; preparing and distributing fund-raising materials, and other activities involved with soliciting contributions. Membership development activities include soliciting for prospective members and membership dues, membership relations, and similar activities.

Individual expenses, such as salaries or rent, are recorded in the respective natural expense accounts in much the same way that they would be recorded in the accounts of profit entities. All expenses are considered reductions in unrestricted net assets. Therefore, when expenses are recorded for purposes stipulated by donors, a reclassification of temporarily restricted to unrestricted net assets is recorded. At the end of the fiscal year, the expenses are allocated to the individual programs conducted and to the supporting services of management, fund raising, and membership development. Allocation of joint costs should be on some rational basis, such as assigning salaries on the basis of time expended, allotting rental charges on the basis of floor space, or apportioning supplies expense on the basis of consumption. However, it is not always simple to allocate costs.

The public has been deluged with informational materials that attempt to educate the reader about proper health habits to avoid disease or infection, birth control and other family planning issues, and the need to protect endangered species or the environment. Included in much of this material is a fund-raising appeal. A question arises as to whether the total cost of sending such literature should be charged to the program publicized or to fund raising, or whether it should be allocated between them. Since board members, donors, and the general public pay particular attention to the percentages of revenue consumed by administrative and fund-raising purposes, the desire to keep those percentages at a minimum is understandable.

One area of concern involves fund-raising costs being "hidden" within the program and management activities. An exposure draft issued on September 10, 1993 would require, among other things, that:

> Costs of all materials and activities that include a fund raising appeal be reported as fund raising costs . . . unless a bona fide program or management function has been conducted in conjunction with the appeal.

> If a bona fide program or management function has been conducted, the joint costs should be allocated.[7]

It also discusses acceptable allocation methods and lists disclosure requirements if joint costs are allocated.

CLOSING ENTRIES

After all expenses have been assigned, an entry is made to close the expense accounts and charge each of the expenses to the individual programs and supporting services. For the environmental protection association used earlier as an example, the following entry might be recorded:

River Pollution Program Expense	XXX	
Animal and Bird Sanctuary Program Expense	XXX	
Management and General Services Expense	XXX	
Fund-Raising Services Expense	XXX	
Salary Expense, Supplies Expense, etc.		XXX

The final closing entries close support and revenue accounts, as well as the program and services accounts, to the appropriate net asset classification. The

---

[7]Exposure Draft, *Accounting for Costs of Materials and Activities of Not-for-Profit Organizations and State and Local Government Entities That Include a Fund-Raising Appeal* (New York: American Institute of Certified Public Accountants, 1993), par. 15.

closing entry for the Unrestricted Net Assets of the environmental protection association might be:

Contributions—Unrestricted	XXX	
Legacies and Bequests—Unrestricted	XXX	
Membership Dues Revenue	XXX	
Investment Revenue—Unrestricted	XXX	
Reclassification In—Unrestricted—Satisfaction of Donor Restrictions:		
River Pollution Program Expense		XXX
Animal and Bird Sanctuary Program Expense		XXX
Management and General Services Expense		XXX
Fund-Raising Services Expense		XXX
Unrestricted Net Assets		XXX

If the board of directors should decide to designate a specified sum of the Unrestricted Net Assets for a future program to reduce air pollution, the following entries are recorded:

Undesignated Net Assets	XXX	
Unrestricted Net Assets—Designated for Air Pollution Program		XXX

Similar entries to close temporarily restricted and permanently restricted accounts are the following:

Contributions—Temporarily Restricted	XXX	
Legacies and Bequests—Temporarily Restricted	XXX	
Investment Revenue—Temporarily Restricted	XXX	
Reclassifications Out—Temporarily Restricted—Satisfaction of		
Donor Restrictions		XXX
Temporarily Restricted Net Assets		XXX
Contributions—Permanently Restricted	XXX	
Legacies and Bequests—Permanently Restricted	XXX	
Permanently Restricted Net Assets		XXX

FINANCIAL STATEMENTS

Consistent with other not-for-profits, the three financial statements for VHWOs are a statement of financial position, a statement of activities, and a statement of cash flows. In addition, VHWOs must provide a statement of functional expenses.

A statement of financial position is prepared either in single-column form or with a column for each asset class. Organization-wide totals of assets, liabilities, and net assets are presented.

An activities statement can be prepared after the expense allocation entry has been recorded. It is structured with a column for each asset class and shows how effectively the organization operated during the period.

Since program costs and not the typical expenses, such as salaries, are shown in an operating statement, a summary of expenses by object-of-expense classification is provided in a separate statement. This statement of functional expenses, as required by the audit guide and FASB Statement No. 117, supplements the operating statement. It presents the total of each functional expense to programs and supporting services.

Day Star Activity and Respite Center serves older adults afflicted with Alzheimer's Disease or other memory impairment and their families. Day Star provides day care for clients at its day care center, which provides a respite from constant caregiving for primary caregivers. Day Star also provides limited home care for clients. The expenses that were incurred by Day Star are shown below:

Expenses:	
Salaries and payroll taxes	$17,000
Crafts and activities	4,000
Meals on Wheels	4,000
Office expenses	2,000
Repairs and maintenance	1,500
Depreciation expense	5,000
Total expenses	$33,500

Day Star management has estimated the allocation of financial resources to organization activities and prepared the following matrix showing the allocation scheme:

	Day Care	Home Care	Management
Operating expenses	40%	35%	25%
Capital-related expenses	90	10	0

Expenses are allocated to programs and supporting services using the allocation matrix in the following manner. Then they are presented in the statement of activities.

	Total	Day Care	Home Care	Management and General
Operating expenses	$28,500	$11,400	$9,975	$7,125
Capital-related expenses	5,000	4,500	500	

Expenses also are allocated to programs and supporting services using the allocation matrix for presentation in the statement of functional expenses. The following example shows this procedure for three object-of-expense categories:

Object of Expense	Total	Day Care	Home Care	Management and General
Salaries and payroll taxes	$17,000	$ 6,800	$ 5,950	$4,250
Crafts and activities	4,000	1,600	1,400	1,000
Meals on wheels	4,000	1,600	1,400	1,000
Office expenses	2,000	800	700	500
Repairs and maintenance	1,500	600	525	375
Depreciation	5,000	4,500	500	
Total expenses	$33,500	$15,900	$10,475	$7,125

ILLUSTRATION OF ACCOUNTING FOR A VOLUNTARY HEALTH AND WELFARE ORGANIZATION

To illustrate the recording of events and the preparation of financial reports for a VHWO, assume the People's Environmental Protection (PEP) Association, a

Illustration 19-4
People's Environmental Protection (PEP) Association
Statement of Financial Position
As of December 31, 19X4

Assets:	
Cash and cash equivalents	$ 253,500
Contributions receivable (net of $3,100 allowance)	21,500
Inventories	10,000
Short-term investments	152,000
Property, plant, and equipment (net of $16,700 accumulated depreciation)	676,000
Long-term endowment investments	253,000
Total assets	**$1,366,000**
Liabilities and net assets:	
Accounts payable	$ 37,000
Notes payable	100,000
Total liabilities	**$ 137,000**
Net assets:	
Unrestricted	**$ 289,000**
Temporarily restricted	**687,000**
Permanently restricted	**253,000**
Total net assets	**$1,229,000**
Total liabilities and net assets	$1,366,000

voluntary community organization, has three programs: Valley Air Pollution, Keep Fish in the Lakes, and Flood Control. The statement of financial position of PEP on December 31, 19X4 is shown in Illustration 19-4.

The following events occur during the calendar year 19X5. They are summarized to conserve space and minimize duplication. Entries are shown following each transaction. Consistent with the new FASB statements, no fund designation is recorded. VHWOs may choose to use fund accounting for donor-restricted resources, plant, and permanently restricted endowments. These are illustrated in the appendix to the chapter.

Event	Entry		
1. As a result of its fund-raising program, cash contributions of $325,000 were received. $315,000 was unrestricted and $10,000 was restricted for valley air project operating costs. In addition, unconditional promises to give totaled $100,000 of which $80,000 was unrestricted and $20,000 restricted for acquisition of equipment.	Cash	325,000	
	Contributions—Unrestricted		315,000
	Contributions—Temporarily restricted		10,000
	Contributions Receivable	100,000	
	Contributions—Unrestricted		80,000
	Contributions—Temporarily Restricted		20,000
2. Based on past experience, 5% of the promises to give were estimated to be uncollectible.	Provision for Uncollectible Contributions	5,000	
	Allowance for Uncollectible Contributions		5,000

(continued)

Event	Entry		
3. During the year, cash was collected from some unconditional promises to give, while others were written off as uncollectible.	Cash....................................... Allowance for Uncollectible Contributions....... Contributions Receivable..................	95,500 5,600 	 101,100
4. A cash donation of $40,000 was received, with the donor stipulation that it be used to acquire equipment that will assist in water quality improvement.	Cash....................................... Contributions—Temporarily Restricted	40,000 	 40,000
5. With the donor's approval, the $40,000 served as a partial payment on the purchase of a filter system costing $50,000. A note was signed for the unpaid balance. PEP chooses to release the donor restriction over the life of the asset.	Land, Building, and Equipment................ Cash....................................... Notes Payable on Equipment	50,000 	 40,000 10,000
6. PEP received $5,000 from an individual who restricted its use to a special project within a save the lakes program. If that special project is not accomplished within six months, the individual requested that the money be returned. PEP has not yet undertaken the project. Two months remain in the time period specified by the donor.	Cash....................................... Refundable Advances	5,000 	 5,000
7. The following bequests were received: $100,000 unrestricted and $20,000 to be invested in an endowment whose earnings are to be unrestricted.	Cash....................................... Legacies and Bequests—Unrestricted .... Legacies and Bequests—Permanently Restricted	120,000 	 100,000 20,000
8. PEP received donated goods with a fair value of $2,350. Of those donated goods, $750 is restricted by the donor for use in the fish in the lakes program; the remaining gifts can be used at management's discretion.	Inventories................................ Contributions—Unrestricted............... Contributions—Temporarily Restricted	2,350 	 1,600 750
9. PEP held a special summer event to promote its activities, the net proceeds of which were unrestricted. Gross revenues totaled $9,000, with direct costs for the event amounting to $2,000.	Cash....................................... Special Events Support—Unrestricted .... Costs of Special Events..................... Cash...................................	9,000 2,000 	 9,000 2,000
10. PEP uses volunteers to distribute brochures about its operations, to assist the staff with routine office work and to make phone calls during the annual fund-raising appeal. The volunteers provided 1,000 hours of service this year. If the volunteers were not available, the tasks would either be performed by existing staff or not be performed at all. PEP estimates the fair value of these services to be $5 per hour.	No entry. Most volunteer services of this type do not meet criteria. This amount should be disclosed in the footnotes.		
11. An annual membership to PEP is $118, permitting members and their families to use lake facilities for swimming, sailing (no motors allowed), and fishing.	Cash....................................... Membership Dues Revenues..............	118,000 	 118,000
12. The local PEP unit receives unrestricted cash of $16,000 as its share of a campaign run by its national affiliate.	Cash....................................... Received from Federated and Nonfederated Campaigns—Unrestricted...............	16,000 	 16,000
13. Earnings on endowment investments total $28,000 of which $21,000 is not restricted and $7,000 is restricted to investment in equipment for flood control.	Cash....................................... Investment Revenue—Unrestricted .... Investment Revenue—Temporarily Restricted	28,000 	 21,000 7,000

Event	Entry		

14. PEP carries its investments in all funds at market value. Endowment investments are sold for $27,000. They had a cost of $20,000 and a carrying value of $25,000 in the investment account. All endowment gains are to be permanently restricted according to donor specifications.

Cash...		27,000	
Investment (at market)......................			25,000
Gain on Sale of Investments—Permanently Restricted			2,000

15. Additional $46,000 of investments are purchased from endowment funds.

Investments—Permanently Restricted		46,000	
Cash..			46,000

16. Unrestricted investments have shown no material change in market value over the year. At year end, the market value of permanently restricted endowment investments has increased from $265,000 to $294,000. All endowment gains are to be permanently restricted according to the donor specification.

Investments		29,000	
Net Increase in Carrying Value of Investments—Permanently Restricted			29,000

17. A lawyer provided five hours of service to PEP to draw up an endowment agreement. She did not charge for her services. She normally would charge a client $500 for consultation on a similar type of agreement. In the absence of the donated professional services, PEP would have hired a lawyer to draft the agreement.

Professional Services.......................		500	
Contributions—Unrestricted			500

18. A special recreational building and dock costing $96,000 were purchased with unrestricted cash.

Land, Building, Equipment....................		96,000	
Cash....................................			96,000

19. Contributions received in the prior period with the stipulation that they be used for expenses of this period are now available.

Reclassification Out—Temporarily Restricted— Satisfaction of Time Requirements		10,000	
Reclassification In—Unrestricted— Satisfaction of Time Requirements			10,000

20. Accounts payable and expenses were paid or established. Operating expenses related to donor-specific programs totaled $103,000.

Accounts Payable (January 1).................		37,000	
Salaries Expense...........................		200,000	
Payroll Taxes		30,000	
Mailing and Postage Expense.................		50,000	
Rent Expense		28,000	
Telephone Expense		6,000	
Research Expense		215,000	
Professional Services: Legal and Audit		34,000	
Supplies Expense		13,000	
Miscellaneous Expense.......................		5,000	
Accounts Payable.........................			32,000
Cash....................................			586,000

Reclassification Out—Temporarily Restricted— Satisfaction of Program Requirements		103,000	
Reclassification In—Unrestricted— Satisfaction of Program Requirements			103,000

21. Contributed goods of $1,450 were used during the year for the fish in the lakes program. This amount includes the $750 donor-restricted contribution in item 8.

Supplies Expense		1,450	
Inventories................................			1,450

Reclassification Out—Temporarily Restricted— Satisfaction of Program Requirements		750	
Reclassification In—Unrestricted— Satisfaction of Program Requirements			750

(continued)

| Event | Entry |

22. Depreciation on equipment purchased with donor-restricted contributions amounted to $22,000 for the year. (Valley air project—$2,000; fish in the lakes program—$3,000; flood control program—$16,000; management and general services—$1,000). An equivalent amount of temporarily unspecified net assets is released from restrictions.

	Dr.	Cr.
Depreciation Expense	22,000	
Accumulated Depreciation		22,000
Reclassification Out—Temporarily Restricted—Satisfaction of Equipment Acquisition Requirements	22,000	
Reclassification In—Unrestricted—Satisfaction of Equipment Acquisition Requirements		22,000

23. Early in the year, cash contributions for current operations were received, but they cannot be used until late in the following year.

	Dr.	Cr.
Cash	2,000	
Contributions—Temporarily Restricted		2,000

24. At year end, the expenses were allocated to the various programs and supporting services.

	Dr.	Cr.
Valley Air Project	132,000	
Fish in the Lakes Program	184,450	
Flood Control Program	251,000	
Management and General Services	29,500	
Fund-Raising Services	11,000	
Membership Development	2,000	
Salaries Expense		200,000
Payroll Taxes		30,000
Mailing and Postage Expense		50,000
Rent Expense		28,000
Telephone Expense		6,000
Research Expense		215,000
Professional Services: Legal and Audit		34,500
Supplies Expense		14,450
Miscellaneous Expense		5,000
Provision for Uncollectible Contributions		5,000
Depreciation Expense		22,000

The direct cost of a special event is not included in the allocation process because it is subtracted from the gross proceeds of that event. The special event is considered an incidental activity and reported "net" in the statement of activities.

With expenses allocated to programs and supporting services, it is now possible to prepare the statement of activities (Illustration 19-5 on page 1068). The sequence of items is suggested by the title. Inflows of resources from public support, revenues, and reclassification are listed first, followed by the expense totals for each program and supporting service, taken directly from the closing and allocation entries. The beginning net asset balance for each class is added, resulting in the net asset balance at the end of the period.

The final entry at year end closes the support and revenue accounts, as well as the program and supporting services expenses, into the appropriate net asset accounts. Using the statement of activity in Illustration 19-5, the following entries close the three net asset accounts, including the cost of special events account and its related resource inflow account:

25. Closing entries. Each class of asset is closed separately.

	Dr.	Cr.
Contributions—Unrestricted	397,100	
Special Events Support	9,000	
Legacies and Bequests—Unrestricted	100,000	
Received from Federated and Nonfederated Campaigns	16,000	
Membership Dues Revenue	118,000	
Investment Revenue	21,000	

(continued)

Reclassifications In—Unrestricted—Satisfaction of Program Restrictions	103,750	
Reclassifications In—Unrestricted—Satisfaction of Equipment Acquisition Restrictions	22,000	
Reclassifications In—Unrestricted—Satisfaction of Time Restrictions	10,000	
Valley Air Project		132,000
Keep Fish in the Lakes Program		184,450
Flood Control Program		251,000
Management and General Services		29,500
Fund-Raising Services		11,000
Membership Development		2,000
Cost of Special Events		2,000
Unrestricted Net Assets		**184,900**
Contributions—Temporarily Restricted	72,750	
Investment Revenue—Temporarily Restricted . . .	7,000	
Temporarily Restricted Net Assets	**56,000**	
Reclassifications Out—Temporarily Restricted—Satisfaction of Program Restrictions		103,750
Reclassifications Out—Temporarily Restricted—Satisfaction of Equipment Acquisition Restrictions		22,000
Reclassifications Out—Temporarily Restricted—Satisfaction of Time Restrictions		10,000
Legacies and Bequests—Endowment—Permanently Restricted	20,000	
Net Increase in Carrying Value of Endowment Investments—Permanently Restricted	29,000	
Gain on Sale of Endowment Investments—Permanently Restricted	2,000	
Permanently Restricted Net Assets		**51,000**

Since the investments account is carried at market value, it is entirely possible that the carrying value may decrease. If this situation occurs, the account Net Decrease in Carrying Value of Investments is debited and the investments account is credited. The closing entry would credit Net Decrease in Carrying Value of Investments and debit unrestricted or permanently restricted net assets depending on donor specifications or law.

The statement of activities of a VHWO provides valuable data on the total cost per period of each program and of supporting services. To provide the reader of its financial statements with additional information, a statement of functional expenses is included in the reports. This statement shows the allocation of each expense (salaries, rent, etc.) and reveals the cost by function of carrying on the organization's activities. The statement of functional expenses for PEP is shown in Illustration 19-6.

The statement of financial position for PEP on December 31, 19X5, is given in Illustration 19-7. The statement of flows shown in Illustration 19-8 includes cash inflows from contributions and investment income restricted by donor for endowment or acquisition of plant under financing activities per FASB statement No. 117.

As is true in reporting for-profit enterprises, financial statements of VHWO would be prepared with comparative figures for the preceding year. The state-

Illustration 19-5

People's Environmental Protection (PEP) Association
Statement of Activities
For Year Ended December 31, 19X5

	Unrestricted	Temporarily Restricted	Permanently Restricted	Total
Public support and revenue:				
Public support:				
Contributions.........................	$397,100	$ 72,750		$ 469,850
Special events (net of $2,000 direct costs)..	7,000			7,000
Legacies and bequests.................	100,000		$ 20,000	120,000
Received from federated and nonfederated				
campaigns	16,000			16,000
Total public support	$520,100	$ 72,750	$ 20,000	$ 612,850
Revenue:				
Membership dues......................	$118,000			118,000
Investment revenue	21,000	7,000		28,000
Net increase in carrying value of				
investments			29,000	29,000
Realized gain on investments............			2,000	2,000
Total revenue	$139,000	7,000	31,000	177,000
Net assets released from restrictions:				
Satisfaction of program restrictions	$103,750	(103,750)		
Satisfaction of equipment acquisition				
restrictions	22,000	(22,000)		
Expiration of time restrictions............	10,000	(10,000)		
Total net assets released from				
restrictions	$135,750	(135,750)		
Total public support and revenue	$794,850	(56,000)	51,000	789,850
Expenses:				
Valley air project	$132,000			132,000
Keep fish in the lakes program.............	184,450			184,450
Flood control program....................	251,000			. 251,000
Management and general.................	29,500			29,500
Fund raising	11,000			11,000
Membership development	2,000			2,000
Total expenses.......................	$609,950			$ 609,950
Change in net assets	**184,900**	**(56,000)**	**51,000**	**179,900**
Net assets beginning of year	**289,000**	**687,000**	**253,000**	**1,229,000**
Net assets end of year......................	**$473,900**	**631,000**	**304,000**	**$1,408,900**

Illustration 19-6
People's Environmental Protection (PEP) Association
Statement of Functional Expenses
For Year Ended December 31, 19X5

		Program Services					Supporting Services		
	Total All Services	Valley Air Project	Fish in the Lake	Flood Control	Total Programs	Manage-ment and General	Fund Raising	Member-ship Develop-ment	Total Supporting
Salaries	$200,000	$ 36,000	$ 60,000	$ 80,000	$176,000	$19,000	$ 4,500	$ 500	$24,000
Payroll taxes	30,000	5,400	9,000	12,000	26,400	3,000	500	100	3,600
Mailing and postage	50,000	10,000	20,000	19,700	49,700		200	100	300
Rent	28,000	8,000	5,000	11,600	24,600	2,000	400	1,000	3,400
Telephone	6,000	1,500	1,300	2,500	5,300		400	300	700
Research	215,000	35,000	80,000	100,000	215,000				
Professional: legal and audit	34,500	24,000	2,000	4,000	30,000	4,500			4,500
Supplies	14,450	10,100	1,450	2,900	14,450				
Provision for uncollectible contributions	5,000						5,000		5,000
Miscellaneous	5,000		2,700	2,300	5,000				
Total expenses before depreciation	$587,950	$130,000	$181,450	$235,000	$546,450	$28,500	$11,000	$2,000	$41,500
Depreciation of buildings and equipment	22,000	2,000	3,000	16,000	21,000	1,000			1,000
Total expenses	$609,950	$132,000	$184,450	$251,000	$567,450	$29,500	$11,000	$2,000	$42,500

ments also should be accompanied by notes that would summarize significant accounting policies.

ACCOUNTING FOR OTHER NOT-FOR-PROFIT ORGANIZATIONS

In 1981, the AICPA issued the audit guide *Audits of Certain Nonprofit Organizations*, which included AICPA Statement of Position (SOP) 78-10, *Accounting Principles and Reporting Practices for Certain Nonprofit Organizations*. SOP 78-10 provided recommended financial reporting practices for certain nonprofit organizations, but the recommendations did not have the status of being "authoritative." This means that the financial report of such an organization could be out of compliance with SOP 78-10 and still receive certification from a CPA that the financial report is in conformance with GAAP. The status of SOP 78-10 received a boost with the issuance of FASB Statement No. 32 which stated that some AICPA SOPs, including SOP 78-10, contain preferable accounting principles for purposes of applying APB Opinion No. 20, *Accounting Changes*. This means that if an organization is classified as a certain nonprofit organization and it changes its accounting principles, it should do so in accordance with SOP 78-10 as superseded by FASB guidance for not-for-profits. Entities that have restricted resources may use fund accounting for internal control and management reporting

Illustration 19-7

People's Environmental Protection (PEP) Association
Statement of Financial Position
As of December 31, 19X5

Assets:
Cash and cash equivalents	$ 268,000
Contributions receivable (net of $2,500 allowance)	21,000
Inventories	10,900
Short-term investments	152,000
Property, plant, and equipment (net of $38,700 accumulated depreciation)	800,000
Long-term endowment investments	304,000
Total assets	**$1,555,900**

Liabilities and net assets:
Accounts payable	$ 32,000
Refundable advances	5,000
Notes payable	110,000
Total liabilities	**$ 147,000**

Net assets:
Unrestricted	**$ 473,900**
Temporarily restricted	**631,000**
Permanently restricted	**304,000**
Total net assets	**$1,408,900**
Total liabilities and net assets	**$1,555,900**

purposes so that they demonstrate compliance with externally imposed restrictions. Financial statements, however, report organization-wide totals for all assets and liabilities. Net assets are classified as unrestricted, temporarily restricted, or permanently restricted. Financial statements include a statement of financial position, a statement of activities, and a statement of cost flows, along with notes for appropriate disclosures of policy.

Among the not-for-profit entities that are affected by this audit guide, as superseded by recent FASB guidance, are the following:

Cemetery organizations	Private elementary and secondary schools
Civic and fraternal organizations	Professional associations
Labor unions	Public broadcasting stations
Libraries and museums	Religious organizations
Performing arts and other cultural organizations	Research and scientific organizations
	Social and country clubs
Political parties	Trade associations
Private and community foundations	Zoological and botanical societies

Illustration 19-8

People's Environmental Protection (PEP) Association
Statement of Cash Flows
For Year Ended December 31, 19X5

Cash flows from operating activities:

Cash received from members.	$ 118,000
Cash received from contributions	402,500
Cash received from special events.	7,000
Cash received from federated and nonfederated campaigns.	16,000
Cash received from legacies and bequests	100,000
Cash received on a refundable advance.	5,000
Interest and dividends received	21,000
Cash paid to employees and suppliers.	(586,000)
Net cash provided by (used for) operating activities	**$ 83,500**

Cash flows from investing activities:

Proceeds from sales and maturities of investments.	$ 27,000
Purchases of investments	$ (46,000)
Purchases of land, building, and equipment	(146,000)
Net cash provided by (used for) investing activities	**$(165,000)**

Cash flow from financing activities:

Proceeds from issuance of notes payable	$ 10,000
Receipts of interest and dividends restricted for reinvestment	7,000
Contributions received restricted for long-term investment	20,000
Contributions received restricted for investment in plant	60,000
Net cash provided by (used for) financing activities	**$ 97,000**

Net increase (decrease) in cash and cash equivalents	**$ 15,500**
Cash and cash equivalents at beginning of year	**253,500**
Cash and cash equivalents at end of year	**$ 268,000**

Reconciliation of change in net assets to net cash provided by
operating activities:

Change in net assets.	$ 179,900
Depreciation.	22,000
Decrease in contributions receivable.	500
Increase in inventories	(900)
Increase in notes payable	10,000
Increase in refundable advances	(5,000)
Decrease in accounts payable.	(5,000)
Increase in net carrying value of investments	(29,000)
Gain on sale of investments	(2,000)
Interest restricted for long-term investment.	(7,000)
Contributions restricted for long-term investment	(20,000)
Contributions restricted for plant.	(60,000)
Net cash provided by operating activities	$ 83,500

*$4,000 of cash at beginning of year and $5,000 of cash at year end are included in the
classification "long-term endowment investments" on the statement of financial position.

SUMMARY: IMPLEMENTING FASB STATEMENT NOS. 116 AND 117

FASB Statement Nos. 116 and 117 represent the most comprehensive change in the history of financial reporting by not-for-profit organizations. The new standards serve to enhance the information provided to readers of the financial statements about financial viability, financial flexibility, liquidity, cash flows, and service efforts.

Use of financial statements based on net asset classifications is a much different concept from fund group reporting, and organizations should begin to reevaluate their current information systems in view of the new requirements. As all not-for-profit entities struggle to implement the new accounting and financial reporting guidelines set forth by the FASB in Statement Nos. 116 and 117, they must determine policies for recognition and valuation of contributions of cash, assets, and services and work toward articulation of internal information systems (fund accounting) with the new external reporting requirements.

The AICPA Not-for-Profit Organizations Committee is in the process of developing a revised audit and accounting guide—combining three not-for-profit guides: *Audits of Voluntary Health and Welfare Organizations*, *Audits of Certain Not-for-Profit Organizations*, and *Audits of Colleges and Universities*. This guide is expected to give further guidance on accounting for contributions and formats of the financial statements. The AICPA Health Care Committee also is revising its guidance to conform to the new FASB Statements.

The FASB has two additional projects on its not-for-profit agenda: (1) accounting for investments and (2) consolidation policies. Finally, the FASB hopes to address the issue of service efforts and accomplishments as a means for external users to evaluate the effectiveness and efficiency of not-for-profit organizations.

APPENDIX: ACCOUNTING AND FINANCIAL REPORTING BY FUNDS

In this appendix, the accounting and financial reporting of a health care organization and a voluntary health and welfare organization are illustrated within their respective existing fund structures. The illustrations include the same events as in the text in order for readers to compare the resulting financial statements with those assuming no funds.

HEALTH CARE ORGANIZATIONS

As described in the text, health care providers receive bequests, gifts, and grants that are restricted by the donor as to use for (1) specific operating purposes, (2) additions to plant, (3) endowments, or (4) annuities or life incomes. A donor-restricted fund is established for accumulating resources in each of these categories until the resources become available for expenditure by the general funds. As feeders to the general funds, donor-restricted funds are classified as temporarily restricted or permanently restricted. When the donor-restricted assets are to be used for their intended purpose, they are reclassified as unrestricted and recorded as a transfer or, more commonly, as a direct debit to the appropriate net asset account.

The *specific purpose fund* records donor-restricted resources available for current but specified operations as temporarily restricted contributions. When the expenditure is to be made in accordance with the donor's wishes, the temporarily restricted net assets are released from restrictions and reclassified to the unrestricted net assets. A transfer is then recorded to the general funds. Similarly, the *plant replacement and expansion fund* accounts for resources that must be used to purchase property or equipment. When an outlay for plant is made by the general funds in compliance with the wishes of the donor, a cash transfer is recorded by reducing the net assets of the plant replacement and expansion fund and increasing the net assets of the general funds. As with other not-for-profit organizations, health care organizations may choose to release the restrictions of donated fixed assets with the acquisition of the asset or over the useful life of the asset. The *endowment fund* accounts for resources that are received to create permanent endowments (whose income only may be expended) or term endowments (whose principal eventually will become available for expenditure). Revenues from permanent endowment investments are recorded as nonoperating revenues in the general fund if unrestricted or in the appropriate donor-restricted fund if restricted for specific operating or plant purposes. As term endowment funds become available for general operations, they are reclassified as unrestricted and transferred to the general fund. Should the term endowments be restricted further, for example, to purchase equipment, they are transferred to the appropriate donor-restricted fund. It is possible that use of other donor-restricted funds, such as annuity funds or loan funds, may become necessary, depending upon the activities of the organization.

The following illustrations record events within the health care organization fund structure. Funds-based financial statements are also presented.

Illustrative Entries for General Funds.   To illustrate the recording of events for a hospital within the current fund structure, the year's affairs of Fitale Hospital's general funds are summarized next. The illustrative entries employ the same broad categories of control accounts as the previous examples in the text. Transactions of the donor-restricted funds and transfers from the donor-restricted funds to the general funds are shown in the matrix on pages 1074–1077. A funds-based statement of activities and a statement of financial position are presented in Illustrations 19A-1 and 19A-2 respectively. The required statement of cash flows cannot be presented on a funds basis and therefore will be the same as the one presented in Illustration 19-3 on page 1054.

General Fund Entries:

Event		Entry		
Gross charges to patients are for:		Accounts Receivable	5,200,000	
		Patient Service Revenue		5,000,000
Daily patient services	$3,200,000	Other Operating Revenue—		
		Unrestricted		200,000
Other nursing services	500,000			
Professional services	1,300,000			
Other nonmedical services	200,000			
Total	$5,200,000			

(continued on page 1079)

Interaction Matrix for Fitale Hospital

Event	Specific Purpose Fund			Endowment Fund		

1. Fitale received $50,000 cash from a donor to cover operating costs of the student nursing unit.	Cash........................
	  Other Operating Revenue—
	    Temporarily Restricted
	    (Contributions)............
		50,000	50,000			

2. Investment earnings are received in the amount of $75,000 restricted for cancer research.	Cash........................
	  Nonoperating Revenues—
	    Temporarily Restricted
	    (Investment Earnings)......
		75,000	75,000			

3. $500,000 was donated to Fitale Hospital for investments in long-term securities as a pure endowment.				Cash........................
				  Nonoperating Revenues—
				    Permanently Restricted
				    (Endowment Contributions)
					500,000	500,000

4. Securities were purchased.				Endowment Investments....... Cash......................	500,000	500,000

5. A term endowment expired. The $150,000 principal is now available for use by the hospital administration.				Reclassification Out—
				  Temporarily Restricted—
				  Satisfaction of Time
				  Restriction...............
				Reclassification In—
				  Unrestricted Satisfaction of
				  Time Restriction..........
				Unrestricted Net Assets—Equity
				  Transfer Out ....
				  Cash......................
					150,000
					
					150,000
						
						150,000
						
						150,000

6. Receipts of $200,000 and an unconditional promise to give $100,000 were recorded. Gifts were to be used for operating room equipment.						
7. Operating room equipment was purchased. The first year depreciation on the above operating equipment was recorded.						

8. A $400,000 grant from a local manufacturer to be used for a patient nutritional study was received. Results of the study will be used to educate the public, not for the benefit of the donor.	Cash........................
	  Other Operating Revenues—
	    Temporarily Restricted
	    (Contributions)............
		400,000	400,000			

9. Expenses were incurred for the patient nutritional study.	Reclassification Out—
	  Temporarily Restricted
	  Satisfaction of Program
	  Restrictions...............
	Reclassification In—
	  Unrestricted—Satisfaction
	  of Program Restrictions ....
	Unrestricted Net Assets—Equity
	  Transfer Out ....
	  Cash......................
		50,000
		
		50,000
			
			50,000
			
			50,000			

Plant Replacement and Expansion			General Fund		
			Cash..........................	150,000	
			Unrestricted Net Assets—		
			Equity Transfer In..........		150,000
Contributions Receivable	100,000				
Cash..........................	200,000				
Other Operating Revenues—					
Temporarily Restricted					
(Contributions)		300,000			
Temporarily Restricted Net			Equipment....................	200,000	
Assets—Equity Transfer			Cash........................		200,000
Out	200,000		Depreciation Expense	40,000	
Cash		200,000	Allowance for Depreciation....		40,000
			Cash........................	200,000	
			Temporarily Restricted Net		
			Assets—Equity Transfer In ..		200,000
			Reclassification Out—		
			Temporarily Restricted—		
			Satisfaction of Plant		
			Acquisition Restrictions.....	40,000	
			Reclassification In—		
			Unrestricted—Satisfaction		
			of Plant Acquisition		
			Restrictions		40,000
			Wages, Salaries, and Benefits ...	25,000	
			Drugs and Supplies Used	10,000	
			Purchased Services	15,000	
			Cash.......................		50,000
			Cash.........................	50,000	
			Unrestricted Net Assets—		
			Equity Transfer In..........		50,000

(continued)

Interaction Matrix for Fitale Hospital

Event	Specific Purpose Fund		Endowment Fund
10. Fitale allocates natural expenses to the functional areas.	Nursing Services 1,774,000		
	Other Professional Services 1,240,000		
	General Services 995,000		
	Fiscal Services 283,000		
	Administrative Services............. 791,000		
	Wages, Salaries, and Benefits	3,045,000	
	Drugs and Supplies Used	730,000	
	Purchased Services	330,000	
	Medical Malpractice Costs	450,000	
	Depreciation Expense	440,000	
	Interest..........................	66,000	
	Provision for Bad Debts...........	22,000	
11. Closing entries—general fund.			
12. Closing entries: specific purpose fund.	Reclassifications In—Unrestricted—Satisfaction of Program Restrictions 50,000		
	Unrestricted net assets...........	50,000	
	Other Operating Revenue—Temporarily Restricted 450,000		
	Nonoperating Revenue—Temporarily Restricted.................... 75,000		
	Reclassifications Out—Temporarily Restricted—Satisfaction of Program Restrictions...........	50,000	
	Temporarily restricted net assets ...	475,000	
13. Closing entries—plant replacement and expansion fund.			
14. Closing entries—endowment fund.			Reclassifications In—Unrestricted—Satisfaction of Time Restrictions 150,000
			Unrestricted net assets 150,000
			Temporarily restricted net assets... 150,000
			Reclassifications Out—Temporarily Restricted—Satisfaction of Time Restrictions 150,000
			Nonoperating Revenue—Permanently Restricted Endowment Contributions 500,000
			Permanently restricted net assets..................... 500,000

Plant Replacement
and Expansion

General Fund

Patient Service Revenue—Unrestricted	5,000,000	
Other Operating Revenue—Unrestricted . . .	222,000	
Nonoperating Revenue—		
Unrestricted	720,606	
Reclassifications In—Unrestricted—		
Satisfaction of Equipment Acquisition		
Restrictions	40,000	
Charity Care		200,000
Contractual Adjustments		380,000
Nursing Services		1,774,000
Other Professional Services		1,240,000
General Services		995,000
Fiscal Services		283,000
Administrative Services		791,000
Unrestricted net assets		**319,606**
Temporarily restricted net assets	**40,000**	
Reclassifications Out—Temporarily		
Restricted—Satisfaction of Equipment		
Acquisition Restrictions.		40,000

Other Operating Revenue—		
Temporarily Restricted	300,000	
Temporarily restricted net assets		**300,000**

Illustration 19A-1
Fitale Hospital
Statement of Activities
For Year Ended December 31, 19X5

	General Fund	Specific Purpose Fund	Plant Fund	Endowment Fund	Total
Changes in unrestricted net assets:					
Revenues, gains, and other support:					
Patient services revenue.........................	$4,420,000				$ 4,420,000
Other operating revenue........................	222,000				222,000
Total unrestricted revenue	$4,642,000				$ 4,642,000
Net assets released from restrictions:					
Satisfaction of program restrictions		$ 50,000			$ 50,000
Satisfaction of equipment acquisition restrictions................................	$ 40,000				40,000
Expiration of time restrictions				$ 150,000	150,000
Total unrestricted revenues and other support.................................	$4,682,000	$ 50,000		$ 150,000	$ 4,882,000
Expenses and losses:					
Nursing services...............................	$1,774,000				$ 1,774,000
Other professional services	1,240,000				1,240,000
General services..............................	995,000				995,000
Fiscal services................................	283,000				283,000
Administrative services........................	791,000				791,000
Total expenses	$5,083,000				$ 5,083,000
Increase (decrease) in net assets from operations	$ (401,000)	$ 50,000		$ 150,000	$ (201,000)
Nonoperating revenue..........................	720,606				720,606
Increase in unrestricted net assets.............	$ 319,606	$ 50,000		$ 150,000	**$ 519,606**
Changes in temporarily restricted net assets:					
Contributions..................................		$450,000	$ 300,000		$ 750,000
Income on long-term investments		75,000			75,000
Net assets released from restriction	$ (40,000)	(50,000)		$ (150,000)	(240,000)
Increase (decrease) in temporarily restricted net assets.....................................	$ (40,000)	$475,000	$ 300,000	$ (150,000)	**$ 585,000**
Changes in permanently restricted net assets:					
Contributions..................................				$ 500,000	$ 500,000
Increase (decrease) in permanently restricted net assets................................				$ 500,000	**$ 500,000**
Transfers among funds—additions (deductions):					
Satisfaction of program restrictions	$ 50,000	$ (50,000)			
Equipment acquisition..........................	200,000		$(200,000)		
Expiration of time restrictions	150,000			$ (150,000)	
Total transfers	$ 400,000	$ (50,000)	$(200,000)	$ (150,000)	
Increase (decrease) in net assets..................	$ 679,606	$475,000	$ 100,000	$ 350,000	**$ 1,604,606**
Net assets at beginning of year...................	4,698,000	250,000	319,000	3,710,000	**8,977,000**
Net assets at end of year	$5,377,606	$725,000	$ 419,000	$4,060,000	**$10,581,606**

Illustration 19A-2
Fitale Hospital
Statement of Financial Position
As of December 31, 19X5

Assets:	General Fund	Specific Purpose Fund	Plant Fund	Endowment Fund	Total
Cash and cash equivalents	$ 260,000	$475,000			$ 735,000
Accounts and interest receivable (net)	908,000				908,000
Inventories	81,000				81,000
Contributions receivable	165,606		$100,000		265,606
Short-term investments	150,000	250,000			400,000
Assets restricted to investment in land, building, and equipment	126,000		319,000		445,000
Assets limited in use under malpractice funding agreement	440,000				440,000
Property, plant, and equipment (net of depreciation)	5,250,000				5,250,000
Long-term investments	540,000				540,000
Endowment investments				$4,060,000	4,060,000
Total assets	**$7,920,606**	**$725,000**	**$419,000**	**$4,060,000**	**$13,124,606**
Liabilities and net assets:					
Accounts payable	$ 53,000				$ 53,000
Current installments of long-term debt	80,000				80,000
Accrued expenses	100,000				100,000
Notes payable	500,000				500,000
Estimated malpractice costs	640,000				640,000
Long-term debt	1,170,000				1,170,000
Total liabilities	**$2,543,000**				**$ 2,543,000**
Net assets:					
Unrestricted	**$5,217,606**				**$ 5,217,606**
Temporarily restricted	160,000	$725,000	$419,000		1,304,000
Permanently restricted				$4,060,000	4,060,000
Total net assets	**$5,377,606**	**$725,000**	**$419,000**	**$4,060,000**	**$10,581,606**
Total liabilities and net assets	**$7,920,606**	**$725,000**	**$419,000**	**$4,060,000**	**$13,124,606**

Event	Entry
Estimates are made for:	Provision for Bad Debts.............. 22,000
	Contractual Adjustments............. 380,000
Contractual adjustments .... $ 380,000	Allowance for Uncollectible
Uncollectibles 22,000	Receivables and Third-Party
Total .... $ 402,000	Contractual Adjustments.......... 402,000
An analysis of accounts receivable shows:	Cash................................ 3,800,000
	Allowance for Uncollectible
Cash collected.................... $3,800,000	Receivables and Third-Party
Contractual adjustments with	Contractual Adjustments........... 290,000
third-party payors 200,000	Accounts Receivable 4,090,000
Uncollectible 90,000	
Total $4,090,000	*(continued)*

(continued)

Event	Entry		
The hospital determined that $200,000 of the services were to patients who met hospital criteria for charity care.	Charity Services . . . . Accounts Receivable	200,000	200,000

Inventory purchases amounted to $700,000; payments totaled $690,000.	Inventories . . . .
	    Cash . . . .
	    Accounts Payable . . . .
		700,000	690,000
			 10,000

Drugs and supplies costing $720,000 are requisitioned.	Drugs and Supplies Used . . . . Inventories	720,000	720,000

Salaries earned (ignore payroll deductions) amounted to $3,000,000, of which $2,950,000 is paid.	Wages, Salaries, and Benefits . . . .
	    Cash . . . .
	    Accrued Expenses . . . .
		3,000,000	2,950,000
			 50,000

Outside professional fees of $300,000 are paid.	Purchased Services . . . . Cash	300,000	300,000

Jacob Pharmaceutical Co. donated $2,000 of medicines to Fitale Hospital. Such contributions constitute a major ongoing activity of the hospital. If not donated, these medicines would have had to be purchased.	Inventories . . . .
	    Other Operating Revenues—
	      Unrestricted (Contributions) . . . .
		2,000	2,000

Unrestricted earnings from endowment funds totaled $540,000.	Cash . . . .
	    Nonoperating Revenues—Unrestricted
	      (Investment Earnings) . . . .
		540,000	540,000

Payments are made on:

		Entry		
Current installment of long-term debt . . .	$ 80,000	Current Installment of Long-Term Debt	80,000	
Notes payable	200,000	Notes Payable	200,000	
Interest expense	66,000	Interest Expense	66,000	
Total	$ 346,000	Cash		346,000

Event	Entry		

A donor promised to give Fitale $50,000 annually for each of the next four years (recorded at present value).	Contributions Receivable . . . .
	    Nonoperating Revenues—Unrestricted
	      (Contributions) . . . .
		165,606	165,606

The hospital was recently served with a malpractice lawsuit. A prominent local trial attorney decided to assist in the defense of the hospital. Normal fees are $150 per hour. 100 total hours were devoted to the case.	Purchased Services . . . .
	    Nonoperating Revenues—Unrestricted
	      (Contributions) . . . .
		15,000	15,000

Equipment costing $110,000 is purchased for cash.	Property and Equipment . . . . Cash	110,000	110,000
Depreciation expense provision for the year is $400,000.	Depreciation Expense . . . . Accumulated Depreciation	400,000	400,000

The current portion of long-term debt is reclassified as current from:

		Entry		
Bonds payable	$ 50,000	Bonds Payable	50,000	
Mortgage note payable	30,000	Mortgage Note Payable	30,000	
Total	$ 80,000	Current Installment of Long- Term Debt		80,000

Professional services donated to the hospital were recognized:

		Entry		
		Wages, Salaries, and Benefits	20,000	
Nursing services	$ 17,000	Other Operating Revenue— Unrestricted		20,000
Other professional medical services	3,000			

Event	Entry		
A provision for medical malpractice costs of $450,000 is recorded. The hospital is self-insured.	Medical Malpractice Costs . . . . Estimated Malpractice Liability	450,000	450,000

A malpractice self-insurance trust at Third Bank is increased by $230,000.	Cash—Limited in Use Under Malpractice
	    Funding Arrangement . . . .
	    Cash . . . .
		230,000	230,000

Third-party payor reimbursements of $250,000 are to be set aside for plant replacement.	Cash—Limited in Use by Agreement with
	    Third-Party Payors for Plant . . . .
	    Cash . . . .
		250,000	250,000

VOLUNTARY HEALTH AND WELFARE ORGANIZATIONS

To segregate resources and demonstrate compliance with restrictions, fund accounting is sometimes used by voluntary health and welfare organizations. As described in the text, voluntary health and welfare organizations have two current funds consisting primarily of current assets and current liabilities, a separate plant fund, and an endowment fund. Unlike health care organizations, where donor-restricted funds act as feeders to the general funds, all funds of voluntary health and welfare organizations record expenses. As a result, there are few interfund transactions compared with the other not-for-profit organizations.

The following matrix relates the funds used by most VHWOs with the "net asset" categories of the new FASB standards:

Funds	Unrestricted Net assets	Temporarily Restricted Net assets	Permanently Restricted Net assets
Current Unrestricted	X		
Current Restricted	X	X	
Land, Building, and Equipment (Plant Fund) . . .	X	X	X
Endowment Fund		X	X
Agency (Custodial) Fund			

Current Unrestricted Fund.   The *current unrestricted fund* accounts are for resources that have no external restrictions and are available for current operations at the discretion of the governing board. The board, however, may place its own limitations on the fund unrestricted net assets. In the same manner that industry appropriates retained earnings, the board of directors of a health and welfare organization may designate a portion of its unrestricted net assets for a special project. To reflect such an action, a subset of unrestricted net assets, Unrestricted Net Assets—Designated, may be displayed provided the total amount of Unrestricted Net Assets is shown.

Current Restricted Fund.   The *current restricted fund* accounts for assets received from outside sources for a current operating purpose specified by the donor. The distinguishing feature between unrestricted and restricted funds is whether or not an externally imposed restriction exists. A contribution received by a health agency to conduct nutrition classes is an example of a restricted resource. When donor-restricted contributions are expensed, the restriction is released or reclassified to offset the expense. Specifically excluded from this fund are contributions of endowments or contributions restricted to the acquisition of plant assets, which are recorded in other appropriate funds.

Some net assets of this fund may be unrestricted, for example, grants, awards, sponsorships, and appropriations have traditionally been recorded in the restricted current fund. These may now be defined as exchange transactions in which the grantor or sponsor expects to receive something of value in return for the grant. Exchange transactions are unrestricted per FASB Statement No. 116.

Land, Building, and Equipment Fund (Or Plant Fund).   The *plant fund* accounts for the activity related to fixed assets, including the accumulation of resources to acquire or replace them, the liabilities related to them, as well as their acquisition, their disposal, and their depreciation. To determine the total cost of rendering service, depreciation of assets employed in providing that service must be recorded in the plant fund, with the typical depreciation entry debiting Depreciation Expense and crediting Accumulated Depreciation.

The plant fund of a VHWO may have all three net asset classes: unrestricted, temporarily restricted, and permanently restricted. Unrestricted net assets may be transfers from current funds at the discretion of the governing board. Assets acquired with unrestricted funds are unrestricted. Donor-restricted contributions specified for property and equipment are temporarily restricted. As with other not-for-profits, a VHWO may choose to release the restriction of these assets upon acquisition or over the useful life. Contributions of land are considered permanently restricted if the land cannot be sold. If no restriction exists, donated land is an unrestricted contribution.

Endowment Fund.   The *endowment fund* accounts for gifts or bequests with the legal restriction that the principal be maintained in perpetuity (permanently restricted) or until the occurrence of a specified event (temporarily restricted). Various conditions are possible, depending upon the desires of the contributor. Unless otherwise specified, net gains or losses on the sale of endowment fund assets are increases or decreases of the fund principal.

Endowment fund investment revenue may be restricted or unrestricted. Income is recorded directly in the fund that is to receive it. Such income not subject to any restrictions by the principal donor may be recorded directly in the current unrestricted fund as unrestricted investment revenue. If the revenue is subject to a restriction, it would be recorded as temporarily or permanently restricted in the appropriate restricted fund.

Agency (Custodian) Fund.   Agency funds of not-for-profit organizations account for assets that do not belong to the organization holding them. They often are established for payroll withholding. Custodian funds are established to account for assets received by an organization to be held or disbursed only on instructions of the person or organization from whom they were received. Flow-through government grants are examples of this latter use of agency funds.

Assets are recorded when received, along with a related liability. Only when the assets are released by the contributor will the assets be recognized as revenue in the appropriate fund.

Pooling of Investments.   If an organization accumulates substantial investments in its various funds, pooling may be advisable. *Pooling of investments* is the process of combining the investments of various funds into one group or pool to provide greater flexibility at lower cost and to provide diversification to spread the risk. Once pooled, individual investments lose their identity as to fund. Each contributing fund merely maintains in its investment account an amount representing its portion of the pool. Before any additions or withdrawals may be made, the market value of the total portfolio must be determined. Realized gains and losses (and unrealized, if investments are carried at market value rather than cost) are allocated to each participating fund on the basis of its share of the total market value at the previous valuation date. The proportion of each fund's market value may be expressed in terms of units or in terms of percentages of the total. The latter method is more flexible and is used in Illustration 19A-3, which shows changes in pooled investments over a period of time.

Illustrative Entries for Voluntary Health and Welfare Organizations. Entries recording the year's events for People's Environmental Protection (PEP) Association within the existing funds structure for voluntary health and welfare organizations are presented in the matrix in Illustration 19A-4 on pages 1084–1091. The statement of financial position as of December 31, 19X4 is shown in Illustration 19A-5. Closing entries are prepared for each fund. Funds-based financial statements are presented for the year ending December 31, 19X5. The statement of activities is shown in Illustration 19A-6. The statement of financial position as of December 31, 19X5, is shown in Illustration 19A-7. The statement of cash flows and statement of functional expense are not presented on a funds basis. Both statements are identical to those illustrated in the chapter.

Illustration 19A-3
Pooling of Investments

Fund	(1) Cash and/or MV of Securities	(2) Original Equity Percent	(3) Total Pool December 31, 19X0 Cost	(4) Total Pool December 31, 19X0 Market	(5) Mkt. Value Including $50,000	(6) Revised Equity Percent	(7) After Withdrawal of $25,000	(8) New Equity Percent
Unrestricted	$ 36,000	20%	$ 40,000	$ 50,000	$ 50,000	16.67%	$ 25,000	9.09%
Plant	54,000	30	60,000	75,000	75,000	25.00	75,000	27.27
Endowment	90,000	50	100,000	125,000	175,000	58.33	175,000	63.64
Total	$180,000	100%	$200,000	$250,000	$300,000	100.00%	$275,000	100.00%

Illustration 19A-4　　Interaction Matrix for PEP

Event	Unrestricted Current Fund			Restricted Current Fund		
1. As a result of its fund-raising program, cash contributions of $325,000 were received. $315,000 were unrestricted and $10,000 were restricted for valley air project operating costs. In addition, unconditional pledges (promises to give) totaled $100,000, of which $80,000 were unrestricted and $20,000 restricted for acquisition of equipment.	Cash . . . . Contributions receivable . . . . Contributions—Unrestricted . .	315,000 80,000	395,000	Cash . . . . Contributions—Temporarily Restricted	10,000	10,000
2. Based on past experience, 5% of the promises to give were estimated to be uncollectible.	Provision for Uncollectible Contributions . . . . Allowance for Uncollectible Contributions	4,000	4,000			
3. During the year, cash was collected from some unconditional promises to give, while others were written off as uncollectible.	Cash . . . . Allowance for Uncollectible Contributions . . . . Contributions Receivable	76,500 4,600	81,100			
4. A cash donation of $40,000 was received, with the donor stipulation that it be used to acquire equipment that will assist in water quality improvement.						
5. With the donor's approval, the $40,000 served as a partial payment on the purchase of a filter system costing $50,000. A note was signed for the unpaid balance. PEP chooses to release the donor-restriction over the life of the asset.						
6. PEP received $5,000 from an individual who restricted its use to a special project within the save the lakes program. This donation was given with the condition that if the special project is not accomplished within six months, the money will be returned to the individual. PEP has not yet undertaken the project. Two months remain in the time period specified by the donor.				Cash . . . . Refundable Advances	5,000	5,000
7. The following bequests were received: $100,000 unrestricted and $20,000 to be invested in an endowment whose earnings are to be unrestricted.	Cash . . . . Legacies and Bequests— Unrestricted	100,000	100,000			
8. PEP received donated goods with a fair value of $2,350. Of those donated goods, $750 is restriced by the donor for use in the fish in the lakes program; the remaining gifts can be used at management's discretion.	Inventories . . . . Contributions—Unrestricted . .	1,600	1,600	Inventories . . . . Contributions—Temporarily Restricted	750	750
9. PEP held a special summer event to promote its activities, the net proceeds of which were unrestricted. Gross revenues totaled $9,000, with direct costs for the event amounting to $2,000.	Cash . . . . Special Events Support— Unrestricted . . . . Cost of Special Events . . . . Cash	9,000 2,000	9,000 2,000			

Plant Fund			Endowment Fund		
Contributions Receivable	20,000				
Contributions—Temporarily					
Restricted.		20,000			

Provision for Uncollectible					
Contributions	1,000				
Allowance for Uncollectible					
Contributions		1,000			

Cash	19,000				
Allowance for Uncollectible					
Contributions	1,000				
Contributions Receivable		20,000			

Cash	40,000				
Contributions—Temporarily					
Restricted.		40,000			

Land, Building, and Equipment . .	50,000				
Cash		40,000			
Notes Payable on Equipment . .		10,000			

			Cash	20,000	
			Legacies and Bequests—		
			Endowment—Permanently		
			Restricted.		20,000

continued

Illustration 19A-4 (continued)

Event	Unrestricted Current Fund		Restricted Current Fund
10. PEP uses volunteers to distribute brochures about its operations, to assist the staff with routine office work, and to make phone calls during the annual fund-raising appeal. The volunteers provided 1,000 hours of service this year. If the volunteers were not available, the tasks would either be performed by existing staff or not be done at all. PEP estimates the fair value of these services to be $5 per hour.	No entry. Most volunteer services of this type do not meet criteria. This amount should be disclosed in the footnotes.		
11. An annual membership to PEP is $118, permitting members and their families to use lake facilities for swimming, sailing (no motors allowed), and fishing.	Cash. . . . . Membership Dues Revenues	118,000 118,000	
12. The local PEP unit receives unrestricted cash of $16,000 as its share of a campaign run by its national affiliate.	Cash. . . . . Received from Federated and Nonfederated Campaigns—Unrestricted . .	16,000 16,000	
13. Earnings on endowment investments total $28,000, of which $21,000 is not restricted and $7,000 is restricted to investment in equipment for flood control.	Cash. . . . . Investment Revenue— Unrestricted	21,000 21,000	
14. PEP carries its investments in all funds at market value. Endowment investments are sold for $27,000. They had a cost of $20,000 and a carrying value of $25,000 in the investment account. Endowment gains are permanently restricted as specified by donor.			
15. Additional $46,000 of investments are purchased from endowment funds.			
16. Unrestricted investments have shown no material change in market value over the year. At year end, the market value of permanently restricted endowment investments has increased from $265,000 to $294,000. Endowment gains are permanently restricted as specified by donor.			
17. A lawyer provided five hours of service to PEP to draw up an endowment agreement. She did not charge for her services. She normally would charge a client $500 for consultation on a similar type of agreement. In the absence of the donated professional services, PEP would have hired a lawyer to draft the agreement.	Professional Services . . . . Contributions—Unrestricted . .	500 500	

18. A special recreational building and dock costing $96,000 were purchased with unrestricted cash.	Unrestricted Net Assets—
	  Transfer Out . . . .
	  Cash. . . . .
		
		96,000
		
		96,000	

Plant Fund   Endowment Fund

Cash	7,000			
Investment Revenue—				
Temporarily Restricted.		7,000		

			Cash	27,000
			Investments (at market).		25,000
			Gain on Sale of Endowment		
			Investments—Permanently		
			Restricted.		2,000

			Endowment Investments—		
			Permanently Restricted	46,000	
			Cash		46,000

			Endowment Investments	29,000	
			Net Increase in Carrying		
			Value of Investments—		
			Permanently Restricted		29,000

Cash	96,000			
Unrestricted Net Assets—				
Transfer In		96,000		
Land Building and Equipment . . .	96,000			
Cash		96,000		

continued

Illustration 19A-4 (continued)

Event	Unrestricted Current Fund			Restricted Current Fund		
19. Contributions received in the prior period with the stipulation that they be used for expenses of this period are now available.				Reclassification Out— Temporarily Restricted— Satisfaction of Time Requirements............	10,000	
				Reclassification In— Unrestricted—Satisfaction of Time Requirements		10,000
20. Accounts payable and expenses were paid or established. Operating expenses related to donor-specific programs totaled $103,000.	Accounts Payable (January 1)...	33,000		Accounts Payable (January 1)...	4,000	
	Salaries Expense..............	180,000		Salaries Expense..............	20,000	
	Payroll Taxes	24,000		Payroll Taxes	6,000	
	Mailing and Postage Expense...	40,000		Mailing and Postage Expense...	10,000	
	Rent Expense.................	23,000		Rent Expense.................	5,000	
	Telephone Expense............	5,000		Telephone Expense............	1,000	
	Research Expense............	165,000		Research Expense............	50,000	
	Professional Services: Legal and Audit	27,000		Professional Services: Legal and Audit	7,000	
	Supplies Expense ....,....	10,000		Supplies Expense	3,000	
	Miscellaneous Expense	4,000		Miscellaneous Expense	1,000	
	Accounts Payable		31,000	Accounts Payable		1,000
	Cash......................		480,000	Cash......................		106,000
				Reclassification Out— Temporarily Restricted— Satisfaction of Program Requirements............	103,000	
				Reclassification In— Unrestricted—Satisfaction of Program Requirements ..		103,000
21. Contributed goods of $1,450 were used during the year for the fish in the lakes program. This amount includes the $750 donor-restricted contribution in item 8 above.	Supplies Expense	700		Supplies Expense	750	
	Inventories		700	Inventories		750
				Reclassification Out— Temporarily Restricted— Satisfaction of Program Requirements............	750	
				Reclassification In— Unrestricted—Satisfaction of Program Requirements ..		750
22. Depreciation on equipment purchased with donor-restricted contributions amounted to $22,000 for the year. (Valley air project—$2,000; Fish in the lakes program—$3,000; Flood control program—$16,000; Management and general services— $1,000.) An equivalent amount of temporarily restricted net assets are released from restriction.						
23. Early in the year, cash contributions for current operations were received, but they cannot be used until late in the following year.				Cash......................	2,000	
				Contributions—Temporarily Restricted		2,000

Plant Fund		Endowment Fund	
Depreciation Expense	22,000		
Accumulated Depreciation		22,000	
Reclassification Out—			
Temporarily Restricted—			
Satisfaction of Equipment			
Acquisition Requirements. . .	22,000		
Reclassification In—			
Unrestricted—Satisfaction			
of Equipment Acquisition			
Requirements		22,000	

continued

Illustration 19A-4 (continued)

Event	Unrestricted Current Fund			Restricted Current Fund		
24. At year end, the expenses were allocated to the various programs and supporting services.	Valley Air Project	117,000		Valley Air Project	13,000	
	Fish in the Lakes Program	131,700		Fish in the Lakes Program	49,750	
	Flood Control Program	204,000		Flood Control Program	31,000	
	Management and General Services	20,500		Management and General Services	8,000	
	Fund-Raising Services	8,000		Fund-Raising Services	2,000	
	Membership Development	2,000		Membership Development		
	Salaries Expense		180,000	Salaries Expense		20,000
	Payroll Taxes		24,000	Payroll Taxes		6,000
	Mailing and Postage Expense		40,000	Mailing and Postage Expense		10,000
	Rent Expense		23,000	Rent Expense		5,000
	Telephone Expense		5,000	Telephone Expense		1,000
	Research Expense		165,000	Research Expense		50,000
	Professional Services: Legal and Audit		27,500	Professional Services: Legal and Audit		7,000
	Supplies Expense		10,700	Supplies Expense		3,750
	Miscellaneous Expense		4,000	Miscellaneous Expense		1,000
	Provision for Uncollectible Contributions		4,000			
25. Closing entries.	Contributions	397,100		Reclassifications In— Unrestricted—Satisfaction of Program Restrictions	103,750	
	Special Events Support	9,000		Reclassifications In— Unrestricted—Satisfaction of Time Restrictions	10,000	
	Legacies and Bequests— Unrestricted	100,000		Valley Air Project		13,000
	Received from Federated and Nonfederated	16,000		Fish in the Lakes Program		49,750
	Membership Dues Revenue	118,000		Flood Control Program		31,000
	Investment Revenue— Unrestricted	21,000		Management and General Services		8,000
	Valley Air Project		117,000	Fund-Raising Services		2,000
	Fish in the Lakes Program		131,700	**Unrestricted Net Assets. . . .**		**10,000**
	Flood Control Program		204,000	Contributions—Temporarily Restricted	12,750	
	Management and General Services		20,500	**Temporarily Restricted Net Assets . . . .**	**101,000**	
	Fund-Raising Services		8,000	Reclassifications Out— Unrestricted—Satisfaction of Program Restrictions		103,750
	Membership Development . . .		2,000	Reclassifications Out— Unrestricted—Satisfaction of Time Restrictions		10,000
	Cost of Special Events		2,000			
	Unrestricted Net Assets.		**175,900**			

QUESTIONS

1. Explain a hospital's rigid adherence to gross revenue determination.
2. Name the three items that are grouped in the account Allowance for Adjustments and Uncollectibles. Briefly describe the function of the account.
3. Name three different procedures that providers of health care follow to cover the cost of malpractice claims. In all procedures, what should the amount of the expense represent?
4. Name the two criteria that must be met for an entity to qualify as a VHWO.
5. Differentiate between the accounts Unrestricted Net Assets—Designated and Unrestricted Net Assets—Undesignated of a VHWO.

Plant Fund			Endowment Fund	
Valley Air Project..............	2,000			
Fish in the Lakes Program.......	3,000			
Flood Control Program	16,000			
Management and General				
Services.................	1,000			
Fund-Raising Services..........	1,000			
Depreciation Expense		22,000		
Provision for Uncollectibles ...		1,000		

Unrestricted Net Assets	**1,000**		Legacies and Bequests—	
Reclassifications In—			Endowment—Permanently	
Unrestricted—Satisfaction			Restricted................	20,000
of Equipment Acquisition			Net Increase in Carrying Value of	
Restrictions	22,000		Endowment Investments—	
Valley Air Project............		2,000	Permanently Restricted.....	29,000
Fish in the Lakes Program.....		3,000	Gain on Sale of Endowment	
Flood Control Program		16,000	Investments—Permanently	
Management and General			Restricted................	2,000
Services.................		1,000	**Permanently Restricted Net**	
Fund-Raising Services........		1,000	**Assets.**..................	**51,000**
Contributions—Temporarily				
Restricted................	60,000			
Investment Revenue—				
Temporarily Restricted	7,000			
Reclassifications Out—				
Temporarily Restricted—				
Satisfaction of Equipment				
Acquisition Restrictions.....		22,000		
Temporarily Restricted Net				
Assets...................		45,000		

6. Compare and contrast accounting and financial reporting for public colleges and universities and VHWOs regarding the following issues:
   (a) Measurement focus and basis of accounting.
   (b) Presenting revenues and expenses or expenditures.
   (c) Presenting depreciation expense.

7. Differentiate between public support and revenues as sources of assets.

8. A VHWO receives a contribution of $25,000 restricted for current operations. By the end of the fiscal period, it spends $5,000 of the contribution. State the amount that is recognized as revenue, and give the journal entries to record the events.

9. Explain the logic (not the process) of pooling of investments.

10. Why does the statement of activity of a VHWO not show expenses by their natural classification, such as salary expense?

11. What is the currently recommended procedure in relation to joint-cost allocation?

Illustration 19A-5

People's Environmental Protection (PEP) Association
Statement of Financial Position
As of December 31, 19X4

	Unrestricted Current Fund	Restricted Current Fund	Plant Fund	Endowment Fund	Total
Assets:					
Cash and cash equivalents	$115,500	$129,000	$ 9,000		$ 253,500
Contributions receivable (net of $3,100 allowance)	21,500				21,500
Inventories	10,000				10,000
Short-term investments......................	70,000	7,000	75,000		152,000
Long-term investments				$253,000	253,000
Property, plant, and equipment (net of $16,700 accumulated depreciation)			676,000		676,000
Total assets	$217,000	$136,000	$760,000	$253,000	$1,366,000
Liabilities and net assets:					
Accounts payable	$ 33,000	$ 4,000			$ 37,000
Notes payable			$100,000		100,000
Total liabilities	$ 33,000	$ 4,000	$100,000		$ 137,000
Net assets:					
Unrestricted................................	$184,000		$105,000		$ 289,000
Temporarily restricted		$132,000	555,000		687,000
Permanently restricted				$253,000	253,000
Total net assets...........................	$184,000	$132,000	$660,000	$253,000	$1,229,000
Total liabilities and net assets...................	$217,000	$136,000	$760,000	$253,000	$1,366,000

EXERCISES

Exercise 1.

1. Inventory donated for use in a hospital should be reported as:
   (a) Other operating revenue.
   (b) Nonoperating revenues.
   (c) Additions to the unrestricted net assets.
   (d) Additions to the restricted net assets.
2. Dee City's community hospital, which uses enterprise fund reporting and chooses to follow FASB guidelines, normally includes proceeds from sale of cafeteria meals in:
   (a) Patient service revenues.
   (b) Other operating revenues.
   (c) Ancillary service revenues.
   (d) Deductions from dietary service expenses.
3. During 1991, Trained Hospital received $90,000 in third-party reimbursements for depreciation. These reimbursements were restricted as follows:

For replacement of fully depreciated equipment	$25,000
For additions to property..	65,000

(continued on page 1094)

Illustration 19A-6

People's Environmental Protection (PEP) Association
Statement of Activities
For Year Ended December 31, 19X5

	Unrestricted Current Fund	Restricted Current Fund	Plant Fund	Endowment Fund	Total
Public support and revenue:					
Public support:					
Contributions	$397,100				$ 397,100
Special events (net of $2,000 direct costs).....	7,000				7,000
Legacies and bequests	100,000				100,000
Received from federated and nonfederated campaigns..............................	16,000				16,000
Total public support......................	$520,100				$ 520,100
Revenue:					
Membership dues	$118,000				$ 118,000
Investment revenue........................	21,000				21,000
Total revenue...........................	$139,000				$ 139,000
Net assets released from restrictions:					
Satisfaction of program restrictions		$ 103,750			$ 103,750
Satisfaction of equipment acquisition restrictions.....................................			$ 22,000		22,000
Expiration of time restrictions		10,000			10,000
Total net assets released from restrictions ..		113,750	22,000		135,750
Total public support and revenues	$659,100	$ 113,750	$ 22,000		$ 794,850
Expenses:					
Valley air project...........................	$117,000	$ 13,000	$ 2,000		$ 132,000
Keep fish in the lakes program	131,700	49,750	3,000		184,450
Flood control program	204,000	31,000	16,000		251,000
Management and general	20,500	8,000	1,000		29,500
Fund raising	8,000	2,000	1,000		11,000
Membership development.....................	2,000				2,000
Total expenses	$483,200	$ 103,750	$ 23,000		$ 609,950
Increase (decrease) in unrestricted net assets	$175,900	$ 10,000	$ (1,000)		**$ 184,900**
Transfers among funds........................	$ (96,000)		$ 96,000		
Changes in temporarily restricted net assets:					
Contributions		$ 12,750	$ 60,000		$ 72,750
Investment income on endowment			7,000		7,000
Net assets released from restrictions...........		(113,750)	(22,000)		(135,750)
Increase (decrease) in temporarily restricted net assets......................................		$(101,000)	$ 45,000		**$ (56,000)**
Changes in permanently restricted net assets:					
Legacies and bequests				$ 20,000	$ 20,000
Net increase in carrying value of investments ...				29,000	29,000
Gain on sale of investments..................				2,000	2,000
Increase (decrease) in permanently restricted net assets......................................				$ 51,000	**$ 51,000**
Change in net assets..........................	$ 79,900	$ (91,000)	$140,000	$ 51,000	$ 179,900
Net assets beginning of year...................	184,000	132,000	660,000	253,000	1,229,000
Net assets end of year	$263,900	$ 41,000	$800,000	$304,000	**$1,408,900**

Illustration 19A-7
People's Environmental Protection (PEP) Association
Statement of Financial Position
As of December 31, 19X5

	Unrestricted Current Fund	Restricted Current Fund	Plant Fund	Endowment Fund	Totals
Assets:					
Cash and cash equivalents...................	$193,000	$40,000	$ 35,000		$ 268,000
Contributions receivable (net of $2,500					
allowance)..............................	21,000				21,000
Inventories................................	10,900				10,900
Short-term investments.....................	70,000	7,000	75,000		152,000
Property, plant, and equipment (net					
of $38,700 accumulated depreciation)			800,000		800,000
Long-term endowment investments...........				$304,000	304,000
Total assets	$294,900	$47,000	$910,000	$304,000	**$1,555,900**
Liabilities and net assets:					
Accounts payable..........................	31,000	1,000			32,000
Refundable advances.......................		5,000			5,000
Notes payable			110,000		110,000
Total liabilities	$ 31,000	$ 6,000	$110,000		$ 147,000
Net assets:					
Unrestricted................................	$263,900	$10,000	$200,000		**$ 473,900**
Temporarily restricted		31,000	600,000		**631,000**
Permanently restricted				$304,000	**304,000**
Total net assets...........................	263,900	41,000	800,000	$304,000	**$1,408,900**
Total liabilities and net assets	$294,900	$47,000	$910,000	$304,000	**$1,555,900**

What amount of these reimbursements should Trained include in revenue for year ended December 31, 19X1?

(a) 0

(b) $25,000

(c) $65,000

(d) $90,000

4. A hospital should report earnings from endowment funds that are restricted to a specific operating purpose as:

(a) Temporarily restricted revenues.

(b) Permanently restricted revenues.

(c) Unrestricted revenues.

(d) Unrestricted revenues when expended.

5. Hospital financial resources are required by a bond indenture to be set aside to finance construction of a new pediatrics facility. In which of the following hospital net asset classes should these resources be reported?

(a) Permanently restricted.

(b) Temporarily restricted.

(c) Unrestricted.

(d) Refundable deposits.

6. Which of the following financial statements should not-for-profit hospitals prepare?
   (a) Balance sheet and income statement.
   (b) Balance sheet, income statement, and statement of changes in financial position.
   (c) Statement of financial position, statement of activities, and statement of cash flows.
   (d) Statement of funds, statement of activities, and statement of cash flows.

7. Land valued at $400,000 and subject to a $150,000 mortgage was donated to Beaty Hospital without restriction as to use. Which of the following entries should Beaty make to record this donation?

   (a) Land $400,000
          Mortgage Payable   150,000
          Endowment Fund Balance   250,000
   (b) Land $400,000
          Mortgage Payable   150,000
          Contributions—Unrestricted   250,000
   (c) Land $400,000
          Debt Fund Balance   150,000
          Endowment Fund Balance   250,000
   (d) Land $400,000
          Mortgage Payable   150,000
          Unrestricted Fund Balance   250,000

8. In hospital accounting, restricted net assets are:
   (a) *Not* available unless the board of directors removes the restrictions.
   (b) Restricted as to use only for board-designated purposes.
   (c) *Not* available for current operating use; however, the income generated by the funds is available for current operating use.
   (d) Restricted as to use by the donor, grantor, or other source of the resources.

(AICPA adapted)

Exercise 2. A hospital has three revenue-controlling accounts: Patient Service Revenue, Other Operating Revenue, and Nonoperating Revenue.
(a) State in general terms the type of revenue found in each controlling account.
(b) Indicate into which of the three controlling accounts each of the following would be placed by using the symbols PS for Patient Service Revenue, OO for Other Operating Revenue, N for Nonoperating Revenue, and N/A if not a revenue item:

   1. Tuition for entry to the nursing school   _____
   2. An unrestricted gift of cash   _____
   3. General nursing fees charged to patients   _____
   4. Charges for physicians' care   _____
   5. A restricted gift used for research on genes   _____
   6. Dividends from the hospital's investments   _____
   7. Revenue from gift shop sales   _____
   8. Patient room and board charges   _____
   9. Proceeds from sales of cafeteria meals   _____
  10. Recovery room fees   _____
  11. Contributions for plant replacement and expansion _____

Exercise 3. Record the following events of Elmbrook Hospital.
(a) Patients were billed for the following gross charges:

   Room and board............................ $480,000
   Physicians' care............................ 220,000
   Laboratory and radiology 110,000

(b) A donation of drugs with a market value of $12,000 was received from a doctor. The drugs are normally purchased.

(c) Revenues were reported from:

Newsstand and snack bar	$16,000
Parking lot charges	3,200
Vending machines	9,800

(d) A charity allowance of $13,000 was granted indigent patients.

(e) Contractual adjustments granted to patients for Medicare charges totaled $48,000.

(f) The hospital recorded an increase in the provision of $26,000 for uncollectible receivables.

Exercise 4. The Pure Air Rehabilitation Hospital has the following balances that are extracted from its December 31, 19X6 trial balance:

Account	Debit	Credit
Nursing Services Expense	$230,000	
Professional Fees Expense	340,000	
General and Administrative Expense	150,000	
Depreciation Expense	90,000	
Interest Expense	13,000	
Assets Whose Use Is Limited	55,000	
Repairs and Maintenance Expense	110,000	
Provision for Uncollectible Accounts	14,000	
Contractual Adjustments	26,000	
Patient Service Revenue		$740,000
Income, Seminars		23,000
Child Day Care Revenue		15,000
Parking Fees		4,500
Endowment Income—Temporarily Restricted		120,000
Interest Income—Unrestricted		3,000
Donations—Temporarily Restricted		18,000
Gains (Distributable) on Sale of Endowments—Temporarily Restricted		56,000
Net Assets—Unrestricted (1/1/X7)		800,000
Net Assets—Temporarily Restricted (1/1/X7)		755,000
Net Assets—Permanently Restricted (1/1/X7)		750,000

From the above information, prepare a statement of activities for the year ended December 31, 19X7.

Exercise 5. Ambulance Service is a not-for-profit health care provider. Prepare the reconciliation of change in net assets to net cash provided by operating activities that would accompany its statement of cash flows under the direct method for the year ended December 31, 19X4.

Decrease in net assets	$ 93,000
Noncash items: Depreciation	117,000
Amortization of premium on bonds payable	22,000
Cash paid for acquisition of property	10,000
Payment to settle long-term note payable	63,000
Net decrease in receivables and supplies	38,000
Net increase in current payables	10,000

Exercise 6. Record the following events of the Chemical Dependency Clinic, a VHWO:

(a) Membership dues of $7,000 were collected.

(b) Cash contributions of $22,000 and pledges for $32,000 were received.

(c) It is estimated that 10% of the above pledges will prove uncollectible.

(d) A fund-raising dinner grossed $8,400 from the sale of 420 tickets. The catered dinner cost $12 each for the 360 people who attended, plus $200 for the rental of the dining room. Payment for these costs was made.

(e) A classic car was donated to the organization. The car has an estimated market value of $75,000. It will be the main attraction of an auction to be held in the next accounting period. The proceeds of the auction are part of the budget for activities in the next period.

(f) To expand the services of the clinic, a professional fund-raising group was hired to undertake a six-month campaign. At the end of the six months, the group submitted the following report:

Cash collected	$ 70,000
Pledges (estimated 95% collectible)	30,000
Total proceeds	$100,000
Less 20% fund-raising fee (regardless of collections)	20,000
Net proceeds from drive	$ 80,000

Exercise 7. Record the following events of the Mental Health Clinic, a VHWO:

(a) A contribution of $10,000 was received and is to be used for the purchase of equipment, but not until an addition to the building is constructed. Construction has begun on the building.

(b) Equipment costing $17,000, with a book value of $8,000, was sold for $10,000. The gain is unrestricted.

(c) Depreciation of $9,000 is recorded on various plant items.

(d) Equipment was purchased for $12,000, with payment due in 30 days from donor-restricted resources. Mental Health Clinic elects to release the donor restriction upon acquisition of the equipment.

(e) The liability for the equipment purchased in (d) was paid.

Exercise 8. Record the following events of Mercy Health Clinic, a VHWO:

(a) In her will, a leading citizen left a bequest of $100,000 to the clinic. Stipulations were that the amount was to become the corpus of a permanent endowment. Any income received would be used first to cover any loss of principal, with the remaining revenue to be used for an educational program on mental problems. The total amount was received and invested in 8% municipal bonds purchased at face value on an interest date.

(b) Investments were carried at cost. Later in the year, half of the bond investment was sold at 101, plus $3,000 of accrued interest.

(c) Other endowment investments earned $11,000. The amount is not subject to any limitations.

Exercise 9. The Better Life Clinic is a VHWO that has three main programs:

Drug rehabilitation
Alcohol recovery
Weight control

Unrestricted public support received during the period was $35,000; revenues from membership services was $12,000. The following expenses and allocations to program and supporting services are shown for 19X0. Better Life elects to release donor restrictions for property, plant, and equipment over the useful life of the asset.

Item	Amount	Distribution				
		Drug Rehab.	Alcohol Recovery	Weight Control	Fund Raising	Gen. & Adm.
Secretarial salary	5,000					100%
Office supplies.............................	6,000	20%	10%	10%	10%	50
Printing...................................	8,000	10	10	20	50	10
Depreciation (all depreciation is on assets acquired with donor-restricted contributions)..	4,000	20	20	20		40
Instruction	9,000	30	25	35	10	
Rent.......................................	10,000	30	20	30		20

Temporarily restricted net assets totaled $30,000 on January 1; the unrestricted net asset balance was $12,000. Prepare a statement of activities for the year.

APPENDIX EXERCISES

Exercise 19A-1. The Health Awareness Club is a not-for-profit organization that conducts meetings and special programs dedicated to promoting better health for members of the community. Members participate in regularly scheduled classes and exercise programs. There are also a variety of community services available to the general population. During the year, various funds flow to the organization. A list of receipts follows. For each item indicate which of the following funds records the item, and indicate the category within which the item is recorded in that fund.

Name of Fund	Category
Current unrestricted fund	Revenue—Unrestricted
Current restricted fund	Public Support—Unrestricted
Plant fund	Deferred Revenue
Endowment fund	Public Support—Temporarily Restricted
	Public Support—Permanently Restricted
	Revenue—Temporarily Restricted

The transactions were:
(a) General membership dues.
(b) Receipts for Pancake Breakfast open to public.
(c) Donation of equipment to be used in exercise room. Restrictions are released when assets are placed in service.
(d) Donation of equipment to be sold; proceeds are to be used to support education program.
(e) Share of federated national fund drive.
(f) Sale of educational books produced by the organization.
(g) Auction of donated services to be used to acquire additional land for expansion.
(h) Receipt of endowment from former president of organization.
(i) Income on endowment that supports youth health program.

(j) Pledge of $5,000 from local corporation for youth health program. The pledge is conditional, in that the organization must match the grant with funds raised from other corporate sponsors.

Exercise19A-2. The Health Awareness Club is a not-for-profit organization that conducts meetings and special programs dedicated to promoting better health for members of the community. Members participate in regularly scheduled classes and exercise programs. There are also a variety of community services available to the general population. During the year, various expenditures are recorded. For each item listed, indicate the fund in which the entry would be made and the nature of the transaction. The available funds and transaction types are:

Name of Fund	Nature of Transaction
Current unrestricted fund	Fund-raising expense
Current restricted fund	General and administrative
Plant fund	Program expense
Endowment fund	Offset to public support

The transactions were:
(a) Cost of brochures asking for donations
(b) Accounting services received.
(c) Office supplies consumed.
(d) Repair and maintenance of exercise room equipment.
(e) Depreciation on exercise room equipment.
(f) Costs associated with pancake breakfast.
(g) Costs of cancer awareness program paid from donations that are restricted to this use.

Exercise 19A-3. On January 2, 19X1, the available cash in the following funds was placed into an investment pool:

Fund	Cash Pooled
Current unrestricted	$ 40,000
Current restricted.	30,000
Plant.	10,000
Endowment	20,000
Total	$100,000

During the next year, no additional cash was placed into the pool, nor was any amount withdrawn. At the end of the year, the pooled investments had a basis of $120,000, representing original contributions plus $20,000 of realized gains that remained in the investment pool. At year end, the market value of the pool amounted to $130,000. Prepare a schedule reflecting pooling activities for the year 19X1.

Exercise 19A-4. The characteristics of VHWOs differ in certain respects from the characteristics of state or local governmental units. As an example, VHWOs derive their revenues primarily from voluntary contributions from the general public, while governmental units derive their revenues from taxes and from services provided to their jurisdictions.
(1) Describe fund accounting and discuss whether its use is consistent with the concept that an accounting entity is an economic unit that has control over resources, accepts responsibilities for making and carrying out commitments, and conducts economic activity.

(2) Discuss how methods used to account for fixed assets differ between VHWOs and governmental units.

(AICPA adapted)

PROBLEMS

Problem 19-1. Select the best answer for each of the following multiple-choice items dealing with hospitals:

1. On March 1, 19X8, A. C. Rowe established a $100,000 endowment fund, the income from which is to be paid to Elm Hospital for general operating purposes. Elm does not control the fund's principal. Rowe appointed West National Bank as trustee of this fund. What journal entry is required by Elm to record the establishment of the endowment?

   (a) Cash $100,000
       Nonexpendable Endowment Fund $100,000

   (b) Cash $100,000
       Nonoperating Revenue $100,000

   (c) Nonexpendable Endowment Fund $100,000
       Endowment Fund Balance $100,000

   (d) Memorandum entry only.

2. In 19X8, Wells Hospital received an unrestricted bequest of common stock with a market value of $50,000 on the date of receipt of the stock. The testator had paid $20,000 for this stock in 19X6. Wells should record this bequest as:
   (a) Nonoperating revenue of $50,000.
   (b) Nonoperating revenue of $30,000.
   (c) Nonoperating revenue of $20,000.
   (d) A memorandum entry only.

3. Cedar Hospital has a marketable equity securities portfolio that is included appropriately in noncurrent assets in unrestricted funds. The portfolio has an aggregate cost of $300,000. It had an aggregate market value of $250,000 at the end of 19X7 and $290,000 at the end of 19X6. If the portfolio was reported properly in the balance sheet at the end of 19X6, the change in the valuation allowance at the end of 19X7 should be:
   (a) 0
   (b) A decrease of $40,000
   (c) An increase of $40,000
   (d) An increase of $50,000

4. Ross Hospital's accounting records disclosed the following information:

   Net resources invested in plant assets (hospital policy is to release
       donor-restrictions when assets are placed in service) $10,000,000
   Board-designated funds   2,000,000

   What amount should be included as unrestricted net assets?

   (a) $12,000,000   (b) $10,000,000   (c) $2,000,000   (d) 0

5. Under Cura Hospital's established rate structure, patient service revenues of $9,000,000 would have been earned for the year ended December 31, 19X7. However,

only $6,750,000 was collected because of charity allowances of $1,500,000 and discounts of $750,000 to third-party payors. For the year ended December 31, 19X7, what amount should Cura record as net patient service revenues?

(a) $6,750,000   (b) $7,500,000   (c) $8,250,000   (d) $9,000,000

6. An organization of high school seniors performs services for patients at Leer Hospital. These students are volunteers and perform services that the hospital would not otherwise provide, such as wheeling patients in the park and reading to patients. These volunteers donated 5,000 hours of service to Leer in 19X7. At the minimum wage rate, these services would amount to $22,500, while it is estimated that the fair value of these services was $27,000. In Leer's 19X7 statement of revenues and expenses, what amount should be reported as nonoperating revenue?

(a) $27,000   (b) $22,500   (c) $6,250   (d) 0

7. In June 19X8, Park Hospital purchased medicines from Jove Pharmaceutical Co. at a cost of $2,000. However, Jove notified Park that the invoice was being canceled, and the medicines were being donated to Park. Park should record this donation of medicines as:
   (a) A memorandum entry only.
   (b) Other operating revenue of $2,000.
   (c) A $2,000 credit to operating expenses.
   (d) A $2,000 credit to nonoperating expenses.

8. Palma Hospital's patient service revenues for services provided in 19X8, at established rates, amounted to $8,000,000 on the accrual basis. For internal reporting, Palma uses the discharge method. Under this method, patient service revenues are recognized only when patients are discharged, with no recognition given to revenues accruing for services to patients not yet discharged. Patient service revenues at established rates using the discharge method amounted to $7,000,000 for 19X8. According to GAAP, Palma should report patient service revenues for 19X8 of:
   (a) Either $8,000,000 or $7,000,000, at the option of the hospital.
   (b) $8,000,000
   (c) $7,500,000
   (d) $7,000,000

9. In 19X6, Pyle Hospital received a $250,000 pure endowment grant. Also in 19X6, Pyle's governing board designated, for special uses, $300,000 which had originated from unrestricted gifts. What amount of these resources should be accounted for as part of the unrestricted net asset class?

(a) 0   (b) $250,000   (c) $300,000   (d) $550,000

10. Cura Hospital's property, plant, and equipment, net of depreciation, amounted to $10,000,000, with related mortgage liabilities of $1,000,000. What amount should be included in the permanently restricted net asset class?

(a) 0   (b) $1,000,000   (c) $9,000,000   (d) $10,000,000
                                                                      (AICPA adapted)

Problem 19-2. Select the best answer for each of the following multiple-choice items. Items 1 through 3 are based on the following:

The Bay Ridge Humane Society, a VHWO caring for lost animals, had the following financial inflows and outflows for the year ended December 31, 19X3:

Inflows:

Cash received from federated campaign	$680,000
Cash received that is designated for 19X4 operations.	30,000
Contributions pledged for 19X3 not yet received	90,000
Contributions pledged for 19X4 not yet received	25,000
Sales of pet supplies	10,000
Pet adoption fees	50,000

Outflows:

Kennel operations.	$350,000
Pet health care.	100,000
Advertising pets for adoption.	50,000
Fund raising.	70,000
Administrative and general.	200,000

1. In the humane society's statement of activities for the year ended December 31, 19X3, what amount should be reported under the classification of public support—unrestricted?

    (a) $740,000   (b) $762,000   (c) $770,000   (d) $825,000

2. In the humane society's statement of activities for the year ended December 31, 19X3, what amount should be reported under the classification of program services expense?

    (a) $770,000   (b) $450,000   (c) $550,000   (d) $500,000

3. In the humane society's balance sheet as of December 31, 19X3, what amount should be reported under the classification public support—temporarily restricted?

    (a) $55,000   (b) $30,000   (c) $25,000   (d) 0

4. Arbor Haven, a voluntary welfare organization funded by contributions from the general public, received unrestricted pledges of $500,000 during 19X6. It was estimated that 12% of these pledges would be uncollectible. By the end of 19X6, $400,000 of the pledges had been collected, and it was expected that $40,000 more would be collected in 19X7, with the balance of $60,000 to be written off as uncollectible. Donors did not specify any periods during which the donations were to be used. What amount should Arbor Haven include under public support in 19X6 for contributions?

    (a) $500,000   (b) $452,000   (c) $440,000   (d) $400,000

5. The following expenditures were among those incurred by a voluntary welfare society during 19X7:

Printing of annual report	$10,000
Unsolicited merchandise sent to encourage contributions	20,000

    What amount should be classified as fund-raising costs in the society's statement of activities?

    (a) 0   (b) $10,000   (c) $20,000   (d) $30,000

6. Apex Inc. donated a computer to Bird Shelter, a voluntary organization. The computer cost Apex $40,000. On the date of donation, it had a book value of $25,000 and a market value of $20,000. Bird Shelter's depreciation expense should be based on:

(a) $40,000   (b) $25,000   (c) $20,000   (d) $15,000

(AICPA adapted)

Problem 19-3. Select the best answer for each of the following multiple-choice questions. (No. 1 is AICPA adapted.)
1. In the statement of activities of a VHWO, depreciation expense should:
    (a) Be included as an element of expense.
    (b) Be included as an element of other changes in fund balances.
    (c) Be included as an element of support.
    (d) Not be included.

2. Donor-restricted contributions that have been given to a VHWO for the purpose of purchasing fixed assets should be recorded as increases to:
    (a) Unrestricted Net Assets.
    (b) Temporarily Restricted Net Assets.
    (c) Permanently Restricted Net Assets.
    (d) Fund Balance—Restricted.

3. The following correct entry is found on the books of a VHWO:

    Unrestricted Net Assets—Undesignated. XXX
       Unrestricted Net Assets—Designated for AIDS Research   XXX

    From the entry, one should conclude that the board of directors has:
    (a) Designated a portion of the unrestricted net assets for a future AIDS research program.
    (b) Designated a portion of the restricted net assets for a future AIDS research program.
    (c) Transferred resources to an AIDS research program.
    (d) Directed that unused resources previously assigned to an AIDS research program be returned to unrestricted net asset classification.

4. To protect the principal of the endowment of a VHWO, unrestricted cash interest received on bond investments purchased at a premium is classified as unrestricted:
    (a) In an amount equal to net earnings after premium amortization.
    (b) In an amount equal to the gross cash interest received.
    (c) Only when the interest received equals the total premium paid.
    (d) Only upon the maturity of the bonds.

5. The investments of a VHWO are pooled and carried at market value. At the end of the period, there is a decrease in total market value. The market value decrease should:
    (a) Not be recorded until the loss is realized.
    (b) Be debited to Realized Loss on Pooled Investments.
    (c) Be debited to Endowment Fund Balance.
    (d) Be debited to Net Decrease in Carrying Value of Investments.

Problem 19-4. Select the best answer for each of the following multiple-choice items:
1. A nonprofit performing arts organization receives a donation that is restricted to its endowment and another donation that is restricted to use in acquiring a performing arts center. How should these donations be reported in the year received, assuming neither donation is expended in that year?

Donation for Endowment	Donation for Performing Arts Center
(a) Contributions—Temporarily Restricted	Contributions—Temporarily Restricted
(b) Deferred Capital Additions	Capital Additions
(c) Contributions—Unrestricted	Contributions—Unrestricted
(d) Capital Additions	Deferred Capital Additions
(e) Contributions—Permanently Restricted	Contributions—Temporarily Restricted

2. Environs, a community foundation, incurred $10,000 in management and general expenses during 19X1. In Environs' statement of activities for the year ended December 31, 19X1, the $10,000 should be reported as:
   (a) A direct reduction of unrestricted net assets.
   (b) Part of supporting services expense.
   (c) Part of program services expense.
   (d) A contra-account to offset revenue and support.

3. Super Seniors is a not-for-profit organization that provides services to senior citizens. Super employs a full-time staff of 10 people at an annual cost of $150,000. In addition, two volunteers work as part-time secretaries replacing last year's full-time secretary who earned $10,000. Services performed by other volunteers for special events had an estimated value of $15,000. These volunteers were employees of local businesses and they received small-value items for their participation. What amount should Super report for salary and wage expenses related to the above items?
   (a) $150,000
   (b) $160,000
   (c) $165,000
   (d) $175,000

4. The League, a not-for-profit organization, received the following pledges:

Unrestricted...............................	$200,000
Restricted for capital additions.................	150,000

   All pledges are legally enforceable; however, the League's experience indicates that 10% of all pledges prove to be uncollectible. What amount should the League report as pledges receivable net of any required allowance account?
   (a) $135,000
   (b) $180,000
   (c) $315,000
   (d) $350,000

5. Midtown Church received a donation of marketable equity securities from a church member. The securities had appreciated in value after they were purchased by the donor, and they continued to appreciate through the end of Midtown's fiscal year. At what amount should Midtown report its investment in marketable equity securities in its year-end balance sheet?
   (a) Donor's cost.
   (b) Market value at the date of receipt.
   (c) Market value at the balance sheet date.
   (d) Market value at either the date of receipt or the balance sheet date.

6. Maple Church has cash available for investments in several different accounting funds. Maple's policy is to maximize its financial resources. How may Maple pool its investments?

(a) Maple may **not** pool its investments.

(b) Maple may pool all investments, but must equitably allocate realized and unrealized gains and losses among participating funds.

(c) Maple may pool only unrestricted investments, but must equitably allocate realized and unrealized gains and losses among participating funds.

(d) Maple may pool only restricted investments, but must equitably allocate realized and unrealized gains and losses among participating funds.

7. When a nonprofit organization combines fund-raising efforts with bona fide educational efforts or program services, the total combined costs incurred are:

(a) Reported as program services expenses.

(b) Allocated between fund-raising and program services expenses using an appropriate allocation basis.

(c) Reported as fund-raising costs.

(d) Reported as management and general expenses.   (AICPA adapted)

Problem 19-5. The following selected events relate to the 19X5 activities of Aires Nursing Home Inc., a not-for-profit agency:

(a) Gross patient service revenue totaled $2,200,000. The provision for uncollectible accounts was estimated at $92,000. The allowance for contractual adjustments was increased by $120,000.

(b) After a conference with representatives of Gold Star Insurance Company, differences between the amounts accrued and subsequent settlements reduced receivables by $60,000.

(c) A grateful patient donated securities with a cost of $20,000 and a market value at date of donation of $75,000. The donation was restricted to expenditure for modernization of equipment. The donation was accepted.

(d) Cash of $37,000 that had been restricted by a donor for the purchase of furniture was used this year. Aires chose to release the donor restriction over the useful life of the asset.

(e) The board voluntarily transferred $50,000 of cash to add to the resources held for capital improvements.

(f) Pledges of $60,000 and cash of $20,000 were received to defer operating expenses. Of the pledges, 10% are considered uncollectible. Term endowments of $10,000 matured and were released to cover operations.

(g) Equipment costing $250,000 was purchased on account. Restricted resources held for that purpose will be released from restriction over the useful life of the asset.

(h) The nursing home uses functional operating expense control accounts. Expenses for the year were for:

Nursing services	$1,120,000
Dietary services	230,000
Maintenance services	115,000
Administrative services	285,000
Interest	160,000
Subtotal (of which $253,000 is unpaid)	$1,910,000
Depreciation [$20,000 from assets purchased with resources in (d) and (g) above]	60,000
Total	$1,970,000

Required:

(1) Omitting explanations, prepare journal entries for the foregoing events.

(2) Prepare a statement of activities for the year ended December 31, 19X5.

Problem 19-6. The following nominal accounts were extracted from the December 31, 19X5 adjusted trial balance of Downs Private Hospital:

Gross patient service revenue		$11,049,200
Research grant revenue to the extent expended		361,000
Revenue from sale of cafeteria meals to guests and employees		108,000
Donated services of nurses and physicians (skilled services otherwise purchased)		145,000
Unrestricted gifts and grants		100,200
Unrestricted endowment income		12,000
Gifts restricted for equipment purchase		540,000
Donor-restricted investments for permanent endowment		150,000
Temporarily restricted endowment income		25,000
Revenue from parking lot		31,000
Revenue from vending machines		68,000
Income on investments whose use is limited by the board for capital improvements		207,000
Contributions restricted by donor for pediatric unit operations		225,000
Reclassifications In—unrestricted—satisfaction of program restrictions		125,000
Reclassifications In—unrestricted—satisfaction of plant acquisition restrictions		220,000
Unrestricted net assets, 1/1/X5		625,000
Temporarily restricted net assets, 1/1/X5		825,000
Permanently restricted net assets, 1/1/X5		2,350,000
Reclassifications Out—temporarily restricted—satisfaction of program restrictions	125,000	
Reclassifications Out—temporarily restricted—satisfaction of plant acquisition restrictions	220,000	
Administrative services (including $30,000 malpractice cost)	112,500	
Contractual adjustments under third-party reimbursement programs	1,328,500	
Charity Care	215,000	
Provision for uncollectibles	341,600	
Nursing services (including $125,000 in pediatric unit)	6,589,100	
Dietary services	1,511,200	
Maintenance services	838,300	
Depreciation and amortization	478,200	
Interest expense	142,200	
Loss on sale of endowment investments	5,300	

Required:

Prepare a statement of activities for the year ended December 31, 19X5.

Problem 19-7. You are provided with a summarized version of the cash account of Lakeside Hospital, a not-for-profit organization. Prepare a statement of cash flows, using the direct method, for the year ended December 31, 19X6.

Cash Account

	Debit	Credit
Cash balance, January 1, 19X6............................	275,900	
Cash received from: Patients..............................	2,061,900	
Third-party payors....................	6,500,000	
Operation of gift shop................	517,700	
Unrestricted gifts	323,500	
Contributions restricted for endowment	500,000	
Donor-restricted contributions for purchase of property and		
equipment..	183,000	
Early repayment of long-term debt		242,300
Cash paid to: Employees		1,151,000
Suppliers		6,200,000
Providers of consultation services.............		800,000
Bank for interest		147,000
Contractor for purchase of property and		
equipment		501,200
Cash balance, December 31, 19X6........................	$1,320,500	

Problem 19-8. Using data from Problem 19-7 and the following additional information, prepare a reconciliation of change in net assets to net cash provided by operating activities that would accompany Lakeside Hospital's statement of cash flows for the year ended December 31, 19X6.

The following condensed statement of activities for the year ended December 31, 19X6, shows:

Total operating revenues	$9,302,400
Total operating expenses....................	8,780,100
Income from operations.....................	$ 522,300
Nonoperating revenue	1,024,000
Excess of revenues over expenses............	$1,546,300

Included in the condensed statement of activities were:

Depreciation and amortization	$ 432,500
Noncash gifts and bequests	17,500
Increase in expense and liability for	
estimated malpractice costs	12,300

An analysis of comparative balance sheet items showed the following changes in balances during 19X6:

Increase in patient accounts receivable........	$ 227,400
Decrease in supplies inventory...............	11,800
Increase in accounts payable	30,100

Problem 19-9. Carolina Hospital's postclosing trial balance at December 31, 19X6, is as follows:

Cash...	$ 370,000	
Investment in U.S. Treasury Bills.........................	400,000	
Investment in Corporate Bonds	500,000	
Interest Receivable	10,000	
Accounts Receivable.....................................	50,000	
Inventory...	30,000	
Land..	100,000	
Building..	800,000	
Equipment	170,000	
Allowance for Depreciation..............................		$ 410,000
Accounts Payable		30,000
Notes Payable		370,000
Permanently Restricted Net Assets		520,000
Unrestricted Net Assets..................................		1,100,000
	$2,430,000	$2,430,000

Carolina, which is a not-for-profit hospital, did not maintain its books using hospital fund accounting. Effective January 1, 19X7, Carolina's board of trustees voted to adjust the December 31, 19X6 general ledger balances and to establish separate funds for the general funds, the endowment fund, and the plant replacement and expansion fund for internal control.

An audit of Carolina's accounts revealed several required adjustments:

(a) Investment in Corporate Bonds pertains to the amount required to be accumulated under a board policy to invest cash equal to accumulated depreciation until the funds are needed for asset replacement. The $500,000 balance at December 31, 19X6, is less than the full amount required because of errors in computation of building depreciation for past years. Included in the allowance for depreciation is a correctly computed amount of $90,000 applicable to equipment purchased with cash donated for that purpose. The hospital elects to release donor restrictions over the useful life of the fixed assets.

(b) Permanently Restricted Net Assets has been credited with the following:

Donor's bequest of cash	$350,000
Gain on sales of securities	50,000
Interest and dividends earned in	
19X4, 19X5, and 19X6—Unrestricted.........	120,000
Total...................................	$520,000

The terms of the bequest specify that the principal, plus all gains on sales of investments, are to remain fully invested in U.S. government or corporate securities. At December 31, 19X6, $400,000 was invested in U.S. Treasury bills. The bequest further specifies that interest and dividends earned on investments are to be used for payment of current operating expenses.

(c) Land comprises the following:

Donation of land 40 years ago, at	
appraised value (land is unrestricted).........	$ 45,000
Appreciation in value of land as determined by	
an independent appraiser 5 years ago........	55,000
Total...................................	$100,000

(d) Building comprises the following:

$$
\begin{array}{lr}
\text{Hospital building completed 40 years ago} & \\
\quad \text{when operations were started (useful life of 50} & \\
\quad \text{years), at cost.\dots\dots\dots\dots\dots\dots\dots\dots} & \$720{,}000 \\
\text{Installation of elevator 20 years ago (estimated} & \\
\quad \text{useful life of 20 years), at cost \dots\dots\dots\dots} & \underline{80{,}000} \\
\qquad\qquad \text{Total\dots\dots\dots\dots\dots\dots\dots\dots\dots} & \underline{\underline{\$800{,}000}}
\end{array}
$$

(e) A fund drive was conducted in 19X6 to offset a possible operating loss. As of December 31, 19X6, there were unrecorded unconditional pledges of $121,000, of which 90% are likely to be collected. $75,000 of these pledges are unrestricted; the remaining $46,000 are donor restricted for cancer research.

(f) $100,000 of the current cash balance is donor restricted for new equipment acquisition.

Required:

Enter the postclosing trial balance on a worksheet. Use the following columnar headings with a debit and credit column for each: Trial Balance, Adjustments, General Funds, Endowment Fund, and Plant Replacement and Expansion Fund.

Enter the adjustments necessary to restate the general ledger account balances properly. Distribute the adjusted balances to establish the separate fund accounts, and complete the worksheet. Formal journal entries are not required, but supporting computations should be referenced to the worksheet adjustments.

(AICPA adapted)

Problem 19-10. Carleton Agency, a VHWO, conducts two programs: Medical Services Program and Community Information Services Program. It had the following transactions during the year ended June 30, 19X9:

(1) Received the following contributions:

Unrestricted pledges.\dots\dots\dots\dots\dots\dots\dots\dots\dots\dots\dots\dots\dots\dots	$800,000
Restricted cash.\dots\dots\dots\dots\dots\dots\dots\dots\dots\dots\dots\dots\dots\dots	95,000
Building fund pledges.\dots\dots\dots\dots\dots\dots\dots\dots\dots\dots\dots\dots\dots	50,000
Endowment fund cash\dots\dots\dots\dots\dots\dots\dots\dots\dots\dots\dots\dots\dots	1,000

(2) Collected the following pledges:

Unrestricted\dots\dots\dots\dots\dots\dots\dots\dots\dots\dots\dots\dots\dots\dots\dots	$450,000
Building fund\dots\dots\dots\dots\dots\dots\dots\dots\dots\dots\dots\dots\dots\dots\dots	20,000

(3) Received the following unrestricted cash flows from:

Theater party (net of direct costs)\dots\dots\dots\dots\dots\dots\dots\dots\dots\dots	$ 12,000
Bequests\dots\dots\dots\dots\dots\dots\dots\dots\dots\dots\dots\dots\dots\dots\dots\dots	10,000
Membership dues\dots\dots\dots\dots\dots\dots\dots\dots\dots\dots\dots\dots\dots\dots	8,000
Interest and dividends\dots\dots\dots\dots\dots\dots\dots\dots\dots\dots\dots\dots\dots	5,000

(4) Program expenses incurred (processed through vouchers payable):

Medical services\dots\dots\dots\dots\dots\dots\dots\dots\dots\dots\dots\dots\dots\dots	$ 60,000
Community information services.\dots\dots\dots\dots\dots\dots\dots\dots\dots\dots	15,000

(5) Services expenses incurred (processed through vouchers payable):

General administration.\dots\dots\dots\dots\dots\dots\dots\dots\dots\dots\dots\dots\dots	$150,000
Fund raising\dots\dots\dots\dots\dots\dots\dots\dots\dots\dots\dots\dots\dots\dots\dots	200,000

(6) Purchased fixed assets:

Fixed assets purchased with donor-restricted cash . . . . $ 18,000

Carleton's policy is to release donor restrictions when assets are placed in service.

(7) Depreciation of all buildings and equipment in the land, buildings, and equipment fund was allocated as follows:

Medical services program . . . . $ 4,000
Community information services program   3,000
General administration.   6,000
Fund raising   2,000

(8) Vouchers paid:

Paid vouchers payable $330,000

(AICPA adapted)

Required:

Record journal entries for the preceding transactions. Number your journal entries to coincide with the preceding transaction numbers.

Problem 19-11. The Super Senior Agency is a VHWO. The following events occurred during the year. The agency uses one control account for its fixed assets, with supporting subsidiary records.

(a) Property was purchased for $200,000. A down payment of $40,000 was made from unrestricted cash and a 14% mortgage was signed for the remainder.

(b) Office furniture was purchased for $9,000 on open account.

(c) A local corporation donated and installed room partitions. The value of the donated items and services was $4,000. Super Senior's policy is to release donor restrictions over the useful life of the assets to match depreciation expense.

(d) At year end, a payment was made covering mortgage interest for one year, plus a $10,000 payment on the principal.

(e) Office equipment costing $3,000, with a book value of $1,000, was sold for $1,800 cash. The gain is unrestricted.

(f) Fully depreciated equipment costing $7,000 was written off. There was no scrap value.

(g) A depreciation schedule was prepared, showing annual depreciation expense of $46,000, which was recorded. Depreciation of $20,000 was for equipment donated or purchased with donated cash.

(h) Two years ago, the will of an agency volunteer granted $50,000 for the acquisition and installation of theater equipment, providing the organization acquired a new building. The amount now was expended in accordance with the stipulations of the will, and payment of $50,000 was made.

(i) The account payable of $9,000 mentioned in item (b) was paid.

Required:

Prepare journal entries to record the preceding events.

Problem 19-12. The June 30, 19X6 adjusted trial balances of the Bloomfield Community Association for Handicapped Children follow. This association is a voluntary welfare organization.

Bayfield Community Association for Handicapped Children
Adjusted Current Funds Trial Balances
June 30, 19X6

	Unrestricted		Restricted	
Cash....................................	11,000		29,000	
Bequest Receivable.......................			5,000	
Pledges Receivable.......................	12,000			
Accrued Interest Receivable	1,000			
Investments (at cost, which approximates market)...............................	140,000			
Endowment Investments...................			250,000	
Accounts Payable and Accrued Expenses ...		50,000		1,000
Refundable Deposits......................		2,000		
Allowance for Uncollectible Pledges........		3,000		
Net Assets, July 1, 19X5:				
Designated, Unrestricted.................		12,000		
Undesignated, Unrestricted..............		26,000		
Temporarily Restricted				3,000
Permanently Restricted				250,000
Endowment Revenue—Temporarily Restricted				20,000
Contributions		300,000		15,000
Membership Dues........................		25,000		
Program Service Fees....................		30,000		
Investment Income		10,000		
Auction Proceeds........................		42,000		
Auction Expenses	11,000			
Deaf Children's Program	120,000			
Blind Children's Program.................	150,000			
Management and General Services	49,000			
Fund-Raising Services	9,000			
Provision for Uncollectible Pledges.........	2,000			
Reclassification In—Satisfaction of Program Restrictions............................		5,000		
Reclassification Out—Satisfaction of Program Restrictions			5,000	
	505,000	505,000	289,000	289,000

Required:

(1) Prepare a statement of activities for the year ended June 30, 19X6. *p. 1093*

(2) Prepare a statement of financial position as of June 30, 19X6. *p. 1092*

(AICPA adapted)

Problem 19-13. Thirty years ago, a group of civic-minded merchants in Mayfair organized the "Committee of 100" for the purpose of establishing the Mayfair Sports Club, a not-for-profit sports organization for local youth. Each of the Committee's 100 members contributed $1,000 toward the Club's capital. In addition, each participant agreed to pay dues of $200 a year for the Club's operations. All dues have been collected in full by the end of each fiscal year, which ends on March 31. Members who have discontinued their participation have been replaced by an equal number of new members by transferring the participation certificates from the former members to the new ones. Following are the Club's trial balances at April 1, 19X2:

	Debit	Credit
Cash...	29,000	
Investments (at market, equal to cost)......................	88,000	
Inventories...	5,000	
Land..	10,000	
Building..	164,000	
Accumulated Depreciation—Building..........................		130,000
Furniture and Equipment...................................	54,000	
Accumulated Depreciation—Furniture and Equipment...........		46,000
Endowment Investments....................................	400,000	
Accounts Payable...		10,000
Participation Certificates (100 @ $1,000)....................		100,000
Unrestricted Net Assets...................................		12,000
Temporarily Restricted Net Assets..........................		52,000
Permanently Restricted Net Assets..........................		400,000
Totals...	750,000	750,000

Transactions and adjustment data for the year ended March 31, 19X3, are as follows:

(a) Collections from participants for dues totaled $20,000.
(b) Snack bar and soda fountain sales amounted to $31,000.
(c) Interest and dividends totaling $6,000 were received. This investment income is unrestricted.
(d) The following additions were made to the voucher register:

House expense	$17,000
Snack bar and soda fountain	26,000
General and administrative....................	11,000

(e) Vouchers totaling $55,000 were paid.
(f) Assessments for capital improvements not yet incurred totaled $10,000. The assessments were made on March 20, 19X3, and were to be collected during the year ending March 31, 19X5.
(g) An unrestricted bequest of $5,000 was received.
(h) Investments are valued at market, which amounted to $95,000 at March 31, 19X3. There were no investment transactions during the year.
(i) Depreciation for the year is as follows:

| Building...................................... | $4,000 |
| Furniture and equipment...................... | 8,000 |

Depreciation is allocated to:

House expense	$9,000
Snack bar and soda fountain	2,000
General and administrative....................	1,000

(j) The actual physical inventory, which was $1,000 at March 31, 19X3, pertains to the snack bar and fountain.
(k) A donor contributed $10,000 to be used to acquire land for expansion.
(l) An unconditional pledge of $100,000 to be permanently restricted is received. Income is to be used to maintain the building.

Required:
(1) Prepare entries for each of the above transactions.
(2) Prepare the statement of activities for the year ended March 31, 19X3.

(AICPA adapted)

Problem 19-14. The Caring Clinic, a VHWO, conducts two programs: Alcohol and Drug Abuse and Outreach to Teens. It has the typical supporting services of management and fund raising. Expense accounts from the preallocation trial balances as of December 31, 19X6 are as follows:

	Funded by Unrestricted Resources	Funded by Donor-Restricted Resources	Total
Salaries and Payroll Taxes	63,000	23,000	86,000
Telephone and Miscellaneous Expenses.	10,000	2,000	12,000
Nursing and Medical Fees	70,000	50,000	120,000
Educational Seminars Expense.	46,000	20,000	66,000
Research Expense	137,000	16,000	153,000
Medical Supplies Expense	65,000	22,000	87,000
Rent Expense		10,000	10,000
Interest Expense on Equipment Mortgage.	4,000		4,000
Depreciation Expense.		20,000	20,000
Provision for Uncollectible Pledges	26,000		26,000
	421,000	163,000	584,000

In preparation for the allocation of expenses to programs and supporting services, a study was conducted to determine an equitable manner for assigning each expense. The study resulted in the following table for percentage allocations.

Percentage of Allocations

	Programs		Supporting Services	
Expenses to Be Allocated	Alcohol and Drug Abuse	Outreach to Teens	Management	Fund Raising
All expenses (other than depreciation) financed by donor-restricted contributions	60%	40%		
Expenses financed by unrestricted resources:				
Salaries and payroll taxes	30	20	30%	20%
Telephone and miscellaneous.	20	20	15	45
Nursing and medical fees.	70	30		
Educational seminars	30	60		10
Research	60	40		
Medical supplies.	90	10		
Equipment-related expenses:				
Interest	50	10	30	10
Depreciation	50	10	30	10

Required:
(1) Using a total of allocable expenses financed by donor-restricted resources, prepare a journal entry to assign those expenses to the programs.
(2) With the following format, prepare a schedule to show the assignment of the allocable expenses financed by unrestricted resources to the various programs and supporting services, using the percentages provided by the problem:

Caring Clinic
Allocation of Expenses
For Year Ended December 31, 19X6

		Programs		Supporting Services	
Expense Allocated	Total Amount	Alcohol and Drug Abuse	Outreach to Teens	Manage- ment	Fund Raising

(3) Using the schedule from requirement (2), prepare a journal entry to record the allocation and closing of expenses financed by unrestricted resources.

(4) Prepare a journal entry to assign plant-related expenses to programs and support services.

Problem 19-15. The Caring Clinic, a VHWO, conducts two programs: Alcohol and Drug Abuse and Outreach to Teens. It has the typical supporting services of management and fund raising. The condensed trial balances after allocable expenses have been assigned are presented as follows:

Caring Clinic
Condensed Postallocation Trial Balances
December 31, 19X6

Debits

Assets.	716,000
Endowment Assets	256,000
Alcohol and Drug Abuse Program	322,200
Outreach to Teens Program.	184,100
Management and General Services.	27,600
Fund-Raising Services	50,100
Cost of Special Events.	18,000
Reclassification Out—Temporarily Restricted—Satisfaction of Program Restrictions.	143,000
Reclassification Out—Temporarily Restricted—Satisfaction of Equipment Acquisition Restrictions	20,000
Totals	1,737,000

Credits

Liabilities	179,000
Unrestricted Net Assets	202,000
Temporarily Restricted Net Assets	196,000
Permanently Restricted Net Assets	201,000
Contributions—Unrestricted	407,000
Contributions—Temporarily Restricted.	254,000
Special Events Support—Temporarily Restricted	48,000
Legacies and Bequests—Permanently Restricted.	30,000
Investment Revenue—Unrestricted.	13,000
Investment Revenue—Temporarily Restricted.	11,000
Gain on Sale of Investments—Temporarily Restricted.	8,000
Gain on Sale of Investments—Permanently Restricted	25,000
Reclassification In—Unrestricted—Satisfaction of Program Restrictions. . . .	143,000
Reclassification In—Unrestricted—Satisfaction of Equipment Acquisition Restrictions	20,000
Totals	1,737,000

Required:
(1) Prepare a statement of activities in the format shown in Illustration 19-3 on page 1054.
(2) Prepare closing entries for each net asset classification.

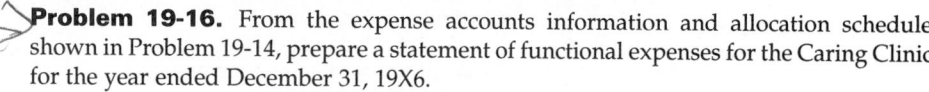

Problem 19-16. From the expense accounts information and allocation schedule shown in Problem 19-14, prepare a statement of functional expenses for the Caring Clinic for the year ended December 31, 19X6.

APPENDIX PROBLEMS

Problem 19A-1. During the calendar year 19X6, the following events occurred at Brown Hospital, a voluntary hospital:

(a) Gross charges for hospital services were debited to Accounts Receivable. The hospital controller wishes to use separate revenue accounts for:

Room and board charges.....................	$800,000
Charges for other professional services.........	300,000
Other nursing services	150,000

(b) Estimated deductions from gross billings were as follows:

Contractual adjustments.....................	$ 60,000
Charity services.............................	18,000
Provision for uncollectible receivables..........	30,000

The accounting system uses a single allowance account.

(c) Charity services accounts receivable of $15,000 were written off.
(d) During the year, the following contributions were received:

From W. Brown for future acquisition of a new X-ray machine	$ 30,000
From J. Sago for an emergency fund to be used if special assistance for burn care services is required	60,000
From various sources, with no restrictions as to use	79,000

(e) Unrestricted investment earnings from endowments totaling $23,000 have been earned and collected.
(f) A new X-ray machine costing $35,000 is acquired with donor-restricted resources. The invoice was vouchered. Brown's policy is to release donor restrictions upon asset acquisition.
(g) The old X-ray machine is sold for $8,000. It cost $27,000 and had a book value of $7,000 when sold. The gain is unrestricted.
(h) The following data are provided regarding accounts receivable collections:

Gross billings................................	$980,000
Less: Contractual adjustments.................	35,000
Uncollectible accounts written off.........	10,000
Cash collected..............................	$935,000

Cash collected includes reimbursement by third-party payors for depreciation of $63,000, which must be accumulated to update facilities.

(i) Vouchers totaling $1,210,000 were issued for the following items:

Administrative services expense...............	$130,000
Fiscal services expense.......................	104,000
General services expense.....................	225,000
Nursing services expense.....................	520,000
Other professional services expense	165,000
Supplies (perpetual inventory is used)..........	60,000
Expenses accrued at December 31, 19X5	6,000

(j) Cash payments on vouchers payable during the year were $925,000.

(k) Supplies of $37,000 were issued to nursing services.

(l) Investments earned $7,000, all of which was received. Earnings are restricted for plant expansion.

(m) Depreciation for the year amounts to $160,000.

(n) Included in the vouchered items was a bill for burn care services of $15,000.

(o) A payment of $27,000 is made, covering $15,000 of mortgage bonds retired at face value and $12,000 for the annual interest. The hospital records interest as part of Administrative Services Expense.

(p) Endowment investments costing $50,000 were sold for $61,000. Gains are unrestricted.

Required:

Prepare journal entries to record events, using the following format:

Event	Fund	Journal Entry
(a)		

Problem 19A-2. Using the data from Problem 19A-1, prepare a statement of activities for Brown Hospital for the year ended December 31, 19X6.

Problem 19A-3. Listed are five independent transactions or events that relate to a local government and to a VHWO:

(a) $30,000 was disbursed from the general fund (or its equivalent) for the cash purchase of new equipment.

(b) An unrestricted cash gift of $100,000 was received from a donor.

(c) A cash gift of $40,000 was received. The use of the funds was restricted to purchase life-saving equipment. $15,000 was used to purchase qualifying equipment.

(d) Listed common stocks with a total carrying value of $50,000 were sold by an endowment fund for $55,000 before any dividends were earned on these stocks.

(e) $1,000,000 (face amount) of general obligation bonds payable were sold at par, with the proceeds required to be used solely for construction of a new building. This building was completed at a total cost of $1,000,000, and the total amount of bond issue proceeds was disbursed in payment.

Required:

(1) For each of the listed transactions or events, prepare journal entries, without explanations, specifying the affected funds and account groups and showing how these transactions or events should be recorded by a local government whose debt is serviced by general tax revenues.

(2) For each of the listed transactions or events, prepare journal entries, without explanations, specifying the affected funds and showing how these transactions or events should be recorded by a VHWO that maintains a separate plant fund.

(AICPA adapted)

Problem 19A-4. The Caring Clinic, a VHWO, conducts two programs: Alcohol and Drug Abuse and Outreach to Teens. It has the typical supporting services of management and fund raising. The trial balances of its various funds as of January 1, 19X6, are as shown.

Debits	Unrestricted Current Fund	Restricted Current Fund	Plant Fund	Endowment Fund	Total
Cash	$ 31,000	$ 5,000	$ 12,000	$ 1,000	$ 49,000
Investments.	120,000	23,000	45,000	200,000	388,000
Accrued Investment Revenue	6,000				6,000
Pledges Receivable	45,000				45,000
Grants Receivable	16,000				16,000
Inventories of Educational Materials	11,000				11,000
Inventories of Medical Supplies	12,000				12,000
Land, Building, and Equipment.			173,000		173,000
Total	$241,000	$28,000	$230,000	$201,000	$700,000

Credits					
Allowance for Uncollectible Pledges	$ 9,000				$ 9,000
Accumulated Depreciation.			$ 22,000		22,000
Accounts Payable.	14,000				14,000
State Grants Refundable	16,000				16,000
10% Mortgage Payable.			40,000		40,000
Unrestricted Net Assets—Undesignated	112,000		70,000		182,000
Unrestricted Net Assets—Designated					
for Research	50,000				50,000
Temporarily Restricted Net Assets	40,000	$28,000	98,000		166,000
Permanently Restricted Net Assets				$201,000	201,000
Total	$241,000	$28,000	$230,000	$201,000	$700,000

During 19X6, the following events related to the clinic occurred. To minimize repetition, similar events for the year are combined.

		Unrestricted	Restricted
(a)	Contribution pledges received	$396,000	$162,000
(b)	Estimated uncollectible pledges	20,000	6,000
(c)	Cash collected on pledges	380,000	148,000
	Pledges written off as uncollectible.	18,000	5,000
(d)	Investment revenue received (including accrued) . . .	9,000	1,000
(e)	Items paid:		
	Accounts payable as of January 1, 19X6.	14,000	
	Salaries and payroll taxes.	60,000	23,000
	Rent expense.		10,000
	Telephone and miscellaneous expenses	10,000	2,000
	Nursing and medical fees	70,000	50,000
	Educational seminars expense	38,000	20,000
	Research expense.	137,000	16,000
	Medical supplies (perpetual inventory is used) . . .	71,000	29,000

(f) The residence of a leading citizen was bequeathed in a will to the clinic. After the person's death, it was found that the building was not suitable for clinical use, and it would be sold as soon as possible. The residence was appraised at $92,000. The will stipulated that proceeds from the sale must be used to expand the clinic building. The will also provided $30,000 in cash to create a fund, the revenue from which must be devoted to an alcohol abuse program.

(g) During the year, a dinner was held to raise additional funds for the clinic building. Gross cash proceeds were $48,000, of which $18,000 was paid for direct costs.

(h) Bids for construction of a wing for the clinic building were sought. The contract was let at a cost of $250,000. The residence received from the citizen was sold for $100,000, which was used as a partial payment on the contract, along with the net proceeds from the dinner mentioned in (g). The wing was completed. A 12%, 20-year mortgage was signed for the remaining $120,000. Caring's policy is to release donor restrictions over the life of the fixed asset to match depreciation.

(i) A grant of $16,000 from the state government, awarded last year for a special drug abuse program, was received. The item originally was recorded as a grant receivable.

(j) At year end, a physical inventory shows $3,000 of educational materials and $18,000 of medical supplies in the unrestricted fund and $7,000 of medical supplies in the restricted fund.

(k) Annual depreciation amounts to $20,000. $10,000 depreciation was for temporarily restricted assets.

(l) A payment of $5,000 was made against the 10% mortgage payable, and a payment of $4,000 for interest was made.

(m) Plant fund investment revenue was $4,000, of which $3,000 was received. Revenue must be used for plant purposes.

(n) Endowment fund investment revenue received amounted to $16,000. There is no restriction on $10,000 of the revenue. The remaining $6,000 must be devoted to alcohol abuse programs. Items are entered directly in recipient funds.

(o) $11,000 of the contributions restricted for future periods in the Restricted Current Fund became available.

(p) The board of directors has decided to increase the Fund Balance Designated for Research from $50,000 to $90,000.

(q) Unpaid and unrecorded items in the unrestricted fund on December 31, 19X6, consist of $3,000 for accrued salaries and $10,000 for previously distributed educational brochures.

(r) Endowment fund investments costing $40,000 were sold for $65,000. The gain is unrestricted.

Required:

(1) Prepare journal entries to record the events, using the following format:

Event	Fund	Journal Entry
(a)		

(2) Prepare preallocation trial balances, reflecting balances immediately after the preceding entries are posted, in the same format as the trial balances at the beginning of the problem.

PART 6

Fiduciary Accounting

Protecting and preserving an individual's estate has become a very important and complex area in which accountants frequently are involved. Special estate tax and accounting considerations are necessary in order to properly protect and administer an estate. The gifting of personal assets and the creation of trusts are important devices to be used in estate planning.

Unlike individuals, corporations are assumed to have an unlimited life, and the going concern assumption is reflected in the accounting for corporations. However, due to a variety of factors, a corporation's existence may be threatened and management must seek ways to correct the situation or face liquidation. Corrective actions often include debt restructuring or corporate reorganizations. If these actions are not successful, a corporation may be liquidated. Corporate reorganizations and liquidations are subject to legal requirements which must be understood by today's practicing accountants.

CHAPTER 20

Estates and Trusts: Their Nature and the Accountant's Role

This chapter examines the basic nature of estates and trusts and how the practicing accountant may be involved. There is a tremendous amount of complexity surrounding the legal and tax aspects of estates and trusts; therefore, this chapter provides only a broad overview.

An estate consists of the net assets of an individual at the time of his/her death. Until these net assets are completely distributed or consumed, the estate also exists as a separate, distinct entity that is governed, managed, and accounted for. Often the net assets of an estate are distributed to a trust, which also is a separate, distinct entity. The trust is an arrangement whereby assets are protected, conserved, and/or distributed by a trustee according to the terms of the trust agreement. Persons who are responsible for the management of the net assets of an estate or trust have a fiduciary responsibility. These persons, called fiduciaries, are held accountable by law and are required to prepare specialized reports that account for their actions. The role of the accountant in the preparation of these reports is discussed in this chapter.

THE ROLE OF ESTATE PLANNING

Estate planning has a primary goal of reflecting the desires of the deceased individual, referred to as the *decedent*. Obviously, such planning can become extremely complex since the circumstances and desires of each individual differ. As the net assets of an estate increase in value and nature, so does the complexity of the necessary estate planning. Many attorneys and accountants specialize in estate planning, which requires special knowledge of law, taxation, and accounting.

As the complexity of an estate increases, so do the goals of estate planning, which should include the following:

1. Discover and clearly communicate the desires and wishes of the decedent.
2. Insure that the estate is administered or managed properly in order to satisfy the desires and wishes of the decedent.
3. Maximize the economic value of the estate's net assets.
4. Minimize the taxes that may be assessed against the assets and income of the estate.
5. Define the necessary liquidity of the estate's assets so that desired conveyances and distributions may be achieved.
6. Provide a proper and timely accounting of the activities of the estate and its fiduciary.

COMMUNICATING THROUGH A WILL

Obviously, a deceased individual is not available to directly communicate his/ her intentions regarding the estate. Therefore, it is critical that prior to death the person communicate through the creation of a valid *will*, a legal declaration containing directions as to the disposition of property. When an individual dies having left a will, the decedent is said to have died *testate*. The will must be presented to a *probate* court, which determines the validity of the will and identifies the fiduciary responsible for administering the will. Generally, probate law is developed by each state; therefore, it may vary significantly throughout the U.S. While the Uniform Probate Code does exist, its adoption by states has been very limited.

A fiduciary responsible for the administration of a will may be named or nominated in the will. This person is referred to as an *executor* and, assuming he/she is able and has the desire to serve, normally will be confirmed by the probate court. If the will does not name an executor or the executor is unable to serve, the court will appoint a party referred to as an *administrator*. Once the will has been probated, the decedent's assets are managed by the fiduciary subject to the oversight or control of the court.

If a decedent has no will or an invalid will, the person is said to have died *intestate*. In this situation the probate court appoints an *administrator* and distributes the net assets of the estate according to state inheritance laws.

IDENTIFYING THE PRINCIPAL OR CORPUS OF AN ESTATE

One of the first responsibilities of the fiduciary of an estate is to identify the assets of the estate. These assets vary in nature and must be measured at their fair market value. The value of certain assets, such as publicly traded securities, is determined with relative ease while other assets, such as an interest in a closely held business, require independent appraisals.

The assets of the estate are referred to as the principal or corpus of the estate. In identifying the principal the fiduciary must identify those assets that were the legal property of the decedent at the time of death. Therefore, the assets will include accrued items such as interest and rents. Items frequently comprising the estate principal include the following:

1. Cash on hand and in bank accounts.
2. Investments such as stocks, bonds, mutual funds, retirement accounts, and money market funds.

3. Accrued interest and declared dividends on the above investments as of the decedent's death.
4. Capital interests in businesses, such as closely held corporations, partnerships, and/or sole proprietorships.
5. Life insurance proceeds that name the decedent's estate as the beneficiary.
6. Investments in real estate, including accrued rents at the date of the decedent's death.
7. Intangible assets, such as patents and royalties including related accrued income at the date of the decedent's death.
8. Loans or notes receivable, including accrued interest at the date of the decedent's death.
9. Unpaid wages and other forms of earned income accruing to the decedent at the date of the decedent's death.
10. Personal valuables, including furniture, fixtures, jewelry, vehicles, boats, and collectible items such as coins, stamps, and artwork.

It is important to note that the preceding inventory of the principal is not reduced by the liabilities of the decedent. These obligations are recognized when they are paid or satisfied through the distribution of estate principal.

Often, it is not possible for the fiduciary to identify all of the assets of an estate initially. Those assets that are discovered subsequently must be included ultimately in the estate principal.

Exempt Property and Special Allowances.   Some state probate laws exempt certain real property from the estate principal. These assets pass directly to the designated beneficiary or joint tenant. Other assets of the decedent are not included in the estate principal by way of a *homestead allowance* and a *family allowance* and, therefore, are exempt from the probate process. Most states provide for the allowances that are described in Uniform Probate Code as follows:

> *A surviving spouse of a decedent . . . is entitled to a homestead allowance of $5,000. If there is no surviving spouse, each minor child and each dependent child of the decedent is entitled to a homestead allowance amounting to $5,000 divided by the number of minor and dependent children of the decedent.*[1]

> *. . . the surviving spouse and minor children whom the decedent was obligated to support . . . are entitled to a reasonable allowance in money out of the estate for their maintenance during the period of administration.*[2]

The family allowance consists of intimate objects of the deceased and an amount of cash or productive property to provide funds for the surviving family until matters are settled. What constitutes a "reasonable allowance" depends upon the circumstances in each case, but the fiduciary may not grant more than $500 per month for one year. If a greater allowance is deemed necessary, a special court order must be obtained.

---

[1]*Uniform Probate Code (U.L.A.)* (St. Paul, MN: West Publishing Company, 1974), Sec. 2-401.
[2]*Ibid.*, Sec. 2-403.

Accounting for the Inventory of an Estate.   After the special exemptions and allowances for estate assets have been provided for, the fiduciary must file a report with the probate court identifying the estate principal, which consists of the initial assets transferred to the estate as well as those assets subsequently discovered. An initial accounting of the estate principal requires an entry debiting the various assets and crediting an estate principal account.

In order to demonstrate the initial accounting for estate principal, assume Jane Jacoby died on June 1, 19X7. Jane Jacoby's will names her attorney Howard Wells as executor of the estate. Through special exemptions and allowances, Jane Jacoby's residence, $2,000 cash, clothing, and furniture passed to her husband Walter Jacoby. Life insurance proceeds of $50,000 also were paid to the beneficiary Robert Williams, Jane Jacoby's son from a prior marriage. The remaining assets of the estate are subject to probate and are recorded as follows:

Principal Cash	81,000	
Investment in XYZ Stock	744,000	
Declared Dividend on XYZ Stock	3,000	
Investment in J&D Partnership	155,000	
Automobile	15,000	
Wages Receivable	2,000	
Estate Principal		1,000,000

An investment in Apex bonds valued at $20,000 along with accrued interest of $1,000 was discovered subsequently and is recorded as follows:

Investment in Apex Bonds	20,000	
Accrued Interest	1,000	
Estate Principal: Assets Subsequently Discovered		21,000

After recording the inventory of the estate principal, the fiduciary would submit a listing of the inventory to the probate court.

Subsequent to the initial recording of the inventory, sales or other dispositions of the assets may occur. Gains on such transactions increase the estate principal, while losses reduce principal. Continuing the above examples for the estate of Jane Jacoby, the following entries account for the sale of estate assets:

Principal Cash	165,000	
Investment in J&D Partnership		155,000
Gain on Realization of Principal Asset		10,000
Principal Cash	19,500	
Loss on Realization of Principal Asset	1,500	
Investment in Apex Bonds		20,000
Accrued Interest		1,000
Principal Cash	5,000	
Wages Receivable		2,000
Declared Dividend on XYZ Stock		3,000

IDENTIFYING CLAIMS AGAINST THE ESTATE

The discovery and identification of claims against the decedent's estate is of equal importance to the discovery and identification of estate principal. Notification of the decedent's death is required by law and valid claims must be identified within a prescribed period of time. The fiduciary must evaluate the validity of claims and place them in an order of priority for payment purposes. Claims accruing to the date of death are charged against estate principal, and the following order of priority generally is observed:

1. Claims having a special lien against property, but not to exceed the value of the property.
2. Funeral and administrative expenses.
3. Taxes: income, estate, and inheritance.
4. Debts due the United States and various states.
5. Judgments of any court of competent jurisdiction.
6. Wages due domestic servants for a period of not more than one year prior to date of death and medical claims for the same period.
7. All other claims.

Within a class, each claim is satisfied on a pro rata basis if funds are inadequate to accomplish total payment for that class.

The following claims against the estate of Jane Jacoby are accounted for as follows:

Funeral Expenses	5,000	
Administrative Expenses	3,000	
Debts of Decedent Paid	23,000	
Medical Expenses	7,000	
Principal Cash		38,000

TAX IMPLICATIONS OF AN ESTATE

A major claim against the assets of an estate may result from the imposition of a federal estate tax and a state inheritance tax. Minimizing the taxes imposed on an estate is a very complex topic and prudent estate tax planning should address the following considerations:

1. Maximizing benefits of the marital deduction.
2. Making gifts during one's lifetime.
3. Taking actions to accomplish a step-up in property basis.
4. Taking actions to benefit from a loss in property values.
5. Maneuvering with charitable deductions.
6. Planning estate liquidity.

To be protected, an estate must have a certain amount of liquid assets to pay death taxes and the probate costs of establishing the validity of the will. Otherwise, a forced sale of estate assets might result. Some form of insurance often is recommended to provide liquidity and flexibility.

FEDERAL ESTATE TAXATION

Significant changes regarding gratuitous transfers of property resulted from the *Tax Reform Act of 1976*. Prior to its enactment, transfers of property during the owner's lifetime were subject to the federal gift tax, while property passing as a result of death was subject to the federal estate tax. The rules and rates for these taxes were different. Most of the distinction was removed by the Tax Reform Act, which substituted a unified transfer tax, commonly referred to as the *federal estate tax*, for life and death transfers made after 1976.

The computation of the federal estate tax may be summarized as follows:

Gross estate	XX
Less deductions allowed	– XX
Taxable estate	XX
Add post-1976 taxable gifts	+ XX
Tax base	XX
Tentative tax on total transfers	XX
Less tax credits	– XX
Estate tax due	XX

[handwritten margin note: the estate FMV owned by the deceased]

The starting point for the computation of the federal estate tax is the determination of the gross estate, which includes the fair market value of property owned by the decedent at date of death, regardless of the nature of the property. Whether it is real or personal, tangible or intangible, business or nonbusiness, the property is includable. Then, the taxable estate is determined by subtracting the total of the following allowable deductions:

1. Allowable expenses, such as funeral expenses and costs of administrating the estate;
2. Indebtedness against property included in the gross estate, such as a mortgage and other debts of the decedent;
3. Unpaid property and income taxes of the decedent to date of death;
4. Losses from casualty or theft of estate assets during the period of settlement;
5. Transfers to charity specified by the will; and
6. Marital deduction, which is unlimited in amount, for estate property that passes to the surviving spouse.

The *Revenue Act of 1978* required that the taxable estate be increased by any taxable gifts made after 1976. Gifts would be taxable to the donor if their fair market value per donee for the tax year exceeded $3,000 ($6,000 for consenting spouse gifts) through 1981. For gifts after 1981, taxable gifts result if they exceed $10,000 ($20,000 for consenting spouse gifts) per donee per year. After taxable gifts are added to the taxable estate, the tax rates found in the *unified rate schedule* are applied to the tax base.

The tax rates on taxable estates are progressive and range from 18% to 55%. Taxable estates up to $10,000 are taxed at 18% while taxable amounts exceeding $3,000,000 are taxed at 55%. For taxable estates in excess of $10,000,000 but not exceeding $21,040,000 the marginal tax rate is 60%. However, estates in excess of $21,040,000 are taxed at 55%. This additional 5% tax has the effect of phasing out the benefits of the graduated tax rates and the unified credit.

The resulting tentative estate tax then is reduced by certain credits. The *unified credit* in substance results from exempting $600,000 of taxable estate from taxation. The maximum amount of the credit is $192,800. Additional credits against the tax due are based on state death or inheritance taxes paid and taxes already paid on taxable gifts made after 1976. After recognizing applicable credits, the net tax due is paid out of the principal of the estate. If the estate principal does not have adequate cash to pay the taxes, other principal assets must be liquidated in order to generate the necessary cash.

ESTATE REDUCTION WITH GIFTS

Estate planning is essential to achieve the maximum benefit provided in the law, especially when the impact of continued inflation is considered. One simple way to reduce an estate is to make gifts annually. Currently, the first $10,000 ($20,000 for consenting spouse gifts) to any one person during any calendar year is excluded in determining taxable gifts. This is an annual exclusion. Consenting spouses who participate for ten years in an annual gift program involving six recipients would be able to transfer $1,200,000 ($20,000 × 6 × 10) without incurring any gift tax. Spouses also can make gifts to each other. No matter what the amount, such gifts between spouses are free of gift taxes.

One might ask, "What is the maximum total gift a husband and wife may give to one individual at one time without incurring any tax?" For gift tax purposes, a gift made by one person to someone other than his or her spouse is considered as having been made one-half by each spouse. Each spouse is entitled to a unified credit of $192,800, or an exemption equivalent gift of $600,000, plus the annual $10,000 exclusion. Therefore, a husband and wife could give $1,220,000 (2 × $610,000) to one person without incurring a tax. The unified credit may be used only one time by each spouse. Once used, a unified transfer tax would be due on gifts above the annual exclusion and eventually on their total remaining taxable estate.

MARITAL DEDUCTION

In the computation of the taxable estate, recall that a marital deduction is allowed for the value of qualifying property passing to a surviving spouse. The amount of the deduction is unlimited. No matter how large the estate, a bequest of all property to one's surviving spouse will eliminate completely federal estate taxes for the decedent. That statement is technically correct, but incomplete. It also should state that the deduction may defer estate taxes only until the death of the other spouse. At that point, it may be discovered that use of the unlimited deduction actually increased the overall estate tax. This can result because the tax rates are progressive (the higher the tax base, the higher the rates) and the effect of the unlimited marital deduction is to channel all assets into the estate of the surviving spouse.

To illustrate, assume Jane Jacoby's will stipulated that her husband Walter was to receive all of the gross estate valued at $1,500,000. Outstanding debts of $150,000 and funeral/administrative expenses totaling $50,000 are paid out of the estate. Also, assume that the following year Walter dies with the estate assets still intact. At the time of Walter's death, debts of his estate total $80,000, and

$20,000 of funeral and administrative costs have been incurred. With an unlimited marital deduction, their estate tax computations are as follows:

	Jane		Walter	
Gross estate.		$1,500,000		$1,300,000
Less deductions:				
Debts	$ 150,000		$80,000	
Funeral and administrative costs . . .	50,000		20,000	
Marital deduction.	1,300,000	1,500,000	0	100,000
Taxable estate		$ 0		$1,200,000
Estate tax before credits.				$ 427,800
Less unified credit				192,800
Estate tax due				$ 235,000

As an alternative strategy, Jane's will could have stipulated that an amount equal to the exemption equivalent ($600,000) be placed in a trust, with Walter as the income beneficiary. If properly designed, the trust would not be included in Walter's estate upon his death. The remainder of Jane's net assets ($700,000) could go directly to him and qualify for the marital deduction. Now their estate computations would be:

	Jane		Walter	
Gross estate.		$1,500,000		$ 700,000
Less deductions:				
Debts	$ 150,000		$80,000	
Funeral and administrative costs . . .	50,000		20,000	
Marital deduction.	700,000	900,000	0	100,000
Taxable estate		$ 600,000		$ 600,000
Estate tax before credits.		$ 192,800*		$ 192,800
Less unified credit		192,800		192,800
Estate tax due		$ 0		$ 0

*This amount of tax is based on the 1994 unified rate schedule for estates.

Failure to do some estate planning could cost the Jacoby family $235,000.

VALUATION OF ESTATE ASSETS

Fair market value must be established for assets included in an estate. Some valuations, such as the values of stocks and bonds traded on recognized exchanges, pose no problems. For other assets, such as property, jewelry, art objects, or antiques, a competent appraisal in writing should be obtained. Assets are included in the estate at their fair market value on the date of death or on an alternate valuation date, if the executor or administrator so elects. If the alternate valuation date is elected, all estate property must be valued as of six months after the decedent's death, except for property sold, distributed, or otherwise disposed of during the six-month period. Such property is valued as of the date of disposition. The alternate valuation date may be used only if it would reduce the total gross estate and decrease the estate tax liability. The alternate valuation date protects estates if there should be a significant decrease in property values during the six-month interval.

Formerly, it would have been possible for a fiduciary, knowing that there would be no estate tax to pay, to select the alternate valuation date if assets increased in value, thereby giving the heirs a higher basis for their inherited property, at no cost to the estate. To prevent this windfall, Congress took an action that permitted election of the alternate valuation date only if it would reduce the total gross estate and decrease the estate tax liability.

Congress felt it was being sufficiently generous by permitting a stepped-up basis. Recall that, to the recipient, the basis of property acquired from a decedent is market value on the date of death or alternate valuation date. That regulation may result in a step-up of basis. For example, assume Jane Jacoby held stock with a cost of $100,000. At the date of her death, it was worth $500,000 and was willed to her nephew, whose basis now becomes $500,000. A subsequent sale by him for $500,000 would result in no taxable gain. Although the value of the stock must be included in the inventory of the estate, which would be subject to the unified transfer tax only if the estate is large enough, the $400,000 gain would escape *federal income taxation* because of the step-up in basis. If Jane had sold the stock before her death, the gain would have been subject to income tax. Tax planning would suggest that, if possible, property that has appreciated substantially in value should be held as part of an estate because of the advantage of the step-up in basis. The opposite is true if there is a substantial decline in value. If Jane's stock had a value of $5,000 on the valuation date, that would become the basis to her nephew. Neither he nor the estate would derive any benefit from the $95,000 loss in value. If Jane had sold the stock prior to death, benefits resulting from the deductibility of the loss for income tax purposes would have materialized.

OTHER TAXES AFFECTING AN ESTATE

In addition to federal estate taxes, most individual states assess an inheritance tax on the value of estate assets to heirs. Certain transfers of assets are exempt while other transfers are partially exempt depending on the amount of the transfer and the relationship of the heir. The taxable amount of nonexempt transfers is reduced further by certain deductions such as funeral and adminis-trative expenses, debts of the decedent, and mortgages on real property.

In certain instances, an estate subsequently will generate income that is not included in the initial estate principal. The estate is viewed as a separate taxable entity. Estate income that is distributed currently and properly to a beneficiary generally is excluded from the taxable income of the estate. Therefore, the estate functions as a conduit through which the income passes to the recipient. Income passing in this manner retains the same character it had in the hands of the estate. For example, if the estate receives and distributes nontaxable income such as interest on municipal bonds, the interest remains tax free in the hands of the recipient. Normally, the beneficiary is taxed on any taxable income that he/she receives, and the estate, as a separate taxable entity, is taxed on any taxable income that it accumulates. Estate income taxes are assessed at the same rates as used for individual taxpayers except that the levels of income at which rates become effective are lower for estates than they are for individuals.

MEASUREMENT OF ESTATE INCOME

The tax incidence with estate income suggests the need for the estate fiduciary to distinguish between transactions affecting principal and those affecting income. Furthermore, a decedent's will may stipulate certain provisions regarding estate income that differ from those regarding principal. For example, a will might stipulate that the interest income earned on bonds subsequent to the decedent's death is to accrue to a particular beneficiary for a period of time. The recipient of the income is referred to as an *income beneficiary* and the party ultimately receiving the principal is referred to as the *remainderman*.

If the will is not clear with respect to the measurement of income, state statutes should be applied. Many states have adopted the *Revised Uniform Principal and Income Act*, which provides guidance as to the measurement of estate principal and income. The determination of estate income does not always parallel generally accepted accounting principles (GAAP). As discussed previously, the gains or losses on the sale of estate assets is considered a component of principal rather than income. When bonds are a part of the estate at the time of death, the premium or discount on the bonds is not amortized. Generally, however, if bonds are purchased subsequently by the fiduciary, a premium is amortized whereas a discount is not amortized.

Unless the will requires it, the common procedure is not to make any charge against income for depreciation. If the decedent wishes to protect principal for the depreciation factor, there should be a statement in the will that depreciation should be charged against income and an amount equal to the depreciation should be transferred from income to principal. For the depletion on wasting assets, the general rule is that income should be charged for the depletion because of the possibility of total consumption of principal.

SETTLING AN ESTATE

After the debts of an estate and the applicable estate taxes have been determined and paid, the fiduciary must focus on carrying out the remaining provisions of the decedent's will as they relate to principal and income. If the decedent dies intestate, distribution of remaining estate principal is governed by applicable state law.

DISTRIBUTIONS OF PROPERTY

If a decedent dies intestate, real property is distributed according to the laws of descent of the state in which the real property is located. Personal property is distributed according to the laws of distribution of the decedent's home state, called the *state of domicile*. In general, only a spouse or blood relative may receive an intestate distribution.

In a testate situation, a distribution of real property is a *devise*, and the recipient of the property is the *devisee*. Distributions of personal property are called bequests or *legacies,* and the recipient of personal property is called the *legatee.*

A devise is usually a distribution of a specific piece of property. In contrast, legacies may include one or more of the following types:

1. A *specific legacy* is a gift of a particular, specified thing, distinguishable from others: my 3-carat diamond ring or the twenty bottles of Romanée Conti Burgundy 1961 on the north wall of my wine cellar.
2. A *demonstrative legacy* is a gift of an amount from a specific source, with the will stipulating that if the amount cannot be satisfied from that source, it shall be satisfied from the general estate: $50,000 from several identified insurance policies. If proceeds are inadequate to meet the amount, the difference shall constitute a general legacy.
3. A *general legacy* is a gift of an indicated amount or quantity of something: $5,000 or twenty bottles of wine. However, the specific source of the payment is not designated.
4. A *residuary legacy* is composed of all estate property remaining after assigning the specific, demonstrative, and general legacies.

If the remaining estate principal, after paying debts and expenses, is not adequate to satisfy the various legacies, a process called *abatement* is followed. Abatement requires that the legacies be satisfied to whatever extent possible in the order in which they are presented above (items 1 through 4).

In order to illustrate the accounting for the distribution of property, the earlier example regarding Jane Jacoby's estate is continued. Those events relating to Jane Jacoby's estate that were discussed previously are included as events numbers 1 through 6 of Illustration 20-1. Events 7 through 13 of Illustration 20-1 relate to the accounting for estate income and property distributions.

THE CHARGE AND DISCHARGE STATEMENT

Periodically, the fiduciary will prepare a report to the court summarizing the results during the period of stewardship. This report is called a *charge and discharge statement.* The preparation of the report is simplified if a double trial balance has been prepared, since the charge and discharge statement is divided into two parts—one as to principal and one as to income. The statement for the estate of Jane Jacoby on December 31, 19X7, appears as Illustration 20-2.

In a more complex estate, each of the items in the charge and discharge statement would be supported by a schedule providing detail. For example, a supporting schedule for gains and losses on realization of principal assets might appear as follows:

Schedule of Gains and Losses on Realization of Principal Assets

	Inventory Value	Proceeds on Realization	Loss	Gain
J&D partnership.	$155,000	$165,000		$10,000
Apex bonds and accrued interest.	21,000	19,500	($1,500)	
Totals.	$176,000	$184,500	($1,500)	$10,000

If the fiduciary had completed his/her responsibilities to the estate, all assets comprising estate principal and income would have been distributed. In this case the charge and discharge statement would reflect zero balances as to estate principal and income. Final distributions of estate principal often are made in the form of a residual legacy and/or a trust for the benefit of designated parties. After all final distributions, the estate records are closed with the estate principal and estate income accounts serving as clearing accounts. The final distributions of the estate of Jane Jacoby, along with necessary closing entries, are recorded as events 14 through 16 of Illustration 20-1.

SUMMARY OF ITEMS AFFECTING ESTATE PRINCIPAL AND INCOME

There are a variety of items that can affect the estate of a decedent and the presence of a valid will certainly provides direction in this regard. The estate's fiduciary must act in a responsible manner and assume that a proper accounting of the items affecting an estate has taken place. A proper accounting will provide better management of the estate and serve as a basis for statutory reporting requirements. Today's professional accountant can support the fiduciary role by understanding the principles of estate administration and accounting. A review of the items affecting estate principal and income will help to ensure a proper accounting.

The items that usually are chargeable against principal and the account debited when each item is recorded are as follows:

Item	Account Debited
Debts of the decedent incurred prior to death	Debts of Decedent Paid
Funeral and administrative expenses	Funeral and Administrative Expenses
Medical expenses	Medical Expenses
Costs incurred in probating the will	Funeral and Administrative Expenses
Final income taxes of decedent	Debts of Decedent Paid
Federal estate tax[3] and any state inheritance tax	Funeral and Administrative Expenses

(continued)

---

[3]The Uniform Probate Code provides that where the will does not stipulate treatment of estate taxes, they are to be prorated to the recipients of estate assets on the basis of the value of the asset received relative to the aggregate value of all assets subject to tax.

Illustration 20-1
Accounting for the Estate of Jane Jacoby

Event	Entry		
1. Recording of the initial estate inventory after special exemptions and allowances.	Principal Cash	81,000	
	Investment in XYZ Stock	744,000	
	Declared Dividend on XYZ Stock.....	3,000	
	Investment in J&D Partnership	155,000	
	Automobile........................	15,000	
	Wages Receivable..................	2,000	
	Estate Principal		1,000,000
2. Subsequent discovery of estate assets.	Investment in Apex Bonds	20,000	
	Accrued Interest...................	1,000	
	Estate Principal: Assets Subsequently Discovered		21,000
3. Sale of estate assets: J&D partnership for $165,000 cash.	Principal Cash	165,000	
	Investment in J&D Partnership		155,000
	Gain on Realization of Principal Asset		10,000
4. Sale of estate assets: Apex bonds plus accrued interest for $19,500.	Principal Cash	19,500	
	Loss on Realization of Principal Asset	1,500	
	Investment in Apex Bonds		20,000
	Accrued Interest		1,000
5. Receipt of accrued wages and dividends receivable.	Principal Cash	5,000	
	Wages Receivable...............		2,000
	Declared Dividend on XYZ Stock...		3,000
6. Payment of claims against the estate.	Funeral Expenses	5,000	
	Administrative Expenses...........	3,000	
	Debts of Decedent Paid	23,000	
	Medical Expenses	7,000	
	Principal Cash		38,000
7. Receipt of interest on cash accounts.	Income Cash	1,000	
	Estate Income		1,000
8. Receipt of dividend declared on XYZ stock subsequent to decedent's death.	Income Cash	3,000	
	Estate Income		3,000
9. Distribution of specific legacy of automobile to Jacoby's nephew.	Legacies Distributed.................	15,000	
	Automobile......................		15,000
10. Distribution of general legacy of $25,000 to Jacoby's sister.	Legacies Distributed.................	25,000	
	Principal Cash		25,000
11. Distribution of specific legacy of 5,000 shares of XYZ stock to Riveredge Nature Center.	Legacies Distributed...............	186,000	
	Investment in XYZ Stock		186,000
12. Payment of administrative expenses of which $100 is traceable to income.	Administrative Expenses............	300	
	Expenses Chargeable Against Income........................	100	
	Principal Cash		300
	Income Cash		100

(continued)

Event	Entry		
13. Distribution of income cash traceable to dividends received to Jane Jacoby's brother.	Distribution to Income Beneficiary ... Income Cash	3,000	3,000
14. Distribution of all estate assets to the Jacoby children's trust administered by the First National Trust Company.	Principal Assets Transferred to Trust .. Income Assets Transferred to Trust ... Principal Cash .... Investment in XYZ Stock .... Income Cash	765,200 900	 207,200 558,000 900
15. Closing of estate principal.	Estate Principal .... Estate Principal: Assets Subsequently Discovered .... Gain on Realization of Principal Asset .... Loss on Realization of Principal Asset .... Funeral Expenses .... Administrative Expenses .... Debts of Decedent Paid .... Medical Expenses .... Legacies Distributed .... Principal Assets Transferred to Trust	1,000,000 21,000 10,000	 1,500 5,000 3,300 23,000 7,000 226,000 765,200
16. Closing of estate income.	Estate Income .... Expenses Chargeable Against Income...................... Distributions to Income Beneficiary .... Income Assets Transferred to Trust........................	4,000	 100 3,000 900

Legal and other professional fees to preserve estate principal	Funeral and Administrative Expenses
Charges applicable to personal property that produces no income	Expenses Chargeable Against Principal
Distributions of legacies or devises in a testate distribution	Legacies Distributed ⎫ often combined or ⎬ in the first Devises Distributed ⎭ account
Distributions to trusts	Principal Assets Transferred to Trust
Disposition of estate assets at a loss	Loss on Realization of Principal Assets (a gain would be credited to Gain on Realization of Principal Assets, with total proceeds on any sale of a principal asset debited to Cash—Principal)

When income cash is received, Estate Income is credited and, if the estate is large, a subsidiary ledger is maintained that details the types of income. The items for which income cash usually is disbursed and the account debited when each item is recorded are as follows:

Illustration 20-2
Charge and Discharge Statement

Estate of Jane Jacoby
Howard Wells, Executor
Charge and Discharge Statement
For the Period June 1, 19X7, to December 31, 19X7

As to Principal

I charge myself with:

Assets per original inventory	$1,000,000	
Assets subsequently discovered	21,000	
Net gain on realization of principal assets	8,500	
Total charges		$1,029,500

I credit myself with:

Funeral and administrative expenses	$ 8,300	
Medical expenses	7,000	
Debts of decedent paid	23,000	
Legacies distributed	226,000	
Total credits		264,300

Balances as to estate principal, consisting of:

Cash—principal	$ 207,200	
XYZ stock	558,000	
		$ 765,200

As to Income

I charge myself with:

Estate income	$ 4,000

I credit myself with:

Expenses chargeable against income	$ 100	
Distributions to income beneficiaries	3,000	
Total credits		3,100

Balances as to estate income, consisting of:

Cash—income	$ 900

Item	Account Debited
Expenses incurred to protect income flow	Expenses Chargeable Against Income
Ordinary repairs to income-producing property	Expenses Chargeable Against Income
Distributions of income cash to beneficiaries	Distributions to Income Beneficiaries
Distributions of income cash to trusts	Income Assets Transferred to Trust

TRUST ACCOUNTING

A trust is a separate, distinct entity that receives assets from an individual for the purpose of managing and distributing them over a period of time. Trusts may be created for several reasons. It is possible that heirs to an estate currently lack the maturity, sophistication, or prudence necessary to receive substantial assets directly. Therefore, a trust is established to manage the asset for the intended heir. Trusts also provide opportunities for assets to be exempt from the probate process and, more important, taxes imposed on an estate. Finally, trusts are used as a means to convey assets to special organizations or causes, such as charities, universities, and other not-for-profit organizations. Rather than conveying estate assets directly to these organizations, a trust presents an opportunity to recognize the needs of individual heirs prior to such distributions.

Trusts may take a variety of forms. The following brief discussion of several types will serve to illustrate the various strategies for creating a trust. A *charitable remainder trust* distributes the income from trust assets to individual beneficiaries over a period of time (often for the rest of their lives) at which time the assets go to the remainderman which must be a charitable organization. Under such an arrangement, a charitable deduction is available to the *grantor* when the trust is created. Upon death of the grantor, the property is excluded from the estate, thereby escaping estate taxes. A *bypass or credit shelter trust* is designed to split assets between a surviving spouse and a trust so that the value of the marital deduction and unified credit are maximized. Generally, the surviving spouse receives income during his/her lifetime after which the trust assets are distributed to surviving children or heirs. A *qualified terminable interest property trust* (Q-TIP trust) is similar to a bypass or credit shelter trust.

Noting that trusts may be designed to accomplish a variety of purposes, they may become operative while the grantor is alive or they may be created through a will to become effective upon the grantor's death. The former type of trust is an *inter vivos*, or *living, trust* while the latter is referred to as a *testamentary trust*. In order to carry out the provisions of a trust, a *trustee* must be appointed. The trustee may be an individual; however, banks frequently serve as trustees. Most major banks have a trust department whose services are available for a fee.

ACCOUNTING FOR TRUSTS

The accounting for a trust is very similar to the accounting for an estate. The distinction between principal and income must be maintained through the use of *trust principal* and *trust income accounts*. The trust agreement should provide direction regarding how income is to be determined. A charge and discharge statement is required periodically for both trust principal and income.

Illustration 20-3 demonstrates the accounting for various events affecting the trust established by Jane Jacoby's will.

To demonstrate adherence to the terms of the trust, the trustee must provide annual, confidential reports to income beneficiaries and remaindermen. For a testamentary trust, a report also must be rendered to the probate court of the county in which the will was admitted to probate. The nature of the report is dependent upon the statutory requirement of the relevant state. Generally within 30 days after the end of each year, a report must be filed that shows:

Illustration 20-3

Accounting for the Jacoby Children's Trust

Event	Entry		
1. Receipt of distribution from the estate of Jane Jacoby.	Principal Cash.......................... Investment in XYZ Stock.............. Trust Principal..................... Income Cash.......................... Trust Income........................	207,200 558,000 900	765,200 900
2. Purchase of mutual funds with principal cash.	Investment in Mutual Fund............. Principal Cash.....................	200,000	200,000
3. Receipt of dividend and interest income.	Income Cash.......................... Trust Income........................	5,300	5,300
4. Payment of trustee's fees and allocation to principal and income.	Administrative Expenses: Principal..... Administrative Expenses: Income....... Principal Cash..................... Income Cash........................	400 200	400 200
5. Distribution of income cash to beneficiaries.	Distribution to Income Beneficiary........................ Income Cash........................	6,000	6,000

1. The trust principal on hand at the beginning of the period.
2. Changes in the trust principal during the period, such as asset acquisitions or dispositions.
3. The trust principal on hand at the end of the period, its composition, and the estimated market values of all investments.

As to trust income, the report shows:

1. The trust income on hand at the beginning of the period.
2. Trust income received during the period, detailing the sources and amounts.
3. Distributions of trust income made during the period to income beneficiaries.
4. The trust income on hand at the end of the period and how it is invested.

These requirements may be met by the periodic filing of a charge and discharge statement, provided that sufficient detail as to principal and as to income is incorporated into the report. At the time of submitting the statement to the court, many trustees prefer to close trust books to have them correspond to the annual time frame used in filing reports. Trust Principal and Trust Income are the clearing accounts used in the closing process, paralleling the procedures for closing an estate.

The trust will terminate when all trust property is distributed in accordance with the trust arrangement. For example, a trust may have been created to provide a beneficiary with income until a certain age is reached, at which time trust principal is released. The trustee's final report will take the same form as the periodic reports but, in addition, will itemize total distribution of trust principal and income to indicate termination of stewardship.

QUESTIONS

1. Estate planning is becoming more important to many individuals. Identify several goals of estate planning.
2. Why are the desires and wishes of a decedent easier to identify if they die testate versus intestate?
3. Assuming a decedent has an investment in stocks, discuss how cash dividends and gains or losses on the disposition of stocks affect estate principal.
4. Outline the steps that are followed to settle the estate of a decedent who left a valid will.
5. An amount equal to the homestead allowance is exempt from the claims against an estate. What is the nature and amount of the homestead allowance?
6. At what point in time are the claims against an estate recognized and how are they satisfied if valid claims against the estate exceed estate assets?
7. After providing for the special reservation of assets because of the estate's family allowance and homestead allowance, the estate does not have sufficient assets to settle all accepted claims. The fiduciary informs the funeral director who handled final arrangements that the funeral expenses will have to be paid on a pro rata basis with all other claims. Is the fiduciary's statement correct?
8. Is it true that federal estate taxes for a married individual may be eliminated completely by use of the unlimited marital deduction? Is the adoption of such a procedure always wise? Explain.
9. State the rule that establishes the alternative valuation date for estate tax purposes.
10. How many gifts prior to one's death may be used to reduce federal estate taxes?
11. An estate is expected to have income that is generated by certain assets of the estate. What purpose would be served by recognizing depreciation on equipment held by the estate?
12. A decedent's will provides for the distribution of certain personal property. How does a specific legacy differ from a general legacy?
13. An estate has $180,000 of estate assets available for distribution to legatees. However, stated legacies total $220,000 in value. How is this problem resolved?
14. Someone once stated that "A trust is of value only if heirs to an estate lack maturity and/or financial responsibility." Do you agree with the statement?

EXERCISES

Exercise 1. Select the best answer for each of the following multiple-choice questions.
1. You have been informed that, under your late aunt's will, you are a legatee. Technically, this means that you will receive:
    (a) Cash.
    (b) Real property.
    (c) Personal property.
    (d) The face value of a life insurance policy.
2. Tim Mietrich, a single man, has accumulated a considerable amount of assets. He wishes to reduce his ultimate estate tax. Over the next twelve years, the maximum total gifts that he could make without incurring any gift tax or consumption of the unified credit is:
    (a) $10,000 × 12.
    (b) $20,000 × 12.

(c) $10,000 × 12 × 10.

(d) Not determinable from the facts provided.

3. Carlota Lopez wishes to donate $10,000 to her church this year. Her estate is large and will be subject to estate tax. She is undecided whether to give $10,000 in cash, donate shares of stock that cost $40,000 with a current market value of $10,000 and little hope of recovery, or sell these shares and donate the proceeds. Considering only these facts, she should:

(a) Sell the stock and donate the proceeds.

(b) Donate $10,000 cash and keep the stock.

(c) Donate the shares of stock.

(d) Make no donation until the market value of the shares has recovered.

4. Julio Doro received 400 shares of stock from his mother as a result of her death on February 1. Her basis for the stock was $12,000. The stock had a market value of $20,000 on February 1, $23,000 six months later, and $25,000 when the estate tax return was filed. The alternate valuation date was not applicable. Julio's basis for the stock is:

(a) $25,000   (b) $23,000   (c) $20,000   (d) $12,000

5. Which one of the following statements in regard to the maximum marital deduction is correct?

(a) Its use could increase the overall estate tax.

(b) It should not be combined with a gift program.

(c) It is of greater tax benefit to the surviving spouse than to the deceased.

(d) It is of greater benefit to taxable estates of $600,000 or less.

6. The valid will of Ginger Hill said, "I leave my friend Chien Yang $10,000." This is an illustration of a:

(a) Specific legacy.

(b) General legacy.

(c) Demonstrative legacy.

(d) Residuary legacy.

7. In most cases, the basis for effective estate planning is dependent upon:

(a) Having a valid and available will.

(b) Using the maximum marital deduction.

(c) Selling securities with a stepped-up basis before death.

(d) Putting the only copy of your will in a safety deposit box.

8. John and Mary, a married couple with no children, hold all of their property jointly. Neither has a will. John is killed in an accident. Mary dies three months later. The estate would be:

(a) Divided one-third to John's family and two-thirds to Mary's family.

(b) Divided equally between John's family and Mary's family.

(c) Inherited by John's family.

(d) Inherited by Mary's family.

Exercise 2. Robert Wagner has become extremely ill and is doing some estate planning in contemplation of his death. Robert is married and has two minor children. It is estimated that Robert's estate would have a value of $3,600,000 and his executor would be responsible for paying $100,000 in medical/funeral expenses and $20,000 in administrative fees. In the event of Mrs. Wagner's death, it is estimated that allowable expenses of her estate would be approximately $60,000. Valid other claims against the estate are estimated to be $800,000. The estate assets are not very liquid and consist primarily of investments in stocks, bonds, and land. Mr. and Mrs. Wagner are considering establishing a trust whereby Mrs. Wagner would be the income beneficiary for the duration of her life, and the children would be the remaindermen.

(1) Considering both Mr. and Mrs. Wagner, determine the minimum measure of estate assets exposed to net federal estate tax if the trust were not established. (Ignore possible homestead and family allowances.)

(2) Considering both Mr. and Mrs. Wagner, determine the minimum measure of trust assets required so that there are no federal estate taxes due. (Ignore possible homestead and family allowances.)

Exercise 3. The following transactions are typical of those incurred by an estate:
(a) Recording of the original assets of the estate.
(b) Sale of capital stock in the original estate at a gain.
(c) Recording receipt of interest (partly accrued at date of death) on bonds in the original estate.
(d) Recording assets subsequently discovered.
(e) Purchase of bonds at a premium, along with accrued interest.
(f) Receipt of first interest check on bonds in (e).
(g) Payment of property taxes on a rental apartment. The taxes became a lien after the date of death.

Assuming no stipulation to the contrary is made in the will, indicate whether the typical accounting treatment of each of the items would affect principal accounts only, income accounts only, or both. Use the following columnar format for your answers, placing an "X" in the appropriate column.

	Would Affect		
Letter of Item	Principal Only	Income Only	Principal and Income

Exercise 4. The will of Donna Kaiser, an unmarried individual, contained the following provisions regarding her estate:
(a) The dairy farm located in Watertown is to be deeded to her nephew James Quade.
(b) The collection of Navajo Indian rugs is to be given to the Museum of Native American Arts.
(c) Michael Kaiser, Donna's brother, is to receive $98,000 in cash.
(d) Michele Kaiser, Donna's sister, is to receive all of the cash deposited in the First Bank of Watertown savings account.
(e) Michele Kaiser shall receive a demonstrative legacy of $150,000 from the net proceeds of insurance policies on Donna Kaiser's life.
(f) All personal effects (clothing, furniture, housewares) are to be given to Goodwill Industries.
(g) All of the IBM stock is to be distributed to the World Wildlife Fund (a charitable organization).
(h) All remaining assets are to be placed in trust for Donna's foster child Emily Natal. Other claims against the estate include:

Heavenly Hands, funeral expenses	$ 10,000
Attorney B. J. Wells, administrative expenses	5,000
Northwestern Mutual Life, insurance policy loans	30,000
Note due to First Bank of Watertown	20,000
Federal and state income taxes due on final tax return	3,000
Watertown Treasurer, accrued property taxes on the farm	12,000

The inventory of Donna Kaiser's estate consists of:

Cash—checking account	$ 3,500
Cash—savings account, First Bank of Watertown	18,000
Cash—savings account, Federal Savings and Loan	73,000
Personal effects	8,000
Navajo rug collection	49,000
Life insurance death benefit	128,000
Watertown dairy farm	370,000
Investment in IBM stock	220,000
Investment in U.S. treasury bonds	20,500
Dividends declared on IBM stock	13,000

As executor of the estate, (a) explain why no federal estate taxes are due, and (b) prepare a listing of all items comprising estate principal, and for each item, indicate who will receive the item and in what amount.

Exercise 5. Jason Jackson was killed in a mountain climbing accident in British Columbia. As Jason's trusted friend and CPA, you have been named executor of his estate and guardian to his minor child, Cody Jackson. Jason's estate consists of the following assets subject to probate:

Cash	15,000
Vacant land in Colorado	130,000
Investment in Merkt stock	54,000
Investment in GTE stock	13,000
Dividend declared on GTE stock	1,000
Investment in Trident Bond Fund	40,000
Accrued interest on Trident Bond Fund	2,000
Royalties receivable	17,000

Prepare journal entries to record the above inventory and the following events related to the estate principal and income:
(a) Final medical and funeral expenses of $22,000 are paid.
(b) An Individual Retirement Account (IRA) naming Jackson's estate as beneficiary and having a value of $37,000 subsequently is discovered.
(c) Cash dividends of $1,000 on the GTE stock and $2,700 on the Merkt stock are received.
(d) The vacant land in Colorado is sold for $150,000 less accrued property taxes of $2,000 and a broker's commission of $8,000.
(e) Interest of $2,400 is received on the Trident Bond Fund and the royalty receivable also is collected.
(f) Income taxes of $4,000 on the decedent's final tax return are paid, along with $24,000 of other claims against the estate.
(g) A legacy of $15,000 is paid to the High Adventure Climbing School.
(h) Administrative expenses of $3,200 are paid, of which $100 is traceable to income.

Exercise 6. Given the facts of Exercise 5, prepare the charge and discharge statement that would have resulted from the above events and prepare the entries to transfer all estate principal and income amounts to a trust for the benefit of Cody Jackson.

Exercise 7. Each of the following situations concerns the making of gifts as it relates to estate planning:
(a) Mr. and Mrs. Herman have two married daughters, an unmarried son, and four grandchildren. During the next six years, they wish to make the maximum total gifts possible to their descendants (including spouses) without incurring any federal gift tax or consuming their unified credit. What would this total amount be for the six years?

(b) Mrs. Gehrig, a widow, has three married children and two grandchildren. What is the maximum amount she can give each year to her descendants and their spouses without incurring any federal gift tax or consuming her unified credit?

(c) Frank Martin, who is single, has two nieces and one nephew. What is the maximum amount he can give each year to these relatives without incurring any federal gift tax or consuming his unified credit?

Exercise 8. Casey Jones died testate on May 1, 19X0. As the approved executor, prepare journal entries to record the following activities related to the estate:

(a) The assets are inventoried, and the following listing is filed with the probate court:

Cash	$ 60,000
Stock of Trains Inc.	40,000
Zip Railroad 10% bonds, interest payable March 1 and September 1, at face value (also market value)	120,000
Accrued interest on Zip bonds.	2,000
Personal and household effects	30,000
Total	$252,000

(b) Funeral expenses paid, $2,800.

(c) Dividends were declared on May 10 by Trains Inc., and the check for $800 was received on June 1.

(d) Interest on Zip Railroad bonds was collected on September 1.

(e) Half of the Zip Railroad bonds were sold on October 1 at 103 plus accrued interest.

(f) Casey was a bachelor. The will stipulates that his personal and household effects be given to his housekeeper, Karen Kay. The executor released the items to her.

(g) On December 1, the executor's fee of $3,000 was approved by the court and paid. Of the total amount, $200 is to be charged against income of the estate.

PROBLEMS

Problem 20-1. Alex Dunn, Jr., died on January 15, 19X7; his records disclose the following estate at fair market value:

Cash in bank	$ 3,750
6% note receivable, including $50 accrued interest	5,050
Stocks	50,000
Dividends declared on stocks.	600
6% mortgage receivable, including $100 accrued interest	20,100
Real estate—apartment house.	35,000
Household effects.	8,250
Total.	$122,750

Subsequent to recording the inventory of the estate, the executor discovered on July 1, 19X7, the late Alex Dunn, Sr., created a trust fund that established his son, Alex Dunn, Jr., as life tenant, and his grandson as remainderman. The assets in the fund consist solely of the outstanding capital stock of Dunn, Inc.; namely, 2,000 shares of common stock. At the creation of the trust, the book value and the market value of these shares was $400,000. At December 31, 19X7, the market value was $500,000. On January 2, 19X7, Dunn, Inc., declared a $1.25 per share cash dividend payable February 2, 19X7, to shareholders of record on January 12, 19X7.

The executor's cash transactions from January 15 to January 31, 19X7, were as follows:

Cash receipts:

Jan. 20	Dividends declared		$ 600
25	6% notes receivable collected.		5,000
	Interest accrued on note		58
	Stocks sold, inventoried at $22,500		20,900
	6% mortgage sold.		20,100
	Interest accrued on mortgage		132
29	Real estate sold		30,250
	Dividends not previously declared		900
			$77,940

Cash disbursements:

Jan. 20	Funeral expenses		$ 750
23	Decedent's debts		8,000
25	Decedent's legacies.		10,000
31	Distribution of income to widow		500
31	Property taxes assessed January 10, 19X7		1,000
			$20,250

Required:

Prepare a charge and discharge statement for the executor for the period from January 15 to January 31, 19X7.

Problem 20-2. The will of Andrew Larsen established a charitable remainder trust. Andrew's wife, Judith, is the trust's income beneficiary. On January 1, 19X9, the remaining income will be distributed to Judith, and the trust principal will be distributed to the Nature Conservancy (a charitable organization). The executor of Andrew Larsen's estate transferred the following assets to the trust on April 10, 19X4:

Cash.	$ 60,000
Investment in McCaw stock	40,000
Investment in Divide, real estate partnership	160,000
Investment in Michigan, tree farm.	200,000
Medical equipment.	600,000

The trust agreement provides that the disposition of trust principal at a loss will be borne by the income beneficiary by way of a transfer of income assets to trust principal. However, gains on the disposition of trust principal will accrue to trust principal but not exceeding 5% of the principal assets carrying value. Gains in excess of this 5% limit accrue to the income beneficiary. With respect to investments in bonds, the discount on bonds purchased is not to be amortized. However, the premium on such bonds is to be amortized with a corresponding amount of the interest received to be recorded as principal cash. The medical equipment included in the inventory is to be leased to a physicians' group. The lease qualifies as an operating lease, and the revenue received is to be allocated between trust income and trust principal. The portion allocated to principal is equal to the depreciation on the asset assuming: a 5-year useful life, straight-line depreciation, and a $100,000 residual value. Any gain or loss on the disposition of the medical equipment accrues to the remainderman. The income beneficiary is to receive distributions at the end of each month equal to the available income cash.

The following events occurred subsequent to April 10, 19X4:

(a) On April 15, 19X4, a $1,200 dividend was declared on the McCaw stock. The dividend will be paid on May 15, 19X4, to holders of record on May 10, 19X4.

(b) On April 29, 19X4, the tree farm in Michigan was sold for $230,000 less brokerage fees of $16,000.

(c) On May 1, 19X4, the medical equipment was leased to a medical group, and the monthly rent of $12,000 was received.

(d) On May 1, 19X4, bonds with a face value of $200,000 were purchased at 103 plus accrued interest. The 9% bonds mature in 5 years. Interest is payable on June 1 and November 1 of each year.

(e) On May 3, 19X4, the investment of McCaw stock was sold for $40,200 including the declared dividend.

(f) On May 10, 19X4, a profit distribution of $15,000 was received on the real estate partnership.

(g) The lease payment of $12,000 on the medical equipment was received on June 1, 19X4, along with the interest on the bonds.

(h) Administrative expenses totaling $1,500 were paid and allocated 40% to principal and 60% to income.

(i) On June 30, 19X4, the necessary distribution was made to the income beneficiary.

Required:

(1) Prepare journal entries to record all events related to the trust through the end of June 19X4.

(2) Explain why the amortization of a premium on a bond investment preserves the principal of the trust.

(3) Explain why the recognition of depreciation on trust assets may be necessary in order to preserve the principal of the trust.

Problem 20-3. Early in 19X0, Alex Bowe dies, leaving a gross estate of $1,400,000. He had outstanding debts of $50,000. Administrative expenses of the estate amounted to $50,000. Later that year, his wife dies, leaving an estate of $250,000, in addition to the property left to her by her husband. Administrative expenses on Mrs. Bowe's estate were $60,000.

You are provided with the following partial unified estate and gift tax table:

Exceeding (A)	Not Exceeding (B)	Tax on Amount in Column (A)	Rate of Tax on Excess over Amount in Column (A)
$ 500,000	$ 750,000	$155,800	37%
750,000	1,000,000	248,300	39
1,000,000	1,250,000	345,800	41
1,250,000	1,500,000	448,300	43

Required:

(1) Ignoring state gift and estate taxes, determine the amount of federal estate tax on both estates:

(a) If Mr. Bowe left his total estate to his wife, exercising the unlimited marital deduction.

(b) If Mr. Bowe left his wife an estate that will equate his taxable estate with the maximum unified credit.

(2) What does the estate tax computation demonstrate in relation to exercising the unlimited marital deduction?

Problem 20-4. The following selected events occurred after the death of Gloria Scott on January 31, 19X1:

(a) The inventory of estate assets as of the date of death included Oklahoma City 5% bonds, paying interest annually on September 1. The face value of the bonds was

$100,000. On the date of death, the market value of the bonds was 95. (The journal entry should show how the bonds and interest would be recorded as part of the original estate.)

(b) On May 31, the fiduciary sold the bonds for 94 plus accrued interest.

(c) An apartment building was part of the estate. The property originally cost the decedent $260,000, of which $20,000 was applicable to the land. The building was 30% depreciated as of the date of death, based on a 40-year estimated life, zero salvage value, and the straight-line depreciation method. The fiduciary agrees with the originally estimated life. Market value of the property as of the date of death is $320,000, of which $40,000 is applicable to the land. (The journal entry should show how the property would be recorded as part of the inventory of the estate.)

(d) Scott's will stipulated that, in regard to the property discussed in (c), the principal of the estate should be protected by assigning rental income equal to depreciation directly to principal. For the ensuing year, gross apartment rentals collected were $60,000. Expenses paid amounted to $17,000.

(e) After the deduction of expenses, the net rental income from the apartment building is to be released to Scott's nephew, but the amount shall not exceed $25,000 per year. The maximum annual amount was paid to the income beneficiary.

Required:

Prepare journal entries to record each of these events.

Problem 20-5. Laurel Rose has been the executrix of her brother's estate since his death on February 1, 19X6. The following events occurred during her administration:

(a) Included in the principal assets were 40, $1,000, 8% City of Pittsburgh bonds, paying interest on January 1 and July 1. The bonds had a market value of 101 on February 1, 19X6. Rose sold the bonds at 103, plus accrued interest, on March 1, 19X6.

(b) On March 1, 19X6, Rose purchased 50, $1,000, 5% City of Detroit bonds at 98, plus accrued interest. The bonds pay interest on April 1 and October 1. The bonds mature on April 1, 19X8.

(c) On March 1, 19X6, she also purchased $10,000 (face value), 7% City of Newark bonds at 102, plus accrued interest. The bonds pay interest on June 1 and December 1. The bonds mature on December 1, 19X7.

(d) On April 1, 19X6, she received a check for the interest on the Detroit bonds.

(e) On June 1, 19X6, she received a check for the interest on the Newark bonds.

(f) On September 1, 19X6, she sold the Detroit bonds at 101, plus accrued interest.

Required:

Prepare journal entries to record each of these events. Use the straight-line method of amortization where applicable.

Problem 20-6. Sheri Shannon died on June 1, 19X3, leaving a valid will that named her friend, Steve Chevalier, the executor of the estate.

(a) Steve prepared the following inventory of assets, listing their market values as of June 1:

Cash	$31,000
1,000 shares of Pal Corp. common stock............................	60,000
2,000 shares of BVD Corp. common stock	40,000
Rapid Transit Corp. (RTC) 8% bonds, interest payable April 1 and October 1, $30,000 face amount	30,300
Time-share condominium unit at Lake Tahoe, used for her two-week vacations	10,000
Sheri's one-half interest in the Sheri Limo Service Co..................	70,000

CHAPTER 20 Estates and Trusts: Their Nature and the Accountant's Role 1145

(b) On June 15, after filing the inventory of assets with the probate court, Steve discovered Sheri's gold-coin collection that was appraised at $18,000.
(c) On June 20, a $250 check was received from Pal Corporation for dividends declared on May 10, 19X3, to owners on record as of May 30.
(d) Steve sold the time-share condominium for $14,000 on July 7.
(e) The following items were paid between June 1 and July 31:

Sheri's charge card purchases	$1,900
Funeral costs	6,000
Lawyer's fee to probate the will	800
Cost to paint condominium prior to sale	1,100
Payment to executor approved by the court	1,700

(f) On July 5, a $15,000 check was received for Sheri's portion of partnership earnings for the quarter ended June 30. Earnings are fairly constant from one month to the next and are available for withdrawal on a monthly basis if a partner so desires. Otherwise, payments are made quarterly.
(g) Sheri's partner offered Steve $90,000 for her interest in the partnership. Steve accepted the offer and received full payment.
(h) On October 1, a check for interest was received from Rapid Transit Corp.
(i) On December 1, Steve completed Sheri's final income tax return, paying the additional tax due of $18,200.

Required:
(1) Prepare journal entries to record the events.
(2) Prepare a charge and discharge statement as of December 31, 19X3.

Problem 20-7. You are given the following trial balance of the estate of Sheri Shannon as of December 31, 19X3. Her will stipulated that the executor should be granted $30,000 from principal cash. The remainder of the estate's principal assets and its income asset are to be transferred to Community Bank, which will act as trustee of an endowment fund. Income from trust assets shall be used for scholarships for accounting majors at a local university.

Trial Balance

Cash—Principal	115,950	
Cash—Income	5,800	
Pal Corp. Stock	60,000	
BVD Corp. Stock	40,000	
Rapid Transit Corp. Bonds	30,300	
Coin Collection	18,000	
Estate Principal		241,700
Estate Income		5,800
Assets Subsequently Discovered		28,250
Gain on Realization of Principal Assets		24,000
Funeral and Administrative Expenses	8,500	
Debts of Decedent Paid	20,100	
Expenses Chargeable Against Principal	1,100	
	299,750	299,750

Required:

(1) Record the payment to the executor and the transfer of all remaining assets to the trustee.

(2) Prepare journal entries to close the executor's records.

(3) Prepare journal entries to record receipt of assets by the trustee. Explain why it was unnecessary to accrue the interest on the Rapid Transit Corp. bonds to the date of actual transfer.

Problem 20-8. The probate court is dissatisfied with the procedures followed by the executor of the estate of Jean O'Brien and demands the records. The executor submits the following:

Journal Entries for the Estate of Jean O'Brien—Died, May 1, 19X6

May 8	Bank Checking Account		14,100	
	Insurance Policy at Cash Surrender Value (face of policy is $100,000 and is payable to the estate)		18,000	
	Shannon Corporation 12% Bonds (interest is payable April 1 and October 1; face value, $100,000; fair market value at date of death, $106,000; recorded at Jean's cost)		124,000	
	O'Brien Corporation Common Stock (10,000 shares of $10 par. Stock was quoted at $18 when Jean died. These shares were a gift from her father, the founder of the corporation, so I've entered them at $1, just to make a record.)		1	
	Condominium (Her condo is just like mine, which cost me $96,000 a week before she died. Her cost was $73,000.)		73,000	
	Paintings (I don't understand these, but a dealer says they are worth $25,000. They cost Jean $9,000.)		25,000	
	Gain on Paintings			16,000
	Total Estate			238,101
	This is a list of the assets I found so far. I made a copy of this entry and filed it with the court. I omitted a Silver Cloud Rolls-Royce, worth about $30,000. I'll keep the car instead of asking for a fee. Jean always said she wanted me to have it. She must have forgotten it when she made out her will.			
9	Cash.		2,000	
	O'Brien Corporation Dividend.			2,000
	Received a check for a dividend declared April 2 to holders of record on April 25.			
June 1	Cash.		100,000	
	Insurance Policy at Cash Surrender Value.			18,000
	Gain on Loss of Jean O'Brien.			82,000
	This is the check from the insurance company.			

(continued)

Journal Entries for the Estate of Jean O'Brien—Died, May 1, 19X6

5	Expenses		44,000
	Cash...................................			44,000
	I issued checks to cover:		
	Funeral expenses......................	$ 5,100	
	Jean's medical bills	300	
	Final income tax payments..............	17,900	
	Jean's charges on American Express	700	
	Partial payment on estate tax. The will		
	says it should be charged against		
	principal, whatever that means.........	20,000	
	Total...........................	$44,000	

30	Expenses		25,000
	Paintings			25,000
	Turned paintings over to Art Institute, as		
	the will said I should do.		

Sept. 10	Loss on O'Brien Corporation Common Stock ...		1
	O'Brien Corporation Common Stock.........			1
	The will stated that the stock should be		
	returned to the corporation, so I did it.		

Oct. 1	Cash....................................		6,000
	Interest Received........................			6,000
	To record check received from Shannon		
	Corporation.		

1	Cash....................................		90,000
	Condominium............................			73,000
	Gain on Sale of Condominium			17,000
	To record sale of condo. The will says the		
	proceeds should be used to establish a		
	Jean O'Brien Scholarship Endowment Fund		
	at State University, her alma mater.		

3	Cash Turned Over to State University..........		90,000
	Cash....................................			90,000
	I sent a check to the university for the		
	scholarship endowment fund.		

31	Expenses		3,000
	Cash....................................			3,000
	The court relieved me as executor and said		
	I could not have the Rolls-Royce. This		
	payment to me is to be charged to		
	principal. I don't think what they did is fair		
	to me.		

Required:

(1) The probate judge is disgusted with the records, terminates the executor's responsibilities, and appoints you as the replacement. Prepare a correct set of entries to date.

(2) Prepare a charge and discharge statement. No supporting schedules are necessary.

Problem 20-9. Arthur Taine died in an accident on May 31, 19X6. His will, dated February 28, 19X4, provided that all just debts and expenses be paid and his property be disposed of as follows:

Personal residence is devised to Bertha Taine, widow.

U.S. Treasury bonds and Puritan Company stock are to be placed in trust. All income is to go to Bertha Taine during her lifetime.

Seneca Company mortgage notes are bequeathed to Elaine Taine Langer, daughter.
A cash bequest of $10,000 is to be made to David Taine, son.

The remainder of the estate is to be divided equally between the two children, Elaine
Taine Langer and David Taine.

The will further provided that, during the administration period, Bertha Taine is to be
paid $300 a month out of estate income. Estate and inheritance taxes are to be borne by the
principal of the estate. David Taine was named as executor and trustee.

An inventory of the decedent's property was prepared. The fair market value of all
items as of the date of death was determined. The preliminary inventory, before the
computation of any appropriate income accruals on inventory items, follows:

Personal residence	$ 45,000
Jewelry—diamond ring.	9,600
York Life Insurance Company—term life insurance policy on life of Arthur	
Taine, with Bertha Taine designated as beneficiary	120,000
Granite Trust Co.—5% savings bank account, in trust for Philip Langer	
(grandchild), interest credited January 1 and July 1; balance May 31	400
Fidelity National Bank checking account balance.	143,000
$100,000 U.S. Treasury bonds, 3%, interest payable March 1 and	
September 1	100,000
$9,700 Seneca Co. first mortgage notes, 6%, interest payable May 31 and	
November 30.	9,900
800 shares Puritan Company common stock	64,000
700 shares Meta Manufacturing common stock.	70,000

The executor opened an estate bank account, to which he transferred the decedent's
checking account balance. Other deposits, through July 1, 19X7, were as follows:

Interest collected on U.S. Treasury bonds:	
September 1, 19X6.	$ 1,500
March 1, 19X7	1,500
Dividends received on Puritan Company stock:	
June 15, 19X6, declared May 7, 19X6, payable to holders of record	
May 27, 19X6.	800
September 15, 19X6.	800
December 15, 19X6	1,200
March 15, 19X7	800
June 15, 19X7	800
Net proceeds of June 19, 19X6 sale of 700 shares of Meta Manufacturing	
common stock.	68,810

Payments were made from the estate's checking account through July 1, 19X7, for the
following:

Funeral expenses	$ 2,000
Assessments for additional 19X4 federal and state income taxes ($1,700)	
plus interest ($110) to May 31, 19X6.	1,810
19X6 income taxes of Arthur Taine for the period January 1 through May	
31, 19X6, in excess of amounts paid by the decedent on Declaration of	
Estimated Tax	9,100
Federal and state fiduciary income taxes, fiscal year ending June 30, 19X6	
($75), and June 30, 19X7 ($1,400)	1,475
Federal and state estate taxes	58,000
Monthly payments to Bertha Taine: 13 payments of $300 each	3,900
Attorney's and accountant's fees	25,000

The executor waived his commission. However, he desired to receive his father's diamond ring in lieu of the $10,000 specific legacy. All parties agreed to this in writing, and the court's approval was secured. All other specific legacies were delivered by July 15, 19X6. On July 2, 19X7, final distributions of the residuary legacies were made to Elaine and David, the latter continuing to function as trustee, establishing separate records for the trust.

Required:

Prepare journal entries to record all events related to the estate of Arthur Taine, including transfer to the trust and final closing entries for the estate.

(AICPA adapted)

Problem 20-10. Using the information detailed in Problem 20-9, prepare a charge and discharge statement and supporting schedules for the period May 31, 19X6, through July 1, 19X7. The following supporting schedules should be included:

Schedule   1—Original principal of the estate
            2—Gains and losses on realization of principal assets
            3—Funeral and administrative expenses
            4—Debts of decedent paid
            5—Legacies distributed
            6—Principal assets on hand, July 1, 19X7
            7—Proposed plan of distribution of estate assets as of July 1, 19X7
            8—Income collected
            9—Expenses chargeable to income
           10—Distributions to income beneficiary

(AICPA adapted)

Problem 20-11. The will of William Kraus, deceased, provided that as soon as possible a trust be established to assist his daughter, Sandy, in continuing voice lessons in New York City in preparation for a career in opera. Providing her progress is satisfactory, she shall receive $1,000 on the first day of each month. An additional $5,000 shall be made available during the summer if she is accepted at a recognized school for opera singers. Payments to Sandy shall be charged against trust income during the year. If income for the year is inadequate to cover expenses chargeable against income and income distributions, the deficiency shall be covered by principal, with no need for reimbursement from later income. If within six years Sandy has made a successful debut, the remaining assets shall be released to her. If she has not made her debut within that period, the payments shall cease, with any remaining assets turned over to UWM University for music scholarships.

The following events occurred that involved the trust:

(a) The will specified that principal and income assets of the estate retain their identity when transferred to the trust. The following assets were accepted by the trustee on January 2, 19X3:

As to principal:	Cash	$40,000	
	AMD common stock	15,000	
	Parrot 6% preferred stock	30,000	
	Rental property	80,000	$165,000
As to income:	Cash		4,000

(b) A $20,000, six-month money market certificate was purchased with principal cash on February 10, when the annual rate was 14%.

(c) On March 15, a dividend of $1,200 was received on the AMD common stock. By year end, the value of the stock increased from $15,000 to $18,000.

(d) Rental income of $4,200 for the first six months of 19X3 was received. Ordinary property expenses of $1,200 were paid. The trustee believed that the net return was not adequate to justify retaining the property in the trust. It was sold for $73,000 on July 1, 19X3.

(e) On July 1, principal cash was invested in 15% industrial bonds with a face value of $80,000, purchased at 105 plus accrued interest from May 1, the last semiannual interest payment date. The bonds mature on November 1, 19X6.

(f) Sandy was notified that she was accepted for the summer session master classes in voice at the La Scala School for Voice in Italy. On July 3, a payment of $5,000 was made to her in accordance with the will.

(g) On August 12, a check for the interest on the money market certificate was received. The trustee renewed the certificate for another six months.

(h) The annual dividend of $1,800 on the Parrot 6% preferred was received on September 2. The trustee believed that the return was minimal. When a takeover bidder offered $42,000 for the stock, the trustee sold. Most of the proceeds were invested in $36,000 (face value) of City of Madison 10% bonds, purchased at 96 and accrued interest on October 1. Semiannual interest payment dates are June 1 and December 1. The bonds mature on December 1, 19X9.

(i) Interest on the industrial bonds was received on November 1. When necessary, the trustee uses pro rata amortization techniques on interest collection dates only. Since Sandy is the only income beneficiary, the trustee does not accrue at calendar year end, which is an acceptable procedure under the circumstances.

(j) On December 1, interest on the City of Madison 10% bonds was received.

(k) During the year, twelve monthly payments of $1,000 were made to Sandy. (Make one entry for the twelve payments.)

(l) The trustee's fee of $4,000, which is to be charged against principal, was paid.

(m) Since trust income was inadequate to meet expenses chargeable against income and income distributions, an entry was to be made to cover the deficiency.

Required:

(1) Prepare journal entries to record the events for the year.

(2) Prepare a charge and discharge statement for the trust for the year ended December 31, 19X3.

CHAPTER 21

Debt Restructuring, Corporate Reorganizations, and Liquidations

The principles of accounting are based on several important underlying assumptions, one of which is the going concern assumption. Since this assumption assumes that a business entity will have a long, extended life as a separate, distinct entity, valuation and classification of account balances are significantly influenced by it. For example, both the valuation of a building at depreciated historical cost, rather than net realizable value, and the classification of a building as a noncurrent asset, rather than a current asset, are in recognition of the going concern assumption. Certainly, without this assumption all assets and liabilities would be classified as current in nature.

However, over time, the going concern assumption may not hold true for all business entities. An entity may decide voluntarily to cease its business purpose. For example, a research and development (R&D) venture may cease operations at the completion of a successful or unsuccessful R&D effort. Unfortunately, a business entity also may face difficulties that cause the going concern assumption to be challenged. A business may suffer from several factors, including poor management, poor accounting controls, uncontrolled growth, loss of market share, resistance to change, government intervention, and/or a declining profit margin. Although many businesses may be able to respond to these factors in a positive manner, other businesses may become troubled or insolvent and they seek corrective action. A business is considered to be insolvent if it is unable to service its liabilities, or if it technically has liabilities in excess of assets. Businesses experiencing such difficulties often are viewed as bankrupt, which is a state of lacking all or part of the means to service debts. This chapter focuses on several corrective actions available to a troubled or insolvent business, including troubled debt restructurings, reorganizations, and liquidations.

No business is immune from the factors that may result in financial difficulty. Large, small, young, and mature companies alike may find themselves having to cope with such difficulties. Along with the expansion of business

---

Exhibit 21-1
Examples of Companies Experiencing Financial Difficulties

CREDITORS FILE FOR LIQUIDATION OF MGM-PATHE

Group Says That It is Owed About $10 Million, Seeks Action Under Chapter 7

LOS ANGELES—After weeks of wrangling, a group of creditors filed a petition in federal bankruptcy court here seeking to force MGM-Pathe Communications Co. into involuntary liquidation under Chapter 7 of the federal Bankruptcy Code.

The creditor group, which includes producer Roger Corman's Concorde-New Horizons Corp., claims it is owed about $10 million, according to the court filing.

The beleaguered movie and television unit has had severe cash shortages since it was acquired by Giancarlo Parretti's Pathe Communications Co. in November for $1.3 billion.

Source: *The Wall Street Journal,* April 1, 1991.

RHODE ISLAND DEVELOPER LAROCHE FORCED INTO BANKRUPTCY FILING BY CREDITOR BANKS

PROVIDENCE, R.I.—David F. LaRoche, developer, bank stock speculator and chairman and major owner of NEO Enterprises Inc., was forced into a bankruptcy filing by several banks.

Mr. LaRoche, who started as a developer of vacation properties, invested millions of dollars in numerous banks during the boom in New England bank stocks in the mid-1980s. He also succeeded in a hostile takeover of NECO, then a sleepy Rhode Island utility, to which he later sold some of his deteriorating investments in controversial transactions.

His investments, concentrated largely in New England, turned sour as both bank stocks and real estate slumped sharply.

Source: *The Wall Street Journal,* February 22, 1991.

FIRST EXECUTIVE FILES PETITION FOR CHAPTER 11

Bankruptcy-Law Protection Aimed at Reorganization By the Parent Company

LOS ANGELES—First Executive Corp., whose two main insurance units were seized by regulators last month, filed for protection from creditors under Chapter 11 of the federal Bankruptcy Code.

The insurance holding company's bankruptcy-law petition had been widely expected since insurance departments in California and New York took control respectively of Executive Life Insurance Co. and Executive Life of New York. In a bit of a surprise, the parent is seeking to reorganize rather than liquidate.

Source: *The Wall Street Journal,* May 15, 1991.

---

comes the inevitable fact that some businesses may become troubled and/or fail. These difficulties are an everyday occurrence, as reflected in the above excerpts from the *Wall Street Journal*.

The accounting profession is involved with troubled businesses in a variety of ways. Providing consulting services and sound financial planning and reporting, accountants may be of invaluable service in thwarting or managing the forces leading to financial difficulty. Accountants also provide an important discovery and reporting function for those businesses seeking relief from their financial difficulties.

RELIEF PROCEDURES NOT REQUIRING COURT ACTION

When a business becomes insolvent or is not able to service its debts on a timely basis, there are several remedies available that do not require court approval. Since several of these remedies are discussed in intermediate textbooks, they will be only highlighted in this section. Seeking relief to financial problems outside of bankruptcy court offers several advantages. The time required to implement relief procedures is significantly less than the time required to seek relief through bankruptcy proceedings. Not requiring court action also allows the debtor's financial problems to be less public and more discreet. Knowledge of a company's financial troubles can affect adversely its ability to generate new business and acquire goods and services from vendors.

TROUBLED DEBT RESTRUCTURINGS

A basic approach to resolving an inability to service debt is to seek some concessions or compromises from major creditors. A troubled debt restructuring is a process whereby creditors grant concessions to the debtor that they would not consider otherwise. However, both the debtor and creditor are faced with a difficult situation, and a restructuring offers the creditor the best opportunity to recover the debt, as compared to nonrestructuring alternatives.

Although not all debt restructurings qualify as troubled debt restructurings, those that do generally take several forms. Troubled debt restructurings are discussed in FASB No. 15. The most common forms of restructuring, along with the appropriate debtor accounting, are summarized as follows.

Transfer of Assets in Full Settlement:

Form: The debtor transfers assets, such as third party receivables, real estate, and other assets, to the creditors in order to satisfy the debt either totally or partially.

Accounting by Debtor: The debtor records a gain on restructuring measured by the excess of the carrying basis of the debt, including related accrued interest, premiums, etc., and the fair market value of the assets transferred. The restructuring gain should be classified as an extraordinary item, if material. The difference between the book value of assets transferred to the debtor and their fair market value results in a gain or loss, which is not part of the gain on restructuring.

Example: Assets with a book value of $100,000 and a fair market value of $120,000 are transferred to a creditor in full settlement of a loan of $130,000 plus accrued interest of $2,000.

```
Loan Payable . . . . . . . . . . . . . . . . . . . . . . . . . . . . . . . . . . . . . . . . . . . . . .   130,000
Accrued Interest Payable . . . . . . . . . . . . . . . . . . . . . . . . . . . . . . . .     2,000
   Gain on Assets . . . . . . . . . . . . . . . . . . . . . . . . . . . . . . . . . . . . . . . . .                 20,000
   Assets . . . . . . . . . . . . . . . . . . . . . . . . . . . . . . . . . . . . . . . . . . . . . . . .                100,000
   Gain on Restructuring . . . . . . . . . . . . . . . . . . . . . . . . . . . . . . . . . .                 12,000
```

Granting an Equity Interest:

Form: Excluding existing terms for converting debt into equity (e.g., convertible debt), an equity interest in the company is granted to the creditor in order to satisfy the debt either totally or partially.

Accounting by Debtor: The debtor records a gain on restructuring measured by the excess of the carrying basis of the debt and the fair market value of the equity interest. The restructuring gain should be classified as an extraordinary item if material.

Example: Preferred stock with a par value of $20,000 and a market value of $120,000 is granted to a creditor in full settlement of a loan of $130,000 plus accrued interest of $2,000.

```
Loan Payable . . . . . . . . . . . . . . . . . . . . . . . . . . . . . . . . . . . . . . . . . . . . . .   130,000
Accrued Interest Payable . . . . . . . . . . . . . . . . . . . . . . . . . . . . . . . .     2,000
   Preferred Stock, at Par . . . . . . . . . . . . . . . . . . . . . . . . . . . . . . . . . . .                 20,000
   Paid-In Capital in Excess of Par . . . . . . . . . . . . . . . . . . . . . . . . . .                100,000
   Gain on Restructuring . . . . . . . . . . . . . . . . . . . . . . . . . . . . . . . . . .                 12,000
```

Modification of Terms:

Form: The terms of the debt are modified in several possible ways involving interest and/or principal. Interest rates may be reduced and/or accrued interest may be reduced. The principal amount of the debt may be reduced and/or the maturity date of the loan may be extended.

Accounting by Debtor: If the total future cash payments (both principal and interest) specified by the restructuring are less than the carrying basis of the debt, a gain on restructuring is recognized. The restructuring gain should be classified as an extraordinary item, if material. After recognizing the gain, all subsequent cash payments made per the terms of the restructuring should be accounted for as a reduction of the debt payable. Therefore, no interest expense shall be recognized on the restructured debt. If the total future cash payments (both principal and interest) specified by the restructuring are more than the carrying basis of the debt, no gain on restructuring is recognized. However, interest expense is recognized between restructuring and maturity. The interest recognized should be based on an effective interest rate that equates the present value of restructured future cash payments to the carrying value of the debt.

Example A: The terms of an outstanding debt of $130,000 plus accrued interest of $2,000 have been modified as follows: payments of $60,000 per year will be made over the next two years in full satisfaction of the debt.

Loan Payable	130,000	
Accrued Interest Payable	2,000	
Restructured Loan Payable		120,000
Gain on Restructuring		12,000
Restructured Loan Payable	60,000	
Cash		60,000
Restructured Loan Payable	60,000	
Cash		60,000

Example B: Same situation as Example A except that the payments are $76,057 each year, which results in an effective interest rate of 10%.

Loan Payable	130,000	
Accrued Interest Payable	2,000	
Restructured Loan Payable		132,000
Restructured Loan Payable	62,857	
Interest Expense (10% × 132,000)	13,200	
Cash		76,057
Restructured Loan Payable	69,143	
Interest Expense (10% × 69,143)	6,914	
Cash		76,057

Combination Restructurings:

Form: A restructuring may involve some combination of the above restructuring features.

Accounting by Debtor: The accounting for a combination restructuring is the same as discussed above except that first, the carrying basis of the debt should be reduced by the fair market value of assets transferred and/or equity interests granted. This step does not result in the recognition of a gain on restructuring. Second, the remaining carrying basis of the debt is compared against the "modification of terms" portion of the restructuring and accounted for accordingly.

Example: Land with a fair market value of $52,000 and a cost basis of $45,000 is transferred to a creditor in partial settlement of a debt of $130,000 plus accrued interest of $2,000. The balance of the debt is satisfied by the payment of $35,000 per year for each of the next two years.

Loan Payable	130,000	
Accrued Interest Payable	2,000	
Gain on Transfer of Land		7,000
Land		45,000
Gain on Restructuring		10,000
Restructured Debt		70,000
Restructured Debt	35,000	
Cash		35,000
Restructured Debt	35,000	
Cash		35,000

As seen from the previous examples, a troubled debt restructuring may be accomplished in a variety of ways. Regardless of the method used, a formal agreement must be reached between the debtor and individual creditors. Generally, such agreements take the form of a creditor agreement or a composition agreement. A creditor agreement is used to extend the terms of a debt or make other concessions regarding future interest rates. A composition agreement is used to scale down a creditor's claims against the debtor. For example, creditors might agree to accept $0.70 per dollar of debt owed to them.

Although the above discussion of troubled debt restructuring has focused on the necessary accounting by the debtor, FASB No. 114 discusses the necessary accounting by the creditor. A creditor in a troubled debt restructuring, involving only a modification of terms of a receivable, should measure the loan receivable based on the present value of the expected future cash flows discounted at the loan's effective interest rate. As a practical matter, the creditor may measure the loan receivable at the loan's observable market price or the fair value of the collateral, assuming the loan is collateral dependent. If the measure of the impaired loan receivable is less than the recorded investment in the loan, the difference is charged to bad-debt expense and a valuation allowance is established.[1]

QUASI-REORGANIZATIONS

A corporation may not be insolvent, but may have accumulated a relatively large deficit as a result of such problems as an excessive investment in plant assets or inventory, or management's inability to recognize and influence market demands. If management is replaced and if profits result from new policies, most state laws still will not permit declaration of dividends until the deficit is eliminated. The turnabout period and deficit elimination may take so long that the investors' interest in the company vanishes, and capital acquisition becomes difficult. To overcome such a handicap, the corporation might seek a *quasi-reorganization*.

Quasi-reorganization does not require court action, nor does it require the consent of creditors since creditor interests are not altered. However, the procedure is described in state laws, many of which require a quasi-reorganization to be approved by two-thirds of the stockholders.

The primary purpose of a quasi-reorganization is to eliminate a large deficit and take such action as will permit successful operations in the future. Excessive plant capacity and equipment may be sold. Plant assets that are retained may be revalued to reflect a lower but fair value, thereby reducing depreciation charges allocated to future periods. For example, as part of the quasi-reorganization process, a corporation's board of directors reduces plant assets from a cost of $1,000,000 to a more realistic fair value of $400,000 and reduces accumulated depreciation from $200,000 to $80,000. Future annual depreciation charges will be reduced from $50,000 to $20,000. The entry to record the revaluation would be:

Accumulated Depreciation	120,000	
Retained Earnings	480,000	
Property, Plant, and Equipment		600,000

[1]FASB Statement No. 114, *Accounting by Creditors for Impairment of a Loan* (Norwalk, CT: Financial Accounting Standards Board, 1993).

It should be noted that the write-down of the assets increases the deficit, which then will be eliminated by subsequent changes in the capital structure.

The deficit is eliminated by charges against the existing paid-in capital in excess of par or stated values. If no such paid-in capital exists, it may be created by altering the capital structure and substituting stock with lower par value or lower stated value for existing shares. To illustrate the manner in which the owners' equity section in the balance sheet is revised by a quasi-reorganization, assume the following stockholders' equity:

Common stock ($10 par, 12,000 shares outstanding)	$120,000
Retained earnings (deficit)	(45,000)
Total stockholders' equity	$ 75,000

On March 1, 19X0, the stockholders approve a reduction in par value to $1. Note that such a maneuver has absolutely no effect on the proportionate interests of each stockholder.

The entries to record the quasi-reorganization are as follows:

Common Stock ($10 par)	120,000	
Common Stock ($1 par)		12,000
Paid-In Capital from Reduction in Stock Par Value		
(or Reorganization Capital)		108,000
To record the reduction in par value.		
Paid-In Capital from Reduction in Stock Par Value	45,000	
Retained Earnings		45,000
To eliminate the deficit.		

Immediately following the quasi-reorganization, the owners' equity section would show:

Common stock ($1 par, 12,000 shares outstanding)	$12,000
Paid-in capital from reduction in stock par value	63,000
Retained earnings (subsequent to March 1, 19X0)	0
Total stockholders' equity	$75,000

In future financial statements, retained earnings must be dated to indicate the starting point of new accumulations. The process of dating retained earnings should be continued for as long a period of time as is deemed advisable, but rarely does it exceed ten years.

CORPORATE LIQUIDATIONS

A corporation may decide to liquidate its assets, distribute available amounts to creditors, and terminate the business. Such a liquidation may be accomplished without a formal bankruptcy proceeding through the use of a general assignment for the benefit of creditors, which generally must be agreed to by all creditors. Shareholders of the corporation receive any net assets remaining after fully satisfying the claims of creditors. Usually, assets are not adequate to fully satisfy creditor claims. In this case, creditors share according to the terms of the general assignment.

BANKRUPTCY REFORM ACT OF 1978 AND THE 1986 BANKRUPTCY CODE AMENDMENTS

If a satisfactory solution cannot be reached under the procedures described in the previous paragraphs, the legal proceedings for bankruptcy may be initiated. Modern bankruptcy procedures attempt to give a debtor a fresh start, unburdened by former obligations, while simultaneously accomplishing an equitable distribution of the debtor's property among creditors.

In an attempt to modernize an antiquated system existing under the Bankruptcy Act of 1898, as amended by the Chandler Act of 1938, Congress passed the *Bankruptcy Reform Act of 1978* (Title 11 of the U.S. Code), which became effective on October 1, 1979. In 1982, the U.S. Supreme Court ruled that the section of the Bankruptcy Reform Act of 1978 (hereafter referred to as the Act) giving bankruptcy judges the power to consider and rule on issues that were not directly part of the bankruptcy proceedings was unconstitutional. Under the Act, bankruptcy judges had the power to consider any issue arising in or related to bankruptcy cases. Thus, if a company had filed in bankruptcy court and another company had a damage suit against it, the damage claim could have been heard in bankruptcy court instead of in a federal district or state court. Under the Supreme Court's decision, bankruptcy judges now must limit their rulings to issues directly related to bankruptcy proceedings. In June, 1984, Congress passed a bill to overhaul the bankruptcy system. The bill limited the powers of bankruptcy judges to comply with the 1982 Supreme Court decision and created 85 new federal trial and appellate judgeships to assist with cases that spill out of bankruptcy courts. The other provisions of the Act remained operative.

Bankruptcy rules were modified effective August 1, 1987, by Bankruptcy Code amendments as detailed in the *Bankruptcy Judges, U.S. Trustees, and Family Farmer Bankruptcy Act of 1986.* The act authorized 52 additional bankruptcy judges to break up the log jam of cases awaiting disposition. It established a U.S. Trustee system under the control of the U.S. Attorney General. Supervisory and administrative duties of the U.S. Trustee were broadened and even include the reporting of any potential crimes to the Attorney General.

A bankruptcy case may be filed under one of the following operative chapters of the code:

Chapter 7: Liquidation. A nonbusiness debtor or any business not wishing to remain in operation, except a railroad, governmental unit, bank, insurance company, or savings and loan association, may file a petition under this chapter.

Chapter 9: Adjustments of Debts of a Municipality is not covered in this text.

Chapter 11: Reorganization. The purpose of Chapter 11 is to assist a company or individual to remain in possession of the business during the judicial process of reorganization, without the appointment of a trustee and without the harassment of creditors. This chapter is used primarily by corporate or partnership debtors. Although the chapter may be used by an individual proprietor, the procedures are more cumbersome and more expensive than those of Chapter 13. Only individuals with substantial assets and liabilities resort to Chapter 11 proceedings.

Chapter 13: Adjustment of Debts of an Individual with Regular Income. This chapter is limited exclusively to individuals, including sole proprietors, with less than $100,000 in unsecured debt and less than $350,000 in secured debt. A joint case of debtor and spouse is permissible if their combined debt does not exceed the two limitations.

There are provisions for the movement or conversion of a case from one chapter to another, such as converting an unsuccessful reorganization (Chapter 11) to a liquidation (Chapter 7). Chapters 9 and 13 of the code will not be specifically discussed in this text.

COMMENCEMENT OF A BANKRUPTCY CASE

The Act states that a debtor must be a person (individual, partnership, or corporation) residing in or having a domicile, business, or property in the United States, or be a municipality. If a debtor initiates the action of filing a petition with the court of bankruptcy under the appropriate chapter of the Act, it is a *voluntary* case. A voluntary petition may seek relief under Chapters 7, 9, 11, or 13. Filing constitutes an *order for relief*, which represents a stay of action by prohibiting commencement or continuation of legal action against the debtor to recover a claim.

If the petition is filed by someone other than the debtor, an *involuntary* proceeding results. Such proceedings may be filed under Chapter 7 (Liquidation) or Chapter 11 (Reorganization), but not under Chapter 13, where the individual debtor is willing to make payments to creditors. Involuntary proceedings may not be initiated against a farmer or a charitable organization. Under Chapters 7 and 11, if a debtor has twelve or more creditors, three or more of them may file an involuntary petition, providing the total of their noncontingent, unsecured claims is $5,000 or more. If there are less than twelve creditors, one or more of them may initiate an involuntary case, but the same limit of $5,000 applies. In an involuntary case, the claims must have arisen before the order for relief was issued. The court will issue such an order if the debtor files no answer to the involuntary petition. If an answer is filed by the debtor, the court will hold a hearing, following which it will either dismiss the case, issue an order for relief, or postpone the decision pending receipt of additional information.

CORPORATE REORGANIZATIONS—CHAPTER 11

The ultimate goal of a reorganization is to restructure the debt and/or equity of a company so that the company may continue to carry on its business purpose and become a financially sound business. Unfortunately, the vast majority of reorganizations never achieve this goal. Such a reorganization often is more attractive than a debt restructuring not involving a bankruptcy proceeding because the reorganization may be more generous toward the debtor company. Generally, a reorganization reduces debt through forgiveness to a greater extent than a conventional debt restructuring. Furthermore, interest on unsecured debt is not accrued during the period of reorganization. The period of reorganization provides a company with an opportunity to delay creditors from bringing suit for delinquent debts as well as to seek protection from a variety of business risks, which may affect a company's ability to continue as a going concern.

Companies have used Chapter 11 procedures to gain court protection for a broad spectrum of purposes. In 1982, front-page headlines announced that Manville Corporation, the largest asbestos company in the world, filed a petition for reorganization and protection. At the time, it ranked 181st in *Fortune's* list of the nation's leading industrial corporations. Amazing was the fact that, with net assets of over $2 billion, it was a financially healthy company. However, lawsuits at the rate of 500 a month were being brought against the company by workers who allegedly had developed lung cancer and other diseases as a result of their exposure to asbestos. Its chairperson, John A. McKinney, estimated that, at the going settlement rate of $40,000 per case, a reserve fund of at least $2 billion would have to be created, virtually wiping out its net worth and crippling operations. The board of directors filed under Chapter 11 to establish an effective method for handling the asbestos claims.

In April 1987, Texaco filed under Chapter 11. Thus began the largest bankruptcy case to date. Texaco had assets of $34 billion and liabilities of $20 billion. It filed to delay and possibly reduce the history-making $10.5 billion judgment against it awarded to Pennzoil Company in 1985. Texaco had been found guilty of improper and illegal action when it disrupted the merger pact that was in process between Pennzoil and Getty Oil. Texaco was trying to prevent possible panic among its creditors if it had to commit billions of dollars of assets as security for payment while it sought relief from the enormous damage award.

Generally, Chapter 11 is not successful in protecting assets outside of the United States. Foreign courts typically do not recognize the concept of bankruptcy reorganization. *Business Week* made the comment that, to foreign creditors, reorganization means "grab the assets."[2] When U.S. Lines, Inc., with its fleet of twenty-seven ships, filed for protection from creditors in 1986, the following events occurred:

Belgium—Local courts placed Lines' Belgium assets under a trustee.

England—British courts froze company assets and bank accounts.

Italy—Courts placed company assets in Italy in receivership.

Hong Kong—Creditors seized four ships and auctioned them for $16 million. The ships cost U.S. Lines $184 million.

---

[2]Todd Vogel, "There's No Word for Chapter 11 in Dutch," *Business Week* (November 30, 1987): p. 62.

Netherlands—Dutch creditors seized Lines' European headquarters building and filed involuntary bankruptcy proceedings.[3]

Recent events have strengthened the position of those who are critical of the manner in which Chapter 11 has been manipulated. It was designed to assist those in difficulty under the conventional interpretation of indebtedness. On the docket of bankruptcy courts have been companies who have filed in order to protect themselves from mass tort litigations (Manville, with its asbestos products, and A.H. Robins Inc., with its Dalkon Shield contraceptive device), to ward off enforcement of huge judgments (Texaco), or to escape funding of pension plans (LTV Corporation). It is doubtful that Congress intended bankruptcy laws to be an umbrella of corporate protection with such serious public consequences.

DEVELOPING A PLAN OF REORGANIZATION

A petition seeking a corporate reorganization may be filed voluntarily or involuntarily to seek an order for relief. Normally, the debtor remains in charge of the business, although in unusual instances, a trustee may be appointed to take control of the company. Those unusual instances include management fraud, deceit, and/or gross mismanagement.

After the filing of the petition, the law provides that the debtor shall not be harassed by creditors or stockholders so that the debtor can devote full energy to the reorganization. For the first 120 days, the debtor has the exclusive right to file a plan of reorganization. Thereafter, a plan may be filed by any party of interest. The court appoints a committee of the creditors holding the seven largest claims against the debtor. A committee of equity security holders also may be appointed. Their primary functions are to consult with the debtor in possession (or the trustee) about the administration of the case and assist in the formulation of a plan of reorganization.

The plan of reorganization must detail the methods and means by which it will achieve its objectives. Possible arrangements will involve eliminating some debt, reducing debt principal and/or interest, reducing interest rates, postponing payment, and exchanging an equity interest for creditor claims or exchanging a lower ranking for a higher equity interest, such as substitution of common stock for preferred stock. The plan identifies the various classes of claims (secured versus unsecured) and classes of interests (stockholders or limited partners). It indicates the claims of interests (stockholders or limited partners). It indicates the claims or interests that are not impaired, as well as the treatment to be accorded those that are impaired. A class is impaired if the plan alters its legal or contractual rights.

If a class is not impaired, it is considered to have accepted the plan. The holder of a claim or interest impaired by the plan may accept or reject it. Parties impaired are provided a description of the reorganizational plan along with a court-approved disclosure statement regarding the plan. After evaluating the plan, the affected parties must vote to approve or reject it. A plan affecting

---

[3]*Ibid.*

impaired creditors is approved if it is accepted by creditors representing at least two-thirds in amount and more than one-half in number of a class of claims. A plan affecting shareholders or equity interests is approved if it is accepted by holders of such interests representing at least two-thirds in amount of the allowed claims of that class.

Upon approval by the impaired parties, confirmation by the bankruptcy court is sought. Before confirmation, the court verifies that under the plan each holder of a claim or interest will receive or retain property of a value that is not less than the amount such holder would receive under a Chapter 7 liquidation.

Once a plan is confirmed by the court, its provisions are binding on the debtor and on all creditors and equity security holders, whether or not they accepted the plan. Confirmation vests property in the debtor company or trustee. Such property is free of all claims of creditors and interests of equity holders, except as stipulated in the provisions of the plan. Under Chapter 11, once a plan is confirmed, the payment obligation on the debtor is fixed, regardless of any subsequent increase in the debtor's net cash inflow. If the reorganization is not accomplishing its intended objectives during the period outlined in the plan, a request for modification may be submitted to the court for approval, or a request may be filed to convert to a Chapter 7 liquidation.

ACCOUNTING FOR THE REORGANIZATION

The accounting professional is involved significantly in providing expertise regarding corporate reorganizations. Accountants may help in the discovery of assets and liabilities or in the determination of the impact of a reorganization. Prospective information also must be generated in order to determine the effect of a reorganization plan on future operations of the company. A plan of reorganization includes debt and/or equity restructuring similar to that discussed in the earlier section of this text involving troubled debt restructurings and quasi-reorganizations.

With respect to the restructuring of debt in a bankruptcy reorganization, the principles set forth in FASB Statement No. 15 generally do not apply to a bankruptcy reorganization; therefore, a different approach is used to measure the gain or loss on restructuring involving a modification of terms. In a bankruptcy reorganization, the gain on restructuring is measured as the difference between the fair market value of the restructured consideration received (its discounted present value) and the carrying basis of the debt being restructured. In FASB Statement No. 15, the gain on restructuring is measured as the difference between the total future cash payments (both principal and interest) to be received and the carrying basis of the debt being restructured. The gain on restructuring in a bankruptcy reorganization is typically recorded as either an extraordinary item or additional paid-in capital. Recognizing the gain as a component of paid-in capital facilitates the reduction of a deficit balance in retained earnings, if appropriate as part of the reorganization plan.

The recognition of subsequent interest on the restructured debt also differs for a bankruptcy reorganization. In this case, the total interest recognized on the restructured debt is imputed at market rates and represents the difference between the fair market value of the new debt (its discounted present value using market rates) and the total of all principal and interest payments. A FASB Statement No. 15 restructuring measures the total interest as the difference between the carrying basis of the debt being restructured and the total of all principal and interest payments. Therefore, under Statement No. 15, no interest is recognized if the total of all principal and interest payments made under the restructuring agreement do not exceed the carrying basis of the original debt being restructured. Other than the above differences, the accounting principles and standards for reorganizations are applicable to both bankruptcy and non-bankruptcy reorganizations.

Companies undergoing corporate reorganizations also are required to submit to the bankruptcy court periodic reports detailing operations, cash flows, and other information that the court may request. The preparation of these statements and reports presents no unusual accounting problems. Balance sheets may distinguish between assets and liabilities existing prior to and subsequent to the approval of the reorganization or appointment of a trustee, if applicable. Generally, the books of record used to account for the company prior to reorganization also are employed during the reorganization. However, if a trustee is appointed, the trustee may elect to establish a new set of books.

If new accounting records are to be established, the assets accepted by the fiduciary are debited at their book values, with a credit to an account called X Corporation in Trusteeship. On the corporate books, the transfer of assets is recorded by debiting an account to charge the fiduciary, such as E. Schenker, Trustee. These new accounts are reciprocal and represent the accountability of the trustee.

The fiduciary is not responsible for commitments made by the corporation prior to the period of stewardship. Therefore, those liabilities remain on the corporate books. However, the courts may direct payment of such liabilities. In this case, the trustee either may debit X Corporation in Trusteeship directly or create a temporary account, such as Accounts Payable—X Corporation, which periodically is closed into the major reciprocal account. The corporation would reflect payment with a debit to Accounts Payable and a credit to the account E. Schenker, Trustee.

The usual accounting procedures are followed by the trustee to record revenues and expenses. At the end of the year or at termination of the period of stewardship, the profit or loss on the trustee's books is closed into the accountability account, X Corporation in Trusteeship. On the corporate books, net income is recorded with a debit to the trustee account and a credit to Retained Earnings, while a net loss is recorded by the reverse procedure. When control is returned to the owners, the trustee eliminates all account balances, including the X Corporation in Trusteeship balance. The corporation records these accounts and eliminates the trustee account.

While the trustee is in control, the corporation's financial story is contained partly in the records of the trustee and partly in those of the corporation. The two records must be combined in order to prepare financial statements. The following skeleton worksheet is designed to accomplish the objective of reuniting the two sets of financial information:

X Corporation in Trusteeship
E. Schenker, Trustee
Worksheet for Combined Trial Balance
For Year Ended June 30, 19X1

Account Title	Trial Balance		Adjustments and Eliminations		Combined Trial Balance
	Trustee	Corporation			
Debits:					
E. Schenker, Trustee		90,000		(a) 90,000	
Total debits	500,000	420,000			
Credits:					
X Corp. in Trusteeship	90,000		(a) 90,000		
Total credits	500,000	420,000			

The worksheet begins with the trial balances of the trustee's records and the corporation's records. These trial balances should be adjusted fully before they are entered on the worksheet. Any additional adjustments discovered subsequently are entered, and the two reciprocal account balances are eliminated. The items then are combined to produce a trial balance from which financial statements may be prepared.

CORPORATE LIQUIDATIONS—CHAPTER 7

The only solution for certain insolvent companies is to liquidate the assets of the company, service its debts, distribute any remaining funds to shareholders, and terminate the business. Unfortunately, corporate reorganizations frequently are not successful and ultimately result in liquidation.

The commencement of a voluntary or involuntary case under Chapter 7 (Liquidation) creates an estate that consists of the assets of the debtor, who must file an inventory of debts and property on a form called the Statement of Assets and Liabilities. This form consists of the following schedules:

1. Schedule A—Statement of All Liabilities of Debtor
    Schedule A-1—Creditors Having Priority (with amount of claim)
    Schedule A-2—Creditors Holding Security (with market value of security and amount of claim)
    Schedule A-3—Creditors Having Unsecured Claims Without Priority (with amount of claim)
2. Schedule B—Statement of All Property of Debtor
    Schedule B-1—Real Property (with market values)
    Schedule B-2—Personal Property (with market values)
    Schedule B-3—Property Not Otherwise Scheduled (includes property transferred for benefit of creditors within four months prior to filing of the petition)

Schedule B-4—Property Claimed as Exempt (with reference to the statute creating the exemption and value claimed as exempt)

APPOINTMENT OF A TRUSTEE IN LIQUIDATION

As soon as possible after issuing the order for relief, the court appoints an interim trustee to take charge until a permanent trustee is selected, and then a meeting of creditors is called. Creditors either may elect a permanent trustee or have the interim trustee serve in that capacity. If desired, creditors may elect a committee of three to eleven creditors to assist and advise the trustee in the administration of the estate. Only creditors who have filed a written proof of claim at or before the meeting are entitled to vote. Proofs of claim are examined by the trustee, who may accept them or, if they are improper, disallow them. To be considered in the settlement, a claim normally must be filed within six months after the date set for the first meeting of creditors.

The debtor is required to be present at the meeting of creditors in order to be subject to examination by the creditors or the trustee and must cooperate with the trustee in the preparation of an inventory of property, the examination of proofs of claim, and the general administration of the estate. To assist the trustee, a debtor files a *statement of affairs,* consisting of answers to a series of stated questions about the identity of the debtor's records and books, transactions, and events affecting the financial condition of the debtor, including any prior bankruptcy proceedings. This *legal* statement of affairs is not to be confused with the *accounting* statement of affairs discussed later in the chapter.

Duties of Trustee.   The trustee shall:

1. Collect and reduce to money the nonexempt property of the estate.
2. Account for all money and property received, maintaining a record of cash receipts and disbursements.
3. Investigate the financial affairs of the debtor, including a review of the forms filed by the debtor.
4. Examine proofs of claim and disallow any improper claim.
5. Furnish information reasonably requested by a party of interest.
6. Operate the business of the debtor, if any, when so authorized by the court if such operation is in the best interest of the estate and consistent with its orderly liquidation.
7. Pay dividends to creditors as promptly as practicable, with regard for priorities. (The law applies the term "dividend" to any payment made to a creditor.)
8. File reports of progress, with the final report accompanied by a detailed statement of receipts and disbursements.

Disposition of Property.   One duty of the trustee is to dispose of property, even if another entity has an allowed claim secured by a lien on the property. The claim is secured to the amount of the value of the property. For example, if a creditor has an allowed claim of $20,000, with a sole lien against real property whose market value is $30,000, the claim is fully secured. Upon realization of the property, the excess of $10,000 would be available to meet unsecured claims in the order of priority. If the creditor in the example has an allowed claim of $35,000, there is a secured claim of $30,000 and an unsecured claim of $5,000.

Priorities for Unsecured Claims.   An order of priority to receive distributions from amounts available to meet unsecured claims has been established by the Act. Each class must be paid in full or provided for before any amount is paid to the next lower class. When the amount is inadequate to pay all claims of a given class, the amount is distributed on a pro rata basis within that class. When the amount is sufficient to pay the claims of all classes, which is highly unlikely, the excess amount is returned to the debtor. The order of priority for allowed unsecured claims is as follows:

Class 1—Expenses to administer the estate. Those who administer the estate should be assured of payment; otherwise, competent attorneys and accountants would not be willing to participate.

Class 2—Debts incurred after the commencement of a case of involuntary bankruptcy but before the order for relief or appointment of a trustee. These items are granted priority in order to permit the business to carry on its operations during the period of legal proceedings.

Class 3—Wages up to $2,000 per individual, earned within 90 days before the filing of the petition or the cessation of the debtor's business, whichever occurs first.

Class 4—Unpaid contributions to employee benefit plans to the extent of $2,000 per employee covered by the plan, less any amount paid to participating employees under priority 3.

Class 5—Deposits up to $900 each for goods or services never received from the debtor.

Class 6—Tax claims of a governmental unit. Since these taxes are nondischargeable (i.e., they still must be met by the debtor after the termination of the case), the arrangement favors the debtor. Whatever funds are available for this priority will reduce the amount the debtor will have to pay later. For this reason, if a governmental unit fails to file a claim for taxes, the Act permits the debtor to do so.

Class 7—Claims of general creditors not granted priority. All remaining unsecured claims fall into this category.

For a successful case under Chapter 11 (Reorganization) or Chapter 13 (Individual), the sequence of priority also has significance. In a Chapter 11 case, the plan of reorganization will not be confirmed unless the court has determined that creditors will receive at least as much as they would under Chapter 7. The same idea is used for Chapter 13 cases, for which the Code states that the court will approve the plan only if the value of the property to be distributed on account of each allowed unsecured claim is not less than the amount that would be paid under Chapter 7.

PREPARATION OF THE STATEMENT OF AFFAIRS

Earlier in this chapter, a reference was made to the legal statement of affairs, which consists of responses to questions regarding a debtor's financial condition. The other report with the same name is the *accounting statement of affairs*, which is discussed in this section of the chapter. The primary purpose of the accounting statement of affairs is to approximate the estimated amounts available to each class of claims. It thereby assists all concerned parties in reaching a decision as to what insolvency action is preferable. It is a balance sheet of a potentially liquidating concern rather than of a going concern. Thus, it shifts the emphasis for assets from historical cost to estimated realizable values and the allocation of proceeds to creditors and stockholders. It is important to note that the statement of affairs is based on estimated values available to creditors, and the actual values realized from the liquidation of assets may differ. Although the statement assumes a liquidation of the insolvent company, the statement also is used to evaluate the reasonableness of a corporate reorganization. Plans for a corporate reorganization will not be confirmed by the court unless creditors will receive at least as much as they would under a liquidation.

In the past, the preparation and the format of the statement of affairs have been cumbersome and confusing. Thus, a revised form is recommended, in which the statement of affairs is split into two sections, one dealing with the assets and the other with the liabilities and the owners' equity. Before the statement of affairs is prepared, however, the account balances should be adjusted fully, an income statement should be prepared, and owners' equity should be adjusted to include the net profit or net loss to date.

The asset portion of the statement of affairs identifies the assets of the liquidating entity and their book value, estimated net realizable value, and estimated gain or loss upon liquidation. Available assets are identified as follows:

1. Assets pledged with fully secured creditors,
2. Assets pledged with partially secured creditors, and
3. Free assets available to unsecured creditors.

For each asset, the net realizable value must be estimated, using whatever information is available. For example, receivables would exclude unrealizable amounts; marketable securities would be based on current market reports; and real estate would reflect current market appraisals. Some assets, such as goodwill, may have no realizable value. For each asset, the difference between realizable value and book value is entered as a gain or loss upon liquidation. The assets available to unsecured creditors also are identified on the asset section of the statement of affairs.

The liability and owners' equity section on the statement of affairs identifies the following components:

1. Fully secured creditors,
2. Partially secured creditors,
3. Unsecured creditors with priority (Class 1 through 6 creditors),

4.   Unsecured creditors without priority (Class 7 creditors), and
5.   Owners' equity deficiency or surplus.

In order to illustrate the statement of affairs, assume Insolve Corporation's adjusted balance sheet as of February 28, 19X8, is as appears in Illustration 21-1.

Illustration 21-1
Insolve Corporation
Balance Sheet
February 28, 19X8

Assets

Current assets:			
Cash		$ 4,000	
Accounts receivable	$ 84,000		
Less allowance for uncollectible accounts	(14,000)	70,000	
Marketable securities		20,000	
Inventories:			
Raw materials	35,000		
Work in process	63,000		
Finished goods	124,000	222,000	$316,000
Property, plant, and equipment:			
Land		110,000	
Building		340,000	
Less accumulated depreciation—building		(158,000)	
Equipment		290,000	
Less accumulated depreciation—equipment		(140,000)	442,000
Goodwill (net of amortization)			48,000
Total assets			$806,000

Liabilities and Owners' Equity

Current liabilities:			
Accounts payable		$240,000	
Accrued liabilities—other		12,000	
Accrued income taxes		6,000	
Accrued mortgage interest		24,000	
Accrued liquidation expenses		13,000	
Accrued payroll taxes		14,000	
Accrued payroll (not exceeding $2,000 per person)		33,000	$342,000
Long-term liabilities:			
Mortgage payable		280,000	
Bank loan payable		200,000	480,000
Total liabilities			$822,000
Owners' equity:			
Common stock		10,000	
Paid-in capital in excess of par		40,000	
Deficit		(66,000)	(16,000)
Total liabilities and owners' equity			$806,000

Prior to liquidation, management has decided to complete the work in process by incurring $12,000 of additional labor costs and $4,000 of additional overhead. It is expected that upon completion the additional finished goods can be sold for $94,000. The mortgage payable is secured by the land and building, and the bank loan is secured by the equipment. Accounts payable totaling $180,000 are secured by inventory with a book value of $180,000 and an estimated net realizable value of $160,000.

The statement of affairs for Insolve Corporation is based on assumed net realizable amounts and appears as Illustration 21-2.

There are several important things to note about the mechanics of the statement of affairs. First, the two major sections of the statement (Assets and Liabilities and Owners' Equity) should be completed in conjunction with each other. For example, when identifying assets pledged with partially secured creditors, the secured and unsecured amounts of liabilities to such creditors should be identified. Second, the statement is constructed to provide crossfootings as a check on the mathematical accuracy and completeness of the schedule. For example, in the asset section the book value of the assets should equal the Assets' estimated net realizable value plus (minus) the estimated loss (gain) on liquidation ($806,000 = $754,000 + $52,000). In the liabilities and owners' equity section, the book value total before the owners' deficiency should equal the total of estimated secured and unsecured liabilities ($822,000 = $582,000 + $66,000 + $174,000). Finally, the deficiency traceable to unsecured creditors without priority ($68,000) should equal the difference between the estimated net realizable value of the assets and the total of estimated secured and unsecured amounts due creditors [$68,000 = $754,000 − ($582,000 + $66,000 + $174,000)]. This deficiency represents the extent to which the net realizable value of assets is inadequate to meet the claims of creditors. Certainly, if the net realizable value of such assets exceeded the creditors' claims, the excess would be available to satisfy the claims of owners/shareholders.

Of interest to the unsecured creditors in Class 7 and the bankruptcy court is a ratio that is referred to as the dividend to general unsecured creditors. This ratio is computed as follows:

$$\text{Dividend} = \frac{\text{Net proceeds available to unsecured creditors in Class 7}}{\text{Total claims of unsecured creditors in Class 7}}$$

The dividend is an estimate of how much will be received by Class 7 unsecured creditors for each dollar owed to them, and it is expressed either in absolute amount or in percentage form.

The approximate dividend in Class 7 unsecured creditors of Insolve Corporation will be:

$$\frac{\$106,000}{\$174,000} = \$0.61 \text{ on one dollar, or } 61\%$$

Illustration 21-2

Insolve Corporation
Statement of Affairs
February 28, 19X8

Book Value	Assets	Estimated Net Realizable Value	Estimated Amount Available for Unsecured Creditors	Estimated Gain or (Loss) on Liquidation
	Assets pledged with fully secured creditors:			
$110,000	Land	$130,000		$ 20,000
182,000	Building (net)	210,000		28,000
		$340,000	$ 36,000	
	Assets pledged with partially secured creditors:			
150,000	Equipment (net)	118,000		(32,000)
	Inventory			
35,000	Raw materials	18,000		(17,000)
63,000	Work in process (less estimated completion costs of $16,000)	78,000		15,000
124,000	Finished goods	112,000		(12,000)
	Total	326,000	48,000	
	Free assets:			
4,000	Cash	4,000	4,000	
70,000	Accounts receivable (net)	70,000	70,000	
20,000	Marketable securities	14,000	14,000	(6,000)
48,000	Goodwill			(48,000)
	Estimated amount available for unsecured creditors with and without priority		$172,000	
	Less unsecured creditors with priority		(66,000)	
	Estimated amounts for unsecured creditors without priority:			
	Net realizable amount available		$106,000	
	Deficiency (to agree with total unsecured amount without priority)		68,000	
$806,000	Totals	$754,000	$174,000	($52,000)

PREPARATION OF OTHER ACCOUNTING REPORTS

The trustee appointed to a company in liquidation is expected to make periodic reports to the bankruptcy court regarding the activities of the trustee. In the absence of specific reporting requirements imposed by the Act, each bankruptcy court identifies the type of accounting reports to be submitted by the trustee.

Book Value	Liabilities and Owners' Equity	Estimated Secured Amount	With Priority	Without Priority
			Estimated Unsecured Amount	
	Fully secured creditors:			
$ 24,000	Accrued mortgage interest................	$ 24,000		
280,000	Mortgage payable	280,000		
	Total.....................................	$304,000		
	Partially secured creditors:			
200,000	Bank loan payable	$118,000		$ 82,000
180,000	Accounts payable........................	160,000		20,000
	Total.....................................	$278,000		
	Unsecured creditors with priority:			
6,000	Accrued income taxes....................		$ 6,000	
13,000	Accrued liquidation expenses		13,000	
14,000	Accrued payroll taxes		14,000	
33,000	Accrued payroll..........................		33,000	
	Unsecured creditors without priority:			
12,000	Accrued liabilities—other.................			12,000
60,000	Accounts payable........................			60,000
$822,000	Totals....................................	$582,000	$66,000	$174,000
(16,000)	Owners' deficiency			
$806,000				

(handwritten: -354,000 ← 48,000)

Generally speaking, a court will require the trustee to provide an accounting regarding the following items pertaining to the insolvent company:

1. Unrealized assets assigned to the trustee including those subsequently discovered.
2. Assets that have been realized or liquidated.
3. Liabilities to be liquidated that have been assigned to the trustee.
4. Liabilities that have been liquidated.

Historically, the preceding information was presented in a report called the realization and liquidation account, which employed a rather cumbersome format. Currently, this information is presented usually in a worksheet format that identifies critical balances and relevant cash receipts and disbursements.

The statement of realization and liquidation differs from the statement of affairs in the following respects:

1. The statement of realization and liquidation reports the actual liquidation results. In contrast, the statement of affairs is of a pro forma nature and is based on estimated rather than actual results.
2. The statement of realization and liquidation provides an ongoing reporting of the trustee's activities and is updated throughout the liquidation process. The statement of affairs is a summary of the estimated results of a completed liquidation.

In order to illustrate the preparation of a statement of realization and liquidation, the balance sheet of Insolve Corporation, which is presented in Illustration 21-1, will be used as a starting point. Assuming the assets and liabilities contained in Insolve's balance sheet were assigned to the trustee, a statement of realization and liquidation for the period March 1, 19X8, to March 31, 19X8, is presented in Illustration 21-3. In reviewing this illustration, note that it reports actual results rather than estimated amounts, as contained in the statement of affairs. Also note that the statement reports liquidation activity to date and may be updated to reflect subsequent activity.

The statement also may be used to reassess the effect of a liquidation on various claims of liabilities. For example, as of March 31, 19X8, Insolve Corporation still has $447,000 of noncash assets to be realized. A statement of these assets and their newly revised estimated net realizable values follows:

Noncash Assets	Book Value	Estimated Net Realizable Value
Accounts receivable (net)	$ 18,000	$ 18,000
Inventories	74,000	70,000*
Land	110,000	130,000
Building (net)	182,000	210,000
Goodwill	48,000	0
Assets subsequently discovered	15,000	17,000
	$447,000	$445,000

*$44,000 of this amount is traceable to partially secured accounts payable.

The estimated net realizable value of noncash assets of $445,000 plus the available existing cash of $108,000 represents a total of $553,000, which would be available to satisfy liabilities and owners' equity. A tentative distribution of this total follows on page 1174:

Illustration 21-3
Insolve Corporation
Statement of Realization and Liquidation
For the Period March 1, 19X8, to March 31, 19X8

| | Assets | | Liabilities | | Unsecured | | |
	Cash	Noncash	Fully Secured	Partially Secured	With Priority	Without Priority	Owners' Equity
Beginning balances, assigned March 1, 19X8..............	$ 4,000	$802,000	$304,000	$380,000	$66,000	$ 72,000	($16,000)
Subsequently discovered and other items:							
Assets.....................		15,000*					15,000
Loans from officers						20,000*	(20,000)
Additional liquidation expenses[1]					2,000		(2,000)
Cash receipts:							
Sale of marketable securities....	16,000*	(20,000)					(4,000)
Partial collection of accounts receivable	52,000	(52,000)					
Sale of equipment............	124,000*	(150,000)					(26,000)
Sale of inventory[2]	134,000*	(148,000)					(14,000)
Cash disbursements:							
Partial payment of bank loan[3]...	(124,000)			(200,000)		76,000	
Partial payment of accounts payable[4]	(98,000)			(135,000)		37,000	
Ending balances................	$108,000	$447,000	$304,000	$ 45,000	$68,000	$205,000	($67,000)

*These amounts differ from the estimated amounts included in the statement of affairs.

[1]Liquidation expenses were originally estimated to be $13,000. However, actual liquidation expenses to date total $15,000.

[2]The sale of inventory consists of the following:

	Book Value	Amount Realized
Raw materials	$ 35,000	$ 18,000
Work in process (less completion costs of $18,000)	63,000	76,000
Finished goods	50,000	40,000
	$148,000	$134,000

[3]The bank loan of $200,000 is secured by the equipment, which was disposed of for $124,000 net of expenses. Therefore, $76,000 of the loan is reclassified as an unsecured liability.

[4]The sale of inventory described in footnote 2 included inventory securing the accounts payable. This inventory had a book value of $135,000 and was sold for $98,000. Therefore, accounts payable with a value of $135,000 were only secured to the extent of $98,000. The unsecured portion of $37,000 ($135,000 – $98,000) is reclassified as such.

Liabilities and Owners' Equity	Book Value	Estimated Distribution	Dividend (Payout) Percentage
Fully secured liabilities	$304,000	$304,000	100%
Partially secured liabilities:			
Book value of $45,000 less unsecured portion of $1,000	44,000	44,000	100
Unsecured liabilities:			
With priority.	68,000	68,000	100
Without priority:			
Book value of $205,000 plus unsecured portion and partially secured liabilities.	206,000	137,000	67
Owners' equity (deficit)	(67,000)		
	$555,000	$553,000	

Although corporate reorganizations and liquidations are significantly influenced by law, the accounting profession also may be significantly involved in the entire process. Accountants assist in the identification and valuation of assets and liabilities traceable to the insolvent company. The activities of a company involved in a Chapter 11 reorganization or a Chapter 7 liquidation must be periodically reported to the bankruptcy courts. This periodic reporting function is a major area involving the expertise of the accounting profession.

QUESTIONS

1. A troubled debt restructuring may take several forms. Identify the various forms of these restructurings.
2. Describe the basic characteristics of a quasi-reorganization and indicate how it may improve a shareholder's ability to receive a dividend.
3. Distinguish between a voluntary and an involuntary case under the Bankruptcy Reform Act.
4. Distinguish between a corporate reorganization and a liquidation as addressed in Chapters 11 and 7, respectively, of the Bankruptcy Reform Act.
5. A plan of reorganization must be approved by impaired parties. Who are these impaired parties, and what approvals are required?
6. What are the responsibilities of a debtor under a Chapter 7 liquidation once a trustee has been appointed?
7. Under the Bankruptcy Reform Act, do all unsecured creditors share pro rata in funds as they become available? Explain.
8. Differentiate between the legal statement of affairs and the accounting statement of affairs.
9. The accounting statement of affairs contains a section identifying available assets and another section dealing with liabilities and owners' equity. Identify the categories of liabilities that are influenced by the value of free assets.
10. What is the nature of the dividend as typically computed from the account statement of affairs? Will all creditors receive this percentage of their claims?
11. Various values on the statement of affairs affect the deficiency traceable to unsecured creditors without priority. Explain how the value of this deficiency is determined.

12. In a corporate liquidation under Chapter 7, a trustee is appointed by the court. Identify several of the duties to be performed by the trustee.
13. A corporate liquidation involves the use of a statement of affairs report and a realization and liquidation account report. Discuss the fundamental differences between these two reports.

EXERCISES

Exercise 1. TBD Corporation has been experiencing difficulties servicing its long-term debt and is seeking to restructure the debt rather than face a potential liquidation of the business. The company is not seeking relief through the bankruptcy courts. However, if the company were liquidated, it estimates that long-term creditors would receive approximately $0.85 for each dollar of outstanding debt. The debt to be restructured has a principal balance of $800,000 and accrued interest payable of $32,000 as of November 1, 19X6, and bears interest at the rate of 12%. Management is proposing to restructure the debt by conveying to the creditors: (1) undeveloped land with a cost basis of $200,000 and a fair market value of $338,935 and (2) a promise to pay $15,000 at the end of each month for the next 36 months.

(1) Assuming the restructuring agreement is accepted on November 1, 19X6, prepare the entries to record the restructuring through December 31, 19X6.
(2) Assuming a market rate of interest for a 36-month debt is 15%, given TBD's risk profile, would you recommend that the long-term creditors accept the restructuring or seek a liquidation?

Exercise 2. In an attempt to avoid liquidating the company, the management of Carter, Inc. is considering a reorganization that calls for the restructuring of $2,100,000 of debt maturing in 3 years and related accrued interest payable of $72,737. The restructuring agreement calls for monthly payments over the next 60 months, a reduction in the interest rate to 8%, and the cancellation of $200,000 of debt. The market rate of interest for such a refinancing would be 13%. In addition to the debt restructuring, management is proposing to reduce the par value of their common stock in order to generate enough paid-in capital in excess of par value to absorb a $500,000 deficit in retained earnings. The present balance of paid-in capital in excess of par value is $80,000.

(1) Prepare a schedule to determine the total gain resulting from the forgiveness and restructuring of debt and the amount of future interest expense assuming: (a) a nonbankruptcy approach and (b) a bankruptcy approach to the reorganization.
(2) Determine by how much the par value of common stock would have to be reduced in order to absorb the deficit in retained earnings assuming: (a) a nonbankruptcy approach and (b) a bankruptcy approach.

Exercise 3. The stockholders of Vegas Corporation have authorized the company to conduct a quasi-reorganization in order to revise asset valuations and eliminate its deficit. A condensed balance sheet at October 1, 19X5, just prior to the quasi-reorganization, is as follows:

Assets		Liabilities and Equity	
Current assets	$ 400,000	Liabilities..................	$ 600,000
Property and equipment		Capital stock ($10 par)	2,200,000
(net)	2,000,000	Deficit.....................	(400,000)
		Total liabilities	
Total assets..............	$2,400,000	and equity.............	$2,400,000

Additional data:
(a) Inventories have been overvalued by $80,000.
(b) Plant assets have been appraised at $1,500,000.
(c) Stockholders have approved a reduction in the par value of capital stock to $5 per share.

(1) Prepare journal entries to record the quasi-reorganization.
(2) Prepare a balance sheet for immediately after the quasi-reorganization.

Exercise 4. Select the best answer for each of the following multiple-choice questions.

1. The primary difference between a balance sheet and an accounting statement of affairs is that:
    (a) A balance sheet reflects book values, while a statement of affairs emphasizes realization values.
    (b) Assets are arranged in a different sequence.
    (c) Liabilities are arranged in a different sequence.
    (d) Owners' equity is not considered in the statement of affairs.

2. An accounting statement of affairs of a corporation in financial difficulty indicates that unsecured creditors would receive $0.40 on the dollar. Which one of the following assets is most likely to realize the smallest percentage of its book value?
    (a) Accounts receivable.
    (b) Inventories.
    (c) Plant and equipment.
    (d) Goodwill.

3. Immediately after the recording of a quasi-reorganization, there will be no balance in the account:
    (a) Accumulated Depreciation.
    (b) Capital Stock.
    (c) Paid-In Capital from Reorganization.
    (d) Retained Earnings.

4. If a dividend of 80% is allocable to Class 7 unsecured creditors based on an accounting statement of affairs, it correctly may be concluded that:
    (a) All unsecured claims will receive the same percentage of return.
    (b) All unsecured claims will be paid in full.
    (c) Class 1 through 6 unsecured claims will be paid in full.
    (d) Stockholders will receive 20% of their equity.

5. An arrangement for creditors to accept an amount less than the amount owed to them is referred to as a:
    (a) Charge and discharge agreement.
    (b) Composition agreement.
    (c) Bankruptcy agreement.
    (d) Chandler agreement.

6. In a liquidation proceeding, if the proceeds on the realization of an asset exceed the lien against that asset, the excess is assigned to:
    (a) The holder of the lien.
    (b) Other lien holders whose assets will not realize a sufficient amount to cover their liens.
    (c) Meet the claims of the unsecured creditors.
    (d) The stockholders of the corporation.

Exercise 5. J. Wachs, CPA, has prepared a statement of affairs. Assets against which there are no claims or liens are expected to produce $70,000, which must be allocated to unsecured claims of all classes totaling $105,000. The following are some of the claims outstanding:

(a) Accounting fees for Wachs, $1,500.

(b) An unsecured note for $1,000, on which $60 of interest has accrued, held by S. Bart.

(c) A note for $3,000, secured by $4,000 of receivables, estimated to be 60% collectible, held by J. Gamble.

(d) A $1,500 note, on which $30 of interest has accrued, held by B. Land. Property with a book value of $1,000 and a market value of $1,800 is pledged to guarantee payment of principal and interest.

(e) Unpaid income taxes of $3,500.

   From this information, determine:

(1) The total amount allocable to unsecured claims with priority.

(2) The dividend per each dollar of Class 7 unsecured claims.

(3) The amount each of the claimants may expect to realize.

Exercise 6. Tabco Industries, Inc. has submitted a plan of reorganization to the bankruptcy courts seeking relief under Chapter 11. In order to evaluate the reasonableness of the plan, it must be evaluated against the alternative of a corporate liquidation. The following condensed trial balance and estimates of net realizable values has been prepared as of July 1, 19X9.

	Book Values		Estimated Net Realizable Value
	Debit	Credit	
Cash	$ 2,000		$ 2,000
Accounts Receivable	158,000		126,400
Inventory	74,000		60,600
Other Current Assets.	16,000		12,000
Property, Plant, and Equipment (net)	420,000		440,000
Other Assets	12,000		0
Accounts Payable.		$180,000	
Other Current Liabilities		134,000	
Mortgage and Related Interest Payable.		300,000	
Other Noncurrent Debt		50,000	
Owners' Equity		18,000	
Totals	$682,000	$682,000	$641,000

   Accounts payable totaling $50,000 are secured by inventory with a book value of $50,000 and a market value of $42,000. The mortgage and the related interest payable is fully secured by land and building having a book value of $284,000 and a net realizable value of $330,000. The other noncurrent debt represents an unsecured loan from officers of the corporation. The other current liabilities in part include:

Unpaid wages (less than $2,000 per individual)	$ 20,000
Customer deposits (less than $900 per customer)	14,000
Real estate taxes (having a lien on the land and building)	18,000
Undeposited payroll taxes	8,000
Accounts receivable assigned (receivables are estimated to be 90% collectible)	64,000
	$124,000

   The trial balance does not include $7,000 of estimated expenses to administer the liquidation.

Prepare a statement of affairs for Tabco and calculate the estimated dividend to general unsecured creditors with and without priority.

Exercise 7. A partially completed statement of realization and liquidation is as follows:

The Rodak Corporation
Statement of Realization and Liquidation
For the Period of July 1, 19X9, to August 12, 19X9

| | Assets | | Liabilities | | | | |
| | | | | | Unsecured | | |
	Cash	Noncash	Fully Secured	Partially Secured	With Priority	Without Priority	Owners' Equity
Beginning balances, assigned July 1, 19X9	$12,000	$590,000	$200,000	$175,000	$ 54,000	$150,000	$ 23,000
Cash receipts: Sale of inventory	30,000	(25,000)					5,000

The following additional transactions have occurred through August 12, 19X9:
(a) Receivables collected amount to $39,000. Receivables with a book value of $15,000 that were not allowed for were written off.
(b) A $12,000 loan that was fully secured was paid off.
(c) A valid claim is received from a leasing company seeking payment of $15,000 for equipment rentals.
(d) Securities costing $18,000 are sold for $23,000, minus brokerage fee of $500.
(e) Depreciation on machinery is $3,200.
(f) Payments on accounts payable total $25,000 of which the entire amount was secured by the inventory sold.
(g) Machinery that originally cost $85,000 and has a book value of $45,000 sold for $36,000.
(h) Proceeds from the sale of machinery in (g) are remitted to the bank, which holds a $50,000 loan on the machinery.

(1) Update the statement of realization and liquidation to properly reflect transactions (a) through (h).
(2) Assuming the remaining noncash assets can be realized for $410,000, determine the estimated dividend to be received by unsecured creditors without priority.

PROBLEMS

Problem 21-1. Milton Company has developed a plan to restructure a major portion of its debt. The provisions of the restructuring of debt existing at February 1, 19X9 are as follows:
(a) Accounts payable with a book value of $800,000 will be paid off within 2 months at the rate of $0.80 on the dollar.
(b) Loans from officers with a book value of $300,000 and accrued interest of $16,000 will be satisfied by conveying land with a market value of $290,000.

(c) A bank note payable with a maturity value of $1,400,000 and delinquent accrued interest of $131,237 will be exchanged for a new note. The new note in the amount of $1,480,000 will be serviced over 5 years with monthly payments reflecting a market interest rate of 12.9%.

(d) An unpaid balance on the corporate line of credit of $112,000, including accrued interest, will be converted into a $100,000, 12-month note payable. Interest for the first 4 months will be waived, after which time the first of 8 monthly payments will begin bearing interest at 12%.

(e) A $500,000 mortgage payable with 5 years to maturity will be refinanced over 15 years at a rate of 10.2%. In addition to the monthly payments, an initial refinancing fee of $5,000 is to be paid.

Required:

(1) Prepare a schedule for management that details the estimated cash outflows over the next 6 months resulting from the debt restructuring.

(2) Prepare a schedule for management that details the estimated effect on net income over the next 6 months resulting from the debt restructuring assuming:

    (a) The restructuring is not part of a formal bankruptcy filing.

    (b) The restructuring is part of a formal bankruptcy filing.

Problem 21-2.   The audit of Shaky Corporation for the year ended December 31, 19X6, has just begun. The president indicates that the company is insolvent and may require liquidation unless a large loan can be obtained immediately. A lender who is willing to advance $450,000 to the company has been located, but the loan will be subject to the following conditions:

(a) A $700,000, 8% mortgage, along with 3 months' accrued interest, will be canceled in exchange for 5,000 shares of $100 par, 6% cumulative, nonparticipating preferred stock with a market value of $660,000.

(b) The $450,000 loan will require that a 12% mortgage be placed on the land and buildings as security. The 12% mortgage principal is payable in equal installments over 15 years.

(c) On May 1, 19X6, the company's trade creditors accepted $360,000 in notes, payable on demand, at 6% interest in settlement of all past due accounts. No payment has been made to date. The company will offer either to settle these liabilities at $0.75 per $1 owed or to replace the notes payable on demand with new notes payable for the full amount of the indebtedness, including accrued interest. The new notes would pay interest at 8% and mature in 5 years. It is estimated that $200,000 of the demand notes will be exchanged for the longer term notes, and the other creditors will accept the offer of a reduced cash settlement.

(d) A new issue of 1,000 shares of $100 par, 5% noncumulative, nonparticipating preferred stock will replace 1,000 shares of $100 par, 7% cumulative, participating preferred stock. Preferred stockholders will forfeit all claims to $14,000 of dividends in arrears. The company never has formally declared the dividends. The new preferred stock has a market value of $200,000.

(e) Common stock with a total par value of $300,000 is to be reduced to a par value of $220,000.

(f) The deficit is to be eliminated.

The president of Shaky Corporation requests that the auditor determine the effect of the foregoing on the company and furnishes the following selected account balances, which the auditor believes are presented fairly:

Bank overdraft		$ 15,000
Other current assets		410,000
Property, plant, and equipment (net)		1,325,000
Trade accounts payable		235,000
Demand notes payable		360,000
Other current liabilities		85,000
Paid-in capital in excess of par on 7% cumulative preferred		125,000
Additional paid-in capital, common stock		160,000
Retained earnings (deficit)		(345,000)

Required:

(1) Prepare pro forma journal entries to become effective as of January 1, 19X7. Key entries to lettered information. Gains on restructuring are to be credited to additional paid-in capital on common stock.

(2) Prepare a pro forma balance sheet as of January 1, 19X7, as if the reorganization had been consummated.

(AICPA adapted)

Problem 21-3. Due to continuing problems that have plagued Falco Corporation, management has voluntarily filed for protection under Chapter 11 of the bankruptcy code and has received confirmation of its plan by the bankruptcy court. Falco's balance sheet prior to the reorganization is as follows:

Falco Corporation
Balance Sheet
March 31, 19X9

Assets

Current assets	$1,080,000
Land	560,000
Buildings (net of $520,000 of accumulated depreciation)	1,410,000
Equipment (net of $430,000 of accumulated depreciation)	950,000
Other assets	240,000
Total assets	$4,240,000

Liabilities and Stockholders' Equity

Current liabilities:		
Accounts payable	$ 840,000	
Other current liabilities	180,000	$1,020,000
Mortgage payable		1,320,000
Equipment loans payable		600,000
Bonds payable		1,500,000
Loans from officers		200,000
Stockholders' equity:		
Common stock	200,000	
Additional paid-in capital	500,000	
Deficit	(1,100,000)	(400,000)
Total liabilities and stockholders' equity		$4,240,000

The plan or reorganization calls for the following provisions:

(a) The bonds payable along with current accrued interest of $75,000 will be exchanged for newly authorized 5%, cumulative preferred stock. The stock has a $300,000 par value and a market value of $1,250,000.

(b) The creditors represented by accounts payable have agreed to accept a payment of $0.75 per dollar to be made within the next 60 days.

(c) Officers who have made personal loans to the corporation have agreed to accept an immediate cash payment of $50,000 with the balance of the loan being repaid with three semiannual payments of $45,000 each, beginning on September 30, 19X9. The fair value or net present value of these payments is $102,745.

(d) The equipment loan plus related current accrued interest of $42,000 is to be restructured. Other assets (land held for speculation) with a book value of $110,000 and a market value of $180,000 is to be conveyed to the creditors. The current accrued interest of $42,000 is to be forgiven. The remaining debt is to be repaid over 60 months, beginning at the end of April 19X9. Payments are to include interest at the market rate of 13.5%.

(e) A warehouse with a net book value of $420,000 ($180,000 of accumulated depreciation) and other assets with a book value of $130,000 are to be revalued to their market value of $220,000 and $52,000, respectively.

(f) Common stock having a par value of $200,000 is to be reduced to a par value of $10,000.

(g) The remaining retained earnings deficit after the above provisions is to be eliminated against additional paid-in capital traceable to common stock.

Required:

(1) Prepare the necessary journal entries to record the preceding provisions called for by the reorganization plan. Gains on restructuring are to be credited to additional paid-in capital on common stock.

(2) Prepare a balance sheet that reflects the recording of the entries in (1).

(3) Calculate the value of each of the following ratios based on balance sheet amounts: (a) prior to the reorganization and (b) after the reorganization.

> Current ratio
> Debt to total assets
> Debt to equity

Problem 21-4.   Creditors of Lap Company are concerned because payments are not being met. On March 15, 19X4, the following balance sheet was prepared:

Lap Company
Balance Sheet
March 15, 19X4

Assets

Cash		$ 10,000
Notes receivable (net of discounted notes)		15,000
Accounts receivable (no allowance for uncollectibles).		24,000
Inventory		20,000
Prepaid expenses.		1,000
Land		16,000
Buildings	$50,000	
Less accumulated depreciation.	20,000	30,000
Machinery.	$30,000	
Less accumulated depreciation.	18,000	12,000
Goodwill		4,000
Total assets		$132,000

(continued)

Liabilities and Stockholders' Equity

Notes payable...		$ 15,000
Accounts payable		20,000
Accrued interest on notes payable........................		450
Accrued interest on mortgage payable.....................		700
Accrued wages payable		6,100
Taxes payable..		2,200
Mortgage payable.......................................		25,000
Total liabilities..		$ 69,450
Capital stock	$80,000	
Deficit..	(17,450)	62,550
Total liabilities and stockholders' equity		$132,000

Additional information:

Bank save cash with penalty if payment doesn't occur

(a) Customers' notes receivable of $7,000 were discounted at the bank with recourse. These notes were due March 10, 19X4. No payments have been made to the bank, nor is the liability reflected in the balance sheet. Accrued interest and protest fees on the dishonored notes will amount to $550. In addition, $11,000 of notes receivable have been pledged to one of the creditors for an account payable of $12,000. All nondiscounted notes are collectible.

(b) Accounts receivable are classified as follows:

	Book Value	Estimated Realization
Good accounts.........................	$ 9,000	$ 9,000
Doubtful accounts......................	10,000	7,000
Bad accounts	5,000	0
Total.................................	$24,000	$16,000

Good accounts receivable of $4,000 have been pledged to the holder of a $3,000 note payable on which there is $100 of accrued interest.

(c) The mortgage payable held by the bank is secured by a lien upon the land and buildings. Lap Company has received an offer to purchase the land and buildings for $36,000.

(d) Machinery will realize about $9,000. Inventory can be sold at 80% of cost. Nothing is realizable from prepaid expenses.

(e) Liquidation expenses are expected to be $1,000, plus a trustee's fee of $2,000.

(f) Wages payable include $2,400 of unpaid salary to the company president. All wages were earned within the preceding 90-day period.

Required:

(1) Prepare a statement of affairs.

(2) Determine the dividend to Class 7 unsecured claims.

   Suggestion: Adjust or create any real accounts necessary, based on the data provided, before entering book values in the statement of affairs.

Problem 21-5. The past several years have been extremely difficult for Avery Manufacturing Company, Inc. During this time, the company lost significant market share and was successfully sued with respect to several product liability cases. In response to those problems, the company filed a voluntary petition to liquidate the company on May 15, 19X9, at which time the company had the following condensed trial balance:

Cash..	$ 30,000	
Noncash Assets..................................	2,958,000	
Liabilities:		
Fully Secured.................................		$1,720,000
Partially Secured.............................		762,000
Unsecured—With Priority.....................		20,000
Unsecured—Without Priority..................		230,000
Owners' Equity		256,000
Totals...	$2,988,000	$2,988,000

The bankruptcy court issued an order of relief on June 1, 19X9. The following liquidation transaction occurred through July 15, 19X9:

(a) The inventory of raw materials was disposed of as follows:

	Cost	Market Value
Returned to fully secured vendors..........................	$180,000	$180,000
Sold to liquidations broker.................................	70,000	50,000
Transferred to work in process	40,000	40,000
	$290,000	$270,000

(b) Work in process with a cost prior to liquidation of $117,000 was completed with the addition of the following costs:

Raw materials per (a)...	$40,000
Additional unpaid labor (individually less than $2,000)...................	17,000
Overhead:	
Depreciation...	1,000
Additional liabilities incurred	4,000*
	$62,000

*These debts were incurred between May 17, 19X9, and May 28, 19X9.

The finished work in process was sold for $160,000.

(c) Remaining finished goods with a cost of $204,000 were sold to a liquidation broker for $154,000.

(d) The company's Indiana manufacturing facility, which had a net book value of $1,240,000, was sold for $1,000,000. The $800,000 mortgage on the property and related accrued interest of $34,000 were paid off with the sales proceeds.

(e) The company's warehouse with a net book value of $430,000 and an appraised value of $380,000 was assigned to the bank that held the $450,000 mortgage on the property.

(f) Equipment with a net book value of $450,000 was sold at auction for $330,000. Lenders with equipment loans of $272,000, including accrued interest, received $220,000 upon sale of the equipment. Leased equipment was returned to the lessors and the company forfeited $15,000 in lease deposits.

(g) Unassigned accounts receivable were realized as follows:

	Book Value	Market Value
Collected in full	$ 72,000	$72,000
Written off:		
Against a $30,000 allowance......................	30,000	0
In excess of allowance...........................	14,000	0
	$116,000	$72,000

(h) Assigned accounts receivable totaling $40,000 were disposed of as follows:

$$
\begin{array}{lr}
\text{Collected in full} \dots\dots\dots\dots\dots\dots\dots\dots\dots\dots & \$32,000 \\
\text{Returned to the company with recourse} \dots\dots\dots & 8,000
\end{array}
$$

(i) Expenses totaling $14,000 have been incurred by the trustee.

(j) The company was just assessed another $15,000 of property taxes, which brings the total amount of taxes owed to governmental units to $35,000.

Required:

(1) Prepare a statement of realization and liquidation for the period June 1, 19X9, to July 15, 19X9.

(2) Determine the amount to be paid to unsecured creditors with and without priority assuming the remaining noncash assets have a net realizable value of: (a) $10,000 and (b) $64,000.

If only unsecured creditors with priority will receive a distribution, indicate which specific class of creditors will be paid.

Problem 21-6. A creditor's committee of Carlton Company has obtained the March 31, 19X5 balance sheet shown below:

Carlton Company
Balance Sheet
March 31, 19X5

Assets

Current assets:			
Cash			$ 11,250
Marketable securities.............................			28,750
Notes receivable.................................	$ 10,000		
Less notes receivable discounted	10,000		0
Accounts receivable............................	$ 15,000		
Less allowance for doubtful accounts	1,000		14,000
Subscriptions receivable......................			20,000
Inventories:			
Finished goods...............................	$ 27,500		
Work in process	11,250		
Materials	15,000	53,750	
Total current assets			$127,750
Property, plant, and equipment:			
Land and building	$112,500		
Equipment......................................	60,000	$172,500	
Less accumulated depreciation................		50,000	
Total property, plant, and equipment.........			122,500
Total assets			$250,250

Liabilities and Stockholders' Equity

Current liabilities:			
Notes payable..............................		$ 87,500	
Accounts payable...........................		60,000	
Salaries payable............................		2,650	
Property tax payable		1,150	
Total current liabilities.....................		$151,300	
Long-term liabilities:			
First mortgage payable......................	$ 37,500		
Second mortgage payable...................	50,000	87,500	
Total liabilities.................................			$238,800
Stockholders' equity:			
Common stock, $100 par (1,000 shares authorized)			
750 shares issued..........................		$ 75,000	
250 shares subscribed......................		25,000	
Total		$100,000	
Retained earnings (deficit)		(88,550)	
Total stockholders' equity......................			11,450
Total liabilities and stockholders' equity			$250,250

An analysis of the company's accounts disclosed the following activities through April 30, 19X5:

(a) Carlton Company started business on April 1, 19X0, with authorized stock of $100 par. Of the 1,000 authorized shares, 750 were paid for in full at par, and 250 were subscribed at par, with a required 20% down payment and the balance payable upon call. All of the subscriptions receivable are due from W. Krueger, president of the company, and are fully collectible.

(b) Marketable securities include the $25,000 cost of U.S. Treasury bonds valued at $23,200 and 25 shares of Groves Company common stock, costing $3,750, with a market value of $3,300.

(c) The land originally cost $10,000, and the building was erected at a cost of $102,500. Of the accumulated depreciation, $30,000 is applicable to the building. The realizable value of the real estate is $75,000.

(d) Notes receivable were endorsed with recourse when discounted and are expected to be dishonored. Of the accounts receivable, $3,000 are considered collectible.

(e) Inventories are shown at cost. Any finished goods are expected to yield 110% of cost. If scrapped, goods in process have a realizable value of only $2,200. It is estimated, however, that the work in process can be completed by the addition of $3,000 of present materials and an expenditure of $3,500 for labor. The materials deteriorate rapidly and will realize only 20% of cost. (Use the cost completion method illustrated in the text.)

(f) Equipment is estimated to have a realizable value of $12,000.

(g) Notes payable include a $25,000 note to Aerotex Company and a $62,500 note to B. Williams. Aerotex holds the U.S. Treasury bonds as security for its loans. It also holds the first mortgage of $37,500 on the company's real estate, interest on which is paid through March 31, 19X5. The note payable to Williams is secured by a chattel mortgage on factory equipment. Interest on the note has been paid through March 31, 19X5. Williams also holds the second mortgage on the real estate.

(h) Any expenses not specifically mentioned need not be considered. All salaries qualify for priority, including labor to complete the work in process.

Required:

Prepare a statement of affairs for Carlton Company.

Problem 21-7. Mayne Manufacturing Co. has incurred substantial losses for several years and has become insolvent. On March 31, 19X5, Mayne petitioned the court for protection from creditors and submitted the following statement of financial position.

Mayne Manufacturing Co.
Statement of Financial Position
March 31, 19X5

Assets	Book Value	Liquidation Value
Accounts receivable.	$100,000	$ 50,000
Inventories.	90,000	40,000
Plant and equipment	150,000	160,000
Totals	$340,000	$250,000

Liabilities and Stockholders' Equity	
Accounts payable—general creditors	$600,000
Common stock outstanding	60,000
Deficit	(320,000)
Total	$340,000

Mayne's management informed the court that the company has developed a new product. A prospective customer is willing to sign a contract for the purchase of 10,000 units of this product during the year ending March 31, 19X6, 12,000 units of this product during the year ending March 31, 19X7, and 15,000 units of this product during the year ending March 31, 19X8, all at a price of $90 per unit. This product can be manufactured using Mayne's present facilities. Monthly production with immediate delivery is expected to be uniform within each year. Receivables are expected to be collected during the calendar month following sales.

Unit production costs of the new product are expected to be as follows:

Direct materials.	$20
Direct labor	30
Variable overhead.	10

Fixed costs (excluding depreciation) will amount to $130,000 per year.

Purchases of direct materials will be paid during the calendar month following purchase. Fixed costs, direct labor, and variable overhead will be paid as incurred. Inventory of direct materials will be equal to 60 days' usage. After the first month of operations, 30 days' usage of direct materials will be ordered each month.

The general creditors have agreed to reduce their total claims to 60% of their March 31, 19X5 balances, under the following conditions:

(a) Existing accounts receivable and inventories are to be liquidated immediately, with the proceeds turned over to the general creditors.

(b) The balance of reduced accounts payable is to be paid as cash is generated from future operations, but in no event later than March 31, 19X7. No interest will be paid on these obligations.

Under this proposed plan, the general creditors would receive $110,000 more than the current liquidation value of Mayne's assets. The court has engaged you to determine the feasibility of this plan.

Required:

Ignoring any need to borrow and repay short-term funds for working capital purposes, prepare a cash budget for the years ending March 31, 19X6, and 19X7, showing the cash expected to be available to pay the claims of the general creditors and payments to general creditors and the cash remaining after payment of claims. Support the cash budget with two schedules showing collections from customers and disbursements for direct materials.

Problem 21-8. FICO Corporation is insolvent, and its board of directors is considering several alternatives being proposed by both creditors and management. The creditors are proposing to seek an involuntary petition to liquidate the corporation. It is estimated that the assets and liabilities of the corporation as of February 1, 19X8, will have the following values:

	Book Value	Market Value
Assets pledged with fully secured creditors	$2,400,000	$2,809,000
Assets pledged with partially secured creditors	1,640,000	1,580,000
Free assets	870,000	740,000
Fully secured creditors	2,300,000	N/A
Partially secured creditors	1,640,000	N/A
Unsecured creditors:		
With priority	80,000	N/A
Without priority	1,200,000	N/A

In addition to the preceding liabilities, it is estimated that the trustee's expenses in connection with the liquidation of the corporation will be $35,000.

Management is proposing to continue operations under the supervision of a court-appointed trustee. Management's plan consists of the following:

(a) Continue operations for the balance of 19X8, which would result in the following:

Sales revenue:		
Collected	$1,480,000	
Uncollected	210,000	
Cost of sales:		
Beginning inventory decrease	60,000	
Current purchases:		
Paid	1,100,000	
Unpaid	150,000	
Selling, general, and administrative (SG&A)		
expenses:		
Paid	80,000	
Unpaid ($20,000 of Class 3 wages)	30,000	

(b) Accounts receivable on February 1, 19X8, of $320,000 would be disposed of as follows:

Written off	$ 30,000	
Assigned as collateral of a new loan of		
$250,000	290,000	

(c) With the exception of (b) above, all accounts receivable are considered free assets. All accounts payable are unsecured.

(d) A $600,000 bank loan, which was partially secured by assets with a book value of $540,000, will be satisfied by the payment of $100,000 cash and the substitution of a new 6-month unsecured loan. The new loan calls for principal payments of $400,000 and interest payments of $24,000 based on a market rate of interest.

(e) Unsecured creditors with claims of $400,000 on February 1, will accept 4,000 shares of 6.5%, cumulative, preferred stock. The preferred stock has an estimated market value of $320,000.

(f) Equipment with a net book value of $640,000 will be sold for $520,000. This equipment is pledged as collateral on a $550,000 note. Holders of the note will accept the sales proceeds as payment in full. Additional equipment necessary for operations will be leased under operating leases. Applicable lease payments are included in cost of sales.

(g) As of December 31, 19X8, management estimated that: assets pledged with fully secured creditors will have a net realizable value of $2,750,000, assets pledged with partially secured creditors will have a net realizable value of 110% of the creditors' balances, and free assets will have a net realizable value equal to 90% of book value.

Required:

(1) The board of directors of FICO Corporation have retained you to evaluate the two competing proposals. Prepare a schedule for each alternative that identifies for each category of liabilities and owners' equity: book values, assets available to satisfy claims, and dividend (recovery) percentages.

Hint: The analysis of management's proposal should include schedules that detail the new balances for liabilities, owners' equity, and available assets as of December 31, 19X8.

(2) As a common shareholder, discuss which proposal would be most attractive to you.

Index

Check Figures for Selected Problems

PROB.	CHECK FIGURES
1-1	Purchase goodwill, $125,000; Pooling retained earnings, $115,000. Net income: purchase, $2,500; Pooling, $49,000
1-2	Total goodwill, $385,000
1-3	Retained earnings: $270,000 Bruce, $145,000 Gramling
1-4	Bond value, $311,983; Goodwill, $147,344
1-5	1) Goodwill, $80,000; 2) Land, $33,000; 3) Deferred credit, $35,000
1-6	Investment in direct financing lease, $710,605; Goodwill, $82,678
1-7	Deferred tax expense, $36,000; Deferred tax liability, $74,571
1-8	1) Land, $390,000; 3) 870 added shares
1-9	Retained earnings: 1) $605,000, 2) $605,000, 3) $585,000
1-10	1) Retained earnings, $1,487,500; 2) Goodwill, $886,625
1-11	1) Balance sheet retained earnings, $846,000; 2) 19X5 Net Income, $330,000
2-1	Goodwill, $70,000
2-2	1) goodwill on balance sheet, $205,000; 2) goodwill on balance sheet, $105,000
2-3	Increase land by $21,667
2-4	Goodwill, $63,000
2-5	1) goodwill $200,000; 2) balance sheet retained earnings, $550,000
2-6	Balance sheet figures: property plant and equipment, $925,000; goodwill, $16,000
2-7	Goodwill, $24,000
2-8	2a) goodwill, $66,400; 2b) retained earnings, $1,040,000
2-9	Goodwill, $44,680; minority interest, $27,320

(Consolidated net income is controlling interest only)

3-1	Original goodwill, $44,000
3-2	Original goodwill, $40,000; Consolidated net income, $169,000
3-3	Original goodwill, $40,000; Consolidated net income, $169,000
3-4	Consolidated net income, $47,500; Goodwill on balance sheet, $92,500

PROB.	CHECK FIGURES
3-5	Consolidated net income, $95,000
3-6	Consolidated net income, $45,000; Net building on balance sheet, $717,000
3-7	Consolidated net income, $73,700; Goodwill on balance sheet, $73,800
3-8	Consolidated net income, $127,000; Balance sheet retained earning for controlling interest, $928,000
3-9	Consolidated net income, $33,600; Goodwill on balance sheet, $30,400
3-10	Consolidated net income, $293,000; Controlling retained earnings on balance sheet, $1,602,000
3-11	Consolidated net income, $243,650; Goodwill on balance sheet, $4,900
3-12	Consolidated net income, $375,800; Controlling retained earnings on balance sheet, $1,851,800
3-13	Goodwill on balance sheet, $1,347,500
3A-1	Original goodwill, $40,000; consolidated net income, $169,000
3A-2	Original goodwill, $76,000; Consolidated net income, $126,400
3A-3	Consolidated net income, $106,600; Goodwill on balance sheet, $34,400
3B-1	Gross original goodwill, $146,286
3B-2	Gross original goodwill, $437,714
3B-3	Gross original goodwill, $114,286; Controlling interest in retained earnings, $685,967

(Consolidated net income is controlling interest only)

4-1	Consolidated cost of goods sold, $7,358,000; consolidated net income, $1,192,000
4-2	Consolidated cost of goods sold, $1,146,020; consolidated net income, $76,740
4-3	Consolidated net income, $986,688
4-4	Goodwill, $100,000; consolidated cost of goods sold, $861,000; consolidated net income, $206,000
4-5	Consolidated accumulated depreciation, $298,650; consolidated net income, $203,960
4-6	Consolidated earned income on long-term contracts, $420,500; consolidated construction in progress, $1,232,000; consolidated net income, $146,525
4-7	Consolidated accounts and other current receivables, $385,000; consolidated cost of goods sold, $1,606,000; consolidated net income, $291,000
4-8	Consolidated cost of goods sold, $1,338,600; consolidated net income, $141,295; purchased income, $35,200
4-9	Consolidated accumulated depreciation, $137,000; consolidated cost of goods sold, $455,000; consolidated net income, $183,000
4-10	Same as Problem 9
4-11	Same as Problem 9
4-12	Distribute $72,000 of excess cost of building; consolidated cost of goods sold, $187,000; consolidated other expenses, $62,400; consolidated net income, $75,840
4-13	Investment in Strand on December 31, 19X1, $6,460,000; December 31, 19X1 retained earnings, $10,850,000
4A-1	Consolidated net income, $334,000, consolidated ending retained earnings, $586,000
4A-2	Goodwill, $80,000; Consolidated cost of goods sold, $210,000; consolidated net income, $612,700
4A-3	Same as Problem 9

PROB.   CHECK FIGURES

(Consolidated net income is controlling interest only)

5-1	Loss on bonds, $1,000; consolidated net income, $807,000
5-2	January 1 loss on bonds, $1,900; consolidated net income, $179,180
5-3	January 1 loss on bonds, $15,000; mortgage interest eliminated, $9,625; consolidated net income, $1,499,400
5-4	March 31 gain on bonds, $8,000; consolidated net income, $1,412,500
5-5	January 1 gain on bonds, $50,188; consolidated net income, $409,812
5-6	January 1 loss on bonds, $15,600; consolidated net income, $119,348
5-7	Goodwill, $20,000
5-8	January 1 gain on bonds $7,023; consolidated net income, $60,412
5-9	Consolidated net income, $1,021,000
5-10	Consolidated net income, $290,800
5-11	Interest on factory lease, $7,587; Interest on equipment lease, $4,476; consolidated net income, $154,125
5-12	Interest on machine lease, $1,417; interest on truck lease, $3,023; consolidated net loss, $4,081
5A-1	Interest on equipment lease, $7,939; consolidated net income, $344,656
5A-2	none

(Consolidated net income is controlling interest only)

6-1	Cash from operations, $404,500
6-2	Cash from operations, $201,700; cash applied to investing activities, $40,000
6-3	Cash from operations, $384,000; cash applied to financing activities, $179,000
6-4	Primary EPS, $4.42; Fully diluted EPS, $4.12
6-5	Consolidated cost of goods sold, $1,126,005; minority interest in income, $5,582
6-6	Combined income (before deduction of minority interest) before tax, $196,000; consolidated net income, $131,740
6-7	Combined income (before deduction of minority interest) before tax, $180,650; consolidated net income, $120,659
6-8	Combined income (before deduction of minority interest) before tax, $123,881; consolidated provision for tax, $56,452
6-9	Investor share of investee net income: 19X6, $5,500; 19X7, $5,875; 19X8, $9,687
6-10	19X7 investment income, $4,950; 19X8 investment income, $5,100
6-11	Investment income from all investments: 19X6, $5,340; 19X7, $5,060; 19X8, $104,145

(Consolidated net income is controlling interest only)

7-1	Consolidated net income, $132,150
7-2	Goodwill: 70% interest, $20,000; 20% interest, $18,000; investment account balance on December 31, 19X2, $412,000; consolidated net income, $165,600
7-3	Goodwill: 20% investment, $10,000, 45% interest, $20,500; consolidated net income, $132,950
7-4	Goodwill: 20% interest, $20,000; 60% interest, $42,000; consolidated net income, $158,600
7-5	Purchased income, $900; consolidated cost of goods sold, $169,000; consolidated net income, $69,015

CHECK FIGURES

PROB.	
7-6	Purchased income, $5,000; consolidated cost of goods sold, $1,783,000; consolidated net income, $226,250
7-7	Gain on sale of 1/9 interest, $11,950; loss on sale of 8/9 interest, $24,000
7-8	Correct investment account balance prior to sale, $31,900
7-9	Preferred claim on retained earnings, $16,000, consolidated net income, $349,440
7-10	No excesses on any investments; purchased income, $12,000; Remaining gain on bonds on January 1, $1,500, consolidated net income, $71,040
7-11	Excess cost to equipment, $24,800; increase in paid-in capital from retirement of preferred stock, $2,000; consolidated net income, $43,810
7-12	Gain on sale of investment, $16,000; consolidated cost of goods sold, $3,893,000; consolidated net income, $861,600
7A-1	Consolidated inventory, $133,100; retained earnings of East, $115,480
7A-2	Goodwill balance on December 31, $13,067; Encanto retained earnings, $487,217
7A-3	Retained earnings, $4,290,000
7A-4	Goodwill on purchase date, $20,000; gain on bond retirement, $1,705; Company P retained earnings, $305,135
8-1	Goodwill on purchase date: Tarman, $4,000; Sarge, $30,000; Tarman subsidiary income; 19X7, $20,000; 19X8, $9,600; Sarge subsidiary income for 19X8, $28,933
8-2	Total retained earnings adjustments: Kantor common stock, $87,000; Saeger common stock, $87,500
8-3	Equity adjustment for subsidiary stock sale, $1,200; goodwill on purchase date, $42,000; consolidated net income, $119,680
8-4	Goodwill on purchase date: 60% interest, $20,000, 4% interest, $5,520; consolidated cost of goods sold, $1,539,300; consolidated net income, $179,716
8-5	Gain on bonds retired, $2,100; consolidated net income, $121,605
8-6	Consolidated cost of goods sold, $1,681,500; consolidated net income, $155,500
8-7	Goodwill on purchase date: investment in Boehm, $33,000; investment in Shelby, $27,380; consolidated cost of goods sold, $1,272,000; consolidated net income, $189,131
8-8	Consolidated cost of goods sold, $1,821,600; consolidated net income, $149,645
8-9	Consolidated net income, $163,000
8-10	Consolidated net income, $160,510
8-11	Goodwill: 40% interest, $3,200; 35% interest, $2,300; consolidated net income, $176,975

Appendices to Chapters 1–8

A-1	Total goodwill, $102,500; consolidated net income (controlling interest), $73,700; minority interest, $69,850
A-2	Total goodwill, $37,500; consolidated net income (controlling interest), $183,000; minority interest, $74,500
A-3	Goodwill, $30,000; consolidated net income, $182,400; no minority interest appears
B-1	Goodwill: 70% investment, $49,000; 10% investment, $2,000
10-1	(1) with hedge: $252,000; (2) recognized loss, $500; (3) $533
10-2	10/25 exchange loss: 50,000
10-3	(2) Income effect with hedge: $1,500

PROB.	CHECK FIGURES
10-4	(3) Contract discount: $6,500; (4) Two contract approach is preferred
10-5	July expense: $19,795; August expense: $4,197
10-6	Assumption 1, Option C income effect: $127,960 expense
10-7	(3) Selling forward rate: $0.00415
11-1	(1) $805,200
11-2	(1) $17,711,000; (2) $468,000
11-3	Cumulative translation adjustment: $104,648
11-4	(1) Remeasurement loss: $2,560; (3) $2,286,340
11-5	Translation adjustment: $26,571
11-6	Remeasurement loss: $73,750
11-7	(2) $301,200; (4) $20,141,840
11-8	(1) $111,600 loss; (2) $45,432 debit
11-9	Tobac cumulative translation adjustment: $(3,287,637); consolidated adjustment: $(3,560,637)
11-10	Remeasurement loss: $297,363
12-1	2nd quarter YTD tax on cumulative effect: $25,000
12-2	Net income: $924,400
12-3	N/A
12-4	Tax benefit on loss B: $28,550
12-5	Qt. 2 effective tax rate: 27.86%
12-6	Qt. 3 restated effective tax rate: 28.89%
12-7	Qt. 1 restated (second time) effective tax rate: 26.10%
12-8	Reportable segments: A, B, & D
12-9	All reportable except F
12-10	F not reportable
13-1	Earnings per common share: $3.59; PEPS: $3.47
13-2	Earnings per common share: $1.96; PEPS: $1.84; FDEPS: $1.76
13-3	(a) PEPS 19X5 IA & SA: 0 and 30,000
13-4	N/A
13-5	Earnings per common share: $2.1899; PEPS: $2.1890
13-6	(1) PEPS: $18.897; FDEPS: $14.735
13-7	Earnings per common share: $2.537; PEPS: $2.436; FDEPS: $2.466
13-8	Earnings per common share: $1.543; PEPS: $1.500; FDEPS: $1.494
13-9	Earnings per common share: $15.02; PEPS: $14.01
14-1	(2) $128,085
14-2	(1) Nichols: $52,682; (2) Nichols: $61,682
14-3	N/A
14-4	(1) Brown: $49,600; (2) Brown: $67,599
14-5	(2) Domer: $37,347
14-6	Carson's adjusted capital: $12,600
14A-1	Net income per tax: $38,000

PROB.   CHECK FIGURES

15-1   (2) goodwill: $20,000
15-2   Flint's 12/31/X8 capital balance: $348,401
15-3   (1) $22,000
15-4   Meyers balance: $57,640
15-5   Accept Baker's offer
15-6   8/1/X7 distribution to Sullivan: $11,000
15-7   (2) distribution A to Knapp: $16,000
15-8   Third month balance for Barker: $25,500
15-9   (2) McCoy receives $28,600
15-10   Part II. Aikens receives $41,500
15-11   January payment of Perry estate: $1,046

16-4   (2) Debit to Fund Balance—Unreserved, Undesignated in closing entry, $52,000; (3) Total actual fund balances June 30, 19X7, $24,000.
16-5   (2) Credit to Fund Balance—Unreserved, Undesignated for closing, $386,100; (3) Actual Fund Balance, $231,000
16-6   (e) credit to taxes receivable delinquent $46,000; (j) debit fund balance—reserved for stores $6,000
16-7   (d) debit to expenditures $48,000 in general fund; debit investment in general fixed assets in GFAAG $35,000; debit machinery and equipment in GFAAG $61,000
16-8   (e) debit to Other Financing Uses $150,000 in general fund; (c) debit Amount Available in debt service fund $150,000
16-9   (2) Total general fixed assets, $6,455,000
16-10   (2) Amount available in debt service funds for serial bonds on December 31, 19X7, $232,662
16-11   (1) Excess of revenues over expenditures, $228,400; (2) Total liabilities and fund equity, $462,400
16-12   (b) debit to revenues and credit to Donated Land $27,000 in general fund; (b) debit Land in GFAAG

17-3   (b) Credit to fund balance to close, $7,600,000; (c) Total liabilities and fund balance, $8,800,000
17-5   May 1 entry: debit to Improvements other than Buildings $896,600 in the GFAAG
17-6   (2) Fund Balance—Unreserved, Undesignated in balance sheet, $150,000
17-7   Capitalized expenditures to date, $676,600
17-8   Cash received by Dane City General Fund, $423,3600
17-9   (2) Decrease in actuarial deficiency, $13,000; (3) Total fund balances, $528,000
17-10   (2) Excess of operating revenues over operating expenses in closing entry, $14,500
17-11   (f) debit to Buildings in GFAAG; (a) credit Other Financing Sources in the debt service fund
17-12   (4) Debit to Residual Equity Transfer Out $5,000 in general fund; (7) credit Encumbrances $75,000 in capital project fund
17-13   Capitalize total expenditures in the General Fixed Asset Account Group; Land $150,000, Buildings $410,000

PROB.   **CHECK FIGURES**

17-14   Cash balances; General Fund—$93,800, Debt Service Fund—$6,000, Capital Projects Fund—$400,000

18-3   (2) Net increase in Unrestricted Current Funds for the year, $117,000
18-4   (d) Debit to Fund Balance—Restricted in Plant Fund for Retirement of Indebtedness
18-5   (2) Total increase in net assets, $282,000
18-6   Total increase in Net Assets, $5,965,000
18-7   Total increase in Net Assets, $85,000
18-8   Total net assets, $4,235,000

18A-2   (15) Debit to Reclassification Out—Temporarily Restricted, $15,000; (16) Debit depreciation expense to Expenses—Operation and Maintenance of Plant, $20,000; increase in unrestricted net assets, $117,609
18A-3   Total net assets for Current Funds, $204,449
18A-4   Net assets end of year, $3,544,200

19-5   (a) Debit to Contractual Adjustments, $120,000; (h) Debit to Reclassification Out—Temporarily Restricted, $20,000; loss from operations, $48,000
19-6   Change in unrestricted net assets, $864,000; change in Temporarily Restricted Net Assets, $445,000; change in Permanently Restricted Net Assets, $150,000
19-7   Net cash provided by operating activities, $1,105,100
19-8   Contributions restricted for endowment, $500,000 and Contributions restricted for purchase of property and equipment, $183,000 added to change in net assets to reconcile to net cash provided by operating activities
19-9   Total unrestricted net assets, $701,900; total temporarily restricted net assets, $236,000; total permanently restricted net assets, $400,000
19-10   (6) Debit to Buildings and Equipment, $18,000; Debit to Reclassification Out—Temporarily Restricted, $18,000
19-11   (g) Debit to Depreciation Expense, $46,000; Debit to Reclassifications Out—Temporarily Restricted, $20,000
19-12   (1) Change in net assets, $101,000; (2) Total net assets, $392,000
19-13   Change in net assets, $109,000
19-14   Total operating expenses allocated to Fundraising Services, $47,700; Total plant-related expenses allocated to Fundraising Services, $2,400
19-15   (1) Change in unrestricted net assets, ($1,000); change in temporarily restricted net assets, $140,000; change in permanently restricted net assets, $55,000
19-16   Total expenses allocated to Alcohol and Drug Abuse, $322,200

19A-1   (d) Credit to Nonoperating Revenues—Temporarily Restricted (Contributions), $30,000; credit to Other Operating Revenues—Temporarily Restricted (Contributions), $60,000; credit to Nonoperating Revenues—Unrestricted, $79,000
19A-2   Change in net assets in General Fund, ($58,000)
19A-3   (c) Debit to Equipment in Plant Fund, $15,000; credit to Reclassification—Unrestricted, $15,000
19A-4   (2) Total debits in Unrestricted Current Fund, $651,000; Total debits for organizations, $1,793,000

PROB.	CHECK FIGURES
20-1	Principal balance: $99,250
20-2	N/A
20-3	(a) Estate tax: 0 and $358,700
20-4	N/A
20-5	N/A
20-6	Principal balance: $264,250
20-7	N/A
20-8	N/A
20-9	N/A
20-10	Principal balance: $281,450
20-11	Trust principal: $164,600
21-1	(1) Cash outflows: $905,336
21-2	(2) Stockholders' equity: $1,095,600
21-3	(2) Total assets: $3,802,000
21-4	(2) 100%
21-5	(2) (b) Payment to unsecured creditors without priority: $30,000
21-6	Total unsecured creditors without priority: $134,800
21-7	Cash balance at year end 19X6: $75,000
21-8	(1) Assets available: $5,129,000